NEW YORK
CONSOLIDATED LAWS*

Abandoned Property
Agricultural Conservation and
   Adjustment
Agriculture and Markets
Alcoholic Beverage Control
Alternative County Government
Banking
Benevolent Orders
Business Corporations
Canal
Civil Practice Law and Rules
Civil Rights
Civil Service
Commerce
Condemnation
Cooperative Corporations
Correction
County
Criminal Procedure
Debtor and Creditor
Domestic Relations
Education
Election
Eminent Domain Procedure Law
Employers' Liability
Energy
Environmental Conservation
Estates, Powers and Trusts
Executive
General Associations
General Business
General City
General Construction
General Municipal
General Obligations
Highway
Indian
Insurance
Judiciary
Labor
Legislative
Lien
Local Finance
Mental Hygiene
Military
Multiple Dwelling
Multiple Residence
Municipal Home Rule
Navigation
Not-for-Profit Corporation

Parks and Recreation
Partnership
Penal
Personal Property
Private Housing Finance
Public Authorities
Public Building
Public Health
Public Housing
Public Lands
Public Officers
Public Service
Railroad
Rapid Transit
Real Property Actions and
   Proceedings
Real Property
Real Property Tax
Religious Corporations
Retirement and Social Security
Rural Electric Cooperative
Salt Springs
Second Class Cities
Social Services
Soil and Water Conservation
   Districts
State Law
State Administrative Procedure Act
State Finance
State Printing and Public
   Documents
Statute of Local Governments
Surrogate's Court Procedure Act
Tax
Town
Transportation
Transportation Corporations
Uniform Commercial Code
Uniform Commercial Code Appendix
Vehicle and Traffic
Village
Volunteer Firemen's Benefit
Workmen's Compensation
Unconsolidated Laws
Constitution of the United States
Constitution of State of New York
Court Acts
Court Rules
Family Court Act
New York City Criminal Court Act

Consult Pocket Supplements for new titles or other changes

CLS

New York Consolidated Laws Service

Annotated Statutes with Forms

Civil Practice
Law and Rules
401–1300

Volume 4B

By the Editorial Staff
of the Publisher

1978

THE LAWYERS CO-OPERATIVE PUBLISHING CO.
Rochester, New York 14603

LCP

Library of Congress Catalog Card Number 50–2674

iii

FOREWORD

The publisher is pleased to present this CLS volume, which with its companion volumes, contain the text of the Civil Practice Law and Rules, with all amendments through the 1977 Session of the New York Legislature down to September 30, 1977. These new volumes provide new and expanded features designed to facilitate the task of the statutory researcher and provide easy access to related information, practice aids, and additional research sources. These include:

Codes, Rules and Regulations.—Wherever appropriate, the statutes or rules are annotated with references to pertinent rules or regulations promulgated for the various courts comprising the New York judicial system.

Federal Aspects.—In these volumes containing the Civil Practice Law and Rules, the statutes or rules are annotated with references designed to call attention to similar federal civil practice statutes and rules, if any, and to refer the user to specific federal sources.

Scope Note.—Brief note at the head of Civil Practice Law and Rules point out the scope and content of the law and point out where statutes governing other related questions may be found.

Research References.—There references give quick and convenient leads to the very extensive research material in such well-known sources as Carmody-Wait 2d, New York Jurisprudence, American Jurisprudence, and the American Law Reports (ALR).

Practice Aids.—Research references are also provided to the practical and useful practice material in sources such as New York Legal Forms, Am Jur Legal Forms, Am Jur Trials, Am Jur Proof of Facts, and the leading New York law reviews.

Format.—The entire contents of the volumes are presented in a new improved format designed to make the New York Consolidated Laws Service an even more effective tool for today's practicing attorneys.

These new and useful features, in modern new typography designed for easy readability, will be included in forthcoming replacement volumes of your Consolidated Laws Service, and will make that service the most up-to-date and useful statutory service available to the New York lawyer.

Besides new features, the present volumes provide the kind of content that has become the hallmark of the Consolidated Laws Service. The material includes—

● History notes showing the source and derivations of sections or rules of the Civil Practice Law and Rules, with any amendments.

● Cross references to other related provisions in other laws appearing in the Consolidated Laws Service, and in the state Constitution.

● Case note annotations abstracted from reported decisions of New York courts and of federal courts sitting in New York which interpret, construe or apply the various provisions of Civil Practice Law and Rules, or the earlier practice statutes or rules from which they derive.

● Forms linked to particular statutes or rules.

THE PUBLISHER

ABBREVIATIONS

Exec.	Executive Law
Family Ct. Act	Family Court Act
F	Federal Reporter
F2d	Federal Reporter, 2d Series
F Supp	Federal Supplement
Gen. Assn.	General Associations Law
Gen. Bus.	General Business Law
Gen. City	General City Law
Gen. Const.	General Construction Law
Gen. Corp.	General Corporation Law (repealed)
Gen. Mun.	General Municipal Law
Gen. Oblig.	General Obligations Law
High.	Highway Law
Indian	Indian Law
Ins.	Insurance Law
Jud.	Judiciary Law
Jus. Ct. Act	Justice Court Act (repealed)
L.	Laws
Labor	Labor Law
L Ed	Lawyers' Edition U.S. Supreme Court Reports
L Ed 2d	Lawyers' Edition U. S. Supreme Court Reports, 2d Series
Legis.	Legislative Law
Lien	Lien Law
Loc. Fin.	Local Finance Law
Mem. Corp.	Membership Corporations Law (repealed)
Men. Hyg.	Mental Hygiene Law
Mil.	Military Law
Misc	Miscellaneous Reports
Misc 2d	Miscellaneous Reports, 2d Series
mod.	modified
modg.	modifying
Mult. D.	Multiple Dwelling Law
Mult. R.	Multiple Residence Law
Mun. H. R.	Municipal Home Rule Law
Nav.	Navigation Law
NE	Northeastern Reporter
NE2d	Northeastern Reporter, 2d Series
Neg. Inst.	Negotiable Instruments Law (repealed)
N-PCL	Not-for-Profit Corporation Law
NY	Court of Appeals Reports
NY2d	Court of Appeals Reports, 2d Series
NYC Civil Ct. Act	New York City Civil Court Act
NYC Crim. Ct. Act	New York City Criminal Court Act
NYCRR	Codes, Rules and Regulations of the State of New York
NY Jur.	New York Jurisprudence
NYS	New York Supplement
NYS2d	New York Supplement, 2d Series
Op. Atty. Gen.	Opinion of the Attorney-General
Op. Co. Gov.	Optional County Government Law (repealed)
Op. Comr. Ed.	Opinion of the Commissioner of Education
Op. Counsel SBEA	Opinion of the Counsel of the State Board of Equalization and Assessment
Op. Counsel State Tax Dept.	Opinion of Counsel of the State Tax Department
Op. St. Compt.	Opinion of the State Comptroller
Op. State Tax Comm.	Opinion of the State Tax Commission
Partn.	Partnership Law
Penal	Penal Law

TABLE OF ABBREVIATIONS

THIS VOLUME CONTAINS

Statutes:

Full text of statutes enacted through the 1977 Regular Session of the Legislature to September 30, 1977

Rules:

Changes in court rules adopted prior to April 1, 1976

Case notes and collateral matters:

The sources of the case notes and collateral matters showing the constructions of the statutes referred to in this volume have been brought down through the following volumes:

393 NYS2d

362 NE2d 625

547 F2d 1177

425 F Supp 289

52 L Ed 2d 171

78 ALR3d

33 ALR Fed

Attorney General and Comptroller General Opinions
down to the most recently published reports

CIVIL PRACTICE LAW AND RULES

•

CITE BY TITLE AND SECTION OR RULE e.g.

CPLR § 101

STATE OF NEW YORK

SENATE and ASSEMBLY

Pursuant to the authority vested in us by section 70-b of the Public Officers Law and upon information and belief, I, Warren M. Anderson, Temporary President of the Senate and I, Stanley Steingut, Speaker of the Assembly, hereby jointly certify that the text of the provisions of law contained in this publication is a correct transcript of the text of such law as last amended as of the date of execution of this certificate, and, in accordance with such section, is entitled to be read into evidence.

Given under my hand and seal of office, in the County of ___Albany___, this 15th day of ___December___ 197 7

_____
Temporary President of the Senate

Given under my hand and seal of office, in the County of ___Albany___, this 15th day of ___December___ 197 7

_____
Speaker of the Assembly

This certification is issued for: (title of publication) The Lawyers Co-Operative Publishing Co.

CLS Vol 4B

CIVIL PRACTICE LAW AND RULES

HISTORY:
Schedule of articles, amd, L 1963, ch 532, § 3, eff Sept 1, 1963.

CIVIL PRACTICE LAW AND RULES

VOLUME 4B

ARTICLE 4

Special Proceedings

HISTORY:

Add, L 1962, ch 308, eff Sept 1, 1963.

ADVISORY COMMITTEE NOTES:

This article is new. It provides a uniform summary mode of procedure for every special proceeding, which is applicable to all aspects of procedure except where, by express provision applicable in a specific special proceeding, other procedure is provided. Under new CPLR § 103(b), procedure not specifically covered by this title or by other statute or rule, will be the same as in an action.

In most proceedings, continuity with the former practice is maintained. Much of the procedure is similar to that on a motion, and where such similarity exists, an effort has been made to conform to the provisions of new CPLR article 22. The major innovations in Article 4 are those provisions giving the court more control than under former law over such elements of practice as discovery, addition of parties and severance; such control is desirable to preserve the summary nature of the proceeding. In addition, because it is essentially similar in function to a traditional judgment, the final determination in a proceeding is a judgment, rather than a final order.

The primary object of this article is to assemble in one place the generally applicable rules of procedure governing a special proceeding. Under former law, such rules were repeated many times; there were procedural provisions for each special proceeding treated in the CPA and there were numerous separate statutes containing procedural provisions scattered throughout the Consolidated Laws. These provisions contained needless minor variations. It is contemplated that eventually provisions duplicating those in this article will be removed from such statutes and that, as far as is justified by the nature of the proceeding, conflicting provisions will be brought into conformity with this article. Often a simple cross-reference to this article would suffice. Moreover, the existence of a uniform body of rules will greatly simplify the task of the Legislature should it see fit to create a new special proceeding or to make any special proceeding procedure applicable to all or certain actions.

CROSS REFERENCES:
This article referred to in CLS Unconsol Laws ch 252-C § 21.

RESEARCH REFERENCES AND PRACTICE AIDS:
2 Carmody-Wait 2d, Actions and Proceedings § 9.4.
8 Carmody-Wait 2d, Judgments § 63:2.
9 Carmody-Wait 2d, Enforcement of Money Judgments § 64:348.
14 Carmody-Wait 2d, Summary Proceeding to Recover Possession of Real Property, §§ 90:1, 90:3.
17 Carmody-Wait 2d, Proceeding for Disposition of Real Property of Infant or Incompetent §§ 106:1 et seq.
21 Carmody-Wait 2d, Actions and Proceedings by and Against Infants and Incompetents § 124:36.
22 Carmody-Wait 2d, Proceeding Relating to Express Trusts §§ 131:1, 131:8.
22 Carmody-Wait 2d, Habeas Corpus §§ 139:3, 139:28 et seq.

§ 401. Parties

The party commencing a special proceeding shall be styled the petitioner and any adverse party the respondent. After a proceeding is commenced, no party shall be joined or interpleaded and no third-party practice or intervention shall be allowed, except by leave of court.

HISTORY:
Add, L 1962, ch 308, eff Sept 1, 1963.
Earlier statutes: CPA § 192; CCP § 1588; 2 RS 387, §§ 6, 7.

ADVISORY COMMITTEE NOTES:
The first sentence of this rule is based upon a similar provision governing actions in the first sentence of CPA § 191. It establishes uniform terminology for the designation of parties in a special proceeding, which avoids the confusing variety of terminology formerly in use and, at the same time, is distinct from that employed in an action. The terms adopted are those used in practice in the greatest number of special proceedings.

The petitioner and respondent in a special proceeding correspond to the plaintiff and defendant in an action. Party provisions of article 10 of the new CPLR are intended to be applicable to special proceedings, except that, because a special proceeding is brought before the court immediately, parties may not be added or interpleaded without leave of court, and such leave is also required for third-party practice and intervention. The court in a special proceeding is thus given the degree of control over parties necessary to preserve the summary nature of the proceeding, but it is still able to utilize the party devices of article 10 to prevent an undesirable multiplicity of suits. Requiring a court order in every instance is not unduly burdensome; even if none were required for this purpose, it would almost always be necessary to secure an order extending the time of the hearing or giving the additional party time to plead.

It is possible that there will be no adverse party in a special proceeding. See, e. g., CPA art 82 (proceeding for disposition of real property of infant or incompetent).

For this reason the term "any adverse party" rather than "the adverse party" is used in the section.

FEDERAL ASPECTS:

United States as a party, 28 USCS §§ 2401 et seq.

Special proceedings in the United States Supreme Court, Rules 53 and 54 of United States Supreme Court Rules, USCS Court Rules.

Parties, Rules 17 to 25 of Federal Rules of Civil Procedure, USCS Court Rules.

Special proceedings (including injunctions, proceedings against sureties, appointment of receivers, and condemnation of real property), Rules 64 to 71A of Federal Rules of Civil Procedure, USCS Court Rules.

Necessity of leave of court to add or drop parties by amended pleading filed before responsive pleading is served, under Rules 15(a) and 21 of the Federal Rules of Civil Procedure. 31 ALR Fed 752.

RESEARCH REFERENCES AND PRACTICE AIDS:

3 Carmody-Wait 2d, Parties §§ 19:1, 19:93, 19:142.

6 Carmody-Wait 2d, Interpleader § 40:18.

14 Carmody-Wait 2d, 90:202, 221, 236. Summary Proceedings to Recover Possession of Real Property §§ 90:202, 90:221.

17 Carmody-Wait 2d, Proceeding for Disposition of Real Property of Infant or Incompetent § 106:8.

22 Carmody-Wait 2d, Arbitration § 141:48.

24 Carmody-Wait 2d, Proceeding Against a Body or Officer § 145:253–145:289.

24 Carmody-Wait 2d, Judicial Review of Tax Assessments and Taxes § 146:74.

25 Carmody-Wait 2d, Fundamentals of Practice in the Surrogate's Court § 149:214.

5 Am Jur Pl and Pr Forms (Rev ed), Certiorari, Forms 11–14.

Law Reviews:

Parties and pleading under the CPLR. 31 Brooklyn L Rev 98.

Biannual survey of New York practice: Part III. 39 St. John's L Rev 178.

Biannual survey of New York practice: Part IV. 39 St. John's L Rev 408.

Biannual survey of New York practice: Part V. 40 St. John's L Rev 125.

1975 survey of New York law—civil practice. 27 Syracuse L Rev 425.

CASE NOTES

A request for a declaratory judgment is properly asserted in a special proceeding. Gunter v Gunter (1965) 47 Misc 2d 861, 263 NYS2d 219.

Civil Court of the City of New York does not have jurisdiction to implead a third-party respondent in a summary proceeding for nonpayment of rent. Gorman v Gorman (1974) 77 Misc 2d 687, 355 NYS2d 902.

Proceeding in which district attorney made application for order directing owner of automobile, which had been seen fleeing scene of shooting, to appear at lineup and be viewed by witnesses was one in nature of civil rather than criminal suit. C.

v Morgenthau (1975) 50 AD2d 97, 376 NYS2d 126, motion den 38 NY2d 801, 381 NYS2d 872, 345 NE2d 344.

Where parents of handicapped pupils brought action to compel county to pay transportation costs to special education schools, county brought motion to hold school districts liable for costs of transportation, and original petitions had not been served on school districts and school districts were not named in petitions, school districts were not parties to special proceeding and thus county's motion would be denied since court lacked jurisdiction over such school districts. Re P. (1976) 87 Misc 2d 423, 384 NYS2d 944.

CASE NOTES

UNDER FORMER CIVIL PRACTICE LAWS

See also Case Notes
under § 1003.

1. Generally
2. Bringing in new parties

3. —Who must be brought in
4. —Who may be joined
5. Substitution
6. Misjoinder of and dropping parties

1. Generally

Although a proceeding may not generally be dismissed for nonjoinder of parties, yet where an application for the addition of the omitted party would have to be denied, because it was too late to bring the proceeding against the omitted party, the proceeding would be dismissed. Baum v Van Keuren (1959) 19 Misc 2d 92, 189 NYS2d 969, wherein court suggested the availability of CPA § 23.

2. Bringing in new parties

Controversy as to which faction of labor union was entitled to administer grievance matters was proper case for intervention by one faction in employer's proceeding to stay arbitration under CPA § 1450 (Real Prop Actions & Proc Law 918, 967 herein). Re American Machine & Foundry Co (1948) 193 Misc 990, 85 NYS2d 456.

Commissioner of Agriculture was necessary or proper party to petition by milk dealer against health commissioner to issue health permit for milk from added milk supply, where both parties believe that meaning of condition placed in extension of petitioner's license by commissioner of agriculture is involved. Dellwood Dairy Co. v Brown (1950, Sup) 101 NYS2d 992.

3. —Who must be brought in

Upon return date of order to show cause to permit occupant of premises to intervene in proceeding to set aside dispossess warrant, justice of Municipal Court has right and power to require service of process upon such additional parties as he deemed necessary to litigation. Radcliffe v Nelson (1955, Sup) 137 NYS2d 725.

4. —Who may be joined

In mandamus against extraordinary trial and special term of supreme court, district attorney could be brought in as proper party so that he might advance any contentions in relation to claimed prerogatives of his office in respect to subject-matter of mandamus. People ex rel. Hirschberg v Extraordinary Trial (1940) 259 AD 890, 19 NYS2d 893.

5. Substitution

Where mandamus proceedings have been instituted against the commissioners of a department of a municipal government to secure the reinstatement of the realtor and the respondent ceases to be such commissioner, the proceedings are abated; the realtor is not entitled to have the respondent's successor substituted, but his remedy is to make a demand for reinstatement upon the successor and to institute a new mandamus proceeding if such successor refuses. People ex rel. Hatch v Lantry (1903) 88 AD 583, 85 NYS 193.

Successor in interest of HOLC acquired all rights obtained by latter by entry of final order in proceeding by it as landlord, and was entitled to be substituted as party landlord. Home Owners' Loan Corp. v McShane (1945) 184 Misc 579, 56 NYS2d 91.

6. Misjoinder of and dropping parties

In an action under the Election Law even though failure to join the successful candidate as a party was not fatal to the proceeding, the defect could not be cured after the time limited for the institution of the proceeding namely ten days after the primary election in question. Suthergreen v Westall (1958) 6 AD2d 1014, 178 NYS2d 546.

Jockey club stewards might appear, if they so desired, and could be brought in by jockey, in his proceeding to review refusal of license by State Racing Commission and Jockey Club. Merritt v Swope (1943, Sup) 43 NYS2d 902, affd on other ground 267 AD 519, 46 NYS2d 944.

Motion to quash writs of certiorari to review tax assessments on ground of misjoinder of parties plaintiff properly denied. People ex rel. American Sugar Ref. Co. v Sexton (1937) 274 NY 304, 8 NE2d 869.

§ 402. Pleadings

There shall be a petition, which shall comply with the requirements for a complaint in an action, and an answer where there is an adverse party. There shall be a reply to a counterclaim denominated as such and there may be a reply to new matter in the answer in any case. The court may permit such other pleadings as are authorized in an action upon such terms as it may specify. Where there is no adverse party the petition shall state the result of any prior application for similar relief and shall specify the new facts, if any, that were not previously shown.

HISTORY:

Add, L 1962, ch 308, amd, L 1965, ch 773, eff Sept 1, 1965.
Earlier statutes: CPA § 1292.

ADVISORY COMMITTEE NOTES:

Under this section, article 30 governs pleadings in a special proceeding as well as in an action. The provisions as to a complaint will apply to a petition. Under former law, pleading provisions were not generally applicable to special proceedings, although pleadings analogous to those in an action were frequently prescribed in particularly special proceedings.

Failure of parties to comply with minimum pleading requirements has made formulation of issues difficult and caused unnecessary problems in some cases. See, e. g., Matter of Meyer, 7 AD2d 60, 180 NYS2d 918 (1st Dept 1958). Although a statute could vary the nature of pleadings in a particular special proceeding or abolish them altogether, the general requirements for pleadings in a special proceeding are similar to those for an action, since both fulfill the purpose of framing issues and of notifying the opponent of the nature of claims and defenses.

To insure that the summary nature of special proceedings is not interfered with by the joinder of claims and the interposition of counterclaims or cross-claims, the court is given broad severance powers. See new CPLR § 407.

New CPLR § 3011 allows a reply only upon court order, except where a counterclaim is involved. The second sentence in this section follows CPA § 1292 governing proceedings against a body or officer, which allows a reply at the petitioner's option. It differs from § 1292 in requiring a reply to a counterclaim, because article 4 permits counterclaims in special proceedings, while article 78 prohibits a counterclaim. See CPA § 1291.

The third sentence requires permission of the court for any pleading after an answer or reply. The theory of special proceedings is that they shall proceed as expeditiously as possible with control by the court at a very early stage. Impleader and cross-claims therefore should be controlled by the court to prevent any unnecessary delay and confusion.

The last sentence of the section is based upon a similar provision as to ex parte motions in new CPLR rule 2217(b). See RCP 61. An ex parte application under former law was sometimes designated as special proceeding by statute, but the general definition of a special proceeding in the former law did not include them, as does new CPLR article 1. There would, of course, be no responsive pleading where there was no adverse party.

CROSS REFERENCES:

Time for service of reply, CPLR 403(b).

FEDERAL ASPECTS:

Service and filing of pleadings and other papers, Rule 5 of Federal Rules of Civil Procedure, USCS Court Rules.

Pleadings and motions, generally, Rules 7 through 16 of Federal Rules of Civil Procedure, USCS Court Rules.

RESEARCH REFERENCES AND PRACTICE AIDS:

4 Carmody-Wait 2d, General Rules of Pleading § 27:6.
4 Carmody-Wait 2d, The Complaint or Petition § 28:1.
5 Carmody-Wait 2d, The Answer § 30:1.
5 Carmody-Wait 2d, Counterclaim § 31:1.
6 Carmody-Wait 2d, Reply §§ 32:1, 32:4.
14 Carmody-Wait 2d, Summary Proceedings to Recover Possession of Real Property §§ 90:193, 90:211.
17 Carmody-Wait 2d, Proceeding for Disposition of Real Property of Infant or Incompetent § 106:11.
20 Carmody-Wait 2d, Actions and Proceedings By and Against Corporations, Their Officers, Directors, and Shareholders § 121:83.
24 Carmody-Wait 2d, Proceeding Against a Body or Officer § 145:298.
24 Carmody-Wait 2d, Judicial Review of Tax Assessments and Taxes §§ 146:73, 146:138.

Law Reviews:

A summary civil remedy for trade-name infringement: the New York experience. 14 Syracuse L Rev 1.

Forms:

See "FORMS" heading following "CASE NOTES", infra.

CASE NOTES

Although the definition of cross-claim contained in CPLR § 3019, subd b includes a claim of a "respondent" against a "judgment debtor" in a special proceeding brought pursuant to CPLR § 5227, counterclaim was not proper in special proceeding where court had not granted garnishee permission to file such counterclaim against judgment creditor, and where counterclaim, set forth in "wherefore" clause of garnishee's answer, failed to comply with separate pleading requirements of CPLR § 3014. Michigan Associates v Emigrant Sav. Bank (1973) 74 Misc 2d 495, 345 NYS2d 329.

Defect in caption in petition by landlord in summary nonpayment proceedings was not necessarily fatal to court's jurisdiction of subject matter, especially where parties and their relationships were clearly defined in petition so that no prejudice could accrue by reason of the inaccurate caption. Presidential Management Co. v Farley (1974) 78 Misc 2d 610, 359 NYS2d 424.

By virtue of statutes which govern petitions and captions, captions should be liberally construed and defects in form should be disregarded unless demonstratively prejudicial or timely objection made. Presidential Management Co. v Farley (1974) 78 Misc 2d 610, 359 NYS2d 424.

In a proceeding under Article 7 of the Real Property Actions and Proceedings Law, where the proceeding was brought by the landlord and the petition was verified by his attorney, such verification was bad where the attorney was not named as the petitioner, and no facts were alleged which showed that the case was one under CPLR 3020(d)(3), where a representative's verification was proper. Hirent Realty Corp. v Mosley (1970) 64 Misc 2d 1011, 317 NYS2d 592.

Verification of summary proceeding pursuant to real Property Actions and Proceedings Law § 741 must be accomplished by such persons as are delineated by a joint reading of CPLR § 402 and § 3020. Teachers College v Wolterding (1973) 75 Misc 2d 465, 348 NYS2d 286, revd on other grounds 77 Misc 2d 81, 351 NYS2d 587.

In the absence of an answer filed by the opposing party to a petition for a declaratory judgment with respect to the validity of a separation agreement, the questions of validity or invalidity and of estoppel cannot be summarily determined on affidavits but should be tried as provided in CPLR § 410. Gunter v Gunter (1965) 47 Misc 2d 861, 263 NYS2d 219.

The exercise of the power of the court to accept newly discovered evidence is not governed by any well defined rules, but depends in a great degree upon the peculiar circumstances of each case, and upon whether substantial justice has been done. Altimari v Meisser (1965) 23 AD2d 672, 257 NYS2d 254.

CASE NOTES

UNDER FORMER CIVIL PRACTICE LAWS

1. Generally
2. Petition for certiorari under prior provisions
3. Petition for mandamus under former provisions
4. —Averment of possession of funds applicable
5. —Charges of favoritism and fraud
6. —Demands in excess of rights
7. —Joining causes of action
8. —Sufficiency of petition
9. Verification
10. Affidavits
11. Amendment of petition
12. Aggrieved persons

1. Generally

Procedure with reference to applications pursuant to CPA Article 78 stated. Doherty v McElligott (1939) 258 AD 257, 16 NYS2d 489.

Injunction, issuable only in action, was not within CPA § 1288. Rivkin v Garbros (1944) Inc. 183 Misc 389, 48 NYS2d 25.

Allegation that officer who heard application of police officer for accidental disability retirement allowance disregarded competent evidence, intermingling conclusions and superfluities, was insufficient to show that action of respondent was capricious or arbitrary. Donohue v McGovern (1952, Sup) 114 NYS2d 581.

Owners of residential property, situated mile from residential property in residential district for which town zoning board of appeals issued building permit for guest house or motel, are not aggrieved persons who may review determination of such board. Blumberg v Hill (1953, Sup) 119 NYS2d 855.

To be aggrieved by decision of zoning board of appeals so as to be entitled to have it reviewed, one must have specific, personal and legal interest in subject matter thereof as distinguished from general interest such as is theoretically shared by all members of community; person is entitled to attack validity of such decision only where he is specially and adversely affected thereby. Blumberg v Hill, supra.

Any interested officer, department, board or bureau of village is expressly authorized by statute to maintain proceeding to review determination of zoning board of appeals, and when such officer or board appeals to court, question is whether particular officer or board has interest in his official capacity in subject matter. Fox v Adams (1954) 206 Misc 236, 132 NYS2d 560.

Professional boxer, who may be prevented from earning livelihood by refusal of State Athletic Commission to grant him license or to approve contract, has sufficient interest to permit him to seek review of actions of such agency. Christensen v Helfand (1955) 208 Misc 302, 143 NYS2d 285.

Where plaintiff brought proceeding for review of variance of zoning ordinance, but the papers did not show that the petitioners were aggrieved parties they could not have maintained CPA Article 78 proceedings. Blum v Board of Zoning & Appeals (1957) 8 Misc 2d 403, 166 NYS2d 32.

2. Petition for certiorari under prior provisions

The petition is the pleading and sets in motion the proceeding; it must show a proper case for the issuing of the order, or it falls. Hall v Hood (1923) 121 Misc 572, 201 NYS 498.

While the verification of a petition for a certiorari order before the son of the petitioner, who was a member of the board of zoning appeals and one of the appellants is not to be commended, it was at most a mere irregularity and did not render the petition void or deprive the court of jurisdiction. Brewster v Wendt (1934) 242 AD 775, 274 NYS 428.

Defect in the petition may be waived by filing a return without moving to quash the writ. People ex rel. Long Island R. Co. v State Board of Tax Comrs. (1921) 231 NY 221, 131 NE 896, modg 193 AD 297, 183 NYS 733; People ex rel. Colgate Inn, Inc. v Assessors of Hamilton (1928) 132 Misc 506, 230 NYS 134.

3. Petition for mandamus under former provisions

The remedy of mandamus, like every other judicial remedy, may be granted only after the suitor has established right to the remedy. His petition must allege facts which if true would establish that right. Durr v Paragon Trading Corp. (1936) 270 NY 464, 1 NE2d 967, affg 246 AD 579, 284 NYS 357.

The petition for a mandamus order is governed as to its form by provisions of statute and rule respecting the statement in a complaint of the facts constituting the cause of action. Universal By-Products Corp. v Schwartz (1926) 216 AD 311, 215 NYS 45.

4. —Averment of possession of funds applicable

Averments in writ in proceeding to compel payment of amount due sewer contractors held not subject to objection that they state that defendant sewer commissioners have not in hand funds applicable to such claim, in view of the express averment that a part of the proceeds of the sale of sewer bonds which were issued for the erection of the sewer is in defendant town board's hands. People ex rel. Desiderio v Conolly (1921) 117 Misc 77, 190 NYS 497.

5. —Charges of favoritism and fraud

Motion denied, which sought to strike portions of a petition for mandamus, which charged public officers with favoritism amounting to fraud in regulating the erection of gas stations. Re Peck (1930) 137 Misc 703, 244 NYS 179, judgment revd 231 AD 99, 246 NYS 280, affd 256 NY 669, 177 NE 186.

6. —Demands in excess of rights

Where the petition asks more than the applicant would be entitled to in any case, the proceeding may be dismissed, even though the applicant is right in all other respects. Moose v Town Board of Health (1921) 116 Misc 459, 190 NYS 161.

7. —Joining causes of action

Where, in order for a payment to be made of the amount due under a sewer contract, it is necessary that successive steps be taken by the board of sewer commissioners and the town board, both boards are properly joined as defendants on a mandamus proceeding by a sewer contractor to compel the payment of an amount claimed to be due under his contract. People ex rel. Desiderio v Conolly (1921) 117 Misc 77, 190 NYS 497.

8. —Sufficiency of petition

Petition insufficient in not setting up the source of petitioner's information and grounds of belief, and the answering affidavits denying all except the formal allegations and setting forth facts which, if true, constituted bad faith on the part of the petitioner; order for writ reversed. Hoffman v Lincoln Smoked Fish Corp (1929) 227 AD 602, 234 NYS 813.

In the absence of any answer, affidavit or evidence controverting petition, facts stated in moving papers on application for order are taken as true for purpose of the motion. O'Malley v Robbins (1931) 142 Misc 305, 255 NYS 161.

Where an objection is raised in point of law, the allegations of the petition must be assumed to be true and must be considered in their most favorable light in support of the petition. Hassett v Barnes (1960) 11 AD2d 1089, 206 NYS2d 606.

Petition to annul determination of state housing commissioner refusing to compel public limited dividend corporation to renew lease of petitioner for membership in tenant's association held insufficient, as alleging no discrimination for "creed." Cummings v Weinfeld (1941) 177 Misc 129, 30 NYS2d 36.

Petition for reinstatement held fatally defective in failing to show that petitioner had originally been appointed in accordance with law. Ballantine v Glen Cove (1942) 264 AD 773, 34 NYS2d 747.

Where petition is neither plain nor concise, and it is impossible for respondent to prepare answer to it, entire petition was struck out with leave to plead anew. Berkon v Mahoney (1943) 180 Misc 610, 42 NYS2d 90.

Mixture of alleged facts, argument, conclusions of law, discussion of statutory provisions, procedure, and determinations in other cases, rendered petition bad. Hines v State Board of Parole (1943) 181 Misc 274, 47 NYS2d 535.

Allegations of fraud and irregularities in petition to recall and reconvene political meeting to elect executive board must be definite and substantial. Balter v Cohen (1944, Sup) 50 NYS2d 526.

Injury to petitioner must be shown in petition. Fitzgerald v Conway (1948) 191 Misc 1048, 78 NYS2d 418.

Petitioner, who was not resident or taxpayer in fire district or town, had no such interest as would entitle him to compel town supervisor to forbid use of fire house for religious worship. Lewis v Mandeville (1951) 201 Misc 120, 107 NYS2d 865.

Allegations highly derogatory and merely conclusions and therefore frivolous, were struck out. Schwartz v Shapiro (1949, Sup) 91 NYS2d 771.

Surplus allegations ordered struck from petition for reinstatement of members expelled from corporation, leaving allegations limited to petitioning member. Briggs v Technocracy (1948, Sup) 85 NYS2d 735.

Petition must contain prayer for specific relief. Fitzgerald v Conway (1948) 191 Misc 1048, 78 NYS2d 418.

Relief granted is relief to which court deems petitioner entitled. Application of Dillon (1948) 193 Misc 6, 85 NYS2d 228, mod on other grounds 274 AD 911, 83 NYS2d 255.

Petition, alleging on information and belief, that determination of acting commissioner was capricious, unreasonable or arbitrary, was insufficient. Re Board of Education (1951) 199 Misc 631, 106 NYS2d 615.

Though petition sounds in mandamus, court may search record and grant relief, without rigidly holding applicant to form of relief applied for. Stafford v Sands Point (1951) 200 Misc 57, 102 NYS2d 910.

Any private citizen may institute mandamus to compel pension board of trustees to rescind illegal resolution retiring deputy police commissioners and placing them on pension roll as chief inspectors. Bergerman v Murphy (1951) 199 Misc 1008, 102 NYS2d 622, mod on other grounds 278 AD 388, 105 NYS2d 642, affd 303 NY 762, 103 NE2d 545.

Proceeding by seven licensed loan companies to annul granting of license to particular loan company on ground that it stipulated to charge less than maximum rate of interest, was dismissed where petitioners failed to allege or show that they were aggrieved, where Superintendent of Banks considered past and prospective rates in determining whether to grant license. Personal Finance Co. v Lyon (1953) 203 Misc 710, 121 NYS2d 72.

Petition need not be signed or subscribed, but it must be verified; failure of attorney or petitioner to subscribe petition is not jurisdictionally fatal. Fox v Adams (1954) 206 Misc 236, 132 NYS2d 560.

Petition by motormen on subways operated by New York City Transit Authority, alleging that latter had suspended former for reporting sick and failing to report for work and resulting in paralyzing transit breakdown, and that latter subjected former to probation for periods of six months without formal hearing, stated cause of action against Transit Authority. Horvath v Patterson (1956) 3 Misc 2d 960, 151 NYS2d 183, affd 3 AD2d 730, 160 NYS2d 816.

In CPA Article 78 proceeding while the petitioner sought a direction to reopen a hearing of the State Harness Racing Commission for the purpose of taking additional proof, an issue within the discretion of respondent and not subject to judicial control, the expression of such abortive purpose was not fatal to the basic prayer that respondent be directed to reopen the hearing. Brennan v Monaghan (1957) 8 Misc 2d 189, 166 NYS2d 190.

A petition for an order directing a city clerk to publish a certain ordinance passed by the city council is defective where it fails to allege a demand and a refusal by the city clerk to publish the ordinance, since such a proceeding may only be maintained after respondent's refusal upon demand to perform his duty. Glen Cove Shopping Center v Suozzi (1957) 8 Misc 2d 247, 166 NYS2d 917.

To be entitled to seek the review of a decision of Zoning Board of Appeals, applicant must allege that he is a person aggrieved thereby specially, personally, and adversely, as distinguished from one who is merely a taxpayer interested in protecting the welfare of the entire community. Hattem v Silver (1959) 19 Misc 2d 1091, 190 NYS2d 752.

An allegation that petitioner was duly appointed sufficiently alleges that he was appointed according to law and that whatever was necessary to constitute a valid appointment was done. Chiodo v Rice (1959) 9 AD2d 688, 191 NYS2d 808.

Where petitioner seeks to compel performance of a duty specifically enjoined by law, formally mandamus, he must allege that respondent owes him a clear legal duty, a breach of that duty, resulting injury to him, a demand by him that respondent perform that duty, a refusal by respondent to act, and due performance by him of all conditions precedent to asserting his right. Hassett v Barnes (1959) 21 Misc 2d 895, 193 NYS2d 254, revd on ground petition was sufficient 11 AD2d 1089, 206 NYS2d 606.

Petition by police officer for reinstatement by Town Board alleging his resignation was involuntary and was obtained by defendants' threat of criminal prosecution was held sufficient. Hassett v Barnes (1960) 11 AD2d 1089, 206 NYS2d 606.

9. Verification

A petition for a writ of certiorari signed by the president of the petitioner, a corporation, may not properly be dismissed for want of jurisdiction on the ground that the president had failed also to sign the verification, though it was duly signed by a notary public before whom the affidavit was taken. Assuming, but not deciding, that such a verification is defective the defect is not jurisdictional and may be corrected on motion. People ex rel. New York City Omnibus Corp v Miller (1939) 282 NY 5, 24 NE2d 722.

Where petition is made, signed and verified by attorney of claimant against city, petition was dismissed. Zelter v Nash (1955) 285 AD 1214, 140 NYS2d 652.

Where verification of petition to review official determination is defective, court may correct mistake or supply omission in absence of showing of prejudice of substantial right. Re Smith (1956) 2 AD2d 67, 153 NYS2d 131.

Court refused to entertain application of Matteawan inmate using a pseudonym to compel county clerk to file petitioner's summons and affidavit of service where petition was unverified. "Today's Peter Zenger!" v County Clerk of New York County (1959) 15 Misc 2d 619, 182 NYS2d 730.

Petitioner must present a verified petition, containing plain and concise statement of material facts, demanding appropriate relief. Hassett v Barnes (1959) 21 Misc 2d 895, 193 NYS2d 254, revd on ground petition was sufficient 11 AD2d 1089, 206 NYS2d 606.

Verification of petition in CPA Article 78 proceeding by only one of several petitioners was sufficient, in view of their unity of interest. Dobler v Kaplan (1961) 27 Misc 2d 15, 211 NYS2d 96.

10. Affidavits

Affidavits may support petition, and may be considered in favor of its allegations. Yonkers Bus v

Maltbie (1940, Sup) 23 NYS2d 87, affd 260 AD 893, 23 NYS2d 91.

Affidavit cannot take place of petition, and proceeding commenced by affidavit will be dismissed. Levine v Lending (1941) 176 Misc 462, 26 NYS2d 775.

Affidavit is not substitute for petition. Stecklow Bros. v Carol Management Corp. (1948, Sup) 78 NYS2d 427, affd without op 273 AD 1013, 79 NYS2d 886.

Affidavits may be attached to petition "in support" thereof, and may be used in support of petition, though tending to destroy its allegations. Martin Epstein Co. v New York (1950) 31 Misc 2d 759, 100 NYS2d 326.

In proceeding to review determination of administrative officer, new matter in petition in form of affidavits which were not before such officer when he made his determination were properly stricken from petition. Fragomeni v Wilson (1952) 280 AD 1023, 116 NYS2d 836.

But see Henderson v Sarle (1960) 23 Misc 2d 334, 197 NYS2d 916, where in mandamus proceeding to obtain inspection of union's books it was held that use of an affidavit rather than a verified petition was an irregularity that could be disregarded.

11. Amendment of petition

See Association for Preservation of Freedom, etc. v Shapiro (1961) 14 AD2d 800, 220 NYS2d 696, where Court of Appeals had reversed with remittitur to Appellate Division for further proceedings, and before Appellate Division could act thereon, petitioner, without leave, filed amended petition containing a new cause of action and Appellate Division, because no prejudice had been shown, overlooked the irregularity.

12. Aggrieved persons

The fact that a licensee may suffer economic injury if similar licenses are granted to others located in his immediate vicinity does not make him an aggrieved person so as to entitle him to initiate a proceeding to annul the granting of such licenses where he does not show either that public officer had acted arbitrarily in granting such licenses or that he is in imminent danger of suffering loss of a legally protected right. Nostrand Check Cashing Co. v Clark (1960) 27 Misc 2d 799, 210 NYS2d 437 (check cashing business license), affd 13 AD2d 922, 218 NYS2d 546.

FORMS

Form 1—Skeleton form of petition
Form 2—Skeleton form of answer
Form 3—Reply

Form 1

Skeleton Form of Petition

Supreme Court, __1____ County.

In the Matter of the Application of
__2_____ for a Judgment __3_____
[state general nature of judgment]
  against
__4_____, Respondent [or "Respondents"]

                          Petition
                          Index No. __5__ [if assigned]

The petition of __6_____ respectfully shows:

1. That petitioner is __7_____ [state facts to show petitioner beneficially interested] and a resident of the City of __8_____, County of __9_____, in the State of __10_____ [add any other allegations necessary to show right of petitioner to institute proceeding].

2. That at all the times herein mentioned respondent was and now is __11_____ [state office held by respondent and any pertinent facts as to his duties, etc.].

3. That __12_____ [state plainly and concisely the material facts on which petitioner relies].

4. [In a proper case.] That __13_____ [respondent] has failed, neglected and refused to __14_____, although demand has been made therefor.

5. That attached hereto, in support of this petition, are the affidavits of __15_____, sworn to __16_____, 19_17_, of __18_____, sworn to __19_____, 19_20_, and __21_____ [state the nature of any other written proof attached].

6. [If there is no adversary.] That no previous application for the relief demanded herein, nor for similar relief, has been made to any court or judge, except [state result of prior application, if any and specify new facts not previously shown, if any].

Wherefore petitioner respectfully prays that this court may grant a judgment directed to said __22_____ [state name and office held], commanding him to __23_____ [or "prohibiting him from __24_____," or "to review and annul the determination made by him as hereinabove set forth," or two or more of above or other appropriate relief], and for such other and further relief as may seem just and proper.

                          __25_____,
                                         Petitioner
              By __26_____,
                      Attorney for Petitioner
                          Address __27_____
                        Telephone No. __28__

[Venue.]

__29_____, being duly sworn, deposes and says that he is the petitioner herein, that he has read the foregoing petition and knows the contents thereof, and that the same is true of his own knowledge except as to the matter therein stated to be alleged on information and belief and as to those matters he believes it to be true.

                                        [Signature]
                          __30_____
                    [Print signer's name below signature]

Sworn to before me this __31__ day of __32_____, 19_33_
                        __34_____, Notary Public, __35_____ County.

[Annex to petition affidavits and other written proof to support the petition, i. e., evidentiary proof of facts stated in petition.]

Form 2

Skeleton Form of Answer

[Title of court and proceeding
as in Form 1, supra.]
                            Answer
                            Index No. __1__ [if assigned]

The respondent, __2_____ [name and official title], answering the petition herein:

1. Denies __3_____ [note that statute reads "proper denials . . . as in an action." Therefore, it seems, denials are properly in the same form as denials in any action, and may include denials on information and belief or of knowledge and information sufficient to form a belief. For forms of denials in actions in general, see § 3018.]

For a separate and distinct defense to the petition herein, respondent alleges:

2. That __4_____ [set forth any "new matter, as in an action, and . . . facts as may be pertinent and material to show the grounds of the action taken by the respondent which is complained of"].

3. That annexed hereto and made a part of this answer is a duly certified transcript of the record of the proceedings subject to review or consideration herein.

4. That served and submitted with this answer are the affidavits of __5_____ and __6_____, sworn to __7_____, 19_8_ [or "written proof"] showing the evidentiary facts entitling petitioner herein to the trial of an issue of fact herein.

Wherefore, respondent prays that the court render a judgment dismissing the proceeding herein on the merits with costs to respondent.

_9_____
Attorney for Respondent
Address __10_____
Telephone No. __11__

[Verification.]

Form 3

Reply

[Title of court and proceeding   Reply
as in Form 1, supra]   Index No. __1__ [if assigned]

The petitioner, replying to the answer herein:

1. Denies __2_____.

2. Alleges [for instance] that the transcript of the record of the proceedings annexed to the answer herein is not accurate [or "complete"] in that __3_____ [state wherein transcript inaccurate or incomplete].

3. That annexed hereto are the affidavits of __4_____ and __5_____, sworn to __6_____, 19_7_ [or "written proof consisting of __8_____"] showing the truth of the allegations in the petition herein and in this reply, and of the denials contained in this reply.

Wherefore, petitioner prays that the prayer of the petition herein be granted.

_9_____
Attorney for Petitioner
Address __10_____
Telephone No. __11__

[Verification if necessary.]

§ 403. Notice of petition; service; order to show cause

(a) **Notice of petition.** A notice of petition shall specify the time and place of the hearing on the petition and the supporting affidavits, if any, accompanying the petition.

(b) **Time for service of notice of petition and answer.** A notice of petition, together with the petition and affidavits specified in the notice, shall be served on any adverse party at least eight days before the time at which the petition is noticed to be heard. An answer and supporting affidavits, if any, shall be served at least one day before such time. A reply, together with supporting affidavits, if any, shall be served at or before such time. An answer shall be served at least five days before such time if a notice of petition served at least ten days before such time so demands; whereupon any reply shall be served at least one day before such time.

(c) **Manner of service.** A notice of petition shall be served in the same manner as a summons in an action.

(d) **Order to show cause.** The court may grant an order to show cause to be served, in lieu of a notice of petition at a time and in a manner specified therein.

HISTORY:

Add, L 1962, ch 308, eff Sept 1, 1963.

Earlier statutes and rules: RCP 21, 60; CCP §§ 433, 780; CPA §§ 1288, 1289, 1292, 1309, 1421, 1469-d; Gen Rules Pr 37.

ADVISORY COMMITTEE NOTES:

Subd (a). A notice of petition accomplishes the purposes of both a summons and a notice of motion. As in the case of a summons, the special proceeding is commenced and jurisdiction is acquired over the respondent by service of the notice of petition. As in the case of a notice of motion, a notice of petition must fix the return date and be accompanied by any supporting affidavits. There is no demand for relief in the notice of petition, however, because the demand is made in the petition—the equivalent of the complaint in an action—which is to be served with the notice.

Subd (b) is based mainly on the provisions controlling motions. The third sentence is derived from part of CPA § 1292 in the article governing proceedings against a body or officer. New CPLR § 402 authorizes a reply in special proceedings; this subdivision simply prescribes the time limits. Since the primary function of a special proceeding is summary disposition, most statutes governing special proceedings provide for short notice. In this respect, a special proceeding is analogous to a motion. Although there is considerable variation, the time periods of the motion provisions are those most frequently employed. See, e. g., CPA §§ 1289, 1461, 1463, 1469-b. Considerable flexibility will be achieved through the court's discretionary power to adjourn the hearing, to allow added time to plead and to require additional proof. The court may also vary the time of service by use of an order to show cause. Affidavits with attached exhibits may be submitted with the petition or answer to facilitate a summary determination on the pleadings and papers in a manner similar to that on a motion for summary judgment.

Subd (c) is derived from RCP § 21. Similar provisions were contained in many of the statutes governing particular special proceedings. See, e.g., CPA §§ 1289, 1309, 1421, 1469-d. Such service is required in order to obtain original jurisdiction. The restriction of RCP 21 to the provision for "personal" service of a summons has been eliminated. If personal service cannot be effected, there is no reason why service by mail or by publication should not be allowed, as in an action. The court may make additional provisions as to the manner of service in an order to show cause as long as the mode of service gives sufficient notice to meet the demands of due process.

Subd (d) is based upon new CPLR rule 2214(d), which applies to motions. See RCP 60. Service of an order to show cause is equivalent to service of a notice of petition for the purposes of the jurisdictional requirements of new CPLR § 304. An order to show cause permits the court to make provisions for special problems that may arise as to time, service and parties, and at the same time grant such provisional relief as may be necessary. Both the affidavits upon which the order to show cause was granted and the petition should be served with the order to show cause, in order to insure notice to the defendant not only of the claims against him but of the reason for proceeding by order to show cause.

CROSS REFERENCES:

Personal service upon court, board, or commission, CPLR 312.
Motions, CPLR 405, 406, 2211–2218.
Petition in proceeding against body or officer, CPLR 7804.

CODES, RULES AND REGULATIONS:

Special proceedings in Appellate Division, Third Judicial Department. 22 NYCRR 800.2 (CLS App. Div. Rules—Third Judicial Dept. § 800.2).
State human rights proceedings (Executive Law, § 298 et seq.) in Appellate Division, Third Judicial Department. 22 NYCRR 800.20 (CLS App. Div. Rules—Third Judicial Dept. § 800.20).

FEDERAL ASPECTS:

Process, Rule 4 of Federal Rules of Civil Procedure, USCS Court Rules.
Service and filing of pleadings and other papers, Rule 5 of Federal Rules of Civil Procedure, USCS Court Rules.

RESEARCH REFERENCES AND PRACTICE AIDS:

1 Carmody-Wait 2d, Officers of Court § 3:12.
3 Carmody-Wait 2d, Commencement of Action; Summons and Service of Process §§ 24:1, 24:4, 24:5, 24:7.
6 Carmody-Wait 2d, Reply § 32:18.
6 Carmody-Wait 2d, Motions Addressed to Pleadings § 37:41.
9 Carmody-Wait 2d, Enforcement of Money Judgments § 64:349.
10 Carmody-Wait 2d, Enforcement of Money Judgments § 64:359.
11 Carmody-Wait 2d, Attachment § 76:149.
22 Carmody-Wait 2d, Habeas Corpus § 139:55.
22 Carmody-Wait 2d, Arbitration § 141:48.
24 Carmody-Wait 2d, Judicial Review of Tax Assessments and Taxes § 146:62.

Law Reviews:

The quarterly survey of New York practice: CPLR 403(c) and (d): care required to fulfill court's specifications as to service of an order to show cause. 41 St. John's L Rev 133.

Forms:

See "FORMS" heading following "CASE NOTES", infra.

CASE NOTES

1. In general; notice of petition
2. Timeliness and limitations
3. Manner of service
4. Order to show cause

1. In general; notice of petition

Actions and special proceedings are independent applications to a court for relief and must be instituted by service of a summons or notice of a petition, thus acquiring jurisdiction over the person of the defendant or respondent. Anderson v Anderson (1967) 54 Misc 2d 916, 283 NYS2d 679.

A proceeding to determine whether a person has been guilty of a criminal contempt by reason of his conduct in connection with the prosecution of a civil action, and which is instituted by an order to show cause, is a civil special proceeding which is governed generally by the provisions of CPLR 403 providing for the initiation of a special proceeding by service of a notice of petition in the same manner as a summons in an action, or by the court granting an order to show cause to be served, in lieu of a notice of petition, at a time and in a manner specified therein. Board of Education v Zeluck (1969) 60 Misc 2d 1090, 304 NYS2d 697.

Special proceeding instituted by service of summons demanding service of answer within twenty days is fatally defective, and will be dismissed.

Montgomery v Olley (1964) 42 Misc 2d 906, 249 NYS2d 205.

While CPLR 7503, subd c provides for an alternate method of service (by registered or certified mail, return receipt requested), it does not change the general rule that initiatory process must be served upon the party over whom jurisdiction is sought to be acquired and not upon his attorney. State-Wide Ins. Co. v Lopez (1968) 30 AD2d 694, 291 NYS2d 928.

The failure of police officers seeking a court order staying a departmental hearing to be held on charges filed against them to file a verified petition constituted a technical irregularity which was waived by a tardy objection thereto. Sardino v Finch (1970) 35 AD2d 686, 314 NYS2d 690.

2. Timeliness and limitations

Petitioners seeking a review of their respective tax assessments, who, within the four-year limitation period, filed and served notes of issue and paid the fees therefor, had done all they could do to bring their petitions on for hearing, and they are not deemed to have abandoned their actions if not heard within four years from date of filing, for § 718 of the Real Property Tax Law must be construed to refer to an order extending time for the petitioners to put their cases on the calendar, and it does not apply to persons situated as the petitioners are. Sturay Realty Corp. v Board of Assessors (1965) 48 Misc 2d 2, 263 NYS2d 991.

Timely service of Article 78 petition upon Attorney General was not sufficient to stop running of statute of limitations as against respondent Tax Commission so as to permit late service upon Commission. Cohen v State Tax Com. (1976) 51 AD2d 79, 378 NYS2d 507.

3. Manner of service

Service by certified mail, instead of service in the same manner as a summons, of notice of application to direct third party to turn over to judgment creditor debts owed to judgment debtor is jurisdictionally defective, in the absence of an order to show cause directing such service (CPLR 403). R. H. Macy & Co. v Geller (1964) 42 Misc 2d 1063, 249 NYS2d 1004.

CPLR 5239 by providing that an adverse claimant to property levied upon by the sheriff may assert his right by serving a notice of petition upon the sheriff and upon the judgment creditor "in the same manner as a notice of motion" constitutes an exception to the general rule of CPLR 403(c), and service upon the judgment creditor's attorney, including service by mail, will serve to expedite the matter and yet provide due process notice; and there is no requirement that the judgment creditor be personally served. Joseph Durst Corp. v Leader (1966) 51 Misc 2d 72, 272 NYS2d 448.

In custody proceeding, service of notice of petition by mail and personal service upon her attorney, without more, will not serve to confer jurisdiction over respondent who was resident of Belgium and maintained no domicil in New York. Application of Kay (1968) 29 AD2d 937, 289 NYS2d 709.

An application for a stay of arbitration is the institution of a special proceeding, rather than a motion in a pending action or proceeding (CPLR 7502(a)). Jurisdiction is obtained in a special proceeding by the service of an order to show cause, in the manner specified therein, or of a notice or petition, which must be served in the same manner as a summons in an action (CPLR 304, 403[c], [d]). When the object of the special proceeding is to stay arbitration, an additional manner of service is provided in CPLR 7503(c)-viz. The notice may be served by registered or certified mail, return receipt requested. Bauer v Motor Vehicle Acci. Indemnification Corp. (1969) 31 AD2d 239, 296 NYS2d 675.

Where service of the application for confirmation of an arbitrator's award was made by ordinary mail upon the attorney for respondent who had appeared at the hearing and such attorney, on return of the application, advised the court that he no longer had authority to represent respondent in the arbitration and suggested direct service on his former client, which suggestion was not followed, process was not obtained against the respondent. Saddler Textiles, Inc. v Winston Uniform Corp. (1972) 39 AD2d 845, 332 NYS2d 650.

Service by mail of beneficiary's motion for delivery of a verified statement was a mere irregularity, not a jurisdictional defect, where lienor trustees received mailed notices, had actual knowledge of the proceedings, were represented by an attorney in said proceeding, and were domiciliaries of New York subject to the in personam jurisdiction of New York courts even without personal service, and where service by mail could have been authorized either originally or nunc pro tunc pursuant to CPLR § 403, subd d. Fagenson v First-York 86th Street Corp. (1973) 73 Misc 2d 1069, 343 NYS2d 774.

Under CPLR § 7502, subdivision a, it was not necessary for jurisdictional purposes to bring a special proceeding with service of petition for order confirming arbitration award in the same manner as service of summons pursuant to CPLR § 403, subdivision c, and thus service of petition by mail was sufficient, where a pending court action had been stayed pursuant to CPLR § 7503, but not continued, pending outcome of arbitration. A & R Constr. Co. v Gorlin-Okun, Inc. (1973) 41 AD2d 876, 342 NYS2d 950.

Although State Tax Commission is a commission having a chairman, personal service of petition to annul determination of Commission was not mandatory, and proper service upon any one of the members of the Commission was sufficient. Harlem River Consumers Cooperative, Inc. v State Tax Com. (1974) 44 AD2d 738, 354 NYS2d 472, affd 37 NY2d 877, 378 NYS2d 363, 340 NE2d 730.

In absence of order authorizing service in a manner other than provided for by rule relating to manner of service of notice of petition, service of notice of petition and petition to annul determination of State Tax Commission by mail on the Commission was insufficient to confer jurisdiction over that body. Harlem River Consumers Cooperative, Inc. v State Tax Com. (1974) 44 AD2d 738, 354 NYS2d 472, affd 37 NY2d 877, 378 NYS2d 363, 340 NE2d 730.

4. Order to show cause

Motion to dismiss petition was denied where, regardless of alleged infirmities in the manner of the service of the order to show cause, there was a showing of actual notice to defendant who, in fact, did appear at the court on the return day of the order to show cause. Caro v Jones (1973) 41 AD2d 829, 342 NYS2d 856.

An order signed on November 8, 1968 to show cause why a second arbitrator should not be appointed, which order was not precluded by the prior dismissal of a petition to stay arbitration on June 14, 1968, and which was properly and timely served upon respondent's attorney was sufficient to effect jurisdiction of respondent. Grant v Koppelman (1969) 59 Misc 2d 271, 298 NYS2d 329.

Service of an order to show cause must be made in the manner specified in the order as required by subd (d) of CPLR § 403, and noncompliance with the order in this respect precludes substantive consideration of the application. Graffagnino v Motor Vehicle Acci. Indemnification Corp. (1965) 48 Misc 2d 441, 264 NYS2d 483.

Attorney General's application for a preliminary injunction considered as one under § 211 of the Civil Service Law, and the trial court had jurisdiction to issue a temporary restraining order as ancillary to the action or proceeding thus instituted and subsequently validly commenced by the service of the order to show cause on defendants. State v Fuller (1968) 31 AD2d 71, 296 NYS2d 37.

Service upon attorney of respondent under rule of American Arbitration Association conferred jurisdiction upon court to vacate arbitrator's interim award and complied with notice provisions of order to show cause to extent that it mandated "personal service" and such service also satisfied requirements of due process. Board of Education v Half Hollow Hills Teachers Asso. (1974) 79 Misc 2d 223, 358 NYS2d 285.

CASE NOTES

UNDER FORMER CIVIL PRACTICE LAWS

A. SERVICE OF NOTICE OF PETITION AND ANSWER

I. IN GENERAL
1. Generally
2. Notice
3. Service
4. Waiver of defects and irregularities

II. DECISIONS UNDER RCP 21

a. COMMENCEMENT OF PROCEEDINGS
5. Generally
6. Injunction
7. Settlement of accounts
8. Invalidation of election designating petition
9. Review of tax assessment
10. Supplementary proceeding

b. SERVICE
11. Generally
12. Enforcement of attorney's lien
13. Injunction
14. Subpoena to attend pre-trial examination
15. Supplementary proceeding

B. ORDER TO SHOW CAUSE
16. Generally
17. Manner of service

A. SERVICE OF NOTICE OF PETITION AND ANSWER

I. IN GENERAL

1. Generally

The notice required by CPA § 1289 had no rela-

tion to an initial application for a writ of certiorari to review a village assessment under § 291 of the Tax Law. People ex rel. Lehigh Valley R. Co. v Clover (1940) 174 Misc 44, 19 NYS2d 865.

Successful bidder, added as necessary party to proceeding to annul resolution of town board awarding public contract and to direct award to lowest bidder, was granted rehearing de novo after service upon him of written notice and copy of petition and supporting papers. Re Cestone Bros. (1950) 276 AD 970, 95 NYS2d 172.

New York City Administrative Code, providing for review of determination of New York City Board of Standards and Appeals, where not specific in its procedural directions, was supplemented by CPA §§ 1288 and 1289 and so petition, in respect of verification, was substantially in same situation as complaint, answer or reply in action. Re Smith (1956) 2 AD2d 67, 153 NYS2d 131.

CPA Article 78 proceeding was duly presented at Special Term within 30-day period, as required by New York City Administrative Code provision governing proceedings against Board of Standards and Appeals, when within that period notice of motion and petition were served, filed, and placed on the calendar, even though return day was beyond the 30-day period. Satin v Board of Standards & Appeals (1960) 12 AD2d 526, 208 NYS2d 518.

2. Notice

Where proceeding brought to review restraint of respondent by board of parole and denial of parole, although permissible, an order to show cause is not necessary to commence such a proceeding. And where there appears in the papers no reason for resorting to order to show cause rather than usual notice, Special Term's denial of ex parte application justified. Harris v New York State Board of Parole (1958) 7 AD2d 662, 179 NYS2d 378.

See Beary v Queens County Bar Asso. (1960) 25 Misc 2d 794, 207 NYS2d 324, where an order to show cause to strike out improper matter in a petition in an Article 78 proceeding was used, not to shorten the notice of motion, but so as to have order to show cause also provide that respondent's time to answer be extended in the event application were denied.

3. Service

Service as prescribed by CPA § 1289 may have been resorted to only where pertinent statute did not prescribe procedure for commencing review proceeding; service on town attorney, not a member of Zoning Board of Appeal, in violation of pertinent statute, was held insufficient. Pearl v Keller (1959) 20 Misc 2d 219, 191 NYS2d 44.

Service is effected and jurisdiction obtained by service of order to show cause. Levine v Lending (1941) 176 Misc 462, 26 NYS2d 775.

On prisoner's application for order to show cause to initiate proceeding to annul judgment of his conviction which could be commenced by notice of application, requiring his presence in court on return day, court denied preliminary orders where there was no merit to prisoner's application and no possibility of ultimate success. Re Cataldo (1942, Sup) 36 NYS2d 783.

Proceeding is instituted by service of petition and notice or order to show cause, and not by signing of such order. Brown v New York (1950) 198 Misc 147, 97 NYS2d 560.

Special proceeding is commenced by service of notice or order to show cause. Re Burge (1952) 203 Misc 677, 118 NYS2d 23, revd 282 AD 219, 122 NYS2d 232, affd 306 NY 811, 118 NE2d 822.

Service by petitioner seeking writ of prohibition was improper since he was a party to the proceeding. Schildhaus v Justices of Court of Special Sessions (1959) 16 Misc 2d 675, 184 NYS2d 366.

Failure to serve petition on objector to nominating petition as well as on election board is fatal to the proceeding. Dyte v Lawley (1959) 20 Misc 2d 988, 190 NYS2d 253.

4. Waiver of defects and irregularities

Where special term did not follow the requirements of CPA § 1289 which required at least eight days' notice in writing and the attorney for respondent corporation was also an officer of that corporation filed an affidavit in opposition to the petition on the merits, any defect on procedure was thus waived and was held to be binding on the corporation. Therefore, since an answering affidavit had already been interposed by respondents, there was no abuse of discretion by the

court in not granting them an adjournment because of actual engagement of another and different counsel. Dewar v Cigarette Service, Inc. (1958) 5 AD2d 764, 170 NYS2d 89.

II. Decisions Under RCP 21

a. Commencement of Proceedings

5. Generally

Issuance of process does not institute special proceeding. Kaplan v Meisser (1949) 196 Misc 6, 91 NYS2d 363.

Attorney for domestic corporation is not person who could receive service of process to commence special proceeding under CPA § 696 to determine title to property levied on under execution and claimed by such corporation, and filing by attorney on its behalf of notice of claim was not commencement of special proceeding thereafter initiated by petitioner. Skotak v Greenway B. Co. (1955) 285 AD 500, 138 NYS2d 215.

6. Injunction

Where wife after obtaining separation moved to enjoin nonresident husband from prosecuting Nevada action for divorce by order to show cause directing service by mail on his New York office and on his attorney in separation action, such service was insufficient. Long v Long (1949) 196 Misc 982, 94 NYS2d 83, affd 277 AD 1033, 100 NYS2d 713.

Application for injunctive relief under PL § 964, by service of copies of petition and notice of motion by ordinary mail, was insufficient; personal service of petition and notice of motion should have been made upon proper officer as provided in CPA § 229 (§§ 311(1), 3012(c), Rule 320(a) herein). International U. Corp. v International Mills, Inc. (1953, Sup) 121 NYS2d 211.

7. Settlement of accounts

In proceeding by trustee for judicial settlement of intermediate accounts Supreme Court obtains jurisdiction of parties by service of order to show cause in the manner provided for the personal service of summons. Hill v Hill (1924) 124 Misc 102, 207 NYS 705.

8. Invalidation of election designating petition

Proceeding under Election L § 330 to invalidate designating petition is instituted by service of process, and not by its mere issuance or signing of order to show cause. Re Tombini (1941) 177 Misc 148, 30 NYS2d 79, affd 262 AD 956, 30 NYS2d 106. See Gallagher v Cohen (1943) 180 Misc 1030, 46 NYS2d 333; Re Walker (1944, Sup) 50 NYS2d 277; Kram v Cohen (1944, Sup) 50 NYS2d 322.

Special proceeding is commenced by service of process, and not by issuance thereof. Dyte v Lawley (1959) 20 Misc 2d 988, 190 NYS2d 253.

9. Review of tax assessment

Certiorari to review tax assessment is commenced by service of writ upon city tax commission, and not by allowing writ. People ex rel. Northchester

Corp. v Miller (1942) 288 NY 163, 42 NE2d 469. Compare Cregg v Brown (1942) 263 AD 1056, 34 NYS2d 336.

10. Supplementary proceeding

Mere signature of order not commencement of supplementary proceedings. Dorfman v Jacobs (1917) 100 Misc 592, 166 NYS 403.

b. SERVICE

11. Generally

Service by party, see Losey v Stanley (1894) 83 Hun 420, 31 NYS 950, revd 147 NY 560, 42 NE 8.

No special provision has been made by law or rule for the manner of service of process in a special proceeding to determine the custody of an infant, and accordingly the provisions of CPA § 235 (§§ 313, 3012(c), Rule 320(a) herein) were applicable thereto. Re Kades (1960) 23 Misc 2d 222, 201 NYS2d 379, affd 10 AD2d 919, 202 NYS2d 792.

12. Enforcement of attorney's lien

The petition in a proceeding to enforce an attorney's lien must be served personally on the defendant. Entenberg v Goodman (1934) 153 Misc 205, 274 NYS 443, affd Fischel v Goodman (1934) 242 AD 825, 275 NYS 974.

Special proceeding by attorney to have his lien fixed must be commenced by personal service. Leis v Shaughnessy (1961, Sup) 219 NYS2d 104.

13. Injunction

An injunction to restrain picketing by defendant labor union will not be granted upon service of order and papers on one who was not and never had been an officer of defendant within § 13 of the General Associations Law. Salitra v Borson (1926) 127 Misc 173, 215 NYS 332.

14. Subpoena to attend pre-trial examination

Subpoena to attend examination held by referee before trial may be served by party to proceeding. Everdyke v Adler (1941) 176 Misc 283, 27 NYS2d 159.

15. Supplementary proceeding

An order for the examination of a third party in proceedings supplementary to execution may not be served by the judgment creditor. Re Dawes (1905) 108 AD 174, 96 NYS 52.

Service of an order for examination of a foreign corporation, licensed in this state, in supplementary proceedings, must be made upon an officer of the corporation. See Meyer v Consolidated Ice Co. 132 AD 265, 116 NYS 906, affd 196 NY 471, 90 NE 54. Mednicoff v Lashing (1929) 135 Misc 485, 237 NYS 695.

B. ORDER TO SHOW CAUSE

16. Generally

Where both corpus of trust and named trustee were outside state, fact that settlor was and is resident did not confer on New York court jurisdiction over subject matter in proceeding to appoint successor trustee of inter vivos trust. Re Saddy (1954, Sup) 129 NYS2d 163.

CPA § 1309 required court to prescribe time and place when order should be returnable, and granted discretion as to manner of service. Re Blake (1955) 208 Misc 22, 141 NYS2d 194.

Since CPA § 1309 required that only representatives of a class of contingent remaindermen be served in an accounting proceeding, while the Surrogate's Court Act required more extensive service, the Supreme Court had to exercise concurrent jurisdiction over testamentary trusts where there were contingent remaindermen. Re Bliss' Will (1957) 9 Misc 2d 596, 164 NYS2d 664.

17. Manner of service

Where court authorized mail service of order to show cause in inter-vivos trust accounting proceeding, only question which might be raised under CPA § 1309 was one concerning reasonableness of directions made by court in its discretion under such statute; if direction for service, including mail service, was reasonable, fact that vendee did not receive mailed notice did not deprive court of jurisdiction. Re Edwards' Trust (1955, Sup) 142 NYS2d 169.

FORMS

Form 1—Notice of petition

Form 2—Order to show cause

Form 1

Notice of Petition

Notice of Application

[Title of court and proceeding]   Index No. __1__ [if assigned]

Please take notice that on the petition of __2_____, verified __3_____, 19_4_, and the affidavit [if any] of __5_____, sworn to __6_____, 19_7_, and __8_____ [recite any further written proof in support of petition], copies of all of which are herewith served on you, an application will be made at __9_____ [continue as in ordinary form of notice of motion], for a judgment that __10_____ [state nature of relief sought as in petition] and for such other and further relief as may be just.

[Date.]

__11_____
Attorney for Petitioner
Address __12_____
Telephone No. __13__

To __14_____ [name and official designation of respondent].

Form 2

Order to Show Cause

[Title of court and proceeding   Order to Show Cause
as in Form 1 under CPLR 402.]   Index No. __1__ [if assigned]

Present: Hon. __2_____, Justice.

On reading the petition of __3_____, verified __4_____, 19_5_, and the affidavit of __6_____, sworn to __7_____, 19_8_, and __9_____ [recite any further written proof in support of the petition], copies of which are herewith served on you, let the respondent or his attorney show cause at __10_____ [continue as in form of ordinary order to show cause] why a judgment should not be entered herein for __11_____ [state relief sought as in petition] and for such other and further relief as may be just.

[Add stay of proceedings and directions as to service of copy of order, as in Form 18 under CPLR 511 substituting word "petitioner" for word "plaintiff".]

Signed this __12__ day of __13_____, 19_14_ at __15_____, New York.

[Signature]
[Print signer's name below signature]
Justice, Supreme Court
__16_____ County

§ 404. Objections in point of law

(a) By respondent. The respondent may raise an objection in point of law by setting it forth in his answer or by a motion to dismiss the petition, made upon notice within the time allowed for answer. If the motion is denied, the court may permit the respondent to answer, upon such terms as may be just; and unless the order specifies otherwise, such answer shall be served and filed within five days after service of the order with notice of entry. The petitioner may re-notice the matter for hearing upon two days' notice.

(b) By petitioner. The petitioner may raise an objection in point of law to new matter contained in the answer by setting it forth in his reply or by moving to strike such matter on the day the petition is noticed or re-noticed to be heard.

HISTORY:

Add, L 1962, ch 308, eff Sept 1, 1963.
Earlier statutes: CPA § 1293.

ADVISORY COMMITTEE NOTES:

Subd (a). This section is patterned upon CPA § 1293 in the CPA article governing proceedings against a body or officer; the section makes it applicable to special proceedings generally. It includes the 1959 amendments proposed by the New York State Bar Association Committee on Administrative Law. NY Laws 1959, c 364. No change in meaning is intended but the language has been conformed to the terminology of the new CPLR. For example, the time limitation of the first sentence of subd (a) is the same as in CPA § 1293 since a motion on notice is "made" when notice of the motion is served.

The section provides a method of summary disposition of the proceeding analogous to the motions to dismiss and for summary judgment that are available in actions. It provides special short time limitations, however, which are particularly suited to the expeditious handling of special proceedings.

In subd (b), corresponding to the last paragraph of CPA § 1293, the words "a defense" are omitted since under the proposed rules the answer may contain, and the motion may be directed toward, a counterclaim as well as a defense. The words "on the face thereof" are also omitted, in accordance with the general policy against testing legal sufficiency on the basis of pleadings alone.

CROSS REFERENCES:

Objections in point of law in a proceeding against a body or officer, CPLR 7804(f).

FEDERAL ASPECTS:

Evidence, Rule 43 of Federal Rules of Civil Procedure, USCS Court Rules.

RESEARCH REFERENCES AND PRACTICE AIDS:

5 Carmody-Wait 2d, The Answer § 30:45.

6 Carmody-Wait 2d, Reply §§ 32:1, 32:23.

6 Carmody-Wait 2d, Motions Addresses to Pleadings § 37:40.

6 Carmody-Wait 2d, Pretrial Motions to Dismiss §§ 38:46–38:48.

14 Carmody-Wait 2d, Summary Proceedings to Recover Possession of Real Property §§ 90:235, 90:259.

24 Carmody-Wait 2d, Proceeding Against a Body or Officer § 145:314.

25 Carmody-Wait 2d, Fundamentals of Practice in the Surrogate's Court §§ 149:201, 149:223.

Forms:

See "FORMS" heading following "CASE NOTES", infra.

CASE NOTES

Where attorneys sought to obtain the value of their services by motion procedure when the primary action was concluded by a judgment of the Court of Appeals, the Supreme Court lacked personal jurisdiction to entertain such a motion. Kreindler v Irving Trust Co. (1969) 60 Misc 2d 441, 303 NYS2d 421.

Where the petitioners alleged that the State Liquor Authority had issued package store licenses without making the necessary determination that public convenience and advantage would thereby be served, the authority's motion to dismiss, pursuant to CPLR 404, was denied, and the authority's contention that the Alcoholic Beverage Control Law did not authorize the instant proceeding and that pursuant to § 2, and § 121 of that law, the action of the authority was not subject to review was rejected. Kaplan v State Liquor Authority (1965) 47 Misc 2d 257, 262 NYS2d 254.

Where the defendant moved to compel arbitration in an action already pending, rather than having commenced a special proceeding, CPLR 404 was not applicable. Olsen & Chapman Constr. Co. v Cazenovia (1970) 33 AD2d 929, 306 NYS2d 560.

Where a settlor's objection in point of law to a petition by the trustee for a determination that the trustee's consent was required in order to revoke the trust had been rejected by the court, there was no merit in his contention he had been denied the "right" to interpose an answer, since CPLR 404(a) provides that upon denial of a motion, the court may permit the respondent to answer. Special Term properly determined no useful purpose could be served by any answer. Re Dodge's Trust (1969) 25 NY2d 273, 303 NYS2d 847, 250 NE2d 849.

Granting an adjournment on the return day of notice of petition waives untimely service of motion to dismiss. Katz v Board of Appeals (1964) 21 AD2d 693, 250 NYS2d 469.

A petition in an Art 78 proceeding which sets forth a triable issue of fact, the resolution of which in petitioners' favor would leave no rational basis for the administrative decision complained of, should not be dismissed under subd (a) of CPLR § 404 or subd (f) of CPLR § 7804. Genesee Bus Service, Inc. v Board of Education (1965) 23 AD2d 624, 257 NYS2d 501.

Objection to the jurisdiction of the court to question certain acts of the state liquor authority may be raised under subd (b) of this section. J. R.

Liquors, Inc. v State Liquor Authority (1965) 46 Misc 2d 867, 261 NYS2d 93, affd 25 AD2d 819, 269 NYS2d 933.

A procedure to enforce a shareholder's right to receive payment for her shares is conditioned upon the shareholder's adherence to the time requirements of the statute. However, equity requires that the court have some discretion to waive absolute compliance where special circumstances justify such determination. Davis v Adirondack Industries, Inc. (1970) 33 AD2d 1100, 308 NYS2d 107.

In proceeding by Attorney General for injunctive and other relief against two corporations and several individuals, given pro se nature of individual defendant's appearance and the request that individual defendant be directed to answer within five days of denial of his dismissal motion, circumstances demanded that defendant be made aware of possibility of a summary disposition by trial court, and summary judgment against defendant was reversed with leave for him to answer. Lefkowitz v Therapeutic Hypnosis, Inc. (1976) 52 AD2d 1017, 383 NYS2d 868, later app 57 AD2d 979, 394 NYS2d 107.

FORMS

Form 1—Notice of motion to dismiss petition raising objection in point of law

Form 2—Order dismissing petition on objections thereto in point of law

Form 3—Another form of order based on motion to dismiss petition

Form 4—Order denying motion to dismiss petition on objection thereto in point of law

Form 1

Notice of Motion to Dismiss Petition Raising Objection in Point of Law

Notice of Motion

[Title of court and proceeding]   Index No. __1__ [if assigned]

Please take notice that on the petition herein, [if not based on defects appearing on face of petition, add reference to affidavit in support of motion], on the return day of this proceeding, at a motion term [Part __2__] of this court to be held in and for the County of __3_____ at the county court house in the City of __4_____, on the __5__ day of __6_____, 19_7_, at __8__ o'clock in the __9_____ noon of that day, or as soon thereafter as counsel can be heard, respondent will apply to this court for a judgment dismissing the petition herein on the ground that __10_____ [state grounds for dismissed], pursuant to section 404 of the Civil Practice Law and Rules, and for such other and further relief as may be just.

__11_____

Attorney for Respondent

Address __12_____

Telephone No. __13__

[Date.]

To __14_____, Attorney for Petitioner

Address __15_____

Form 2

Order Dismissing Petition on Objections Thereto in Point of Law

Supreme Court, __1_____ County.

Order

[Title of proceeding]   Index No. __2__

Present: Hon. __3_____, Justice.

Petitioner herein having presented a petition, verified __4_____, 19_5_, praying for __6_____ [state relief demanded], and the respondent above named having filed and served upon petitioner on __7_____, 19_8_, a notice of motion to dismiss the petition as a matter of law on the ground that __9_____, and after hearing __10_____, attorney for respondent, in support of this application to dismiss the petition herein, pursuant to Civil Practice Law and Rules 404, and __11_____, attorney for petitioner, in opposition thereto,

Now, on motion of __12_____, attorney for respondent, and after reading and filing __13_____ [recite motion papers], it is

Ordered, that this proceeding be dismissed [with leave to petitioner to renew said application if he be so advised, on condition that __14_____], and that judgment be entered accordingly.

Signed this __15__ day of __16_____, 19_17_, at __18_____, New York.

Enter

__19_____

[Signature, with name
printed underneath]
Justice, Supreme Court
__20_____County

[Name and address of attorney or party serving or filing order]

[Certification and notice of entry]

Form 3

Another Form of Order Based on Motion to Dismiss Petition

Supreme Court, __1_____ County.

Order

[Title of proceeding]   Index No. __2__

Present: Hon. __3_____, Justice.

The respondent above named having duly moved for an order dismissing the petition in the above-entitled proceeding, under Civil Practice Law and Rules 404, on the ground that [state grounds specified in the notice of motion].

Now on reading and filing the notice of motion dated the __4__ day of __5_____, 19_6_, with due proof of service thereof on the attorney for petitioner, and the petition herein, verified the __7__ day of __8_____, 19_9_, and after hearing __10_____, attorney for respondent, in favor of said motion, and __11_____, attorney for petitioner in opposition thereto, and due deliberation having been had,

Now, on motion of __12_____, attorney for respondent, and on the decision filed herein it is hereby

Ordered, that said motion be and the same hereby is granted, and that the petition herein be dismissed with costs to respondent and __13_____ dollars costs of this motion [upon condition, however, that within twenty days after the service of a copy of this order with notice of entry thereof on petitioner's attorney, petitioner may serve an amended petition, upon payment of ten dollars costs, and upon the failure of petitioner to pay said costs and serve said amended petition within said time, the order dismissing the petition shall become absolute and judgment shall be entered dismissing the petition with the costs of the action and __14_____ dollars costs of this motion].

Signed this __15__ day of __16_____, 19_17_, at __18_____ New York.

Enter

__19_____

[Signature, with name
printed underneath]
Justice, Supreme Court
__20_____ County

[Name and address of attorney or party serving or filing order]

[Certification and notice of entry]

21

Form 4

Order Denying Motion to Dismiss Petition on Objection Thereto in Point of Law

Supreme Court, __1_____ County.

Order

[Title of proceeding]   Index No. __2__

Present: Hon. __3_____, Justice.

Petitioner herein having presented a petition, verified on the __4__ day of __5_____, 19_6_, praying for __7_____ [state relief demanded], and the respondent above-named having filed and served upon petitioner, on the __8__ day of __9_____, 19_10_, a notice of motion to dismiss the petition as a matter of law on the ground that __11_____, and after hearing __12_____, attorney for respondent in support of said motion to dismiss the petition herein, pursuant to Civil Practice Law and Rules 404, and __13_____, attorney for petitioner, in opposition thereto,

Now, on motion of __14_____, attorney for petitioner, and after reading and filing __15_____ [recite motion papers], it is

Ordered, that the motion of the respondent to dismiss the petition as a matter of law be, and the same is hereby, denied, and it is further

[Ordered, that __16_____ shall serve and file his answer herein within __17__ days after service of this order, with notice of entry thereof.]

Signed this __18__ day of __19_____, 19_20_ at __21_____, New York.

Enter

__22_____

[Signature, with name
printed underneath]
Justice, Supreme Court
__23_____ County

[Name and address of attorney or party serving or filing order]

[Certification and notice of entry]

§ 405. Correction of defects in papers

(a) Motion to correct. Either party may move to cure a defect or omission in the record, or to strike scandalous or prejudicial matter unnecessarily inserted in a pleading, or for a more definite statement of a pleading which is so vague or ambiguous that he cannot reasonably be required to frame a response.

(b) Time limits; pleading after disposition. A party shall make a motion under this section by serving a notice of motion or order to show cause within the time allowed for his responsive pleading. Unless the court so orders on motion made without notice on the ground that the party is unable to plead until the papers are corrected, the motion shall not extend the time for such responsive pleading. If the motion is granted, the party who made the motion shall serve and file his responsive pleading within five days after service of the amended pleading. If the motion is denied and the time to serve a responsive pleading has been extended, the party shall serve and file his responsive pleading within two days after service of the order denying the motion with notice of entry, unless the order specifies otherwise. A party may re-notice the matter for hearing upon two days' notice.

(c) Petitioner's motion. The petitioner may raise the objections specified in subdivision (a) in his reply or by motion on the day on which the petition has been noticed or re-noticed to be heard.

HISTORY:

Add, L 1962, ch 308, eff Sept 1, 1963.
Earlier statutes: CPA § 1294.

ADVISORY COMMITTEE NOTES:

This section is based upon CPA § 1294, as amended in 1958 upon recommendation of the New York State Bar Association Committee on Administrative Law. NY Laws 1958, c 885. This section extends it to all special proceedings.

Subd (a) varies slightly from the first sentence of CPA § 1294. The statement of the defects in pleadings that may be reached by the motion has been conformed to that in new CPLA rule 3024, governing motions to correct pleadings in an action. Thus, it does not allow a motion to strike irrelevant, immaterial or redundant matter unless such matter is also prejudicial; and it states more clearly than CPA § 1294 that the motion may be used to correct a vague or ambiguous pleading. Since the motion may also be based upon a "defect or omission in the record" there is no need to retain CPA § 112. Section 112 is a holdover from the pre-article 78 proceedings to review the determination of a body or officer. In the Throop Code it appeared, together with the other provisions relating to certiorari to review, as § 2124; at that time it authorized an appellate court reviewing the determination of a body or officer. In the Throop Code it appeared, together with the other provisions relating to certiorari to review, as § 2124; at that time it authorized an appellate court reviewing the determination of a body or officer to issue a writ of certiorari requiring the body or officer to supply any "diminution, variance, or other defect, in the record or other papers." The authors of the CPA substituted the use of an ordinary order for the same purpose and removed the section to its position in the article governing "Mistakes, Defects and Irregularities," while the rest of the provisions governing certiorari, mandamus and prohibition were placed in former articles 78–80. See Report of the Joint Legislative Committee on the Simplification of Civil Practice 111 (1919). The 1937 revision which produced CPA article 78 took no account of § 112. See 3 NY Jud Council Rep 129-98 (1937). According to Throop's note the section served a purpose analogous to that of the provision permitting a respondent in an ordinary appeal to transmit the papers to the appellate court, if the appellant failed to do so, and tax the expense thereof as disbursements. See NY Code Civ Proc § 2124, note (Throop ed 1880); id. § 1315; cf. CPA § 607-d. Apart from the question of costs, there is no problem of "diminution, variance, or other defect" under former appeals practice or new CPLR article 55, since both parties have equal access to the papers and there is ample provision for settlement of a transcript of the proceedings below.

Subds (b) and (c) are taken from the 1958 additions to CPA § 1294 with only minor verbal changes. Like the 1959 amendments to CPA § 1293, they insure expeditious handling of the motion and the committee has extended them to special proceedings generally. **Subd (b)** has been reworded to reflect the fact that a motion may be made by either party. Time to serve and file a responsive pleading, if the motion is denied and the party's time to serve such pleading has been extended, has been shortened from five to two days.

FEDERAL ASPECTS:

Amendment of pleadings to show jurisdiction, 28 USCS § 1653.
Pleadings and motions, generally, Rules 7 through 16 of Federal Rules of Civil Procedure, USCS Court Rules.
Amended and supplemental pleadings, Rule 15 of Federal Rules of Civil Procedure, USCS Court Rules.
Motion day in Federal District Courts, Rule 78 of Federal Rules of Civil Procedure, USCS Court Rules.

RESEARCH REFERENCES AND PRACTICE AIDS:

5 Carmody-Wait 2d, The Answer § 30:4.

6 Carmody-Wait 2d, Reply § 32:22.

6 Carmody-Wait 2d, Motions Addressed to Pleadings §§ 37:2, 37:3, 37:40, 37:41.

14 Carmody-Wait 2d, Summary Proceedings to Recover Possession of Real Property § 90:259.

25 Carmody-Wait 2d, Fundamentals of Practice in the Surrogate's Court §§ 149:200, 149:201.

Law Reviews:

Parties and pleading under the CPLR. 31 Brooklyn L Rev 98.

CASE NOTES

Where the allegations of a petition sufficiently advised the respondent that the proceeding was against him in his official capacity, and there was no indication that he would be prejudiced by an amendment of the title of the proceeding, petitioner's motion for an order correcting the caption of the proceeding by adding to the name of the respondent the words "as Commissioner of the Department of Public Welfare of the County of Albany" was granted. Albany Medical Center Hospital v Breslin (1965) 47 Misc 2d 208, 262 NYS2d 285.

CASE NOTES

UNDER FORMER CIVIL PRACTICE LAWS

1. Generally
2. Amendments
3. Striking out matter
4. Extension of time to answer

1. Generally

CPA § 1294 cited generally in Re Crown Heights Hospital (1944) 183 Misc 563, 49 NYS2d 658.

2. Amendments

Absence of pleadings, such as petition, answer and reply, cannot be supplied, where proceeding was attempted to be commenced by affidavit. Levine v Lending (1941) 176 Misc 462, 26 NYS2d 775.

Amendment of petition must be made on notice to all parties, including intervenors, though original parties stipulated against amendment. Tru-matic Mach. & Tool Co. v Bantz (1949) 196 Misc 82, 91 NYS2d 414.

Caption of proceeding on behalf of "herself and 26 other petitioners" was amended to read "29 other petitioners". Cashman v Conway (1951) 106 NYS2d 668.

Where petition was verified in manner in which certificate of acknowledgment would be executed, such defect may be cured by substitution, nunc pro tunc, of corrected verification in place of defective one. Re Dairymen's League Co-op Asso. (1952) 201 Misc 354, 109 NYS2d 867, affd 282 AD 69, 121 NYS2d 857.

Where title and body of petition against town zoning board of appeals clearly indicates that it is made on behalf of corporate owners by owners of development, such petition may be amended to state that it is made by such owners. Lake Mohopac Heights, Inc. v Zoning Board of Appeals (1952, Sup) 119 NYS2d 809.

Where petition to review determination of zoning board failed to allege that officials suing were authorized to do so in their official capacity, petition was insufficient as matter of law, but amendment was allowed to supply such allegation. Fox v Adams (1954) 206 Misc 236, 132 NYS2d 560.

In proceeding to annul revocation of building permit, commissioner of public works was allowed to extend his time to answer where papers raised issue whether petitioner's failure to proceed with construction was due to wilful delay in issuing permit. Claremont Gardens v Barker (1953) 282 AD 1069, 126 NYS2d 640.

In proceeding to reverse determination of town board denying zone change, petitioner's claim that statement of town clerk as to filing of decision in his office was not sworn to could have been met and corrected by court under CPA § 1294. Firestone v Oyster Bay (1954, Sup) 134 NYS2d 882.

Where attorney for petitioners submitted affidavit indicating that subsequent to dismissal of petitioners there was some demand for their reinstatement as exempt fireman and that respondent's final refusal to reinstate was within four months of date proceeding was instituted, they were permitted to amend petition and to plead any facts tending to show that proceeding was timely brought. McDermott v Johnson (1955) 1 Misc 2d 55, 145 NYS2d 247.

That notice of motion served following dismissal of original petition with leave to replead included a prayer for relief not contained in the original notice of motion was an irregularity not requiring dismissal of the notice. Bettman v Michaelis (1961) 27 Misc 2d 1008, 212 NYS2d 347.

Service of notice of motion, petition and affidavits, rather than simply an amended petition, following dismissal of original petition with leave to replead was an irregularity and did not warrant dismissal of the notice. Bettman v Michaelis, supra.

Prayer in notice of motion served following dismissal of original petition with leave to replead that proceeding be transferred to Appellate Division was surplusage not warranting dismissal of the notice. Bettman v Michaelis, supra.

3. Striking out matter

Where petition was neither plain nor concise as required by CPA § 1288 (§§ 403, 7804(a) herein) and it was impossible for respondent to prepare answer to it, court struck out entire petition with leave to plead anew. Berkon v Mahoney (1943) 180 Misc 610, 42 NYS2d 90.

Petitioner's motion to strike allegations of answer as immaterial should be denied unless immateriality is clear. Re Chanel (1947, Sup) 74 NYS2d 211.

An unresponsive answer to a demand for admission as to ratio of full value at which realty was assessed, will not be deemed to be an admission, but will be stricken with leave to file a proper answer. Re Putnam Theatrical Corp (1960) 11 AD2d 1090, 206 NYS2d 706.

Instead of answering as provided by CPA § 1291 (§ 7804(c) herein), respondent could have moved to correct petition under CPA § 1294. Beary v Queens County Bar Asso. (1960) 25 Misc 2d 794, 207 NYS2d 324.

4. Extension of time to answer

An order to show cause initiating an application to strike out improper matter in the petition may also include a provision extending respondent's time to answer, if motion be denied, and if based on attorney's affidavit that respondent cannot answer until the petition be corrected, will suffice to constitute the order extending respondent's time to answer contemplated by this section. Beary v Queens County Bar Asso. (1960) 25 Misc 2d 794, 207 NYS2d 324.

When motion is made to strike out improper matter in the petition, respondent's time to answer, in the event of denial of motion, can be extended by order on the ground that respondent is unable to answer until the petition is corrected, and an affidavit of merits is unnecessary, CPR 88 not being applicable to an Article 78 proceeding. Beary v Queens County Bar Asso., supra.

Rule 406. Motions

Motions in a special proceeding, made before the time at which the petition is noticed to be heard, shall be noticed to be heard at that time.

HISTORY:

Add as § 406, L 1962, ch 308, renumbered Rule 406, L 1962, ch 318, § 2, eff Sept 1, 1963.

ADVISORY COMMITTEE NOTES:

This rule shortens the time for notice of pre-hearing motions, so that they may be heard at the hearing on the petition. Otherwise, the general motion practice rules apply to special proceedings. Certain specific motions, however, are not adapted for use in special proceedings. There is no need, for example, for a motion for summary judgment, since, under new CPLR rule 409(b), the court must make a summary determination upon the pleadings and papers where it is possible to do so. This is the equivalent of a motion for summary judgment in an action.

FEDERAL ASPECTS:

Time for motions in United States District Courts, Rule 6(d) of Federal Rules of Civil Procedure, USCS Court Rules.

Pleadings and motions, generally, Rules 7 through 16 of Federal Rules of Civil Procedure, USCS Court Rules.

Motions and other papers in United States District Courts, Rule 7(b) of Federal Rules of Civil Procedure, USCS Court Rules.

Motion day in Federal District Courts, Rule 78 of Federal Rules of Civil Procedure, USCS Court Rules.

RESEARCH REFERENCES AND PRACTICE AIDS:

2 Carmody-Wait 2d, Motions, Petitions, and Orders § 8:1 et seq.

17 Carmody-Wait 2d, Proceeding for Disposition of Real Property of Infant or Incompetent § 106:17.

Law Reviews:
Motion practice under the CPLR. 9 NY L F 317.

§ 407. Severance

The court may at any time order a severance of a particular claim, counterclaim or cross-claim, or as to a particular party, and order that, as to such claim or party, the special proceeding continue as an action or as a separate special proceeding.

HISTORY:

Add, L 1962, ch 308, eff Sept 1, 1963.
Earlier statutes: CPA §§ 85, 96; CCP §§ 758, 817, 819, 1220; 2 RS 383, §§ 1, 36, 38.

ADVISORY COMMITTEE NOTES

Provisions as to joinder of claims, counterclaims and cross-claims, under former law applicable generally only to an action, are applicable under new CPLR § 103(b) to special proceedings. It is essential, therefore, that the court have broad powers of severance where the joinder or interposition of such claims would interfere with the summary nature of the special proceeding. The provisions of new CPLR §§ 603 and 1003 as to severance and separate trials provide appropriate power. This section gives the court the additional power to sever as to a claim or party and require the severed portion to proceed as an action or as a separate special proceeding. This power is especially important if two claims are governed by different statutes.

CROSS REFERENCES:

Definition of special proceeding, CPLR 105(b).
Severance and separate trials generally, CPLR 603.

FEDERAL ASPECTS:

Consolidation and separate trials in United States District Courts, Rule 42 of Federal Rules of Civil Procedure, USCS Court Rules.

RESEARCH REFERENCES AND PRACTICE AIDS:

9 NY Jur, Contempt § 35.
14 NY Jur (Rev ed), Damages §§ 26, 32.
24 NY Jur, Fraud and Deceit § 229.
3 Carmody-Wait 2d, Severance of Actions §§ 18:1, 18:3.
5 Carmody-Wait 2d, The Answer § 30:78.
21 Carmody-Wait 2d, Actions Against Persons Jointly Liable § 123:22.
25 Carmody-Wait 2d, Fundamentals of Practice in the Surrogate's Court § 149:327.
1 Am Jur Pl and Pr Forms (Rev ed), Actions, Forms 41 et seq.

CASE NOTES

Where counterclaim has nothing whatever to do with the issue of whether the landlord is entitled to the immediate possession of his property, the court should sever the counterclaim from the proceeding. Great Park Corp. v Goldberger (1964) 41 Misc 2d 988, 246 NYS2d 810.

The defendant's counterclaims for conversion of underground gas and trespass to land in an action to condemn underground storage space beneath defendant's land could and should be severed. Home Gas Co. v Banach (1966) 26 AD2d 758, 272 NYS2d 183.

It was an abuse of discretion to deny a landlord's motion to sever a counterclaim for personal injuries from the landlord's nonpayment summary proceedings. Tankoos-Yarmon Hotels, Inc. v Smith (1968) 58 Misc 2d 1072, 299 NYS2d 937.

Village trustee's counterclaim, in Article 78 proceeding, predicated on alleged encroachment on public highway by gasoline pumps was properly removed from Article 78 proceeding reviewing village board's determination, but counterclaim should have been severed rather than dismissed.

Nodine v Board of Trustees (1974) 44 AD2d 764, 354 NYS2d 248.

Counterclaim interposed by defendant in a proceeding pending in the Justice Court severed where it appeared that the defendant did not intend to waive its claim of any amount in excess of $1,000 as it had an action pending thereon in the Supreme Court. Harlee-Mitchell Camp Corp. v Granite Lake Camp, Inc. (1970) 35 AD2d 551, 313 NYS2d 184.

CASE NOTES

UNDER FORMER CIVIL PRACTICE LAWS

1. Generally
2. Severance after proper consolidation
3. Remedy for improper joinder
4. Severance of causes, not issues
5. Action for different causes
6. Contract and negligence
7. Tort action and equity action
8. Installment contract
9. No defense to one cause of action
10. Land contract
11. Insurance
12. Partnership
13. Damage caused by all defendants
14. Effect of reversal of order of dismissal
15. Severance on appellate review
16. Court of Claims, actions in
17. Tax assessments, proceedings to review

1. Generally

Court should not hesitate to sever issues or grant separate trials when by doing so it expedites the findings embraced in the controversy. Gould v Gould (1924) 124 Misc 240, 207 NYS 137.

The purpose of this statute is to eliminate technicalities, multiplicities of action and delays and to protect substantial rights. Datz v Economy Cotton Goods Stores, Inc. (1934) 263 NY 252, 188 NE 728.

The liberal provisions of the statute are not to be limited by strict or literal construction, or by reason of mechanical difficulties. Its purpose is to commit to the courts a wide discretion in the administration of litigated business. Uterhart v National Bank of Far Rockaway (1938) 255 AD 859, 7 NYS2d 507.

The effect of CPA § 96, especially when read with CPA § 258 (§§ 601, 603, Rule 3014 herein), was to liberalize practice as much as possible and to remove technical restrictions upon administration of justice. Wegner Canning Corp. v Wegner (1942, Sup) 33 NYS2d 443.

Divergent decision in each separate case is prevented. Philip Shlansky & Bro. Inc. v Grossman (1948) 273 AD 544, 78 NYS2d 127.

Power of court to sever actions must be administered in accord with policy of law to avoid rather than to encourage multiplicity of actions; and so sound judicial discretion requires that such power should not be exercised unless failure to sever will place some substantial right in jeopardy. C. W. Lauman & Co. v State (1956) 2 Misc 2d 693, 153 NYS2d 813.

Severance cannot be had without prejudicing a substantial right where the defendant's counterclaims are so united with the action that they would exceed and defeat the plaintiff's demand, if proved. Dietz v Glynne (1927) 221 AD 329, 223 NYS 221.

Where a sum larger than plaintiff's claim was demanded by counterclaim it was error to grant plaintiff a partial summary judgment and sever the action, with a proviso that the judgment should be subject to any judgment recovered on the counterclaim. Aetna Life Ins. Co. v National Dry Dock & Repair Co. (1930) 230 AD 486, 245 NYS 365.

Where plaintiff seeks recovery in amount in excess of amount of defendant's counterclaim, it would prejudice plaintiff to deny him opportunity, in event of ultimate success, to deduct amount which defendant recovers. Lipman v New York Herald Tribune (1952, Sup) 114 NYS2d 7.

Severance of action held not prejudicial to rights of parties. Prescott v Guibord (1932) 236 AD 170, 258 NYS 133.

Where issue appears to be single, intergrated controversy, which should be disposed of at one time, and in one action, severance is improper. Lipman v New York Herald Tribune (1952, Sup) 114 NYS2d 7.

Where plaintiff's application for a severance is unduly delayed, it will be granted only on condition that he pay the costs of the action to date. McGowan v 147 W. 105th St. (1949) 95 NYS2d 94.

CPA § 85 was not confined to cases where the contract liability was in terms several as well as joint, the matter of several liability was only referred to in the section in connection with a severance of the action. First Nat. Bank v Lenk (1890, Sup) 10 NYS 261, affd 123 NY 638, 25 NE 953.

Where one of the parties, upon a cause of action which is both joint and several, dies pending suit, it is discretionary with the court whether, after reviving the action against the personal representative of the decedent, it orders a severance of the action. Hobart v Peck (1888, Sup) 1 NYS 623. And see Union Bank v Mott (1863) 27 NY 633; Arthur v Griswold (1874) 2 Hun 606, affd 60 NY 143; Pierson v Morgan (1889, Sup) 4 NYS 898, affd 121 NY 705, 24 NE 1100.

In death action for negligence where codefendant dies before trial, action should be severed against deceased defendant, or administrator substituted as party defendant. Wanamaker v Springstead (1948) 274 AD 1008, 85 NYS2d 27.

Severance will be denied where it is not established that the prejudice to defendant would outweigh the convenience of disposing of all issues in one trial. Kidder, Peabody & Co. v Loewe (1961) 12 AD2d 917, 210 NYS2d 553.

In an action by plaintiff to recover attorney fees paid out to defend against a chattel mortgage alleged to have been placed on goods bought from defendant, by the latter, plaintiff's complaint was dismissed on proof there was no chattel mortgage, and the defendant's counterclaim for the value of the goods was severed and a new trial granted thereon and the reply thereto. Allen v Hurum (1927) 220 AD 273, 221 NYS 171.

In a condemnation proceeding to acquire certain parcels for water front improvement, wherein it was necessary to prove title in numerous claimants as well as the damages sustained by them, and it appeared that two of the claimants claimed title to all of the property in the condemnation area under an early grant, held that the court properly severed the proceeding as to the grant and first took up the determination of its validity and extent. Re New York (1923) 237 NY 275, 142 NE 662.

If the complaint makes a release of liability an integral part of the action, the validity thereof should not be tried separately from the question of liability itself. Willett v Chase Nat. Bank (1926) 219 AD 41, 219 NYS 289.

Where defendant raises the objection that two causes of actions have been improperly joined in one complaint, the court cannot, before ruling upon the objection, permit the plaintiff to sever the actions and serve an amended complaint, even though his time to amend as of course had not expired. Neun v B. H. Bacon Co. (1910) 137 AD 397, 121 NYS 718.

In action by landlord against tenants to compel removal of television aerials, action was severed as to tenants who defaulted in answering and in appearing for trial. West Holding Corp. v Cordero (1952, Sup) 114 NYS2d 668.

Action by passenger of city bus against city and bus driver was severed from action by passenger against owners of other two colliding cars. Goldstein v New York (1952) 281 AD 712, 118 NYS2d 48.

In action against cab driver and company for injuries due to his negligence, where driver defaulted, granting of proposed severance so that plaintiff may immediately proceed to take inquest and default judgment against cab driver and then sue cab owner and insurer would prejudice substantial right of defendant and its insurer. Frenkel v Kress Taxi, Inc. (1955) 208 Misc 374, 144 NYS2d 413.

In action on written contract for services in burying relative of two of three defendants, where court granted summary judgment against such two defendants, action was severed as to them. Kearns v Ceretta (1955, Sup) 139 NYS2d 3.

Where factual issues to be tried in third-party action and main action are practically same, it was advisable that there be one rather than two separate trials, possibly with inconsistent results, despite possible delay arising from lack of severance. A/S Grindstedvaerket v European C. Co. (1956) 2 AD2d 672, 152 NYS2d 797.

The convenience of one trial does not overcome the prejudice that may result to two defendants and the confusion which the jury will encounter in trying to determine the extent of injuries attributable to each and compensation therefor, where plaintiff's injuries were aggravated in a second accident. Pride v Perras (1958) 6 AD2d 842, 176 NYS2d 573.

Plaintiff's personal injury action against driver of automobile which struck him could not be consolidated with his personal injury action against owners and operators of ambulance and truck which collided while he was being taken to the hospital in the ambulance after the first accident. Abbatepaolo v Blumberg (1959) 7 AD2d 847, 182 NYS2d 83.

Severance was denied where though the wrongful acts of the two defendants were not precisely concurrent in point of time, they might nevertheless be joint tortfeasors where their several acts of neglect concurred in producing the injury. Misiano v Rosen (1960) 22 Misc 2d 289, 203 NYS2d 561.

Where personal injury action was brought against several joint tortfeasors, and plaintiff was held entitled to summary judgment against one but not all, the court granted summary judgment against the one, and to protect his rights of contribution denied severance, granted plaintiff a preference, and restricted such joint tortfeasors' participation in trial to issue of damages only. Sonnenthal v Hodes (1960) 11 AD2d 645, 201 NYS2d 547.

Where contract and tort liability arose out of a single transaction, severance of tort causes which would subject defendant to separate trials involving a single state of facts should not have been granted. Eugene J. Busher Co. v Galbreath-Ruffin Realty Co. (1962) 16 AD2d 750, 227 NYS2d 532.

2. Severance after proper consolidation

Actions having been properly consolidated, it is error to sever the actions and render judgment in one of the actions, less one of the counterclaims, leaving the action to proceed as to the balance. Colt v Davis (1888) 50 Hun 366, 3 NYS 354.

The fact that some parties were represented by different attorneys in their capacities as plaintiffs and defendants, does not warrant serverance of actions consolidated by outstanding order of court of co-ordinate jurisdiction. Olson v New York (1955) 285 AD 1155, 140 NYS2d 231.

3. Remedy for improper joinder

A complaint will not be dismissed for improperly joining causes of action, since other remedies are now furnished. New Amsterdam Casualty Co. v

Mobinco Brokerage Co. (1927) 219 AD 486, 220 NYS 340.

Plaintiff's claim that injuries received in first automobile accident were aggravated by second automobile accident which occurred 13 months later did not justify joinder of causes of action against different defendants based on respective accidents, and a severance will be ordered. Cipolla v La Franco (1960) 24 Misc 2d 30, 202 NYS2d 337.

4. Severance of causes, not issues

The severance contemplated by CPA § 96 was that of one or more causes of action from one or more other causes of action, or of claims by or against one or more parties from claims by or against one or more other parties, but the segregation from pleadings in a single cause of action of certain issues for trial in advance of other issues was governed by CPA § 443 (§ 603, Rule 4011 herein). New York v Interborough Rapid Transit Co. (1929) 134 Misc 827, 236 NYS 449.

Plaintiff's claim that injuries received in first automobile accident were aggravated by second automobile accident which occurred 13 months later did not justify joinder of causes of action against different defendants based on respective accidents, and a severance will be ordered. Cipolla v La Franco (1960) 24 Misc 2d 30, 202 NYS2d 337.

5. Action for different causes

Causes of action, stated in one complaint, by which a corporation seeks damages for interference with its business by an alleged combination in restraint of trade, and its president seeks damages to his reputation and financial standing, will be severed on defendant's motion. Gerseta Corp. v Silk Asso. of America (1927) 220 AD 302, 222 NYS 7.

Where complaint connects all defendants with all causes, severance was denied. Abelow v Chazen (1947, Sup) 75 NYS2d 128, affd 277 AD 973, 100 NYS2d 227.

Where plaintiff set up two causes of action in the same complaint, both for breaches of the same contract and provable by the same evidence, severance was improperly granted although one cause of action was for liquidated damages and the other for unliquidated damages, and the amounts recoverable were different. Posner v Rosenberg (1912) 153 AD 249, 137 NYS 1084.

Cause of action of infant bus passenger for injuries and father's action for loss of services, against bus company and colliding motorist, were severed from infant's cause of action for assault and battery and false imprisonment against bus company alone. Vuolo v North Shore Bus Co. (1943, Sup) 41 NYS2d 453.

Where parent's cause of action arose out of one accident and infant's cause arose out of another three months later, economy of time resulting from single trial, is overcome by danger of prejudice from joint trial of unrelated though similar accidents. McGowan v 147 W. 105th St. (1949) 95 NYS2d 94.

An action for several libels, alleged as separate causes of action, but for which one entire sum without apportionment is demanded as damages, was held severable under this section, after damages had been ascertained by a sheriff's jury as to one of the causes of action to which defendant had failed to answer over on the overruling of his demurrer thereto, so as to allow final judgment to be entered as to the cause of action demurred to, and the other causes of action to be proceeded on in a separate action. Stokes v Stokes (1894) 62 NYSR 39, 30 NYS 153.

Action for fraud and false arrest was severed. Murphy v Appelli (1948) 273 AD 261, 77 NYS2d 199.

Where claim for an accounting was improperly combined with claim for separation, which was ready for trial, and which involved only alimony, action was severed. Carr v Carr (1950) 277 AD 861, 97 NYS2d 900.

6. Contract and negligence

Where the complaint stated a cause of action sounding in contract for breach thereof and for unjustifiable deviation sounding in negligence, alleging liability in the alternative, motion to compel separation was granted. Winslow Bros. & Smith Co. v Grace S. S. Co. (1929) 133 Misc 902, 233 NYS 448.

7. Tort action and equity action

The severance of an action for tort and an equity action made it unnecessary to serve a second summons or amended complaints. Rosen v Goldstein (1931) 234 AD 872, 254 NYS 71.

8. Installment contract

When severance proper as to causes of action arising on instalments growing out of one contract. A. A. Levy Co. v Columbia Overseas Corp. (1922) 202 AD 674, 195 NYS 613.

9. No defense to one cause of action

Severance proper where there was no defense to the first cause of action and the defenses and counterclaims pertained to the second cause only. Bimberg v Rothenfeld (1931) 233 AD 861, 250 NYS 1010.

10. Land contract

In action for return of down payment on a land contract on the ground that mortgage provided for in the contract contained acceleration clause in violation of its terms, motion for summary judgment by severance was granted. Reich v Muss (1928) 132 Misc 699, 230 NYS 150.

11. Insurance

Where proceeds of an insurance policy were payable to surviving wife and children, and wife settled with insurer, action on the policy was severed. Killian v Metropolitan Life Ins. Co. (1929) 251 NY 44, 166 NE 798, 64 ALR 956.

In action based on a policy of life insurance, in

which the defendant insurer counterclaimed for the rescission of the policy, the defendant's motion for an order severing the issues and directing a separate and prior trial of the issues raised by the counterclaim and staying the trial of the issues raised by the complaint, was denied, even though the defendant stated that it was willing, if the relief asked was granted, to stipulate that in the event plaintiff prevailed at the trial, judgment could be entered against it for the proceeds of a policy as prayed for in the complaint. Schenck v Prudential Ins. Co. (1938) 167 Misc 282, 3 NYS2d 856.

Tort action by insured's wife for maliciously inducing breach of contract and action on insurance policy for proceeds brought by insured's brother, should not be consolidated. Cramer v Travelers Ins. Co. (1943) 180 Misc 464, 40 NYS2d 934.

Fact that one defendant insurer had made disability payments, while other defendant insurers had not, would prejudice jury against latter, entitling them to severance. Framer v Travelers Ins. Co. (1944) 181 Misc 661, 47 NYS2d 451.

Where a third party defendant insurance company would be subjected to some prejudice if both the main and third party actions were tried before the same jury and the severance would not injure any party, severance properly directed. Kelly v Yannotti (1958) 4 NY2d 603, 176 NYS2d 637, 152 NE2d 69, conformed to 6 AD2d 1046, 179 NYS2d 653.

Where terms of an insurance policy did not constitute a waiver barring a third party action under CPA section 193-a, a motion to dismiss third party complaint was denied and an application by the third party defendant for severance of trial was denied. Eastling v Federated Dept. Stores, Inc. (1958) 12 Misc 2d 795, 173 NYS2d 61.

Severance of third-party action against insurance company was denied where defendant-third-party plaintiff's consent to waive jury trial in the main action and plaintiffs' statement that they would not demand a jury trial had eliminated the possibility of prejudice to third-party defendant. Levine v Arthur Rosenbaum, Inc. (1958) 16 Misc 2d 980, 182 NYS2d 135.

In automobile personal injury negligence action where defendant impleads disclaiming insurance carrier, carrier is entitled to severance and separate trial, to avoid possible prejudice, even though jury because of compulsory insurance requirement in New York would be aware that there is insurance. Santonocito v Suburban Oil Co. (1961) 27 Misc 2d 697, 211 NYS2d 571.

Severance of third-party action against insurance carrier for defendant in primary action was granted because of probable and improper prejudice likely from disclosure of insurance coverage from name of third-party defendant to jury if the two actions were tried together. May v Heiney (1960) 26 Misc 2d 61, 207 NYS2d 828, revd conditionally on other grounds 15 AD2d 580, 223 NYS2d 73, affd 12 NY2d 683, 233 NYS2d 474, 185 NE2d 910.

12. Partnership

Action against copartners to recover for goods sold and delivered cannot be severed. Nathan v Zierler (1928) 223 AD 355, 228 NYS 170.

13. Damage caused by all defendants

It is error to direct a severance of a cause of action under a complaint which alleges that the damaged condition of goods was caused by the acts of all the defendants. Kalm v Westmoreland Glass Co. (1927) 129 Misc 238, 221 NYS 9.

14. Effect of reversal of order of dismissal

Order of severance and continuance against one defendant will not survive reversal of prior order and judgment whereunder the complaint was dismissed as to other defendants. Warshawsky v Ward (1931) 233 AD 390, 253 NYS 246.

15. Severance on appellate review

Where the verdict cannot be sustained as to one of two causes of actions combined in a complaint, but can be as to the other, the judgment will be affirmed as to the latter and the action will be severed to permit a new trial of the former cause of action. Ashmead v Sullivan (1921) 198 AD 885, 191 NYS 205.

Where the trial court directed a verdict for plaintiffs, and for defendant on his counterclaim, and the verdict on the counterclaim cannot be sustained, the action may be severed and judgment ordered for plaintiffs for the difference between the counterclaim and the verdict in their favor. Wrenn v Moskin (1932) 236 AD 226, 258 NYS 703, affd 262 NY 619, 188 NE 91.

Where actions by husband, wife and infant for injuries in automobile collision were consolidated and jury gave verdict for husband but was silent as to wife and infant, action was severed and wife and infant were granted new trial. Gross v Schlossberg (1941) 178 Misc 84, 32 NYS2d 180.

16. Court of Claims, actions in

Most frequent use of severance occurred as incident to summary judgment pursuant to RCP 113 and 114 (Rules 3212(a)–(f), 3212(e), 5012 herein), but since such Rules were not available to claimant in Court of Claims inasmuch as State was not required to answer, severance could not generally be used in Court of Claims as incident to utilization of RCP 113 and 114. (Rules 3212(a)–(f), 3212(e), 5012 herein). C. W. Lauman & Co. v State (1956) 2 Misc 2d 693, 153 NYS2d 813.

Where claimant in Court of Claims made no showing that failure to sever his two causes of action or claims against State will in any way prejudice any of his rights, and he in effect is actually seeking two trials instead of one and asking court in first trial to determine question which is essentially part of State's defense to first cause of action, and he made no showing as to why court should utilize two trials when all of questions can just as well be determined in one trial, or as to why all issues cannot be tried just as rapidly as first cause of action alone, severance was denied. Lauman & Co. v State, supra.

17. Tax assessments, proceedings to review

The provisions of CPA § 96 applied to severance of proceedings to review tax assessments, as well as to their consolidation. Allen v Rizzardi (1959) 5 NY2d 493, 186 NYS2d 225, 158 NE2d 813; O'Brien v Village Assessor of Larchmont (1962) 35 Misc 2d 204, 225 NYS2d 389.

§ 408. Disclosure

Leave of court shall be required for disclosure except for a notice under section 3123. A notice under section 3123 may be served at any time not later than three days before the petition is noticed to be heard and the statement denying or setting forth the reasons for failing to admit or deny shall be served not later than one day before the petition is noticed to be heard, unless the court orders otherwise on motion made without notice. This section shall not be applicable to proceedings in a surrogate's court, nor to proceedings relating to express trusts pursuant to article 77, both of which shall be governed by article 31.

HISTORY:

> Add as Rule 408, L 1962, ch 308, renumbered § 408, L 1962, ch 318, § 2, amd, L 1964, ch 477, L 1976, ch 193, eff Sept 1, 1976.

ADVISORY COMMITTEE NOTES:

> This section is contrary to former law. See CPA § 308; RCP 121. It is also contrary to the provisions covering actions in the new CPLR, which allow all disclosure to be obtained on notice. CPLR § 3102(b).
>
> The requirement of an order for disclosure is designed to preserve the summary nature of a special proceeding. To allow disclosure on notice before the hearing, even with the five-day notice provided for in RCP 121, would almost certainly extend the eight-day notice of petition period. Since a hearing always involves the possibility of a summary determination, the policy of new CPLR § 3214(b), staying disclosure upon service of a notice of motion for summary judgment, applies here. In the event that the court orders a trial, it could include a provision for disclosure in its order.
>
> The section excepts requests for admissions from the requirement of obtaining leave of court and provides a speedy procedure for utilizing such requests in special proceedings.

FEDERAL ASPECTS:

> Depositions, 28 USCS §§ 1781 et seq.
> Depositions and discovery, Rules 26 to 37 of Federal Rules of Civil Procedure, USCS Court Rules.

RESEARCH REFERENCES AND PRACTICE AIDS:

> 9 NY Jur, Contempt § 50.
> 7 Carmody-Wait 2d, Disclosure § 42:6.
> 7 Carmody-Wait 2d, Admissions §§ 53:2, 53:3, 53:6, 53:8.
> 14 Carmody-Wait 2d, Summary Proceedings to Recover Possession of Real Property § 90:257.
> 17 Carmody-Wait 2d, Proceeding for Disposition of Real Property of Infant or Incompetent § 106:17.
> 23 Carmody-Wait 2d, Arbitration § 141:111.
> 24 Carmody-Wait 2d, Judicial Review of Tax Assessments and Taxes § 146:79.
> 25 Carmody-Wait 2d, Fundamentals of Practice in the Surrogate's Court § 149:240.

Law Reviews:

> Disclosure in New York. 37 NYSBJ 49.

CASE NOTES

Particularization of a claim is not disclosure as that word is employed in § 408 and Article 31 of CPLR; disclosure is designed to produce evidentiary matter while a bill of particulars is a pleading that amplifies and explains the claim but does not contain the evidence that will be adduced to support the claim. Western Printing & Lithographing Co. v McCandlish (1967) 55 Misc 2d 607, 286 NYS2d 59.

In a habeas corpus proceeding instituted to determine the custody of the parties' three children, petitioner's application for an order requiring his wife to furnish authorization permitting him to make copies of hospital records from January of 1963 to date was denied, since in awarding custody of the children the court was concerned only with respondent's present mental condition and the records sought would not disclose the present mental condition of respondent and were material only upon a showing reflecting a relationship between her past and present mental condition. Application of Do Vidio (1968) 56 Misc 2d 79, 288 NYS2d 21.

Where tax assessments were increased by a village tax assessor after the close of the normal grievance period, it was proper to allow examination of the assessor before trial under CPLR § 408 to determine whether the assessor actually made a mistake in the original assessment, and whether he intended to place the property on the rolls at the increased rate complained of. New York Tel. Co. v Board of Trustees (1972) 70 Misc 2d 559, 334 NYS2d 462.

Trial court properly exercised its discretion in denying request of applicant for liquor license, which sought review of denial of license, to examine two commissioners of the State Liquor Authority, before trial. Pasta Chef, Inc. v State Liquor Authority (1975) 47 AD2d 713, 364 NYS2d 638.

Motion of applicant for liquor license, which sought review of denial of license, to examine, before trial, two commissioners of the State Liquor Authority should have been brought pursuant to provision relating to disclosures in special proceedings rather than provision relating to discovery in

actions. Pasta Chef, Inc. v State Liquor Authority (1975) 47 AD2d 713, 364 NYS2d 638.

In probate proceeding, wherein contention was only that testator lacked testamentary capacity, motion to examine nominated executor, a bank, and for production by bank of all papers of any nature in its possession in any capacity was far too broad, and surrogate properly limited examination to documents or papers pertaining to investment or banking records of decedent whether in his individual, fiduciary or any other capacity, and any and all income tax records of decedent. Regan v State (1975) 50 AD2d 619, 374 NYS2d 738.

In probate proceeding, wherein contention was only that testator lacked testamentary capacity, motion to examine nominated executor, a bank, and for production by bank of all papers of any nature in its possession in any capacity was far too broad, and surrogate properly limited examination to documents or papers pertaining to investment or banking records of decedent whether in his individual, fiduciary or any other capacity, and any and all income tax records of decedent. Re Will of Schneier (1975) 50 AD2d 715, 374 NYS2d 872.

Where only issue to be tried is whether claimants gave notice of their claims within 90 days after accident, an issue which turns solely on claimants' diligence and on facts within their knowledge, they are not entitled to an examination before trial of Motor Vehicle Accident Indemnification Corporation's internal procedures in processing claims. Seasonwein v Motor Vehicle Acci. Indemnification Corp. (1965) 23 AD2d 732, 258 NYS2d 126.

Assuming that motion for disclosure of names and addresses of witnesses to transactions involved in special proceedings seeking to enjoin corporations from committing allegedly deceptive business practices was one for discovery and that a special proceeding is not exempt from discovery relief, it was an abuse of discretion to grant such relief since defendants' purpose, barely concealed, was to uncover scope of Attorney General's investigation and to perhaps discourage prospective witnesses; record provided ample detail and definition of the practices attacked as fraudulent. People v Bestline Products, Inc. (1977) 41 NY2d 887, 393 NYS2d 984, 362 NE2d 614.

Rule 409. Hearing

(a) Furnishing of papers; filing. Upon the hearing, each party shall furnish to the court all papers served by him. The petitioner shall furnish all other papers not already in the possession of the court necessary to the consideration of the questions involved. Where such papers are in the possession of an adverse party, they shall be produced by such party at the hearing on notice served with the petition. The court may require the submission of additional proof. All papers furnished to the court shall be filed unless the court orders otherwise.

(b) Summary determination. The court shall make a summary determination upon the pleadings, papers and admissions to the extent that no triable issues of fact are raised. The court may make any orders permitted on a motion for summary judgment.

HISTORY:

Add, L 1962, ch 308, eff Sept 1, 1963.
Earlier statutes: CPA § 101; CCP § 825; chap 470 of 1847, § 20.

ADVISORY COMMITTEE NOTES:

Subd (a) is based upon new CPLR rule 2214(c) as to motions. Cf. RCP 65. The hearing in a special proceeding closely resembles the hearing on a motion and the reasons for the provisions of the motion rule apply here. The rule will facilitate the submission to the court upon the hearing of all relevant documentary evidence necessary for a summary determination. It is contemplated that where additional proof is required, the court may adjourn the hearing or allow the submission of such proof after the hearing. The next to the last sentence expresses the former practice in special proceedings and on motions. CPA § 101; RCP 71. Provision that court may dispense with filing of a paper added to conform to motion practice.

Subd (b) requires the equivalent of a summary judgment in every case. Since there is no necessity of a motion for such relief, the provision of new CPLR rule 3212, except as specifically retained, would be inapplicable to special proceedings. The last sentence of this subdivision, by allowing a partial determination, affords an opportunity for the summary disposition of as great a portion of the case as possible. If a trial is necessary, an order limiting issues for trial in the nature of a pre-trial order is permitted. Such order should be based upon an examination of the papers and a conference similar to a pre-trial conference.

RESEARCH REFERENCES AND PRACTICE AIDS:

3 Carmody-Wait 2d, Service and Filing of Papers § 20:33.
6 Carmody-Wait 2d, Summary Judgment § 39:3.
6 Carmody-Wait 2d, Tender and Offer; Payment into Court § 41:86.
14 Carmody-Wait 2d, Summary Proceedings to Recover Possession of Real Property §§ 90:259, 90:260.
23 Carmody-Wait 2d, Arbitration §§ 141:163, 141:174.
24 Carmody-Wait 2d, Proceeding Against a Body or Officer § 145:334.

CASE NOTES

1. In general; sufficiency of supporting papers
2. Summary determination in special proceedings
3. —Proceedings involving real property; condemnation

1. In general; sufficiency of supporting papers

Standards of summary judgment should be applied by the court to proceedings governed by this section. Port of New York Authority v 62 Cortlandt Street Realty Co. (1966) 18 NY2d 250, 273 NYS2d 337, 219 NE2d 797, cert den 385 US 1006, 17 L Ed 2d 544, 87 S Ct 712.

In proceeding pursuant to Mental Hygiene Law § 78.03, subd 3, governed by CPLR § 409, affidavits in support, comprising conclusory statements of respondent's brothers and sisters alleging that respondent had delusions of seeing her deceased parents in her residence, that she had fits of temper, wandered from subject to subject in her conversation, had exposed herself naked on her porch, and was filthy in her appearance, were insufficient to support conclusion that respondent was incapable of handling her own affairs, where overwhelming evidence was submitted from respondent's doctor, banker, real estate broker, neighbor, and brother indicating that respondent was intelligent, coherent, fully competent, and capable of handling her own affairs. Re Javarone (1973) 76 Misc 2d 20, 350 NYS2d 87, affd 49 AD2d 788, 372 NYS2d 745.

In view of affidavit of attending physician that respondent was competent and able to manage her affairs, affidavit of real estate broker who appraised property sold by respondent and concluded that sale price was adequate, and affidavit of local banker stating that he had done business with respondent and that she was capable of managing her own affairs, petition, which sought to have respondent declared incompetent and to have committee of her person and property appointed, and which alleged, inter alia, that respondent had exposed herself naked in public, that she had delusions of seeing her deceased parents, that she had uncontrollable fits of temper and that whe was filthy in her appearance was properly dismissed. Re Javarone (1975) 49 AD2d 788, 372 NYS2d 745.

Although case turned largely on documentary proof, oral motion for summary judgment of dismissal was denied where critical documents in case could best be construed in light of facts in respect of surrounding circumstances. Gumper v Biggane (1975) 81 Misc 2d 947, 367 NYS2d 677.

Attorney General's petition to enjoin corporation engaged in business of selling water conditioning equipment from engaging in continued fraudulent and illegal acts by making false representations to prospective customers regarding warranty of equipment being sold would be granted where allegations of petition were factually supported by affidavit of assistant Attorney General with documentary evidence attached thereto and where only papers submitted by respondent, which was verified answer consisting of general denial, failed to raise any factual issue. State v Waterfine Water Conditioning Co. (1975) 87 Misc 2d 18, 384 NYS2d 348.

2. Summary determination in special proceedings

In a special proceeding if no triable issues of fact are raised the court has power to make a summary determination. Kavares v Motor Vehicle Acci. Indemnification Corp. (1967) 29 AD2d 68, 285 NYS2d 983, affd 28 NY2d 939, 323 NYS2d 431, 271 NE2d 915.

Where, in proceedings to review reapportionment legislation subd (b) of CPLR Rule 409 does not apply and motions for summary judgment under CPLR 3212 were denied. Petition of Orans (1965) 45 Misc 2d 616, 257 NYS2d 839, affd 15 NY2d 339, 258 NYS2d 825, 206 NE2d 854, app dismd 382 US 10, 15 L Ed 2d 13, 86 S Ct 75, reh den 382 US 934, 15 L Ed 2d 346, 86 S Ct 311.

Garnishee bank could not avoid judgment against it pursuant to CPLR § 409, subd b by suggesting that funds in Totten Trust Bank account from which it had permitted withdrawals after notice from judgment creditor had vested in beneficiary, where bank offered no evidence at hearing that the funds had in fact vested. Michigan Associates v Emigrant Sav. Bank (1973) 74 Misc 2d 495, 345 NYS2d 329.

In proceeding brought to have person declared incompetent and for appointment of committee, court is authorized, within its discretion, to grant summary determination upon papers alone if no triable issues of fact are raised. Re Javarone (1975) 49 AD2d 788, 372 NYS2d 745.

Article 78 proceeding was inappropriate vehicle for obtainment of relief by discharged civil service employee where he had not exhausted his administrative remedies, but where a proceeding to compel arbitration would be available to such employee, who had improperly been denied his appeal to arbitration, and since further relief could be granted summarily where there was no dispute as to the facts, employee was entitled to judgment as a matter of law affording him an opportunity to appeal to arbitration from the termination of his employment. Bursor v Levitt (1976) 55 AD2d 730, 389 NYS2d 186.

3. —Proceedings involving real property; condemnation

In an action to recover property in which a judgment debtor has an interest, a hearing is mandated if a court order is based upon a determination that the provisions of a restraining order has been violated, and summary judgment may not be entered if there are disputed issues of fact. V P Supply Corp. v Normand (1967) 27 AD2d 797, 279 NYS2d 124.

Condemnation proceedings are special proceedings, and accordingly the court is under a duty to make a summary determination upon the pleadings, papers, and admissions to the extent that no triable issues of fact are raised. Iroquois Gas Corp. v Gernatt (1966) 50 Misc 2d 1028, 272 NYS2d 291, affd 28 AD2d 811, 281 NYS2d 896, affd 22 NY2d 694, 291 NYS2d 806, 238 NE2d 916.

CASE NOTES

UNDER FORMER CIVIL PRACTICE LAWS

The examination of a judgment debtor in supplementary proceedings is a record of the court, in which the judgment debtor has sufficient interest to require the judgment creditor to file it for future use or reference. Renner v Meyer (1889, City Ct) 6 NYS 535.

Proceedings supplementary to execution were special proceedings within CPA § 101, and depositions taken therein had to be filed with the county clerk, though not used in procuring the order and though taken by a stenographer paid by plaintiff's attorney. Fiske v Twigg, 50 Super Ct (18 Jones & S) 69; Falkenberg v Frank (1897) 20 Misc 692, 46 NYS 675.

§ 410. Trial

If triable issues of fact are raised they shall be tried forthwith and the court shall make a final determination thereon. If issues are triable of right by jury, the court shall give the parties an opportunity to demand a jury trial of such issues. Failure to make such demand within the time limited by the court, or, if no such time is limited, before trial begins, shall be deemed a waiver of the right to trial by jury.

HISTORY:

Add, L 1962, ch 308, eff Sept 1, 1963.

ADVISORY COMMITTEE NOTES:

In the event of partial summary determination under new CPLR rule 409(b), the issues remaining would be tried under this section. The court could make an order in the nature of a pretrial order which would specify the issues to be tried, define the scope of trial and remove from the case facts which are not in dispute or which are incontrovertible. Unlike new CPLR § 2218 which requires the court to specify the issues to be tried, rule 409(b) is permissive.

Thus limited, the trial should proceed forthwith, i.e., at the earliest possible date. It is contemplated that special proceedings would be given preference on trial calendars, depending upon their nature. The provisions of this rule for demand of a jury, based upon the language of new CPLR § 2218 as to the trial of an issue of fact raised on a motion, are applicable only where there is a right to trial by jury.

FEDERAL ASPECTS:

Trials, Rules 38 to 55 of Federal Rules of Civil Procedure, USCS Court Rules.

RESEARCH REFERENCES AND PRACTICE AIDS:

6 Carmody-Wait 2d, Tender and Offer § 41:86.
7 Carmody-Wait 2d, Trial in General § 45:1 et seq.
11 Carmody-Wait 2d, Attachment § 76:152.
17 Carmody-Wait 2d, Committee for an Incompetent or a Mental Patient § 109:30.
22 Carmody-Wait 2d, Arbitration § 141:82.
23 Carmody-Wait 2d, Arbitration §§ 141:163, 141:174.
24 Carmody-Wait 2d, Proceeding Against a Body or Officer § 145:341.

CASE NOTES

Proceedings for judgment directing insurer as garnishee to turn over to sheriff some of money to satisfy judgment to be entered upon jury verdict was, in lieu of a separate plenary action brought against insurer, proper and within compass of statute. Simpson v Loehmann (1975) 81 Misc 2d 386, 365 NYS2d 368.

In an action for a declaratory judgment with respect to the validity of a separation agreement the issues of validity and invalidity and of estoppel cannot be summarily determined on affidavits, but must be tried as provided in this section. Gunter v Gunter (1965) 47 Misc 2d 861, 263 NYS2d 219.

In an action to recover property in which a judgment debtor has an interest, a hearing is mandated if a court order is based upon a determination that the provisions of a restraining order has been violated, and summary judgment may not be entered if there are disputed issues of fact. V P Supp Corp. v Normand (1967) 27 AD2d 797, 279 NYS2d 124.

In action by decedent's wife to impose a trust on death benefits, summary judgment was precluded by issue of whether decedent, who changed the beneficiary after leaving wife, had acted with actual intent to defraud his wife and children who were his creditors under court orders of support. Huston v NYSA-ILA Welfare Fund (1973) 43 AD2d 590, 349 NYS2d 764.

The nature of the issue of the validity of a disclaimer of coverage raised in an application for a stay of arbitration demanded under an uninsured automobile policy endorsement does not call for a trial earlier than the usual issues on the general non-jury calendar of the Supreme Court. Blondo v All City Ins. Co. (1968) 56 Misc 2d 516, 288 NYS2d 765.

Rule 411. Judgment

The court shall direct that a judgment be entered determining the rights of the parties to the special proceeding.

HISTORY:

Add, L 1962, ch 308, eff Sept 1, 1963.

ADVISORY COMMITTEE NOTES:

Under this section the final determination in a special proceeding is made in the form of a judgment rather than a final order. A judgment in a special proceeding is, for all purposes, the same as a judgment in an action. The provisions of the new CPLR as to the form, entry, filing, docketing, satisfaction, interest, lien effect and enforcement of a judgment are therefore applicable. The disposition of motions, however, may be by order, if the court considers it necessary.

Provisions previously drafted will be conformed to this changed terminology. It is intended that, until existing statutes are conformed in terminology, a "final order" required in a special proceeding should be treated as if it were a judgment.

The function of a final order and a judgment under former law were identical. Both finally determined a judicial proceeding, fixed the rights of the parties, and either granted, or denied the relief applied for. In several respects, however, they were treated differently under former law. No justification has been found for such difference in treatment. The difference is essentially a formal one. The important elements of docketing and enforcement are equally available in special proceedings and actions, although different procedures and modes of enforcement may be required for final orders in special proceedings. There is no reason why two court directions having identical functions and essentially enforceable in the same manner, should be treated differently because one is made in an action and another in a special proceeding. The reason for distinguishing a special proceeding from an action is simply to provide for a summary mode of procedure in certain cases. The form and effect of the final determination bears no relationship to the summary nature of the proceeding.

The word "final" has been deleted before "judgment" so that the provision now authorizes interlocutory as well as final judgments.

FEDERAL ASPECTS:

Judgment, Rules 54 to 63 of Federal Rules of Civil Procedure, USCS Court Rules.

RESEARCH REFERENCES AND PRACTICE AIDS:

35 NY Jur, Limitations and Laches § 48.

2 Carmody-Wait 2d, Motions, Petitions, and Orders § 8:2.

2 Carmody-Wait 2d, Limitation of Actions § 13:96.

8 Carmody-Wait 2d, Judgments §§ 63:1 et seq.

9 Carmody-Wait 2d, Judgments § 63:103.

14 Carmody-Wait 2d, Summary Proceedings to Recover Possession of Real Property § 90:265.

17 Carmody-Wait 2d, Proceeding for Disposition of Real Property of Infant or Incompetent § 106:27.

22 Carmody-Wait 2d, Habeas Corpus § 139:73.

24 Carmody-Wait 2d, Proceeding Against a Body or Officer § 14:372.

24 Carmody-Wait 2d, Judicial Review of Tax Assessments and Taxes § 146:110.

25 Carmody-Wait 2d, Fundamentals of Practice in the Surrogate's Court § 149:328.

Forms:

See "FORMS" heading following "CASE NOTES", infra.

CASE NOTES

The purpose of a summary proceeding is to afford a means of obtaining a swift determination of disputes between landlord and tenant as to the right of possession, and such a proceeding may not be used to adjudicate constitutional questions raised by tenant. Lincoln Square Apartments, Section 1, Inc. v Davis (1968) 58 Misc 2d 292, 295 NYS2d 358, affd 64 Misc 2d 859, 316 NYS2d 130.

Enforcement in summary proceedings which presently culminate in judgment pursuant to CPLR 411 are included in the automatic stay provisions of CPLR 5519(a) where the property is still in the possession of the tenant. Oleck v Pearlman (1966) 49 Misc 2d 202, 267 NYS2d 76.

Proceeding resulting in judgment denying a permanent stay of arbitration was a special proceeding in which costs might be granted. Douglas v Motor Vehicle Acci. Indemnification Corp. (1966) 50 Misc 2d 1099, 272 NYS2d 680.

The order in a proceeding pursuant to Mental Hygiene Law § 206 must be classified as a judgment. Narcotic Addiction Control Com. v Couloufacos (1968) 29 AD2d 199, 287 NYS2d 238.

In an action for false arrest and imprisonment, where the jury found in a special finding that there were reasonable grounds for detaining plaintiff and the detention was for a reasonable time, but nevertheless in a general verdict found for the plaintiff, awarding him $1,600, a trial judge erred in not directing the entry of a judgment for the defendant dismissing the complaint in view of the overwhelming evidence in support of the jury's special finding. Jacques v Sears Roebuck & Co. (1971) 37 AD2d 121, 322 NYS2d 941.

Order directing settlement of judgment for arbitration sought under written contract would not be modified to direct settlement of an order rather than a judgment on theory that further applications to court could be necessary and that there was no need for each such application to be by special proceeding rather than by application in the pending special proceeding, since speculation as to future applications did not justify a court directive that the proceeding remain in limbo and since if an arbitrator was not appointed, relief could be obtained by application to enforce the judgment. Miller v Ives (1974) 79 Misc 2d 184, 359 NYS2d 640.

Statute providing summary proceeding for recovery of possession of realty prescribes its own procedure, and its procedures, unlike those of the article providing procedures for special proceedings generally, are to be construed strictly. Allyn v Markowitz (1975) 83 Misc 2d 250, 373 NYS2d 293.

In special proceeding for recovery of possession of realty, court has no jurisdiction to adjudicate monetary claim other than rent allegedly due, and no jurisdiction to adjudicate claim for damage to the real property. Allyn v Markowitz (1975) 83 Misc 2d 250, 373 NYS2d 293.

FORMS

Order Directing Entry of Judgment Where No Issue of Fact Presented

Supreme Court, __1____ County

Order

[Title of proceeding]   Index No. __2__ [if assigned]

Present: Hon. __3____ , Justice.

On reading and filing the petition herein, verified __4____, 19_5_, praying for entry of a judgment directing [or as the case may be] __6____ [state nature of relief sought in the petition], the affidavit of __7____, sworn to __8____, 19_9_, and __10____ [recite any other written proof presented by petitioner], the written notice of petition with proof of due service thereof on respondent, and the reply of petitioner herein, verified __11____, 19_12_, and __13____ [recite any affidavits or other written proof accompanying the reply], in support of this petition, and the answer of respondent, verified __14____, 19_15_, duly served on petitioner and filed herein, together with the affidavit of __16____, sworn to __17____, 19_18_, and __19____ [recite any other written proof served and submitted with the answer], in opposition thereto, and it appearing to this court from the pleadings and accompanying papers that no triable issue of fact is raised thereby, now, on motion of __20____, attorney for petitioner, and after hearing __21____, attorney for petitioner, in support of this motion, and __22____, attorney for respondent, in opposition thereto, it is

ORDERED that a judgment be entered directing [state relief to be granted or as the case may be]

Signed this __23__ day of __24_____, 19_25_ at __26_____, New York.
Enter

                                                    _27_____
                                            [Print signer's name below signature]
                                                    Justice, Supreme Court
                                                    __28_____County

**[CPLR 412–500 have been reserved for future use.
Please check your supplement.]**

ARTICLE 5

Venue

HISTORY:

Add, L 1962, ch 308, eff Sept 1, 1963.

ADVISORY COMMITTEE NOTES:

The basic theory of New York venue practice is that mistakes do not affect jurisdiction. Thus, a change in venue does not require commencement of a new action and the question may be waived by failure to raise it promptly. This eminently sound approach has been retained. The changes have been designed to simplify practice and to clarify procedure. Foreign corporations locally engaged in business, as well as individual proprietors, have been treated in a way consistent with other business enterprises in order to make commercial litigation practice more uniform. An attempt has been made to consolidate and simplify the scattered provisions covering venue where a governmental agency or municipality is involved.

CROSS REFERENCES:

Proceeding for appointment of conservator, Men Hyg Law § 77.05.
Proceeding for declaration of incompetency and appointment of committee, Men Hyg Law §§ 78.03(b), 78.07.

§ 501. Contractual provisions fixing venue

Subject to the provisions of subdivision two of section 510, written agreement fixing place of trial, made before an action is commenced, shall be enforced upon a motion for change of place of trial.

HISTORY:
    Add, L 1962, ch 308, amd, L 1963, ch 532, § 8, eff Sept 1, 1963.

NOTE:
    Laws 1963, ch 532, made two types of changes: first, some provisions were designed to correct the typographical errors which existed in the CPLR. Second, other provisions incorporated into the CPLR, without any change in substance, all pertinent amendments to the C.P.A. which were passed and approved during the 1962 legislative session. In this connection, only changes in language were made to conform to the style and format of the CPLR. Those C.P.A. amendments of 1962 essentially covered by original provisions of the CPLR, and those C.P.A. amendments pertaining to areas transferred on September 1, 1963, to laws other than the CPLR, were not incorporated into this act.

ADVISORY COMMITTEE NOTES:
    This provision is new and codifies the rule of Syracuse Plaster Co. v Agostini Bros. Bldg. Corp. (Sup Ct 1938) 169 Misc 564, 7 NYS2d 897, that a contractual provision fixing venue may be the basis for a motion for a change of venue to the county agreed upon. It does not affect the rule that such a contractual provision is not a defense to the action where venue is placed in a county other than that agreed upon. See Graziano v Indemnity Ins. Co. (2d Dept 1955) 286 App Div 867, 142 NYS2d 44.

FEDERAL ASPECTS:
    Venue in United States District Court, 28 USCS §§ 1391 et seq.
    Venue as unaffected by Federal Rules of Civil Procedure, Rule 82 of Federal Rules of Civil Procedure, USCS Court Rules.

RESEARCH REFERENCES AND PRACTICE AIDS:
    7 Carmody-Wait 2d, Place of Trial or Venue §§ 48:3, 48:21.
    77 Am Jur 2d, Venue §§ 1 et seq.
    24 Am Jur Pl and Pr Forms (Rev ed), Venue, Forms 1–21.

Annotations:
    Retroactive operation and effect of venue statute. 41 ALR2d 798.
    Validity of contractual provision limiting place or court in which action may be brought. 56 ALR2d 300.
    Sufficiency of contractual designation of place of performance to fix venue at that place, under statute authorizing or requiring such venue. 97 ALR2d 934.
    Construction and application of federal statute (28 USCS § 1406) providing for dismissal or transfer of cases for improper venue. 3 ALR Fed 467.

Law Reviews:
    New York Civil Practice Law and Rules: venue. 27 Albany L Rev 181.
    Biannual survey of New York practice: Part V. 40 St. John's L Rev 125.
    Biannual survey of New York practice: Part III. 39 St. John's L Rev 178.
    Biannual survey of New York practice: Part IV. 39 St. John's L Rev 408.
    Biannual survey of New York practice: Part IV: federal venue statute regarding national banking associations deemed controlling. 39 St. John's L Rev 426.
    1975 survey of New York law—civil practice. 27 Syracuse L Rev 425.

CASE NOTES

1. In general; public policy and the like
2. Availability of impartial trial
3. Agreements enforceable
4. Agreements not enforceable

1. In general; public policy and the like

Stipulations and contracts as to venue will be sustained where no question of public policy is involved. Rivers v Ben Constr. Corp. (1967) 53 Misc 2d 299, 278 NYS2d 478, mod on other grounds 29 AD2d 1048, 289 NYS2d 866.

Court should not enforce contract provision respecting venue if it is unconscionable, unreasonable or contrary to public policy and good morals. Gardner & North Roofing & Siding Corp. v Demko (1974) 82 Misc 2d 922, 370 NYS2d 294.

2. Availability of impartial trial

Written agreement fixing place of trial made before action is commenced may be enforced if impartial trial can be had in proper county. Flush Metal Partition Corp. v Guy H. Nuovo Corp. (1968) 57 Misc 2d 900, 293 NYS2d 867.

A written agreement fixing the place of trial is to be given effect, subject only to the court's power to change venue if an impartial trial cannot be had in the stipulated county. National Equipment Rental, Ltd. v Sanders (1967, DC NY) 271 F Supp 756.

3. Agreements enforceable

That defendant proposes to call seven witnesses resident of Oneida County is insufficient to override agreement of parties fixing venue of actions arising out of breach of agreement in Onondaga County where plaintiff's place of business was located. Kenron Awning & Window Corp. v Abbott (1964) 43 Misc 2d 552, 251 NYS2d 593.

The surety of a contractor was entitled to an order changing the venue of an action by a subcontractor, who contended it was wrongfully discharged, from Erie County to New York county pursuant to the contract between the parties which contained a clause providing that the venue of any action arising out of or relating to the contract would be in New York county. Frontier Excavating, Inc. v St. Paul Fire & Marine Ins. Co. (1966) 50 Misc 2d 232, 269 NYS2d 782.

Plaintiff was bound by clause in contract stipulating venue, even though she may not have understood the meaning and importance thereof. Grey v Colonial Home Improv. Co. (1967) 57 Misc 2d 321, 292 NYS2d 731.

A written agreement fixing the place of trial made before an action is commenced may be enforced, if an impartial trial can be had in the proper county. Flush Metal Partition Corp. v Guy H. Nuovo Corp. (1968) 57 Misc 2d 900, 293 NYS2d 867, holding that where bond, upon which action was brought, provided that no action thereon should be commenced except in the state court of competent jurisdiction in and for the county or other political subdivisions of state in which the project (being the subject of the bond) or any part thereof was situated, such action should be brought in such county.

Defendant was entitled to change of venue to county of its residence where contract out of which cause of action arose provided that venue of any such action shall be in the county where the home office of defendant was located. Harvey v Colonial Home Improv. Co. (1965) 57 Misc 2d 196, 291 NYS2d 755.

Where construction subcontract under which suit was brought specifically provided that any action resulting from contract would be commenced in courts of specified county and that subcontractor expressly waived any and all right it might have by reason of surety bonds, trial court did not abuse its discretion in granting contractor's motion to change venue to specified county. Callanan Industries, Inc. v Sovereign Constr. Co. (1974) 44 AD2d 292, 354 NYS2d 486.

Provision in construction subcontract that any action resulting from contract would be commenced in courts of specified county was not against public policy, providing that action was brought in court having sufficiently broad jurisdiction to entertain same. Callanan Industries, Inc. v Sovereign Constr. Co. (1974) 44 AD2d 292, 354 NYS2d 486.

4. Agreements not enforceable

Contractual provisions for venue in Onondaga County did not require change of venue to such County in action for rescission of contract on ground of alleged fraud, which action had been brought in Tioga County and alleged fraud occurred in such County and plaintiff was a resident of Tioga County. Colby v Ben Constr. Corp. (1968) 57 Misc 2d 850, 293 NYS2d 759.

Although home improvements contract provided that venue should be in Onondaga County, venue of action would be transferred from Onondaga County to Oneida County, where defendant, a resident of Oneida County, was 75 years old, had great difficulty in speaking English, and was unable to read in any language. Gardner & North Roofing & Siding Corp. v Demko (1974) 82 Misc 2d 922, 370 NYS2d 294.

Where neither of parties reside in contracted county, and property is not located in that county, traditional rules should prevail and the court should select the proper venue. Gardner & North Roofing & Siding Corp. v Demko (1974) 82 Misc 2d 922, 370 NYS2d 294.

Where defendant's motion to place venue of two actions which had been consolidated for joint trial in Warren County was made under provision relating to consolidation and where Warren County courthouse was within 30 miles of courthouse in county selected by plaintiffs for trial, requisite special circumstances that would compel designation of county other than one of those selected by plaintiffs as place for trial did not exist and motion was properly denied. Newell v Niag-

ara Mohawk Power Corp. (1976) 52 AD2d 664, 381 NYS2d 908.

§ 502. Conflicting venue provisions

Where, because of joinder of claims or parties, there is a conflict of provisions under this article, the court, upon motion, shall order as the place of trial one proper under this article as to at least one of the parties or claims.

HISTORY:

Add, L 1962, ch 308, eff Sept 1, 1963.

ADVISORY COMMITTEE NOTES:

This provision is new. It is designed to make it clear that where an otherwise proper joinder of claims or parties results in a conflict in the applicable venue provisions, this is not an objection to the joinder and the court may make an appropriate order as to venue.

FEDERAL ASPECTS:

Venue in United States District Court, 28 USCS §§ 1391 et seq.

Venue as unaffected by Federal Rules of Civil Procedure, Rule 82 of Federal Rules of Civil Procedure, USCS Court Rules.

Rights of parties as to contested venue requests in United States Customs Courts Act of 1970 (28 USCS §§ 253, 256) and Rules of Customs Court. 30 ALR Fed 781.

RESEARCH REFERENCES AND PRACTICE AIDS:

7 Carmody-Wait 2d, Place of Trial or Venue § 48:11.

Law Reviews:

New York Civil Practice Law and Rules: venue. 27 Albany L Rev 181.

Biannual survey of New York practice: Part IV: federal venue statute regarding national banking associations deemed controlling. 39 St. John's L Rev 426.

CASE NOTES

Although as a general rule the venue of the action first commenced should be deemed the place of a joint trial, special circumstances may properly be found to negate the choice. Such special circumstances may arise when the cause of action arises in the county where the second action has been commenced; hospitalization and treatment of injured persons occur in the county where the second action has been commenced; convenience of witnesses point toward trial in the county where the second action has been commenced; or court calendars are less congested in the county where the second action has been commenced. Boyea v Lambeth (1970) 33 AD2d 928, 306 NYS2d 481.

Where cogent reasons were advanced on both sides as to whether venue should be changed from Sullivan County in auto accident case, special term's decision was warranted. Palmer v Chrysler Leasing Corp. (1965) 24 AD2d 820, 263 NYS2d 882.

Where all defendants but one were residents of

New York County action against Mayor of the City of New York and others to enjoin construction of federally subsidized public housing in Queens County would be changed to New York County. Cohen v Lindsay (1968) 57 Misc 2d 840, 293 NYS2d 664.

Cross motion by defendant corporation and its president for change of venue denied where the proceeding was brought in the proper county as to the individual defendant and the convenience of the material witnesses was promoted by the court's retaining jurisdiction. State v Remedial Education, Inc. (1972) 70 Misc 2d 1068, 335 NYS2d 353.

Where parties consented to joint trial of medical malpractice actions brought against physicians in Kings County and against Nassau County in Nassau County, because of venue conflict under statute and in the interests of justice, court properly directed that joint trial proceed in Kings County. Ferrara v Leventhal (1974) 46 AD2d 656, 359 NYS2d 1005.

Right of party to contested probate proceeding to trial by jury is substantial right which should not be lost by mere inadvertence. Re Estate of Mirsky (1975) 81 Misc 2d 9, 365 NYS2d 122.

§ 503. Venue based on residence

(a) Generally. Except where otherwise prescribed by law, the place of trial shall be in the county in which one of the parties resided when it was commenced; or, if none of the parties then resided in the state, in any county designated by the plaintiff. A party resident in more than one county shall be deemed a resident of each such county.

(b) Executor, administrator, trustee, committee, general or testamentary guardian, or receiver. An executor, administrator, trustee, committee, general or testamentary guardian, or receiver shall be deemed a resident of the county of his appointment as well as the county in which he actually resides.

(c) Corporation. A domestic corporation, or a foreign corporation authorized to transact business in the state, shall be deemed a resident of the county in which its principal office is located; except that such a corporation, if a railroad or other common carrier, shall also be deemed a resident of the county where the cause of action arose.

(d) Unincorporated association, partnership, or individually-owned business. A president or treasurer of an unincorporated association, suing or being sued on behalf of the association, shall be deemed a resident of any county in which the association has its principal office, as well as the county in which he actually resides. A partnership or an individually-owned business shall be deemed a resident of any county in which it has its principal office, as well as the county in which the partner or individual owner suing or being sued actually resides.

(e) Assignee. In an action for a sum of money only, brought by an assignee other than an assignee for the benefit of creditors or a holder in due course of a negotiable instrument, the assignee's residence shall be deemed the same as that of the original assignor at the time of the original assignment.

(f) Consumer credit transaction. In an action arising out of a consumer credit transaction where a purchaser, borrower or debtor is a defendant, the place of trial shall be the residence of a defendant, if one resides within the state or the county where such transaction took place, if it is within the state, or, in other cases, as set forth in subdivision (a).

HISTORY:

> Add, L 1962, ch 308, eff Sept 1, 1963.
> Subd (e), amd, L 1965, ch 114, eff Sept 1, 1965.
> Sub (f), add, L 1973, ch 238, eff Sept 1, 1973.
> Earlier statutes: CPA §§ 182, 184-a; CCP §§ 984, 991.

ADVISORY COMMITTEE NOTES:

> The provision of subd (a) is taken from the first, third, and fourth sentences of CPA § 182 without substantial change. It continues the former New York rule that, subject to special exceptions, venue in transitory actions is determined by residence of the parties.
> The provision of subd (b) is taken from the second sentence of CPA § 182 with the addition of committee and general and testamentary guardian. These were added

because the same considerations apply to them as to the persons presently included.

The provision of subd (c) codifies former New York law with respect to domestic corporations. It changes the former law by making a foreign corporation a resident of the state for venue purposes if it has obtained authority to transact business in New York. The provision also is intended to apply to railroad corporations, contrary to the former rule that, for purposes of venue, such corporations are deemed to be residents of every county in which they operate a railroad or otherwise transact business. Last clause added to cover peculiar problems involved in such actions. It is designed to avoid requiring nonresidents injured in upstate counties either to sue in New York City or to obtain New York City counsel to move for a change of venue.

The provision of subd (d) is designed to place a partnership, an individual owner of a business and an unincorporated association suing or being sued through an officer on substantially the same basis as a corporation for venue purposes. Residence of an association officer, partner, or individual owner as the basis for venue is not affected by this subdivision, which merely provides an alternative basis. Thus, for example, if an individual conducts a business in New York County and lives in Suffolk County, a resident of Erie County may fix venue of a transitory action involving the business in Erie, New York or Suffolk County.

The provision of subd (e) is derived from CPA § 184-a but with simplification of language and omission of the provisions relating to a suit in the county where the contract was made or to be performed or the cause of action or part of it arose. It accomplishes in a simpler manner the purpose of preventing assignments designed to circumvent the venue rules. The phrase "only" has been added to the words "an action for a sum of money." This makes it clear that the provision is not applicable to a claim for a sum of money joined to a nonmonetary claim.

CROSS REFERENCES:

Applications affecting corporations, Bus Corp Law § 1113.
For insolvency proceedings, Dr & Cr Law § 2.
Action to recover milk cans, Gen Bus Law § 271.
Enforcement of mortgage tax, Tax Law § 266.
Actions against towns, Town Law § 66.
Venue in certain courts, NYC Civil Ct Act § 301.

CODES, RULES AND REGULATIONS:

Preference claim in note of issue in Supreme Court, Bronx and New York Counties, First Judicial Department. 22 NYCRR 660.9(c)(1) (CLS Supreme Ct. Rules— Bronx and New York Counties § 660.9(c)(1)).
Preference claim in note of issue in Supreme Court, Bronx and New York Counties, First Judicial Department. 22 NYCRR 660.9(c)(1)(ii) (CLS Supreme Ct. Rules— Bronx and New York Counties § 660.9(c)(1)(ii)).
Preferences in Supreme Court, Kings County, Second Judicial Department. 22 NYCRR 752.6 (CLS Kings County Supreme Ct. Rules § 752.6).
Preference in trial of commercial and other actions on Trial Term calendar of Supreme Court, Nassau County, Second Judicial Department. 22 NYCRR 785.4 (CLS Nassau County Supreme Ct. Rules § 785.4).
Preference in trial of commercial and other actions on Trial Term calendar in Supreme Court, Queens County, Second Judicial Department. 22 NYCRR 795.4 (CLS Queens County Supreme Ct. Rules § 795.4).
Preferences in Supreme Court, Richmond County, Second Judicial Department. 22 NYCRR 755.3(b) (CLS Richmond County Supreme Ct. Rules § 755.3(b)).

FEDERAL ASPECTS:

Venue in United States District Court, 28 USCS §§ 1391 et seq.
Venue as unaffected by Federal Rules of Civil Procedure, Rule 82 of Federal Rules of Civil Procedure, USCS Court Rules.

RESEARCH REFERENCES AND PRACTICE AIDS:

1 Carmody-Wait 2d, Courts and their Jurisdiction § 2:138.

7 Carmody-Wait 2d, Place of Trial or Venue §§ 48:5, 48:12, 48:14, 48:16.

18 Carmody-Wait 2d, Annulment of Marriage § 113:100.

18 Carmody-Wait 2d, Absolute Divorce § 114:112.

19 Carmody-Wait 2d, Separation § 117:143.

20 Carmody-Wait 2d, Actions and Proceedings By and Against Corporations, Their Officers, Directors, and Shareholders §§ 121:90–121:93.

20 Carmody-Wait 2d, Actions and Proceedings By or Against, or in Reference to, Partnerships and Associations § 122:7.

21 Carmody-Wait 2d, Actions and Proceedings By and Against Infants and Incompetents § 124:30.

21 Carmody-Wait 2d, Litigation By and Against Fiduciaries § 129:59.

21 Carmody-Wait 2d, Action for Wrongful Death § 130:73.

23 Carmody-Wait 2d, Actions By and Against Public Bodies and Public Officers § 144:98.

19 Am Jur 2d, Corporations §§ 1456–1461.

5 Am Jur Pl and Pr Forms (Rev ed), Captions, Prayers, and Formal Parts, Forms 251–262.

24 Am Jur Pl and Pr Forms (Rev ed), Venue, Forms 1–21.

Annotations:

Venue of suit to enjoin nuisance. 7 ALR2d 481.

Relationship between "residence" and "domicil" under venue statutes. 12 ALR2d 757.

Jurisdiction of suit involving trust as affected by location of res, residence of parties to trust, service, and appearance. 15 ALR2d 610.

What is an action for damages to personal property within venue statute. 29 ALR2d 1270.

Construction and effect of statutes providing for venue of criminal case in either county, where crime is committed partly in one county and partly in another. 30 ALR2d 1265.

Acquisition of domicile by sending wife or family to new home. 31 ALR2d 775.

Venue of action for partnership dissolution, settlement, or accounting. 33 ALR2d 914.

Venue of wrongful death action. 36 ALR2d 1146.

Venue of action against nonresident motorist served constructively under statute. 38 ALR2d 1198.

Venue of divorce action in particular county as dependent on residence or domicil for a specified length of time. 54 ALR2d 898.

Place of personal representative's appointment as venue of action against him in his official capacity. 93 ALR2d 1199.

Provision in 28 USC § 1391(c) for laying venue of an action against a corporation in district in which it is doing business as referring to date of filing suit or of accrual of cause of action. 2 ALR Fed 995.

Law Reviews:

New York Civil Practice Law and Rules: venue. 27 Albany L Rev 181.

Biannual survey of New York practice: Part IV: federal venue statute regarding national banking associations deemed controlling. 39 St. John's L Rev 426.

Biannual survey of New York practice: Part V: CPLR 503(c): residence of a foreign corporation. 40 St. John's L Rev 143.

The quarterly survey of New York practice: CPLR 503(c): corporation's office as filed with Secretary of State recognized proper for venue purposes. 41 St. John's L Rev 135.

CASE NOTES

1. In general
2. Multiple residences of parties
3. Conflict and change of venue
4. Domestic corporations
5. Foreign corporations
6. Associations, partnerships, and proprietorships
7. Assignees
8. Consumer credit transactions

1. In general

Where husband's motion for change of venue in separation action was unnecessary under this section, such fact would be considered in awarding counsel fees for unsuccessful plaintiff wife. Becker v Becker (1965) 46 Misc 2d 858, 260 NYS2d 879.

A physician who resided in New Jersey and practiced medicine in New York was not a resident of New York under CPLR 8501 for the purpose of exempting him from furnishing security for costs in an action in which he was the plaintiff. Gottlieb v Paysner (1965) 46 Misc 2d 388, 259 NYS2d 468.

Provision in construction subcontract that any action resulting from contract would be commenced in courts of specified county was not against public policy, providing that action was brought in court having sufficiently broad jurisdiction to entertain same. Callanan Industries, Inc. v Sovereign Constr. Co. (1974) 44 AD2d 292, 354 NYS2d 486.

Statutes governing actions against cities, inter alia, and real property actions, rather than provisions of statute governing venue based on residence, controlled action to enjoin municipality from discharging sewage into harbors and waters surrounding municipality, which sewage allegedly washed ashore onto public beaches of plaintiff municipalities. Hempstead v New York (1976) 88 Misc 2d 366, 388 NYS2d 78.

2. Multiple residences of parties

CPLR 503(a) recognizes the principle that a party may have more than one residence. Fleck v Fleck (1965) 47 Misc 2d 454, 262 NYS2d 789.

Subdivision (d) of this section is designed to give additional county residences to residents of the state, not to confer upon a nonresident the status of a resident. Gottlieb v Paysner (1965) 46 Misc 2d 388, 259 NYS2d 468.

3. Conflict and change of venue

The plaintiff in a libel action is entitled to bring suit in the county in which he resides, and where defendant made no showing that it could not receive an impartial trial in that county and failed to indicate the names and addresses of witnesses whose convenience would be served by a change of trial and the substance of any testimony sought to be elicited from those witnesses, defendant's motion for a trial change was denied. Rae v Advance Publications, Inc. (1969) 60 Misc 2d 792, 303 NYS2d 911.

In action brought in Kings County to recover damages for wrongful death and conscious pain and suffering of plaintiff's decedent who while employed as roofer fell through hole in roof at construction site in Rockland County, circumstances of case from standpoint of convenience indicated propriety of retaining venue in Kings County wherein plaintiff and her family had moved into residence of her parents for duration of husband's employment in Rockland County, where only nexus with Suffolk County was residence of plaintiff whereas many of plaintiff's husband's coworkers resided in or near Kings County and other parties had their places of business in New Jersey and at White Plains, New York. Fitzpatrick v Sullivan, Magee & Sullivan, Inc. (1975) 49 AD2d 902, 373 NYS2d 381.

Proper venue for trial of State's action against town for contribution to the State with respect to liability of the State to injured motorist would be the county in which the town was located rather than Albany County. State v County of Sullivan (1976) 54 AD2d 29, 386 NYS2d 253.

Where venue chosen is county where accident occurred, where all persons involved reside, and where physicians who treated plaintiff and police officers who investigated the accident reside, venue will not be changed solely because infant plaintiff was placed in custody of an organization whose home office was in another county. Lada v Cester (1964) 22 AD2d 642, 252 NYS2d 874.

In an action where residence controls venue and plaintiff lays the venue in a county of which he is not a resident, the defendant is entitled, as a matter of right, to have the venue changed to the county of his residence. Konigsberg v Long Island Daily Press Publishing Co. (1968) 57 Misc 2d 911, 293 NYS2d 861.

Where proceeding to nullify result of primary election involved congressional district including portions of three counties, petitioner's election of venue in the one of the three counties where he resided was proper; tabulation in bill of particulars indicating that 80% of the alleged irregularities occurred in Bronx County did not establish requisite factual basis for change of venue from Queens County on grounds of convenience of material witnesses and the ends of justice. Vallone v Power (1970) 35 AD 655, 315 NYS2d 315.

Although action for divorce and counterclaim that certain real property in Nassau County, which property was held by the parties as tenants by the entirety, be the sole property of the defendant could have been tried in the matrimonial proceeding in Warren County, special term did not abuse its discretion in severing the real property cause of action and transferring it to Nassau County for trial. Forde v Forde (1976) 53 AD2d 779, 384 NYS2d 547.

4. Domestic corporations

For venue purposes a domestic corporation is deemed a resident of the county designated in its certificate of incorporation as the place where the office of the corporation is to be located, and the mere fact that a corporation has an office in a county other than that designated in its certificate does not change its residence for purpose of legal procedure. McNamara Realty, Inc. v Hutchinson (1967) 54 Misc 2d 810, 283 NYS2d 422.

For purposes of venue, the residence of a corporation is in the county set forth in its certificate of incorporation as its principal place of business. Wegorzewski v Macrose Lumber & Trim Co. (1967) 28 AD2d 713, 280 NYS2d 994; Davis Aircraft Products Co. v Bankers Trust Co. (1969) 32 AD2d 832, 302 NYS2d 379; Bryan v Hagemann (1969) 31 AD2d 905, 298 NYS2d 101; Reliable Displays Corp. v Maro Industries, Inc. (1971) 67 Misc 2d 747, 325 NYS2d 616.

Although plaintiff corporation relocated its entire office and manufacturing facility to another county, the residence of the corporation for purposes of venue was in the county set forth in its certificate of incorporation as its principal place of business. Reliable Displays Corp. v Maro Industries, Inc. (1971) 67 Misc 2d 747, 325 NYS2d 616.

Venue for a proceeding to stay arbitration is maintainable not only "in a court in the county in which one of the parties resides" but also in a court in the county in which one of the parties "is doing business". Manitt Constr. Corp. v J. S. Plumbing & Heating Corp. (1966) 50 Misc 2d 502, 270 NYS2d 716 (disapproved on other grounds Sommer v Anthony J. Quarant Contracting, Inc. 40 AD2d 95, 337 NYS2d 957, 73 ALR3d 1063).

5. Foreign corporations

The venue of an action brought by a foreign corporation is the place named in its "statement and designation" filed with the secretary of state, and this may not necessarily be the place where it conducts its principal business activities, under the provisions of subd (c) of this section. General Precision, Inc. v Ametek, Inc. (1965) 45 Misc 2d 451, 257 NYS2d 120, affd 24 AD2d 757, 263 NYS2d 470.

Where both parties to a commercial action were foreign corporations authorized to do business in New York, the proper venue of the suit was the county designated by the plaintiff in its statement as the county where its office was to be located, and the mere fact that the corporation has its office in a county other than that designated does not change its residence for the purpose of legal procedure. General Precision, Inc. v Ametek, Inc. (1965) 24 AD2d 757, 263 NYS2d 470.

The residence of a foreign corporation authorized to do business in this state means the location of its office within the state designated in its application for authority to do business filed with the secretary of state. General Acci. Fire & Life Assur. Corp. v Allcity Ins. Co. (1967) 53 Misc 2d 596, 279 NYS2d 422.

Where the defendant-foreign corporation, who was no longer resident in any county for venue purposes, moved for a change of venue to New York County as a matter of right, correctly alleging that Westchester County had been improperly designated for venue purposes by the plaintiff-domestic corporation, the motion was denied; although Queens County was only proper county for venue purposes, since the defendant had not sought the case's transfer there, the court declined to do so sua sponte. Reliable Displays Corp. v Maro Industries, Inc. (1971) 67 Misc 2d 747, 325 NYS2d 616.

6. Associations, partnerships, and proprietorships

The New York courts obtained personal jurisdiction over a limited partnership organized under New Jersey law with principal offices in New Jersey which did not transact business in this state by service of a summons upon a general partner of the defendant who resided in New York. It was also held the fact that the partnership was sued in the partnership name was of no consequence. Rait v Jacobs Bros. (1966) 49 Misc 2d 903, 268 NYS2d 750.

7. Assignees

Where plaintiff was not a holder in due course of negotiable instruments sued on and plaintiff's assignor was not a resident of the county in which action was brought, defendant was entitled to change of venue to his county of residence. Gerdon Credit Corp. v Fletcher (1968) 30 AD2d 688, 292 NYS2d 327.

8. Consumer credit transactions

Record established that action based upon a consumer credit transaction was commenced in Orange County in direct violation of statutory provision mandating that actions based on consumer credit transactions be brought in the county of defendant's residence, if he resides in the state, or in the county where the transaction took place, if it took place in the state; accordingly, vindication of the remedial statute's salutary purpose dictated that defendant be relieved of her default and afforded an opportunity to defend the action on the merits. Empire Nat. Bank (Bankamericard Div.) v Olori (1976) 87 Misc 2d 320, 384 NYS2d 948.

CASE NOTES

UNDER FORMER CIVIL PRACTICE LAWS

A. IN GENERAL

1. Generally
2. Waiver

B. ACTIONS WITHIN STATUTE

3. Generally
4. Transitory actions
5. Personal injury and death
6. Libel
7. Malpractice
8. Matrimonial actions

C. PARTIES

9. Generally
10. Agents
11. Assignees
12. Bankrupts
13. Brokers
14. National banks
15. Municipal corporations
16. Public officers

D. RESIDENCE OF PARTIES

17. Generally
18. Domicile distinguished from residence
19. Pleading as determining residence
20. Proof of residence
21. Plaintiff's residence
22. Defendant's residence
23. Executors and administrators
24. Committee for incompetent
25. Guardians
26. Domestic corporations
27. Foreign corporations
28. Common carriers
29. Partnerships

E. PLACE OF TRIAL OF ASSIGNED CAUSE OF ACTION

30. Generally
31. Foreign corporations
32. Money lent
33. Goods sold and delivered

A. IN GENERAL

1. Generally

CPA § 182 did not control a case which fell within the exceptions stated therein; thus, where some of the real estate as to which an action was brought was within the county of New York, the venue of the action should have been laid in that county even though personal property was also involved, and none of the parties resided in the county where the real estate was located. Hall v Gilman (1902) 77 AD 464, 79 NYS 307.

A demand by defendant to change the place of trial upon the grounds stated in CPA § 183 was not sufficient upon which to found a motion to change the place of trial upon the grounds stated in CPA § 182. Whitehead Bros. Co. v Dolan (1910) 69 Misc 208, 126 NYS 414.

Where plaintiff maintained two residences one of which was in county where action was brought, defendant's motion to change venue was denied. Schwartz v Schwartz (1949) 274 AD 1082, 85 NYS2d 616.

Opening sentence of CPA § 182 was mandatory. Defendant was entitled to change of venue to the county of his residence where the cause was not within the specified following sections. Universal Film Exchanges, Inc. v Perriello (1931) 140 Misc 177, 250 NYS 126.

Supreme court action other than those enumerated in the sections excepted in CPA § 182 must be venued in resident county of one of the parties. Joyce v Daniels & Kennedy (1943) 180 Misc 233, 41 NYS2d 793.

CPA § 182 was not violated by granting preference to nonresident of state under Rule 151. Yates v John J. Casale (1949, Sup) 89 NYS2d 583.

CPA § 182 governed actions under the Federal Employers' Liability Act, when such actions brought in the state court. Barton v Delaware, L. & W. R. Co. (1926) 218 AD 748, 218 NYS 171. County first invoked was proper venue of consolidated actions arising from same automobile accident. Casey v Lavut (1947, Sup) 75 NYS2d 673.

CPA § 182 cited generally in Penniman v Fuller & Warren Co. (1892) 133 NY 442, 31 NE 318; Zeimer v Rafferty (1897) 18 AD 397, 46 NYS 345; Binder v Metropolitan S. R. Co. (1902) 68 AD 281, 74 NYS 54.

CPA § 182 cited in reversing order changing place of trial. Gelderman v Fisher (1924) 211 AD 862, 207 NYS 841.

An issue of fact must be tried in the county of residence of a party or in a county in the same judicial district as that county. Shippey v Berkey (1958) 6 AD2d 473, 179 NYS2d 366.

General Municipal Law, § 50-e subd. 5, providing infant's application to serve notice of claim against public corporation, such as New York City Housing Authority, after expiration of period for filing such claim shall be made returnable at trial or special term of Supreme Court, in county where action on claim could properly be brought for trial, raised question of venue but not of jurisdiction, under CPA §§ 182–187. Musarra v New York City Housing Authority (1955, Sup) 141 NYS2d 267.

Subd. 5 of Trial Term Rule V of New York County Supreme Court, giving trial preference to resident plaintiffs and giving plaintiff choice of venue if parties do not reside in same county, did not conflict with CPA § 182. Shapiro v New York City Omnibus Corp. (1956, Sup) 151 NYS2d 252.

2. Waiver

Court may not of its own motion refuse to try the action although brought in county where neither party resides, as venue of transitory action may be waived. Anderson v Nassau E. R. Co. (1910) 138 AD 816, 123 NYS 374; Block v Bacon Coal Co. (1921) 196 AD 958, 188 NYS 911.

A motion to consolidate a transitory action waives the right to trial in the county where it was brought originally. Gruber v Alpert (1939) 257 AD 1007, 13 NYS2d 771.

Failure to move to change venue to proper county constitutes waiver, and such waiver applies not only to question to trial but to proceedings which are similar in nature, such as infant's application to serve notice of claim against public corporation. Musarra v New York City Housing Authority (1955) 141 NYS2d 267.

B. Actions Within Statute

3. Generally

Actions under CPA §§ 182-a, 182-b, 183, 184, 184-a (§§ 503(e), 504, 505(b), 507, 508 herein) are excepted from CPA § 182 providing specified actions must be tried in county of residence of party. Weber v Lacey (1953) 281 AD 290, 120 NYS2d 88.

An action for damages to land in one county caused by a diversion of a stream of water by a dam in another county, where both parties reside, was properly tried according to CPA § 182. Thompson v Attica Water Co. 1 Civ Proc 345.

Action by Onondaga resident against Kansas resident to collect debts of intestate out of realty located in Broome County, claimed by defendant as sole heir, was properly brought in latter county. Titus v Titus (1941) 175 Misc 970, 25 NYS2d 936.

An action by a conditional seller to replevin chattels is triable in the county of the residence of one of the parties. United Projector & Film Corp. v Brown (1932) 145 Misc 412, 260 NYS 269.

An action in the nature of a quo warranto may be tried in any county. People v Cook, 6 How Pr 448.

Where as result of automobile accident in Tompkins County three different negligent actions were commenced, one by plaintiff in Queens County where he resides and two other actions by other parties against plaintiff were commenced in Broome County, and later all three actions were consolidated and place of trial fixed in Broome County, but said two actions were settled and discontinued before order of consolidation was filed in Queens County, venue of single remaining action was restored to Queens County. Intner v Morton (1955) 1 AD2d 723, 146 NYS2d 726.

Where consolidation of two actions is desired, special term should follow the general rule that venue of consolidation of separate actions begun in different counties between the same parties upon

related transactions is to be fixed in the county wherein jurisdiction was first invoked. Efco Products, Inc. v Long Island Baking, Inc. (1958) 6 AD2d 832, 176 NYS2d 46.

4. Transitory actions

Transitory actions should be tried in the county where the transactions involved took place, unless a large preponderance of the witnesses live in another county. Spanedda v Murphy (1911) 144 AD 58, 128 NYS 884; Red Hook Light & Power Co. v Rightmyer (1912) 150 AD 663, 135 NYS 725; Van Alstine v Burt (1912) 151 AD 81, 135 NYS 779; Veeldorano v Union R. Co. (1918) 183 AD 575, 171 NYS 5.

Where a transitory action is brought on for trial the judge presiding may not, of his own motion, without any request from either of the parties, strike the case from the calendar simply because it appears that both the parties are residents of another county. Phillips v Tietjen (1905) 108 AD 9, 95 NYS 469.

In transitory actions in the supreme court, parties may lay the venue in any county and have the issues there tried if they so desire; the court of its own motion cannot strike such cause from the calendar upon the ground that the parties are residents of another county where the cause arose. Anderson v Nassau E. R. Co. (1910) 138 AD 816, 123 NYS 374.

Action by lienor against contractor and surety on former's bond to establish claim for materials furnished for public improvement held transitory and not an action to foreclose a lien on realty within subdivision 9 of CPA § 183 (§ 507 herein). Shelt Co. v Simiele Constr. Co. (1941) 176 Misc 730, 28 NYS2d 794.

A transitory action as a general rule should be tried where it arose, other things being equal. Hahn v Unverdorben (1959) 9 AD2d 9, 189 NYS2d 440; Goldman v Isgood Stottville Realty Corp. (1961) 14 AD2d 759, 220 NYS2d 491.

Although the accident occurred in Suffolk County, an action commenced there was consolidated with multiple actions in New York County and transferred to New York County because New York court's jurisdiction had been first invoked, the New York personal injury calendar was months ahead of the Suffolk calendar, and most of the plaintiffs and attorneys participating in the action were located in New York County. Fernandez v Jagoda (1959) 21 Misc 2d 545, 196 NYS2d 24.

5. Personal injury and death

Actions for damages for death caused by negligence may be brought wherever jurisdiction of the party can be obtained, being transitory. Robinson v Oceanic Steam Nav. Co. (1889) 112 NY 315, 19 NE 625.

An action by a resident of New York City, against a corporation of Massachusetts working a mine in Dutchess county, being for personal injuries received by the plaintiff while working in the mine, should be tried in Dutchess county and not in

New York county. Gorman v South Boston Iron Co. (1884) 32 Hun 71.

Venue of action for personal injury was properly laid in county where one of parties resided. Liebowitz v Hudson Transit Corp. (1945, Sup) 59 NYS2d 313.

Death action must be tried in county in which one of parties resided at commencement of action. Linder v Elmira Ass'n of Commerce, Inc. (1948) 192 Misc 830, 81 NYS2d 132. See also Gray v Compania Naviera Limitada (1949) 196 Misc 903, 96 NYS2d 293.

Action to recover for personal injury and death resulting from malpractice is a transitory action, and the residence of the parties, rather than place where cause of action arose, is determinative of venue. Koslow v Fine (1960) 21 Misc 2d 642, 196 NYS2d 49.

6. Libel

Plaintiff in action for libel could lay the venue in the county of his residence. Barnes v Roosevelt (1914) 87 Misc 55, 149 NYS 291, revd 164 AD 540, 150 NYS 30, to avoid partiality on part of jury due to peculiar circumstances.

When the complaint in an action for libel makes no allegation that there was any publication thereof outside of the county where the newspaper was printed and circulated, the action should be tried in that county. MacCormac v Tobey (1905) 109 AD 581, 96 NYS 302.

Where libeling newspaper was published and circulated in Kings county, where individual parties reside, venue was properly laid in Kings county, though newspaper was circulated and plaintiff was damaged in New York county. Alexander v Brooklyn Eagle (1952, Sup) 114 NYS2d 5, affd 280 AD 929, 116 NYS2d 500.

In libel and slander action where plaintiff resides in New York County and all but one defendant reside in Suffolk County, either county is "proper" county within meaning of this section. Condon v Schwenk (1960) 10 AD2d 822, 199 NYS2d 238.

7. Malpractice

Action to recover for personal injury and death resulting from malpractice is a transitory action, and the residence of the parties, rather than place where cause of action arose, is determinative of venue. Koslow v Fine (1960) 21 Misc 2d 642, 196 NYS2d 49.

8. Matrimonial actions

An action for divorce may be brought in the county where one of the parties resides. Jewitt v Jewitt (1888, Sup) 2 NYS 250.

Motion by defendant to change place of trial of divorce action from Rockland county to New York county granted, where plaintiff at the time of the commencement of the action was a resident of New York county and the defendant a resident of Queens county. Goldstein v Goldstein (1935) 243 AD 777, 277 NYS 643.

Action to annul marriage should be brought in county where one or both parties reside. Casale v Casale (1948, Sup) 81 NYS2d 209.

In annulment action, county residence of either party fixes venue. Fenicchia v Fenicchia (1952, Sup) 110 NYS2d 110.

In an action for separation, county of residence of wife at time of trial fixed venue, where because of husband's cruelty she was compelled to leave him. Generous v Generous (1950) 197 Misc 651, 99 NYS2d 416.

Actual residence, as distinguished from domicile, of wife in Kings county entitled her to sue in such county for separation for cruelty of husband. Lawson v Lawson (1946, Sup) 64 NYS2d 356.

An action for money had and received by a wife living apart from her husband, under an agreement of separation, cannot be removed from the county where the wife lives to that of the residence of the husband. Lyon v Lyon (1883) 30 Hun 455.

C. Parties

9. Generally

"One of the parties" does not embrace all of the plaintiffs or defendants, but means that "an action must be tried in the county in which one of the persons who is a party resided." Shepard v Squire (1894) 76 Hun 598, 28 NYS 218.

It was held under the corresponding section of the judiciary act that "parties" meant parties in interest and not simply parties to the record. Henry v Bank of Salina, 5 Hill 523; Stevens v White, 5 Hill 548; Hart v Oatman, 1 Bard 229. But where action was brought in the name of the treasurer of an express company against the president of another express company, the question was governed by the residence of the parties named. Bacon v Dinsmore, 42 How Pr 368.

10. Agents

The place of trial of an action brought by an agent residing in Queens county against a defendant residing in Kings county cannot be properly laid in Madison county where the owner resides, and the defendant may require the place of trial to be changed to Kings county. Walsh v Maroney (1907) 53 Misc 369, 104 NYS 758.

11. Assignees

Assignee is a party to the action within the meaning of CPA § 182. Bartrop v Sobel Realty Co. (1925) 214 AD 799, 210 NYS 491.

12. Bankrupts

The place of trial will be changed to the county of the principal office and place of business of the bankrupt corporation, where the venue has been laid in another county which was the residence of the trustee in bankruptcy. Allen v McCormick (1919) 110 Misc 254, 180 NYS 116.

13. Brokers

Action for broker's commissions should be brought in county where plaintiff resides. Nevelson v Piesner (1947) 272 AD 555, 74 NYS2d 105.

14. National banks

In an action against a national bank, the place of trial may be laid in any county where it could be laid in an action for the same cause against an individual. Talmadge v Third Nat. Bank (1883) 91 NY 531.

A national bank is a foreign corporation so that a domestic corporation sued by a national bank has an absolute right to have the place of trial changed to the county of the corporation's principal office. Remington & Sherman Co. v Niagara County Nat. Bank (1900) 54 AD 358, 66 NYS 560.

The plaintiff national bank being a foreign corporation with no residence in the county, the defendant is entitled as a matter of right to have trial in his home county. Philadelphia Nat. Bank v McAllister (1931) 234 AD 883, 254 NYS 358.

National banking association, having no office or place of business in New York county, was not immune from suit in New York Supreme Court having state wide jurisdiction. Chaffee v Glens Falls Nat. Bank & Trust Co. (1953) 204 Misc 181, 123 NYS2d 635, affd 128 NYS2d 539.

15. Municipal corporations

CPA § 182 did not prevent change of venue of an action against a city and its officials, under the second-class cities' law, to the county in which such municipality was located. Colonial Motor Coach Corp. v Albany (1930) 229 AD 309, 242 NYS 689, decided before the enactment of CPA § 182-a.

Prior to the enactment of § 66 of the Town Law there was no statute excluding towns from the general provisions of the Civil Practice Act, which regulated the place of trial in actions against towns for negligence. Foley v Hempstead (1934) 241 AD 1, 270 NYS 655.

Board of education of school district embracing 4 towns and central school in Washington county and one town in Rensselaer county, was deemed resident of Washington in action against board for negligence. Schoen v Board of Education (1949) 274 AD 682, 87 NYS2d 589.

Proper venue for infant's application to serve notice of claim against New York City Housing Authority, pursuant to General Municipal Law § 50-e subd. 5, is New York County where infant resides. Musarra v New York City Housing Authority (1955, Sup) 141 NYS2d 267.

Venue of declaratory judgment action brought by New York City against Delaware County to test validity of statutory amendment affecting city's snow-removal obligations was properly laid in New York County since provisions of County Law § 52 governing venue in actions against a county is not applicable to declaratory judgment actions. New York v Colchester (1961) 28 Misc 2d 426, 212 NYS2d 667, affd 16 AD2d 772, 228 NYS2d 462.

Defendant-towns in New York City's declaratory judgment action to test validity of statutory amendment waived their rights to change of venue (Town L § 66) by interposing counterclaims

against the city which were required by CPA § 182-a (§ 504 herein) to be tried in New York County. New York v Colchester, supra.

16. Public officers

Action against public officers for conspiracy fell clearly within CPA § 182, and must have been tried within the county in which one of the parties resided at the commencement of the action. Metropolitan By-Products Co. v Van Name (1917) 176 AD 545, 163 NYS 592.

Where the superintendent of insurance sues in his official capacity as liquidator of an insolvent insurance company the venue is properly laid in Albany County. Stoddard v Manzella (1924) 207 AD 519, 203 NYS 136.

An action for damages against a lawyer for malpractice is not within the subd 2 of § 184 of the Civil Practice Act. Locke v Singer (1952) 279 AD 1097, 112 NYS2d 676.

D. RESIDENCE OF PARTIES

17. Generally

Residence of party, for purposes of venue, must be determined as of time of commencement of action. Jonas Equities, Inc. v 614 E. 14th St. Realty Corp. (1953) 282 AD 773, 123 NYS2d 44.

For the purposes of CPA § 182 a party to an action was not confined to a single residence. The word "residence" did not involve the intention never to leave the place where one settled. Hurley v Union Trust Co. (1935) 244 AD 590, 280 NYS 474.

Residence means "permanent residence," as distinguished from stopping place for business or pleasure; likened to term as used in § 1522. Harshbarger v Sherron Metallic Corp. (1943) 179 Misc 1037, 40 NYS2d 651.

That one home is regular or nine months a year residence and the other only a permanent summer residence, or a claimed permanent hotel residence, does not make the latter the less a residence for purposes of venue, or even for domicile and voting rights. Fromkin v Loehmann's Hewlett, Inc. (1959) 16 Misc 2d 117, 184 NYS2d 63.

18. Domicile distinguished from residence

"Resided" as used in § 182 meant actual residence and not necessarily domicil of one party. Cincinnati H. & D. R. Co. v Ives (1889, Sup) 3 NYS 895; General Motors Acceptance Corp. v Barnett (1931) 142 Misc 192, 254 NYS 166; Gelband v Gelband (1946, Sup) 65 NYS2d 710; Generous v Generous (1950) 197 Misc 651, 99 NYS2d 416.

The term "residence," formerly used in CPA § 182 was construed as synonymous with "domicile," to conform with the construction of that term in former CPA § 1162. Washington v Thomas (1905) 103 AD 423, 92 NYS 994; Kleinrock v Nantex Mfg. Co. (1922) 201 AD 236, 194 NYS 142.

Under CPA § 182, residence and domicile were not synonymous; party might have more than one residence. Fromkin v Loehmann's Hewlett, Inc. (1959) 16 Misc 2d 117, 184 NYS2d 63.

19. Pleading as determining residence

Residence of party, where the summons lays the venue in one county and the complaint in another county, is controlled by the complaint. Jacobs v Callan (1911) 143 AD 827, 128 NYS 295, affd 307 NY 709, 121 NE2d 537.

Allegations by plaintiff in her complaint as to her residence will take precedence over inconsistent statements in an affidavit, and the defendant's motion to change the place of trial to the county alleged in the complaint may be granted. Barnes v Barnes (1927) 219 AD 759, 219 NYS 773.

The rule, that where there is a difference between the summons and complaint as to the place of trial, the complaint controls is subject to the exception that, where it appears that the statement of a different place of trial in the complaint from that named in the summons was due to the inadvertence of the plaintiff's attorney, the place of trial is not changed to the county named in the complaint, provided the plaintiff's attorney moves promptly in the matter to correct the error, so as not to permit his adversary to presume that the charge was intentional. Bell v Polymero (1904), 99 AD 303, 90 NYS 920.

The venue of a case in the supreme court depends upon the nature of the action, determinable from the complaint and demand for judgment. Page Belting Co. v Joseph (1928) 131 Misc 373, 226 NYS 723, revd on other grounds 224 AD 720, 229 NYS 893.

20. Proof of residence

A plaintiff who comes to a particular county for the sole purpose of bringing an action to recover for personal injuries and with no intention of remaining there permanently is not a resident of that county. Hislop v Taaffe (1910) 141 AD 40, 125 NYS 614.

Bona fide intention to choose a residence, characterized by element of permanency and actual abiding there with intention of remaining, constituted compliance with § 182. Bradley v Plaisted (1951) 277 AD 620, 102 NYS2d 295.

One who is keeping a boardinghouse at Saratoga at the time when a motion for change of venue is made, and who does so each year from May to October, is a resident of Saratoga for the purposes of the motion. Stacom v Moon (1881) 25 Hun 452.

A person will be held to be a resident of Nassau county where he merely had an apartment in New York, temporarily, and continued to vote in Nassau county, and before commencement of present action surrendered his apartment, dismissed his servants and moved back to Nassau county. Dresser v Mercantile Trust Co. (1907) 53 Misc 18, 102 NYS 569, affd 118 AD 922, 103 NYS 1124.

That nonresident defendant maintains living quarters in hotel in New York county and has office to transact business there, may not be considered, where he actually resides outside state. Levine v Grey (1946) 63 NYS2d 284.

Renting room in dwelling shortly before instituting action does not make plaintiff resident of that place. Oelkers v Hulseberg (1951) 200 Misc 352, 107 NYS2d 144, affd 279 AD 669, 108 NYS2d 982.

Person cannot reside where he has no room and never spends a night. Marine Midland Trust Co. v Dugan (1952) 202 Misc 847, 119 NYS2d 714.

Trailer occupant was resident of county where trailer was located, where he slept in it and voted from it. Vrooman v Vrooman (1944) 183 Misc 233, 50 NYS2d 694.

Moving affidavits for change of venue attacking residence but based on information and belief without disclosing sources and grounds was not sufficient especially in face of opposing affidavits definitely establishing residence. McDermott v McDermott (1943) 267 AD 171, 45 NYS2d 321.

Where plaintiff's affidavit, opposing defendant's motion to change venue in action for libel from Kings to Westchester County, asserts that plaintiff resides in Kings County, and such assertion is not denied by defendant, venue was properly laid in Kings County. Klein v O'Connell (1956, Co Ct) 152 NYS2d 729.

Mere assertion by plaintiffs that they reside where they have a place of business is not sufficient. Residence requires more stability than occasional stopovers at a hotel, and the mere fact that the plaintiffs rent premises on a year round basis where they sleep while on business does not establish a residence. Hammerman v Louis Watch Co. (1958) 7 AD2d 817, 181 NYS2d 65.

21. Plaintiff's residence

The county in which plaintiff resided at the time the action is brought is the proper county in which to bring the action. Abbott Bread Co. v Schlansky (1934) 242 AD 774, 274 NYS 587.

The proper place for the trial of an action is the county where plaintiff resides, and the place of trial of the action can be changed from that county only for one of the reasons stated in former CPA § 187 subds 2 and 3. Gelderman v Fisher (1924) 211 AD 862, 207 NYS 841.

In action for breach of employment plaintiff's residence fixes venue there, though defendant was doing business in another county. Baker v Julius Pollak & Sons (1950) 277 AD 11, 97 NYS2d 694.

Where plaintiff is resident of county where action is brought, burden of justifying transfer of action to some other place is upon him who seeks change of venue. Horstmann v Freemire (1953, Sup) 124 NYS2d 243.

An action on a promissory note was properly brought in the county where two of the plaintiffs reside at the time of the commencement of the action. Searle v Foltis-Fisher Corp. (1935) 246 AD 620, 282 NYS 981.

In action for work and labor, change of venue from county of plaintiff's residence to county where work was performed was properly denied. Cornyn v University Chevrolet Inc. (1954) 283 AD 969, 130 NYS2d 605.

Residence and place of business of both plaintiffs in county fixed venue there. Samuels v Empire Paper Goods Co. (1949) 194 Misc 871, 91 NYS2d 67.

Where one plaintiff in action for personal injuries was county resident, joinder of nonresident co-plaintiff did not make CPA § 182 inapplicable. Smith v Spencer (1943) 182 Misc 767, 45 NYS2d 242.

Court would not remove action to recover rent out of county where landlord had its principal office, even though demised premises, the tenants, and landlord's managing agent were residents of or located in another county. Rocal Realty Corp. v Magee (1957) 7 Misc 2d 514, 163 NYS2d 846.

Action of interpleader against three defendants one of whom resides in Monroe County was properly brought in such county. John Hancock Mut. Life Ins. Co. v Breen (1955, Sup) 146 NYS2d 561.

In action on guarantee of payment of check given plaintiff in payment of merchandise bought in Montgomery County, where both defendants reside in Oneida County and plaintiff resides in Herkimer County, and maintains his business in Montgomery County, venue is improperly laid in Montgomery County. Du Pont v Bank of Utica (1959) 9 AD2d 807, 192 NYS2d 948.

22. Defendant's residence

Change of venue granted to county of defendant's residence, plaintiffs being non-residents. Van Der Wiele v Van Baalen (1930) 230 AD 715, 242 NYS 894; Dodds v Whitcomb (1943, Sup) 45 NYS2d 441.

Where the plaintiff in a negligence action lays the venue in a county of which he is not a resident, the defendant is entitled as a matter of right to have the venue changed to the county of its residence. Lageza v Chelsea Fibre Mills (1909) 135 AD 731, 119 NYS 906.

If the plaintiff is a nonresident he may lay the venue in the county of the residence of either of the defendants. Forehand v Collins (1874) 1 Hun 316.

If one of the defendants resides in the county it will be sufficient, although he is not served; that the other defendant was not a resident of the county and was the only one who appeared and answered does not affect the question. Forehand v Collins, supra.

An action by a resident of New Jersey upon a written contract executed and to be performed in New York County, in which the original defendant and one of others brought in on plaintiff's motion reside in New York County, while the other defendants are nonresidents, defendant's motion to change the place of trial from Queens County, where instituted, to New York County, should have been granted, in view of the provisions of §§ 182, 183–187 (§§ 503(a), 503(b)(e), 504, 505(b), 507, 508, 509, 510, 602(b), Rule 512

herein). Pond v Cadwell (1923) 206 AD 623, 199 NYS 21.

In an action by a nonresident brought in New York county for personal injuries resulting from an accident which occurred in Queens county against a resident of Jefferson county, a motion by the defendant for a change of venue to the county of his residence is granted. A cross-motion by the plaintiffs for a change of venue to Queens county could not be entertained in New York county and is, therefore, denied. Reed v Ross (1940) 260 AD 596, 23 NYS2d 341.

Place of trial of two actions for negligence is changed from Franklin county, where they arose, to Bronx county, where it appears that defendant resides in that county and plaintiffs are residents of New York county. Dunlap v Paterno (1933) 147 Misc 393, 263 NYS 195.

Defendant is entitled as matter of right to have venue changed to county where he resides, when plaintiff has no residence in county where action is brought. McCarthy v Andrews (1950) 199 Misc 656, 103 NYS2d 170.

Where infant plaintiff was resident of foreign state and defendant was resident of Herkimer county, defendant's motion to change venue to his county was granted, over plaintiff's motion to retain action in Kings county, where witnesses were equally balanced. Safran v Elias (1951, Sup) 104 NYS2d 616.

Where neither plaintiff nor defendant resided in the county where the venue was laid, at the commencement of the action, motion to change place of trial to residence of defendant should be granted. General Baking Co. v Daniell (1918) 181 AD 501, 170 NYS 365.

Purely technical objection raised by plaintiff that defendant, having failed to file a certificate of doing business in county in which he does business, so misled plaintiff that defendant should be estopped from designating place of trial was not valid. The only test within the purview of CPA § 182 was the residence of the parties. Midwest Mower Corp. v Lober (1956) 31 Misc 2d 191, 157 NYS2d 307.

Where a nonresident is suing a New York resident, the proper venue is in the county where the defendant resides. Carnes v Zanghi (1956) 4 Misc 2d 815, 157 NYS2d 331.

In action by minority stockholder for accounting, where neither plaintiff nor any defendant resides in Kings county, venue was changed to New York county where several defendants reside, despite plaintiff's disputed claim of oral stipulation retaining venue in Kings county. Wohl v Miller (1954) 284 AD 1062, 135 NYS2d 890.

Where liquidating trustees of dissolved corporation resided in Nassau county, but principal place of business of corporate defendant was in Kings county, action to set aside release for fraud was properly brought in Kings county. Searing v Randall Cadillac Corp. (1956) 3 Misc 2d 594, 151 NYS2d 163, adhered to 3 Misc 2d 594, 158 NYS2d 358.

53

Where none of the plaintiffs resided in county in which action was instituted, defendants were entitled to a change of venue to county wherein all defendants and one of the plaintiffs resided and the motion for change was properly made in that county where plaintiffs' opposing affidavit was insufficient. Chason v Airways Hotel, Inc. (1959) 18 Misc 2d 96, 184 NYS2d 125.

In action on guarantee of payment of check given plaintiff in payment of merchandise bought in Montgomery County, where both defendants reside in Oneida County and plaintiff resides in Herkimer County, and maintains his business in Montgomery County, venue is improperly laid in Montgomery County. Du Pont v Bank of Utica (1959) 9 AD2d 807, 192 NYS2d 948.

23. Executors and administrators

Prior to the 1924 amendment to former CPA § 182 the residence of an executor was held to be his personal residence. Dayton v Farmer (1922) 200 AD 737, 193 NYS 331; Rathbun v Brownell (1904) 43 Misc 307, 88 NYS 833.

CPA § 182 entitled ancillary administrator, to fix the venue of his action in the county in which the ancillary letters were issued. Waterworth v Franz (1933) 146 Misc 668, 262 NYS 660.

In an action by a nonresident against two executors, in which the second executor is in default, a motion by the first executor for a change of the place of trial to the county of his appointment, rather than to the county in which he resides, is granted in the interests of justice. Bahnsch v Andrews (1939) 172 Misc 61, 14 NYS2d 578.

Administrator is entitled to elect whether action will be instituted in county where administrator resides or in county of his appointment. McNamara v Penner (1953, Sup) 123 NYS2d 576.

Nonresident of state is not deemed resident of county of appointment in action against administratrix for negligent death. Central Greyhound Lines, Inc. v Faust (1949) 196 Misc 53, 91 NYS2d 609, affd Re Roop's Estate (1951) 278 AD 1012, 105 NYS2d 1010.

24. Committee for incompetent

Committee of incompetent who was simply the designated person to sue on behalf of the incompetent was not a "party to the action" and his residence did not control for the purposes of determining the place of trial. Mahan v Wyman (1957) 6 Misc 2d 81, 161 NYS2d 929.

25. Guardians

Residence of guardian ad litem does not control venue of action by infant, since guardian is not a party. Levey v United States Life Ins. Co. (1940) 259 AD 909, 20 NYS2d 157.

26. Domestic corporations

For the purpose of determining the venue, a corporation is a resident of the place designated in its articles of incorporation as its principal place of business. Speare v Troy Laundry Mach. Co.

(1899) 44 AD 390, 60 NYS 1080; Dairymen's League Co-op. Ass'n v Brundo (1927) 131 Misc 548, 227 NYS 203; Keehn v S. & D. Motor Lines Inc. (1943, Sup) 41 NYS2d 521.

The 1925 amendment to former CPA § 182 did not include in the word "party" a corporation so that it would be given the right to have other residence than that it selects with its franchise. Ajax Rubber Co. v J. P. Devine Co. (1926) 126 Misc 341, 214 NYS 311.

On a motion of a change of venue, a domestic corporation is deemed to be a resident of the county in which it has its principal office and place of business. Finch School v Finch (1911) 144 AD 687, 129 NYS 1.

A domestic corporation sued by a non-resident has the right to have the trial in the county of its principal place of business. Duche v Buffalo Grape Sugar Co. 63 How Pr 516.

Unlike a railroad, a baking corporation does not reside in every county in which it operates and has branches. General Baking Co. v Daniell (1918) 181 AD 501, 170 NYS 365.

The place of residence of a corporation is where its principal business is to be carried on as designated by its charter, though in fact it may have an office and conduct a large part of its business in another county. Rossie Iron-Works v Westbrook (1891) 59 Hun 345, 13 NYS 141.

It has been held that where prevailing proof indicated that corporate plaintiff is actively present and conducted its true residence and business in Kings county, it was improper to change venue to New York county, regardless of plaintiff's certificate of incorporation. Golfbay Country Club, Inc. v Oceanside Golfers Ass'n, Inc. (1952, Sup) 114 NYS2d 175.

Where plaintiff's certificate of incorporation was amended prior to and presumably in contemplation of commencing action but was filed after service of defendant's demand to change place of trial to county of latter's incorporation, defendant's demand was granted. Jonas Equities, Inc. v 614 E. 14th St. Realty Corp. (1953) 282 AD 773, 123 NYS2d 44.

Change of principal place of business of domestic corporation two days after service of summons was ineffective to defeat CPA § 182. American Millwork Corp. v Roskin Bros. Inc. (1952, Sup) 112 NYS2d 15.

Action by lienor against contractor and surety on former's bond, to establish claim for materials furnished for public improvements, was properly tried in the county where plaintiff corporation had its principal place of business. Shelt Co. v Simiele Constr. Co. (1941) 176 Misc 730, 28 NYS2d 794.

An action by a judgment debtor for the sequestration of the property of a corporation comes within CPA § 182, and so does a motion for a receiver or any other judicial relief. Smith v Danzig, 3 Civ Proc 127.

A party can have for venue-of-action purposes a residence in more than one county, but where a certificate of incorporation expressly fixes the location of a place of business as in one named county, that is the residence of such business. Yonkers Raceway, Inc. v National Union Fire Ins. Co. (1957) 9 Misc 2d 412, 170 NYS2d 205, affd 6 AD2d 846, 176 NYS2d 241, affd 6 NY2d 756, 186 NYS2d 656, 159 NE2d 203; Circle Bake Shop, Inc. v Demand Oil Corp. (1959) 21 Misc 2d 643, 196 NYS2d 47.

A motion for a change of venue will be denied where the plaintiff conducts a business in the county in which the action is laid and is deemed to be a resident thereof where it has designated that county in the certificate of incorporation as its place of business. Yonkers Raceway, Inc. v National Union Fire Ins. Co. (1957) 9 Misc 2d 412, 170 NYS2d 205, affd 6 AD2d 846, 176 NYS2d 241, affd 6 NY2d 756, 186 NYS2d 656, 159 NE2d 203.

Certificate of incorporation designating New York County as county in which plaintiff's office is located is conclusive evidence of its residence for venue purposes, and defendant was entitled to have venue changed from Kings to Westchester County where defendant resided. Acme Kalamein Door & Sash Co. v Bronxville-Devon Corp. (1954, Sup) 135 NYS2d 184.

Where certificate of incorporation provides that its principal business office is located in New York County and location for conduct of business is in Westchester County, defendant's motion to change place of trial from Westchester County to New York County denied. Yonkers Raceway, Inc. v National Union Fire Ins. Co. (1958) 6 AD2d 846, 176 NYS2d 241, affd 6 NY2d 756, 186 NYS2d 656, 159 NE2d 203.

County in which plaintiff corporation has its principal place of business is proper venue of action involving contract to be performed in another county. Gardner & North Roofing & Siding Corp. v Deaton (1955) 1 Misc 2d 90, 146 NYS2d 577, affd 286 AD 992, 144 NYS2d 744.

In stockholder's derivative action against corporation, stockholder is party plaintiff and his county residence fixes venue of action. Feldmeier v Webster (1955) 208 Misc 996, 145 NYS2d 365, affd 1 AD2d 938, 150 NYS2d 581.

A corporation has its residence for venue purposes in the county designated in its certificate of incorporation as the place in which its office is located, and not in the county in which it actually maintains its place of business. Boro Kitchen Cabinets, Inc. v Spalt (1959) 9 AD2d 925, 195 NYS2d 87.

In breach of contract action, corporation was granted change of venue from New York County to Kings County, the county designated in its certificate of incorporation as the location of its principal office. Hoffman v Oxford Developments, Inc. (1959) 9 AD2d 937, 195 NYS2d 484.

Corporation's residence is in the county in which its principal office as designated in its certificate of incorporation is located, and fact that it also has an office in another county does not change its residence for purpose of venue. Hoffman v Oxford Developments, Inc., supra.

In action by director against corporation and majority stockholder for corporation's failure to pay dividends, director's residence, rather than residence of corporate defendant, controlled venue of action. Blum v Gleitsman (1960) 25 Misc 2d 740, 203 NYS2d 38.

In proceedings to set aside election of directors, denial of corporate defendant's motion for change of venue from Queens to Erie County, situs of its principal place of business and where the election was held was reversed as an improvident exercise of discretion. Scharf v Irving Air Chute Co. (1961) 15 AD2d 563, 223 NYS2d 307.

27. Foreign corporations

A foreign corporation cannot be a resident of the state. Shepard & Morse Lumber Co. v Burleigh (1898) 27 AD 99, 50 NYS 135.

In an action by a foreign corporation against a resident, defendant is entitled as a matter of right to have trial in his home county. Dan W. Feitel Bag Co. v Bobinski (1931) 234 AD 879, 254 NYS 357; Philadelphia Nat. Bank v McAllister (1931) 234 AD 883, 254 NYS 358; New Haven Clock Co. v Hubbard (1891, Sup) 16 NYS 125.

A domestic corporation having its principal office in the county of Niagara, when sued by a foreign corporation, has an absolute right to have the place of trial changed to Niagara county. Remington & Sherman Co. v Niagara County Nat. Bank (1900) 54 AD 358, 66 NYS 560.

Business place of foreign corporation in particular county did not bar change of venue to county of defendant's residence. Nash Kelvinator Sales Corp. v Clark (1950) 276 AD 1056, 96 NYS2d 354.

When a foreign corporation doing business in this state, sued resident defendants in an action upon contract not specified in CPA § 183 or § 194, the trial should have been laid in the county in which one of the defendants resided; the residence of a citizen of this state is not affected by the place of his business interests or official position. When such defendant moves to change the venue to the county of his residence, the court is without authority to consider the convenience of witnesses at the instance of the plaintiff. Mills & Gibb v Starin (1907) 119 AD 336, 104 NYS 230.

Where individual plaintiff was nonresident and defendant was foreign corporation, plaintiff may fix venue in any county of New York, provided the court accepts jurisdiction. Gray v Compania Naviera Limitada (1949) 196 Misc 903, 96 NYS2d 293.

Where plaintiff is a foreign corporation, proper venue is determined by residence of defendant president or treasurer as such. Republic Aviation Corp. v Republic Lodge, etc. (1957) 10 Misc 2d 783, 169 NYS2d 651.

Where New Jersey corporation was authorized to do business in New York and had its only place of business in Kings County, its only domicile and residence was in New Jersey, and proper venue of its action against defendant for money lent was county of defendant's residence. Taller & Cooper,

Inc. v Rand (1955) 286 AD 1096, 145 NYS2d 557.

In an action in which a resident of this state and a foreign corporation are parties, the county of the resident is the proper county. Twentieth Century-Fox Corp. v Papayanokos (1957) 8 Misc 2d 1079, 171 NYS2d 526.

28. Common carriers

A railroad company is considered as having a residence in every county through which its railroad runs. Poland v United Traction Co. (1903) 88 AD 281, 85 NYS 7, affd 177 NY 557, 69 NE 1125; Polley v Lehigh Valley R. Co. (1910) 138 AD 636, 122 NYS 708, affd 200 NY 585, 94 NE 1098; Levey v Payne (1922) 200 AD 30, 192 NYS 346; De Groat v New York C. R. Co. (1932) 235 AD 816, 256 NYS 853; People ex rel. Buffalo & S. L. R. Co. v Barker (1871) 48 NY 70.

In an action to recover damages for personal injuries against a railroad company, the place of trial is properly laid in a county through which its road is operated in which it owns property and has a place for the regular transaction of business. Mole v New York, O. & W. R. Co. (1907) 53 Misc 22, 102 NYS 308.

Where a railroad is sued in a county in which it does not operate or has no property, venue may be changed to a county in which it has property and is doing business. Gaboury v Central V. R. Co. (1928) 225 AD 145, 231 NYS 630, revd on other grounds 250 NY 233, 165 NE 275.

Where plaintiff, a resident of Kings County, brought suit against the Director General of Railroads in New York County on a cause of action arising in Sullivan County, where the defendant operated his railroad, and the defendant moved for a change of venue to Sullivan County, it was error for the court, on its own motion, to direct the trial to be had in Kings County, and to deny defendant's motion for a change of venue to Sullivan County, in view of CPA § 182 and § 187 (§§ 510, 602(b) herein). Levey v Payne (1922) 200 AD 30, 192 NYS 346.

Bus corporation, a common carrier, is entitled to change venue of action against it from Queens to Nassau county, where plaintiff resided and where corporation resides, as fixed by its certificate of incorporation. Ray v Bee Line, Inc. (1943) 180 Misc 172, 40 NYS2d 447.

Fact that steamship corporation has pier in certain county does not make it a resident of such county; it is resident of county where its principal place of business is located. Hearn v Farrell Lines (1951) 278 AD 829, 104 NYS2d 227.

Railroads which operate through Westchester County could properly lay venue of their action for declaratory judgment that certain provisions of Railroad Law are void in that county and fact that they sought, as incidental relief, a permanent injunction against Public Service Commission did not require change of venue to Albany County. New York C. R. Co. v Lefkowitz (1962, Sup) 227 NYS2d 302, affd 17 AD2d 638, 230 NYS2d 678,

affd 12 NY2d 305, 239 NYS2d 341, 189 NE2d 695.

29. Partnerships

In action for breach of construction contract, where principal office of partnership and of one individual partner were in New York county, such county was proper venue. Minskoff v Henderson-Johnson Co. (1951, Sup) 112 NYS2d 74.

Action on account instituted by limited partnership triable in county of residence of single partner, though certificate of formation fixes principal place of business in another county. Bulkley v O'Donnell (1933) 148 Misc 186, 265 NYS 495, affd 240 AD 929, 267 NYS 983.

E. PLACE OF TRIAL OF ASSIGNED CAUSE OF ACTION

30. Generally

CPA § 184-a is subject to power afforded by CPA § 187 to change place of trial for convenience of witnesses. Weber v Lacey (1953) 281 AD 290, 120 NYS2d 88.

It was held before the enactment of CPA § 184-a that the ends of justice would be promoted by trying the assigned issues in the county where plaintiff's assignors resided and rendered the services sued for, and that the court must consider the county where the cause of action arose rather than the convenience of an assignee. Brecht v Jagger (1916) 172 AD 880, 158 NYS 1017.

An action upon contract made in New York City, and to be performed there, is properly brought in New York County, although the claims were assigned to the resident of another county who sued on them; especially in view of the fact that the assignee was employed by the assignor and himself was in business in New York City. Brady v Hogan (1907) 117 AD 898, 102 NYS 962 (decided before enactment of § 184-a).

CPA § 182 construed with CPA § 184-a in holding that stockholder's derivative action is not excepted from provisions of CPA § 182. Feldmeier v Webster (1955) 208 Misc 996, 145 NYS2d 365, affd 1 AD2d 938, 150 NYS2d 581.

In a case where the plaintiff is an assignee and merely a nominal party in interest, the usual requirements to effectuate a change of venue need not be strictly enforced. Saphir v Kruse (1957) 5 Misc 2d 415, 158 NYS2d 620.

Assignee of accounts receivable does not come within the terms of the exception clause in favor of holders in due course of negotiable instruments. Sterling Factors Corp. v Sad Sam's Furnitureland Inc. (1960) 21 Misc 2d 837, 195 NYS2d 55.

Action to recover royalties payable on a percentage basis, in the absence of allegations of fiduciary relationship is an action to recover money only, even though plaintiff also prays for an accounting. Jernberg v Virtus Co. (1961) 32 Misc 2d 820, 225 NYS2d 180.

31. Foreign corporations

A foreign corporation, authorized to do business

in New York, is not resident of any county for purpose of venue, and action by plaintiff-assignee was properly brought in county designated by plaintiff. Meyer v Anselm & Co. (1949) 196 Misc 736, 94 NYS2d 613.

A foreign corporation authorized to do business here is not a resident of any county for purpose of venue, and therefore, an action by assignee of such corporation must be brought in the county of defendant's residence. Sterling Factors Corp. v Sad Sam's Furnitureland Inc. (1960) 21 Misc 2d 837, 195 NYS2d 55.

32. Money lent

In action by assignee for money lent, where de-

fendants resided in New York county and had their principal place of business there, defendants had procedural right to change venue to New York county, but they waived their privilege by failing to move for change of venue under RCP 146. Shapiro v Leslie Fay Corp. (1954, Sup) 138 NYS2d 606.

33. Goods sold and delivered

In action by assignee of claim for goods sold and delivered, motion setting aside service of summons properly denied where motion on ground that service not made on proper officer of corporation and action not within jurisdiction of City Court of White Plains. Monea v Refrigeration Corp. of America (1958) 7 AD2d 639, 179 NYS2d 850.

§ 504. Actions against counties, cities, towns, villages, school districts and district corporations

Notwithstanding the provisions of any charter heretofore granted by the state and subject to the provisions of subdivision (b) of section 506, the place of trial of all actions against counties, cities, towns, villages, school districts and district corporations or any of their officers, boards or departments shall be, for:

1. a county, in such county;

2. a city, except the city of New York, town, village, school district or district corporation, in the county in which such city, town, village, school district or district corporation is situated, or if such school district or district corporation is situated in more than one county, in either county; and

3. the city of New York, in the county within the city in which the cause of action arose, or if it arose outside of the city, in the county of New York.

HISTORY:

> Add, L 1962, ch 308, amd, L 1966, ch 444, eff Sept 1, 1966.
> Section heading, amd, L 1966, ch 444, eff Sept 1, 1966.
> Earlier statutes: CPA §§ 182-a, 182-b.

ADVISORY COMMITTEE NOTES:

> Subject to § 506, which deals with CPA article 78 proceedings, this provision aims at a uniform rule governing actions against counties, cities, towns and villages or any of their officers, boards or department. It consolidates CPA §§ 182-a and 182-b, County Law § 52, Second Class Cities Law § 242, Town Law § 66(1) and Village Law § 341-e. It is also designed to override any charter provisions to the contrary. Cf. County of Westchester v Department of Health of the City of New York, 297 NY 491, 74 NE2d 190 (1947). Suits by a municipality are governed by §§ 503(a) and 503(c), but if one municipality sued another § 504, and not § 503, would control.

CROSS REFERENCES:

> Action by city under Public Markets Law, Agr & M Law § 270-e(1).
> Compare action against county, County Law § 52(1).
> Venue of proceedings against second class city, Sec Cl Cities Law § 242.

FEDERAL ASPECTS:

> Venue in United States District Court, 28 USCS §§ 1391 et seq.

United States as defendant, 28 USCS § 1402.

Venue as unaffected by Federal Rules of Civil Procedure, Rule 82 of Federal Rules of Civil Procedure, USCS Court Rules.

RESEARCH REFERENCES AND PRACTICE AIDS:

7 Carmody-Wait 2d, Place of Trial or Venue §§ 48:12, 48:28.

23 Carmody-Wait 2d, Actions By and Against Public Bodies and Public Officers § 144:98.

56 Am Jur 2d, Municipal Corporations, Counties, and Other Political Subdivisions §§ 855–858.

Law Reviews:

New York Civil Practice Law and Rules: venue. 27 Albany L Rev 181.

Biannual survey of New York practice: Part IV: federal venue statute regarding national banking associations deemed controlling. 39 St. John's L Rev 426.

CASE NOTES

In an action against a county, venue may be transferred out of the county against whom such action is commenced, but such procedure requires a motion by plaintiff for that relief. Braver v County of Nassau Office of Administrative Services (1971) 67 Misc 2d 120, 323 NYS2d 630.

Where all parties and witnesses lived in New York City, witnesses in action against Nassau County for personal injuries could not be so inconvenienced by a trial in that county as to defeat its venue right. Braver v County of Nassau Office of Administrative Services (1971) 67 Misc 2d 120, 323 NYS2d 630.

The Brooklyn Public Library, sued for negligence, is not a branch of the city of New York within the meaning of statute providing that the place of trial of all actions against the city shall be in the county within the city in which the cause of action arose. Flawless Realty Co. v Brooklyn Public Library (1975) 48 AD2d 891, 369 NYS2d 502.

Proper venue for trial of State's action against town for contribution to the State with respect to liability of the State to injured motorist would be the county in which the town was located rather than Albany County. State v County of Sullivan (1975) 84 Misc 2d 765, 376 NYS2d 786, revd on other grounds 54 AD2d 29, 386 NYS2d 253.

The venue of an action brought by New York City sanitation workers to recover unpaid wages lay in the county within the city in which they performed work for which they allege they were not paid, and it does not lie in the county in which the city comptroller has an office and where he determined the plaintiffs were not entitled to the wages claimed, under subd 3 of CPLR § 504. McElroy v New York (1965) 45 Misc 2d 713, 257 NYS2d 376, affd 25 AD2d 498, 267 NYS2d 484.

Venue properly lies in the county where the zoning authority complained of is located. Lerner v Islip (1967, DC NY) 272 F Supp 664.

Proper venue for trial of State's action against town for contribution to the State with respect to liability of the State to injured motorist would be the county in which the town was located rather than Albany County. State v County of Sullivan (1976) 54 AD2d 29, 386 NYS2d 253.

Statutes governing actions against cities, inter alia, and real property actions, rather than provisions of statute governing venue based on residence, controlled action to enjoin municipality from discharging sewage into harbors and waters surrounding municipality, which sewage allegedly washed ashore onto public beaches of plaintiff municipalities. Hempstead v New York (1976) 88 Misc 2d 366, 388 NYS2d 78.

Where it was alleged that municipality had continuously permitted public nuisance and trespass to occur by virtue of discharge of sewage into surrounding harbors and waters, which acts or omissions to act affected other municipalities' use and enjoyment of their real property due to fact that sewage allegedly washed ashore onto their public beaches, venue of action belonged in county where real property was located. Hempstead v New York (1976) 88 Misc 2d 366, 388 NYS2d 78.

CASE NOTES

UNDER FORMER CIVIL PRACTICE LAWS

1. Generally
2. Actions against city officials
3. Waiver or loss of right to change of venue
4. Joint trial of actions

5. Action against City of New York
6. Action against NYC officials
7. Action by outside county

1. Generally

CPA § 182-a was subject to power afforded by CPA § 187 (§§ 510, 602(b), herein) to change place of trial for convenience of witnesses. Weber v Lacey (1953) 281 AD 290, 120 NYS2d 88.

Right conferred by CPA § 182-a upon city and officers was personal to it and them; it was not available to any other defendant. Shelt Co. v Simiele Constr. Co. (1941) 176 Misc 730, 28 NYS2d 794.

In action against Schenectady and others, proper place of trial in first instance was Schenectady county, where there was no claim that convenience of witnesses required change of venue. Bagan v Fritz (1949) 274 AD 1082, 85 NYS2d 530.

CPA § 182-a applied to every city in New York State, including City of New York. Reeve v O'Dwyer (1950) 199 Misc 123, 98 NYS2d 452.

Venue of an action against a city, its common council and mayor was changed to the county in which the municipality was situated under Second Class Cities Law, before the enactment of CPA § 182-a. Colonial Motor Coach Corp. v Albany (1930) 229 AD 309, 242 NYS 689.

CPA § 182 construed with § 182-a in holding stockholder's derivative action was not excepted from provisions of CPA § 182. Feldmeier v Webster (1955) 208 Misc 996, 145 NYS2d 365, affd 1 AD2d 938, 150 NYS2d 581.

Where action is brought by Commissioners of State Insurance Fund, such action is to be brought in county in which fund maintains office but venue can be changed for convenience of witnesses and in interests of justice. Commissioners of State Ins. Fund v Alexander (1956) 4 Misc 2d 309, 157 NYS2d 244.

Where one of defendants was a city in Orange County and others were police officers in that city their motion to change venue to Orange County was granted where plaintiffs, on their cross-motion to retain venue in New York County, failed to produce sufficient evidence to establish inconvenience of witnesses or impossibility of securing a fair trial in Orange County. Levine v Port Jervis (1958) 15 Misc 2d 574, 182 NYS2d 705, affd 11 AD2d 1016, 210 NYS2d 478.

Where no prejudice resulted to plaintiff, defendant city's demand for change of venue to county in which it is situated served with its amended answer conforming the venue in the answer to that of the complaint was granted. Ross v Rochester (1959) 8 AD2d 925, 187 NYS2d 929, affd 8 NY2d 1067, 207 NYS2d 282, 170 NE2d 413.

2. Actions against city officials

CPA § 182-a applied to action against officials of City of New York, though City itself was not sued. Reeve v O'Dwyer (1950) 199 Misc 123, 98 NYS2d 452.

Defendant-towns in New York City's declaratory judgment action to test validity of statutory amendment waived their rights to change of venue (Town L § 66) by interposing counterclaims against the city which are required by CPA § 182-a to be tried in New York County. New York v Colchester (1961) 28 Misc 2d 426, 212 NYS2d 667, affd 16 AD2d 772, 228 NYS2d 462.

3. Waiver or loss of right to change of venue

City's two years' acquiescence in plaintiff's designation of venue in the county of his residence, and its failure to show prejudice, warranted denial of its motion for change of venue. Godley v New York (1961) 31 Misc 2d 841, 220 NYS2d 260.

4. Joint trial of actions

Where two actions arising out of automobile collision in New York County were pending in Bronx County and New York County, and the Bronx action had been begun first and was ready to be reached for trial, the fact that New York City was a defendant in the New York action did not prevent the court, in the exercise of its discretion, from fixing venue for the joint trial of the action in Bronx County. Spadaccini v New York (1960) 9 AD2d 502, 195 NYS2d 666.

5. Action against City of New York

CPA § 182-b and the preceding one, CPA § 182-a, when read together meant that any action brought against any city should have been in the county in which the city was located and since, except for the city of New York, every city is contained within a single county, special provision had to be made for the city of New York, with respect to which one of the five counties, in which the city is located, should be the venue of actions against it. Reeve v O'Dwyer (1950) 199 Misc 123, 98 NYS2d 452.

An action against New York City for personal injuries received in automobile collision in Queens county was properly removed from New York to Queens county. Masch v New York (1945) 270 AD 182, 59 NYS2d 2.

Right to preference in contract action accorded to resident of Kings county may only be considered in respect of action begun in first instance as matter of right in such county, and may not be considered when begun in disregard of CPA § 182-b. Barash v New York (1946) 270 AD 945, 62 NYS2d 264.

CPA § 182 (§ 502(a)(b), herein) construed with CPA § 182-b in holding that stockholder's derivative action is not excepted from provisions of CPA § 182 (§ 502(a)(b), herein). Feldmeier v Webster (1955) 208 Misc 996, 145 NYS2d 365, affd 1 AD2d 938, 150 NYS2d 581.

CPA § 182-b must be construed to harmonize with the purposes of CPA § 96-a (§ 602(a) herein) governing joint trials. Spadaccini v New York (1960) 9 AD2d 502, 195 NYS2d 666.

Under provisions of CPA § 182-b Supreme Court of New York County had jurisdiction to entertain petition of infant for leave to file late claim though cause of action accrued in Kings County. Manceri v New York (1960) 23 Misc 2d 94, 198 NYS2d 388.

CPA § 182-b was a venue statute designating where an action was to be commenced, but it did not impinge upon the jurisdiction of the Supreme Court to change the venue of an action. Spadaccini v New York (1960) 9 AD2d 502, 195 NYS2d 666.

6. Action against NYC officials

CPA § 182-b applied to action against officials of New York City, though City itself was not sued.

Reeve v O'Dwyer (1950) 199 Misc 123, 98 NYS2d 452.

7. Action by outside county

Action by Westchester county against Department of Health of City of New York for judgment declaring regulation of such Department illegal, was properly brought in Westchester county. Westchester County v Department of Health (1947) 297 NY 491, 74 NE2d 190.

§ 505. Actions involving public authorities

(a) Generally. The place of trial of an action by or against a public authority constituted under the laws of the state shall be in the county in which the authority has its principal office or where it has facilities involved in the action.

(b) Against New York city transit authority. The place of trial of an action against the New York city transit authority shall be in the county within the city of New York in which the cause of action arose, or, if it arose outside of the city, in the county of New York.

HISTORY:
> Add, L 1962, ch 308, eff Sept 1, 1963.
> Earlier statutes: CPA § 182-b.

ADVISORY COMMITTEE NOTES:
> **Subd (a)** of this section provides a new and uniform rule to govern actions by or against public authorities. It conforms in large part to the pattern found in special venue provisions in the Public Authorities Law. All such special venue provisions are to be repealed.

FEDERAL ASPECTS:
> Venue in United States District Court, 28 USCS §§ 1391 et seq.
> United States as defendant, 28 USCS § 1402.
> Venue as unaffected by Federal Rules of Civil Procedure, Rule 82 of Federal Rules of Civil Procedure, USCS Court Rules.

RESEARCH REFERENCES AND PRACTICE AIDS:
> 7 Carmody-Wait 2d, Place of Trial or Venue § 48:12.
> 23 Carmody-Wait 2d, Actions By and Against Public Bodies and Public Officers § 144:98.

> **Annotations:**
> > Construction and application of 28 USCS § 1391(e) providing for venue and process in civil actions against federal officers, employees, or agencies. 9 ALR Fed 719.

> **Law Reviews:**
> > New York Civil Practice Law and Rules: venue. 27 Albany L Rev 181.
> > Biannual survey of New York practice: Part IV: federal venue statute regarding national banking associations deemed controlling. 39 St. John's L Rev 426.
> > Survey of New York law venue. 15 Syracuse L Rev 401.

CASE NOTES

Where action was brought against state agency which had a principal office in New York County, and also against a village, and plaintiff filed affidavit that New York County was the proper place for trial, an order changing the place of trial to Nassau County was improper and motion should properly have been made returnable in New York County. Meyers v New York State Div. of Housing & Community Renewal (1969) 32 AD2d 818, 302 NYS2d 287.

Summary judgment is not a "trial" within the meaning of CPLR § 505(a). Vizzi v Islip (1972) 71 Misc 2d 483, 336 NYS2d 520.

CASE NOTES

UNDER FORMER CIVIL PRACTICE LAWS

1. Generally
2. Action against NYC officials
3. Action by outside county

1. Generally

CPA § 182-b is subject to power afforded by CPA § 187 (§§ 510, 602(b) herein) to change place of trial for convenience of witnesses. Weber v Lacey (1953) 281 AD 290, 120 NYS2d 88.

CPA § 182-b and the preceding one, CPA § 182-a, when read together, meant that any action brought against any city should be in the county in which the city is located and since, except for the city of New York, every city is contained within a single county, special provision had to be made for the city of New York, with respect to which one of the five counties, in which the city is located, should be the venue of actions against it. Reeve v O'Dwyer (1950) 199 Misc 123, 98 NYS2d 452.

An action against New York City for personal injuries received in automobile collision in Queens county was properly removed from New York to Queens county. Masch v New York (1945) 270 AD 182, 59 NYS2d 2.

Right to preference in contract action accorded to resident of Kings county could only be considered in respect of action begun in first instance as matter of right in such county, and could not be considered when begun in disregard of CPA § 182-b. Barash v New York (1946) 270 AD 945, 62 NYS2d 264.

2. Action against NYC officials

CPA § 182-b applied to action against officials of New York City, though City itself was not sued. Reeve v O'Dwyer (1950) 199 Misc 123, 98 NYS2d 452.

3. Action by outside county

Action by Westchester county against Department of Health of City of New York for judgment declaring regulation of such Department illegal, was properly brought in Westchester county. Westchester County v Department of Health (1947) 297 NY 491, 74 NE2d 190.

§ 506. Where special proceeding commenced

(a) Generally. Unless otherwise prescribed in subdivision (b) or in the law authorizing the proceeding, a special proceeding may be commenced in any county within the judicial district where the proceeding is triable.

(b) Proceeding against body or officer. A proceeding against a body or officer shall be commenced in any county within the judicial district where the respondent made the determination complained of or refused to perform the duty specifically enjoined upon him by law, or where the proceedings were brought or taken in the course of which the matter sought to be restrained originated, or where the material events otherwise took place, or where the principal office of the respondent is located, except that

1. a proceeding against a justice of the supreme court or a judge of a county court or the court of general sessions shall be commenced in the appellate division in the judicial department where the action, in the course of which the matter sought to be enforced or restrained originated, is triable, unless a term of the appellate division in that department is not in session, in which case the proceeding may be commenced in the appellate division in an adjoining judicial department; and

2. a proceeding against the regents of the university of the state of New York, the commissioner of education, the state tax commission, the public

service commission, the commissioner or the department of transportation relating to articles three, four, five, six, seven, eight, nine or ten of the transportation law or to the railroad law, the water resources board, the comptroller or the department of agriculture and markets, shall be commenced in the supreme court, Albany county.

HISTORY:

Add, L 1962, ch 308, eff Sept 1, 1963.
Sub (b), par 2, amd, L 1962, ch 318, § 3, L 1970, ch 267, § 8, eff Mar 1, 1971.
Earlier statutes and rules: CPA § 1287; RCP 295; CCP § 2349, in part; from portions of 2 RS 194, 195, §§ 167, 170, 175; 2 RS 53–55, §§ 11, 16, 19, 22; ch 417 of 1864, §§ 1, 5; ch 627 of 1869; ch 37 of 1870; ch 446 of 1874, tit 1, §§ 6, 9, 17, 23.

ADVISORY COMMITTEE NOTES:

Subd (a), applying to special proceedings generally, is new. It is modeled on CPA § 1287. Since special proceedings are brought on in much the same manner as a motion, the special proceeding may be brought in any county within the judicial district where the proceeding is triable.

Subd (b) is derived from CPA § 1287. Minor changes have been made in terminology and the following provision has been omitted as unnecessary: "The special term at which relief is applied for may, in the exercise of its discretion, transfer the proceeding to the county wherein the principal office of the respondent is located."

CROSS REFERENCES:

This section referred to in 504, 7804.

FEDERAL ASPECTS:

Venue in United States District Court, 28 USCS §§ 1391 et seq.
Venue as unaffected by Federal Rules of Civil Procedure, Rule 82 of Federal Rules of Civil Procedure, USCS Court Rules.

RESEARCH REFERENCES AND PRACTICE AIDS:

23 Carmody-Wait 2d, State Warrants for Collection of Taxes and Other Charges § 143:20.
24 Carmody-Wait 2d, Proceeding Against a Body or Officer §§ 145:248–145:252.
24 Carmody-Wait 2d, Judicial Review of Tax Assessments and Taxes § 146:136.
5 Am Jur Pl and Pr Forms (Rev ed), Certiorari, Forms 11–14.

Law Reviews:

New York Civil Practice Law and Rules: venue. 27 Albany L Rev 181.
Biannual survey of New York practice: Part IV: federal venue statute regarding national banking associations deemed controlling. 39 St. John's L Rev 426.

CASE NOTES

1. In general
2. Proceeding against body or officer
3. —Judicial officers
4. —Proceedings commenced in Albany County

1. In general

Improper venue is not jurisdictional and is not destructive to the action. Hvac & Sprinkler Contractors Asso. v State University Constr. Fund (1975) 80 Misc 2d 1047, 364 NYS2d 422.

Habeas corpus, a special proceeding, is subject to the practice provisions governing venue generally. Greene v Supreme Court, Westchester County (1968) 31 AD2d 649, 297 NYS2d 599.

2. Proceeding against body or officer

Article 78 proceeding brought in Nassau County to annul determination of Superintendent of Banks authorizing establishment of branch bank in Nassau County, was transferred in court's discretion to New York County, where the principal office of the bank was located, the acts complained of occurred, and all the acts required to be done by petitioner would have to be performed. Franklin Nat. Bank v Superintendent of Banks (1963) 40 Misc 2d 315, 243 NYS2d 214.

Venue properly lies in the county where the zoning authority complained of is located. Lerner v Islip (1967, DC NY) 272 F Supp 664.

Petitioner which initially chose forum for Article 78 proceeding could not complain of venue. Hvac & Sprinkler Contractors Asso. v State University Constr. Fund (1975) 80 Misc 2d 1047, 364 NYS2d 422.

A motion to quash a nonjudicial subpoena is akin to a proceeding against an officer, and the proper court for venue purposes is where the subpoena originated or in the county where the principal office of the officer is located. Re Associated Homeowners & Businessmen's Organization, Inc. (1976) 85 Misc 2d 676, 381 NYS2d 191, transf 87 Misc 2d 67, 385 NYS2d 449.

Proper venue for motion to quash subpoena duces tecum issued by deputy Attorney General in connection with investigation of nursing homes was in New York County, not Kings County, where subpoena was returnable in New York County. Deutsch v Yagman (1975) 85 Misc 2d 681, 381 NYS2d 369.

3. —Judicial officers

Special Term had no jurisdiction to enter order of prohibition against the County Court and the district attorney of the county to prevent further prosecution of defendant. Snee v County Court of County of Cayuga (1969) 31 AD2d 303, 297 NYS2d 414.

Proceeding to enjoin county court judges from proceeding with prosecution of an indictment and to compel judges of district court to reinstate accused's previous plea of guilty to crime of sexual abuse which had been vacated without his consent was required to be commenced in the appropriate special term of the Supreme Court and not in the Appellate Division. Green v Judges of County Court (1976) 51 AD2d 968, 380 NYS2d 296.

Where parties seeking redress from execution of allegedly illegal search warrant sought prohibition against a county court judge as well as against a public prosecutor, proceeding was properly commenced in the Appellate Division. B. T. Productions, Inc. v Barr (1976) 54 AD2d 315, 388 NYS2d 483.

4. —Proceedings commenced in Albany County

Since a garnishment proceeding against the state of New York was not a direct proceeding against the Comptroller, § 506(b)(2) of the CPLR is not applicable. Butler v State (1965) 47 Misc 2d 365, 262 NYS2d 705.

In action to declare Transportation Law § 15 and Public Service Law § 89-b unconstitutional, and to enjoin public utilities from discontinuing service on basis of alleged nonpayment, such discontinuance involved state action, and procedure for discontinuance under aforementioned statutes and regulations promulgated pursuant thereto provided due process, but Public Service Commission's alleged refusal to hold a "formal hearing" on discontinuance pursuant to regulation was reviewable only by Article 78 proceeding, and was accordingly transferred to Supreme Court in accordance with requirements of CPLR § 506(b), subd 2. Levine v Long Island Lighting Co. (1973) 76 Misc 2d 247, 349 NYS2d 963.

An action, in the nature of prohibition, to prevent the closing of a state school because of budgetary reasons, was required to be brought in Albany County, where the determination was made and the material events took place. Semple v Miller (1971) 67 Misc 2d 545, 324 NYS2d 369, affd 38 AD2d 174, 327 NYS2d 929.

The reference in CPLR 506 to the Water Resources Board (water resources commission) must be deemed a reference to the Department of Environmental Conservation, and an action to review a determination of such Department must be brought in Albany County. Hamilton v Diamond (1972) 69 Misc 2d 492, 330 NYS2d 199.

Venue properly lay in Albany County in an Article 78 proceeding brought against Attorney General of state, since principal office of Attorney General was necessarily located at seat of state government in capitol at Albany. Normandy Village Co. v Lefkowitz (1976) 88 Misc 2d 363, 388 NYS2d 64.

CASE NOTES

UNDER FORMER CIVIL PRACTICE LAWS

A. IN GENERAL

1. Generally

A proceeding by an assignee for the benefit of creditors against a state department should be brought in the third judicial district wherein the department was located and conducted its business, although the assignee was appointed and the debtor resided in Kings county. Re 1200 Ocean Parkway, Inc. (1938) 170 Misc 129, 9 NYS2d 22.

CPA § 1287 authorized the supreme court at special term to review an order suspending automobile licenses where the term was held in the county where the alleged violation occurred, where the conviction was had and where the petitioner resided. Application of Gardiner (1938) 168 Misc 349, 5 NYS2d 942, affd 255 AD 106, 6 NYS2d 385.

Supreme court has jurisdiction to restrain by prohibition county court from granting defendant charged with murder inspection of medical examiner's report to district attorney. Application of Hughes (1943) 181 Misc 668, 41 NYS2d 843.

CPA § 1287 referred only to venue; and was not intended to affect jurisdiction of supreme court. Application of Avon Dairies, Inc. (1952) 280 AD 116, 111 NYS2d 272.

CPA § 1287 which required that CPA Article 78 (Article 78 herein) proceedings against the State Tax Commission had to be brought in the Third Judicial District, applied only to article 78 proceedings, and was not applicable to plenary actions. Hudson Transit Lines, Inc. v Bragalini (1958) 11 Misc 2d 1094, 172 NYS2d 423.

Jurisdiction of CPA Article 78 (Article 78 herein) proceeding to remedy removal in violation of Civil Service Law § 22 would lie in the Fifth Judicial District. Hook v State (1958) 15 Misc 2d 672, 181 NYS2d 621.

CPA § 1287 required petitioner to seek relief at Special Term of Supreme Court. The County Court had no jurisdiction of CPA Article 78 (Article 78 herein) proceeding and where a City Court denied District Attorney an adjournment, the County Court had no authority to prohibit the City Court from continuing to assume jurisdiction and its order to that effect must be reversed without prejudice to the bringing of an Article 78 proceeding in the Supreme Court. Application of Sovocool (1959) 7 AD2d 262, 182 NYS2d 553.

Court of General Sessions had no jurisdiction over CPA Article 78 (Article 78 herein) proceeding against the district attorney for failure of official duty, since its jurisdiction was exclusively criminal. People v Moore (1961) 31 Misc 2d 1014, 220 NYS2d 990.

2. Place of trial

Where according to petition material facts took place within named county, such county is the proper county in which application to annul determination should be made and where such county is in the Fifth Judicial District, referral of the matter should be made to the Appellate Division, Fourth Department. Eldred v Monaghan (1958) 11 Misc 2d 701, 175 NYS2d 223.

A proceeding may be brought in Kings county wherein it is alleged "material facts otherwise took place" although the "determination complained of" was made in New York county. Rosenberg v Board of Estimate (1938) 170 Misc 359, 9 NYS2d 635.

There was nothing in CPA § 1287 to indicate that any of the three alternatives as to the county wherein application for relief may have been made had priority over the others. Rosenberg v Board of Estimate, supra.

A proceeding to review determinations involving an application for death benefits under the New York city retirement system may be maintained in Queens county, where the decedent was employed, and where the accident on which the claim is based occurred. The claim that the proceeding is maintainable only in a county embraced within the First Judicial District, wherein the public body or officer performing the act complained of, is not sustained. Daley v Board of Estimate (1939) 258 AD 165, 15 NYS2d 868.

A proceeding to review determination of agriculture commissioner may be commenced in county wherein occurred underlying events giving rise to official act complained of, though actual determination was made in county of another judicial district. Rochester Co-op. Milk Producers Bargaining Agency, Inc. v Du Mond (1945) 185 Misc 522, 57 NYS2d 321, transf 271 AD 769, 65 NYS2d 437.

County of origin of materials facts is proper county for institution of proceedings. Zorach v Clauson (1949) 275 AD 774, 87 NYS2d 639, affd 300 NY 613, 90 NE2d 68.

Where income taxpayer resided in Kings county, where he conducted his realty business and made and verified his tax return, he may institute proceeding in Kings county to review determination of tax commission having office in such county. Brown v Bates (1951, Sup) 102 NYS2d 859.

In proceeding by city employees to review determination of comptroller of City of New York of prevailing wage rates, motion to change place of trial from Queens to New York was granted, where comptroller maintains office in New York county at which he renders all determinations as to Labor Law complaints. Application of Kiernan (1952, Sup) 114 NYS2d 445.

In proceeding to review revocation of retail liquor license by state liquor authority, venue is properly laid in county where material facts took place. Lacqua v O'Connell (1952) 280 AD 31, 111 NYS2d 777.

Where taxpayer seeks to review assessments and his petition is directed against State Tax Commission, application must be made at Special Term of supreme court in third judicial district. Application of State Tax Com (1953) 203 Misc 404, 122 NYS2d 647.

Proceeding to review determination of Classified and Appeals Board of State Department of Civil Service, denying petitions for upward reallocation of salary grades in positions of Senior Underwriters State Insurance Fund, was properly transferred from New York to Albany county. Mahony v Conway (1953) 281 AD 1057, 121 NYS2d 556.

In proceeding to compel restoration of exempt firemen to their former employment, where petitioners were all residents of Monroe County, performed their work there and their status as exempt firemen arose there, such proceeding was properly brought in Monroe County. McDermott v Johnson (1955) 1 Misc 2d 55, 145 NYS2d 247.

CPA § 1287 specifically provided for the venue of CPA Article 78 (Article 78 herein) proceedings and where petitioner alleged police commissioner in New York county arbitrarily refused to appoint him, venue was improperly laid in Kings County and matter should have been transferred to New York County. De Riso v Kennedy (1958) 13 Misc 2d 322, 176 NYS2d 444.

Venue of proceeding to review determination of Rent Commission was changed to Queens County where the determination was made there, the material facts took place there, and the apartment in question was located there. Caro v Weaver (1958) 15 Misc 2d 558, 182 NYS2d 630.

Venue in CPA Article 78 (Article 78 herein) proceedings lay in judicial district wherein occurred the material facts, or the underlying events giving rise to the official action complained of; consequently review of determination of Parole Board as matter of law that prisoner's sentence ran consecutively may properly have been had in district where the sentences were originally imposed, and not in district where Parole Board rendered its ruling. Browne v State Board of Parole (1960) 25 Misc 2d 1050, 207 NYS2d 488, affd 12 AD2d 800, 211 NYS2d 1014, revd on other grounds 10 NY2d 116, 218 NYS2d 33, 176 NE2d 492.

On motion to change venue, a county within the judicial district embracing the county wherein the material facts took place is favored over a county in the judicial district wherein respondent's principal office is located. Manzi v Kaplan (1962) 33 Misc 2d 62, 224 NYS2d 409.

Prohibition proceeding against Court of General Sessions and District Attorney to restrain them from retrying petitioner on indictment should be made returnable to the Appellate Division, not Special Term. Application of Nolan (1961) 15 AD2d 78, 222 NYS2d 635, affd 11 NY2d 114, 227 NYS2d 1, 181 NE2d 751.

Special term does not have jurisdiction to hear prohibition proceeding against County Court judges; the proceeding must be brought in the Appellate Division. Wapnick v County Court of State (1962) 34 Misc 2d 357, 228 NYS2d 201.

3. —Schools

Proceeding by school district trustees of certain school district in Saratoga county to review determination of education commissioner, directing them to provide transportation of elementary school children, should be brought in Third Judicial District wherein was his office. Re Trustees of School Dist (1941) 261 AD 1016, 25 NYS2d 845.

Proceeding to review reinstatement of director of physical education of schools of Beacon by State Department of Education, was properly brought in Dutchess county where events occurred. Board of Education v State Dept. of Education (1949) 275 AD 1041, 91 NYS2d 894.

Where petition signed by qualified voters requesting that special meeting be called was presented to Board of Education of such district and was rejected, and then petitioners appealed to Commissioner of Education in Albany, they may bring proceedings to review his decision within Third Judicial District, since decision appealed from was made in Albany County. Knapp v Chisholm (1955, Sup) 144 NYS2d 191.

Proceeding against Board of Education to annul its determination confirming decision of Superintendent of Schools to transfer certain pupils in Brooklyn school to schools in Queens County, should be brought in Queens Court where the main investigation by the Superintendent was made in Queens County, and the locale of the Queens schools was also a material fact underlying his decision. Anderson v Board of Education (1959) 19 Misc 2d 873, 192 NYS2d 941.

4. —Prisons

On certiorari to review determination of parole board denying parole to inmate of Sing Sing in Westchester county, Albany county supreme court properly changed place of hearing to Westchester county supreme court. Hines v State Board of Parole (1943) 267 AD 99, 44 NYS2d 655.

5. Power of special term

Special term may pass on availability of other relief although required to transfer proceedings to appellate division. Re City Ice & Fuel Co. (1940)

260 AD 537, 23 NYS2d 376, app den 261 AD 847, 25 NYS2d 1011.

Where it did not appear from papers submitted that proceeding to review determination of commissioner of motor vehicles had been commenced at Special Term or that it had been transferred to Appellate Division, jurisdiction was lacking. Application of Bieder (1954) 283 AD 725, 127 NYS2d 645.

After transfer of CPA Article 78 (Article 78 herein) proceeding to Appellate Division, Special Term had no jurisdiction to take any other action in regard to it without permission of Appellate Division. Desimone v New York State Liquor Authority (1961) 12 AD2d 998, 211 NYS2d 481.

6. Waiver

In absence of motion to change venue, village's statutory right to have venue changed to county where village is situated will be waived. Herricks Road Corp. v Godfrey (1946, Sup App T) 63 NYS2d 447.

B. DECISIONS PRIOR TO ENACTMENT OF ARTICLE 78

7. District

Application for mandamus made in the wrong district, reversed. Buffalo Dump Truck Owners' Ass'n v Condon (1931) 232 AD 273, 249 NYS 602.

8. Place of trial

Where transaction took place in another county, order was reversed. Buffalo Dump Truck Owners' Ass'n v Condon (1931) 232 AD 273, 249 NYS 602.

C. CERTIORARI; DECISIONS UNDER FORMER § 1296 PRIOR TO CIVIL PRACTICE ACT

9. Generally

The practice as to a certiorari to review an assessment is regulated by chap. 269 of 1880, and not by the Civil Prac. Act. People ex rel. New York L. E. & W. R. Co. v Low (1886) 40 Hun 176.

10. Term at which returnable

A certiorari issued under chap. 269 of 1880, must be made returnable at a special term in the judicial district in which the assessment complained of was made. People ex rel. Church of Holy Communion v Assessors of Greensburgh (1887) 106 NY 671, 12 NE 794.

11. Amendment

Under the Tax Law, a petition for the writ of certiorari to review certain franchise assessment upon property in New York state may be made to and the writ allowed by the supreme court in the first judicial district, but under this section the writ should be returnable in the third judicial district at the office of the clerk of the county of Albany, where the assessment is made, and if made returnable in the first district it should not be quashed but should be amended and made returnable in the third district. People ex rel. New York C. & H. R. R. Co. v Priest (1902) 169 NY 432, 62 NE 567, modg 63 AD 128, 71 NYS 390.

12. Waiver of objections

A certiorari issued under chap. 269 of 1880, for reviewing an assessment of personal property, was made returnable to the office of the clerk of Onondaga county instead of at special term, and both parties appeared before such clerk and agreed that the matter be referred to referee. Held to be a waiver of the objection. People ex rel. Paddock v Lewis (1890) 55 Hun 521, 9 NYS 333.

D. MANDAMUS; DECISIONS UNDER FORMER § 1317 PRIOR TO CIVIL PRACTICE ACT

13. Generally

See People ex rel. Thaw v Grifenhagen (1915, Sup) 154 NYS 965.

This section does not take the application for a mandamus out of the general provision of § 116, the object of which was to give the judges of the first judicial district all the powers of a court without the formality of being in court. People ex rel. Lower v Donovan (1892) 63 Hun 512, 18 NYS 501, revd 135 NY 76, 31 NE 1009.

The provisions of this section, that a writ of mandamus can only be granted at a special term, apply only to the original application for the writ, and under §§ 105, 106, 584, the appellate division may, upon appeal from order denying the writ, grant the writ. People ex rel. Kavanagh v Grady (1897) 20 AD 27, 46 NYS 645.

14. Adjourned special term

As an alternative writ of mandamus may be granted with or without notice, as the court thinks proper, the order directing the issue of the writ may be granted at an adjourned special term. People ex rel. Fulton v Board of Supervisors (1888) 50 Hun 105, 3 NYS 751.

An alternative writ of mandamus, where it is granted without notice, may properly be granted at an adjourned special term—i. e., a special term adjourned to a judge's chambers—but it seems that it should not be granted upon notice at such a term. People ex rel. Fulton v Board of Supervisors, supra.

15. Judge at chambers

A writ of mandamus cannot be issued by a judge at chambers in the city of New York, or elsewhere within the state. People ex rel. Lower v Donovan (1892) 135 NY 76, 31 NE 1009, revg 63 Hun 512, 18 NYS 501.

16. Proper district

In order to entitle the appellant to the writ, it was

necessary to establish a legal equalization of the valuation of the respective counties by the board of equalization, filing of the statement or certificate of such equalization by the board of equalization, the notification of the proper officers in the respective counties of the valuation fixed by said board, and the nonpayment of the taxes into the treasury of the state. These acts were actually or constructively performed in the city of Albany; therefore, a motion for a writ of mandamus was properly made in the third judicial district. People v Myers (1888) 50 Hun 479, 3 NYS 365, affd without op 112 NY 676, 20 NE 417.

An application for a writ of mandamus against public officers must be made within the judicial district in which the action resulting from the issue of such a writ would be triable, or in a county adjoining. People ex rel. Cagger v Supervisors of Schuyler County, 2 Abb Pr NS 78; Mason v Willers (1876) 7 Hun 23.

Application for a writ of mandamus to reinstate the relator to the place of state oyster protector must be made in Albany county, where the forest, fish and game commission has its office, the material fact being the removal from office. People ex rel. Overton v Whipple (1908) 61 Misc 112, 114 NYS 307.

17. Waiver

When a motion is made to quash an alternative writ of mandamus, a respondent waives his right to have it argued at a term of the appellate division by arguing the question without objection at the trial term. People ex rel. Ajas v Department of Health (1910) 138 AD 559, 123 NYS 294.

E. MANDAMUS; DECISIONS UNDER FORMER § 1318 PRIOR TO CIVIL PRACTICE ACT

18. Waiver

When a motion is made to quash an alternative writ of mandamus, a respondent waives his right to have it argued at a term of the appellate division by arguing the question without objection at the trial term. People ex rel. Ajas v Department of Health (1910) 138 AD 559, 123 NYS 294.

F. MANDAMUS; DECISIONS UNDER FORMER § 1334 PRIOR TO CIVIL PRACTICE ACT

19. Where material facts arose

In determining where an issue or an alternative writ of mandamus should be tried, when the affidavit fails to disclose where the "material facts" arose, legal inferences cannot be substituted for facts; as in an action involving the discharge of a barge canal laborer, it cannot be assumed as a matter of law that the removal took place in Albany county. People ex rel. Arnold v Skene (1909) 194 NY 186, 87 NE 432, affg 128 AD 883, 112 NYS 1141.

20. State comptroller as defendant

An application for a writ of mandamus requiring the state comptroller to approve an assessment roll containing assessments of forest lands against the state, should be made within the third judicial district where the office of the comptroller is located. People ex rel. Brighton v Williams (1911) 145 AD 8, 129 NYS 457.

21. Return of verdict

The verdict must be returned to, and the final order which is to be deemed a final judgment must be made, by the special term; and the judgment is to be entered, docketed and enforced, as prescribed by § 1332. People ex rel. Neftaniel v Order of American Star, 53 Super Ct (21 Jones & S) 66; People v Myers (1888) 50 Hun 479, 3 NYS 365, affd without op 112 NY 676, 20 NE 417.

On the trial of issues of fact joined on an alternative writ of mandamus, the trial term may direct a verdict as in other cases, but is without power to grant a final order thereon; the verdict or decision "must be returned to and the final order thereupon must be made by the appellate division or special term as the case requires," and these tribunals alone have power to make the final order. People ex rel. Blank v Supreme Lodge, K. & L. of H. (1908) 126 AD 86, 110 NYS 148.

G. PROHIBITION; DECISIONS UNDER FORMER § 1343 PRIOR TO CIVIL PRACTICE ACT

22. Generally

A special term has no power to issue an alternative writ of prohibition, prohibiting a referee appointed under the act to prevent monopolies, chap. 690 of 1899, to secure testimony before proceeding in the matter; this is a power which under §§ 1343 and 1344 has been reserved to the appellate division. Re Atty. Gen. 32 Misc 1, 66 NYS 129, revd on other grounds People ex rel. Morse v Nussbaum, 55 AD 245, 67 NYS 492, revd on other grounds 168 NY 89, 61 NE 118.

H. PROHIBITION; DECISIONS UNDER FORMER § 1344 PRIOR TO CIVIL PRACTICE ACT

23. Generally

As to power of special term to issue writ against referee appointed by another special term, see Re Atty. Gen. 32 Misc 1, 66 NYS 129, revd People ex rel. Morse v Nussbaum, 55 AD 245, 67 NYS 492, revd 168 NY 89, 61 NE 118.

Where on the day application to the first department was made for a writ to a justice of the second department, the term of the appellate division for that department had not adjourned, but had previously recessed, and on the date of the application the court had handed down opinions and five justices, while, not on the bench, were actually in the courthouse prepared to handle judicial business, a term of the court was in session and the first department was without jurisdiction to issue the writ. People ex rel. Whitman v Woodward (1912) 150 AD 180, 134 NYS 910.

§ 507. Real property actions

The place of trial of an action in which the judgment demanded would affect the title to, or the possession, use or enjoyment of, real property shall be in the county in which any part of the subject of the action is situated.

HISTORY:

    Add, L 1962, ch 308, eff Sept 1, 1963.
    Earlier statutes: CPA § 183; CCP § 982.

ADVISORY COMMITTEE NOTES:

    This provision is based upon CPA § 183(9). No change of substance is intended. The listing of specific types of real property actions found in § 183 seems unnecessary, since the language is broad enough to cover all of the specific listings.

CROSS REFERENCES:

    Mechanics' liens, Lien Law §§ 24, 40–64.
    Lien on vessels, Lien Law §§ 85–107.
    Other liens, Lien Law §§ 122, 160, 205–210.
    Land without state, Real P Actions & Pr Law § 121.

FEDERAL ASPECTS:

    Venue in United States District Court, 28 USCS §§ 1391 et seq.
    Venue as unaffected by Federal Rules of Civil Procedure, Rule 82 of Federal Rules of Civil Procedure, USCS Court Rules.

RESEARCH REFERENCES AND PRACTICE AIDS:

    1 Carmody-Wait 2d, Courts and their Jurisdiction § 2:165.
    3 Carmody-Wait 2d, Stays § 22:21.
    7 Carmody-Wait 2d, Place of Trial or Venue §§ 48:4, 48:12.
    13 Carmody-Wait 2d, Real Property Actions Generally §§ 86:12 et seq.
    14 Carmody-Wait 2d, Partition § 91:111.
    14 Carmody-Wait 2d, Foreclosure of Mortgages on Real Estate § 92:77.
    16 Carmody-Wait 2d, Establishment, Discharge, and Enforcement of Mechanics' Liens § 97:300.
    17 Carmody-Wait 2d, Actions Respecting Dower § 104:19.
    17 Carmody-Wait 2d, Proceeding for Disposition of Real Property of Infant or Incompetent § 106:7.
    17 Carmody-Wait 2d, Actions for Waste, Nuisance, and Trespass §§ 107:23, 107:65, 107:84.
    23 Carmody-Wait 2d, State Warrants for Collection of Taxes and Other Charges § 143:20.
    24 Carmody-Wait 2d, Proceeding Against a Body or Officer §§ 145:248–145:252.
    24 Carmody-Wait 2d, Judicial Review of Tax Assessments and Taxes § 146:136.
    25 Am Jur 2d, Ejectment § 74.

Annotations:

    Lien as estate or interest in land within venue statute. 2 ALR2d 1261.
    Venue of suit to enjoin nuisance. 7 ALR2d 481.
    Venue of action to set aside as fraudulent conveyance of real property. 37 ALR2d 568.
    Venue of damage action for breach of real-estate sales contract. 8 ALR3d 489.

Law Reviews:

    New York Civil Practice Law and Rules: venue. 27 Albany L Rev 181.
    Biannual survey of New York practice: Part IV: federal venue statute regarding national banking associations deemed controlling. 39 St. John's L Rev 426.

CASE NOTES

1. In general
2. "Affecting" title distinguished from "involving" title
3. Waiver
4. Consolidation
5. Contracts, foreclosures, liens and the like
6. Damage to property; nuisance
7. Matrimonial actions

1. In general

Statute providing that real property actions are to be tried in the county where the real property is found has its application in venue and not jurisdiction. Drachman Structurals, Inc. v Anthony Rivara Contracting Co. (1974) 78 Misc 2d 486, 356 NYS2d 974.

Statutory provision that place of trial in action in which judgment demanded would affect title to, or possession, use or enjoyment of, real property shall be in county in which any part of subject of action is situated precludes trial of an action affecting real property from taking place in a county other than one in which real property is located. Inspiration Enterprises, Inc. v Inland Credit Corp. (1976) 54 AD2d 839, 388 NYS2d 578, motion dismd 40 NY2d 1014, 391 NYS2d 573, 359 NE2d 1367.

2. "Affecting" title distinguished from "involving" title

This section applies only to actions which would affect the title to, or the possession, use or enjoyment of, real property, and is inapplicable to an action which merely "involves" title but does not actually "affect" it. McNamara Realty, Inc. v Hutchinson (1967) 54 Misc 2d 810, 283 NYS2d 422.

The line of demarcation in applying this section and its predecessor is whether the action "involves" title to real property or "affects" title to realty, and the section extends only to the latter class of actions. Accordingly, defendant's motion to move the venue from Monroe to Ontario County should have been granted in an action seeking a decree directing defendant to execute and deliver to plaintiff a mortgage upon realty situated in Ontario County, since in the interest of orderly procedure and for the sake of facility and certainty in title records trial in the county of the realty is favored. Craig v Clifton Springs Country Club, Inc. (1966) 26 AD2d 903, 274 NYS2d 455.

3. Waiver

Owners and lessee of real property who failed to object or to move against venue in actions to foreclose mechanic's liens waived objections to venue. Drachman Structurals, Inc. v Anthony Rivara Contracting Co. (1974) 78 Misc 2d 486, 356 NYS2d 974.

4. Consolidation

While complaint in third action was virtually identical to complaint in first action, based on alleged fraud of defendants in instituting a foreclosure action against property formerly owned by plaintiff in New York County, and sought identical relief, where it pertained to a foreclosure of real property in Suffolk County, and foreclosures in both counties had no connection with each other except that most of the parties were the same in both actions, denial of motions to remove and consolidate action pending in Suffolk County with action pending in New York County and to enjoin defendants from maintaining action in Suffolk County while action in New York County was pending was not an abuse of discretion inasmuch as consolidation would adversely affect substantial rights of parties. Inspiration Enterprises, Inc. v Inland Credit Corp. (1976) 54 AD2d 839, 388 NYS2d 578, motion dismd 40 NY2d 1014, 391 NYS2d 573, 359 NE2d 1367.

5. Contracts, foreclosures, liens and the like

Proper venue of action, in form of stockholder's derivative action brought to require reconveyance of certain real estate to corporations and to enjoin the transfer of the property or the creation of liens or encumbrances thereof, was in county in which real property was situated. Winston v Krinsky (1968) 30 AD2d 524, 290 NYS2d 247.

Where the plaintiff alleged that defendant had misappropriated his funds and used the money to purchase real estate, and asked that the property be subjected to a lien, the action must be brought in the county in which the real property is located. John H. Dair Bldg. Constr. Co. v Mayer (1966) 27 AD2d 535, 275 NYS2d 724.

Where plaintiff, who had obtained option to purchase real property but found such title to be unmarketable, brought action to cancel the executory contract to purchase and to impress a lien on the real property for the amount of its damages and for a decree directing sale of premises to satisfy said lien, such action was one affecting an interest in real property and county in which real property was situated was proper place for trial despite fact that both parties were nonresidents. Merrill Realty Co. v Harris (1974) 44 AD2d 629, 353 NYS2d 570.

This section does not apply to an action at law to recover damages for breach of a contract for payment of real estate commissions, although that contract relates to real property, for in such a case the judgment which plaintiff seeks is a simple money judgment and does not affect the title to real property. McNamara Realty, Inc. v Hutchinson (1967) 54 Misc 2d 810, 283 NYS2d 422.

Subcontractor's cause of action, which was phrased in terminology normally employed in mechanic's lien foreclosure proceeding, but which requested judgment adjusting and determining equities of all parties to action, determining extent and priority of each and all liens and claims presented and asserted, and foreclosing defendants and all persons claiming by or through them of all equity of redemption or other lien, claim or interest in subject property, was not action which could be maintained only in county wherein subject property was located, was not action which affected title, possession or enjoyment of real property, but was transitory action of which Suffolk County Supreme Court, where action was initially brought had jurisdiction. Axinn & Sons Lumber Co. v Northwood Projects, Inc. (1976) 86 Misc 2d 890, 385 NYS2d 487.

6. Damage to property; nuisance

An action in which damages are sought for the cutting of trees and damage to other property located in St. Lawrence County is a real property action, and although the plaintiff is a resident of both Nassau and St. Lawrence counties and filed his action in Nassau County the proper venue was in St. Lawrence County where the alleged damage occurred. Geidel v Niagara Mohawk Power Corp. (1965) 46 Misc 2d 990, 261 NYS2d 379.

Statutes governing actions against cities, inter alia, and real property actions, rather than provisions of statute governing venue based on residence, controlled action to enjoin municipality from discharging sewage into harbors and waters surrounding municipality, which sewage allegedly washed ashore onto public beaches of plaintiff municipalities. Hempstead v New York (1976) 88 Misc 2d 366, 388 NYS2d 78.

Where it was alleged that municipality had continuously permitted public nuisance and trespass to occur by virtue of discharge of sewage into surrounding harbors and waters, which acts or omissions to act affected other municipalities' use and enjoyment of their real property due to fact that sewage allegedly washed ashore onto their public beaches, venue of action belonged in county where real property was located. Hempstead v New York (1976) 88 Misc 2d 366, 388 NYS2d 78.

7. Matrimonial actions

Where wife in matrimonial action instituted in Albany County demanded judgment granting her exclusive possession of marital residence, statute mandated that place of trial be in Suffolk County in which marital residence was located. Turner v Turner (1974) 84 Misc 2d 229, 375 NYS2d 718.

Although action for divorce and counterclaim that certain real property in Nassau County, which property was held by the parties as tenants by the entirety, be the sole property of the defendant could have been tried in the matrimonial proceeding in Warren County, special term did not abuse its discretion in severing the real property cause of action and transferring it to Nassau County for trial. Forde v Forde (1976) 53 AD2d 779, 384 NYS2d 547.

CASE NOTES

UNDER FORMER CIVIL PRACTICE LAWS

A. IN GENERAL
 1. Generally
 2. Other statutes
 3. Land in different counties
 4. Land in another state
 5. Inferior courts
 6. Third-party action

B. SPECIFIC ACTIONS
 7. Generally
 8. Ejectment
 9. Foreclosure of mortgage
10. Waste
11. Nuisance
12. Specific performance

C. ACTIONS AFFECTING OTHER INTERESTS IN REAL PROPERTY
13. Generally
14. Trespass
15. Establishment of mortgage
16. Annulment of mortgage
17. Enforcement of mechanic's lien on real property
18. Condemnation of land

19. Rescission, reformation, cancellation
20. For cutting timber
21. Assignments for benefit of creditors
22. Enforcement of judgments
23. Water rights

D. ACTIONS NOT WITHIN STATUTE
24. Generally
25. Assignment of mortgage
26. Breach of contract relating to real property
27. Covenants in deed
28. Diversion of water
29. Enforcement of mechanics' liens against public improvements, or substitution bond generally
30. On municipal bonds
31. Partnership accounting
32. Rent or income
33. To compel satisfaction of money judgment where a lien on real property
34. Matrimonial litigation involving realty

A. IN GENERAL

1. Generally

CPA § 183 did not affect the jurisdiction of the Supreme Court, but determined only the county of trial. If the defendant did not avail himself of the provisions of the Civil Practice Act to have the cause moved to the proper county for trial, a judgment in an action affecting real property brought in a county other than that designated as the proper county was valid. Railroad Co-operative Bldg. & Loan Ass'n v Cocks (1936) 248 AD 905, 290 NYS 611; Railroad Federal Sav. & Loan Asso. v Rosemont Holding Corp. (1936) 248 AD 909, 290 NYS 609.

The territory annexed to the county of New York is part of the county of New York for the purpose of determining the place of trial of one of the class of actions specified in CPA § 183. Hawkins v Pelham Electric Light & Power Co. (1899) 158 NY 417, 53 NE 162; Zeimer v Rafferty (1897) 18 AD 397, 46 NYS 345.

A statute governing the place of trial of actions against cities of the second class is in the nature of an act affecting forms of procedure only, and governs a motion to change the place of trial, although the act took effect after the commencement of the action. People v Syracuse (1908) 128 AD 702, 113 NYS 707.

The ineligibility of some of the judges in a county where real property affected by the action is situated, does not prevent trial in that county. Sherwood v Verplanck, 10 Reporter 608.

CPA § 183 was mandatory as to requirements contained therein. Katzen v Central Park Towers, Inc. (1955) 207 Misc 181, 138 NYS2d 615.

One discernible purpose of legislative intent in choosing mandatory language in enacting statute as to venue of action relating to land is to have records of county, in which land involved is situated, show all matters that in any way affect title to such land. Katzen v Central Park Towers, supra.

CPA § 182 (§ 503(a)(b) herein) construed with CPA § 183 in holding that stockholder's derivative action was not excepted from provisions of former CPA § 182 (§ 503(a)(b) herein). Feldmeier v Webster (1955) 208 Misc 996, 145 NYS2d 365, affd 1 AD2d 938, 150 NYS2d 581.

2. Other statutes

Where some of the real estate as to which the action is brought is without the state but some is in the county of New York, the venue should be laid in that county; CPA § 182 (§ 503(a)(b) herein) related to other actions than those specifically provided for in CPA §§ 183, 184; an action specifically provided for in CPA § 183 did not fall within the provisions of CPA § 182, even though it involved personalty as well, and none of the parties resided in the county where the real estate was located. Hall v Gilman (1902) 77 AD 464, 79 NYS 307.

Action against public officers for damages for conspiracy did not come within the provisions of CPA § 183 and is not one for the application of CPA § 184, subd 2, but fell clearly within CPA § 182, and was to be tried within the county in which one of the parties resided at the commencement of the action. Metropolitan By-Products Co. v Van Name (1917) 176 AD 545, 163 NYS 592.

CPA § 183 providing that actions affecting real estate were to be tried in a county in which the real estate was situated was not affected by the charter of cities of the second class as to the place of trial of actions against the city. Czamowsky v Rochester (1900) 55 AD 388, 66 NYS 931, affd 165 NY 649, 128 AD 704, 59 NE 1121.

The various statutes contained in the city charters, similar to § 242 of the Greater New York charter, providing that actions against the city shall be tried in the county in which the city is located, relate to transitory actions and not to actions mentioned in CPA § 183. See Czamowsky v Rochester, supra.

While on motion under CPA § 183 to change the place of trial of an action to the county in which the land involved was situated, it was improper to permit the plaintiff to read affidavits tending to show that the greater convenience of witnesses would be served by retaining the cause in the county where instituted, especially where he failed to serve the notice required by CPA § 117 (Rules 2214(a), (b), 2215 herein), after the venue has been changed the court could entertain his motion to change the venue for the convenience of witnesses, under CPA § 187. Johnson v Millard (1921) 199 AD 73, 190 NYS 865.

Where a litigant bringing an action affecting title to land or an interest in real estate fails to comply with the statutory requirement as to the place of trial, any defendant may at any time before trial apply for a change of venue, and such application, although made too late for relief as a matter of right, may be granted in the court's discretion when no prejudice has been caused by the delay. In cases of this class, the court has inherent power to order the change. Reichenbach v Corn Exchange Bank Trust Co. (1936) 249 AD 539, 292 NYS 732.

CPA § 183 is subject to power afforded by CPA § 187 (§§ 510, 602(b) herein) to change place of trial for convenience of witnesses. Weber v Lacey (1953) 281 AD 290, 120 NYS2d 88.

A demand by defendant to change the place of trial upon the grounds stated in CPA § 183 was not sufficient upon which to found a motion to change the place of trial upon the grounds stated in CPA § 182. Whitehead Bros. Co. v Dolan (1910) 69 Misc 208, 126 NYS 414.

3. Land in different counties

An action for the specific performance of a contract to exchange land in one county for land in another may be brought in either county. Smith v Van Veighten (1918) 184 AD 813, 172 NYS 697.

Where both the plaintiffs' bulkhead and pier in Kings County, and under water lands of the defendant in New York County was affected by the judgment in an action, the gravamen of which was that the proximity of ferry structures maintained by the defendant interferes with access to plaintiffs' pier and bulkhead, the venue of the action was properly laid in either county, in view of CPA § 183, and defendant's motion to change the venue from Kings County to New York County was denied. Fairchild v Union Ferry Co. (1921) 117 Misc 470, 192 NYS 550, affd 202 AD 825, 194 NYS 932, affd 235 NY 84, 138 NE 745.

4. Land in another state

The New York court will decline to restrain an action in Pennsylvania where every issue presented in the action here can be litigated in the Pennsylvania action where the real property is located and where the defendant resided and the purchaser of property under the contract in question is a party to the Pennsylvania action. Pitsanis v Bitsanis (1958) 11 Misc 2d 790, 173 NYS2d 956.

5. Inferior courts

This section has no application to actions brought in justice's court or in the municipal court in the city of New York. Eaton v Hall (1903) 78 AD 542, 79 NYS 887.

6. Third-party action

Where a main action by landlords seeks a declaration affecting landlord's property located in Kings County and a defendant by third-party complaint seeks to eject a third-party defendant and also seeks declaratory relief affecting the real property, a motion by the third-party defendant to change the place of trial from New York County to Kings County will be granted and the action in its entirety, the main action as well as the issues raised by the third-party complaint, should be transferred to Kings County. Franco v Tawil (1958) 13 Misc 2d 713, 178 NYS2d 750.

B. SPECIFIC ACTIONS

7. Generally

The alleging in a counterclaim of an action specified in CPA § 183 will not bring the action within CPA § 183, where the complaint set out a cause of action not within CPA § 183, such as a complaint for a money judgment. Taconic Inn Corp. v Holsapple (1946) 188 Misc 322, 65 NYS2d 262. But compare Nicoletto v Pettit Supply Corp. (1938) 254 AD 750, 4 NYS2d 231.

8. Ejectment

Where a main action by landlords seeks a declaration affecting landlord's property located in Kings County and a defendant by third-party complaint seeks to eject a third-party defendant and also seeks declaratory relief affecting the real property, a motion by the third-party defendant to change the place of trial from New York County to Kings County will be granted and the action in its entirety, the main action as well as the issues raised by the third-party complaint, should be transferred to Kings County. Franco v Tawil (1958) 13 Misc 2d 713, 178 NYS2d 750.

9. Foreclosure of mortgage

An action to foreclose a mortgage must be tried in the county in which the property is situated.

Manufacturers' Trust Co. v Roerich Museum (1932) 236 AD 76, 258 NYS 284.

An action to foreclose a mortgage on real property must be tried in the county wherein the property is situated, and there is no authority for the appointment of a receiver in any other county. Railroad Federal Sav. & Loan Ass'n v Zelkind (1936) 247 AD 110, 286 NYS 158.

A foreclosure action is entirely triable in the county where the premises are situated, and the trial cannot be adjourned to another county. Gould v Bennett (1874) 59 NY 124.

An action to foreclose a mortgage on land in another state is within the jurisdiction of the court where the parties are, and are served with process, and, answering, contest the right of the plaintiff to maintain the action. House v Lockwood (1886) 40 Hun 532, later app 137 NY 259, 33 NE 595; see as to foreclosure generally, Gould v Bennett, supra.

The supreme court has jurisdiction of an action to foreclose a mortgage upon land located partly in this state and partly in Connecticut, and may, when the mortgagors are residents of New York and have been served personally, provide in the decree that a referee shall sell all the mortgaged land. Mead v Brockner (1903) 82 AD 480, 81 NYS 594.

Surplus money, arising upon a sale under a decree in a foreclosure action, commenced after the death of the mortgagor and owner of the equity of redemption, is regarded as real property; and an action by a person claiming a lien thereupon, to have the lien established and the money divided accordingly, must be brought in the county where the land is situated. Fliess v Buckley (1880) 22 Hun 551.

Plaintiff was permitted to retain in Dutchess County action to foreclose two mortgages, although they covered property in Dutchess County and Ulster County respectively, where the mortgages were between the same parties, arose out of the same transaction, and the defense of fraud was raised as to both mortgages. Coppola v Whitaker (1959) 19 Misc 2d 145, 194 NYS2d 294.

10. Waste

An action to recover the value of the interest which plaintiff had in liens on certain real property in Orange county as a consequence of the ownership of two mortgages thereon, the value of the security thereof being allegedly impaired, and also to recover damages for alleged waste affects a lien or interest in real property situated in said county and under CPA § 183 had to be tried in that county. Labes v P. Delany & Co. (1939) 258 AD 913, 16 NYS2d 481.

An action for waste on land in another state will not lie here. Cragin v Lovell (1882) 88 NY 258, 2 Civ Proc (Browne) 128.

11. Nuisance

CPA § 183 applied to all actions whether legal or equitable to abate a nuisance; but an action for a nuisance had to be tried in the county in which the subject matter of the action was situated. The county in which the foul substances were deposited in the river, and not in the county where the nuisance was caused thereby, was the county in which the venue should have been laid. Horne v Buffalo (1888) 49 Hun 76, 1 NYS 801.

It has been held that an action for a nuisance is a common law action enumerated in CPA § 425 (§ 4101 herein), Trial by Jury, and that CPA § 183 did not apply to an equitable action to restrain a nuisance. Litchfield v International Paper Co. (1899) 27 Misc 8, 57 NYS 275. This case however was reversed on the ground that the action in question was to restrain a trespass. 41 AD 446, 58 NYS 856.

Where plaintiff claimed that defendant's ferry structures interfered with plaintiff's access to his pier and bulkhead, and the properties of the plaintiff and defendant were in different counties, the action could properly be brought in either county. Fairchild v Union Ferry Co. (1921) 117 Misc 470, 192 NYS 550, affd 202 AD 825, 194 NYS 934, affd 235 NY 84, 138 NE 745.

An action under the National Prohibition Act to enjoin a nuisance alleged to be the possession and sale of intoxicating liquors in a certain building was not an action "for a nuisance" within the meaning of CPA § 183. United States v Myers (1926) 215 AD 624, 214 NYS 438.

Prayer for injunction is consistent with and generally includible in nuisance actions, and does not change basic cause of action. Tenperal Homes, Inc. v Italiano (1955, Sup) 140 NYS2d 148.

Where complaint alleged that defendant posted signs on house purchased from plaintiff, reading "This house is a lemon" and "We sure got stuck" and that such posting was nuisance, and prayed for injunction to restrain maintenance of such signs, venue was changed to county where house was located. Tenperal Homes v Italiano, supra.

12. Specific performance

Specific performance action must be tried in county where realty is situated. Brunner v Steinhardt (1952) 4 Misc 2d 923, 111 NYS2d 887.

An action brought to compel the vendee in a land contract to accept the title tendered by the vendor and to pay the contract price therefor is an action brought "to procure a judgment establishing, etc., or affecting an estate, etc., interest in real property." Turner v Walker (1902) 70 AD 306, 75 NYS 260.

Counterclaim for specific performance does not govern venue of action for money only. Taconic Inn Corp. v Holsapple (1946) 188 Misc 322, 65 NYS2d 262.

An action for specific performance of a contract to exchange lands in one county for lands in another is triable in either county. Smith v Van Veighten (1918) 184 AD 813, 172 NYS 697.

An action which seeks a conveyance of land in one county in specific performance of an agreement to exchange lands in another county therefor must be brought in the county where the first land is situated. Kearr v Bartlett (1888) 47 Hun 245.

Where, under a contract to buy realty situated in Delaware County, the purchaser sued in Supreme Court, Queens County, to recover the deposit and the seller sued in Supreme Court, Delaware County, for specific performance, the actions were consolidated for trial in Delaware County. Brunner v Steinhardt (1952) 4 Misc 2d 923, 111 NYS2d 887.

C. ACTIONS AFFECTING OTHER INTERESTS IN REAL PROPERTY

13. Generally

An action affecting "an estate, right, title, lien or other interest" is a local one and should be tried in the county in which the lands are situated. Iron Nat. Bank v Dolge (1899) 46 AD 327, 61 NYS 680.

Subd 9 of CPA § 183 applied only if judgment demanded involved change in title. Greenberg v Refined Gas Stations, Inc. (1948, Sup) 83 NYS2d 761.

While realty may be affected by ultimate determination, action contemplated must be of such nature as directly affects realty. Reeve v O'Dwyer (1950) 199 Misc 123, 98 NYS2d 452.

Change of venue granted pursuant to subdivision 9 of CPA § 183. Nicoletto v Pettit Supply Corp. (1938) 254 AD 750, 4 NYS2d 231.

The alleged right of a riparian owner to the flow of water in a stream along its land is an interest in real property. Hence action by the State Water Power and Control Commission to restrain defendant power company from withdrawing from the waters of the Niagara river more than a certain amount of water without first receiving a license, and for other relief, must be tried in the county of Niagara, where the property is located. Water Power & Control Com. v Niagara Falls Power Co. (1938) 166 Misc 10, 1 NYS2d 915, mod 289 NY 353, 45 NE2d 907.

Action by Onondaga resident against Kansas resident to collect debts of intestate out of realty, located in Broome county, claimed by decedent as intestate's sole heir, held one within subd. 9, of CPA § 183 and so triable in Broome county. Titus v Titus (1941) 175 Misc 970, 25 NYS2d 936.

An action to restrain the erection of a bridge between buildings over a highway on the ground of the injury to light and air is local. Leland v Hathorn (1870) 42 NY 547.

Where plaintiff seeks judgment which involves change in title to realty, action is one within CPA § 183. Rothenberg v Fields (1953) 204 Misc 86, 118 NYS2d 822.

Action by alleged descendant of former holder of title to land on which Trinity Church now stands for declaratory judgment that Trinity Church was prohibited by charter from pleading statute of limitations and of acquiring title by adverse possession, is action affecting title or interest in realty. McClatchie v Trinity Church (1953, Sup) 118 NYS2d 648.

It cannot be said that case came within subd. 9 of CPA § 183 where there were no facts alleged in complaint which, if taken as true, sustained finding that alleged agreement affected realty, under terms of agreement itself. Deitch v Atlas (1954, Sup) 132 NYS2d 803.

Where alternative relief prayed for in complaint affects estate, title or other interests in realty, venue was changed to county where realty is located. Katzen v Central Park Towers, Inc. (1955) 207 Misc 181, 138 NYS2d 615.

14. Trespass

An action for trespass quaere clausum is local and must be tried in the court where the trespass occurred. Easton v Booth (1884) 32 Hun 464; Freeman v Thompson (1888) 50 Hun 340, 3 NYS 93.

Actions for trover and trespass on real estate are not included. Polley v Wilkisson, 5 Civ Proc 135.

An action to restrain defendants from raising and maintaining a dam in an action for trespass and hence within the provisions of CPA § 183. Litchfield v International Paper Co. (1899) 41 AD 446, 58 NYS 856.

An action for trespass on demised premises brought by tenant against his landlord must be tried in the county where the premises are situated. Rothlein v Hewitt (1899) 29 Misc 664, 61 NYS 97.

An order changing the place of trial in an action for trespass on lands to the county where such lands are situated will be sustained, especially where the value of the land is small, and the convenience of witnesses and the ends of justice will be promoted and the expenses of trial reduced by the change. Dexter v Alfred (1890, Sup) 12 NYS 365.

Action in trespass against gas transmission company, claiming easement over realty involved, must be tried in county where realty is located, since issue affects interest in realty and since action in trespass must be tried in county where trespass was committed. Jacoby v Algonquin Gas Transmission Co. (1955) 285 AD 941, 139 NYS2d 43.

Trespass action must be tried in county where trespass was committed. Fontana v Hempstead (1961) 30 Misc 2d 522, 223 NYS2d 732.

15. Establishment of mortgage

A cause of action for judgment that a bond and mortgage be declared to be valid obligations of the defendant, with a counterclaim praying for a declaration to the contrary, was within subdivision 9 of CPA § 183. Nicoletto v Pettit Supply Corp. (1938) 254 AD 750, 4 NYS2d 231.

Action to declare bond and mortgage to be valid obligations was within CPA § 183. Taconic Inn Corp. v Holsapple (1946) 188 Misc 322, 65 NYS2d 262.

16. Annulment of mortgage

Where the venue of an action brought to annul a mortgage upon real property is not laid in the county in which the real property is situated, the defendant mortgagee is entitled to an order changing the venue to the latter county, notwithstanding the fact that no notice of his application for such order has been given to the defendant mortgagor who has not answered or appeared in the action and whose time to do so has not expired. North Shore Industrial Co. v Randall (1905) 108 AD 232, 95 NYS 758.

17. Enforcement of mechanic's lien on real property

Enforcement of mechanics' liens directly upon real property was governed by CPA § 183. H. W. Palen's Sons v Nelson & Caulkins, Inc. (1928) 222 AD 357, 226 NYS 350.

18. Condemnation of land

In a proceeding for the condemnation of land, the venue is properly laid in the county in which the land or some part thereof is situated. New York C. & H. R. R. Co. v Matthews (1911) 70 Misc 567, 128 NYS 138, affd 144 AD 732, 129 NYS 828.

19. Rescission, reformation, cancellation

A suit in equity to rescind the executed contract for the sale of land and to recover the consideration paid on account of false representations must be tried in the county where the real estate is situated. Birmingham v Squires (1910) 139 AD 129, 123 NYS 906.

But an action to rescind an executory written contract to purchase realty, for lien on said premises, for down payment and for judgment for $1500 and interest, was held not within subd 9 of CPA § 183. MacCabee v Lipman (1946) 4 Misc 2d 917, 83 NYS2d 545.

The mere fact that title to real estate is involved in an action does not necessarily bring case within provisions of CPA § 183, but CPA § 183 applied if the judgment demanded involved a change in the title, and an action to rescind an executed contract of sale of land, the necessary effect of which was to effect the change of title, was within CPA § 183. Nassau Hotel Co. v Barnett (1914) 164 AD 203, 149 NYS 645.

Where defendants sold all the sawing timber on certain land to plaintiffs, and plaintiffs brought action alleging that defendants did not own all the timber sold, and asked that the instrument be reformed by striking therefrom the timber not owned by defendants, and that defendants be adjudged to pay plaintiffs the value of such timber not owned by them, defendants were entitled to change place of trial to county where the land was located, as the judgment would affect title to real property or a chattel real. Stull v Norton (1916, Sup) 161 NYS 237, affd 176 AD 950, 162 NYS 1146.

In action for removal of defendant bank as testamentary trustee, appointment of successor, accounting and cancellation of record of deed of real property located in Franklin county, place of trial changed from Warren to Franklin county. Re McCarthy's Will (1941) 262 AD 1049, 30 NYS2d 344.

20. For cutting timber

When an action for damages for unlawfully cutting timber was commenced in a county other than that in which the land involved was situated, the place of trial should have been changed, on motion, to the proper county under CPA § 183. Johnson v Millard (1921) 199 AD 73, 190 NYS 865.

21. Assignments for benefit of creditors

When property assigned for the benefit of creditors consists in part of real property, an action to set aside the assignment must be tried in the county where the real estate is situated. Acker v Leland (1884) 96 NY 383; Wyatt v Brooks (1886) 42 Hun 502; Moss v Gilbert, 18 Abb NC 202.

22. Enforcement of judgments

An action to recover the interest of a defendant in his father's real estate, to set aside an assignment of it and procure the application of it on a judgment, came within CPA § 183. Thompson v Heidenrich, 66 How Pr 391.

An action to restore a lien by judgment upon real property should be brought within the county wherein such real estate is situated. Mahoney v Mahoney (1893) 70 Hun 78, 23 NYS 1097.

23. Water rights

Action to compel determination of conflicting claims to the use of water of a lake, which is wholly situated within one county, must be brought in that county where controversy does not involve any claim to real property situated in any other county. New York Water Service Corp. v Palisades Interstate Park Com. (1960) 12 AD2d 646, 208 NYS2d 460.

D. Actions Not Within Statute

24. Generally

Where action was merely for money damages measured by claim for asserted injury to realty, it did not affect any estate or interest in realty. Pasher v Reisenberg (1949, Sup) 87 NYS2d 872.

An action in equity against a cemetery corporation in which the mother of the plaintiffs had been interred, to compel the cemetery corporation to allow the plaintiffs to disinter the body for the purpose of reinterring it in another cemetery, does not affect any right or interest in real property, and is consequently not a local action. Cohen v Congregation Shearith Israel (1903) 85 AD 65, 82 NYS 918.

An action to compel contribution toward the expenses of a real estate transaction was not an action "to recover real property" under CPA § 183 and therefore need not be tried in the county where the real estate was situated. Barnes v Barnhart (1905) 102 AD 424, 92 NYS 459.

An action to enforce an agreement for the transfer of corporate stock did not affect title to real property within CPA § 183 merely because of the fact that the owner of the stock may bring a stockholder's action to recover real property on behalf of the corporation. Deitch v Atlas (1954, Sup) 132 NYS2d 803.

Malpractice action did not come within purview of CPA § 183. Locke v Singer (1952) 279 AD 1097, 112 NYS2d 676.

Where the complaint set out a cause of action not within CPA § 183, as for a sum of money only, a counterclaim might not have brought the action within the section by alleging a cause of action, such as one for specific performance of a contract for the sale of land. The relief sought by a defendant in a counterclaim might have brought the action within the scope of subd 9 of CPA § 183. Nicoletto v Pettit Supply Corp. (1938) 254 AD 750, 4 NYS2d 231.

25. Assignment of mortgage

This section did not include an action to compel an assignment of a mortgage. Yates County Nat. Bank v Blake (1887) 43 Hun 162.

26. Breach of contract relating to real property

The mere fact that a question of title to real estate might have had to be passed upon in a suit did not make it imperative that the case be tried in the county where the land was situated. CPA § 183 did not apply to an action for damages for breach of contract, although the contract referred to real property, and the breach was due to inability to give a good title thereto. Hogg v Mack (1889) 53 Hun 463, 6 NYS 301.

An action to recover damages for the breach of a contract upon the sale of real estate under an agreement that the defendant would purchase, if the plaintiff was unable to sell at the expiration of a certain period, does not affect any interest in the real estate and need not be brought in the county in which the real estate is situated. Maier v Rebstock (1902) 68 AD 481, 73 NYS 817, later app 95 NYS 1144.

An action to recover back part of the purchase price of land, on the ground of deficiency in the area agreed to be conveyed, the complaint containing no allegations as to title, is not to compel the determination of a claim to real property. Oakes v De Lancey (1890, Sup) 12 NYS 840.

Action for breach of construction contract, relating to work and labor, does not involve title to realty. Minskoff v Henderson-Johnson Co. (1951, Sup) 112 NYS2d 74.

27. Covenants in deed

Action for breach of covenant in deed to real estate was not an action affecting title to realty within the meaning of subd 9 of CPA § 183, entitling plaintiff to have the place of trial changed to the county where the real estate referred to in the complaint was situated. Lawyers' Title & Trust Co. v Hewlett (1924) 210 AD 793, 207 NYS 92.

28. Diversion of water

An action for damages for diverting the flow of water in a creek from certain lands is not one affecting an interest in real property and triable in the county where such land is situated, but rather in the county of the residence of the parties and where the dam causing the diversion is situated. Thompson v Attica Water Co. 1 Civ Proc 368.

Action to compel determination of conflicting claims to the use of water of a lake, which is wholly situated within one county, must be brought in that county where controversy does not involve any claim to real property situated in any other county. New York Water Service Corp. v Palisades Interstate Park Com. (1960) 12 AD2d 646, 208 NYS2d 460 reh and app den 12 AD2d 817, 211 NYS2d 706.

29. Enforcement of mechanics' liens against public improvements, or substitution bond generally

Unlike the enforcement of a mechanic's lien directly on real property, proceedings to enforce a mechanic's lien for the construction of a public improvement were directed against the fund alone, and so the venue was transitory, unaffected by CPA § 183. H. W. Palen's Sons v Nelson & Caulkins, Inc. (1928) 222 AD 357, 226 NYS 350.

Action by plaintiff-lienor against contractor and surety on former's bond to establish claim for materials furnished for public improvement held transitory and not action to foreclose lien on realty within subd 9 of CPA § 183. Shelt Co. v Simiele Constr. Co. (1941) 176 Misc 730, 28 NYS2d 794.

Where a bond has been substituted for a mechanic's lien filed against realty the place of trial of an action on the bond is not controlled by the situs of the realty. People ex rel. Jenkins v Neff (1899) 29 Misc 59, 60 NYS 582, affd 47 AD 394, 62 NYS 321, affd 163 NY 320, 57 NE 408, affd 186 US 230, 46 L Ed 1140, 22 S Ct 905.

Motion to discharge undertaking to discharge notice of mechanic's lien filed in Nassau county, may be brought in Queens county. Application of Stephen Manor Homes, Inc. (1951) 201 Misc 721, 108 NYS2d 469.

30. On municipal bonds

An action to recover the amount due on town bonds, where the only question in issue was whether or not the bonds were duly issued and were valid obligations, was not within CPA § 183, even though a recovery was to be chargeable upon the real and personal property in the town subject to taxation. Becker v Cherry Creek (1893) 70 Hun 6, 24 NYS 19, affd 139 NY 658, 35 NE 208.

31. Partnership accounting

An action by executors of a deceased partner for an accounting and that a certain lease should be included in the partnership assets is not an action to determine the title to real property. Simpson v Simpson (1899) 41 AD 449, 58 NYS 882.

32. Rent or income

An action to recover of trustees holding real estate, a dividend on the income thereof according to the terms of a certificate declaring the plaintiff's interest in such property and its income, was for money had and received and not within CPA § 183. Roche v Marvin (1883) 92 NY 398.

Tenant's action to recover excess rent paid by tenant on premises located in Queens county, not relating to realty, was transferred to New York county where both parties, domestic corporations, had principal places of business. Jaylo Realty Corp. v Bobnor Realty Corp. (1947) 189 Misc 990, 73 NYS2d 439.

Action by owner of realty for declaratory judgment to determine effect of two lease contracts between parties and that major lease contract was not subject to commercial rent laws, was not within subd 9 of CPA § 183. Greenberg v Refined Gas Stations, Inc. (1948, Sup) 83 NYS2d 761.

Municipal court of the City of New York lacked jurisdiction of action to recover rent under lease of premises located in Binghamton, New York. The court declined to decide the issue of the applicability of CPA § 183 to the litigation. 43-49 Chanango Street Corp. v Metropolitan Life Ins. Co. (1957) 6 Misc 2d 788, 162 NYS2d 802.

33. To compel satisfaction of money judgment where a lien on real property

An action was brought in New York county to compel the defendant J, who had in his possession a satisfaction piece of a judgment in favor of the plaintiff against the defendant N, to deliver it up to the plaintiff to be canceled. Upon an affidavit that N had real property in Kings county, upon which the judgment was a lien, one of the defendants moved to change the place of trial to that county. Held, that this was not an action affecting real property, within the meaning of CPA § 183, and that the motion was therefore properly denied. Knickerbocker Life Ins. Co. v Clark (1880) 22 Hun 506.

34. Matrimonial litigation involving realty

In action for judgment declaring marital status of the parties, prayer for possession of premises owned by them by the entirety does not transform the action into a real property action for purposes of venue. Zaczek v Zaczek (1961) 27 Misc 2d 740, 212 NYS2d 588, affd 14 AD2d 808, 218 NYS2d 529 and revd 20 AD2d 902, 249 NYS2d 490.

§ 508. Actions to recover a chattel

The place of trial of an action to recover a chattel may be in the county in which any part of the subject of the action is situated at the time of the commencement of the action.

HISTORY:

Add, L 1962, ch 308, eff Sept 1, 1963.
Earlier statutes: CCP § 983; CPA § 184.

ADVISORY COMMITTEE NOTES:

This provision changes former law, which treated a replevin action as transitory only. Commencement of replevin actions should be permitted in the county where the property is found since the property may be seized in that county. Residence of the parties remains an alternative basis for venue, this section being only permissive.

FEDERAL ASPECTS:

Venue in United States District Court, 28 USCS §§ 1391 et seq.
Venue as unaffected by Federal Rules of Civil Procedure, Rule 82 of Federal Rules of Civil Procedure, USCS Court Rules.

RESEARCH REFERENCES AND PRACTICE AIDS:

7 Carmody-Wait 2d, Place of Trial or Venue § 48:12.
12 Carmody-Wait 2d, Action to Recover a Chattel (Replevin) § 82:150.
66 Am Jur 2d, Replevin § 57.

Annotations:

What is an action for damages to personal property within venue statute. 29 ALR2d 1270.
Proper county for bringing replevin, or similar possessory action. 60 ALR2d 487.

Law Reviews:

New York Civil Practice Law and Rules: venue. 27 Albany L Rev 181.
Biannual survey of New York practice: Part IV: federal venue statute regarding national banking associations deemed controlling. 39 St. John's L Rev 426.

CASE NOTES

UNDER FORMER CIVIL PRACTICE LAWS

1. Generally
2. Replevin
3. Attachment

1. Generally

An action by a person claiming to be the owner of property by virtue of an assignment for the benefit of creditors, was not within subd 3 of CPA § 184. Ackerman v Delude (1883) 29 Hun 137.

History of subd 3 of CPA § 184 and development of legislation pertaining to the designation of venue in replevin and distress actions reviewed. United Projector & Film Corp. v Brown (1932) 145 Misc 412, 260 NYS 269.

Cause of action to determine ownership of tools and to recover damages for wrongful detention arose in county where tools were, and was triable there. Lieberman v Sargent & Greenleaf, Inc. (1946, Sup) 97 NYS2d 686.

An action brought under the provisions of Personal Property Law §§ 65 and 66 was one for the recovery of a penalty for noncompliance therewith, and not an action for damages for the taking, keeping or withholding a chattel within the meaning of subd 3 of CPA § 184, and hence was triable in the county of which the plaintiff was a resident. Adie v William Knabe & Co. Mfg. Co. (1925) 124 Misc 655, 208 NYS 160.

2. Replevin

An ordinary action for replevin was not an action to recover a chattel distrained, or for damages for distraining a chattel, within CPA § 184, but is one which should have been tried in the county which was the residence of one of the parties at the commencement of the action. Universal C.I.T. Credit Corp. v Horton (1942) 179 Misc 222, 38 NYS2d 655.

Action by conditional seller to replevin chattels was not action to recover chattel distrained within the meaning of subd 3 of CPA § 184 and was not a local action. United Projector & Film Corp. v Brown (1932) 145 Misc 412, 260 NYS 269.

3. Attachment

A seizure of property pursuant to the statutory

provisional remedy of attachment did not constitute a distress of property within the meaning of subd 3 of CPA § 184. P. F. Scheidelman & Sons, Inc. v Webster Basket Co. (1932) 143 Misc 836, 257 NYS 552, affd 236 AD 774, 259 NYS 963.

§ 509. Venue in county designated

Notwithstanding any provision of this article, the place of trial of an action shall be in the county designated by the plaintiff, unless the place of trial is changed to another county by order upon motion, or by consent as provided in subdivision (b) of rule 511.

HISTORY:

> Add, L 1962, ch 308, amd, L 1965, ch 773, eff Sept 1, 1965.
> Earlier statutes: CPA § 186; CCP § 985.

ADVISORY COMMITTEE NOTES:

> This provision is derived from CPA § 186, with some changes in phraseology but none in substance. The provision preserves the present New York rule that venue relates merely to place of trial and not jurisdiction and that improper venue may be waived unless objection is properly and timely made. An action may be tried in the venue designated even though improper if there is no motion for change of venue.

FEDERAL ASPECTS:

> Venue in United States District Court, 28 USCS §§ 1391 et seq.
> Pleadings and motions, generally, Rules 7 through 16 of Federal Rules of Civil Procedure, USCS Court Rules.
> Motion day in Federal District Courts, Rule 78 of Federal Rules of Civil Procedure, USCS Court Rules.
> Venue as unaffected by Federal Rules of Civil Procedure, Rule 82 of Federal Rules of Civil Procedure, USCS Court Rules.

RESEARCH REFERENCES AND PRACTICE AIDS:

> 7 Carmody-Wait 2d, Place of Trial or Venue §§ 48:2, 48:13, 48:28.
> 24 Am Jur Pl and Pr Forms (Rev ed), Venue, Forms 31 et seq.

Law Reviews:

> New York Civil Practice Law and Rules: venue. 27 Albany L Rev 181.
> Biannual survey of New York practice: Part IV: federal venue statute regarding national banking associations deemed controlling. 39 St. John's L Rev 426.

Forms:

> See "FORMS" heading following "CASE NOTES", infra.

CASE NOTES

Venue, even if improper, does not result in a jurisdictional defect. Re Ronan (1973) 73 Misc 2d 35, 341 NYS2d 176.

Where habeas corpus proceeding was properly brought in Westchester County by inmate confined in an institution therein, though it was irregular that the proceeding be transferred to the Supreme Court, Clinton County (to which county the prisoner had been transferred) without a motion for that transfer, the removal of petitioner from one state institution to another in the exercise of an appropriate administrative power suspended the jurisdiction of the Supreme Court, Westchester County to continue the proceeding under normal circumstances. Greene v Supreme Court, Westchester County (1968) 31 AD2d 649, 297 NYS2d 599.

Where construction subcontract under which suit was brought specifically provided that any action resulting from contract would be commenced in courts of specified county and that subcontractor expressly waived any and all right it might have by reason of surety bonds, trial court did not abuse its discretion in granting contractor's motion to change venue to specified county. Callanan Industries, Inc. v Sovereign Constr. Co. (1974) 44 AD2d 292, 354 NYS2d 486.

Improper venue is not jurisdictional and is not destructive to the action. Hvac & Sprinkler Contractors Asso. v State University Constr. Fund (1975) 80 Misc 2d 1047, 364 NYS2d 422.

Where defendants failed to serve a written demand that action be tried in proper county, specifying such county, before filing of their answer, and failed to move to change place of trial within 15 days after service of demand for venue change, they were not entitled to change of venue as matter of right, but their motion became one addressed to court's discretion. Callanan Industries, Inc. v Sovereign Constr. Co. (1974) 44 AD2d 292, 354 NYS2d 486.

Petitioner which initially chose forum for Article 78 proceeding could not complain of venue. Hvac & Sprinkler Contractors Asso. v State University Constr. Fund (1975) 80 Misc 2d 1047, 364 NYS2d 422.

CASE NOTES

UNDER FORMER CIVIL PRACTICE LAWS

1. Generally
2. Demand
3. Striking case from calendar
4. Waiver
5. Corporations

1. Generally

County for motion under CPA § 186 was governed by RCP 63 (§ 2213(a) herein). Nevelson v Piesner (1947) 272 AD 555, 74 NYS2d 105.

Statutory direction in CPA § 186 as to place of trial of action specified in CPA §§ 182-a, 182-b, 183, 184 and 184-a (§§ 503(e), 504, 505(b), 507, 508 herein) was not jurisdictional, and did not curtail general jurisdiction of supreme court. Weber v Lacey (1953) 281 AD 290, 120 NYS2d 88.

Where the cause of action arose and the parties and witnesses all resided in the same county, and the venue was laid in another county, the latter became the proper county until the court entertained a motion for change of venue. Marcus v Greenblaum (1928) 132 Misc 500, 230 NYS 478.

2. Demand

The provisions of CPA § 186 were directory only and did not preclude an application to the court under CPA § 187 (§§ 510, 602(b) herein), when a demand had not been made. McConihe v Palmer (1894) 76 Hun 116, 27 NYS 832.

Service of written demand upon plaintiff's attorney was a necessary prerequisite to motion for change of place of trial under CPA § 186. Hoffman v Hoffman (1912) 153 AD 191, 138 NYS 356.

Attorney's demand was sufficient. CPA § 186. Berwick v Berwick (1944, Sup) 47 NYS2d 86.

Demand for change was necessary to have venue changed under CPA § 186. Frank v Herman (1944) 183 Misc 678, 53 NYS2d 559.

A demand for change of venue served for the first time with an amended answer, under CPA § 186, would be deemed timely unless it was shown that amendment of answer was for purposes of delay. Boro Kitchen Cabinets, Inc. v Spalt (1959) 9 AD2d 925, 195 NYS2d 87.

3. Striking case from calendar

Where a transitory action is brought on for trial at a term of court, held in the county in which the venue is laid, the judge presiding at such court may not, of his own motion and without a request from either of the parties, strike the case from the calendar simply because it appears that both of the parties are residents of another county. Phillips v Tietjen (1905) 108 AD 9, 95 NYS 469.

4. Waiver

Where parties by their conduct acquiesced in trial in county where suit was brought, a subsequent motion for change should have been denied. Hull v Trainor (1931) 233 AD 350, 252 NYS 845.

Although the venue of an action is not laid in the proper county, it may be tried in that county, if the defendant does not take proper steps to have the venue changed, and defendant may waive his rights to have the venue changed by laches. Dembitz v Orange County Traction Co. (1911) 147 AD 583, 132 NYS 593.

Where defendant failed to demand change of venue from Kings to New York county where all parties resided and accident happened, court in exercise of its discretion granted defendant's motion to change venue to New York county. Joyce v Daniels & Kennedy, Inc. (1943) 180 Misc 233, 41 NYS2d 793.

Village must move promptly for change of place of trial to county where village is situated. Herricks Road Corp. v Godfrey (1946, Sup App T) 63 NYS2d 447.

Failure on part of objector to make appropriate motion for change of venue constitutes waiver; such waiver applies not only to question of trial but to proceedings such as application to file notice of claim against New York City Housing Authority. Musarra v New York City Housing Authority (1955, Sup) 141 NYS2d 267.

Where action on contract is commenced in improper county it nevertheless may be tried there, though venue is not properly placed there, and such action is not entitled to preference under Rule 6 of Queens County Supreme Court Rules. Carbide & Carbon Chemicals Co. v Northwest

Exterminating Co. (1955) 207 Misc 548, 139 NYS2d 480.

Where plaintiff is a foreign corporation, proper venue for the action is determined by the residence of defendant president or treasurer of the union, as such and where plaintiff has brought the action in the Supreme Court defendant waived defect by failing to demand change of venue under CPA § 186 and RCP 146 (Rule 511(a)(b) herein). Republic Aviation Corp. v Republic Lodge, etc. (1957) 10 Misc 2d 783, 169 NYS2d 651.

5. Corporations

Where a corporation sued in a county other than that designated by its charter as its principal place of business, the court not having jurisdiction otherwise, the defendant was entitled to an order changing the place of trial under CPA § 186.

Rossie Iron Works v Westbrook (1891) 59 Hun 345, 13 NYS 141.

Action by plaintiff-lienor against contractor and surety on former's bond to establish claim for materials furnished for public improvement, was properly tried in county where plaintiff corporation has its principal place of business. Shelt Co. v Simiele Constr. Co. (1941) 176 Misc 730, 28 NYS2d 794.

CPA § 186 cited in connection with construction of § 17, par. 2 of the Municipal Court Act, and holding that where an action was brought in the wrong district it should have been transferred on motion of the defendant to the district in which he resided, and that it was error to grant plaintiff's cross-motion to transfer the case to the district in which both parties had their business address and in which plaintiff alone resided. Prince v Weiland (1924) 124 Misc 179, 207 NYS 225.

FORMS

Designation of Place of Trial in Title of Complaint

Supreme Court __1_____ County.

§ 510. Grounds for change of place of trial

The court, upon motion, may change the place of trial of an action where:

1. the county designated for that purpose is not a proper county; or

2. there is reason to believe that an impartial trial cannot be had in the proper county; or

3. the convenience of material witnesses and the ends of justice will be promoted by the change.

HISTORY:

> Add, L 1962, ch 308, eff Sept 1, 1963.
> Earlier statutes: CPA § 510; CCP § 987.

ADVISORY COMMITTEE NOTES:

> This provision is taken from CPA § 187. Words "upon motion" inserted in opening paragraph to avoid implication that the court may change the place of venue on its own motion.

CROSS REFERENCES:

> This section referred to in 501.
> Grounds for removal and procedure on removal, CPLR 325, 326.
> Procedure for change of place of trial, CPLR 511.
> Consolidation of cases pending in different courts, CPLR 602(b).
> Change by supreme court of place of trial of action pending in another court, CPLR 604.
> Change of venue in delinquency proceedings against insurer, Ins Law § 530.
> Change of venue in tax proceedings, to review special franchise assessments, Real P Tax Law § 744.
> Venue of action against Port of New York Authority, CLS Unconsol Laws ch 179, § 6.

FEDERAL ASPECTS:

> Venue in United States District Court, 28 USCS §§ 1391 et seq.
> Change of venue in United States Courts, 28 USCS § 1404.

Pleadings and motions, generally, Rules 7 through 16 of Federal Rules of Civil Procedure, USCS Court Rules.

Motion day in Federal District Courts, Rule 78 of Federal Rules of Civil Procedure, USCS Court Rules.

Venue as unaffected by Federal Rules of Civil Procedure, Rule 82 of Federal Rules of Civil Procedure, USCS Court Rules.

RESEARCH REFERENCES AND PRACTICE AIDS:

2 Carmody-Wait 2d, Motions, Petitions, and Orders § 8:23.

7 Carmody-Wait 2d, Place of Trial or Venue §§ 48:2, 48:3, 48:13, 48:16, 48:18–48:28, 48:30.

18 Carmody-Wait 2d, Annulment of Marriage § 113:100.

18 Carmody-Wait 2d, Absolute Divorce § 114:112.

19 Carmody-Wait 2d, Separation § 117:143.

23 Carmody-Wait 2d, Actions By and Against Public Bodies and Public Officers § 144:98.

24 Am Jur Pl and Pr Forms (Rev ed), Venue, Forms 231–234, 241, 242, 251–257.

2 Am Jur Proof of Facts p 495, Bias or Prejudice.

Annotations:

Right of accused in misdemeanor prosecution to change of venue on grounds of inability to secure fair trial and the like. 34 ALR3d 804.

Choice of venue to which transfer is to be had, where change is sought because of local prejudice. 50 ALR3d 760.

Question as to convenience and justice of transfer under forum non conveniens provision of Judicial Code (28 USC § 1404(a)). 1 ALR Fed 15.

Law Reviews:

New York Civil Practice Law and Rules: venue. 27 Albany L Rev 181.

Biannual survey of New York practice: Part IV: federal venue statute regarding national banking associations deemed controlling. 39 St. John's L Rev 426.

CASE NOTES

1. In general; discretion
2. Motion
3. Action not brought in proper county
4. Fair trial not available in proper county
5. Convenience of witnesses and ends of justice
6. Stipulations and agreements as to venue

1. In general; discretion

Determination of motion for change of venue normally depends not on one controlling factor but on evaluation of various criteria, some statutory and some judicial in origin. Palmer v Chrysler Leasing Corp. (1965) 24 AD2d 820, 263 NYS2d 882.

Special Term has wide discretion in selecting the venue when actions commenced in different counties are consolidated or joined for trial, and all of the factors relevant to a motion for a change of venue pursuant to CPLR 510 may be considered in exercising that discretion. Linton v Lehigh V. R. Co. (1969) 32 AD2d 148, 300 NYS2d 468.

Generally, the condition of the court calendar is a factor to be considered in fixing the venue of actions. Poly Const. Corp. v Oxford Hall Contracting Corp. (1965) 24 AD2d 637, 262 NYS2d 206.

In an action against a county, venue may be transferred out of the county against whom such action is commenced, but such procedure requires a motion by plaintiffs for that relief. Braver v County of Nassau Office of Administrative Services (1971) 67 Misc 2d 120, 323 NYS2d 630.

On motion pursuant to CPLR 510 for a change of venue, predicated on the convenience of material witnesses and the ends of justice, respondent failed to sustain his burden of establishing the requisite factual basis for the motion on the grounds alleged and the mere tabulation in a bill of particulars indicating that 80 percent of the alleged irregularities occurred in Bronx County did not so substantially sustain the moving party's burden of proof and hence the granting of the motion to change venue was erroneous, as it constituted an invalid exercise of discretion. Vallone v Power (1970) 35 AD2d 678, 315 NYS2d 317.

Although testator was resident of Connecticut and certain claimed misrepresentations took place there, where one of her sons and corporate defendant were New York residents and corporate coexecutor was New York bank, special term improperly dismissed, sua sponte on ground of forum non conveniens, testator's sons' action alleging that testator's financial advisors fraudulently and negligently represented to testator and to them that she owned, when in fact she did not, sufficient property to satisfy all bequests in her will without necessity of her further exercising testamentary power of appointment. Wierdsma v Markwood Corp. (1976) 53 AD2d 581, 384 NYS2d 836.

2. Motion

Where defendants failed to serve a written demand that action be tried in proper county, specifying such county, before filing of their answer, and failed to move to change place of trial within 15 days after service of demand for venue change, they were not entitled to change of venue as matter of right, but their motion became one addressed to court's discretion. Callanan Industries, Inc. v Sovereign Constr. Co. (1974) 44 AD2d 292, 354 NYS2d 486.

Where an action is instituted in the Supreme Court, a notice of motion for change of venue must be held in the judicial district where the action was triable or in a county adjoining the county where the action is triable. Commissioners of State Ins. Fund v Hoyt (1966) 53 Misc 2d 342, 278 NYS2d 472.

Subdivision (b) of CPLR § 511 applies only to motions for a change of venue on the ground that the county designated in the complaint is not a proper one and does not apply when the motion for change of venue is upon either of the other two grounds contained in this section. People v Archie (1966) 52 Misc 2d 129, 275 NYS2d 217.

The procedures specified in CPLR 511(b) have no application to motions under CPLR 510(2) and 510(3) and there is no means of having the motion heard in the county to which movant seeks to have the venue changed, unless it is one of the alternative counties permitted for motions generally by CPLR 2212(2). Furie v Furie (1967) 54 Misc 2d 966, 283 NYS2d 709.

Where after an action brought in Queens County was consolidated with another action brought in Sullivan County, and transferred to Sullivan County, the action originally brought in Sullivan County was settled and discontinued, an application to transfer the Queens County action to Queens County, even if labelled as a motion for "remand to its original venue", is a motion for change of venue addressed to the discretion of the court. Yeomans v Malen (1963) 20 AD2d 615, 245 NYS2d 431.

Where main plaintiff was New Jersey resident and accident occurred in Warren County, and change of venue from New York County to Warren County was sought with due diligence when counsel for defendants discovered that plaintiff's claim of residence in New York County was specious, and where answer had pleaded separate defense with respect to residence of parties and place of accident, there was no abuse of discretion in transferring venue to Warren County though no formal demand for change of venue was served

with or before answer. De Litta v Milde (1976) 52 AD2d 548, 382 NYS2d 74.

Where motion for change of venue upon grounds that designated county was not proper one and that convenience of witnesses and ends of justice would be promoted by change was made under procedure established for hearing of motions for change of venue on grounds that county designated for trial is improper one, court could not consider part of motion being made on other grounds. Axinn & Sons Lumber Co. v Northwood Projects, Inc. (1976) 86 Misc 2d 890, 385 NYS2d 487.

On motion for change of venue, court may look to subject matter of lawsuit, identity of parties, and convenience of witnesses and interests of justice. Hempstead v New York (1976) 88 Misc 2d 366, 388 NYS2d 78.

3. Action not brought in proper county

A motion, timely made, by a national banking corporation defendant for a change of venue from Sullivan to Nassau County on the ground that it is established or located in the latter county with no office or branch in the former should be granted. Blank v Meadow Brook Nat. Bank (1964) 44 Misc 2d 448, 254 NYS2d 56.

A national banking association "established" or "located" in Nassau County, being sued in Sullivan County where it has no branch or office, is entitled to change of venue to Nassau County by reason of federal statute so requiring. Blank v Meadow Brook Nat. Bank (1964) 44 Misc 2d 448, 254 NYS2d 56.

Where plaintiff was not a holder in due course of negotiable instruments sued on and plaintiff's assignor was not a resident of the county in which action was brought, defendant was entitled to change of venue to his county of residence. Gerdon Credit Corp. v Fletcher (1968) 30 AD2d 688, 292 NYS2d 327.

In an action on a promissory note in which defendant counterclaimed to cancel a real property mortgage securing a note, the action was properly transferred to Onondaga County where the mortgaged property was situated, since the demand for judgment by defendants affected the title to real estate. Sterling Commercial Corp. v Bradford (1969) 32 AD2d 952, 303 NYS2d 757.

Although property in dispute was situated in Cayuga County, proper venue was in Broome County, where all of parties resided, the action, based on agreement made after execution of sales contract which agreement was not signed by all parties to contract, being transitory in nature. Pezzuti v Vining (1974) 44 AD2d 651, 352 NYS2d 739.

Where a motion for a change of venue is founded upon more than one of the permitted grounds in this section, and one of the grounds is that the designated county is not the proper one and the other ground is either the convenience of witnesses or inability to obtain an impartial trial, the court in the new and otherwise improper county would under CPLR § 2212(a) be permitted to consider only that part of the motion based on the ground that the county designated is not the proper county, and should deny that part of the motion being made on the other grounds, but without prejudice to the motion's being re-made in the proper county. People v Archie (1966) 52 Misc 2d 129, 275 NYS2d 217.

Where habeas corpus proceeding was properly brought in Westchester County by inmate confined in an institution therein, though it was irregular that the proceeding be transferred to the Supreme Court, Clinton County (to which county the prisoner had been transferred) without a motion for that transfer, the removal of petitioner from one state institution to another in the exercise of an appropriate administrative power suspended the jurisdiction of the Supreme Court, Westchester County to continue the proceeding under normal circumstances. Greene v Supreme Court, Westchester County (1968) 31 AD2d 649, 297 NYS2d 599.

4. Fair trial not available in proper county

Mere belief, suspicion, or feeling that fair trial has been rendered impossible because of circumstances are not sufficient grounds for a granting of motion for change of venue. Clausi v Hudson Cement Co. (1966) 26 AD2d 872, 273 NYS2d 906.

The mere expression of belief or opinion by a party that he will not be afforded a fair trial has never been held a valid ground for changing the place of trial. Cabannis v Reich (1969) 59 Misc 2d 821, 300 NYS2d 416.

The fact that plaintiff, in an action for specific performance or damages, laid the venue of its action in a proper county under 504, subd 1 does not constitute a waiver of its right to move for a change of venue on the ground of inability to obtain an impartial trial in the county in which the action was commenced. Kenford Co. v County of Erie (1972) 38 AD2d 781, 328 NYS2d 69.

Where plaintiff, by virtue of the fact that he was seeking equitable relief, had no right to trial by jury, he was not entitled to a change of venue on the ground that there was reason to believe that an impartial trial could not be had in the county in which the action was commenced, as there was no sufficient showing to support a determination that impartial trial could not be had by a judge without a jury. Kenford Co. v County of Erie (1972) 38 AD2d 781, 328 NYS2d 69.

Change of venue in action by power company to recover alleged overcharges from petroleum supplier was not required in response to contention that judges resident and sitting in county where suit was brought, which county was served by power company, would be unable to provide fair trial by reason of "pecuniary interest" in action resulting from their having to pay higher electricity charges or from possibility that amounts recovered by power company might be rebated to customers. Long Island Lighting Co. v New England Petroleum Corp. (1974) 80 Misc 2d 183, 362 NYS2d 350.

Change of venue would be granted in action filed by power company against petroleum supplier to recover $56,000,000 in damages for alleged breach of contract and overcharges for petroleum supplied, in view of possibility that jurors selected from county in which suit originally was brought, which county was served by power company, would be influenced by higher electricity charges allegedly occasioned by defendant's activities and by possibility that amounts recovered by plaintiff might be ordered rebated to power company's customers. Long Island Lighting Co. v New England Petroleum Corp. (1974) 80 Misc 2d 183, 362 NYS2d 350.

Belief that a fair trial cannot be had in the County because plaintiff's attorney is employed by one of the justices in the judicial district is insufficient to warrant change of venue. Fishman v Fishman (1964) 20 AD2d 941, 248 NYS2d 916, app dismd 15 NY2d 621, 255 NYS2d 665, 203 NE2d 918.

Order in medical malpractice action denying defendant's motion for change of venue, based on adverse newspaper publishing, without prejudice and with leave to renew before trial charge would be affirmed because it might well be that a jury could readily be selected from persons who had never heard of defendant or who had not read any of the articles in question. Wiedemann v Smithtown General Hospital (1977, AD) 392 NYS2d 42.

5. Convenience of witnesses and ends of justice

Although changes of venue pursuant to CPLR 510 have been termed a "right", even where the defendant moves "as of right," the plaintiff may cross-move to retain the action for the convenience of witnesses. Maxon Pontiac, Inc. v Weisberger (1971) 65 Misc 2d 825, 319 NYS2d 325.

That defendant proposes to call seven witnesses resident of Oneida County is insufficient to override agreement of parties fixing venue of actions arising out of breach of agreement in Onondaga County where plaintiff's place of business was located. Kenron Awning & Window Corp. v Abbott (1964) 43 Misc 2d 552, 251 NYS2d 593.

Where the convenience of the witnesses of the respective parties is fairly evenly balanced, a transitory action should be tried in the county where the cause arose. Strosberg v Kiamesha Concord, Inc. (1966) 26 AD2d 723, 271 NYS2d 767.

A defendant cannot serve a demand for a change of venue and upon plaintiff's failure to respond with an affidavit, move in the county of defendant's choice for a change upon the ground of convenience of witnesses and the ends of justice. Furie v Furie (1967) 54 Misc 2d 966, 283 NYS2d 709.

Ends of Justice were best served by retaining venue in county in which cause of action arose rather than county where action was commenced, where there was no preponderance of witnesses for either side and where trial would be reached in about the same time in either county. Morris v Treadway Inn & Resorts, Inc. (1973) 43 AD2d 621, 349 NYS2d 171.

In personal injury action commenced in St. Lawrence county arising out of automobile collision which occurred in Suffolk county, it was not an abuse of discretion to refuse change of venue to Suffolk county despite fact that all witnesses resided in said county, where St. Lawrence county trial would be reached in 6 months as opposed to 32 months in Suffolk county. Edwards v Lamberta (1973) 42 AD2d 1003, 348 NYS2d 225.

Where all of the witnesses as to the operative facts concerning a cause of action were residents of Nassau County, that county was the proper forum for trial. John H. Dair Bldg. Constr. Co. v Mayer (1966) 27 AD2d 535, 275 NYS2d 724.

"Merit" must be shown by affidavit in order to obtain a change of venue for the convenience of material witnesses. People v Archie (1966) 52 Misc 2d 129, 275 NYS2d 217.

Motion to change the place of trial of the action from one county to another upon the ground that convenience of material witnesses and the ends of justice will be promoted thereby must be denied where (a) defendants failed to justify that grounds of convenience of witnesses and ends of justice in that their moving papers did not set forth as required, an affidavit of merit and a showing of what was expected to be proved by the witnesses, and the necessity and materiality of the testimony to be given by them; (b) the preponderance and character of plaintiff's material witnesses and (c) defendants failed to establish as required by the statute that the convenience of witnesses and the ends of justice would be served by a change of venue. Lewandowski v Ambrosetti (1969) 32 AD2d 660, 301 NYS2d 690.

The plaintiff in a libel action is entitled to bring suit in the county in which he resides, and where defendant made no showing that it could not receive an impartial trial in that county and failed to indicate the names and addresses of witnesses whose convenience would be served by a change of trial and the substance of any testimony sought to be elicited from those witnesses, defendant's motion for a trial change was denied. Rae v Advance Publications, Inc. (1969) 60 Misc 2d 792, 303 NYS2d 911.

Where real property which was subject of action was located in Columbia County and where most of the parties to the action resided in Columbia County or spent considerable time in such county, and most of the material witnesses resided in Columbia County, motion of change of venue from Kings to Columbia County would be granted in the interest of satisfying the convenience of witnesses and the interest of justice. National Biochemical Corp. v Hudson-Michael Realty, Inc. (1973) 74 Misc 2d 628, 344 NYS2d 780.

Claim that venue should be transferred from Sullivan County to New York County to facilitate the testimony of nine medical witnesses did not require change of venue in view of fact that nonparty liability witnesses presumably resided in Sullivan County. Palmer v Chrysler Leasing Corp. (1965) 24 A2d 820, 263 NYS2d 882.

Change of venue from Kings County to Monroe County was in interest of justice where transitory action arose in Monroe County, several of witnesses were officials of Monroe County and should not be kept from their duties unnecessarily, and where trial calendar of Monroe County was less crowded and speedier trial could be afforded. McComb v Hilton Heights Apartments, Inc. (1974) 43 AD2d 972, 352 NYS2d 226.

Where number of material and necessary witnesses in Monroe County clearly outnumbered those in Kings County, it would serve convenience of preponderance of witnesses to change venue to Monroe County. McComb v Hilton Heights Apartments, Inc. (1974) 43 AD2d 972, 352 NYS2d 226.

Upon appeal from an order which granted consolidation of three separate actions and fixed New York County as the place of trial of the actions which arose from the collision of a Greyhound bus and an automobile at a thruway interchange in Seneca County, about 35 miles from the county seat of Onondaga County, the order was reversed and petitioner's motion granted to the extent of ordering a joint trial of the three actions to be held in Onondaga County, where that County was the venue of the action first commenced, a much earlier trial could be held in that county, all of plaintiffs who survived the accident were examined and treated in hospitals nearby, the police officers who investigated the accident and their reports were filed in a police substation only 35 miles from the courthouse in Onondaga County and the only known non-party eyewitnesses to the accident resided in nearby Monroe and Erie Counties. Padella v Greyhound Lines, Inc. (1968) 29 AD2d 495, 288 NYS2d 641.

Where, following a golf cart accident, plaintiff brought suit for her injuries in New York County and defendant instituted an action for property damage to its golf cart in Sullivan County, and undisputed proof revealed that plaintiff was paralyzed from the waist down as a result of the accident and that a great hardship would result if she must travel to a distant place and live there during the trial, New York County was selected as the proper venue. The court held that Special Term had great discretion in selecting the venue when consolidation is granted pursuant to CPLR 602, and that all of the factors which relate to a discretionary change of venue under CPLR 510 are relevant to the exercise of such discretion. Kiamesha Concord, Inc. v Greenman (1968) 29 AD2d 904, 287 NYS2d 972.

Fact that one of several actions arising out of automobile accident was commenced first in another county, while a recognized factor in determining motion for change of venue, did not mandatorily determine the issue where there was only one day difference in the commencement of action in county of venue. Palmer v Chrysler Leasing Corp. (1965) 24 AD2d 820, 263 NYS2d 882.

Where venue chosen is county where accident occurred, where all persons involved reside, and where physicians who treated plaintiff and police officers who investigated the accident reside, venue will not be changed solely because infant plaintiff was placed in custody of an organization whose home office was in another county. Lada v Cester (1964) 22 AD2d 642, 252 NYS2d 874.

Where medical affidavit in support of assertion that mental and physical health of parties would be seriously impaired by trial in Sullivan County did not demonstrate any physical incapacity which would preclude requiring the trial in Sullivan County, change of venue from Sullivan County to New York County was not required. Palmer v Chrysler Leasing Corp. (1965) 24 AD2d 820, 263 NYS2d 882.

In action for defamation, on motion for change of venue, venue should be changed to county in which defamation occurred and in which anticipated business transactions related to alleged damages were to take place where the number of material witnesses was fairly equal for each side. Ryan v Great Atlantic & Pacific Tea Co. (1968) 30 AD2d 549, 290 NYS2d 849, holding that the rule that a transitory cause of action, all other things being equal, should be tried in the county in which it arose is particularly applicable in defamation cases.

Change of venue from Kings County to Monroe County was in interest of justice where transitory action arose in Monroe County, several of witnesses were officials of Monroe County and should not be kept from their duties unnecessarily, and where trial calendar of Monroe County was less crowded and speedier trial could be afforded. McComb v Hilton Heights Apartments, Inc. (1974) 43 AD2d 972, 352 NYS2d 226.

Motion for change of venue was properly denied where it alleged the impossibility of a fair trial within certain county because of adverse newspaper articles and radio editorials which were asserted to have aroused hostile public opinion, and no proof was offered to show that such articles and editorials had in fact affected public opinion, since such conclusion without evidence would be purely conjectural and speculative. Clausi v Hudson Cement Co. (1966) 26 AD2d 872, 273 NYS2d 906.

6. Stipulations and agreements as to venue

Plaintiff was bound by clause in contract stipulating venue, even though she may not have understood the meaning and importance thereof. Grey v Colonial Home Improv. Co. (1967) 57 Misc 2d 321, 292 NYS2d 731.

Stipulations and contracts as to venue will be sustained where no question of public policy is involved. Rivers v Ben Constr. Corp. (1967) 53 Misc 2d 299, 278 NYS2d 478, mod on other grounds 29 AD2d 1048, 289 NYS2d 866.

A written agreement fixing the place of trial is to be given effect, subject only to the court's power to change venue if an impartial trial cannot be had in the stipulated county. National Equipment Rental, Ltd. v Sanders (1967, DC NY) 271 F Supp 756.

Provision in construction subcontract that any action resulting from contract would be commenced in courts of specified county was not against public policy, providing that action was brought in court having sufficiently broad jurisdiction to entertain same. Callanan Industries, Inc. v Sovereign Constr. Co. (1974) 44 AD2d 292, 354 NYS2d 486.

Where construction subcontract under which suit was brought specifically provided that any action resulting from contract would be commenced in courts of specified county and that subcontractor expressly waived any and all right it might have by reason of surety bonds, trial court did not abuse its discretion in granting contractor's motion to change venue to specified county. Callanan Industries, Inc. v Sovereign Constr. Co. (1974) 44 AD2d 292, 354 NYS2d 486.

Court should not enforce contract provision respecting venue if it is unconscionable, unreasonable or contrary to public policy and good morals. Gardner & North Roofing & Siding Corp. v Demko (1974) 82 Misc 2d 922, 370 NYS2d 294.

Although home improvements contract provided that venue should be in Onondaga County, venue of action would be transferred from Onondaga County to Oneida County, where defendant, a resident of Oneida County, was 75 years old, had great difficulty in speaking English, and was unable to read in any language. Gardner & North Roofing & Siding Corp. v Demko (1974) 82 Misc 2d 922, 370 NYS2d 294.

Where neither of parties reside in contracted county, and property is not located in that county, traditional rules should prevail and the court should select the proper venue. Gardner & North Roofing & Siding Corp. v Demko (1974) 82 Misc 2d 922, 370 NYS2d 294.

CASE NOTES

UNDER FORMER CIVIL PRACTICE LAWS

A. IN GENERAL

1. Generally

The proper place for the trial of an action in the county where plaintiff resides, and the place of trial of the action can be changed from that county only for one of the reasons stated in subd 2 and 3 of this section. Gelderman v Fisher (1924) 211 AD 862, 207 NYS 841.

The main transactions out of which the action arose may be considered in determining a motion for change of venue. Ackerman v Delude (1883) 29 Hun 137.

Where plaintiff, a resident of Kings County, brought suit against the Director General of Railroads in New York County on a cause of action arising in Sullivan County, and the defendant moved to change the venue to Sullivan County, the court was without power, on its own motion, to direct the trial to be had in Kings County, and to deny defendant's motion for a change of venue to Sullivan County, in view of CPA § 187 and CPA § 182 (§ 503(a)(b) herein). Levey v Payne (1922) 200 AD 30, 192 NYS 346.

It is not a practice to be approved for a plaintiff to lay a place of trial in a distant county for the purpose of moving a reference though the defendant had demanded a change to the proper county, but it cannot be held to be erroneous. Elting v Dayton, 4 NYSR 481.

Change of venue in an action for conversion. Newgold v Weller Bottling Works (1911) 143 AD 381, 128 NYS 499.

The place of trial of an action brought in the supreme court may be changed only in those cases mentioned. Birmingham Iron Foundry v Hatfield (1870) 43 NY 224.

CPA § 187 modified the language of CPA §§ 182–184 (§§ 503(a)(b)(c), 504, 505(b), 507, 508 herein). Gorman v South Boston Iron Co. (1884) 32 Hun 71.

The provisions of Laws 1888, ch 577, § 3, do not deprive the supreme court of its power to change the place of trial of an action for the penalty for a violation of the game laws. People v Rouse (1891, Sup) 15 NYS 414; and see People v Coughtry (1890) 58 Hun 245, 12 NYS 259, affd 125 NY 723, 26 NE 756.

On a motion for change of venue consideration may be given to the location of various records which will be used on the trial. Hilgers v Hyde (1958) 6 AD2d 963, 176 NYS2d 522.

Where no grounds for change are shown, venue of libel action properly brought in county of plaintiff's residence will be upheld on motion to remove to venue of defendant-newspaper's principal place of circulation. Scheinblum v Long Island Daily Press Publishing Co. (1959) 19 Misc 2d 134, 190 NYS2d 586.

That the court will be burdened by adding the case to its overcrowded calendar is not a significant reason for changing venue. Condon v Schwenk (1960) 10 AD2d 822, 199 NYS2d 238.

2. Other courts

In the absence of a specific provision in the Municipal Court Code, CPA § 187 and RCP 146 (Rule 511(a)(b) herein) would govern transfer of cases. Grady v Selden Truck Corp. (1928) 133 Misc 97, 231 NYS 255.

Surrogate cannot make order changing place of jury trial in contested probate proceeding to another county. Re Corey's Will (1949) 275 AD 53, 87 NYS2d 208.

Court of Claims applied provisions of CPA § 187, relating to venue. Richards v State (1953) 281 AD 947, 119 NYS2d 814; Joseph Davis, Inc. v State (1954) 204 Misc 1050, 127 NYS2d 12.

3. Court of claims

Where action brought in the Court of Claims and claimant moved for order directing trial at regular term of court held in New York city, motion treated as governed by subdivision 3 of CPA § 187, and claimants not precluded from removing motion on showing facts necessary to determine question of materiality and actual convenience of witnesses weighed against similar considerations applied to witnesses called by the state. Feiden v State (1958) 5 AD2d 926, 171 NYS2d 931.

4. Codefendants

Either defendant, in action against the maker and endorser of a note, may have the venue changed as to himself without the other's consent. Sherman v Gregory, 42 How Pr 481.

That one defendant has been denied a change of venue does not prejudice the motion of another. New Jersey Zinc Co. v Blood, 8 Abb Pr 147.

Venue is properly laid in county in which one of parties resides where one of the persons named in action as a defendant is treasurer of the union and has been named in his individual capacity as well as in his capacity as such officer since he consented to acts of union and was responsible as member of union for picketing. B. & D. Luncheonette, Inc. v Dallas (1958) 6 AD2d 805, 176 NYS2d 229.

5. Nonresident's right to change

The fact that the defendant was not a resident of the state did not preclude him from demanding a change of venue in accordance with CPA § 182 (§ 503(a)(b) herein). Dayton v Farmer (1922) 200 AD 737, 193 NYS 331.

6. Change of residence

Where plaintiff in a negligence action did not, when injured, reside in the county in which the venue is laid, but subsequently acquired a residence therein, a motion to change the place of trial upon the ground that neither of the parties reside in that county will be denied. Gilmartin v George A. Fuller Co. (1911) 147 AD 697, 132 NYS 553.

7. Class action

One of a class, for whose benefit an action had been brought under former CPA § 195 but who had not been named in the summons or complaint, and who had not been made a party to the action, was not to be regarded as a party for the purpose of influencing the disposition of a motion to change the venue of the action. Brown v Bache (1901) 66 AD 367, 72 NYS 687.

8. Federal Employers' Liability cases

The Federal Employers' Liability Act, § 6, providing the place of trial for actions brought under the act in a United States court, had no application to such actions brought in the state court. In the latter case the Civil Practice Act governed. Barton v Deleware, L. & W. R. Co. (1926) 218 AD 748, 218 NYS 171.

9. Discretion of court

The appellate court will not interfere with the sound discretion which the court below has in such a matter, unless there has been a plain abuse of discretion. Lane v Hancock (1890, Sup) 9 NYS 97; Fitzgerald v Payn (1894) 78 Hun 38, 28 NYS 1033.

Or unless it clearly appears that the court erred in its conclusion. Schmidt v Rochester Lithographic & Printing Co. (1890, Sup) 9 NYS 267.

The disposition to be made of a motion to change the venue of a transitory action rests largely in the discretion of the special term. Pattison v Hines (1905) 105 AD 282, 93 NYS 1071.

Order changing place of trial of action by automobile guests for injuries in collision between automobile and truck against truck owner and driver, from Schoharie to Otsego county where collision occurred, was discretionary. McDougall v Colebeck (1940) 259 AD 953, 20 NYS2d 1.

In action by husband and wife for injuries to her while riding in automobile, denial of change of venue from Delaware where plaintiffs resided to Cortland where accident occurred, held not abuse of discretion. Armstrong v Bero Engineering Constr. Co. (1940) 259 AD 1111, 21 NYS2d 224.

Change of venue on ground that impartial trial cannot be had is on sound discretion of special term; mere belief is insufficient in the absence of facts showing the belief well founded; nor that the defendant and his attorneys have business and political prominence; nor that the action was widely discussed, when nothing indicates unfair reports. Noonan v Luther (1908) 128 AD 673, 112 NYS 898.

Though defendant is not entitled to change of venue as matter of right, court may grant such relief as matter of discretion. Searing v Randall Cadillac Corp. (1956) 3 Misc 2d 594, 151 NYS2d 163, adhered to 3 Misc 2d 594, 158 NYS2d 358, app dismd 6 AD2d 1048, 179 NYS2d 656.

In action for death of Ulster County resident who died in defendant hospital in Middletown from negligent treatment by defendant's employees, order granting defendant's motion to change venue from Ulster to Orange County, for convenience of witnesses and in "interest of conserving witnesses' expenses and expediting trial", was discretionary and no persuasive reason was found for interfering with it. Reichenthaler v Elizabeth A. Horton Memorial Hospital (1956) 2 AD2d 630, 151 NYS2d 747.

Special Term was held justified in the exercise of its discretion in changing venue on grounds of improbability of securing impartial trial of action by dairy farmers against creameries where county in which venue was laid was primarily a dairy-farming county. Althiser v Richmondville Creamery Co. (1961) 13 AD2d 162, 215 NYS2d 122.

10. Waiver and admissions

Where a defendant receives an extension of time upon a stipulation to take short notice of trial at a certain circuit, he waives the right to have a change in the place of trial to the proper county. Haiz v Starin, 1 NYSR 553.

If a motion to change the place of trial of an action to the proper county is not made in the manner and within the time prescribed, the right to have it changed is waived and the motion should be denied. Duche v Buffalo Grape Sugar Co. 2 Civ Proc (McCarty) 268, 63 How Pr 316.

Although a defendant may be entitled to a change of place of trial for convenience of witnesses, he waives that right by noticing the case for trial in the other county, by stipulating that the case be tried at certain dates, by accepting the favor of opening defaults on agreement that the case be placed on the calendar for trial at early dates, by appearing in court apparently ready for trial and by general laches. Schaaf v Denniston (1907) 121 AD 504, 106 NYS 168.

The defendants have waived their right to have the place of trial changed, and, in any event, are guilty of laches, where it appears that on the granting of an application for the postponement of the trial about one year prior to the motion to change the place of trial the defendants did not indicate that it would be inconvenient for them, or their witnesses, to attend on the trial. Schwartz v Cuyler (1939) 256 AD 1041, 10 NYS2d 936. See also Levine Bros. v Cuyler (1939) 256 AD 1042, 10 NYS2d 937.

Where plaintiff in action for personal injuries in automobile accident is county resident, defendant is not entitled as of right to change venue to county of his residence. Smith v Spencer (1943) 182 Misc 767, 45 NYS2d 242.

If a clear case for the change of place of trial on account of the residence and convenience of witnesses is made out, it should not be refused merely because the other party to the action offers to admit the chief facts expected to be proved by such witnesses. Metropolitan Life Ins. Co. v McCoy, 12 NY Week Dig 100.

Defendant-towns in New York City's declaratory judgment action to test validity of statutory amendment waived their rights to change of venue (Town L § 66) by interposing counterclaims against the city which were required by CPA § 182-a (§ 504 herein) to be tried in New York County. New York v Colchester (1961) 28 Misc 2d 426, 212 NYS2d 667, affd 16 AD2d 772, 228 NYS2d 462.

B. ACTION NOT BROUGHT IN PROPER COUNTY

11. Generally

The proper county within this subdivision is one in which one of the parties resides. Lynch v Mosher, 4 How Pr 86. The change to such county is a matter of right. Starks v Bates, 12 How Pr 465; see Christy v Kierstad, 47 How Pr 467.

Defendant entitled as matter of right to have venue changed to county where he resides where action was not one specified in either CPA §§ 183 (§ 507 herein) or 184 (§ 508 herein) and plaintiff had no residence in county where action was brought. Dan W. Feitel Bag Co. v Bobinski (1931) 234 AD 879, 254 NYS 357. See also Philadelphia Nat. Bank v McAllister (1931) 234 AD 883, 254 NYS 358.

Order granting change of venue reversed since defendant did not establish that plaintiff was a nonresident of the county. Sanders v Prescott (1931) 234 AD 899, 254 NYS 535.

Judiciary L § 147 did not limit absolute right to change venue to residence of party under CPA § 182 (§ 503(a)(b) herein). McCarthy v Andrews (1950) 199 Misc 656, 103 NYS2d 170.

While plaintiff and defendant in an action for death both resided in one county, but action was brought in county where death occurred, the court of that county could properly refuse to grant a change of place of trial if it was reasonable to believe that an impartial trial could not be had in the proper county, and convenience of witnesses and ends of justice would be promoted by allowing the case to remain there. Buxbaum v Paulsen (1916) 95 Misc 717, 159 NYS 427, mod 167 NY 1091.

Where the venue in a suit for an accounting and a money judgment is laid in a county where neither of the parties reside, the defendant, having made a demand, is entitled to have the venue changed to the county where both parties reside as a matter of absolute right. Finch School v Finch (1911) 144 AD 687, 129 NYS 1.

Where defendant moves to change venue from improper to proper county, he is entitled to have venue changed to such county and none other. Yachwak v Conlen (1940) 260 AD 976, 23 NYS2d 313.

Where an action was instituted in a county wherein none of the parties resided, defendant was entitled to have the venue changed to the county wherein he resided since there was no showing as to the convenience of witnesses. Commercial State Bank & Trust Co. v Ritz (1957) 4 AD2d 674, 163 NYS2d 428; Boro Kitchen Cabinets, Inc. v Spalt (1959) 9 AD2d 925, 195 NYS2d 87.

Defendant's motion for change of venue from Suffolk to New York County was denied where it appeared that plaintiff had a home in Suffolk which he considered his permanent home though he also maintained an apartment in New York County. Garfield v Lowy (1960) 22 Misc 2d 110, 202 NYS2d 331.

In proceedings to set aside election of directors,

denial of corporate defendant's motion for change of venue from Queens to Erie County, situs of its principal place of business and where the election was held was reversed as an improvident exercise of discretion. Scharf v Irving Air Chute Co. (1961) 15 AD2d 563, 223 NYS2d 307.

Venue was properly changed from New York County to Albany County where affidavit of individual plaintiff suing as treasurer of unincorporated association while denying assertion that he resided in Albany County also negatived his own prior assertion that he resided in New York County and failed to negate assertions that principal offices of association and of defendant corporation were located in Albany County, and thus failed to set forth facts showing either that Albany County was not proper, or that New York County was the proper one. Payne v Civil Service Employees (1961) 15 AD2d 265, 222 NYS2d 725.

12. Effect of stipulation of facts; or pleading

That the plaintiff has omitted in his complaint any averments that the assignment asked to be set aside embraces real property will not defeat defendant's right to have the trial in the proper county. Acker v Leland (1884) 96 NY 383.

A police officer sued for false imprisonment, whose answer did not allege facts showing that the arrest was made in virtue of his office, was not entitled to a change of venue so that the trial might be had in the county where the arrest was made as provided in subd 2 of former CPA § 184. Phillips v Leary (1906) 114 AD 871, 100 NYS 200.

A complaint not alleging that the parties were engaged in a definite business in which they were to share the profits, does not sufficiently allege a partnership; a defendant denying the allegations of the complaint as to the partnership and alleging that the parties are tenants as to real property situated in the defendant's county is entitled to a change of venue. Chappell v Chappell (1908) 125 AD 127, 109 NYS 648, affd 193 NY 653, 86 NE 1122.

A motion to remove to a county where the real estate is situated cannot be defeated by a stipulation that the plaintiff will not attempt to reach the assignor's real estate. Wyatt v Brooks (1886) 42 Hun 502.

C. Impartial Trial

13. Generally

The rule that transitory actions will be tried in county where cause arose does not apply where "other things" are not equal. Averbach v Totem Lodge & Country Club, Inc. (1945, Sup) 57 NYS2d 750.

To obtain a change of place of trial under subd 2 of CPA § 187 it was not necessary "conclusively" that an impartial trial could not be had in the proper county. The statute authorized a change where there was "reason to believe" that an impartial trial could not be had in the proper county. Jacob v Oyster Bay (1907) 119 AD 503, 104 NYS 275.

Evidence held insufficient to induce a belief that an impartial trial could not be had in county where actions were brought. Tongate v Erie R. Co. (1924) 123 Misc 580, 205 NYS 768.

Inability to obtain an impartial trial must be clearly established, ordinarily by actual experiment in trying to obtain a jury or in trying the case. People v Wright, 5 How Pr 23, 3 NY Code R 75; for facts and circumstances must appear, a belief simply is not sufficient. People v Sammis (1875) 3 Hun 560; see also People v Webb, 1 Hill 179; Budge v Northam, 20 How Pr 248; and see Corporation of New York v Dawson, 2 Johns Cas 335; Zobieski v Bauder, 1 Caines 487; Baker v Sleight, 2 Caines 46; New Windsor Turnpike Co. v Wilson, 3 Caines 127; generally, Messenger v Holmes, 12 Wend 203.

The president-justice of the Municipal Court of the city of New York has authority to transfer a summary proceeding from one district court to another where a fair trial may not be had in the district where the property is located. Millhauser v Schwach (1934) 152 Misc 546, 273 NYS 944.

Mere belief or feeling of party that he cannot have impartial trial is not ground for changing place of trial. Bristol v Volney Volunteer Fire Corp. (1955, Sup) 140 NYS2d 429.

14. Bias of neighborhood

Change of venue was ordered in individual's action against a town, involving valuable land in the town, because of bias of jurors. Jacob v Oyster Bay (1907) 119 AD 503, 104 NYS 275.

An affidavit by the people, plaintiffs, setting out that a complaint against the defendant for fraud in repairing the capitol building, was presented to two grand juries of the county, and each failed to find a bill of indictment, that the defendant resided in the county, employed many men, and had business relations with many more, and that from the many rumors and insinuations of the press and citizens of the capital city the plaintiffs believed that an impartial trial could not be had in that county, and that justice would be promoted by a trial in Oneida County, was not sufficient to prevent a removal under CPA § 187, subd 3. People v Snaith (1889, Sup) 8 NYS 668, affd (Sup) 8 NYS 943.

Where cause of action arose in King's County where plaintiff was a justice of the supreme court performing his duties almost entirely in that county, the venue of the action was properly removable from King's County but in view of the convenience of witnesses should be heard in the adjoining county of New York the possibility of unconscious bias due to the position of the plaintiff, being sufficient to satisfy the requirement of reasonable grounds for belief required by CPA § 187. Arkwright v Steinbugler (1954) 283 AD 397, 128 NYS2d 823, reh and app den 283 AD 873, 129 NYS2d 775.

In will contest, bequests to charity did not show that impartial trial could not be had in county of decedent's residence. Re Corey Will (1948) 192 Misc 932, 82 NYS2d 494, affd 275 AD 53, 87 NYS2d 208.

Defendant's motion for change of venue on ground that a fair and impartial trial could not be had in the county was erroneously denied, since attorney for plaintiff was responsible for newspaper publication of matter prejudicial to an impartial trial. Niven v Stoddard (1928) 225 AD 705, 231 NYS 831.

Special Term was held justified in the exercise of its discretion in changing venue on grounds of improbability of securing impartial trial of action by dairy farmers against creameries where county in which venue was laid was primarily a dairy-farming county. Althiser v Richmondville Creamery Co. (1961) 13 AD2d 162, 215 NYS2d 122.

Where volunteer fire company was involved in automobile accident and carried no insurance, and where people of town would be liable by law for damages in case judgment was obtained against it, change of venue to another county was not warranted on ground that impartial trial could not be had in county where accident occurred, since voluntary fire companies existed in county to which venue was sought to be changed. Bristol v Volney Volunteer Fire Corp. (1955, Sup) 140 NYS2d 429.

15. Prejudice from judge's remarks

Judge's remarks were prejudicial, defendants' motion for change should have been granted. Sherk v Catena (1932) 235 AD 686, 255 NYS 315.

16. Action involving local official

In an action in Westchester county against a sheriff and others, a motion to change the place of trial to some other county is denied. A medical examiner of the county can take the place of the sheriff in directing the drawing, notification and taking charge of the jurors. Ingo v Casey (1940) 175 Misc 805, 25 NYS2d 384, affd 260 AD 1024, 25 NYS2d 413.

The fact that plaintiff's son had been elected sheriff of the county where the venue was laid was not sufficient ground on which to change the venue, under subd 2 of CPA § 187. Weiant v Rockland Lake Trap Rock Co. (1902) 74 AD 24, 76 NYS 699.

Where defendant was President Justice of New York City Municipal Court, venue of action was changed beyond territorial limits of the First and Second Departments to protect court's reputation from the slightest suspicion of bias. Seifert v McLaughlin (1961) 15 AD2d 555, 223 NYS2d 18.

D. Convenience of Witnesses

17. Generally

CPA § 187 distinguished between motion to change venue where county designated is improper, and motion to change for convenience of witnesses. Bond v New England Industries, Inc. (1948, Sup) 82 NYS2d 456.

CPA § 182-a (§ 504 herein) was limited by CPA § 187, authorizing change of place of trial for convenience of witnesses. Weber v Lacey (1953) 281 AD 290, 120 NYS2d 88.

The venue of an action will not be changed for the convenience of witnesses where a fair trial cannot be had in the county where they reside. Tuomey v Kingsford (1902) 68 AD 180, 74 NYS 13.

This section does not limit to the defendant the right of having the place of trial changed for convenience of witnesses, and the method of applying for the change is by motion. Lindsley v Sheldon (1904) 43 Misc 116, 88 NYS 192.

Convenience of witnesses who do not reside in either county will not be considered. Sanders v Prescott (1931) 234 AD 899, 254 NYS 535.

Motion for change of venue granted on account of the greater convenience of witnesses. Mesler v Richland Basket Co. (1923) 206 AD 654, 198 NYS 932.

Where defendant in one of consolidated actions has produced overwhelming proof of convenience of material and necessary witnesses who reside in Cortland county, it was error not to transfer trial from Sullivan to Cortland. Scott v Van Patten (1951) 278 AD 1038, 106 NYS2d 893.

While on motion under CPA § 183 (§ 507 herein) to change the place of trial of an action to the county in which the land involved is situated, it was improper to permit the contesting party to read affidavits tending to show that the greater convenience of witnesses would be served by retaining the cause in the county where instituted, especially where he had failed to serve the notice contemplated by CPA § 117 (Rule 2214(a)(b), 2215 herein), after the venue had been changed on such motion the court might entertain a motion to change the venue for the convenience of witnesses under CPA § 187. Johnson v Millard (1921) 199 AD 73, 190 NYS 865.

On a motion to change the place of trial to the proper county the convenience of witnesses may not be considered, but after the change has been made, it may be considered, upon a motion to return the case to the original county, even though that county is one wherein none of the parties reside. Culver v Union Nat. Bank, Troy (1925) 212 AD 766, 210 NYS 370.

Where cause of action arose in Orange county record established that convenience of witnesses will be better served there, motion for change of venue to such county should have been granted. Murray v Wright (1953) 282 AD 855, 124 NYS2d 294.

Business firms and corporations are not witnesses whose convenience will be considered. White v Mayer (1952) 112 NYS2d 253.

Corporations are not "witnesses" whose convenience is considered on motion to change venue. Potolski Int'l. v Parsons & Whittemore (1953) 282 AD 99, 125 NYS2d 485.

Venue of stockholder's derivative action against corporation was properly laid in county of residence of stockholder, but any inconvenience to defendants might be raised by motion for change of venue under CPA § 187. Feldmeier v Webster (1955) 208 Misc 996, 145 NYS2d 365, affd 1 AD2d 938, 150 NYS2d 581.

Where action is brought by Commissioners of State Insurance Fund, such action is to be brought in county in which fund maintains office. But venue can be changed for convenience of witnesses and in the interests of justice. Commissioners of State Ins. Fund v Alexander (1956) 4 Misc 2d 309, 157 NYS2d 244.

Resident of Niagara County, injured in New York County, and hospitalized and treated in New York County, entitled to change of venue was changed to New York County in the interests of justice and the convenience of witnesses. Larson v Bristol Corp. (1958) 7 AD2d 829, 180 NYS2d 794.

In absence of showing nature of testimony of witnesses, whose convenience is the basis for change of venue, as well as the materiality or necessity of their testimony, it is improvident exercise of discretion to change venue from county where plaintiff maintains business, where the transaction involved occurred, and where an earlier trial may be had. Du Pont v Bank of Utica (1959) 9 AD2d 807, 192 NYS2d 948.

On motion for change of venue for convenience of material witnesses, court must be factually advised as to what the witness' testimony will be so that it can decide materiality; it is not enough merely to state that the witness was present at the controverted event and had the opportunity to observe, since that does not necessarily mean that he will give material testimony. Condon v Schwenk (1960) 10 AD2d 822, 199 NYS2d 238.

18. Necessity that prior venue be proper

Motion to change the place of trial for convenience of witnesses will only be considered when the venue has been laid in or changed to the proper county. Convenience of witnesses will not be considered on a motion to remove a case to the proper county. Page Belting Co. v Joseph (1928) 131 Misc 373, 226 NYS 723, revd on other grounds 224 AD 720, 229 NYS 893.

After change of place of trial to proper county, court may change place of trial for convenience of witnesses. Johnson v Papen (1932) 236 AD 601, 260 NYS 479; Dunlap v Paterno (1933) 147 Misc 393, 263 NYS 195.

19. Condition of calendar

The venue of an action will not be changed from Saratoga to New York County because of the condition of the calendar in that county; an action should not be changed to a county adjacent to the county of New York, as the trial of an action will not be changed to a county in which neither of the parties nor any of the witnesses reside unless under unusual circumstances; that on a motion to change the place of trial for the convenience of witnesses, the convenience of the defendants in the action will not be considered. Kavanaugh v Mercantile Trust Co. (1904) 94 AD 575, 88 NYS 113.

The place of trial will not be changed from a rural county to the county of New York or Kings merely to subserve the convenience of witnesses, because the ends of justice must likewise be promoted, and this is best subserved by retaining the venue in a county where a speedy trial may be had. Mills v Sparrow (1909) 131 AD 241, 115 NYS 629.

Change of venue to New York county upon ground of convenience of witnesses was denied where some of plaintiff's witnesses resided in rural county where action was brought, in which county the case could be disposed of at the next term. Olinsky v Weinstein (1917) 166 NYS 613.

On a motion for change of venue where plaintiff claims ends of justice will be promoted by speedier trial in county in which venue laid, and consequently defendant's motion denied where party has an equal number of witnesses and convenience of travel is the same. Scaccia v Onondaga (1957) 11 Misc 2d 907, 175 NYS2d 120.

Calendar congestion as a factor, see Slavin v Whispell, 5 AD2d 296, 171 NYS2d 892; Efco Products, Inc. v Long Island Baking, Inc. (1958) 6 AD2d 832, 176 NYS2d 46.

In absence of showing nature of testimony of witnesses, whose convenience is the basis for change of venue, as well as the materiality or necessity of their testimony, it is improvident exercise of discretion to change venue from county where plaintiff maintains business, where the transaction involved occurred, and where an earlier trial may be had. Du Pont v Bank of Utica (1959) 9 AD2d 807, 192 NYS2d 948.

20. Effect of residence of parties

The court has the power to change the place of trial to a county convenient to the witnesses although such county is not one in which either party resides. Herbert v Griffith (1896) 2 AD 566, 37 NYS 1098.

Mere fact that defendant did not reside in county to which he desires change of place of trial for convenience of witnesses is immaterial. Wright v Stall (1918) 171 NYS 961.

Plaintiff's proofs being by deposition, venue of action by assignee was changed from the county of his residence for convenience of witnesses. Achilles v Union Produce Export Co. (1928) 224 AD 620, 232 NYS 93.

Where a motion is being heard to change the place of trial to the county where both parties reside, one party should not be allowed to read affidavits as to the convenience of witnesses. Sylvester v Lewis (1900) 55 AD 470, 67 NYS 176.

When a foreign corporation doing business in this state, sued resident defendants in an action upon contract not specified in CPA § 183 (§ 507 herein) or § 184 (§ 508 herein), the trial should have been laid in the county in which one of the defendants resided; the residence of a citizen of this state is not affected by the place of his business interests or official position. When such defendant moves to change the venue to the county of his residence, the court is without authority to consider the convenience of witnesses at the instance of the plaintiff. Mills & Gibb v Starin (1907) 119 AD 336, 104 NYS 230.

Where plaintiff, resident of Monroe county, sued defendants, residents of Pennsylvania, in said county for damages from accident in Cattaraugus county, motion by defendants to change place of trial to latter county for convenience of witnesses granted. Ackerman v Cummiskey (1932) 236 AD 519, 259 NYS 489.

21. Witness' residence outside of county to which transfer is sought

Witnesses residing outside county to which transfer is sought should not be considered. Averbach v Totem Lodge & Country Club (1945) 57 NYS2d 750.

On a motion for a change of venue from Oneida County to Lewis County, resisted by plaintiff on the ground that she has six witnesses in Lewis County who reside closer to the county seat of Oneida County than to that of Lewis County, the convenience of such witnesses cannot be considered. Johnson v Millard (1922) 200 AD 734, 193 NYS 333.

Where all persons on whose testimony plaintiff appears to be relying reside outside of county to which plaintiff seeks to change venue, their convenience may not be considered on motion to change venue to such county. Delair v T. Southworth T. & M. Co. (1955) 142 NYS2d 449.

On a motion to change venue from one county to another, convenience of witnesses residing outside both counties should not be considered. Slavin v Whispell (1958) 5 AD2d 296, 171 NYS2d 892.

22. Sufficiency of grounds of convenience

Change of venue on the ground of convenience of witnesses is properly denied where the facts sought to be proved by them are admitted by stipulation. Tavener v Burke (1923) 206 AD 645, 198 NYS 737; Geneva Trust Co. v Boston & M. R. Co. (1925) 212 AD 695, 209 NYS 557.

Motion to change place of trial for convenience of witness denied. Evans v Gardiner (1933) 238 AD 868, 263 NYS 927.

Where slight difference in mileage between residence of witnesses and courthouses would not affect convenience of any witness materially, court will not change venue, where action was commenced in proper county. Cartwright v Harry R. Drake & Sons (1953) 122 NYS2d 737.

Application to change venue of action to recover for services as an architect from Albany county to Kings county on the grounds of convenience of witnesses, denied. Simpson v Parkville Amusement Corp. (1936) 247 AD 845, 286 NYS 350.

Motion to change place of trial of action for alienation of affections from Ulster county to Kings county on ground of convenience of witnesses, denied. Engel v Engel (1936) 247 AD 833, 286 NYS 178.

Motion to change place of trial from Warren county to Saratoga county, adjoining county, of actions involving automobile accident which happened in Saratoga county, on ground of convenience of witnesses, denied. Micks v Bogle (1937) 252 AD 236, 298 NYS 927.

Where accident occurred in Monroe county and all witnesses on issue of liability resided there, and witnesses residing in Albany county could testify only as to amount of damages, venue was properly changed from Albany to Monroe county. Kalteux v C. P. Ward, Inc. (1953) 282 AD 847, 124 NYS2d 338.

Where only three witnesses resided in county to which plaintiff sought transfer of case, doctor, druggist who supplied medicines, and automobile mechanic who it was stated would testify to damages to automobile, change of venue for convenience of witnesses was denied. McLaren v Mayer (1953) 282 AD 754, 121 NYS2d 925.

Where moving papers to change venue from St. Lawrence to Cortland county disclosed that only witness whose convenience will be served by such change was State Trooper, alleged on information and belief to be eye-witness to accident involved, without stating substance of his testimony or whether he would be called by movant as witness, motion was denied. McCadam v Spahalski (1953) 123 NYS2d 157.

In action for automobile negligence between nonresidents, convenience of witness will be better served by transferring case to county where accident occurred. Linman v Lynch (1953) 282 AD 848, 124 NYS2d 293.

Motion to change place of trial of action to restrain unfair alleged business competition from Oneida county to New York county, denied. Augusta Knitting Corp. v Ogust (1938) 255 AD 827, 7 NYS2d 1.

Place of trial changed from Erie county to Kings county where removal of defendant's books and records from Kings county was likely to cause serious embarrassment in the conduct of its business and contract of hiring was made in Kings county and defendant's officers and employees were necessary and material witnesses. Rosenbloom v Springdale Distilling Co. (1938) 255 AD 1031, 8 NYS2d 844.

Concessions by plaintiff as to certain witness held not to bar change of venue on defendant's showing that convenience of witnesses required change. Schwartz v Haight (1940) 259 AD 911, 20 NYS2d 164.

Change of venue refused, on ground that the convenience of witnesses will be better served by retaining the action in the county where commenced. Meulendyke v Schell (1922) 196 NYS 410.

Only if real hardship is involved and there exists a probability of loss of material evidence will residence of witnesses effect change of venue. Will v Will & B. Candle Co. (1943) 40 NYS2d 321, revd 266 AD 765, 41 NYS2d 950, 951.

Action by residents of Ulster county against officials of New York City, was properly transferred to New York county, and inconvenience to plaintiffs' witnesses, measured against inconvenience to defendants' witnesses and production of records, did not justify retaining venue in Ulster county. Reeve v O'Dwyer (1950) 199 Misc 123, 98 NYS2d 452.

The motion will not be denied because the other party offers to admit the facts expected to be proved by the witnesses to be convenienced. Metropolitan Life Ins. Co. v McCoy (1881) 24 Hun 382; but see Smith v Averill, 1 Barb 28. As to his bearing expenses of such witnesses, see Worthy v Gilbert, 4 Johns 492; Rathbone v Harman, 4 Wend 208.

Under this section the place of trial of a Monroe County action will not be changed to New York County, where the affidavits do not state the facts that the witnesses will testify to sufficiently to balance up the convenience of witnesses, where the property and business covered by an alleged fraudulent chattel mortgage are located in Queens County, in which county the chattel mortgage is also filed, and the interests of a speedy trial can best be served by retaining the present place of trial. Goodman & Suss, Inc. v David Cohen Sales Co. (1923) 198 NYS 808, affd 207 AD 886, 201 NYS 906.

In personal injury action, in absence of convenience of witnesses, place where accident occurred is proper venue for such action. Gruneisen v Gruber (1955) 141 NYS2d 327.

Where witnesses for defendant would testify as to liability, and witnesses for plaintiff would testify only to special damages, which it not stipulated, would be proven either by deposition or by doctors whom plaintiff asserted he would call, witnesses for defendant were entitled to greater consideration as to convenience. Hahn v Unverdorben (1959) 9 AD2d 9, 189 NYS2d 440.

In absence of showing nature of testimony of witnesses, whose convenience is the basis for change of venue, as well as the materiality or necessity of their testimony, it is improvident exercise of discretion to change venue from county where plaintiff maintains business, where the transaction involved occurred, and where an earlier trial may be had. Du Pont v Bank of Utica (1959) 9 AD2d 807, 192 NYS2d 948.

23. Materiality not established

Where the answer contains a long and confusing statement of facts and the issues raised thereby are in doubt, the venue should not be changed for the convenience of the defendant's witnesses as their materiality cannot be determined. Neither will the venue be changed for the convenience of possible witnesses to the facts alleged in a defective counterclaim as their convenience is best served by leaving them at home. Hurley v Roberts (1907) 117 AD 837, 102 NYS 963.

Venue of consolidated actions involving collisions of two automobiles was not changed from Essex to Clinton where collisions occurred, where moving papers specified no facts to which Clinton witnesses will testify. Gough v Estes (1951) 278 AD 734, 103 NYS2d 52.

Where the affidavits of most of the witnesses named as material in an affidavit for change of venue, state that they know nothing of the matters in such moving affidavit, the motion must be denied. Cunningham v Turney, 9 NYSR 645.

Change of place of trial for convenience of witnesses denied, since the proposed testimony was immaterial and inadmissible. Matthews v Murphy (1929) 133 Misc 782, 233 NYS 517.

24. Preponderance of witnesses in number

If a majority of witnesses will be convenienced by trial in the county where the cause of action arose, an order changing it thereto will not be disturbed. Lyon v Davis (1889) 27 NYSR 517, 7 NYS 564; or the venue will be left in such county. Fowler v Third Ave. R. Co. (1890) 29 NYSR 285, 8 NYS 762.

A motion for change of venue will be denied if the opposing party has the greater number of witnesses. Anker v Darling, 14 NYSR 541.

The venue was changed to the county where the greater number of important witnesses resided upon defendant's stipulating that plaintiff might take the evidence of any of his witnesses before a referee to be read on the trial with the same effect as though the witnesses were present. Smith v Servis (1888) 19 NYSR 338, 2 NYS 865.

If the witnesses to an action for wood bought in one county to be delivered in another county live in the latter, the venue will be changed thereto. Tuthill v Felter (1889) 25 NYSR 151, 6 NYS 173.

On a motion to change the place of trial, where the cause of action arose in the county to which the change is sought to be made, and the case is one where that consideration should have great weight, and the moving affidavits show that all the witnesses who knew anything about the matter lived there and that defendants had talked with "some" of their witnesses and they would testify to the facts stated, and plaintiff swears to no witnesses in the county where the action is brought, the motion should be granted. Hurn v Olmstead (1907) 55 Misc 504, 105 NYS 1091.

Where, upon a motion to change the place of trial for the convenience of witnesses, the opposing affidavits show not only that the plaintiff is an old resident of the county where the venue was laid but that four out of seven of his intended witnesses reside in said county, one in Westchester county, one in Orange county and only one in New York county where the cause of action arose, the motion will be denied in accordance with the settled practice in the ninth judicial district. Brady v Cohen (1908) 57 Misc 358, 109 NYS 628.

Venue changed from Orange to Rockland where preponderance of witnesses resided and where courthouse was nearer to all witnesses. Antonucci v Kelly (1949) 91 NYS2d 131, affg 275 AD 944, 90 NYS2d 677.

It is the common experience that affidavits for

change of venue are swelled with lists of witnesses never called. Fiske v Bardeen, 12 NYSR 869.

Where the number of witnesses is nearly equal upon each side a change of venue will not be granted or the decision of the court below disturbed. Green v Weston (1890) 31 NYSR 478, 10 NYS 948; or the venue will be controlled by the place of the transactions. Whitall v Moshier, 7 NYSR 390; see Maynard v Chase (1890) 30 NYSR 348, 8 NYS 746.

Where plaintiff has selected the county of his residence in which to sue, place of trial should not be changed to county of defendant's residence for convenience of witnesses, where the balance of convenience is about equal. Harris v Regorson Corp. (1918) 170 NYS 866.

A motion to change the place of the trial of an action upon the ground of the convenience of the witnesses is addressed to the discretion of the court and will not be granted merely because the defendant swears to the greater number of necessary witnesses. O'Beirne v Miller (1901) 35 Misc 337, 71 NYS 946.

When it appears that a contract was to be performed in a defendant's county, and that the greater number of witnesses to prove a counterclaim reside there, the venue should be changed to said county. Aldine Mfg. Co. v Duffy-McInnerney Co. (1908) 124 AD 751, 109 NYS 596.

Place of trial, in action on fire policy, was changed from Kings to Westchester county for convenience of material witnesses, 13 in number. Kotz v United States F. Ins. Co. (1946) 270 AD 1029, 63 NYS2d 33.

Where notes sued on were made and were payable in Nassau County and the defendant and nearly all the witnesses resided in that county, and only the plaintiff resided in Onondaga County, where he instituted the action, held that the place of trial should have been changed to Nassau County on the defendant's motion. Moir v Johnson (1925) 211 AD 427, 207 NYS 380.

When in an action for the value of goods sold and delivered the plaintiff shows four necessary witnesses whose convenience will be subserved by retaining the place of trial, while the defendant, making a general denial, has no witnesses, the place of trial will not be changed, although the goods were sold and delivered in the defendant's county. Lewis Co. v Phoenix Car Co. (1906) 115 AD 188, 100 NYS 669.

Where, in an action for goods sold and delivered, brought in Saratoga county by the assignee of a foreign corporation doing business in New York City, the answer alleges a breach of warranty and it appears that all the witnesses resided in or about New York county where the cause of action arose, a motion to change the venue to the latter county should be granted. Belden v Schapiro (1910) 138 AD 669, 123 NYS 53.

Where, in an action for breach of warranty as to the condition of a horse purchased by the plaintiff from the defendant, the latter denied the warranty or that the animal was unsound when sold, the

venue in such action should not be changed to the county of the defendant's residence on the ground of convenience of witnesses, where the greater number of disinterested witnesses reside in or near the county where the venue is laid. Burroughs v Foster (1911) 145 AD 702, 130 NYS 530.

In an action for professional services a motion to change the venue to the county in which defendant resides on the ground of convenience of witnesses should be granted when it is shown that nearly all the services rendered by plaintiff were performed in that county, and the larger number of material witnesses reside there. Harrison v Holahan (1907) 122 AD 740, 107 NYS 741.

The venue of an action to recover damages for personal injuries caused by negligence should be changed to the county where the accident occurred, and where the defendants and the greater number of witnesses reside. Fluckiger v Haber (1911) 144 AD 65, 128 NYS 739.

Venue changed to county where accident involved occurred, for convenience of greater number of witnesses. Huber v Waters (1931) 234 AD 729, 252 NYS 897.

Where defendant has twenty-four witnesses in the vicinity of the accident, and plaintiff only nineteen where the action was brought, the place of trial may be changed. Neeley v Erie R. Co. (1909) 134 AD 781, 119 NYS 953.

Venue changed from Onondaga to Genesee county, where accident occurred and greater number of witnesses resided. Warner v Heimerl Trucking Corp. (1950) 276 AD 1052, 96 NYS2d 265.

Where automobile collision occurred in Orange county where greater number of witnesses reside, venue changed from Kings county. Maricondo v Bradner (1950) 276 AD 908, 94 NYS2d 8.

In action against a dentist for negligent operation, performed in the county of his residence, change from the county of plaintiff's residence, where he was treated for the injury and most of the witnesses resided, was denied. Smith v Flagg (1929) 134 Misc 862, 236 NYS 342.

Where plaintiff's witnesses will testify on main issue of defendant driver's negligence by testifying to actual collision, and where defendant's witnesses will testify only as to his sobriety and whereabouts at particular time, convenience of former witnesses controls. Costa v Randall (1944) 46 NYS2d 300.

Change of place of trial granted on account of convenience of witnesses in an action for assault committed in defendant's store and where defendant specifies eight witnesses, six of whom were present, and plaintiff merely alleges that none of these witnesses were present. Fuchs v Fitzer (1908) 125 AD 917, 109 NYS 1024.

The venue of an action for assault should be changed to the county where the assault occurred and where the greater number of witnesses reside. Orkin v Machan (1911) 148 AD 197, 132 NYS 1003.

A change may be made for witnesses to defendants' condition after an assault at which no witnesses were present. Banks v Bensky (1889) 27 NYSR 135, 7 NYS 518.

An action for damages for forcible ejection from a train should be changed to the county where the alleged tort was committed, where defendant has twenty-four witnesses in that vicinity, and plaintiff only nineteen where the action was brought. Neeley v Erie R. Co. (1909) 134 AD 781, 119 NYS 953.

The trial of a cause of action for false imprisonment should be changed to the county where the arrest was made and a large number of necessary witnesses reside, when the plaintiff is unable to name witnesses residing in the county where the venue is laid. Lutfy v Sullivan (1907) 119 AD 506, 104 NYS 177.

In action for fraud in execution of lease, brought as of right in Kings county, venue was not changed to Sullivan county where cause arose, where it was not shown that material witnesses resident in Sullivan sufficiently outnumbered those resident in Kings county to justify change. Mau-Ste Fallsburg Corp. v Cohen (1951) 278 AD 770, 103 NYS2d 490.

Where resident of Westchester commences libel action in Bronx County against newspaper published and circulated in Westchester County, granting motion to change place of trial from Bronx to Westchester was mandatory where convenience of witnesses predominates in favor of Westchester County, though newspaper president resided in Bronx County near boundary line between two counties. Armbruster v Brady (1956) 154 NYS2d 678.

Where automobile accident occurred in Jefferson County and defendant's moving papers set forth names of five witnesses residing in such county and adequately indicate materiality of their testimony, and plaintiff gives names of no witnesses residing in Lawrence County, venue was changed from Lawrence to Jefferson County. Van Etten v Niagara M. P. Corp. (1955) 1 AD2d 724, 147 NYS2d 111.

Where defendant moved for change of venue and preponderance of convenience of witnesses favors defendant, motion granted. Conner v Jacobs (1958) 5 AD2d 1046, 173 NYS2d 472.

Where a large preponderance of witnesses reside in a county other than that in which the cause of action arose, than the place of the trial should be in that county. Hilgers v Hyde (1958) 6 AD2d 963, 176 NYS2d 522.

Libel and slander action involving group of defendants residing in Suffolk and stemming from local zoning board hearing in Suffolk should be tried in Suffolk especially since essential witnesses, the stenographers, recording technicians, spectators and village officer present at hearing, were all Suffolk residents, and change of venue from New York to Suffolk on ground of convenience of witnesses was proper. Condon v Schwenk (1960) 10 AD2d 822, 199 NYS2d 238.

25. Parties and experts

The words "party to an action" includes parties to the record and no one else, and the residence of a party in interest who is not a party to the record cannot be considered; on a motion to change the venue of an action on the ground of convenience to witnesses, the convenience of witnesses whose testimony will be material and competent can alone be considered. Lane v Bochlowitz (1902) 77 AD 171, 78 NYS 1072.

In an action for an accounting, a motion by the individual defendant a nonresident to change the place of trial from Westchester county to New York county, on the ground that both plaintiff and the defendant corporation were residents of the latter county, denied. Rainbow v Winter Conenara Corp. (1936) 247 AD 889, 286 NYS 769.

Although on a motion for the change of place of trial of an action, the rule, that the convenience of parties and of expert witnesses will not be consulted, does not apply to expert witnesses who will testify from their personal knowledge of the matter in controversy, the court is unable to determine on this application that the doctors for the plaintiffs are not material witnesses on matters of personal knowledge. Roche v Holbrook (1936) 159 Misc 796, 287 NYS 829.

Convenience of expert witnesses will not be considered. Solberg v Ft. Orange Constr. Co. (1913) 142 NYS 228.

Physicians, who are nonresidents, of nonresident plaintiff, should not be considered on motion to change venue for convenience of witnesses. Dobbs v Whitcomb (1943) 45 NYS2d 441.

Physician and nurse were regarded as expert witnesses, in action for negligence predicated on automobile accident. Bushnell v Reay (1949) 276 AD 813, 93 NYS2d 143.

Rule excluding convenience of expert witnesses from consideration applies only to witnesses who are called solely to give expert opinion; it does not apply to witnesses who are not called solely as experts, but to testify to essential and material facts. Laduke v Bond (1954) 284 AD 859, 134 NYS2d 155.

Convenience of expert witnesses, parties or their employees, cannot be considered on motion for change of venue in stockholder's derivative action. Benson v Braun (1955) 141 NYS2d 286, affd 286 AD 1098, 145 NYS2d 711.

Where motion is made for change of venue on ground of convenience of witnesses but plaintiff's affidavit shows great personal difficulties and hardship attendant upon her going to other county, motion must be denied. Sparklin v Jackson & Perkins Co. (1957) 6 Misc 2d 559, 160 NYS2d 315.

In the absence of other compelling circumstances, the witnesses whose convenience is required to be considered on an application of change of venue granted thereon are those other than the parties, their employees and members of their families. Slavin v Whispell (1958) 5 AD2d 296, 171 NYS2d 892.

Convenience of expert witnesses is not a persuasive

factor to be considered in change of venue. Efco Products, Inc. v Long Island Baking, Inc. (1958) 6 AD2d 832, 176 NYS2d 46.

The convenience of busy medical practitioners has real significance, and to the extent that they give testimony as to their personal observation and treatment they are not to be deemed expert witnesses. Hilgers v Hyde (1958) 6 AD2d 963, 176 NYS2d 522.

In action to recover for negligence convenience of anticipated witnesses who are parties to action or are employees of such parties is entitled to subordinate consideration only. Gerber v B. C. R. Hotel Corp. (1960) 10 AD2d 956, 201 NYS2d 749.

In balancing conveniences between two medical witnesses, one a Sullivan County resident and the other who treated plaintiff in Queens County, but whose name and address are not disclosed, fact that Sullivan County physician was first one to treat plaintiff in Sullivan County immediately after the accident is entitled to consideration in granting change of venue from Queens to Sullivan County. Gerber v B. C. R. Hotel Corp., supra.

26. Employees of parties

The change of venue in an action must be denied where the defendant's witnesses were his own employees and the plaintiffs were laborers who could attend in another county only with serious loss. Sparks v United Traction Co. (1901) 66 AD 204, 73 NYS 108.

In an action for the breach of warranty on the sale of goods where the plaintiffs reside in the county where the contract was made and executed, the place of trial should not be changed to another county where the defendant has thirteen witnesses, all employees, while the plaintiff has sixteen witnesses, six of whom are not employees; the convenience of witnesses not employees will be given greater consideration than those who are employees. Hays v Faatz Reynolds Felting Co. (1906) 112 AD 487, 98 NYS 386.

The convenience of witnesses who are employees of the party intending to call them, should be considered on the motion as much as the convenience of other witnesses. Deutsch v E. M. Upton Cold Storage Co. (1911) 146 AD 588, 131 NYS 273.

Convenience of defendant's officers and employees may be considered where necessary and material witnesses. Rosenbloom v Springdale Dist. Co. (1938) 255 AD 1031, 8 NYS2d 844.

Where witnesses were employees of movant and nonresident, change of venue to county where railroad crossing collision occurred was denied in court's discretion. Hoffman v Boston & Maine R. Co. (1940) 259 AD 958, 20 NYS2d 460. See Kingsboro Silk Mills v Auburn Fabrics (1940) 259 AD 1108, 21 NYS2d 316; Walker v Hotel Syracuse (1944) 267 AD 935, 46 NYS2d 770.

Convenience of employees considered along with other factors. National Equipment Corp. v McPhail Candy Corp. (1950) 97 NYS2d 687.

Where party opposing change of venue has no witness in county he selects and other party shows material witnesses in another county, consideration will be given to their convenience though they are employees. Seeley v New York Tel. Co. (1951) 278 AD 613, 102 NYS2d 277.

In the absence of exceptional circumstances courts look with disfavor upon applications to change the place of trial to accommodate the convenience of witnesses in the employ of the moving party. Adie v William Knabe & Co. Mfg. Co. (1925) 124 Misc 655, 208 NYS 160.

Directors and employees of party, seeking change of venue for their convenience as witnesses, cannot be considered. Champlain Creameries v Hovey, S. & Co. (1955) 141 NYS2d 271.

In action for money lent to resident of Jefferson County by New Jersey corporation authorized to do business in New York and having its only place of business in New York, it was abuse of discretion to retain venue in Kings County instead of changing venue to Jefferson County, where all of plaintiff's witnesses were employees or officers of whom four resided outside Kings County. Taller & Cooper v Rand (1955) 286 AD 1096, 145 NYS2d 557.

27. Witnesses engaged in official or government work

In action for false arrest, convenience of law enforcement officials would be served by transferring action from Kings to Chautauqua county where cause arose. Stevens v Bancroft (1949) 275 AD 864, 89 NYS2d 285.

Where records and employees in office of county clerk of Erie would be available in Erie county where cause of action arose, venue was changed from Putnam to Erie. Carlson v Serrone (1945) 268 AD 1060, 52 NYS2d 487.

In an action against a village for personal injuries resulting from a fall upon an icy sidewalk, wherein with the exception of plaintiff, her husband, and her mother-in-law, all the witnesses to the accident and to the weather and other conditions at the time, reside in the defendant village, and amongst these are municipal employees, venue should be changed to the county in which the village is situated. Rice v Peekskill (1924) 211 AD 814, 206 NYS 801.

In action by domestic corporation in county where it has its place of business against a foreign corporation, motion for change of place of trial will be granted for convenience of witnesses, some of whom are engaged in important government work. Spencer Kellogg & Sons v Barber & Co. (1919) 106 Misc 297, 174 NYS 438.

Where two of defendant's witnesses are law enforcement officials the court is entitled to consider their convenience. Slavin v Whispell (1958) 5 AD2d 296, 171 NYS2d 892.

28. Corporations

Corporations are not "witnesses" within meaning of statutory provisions authorizing change of venue for convenience of witnesses. Saranac Truck

Rental, Inc. v Davis White Co. (1961) 12 AD2d 876, 209 NYS2d 664.

29. Financial difficulties

Where defendant had ten witnesses and not the means to take them to county of plaintiff's residence, he was entitled to have trial changed to county of accident where his witnesses resided, though plaintiff had eight witnesses. Wright v Stall (1918) 171 NYS 961.

Financial condition of plaintiff considered with physical condition in determining change of venue. Lawson v Lawson (1946) 64 NYS2d 356.

Extraneous facts, irrelevant and inadmissible on the trial, which make an appeal merely to the sympathies of the court such as plaintiff's plea of financial hardship in provision for transportation and maintenance of witnesses may not ordinarily be considered in arriving at the ends of justice on a motion to change venue unless a complete denial of justice would follow. Slavin v Whispell (1958) 5 AD2d 296, 171 NYS2d 892.

30. Physical disability

Physical and financial condition of plaintiff wife warranted denial of change from Kings to Delaware county. Lawson v Lawson (1946) 64 NYS2d 356.

Motion to change place of trial from Albany County to Niagara County denied, where, although the action is brought to recover damages for personal injuries suffered by plaintiff while she was a guest in the defendants' hotel in Niagara Falls and the defendants assert that they have nine material witnesses residing in the county where the accident happened, it appears that the plaintiff is a woman more than eighty years of age and, according to an affidavit of her physician, it would seriously impair her health to travel from Albany to Niagara County for the purpose of the trial. Foley v Phelps (1939) 257 AD 896, 12 NYS2d 445.

Venue of transitory action would not be changed for convenience of witnesses where medical affidavit established that plaintiff's health would be seriously impaired by travel, and where motion was made by only one of the defendants without explanation as to why the others did not join therein. Goldman v Isgood Stottville Realty Corp. (1961) 14 AD2d 759, 220 NYS2d 491.

31. Transportation facilities

It is no answer to a motion to change the place of trial for the convenience of witnesses to say that because of facilities for transportation it is as convenient for the majority of witnesses to come to New York where the venue is laid as to go to the county seat of their residence. Lambert Snyder Co. v Smith (1908) 124 AD 412, 108 NYS 992.

When the question of convenience of witnesses is under consideration the court will give due weight to the improvements in transportation which serve that convenience. Micks v Bogle (1937) 252 AD 236, 298 NYS 927.

32. Examination before referee in another county

The place of trial may be changed unless the parties stipulate to examine before a referee witnesses in another county. Thomas v Mutual Reserve Fund Life Ins. Co. 43 Hun 636, 6 NYSR 864.

But a refusal to change to the county where the more important and numerous witnesses live, is not cured by a condition that such witnesses might be examined before a referee. Belding v Ladd (1889) 27 NYSR 296, 7 NYS 379.

E. LOCUS OF CAUSE; ENDS OF JUSTICE

33. Generally

The place of trial will not be changed from a rural county to the county of New York or Kings merely to subserve the convenience of witnesses, because the ends of justice must likewise be promoted, and this is best subserved by retaining the venue in a county where a speedy trial may be had. Mills v Sparrow (1909) 131 AD 241, 115 NYS 629.

Speedy trial of action promotes ends of justice. Averbach v Totem Lodge & Country Club (1945) 57 NYS2d 750.

County where trial may be had more speedily will promote ends of justice. Cartwright v Harry Drake & Sons (1953) 122 NYS2d 737.

Where action for death was properly commenced in Oneida county where administrator was appointed, action was not transferred to Madison county where accident occurred and where parties resided, since action was more speedily triable in Oneida county. McNamara v Penner (1953) 123 NYS2d 576.

The fact that the ends of justice will best be served by granting an application for a change of venue in that a preference and a speedier trial will result, is not sufficient without proof that the convenience of material witnesses will be promoted by the change. Bonnano v National Foundry of New York, Inc. (1953) 127 NYS2d 70.

When the answer in an action for breach of contract justifies the discharge because of the incompetency of the plaintiff, who was employed at defendant's factory in another county than that in which the venue was laid, the place of trial should be changed. Pinkus v United Cloak & Suit Co. (1908) 124 AD 535, 108 NYS 932.

In action for death resulting from hay harvesting accident, ends of justice would not be served by transferring action from Bronx county to Schoharie county on ground that rural jurors would better understand harvesting than city jurors. Horstmann v Freemire (1953) 124 NYS2d 243.

In an action by a nonresident against two executors, in which the second executor is in default, a motion by the first executor for a change of the place of trial to the county of his appointment, rather than to the county in which he resides, is granted in the interests of justice. Barnsch v Andrews (1939) 172 Misc 61, 14 NYS2d 578.

Nonresident defendant may have venue changed to

county in which plaintiff resides. Dreskin v Dreskin (1947) 73 NYS2d 764.

Where plaintiff is nonresident of state, defendant is entitled to change of venue to county where he has his business place. Keehn v S. & D. Motor Lines (1943) 180 Misc 91, 41 NYS2d 518.

Subdivision 1 of section 52 of the County Law provides that "The place of trial shall be in the county against which the action is brought." That statute, however, had to be read in conjunction with subdivision 3 of section 187 of the Civil Practice Act which indicated that the court might change the place of trial for the convenience of witnesses and to permit the ends of justice. Scaccia v Onondaga (1957) 11 Misc 2d 907, 175 NYS2d 120.

34. Transitory actions; generally

Other things being equal actions of a transitory character will be tried in the county where the cause of action arose. Mencke v Goldberg (1924) 208 AD 820, 204 NYS 78; Schwartz v Wilbur (1924) 211 AD 806, 206 NYS 852; Page Belting Co. v Joseph (1928) 131 Misc 373, 226 NYS 723, revd on other grounds 224 AD 720, 229 NYS 893.

Transitory actions should be tried in the county where the transactions involved took place unless a large preponderance of the witnesses live in another county. Spanedda v Murphy (1911) 144 AD 58, 128 NYS 884.

Where a transitory action is brought on for trial at a term of court held in the county in which the venue is laid, the judge presiding at such court may not, of his own motion and without a request from either of the parties, strike the case from the calendar simply because it appears that both the parties are residents of another county. Phillips v Tietjen (1905) 108 AD 9, 95 NYS 469.

If it be assumed that no preponderance of witnesses for either of the parties is shown, the controlling factor is that the cause of action arose in a named county and, other things being equal, a transitory action should be tried in the county where the cause of action arose. In addition, a rural county where calendars are not congested is to be preferred to an urban county. Bernstein v McKane (1957) 3 AD2d 764, 160 NYS2d 507.

35. Ends of justice; generally

Extraneous facts, irrelevant and inadmissible on the trial, which make an appeal merely to the sympathies of the court, may not ordinarily be considered in arriving at the ends of justice on a motion to change the venue unless a complete denial of justice would follow. Parkhill v New England Furniture & Carpet Co. (1924) 211 AD 871, 207 NYS 890.

Place of trial will not be changed merely for convenience of greater number of witnesses where court is not satisfied that ends of justice would be promoted by the change. Scheu v Haner (1917) 164 NYS 947, revd on other grounds 180 AD 885, 166 NYS 1113.

Venue changed to the county in which the cause of action arose and where the majority of witnesses resided, on grounds of convenience of witnesses and promotion of cause of justice. Friedman v Birnbaum (1929) 226 AD 770, 234 NYS 794.

Convenience of witnesses and interests of justice required a change of venue. Gest v Whitehead (1929) 227 AD 752, 236 NYS 801.

Change of venue granted where the convenience of the greatest number of material witnesses would be served and the ends of justice promoted. Friedman v Jones (1931) 232 AD 776, 248 NYS 844.

Venue changed from Albany county to Washington county where cause of action arose in latter county and convenience of material witnesses and ends of justice will be promoted. Killian v Cottrell (1931) 234 AD 901, 253 NYS 1042.

Where a contract for the sale of goods by sample was negotiated by the vendor's traveling salesman at the place of business of the vendee, and the vendors on receiving the order from their salesman confirmed the same by writing, and the goods were delivered at the vendee's place of business, a motion to change the place of trial to the vendee's county should be granted, where the moving papers show that the convenience of witnesses and ends of justice will be subserved thereby. Denzer v Grewen (1909) 133 AD 706, 118 NYS 230.

Where plaintiff was arrested in Onondaga on warrant issued in Erie county where he was discharged, change of venue from Onondaga to Erie for convenience of witnesses was denied. Wilbur v Hotel Buffalo (1950) 198 Misc 831, 100 NYS2d 587.

Where plaintiff and defendant in action for death both resided in one county, but action was brought in county where death occurred, the court of that county could properly refuse to grant a change of place of trial if it was reasonable to believe that an impartial trial could not be had in the proper county, and convenience of witnesses and ends of justice would be promoted by allowing the case to remain there. Buxbaum v Paulsen (1916) 95 Misc 717, 159 NYS 427.

Where injury to incompetent occurred in Jefferson county where all witnesses resided, and committee of incompetent alone resided in Genesee county, place of trial was changed from latter to former to promote ends of justice. Griffith v New York C. R. Co. (1946) 271 AD 809, 64 NYS2d 801.

Place of trial changed to county in which defendant village is located and in which village records may more conveniently and without injury to the public business be produced. Brooklyn Nat. Bank v Rockville Centre (1932) 236 AD 812, 259 NYS 979.

Change of venue from a county adjoining that in which was defendant's principal office and where the contract sued on was breached to New York county where it was made, on grounds of convenience of witnesses, prejudice and furtherance of justice, was denied. St. Regis Paper Co. v Hano (1931) 141 Misc 75, 252 NYS 174, affd St. Regis Paper Co. v Harrisville File Folder Corp. (1932) 235 AD 653, 255 NYS 845, 846.

Place of transaction not controlling where ends of justice are involved. Roberge v Millard (1929) 226 AD 701, 234 NYS 136.

The rule that transitory actions will be tried in county where cause arose does not apply where "other things" are not equal. Averbach v Totem Lodge & Country Club (1945) 57 NYS2d 750.

In absence of showing of greater convenience of witnesses, motion for change of venue to the county wherein the cause of action arose should be granted. Gilliland v Konta (1923) 206 AD 685, 199 NYS 829; Weckline v Musgrave (1929) 227 AD 796, 237 NYS 211.

Upon a motion to change the place of trial for the convenience of witnesses, the court must inquire not alone as to the convenience of witnesses but also whether the ends of justice will be promoted by a change; it is not a hard and fast rule that, where the number of witnesses is equally divided between the county in which the venue is laid and that in which the transaction occurred, the place of trial will be changed to the latter county. Larkin v Sheldon (1908) 59 Misc 406, 109 NYS 1105, affd 128 AD 883, 112 NYS 1134.

Cross-motion to retain place of trial in county where accident happened and witnesses convenienced was granted. Brady v Rockland Coaches (1945) 55 NYS2d 588.

In action for failure to deliver lumber to be shipped from certain point at specified price on cars, held that delivery was point of shipment and defendant was entitled to have case tried in that county, subject to convenience of witnesses and ends of justice. Woodland Lumber & Mfg. Co. v Barnett (1918) 185 AD 572, 173 NYS 4.

Venue changed from county where the only material witnesses, plaintiff and husband, resided to county in which all the parties resided when the transactions involved occurred, where defendant resided and where the action was entitled to preference. Booth v Weinstein (1931) 233 AD 329, 252 NYS 775.

Where automobile accident occurred in Clinton county where plaintiff and preponderance of his material witnesses resided, change of place of trial of automobile negligence action from Franklin to Clinton county, for convenience of witnesses and ends of justice, was not abuse of discretion. La Duke v Bond (1955) 285 AD 1109, 139 NYS2d 326.

36. Change to place of transaction

Venue changed to county where plaintiff resided and cause of action arose. Calonie v Smith (1929) 133 Misc 901, 235 NYS 6.

Where estate assets upon which trust was sought to be impressed were located in New York county where all records relating to estate were located, venue was changed from Onondaga to New York county, where cause arose. Latham v Father Divine (1949) 276 AD 824, 93 NYS2d 201.

Action by state against county for support of patient in state tuberculosis hospital arose in county where hospital was located, and venue was changed to such county. People v Chenango County (1943) 39 NYS2d 785.

On an application for change of venue for convenience of witnesses, where it appears that all the transactions arose in defendant's county, the venue should be changed to that county, especially where the action must have been brought there except for an assignment of the claim. Ludlow v Single Paper Co. (1909) 132 AD 601, 116 NYS 1095.

An action to set aside an assignment for creditors should be removed to the county in which all the transactions in question took place, where it appears that a large number of the witnesses on the question of the good faith of the transaction resided in that county. Claflin v Eagan (1891) 38 NYSR 6, 14 NYS 240.

In an action for breach of contracts made and to be performed in the city of New York by parties engaged in business there an assignee of one party who resides in Rockland county, but who is engaged in business in New York, and who is in the employ of his assignor, is not entitled to retain the venue in Rockland county. This, not on the ground of convenience of witnesses, but because the cause of action arose in New York county. Brady v Hogan (1907) 117 AD 898, 102 NYS 962.

On a motion to change the venue of an action to recover for a breach of contract to sell and deliver goods made on the ground of convenience of witnesses, the county where the contract was made and to be performed may be considered. Jacobson v German-American Button Co. (1908) 124 AD 251, 108 NYS 795.

Where contract sued on was entered into in Warren county where defendants reside and related to realty located there, venue was changed from Onondaga to Warren. Community Home Improvement Co. v Harris (1949) 85 NYS2d 824.

Where contract sued on was entered into in Warren county wherein defendant resided and contract related to improvement of realty in such county, venue was changed from Onondaga to Warren county. Community Home Improvement Co. v Stanton (1949) 86 NYS2d 13.

The place of trial should be changed to the county where a contract was made and goods sold thereunder, and the examination of the goods on delivery was made, even though each party had witnesses in their respective counties; two or three witnesses each, as to the condition of goods when delivered, are sufficient. Shaff v Rosenberg (1906) 116 AD 366, 101 NYS 892.

Where, in an action for goods sold and delivered the principal issues to be tried are whether the goods were ever delivered, a motion for a change of the place of trial to the county in which the transaction arose should be granted. Neiman v Gardner (1911) 145 AD 197, 129 NYS 913.

County in which goods were manufactured and in which order was accepted held most convenient for witnesses as against county in which order was taken. Rochester Quality Shoes, Inc. v Bartoli (1921) 190 NYS 793.

The venue in an action will be changed from New York county to Albany county for the convenience of witnesses, where it appears that the services rendered by the plaintiff, the subject of the action, were performed in Albany county. Roberts v Lansing (1901) 60 AD 81, 69 NYS 736.

Venue changed from New York to Oswego; defense of breach of warranty of machinery in action for balance due. National Equipment Corp. v McPhail Candy Corp. (1950) 97 NYS2d 687.

Trial of action by plaintiff-lienor against contractor and surety on former's bond to establish claim for materials furnished for public improvement was properly tried in county where plaintiff corporation had its principal place of business. Shelt Co. v Simiele Constr. Co. (1941) 176 Misc 730, 28 NYS2d 794.

Where plaintiff, resident of Monroe county, sued defendants, residents of Pennsylvania, in said county for damages from accident in Cattaraugus county, motion by defendants to change place of trial to latter county for convenience of witnesses granted. Ackerman v Cummiskey (1932) 236 AD 519, 259 NYS 489.

Motion to change place of trial to county where the accident happened, granted for the convenience of witnesses. Miles v Proper (1938) 255 AD 793, 7 NYS2d 71. See Levine v Poughkeepsie Recreation (1941) 261 AD 907, 25 NYS2d 193.

Where accident occurred in Jefferson county and convenience of witnesses required trial there, venue was changed from Onondaga to Jefferson. Jones v Marchese (1949) 274 AD 1089, 86 NYS2d 235.

Personal injury action could be brought in county of plaintiff's residence, but for convenience of witnesses change of venue could be granted to county where cause of action arose. Solberg v Ft. Orange Constr. Co. (1913) 142 NYS 228.

The trial of a cause of action for false imprisonment should be changed to the county where the arrest was made and a large number of necessary witnesses reside, when the plaintiff is unable to name witnesses residing in any county where the venue is laid. Lutfy v Sullivan (1907) 119 AD 506, 104 NYS 177.

On a motion to change the venue of an action for goods sold and delivered, where there is no such preponderance of witnesses that the motion can be decided on that ground alone, the trial should be had in the county where the contract of sale was made. Brody v C. A. Weed & Co. (1910) 137 AD 754, 122 NYS 625.

In an action for goods sold, the trial should be had where the contract was made, if the number of witnesses on both sides are substantially the same. Studebaker Bros. Co. v Western New York & P. Traction Co. (1910) 140 AD 308, 125 NYS 224.

Where upon a motion for a change of venue of an action on contract the terms of which are in dispute, the number of material witnesses in each county seems to be about equal, the trial should be had in the county in which the contract was made

and was to have been performed. Mullin v Curtis (1911) 145 AD 441, 129 NYS 916.

Where there are conflicting claims as to the number and materiality of witnesses, the place where the cause of action arose and where the conditions and transactions to be inquired into existed and took place form a most important, if not a controlling, consideration. Schulz v Hudson Val. R. Co. (1911) 147 AD 788, 131 NYS 995.

Where it appears that the number of material witnesses necessary to be called on either side is substantially the same the place of trial should be changed to the county where the cause of action arose, unless some special reason exists for retaining the place of trial in the county of plaintiff's residence. Rose v Richmond (1925) 214 AD 142, 211 NYS 721.

Venue changed from Queens to Sullivan county, where cause of action arose; there was no preponderance of witnesses for either party. Wilson v Winco Estates, Inc. (1943) 266 AD 795, 41 NYS2d 684.

In an action by the transferee of promissory notes brought in the county where plaintiff resides, a change of venue will be granted to the defendant's county, where the convenience of witnesses is nearly balanced and where the fraud which is set up in the answer is alleged to have arisen in the defendant's county where the contract originated. Selden Truck Corp. v Burns (1924) 123 Misc 103, 203 NYS 784.

In absence of showing of greater convenience of witnesses, the action should be tried in the county where the transactions between the parties occurred. Remo v Crouse (1928) 132 Misc 873, 230 NYS 719.

Where it appeared that an assignment had been made for purpose of suit, defendants were entitled to change of venue of action to county in which contract was entered into and performed. Saphir v Krause (1957) 5 Misc 2d 415, 158 NYS2d 620.

37. Change from rural to urban county

The rule that in transitory actions, other things being equal, the place where the cause of action arose is the proper county in which to try it, is not universal, but must yield to the rule denying a change from a rural to a metropolitan county. Dairymen's League Co-op Asso. v Brundo (1927) 131 Misc 548, 227 NYS 203.

Venue will ordinarily not be changed from rural to urban county, despite rule that transitory actions should usually be tried in county where cause arose. Dairymen's L. C. Asso. v Eastern F. Products (1950) 198 Misc 798, 100 NYS2d 855.

A speedy trial promotes the ends of justice, so since delay is less likely in a rural than in an urban county, a change from former to latter is generally disapproved. Roberge v Millard (1929) 226 AD 701, 234 NYS 136; St. Regis Paper Co. v Hano (1931) 141 Misc 75, 252 NYS 174, affd St. Regis Paper Co. v Harrisville File Holder Corp. (1932) 235 AD 653, 255 NYS 845, 846.

Ordinarily a change of venue will not be granted

from a rural to a metropolitan county for the accommodation of witnesses. Mills v Sparrow (1909) 131 AD 241, 115 NYS 629; Dairymen's League Co-op. Asso. v Brundo (1927) 131 Misc 548, 227 NYS 203; Lesser v Cohen (1927) 131 Misc 80, 225 NYS 346, affd 223 AD 862, 228 NYS 835.

To justify a change of place of trial the ends of justice must be promoted as well as convenience of witnesses. Rule applied in denying change from rural to metropolitan jurisdiction. Clarke v Schumacher (1928) 223 AD 860, 228 NYS 547; Page Belting Co. v Joseph (1928) 131 Misc 373, 226 NYS 723, revd on other grounds 224 AD 720, 229 NYS 893.

In a transitory action no preference was given a suburban over an urban county where trial in the latter county would be more convenient for witnesses. Dolan v Mohn & Hunter Co. (1930) 229 AD 342, 242 NYS 63.

Change from Allegany to New York county held proper where all witnesses resided in New York city and transaction arose there. Eisenberg Farms v Weiner (1940) 24 NYS2d 397.

Venue of action changed from rural to urban county where the greater number of defendant's material witnesses reside and where the alleged contract sued upon was made and breached and where plaintiff spent much of his time in business. Dwyer v Madison Square Garden Corp. (1932) 235 AD 895, 258 NYS 997.

Where automobile accident occurred in Oswego county where all parties reside, and where case can be reached for trial more quickly than in Onondaga county, plaintiff's motion to change venue from Oswego to Onondaga was denied. Bristol v Volney Vol. Fire Corp. (1955) 140 NYS2d 429.

In the case of an automobile collision in Sullivan County, all plaintiffs in three actions resided in Tompkins County. All actions were consolidated in Tompkins County, where an early and speedy trial could be had and the ends of justice would best be served by retaining venue in that county. Wanderstock v Simke (1955) 286 AD 912, 142 NYS2d 173.

Where plaintiff was injured in accident in Schoharie county and he laid his venue in Franklin county where trial can be had on almost any day that parties are ready, ends of justice were promoted by retaining venue in such county instead of changing venue to Albany county where trial cannot be reached short of eight months to year. Delair v T. Southworth T. & M. Co. (1955) 142 NYS2d 449.

On motion for change of venue fact one county's calendar is less congested is to be considered where the proof is balanced as to the location where a speedier trial may be expected; a rural county where calendars generally are not congested is to be preferred to an urban county where conditions usually are otherwise. Efco Products, Inc. v Long Island Baking, Inc. (1958) 6 AD2d 832, 176 NYS2d 46.

When a discretionary motion for a change of venue is involved a rural county, where calendars are not congested, is to be preferred to an urban one where conditions are otherwise. A speedy trial operates to the convenience of witnesses. Slavin v Whispell (1958) 5 AD2d 296, 171 NYS2d 892.

Although accident causing injury occurred in Onondaga County, but was brought in New York County, where plaintiff resided, action for personal injuries resulting therefrom would be transferred to Onondaga County, where it appeared that such actions were 21 months behind in New York County, but current in Onondaga County, and the preponderance of witnesses as well as defendant resided in Onondaga County. Fisher v Rothrum (1959) 9 AD2d 734, 192 NYS2d 198.

The comparative condition of both calendars is to be given great weight in determining the appropriate county of the supreme court in which a consolidated action should be tried, and it was held to be an improper exercise of discretion to remove a Bronx county action to Westchester county in view of the four-year delay in Westchester as compared to the two-year delay in the Bronx. Mallack v White Mountain Laundry, Inc. (1960) 12 AD2d 503, 207 NYS2d 62.

F. MOTION FOR CHANGE OF VENUE; PROCEDURE

38. Generally

On reargument by consent of motion by defendant to change place of trial for convenience of witnesses, under subd 3 of CPA § 187, court might change place of trial to proper county under CPA § 182 (§ 503(a)(b) herein). Johnson v Papen (1932) 236 AD 601, 260 NYS 479.

Rule of Civil Practice 145 (Rule 511(c) herein), relative to stay of proceedings, did not apply to cases where the motion was made upon ground that county designated for purpose of trial was not the proper county. Magee v Beach (1914) 87 Misc 18, 149 NYS 933, affd 165 AD 949, 150 NYS 1095.

The power to change the place of trial to the proper county at any time, should not be exercised where the attempted defense seems to have been put in for the mere purpose of delay. Taylor v Smith (1890) 32 NYSR 843, 11 NYS 29.

39. Demand

Service of written demand upon plaintiff's attorney was a necessary prerequisite to a motion for change of place of trial. Hoffman v Hoffman (1912) 153 AD 191, 138 NYS 356.

If sheriff sued in wrong county desired that action be tried in proper county, he should have served upon plaintiff's attorney with his answer or before service of answer a written demand accordingly, the officer not having absolute right to try in county where cause of action arose. Hudson County Consumers' Brewing Co. v Odell (1920) 190 AD 866, 181 NYS 62.

It was not necessary to serve a demand to change the place of trial "with or before service of the answer" where the motion was made on the ground of the convenience of witnesses under subd 3 of CPA § 187. Larkin v Watson Wagon Co. (1902) 68 AD 86, 74 NYS 73.

The court on motion to change the place of trial for convenience of witnesses may change the trial to the proper county, although no demand has been made. Cronin v Manhattan Transit Co. (1908) 124 AD 543, 108 NYS 963.

Where action was brought in wrong county, motion for change of place of trial should not be denied on ground that it was not made in time, statute being directory merely and court having power to change place of trial without demand. Goldfeder v Greenberg (1919) 189 AD 184, 178 NYS 581.

It was no defense to a motion to change the venue of an action for the convenience of witnesses that a demand for a change had not been served with or before the service of the answer as provided by RCP 146 (Rule 511(a)(b) herein). Saal Products Sales, Inc. v Schatz Mfg. Co. (1926) 216 AD 544, 215 NYS 530.

The court may order the place of trial to be changed to the proper county notwithstanding a failure of the defendant to make a demand that the place of trial be changed. McConihe v Palmer (1894) 76 Hun 116, 27 NYS 832.

40. Place for motion

County for motion under CPA § 187 was governed by Rule 63. Nevelson v Piesner (1947) 272 AD 555, 74 NYS2d 105.

Motion in proper county, see Combined Century Theatres v Empire State Motion Picture Operators Union (1943) 181 Misc 323, 42 NYS2d 541.

Where action was commenced in proper county where plaintiff resided, motion under CPA § 187 to change venue for convenience of witness could be made only in such county. Minskoff v Henderson-Johnson Co. (1951) 112 NYS2d 74.

It is against public policy to permit parties to contract generally to remove from courts discretionary authority under CPA § 187 subds. 2 and 3 by contracting to fix venue in particular county despite CPA § 187. Gardner & North R. & S. Corp. v Deaton (1955) 1 Misc 2d 90, 146 NYS2d 577, affd 286 AD2d 992, 144 NYS2d 744.

County for motion to change venue for convenience of witnesses, see RCP 63 (§ 2213(a) herein). John Hancock M. L. I. Co. v Breen (1955) 146 NYS2d 561.

In action by an individual as treasurer of an unincorporated association, the submission of an affidavit of the residence of the treasurer, but not of the association, was not a compliance with RCP 146 (Rule 511(a)(b) herein), and permits defendant, at his election, to move for change of venue in the county which he claims is the proper one. Payne v Civil Service Employees Asso. (1961) 27 Misc 2d 1006, 218 NYS2d 871, affd 15 AD2d 265, 222 NYS2d 725.

Where plaintiff's affidavit, served in answer to demand for change of venue, fails to set forth any facts showing either that the demanded venue is improper or that the venue chosen is proper, such affidavit is equivalent to no affidavit at all, and enables defendant to move for change of venue in the county claimed to be the proper one. Payne v Civil Service Employees Asso. (1961) 15 AD2d 265, 222 NYS2d 725 (pointing out that this ruling is not in conflict with rule in First Department since defendant is not being permitted to weigh the sufficiency of the averments because there are no averments to weigh).

41. Time of motion

Court could grant motion made after service of answer for change of venue to proper county. Palmer v Schwarzenback (1912) 151 AD 916, 136 NYS 85.

An application for a change of venue for such a cause made before issue joined, is premature. Briasco v Lawrence (1889) 21 NYSR 964, 4 NYS 94; Stimson v Stimson (1890) 29 NYSR 21, 9 NYS 238.

Change of venue in an action by foreign corporation against a resident after extension of time to answer should be granted. Molson's Bank v Marshall (1900) 32 Misc 602, 67 NYS 220, affd 57 AD 629, 68 NYS 1143.

Motion for change of venue on ground of convenience of witnesses cannot be determined until the answer has been served. Page Belting Co. v Joseph (1928) 131 Misc 373, 226 NYS 723, revd on other grounds 224 AD 720, 229 NYS 893.

Where the cause of action arose and the parties and witnesses all resided in the same county, the venue being laid in another county, the latter became the proper county in absence of motion for change within the proper time, still after that a motion to change for convenience of witnesses was properly entertained and granted. Marcus v Greenblaum (1928) 132 Misc 500, 230 NYS 478.

A demand for change of venue served for the first time with an amended answer, will be deemed timely unless it is shown that amendment of answer was for purposes of delay. Boro Kitchen Cabinets, Inc. v Spalt (1959) 9 AD2d 925, 195 NYS2d 87.

42. Condition of cause

Amendment of complaint at trial to change date of sale; defendant should be allowed to amend his answer and move for change of venue without costs. Danzig v Baroody (1910) 140 AD 542, 125 NYS 797.

In action on promissory notes entitled to place upon special calendar, the fact that defendant has commenced an action against the plaintiff, or has interposed an equitable defense, is no ground for denying plaintiff a speedy trial, defendant's remedy, if he desires a separate trial of issue, being under this section. Wasserman v Pfizer (1912) 151 AD 724, 136 NYS 203.

That the plaintiff will lose a term if the place of trial is changed, is no defense to a motion therefor if the defendant has been guilty of no laches. Garlock v Dunkle, 22 Wend 615; Lynch v Mosher, 4 How Pr 86.

That the defendant has withdrawn his answer is no reason for vacating the order changing the venue. Beard v Kipp, 5 NYSR 66.

43. Laches

Motion for a change of venue on the ground of convenience of witnesses should be denied where not made for more than fourteen months after issue was joined. Thatcher v Kitzing (1934) 242 AD 640, 272 NYS 97.

Defendants are guilty of laches or have waived right to change place of trial where they did not assert alleged inconvenience on postponement of trial about a year before. Schwartz v Cuyler (1939) 256 AD 1041, 10 NYS2d 936. See also Levine Bros. v Cuyler (1939) 256 AD 1042, 10 NYS2d 937.

The court has the power and will, in a proper case, to relieve the defendant from the charge of laches in not serving notice of motion. Thompson v Heidenrich, 66 How Pr 391.

Plaintiff's delay of five months held not to bar motion to change place of trial from Monroe to Essex county where accident occurred and where all 15 witnesses for plaintiff reside and where defendant's witnesses reside and where case could be tried within month, where it could not be reached for trial in six months in Monroe county. Gruneisen v Gruber (1955) 141 NYS2d 327.

44. Parties to motion

Those of the defendants moving for a change of venue for the convenience of witnesses must show why the others did not join in the motion. Bergman v Noble, 10 Civ Proc 190, 1 NYSR 543.

Where the action is against several, those served may move without notice to the unserved defendants. See note to Brittan v Peabody, 4 Hill 61.

Motion for change of venue for convenience of witnesses must be made by all the defendants who defend, unless some reason is shown why all did not join. Goldman v Isgood Stottville Realty Corp. (1961) 14 AD2d 759, 220 NYS2d 491.

45. Sufficiency of motion papers

Where moving papers do not contain necessary information or requirements to comply with statutory provisions authorizing change of place of trial from one county to another, motion will be denied. Stafford v Johnson (1953) 122 NYS2d 779.

Moving papers on motion to change venue for convenience of witnesses must contain affidavit of merits, names and addresses and occupations of witnesses whose convenience will be served, and must disclose substance of their expected testimony and its materiality. McCadam v Spahalski (1953) 123 NYS2d 157.

To support motion for change of venue for convenience of witnesses movant's proof must affirmatively disclose substance of testimony which each proposed witness will give at trial, in sufficient detail to enable court to determine if such evidence will be material and necessary. Hortsmann v Freemire (1953) 124 NYS2d 243.

A party moving for change of venue for convenience of witnesses should disclose to the court the facts to which they will testify to enable the court to determine whether the witnesses are material and necessary. He should also show that he has good ground for the belief that the witnesses will testify as stated, not that he expects to prove certain facts by them. Dairymen's League Co-op. Asso. v Brundo (1927) 131 Misc 548, 227 NYS 203.

A party seeking change of venue for convenience of witnesses must show that he has fairly stated to his counsel what he expects to prove by the witnesses, and that he has been advised that he cannot safely proceed to trial without their testimony. Dairymen's League Co-op. Asso. v Brundo, supra.

Motion under CPA § 187 should have been denied where moving papers failed to set forth names of witnesses or relevancy of their testimony. E. P. Lawson Co. v Browne (1943) 266 AD 183, 41 NYS2d 804.

In an action for negligence between non-residents, claim that plaintiff might be prejudiced if place of trial was changed to county where automobile accident occurred was held to be speculative and not sufficient to bar change of venue. Linman v Lynch (1953) 282 AD 848, 124 NYS2d 293.

Where plaintiff fails to give names and addresses of his proposed witnesses or to indicate substance of their testimony and its materiality to issues, change of venue was denied. Rothenberg v Fields (1953) 204 Misc 86, 118 NYS2d 822.

Where application for change of venue from Nassau to Onondaga county was founded on fact that company books and records are in Syracuse, New York, various witnesses to be called by defendant reside there, and other derivative stockholders' actions are pending in Onondaga county, papers were insufficient, where there was no affidavit of merits and substance of testimony of proposed witnesses is not given. Benson v Braun (1955) 141 NYS2d 286, affd 286 AD 1098, 145 NYS2d 711.

Moving papers for change of venue must include affidavit of merits, names, addresses and occupations of witnesses demonstrating that county sought would serve their convenience, what movant expects to prove by named witnesses and substance of their testimony and how it is material. Searing v Randall Cadillac Corp. (1956) 3 Misc 2d 594, 151 NYS2d 163, 158 NYS2d 358.

Where moving papers of one defendant reveal relevancy and materiality of three named witnesses residing in Nassau county and plaintiff's opposing affidavits fail to make similar showing, merely setting forth generalities without specific facts, to which witnesses will testify, court granted defendant's motion to change venue to county sought. Searing v Randall Cadillac Corp. (1956) 3 Misc 2d 594, 151 NYS2d 163, 158 NYS2d 358.

46. Statement of grounds

Where the affidavit in support of a motion for a change of venue does not state specifically the grounds relied on to show that the witnesses whose testimony is sought for will testify as detailed in the affidavit, the refusal of the special term to grant the motion will not be disturbed on appeal. Gilbert v Shortsville Cart Co. (1891) 39 NYSR 763, 15 NYS 316.

Upon a motion to change the place of trial for the convenience of witnesses, affidavits which state that the moving party expects to prove certain facts by the witnesses named, without stating or disclosing grounds showing that such facts can be proved by them, are insufficient. Mole v New York, O. & W. R. Co. (1907) 53 Misc 22, 102 NYS 308.

Adequate reason for removal must be shown in moving papers where both parties resided in county where action was brought. Hale v Decker (1950) 276 AD 1047, 95 NYS2d 620.

47. Affidavits for change

An affidavit so indefinite that it is impossible to say whether the testimony of the witnesses would be material is insufficient. Rochester Quality Shoes, Inc. v Bartoli (1921) 190 NYS 793.

An affidavit on motion to change venue for convenience of witnesses which consists merely of generalities will not support a motion for that relief. Joseph Davis, Inc. v State (1954) 204 Misc 1050, 127 NYS2d 12.

Where moving affidavit characterized in general terms subject matter of testimony of witnesses, without stating its substance or materiality, it was insufficient. Lawson v Lawson (1946) 64 NYS2d 356.

Where affidavits set forth general conclusions as to prospective testimony of witnesses, and not facts to which they are expected to testify, affidavits were insufficient. Frenk v Katz (1951) 104 NYS2d 393.

See Combined Century Theatres v Empire State Motion Picture Operators Union (1943) 181 Misc 323, 42 NYS2d 541.

A critical examination of the affidavits may test the good faith in which they are made. Myers v Lansingburgh (1889) 28 NYSR 250, 8 NYS 92.

On a motion to change the venue of an action, affidavits in regard to residence are defective unless the averments relate to the time of the commencement of the action, and where there is no evidence before the court as to the residence of the parties at the time the action was commenced, the plaintiff is entitled to designate any county. Burke v Frenkel (1904) 97 AD 19, 89 NYS 621.

It is not absolutely necessary in the third department that an affidavit, used on a motion for a change of venue for the convenience of witnesses, which states that the witnesses referred to will testify to certain material facts, should also state the reason why the affiant believes they will so testify. Ballston Refrigerating Storage Co. v Defeo (1901) 67 AD 341, 73 NYS 772.

On a motion to change the place of trial for convenience of witnesses, the moving party is not compelled to disclose the ground of his expectation, that the witnesses will testify to the material facts claimed, though a failure to disclose the grounds may be considered in determining the motion upon the merits; when the moving party swears to the facts which "he will prove by the said witnesses on the trial of this cause," the affidavit is sufficient to require the court to consider the application on its merits. Kalbfleisch v Rider (1907) 120 AD 623, 105 NYS 539.

Order granting change of venue reversed because the moving affidavit did not give the names and addresses of the proposed witnesses nor the substance of the testimony to be given by them, nor show its materiality. Sanders v Prescott (1931) 234 AD 899, 254 NYS 535.

The affidavit need not show how the affiant is able to state that the several persons named as necessary witnesses will be able to testify to the facts set forth therein. Myers v Lansingburgh (1889) 28 NYSR 250, 8 NYS 92.

Affidavit as to convenience of witnesses was fatally defective, in that it failed to name the witnesses, or state any facts upon which the court could base a decision as to the materiality of their testimony. Gainer v Donner (1931) 140 Misc 841, 251 NYS 713.

Where application for change of venue fails to refer to convenience of material witness, change of venue was denied, because moving papers failed to refer to necessary element of application. Bonnano v Nat. Foundry (1953) 127 NYS2d 70.

A motion for change of venue on the ground of convenience of witnesses must be accompanied by an affidavit of merits. Dairymen's League Co-op. Asso. v Brundo (1927) 131 Misc 548, 227 NYS 203.

A reference to the pleadings may be had to ascertain the merits of the motion when the affidavits evidently overstate the number of witnesses to be convenienced. Smith v Servis (1888) 19 NYSR 338, 2 NYS 865.

Affidavit must show merit, names and addresses and occupations of witnesses, statement to counsel and his advice that such witnesses are material and necessary, disclosure of facts witnesses will testify to, and affiant's belief that witnesses will so testify. Liebowitz v Hudson Transit Corp. (1945) 59 NYS2d 313.

A change of place of trial to the county where the statute requires an action to be tried is a matter of right and an affidavit of merits, upon the motion to change the venue, is unnecessary. Packard v Hesterberg (1905) 48 Misc 30, 96 NYS 72.

A formal affidavit of merits is not necessary where the affidavit alleges that the defendant fairly stated to his counsel the facts, which he expected to prove by the witnesses named. Agne v Schwab (1908) 127 AD 67, 111 NYS 8.

An affidavit to change the place of trial for the convenience of witnesses is defective unless it alleges that plaintiff is advised by counsel that the testimony of such witnesses is material. Rieger v Pulaski Glove Co. (1906) 114 AD 174, 99 NYS 558.

Motion to change the place of trial denied because the affidavit failed to disclose the expected testimony, that plaintiff had been advised by an attorney that the testimony was necessary, and had failed to show that the witness would testify as affiant assumed. Kramer v Harder Mfg. Corp. (1926) 218 AD 745, 218 NYS 47.

The affidavit must state that without the testimony of each and every one of the witnesses named the party cannot safely go to trial, as he is advised by his counsel and verily believes, except where the court can see from the affidavit itself that such is the case. Carpenter v Continental Ins. Co. (1883) 31 Hun 78.

The affidavit upon the motion as founded should state that the party has fully and fairly stated the case to his counsel, giving the name and residence of such counsel. Briasco v Lawrence (1889) 21 NYSR 964, 4 NYS 94.

But where a party is himself an attorney and acts for himself he need not swear to any statement of facts to counsel. Ackerman v Delude (1883) 29 Hun 137.

The affidavit should state that the party has talked with the witnesses and told his counsel what they would say. Rochester Quality Shoes, Inc. v v Bartoli (1921) 190 NYS 793.

An affidavit for change of venue is sufficient in stating that the defendant has ten witnesses in another county material to his case, giving their names and residences, and that his counsel advises him he has a good defense to the action, even though it did not state that he had fully revealed to his counsel the facts he intended to prove by such witnesses, if such act may be inferred from the affidavit as a whole. Rubin v Sheldon (1927) 130 Misc 736, 225 NYS 22.

Where application for change of venue was based on acknowledged statement rather than on affidavit, and movant failed to set forth substance of testimony to be given at trial by each witness whose convenience is urged to induce change of venue, change of venue was denied. Champlain Creameries v Hovey, S. & Co. (1955) 141 NYS2d 271.

Where moving papers to change venue from Monroe to Wayne county do not disclose that convenience of witnesses on either side will be promoted, no sufficient basis for exercise of court's discretion was shown for changing venue. Creighton v Kuttruff (1955) 286 AD 987, 144 NYS2d 450.

Defendant's motion for change of venue could not be summarily decided where questions arose as to whether plaintiff's alleged additional residence at hotel was bona fide. Fromkin v Loehmann's Hewlett, Inc. (1959) 16 Misc 2d 117, 184 NYS2d 63.

48. Affidavits against change

Where the defendant moved under subd 3 of CPA § 187, the plaintiff could not defeat the motion by affidavits showing that there is no real defense. Wiggin v Phelps (1877) 10 Hun 187.

An affidavit in opposition to a motion to change the place of trial for the convenience of witnesses stated that it would be necessary to examine four witnesses for plaintiffs and also the managers of three mercantile agencies to prove representations made by defendants which were repeated to plaintiffs, but did not disclose what the representations were, in what their falsity consisted, nor that any communication had been made to counsel as to what the witnesses were expected to testify. Held, that such affidavit was defective and presented no answer to the application to change the place of trial. Sawyer v Clark (1891) 37 NYSR 932, 14 NYS 252.

Affidavits used in opposition to a motion to change the venue of an action for the convenience of witnesses which fail to show the advise of the counsel that the testimony of the witnesses enumerated is material and necessary for the establishment of the plaintiff's case, are fatally defective and cannot countervail the allegations of the moving party. Fish v Fish (1901) 61 AD 572, 70 NYS 900.

Where affidavits in opposition to motion to change venue for convenience of witnesses fail to state names of alleged eyewitnesses and substance of their testimony, they are inadequate. Laduke v Bond (1954) 284 AD 859, 134 NYS2d 155.

In affidavit opposing defendant's motion for change of venue on ground of convenience of witnesses, plaintiff was required to specify facts to which his witnesses would testify and materiality and necessity for their testimony. Searing v Randall Cadillac Corp. (1956) 3 Misc 2d 594, 151 NYS2d 163, 158 NYS2d 358.

In action by an individual as treasurer of an unincorporated association, the submission of an affidavit of the residence of the treasurer, but not of the association, was not a compliance with RCP 146, and permitted defendant, at his election, to move for change of venue in the county which he claimed was the proper one. Payne v Civil Service Employees Asso. (1961) 27 Misc 2d 1006, 218 NYS2d 871, affd 15 AD2d 265, 222 NYS2d 725.

49. Cross motion

On a motion under subd 1 of CPA § 187 to change the place of trial to the proper county, the court might consider a cross motion made under subd 3 of CPA § 187 to change the place of trial for the convenience of witnesses. Waterworth v Franz (1933) 146 Misc 668, 262 NYS 660.

50. Amendment of pleading

A motion for a change of venue renewed after an amended complaint cannot be denied because the former complaint was held bad on demurrer, a motion for change of venue having fallen with it. Veeder v Baker (1880) 83 NY 156.

Where defendant serves demand for change of venue, and plaintiff serves an amended complaint changing venue to a county other than that demanded by defendant, such amendment does not bar defendant from pursuing his original demand for change of venue. Payne v Civil Service Employees Asso. (1961) 15 AD2d 265, 222 NYS2d 725.

51. Injunction to obtain change

A change of venue cannot be effected by commencing an action and procuring an injunction restraining the prosecution of a prior proceeding. Colson v Pelgram (1932) 259 NY 370, 182 NE 19.

A change of venue should be obtained by motion in the action rather than by an injunction in another action. Reis v Graham (1907) 122 AD 312, 106 NYS 645.

52. Convenience of judge

The judge cannot change the place of trial for his own convenience. Birmingham Iron Foundry v Hatfield (1870) 43 NY 224; Gould v Bennett, 59 NY 124.

That the court will be burdened by adding the case to its overcrowded calendar is not a significant reason for changing venue. Condon v Schwenk (1960) 10 AD2d 822, 199 NYS2d 238.

Defendant's motion for change of venue from New York County to Bronx County on theory that all parties to the action were Bronx residents was denied where defendant failed to show what county plaintiff's certificate of incorporation designated as its principal place of business. Circle Bake Shop, Inc. v Demand Oil Corp. (1959) 21 Misc 2d 643, 196 NYS2d 47.

53. Court's own motion

Although the defendant, after having served a demand for the change of venue by mail, failed to make a motion therefor within the statutory time owing to a reliance upon decisions of doubtful authority, the court nevertheless has inherent power to change the venue to the proper county. State Board of Pharmacy v Rhinehardt (1906) 116 AD 495, 101 NYS 769.

Under the proof in the instant case the court had no power of its own motion to change the venue of an action to a county where neither party resided after it had been started by the plaintiff in the county of his own residence and the defendant had moved to change the venue to the county of his residence. Wetmore v Saunders (1927) 219 AD 842, 221 NYS 923.

Court may not change place of trial to county not asked for by any party. Hull v Trainor (1931) 233 AD 350, 252 NYS 845.

54. Burden of proof

On motion for a change of venue from the county where the action is properly pending the burden rests upon the movant to establish the propriety of a change to another county. Geneva Trust Co. v Boston & M. R. Co. (1925) 212 AD 695, 209 NYS 557.

Some undue difficulty or burden must be shown to which proponent or his witnesses will be subjected unless transfer be effectuated, to entitle proponent to change of venue. Horstmann v Freemire (1953) 124 NYS2d 243.

Defendant's motion to change venue of malpractice action was denied where he failed to state his own residence, and failed to state whether codefendant hospital was a corporation, and if so, what its certificate of incorporation stated as to its principal place of business. Koslow v Fine (1960) 21 Misc 2d 642, 196 NYS2d 49.

55. Imposing conditions to change

The court has no power, as a condition of granting a change of venue for the convenience of witnesses, to require the moving party to consent to a reference. L'Amoureux v Erie R. Co. (1901) 62 AD 505, 71 NYS 70.

When the defendants have shown that a larger number of necessary and material witnesses reside in the county to which they desire the trial changed, a condition imposed by the special term in refusing the change of venue that the plaintiffs admit the validity of signatures to certain instruments is not sufficient to destroy the necessity of the witnesses, because a party should not be compelled on such a motion to disclose his evidence to his adversary. Nichols v Riley (1906) 112 AD 102, 98 NYS 346.

Motion to change venue from Saratoga to St. Lawrence county where accident happened was denied upon condition that plaintiff consent that defendant may present by deposition testimony of witnesses residing in latter county. Reed v Huckel (1943) 265 AD 1029, 39 NYS2d 19.

Where a sheriff has acted in good faith and with diligence, and the action against him is based upon technical grounds, he should not be required to admit away any legal defense as a condition to retaining the venue in his county. Roach v Odell (1883) 30 Hun 478.

56. Subsequent change

It seems that where the place of trial had been changed by the court under CPA § 186 (§ 509 herein) and subd 1 of CPA § 187, the plaintiff might, after issue joined, move to change it back or to some other county, under subd 3 of CPA § 187. Veeder v Baker (1880) 83 NY 156.

After change of place of trial to proper county, court may again change place of trial for convenience of witnesses. Johnson v Papen (1932) 236 AD 601, 260 NYS 479.

Where each of three actions arose out of same automobile accident, fact that prior order had changed venue of one action from Broome to Fulton did not deprive special term of power to change venue of two actions from Fulton to Oneida and to retain venue of third action in Oneida. McKeeby v Baer (1940) 260 AD 826, 22 NYS2d 349.

An action removed to a county where it had been twice tried ineffectually, after the death of the defendant removing it, may be remanded to the county where the cause of action arose and a large number of witnesses resided. Abrahams v Bensen (1880) 22 Hun 605.

57. Terms of order

Where motion for change of venue granted under CPA § 187, the order should have provided that subsequent proceedings in the action be had as though the county to which venue was changed had been designated in the complaint as the place of trial. Simon v Catalan (1958) 6 AD2d 1052, 179 NYS2d 518.

Rule 511. Change of place of trial

(a) Time for motion or demand. A demand under subdivision (b) for change of place of trial on the ground that the county designated for that purpose is not a proper county shall be served with the answer or before the answer is served. A motion for change of place of trial on any other grounds shall be made within a reasonable time after commencement of the action.

(b) Demand for change of place of trial upon ground of improper venue, where motion made. The defendant shall serve a written demand that the action be tried in a county he specifies as proper. Thereafter the defendant may move to change the place of trial within fifteen days after service of the demand, unless within five days after such service plaintiff serves a written consent to change the place of trial to that specified by the defendant. Defendant may notice such motion to be heard as if the action were pending in the county he specified, unless plaintiff within five days after service of the demand serves an affidavit showing either that the county specified by the defendant is not proper or that the county designated by him is proper.

(c) Stay of proceedings. No order to stay proceedings for the purpose of changing the place of trial shall be granted unless it appears from the papers that the change is sought with due diligence.

(d) Order, subsequent proceedings and appeal. Upon filing of consent by the plaintiff or entry of an order changing the place of trial by the clerk of the county from which it is changed, the clerk shall forthwith deliver to the clerk of the county to which it is changed all papers filed in the action and certified copies of all minutes and entries, which shall be filed, entered or recorded, as the case requires, in the office of the latter clerk. Subsequent proceedings shall be had in the county to which the change is made as if it had been designated originally as the place of trial, except as otherwise directed by the court. An appeal from an order changing the place of trial shall be taken in the department in which the motion for the order was heard and determined.

HISTORY:

> Add, L 1962, ch 308, eff Sept 1, 1963.
> Sub (b), amd, L 1964, ch 388, L 1965, ch 773, eff Sept 1, 1965.
> Subd (d), amd, by Judicial Conference, eff Sept 1, 1965.

NOTE:

> The 1965 amendment to subd (d) was designed to preclude uncertainty as to proper place for appeal from order changing venue.
> Earlier statutes and rules: CPA § 188; RCP Rules 145–147; CCP §§ 986, 988, 989; Code Proc § 126; Gen Rules Pr 48.

ADVISORY COMMITTEE NOTES:

> **Subds (a) and (b)** are derived from RCP 146.
> **Subd (c)** is derived from RCP 145 with changes in terminology designed to impose a general standard of due diligence.

The first sentence of subd (d) is the second sentence of CPA § 188. The second sentence is the first sentence of CPA § 188, with the omission of the concluding words "or provided by the written consent of the parties, filed with the clerk."

CROSS REFERENCES:

Grounds for removal and procedure on removal, CPLR 325, 326.

Grounds for change of place of trial, CPLR 510.

Consolidation of cases pending in different courts, CPLR 602(b).

Change by supreme court of place of trial of action pending in another court, CPLR 604.

Stays generally, CPLR 2201.

FEDERAL ASPECTS:

Venue in United States District Court, 28 USCS §§ 1391 et seq.

Change of venue, 28 USCS § 1404.

Removal of cases from state court to United States District Courts, 28 USCS §§ 1441 et seq.

Pleadings and motions, generally, Rules 7 through 16 of Federal Rules of Civil Procedure, USCS Court Rules.

Motion day in Federal District Courts, Rule 78 of Federal Rules of Civil Procedure, USCS Court Rules.

Venue as unaffected by Federal Rules of Civil Procedure, Rule 82 of Federal Rules of Civil Procedure, USCS Court Rules.

RESEARCH REFERENCES AND PRACTICE AIDS:

2 Carmody-Wait 2d, Motions, Petitions, and Orders § 8:23.

7 Carmody-Wait 2d, Place of Trial or Venue §§ 48:28–48:43, 48:45, 48:52.

24 Carmody-Wait 2d, Proceeding Against a Body or Officer § 145:247.

24 Am Jur Pl and Pr Forms (Rev ed), Venue, Forms 221 et seq.

Annotations:

Res judicata effect of judgment dismissing action, or otherwise denying relief, for lack of jurisdiction or venue. 49 ALR2d 1036.

Prohibition as appropriate remedy to restrain civil action for lack of venue. 93 ALR2d 882.

Construction and application of change of venue or transfer provision of Judicial Code (28 USC § 1404(a)), apart from questions of convenience and justice of transfer. 7 ALR Fed 9.

Civil actions removable from state court to Federal District Court under 28 USCS § 1443. 28 ALR Fed 488.

Law Reviews:

New York Civil Practice Law and Rules: venue. 27 Albany L Rev 181.

Motion practice under the CPLR. 9 NY L F 317.

Biannual survey of New York practice: Part IV: federal venue statute regarding national banking associations deemed controlling. 39 St. John's L Rev 426.

Forms:

See "FORMS" heading following "CASE NOTES", infra.

CASE NOTES

1. In general; discretion of court
2. Sua sponte transfer of cause
3. Applicability; effect of other laws
4. Timeliness
5. Waiver
6. Controverting affidavit
7. Venue and jurisdiction of motion
8. Conflict of venue and balancing of interests
9. Convenience of parties and witnesses
10. Place where cause of action arose
11. Calendar congestion

1. In general; discretion of court

Venue motions are directed to the discretion of the

trial court. Palmer v Chrysler Leasing Corp. (1965) 24 AD2d 820, 263 NYS2d 882.

Where after an action brought in Queens County was consolidated with another action brought in Sullivan County, and transferred to Sullivan County, the action originally brought in Sullivan County was settled and discontinued, an application to transfer the Queens County action to Queens County, even if labelled as a motion for "remand to its original venue", is a motion for change of venue addressed to the discretion of the court. Yeomans v Malen (1963) 20 AD2d 615, 245 NYS2d 431.

Where construction subcontract under which suit was brought specifically provided that any action resulting from contract would be commenced in courts of specified county and that subcontractor expressly waived any and all right it might have by reason of surety bonds, trial court did not abuse its discretion in granting contractor's motion to change venue to specified county. Callanan Industries, Inc. v Sovereign Constr. Co. (1974) 44 AD2d 292, 354 NYS2d 486.

Attorneys who represented alleged incompetent in proceedings which resulted in adjudication of her incompetency had authority to prosecute appeal from such adjudication and therein to seek review of the denial of motion for change of venue. Re Aho (1976) 39 NY2d 241, 383 NYS2d 285, 347 NE2d 647.

A motion, timely made, by a national banking corporation defendant for a change of venue from Sullivan to Nassau County on the ground that it is established or located in the latter county with no office or branch in the former should be granted. Blank v Meadow Brook Nat. Bank (1964) 44 Misc 2d 448, 254 NYS2d 56.

Where the plaintiff designates an improper county, the cause need not be sent to any county specified by the defendant as proper whether or not the county specified is proper in fact. Reliable Displays Corp. v Maro Industries, Inc. (1971) 67 Misc 2d 747, 325 NYS2d 616.

In an action where residence controls venue and plaintiff lays the venue in a county of which he is not a resident, the defendant is entitled, as a matter of right, to have the venue changed to the county of his residence. Konigsberg v Long Island Daily Press Publishing Co. (1968) 57 Misc 2d 911, 293 NYS2d 861.

Order denying motion of defendant for change of venue of action for goods sold and delivered constituted a proper exercise of discretion by court after considering defendant's physical disability and the convenience of plaintiff's nonresident witnesses. Karassik v Bereskin (1976) 54 AD2d 557, 387 NYS2d 10.

Having determined that the venue should be changed, the order of special term should have been without prejudice to renewal of plaintiff's motion for a default judgment. Garrow v Holcombe (1977) 56 AD2d 671, 391 NYS2d 481.

2. Sua sponte transfer of cause

Where the defendant-foreign corporation, who was no longer resident in any county for venue purposes, moved for a change of venue to New York County as a matter of right, correctly alleging that Westchester County had been improperly designated for venue purposes by the plaintiff-domestic corporation, the motion was denied; although Queens County was only proper county for venue purposes, since the defendant had not sought the case's transfer there, the court declined to do sua sponte. Reliable Displays Corp. v Maro Industries, Inc. (1971) 67 Misc 2d 747, 325 NYS2d 616.

In view of the case load, the trial judge of the Civil Court of the City of New York on his own motion, pursuant to § 306 of NYC Civil Court Act, ordered the transfer of an improperly venued case to the proper county. Towers v Long Island Properties, Inc. (1971) 67 Misc 2d 1062, 325 NYS2d 605.

3. Applicability; effect of other laws

The procedure for a change of venue in the New York Civil Court is governed by City Court Act § 306 rather than CPLR § 511 subds a and b, and therefore where an action was commenced in the Civil Court of the city of New York, the motions for change of venue should have been brought in the New York City Civil Court rather than the Supreme Court of the county where venue was sought to be had, since the Supreme Court was without jurisdiction to hear this motion. Commissioners of State Ins. Fund v Hoyt (1966) 53 Misc 2d 342, 278 NYS2d 472.

A national banking association "established" or "located" in Nassau County, being sued in Sullivan County where it has no branch or office, is entitled to change of venue to Nassau County by reason of federal statute so requiring. Blank v Meadow Brook Nat. Bank (1964) 44 Misc 2d 448, 254 NYS2d 56.

Subdivision (b) of this section applies only to motions for a change of venue on the ground that the county designated in the complaint is not a proper one and does not apply when the motion for change of venue is upon either of the other two grounds contained in § 510 of the CPLR. People v Archie (1966) 52 Misc 2d 129, 275 NYS2d 217.

Following removal of an action from the Supreme Court of New York County to the Civil Court of the City of New York of Kings County under the provisions of subd (c) of CPLR § 325, the Civil Court, as transferee, had, under the provisions of subd (b) of CPLR Rule 326 and subd (d) of CPLR Rule 511, exclusive jurisdiction of all subsequent proceedings therein, and the transferor court was without jurisdiction to hear a motion for judgment dismissing the complaint on the grounds stated in ¶ 2 of subd (a) of CPLR § 3211. Mather v Ginsroe, Inc. (1965) 45 Misc 2d 674, 257 NYS2d 472.

4. Timeliness

When a motion to change venue on ground that

county designated is not a proper county is untimely, motion is addressed to court's discretion and is not based on right. Fitzpatrick v Sullivan, Magee & Sullivan, Inc. (1975) 49 AD2d 902, 373 NYS2d 381.

In the absence of the timely service of a demand and consent and after the expiration of the period designated for the defendant to move, a motion to change the place of trial to a proper one should be denied for laches. Preisler v Velasquez (1971) 65 Misc 2d 703, 318 NYS2d 977.

The laches of the state would preclude its motion for a change of venue in an action by a judge who had been removed for cause for payment of his salary, where claimant had filed his notice of intention on August 16, 1963, and his claim on February 18, 1965, and the state had answered the New York District Calendar Call "ready" on two separate occasions before making the instant motion two years and one month later. Friedman v State (1966) 52 Misc 2d 454, 276 NYS2d 68.

Where defendants failed to serve a written demand that action be tried in proper county, specifying such county, before filing of their answer, and failed to move to change place of trial within 15 days after service of demand for venue change, they were not entitled to change of venue as matter of right, but their motion became one addressed to court's discretion. Callanan Industries, Inc. v Sovereign Constr. Co. (1974) 44 AD2d 292, 354 NYS2d 486.

The time provisions of CPLR 511, subd b are directory only, and in a case where neither party resides in the county of designated venue, a motion for change of venue to the county wherein the parties reside and the tort occurred made after the 15 day period may be granted by the court without further showing. Beardsley v Wyoming County Community Hospital (1973) 42 AD2d 821, 345 NYS2d 790.

5. Waiver

Defendant does not waive his right to move for change of venue by obtaining a stipulation extending his time to answer the complaint "on the merits." Lofts v Empire Bituminous Products, Inc. (1964) 20 AD2d 693, 246 NYS2d 781.

Where a venue is fixed by statute, for a waiver to exist, the defendant's conduct must be so indicative of an intent to relinquish the statutory privilege that all other reasonable explanations of its conduct are negated. Prince v Franklin Nat. Bank (1970) 62 Misc 2d 855, 310 NYS2d 390.

6. Controverting affidavit

Where plaintiff's affidavit in response to demand for change of venue fails to set forth any facts supporting his contention, it is a nullity, and defendant may make the motion in the judicial district embracing the county which he claims to be proper. Hardenburg v Hardenburg (1963) 41 Misc 2d 143, 245 NYS2d 230.

Where plaintiff within five days of service of demand for change of venue serves an affidavit showing that the specified venue is proper, he has complied with CPLR 511(b), and defendant must make his motion for a change of venue in the Court from which he desires to move. National Can Corp. v Sunset Frozen Foods, Inc. (1964) 44 Misc 2d 429, 253 NYS2d 792.

7. Venue and jurisdiction of motion

Defendant's motion for change of venue was properly noticed to be heard in Madison County, which adjoins Onondaga County wherein plaintiff commenced action, even though plaintiff filed affidavit controverting defendant's motion within 5 days as required by CPLR § 511, subd b. Pickard v Krugger (1973) 74 Misc 2d 618, 344 NYS2d 496.

The procedures specified in CPLR 511(b) have no application to motions under CPLR 510(2) and 510(3) and there is no means of having the motion heard in the county to which movant seeks to have the venue changed, unless it is one of the alternative counties permitted for motions generally by CPLR 2212(2). Furie v Furie (1967) 54 Misc 2d 966, 283 NYS2d 709.

Where an action is instituted in the Supreme Court, a notice of motion for change of venue must be held in the judicial district where the action was triable or in a county adjoining the county where the action is triable. Commissioners of State Ins. Fund v Hoyt (1966) 53 Misc 2d 342, 278 NYS2d 472.

Affidavit in response to demand for change of venue, failing to set forth any facts supporting plaintiff's contention, is a nullity and will be disregarded on motion for change of venue. Hardenburg v Hardenburg (1963) 41 Misc 2d 143, 245 NYS2d 230.

Where Special Term decided that venue should be changed to a county outside of the Department it should have relegated all motions to the transferee court. Rosenblatt v Sait (1970) 34 AD2d 238, 310 NYS2d 790.

Where suit was initially instituted in New York County but defendant moved for change of venue to Delaware County, Delaware County Court had no jurisdiction to decide motion for change of venue where, within five days after demand for change of venue was served, plaintiffs replied with affidavit opposing change in venue and setting forth bases for venue in New York County. Quinn v Stuart Lakes Club, Inc. (1976) 53 AD2d 775, 384 NYS2d 548.

Before determining proper venue of action, determination must be made with regard to proper venue of motion for change of venue. Axinn & Sons Lumber Co. v Northwood Projects, Inc. (1976) 86 Misc 2d 890, 385 NYS2d 487.

8. Conflict of venue and balancing of interests

Where action for goods sold and delivered was brought in the Nassau County District Court, there was no statutory authority for a change of venue to the New York City Court in Queens County, even though the plaintiffs were in Suffolk

County, and the transaction occurred in Queens. De Lea v Clinco (1970) 63 Misc 2d 586, 313 NYS2d 262.

Where action was brought against state agency which had a principal office in New York County, and also against a village, and plaintiff filed affidavit that New York County was the proper place for trial, an order changing the place of trial to Nassau County was improper and motion should properly have been made returnable in New York County. Meyers v New York State Div. of Housing & Community Renewal (1969) 32 AD2d 818, 302 NYS2d 287.

Where cogent reasons were advanced on both sides as to whether venue should be changed from Sullivan County in auto accident case, special term's decision was warranted. Palmer v Chrysler Leasing Corp. (1965) 24 AD2d 820, 263 NYS2d 882.

9. Convenience of parties and witnesses

Forum non conveniens is equitable doctrine and requires showing based upon balancing of interests that action is better adjudicated in another forum. Abkco Industries, Inc. v Lennon (1975) 85 Misc 2d 465, 377 NYS2d 362, affd in part and mod in part on other grounds 52 AD2d 435, 384 NYS2d 781.

In action brought in Kings County to recover damages for wrongful death and conscious pain and suffering of plaintiff's decedent who while employed as roofer fell through hole in roof at construction site in Rockland County, circumstances of case from standpoint of convenience indicated propriety of retaining venue in Kings County wherein plaintiff and her family had moved into residence of her parents for duration of husband's employment in Rockland County, where only nexus with Suffolk County was residence of plaintiff whereas many of plaintiff's husband's coworkers resided in or near Kings County and other parties had their places of business in New Jersey and at White Plains, New York. Fitzpatrick v Sullivan, Magee & Sullivan, Inc. (1975) 49 AD2d 902, 373 NYS2d 381.

Action for breach of managerial contract against British musical group and corporations engaged in recording and distribution of its music would not be dismissed or stayed because action had been instituted in England by group charging management corporation with breach of its management agreement and violation of its fiduciary duties, in that foreign suit was not for same cause, and defendants demonstrated no undue hardship in marshalling proof or requiring attendance of witnesses warranting dismissal or stay on ground of forum non conveniens. Abkco Industries, Inc. v Lennon (1975) 85 Misc 2d 465, 377 NYS2d 362, affd in part and mod in part on other grounds 52 AD2d 435, 384 NYS2d 781.

In order for defendant to carry its burden to demonstrate that the convenience of witnesses required change of venue to its county of residence, it must make a bona fide showing and must not only name its witnesses but make it clear to the court that the witnesses have been contacted and will testify in behalf of the defendant and defendant should specify the substance of the testimony which it is claimed each such witness will give and state that upon advice of counsel it is believed that such testimony will be material and necessary upon the trial of the action. Radatron, Inc. v Z. Z. Auto Tel., Inc. (1968) 30 AD2d 760, 292 NYS2d 207.

A defendant cannot serve a demand for a change of venue and upon plaintiff's failure to respond with an affidavit, move in the county of defendant's choice for a change upon the ground of convenience of witnesses and the ends of justice. Furie v Furie (1967) 54 Misc 2d 966, 283 NYS2d 709.

10. Place where cause of action arose

The venue of an action brought by New York City sanitation workers to recover unpaid wages lies in the county within the city in which they performed work for which they allege they were not paid, and it does not lie in the county in which the city comptroller has an office and where he determined the plaintiffs were not entitled to the wages claimed, under subd 3 of CPLR § 504. McElroy v New York (1965) 45 Misc 2d 713, 257 NYS2d 376, affd 25 AD2d 498, 267 NYS2d 484.

In an action for libel, the action should be tried in the county in which the newspaper is published and circulated even if, at the time of the commencement of the action, plaintiff resides in another county. Konigsberg v Long Island Daily Press Publishing Co. (1968) 57 Misc 2d 911, 293 NYS2d 861.

Where main plaintiff was New Jersey resident and accident occurred in Warren County, and change of venue from New York County to Warren County was sought with due diligence when counsel for defendants discovered that plaintiff's claim of residence in New York County was specious, and where answer had pleaded separate defense with respect to residence of parties and place of accident, there was no abuse of discretion in transferring venue to Warren County though no formal demand for change of venue was served with or before answer. De Litta v Milde (1976) 52 AD2d 548, 382 NYS2d 74.

11. Calendar congestion

In the absence of a showing of prejudice, motion for change of venue made within five months after joinder of issue was not unreasonably delayed where request was for transfer from an urban county where the trial calendar was congested to a rural county where there was no delay in reaching trial. Ryan v Great Atlantic & Pacific Tea Co. (1968) 30 AD2d 549, 290 NYS2d 849.

In view of the case load, the trial judge of the Civil Court of the City of New York on his own motion, pursuant to § 306 of NYC Civil Court Act, ordered the transfer of an improperly venued case to the proper county. Towers v Long Island Properties, Inc. (1971) 67 Misc 2d 1062, 325 NYS2d 605.

CASE NOTES

UNDER FORMER CIVIL PRACTICE LAWS

A. In General

1. Generally
2. Courts
3. Service of amended complaint after demand or notice of motion
4. Default of answer as bar to demand or motion
5. Waiver

B. Grounds for and Against Change

6. Generally
7. Place where cause of action arose
8. Convenience of witnesses
9. Right to move on ground other than that on which demand was based

C. Demand

10. Generally
11. Time for service of demand
12. Effect of striking answer
13. Venue for appointment of receiver pending action on demand

D. Motion

14. Generally
15. Motion sua sponte
16. Demand as condition to motion
17. Venue of motion for change of place of trial
18. Time for service of motion
19. —Where demand served by mail
20. Affidavits
21. —Opposing affidavits
22. Grant or denial of motion
23. —Effect of stipulation for continuance

E. Order and Subsequent Proceedings

24. Generally
25. Change by naming different county in complaint
26. Terms of order

A. In General

1. Generally

Venue changed from Kings to Suffolk county, where defendant was appointed executor, plaintiff being resident of New York County. Epstein v Tausch (1950) 95 NYS2d 679.

Where the venue of an action brought to annul a mortgage upon real property is not laid in the county in which the real property is situated, the defendant mortgagee is entitled to an order changing the venue to the latter county; notwithstanding the fact that no notice of his application for such order has been given to the defendant mortgagor, who has not answered or appeared in the action, and whose time to do so has not expired. North

Shore Industrial Co. v Randall (1905) 108 AD 232, 95 NYS 758.

RCP 146 (Rule 511 herein) which provided that if a defendant demanded an action be tried in a proper county, he must serve a written demand with the answer or before the answer was served, applied to a special proceeding and there was no separate provision in Article 78 which prescribed the procedure to be followed in seeking a change in venue. Application of De Riso v Kennedy (1958) 13 Misc 2d 322, 176 NYS2d 444.

Venue properly laid in county in which one of parties resides where one of the persons named in action as a defendant is treasurer of the union and has been named in his individual capacity as well as in his capacity as such officer since he consented to acts of union and was responsible as member of union for picketing. B & D Luncheonette, Inc. v Dallas (1958) 6 AD2d 805, 175 NYS2d 493.

A corporation has its residence for venue purposes in the county designated in its certificate of incorporation as the place in which its office is located, and not in the county in which it actually maintains its place of business. Boro Kitchen Cabinets, Inc. v Spalt (1959) 9 AD2d 925, 195 NYS2d 87.

2. Courts

RCP 146 (Rule 511 herein) was applicable to actions in the City Court of New York by virtue of § 36 of the New York City Court Act. Strauss v Ocean Acci. & Guaranty Corp. (1933) 146 Misc 766, 262 NYS 807.

RCP 146 (Rule 511 herein) was inapplicable to City Court. Continental Gummed Products Co. v Fingerhut (1945) 185 Misc 387, 58 NYS2d 16.

An application for a change of venue under § 48 of the New York City Court Act was denied where no demand specifying the county where the defendant required the action to be tried was served with or before the service of the answer. Strauss v Ocean Acci. & Guaranty Corp. (1933) 146 Misc 766, 262 NYS 807.

On a motion in the City Court of New York for a change of venue, it was not necessary for the defendant to serve a demand pursuant to RCP 146 (Rule 511 herein). Seligman Fabrics Corp. v Bur-Lee Frocks, Inc. (1934) 150 Misc 537, 269 NYS 649.

Renewal of motion in Municipal Court of City of New York for change of venue was not required to be made within ten days after original demand for change of venue was served as prescribed by RCP 146 (Rule 511 herein). Blackstone Institute v Agnelli (1934) 153 Misc 760, 276 NYS 713.

In the absence of a specific provision for transfer of actions in the New York Municipal Court Code, RCP 146 (Rule 511 herein) and CPA § 187 (§§ 510, 602(b) herein) governed. Grady v Selden Truck Corp. (1928) 133 Misc 97, 231 NYS 255.

3. Service of amended complaint after demand or notice of motion

The plaintiff might amend his complaint by voluntarily inserting the proper county at any time within that allowed for amendments of course within CPA § 244 (§ 3025(a) herein). If he did not do so, he must make a motion for leave to amend his complaint. Fish v Lyon, 1 How Pr 234; Toll v Cromwell, 12 How Pr 79; Stryker v New York Exch. Bank, 42 Barb 511, 28 How Pr 20. See Wakeman v Sprague, 7 Cow 164.

Where an action was begun in a county in which neither party was a resident, and defendant with his answer served a demand that change be made to the county of his residence, and plaintiff thereupon served an amended summons and complaint with the venue laid in another county than that of his own residence, the defendant's demand was held good, and the plaintiff's change too late. Rector v Ridgewood Ice Co. (1885) 38 Hun 293, affd 101 NY 656.

The summons and complaint in an action named Fulton county as the place of trial. After service of an answer the plaintiff served an amended and fuller complaint, naming New York county as the place of trial. The action could be tried in the latter county. Held that the plaintiff had the right in this manner to change the place of trial. McCosker v Smith (1891) 38 NYSR 227, 14 NYS 615.

The plaintiff may, after service of notice of motion to change the place of trial, amend his complaint, if the time therefor has not expired, by changing the county designated as the place of trial; but as such amendment must be without prejudice to the former proceedings, it will not prevent the court from hearing the motion in the county designated in the amended complaint, and changing the place of trial to another county. See Faherty v Schuyler Steam Tow-Boat Line (1887) 43 Hun 432.

Where defendant serves demand for change of venue, and plaintiff serves an amended complaint changing venue to a county other than that demanded by defendant, such amendment does not bar defendant from pursuing his original demand for change of venue. Payne v Civil Service Employees Asso. (1961) 15 AD2d 265, 222 NYS2d 725.

4. Default of answer as bar to demand or motion

A defendant in default for want of an answer cannot serve a demand to, or make a motion for, a change of the place of trial. Vale v Brooklyn Crosstown R. Co. 12 Civ Proc 102.

5. Waiver

Objection to venue of application to disinter remains of petitioner's wife and son was waived by objector not appearing specially for purpose of transferring proceeding to proper county and serving demand under RCP 146 (Rule 511 herein). Re Glasser (1942) 180 Misc 311, 41 NYS2d 733.

See Gray v Compania Naviera Limitada of I anama (1949) 196 Misc 903, 96 NYS2d 293.

Failure of plaintiff to permit defendant at his option to move for change of venue in accord with provisions of RCP 63 (§ 2213(a) herein) was waiver. Gray v Compania Naviera Limitada of Panama, supra.

In action by assignee for money lent, where defendants resided in New York county and had their principal place of business there, they had procedural right to change venue to New York county, but they waived their right by failing to take procedural steps under RCP 146 (Rule 511 herein). Shapiro v Leslie Fay Corp. (1954) 138 NYS2d 606.

Making demand for change of venue and moving for change was waiver, despite attempted special appearance. Dreskin v Dreskin (1947) 73 NYS2d 764.

Where neither city nor officers demanded change of venue under CPA § 182-a (§ 504 herein), such right was waived. Shelt Co. v Simiele Const. Co. (1941) 176 Misc 730, 28 NYS2d 794.

Failure to make timely demand constitutes waiver of "right" to insist that venue be changed to proper county, though court may order such change as matter of discretion. Carbide & C. C. Co. v Northwest E. Co. (1955) 207 Misc 548, 139 NYS2d 480.

Although the venue of an action is not laid in the proper county, it may be tried in that county, if the defendant does not take proper steps to have the venue changed, and defendant may waive his right to have the venue changed by laches. Dembitz v Orange County Traction Co. (1911) 147 AD 583, 132 NYS 593.

Where plaintiff was a foreign corporation, proper venue for the action was determined by the residence of defendant president or treasurer of the union, as such and where plaintiff had brought the action in the Supreme Court defendant waived defect by failing to demand change of venue under CPA § 186 (§ 509 herein) and RCP 146 (Rule 511 herein). Republic Aviation Corp. v Republic Lodge, International Asso. (1957) 10 Misc 2d 783, 169 NYS2d 651.

B. GROUNDS FOR AND AGAINST CHANGE

6. Generally

RCP 146 (Rule 511 herein) applied only to motion based on claim that county in which action was entitled was not proper county, pursuant to CPA §§ 182–185 (§§ 503(a)(b)(e), 504, 505(b), 507, 508, Rule 512 herein). Bond v New England Industries (1948) 82 NYS2d 456.

Convenience of witnesses did not control question of proper county under RCP 146 (Rule 511 herein). Baker v Julius Pollak & Sons (1950) 277 AD 11, 97 NYS2d 694.

If any of the defendants have the right to have the trial take place in a particular county, their motion therefor must be granted; and the plaintiff cannot defeat such right by joining a defendant who has no such right. Horne v Buffalo (1888) 49 Hun 76, 1 NYS 801.

Where venue was laid in improper county, defendant is entitled to have venue changed to county of his residence. Jonas Equities v 614 E. 14th St. R. Corp. (1953) 282 AD 773, 123 NYS2d 44.

On compliance with provisions of RCP 146 (Rule 511 herein), venue was changed from Kings County, where office of plaintiff corporation was located in New York County, to Westchester County where defendant resided. Acme Kalamein D&S Co. v Bronxville-Devon Corp. (1954) 135 NYS2d 184.

CPA § 183 (§ 507 herein) construed with RCP 146 (Rule 511 herein) in holding that where alternative relief prayed for in complaint affected realty, application to change venue to county where realty was located would be granted. Katzn v Central Park Towers (1955) 207 Misc 181, 138 NYS2d 615.

Where certificate of incorporation provides that its principal business office is located in New York County and location for conduct of business is in Westchester County, defendant's motion to change place of trial from Westchester County to New York County denied. Yonkers Raceway, Inc. v National Union Fire Ins. Co. (1958) 6 AD2d 846, 176 NYS2d 241, affd 6 NY2d 756, 186 NYS2d 656, 159 NE2d 203.

7. Place where cause of action arose

Where it appears that the number of material witnesses necessary to be called on either side is substantially the same, the place of trial should be changed to the county where the cause of action arose, unless some special reason exists for retaining the place of trial in the county of plaintiff's residence. Rose v Richmond (1925) 214 AD 142, 211 NYS 721.

Motion by defendant for change of place of trial from Albany County to Niagara County, was granted in action by State Water Power and Control Commission to restrain defendant power company from withdrawing from waters of Niagara river certain amount of water without first receiving license. Water Power & Control Com. v Niagara Falls Power Co. (1938) 166 Misc 10, 1 NYS2d 915.

Since an action to rescind an executory contract for the purchase of real property and for a lien for the down payment was not an action to determine title or to establish a lien within the meaning of CPA § 183(9) (§ 507 herein), the defendant was not entitled to have the venue changed to the county where the real property was situated. Maccabee v Lipman (1946) 4 Misc 2d 917, 83 NYS2d 545.

8. Convenience of witnesses

RCP 146 (Rule 511 herein) had no application to motion to change venue for convenience of witnesses. Cartwright's Estate (1953) 122 NYS2d 737; McCadam v Spahalski (1953) 123 NYS2d 157.

RCP 146 (Rule 511 herein) had no application to motion to change place of trial from New York to Monroe County for convenience of witnesses. Cohen v Ring (1946) 186 Misc 122, 60 NYS2d 379.

See Bond v New England Industries, 82 NYS2d 456.

Fact that cause of action arose in New York County not sufficient reason for changing place of trial where witnesses would not be unduly inconvenienced. Luhrs v Heim (1922) 203 AD 864, 196 NYS 937.

Venue of wife's action for separation was changed on defendant's motion from Queens to Fulton where parties resided. David v David (1939) 21 NYS2d 468, affd 259 AD 905, 20 NYS2d 1008.

A motion to retain the venue for the convenience of witnesses cannot overcome the right of the defendant to have it changed to the proper county. Stimson v Stimson (1890) 9 NYS 238.

After change of place of trial to proper county, court may change place of trial for convenience of witnesses. Johnson v Papen (1932) 236 AD 601, 260 NYS 479.

Where the cause of action arose and the parties and witnesses all resided in the same county, the venue being laid in another county, the latter became the proper county in absence of motion for change within the proper time, still after that a motion to change for convenience of witnesses was properly entertained and granted. Marcus v Greenblaum (1928) 132 Misc 500, 230 NYS 478.

No case for changing place of trial for convenience of witnesses shown by affidavits. Luhrs v Heim (1922) 203 AD 864, 196 NYS 937.

9. Right to move on ground other than that on which demand was based

A change of the place of trial may be made on the ground that the parties resided in the county to which the venue was sought to be changed, although the demand for a change of venue is made on the ground of the convenience of the witness. Navratil v Bohm (1898) 26 AD 460, 50 NYS 225.

C. DEMAND

10. Generally

If sheriff, sued in wrong county, desired that action be tried in proper county, he should serve upon plaintiff's attorney with his answer or before service of answer a written demand accordingly, the officer not having absolute right to try in county where cause of action arose. Hudson County Consumer's Brewing Co. v Odell (1920) 190 AD 866, 181 NYS 62.

RCP 146 (Rule 511 herein) had no application to change of venue based on convenience of witnesses, and no demand for change upon such ground is necessary. Searing v Randall Cadillac Corp. (1956) 3 Misc 2d 594, 151 NYS2d 163, 158 NYS2d 358.

11. Time for service of demand

The written demand that the action be tried in the proper county may be served with, or before the service of, the original or amended answer. Penniman v Fuller & W. Co. (1892) 133 NY 442, 31 NE 318; Shepard v Squire (1894) 76 Hun 598, 28 NYS 218.

Where demand for change of venue is served with answer and accepted by plaintiff, service of demand is timely. Rothenberg v Fields (1953) 204 Misc 86, 118 NYS2d 822.

Demand for a change of place of trial is not too late if served with an amended answer which is served as of course. Penniman v Fuller & Warren Co. (1892) 133 NY 442, 31 NE 318.

Where the demand that the place of trial be changed was served with the answer, the defendant was entitled on his motion to have the place of trial changed as a matter of right. New Haven Clock Co. v Hubbard (1891) 40 NYSR 654, 16 NYS 125.

Where defendant city had an absolute right to amend its answer to conform the venue in the answer to that of the complaint, it could properly serve its demand for change of venue with its amended complaint. Ross v Rochester (1959) 8 AD2d 925, 187 NYS2d 929, affd 8 NY2d 1067, 207 NYS2d 282, 170 NE2d 413.

A demand for change of venue served for the first time with an amended answer, will be deemed timely unless it is shown that amendment of answer was for purposes of delay. Boro Kitchen Cabinets, Inc. v Spalt (1959) 9 AD2d 925, 195 NYS2d 87.

12. Effect of striking answer

Where pending a motion for change of venue the defendant's answer was stricken out and he took no further action upon the motion, he could not after reversal of the striking out of the answer, make a new motion, for the right to the change of venue was barred by the limitation in RCP 146 (Rule 511 herein). Taylor v Smith (1890) 32 NYSR 843, 11 NYS 29, affd 128 NY 678, 29 NE 149.

13. Venue for appointment of receiver pending action on demand

A motion for a temporary receiver, made by the plaintiff in an action brought in the county of New York to foreclose property situate in the counties of Otsego and Herkimer, was denied when it appeared that the defendant had before answer duly demanded, under RCP 146 (Rule 511 herein), that the action be tried in the proper county and that the five days allowed the plaintiff to consent to such demand had not expired; an order appointing a receiver in a foreclosure action must be made in the county where the action is triable. Knickerbocker Trust Co. v Oneonta, C. & R. S. R. Co. (1903) 41 Misc 204, 83 NYS 930.

D. MOTION

14. Generally

Where a stipulation between a loan association and certificate holder provides that any action brought by the latter shall be commenced in a certain county, the remedy when commenced elsewhere is by motion to change the venue and not to dismiss the complaint. Benson v Eastern Bldg. & Loan Asso. (1903) 174 NY 83, 66 NE 627.

That the plaintiffs agree to abandon that part of the relief asked affecting real estate cannot defeat a motion to change the place of trial. Wyatt v Brooks (1886) 42 Hun 502; Sweetser v Smith (1889) 22 Abb NC 319, 5 NYS 378, revd on another ground 21 NYSR 982, 5 NYS 951.

Discontinuance of action, on denial of motion to change venue, was denied, as attempt to do by indirection what plaintiff was unable to do by direct motion. Zuckerbrow v Lombardy Dresses (1949) 197 Misc 39, 93 NYS2d 831.

15. Motion sua sponte

Where a transitory action is brought on for trial at a term of court held in the county in which the venue is laid, the judge presiding in such court may not, of his own motion and without any request from either of the parties, strike the case from the calendar simply because it appears that both parties are residents of another county. Phillips v Tietjen (1905) 108 AD 9, 95 NYS 469.

Where defendant moved to change venue to county of his residence as being proper county, court cannot grant motion on another ground. Diamond Star Timber Corp. v Noyes (1944) 267 AD 930, 46 NYS2d 782.

16. Demand as condition to motion

The provisions of this rule are not directory merely, but the demand prescribed is a necessary condition precedent to a change of the place of trial to the proper county upon a motion for that purpose. Whitehead Bros. Co. v Dolan (1910) 69 Misc 208, 126 NYS 414.

Service of written demand upon plaintiff's attorney was a necessary prerequisite to a motion for change of place of trial under CPA §§ 182 (§ 503(a)(b) herein), 186 (§ 509 herein). Hoffman v Hoffman (1912) 153 AD 191, 138 NYS 356.

It was no defense to a motion to change the venue of an action for the convenience of witnesses, under former CPA § 187(3), that a demand for a change had not been served with or before the service of the answer as provided by RCP 146 (Rule 511 herein). Saal Products Sales v Schatz Mfg. Co. (1926) 216 AD 544, 215 NYS 530.

Defendant was deprived of obtaining a change of venue as a matter of right where it failed to make the demand within the time specified by this rule, but was not precluded from applying for a change in the court's discretion. Reichenbach v Corn Exchange Bank Trust Co. (1936) 249 AD 539, 292 NYS 732.

Where defendant failed to demand change of venue from Kings to New York county where all parties resided and accident happened, court in its discretion may grant defendant's motion to change venue to New York county. Joyce v Daniels & Kennedy, Inc. (1943) 180 Misc 233, 41 NYS2d 793.

A defendant who makes no demand for a change of venue but, instead, serves an answer containing a counterclaim and notices the case for trial in the county in which the action is brought, the case being on the trial calendar there, makes out no case for a change of venue as a matter of right. Furia v Colletti-Reina (1924) 208 AD 741, 202 NYS 791, 792.

Motion for change of venue made eleven months after commencement of action, without previous demand, forfeits defendant's right to change venue as of right. Du Pont v Bank of Utica (1959) 9 AD2d 807, 192 NYS2d 948.

Defendant's motion for change of venue was denied where he failed to show whether an answer had been served, and whether a demand for a change of venue had been served either before the answer or with it. Koslow v Fine (1960) 21 Misc 2d 642, 196 NYS2d 49.

17. Venue of motion for change of place of trial

Motion by defendant, having its business place in Oswego county, to change venue from New York county, to Oswego county, plaintiff being state nonresident, might be made in Onondaga county, adjoining Oswego county, under RCP 63 (§ 2213(a) herein). Keehn v S. & D. Motor Lines (1943) 180 Misc 91, 41 NYS2d 518.

Motion to change venue to Tioga from New York county is properly made at special term in Broome county. Dodds v Whitcomb (1943) 45 NYS2d 441.

Where defendant moves in New York county to change place of trial to that county from Kings county for nonresidence of parties, mere service of plaintiff's contravening affidavit, stating that Kings is proper county, precludes hearing of motion in New York county. Combined Century Theatres v Empire State Motion Picture Operators Union (1943) 181 Misc 323, 42 NYS2d 541.

Motion to change venue to Tioga from New York county was properly made at special term in Broome county. Dodds v Whitcomb (1943) 45 NYS2d 441.

Where defendants demanded change of venue from New York to Kings county on ground that both plaintiff and defendants resided in Kings county and where plaintiff failed to serve affidavit, defendants might at their option regard county which they claim was proper one as county in which action was triable within meaning of RCP 63 (§ 2213(a) herein), and they accordingly might make motion in judicial district embracing Kings county. Matthews v Ruggieri (1954) 135 NYS2d 117.

Motion to change venue from Onondaga to New York county was improperly made in latter county. Bond v New England Industries (1948) 82 NYS2d 456.

RCP 63 (§ 2213(a) herein) governed county for motion. Nevelson v Piesner (1947) 272 AD 555, 74 NYS2d 105.

Where county improper, motion to change venue from New York to Albany county was properly brought in Third District. Samuels v Empire Paper Goods Co. (1949) 194 Misc 871, 91 NYS2d 67.

Where plaintiff failed to serve written consent to change of venue from Kings to Westchester and defaulted in serving affidavit showing that defendant's county is improper one or that plaintiff's county is proper one, defendant's motion to change venue, from Kings as being improper county to Westchester as being proper county, is properly brought in Westchester County. Klein v O'Connell (1956) 152 NYS2d 729.

Motion to change venue for convenience of witnesses should be brought in Second Judicial District where plaintiff resided in Kings County where action for libel was triable, and not in Westchester County in Ninth Judicial District. Klein v O'Connell, supra.

Where motion to change venue from Kings to Westchester is based on ground that county designated is improper one and on ground of convenience of witnesses and court determines that Kings is proper county because plaintiff resides there, entire motion fails, since latter portion of motion must be made in Second Judicial District wherein Kings is located, though former portion of motion is properly brought in Ninth Judicial District wherein Westchester is located. Klein v O'Connell, supra.

Where court determines that Kings County is proper county for trial of action for libel because plaintiff resides there, entire motion based on grounds that designated county is improper one and on ground of convenience of witnesses. Klein v O'Connell, supra.

Where none of the plaintiffs resided in county in which action was instituted, defendants were entitled to a change of venue to county wherein all defendants and one of the plaintiffs resided and the motion for change was properly made in that county where plaintiffs' opposing affidavit was insufficient. Chason v Airways Hotel, Inc. (1959) 18 Misc 2d 96, 184 NYS2d 125.

Defendant was entitled to make his motion to change venue from New York County to Broome County in Broome County where plaintiff's opposing affidavit was devoid of any facts showing that Broome County was not the proper one or that New York County was the proper one. Sterling Factors Corp. v Sad Sam's Furnitureland (1960) 21 Misc 2d 837, 195 NYS2d 55.

Motion to change venue from Albany County, as not the proper county, to Jefferson County was properly heard and determined in Jefferson County where, after demand, plaintiff failed either to consent or to serve affidavit required by RCP 146 (Rule 511 herein). Socony-Mobil Oil Co. v Macaluso (1961) 13 AD2d 575, 212 NYS2d 181.

In action by an individual as treasurer of an unincorporated association, the submission of an affidavit of the residence of the treasurer, but not of the association, was not a compliance with RCP 146 (Rule 511 herein) and permitted defendant, at his election, to move for change of venue in the county which he claimed was the proper one. Payne v Civil Service Employees Asso. (1961) 27 Misc 2d 1006, 218 NYS2d 871, affd 15 AD2d 265, 222 NYS2d 725.

The rule in the First Department is that the mere

service of an affidavit in response to demand for change of venue precludes defendant from making his motion for change of venue in the county claimed to be the proper place, and the sufficiency of the affidavit will not be tested. Ludlow Valve Mfg. Co. v S. S. Silberblatt, Inc. (1961) 14 AD2d 291, 220 NYS2d 239.

18. Time for service of motion

A defendant has no absolute right to such change, where he has failed to make his motion before service of answer. Taylor v Smith (1890) 32 NYSR 843, 11 NYS 29, affd 128 NY 678, 29 NE 149.

Court could grant motion made after service of answer for change of venue to proper county. Palmer v Schwarzenback (1912) 151 AD 916, 136 NYS 85.

A defendant's attorney who moves the court for change of venue two days after he receives notice by mail from plaintiff's attorney that he will not consent to the change does so in time in view of the plaintiff, a foreign corporation, having laid the venue in a county other than that of defendant's residence and the three extra days allowed for notices by mail making defendant's motion within time. Peerless Motor Co. v Hambleton (1927) 219 AD 268, 219 NYS 641.

A motion to change the venue because the action is not in the proper county may be made before service of answer. Stimson v Stimson (1890) 9 NYS 238.

Ex parte order requiring nonresident plaintiff to post security for costs, and staying him from filing affidavit permitted under this rule until compliance with order, held not to avail plaintiff, where he delayed 30 days to file affidavit opposing defendant's motion to change venue to county of his residence. Keehn v S. & D. Motor Lines (1943) 41 NYS2d 521.

Defendant's motion for change of venue to another district of the municipal court denied because not timely made. Rubenstein v Cohen (1930) 138 Misc 305, 246 NYS 692.

Where action was brought in wrong county, motion for change of place of trial should not be denied on ground that it was not made in time, statute being directory merely and court having power to change place of trial without demand. Goldfeder v Greenberg (1919) 189 AD 184, 178 NYS 581.

Where plaintiff instituted his action for personal injuries eight months after accrual and allowed one year to elapse after joinder of issue before moving for change of venue, he was guilty of laches and delay and has waived any rights which he might otherwise have had, where no exceptional circumstances appeared. Delair v T. Southworth T. & M. Co. (1955) 142 NYS2d 449.

Defendant's notice of motion to change venue was untimely when not served within the prescribed ten days after plaintiff's failure to consent to change. Circle Bake Shop, Inc. v Demand Oil Corp. (1959) 21 Misc 2d 643, 196 NYS2d 47.

Defendant's motion for change of venue was denied where he failed to show whether an answer had been served, and whether a demand for a change of venue had been served either before the answer or with it. Koslow v Fine (1960) 21 Misc 2d 642, 196 NYS2d 49.

19. —Where demand served by mail

The ten days given by RCP 146 (Rule 511 herein) to a defendant in which to move for a change of venue in case the plaintiff does not consent to such a change within five days after service of a demand for such change, was extended to twenty days by virtue of Code Civ Proc § 798, where the demand was served by mail. Binder v Metropolitan Street R. Co. (1902) 68 AD 281, 74 NYS 54. [Under CPA § 164 (Rule 2103(b)(2) herein) which replaced that section, the time for such service was extended to thirteen days instead of twenty.]

Service of motion by defendant for change of venue over month after service of demand therefor was not timely, though his original demand was served by mail. Crawford Bros. v Holdridge (1955) 144 NYS2d 202.

Plaintiff's service by mail of answering affidavit to defendant's demand for change of venue extended defendant's time to move for change three days. Chason v Airways Hotel, Inc. (1959) 18 Misc 2d 96, 184 NYS2d 125.

20. Affidavits

Moving affidavit relating to convenience of witnesses should give their names and addresses and the substance of the testimony to be given by them, showing its materiality. Sanders v Prescott (1931) 234 AD 899, 254 NYS 535.

Motion to change the place of trial denied because the affidavit failed to disclose the expected testimony, that plaintiff had been advised by an attorney that the testimony was necessary, and had failed to show that the witness would testify, as affiant assumed. Kramer v Harder Mfg. Corp. (1926) 218 AD 745, 218 NYS 47.

Where the affidavits failed to show that either of defendants resided in New York County the requirements of RCP 146 (Rule 511 herein) were not complied with. Luhrs v Heim (1922) 203 AD 864, 196 NYS 937.

Failure to serve affidavit did not preclude plaintiff from contesting merits of claim for change of venue. McDermott v McDermott (1943) 267 AD 171, 45 NYS2d 321. See Malagese v H. G. Munger & Co. (1951) 107 NYS2d 455.

Affidavit of attorney for moving party is sufficient, where it recites that he has records in his office pertaining to case and is familiar with proceeding therein. Rothenberg v Fields (1953) 204 Misc 86, 118 NYS2d 822.

A change of place of trial to the county where the statute requires an action to be tried is a matter of right and an affidavit of merits, upon the motion to change the venue is unnecessary. Packard v Hesterberg (1905) 48 Misc 30, 96 NYS 72.

In action for divorce, moving papers were held

insufficient. Clark v Clark (1947) 272 AD 1035, 74 NYS2d 671.

Affidavit in support of defendant's motion to change venue cannot be construed as demand, as demand must first be made. Continental Gummed Products Co. v Fingerhut (1945) 185 Misc 387, 58 NYS2d 16.

Where defendant served demand to change venue and plaintiff filed affidavit showing that one of three defendants sued resided in county where venue was laid, such affidavit complied with RCP 146 (Rule 511 herein). John Hancock M. L. I. Co. v Breen (1955) 146 NYS2d 561.

Where plaintiff defaulted in serving affidavit showing defendant's county as improper one or plaintiff's county as proper one, he is not precluded, on hearing of motion, from contesting merits of claim for change of venue by showing that he resides in county named in summons. Klein v O'Connell (1956) 152 NYS2d 729.

An affidavit to comply with RCP 146 (Rule 511 herein) must set forth facts showing either that defendant's county is not the proper county or that plaintiff's county is the proper one and an affidavit which failed to set forth such facts was a nullity. 20th Century-Fox Corp. v Papayanokos (1957) 8 Misc 2d 1079, 171 NYS2d 526.

In action by an individual as treasurer of an unincorporated association, the submission of an affidavit of the residence of the treasurer, but not of the association, was not a compliance with RCP 146 (Rule 511 herein) and permitted defendant, at his election, to move for change of venue in the county which he claimed was the proper one. Payne v Civil Service Employees Asso. (1961) 27 Misc 2d 1006, 218 NYS2d 871, affd 15 AD2d 265, 222 NYS2d 725.

21. —Opposing affidavits

Plaintiff's timely service of opposing affidavit deprived defendant of option granted by RCP 146 (Rule 511 herein) and rendered 1942 addition to RCP 146 wholly inoperative, applicability of which did not affect Rule 63 (§ 2213(a) herein). Bradley v Plaisted (1951) 277 AD 620, 102 NYS2d 295.

Where defendant served demand to change venue of divorce action from Erie to Onondaga and plaintiff failed to serve any counteraffidavit, defendant was entitled to make his motion in Onondaga county. Berwick v Berwick (1944) 47 NYS2d 86.

Opposing affidavit must show that defendant's county is not proper one or that plaintiff's county is proper one, else it is nullity. Linder v Elmira Asso. of Commerce (1948) 192 Misc 830, 81 NYS2d 132.

Where plaintiff's affidavit, opposing defendant's demand to change venue from New York to Washington county, showed that preponderance of plaintiff's business was transacted in New York county despite fact that its certificate of incorporation states that its office and principal place of business was in Washington county, and failed to show that any party to action was resident of New York county and that defendant was not resident of Washington county, its affidavit failed to comply with RCP 146 (Rule 511 herein). Hicks & Goldman v Hicks (1954) 134 NYS2d 803.

Affidavit of plaintiff in opposition to motion for change of venue defective in failing to state names of witnesses and their materiality. Edelstein v Shapiro (1928) 224 AD 751, 230 NYS 830.

An affidavit submitted in opposition to a motion to change the place of trial, on the ground of the convenience of witnesses, need not show that the opposing party has talked with the witnesses on whom he relies and has so received their assurances that they will testify as he expects. Avery v Allen (1903) 78 AD 540, 79 NYS 886.

Where an affidavit of a plaintiff served in an attempt to satisfy RCP 146 (Rule 511 herein) was completely lacking in facts bearing upon the question as to which county was the proper place for trial based on actual residence of the parties, it was not sufficient to invoke RCP 146 (Rule 511 herein). Such affidavit was the equivalent of none at all. Midwest Mower Corp. v Lober (1956) 157 NYS2d 307.

Defendant's motion for change of venue was granted where plaintiff's opposing affidavit failed to state his street and number of residence or other specific information. Cohen v O'Dette (1957) 7 Misc 2d 476, 165 NYS2d 268.

Defendant was entitled to make his motion to change venue from New York County to Broome County where plaintiff's opposing affidavit was devoid of any facts showing that Broome County was not the proper one or that New York County was the proper one. Sterling Factors Corp. v Sad Sam's Furnitureland (1960) 21 Misc 2d 837, 195 NYS2d 55.

22. Grant or denial of motion

Motion for change of venue denied for laches where trial was not had until two years and two months after issue during which time the cause was noticed for trial. Haines v Reynolds (1904) 95 AD 275, 88 NYS 589.

Where, after noticing a case for trial, and after it was upon the calendar the defendant procured a delay of more than twenty months before moving to change the place of trial the motion will be denied upon the ground of laches. Assets Collecting Co. v Equitable Trust Co. (1915) 168 AD 145, 153 NYS 109.

23. —Effect of stipulation for continuance

Where a party has stipulated for a continuance of a case to the next term, consent thereto having been procured from the other party as a favor, it is too late for him thereafter to move for a change of venue; the legal effect of the agreement was an understanding that the cause should be continued for trial in the same court, and having had the benefit of the delay the party will not be heard to repudiate any agreement. Rodie v Verdon (1898) 22 Misc 409, 49 NYS 178.

E. ORDER AND SUBSEQUENT PROCEEDINGS

24. Generally

Appeal from order, made in Cayuga county, and filed in New York county, removing action therefrom to Onondaga county, was properly taken in First Department. McDermott v McDermott (1943) 267 AD 171, 45 NYS2d 321.

Order changing venue from Dutchess County to Ulster County and entered in Ulster County where motion had been made, and copy of which order with notice of entry was filed in Dutchess County, is property appealed to Appellate Division, Second Department. Ruzzo v Kingston Trust Co. (1959) 9 AD2d 692, 192 NYS2d 346.

Haines v Bresky (1933) 239 AD 906, 265 NYS 940; Gould v Auburn Trust Co. (1935) 243 AD 589, 277 NYS 487; Singer v J. F. Friedel Co. (1939) 258 AD 862, 16 NYS2d 536.

25. Change by naming different county in complaint

The service of a complaint, subsequent to the service of the summons, stating a different place of trial from that stated in the summons, operates, particularly where the defendant's attorney admits service of such complaint and retains it without objection, to change the place of trial to the county named in the complaint. Tolhurst v Howard (1904) 94 AD 439, 88 NYS 235.

26. Terms of order

Where motion for change of venue was granted under CPA § 187 (§§ 510, 602(b) herein) the order should have provided that subsequent proceedings in the action be had as though the county to which venue was changed had been designated in the complaint as the place of trial. Simon v Catalan (1958) 6 AD2d 1052, 179 NYS2d 518.

FORMS

Form 1—Demand of defendant for change of place of trial to proper county

Form 2—Consent of plaintiff to change of place of trial to proper county

Form 3—Order changing place of trial on consent of plaintiff's attorney

Form 4—Plaintiff's affidavit after service of demand

Form 5—Notice of motion to change place of trial to proper county

Form 6—Affidavit of defendant in support of motion to change place of trial to proper county

Form 7—Affidavit of attorney in connection with preceding affidavit, in support of motion to change place of trial to proper county

Form 8—Another form of affidavit of officer of defendant corporation in support of motion to change place of trial to proper county

Form 9—Affidavit of attorney for defendant in support of motion to change place of trial to proper county

Form 10—Notice of cross motion to retain venue for convenience of witnesses

Form 11—Order [on motion] changing place of trial to proper county

Form 12—Another form of order

Form 13—Particular clauses in order changing place of trial to proper county where plaintiff has filed a cross motion to retain place of trial for convenience of witnesses, etc.

Form 14—Affidavit for order to show cause why venue should not be changed with request for a stay

Form 15—Order directing plaintiff to show cause why venue should not be changed and containing a stay of proceedings

Form 16—Notice of motion to change place of trial on ground of convenience of witnesses

Form 17—Notice of motion to change place of trial on ground that impartial trial cannot be had in county

Form 18—Order to show cause why place of trial should not be changed on ground of convenience of witnesses

Form 19—Affidavit for change of place of trial on ground of convenience of witnesses

Form 20—Supporting affidavit of defendant where change of place of trial is sought for convenience of witnesses

Form 21—Affidavit in support of motion to change place of trial on ground that impartial trial cannot be had in proper county

Form 22—Order changing place of trial on ground of convenience of witnesses or for purpose of impartial trial

Form 1

Demand of Defendant for Change of Place of Trial to Proper County

	Demand for change of venue
[Title of court and cause]	Index No. __1__

PLEASE TAKE NOTICE that defendant hereby demands that the place of trial of this action be changed from __2_____ County, which is designated for that purpose and is not a proper county therefor, to __3_____ County, which defendant specifies as proper therefor.

Dated: __4_____

__5_____

Attorney for defendant

[Address]

[Telephone No.]

To: __6_____, Esq. Attorney for plaintiff
[Address]

Form 2

Consent of Plaintiff to Change of Place of Trial to Proper County

SUPREME COURT __1_____ COUNTY

	Consent to Change of Venue
[Title of cause]	Index No. __2__ [if assigned]

The plaintiff hereby consents that the place of trial of the above-entitled action be changed from __3_____ County to __4_____ County, and that an order to that effect may be entered without further notice.

[Date.]

__5_____

[Print signer's name below signature]

Attorney for Plaintiff

Address __6_____

Telephone No. __7__

To __8_____ Attorney for Defendant
Address __9_____

Form 3

Order Changing Place of Trial on Consent of Plaintiff's Attorney

[Caption of court order]

SUPREME COURT __1_____ COUNTY

	Order
[Title of cause]	Index No. __2__ [if assigned]

Present: Hon. __3_____, Justice.

On reading and filing the demand of the attorney for the defendant, dated the __4__ day of __5_____, 19_6_, and the consent of the plaintiff's attorney hereto annexed, dated the __7__ day of __8_____, 19_9_, it is

ORDERED, that the place of trial of the above-entitled action be changed from the County of __10_____ to the County of __11_____, and that the clerk of the Supreme Court, __12_____ County, be and he hereby is directed to transmit all papers in the action and certified copies of all minutes and entries relating thereto to the clerk of the Supreme Court, __13_____ County.

Signed this __14__ day of __15_____, 19_16_ at __17_____, New York.

Enter.

                __18_____

[Print signer's name below signature]

Justice, Supreme Court

__19_____ County

Form 4

Plaintiff's Affidavit After Service of Demand

SUPREME COURT, __1_____ COUNTY.

               Affidavit

[Title of action]   Index No. __2__ [if assigned]

STATE OF NEW YORK

COUNTY OF __3_____   ss.

__4_____ being duly sworn, deposes and says that:

1. He is the plaintiff in the above-entitled action.

2. The attorney for the defendant has served upon plaintiff's attorney a demand that the venue of the above entitled action be changed from the County of __5_____ which was designated in the summons and complaint to the County of __6_____ on the grounds that none of the parties to said action reside in the County of __7_____ [or specify other ground upon which demand was made].

3. [Set forth facts showing that the county designated in the summons and complaint as the place of trial is the proper one, as] Deponent legally resides within the said County of __8_____ which County was designated in the summons and complaint herein as the place of trial of the above entitled action. On or about the __9__ day of __10_____, 19_11_, the plaintiff moved with his family to the said County of __12_____, where he has since resided at premises known as No. __13__ __14_____ Street in the City of __15_____ County of __16_____. Plaintiff is now working in the said County of __17_____ and intends to reside in the said county indefinitely. The above-entitled action was commenced on the __18__ day of __19_____, 19_20_ and at that time plaintiff did reside in the said County of __21_____.

                 [Signature of deponent]

        [Print signer's name below signature]

[Jurat]

Form 5

Notice of Motion to Change Place of Trial to Proper County

SUPREME COURT, __1_____ COUNTY.

             Notice of Motion

[Title of cause]   Index No. __2__ [if assigned]

PLEASE TAKE NOTICE, that, on the annexed affidavits of __3_____ and __4_____, sworn to the __5__ day of __6_____, 19_7_, and upon the pleadings in this action, and the demand, dated __8_____, 19_9_, to change the place of trial heretofore served on you, the undersigned will move this court at a motion term thereof, to be held at the county courthouse, at __10_____, on the __11__ day of __12_____, 19_13_, at __14__ o'clock in the forenoon of said day, for an order directing that the place of trial in this action be changed from the County of __15_____ to the County of __16_____, pursuant to paragraph 1 of section 510 of the Civil Practice Law and

Rules on the ground that __17____ [state ground for change], and for such other and further relief as may be just, with the costs of this motion.

Dated the __18__ day of __19_____, 19_20_.

__21_____,
Attorney for Defendant
Address __22_____
Telephone No. __23__

To __24_____, Attorney for Plaintiff
Address __25_____

Form 6

Affidavit of Defendant in Support of Motion to Change Place of Trial to Proper County

SUPREME COURT, __1_____ COUNTY.

[Title of cause]	Affidavit Index No. __2__ [if assigned]

STATE OF NEW YORK
COUNTY OF __3_____   ss.

__4_____, being duly sworn, deposes and says that:

1. He is the defendant in the above-entitled action.

2. The above-entitled action is in the nature of a negligence action for the recovery of damages for personal injury allegedly suffered by plaintiff as a result of a collision between an automobile owned and operated by plaintiff and an automobile owned and operated by the defendant.

3. This action was commenced by the service of a summons and complaint on deponent on __5_____, 19_6_.

4. Deponent served his answer in this action on plaintiff's attorney on __7_____, 19_8_.

5. With the said answer [or "before the service of said answer"] deponent caused a written demand, dated __9_____, 19_10_, for a change of place of trial from __11_____ County to __12_____ County to be served on the attorneys for the plaintiff, as appears from a copy of said demand with admission of service thereon, attached hereto and made a part hereof.

6. Plaintiff's attorney has not served his written consent to the said change as demanded by defendant, and more than five days have elapsed since the service of such demand as appears from the affidavit, sworn to __13_____, 19_14_ of __15_____, attorney for defendant, annexed hereto.

7. Ten days have not elapsed since the expiration of the five-day period allowed the plaintiff to consent to the demand for a change of venue served as aforesaid.

8. [State facts to show that proper county for trial was not designated in summons and complaint, by showing that county is not the proper one for trial because of the provisions of either section 503, 504, 505, 506, 507 or 508 of the Civil Practice Law and Rules.]

9. [If order to show cause is sought, add clauses stating reason for applying for such an order and that no previous application for order or for similar order has been made. If stay of proceedings is sought, add provisions required by Rule 511(c) of the Civil Practice Law and Rules.]

WHEREFORE, deponent requests that the place of trial of this action be changed from the County of ⎯16⎯⎯⎯⎯ to the County of ⎯17⎯⎯⎯⎯.

[Signature of deponent]
[Print signer's name below signature]

[Jurat]

Form 7

Affidavit of Attorney in Connection with Preceding Affidavit, in Support of Motion to Change Place of Trial to Proper County

SUPREME COURT, ⎯1⎯⎯⎯⎯ COUNTY.

Affidavit
[Title of cause]   Index No. ⎯2⎯ [if assigned]

STATE OF NEW YORK
COUNTY OF ⎯3⎯⎯⎯⎯   ss.

⎯4⎯⎯⎯⎯, being duly sworn, deposes and says that:

1. He is employed as an attorney and counsellor-at-law in the office of ⎯5⎯⎯⎯⎯, attorneys for the defendant herein, and as such has charge of the preparation of the defense of the above case.

2. Deponent had the annexed demand in writing, dated ⎯6⎯⎯⎯⎯, 19⎯7⎯, served with the defendant's answer on the attorney for the plaintiff, on the ⎯8⎯ day of ⎯9⎯⎯⎯⎯, 19⎯10⎯, as appears by the admission of service thereon; and the plaintiff's attorney has not consented to change the place of trial, and that the time to file such consent has expired.

[Signature of deponent]
[Print signer's name below signature]

[Jurat]

Form 8

Another Form of Affidavit of Officer of Defendant Corporation in Support of Motion to Change Place of Trial to Proper County

Affidavit
[Title, venue, etc., as in preceding form]   Index No. ⎯1⎯ [if assigned]

⎯2⎯⎯⎯⎯, being duly sworn, says that:

1. He is the secretary and treasurer of the ⎯3⎯⎯⎯⎯ Company, the defendant above named.

2. The summons and complaint were served on this defendant by delivering to and leaving a copy of the same with this deponent.

3. Deponent caused the annexed written demand, dated ⎯4⎯⎯⎯⎯, 19⎯5⎯, to be served with the defendant's answer on the attorney for the plaintiff on the ⎯6⎯ day of ⎯7⎯⎯⎯⎯, 19⎯8⎯, as appears by the admission of service thereon.

4. Plaintiff's attorney has not consented to change the place of trial, as appears by the annexed affidavit of ⎯9⎯⎯⎯⎯, sworn to ⎯10⎯⎯⎯⎯, 19⎯11⎯, who is employed as an attorney and counselor-at-law in the office of ⎯12⎯⎯⎯⎯, attorneys for the defendant.

5. The defendant above named is a corporation, organized and existing under and by virtue of the laws of the State of New York and having its office and principal place of business at No. ⎯13⎯, ⎯14⎯⎯⎯⎯ Street, in the City of ⎯15⎯⎯⎯⎯, County of ⎯16⎯⎯⎯⎯, State of New York; and it is, and was at all the times herein mentioned, engaged in the general business of ⎯17⎯⎯⎯⎯; said defendant did not maintain an office nor transact any business in the County of ⎯18⎯⎯⎯⎯, the county in which this action is brought.

6. As appears from the allegations of the complaint, the plaintiff is a nonresident of the State of New York, and resides at __19_____, in the State of __20_____.

Deponent respectfully requests that, pursuant to paragraph 1 of section 510, of the Civil Practice Law and Rules, an order be granted changing the place of trial of this action from the County of __21_____ to the County of __22_____, and for such other and further relief as may be just, with the costs of this motion.

[Signature of deponent.]
[Print signer's name below signature]

[Jurat]

Form 9

Affidavit of Attorney for Defendant in Support of Motion to Change Place of Trial to Proper County

SUPREME COURT, __1_____ COUNTY.

Affidavit
[Title of cause]   Index No. __2__ [if assigned]
STATE OF NEW YORK
COUNTY OF __3_____   ss.

__4_____, being duly sworn, deposes and says that:

1. He is the attorney for the defendant in this action.

2. This is an action to recover the sum of __5_____ dollars, for goods sold and delivered. The complaint herein was served on the __6__ day of __7_____, 19_8_.

3. As more fully appears from the affidavit of __9_____, duly sworn to the __10__ day of __11_____, 19_12_, with the answer herein, there was served [or "before the answer there was served"] on the attorney for the plaintiff a demand, dated __13_____, 19_14_, that the place of trial of the action be changed from __15_____ County to __16_____ County, and a copy of said demand is hereunto annexed, and made a part of this affidavit.

4. The plaintiff's attorney did not serve a written consent to change the place of trial as demanded by the defendant's attorney within five days after the service of said demand and ten days have not elapsed since the expiration of said five days within which the plaintiff had to serve said consent.

Deponent therefore prays that an order may be made changing the place of trial of this action from __17_____ County to __18_____ County, with the costs of this motion, and that the defendant have such other, further and different relief as may be proper.

[Signature]
[Print signer's name below signature]

[Jurat]

Form 10

Notice of Cross Motion to Retain Venue for Convenience of Witnesses

SUPREME COURT, __1_____ COUNTY.

Notice of Motion
[Title of cause]   Index No. __2__ [if assigned]

PLEASE TAKE NOTICE that upon the annexed affidavit of __3_____, duly sworn to the __4__ day of __5_____, 19_6_, and upon all the proceedings heretofore had, the plaintiff will make a motion upon the argument of a motion for a change of venue made by the defendant in the above-entitled action and returnable at a motion term of the Supreme Court to be held in and for the County of __7_____ on the __8__ day of

__9_____, 19_10_ for an order retaining the place of trial in __11_____ County on the ground that the convenience of witnesses and the ends of justice will be promoted thereby.

[Date.]

__12_____
Attorney for plaintiff
__13_____ Address
Telephone No. __14__

To: __15_____, Attorney for defendant
     __16_____ Address

Form 11

Order [on motion] Changing Place of Trial to Proper County

SUPREME COURT, __1_____ COUNTY.

Order

[Title of cause]   Index No. __2__ [if assigned]

Present: Hon. __3_____, Justice.

Upon reading and filing the affidavits of __4_____ and __5_____, sworn to the __6__ day of __7_____, 19_8_, in support of the motion to change the place of trial of this action from __9_____ County to __10_____ County, and upon the pleadings in this action, and the demand, dated __11_____, 19_12_, to change the place of trial, and on proof of due notice of this motion given to the plaintiff's attorney, and upon reading and filing the affidavit of __13_____, sworn to __14_____, 19_15_, in opposition to said motion,

And after hearing __16_____, attorney for the defendant, __17_____, of counsel, in support of said motion, and __18_____, attorney for the plaintiff, in opposition thereto, and after due deliberation being had thereon,

Now, on motion of __19_____, attorney for the defendant, it is

ORDERED, that the place of trial of this action be, and it hereby is changed from the County of __20_____ to the County of __21_____, on the ground that the county designated for that purpose in the complaint is not the proper county; and it is further

ORDERED, that the defendant recover from the plaintiff ten dollars costs of this motion (to abide the event) and it is further

ORDERED, that this order be filed in the office of the Clerk of the County of __22_____ in the State of New York.

Signed this __23__ day of __24_____, 19_25_ at __26_____, New York.

Enter.

__27_____,
[Print signer's name below signature]
Justice, Supreme Court
__28_____ County

Form 12

Another Form of order

SUPREME COURT, __1_____ COUNTY.

Order

[Title of cause]   Index No. __2__ [if assigned]

Present: Hon. __3_____, Justice.

A motion having been duly made by the defendant to change the place of trial of the above-entitled action from ___4_____ County to ___5_____ County, on the ground that neither of the parties to the action resides in ___6_____ County [or otherwise state the ground in accordance with the preceding notice of motion and affidavits].

On reading and filing the demand by defendant's attorney on the plaintiff's attorney dated the ___7__ day of ___8_____, 19_9_, with due proof [or "admission"] of service thereof on the plaintiff's attorney, the notice of motion dated the ___10__ day of ___11_____, 19_12_, the affidavit of ___13_____, attorney for the defendant, sworn to the ___14__ day of ___15_____, 19_16_, with due proof [or "admission"] of service thereof on the plaintiff's attorney, in support of said motion, and the affidavit of ___17_____, sworn to the ___18__ day of ___19_____, 19_20_, in opposition thereto, and after hearing ___21_____, attorney for the defendant, in favor of said motion, and ___22_____, attorney for the plaintiff, in opposition thereto, and due deliberation having been had,

Now, on motion of ___23_____, attorney for the defendant, and on the decision of the court filed herein, it is hereby

ORDERED, that the place of trial of the above-entitled action be and the same hereby is changed from ___24_____ County to ___25_____ County, with ten dollars costs to the defendant against the plaintiff, and that the clerk of the County of ___26_____ is hereby directed to transmit all papers in the action to the clerk of the County of ___27_____, in accordance with Rule 511(d) of the Civil Practice Law and Rules.

Signed this ___28__ day of ___29_____, 19_30_ at ___31_____, New York.

Enter.

___32_____

[Print signer's name below signature]

Justice, Supreme Court

___33_____ County

Form 13

Particular Clauses in Order Changing Place of Trial to Proper County Where Plaintiff Has Filed a Cross Motion to Retain Place of Trial for Convenience of Witnesses, Etc.

Now on reading and filing ___1_____, and plaintiff having filed a notice of cross motion, supported by the affidavit of ___2_____, sworn to ___3_____, 19_4_, to retain the place of trial in ___5_____ County for convenience of witnesses and promotion of the ends of justice, and after hearing, etc.,

ORDERED that the cross motion of plaintiff be and the same is hereby denied.

Form 14

Affidavit for Order to Show Cause Why Venue Should Not Be Changed With Request for a Stay

SUPREME COURT, ___1_____ COUNTY.

[Title of cause]

Affidavit

Index No. ___2__ [if assigned]

STATE OF NEW YORK

COUNTY OF ___3_____   ss.:

___4_____, being duly sworn, deposes and says:

1. He is the defendant named in the above entitled action.

2. This action was commenced by the service of a summons and complaint personally upon the defendant on the ___5__ day of ___6_____, 19_7_. Thereafter, issue was duly joined by the service of defendant's answer on the ___8__ day of ___9_____, 19_10_. A note of issue was filed on the ___11__ day of ___12_____, 19_13_ and this action is now on the trial calendar of this court as No. ___14__.

3. At the time of the commencement of this action, and at the present time, the plaintiff resides at No. __15__ __16_____ Street in the City of __17_____, County of __18_____ and State of New York. He is engaged in a business activity within the County of __19_____ but does not maintain a residence in the said county. The statement in the summons served in this action that plaintiff resides in the County of __20_____ is erroneous.

4. The defendant resides in the County of __21_____.

5. The defendant was not aware of the true residence address of the plaintiff until on or about the __22__ day of __23_____, 19_24_ when __25_____ [describe circumstances under which knowledge was first acquired of the plaintiff's residence address]. Thereafter, the defendant proceeded with due diligence in preparing this motion for a change of venue to a proper county.

6. The defendant caused the annexed written demand for a change of venue, dated the __26__ day of __27_____, 19_28_, to be served on the attorney for the plaintiff on the __29__ day of __30_____, 19_31_. Plaintiff's attorney has not consented to a change in the venue of this action as appears from the annexed affidavit of __32_____, sworn to the __33__ day of __34_____, 19_35_ and served on the defendant in answer to his demand for a change of venue.

7. The defendant will be seriously inconvenienced and prejudiced if he is required to try his action in the County of __36_____ for the reasons that __37_____ [set forth facts showing that the interests of justice will be served by changing the venue of the action].

8. This action has been at issue for more than __38__ months and might be placed on the alarm calendar of this court at any time. The defendant might be required to prepare for trial in the County of __39_____ and might be required to proceed to trial in the said county if further proceedings on the part of the plaintiff are not stayed pending the determination of this motion.

9. No prior application for the relief prayed for herein has been made to any court or judge.

WHEREFORE, deponent respectfully asks that an order to show cause be issued, requiring the plaintiff or his attorney to show cause why an order should not be made changing the venue of this action from the County of __40_____ to the County of __41_____ and why the defendant should not be granted such other and further relief as may be just and proper; and, in order that the trial may not proceed forthwith, deponent respectfully requests that all proceedings on the part of the plaintiff, except to vacate or review this order, be stayed until the final determination of this motion.

[Signature of deponent]
[Print signer's name below signature]

[Jurat]

Form 15

Order Directing Plaintiff to Show Cause Why Venue Should Not be Changed and Containing a Stay of Proceedings

SUPREME COURT, __1_____ COUNTY.

Order
[Title of cause]   Index No. __2__ [if assigned]

Present: Hon. __3_____, Justice.

On reading and filing the affidavits of __4_____ and __5_____, hereunto annexed, both sworn to on the __6__ day of __7_____, 19_8_, and upon the pleadings and all the proceedings had herein, and sufficient reason appearing therefor, it is

ORDERED that the plaintiff herein, or his attorney, show cause at a motion term of this court appointed to be held in and for the County of __9_____ at the County

Court House in the City of __10_____ on the __11__ day of __12_____, 19_13_ at __14__ o'clock in the __15__ noon of that day or as soon thereafter as counsel can be heard why an order should not be made changing the place of trial of the above-entitled action from the County of __16_____ to the County of __17_____ on the ground that the County of __18_____ is the proper county for the trial of said action and that the interests of justice will be served by such a change, and it is further

ORDERED that personal service of a copy of this order and the papers hereto annexed, on the plaintiff's attorney, either personally or at his office or at his residence, in accordance with the provisions of Rule 2103 of the Civil Practice Law and Rules, on or before __19__ p.m. on the __20__ day of __21_____, 19_22_ shall be sufficient, and it is further

ORDERED that all proceedings herein on behalf of the plaintiff, except to vacate or review this order and particularly __23_____ [state any proceedings other than subpoenaing witnesses—Rule 511(c) of Civil Practice Law and Rules], be and the same hereby are stayed until the final determination of this motion.

Signed this __24__ day of __25_____, 19_26_ at __27_____, New York.

Enter.

___28_____
[Print signer's name below signature]
Justice, Supreme Court
__29_____ County

Form 16

Notice of Motion to Change Place of Trial on Ground of Convenience of Witnesses

SUPREME COURT, __1_____ COUNTY.

                   Notice of Motion
[Title of cause]   Index No. __2__ [if assigned]

PLEASE TAKE NOTICE that on the annexed affidavit of __3_____, sworn to the __4__ day of __5_____, 19_6_, and on the pleadings herein, a motion will be made at motion term [Part I] of this court, to be held in and for the County of __7_____, at the county courthouse therein, on the __8__ day of __9_____, 19_10_, at the opening of court on that day, or as soon thereafter as counsel can be heard, for an order changing the place of trial of the above-entitled action from __11_____ County to __12_____ County, pursuant to section 510 of the Civil Practice Law and Rules, on the ground that the convenience of witnesses and the ends of justice will be promoted by the change, and for such other, further and different relief as may be proper, with the costs of this motion.

Dated the __13__ day of __14_____, 19_15_.

___16_____
Attorney for Defendant
Address __17_____
Telephone No. __18__

To __19_____, Attorney for Plaintiff
    Address __20_____

Form 17

Notice of Motion to Change Place of Trial on Ground That Impartial Trial Cannot Be Had in County

[Same as preceding form except to substitute as ground for the motion the following:] upon the ground that there is reason to believe an impartial trial cannot be had in the County of __1_____.

Form 18

Order to Show Cause Why Place of Trial Should Not Be Changed on Ground of Convenience of Witnesses

SUPREME COURT, __1_____ COUNTY.

Order

[Title of cause]   Index No. __2__ [if assigned]

Present: Hon. __3_____, Justice.

On reading and filing the affidavits of __4_____ and __5_____, hereto annexed, both duly sworn to on the __6__ day of __7_____, 19_8_, and upon the pleadings and all the proceedings had herein, and sufficient reason therefor appearing, let the plaintiff herein or his attorney show cause at a motion term of this court, appointed to be held in and for the County of __9_____, at the county courthouse in the City of __10_____, on the __11__ day of __12_____, 19_13_, at __14__ o'clock in the forenoon of that day, or as soon thereafter as counsel can be heard, why an order should not be made changing the place of trial of the above-entitled action from the County of __15_____, to the County of __16_____, on the ground of convenience of witnesses, and for such other and further relief as to this court may seem just and proper.

Cause having been shown therefor, personal service of a copy of this order and the papers hereto annexed, on the plaintiff's attorney, either personally, or at his office, or at his residence, in accordance with the provisions of Rule 2103 of the Civil Practice Law and Rules, on or before __17__ p.m. on __18_____, the __19__ day of __20_____, 19_21_, shall be sufficient, and it is further

ORDERED, that all proceedings herein on behalf of the plaintiff, except to vacate or review this order, and particularly __22_____ [state any proceedings other than subpoenaing witnesses—Rule 511(c) of Civil Practice Law and Rules], be, and the same hereby are stayed until the determination of this motion.

Signed this __23__ day of __24_____, 19_25_ at __26_____, New York.

__27_____

[Print signer's name below signature]

Justice, Supreme Court

__28_____ County

Form 19

Affidavit for Change of Place of Trial on Ground of Convenience of Witnesses

SUPREME COURT, __1_____ COUNTY.

Affidavit

[Title of cause]   Index No. __2__ [if assigned]

STATE OF NEW YORK

COUNTY OF __3_____   ss.

__4_____, being duly sworn, deposes and says that:

1. He is the defendant in the above-entitled action.

2. As more fully appears from a copy of the pleadings annexed hereto and made a part hereof this action was brought to recover damages for personal injuries sustained by the plaintiff allegedly as a result of the negligence of the defendant. The negligence alleged in the said complaint consisted of the erection and maintenance of a defective appliance which allegedly gave way causing injury to the plaintiff, the failure to take proper precautions to prevent accidents and the failure to employ competent workmen in the business of logging and hauling. The answer filed by the defendant herein denies all the material allegations of the complaint and denies the aforesaid allegations of negligence.

3. This action was commenced by the service of a summons and [verified] complaint

upon the defendant on __5_____, 19_6_. That thereafter issue was joined in this action by the service of the defendant's answer on plaintiff's attorney on __7_____, 19_8_. That __9_____ [state condition of cause as to notice of trial, if any, etc.].

4. __10_____ [State facts to show county in which the cause of action arose].

5. The defendant, upon the trial of this action, will be compelled, in order to meet and disprove the various allegations of __11_____ in the said complaint, to call as witnesses a large number of people, and that all of such witnesses are residents of __12_____ County.

6. The following persons, whose names and residences and occupations are hereafter stated, are material and necessary witnesses for the defendant upon the trial of this action and that they will be produced and examined by the defendant at the said trial, viz.: __13_____ [state name, occupation and residence of each of said witnesses].

7. The witness __14_____ will testify that __15_____.

8. The witness __16_____ will testify that __17_____.

9. [Continue in separately numbered paragraphs to state what each witness will testify to.]

10. [All these men were workmen employed at the scene of the accident at __18_____, at the time and place set forth in the complaint. That several of them were eyewitnesses to the accident to __19_____, and that they are familiar with the conditions that existed at the time and place set forth in the complaint, and their testimony will contradict the specifications of negligence contained in the complaint. The defendant can prove by these witnesses that the appliance which it is alleged gave way was in good and safe condition, and that there was no defect in the same. The defendant will also prove that proper precautions were taken to prevent accidents and that safe methods of doing the work were adopted and applied, and that competent workmen were employed at all of the different steps in the business of logging and hauling.]

11. Upon information and belief, that all of the witnesses above named reside in __20_____ County [and are all working men] for whom it will be a great hardship to be compelled to come to the County of __21_____ to attend the trial of this action, with the expense and inconvenience incidental thereto.

12. The sources of deponent's information and the grounds of his belief are statements of witnesses whom deponent has caused to be interviewed, and the results of investigations which deponent has caused to be made with regard to the subject-matter of this action.

13. [So far as deponent is aware the only witness for the plaintiff who resides in the County of __22_____ where the venue of this action is at present laid is the plaintiff himself.]

14. Deponent has fully and fairly stated to his counsel the facts which the defendant expects to prove by each and every one of the witnesses hereinbefore mentioned; that each and every one of them is a material witness for defendant's defense on the trial of this cause, as deponent is advised by said counsel after such statement of facts to him, and verily believes; that all the witnesses above named are necessary to the defense and that without the testimony of each and every one of said witnesses this defendant cannot safely proceed to the trial of this cause, as deponent is also advised by said counsel and verily believes.

15. Deponent has fully and fairly stated this case to __23_____, his attorney who resides at No. __24__ __25_____ street, and has his office at No. __26__ __27_____ street, in the City of __28_____; and that the defendant has a good and substantial defense on the merits to this action as he is advised by said counsel after such statement and verily believes to be true. That deponent intends to show on the trial

herein as his defense in this action that __29_____ [state facts to show a meritorious defense.]

16. The next trial term in the County of __30_____ is appointed to be held on the __31__ day of __32_____, 19_33_. That the next trial term in the County of __34_____ is appointed to be held on the __35__ day of __36_____, 19_37_.

17. [State any other facts tending to show that a change will promote "the convenience of witnesses and the ends of justice."]

18. [If stay of proceedings is sought.] That by reason of the fact that this action has been noticed for trial for the __38_____ term of this court [and by reason of the fact that in addition thereto the plaintiff has applied to this court for a preference], it is indispensable that the defendant be given an immediate hearing upon the application herein for a change of venue for the convenience of witnesses. That by reason of the remoteness of the scene of the accident from the County of __39_____, and by reason of the fact that numerous witnesses had to be interviewed before the application herein for a change of venue could be made, it was impossible for the defendant to apply at any earlier date than the present for said change of venue. That if the defendant is not given an immediate hearing, and if his claims for a change of venue are not determined before the trial of this cause, the defendant will be materially prejudiced thereby, and he may thereby be prevented from obtaining the relief herein asked for.

19. [In the affidavit of __40_____, submitted with the notice of motion for a preference, there are no sufficient reasons furnished for an immediate preference, and in consequence thereof your deponent respectfully submits that if any preference is granted, this preference should be one over the issues of the __41_____ term of this court only. That the next term of the Supreme Court for __42_____ County will convene in __43_____, 19_44_, and deponent respectfully submits that, as this date is but two months away, the plaintiff cannot be prejudiced by the transfer of this cause to the County of __45_____, by reason of the fact that the plaintiff will have an immediate trial, at the __46_____ term of the __47_____ County Supreme Court. That in the event of a preference being granted by this court, the defendant consents that the said preference shall obtain and control upon the trial of the cause in the County of __48_____.]

20. [If affidavit is made by one other than defendant.] That the reason why this application is made by your deponent and not by the defendant is because your deponent is the agent of the defendant and the general manager of the business conducted by him, under the name of __49_____ Co. That your deponent in his capacity as such agent and manager is fully conversant with all the business transactions of the defendant, and that his knowledge of the matters hereinbefore recited is gained from statements of witnesses to the accident in which the deponent was injured, and that, in his capacity as such agent and manager, he is more fully conversant with the affairs of the defendant's business, appertaining particularly to this matter, than is the defendant.

21. [If order to show cause is asked, state reason for asking for such an order instead of regular notice of motion, and that no previous application has been made for the order or for a similar order.]

WHEREFORE, deponent requests that the place of trial of this action be changed from the County of __50_____ to the County of __51_____ [or if order to show cause is sought, substitute the following if stay of proceedings is desired:]

WHEREFORE, deponent respectfully asks that an order to show cause issue, requiring the plaintiff or his attorney to furnish reason why an order should not be made, changing the place of trial of this action from the County of __52_____ to the County of __53_____, and for such other and further relief as may be just and proper; and in order that the trial may not proceed forthwith and the defendant thereby be prevented from obtaining the relief herein prayed for, to wit, a change of venue to __54_____ County, deponent asks that all proceedings on the part of the plaintiff, except to vacate or review this order, be stayed until the final determination of this motion, and until five days thereafter.

[Signature of deponent]
[Print signer's name below signature]

[Jurat]

Form 20

Supporting Affidavit of Defendant Where Change of Place of Trial is Sought for Convenience of Witnesses

SUPREME COURT, __1_____ COUNTY.

Affidavit
[Title of cause]   Index No. __2__ [if assigned]

STATE OF NEW YORK
COUNTY OF __3_____   ss.

__4_____, being duly sworn, deposes and says that:

1. He is the defendant in the above entitled action.

2. Deponent has fully and fairly stated to his attorney the facts which he expects to prove by each and every one of the witnesses hereinbefore mentioned in the affidavit of __5_____, sworn to the __6__ day of __7_____, 19_8_; that each and every one of them is a material witness for the defendant's defense, on the trial of this cause, as defendant is advised by said counsel after such statement of facts to him, and verily believes; that all the witnesses above mentioned are necessary to the defense, and that without the testimony of each and every one of said witnesses, this defendant cannot safely proceed to the trial of this cause, as the deponent is also advised by said counsel, and verily believes.

3. Deponent has fully and fairly stated the case to __9_____, his attorney, who resides at No. __10__ __11_____ street, and has his office at No. __12__ __13_____ street in the City of __14_____, and deponent has a good and substantial defense on the merits of this action, as he is advised by said counsel after such statement, and verily believes to be true.

[Signature of deponent.]
[Print signer's name below signature]

[Jurat]

Form 21

Affidavit in Support of Motion to Change Place of Trial on Ground That Impartial Trial Cannot Be Had in Proper County

SUPREME COURT, __1_____ COUNTY.

Affidavit
[Title of cause]   Index No. __2__ [if assigned]

STATE OF NEW YORK
COUNTY OF __3_____   ss.

__4_____, being duly sworn, deposes and says that:

1. He is the defendant in the above-entitled action.

2. This action is for __5_____ [state cause of action].

3. This action was commenced by the service of a summons and complaint on defendant on __6_____, 19_7_. Issue was joined herein by the service of an answer on plaintiff's attorney on __8_____, 19_9_. No further proceedings have been had herein.

4. There is reason to believe that an impartial trial cannot be had in __10_____ County for the following reasons: __11_____ [Include very complete and strong statement of the reasons why it is believed an impartial trial cannot be had in the county where the venue is laid. Motions under this section are rarely granted, and each case depends on its special circumstances, so precedents are of little value.]

5. [State facts showing merits of defense.]

WHEREFORE, deponent prays that an order may be made changing the place of trial of the above-entitled action from __12_____ County to __13_____ County, and that the defendant have such other, further and different relief as may be proper, with the costs of this motion.

[Signature of deponent.]
[Print signer's name below signature]

[Jurat]

Form 22

Order Changing Place of Trial on Ground of Convenience of Witnesses or For Purpose of Impartial Trial

SUPREME COURT, __1_____ COUNTY.

	Order
[Title of cause]	Index No. __2__ [if assigned]

Present: Hon. __3_____, Justice.

A motion having been duly made by the defendant to change the place of trial of the above-entitled action from __4_____ County to __5_____ County on the ground that the convenience of material witnesses and the ends of justice will be promoted by the change [or "that there is reason to believe that an impartial trial cannot be had in __6_____ County"].

Now, on reading the pleadings, and on reading and filing the notice of motion dated the __7__ day of __8_____, 19_9_, and the affidavit of __10_____, sworn to the __11__ day of __12_____, 19_13_, with due proof [or "admission"] of service thereof on the plaintiff's attorney, in favor of said motion, and the affidavit of __14_____, sworn to the __15__ day of __16_____, 19_17_, in opposition to said motion, and after hearing __18_____, attorney for the plaintiff, in opposition thereto, and due deliberation having been had,

Now, on motion of __19_____, attorney for the defendant, and on the decision of the court filed herein, it is hereby

ORDERED, that said motion be and the same hereby is granted with ten dollars costs to the plaintiff, and that the place of trial of this action be changed from the County of __20_____ to the County of __21_____, and that the clerk of the County of __22_____ be and hereby is directed to transmit all the papers on file in his office in said action to the clerk of the County of __23_____ in accordance with Rule 511(d) of the Civil Practice Law and Rules.

[Or:] ORDERED, that said motion be and the same hereby is denied, with ten dollars costs to the plaintiff against the defendant.

Signed this __24__ day of __25_____, 19_26_ at __27_____, New York.

Enter.

__28_____
[Print signer's name below signature]
Justice, Supreme Court
__29_____ County

Rule 512. Change of place of trial of action or issue triable without a jury

The place of trial of an action or any issue triable without a jury may be, in the discretion of the court, in any county within the judicial district in which the action is triable. After the trial, the decision and all other papers relating to the trial shall be filed and the judgment entered in the county where the action is pending.

HISTORY:

Add, L 1962, ch 308, eff Sept 1, 1963.
Earlier statutes: CPA § 185; CCP § 990.

ADVISORY COMMITTEE NOTES:

This section is derived without substantial change from CPA § 185.

FEDERAL ASPECTS:

Venue in United States District Court, 28 USCS §§ 1391 et seq.
Change of venue, 28 USCS § 1404.
Venue as unaffected by Federal Rules of Civil Procedure, Rule 82 of Federal Rules of Civil Procedure, USCS Court Rules.

RESEARCH REFERENCES AND PRACTICE AIDS:

7 Carmody-Wait 2d, Place of Trial or Venue § 48:4.
8 Carmody-Wait 2d, Trial by Court Without a Jury § 60:20.
77 Am Jur 2d, Venue §§ 48–92.

Annotations:

Construction and application of federal statute (28 USCS § 1406) providing for a dismissal or transfer of cases for improper venue. 3 ALR Fed 467.
Construction and application of change of venue or transfer provision of Judicial Code (28 USCS § 1404(a)), apart from questions of convenience and justice of transfer. 7 ALR Fed 9.

Law Reviews:

New York Civil Practice Law and Rules: venue. 27 Albany L Rev 181.
Biannual survey of New York practice: Part IV: federal venue statute regarding national banking associations deemed controlling. 39 St. John's L Rev 426.

CASE NOTES

A county clerk other than the county clerk who is the clerk of the court in which an action is pending may not assign an index number to such action, and is not entitled to a fee for assigning an index number for such action. 1977 Ops Atty Gen Feb 8 (Informal).

CASE NOTES

UNDER FORMER CIVIL PRACTICE LAWS

1. Generally
2. Necessity of objection
3. Giving preference on calendar
4. Elections

1. Generally

Under CPA § 185, an issue of law might be tried in any county within the judicial district, embracing the county wherein the action is tried. Kissam v Bremmerman (1899) 27 Misc 14, 57 NYS 890, affd 39 AD 638, 57 NYS 1140.

Venue of trial by court of issues of law or fact. Armstrong v Corcoran (1915) 166 AD 583, 152 NYS 65.

An issue of fact to be tried either by court or jury must be tried in the county of residence of a party or in a county in the same judicial district as that county. Shippey v Berkey (1958) 6 AD2d 473, 179 NYS2d 366.

2. Necessity of objection

The contention that a judgment is void because the trial was concluded at a time and place where no trial or special term was appointed to be held, will not be sustained after the parties have participated without objection and have appealed from the judgment and remained silent during the sale thereunder. McLear v Balmat (1927) 129 Misc 805, 223 NYS 76, revd on other grounds 224 AD 306, 230 NYS 259, mod on reh 224 AD 366, 231 NYS 581.

3. Giving preference on calendar

While under CPA § 185 it was within the discretion of the court to direct the trial of an action in either of two counties in the district, such discretion did not include the power to give the case preference over issues on the Special Term calendar in one of them. Bay Court Estates Co. v Dickerson (1922) 194 NYS 190, affd 202 AD 731, 194 NYS 917.

4. Elections

Special proceeding under Election Law is required to be tried in county in which election controversy arises where there is in session in such county Trial or Special Term or where one is appointed to be held in time adequate for determination of controversy within time limited by statute; where there is no such term in session or thus appointed to be held, proceeding may be tried in any Special Term in judicial district, including Special Term held at chambers. Doyle v Supreme Court (1955) 286 AD 469, 145 NYS2d 19.

§ 513. Misplacement of venue in consumer credit transactions

(a) In an action arising out of a consumer credit transaction, the clerk shall not accept a summons for filing when it appears upon its face that the proper venue is a county other than the county where such summons is offered for filing.

(b) The clerk shall indicate upon the summons the date of the rejection and shall enter such date in a register maintained by him together with the name of the counties in which the summons may properly be filed.

(c) Notwithstanding subdivisions one and three of section three hundred eight, where a summons has been rejected for filing by virtue of this section, service is complete ten days after such summons is filed in the proper county with proof of service upon the defendant of the summons, together with proof of service upon the defendant by registered or certified mail of a notice setting forth the following:

1. the proper county,

2. the date of filing of the summons,

3. the date within which the answer or notice of appearance is to be filed, and

4. the address at which it is to be filed.

HISTORY:

Add, L 1973, ch 238, eff Sept 1, 1973.

CROSS REFERENCES:

Consumer credit transaction defined, 105(f).

FEDERAL ASPECTS:

Truth in Lending Act, 15 USCS §§ 1601 et seq.
Venue in United States District Court, 28 USCS §§ 1391 et seq.
Venue as unaffected by Federal Rules of Civil Procedure, Rule 82 of Federal Rules of Civil Procedure, USCS Court Rules.

RESEARCH REFERENCES AND PRACTICE AIDS:

Am Jur 2d, New Topic Service, Consumer Credit Protection § 229.

Annotations:

Construction and application of federal statute (28 USCS § 1406) providing for dismissal or transfer of cases for improper venue. 3 ALR Fed 467.

Law Reviews:

New York Civil Practice Law and Rules: venue. 27 Albany L Rev 181.

Biannual survey of New York practice: Part IV: federal venue statute regarding national banking associations deemed controlling. 39 St. John's L Rev 426.

**[CPLR 514–600 have been reserved for future use.
Please check your supplement.]**

ARTICLE 6

Joinder of Claims, Consolidation and Severance

HISTORY:

Add, L 1962, ch 308, eff Sept 1, 1963.

ADVISORY COMMITTEE NOTES:

This article combines several related matters treated in different sections of the CPA. The former provisions were liberal and their substance and much of the language is preserved. If a new constitutional provision permits, it may be desirable to allow removal of cases pending in any lower court by any higher court even in another county.

RESEARCH REFERENCES AND PRACTICE AIDS:

14 Carmody-Wait 2d, Partition § 91:77.

§ 601. Joinder of claims

The plaintiff in a complaint or the defendant in an answer setting forth a counterclaim or cross-claim may join as many claims as he may have against an adverse party. There may be like joinder of claims when there are multiple parties.

HISTORY:

Add, L 1962, ch 308, eff Sept 1, 1963.
Earlier statutes: CPA § 258; CCP § 484.

ADVISORY COMMITTEE NOTES:

This provision is based upon CPA § 258.

Since 1949 there has been no difficulty with the problem of joinder of claims where there are multiple parties; apparently this matter has been set at rest by the liberal decision in Great Northern Telegraph Co. v Yokohama Specie Bank, 297 NY 135, 76 NE2d 117 (1947), decided under earlier provisions, although they lacked some of the broad mandates of the CPA § 258. See 15 NY Jud Council Rep 213, 226 (1949).

CROSS REFERENCES:

As to severance or separate trial, CPLR 603.
Joinder of personal and representative causes, see EPTL §§ 11-4.1, 11-4.2.
Foreclosure of tax sale certificates, Real P Tax Law § 1116.
Conflicting claims to tax sale surplus, Real P Tax Law § 926(4).

FEDERAL ASPECTS:

Joinder of claims and remedies, Rule 18 of Federal Rules of Civil Procedure, USCS Court Rules.

RESEARCH REFERENCES AND PRACTICE AIDS:

57 NY Jur, Suretyship and Guaranty § 268.
3 Carmody-Wait 2d, Joinder of Causes of Action §§ 15:7, 15:8, 15:10, 15:11.
4 Carmody-Wait 2d, The Complaint or Petition § 28:24.
5 Carmody-Wait 2d, The Answer § 30:81.
5 Carmody-Wait 2d, Counterclaim § 31:1.
12 Carmody-Wait 2d, Action to Recover a Chattel (Replevin) § 82:123.
13 Carmody-Wait 2d, Real Property Actions Generally § 86:6.
13 Carmody-Wait 2d, Action to Recover Real Property § 89:6.
18 Carmody-Wait 2d, Absolute Divorce § 114:93.
1 Am Jur 2d, Actions §§ 100–126.
21 Am Jur 2d, Creditors' Bills § 76.
65 Am Jur 2d, Receivers § 476.
3 Am Jur Trials p 637, Selecting the Remedy.
3 Am Jur Trials p 681, Tactics and Strategy of Pleading.

Annotations:

Joinder or representation of several claimants in action against carrier or utility to recover overcharge. 1 ALR2d 160.

Joinder of insurer and insured under policy of compulsory indemnity or liability insurance in action by injured third person. 20 ALR2d 1097.

Aggregation of claims to make jurisdictional amount in injunction suits. 30 ALR2d 655.

Joinder of cause of action for pain and suffering of decedent with cause of action for wrongful death. 35 ALR2d 1377.

Right to join principal debtor and guarantor as parties defendant. 53 ALR2d 522.

Construction, application, and effect of Rule 18 pertaining to joinder in a single action of two claims although one was previously cognizable only after the other had been prosecuted to a conclusion. 61 ALR2d 688.

Simultaneous injury to person and property as giving rise to single cause of action. 62 ALR2d 977.

Modern status of rules as to pendent federal jurisdiction over nonfederal claims. 5 ALR3d 1040.

Right of defendant under Rule 14(a) and 18(a) of Federal Rules of Civil Procedure to assert against third party properly in case, claim for damages in excess of, or different from, those sought by original plaintiff. 12 ALR Fed 877.

Appealability of federal court order granting or denying consolidation, severance, or separate trials, 30 ALR Fed 393.

Law Reviews:

Biannual survey of New York practice: Part III. 39 St. John's L Rev 178.
Biannual survey of New York practice: Part IV. 39 St. John's L Rev 408.
Biannual survey of New York practice: Part V. 40 St. John's L Rev 125.
1975 survey of New York law—civil practice. 27 Syracuse L Rev 425.

Forms:

See "FORMS" heading following "CASE NOTES", infra.

CASE NOTES

While a special proceeding and an action may be joined and a civil proceeding is not to be dismissed for error in form, it is still necessary that there be a pleading setting forth the elements of the action on the basis of which the remedy is sought. Levine v Pat-Plaza Amusements, Inc. (1971) 67 Misc 2d 485, 324 NYS2d 145.

A broad discretion is given court to make determinations as to which claims should be tried together and which should be severed, and as a general principle all issues having common questions of law or fact should be tried together; however, issues which might prejudice proper consideration of other issues or which by their very nature will inconvenience the court and the principal litigation should be severed. Axelrod & Co. v Telsey (1973) 77 Misc 2d 1035, 353 NYS2d 596.

The salutory purpose of this section is to avoid a

multiplicity of suits so that the aggrieved party can obtain complete relief in one action. Saunders v Saunders (1967) 54 Misc 2d 1081, 283 NYS2d 969.

Pleading of inconsistent theories does not render the causes of action insufficient. Severino v Salisbury Point Cooperatives, Inc. (1964) 21 AD2d 813, 250 NYS2d 896.

Affirmative defenses and counterclaims alleging the wrongful diversion of assets of a bankrupt mortgagor to the mortgagee at a time when members of a named family were officers and directors and held controlling stock interests in both corporations by the mortgagor's trustee in bankruptcy who entered no defense to the mortgage claim, where the allegations might constitute a valid counterclaim or setoff against the petitioner if, as transferee, it was chargeable with knowledge of the alleged fraudulent acts, could be asserted in

view of the broad principles of adjudicating the rights of the parties in one action, although the members of the named family were not parties to a proceeding by the mortgagee to adjust a condemnation award. Utica v Gold Medal Packing Corp. (1967) 54 Misc 2d 721, 283 NYS2d 603, mod on other grounds 31 AD2d 730, 297 NYS2d 166.

Where defendant trial counsel had been designated as stakeholder of one-third of counsel fee derived from litigation which was settled and the controversy was between another attorney who originally had been retained in matter and plaintiff who had claim in quantum meruit against that attorney for any work he may have done in case at attorney's request, there was a joinder of claims for equitable and legal relief and a jury trial must be considered waived. Geller v Julien (1976) 52 AD2d 808, 383 NYS2d 334.

CASE NOTES

UNDER FORMER CIVIL PRACTICE LAWS

A. IN GENERAL

1. Generally

2. Construction with other statutes or rules

3. Inconsistent, unrelated, or mutually exclusive causes

4. —Mutually destructive causes

5. —Compelling election

6. Multiple parties; representative and individual capacity

B. PARTICULAR CAUSES

7. Contract or implied contract

8. Contract and tort or other cause

9. Rescission and enforcement of contract

10. Reformation and other causes

11. Matrimonial causes

12. Tort causes generally

13. Tort and other causes

14. —Defamation and other causes; libel and slander

15. —Fraudulent acts and fraudulent conveyances

16. Causes concerning corporate matters

17. —Stockholders' actions

18. Real property

19. Taxpayers' actions

20. Other common-law causes

(Due to the liberalizing changes made in 1935 and 1949 to the practice on joinder of causes, decisions, especially those denying joinder, which were decided under the codes or under former § 258 of the Civil Practice Act are often of little value today. Consequently many such earlier decisions are omitted.)

A. IN GENERAL

1. Generally

CPA § 258 gave complete freedom in the joinder of causes of action if the matters could conveniently be tried together subject to severance or separate trials when required in the interest of justice. St. James Realty Corp. v Level Realty Corp. (1956) 3 Misc 2d 934, 155 NYS2d 44.

L 1949, ch 147, amending CPA § 258, gave equal freedom to joinder of causes of action and joinder of parties. St. James R. Corp. v Level R. Corp., supra.

Modern practice favors joinder of causes of action wherever possible. De Oteris v Mario (1945) 185 Misc 1029, 60 NYS2d 674, affd 270 AD 820, 60 NYS2d 297.

A misjoinder of causes of action is not now such defect in pleading as will make it vulnerable to attack. Metropolitan Life Ins. Co. v Union Trust Co. (1938) 167 Misc 262, 5 NYS2d 99.

Proposed joinder of causes of action, as authorized by L 1949 ch 147, was permissive. St. James R. Corp. v Level Realty Corp. (1956) 3 Misc 2d 934, 155 NYS2d 44, as was the case also under former CPA § 258, and §§ 211 and 212, and under the former sections plaintiff was entitled to recover costs as to each of several actions, although by stipulation the question of fact common to all was tried in but one and verdicts directed in the remainder pursuant to the determination in the one tried. Kranzer v Automobile Ins. Co. (1925) 124 Misc 866, 209 NYS 566.

Cited in connection with statement that the practice as to joinder under former Code of Civ Proc § 484, had been superseded by former CPA § 258. Ellicott v Archibald McNeil & Sons Co. (1923) 206 AD 441, 201 NYS 500.

Subdivision 9 of former CPA § 258 did not differ in its effect from subdivision 9 of section 484 of the Code of Civil Procedure, hence cases construing the latter were applicable when the former was to be construed. Turner v Edison Storage Battery Co. (1928) 222 AD 826, 226 NYS 394, app dismd 248 NY 73, 161 NE 423.

The only effect of former CPA § 258 was to limit the character of the causes of action which may be joined. S. L. & Co. v Bock (1922) 118 Misc 756, 194 NYS 773.

Causes of action were held to be properly joined under subd 9, of former CPA § 258 in that they relate to "transactions connected with the same subject of action" Sherlock v Manwaren (1924) 208 AD 538, 203 NYS 709; Holliger v Sweet (1934) 241 AD 698, 270 NYS 944, and two or more such causes of action could be joined, though having different statutes of limitation, some barred, and others not. Conklin v Draper (1930) 229 AD 227, 241 NYS 529, affd 254 NY 620, 173 NE 892.

Prior action to foreclose one of ten mortgages was not splitting cause of action under the circumstances. Zalkin v Sunshine Sales Corp. (1928) 224 AD 475, 231 NYS 571.

Where two or more claims arising out of the same contract were in existence when an action was brought upon one, a judgment in that action was a bar to an action upon the other under former § 248. Kaufman v Walter (1925) 125 Misc 908, 211 NYS 649.

Former CPA § 258 was not applicable to the Municipal Court of the City of New York. Gunner v E. R. Squibb & Sons (1934) 150 Misc 83, 269 NYS 661.

Code Civil Proc § 484, was not applicable to the municipal court of the city of New York. Mackey v Royal Bank of New York (1912) 78 Misc 145, 137 NYS 929.

Compare the rule against splitting causes of action which is in the nature of a rule to prevent vexatious and oppressive litigation. To permit the opening of the original judgment many years after it was paid and long after the second action was tried would defeat the purpose of the rule. Broderick v Aaron (1940) 260 AD 907, 24 NYS2d 140.

Where complaint states facts in one count which are sufficient to constitute separate cause of action against one defendant and separate cause of action against another defendant who before answering did not move to have causes of action separately stated but did move against whole complaint, such motion was properly denied. Trillard v Horowitz (1955) 1 AD2d 680, 146 NYS2d 512.

For denial of consolidation of causes for inducing breach of a lease, and for rents thereunder, see Contract and tort or other cause 8 infra, Brody v Madson Lunch, Inc. (1922) 199 AD 640, 192 NYS 10.

Decisions prior to the Civil Practice Act (largely obsolete)

Prior to the Civil Practice Act two causes of action could be joined in the same complaint, one triable by and one without a jury. Porter v International Bridge Co. (1899) 45 AD 416, 60 NYS 819, affd 163 NY 79, 57 NE 174.

For the definition, under the codes before the Civil Practice Act, of causes arising out of the same transaction or subject of action, see: Lamming v Galusha (1892) 135 NY 239, 31 NE 1024; Reilly v Sicilian Asphalt Paving Co. (1902) 170 NY 40, 62 NE 772; Jacobus v Colgate (1916) 217 NY 235, 111 NE 837; Whiting v Elmira Industrial Ass'n (1899) 45 AD 349, 61 NYS 27; McInerney v Main (1903) 82 AD 543, 81 NYS 539; Rogers v Wheeler (1903) 89 AD 435, 85 NYS 981; People v Equitable Life Assur. Soc. (1908) 124 AD 714, 109 NYS 453; Kaufman v Morris Bldg. Co. (1908) 126 AD 388, 110 NYS 663; Todaro v Somerville Realty Co. (1910) 138 AD 1, 122 NYS 509; Kelly v Webster (1911) 143 AD 737, 128 NYS 58; Cass v Realty Secur Co. (1911) 148 AD 96, 132 NYS 1074, affd 206 NY 649, 99 NE 1105; Metropolitan Trust Co. v Stallo (1915) 166 AD 649, 152 NYS 173, affd 215 NY 710, 109 NE 1084; Griffith v Friendly (1900) 30 Misc 393, 62 NYS 391, affd 47 AD 635, 62 NYS 1138; Barkley v Williams (1900) 30 Misc 687, 64 NYS 318; Letson v Evans (1900) 33 Misc 437, 68 NYS 421; Egan v New York Transp. Co. (1902) 39 Misc 111, 78 NYS 209; Campbell v Hallihan (1904) 45 Misc 325, 90 NYS 432; Warren v Parkhurst (1904) 45 Misc 466, 92 NYS 725, affd 105 AD 239, 93 NYS 1009, affd 186 NY 45, 78 NE 579; Union Transit Co. v Erie R. Co. (1906) 52 Misc 293, 102 NYS 149, affd 123 AD 316, 108 NYS 1; Leslie v Firemen's Ins. Co. (1908) 60 Misc 558, 112 NYS 496; Hill v McKane (1911) 71 Misc 581, 128 NYS 819; Mitchell v Niagara, Lockport & Ontario Power Co. (1917) 99 Misc 366, 163 NYS 999, affd 180 AD 919, 166 NYS 1104; Carter v DeCamp (1886) 40 Hun 258; Kent v Crouse (1886) 5 NYSR 141; Zimmerman v Kinkel (1888) 108 NY 282, 15 NE 407; Farmers' & Mechanics' Nat. Bank v Rogers (1888, Super Ct) 1 NYS 757; Holmes v Abbott (1889) 53 Hun 617, 6 NYS 943; Newcombe v Chicago & N. W. R. Co. (1890, Sup) 8 NYS 366; Spliess v Meyer (1891, Sup) 13 NYS 70; Rosenberg v Staten Island R. Co. (1891, CP Ct) 14 NYS 476; Rothchild v Grand T. R. Co. (1891, Sup) 14 NYS 807; Grimshaw v Woodfall (1891, CP Ct) 15 NYS 857, affd (CP Ct) 19 NYS 1013; Jackson v Brown (1893) 74 Hun 25, 26 NYS 156; Polley v Wilkisson, 5 Civ Proc 135; Sullivan v New York, N. H. & H. R. R. Co. 11 Civ Proc 285.

It was held prior to the Civil Practice Act that misjoinder of causes of action was waived unless objection was properly taken. Doty v Doty (1918, Sup) 171 NYS 852.

2. Construction with other statutes or rules

CPA § 96 (§§ 407, 602(a) herein) construed with CPA § 258 in declaring effect of CPA § 96 was to liberalize practice and to remove technical restrictions upon administration of justice. Wegner Canning Corp. v Wegner (1942, Sup) 33 NYS2d 443; First Trust & Deposit Co. v Dent (1942, Sup) 36 NYS2d 664.

Under former CPA § 258 the court took into

consideration that causes of action sought to be joined under CPA § 96 could be joined under the provisions of CPA § 258 but such fact was not conclusive upon the question of denying their union under CPA § 96 (§§ 407, 602(a) herein). Crandall v A. B. Leach & Co. (1927) 222 AD 292, 225 NYS 649.

CPA § 211 was not limited by CPA § 258 with respect to parties. Great Northern Tel. Co. v Yokohama Specie Bank, Ltd. (1948) 297 NY 135, 76 NE2d 117.

CPA §§ 212–213 (§§ 1002(a)(b), 1022, Rule 5012 herein) construed with CPA § 258, in considering joinder of defendants. Great Northern Tel. Co. v Yokohama Specie Bank, supra.

3. Inconsistent, unrelated, or mutually exclusive causes

Complaint not insufficient because inconsistent theories pleaded. Vendall, Inc. v Statler Mfg. Corp. (1958) 5 AD2d 882, 171 NYS2d 938.

Motion addressed to complaint on grounds that inconsistent and mutually exclusive causes are therein pleaded may no longer be made. Warren v Putnam (1942) 263 AD 474, 33 NYS2d 635.

The former existing bar against the pleading of inconsistent causes of action in a single complaint was removed by the enactment of CPA § 258 by L 1935, chapter 339. Epp v Title Guarantee & Trust Co. (1935) 160 Misc 554, 289 NYS 896.

Inconsistent and mutually exclusive causes of action may be joined. Prosswimmer v Prosswimmer (1944) 182 Misc 807, 50 NYS2d 46; Finestone v Alcroft Studios, Inc. (1946, Sup) 69 NYS2d 396; Bell v Yagur (1951) 201 Misc 171, 104 NYS2d 467.

Plaintiff may plead independent and unrelated legal and equitable causes of action in one complaint. Riesenberger v Sullivan (1956) 1 AD2d 1049, 152 NYS2d 783.

CPA § 258 prior to the 1949 amendments, did not supersede rule 102 of the Rules of Civil Practice, and while, under it a plaintiff could "unite in the same complaint two or more causes of action whether they are such as were formerly denominated legal or equitable," the joinder in one complaint of mutually exclusive causes of action was not permitted. Dickler v National City Bank (1935) 160 Misc 317, 289 NYS 810.

For cause to declare existing divorce valid, and cause for new divorce, see 11 infra, McCloskey v McCloskey (1952, Sup) 117 NYS2d 770.

For action for rent, use and occupation, damages for breach of lease, and waste, see 8 infra, Ribner v Babyatsky (1951, Sup) 103 NYS2d 599.

Prior to the Civil Practice Act joinder of inconsistent causes of action was not permitted. Drexel v Hollander (1906) 112 AD 25, 98 NYS 104; Kranz v Lewis (1906) 115 AD 106, 100 NYS 674, app dismd 188 NY 579, 80 NE 944. Edison Electric Illuminating Co. v Franklin H. Kalbfleisch Co. (1907) 117 AD 842, 102 NYS 1039; Hoag v Lehigh V. R. Co. (1907) 55 Misc 388, 105 NYS

200; Siefken v Erie R. Co. (1907) 57 Misc 222, 107 NYS 1060. Except that causes were not inconsistent within this rule where they arose out of the same transaction. France & Canada S.S. Corp. v Berwind White Coal Mining Co. (1920) 229 NY 89, 127 NE 893; Menzies v Rasker-Halsted Realty Co. (1917, Sup App T) 164 NYS 403.

Inconsistent causes of action may be brought separately or even in the same action. Cassano v Cassano (1959) 18 Misc 2d 981, 187 NYS2d 924, affd 9 AD2d 693, 192 NYS2d 315.

Cause of action for libel and one for injurious falsehood grounded in negligence may be pleaded, though inconsistent. Henkin v News Syndicate Co. (1960) 27 Misc 2d 987, 210 NYS2d 302, affd 19 AD2d 862, 243 NYS2d 667.

4. —Mutually destructive causes

Second cause of action, inconsistent with first cause in that it alleges facts to be so different from facts alleged in first cause that both cannot be true and one is necessarily destructive of other, is improper. Baksi v Wallman (1946, Sup) 62 NYS2d 26, affd 270 AD 995, 63 NYS2d 215 and mod 271 AD 422, 65 NYS2d 894, affd 297 NY 456, 74 NE2d 172.

Under former CPA § 258 antagonistic individual and administrative causes of action could not be joined. Pitzalis v Prudential Ins. Co. (1933) 240 AD 748, 265 NYS 990.

For malicious prosecution and want for probable cause and allegations that plaintiff was held for the grand jury as mutually destructive see Other common-law causes, 20 infra, Graham v Buffalo General Laundries Corp. (1932) 235 AD 246, 257 NYS 101, affd 261 NY 165, 184 NE 746.

For rescission as barring specific performance of same contract, see 9 infra, Bell v Yagur (1951) 201 Misc 171, 104 NYS2d 467.

5. —Compelling election

A motion before answer is unauthorized to require plaintiff to elect between inconsistent and mutually exclusive causes of action. Ikle v Ikle (1939) 257 AD 635, 14 NYS2d 928.

A complaint would not be dismissed under former CPA § 258 for improperly joining causes of action since other remedies were furnished. New Amsterdam Casualty Co. v Parsons (1927) 219 AD 486, 220 NYS 340.

Where inconsistent causes of action were pleaded the most that could be required of plaintiff under former CPA § 258 was to elect upon which he would proceed. Reeve v Cromwell (1929) 227 AD 32, 237 NYS 20; Jersey Silk & Lace Stores, Inc. v Best Silk Shops, Ltd. (1929) 134 Misc 315, 235 NYS 277.

Under former CPA § 258, where plaintiff attempted to plead a cause of action based on breach of warranty where no privity of contract existed, the pleading was so incontrovertibly bad that it was not necessary to decide the question of misjoinder. Turner v Edison Storage Battery Co. (1928) 248 NY 73, 161 NE 423.

A cause of action for money loaned and another for an account stated are not mutually exclusive and plaintiff should not have been compelled to make an election since at most a severance should have been directed. Block v Breindel (1958) 5 AD2d 1007, 174 NYS2d 389.

For compelling election among causes for slander of title, unjust enrichment and services rendered, see 8, infra, Carroll v Warner Bros. Pictures, Inc. (1937, DC NY) 20 F Supp 405.

An election of inconsistent remedies occurs not by the bringing of one action which is inconsistent with another, but by the prosecution of one of such actions to the point of judgment. Cassano v Cassano (1959) 9 AD2d 693, 192 NYS2d 315.

6. Multiple parties; representative and individual capacity

Where there are multiple parties plaintiffs and defendants, causes of action may be joined only where they assert right to relief arising out of same transaction and they must present common questions of law or fact. O'Hara v Gannon (1951) 198 Misc 929, 103 NYS2d 913.

Two causes of action, each for different relief against separate defendants, could be united in the same complaint under former CPA § 258, where they arose out of the same transaction. Boylan v Vogel (1933) 147 Misc 554, 264 NYS 209, revd on other grounds 240 AD 756, 265 NYS 990.

Construed in the light of former CPA § 258 and § 96, CPA §§ 209 and 211–213 of that action were held to authorize inclusion in a single complaint of three causes of action based upon: (1) the lease by the plaintiff to the defendants L and D of certain premises for a term of years ending September 30, 1920; (2) the lease thereof to defendant C for a term of years from October 1, 1920; (3) the refusal of the defendants L and D to surrender the premises at the expiration of their term and their retention thereof, without paying rent, until June 30, 1921; (4) the refusal of defendant C to accept the premises upon the vacation thereof by L and D, or to perform any of the covenants of the lease to him; (5) the re-lease of the premises from October 1, 1921, for the remainder of the term of the lease to C, but at a reduced rental; and (6) the payment of brokerage to procure the re-lease aforesaid; the first of such causes of action being the loss of the rental value of the premises from October 1, 1920, to September 30, 1921, the second being such loss and the loss due to the re-lease at a reduced rental, and the third being the expense noted in clause (6) above; all of which causes were alleged as against the defendants, L, D and C, in the alternative, plaintiff being in doubt as to which of them would be liable thereunder. 137 East 66th St. v Lawrence (1922) 118 Misc 486, 194 NYS 762.

It was held under former CPA § 258, in an action against a number of defendants to recover damages for being deprived of several separate pieces of property by a series of wholly unrelated torts committed by defendants, the plaintiff should be required to separately state and number the different causes of action. Bob v Hecksher (1932) 235 AD 82, 256 NYS 126.

In an action by the administrator of a decedent to recover damages for his wrongful death plaintiff, under former CPA § 258, could not join as defendants two or more parties who were alleged to have been responsible for such death, but whose alleged wrongful acts, neglect or breaches of duty were separate and distinct. Ader v Blau (1925) 241 NY 7, 148 NE 771 (changed by statute as stated in Great Northern Tel. Co. v Yokohama Specie, Ltd. 297 NY 135, 76 NE2d 117).

In an action to recover commissions for sale of real property the action against one of the defendants who held certain money in escrow was properly joined with the action against the person who sold the property and the stakeholder was properly before the court as a conditionally necessary party. Cammarata v Conley (1958) 13 Misc 2d 349, 179 NYS2d 923.

Decisions prior to the Civil Practice Act (largely obsolete)

Before the Civil Practice Act a cause of action existing in favor of plaintiff, as an individual, could not be properly united with the cause of action existing in his favor in a representative capacity as corporate officer or stockholder, or personal representative. Pugsley v Aikin (1954) 11 NY 494; Young v Hyde (1906) 112 AD 760, 98 NYS 1052; Motley v Pratt (1895) 13 Misc 758, 35 NYS 184; Moss v Cohen (1895) 15 Misc 108, 36 NYS 265, revd 158 NY 240, 53 NE 8 (on ground there was only one cause of action); Sortore v Scott, 6 Lans 271; Stanton v Missouri Pac. R. Co. 15 Civ Proc 296, 2 NYS 298; Clark v Coles, 50 How Pr 178; Newcombe v Chicago & N. W. R. Co. (1890, Sup) 8 NYS 366.

Plaintiff could not, before the Civil Practice Act, unite a cause of action for negligence, causing death of one person of whose estate he is the administrator, with a cause of action for the death of another person of whose estate he is also administrator. Danaher v Brooklyn, 4 Civ Proc 286.

Several creditors of a common debtor, who have been induced to sell separate bills of goods through similar although not the same representations, could not, prior to the Civil Practice Act, unite in a common action to recover damages for the deceit. Gray v Rothschild (1889) 112 NY 668, 19 NE 847.

A creditor's suit could not, prior to the Civil Practice Act, unite a cause of action to avoid certain mortgages made by the debtor, on the ground of usury, with one to set aside conveyances of different property to other persons on the ground of fraud, where the two transactions were entirely separate and disconnected. Marx v Tailer, 12 Civ Proc 226, 9 NYSR 22. See also, Church v Stanton, 15 NYSR 1006.

As to causes of action concerning trusts and trustees, see: Garner v Thorn, 56 How Pr 452, affd 6 Abb NC 212; Price v Brown 60 How Pr 511, 10

Abb NC 67; Weeks v Cornwall (1886) 39 Hun 643, affd 104 NY 325, 10 NE 431.

Causes of action on behalf of a stockholder as an individual and on behalf of the corporation may be joined. Solmo v Rosenberg (1961) 31 Misc 2d 911, 221 NYS2d 56.

B. PARTICULAR CAUSES

7. Contract or implied contract

Where an action was brought on a contract by the complaint of a holder of a bill of lading who sues for nondelivery and for damages based on such nondelivery, it was held that it would have been wise for the plaintiff to plead causes of action on both theories utilizing the liberality authorized by CPA § 258. Leo Hess International Corp. v Isthmian S.S. Co. (1958) 5 AD2d 250, 170 NYS2d 705, reh and app den 5 AD2d 982, 173 NYS2d 985.

It was held under former CPA § 258 that all causes of action for breach of same contract existing when action brought should be united. Advance Lamp Shade Corp. v Bloom (1925) 125 Misc 829, 211 NYS 568.

Causes of action on contract and in assumpsit held properly joined under former CPA § 258. Hoffman v Mittlemann (1933) 147 Misc 442, 263 NYS 899.

Under former CPA § 258 causes of action could be pleaded on express contract and for reasonable value and the plaintiff could offer proof in support of both theories and submit both for determination to the court or jury. Etna Heating Co. v Wright (1933) 146 Misc 769, 262 NYS 794.

Action for breach of warranty and for seller's refusal to accept return and pay for defective goods, both founded on contract, held under former CPA § 258 to be properly joined. Neuss, Hesslein & Co. v Meadow (1931) 232 AD 156, 249 NYS 402.

Claim for work, labor and services and one for breach of warranty were held under former CPA § 258 to be inconsistent. Freund Coat Corp. v Lipschutz (1929) 135 Misc 553, 238 NYS 239.

Cause of action for price of goods sold and delivered could be joined with one on a guaranty of payment under former CPA § 258, but had to be separately stated and numbered. Winter v Maple City Mfg. Co. (1928) 132 Misc 631, 230 NYS 458.

Where a guaranty was made as a part or in extension of the contract making the debt, it was a part of the same transaction, and properly joined under former CPA § 258 with an action on the principal debt, but otherwise when made as a part of an assignment of the principal debt by the creditor to a third party. Winter v Maple City Mfg. Co., supra.

Action to recover back moneys paid on contract repudiated by plaintiff for fraud, and one to recover moneys paid on the ground that defendant refused to perform, could be united before the Civil Practice Act. Freer v Denton (1875) 61 NY 492.

It was proper before the Civil Practice Act to unite in a single action claims to recover back moneys paid on several separate purchases of lottery tickets. Grover v Morris (1878) 73 NY 473.

It was formerly held, before the Civil Practice Act, that causes of action arising on contract but inconsistent with each other cannot be joined. Nichols v Drew (1883) 94 NY 22.

A complaint in an action for services or materials furnished, or for goods sold, which alleged both value and agreed price, did not state two causes of action, and even where it contained two counts for the same services, one on special contract and the other on quantum meruit, the plaintiff should not be compelled in advance of trial to elect upon which count he will proceed. Rubin v Cohen (1908) 129 AD 395, 113 NYS 843 (prior to Civil Practice Act).

8. Contract and tort or other cause

Mere fact that one action is on contract and other is in tort does not prohibit joinder of causes. Friedman v December Corp. (1954, Sup) 137 NYS2d 154.

Under former CPA § 258 a cause of action in tort arising out of a contract was properly united with action on the contract. Axelrad v 77 Park Ave. Corp. (1929) 225 AD 557, 234 NYS 27.

Cause of action against corporation for breach of contract of employment of plaintiff, and cause of action against two employees of corporation for wrongfully inducing corporate president to discharge plaintiff, are properly joined where both causes of action arose out of same transaction and will largely be established by same evidence and witnesses. Friedman v December Corp. (1954, Sup) 137 NYS2d 154.

Plaintiff cannot properly commingle two causes of action, one upon a guarantee for breach of performance of a contract, and the other for damages for unlawfully urging or inducing breach of contract and plaintiff directed to serve amended complaint separately stating and numbering. Kasen v Morrell (1957) 10 Misc 2d 176, 167 NYS2d 322.

A party fraudulently induced to enter into a contract may join an action for damages sustained as result of the fraud with an action for breach of the same contract. Teepell v Jefferson County Sav. Bank (1956) 3 Misc 2d 508, 148 NYS2d 347.

Although two causes of action could be included in the same complaint even though they appeared to be inconsistent since the first cause of action was based on the premise that the contract's performance was impossible because of the operation of law and, therefore, there was no contract, whereas the second cause of action was based upon an existing contract which was revocable because of defendants' fraud and which plaintiff had elected to rescind, a determination of both causes could hardly be reached in the same trial whereas plaintiff's success on the first cause would make the second cause academic but his failure thereon would leave the second cause still open. Forgan v McKenzie (1958) 12 Misc 2d 508, 175 NYS2d 322.

Cause of action based on alleged negligence in manufacture and sale of bread and cause of action based on alleged breach of warranty in manufacture and sale of the same may be joined. Buck v Jones Bakery, Inc. (1936) 160 Misc 101, 289 NYS 386.

The joinder in the same complaint of (1) a cause of action in tort for damages for false representations inducing the purchase of bonds, and (2) a cause of action to rescind the purchase and to recover the price, and (3) a cause of action in tort for damages in the amount of the bonds by reason of the defendants' alleged negligence as fiduciaries for the plaintiff, is obviously improper. Dickler v National City Bank (1935) 160 Misc 317, 289 NYS 810.

Where defense by insurer in action by the insured on the policy was that answers to questions contained in the application were false, the plaintiff was entitled to sue, in the alternative, the insurance agency in tort, which he claimed made such answers in the application, in the same complaint in which he brought action against the insurer on contract. Lee v American Bonding Co. (1937) 162 Misc 757, 295 NYS 546.

In infant's action for injuries from student activities at university, cause of action in contract may be joined with cause of action in negligence. Oates v Rochester (1955) 207 Misc 420, 137 NYS2d 586.

Where parked automobile and owner were struck and both injured by codefendant's car and where injured car was burned while being towed away, it was proper to join causes of action for personal injury and property damage against injuring driver and cause of action against fire insurer. Better v Butuola (1952) 203 Misc 723, 115 NYS2d 139.

Under former CPA § 258 a cause of action against two for alleged breach of contract was improperly joined with a cause against two others for fraud and deceit, and a third cause, charging several with conspiring to commit an actionable wrong, but setting forth no tortious acts did not state a cause of action and was subject to dismissal. Miller v Spitzer (1928) 224 AD 39, 229 NYS 526.

Inconsistency of cause of action for rent, use and occupation, damages for breach of covenants in lease and for waste, was not fatal to complaint. Ribner v Babyatsky (1951, Sup) 103 NYS2d 599.

A complaint in an action for slander of title was not subject to dismissal, though it sets out causes of action for unjust enrichment and for services rendered. Defendants, however, on the trial could be required to elect. Carroll v Warner Bros. Pictures, Inc. (1937, DC NY) 20 F Supp 405.

An action under § 51 of the Civil Rights Law for the use of plaintiff's name for advertising or trade purposes and an action based on quasi-contract and the unjust enrichment of the defendant by the alleged unlawful use of plaintiff's name are not inconsistent. Bunnell v Keystone Varnish Co. (1938) 167 Misc 707, 4 NYS2d 601, affd on other ground 254 AD 885, 5 NYS2d 415. Compare joinder of causes under Civil Rights Law §§ 50 and 51 with causes for libel and slander. Tort and

other causes, 13 infra. Franklin v Columbia Pictures Corp. (1935) 246 AD 35, 284 NYS 96, affd 271 NY 554, 2 NE2d 691.

It was permissible under former CPA § 258 to plead liability on two different theories in the same complaint, as in actions for conversion and money had and received. Virdone v Globe Bank & Trust Co. (1932) 235 AD 125, 256 NYS 421.

In view of former CPA § 258, CPA § 96 (§§ 407, 602(a) herein) construed not to authorize consolidation of an action in the Supreme Court by a lessee against his lessor and its president for conspiring to cause and causing a third person to breach his agreement to sublease the premises, with an action thereafter commenced in the City Court of New York by the lessor's assignee to recover the rent due from plaintiff under his lease. Brody v Madison Lunch, Inc. (1922) 199 AD 640, 192 NYS 10.

In view of former CPA § 258 it was improper to join a cause of action against tenants for rent and another cause of action against part of them for damages done to the premises before the occupancy thereof by the other tenant. 137 East 66th St. v Lawrence (1922) 118 Misc 486, 194 NYS 762.

For breach of warranty and rescission see Rescission and enforcement of contract, 9 infra, Joannes Bros. Co. v Lamborn (1923) 237 NY 207, 142 NE 587, remittitur den 237 NY 604, 143 NE 760; Seggerman Bros., Inc. v Rosenberg Bros. & Co. (1926) 217 AD 7, 216 NYS 61.

For joinder of rescission for breach of contract with rescission for fraud see 9 infra, Warren v Putnam (1942) 263 AD 474, 33 NYS2d 635.

For slander and interference with contract obligations see Defamation and other causes 14 infra, G. Weiss Sons, Inc. v Hesse (1934) 242 AD 640, 272 NYS 244.

9. Rescission and enforcement of contract

Complaint for rescission of contract because of its breach and for accounting may be amended by adding cause of action for rescission for fraud inducing execution of contract, since two causes are consistent. Warren v Putnam (1942) 263 AD 474, 33 NYS2d 635.

Action for rescission of contract for fraud was held to bar action for specific performance, on ground that causes were mutually exclusive, 3, supra. Bell v Yasgur (1951) 201 Misc 171, 104 NYS2d 467.

A cause of action seeking rescission by judicial decree of the purchase of mortgage certificates was properly joined in a single complaint with alternative causes of action founded on affirmance of purchase of the certificates pleaded only for the purpose of enabling plaintiffs to recover in the event rescission should prove impossible. Epp v Title Guarantee & Trust Co. (1935) 160 Misc 554, 289 NYS 896.

An action to recover sums paid as commissions to brokers was properly united with an action for rescission where the commissions paid were directly connected with the main transactions involved. Pink v Title Guarantee & Trust Co. (1937) 164 Misc 128, 298 NYS 544.

A cause of action for rescission of a contract of sale, as for the recovery of the price paid, could not be joined under former CPA § 258, with one for breach of warranty in the contract, as the latter is based upon an affirmance of the contract. Joannes Bros. Co. v Lamborn (1923) 237 NY 207, 142 NE 587, remittitur den 237 NY 604, 143 NE 760; Seggerman Bros., Inc. v Rosenberg Bros. & Co. (1926) 217 AD 7, 216 NYS 61.

A demand for rescission of a contract of sale and recovery of the purchase price was held under former CPA § 258 to be inconsistent with one for damages for the difference between the purchase price of the goods and their market value, and the two causes of action could not be united in the same complaint. Tilton v Schwarz (1922) 199 AD 607, 191 NYS 862.

Under former CPA § 258, a complaint seeking equitable relief to obtain a rescission of a contract for the purchase of real estate and to recover monies paid thereon from particular defendants who had received the same, alleges but a single cause of action. Ressler v Samphimor Holding Corp. (1922) 201 AD 344, 194 NYS 363.

For divorce or separation and setting aside separation agreement see 11 infra, De Oteris v Mario (1945) 185 Misc 1029, 60 NYS2d 674, affd without op 270 AD 820, 60 NYS2d 297; Friedlander v Friedlander (1947, Sup) 73 NYS2d 423.

For separation and rescission of separation agreement see 11 infra, Dolan v Dolan (1940) 259 AD 1115, 21 NYS2d 230; De Oteris v Mario (1945) 185 Misc 1029, 60 NYS2d 674, affd without op 270 AD 820, 60 NYS2d 297; Friedlander v Friedlander (1947, Sup) 73 NYS2d 423.

For joinder of contract, rescission and tort in three counts see 8 supra, Dickler v National City Bank (1935) 160 Misc 317, 289 NYS 810.

For joinder of cause by stockholders for rescission of releases and consents to exchange of stock with derivative action for accounting see Stockholders' derivative actions 17 infra, Abrahams v Bachmann (1933) 238 AD 320, 264 NYS 131.

A cause of action to set aside a contract and a cause of action to compel an accounting for injuries sustained under such contract could be joined before the Civil Practice Act. Bosworth v Allen (1901) 168 NY 157, 61 NE 163.

10. Reformation and other causes

Plaintiff may seek impressment of trust and accounting in enforcement of contract and join such cause of action with cause of action for reformation. Cole Steel Equipment Co. v Kardwheel Corp (1956, Sup) 150 NYS2d 415.

A cause of action to foreclose a junior participating interest in a mortgage and a cause of action to reform an agreement concerning the purchase of an indebtedness secured by an assignment of a portion of the junior interest of the bond and mortgage, sought to be foreclosed, were properly

joined under former CPA § 258. Beaumel, Inc. v F. B. & W. Realty Corp. (1934) 152 Misc 631, 274 NYS 56.

Joinder of reformation, an equitable remedy, was not permitted with legal causes under former CPA § 258, not expressly providing as present section does for joinder of legal and equitable causes. Bammon v Holeproof Hosiery Co. (1931) 233 AD 699, 249 NYS 569; Kuhn v Title Guarantee & Trust Co. (1934) 241 AD 874, 271 NYS 377, affd 264 NY 692, 191 NE 630.

As to claim to have a contract reformed, and enforced as reformed prior to the Civil Practice Act, see Bidwell & Banta v Astor Mut. Ins. Co. (1857) 16 NY 263; New York Ice Co. v North Western Ins. Co. (1861) 23 NY 357.

11. Matrimonial causes

Equity and tort causes with reference to marital status may be joined. Friedlander v Friedlander (1947, Sup) 73 NYS2d 423.

Annulment and separation causes may be united in same complaint. Prosswimmer v Prosswimmer (1944) 182 Misc 807, 50 NYS2d 46.

See De Oteris v Mario (1945) 185 Misc 1029, 60 NYS2d 674, affd without op 270 AD 820, 60 NYS2d 297.

Actions for annulment of marriage and for damages for fraud may be joined. Lee v Lee (1945) 184 Misc 686, 57 NYS2d 97.

A cause of action for separation may be joined with a cause of action to set aside a separation agreement. Brock v Brock (1958) 5 AD2d 1002, 173 NYS2d 834.

Wife's causes of action for separation, for setting aside separation agreement and for foreign divorce, and for damages for conspiracy against husband and his attorney, were properly joined. Friedlander v Friedlander (1974, Sup) 73 NYS2d 423.

It was held under former CPA § 258 and earlier provisions before the Civil Practice Act that causes of action for divorce and for separation could not be joined. Galusha v Galusha (1893) 138 NY 272, 33 NE 1062; Hofmann v Hofmann (1921) 232 NY 215, 133 NE 450; Conrad v Conrad (1908) 124 AD 780, 109 NYS 387; People v Berkowitz (1923) 121 Misc 40, 200 NYS 823.

An action for separation and an action to set aside a separation agreement may be joined. Dolan v Dolan (1940) 259 AD 1115, 21 NYS2d 230.

Causes of action for separation, or for divorce, and for setting aside separation agreement may be joined. De Oteris v Mario (1945) 185 Misc 1029, 60 NYS2d 674, affd 270 AD 820, 60 NYS2d 297.

Divorced husband may sue for judgment to declare that his Florida divorce is valid and plead also inconsistent cause of action for divorce. McCloskey v McCloskey (1952, Sup) 117 NYS2d 770.

Pendency of divorce action in same court did not bar action for declaration of invalidity of defendant's foreign divorce and subsequent marriage to other defendant and for annulment of defendant's marriage. Cassano v Cassano (1959) 18 Misc 2d

981, 187 NYS2d 924, affd 9 AD2d 693, 192 NYS2d 315.

12. Tort causes generally

Joinder of causes of action for personal injuries from fall of bathroom ceiling and later from fall of kitchen ceiling, under CPA § 245-a (§ 3025(b) herein), would warrant severance of action in court's discretion, as jury would be influenced by similarity of accidents. Stein v Baff (1950) 197 Misc 509, 95 NYS2d 298.

City court of New York had jurisdiction of action for personal injuries sustained by plaintiff and her husband, and for consequential damages, where each of the causes of action did not exceed $6,000. Robles v Rushfield (1957) 7 Misc 2d 734, 166 NYS2d 612.

Under former CPA § 258 motion for permission to serve amended complaint denied where proposed amendment contemplates uniting in single complaint causes of action by consignors of merchandise for damages due to delay and improper handling in transportation, and causes of action by the consignees of such merchandise for damages due to the same reasons, notwithstanding the assignment of the consignees' causes of action to the consignors. Branch v New York C. R. Co. (1924) 124 Misc 555, 209 NYS 270.

Where the facts stated in the complaint in an action against several physicians for malpractice were so related that in the event of separate trials they would necessarily have to be proved on each trial, and where the substantive law applicable to each cause of action was the same, held under former CPA § 258 that the parties and causes of action were properly joined in an action and one complaint. Sherlock v Manwaren (1924) 208 AD 538, 203 NYS 709.

13. Tort and other causes

Where complaint alleged causes of action based on violation of Civil Rights Law §§ 50 and 51, libel, and slander, award predicated on three causes of action not error under former CPA § 258, where but one judgment was entered. Plaintiff could have obtained all the damages he suffered in a cause of action based solely on a violation of his civil rights. Franklin v Columbia Pictures Corp. (1935) 246 AD 35, 284 NYS 96, affd 271 NY 554, 2 NE2d 691.

For joinder of causes under Civil Rights Law § 51, quasi-contract and unjust enrichment see Contract and tort or other cause, 8, supra, Bunnell v Keystone Varnish Co. (1938) 167 Misc 707, 4 NYS2d 601, affd 254 AD 885, 5 NYS2d 415.

A cause of action for damages caused by blasting in the work of construction and one for intrusion upon plaintiff's premises were properly united in one complaint under former CPA § 258, subd 4, but the complaint was subject to a motion under rule 90 of the Rules of Civil Practice, requiring causes of action to be separately stated and numbered. First Const. Co. v Rapid Transit Subway Const. Co. (1923) 122 Misc 145, 203 NYS 359, affd 211 AD 184, 206 NYS 822.

An administratrix, seeking recovery of damages for personal injuries sustained by her intestate, under circumstances such that had the deceased survived he could have proceeded against the defendants either for maintaining a nuisance or for negligence, was entitled under former CPA § 258 to unite the two causes of action in a single complaint, nor could the defendants complain, in view of CPA §§ 211–213 (§§ 1002(a)(b), 1022, Rule 5012 herein), of the fact that all of them might not be liable on both such causes of action. Smith v Earle (1922) 202 AD 305, 195 NYS 342.

Where both causes, one for nuisance, arose from neglect of defendants, on the same state of facts, and sought recovery for injury to personal property, they were properly joined under former CPA § 258. Millens v Greenport (1931) 139 Misc 555, 249 NYS 655.

14. —Defamation and other causes; libel and slander

It is improper to unite in one count a cause of action on slander with one in libel. Brown v Reed (1957) 10 Misc 2d 8, 167 NYS2d 41.

Actions for slander and for assault, if united in a counterclaim subjected it to dismissal under former CPA § 258; and allegations thereof in the answer by way of evidentiary pleading will be stricken with leave to serve an amended answer. Raspaulo v Ragona (1926) 127 Misc 160, 215 NYS 407.

Under former CPA § 258 it was held causes of action for slander and for malicious prosecution could not be joined in the same complaint but a cause of action for interference with contractual obligations could be joined with a cause of action for slander. G. Weiss Sons, Inc. v Hesse (1934) 242 AD 640, 272 NYS 244.

Cause of action for libel and one for injurious falsehood grounded in negligence may be pleaded, though inconsistent. Henkin v News Syndicate Co. (1960) 27 Misc 2d 987, 210 NYS2d 302, affd 19 AD2d 862, 243 NYS2d 667.

Decisions prior to Civil Practice Act (largely obsolete)

De Wolfe v Abraham (1896) 151 NY 186, 45 NE 455; Green v Davies (1905) 182 NY 499, 75 NE 536; Haughie v New York & N. J. Tel. Co. (1901) 34 Misc 634, 70 NYS 584.

15. —Fraudulent acts and fraudulent conveyances

Where there was only one subject of the action, to wit, the fraudulent acts by which plaintiff claimed to have been injured, it was proper under former CPA § 258 to unite the causes; and motion to compel plaintiff to serve an amended complaint separately stating and numbering the causes of action and directing a division into several actions, should be denied. Mende v Mende (1926) 218 AD 791, 218 NYS 283.

Complaint uniting cause of action based upon common-law count of fraud and one based upon fraudulent issue of bill of lading in violation of statute, both being based upon deceit and the alleged fraudulent issue of the same bill of lading, held proper under former CPA § 258. Slutzkin v Gerhard & Hey, Inc. (1921) 199 AD 5, 191 NYS 104.

Complaint considered and held, under former CPA § 258, to allege one cause of action for damages for fraud and conspiracy against all of the defendants. Moore v Bonbright & Co. (1922) 202 AD 281, 195 NYS 854.

For breach of contract and fraud see Contract and tort or other cause, 8, supra, Miller v Spitzer (1928) 224 AD 39, 229 NYS 526.

For joinder of causes for fraud or fraudulent conveyances with other causes prior to the Civil Practice Act see: Lattin v McCarty (1869) 41 NY 107; People v Tweed, 63 NY 194; Getty v Devlin (1877) 70 NY 504; but see Powers v Benedict (1882) 88 NY 605; France & Canada S. S. Corp. v Berwind White Coal Mining Co. (1920) 229 NY 89, 127 NE 893; Taft v Bronson (1917) 180 AD 154, 167 NYS 433; Coleman v Phelps, 57 How Pr 393; Royer Wheel Co. v Fielding, 61 How Pr 437; Mahler v Smith (1887) 43 Hun 512; Palmer v Searing, 12 NYSR 559; Keenan v Keenan (1890, Sup) 12 NYS 747; Beecher v Schieffelin, 4 Civ Proc 230–239.

16. Causes concerning corporate matters

Causes of action to recover certain stock or its value, although brought on different theories of liability, are consistent with each other and could be joined under former CPA § 258. Ritter v Nirenberg (1934) 243 AD 542, 275 NYS 885.

Where plaintiff sought to be adjudged owner of corporate stock, for entry on the books accordingly, and for removal of directors for mismanagement and misconduct, relief could be granted upon a single complaint under former CPA § 258. Berger v 48th & 56th Streets Realty Corp. (1931) 232 AD 571, 251 NYS 33.

A fatal defect in the joinder of causes of action under former CPA § 258 did not result by reason of the fact that three of the plaintiffs were foreign corporations, where such corporations had places of business in the county wherein the action was brought. United States Fidelity & Guaranty Co. v Worcester Salt Co. (1933) 149 Misc 431, 267 NYS 450, affd 241 AD 673, 269 NYS 1023.

In a trustee's action against directors of a corporation to secure return to it of salaries illegally voted and paid to themselves, it was not improper, under former CPA § 258, to include a demand for the payment of the money so restored to the stockholders in dividends. People's Trust Co. v O'Mera (1923) 204 AD 268, 197 NYS 795, app dismd 236 NY 508, 142 NE 262.

In a case before the Civil Practice Act the complaint in an action against a corporation and five other parties, three of whom were directors, another of whom was a judgment creditor, and the other a grantee of the corporation, alleging that the plaintiff's assignor had recovered a judgment against a corporation and that an execution issued thereon had been returned unsatisfied, ask: First, to have set aside a mortgage and bill of sale executed by the corporation, as alleged, in contemplation of insolvency and with intent to hinder and defraud creditors; second, to have set aside a judgment recovered, as alleged, collusively by one of the defendants against the corporation; third, to have enforced the liability of three of the defendants for their failure as directors to file an annual report; finally, it prayed for a sequestration of the property of the corporation and a division thereof among its creditors and also made a general demand for costs against all the defendants. Upon the hearing upon demurrers interposed by several of the defendants, setting up a misjoinder of causes of action, held, that under the provisions of the Code of Civil Procedure the first and second causes of action were properly joined in one complaint; that the third cause of action could not be joined with the other two under the provisions of said section alone, but that reading that section with General Corp. Law, § 109, providing that where an action is brought by a creditor of a corporation and the directors are made liable by law, in any event or contingency, for the payment of his debt the persons so made liable may be made parties defendant by the original or by a supplemental complaint, the joinder was proper; that while the plaintiff sued alone and there might be other creditors of the corporation not entitled to enforce the liability of the directors for their failure to file an annual report, that difficulty was obviated by §§ 111 and 112, providing for the distribution of the assets of a corporation among its creditors. Cummings v American Gear & Spring Co. (1895) 87 Hun 598, 34 NYS 541.

Stockholder's personal action against one of the defendants individually for breach of agreement was ordered severed from his derivative actions on behalf of multiple corporations for waste and to compel declaration of dividends. Tomasello v Trump (1959) 22 Misc 2d 484, 194 NYS2d 956.

Decisions prior to the Civil Practice Act (largely obsolete)

Wiles v Suydam (1876) 64 NY 173; Mack v Latta (1903) 83 AD 242, 82 NYS 130, revd 178 NY 525, 71 NE 97; Hutchinson v Young (1904) 93 AD 407, 87 NYS 678; Young v Hyde (1906) 112 AD 760, 98 NYS 1052; Sherwood v Holbrook (1917) 98 Misc 668, 163 NYS 326, affd 178 AD 462, 165 NYS 514, later app 188 AD 712, 177 NYS 330, affd 231 NY 533, 132 NE 876; Mappier v Mortimer, 11 Abb Pr 455; Sterne v Herman, 11 Abb Pr NS 371; Stanton v Missouri P. R. Co. (1888, Sup) 2 NYS 298; Bonnell v Wheeler (1874) 1 Hun 332, affd 68 NY 294; Lovelace v Doran (1891, Sup) 15 NYS 278. See also, Bonnell v Griswold (1877) 68 NY 294.

17. —Stockholders' actions

Stockholder's derivative action may be joined with his action for individual damages. Young v Taber (1954) 284 AD 829, 132 NYS2d 431, app dismd 307 NY 841, 122 NE2d 334 and affd 308 NY 687, 124 NE2d 322.

Joinder of transfer action with a derivative stockholder's suit proper. Gertenbach v Rodnon (1939) 171 Misc 302, 12 NYS2d 518.

Action by stockholders for rescission of releases and consents to exchange and reclassification of stock properly joined under former § 258, with derivative action for accounting. Abrahams v Bachmann (1933) 238 AD 320, 264 NYS 131.

Stockholder's representative action against corporate officers was improperly joined under former CPA § 258, with action against officers individually for plaintiff's individual benefit. Sweeney v National Assets Corp. (1930) 139 Misc 223, 246 NYS 315.

In a stockholder's action brought to restore to the corporation property claimed to have been diverted from the corporation by the negligent or wrongful acts of the defendants, there is no misjoinder of causes of action under former CPA § 258, where a part of the allegations of the complaint as to misconduct relate only to part of the defendants, all of the allegations being part of the general transactions of the corporation out of which the alleged negligence and wrongful acts arose. Baker v Baker (1924) 122 Misc 757, 204 NYS 11, affd 212 AD 850, 207 NYS 809.

Actions brought by a stockholder in the right of the corporation may properly be joined with actions brought by him in his right as a stockholder. Bleakney v Schrauff (1959) 18 Misc 2d 919, 186 NYS2d 412.

Causes of action on behalf of a stockholder as an individual and on behalf of the corporation may be joined. Solmo v Rosenberg (1961) 31 AD 911, 221 NYS2d 56.

Decisions prior to the Civil Practice Act (largely obsolete)

Case v New York Mut. Sav. & Loan Ass'n (1903) 88 AD 538, 85 NYS 104; Searles v Gebbie (1906) 115 AD 778, 101 NYS 199, affd 190 NY 533, 83 NE 1122, adhered to 192 NY 588, 85 NE 1105; Brown v Utopia Land Co. (1907) 118 AD 364, 103 NYS 50; Snyder v Bender (1919, Sup) 173 NYS 401.

18. Real property

Review of assessments on thirty-seven separate parcels of property were properly joined in single proceeding to review assessments by certiorari. People ex rel. Michael J. Adrian Corp. v Sexton (1937) 251 AD 181, 295 NYS 542.

The owner of four mortgages, each covering separate parcels of land, may bring a single action for the foreclosure thereof. Poughkeepsie Sav. Bank v Berler (1937) 163 Misc 880, 296 NYS 138.

Under former CPA § 258, and CPA § 8 (§ 103(a) herein), several actions to foreclose mortgages were consolidated under CPA § 96 (§§ 407, 602(a) herein). Down Town Realty Co. v Simpson (1929) 227 AD 803, 237 NYS 228.

Fact that under common law procedure damage to freehold could not be recovered until plaintiff's right to property was established by judgment in ejectment, no longer applied under CPA § 258. Dold v Niagara County (1946) 270 AD 344, 59 NYS2d 426.

For blasting and trespass, see Tort and other causes, 13 supra, First Const. Co. v Rapid Transit Subway Const. Co. (1923) 122 Misc 145, 203 NYS 359, affd 211 AD 184, 206 NYS 822.

Decisions prior to the Civil Practice Act (largely obsolete)

An action to remove a cloud upon title by a deed given by mistake by a third party and a claim to recover possession of the premises fraudulently obtained could be united before the Civil Practice Act. Lattin v McCarty (1869) 41 NY 107.

The complaint might, before the Civil Practice Act, set forth a cause of action for specific performance of a contract to convey land, and also a cause of action for damages for breach of the contract, if for any reason it cannot be performed, and if it turns out that the equitable relief cannot be granted, the plaintiff could recover his damages, if entitled to any. Sternberger v McGovern (1874) 56 NY 12; Margraf v Muir (1874) 57 NY 155.

A claim for damages for withholding possession of real estate did not include rents and profits, a claim for which is a separate and distinct cause of action under Code before the Civil Practice Act. Larned v Hudson (1874) 57 NY 151.

An action for injuries to real property and one for penalties incurred under the fisheries, game and forest law, could not be joined in the same complaint before the Civil Practice Act. People v Wells (1900) 52 AD 583, 65 NYS 319.

Under CCP a landowner could have united in one complaint an action for permanent injury from construction of subway and one for temporary injury resulting from temporary structures in street. Stines v New York (1912) 154 AD 276, 138 NYS 962.

It was held, before the Civil Practice Act, that a cause of action for trespass to lands could not be joined with a cause of action for slander of title of such lands. Dodge v Colby (1885) 37 Hun 515, mod in other respects, 108 NY 445, 15 NE 703.

As to mechanics liens: Cehio v Fischer (1911) 143 AD 577, 128 NYS 289; Whisten v Kellogg (1906) 50 Misc 409, 100 NYS 526.

Ejectment and other causes: Vandevoort v Gould (1867) 36 NY 639; Lattin v McCarty (1869) 41 NY 107; Hubbell v Lerch (1874) 58 NY 237; Compton v The Chelsea (1893) 139 NY 538, 34 NE 1090; Porter v International Bridge Co. (1900) 163 NY 79, 57 NE 174; Wait v Hudson V. R. Co. (1904) 43 Misc 304, 88 NYS 825.

As to mortgage foreclosure: Fleischmann v Tilt (1896) 10 AD 271, 42 NYS 506; Campbell v Campbell (1889, Sup) 5 NYS 171; Selkirk v Wood, 9 Civ Proc 141; Morrissey v Leddy, 11 Civ Proc 438.

As to partition: Schenck v Furst (1910) 140 AD 432, 125 NYS 506; Diehl v Lambart, 9 Civ Proc 267.

19. Taxpayers' actions

A taxpayer's action to restrain certain city officials and certain contractors from carrying out alleged illegal contracts, to prevent further payments thereunder and to require the defendants to restore and repay to the city certain monies alleged to have been illegally wasted and diverted, all having to do with a single department of the city government and arising out of the conduct and management thereof, is not objectionable as a misjoinder of causes of action. Grace v Scott (1922) 201 AD 859, 193 NYS 69.

It was held prior to the Civil Practice Act that a taxpayer's action asking a separate judgment against each of several supervisors, defendants, should state, in each paragraph setting out a separate cause of action, the official position of the defendant against whom judgment was demanded, the capacity in which he acted and all the facts necessary to make that cause of action complete in itself. Wallace v Jones (1902) 68 AD 191, 74 NYS 116.

20. Other common-law causes

A complaint alleging that defendants conspired to slander plaintiff and that each uttered slander in pursuance of conspiracy, properly joined such causes. Duske v Lukas (1946, Sup) 64 NYS2d 389.

Where a series of acts committed by conspirators acting in pursuance of a common scheme result in damages the facts could be set up as one cause of action under former § 258. Travelers' Ins. Co. v Chiarello Stevedoring Co. (1932) 236 AD 468, 260 NYS 18.

Conversion and replevin may be joined where plaintiff does not know whether defendant still has merchandise sold to him, subject to election at trial at close of evidence. Biltmore Knitwear Corp. v Chalfin (1940) 176 Misc 197, 25 NYS2d 947.

For conversion and money had and received see Contract and tort or other cause, 8 supra, Virdone v Globe Bank & Trust Co. (1932) 235 AD 125, 256 NYS 421.

The joinder in counterclaim of causes of action for assault growing out of the transaction on which plaintiff sues and for malicious prosecution was not forbidden under former § 258. Schechner v Wittner (1967) 130 Misc 424, 224 NYS 66.

In an action for malicious prosecution allegations of want of probable cause and that plaintiff was held for the grand jury were contrary, repugnant and mutually destructive under former § 258. Graham v Buffalo General Laundries Corp. (1932) 235 AD 246, 257 NYS 101, affd 261 NY 165, 184 NE 746.

For slander and malicious prosecution see Defamation and other causes 14 supra, G. Weiss Sons, Inc. v Hesse (1934) 242 AD 640, 272 NYS 244.

For slander and assault see Defamation and other causes 14 supra, Raspaulo v Ragona (1926) 127 Misc 160, 215 NYS 407.

For negligence and nuisance see Tort and other causes 13 supra, Smith v Earle (1922) 202 AD 305, 195 NYS 342; Millens v Greenport (1931) 139 Misc 555, 249 NYS 655.

Decisions prior to the Civil Practice Act (largely obsolete)

It was held prior to the Civil Practice Act that false imprisonment and malicious prosecution could be united in one complaint and tried together. Marks v Townsend (1885) 97 NY 590; Castro v Uriarte, 2 Civ Proc R 210; but where they were joined in a complaint, plaintiff would be compelled to elect under which cause of action he will proceed. Thorp v Carvalho (1895) 14 Misc 554, 36 NYS 1, contra; Nebenzahl v Townsend, 61 How Pr 353.

Prior to the Civil Practice Act, in an action to restrain defendant from pumping a mineral spring to accelerate its natural flow, and thus injure plaintiff, the statement of a cause of action under Chap. 429 of 1908 and also one at common-law action, were not open to the objection of misjoinder. Hathorn v Natural Carbonic Gas Co. (1908) 60 Misc 341, 113 NYS 458, mod 128 AD 33, 112 NYS 374, affd 194 NY 326, 87 NE 504.

FORMS

Form 1—Complaint containing two or more causes of action

Form 2—Complaint containing two or more causes of action—another form

Form 1

Complaint Containing Two or More Causes of Action

Complaint

[Title of court and cause]   Index No. __¹__ [if assigned]

Plaintiff complaining of defendants alleges:

    FOR A FIRST CAUSE OF ACTION AGAINST DEFENDANT JOHN DOE ONLY

1. [state facts constituting first cause of action]

    FOR A SECOND CAUSE OF ACTION AGAINST ALL DEFENDANTS

10. Plaintiff repeats and realleges each and every allegation contained in paragraphs

["1", "3", and "5"] of this complaint with the same force and effect as if herein set forth anew.

11. [state facts constituting second cause of action.]

WHEREFORE plaintiff demands judgment against defendant John Doe for [here set forth relief demanded], and demands judgment against all defendants for [here set forth relief demanded].

____2_____

[Print signer's name below signature]
Attorney for plaintiff
Address __3_____
Telephone No. __4__

[Verification]

Form 2

Complaint Containing Two or More Causes of Action—Another Form

SUPREME COURT OF THE STATE OF NEW YORK
COUNTY OF ERIE

_____X
JOHN DOE and ANNA DOE
    Plaintiffs,
  —against—   Complaint
RICHARD ROE   Index No. __1__ [if assigned]
    Defendant.
_____X

AS A FIRST CAUSE OF ACTION
PLAINTIFF ANNA DOE ALLEGES:

1. That at all the times herein mentioned plaintiff John Doe was the owner of a 1963 station wagon bearing New York registration number ____2_____, 1965.

2. That at all the times herein mentioned, plaintiff Anna Doe was and still is a duly registered graduate nurse.

3. Upon information and belief that at all times herein mentioned, defendant was the owner of a 1958 Buick sedan bearing New York registration number __3_____, 1965.

4. That at all the times herein mentioned, Clinton Street in the Town of Gardenville, New York, was and still is a public highway.

5. That on or about January 21, 1965, at about 4:50 o'clock in the afternoon, while plaintiff Anna Doe was driving said station wagon in a westerly direction on said Clinton Street, at about a half mile west of Union Road and on the overpass, the said sedan owned and operated by defendant was so carelessly and negligently managed, operated, and controlled that the same was caused to come in violent contact with, and to collide with said station wagon, and to cause the personal injuries and property damage complained of herein.

6. That plaintiff Anna Doe was driving said station wagon at the time and place aforesaid with the knowledge and consent of plaintiff John Doe.

7. That defendant was negligent and careless in the operation of his said sedan in proceeding in the same direction as plaintiff Anna Doe at an excessive, reckless and imprudent rate of speed; in attempting to pass plaintiff's station wagon in a no passing zone, and cutting directly into plaintiff's said automobile at a time and place when and where there was not sufficient room to pass in safety; in failing to give any signal or warning of his intention to pass plaintiff's station wagon; in failing to take reasonable steps or precautions to avoid said collision; in failing to have a proper lookout in the direction he was going; in failing to have his sedan under proper control at the said

time and place; and in failing to provide same with good and sufficient brakes, and other necessary appliances and equipment, and/or, in failing to properly and adequately apply the same at the time of said collision.

8. That the said collision and resulting property damage and personal injuries were due solely to the negligence of defendant without any negligence of plaintiff Anna Doe or of plaintiff John Doe in any wise contributing thereto.

9. That solely by reason of defendant's negligence as aforesaid plaintiff Anna Doe was caused to suffer severe and painful injuries, both internal as well as external, some of which, upon information and belief, are permanent; extreme nervous shock; a miscarriage of her pregnancy; and further to be rendered unable to engage in her occupation and business as a registered nurse, all of which endured for a long period of time.

10. That by reason of the foregoing, plaintiff, Anna Doe, has been damaged in the sum of $__4__.

AS A SECOND CAUSE OF ACTION
PLAINTIFF JOHN DOE ALLEGES:

11. That plaintiff John Doe realleges each and every allegation contained in the paragraphs of this complaint numbered "1" to "9" inclusive, with the same force and effect as if fully set forth herein.

12. That prior to and at all the times herein mentioned plaintiff Anna Doe was and still continues to be this plaintiff's wife, and as such wife then and ever since has lived and cohabited with this plaintiff; that this plaintiff then and ever since has been providing for his said wife; that prior to the time herein mentioned she had been in good health and fully capable of performing and actually did perform all the usual duties of housewife in their dwelling.

13. That by reason of the foregoing and solely because of the negligence of the defendant as hereinbefore alleged this plaintiff's said wife was severely and upon information and belief permanently injured and was confined to her bed and to plaintiff's house for many weeks; that this plaintiff was obliged to and did necessarily pay and become liable therefor for nursing and medicines and upon information and belief will necessarily continue to pay and become liable for additional sums of money for medical care, aid and attention; that this plaintiff's said wife has been unable to perform the duties aforesaid which she theretofore had performed for this plaintiff; that this plaintiff also has been deprived of the services of his said wife and his comfort and happiness in her society and companionship have been impaired and upon information and belief such deprivation and impairment will necessarily continue for a long time to come, all to this plaintiff's damage in the sum of $__5__.

AS A THIRD CAUSE OF ACTION
PLAINTIFF JOHN DOE ALLEGES:

14. That plaintiff John Doe realleges each and every allegation contained in the paragraphs of this complaint numbered "1", "3", "4", "5", "6", "7", "8", with the same force and effect as if herein set forth anew.

15. That by reason of the foregoing and solely because of the negligence of defendant as hereinbefore alleged this plaintiff's said station wagon was damaged, and he was deprived of the use thereof all to his damage in the sum of $__6__.

WHEREFORE plaintiff Anna Doe demands judgment against defendant in the sum of $__7__ together with the costs and disbursements of this action; and plaintiff John Doe demands judgment against defendant in the sum of $__8__ together with the costs and disbursements of this action.

Richard Roe
Attorney for Plaintiffs
[Office & P. O. Address]
[Telephone No.]

§ 602. Consolidation

(a) Generally. When actions involving a common question of law or fact are pending before a court, the court, upon motion, may order a joint trial of any or all the matters in issue, may order the actions consolidated, and may make such other orders concerning proceedings therein as may tend to avoid unnecessary costs or delay.

(b) Cases pending in different courts. Where an action is pending in the supreme court it may, upon motion, remove to itself an action pending in another court and consolidate it or have it tried together with that in the supreme court. Where an action is pending in the county court, it may, upon motion, remove to itself an action pending in a city, municipal, district or justice court in the county and consolidate it or have it tried together with that in the county court.

HISTORY:

> Add, L 1962, ch 308, eff Sept 1, 1963.
> Earlier statutes: CPA §§ 95–97a; CCP §§ 346, 817–819, 1220; 2 RS 383, §§ 36–38.

ADVISORY COMMITTEE NOTES:

> **Subd (a)** incorporates the provisions of CPA §§ 96, 96-a. See also Fed R Civ P 42(a).
> **Subd (b)** follows CPA § 97. See also CPA §§ 97-a, 187(3); 19 NY Jud Council Rep 79 (1953).

CROSS REFERENCES:

> Consolidation of Mechanic's lien actions, Lien Law § 43.
> Consolidation of appeals, Vill Law § 14-1420.

FEDERAL ASPECTS:

> Pleadings and motions, generally, Rules 7 through 16 of Federal Rules of Civil Procedure, USCS Court Rules.
> Joinder of claims and remedies, Rule 18 of Federal Rules of Civil Procedure, USCS Court Rules.
> Consolidation and separate trials in United States District Courts, Rule 42 of Federal Rules of Civil Procedure, USCS Court Rules.
> Motion day in Federal District Courts, Rule 78 of Federal Rules of Civil Procedure, USCS Court Rules.

RESEARCH REFERENCES AND PRACTICE AIDS:

> 3 Carmody-Wait 2d, Consolidation of Actions §§ 17:1, 17:2, 17:5, 17:7, 17:8, 17:10, 17:12, 17:24.
> 6 Carmody-Wait 2d, Interpleader §§ 40:21, 40:29.
> 7 Carmody-Wait 2d, Order of Disposition of Issues; Joint and Separate Trials §§ 52:9, 52:11.
> 14 Carmody-Wait 2d, Summary Proceedings to Recover Possession of Real Property § 90:188.
> 17 Carmody-Wait 2d, Committee for an Incompetent or a Mental Patient § 109:3.
> 21 Carmody-Wait 2d, Actions By or Against the State § 126:61.
> 22 Carmody-Wait 2d, Arbitration § 141:9.
> 1 Am Jur 2d, Actions §§ 156–161.
> 1 Am Jur Pl and Pr Forms (Rev ed), Actions, Forms 1 et seq.
> 23 Am Jur Pl and Pr Forms (Rev ed), Trial, Forms 41–51.
> 3 Am Jur Trials p 553, Selecting the Forum—Plaintiff's Position.
> 8 Am Jur Trials p 173, Airline Passenger Death Cases.

Annotations:

Right to appellate review, on single appellate proceeding, of separate actions consolidated for trial together in lower court. 36 ALR2d 823.

Propriety of consolidation for trial of actions for personal injuries, death, or property damages arising out of same accident. 68 ALR2d 1372.

Time for making application for consolidation of actions. 73 ALR2d 739.

State court's power to consolidate arbitration proceedings. 64 ALR3d 528.

Appealability of state court order granting or denying consolidation, severance, or separate trials. 77 ALR3d 1082.

Consolidation in federal court of separate personal injury or death actions arising out of single accident. 1 ALR Fed 229.

Appealability of federal court order granting or denying consolidation, severance, or separate trials. 30 ALR Fed 393.

Necessity of leave of court to add or drop parties by amended pleading filed before responsive pleading is served, under Rules 15(a) and 21 of the Federal Rules of Civil Procedure. 31 ALR Fed 752.

Law Reviews:

The quarterly survey of New York practice: CPLR 602: consolidation of actions pending in different inferior courts refused by the supreme court. 41 St. John's L Rev 135.

Forms:

See "FORMS" heading following "CASE NOTES", infra.

CASE NOTES

1. In general
2. Conservation of time and expense
3. Effect of possible prejudice
4. Common questions of law or fact, generally
5. Causes and proceedings joinable
6. Causes and proceedings not joinable
7. Joint trial without consolidation
8. Removal to or from supreme court
9. Removal to or from county or other local court
10. Venue
11. Jurisdiction
12. Right to open or close

1. In general

The consolidation statute should be liberally construed to secure the just, speedy and inexpensive termination of the proceeding. Tucker v Iwaziewicz (1969) 61 Misc 2d 219, 305 NYS2d 137.

The consolidation of two actions gives rise to a new action displacing the actions affected thereby. Rosado v Valvo (1969) 58 Misc 2d 944, 297 NYS2d 230.

Only question to be determined on appeal from grant of consolidation of actions was whether court had abused its discretion in making order of consolidation. Maigur v Saratogian, Inc. (1975) 47 AD2d 982, 367 NYS2d 114.

Although a court has broad powers to order consolidation, they should not have been exercised in a situation where neither side requested such action, where approximately five months had elapsed since both sides offered their proof in action number one and where action number two had not yet been reached for trial. Singer v Singer (1970) 33 AD2d 1054, 308 NYS2d 714.

Where positions of various parties to consolidated arbitration were intertwined and situations were dependent to some extent on results in other of consolidated arbitrations, counterclaims would be restored and stay vacated so that arbitrators could have all claims and contentions before them. Beanuit Corp. v Solarset, Inc. (1976) 51 AD2d 926, 381 NYS2d 243, motion den 39 NY2d 825, 385 NYS2d 767, 351 NE2d 434.

Where individuals who made up partnership did not, other than as a partnership, agree to arbitrate, such individuals would be deemed excluded from consolidated arbitration to the extent any claims were asserted against them by corporation. Beanuit Corp. v Solarset, Inc. (1976) 51 AD2d 926, 381 NYS2d 243, motion den 39 NY2d 825, 385 NYS2d 767, 351 NE2d 434.

2. Conservation of time and expense

Under CPLR § 602, subd a and Real Property Tax Law § 710, a joint trial was ordered on issue of inequality to avoid delay inherent in trial of 24 separate actions, in all of which the same experts and essentially the same proof would be introduced on issues of inequality and value of property under review. 860 Executive Towers, Inc. Board of Assessors (1973) 75 Misc 2d 381, 347 NYS2d 795.

Where each complaint filed in two different counties alleged that subcontractor provided labor and services in connection with installation of baggage-handling system at airport but that contractor had failed to fully compensate the subcontractor, where one action was brought on main contract and the other on a contract for the performance of additional work, and where contractor's counterclaims in both actions alleged that the subcontractor breached the terms of the agreement and was negligent, and where contractor asserted in one of the actions that subcontractor, in total, owed more to contractor than was sought by subcontractor, joint trial was appropriate to avoid duplication. H. C. H. Contractors, Inc. v Docutel Corp. (1975) 47 AD2d 539, 363 NYS2d 112.

3. Effect of possible prejudice

A broad discretion is given court to make determinations as to which claims should be tried together and which should be severed, and as a general principle all issues having common questions of law or fact should be tried together; however, issues which might prejudice proper consideration of other issues or which by their very nature will inconvenience the court and the principal litigation should be severed. Axelrod & Co. v Telsey (1973) 77 Misc 2d 1035, 353 NYS2d 596.

A joint trial would not prejudice the substantial rights of any of the parties and consolidation was therefore granted where both causes of action arose from the same occurrence or series of occurrences and witnesses in both actions would be substantially the same. Sorrentino v First Nat. City Bank (1972) 40 AD2d 820, 338 NYS2d 233.

Circumstances surrounding first action which was for the recovery of damages for personal injuries allegedly sustained by plaintiff while a passenger in defendant's automobile and second to recover damages based on alleged fraud by the liability insurer of defendant motorist in obtaining an infant's compromise settlement were such as to mandate separate trials of the two actions, since the specific knowledge of dispute over insurance coverage would of necessity temper thinking of jury and unduly influence their verdict. McDavid v Gunnigle (1975) 50 AD2d 737, 377 NYS2d 5.

Where by consolidating two actions, evidence of defendant's settlement of one of them may be admissible upon the trial of the consolidated actions, and may impair his right to a fair trial, such consolidation should not be allowed. Bove v Medeo (1963) 19 AD2d 646, 241 NYS2d 907.

4. Common questions of law or fact, generally

In granting a joint trial, it is not required that all questions of law or fact be common to the various actions. Thayer v Collett (1973) 41 AD2d 581, 340 NYS2d 16.

Where plaintiff instituted separate actions to recover injuries allegedly resulting from two automobile accidents but was complaining of similar injuries from both accidents, trial court did not abuse its discretion in granting motion of one of

defendants for a joint trial. Thayer v Collett (1973) 41 AD2d 581, 340 NYS2d 16.

Where there are questions of law and fact, identical to both actions, the actions may be consolidated. Keenan v American Bridge Division-United States Steel Corp. (1968) 31 AD2d 637, 295 NYS2d 991.

Under this section consolidation cannot be ordered where there is no common question of law or fact between the two actions involved although a multiplicity of actions will be avoided and costs and expenses will be saved by the parties without any prejudice to either litigant. While it is not necessary that all rules and all facts be common to both actions, there must at least be some important rules of law and some substantial issues of fact to be determined that are common to both actions. Gibbons v Groat (1964) 22 AD2d 996, 254 NYS2d 843.

Consolidation of two actions was proper exercise of discretion where both involved determination of a central factual issue, namely the cause of a fire. Rockaway Boulevard Wrecking & Lumber Co. v Raylite Electric Corp. (1966) 25 AD2d 842, 270 NYS2d 1.

Consolidation of an action with a special proceeding under § 602(a) is proper when common questions of law or fact exist. Re Elias (1967) 29 AD2d 118, 286 NYS2d 371.

It was error to consolidate actions which involved different questions of law and fact, and which, although involving the same individuals, involved different corporations. Tylan, Ltd. v Cramer (1973) 41 AD2d 883, 342 NYS2d 926, app dismd 33 NY2d 1006, 353 NYS2d 967, 309 NE2d 429.

5. Causes and proceedings joinable

Action by contractor for reformation of construction contract on the ground of unusual, unforeseeable, and unknown conditions constituting a mutual mistake by the parties to the contract and cause of action set forth in cross claim incident to lien foreclosure action stated the same grounds for relief and should be consolidated rather than ordering dismissal of action for reformation. Stewart-Scott Constr. Corp. v F. & M. Schaefer Brewing Co. (1973) 41 AD2d 788, 341 NYS2d 269.

Claims of owner of building against building contractor and architect should be tried together. System Structures, Inc. v Blair Chevrolet, Inc. (1965) 24 AD2d 457, 260 NYS2d 396.

Where common questions of law and fact existed in plaintiff's action in Supreme Court for specific performance and in his summary proceeding to evict tenant of premises the two actions would be consolidated in the Supreme Court and tried together. Notarius v Hess Oil & Chemical Corp. (1968) 30 AD2d 663, 292 NYS2d 1.

While a motion to try three actions together established common question of law and fact between two actions for false arrest and malicious prosecution, but did not allude to any common question between them and the third action alleging the tort of interfering in contract, the Court of

Claims should have granted the motion for joint trials of false arrest and malicious prosecution, but not for a joint trial of the tort action. Perina v State (1971) 37 AD2d 882, 325 NYS2d 323

Where issue of title to premises in which partnership conducted its medical practice was involved in both action for dissolution of partnership and an accounting and summary proceeding pending in another court and plaintiff's claim as to title of premises was crucial to determining both actions, consolidation was proper to avoid multiplicity of suits. Weiss v Blau (1973) 42 AD2d 913, 347 NYS2d 603.

Four actions which all involved relationship of plaintiff and his corporation in an attempt to establish a medical clinic in real estate development were properly consolidated. Maigur v Saratogian, Inc. (1975) 47 AD2d 982, 367 NYS2d 114.

Where two actions for personal injuries and deaths arose out of the same accident and both actions, except as to damages, involve substantially the same issues of law and fact and if they were tried separately virtually the same witnesses would testify at both trials, the defendant's motion to consolidate the actions should be granted upon appropriate terms and conditions, where the plaintiffs fail to show that consolidation would prejudice any of their substantial rights. Burger v Long Island R. R. Co. (1965) 24 AD2d 510, 261 NYS2d 575, later app 28 AD2d 871, 281 NYS2d 944, app dismd 21 NY2d 716, 287 NYS2d 680, 234 NE2d 703.

Five personal injury actions arising out of a collision between an automobile and a bus should be consolidated, as they all arose out of the same accident, involved the same issues, except for the question of damages, and presumably the same witnesses. Pace v New York City Transit Authority (1963) 19 AD2d 630, 241 NYS2d 303.

Two actions, which embraced the same set of promissory notes, an action to cancel the notes and an action to recover upon them, were properly consolidated. Rae v Hotel Governor Clinton, Inc. (1965) 23 AD2d 564, 256 NYS2d 741.

An order directing the consolidation of three separate causes of action for trial was reversed, where certain issues in one of the actions differed from those in the other actions, and the motion for consolidation was not made until the first cause of action was ready for trial. Jacobson v Harte & Co. (1965) 23 AD2d 843, 259 NYS2d 467.

Although Supreme Court action had been instituted by service of summons without complaint and no complaint had been filed at time of filing of motion of defendant former husband to remove Family Court proceeding to Supreme Court and to consolidate it with pending plenary action, inasmuch as Supreme Court would have jurisdiction over whatever issues were raised and common questions of law and fact were clearly involved, the motion would be granted. Millard v Millard (1974) 44 AD2d 812, 355 NYS2d 610.

Where there existed common questions of law and fact in various arbitrations between partnership and corporations, consolidation was particularly appropriate. Beaunit Corp. v Solarset, Inc. (1976) 51 AD2d 926, 381 NYS2d 243, motion den 39 NY2d 825, 385 NYS2d 767, 351 NE2d 434.

Where insurer brought actions in name of tractor trailer owner, pursuant to subrogation agreement, against retailer and manufacturer of tractor trailer for moneys expended in repair and lost profits and tractor trailer owner brought action against the insurer for lost profits based on delay caused by insurer's decision to repair insured tractor rather than replace it, issue as to ultimate responsibility to owner of vehicle for alleged lost profits was a common question of fact common to both actions, and since insurer's mere allegation that its identity as insurance company would be disclosed upon joinder failed to demonstrate necessary prejudice, joint trial of both actions was proper. Wilhelmsen v Frank J. Bolan Sales, Inc. (1976) 54 AD2d 615, 387 NYS2d 756.

As both Article 78 proceedings, respectively brought in New York County and Albany County, involved common questions of law and fact concerning approval by health commissioner and insurance superintendent of Blue Cross rates of payment to petitioner hospitals for 1974 and the underlying determination of such rates by Blue Cross, as petitioners in the New York proceeding were voluntary hospitals in the metropolitan area, whereas petitioners in the Albany proceeding were proprietary hospitals in the same area, and as petitioners not only challenged the same administrative determinations but also based their claims on the same settlement agreement with Blue Cross, the Albany County proceeding would be ordered transferred to New York County and consolidated with the proceeding there. Beekman-Downtown Hospital v Whelan (1976) 88 Misc 2d 324, 387 NYS2d 758, revd on other grounds 57 AD2d 1, 392 NYS2d 878.

Trial court, in actions brought by owner of real property and principal tenant against several fire insurance companies, did not abuse discretion by directing joint trial of actions where all actions arose out of single incident and there were common questions of law and fact, and where defendants did not meet burden of establishing their claim of prejudice. 146 North Salina Street, Inc. v Unigard Jamestown Mut. Ins. Co. (1976) 54 AD2d 1129, 388 NYS2d 805.

6. Causes and proceedings not joinable

In Article 78 proceeding to direct city to issue a certificate of occupancy, to obtain a stay of landlord's summary proceeding, and for declaration of petitioner-tenant's right to quiet enjoyment, petition against non-city respondent was properly dismissed, there being a pending declaratory judgment action against landlord alone, properly denied further stay of summary proceeding, and properly required city to give notice whether a certificate of occupancy would issue; under such circumstances, joinder of declaratory judgment action with Article 78 proceeding would not ameliorate the procedural morass engendered by petitioner. Harlem River Consumers Cooperative, Inc. v Stein (1974) 44 AD2d 546, 353 NYS2d 768, app dismd 34 NY2d 993, 360 NYS2d 418, 318 NE2d 607.

This statute permits joinder only when a common question of law or fact is involved in the two actions, and court will not permit joinder of an action by liability insurance carrier against its insured for a declaratory judgment of nonliability based on failure of notice together with an action against the insured for personal injuries sustained. Bogucki v Mednis (1967) 54 Misc 2d 342, 282 NYS2d 814.

Where a question is raised as to the validity of a release or covenant not to sue in a negligence action, it is improper to join the adjudication of that claim with the primary claim for damages in negligence. Polmanteer v Nationwide Mut. Ins. Co. (1969) 60 Misc 2d 371, 303 NYS2d 146.

Where plaintiff's intestate suffered two identical falls from beds within twenty-four hours, the first occurring in a nursing home, and the second in a hospital, it was error to order that the two actions brought by the executor be tried together without consolidation, since there is no causality between the two accidents, and may involve different standards of care. Korn v Duhl (1964) 22 AD2d 793, 253 NYS2d 874.

Trial court did not abuse its discretion in denying a motion for joinder of an accounting proceeding with an involved fraud and conversion action. Re Houston's Trust (1968) 30 AD2d 999, 294 NYS2d 225.

Action for legal services in defending defendant in divorce action and action for legal services in prosecuting contract action for defendant cannot be consolidated under CPLR, because no important question of law or substantial issue of fact is common to both of them, no matter how desirable consolidation might be otherwise. Gibbons v Groat (1964) 22 AD2d 996, 254 NYS2d 843.

While a motion to try three actions together established common question of law and fact between two actions for false arrest and malicious prosecution, but did not allude to any common question between them and the third action alleging the tort of interfering in contract, the Court of Claims should have granted the motion for joint trials of false arrest and malicious prosecution, but not for a joint trial of the tort action. Perina v State (1971) 37 AD2d 882, 325 NYS2d 323.

Action to foreclose mortgage and previous action by another creditor to set aside deed of subject property as being in fraud of creditors did not involve common questions of law or fact, and where consolidation could not be ordered, in court's opinion, without prejudice to rights of plaintiff in foreclosure action, consolidation would not be ordered. Citibank (Mid-Hudson), N.A. v Rohdie (1975) 82 Misc 2d 372, 368 NYS2d 109.

Despite § 105(b) of the CPLR, context of this section requires that action should not be consolidated with special proceeding. Hanft v Hanft (1965) 46 Misc 2d 548, 260 NYS2d 104.

Arbitration under CPLR is not a special proceeding. Chariot Textiles Corp. v Wannalancit Textile Co. (1964) 21 AD2d 762, 250 NYS2d 493, revd on other grounds 18 NY2d 793, 275 NYS2d 382, 221 NE2d 913.

In the absence of medical proof showing the causal relationship between an accident and the subsequent death of plaintiff's intestate, a motion to consolidate a personal injury action and a wrongful death action may not be granted. Rubin v Grossman (1970) 34 AD2d 680, 310 NYS2d 395.

Supreme Court would not consolidate proceeding in Family Court for enforcement of New Jersey support order with action in Supreme Court for separation where different questions of law were involved in view of limitation placed by Domestic Relations Law § 236 on Supreme Court to order support of the wife only as an adjunct to the matrimonial action. Hanft v Hanft (1965) 46 Misc 2d 548, 260 NYS2d 104.

7. Joint trial without consolidation

Even though actions did not share common questions of law in fact which would permit them to be consolidated under statute, where it appeared that no prejudicial delay would result from a joint trial, interests of justice and judicial economy required that in particular instance all issues between parties be resolved as expeditiously as possible in one forum, and thus an immediate joint trial was directed. Gindi v Gindi (1974) 46 AD2d 650, 359 NYS2d 689.

Joint trial without consolidation of two actions wherein plaintiff sought recovery for injuries received in separate automobile accidents was properly allowed in the trial court's discretion since there was no showing of prejudice and since only five days separated the two accidents. Wyatt v Jensen (1966) 25 AD2d 388, 270 NYS2d 156.

Although claimant's motion to consolidate seven claims arising out of seven separate highway contracts was denied, where questions of fact as to at least part of each claim would be substantially the same and it could be assumed that the same witnesses may be used and identical questions of law may be determined in the various claims, it was ordered the claims be tried jointly with the understanding that the law and facts in each case would be considered separately and separate decisions made. Amadeus, Inc. v State (1967) 52 Misc 2d 834, 277 NYS2d 6.

8. Removal to or from supreme court

Supreme Court of Ulster County where one action was venued had jurisdiction to order joint trial, without consolidation, of five actions, four of which were venued in other counties, and to determine venue for trial. Velasquez v Pine Grove Resort Ranch, Inc. (1974) 77 Misc 2d 329, 354 NYS2d 65.

Supreme Court may remove to itself an action pending in another court for joint trial even though it is pending in another judicial department. Blank v Meadow Park Clothes, Inc. (1968) 57 Misc 2d 305, 292 NYS2d 581.

The Supreme Court's power of removal is limited to cases where the court in which the action is pending lacks jurisdiction to grant the relief sought, and the Supreme Court may consolidate inferior actions only where one of them is removed to the Supreme Court. Currierc v Roeill (1967) 55 Misc 2d 1049, 287 NYS2d 747.

9. Removal to or from county or other local court

Trial court was justified in granting defendant's motion to remove action to Queens County so as to permit it to be tried jointly with two other pending actions where there was sufficient questions of law or fact common to all actions and where plaintiff failed to establish that it would be substantially prejudiced by a joint trial. Washington Federal Sav. & Loan Asso. v Village Mall Townhouse, Inc. (1976) 53 AD2d 611, 384 NYS2d 18.

Special term did not abuse its discretion in denying plaintiff's motion to remove from Civil Court two personal injury negligence actions arising out of two unrelated automobile accidents and to consolidate such actions for joint trial in the Supreme Court and to increase the ad damnum to $1,000,000, since argument that inordinate delay in bringing motion was due to his failure to receive an updated medical report was unpersuasive; also, the Civil Court was proper forum to apply for a joint trial if plaintiff could persuade that court that such action would obviate a waste of judicial time and expense. Hill v Smalls (1975) 49 AD2d 724, 373 NYS2d 134, app dismd 38 NY2d 893, 382 NYS2d 749, 346 NE2d 550.

Where, after defendant had commenced action for breach of construction contract against plaintiff in justice court, plaintiff brought action against defendant in county court seeking to recover $5,500 for defendant's alleged breach of the same contract and defendant failed to show that granting of plaintiff's motion to have action pending in justice court removed to county court and consolidated with action pending therein would result in delay prejudicial to defendant, plaintiff was equitably entitled to the removal and consolidation and granting of plaintiff's motion did not constitute abuse of discretion. Spycher v Andrew (1976) 55 AD2d 715, 388 NYS2d 725.

10. Venue

Where action brought in Orange County and action brought in Sullivan County one year earlier had both arisen out of same accident in Sullivan County, and presented common factual questions, it was a proper exercise of discretion to direct a joint trial in Sullivan County. Liotta v Pollack (1964) 21 AD2d 934, 251 NYS2d 59.

Even though first action was commenced in Kings County and plaintiffs alleged that they and other witnesses resided within Kings County, where cause of action arose in Ulster County, law enforcement and public officials whom defendants sought to call as witnesses lived in Ulster County

and calendar in Ulster County was less congested than calendars in New York County or Kings County, venue for joint trial of actions would be in Ulster County. Velasquez v Pine Grove Resort Ranch, Inc. (1974) 77 Misc 2d 329, 354 NYS2d 65.

Where, following a golf cart accident, plaintiff brought suit for her injuries in New York County and defendant instituted an action for property damage to its golf cart in Sullivan County, and undisputed proof revealed that plaintiff was paralyzed from the waist down as a result of the accident and that a great hardship would result if she must travel to a distant place and live there during the trial, New York County was selected as the proper venue. The court held that Special Term had great discretion in selecting the venue when consolidation is granted pursuant to CPLR 602, and that all of the factors which relate to a discretionary change of venue under CPLR 510 are relevant to the exercise of such discretion. Kiamesha Concord, Inc. v Greenman (1968) 29 AD2d 904, 287 NYS2d 972.

In consolidating three causes of action arising from a truck-train collision for trial in Erie County, the Special Term properly considered that no note of issue had been filed in the first action pending in Tioga County and could not be filed until all depositions were completed, that no party or witness resided in Tioga County, that decedent at the time of the accident was a resident of Erie County, that decedent's administratrix was a resident of and appointed by Erie County Court, and that calendar procedure in Erie County would permit immediate filing of a note of issue and less elapsed time until trial. Linton v Lehigh V. R. Co. (1969) 32 AD2d 148, 300 NYS2d 468.

Where consolidation of actions begun in different counties is laid, the venue should be in the county where jurisdiction was first invoked. Maccabee v Nangle (1970) 33 AD2d 918, 307 NYS2d 509.

Consolidation of two related actions between the parties for trial in the county in which jurisdiction was first invoked, where the trial date was only delayed three months, was proper, although the case could have been brought to trial in approximately six weeks in the second county. Poly Constr. Corp. v Oxford Hall Contracting Corp. (1965) 24 AD2d 637, 262 NYS2d 206.

In general the consolidation involving actions pending in different counties shall be effectuated in the county which first obtained jurisdiction. Rae v Hotel Governor Clinton, Inc. (1965) 23 AD2d 564, 256 NYS2d 741.

It was improper to place venue of consolidated action in county different than that in which jurisdiction of original action had been invoked. Tylan, Ltd. v Cramer (1973) 41 AD2d 883, 342 NYS2d 926, app dismd 33 NY2d 1006, 353 NYS2d 967, 309 NE2d 429.

Where defendant's motion to place venue of two actions which had been consolidated for joint trial in Warren County was made under provision relating to consolidation, and where Warren

County courthouse was within 30 miles of courthouse in county selected by plaintiffs for trial, requisite special circumstances that would compel designation of county other than one of those selected by plaintiffs as place for trial did not exist, and motion was properly denied. Newell v Niagara Mohawk Power Corp. (1976) 52 AD2d 664, 381 NYS2d 908.

11. Jurisdiction

Trial court's granting of motion to consolidate a summary proceeding instituted against it with plaintiff's court action for a declaratory judgment was improper where the civil court had jurisdiction over plaintiff's defense. Lun Far Co. v Ayles-bury Associates (1972) 40 AD2d 794, 338 NYS2d 84.

12. Right to open or close

Appellant electric corporation's greater diligence in the substantial prosecution of its action entitled it to open and close in consolidated action. Rockaway Boulevard Wrecking & Lumber Co. v Raylite Electric Corp. (1966) 25 AD2d 842, 270 NYS2d 1.

It is usual practice for a judge who directs consolidation, as distinguished from direction for joint trial, to also determine order of opening and closing statements. Rockaway Boulevard Wrecking & Lumber Co. v Raylite Electric Corp. (1966) 25 AD2d 842, 270 NYS2d 1.

CASE NOTES

UNDER FORMER CIVIL PRACTICE LAWS

A. IN GENERAL

1. Generally

CPA §§ 96 and 97 were to be read together and the provisions of CPA § 96 safeguarding the substantial rights of a party were to be read into CPA § 97, and made to apply to all consolidations. Brink's Express Co. v Burns (1930) 230 AD 559, 245 NYS 649.

CPA § 110-a (§ 325(b) herein) dealt with removal of action to Supreme Court where no action was pending, whereas CPA § 97 dealt with motion to transfer to Supreme Court, and to consolidate with action already there, cause previously instituted and pending in another court. Helfgott v Tannen (1955) 208 Misc 335, 141 NYS2d 307.

CPA §§ 96, 96-a and 97 controlled procedure for consolidation of trial together of actions or special proceedings, and were to be read together. Hartmann v Dakins (1953, Sup) 123 NYS2d 441.

Proceeding in Surrogate's Court of Onondaga County for construction of will and for accounting in trust involved by trustees of Syracuse University was consolidated with proceeding in Supreme Court on application by Syracuse University for authority to pay to State University income from endowment bequeathed in said will to petitioner. Re Hendricks' Will (1955) 1 Misc 2d 904, 148 NYS2d 245, affd 3 AD2d 890, 161 NYS2d 855, affd 4 NY2d 744, 171 NYS2d 863, 148 NE2d 911.

2. Purpose of section

The purpose of CPA § 96 was to eliminate technicalities, multiplicities of action and delays and to protect substantial rights. Datz v Economy Cotton Goods Stores, Inc. (1934) 263 NY 252, 188 NE 728.

The liberal provisions of this section are not to be limited by strict or literal construction, or by reason of mechanical difficulties. The purpose of CPA § 96 and many others was to commit to the courts a wide discretion in the administration of litigated business. Uterhart v National Bank of Far Rockaway (1938) 255 AD 859, 7 NYS2d 507.

The effect of CPA § 96, especially when read with CPA § 258 (§§ 601, 603, Rule 3014 herein), was to liberalize practice as much as possible and to remove technical restrictions upon administration of justice. Wegner Canning Corp. v Wegner (1942, Sup) 33 NYS2d 443.

Divergent decision in each separate case is prevented. Philip Shlansky & Bro., Inc. v Grossman (1948) 273 AD 544, 78 NYS2d 127.

Intent of Legislature in permitting severance and consolidation of actions wherever it can be done without prejudice to substantial right was to provide for greater flexibility and freedom for prompt administration of justice within sound discretion of court. C. W. Lauman & Co. v State (1956) 2 Misc 2d 693, 153 NYS2d 813.

The court has power in a proper case to consolidate actions whether equitable or legal. Wooster v Case (1890, Sup) 12 NYS 769.

Present tendency is to permit consolidation whenever possible and irrespective of diversity of issues involved. Hartmann v Dakins (1953, Sup) 123 NYS2d 441.

Present tendency is to permit consolidation unless it be shown that same will cause party to suffer loss of substantial right, and burden of proving prejudice rests upon party objecting to consolidation. Edelstein v Hacker (1956, Co Ct) 152 NYS2d 525.

B. JOINT TRIAL OF ACTIONS

3. Generally

Whether joint trial of separate actions will be ordered depends upon discretion of court; joint trial will usually not be ordered if substantial right of one of parties is placed in jeopardy, or if actions do not grow out of same set of facts. Neuwirth v Feeley (1956, Sup) 148 NYS2d 678, affd 1 AD2d 879, 150 NYS2d 773.

CPA § 96-a was not applicable to actions by materialman or laborers under Heard Act. United States use of Johnson v Morley Constr. Co. (1935, DC NY) 20 F Supp 606.

An attempt to combine proceedings for leave to sell property of an incompetent, under article 82 of the Civil Practice Act, with proceedings for the exchange, under section 116 of the Real Property Law, was not unauthorized. Seitz Estates, Inc. v Medico Bros., Inc (1936) 247 AD 71, 286 NYS 833, affd 272 NY 492, 3 NE2d 884.

Wife's action for purchase price of sheep sold and husband's action for work and labor, both against same defendant, held not to grow out of same set of facts, and were improperly ordered tried together. Newton v Newton (1942) 263 AD 197, 33 NYS2d 252.

In proceedings against many physicians to revoke for their misconduct authorization to render medical care under Work Comp L involving common questions of fact, all physicians affected may be grouped in single proceeding and on hearing witnesses may testify only once. Sacharoff v Murphy (1943) 182 Misc 235, 44 NYS2d 117, affd 268 AD 765, 50 NYS2d 168, revd on other grounds Sacharoff v Corsi (1945) 294 NY 305, 62 NE2d 81, cert den 326 US 744, 90 L Ed 445, 66 S Ct 59.

Action in county court was ordered tried without consolidation with later action in supreme court by occupant of colliding car, suing individually and as administratrix of husband. Sternlicht v Wesling (1947) 188 Misc 567, 68 NYS2d 390.

Where many tenants sue landlord for damages from same act or omission, but some leases waived jury trial, individual summons should be served, followed by motion for joint trial. Kushin v Delbro Estates, Inc. (1948, Mun Ct) 78 NYS2d 446.

Where actions were pending in different counties, order directing joint trial should fix venue in county first invoked. James v Buhrmaster (1948) 273 AD 836, 75 NYS2d 777.

CPA §§ 96, 96-a, 97 controlled procedure for consolidation or trial together of actions or special proceedings, and were read together. Hartmann v Dakins (1953, Sup) 123 NYS2d 441.

Consolidation of default action was not within meaning or intent of CPA § 96-a. Stafford v Johnson (1953, Sup) 122 NYS2d 779.

Where rights of respective defendants can more easily be presented to jury, it is better practice to try together separate actions for death against drivers of colliding cars, rather than to consolidate them, where defendants are represented by different counsel. McNamara v Penner (1953, Sup) 123 NYS2d 576.

State's motion to consolidate claims against state for taking of property for highway purposes, or for joint trial thereof, was denied where some of the claimants showed that they would be prejudiced by resulting delay. Levin v State (1960) 22 Misc 2d 443, 201 NYS2d 915.

Because claims by manufacturer against supplier necessarily differed from those of its customer against it, since the warranties made by each of the parties differed, consolidation was not appropriate, but a joint trial would be ordered in the interests of justice. Hercz v Geo. W. Millar & Co. (1960) 10 AD2d 611, 196 NYS2d 159.

Where two actions arose out of same automobile action, and plaintiffs in first action were granted summary judgment and date had been set for assessment of damages, court denied motion for plaintiffs in second action for permission to intervene, or for consolidation, or joint trials, or for stay of assessment until second action was brought to judgment since to do so would prejudice rights of plaintiffs in first action. David v Bauman (1960) 24 Misc 2d 67, 196 NYS2d 746.

Although motion requested consolidation but concluded with prayer "for such other and further relief as may be just and proper", court ordered joint trial where it believed cases would be more easily understood by jury if tried jointly rather than being organically consolidated. Smith v Witteman Co. (1960) 10 AD2d 793, 197 NYS2d 877.

A special proceeding and an action cannot be jointly tried, there being no statutory authority therefor. Hewlett Developers, Inc. v Frisina (1962) 32 Misc 2d 911, 224 NYS2d 587.

4. Matrimonial actions

A husband's action for annulment and a wife's action for separation may properly be tried together. White v White (1936) 246 AD 879, 284 NYS2d 857.

Divorce actions between different parties, cannot be said to have grown "out of same set of facts," and so cannot be tried together. Hoffman v Hoffman (1945) 269 AD 759, 54 NYS2d 896.

5. Review of assessments

Review of assessments on thirty-seven separate parcels of property properly joined in single proceeding to review assessments by certiorari. People ex rel. Michael J. Adrian Corp. v Sexton (1937) 251 AD 181, 295 NYS 542.

The provisions of CPA § 96(a) applied to proceedings to review tax assessments. Allen v Rizzardi (1959) 5 NY2d 493, 186 NYS2d 225, 158 NE2d 813; O'Brien v Village Assessor (1962) 35 Misc 2d 204, 225 NYS2d 389.

6. Costs

Separate bills of cost are allowable in cases tried together but not consolidated. Benjamin v Walch (1936) 160 Misc 39, 288 NYS 458.

Costs are taxed in joint trial of separate actions as in initial causes and courts. Vidal v Sheffield Farms Co. (1955) 208 Misc 438, 141 NYS2d 82.

Defendant, in whose favor a jury returned verdicts of no cause of action in each of six actions, was entitled to separate bills of costs in each action where actions, which arose out of the same set of facts, were not consolidated but were tried together, as provided by CPA § 96-a. Plaintiffs could have avoided that liability by becoming co-plaintiffs in one action. Brown v Cohan (1938) 254 AD 20, 4 NYS2d 883.

7. Joint tort feasors

Two separate actions by same plaintiff against two separate defendants involving two independent accidents occurring nine months apart, where issues are not precisely same and where liability problem in each accident is unique and separate, should not be tried together. Gamble v Fraleigh (1955) 1 Misc 2d 347, 146 NYS2d 146.

Where plaintiff may sue one or more joint tortfeasors, one such defendant is not entitled to joint trial with codefendant. Turk v Beebe Service Corp. (1943) 267 AD 767, 45 NYS2d 224.

Plaintiff's action against driver of automobile which struck him and his action against the owners and operators of ambulance and truck which collided while he was being taken to the hospital in the ambulance after the first accident were not two actions growing out of the same set of facts and could not be tried jointly. Abbatepaolo v Blumberg (1959) 7 AD2d 847, 182 NYS2d 83.

8. Stockholders' suits

Where derivative stockholders' actions were distinct causes, arising out of interrelated facts, they were directed to be tried jointly. Hayman v Morris (1943, Sup) 46 NYS2d 482.

Stockholders' derivative actions were ordered to be tried jointly without consolidation where attorneys could not agree as to general counsel. Price v Creole Petroleum Corp (1944, Sup) 51 NYS2d 783.

Chronology or priority in commencement of stockholders' derivative actions should not be decisive in determining which party or group of attorneys is to control progress of respective cases. Neuwirth v Feeley (1956, Sup) 148 NYS2d 678, affd 1 AD2d 879, 150 NYS2d 773.

9. Opening and closing

The right to open and close in joint trial of separate issues may be left to determination at trial. Vidal v Sheffield Farms Co. (1955) 208 Misc 438, 141 NYS2d 82.

Opening and closing may follow in reverse order. Sternlicht v Wesling (1947) 188 Misc 567, 68 NYS2d 390.

Where as result of an automobile collision two actions were commenced, the first in Bronx county and the second some time later in New York county, joint trial was ordered in Bronx county, and plaintiffs in Bronx action were accorded opportunity to open and close. Spadaccini v New York (1960) 9 AD2d 502, 195 NYS2d 666.

10. Preferences

Preference of one action extends to and includes all other actions tried together. Sternlicht v Wesling (1947) 188 Misc 567, 68 NYS2d 390.

11. Identity of issues

The fact that all issues are not identical is no bar to consolidation for trial. Rhode Island Hospital Trust Co. v Claude Neon, Inc. (1952) 203 Misc 531, 117 NYS2d 83.

Substantial identity of factual issues makes consolidation for trial desirable, as where one action is to recover on promissory notes and other is for return of shares of stock and there is fraud counterclaim in each which is identical against principal and agent as tort-feasors. Rhode Island Hospital Trust Co. v Claude Neon, Inc., supra.

Where evidentiary proof involved in one case differs radically from evidence to be deduced in another case, claims involved are dissimilar with respect to issues involved and basis of liability, barring joint trial. Neuwirth v Feeley (1956, Sup) 148 NYS2d 678, affd 1 AD2d 879, 150 NYS2d 773.

Action by tenant against subtenant for breach of covenant for return of property, subject only to wear and tear, and action by subtenant against insurers on floater policies covering all risks of loss or damage to subtenant's personal effects in leased premises, presented divergence of issues barring joint trial of actions. Blum v Arnstein (1954) 284 AD 682, 134 NYS2d 565.

Where the claims asserted by one defendant do not grow out of the same set of facts as the breaches alleged against defendant by its customer in another action, there is not sufficient identity of the issues to warrant consolidation for the purposes of trial where even if all the claims arose out of the same defects, the warranties made by each of the parties differed. Texilon Co. v Kaiserman (1957) 3 AD2d 743, 160 NYS2d 556.

While there may be one fundamental issue common to each complaint, where there are different transactions involving each plaintiff which may override the one issue that is common to all of them in a contract action, granting of relief provided for under CPA § 96-a as a matter of discretion was not warranted. Tannenbaum v Bangor Mills, Inc. (1957) 3 AD2d 698, 159 NYS2d 76.

Where it is apparent from pleadings that both cases have closely related questions of law and fact, a joint trial will serve the interests of justice and will not prejudice any substantial rights of the parties. South Ridge Corp. v Amsinck Sonne Corp. (1958) 6 AD2d 776, 174 NYS2d 1018, reh and app den 6 AD2d 866, 175 NYS2d 1023.

Joint trial of action for damages for breach of contract to purchase drug store and action by purchaser to recover deposit because of fraud in the inducement to said contract, may be directed without consolidation, in the interests of economy of time, upon condition that the joint trial proceed immediately if plaintiff so elects. Goldsleger v Weiss (1959) 9 AD2d 58, 190 NYS2d 824.

Where issue of fraud is common to two actions, they can properly be directed to be tried together, but to avoid prejudice such common issue should be separated from other issues and tried first. Abelow v Equitable Life Assur. Soc. (1959) AD2d 745, 192 NYS2d 663.

Where two actions arising out of same automobile collision and involving same questions of fact were pending in Supreme Court of different counties, court ordered a joint trial. Spadaccini v New York (1960) 9 AD2d 502, 195 NYS2d 666.

Joint trial of actions for brokers' commissions will be ordered where both actions involve common issues, the same witnesses and same property, and no prejudicial delay will result. David Vogel, Inc. v Spraker (1961) 12 AD2d 744, 209 NYS2d 87.

12. County for trial

County of accident is proper county for joint trial of two actions for same automobile accident against same defendant where defendant first invoked joint trial in such county. Seekamp v Derdiger (1954, Sup) 133 NYS2d 528.

Where two actions arising out of automobile collision in New York County were pending in Bronx County and New York County, and the Bronx action had been begun first and was ready to be reached for trial, the fact that New York City was a defendant in the New York action did not prevent the court, in the exercise of its discretion, from fixing venue for the joint trial of the action in Bronx County. Spadaccini v New York (1960) 9 AD2d 502, 195 NYS2d 666.

13. Titles of actions

Where parties desire joint trial as distinguished from organic joinder, respective titles of several actions, are continued as in each separate action, and same parties are continued as plaintiffs and defendants without change. Vidal v Sheffield Farms Co. (1955) 208 Misc 438, 141 NYS2d 82.

14. Verdict

In joint trial of separate actions separate verdicts

are necessarily rendered. Vidal v Sheffield Farms Co. (1955) 208 Misc 438, 141 NYS2d 82.

15. Judgment

Individual judgments are entered in each action, on joint trial of separate actions. Vidal v Sheffield Farms Co. (1955) 208 Misc 438, 141 NYS2d 82.

16. Prejudice developing at trial

Where a situation of prejudice arises at a joint trial of two actions, the trial judge can direct separate trials if that will solve the problem, notwithstanding special term's order of joint trial. Bivins v Bivins (1960) 10 AD2d 739, 197 NYS2d 490 (where judgment was reversed and new trial ordered).

C. CONSOLIDATION OF ACTIONS

17. Generally

CPA § 96 was to be liberally construed to eliminate technicalities and multiplicity of suits. Hartmann v Dakins (1953, Sup) 123 NYS2d 441; and so as to permit consolidation wherever possible without injustice to any party. Bershadsky v Harvilla (1951) 279 AD 701, 108 NYS2d 329.

Consolidation of actions should only be granted in cases where issues are so similar or are between same parties, or such similar parties, that consolidation will not work injustice to any of litigants who may be involved, no matter how large or small claim of that litigant may be. Garber v Glassman (1956, Sup) 154 NYS2d 479.

The only limitation upon the power of courts to consolidate actions is where it prejudices a substantial right. Priority of action and right to open and close are to be taken into consideration. Lee v Schmeltzer (1930) 229 AD 206, 242 NYS 34; Scocil v Moab Realty Corp. (1930) 229 AD 756, 242 NYS 39.

CPA §§ 96, 96-a, 97 controlled procedure for consolidation or trial together of actions and special proceedings, and should be read together. Hartmann v Dakins (1953, Sup) 123 NYS2d 441.

Object of consolidating actions is to avoid a multiplicity of suits, to guard against oppression or abuse, to prevent delay and to save unnecessary costs and expenses. Hull v Shannon (1931) 139 Misc 564, 249 NYS 33, mod 234 AD 648, 251 NYS 960.

Consolidation of actions is proper whether it may prevent duplication of trials or parts thereof and no substantial right is prejudiced. Scherman v Scherman (1941) 261 AD 908, 25 NYS2d 301.

The purpose of CPA § 96 was to facilitate and expedite trials and the court had a wide latitude of discretion in its application, which should not be exercised to defeat the purpose unless consolidation would result in prejudice to some party. Boyce v Mariano (1928) 132 Misc 623, 230 NYS 408.

Under former CPA 96 the fact that actions involve different principles of law did not preclude consolidation. Hartmann v Dakins (1953, Sup) 123 NYS2d 441; White v Boston & M. R. R. Co.

(1953) 204 Misc 672, 126 NYS2d 787, affd 283 AD 482, 129 NYS2d 15.

Consolidation is peculiarly appropriate where relief sought in one action can constitute offset to that in second action. Tufor Realty Corp. v Equity Express, Inc. (1953, City Ct) 120 NYS2d 693.

Consolidations are naturally favored by courts to save time of litigants, witnesses, attorneys and courts themselves in unnecessary duplicative proceedings and trials, thus expediting easing of calendar congestion, and at same time avoiding possible inconsistency of verdicts or decisions resulting from separate trials. Witzke v Doyle (1955) 3 Misc 2d 323, 146 NYS2d 515.

Consolidation is permissible where common questions of law and fact are involved when it may be done without prejudice to a substantial right. Lamborn v Czarnikow-Rionda Co. (1929) 227 AD 72, 237 NYS 69.

Consolidation should be permitted where the issues are the same. Erlandsen v Weise (1930) 231 AD 846, 246 NYS 488; Brown v Martin (1930) 231 AD 845, 246 NYS 803.

Under the peculiar circumstances of the case, plaintiff's motion to consolidate would have expedited matters and should have been granted. Von Wilmowsky v Prindle (1929) 225 AD 594, 234 NYS 15.

Consolidation ordered, to escape the necessity of two trials involving the same parties and the same cause of action, and to avoid giving to either party the advantage of a first trial of his action. Kelly v Hilbert (1922) 200 AD 489, 193 NYS 263.

Review of assessments on thirty-seven separate parcels of property properly joined in single proceeding to review assessments by certiorari. People ex rel. Michael J. Adrian Corp. v Sexton (1937) 251 AD 181, 295 NYS 542.

Where it is affirmatively shown that substantial prejudice to any party may result from consolidation or joint trial, consolidation will not be permitted. Witzke v Doyle (1955) 3 Misc 2d 323, 146 NYS2d 515.

An action by stockholders for rescission of releases and consents to exchange and reclassification of stock may be consolidated with a derivative action for an accounting. Abrahams v Bachmann (1933) 238 AD 320, 264 NYS 131.

Action for goods sold and money loaned to defendants developing property and action for services rendered and equipment furnished to defendants properly consolidated. Hurley v Rose (1934) 264 NY 484, 191 NE 527.

Action to rescind contract for fraud should not be consolidated with special proceeding to compel arbitration where party's rights to immediate trial of preliminary issue of fraud in making of contract to arbitrate would be lost. Big W. Constr. Corp. v Horowitz (1951) 278 AD 977, 105 NYS2d 827.

Two causes of action brought by the same plaintiff, one action based on breach of contract against one of the defendant companies, the stock ownership of which is controlled by the other corporate defendant, and the second action based on the second defendant's alleged inducement of the claimed breach, will be consolidated. Consolidated Dairy Products Co. v Loft (1935) 155 Misc 771, 280 NYS 935.

Where two actions have been brought against the same defendant the court had power under CPA § 96 to consolidate them before an answer was interposed upon an affidavit by the defendant that there was a counterclaim which existed, and going to the whole of plaintiff's demand. Perkins v Merchants' Lithographing Co. (1897) 21 Misc 516, 47 NYS 712, affd 21 Misc 793, 51 NYS 1148.

Where different actions have been brought by creditors, in behalf of themselves and the other creditors, against an assignee for the benefit of creditors, for an accounting and closing of the trust, the court has power to make an order to compel all the creditors to come in and prove their claims in the action first brought, or the action wherein interlocutory judgment is first obtained, and to stay all proceedings in the other actions. Travis v Myers (1876) 67 NY 542.

Where several causes of action, made the basis of separate suits between the same parties, are essentially the same, arising out of the same contract and are to be proved by substantially the same evidence, a consolidation of such actions will be required to prevent unnecessary harassment of the defendant, particularly where such defendant makes affidavit that it does not intend to defend any of such actions. Sullivan County v Downie (1917) 102 Misc 348, 168 NYS 923, affd 185 AD 918, 171 NYS 1082, affd 171 NYS 1082.

Causes of actions of individual plaintiffs, suing for overtime compensation, may be united in one action, although no one individual had any financial interest in recovery of any other. Mabee v White Plains Pub. Co. (1943) 180 Misc 8, 41 NYS2d 534, revd on other grounds 267 AD 284, 45 NYS2d 479, affd 293 NY 781, 58 NE2d 520, remittitur amd 295 NY 937, 68 NE2d 38 and amd 296 NY 527, 68 NE2d 604 and revd on other grounds 327 US 178, 90 L Ed 607, 66 S Ct 511, conformed to 271 AD 1026, 68 NYS2d 906.

In proceedings against many physicians to revoke for their misconduct authorization to render medical care under Workmen's CA, involving common questions of fact, all physicians affected may be grouped in single proceeding and on hearing witnesses may testify only once. Sacharoff v Murphy (1943) 182 Misc 235, 44 NYS2d 117, affd 268 AD 765, 50 NYS2d 168, revd on other grounds Sacharoff v Corsi (1945) 294 NY 305, 62 NE2d 81, cert den 326 US 744, 90 L Ed 445, 66 S Ct 59.

Motion to consolidate actions was denied, where complaint in one action failed to state cause of action. Sommer v Kenin (1945, Sup) 58 NYS2d 763.

Where defendant in one action is in default, and trial is unnecessary, plaintiff may introduce proof and obtain default judgment. Stafford v Johnson (1953, Sup) 122 NYS2d 779.

An action and a special proceeding involving entirely different issues and between different parties may not be consolidated. Re Murray's Estate (1936) 248 AD 167, 288 NYS 346, revd on other grounds 272 NY 228, 5 NE2d 717.

Diversity of parties and of claims, and lack of relation between transaction out of which claims arose, and lack of cause of action in particular plaintiffs, barred consolidation of actions in supreme and municipal courts. Sommer v Kenin (1945, Sup) 58 NYS2d 536.

CPA §§ 96 and 97 were to be read together and the provision safeguarding the substantial rights of a party were to be read into CPA § 97, and made to apply to all consolidations. Brink's Express Co. v Burns (1930) 230 AD 559, 245 NYS 649.

Under CPA § 96 plaintiff who failed to consolidate actions susceptible, was entitled to costs of but one action. Tubin v Springfield Fire & Marine Ins. Co. (1928) 222 AD 852, 227 NYS 173.

Where defendant contends that claimant's rights are joint, motion to add party under Rule CP 102 (Rule 3024(a) herein) and not motion to consolidate actions under CPA § 96 was proper remedy. Donzella v New York State Thruway Authority (1958) 7 AD2d 771, 180 NYS2d 108.

The provisions of CPA § 96 applied to consolidation of proceedings to review tax assessments, as well as to their severance. Allen v Rizzardi (1959) 5 NY2d 493, 186 NYS2d 225, 158 NE2d 813; O'Brien v Village Assessor (1962) 35 Misc 2d 204, 225 NYS2d 389.

An action and a special proceeding may not be consolidated, there being no statutory authority therefor. Hewlett Developers, Inc. v Frisina (1962) 32 Misc 2d 911, 224 NYS2d 587.

Ordinarily where trial of one action, which was diligently commenced, is imminent, a motion to consolidate other actions with it will be denied; but where no lengthy delay or prejudice will result, consolidation will be permitted. Simplex Plumbing Supply Co. v Bonded Heat & Power Corp. (1959) 20 Misc 2d 652, 193 NYS2d 894.

Because claims by manufacturer against supplier necessarily differed from those of its customer against it, since the warranties made by each of the parties differed, consolidation was not appropriate, but a joint trial would be ordered in the interests of justice. Hercz v Geo. W. Millar & Co. (1960) 10 AD2d 611, 196 NYS2d 159.

CPA § 96 had been construed as applying only to consolidation with actions pending in same court. Application of Elliotte (1960) 28 Misc 2d 677, 209 NYS2d 506.

18. Motions to consolidate

Notice of motion to consolidate actions is necessary. Williams v Williams (1945) 268 AD 1070, 52 NYS2d 813.

Although the usual procedure is to bring motions to consolidate before Special Term, there is nothing in the law which prohibits the making of such motion at the Trial Term. Nor must a motion to consolidate necessarily be made by the defendant, although customarily made by such party. Consolidated Dairy Products Co. v Loft (1935) 155 Misc 771, 280 NYS 935.

The moving party, if defendant, must disclose the nature of the defenses in the suits, or that they were the same in each action, or fully set forth that the questions involved were the same in each action. Campbell Printing Press & Mfg. Co. v Lyddy, 1 Civ Proc 364.

Pending the determination of defendant's motion to consolidate two actions brought against him by plaintiff, plaintiff moved for judgment in each case upon the ground that the answers were frivolous. Plaintiff's motions for judgment were granted and defendant's motion for consolidation denied at the same time. On appeal the orders for judgment were reversed, after which amended answers were served, materially changing the facts relevant to the matter of consolidation. Held, that defendant was entitled to renew his motion for consolidation, notwithstanding his omission to appeal from the denial of the former order. German Exchange Bank v Kroder (1895) 14 Misc 179, 35 NYS 380.

Although motion requested consolidation but concluded with prayer "for such other and further relief as may be just and proper", court ordered joint trial where it believed cases would be more easily understood by jury if tried jointly rather than being organically consolidated. Smith v Witteman Co. (1960) 10 AD2d 793, 197 NYS2d 877.

19. Discretion of court

Independently of statute, the court, in the exercise of discretion, may consolidate actions or stay one or more actions pending the determination of other actions. Pollak v Long Island Lighting Co. (1935) 246 AD 765, 283 NYS 913.

— The discretion of the court in granting or denying motions to consolidate causes of action should not be interfered with unless it is clear that substantial injustice will be done by allowing the consolidation. The burden of showing that substantial injustice will follow a consolidation of causes of action rests upon the party objecting to the consolidation. Crandall v A. B. Leach & Co. (1927) 222 AD 292, 225 NYS 649.

The consolidation of actions between the same parties, under CPA § 96 and § 97 rested in the sound discretion of the court to which application is made. Argyle Co. v Griffith (1908) 128 AD 262, 112 NYS 773.

The problem of consolidation is discretionary, but exercise of discretion should properly be limited to tribunal which will try action. Application of Comfort-Zone Corp. (1955, Sup) 140 NYS2d 76.

In actions by two insurance agents for commissions on same insurance premiums, denial of insurer's motion to consolidate two actions was not improvident abuse of discretion where finding in prior action had different effects on plaintiffs' actions. Hauth v Equitable Life Assur. Soc. (1942) 263 AD 1018, 33 NYS2d 930.

Denial of motion to consolidate three actions based on slander and libel was not improvident

exercise of discretion under facts and circumstances of case. Cullom v Kadel (1954) 283 AD 964, 130 NYS2d 660.

A motion to consolidate two actions by force of the provisions of CPA § 96 was addressed to the sound discretion of the court which could impose such conditions as the plaintiff be permitted to elect with which action the other be consolidated and that defendant stipulate that he would not raise the question that the two causes of action were improperly joined. Mason v Evening Star Newspaper Co. (1901) 35 Misc 77, 71 NYS 203, affd 67 AD 619, 73 NYS 1140.

Where one action is commenced by majority stockholders and a second action is commenced by minority stockholders but on the issues the minority stockholders' action has been or will become academic, a motion to consolidate such actions denied. Marine Midland Trust Co. v Forty Wall Street Corp. (1958) 10 Misc 2d 34, 171 NYS2d 784.

It was an improvident exercise of discretion to order trial of consolidated personal injury action and property damage action to be held in Orange County where the personal injury action pending in New York County was prior in issuance and service of the complaint and in joinder of issue and where the convenience of witnesses would best be served by having trial in New York County. Babcock v Lowy (1959) 7 AD2d 930, 183 NYS2d 777.

Consolidation of Municipal Court action with Supreme Court action granted on condition that nonresident seeking consolidation appear for examination. Reuss v Moiseenko (1959) 17 Misc 2d 424, 184 NYS2d 494.

Possibility that one of causes sought to be consolidated may be settled is in of itself no ground for denial of motion to consolidate. Davis v Williams (1959) 17 Misc 2d 888, 191 NYS2d 731.

Court has power to order consolidation or joint trial of actions pending in two counties, and to direct trial to be held in one of the counties, thus incidentally changing venue of actions pending in other county without necessarily requiring a showing of circumstances which would have independently justified change of venue. Smith v Witteman Co. (1960) 10 AD2d 793, 197 NYS2d 877.

Although motion requested consolidation but concluded with prayer "for such other and further relief as may be just and proper", court ordered joint trial where it believed cases would be more easily understood by jury if tried jointly rather than being organically consolidated. Smith v Witteman Co., supra.

The convenience of witnesses is immaterial in determining the propriety of consolidation. Pembroke v Sarkisian (1961, Sup) 219 NYS2d 424.

20. Actions involving the same event or transactions—In general

Where both actions arise out of same series of transactions between original parties, actions should be consolidated in court's discretion and in interests of justice and economy. Edelstein v Hacker (1956, Co Ct) 152 NYS2d 525.

Actions the causes of which have arisen out of the same transaction may be consolidated where the rights of none of the parties will be affected. Priority in time of commencement is important but is not conclusive of the question of consolidation. Brink's Express Co. v Burns (1930) 230 AD 559, 245 NYS 649.

Action by physician for his fee for services and action against him by patient for malpractice should not be consolidated, since physician would be required to take witness stand to prove his claim when he could then be cross-examined unfairly as to his alleged negligence. Perlman v Perlman (1941) 178 Misc 223, 33 NYS2d 29.

Action by hospital against patient's husband for services rendered to patient, was not consolidated with action by patient against hospital and physicians for damages for surgical operation and by husband for loss of services, where in latter action neither complaint nor bill of particulars states facts constituting cause of action against hospital. Knaup v Horace Harding Hospital (1956) 1 AD2d 849, 150 NYS2d 551.

Action for damages for fraud based on conspiracy and action in equity for injunction are properly consolidated, where plaintiff is same in both actions and corporate defendant is same except five individual defendants, joined with corporate defendant in first action, are officers or employees, and actions involve same transaction and allegations of fact are same. Wegner Canning Corp. v Wegner (1942, Sup) 33 NYS2d 443.

Supreme court actions brought in different counties and involving right to stock dividends and same dispute, were properly consolidated, although process had not been served on one defendant who was plaintiff in one action. Sodus Fruit Farm, Inc. v Williams (1943) 181 Misc 397, 41 NYS2d 49.

Stockholders' derivative action against officers and directors for waste of assets, accounting of illegal profits and return of excessive compensation paid to themselves, was properly consolidated with similar action, pending in another court, which was consolidation of several similar suits, where all actions grew out of misconduct of corporate officers and directors. Meyers v Cowdin (1941) 263 AD 730, 30 NYS2d 902.

Stockholders' derivative actions, having in main same issues, against same defendants in Kings and New York counties, should be consolidated. Weis v Coe (1943) 265 AD 471, 39 NYS2d 470.

Where in fraud action and in counterclaim in foreclosure, purchasers affirmed contract of sale and sought damages for fraudulent representations, consolidation was proper. Samworth v Frankenhoff (1947) 272 AD 831, 70 NYS2d 284.

Actions by two plaintiffs, each claiming brokerage commissions for leasing premises owned by same person, should be consolidated, as both actions arose out of same transaction. Cross & Brown v Cimbar Corp. (1949) 275 AD 680, 86 NYS2d 481.

Action in City Court by landlord for tenant's breach of commercial space lease and refusal to pay landlord any part of gross rents received, was properly consolidated with action in Municipal Court arising out of identical landlord-tenant relationship, and involving same central question whether landlord received more than he was entitled to receive from tenant. Tufor Realty Corp. v Equity Express, Inc. (1953, City Ct) 120 NYS2d 693.

Where an action was brought in the municipal court in the borough of Bronx, second district, for property damage arising out of an automobile collision and thereafter the defendant brought an action against the plaintiff for property damage arising out of the same collision in the same borough but in the first district, the municipal court would consolidate the action brought in the first district with that in the second district and would direct that they be tried in the latter district. Krohe v Goldman (1938) 167 Misc 930, 4 NYS2d 851.

Where principal issues in separate actions, arising out of building of same structure, relate to allocation of responsibility between respondents for allegedly improper construction, and where if separate trials were to be had each respondent might separately prevail on claim that fault was that of other, such contradictory result would prejudice appellant, and it was improvident exercise of discretion to deny consolidation. Heimov v 15 Pleasantville Road Corp. (1956) 1 AD2d 967, 150 NYS2d 377.

Proceeding in Surrogate's Court of Onondaga County for construction of will was consolidated with proceeding in Supreme Court on application by Syracuse University for authority to pay to State University income from endowment bequeathed in said will to petitioner. Re Hendricks' Will (1955) 1 Misc 2d 904, 148 NYS2d 245, affd 3 AD2d 890, 161 NYS2d 855, affd 4 NY2d 744, 171 NYS2d 863, 148 NE2d 911.

An action for annulment may be consolidated with an action for separation. White v White (1936) 246 AD 879, 284 NYS 857.

Order granting consolidation reversed where there does not appear any right to relief in respect to or arising out of the same transaction or that any question of law or fact common to all of them would arise in the action if consolidated. Pride v Perras (1958) 6 AD2d 842, 176 NYS2d 573.

In ordering consolidation of plaintiffs' law action against corporation for salary with corporation's equity action for accounting against plaintiffs, as officer, and director of corporation, for alleged waste and malfeasance the court stated that the issues in the two actions were substantially the same and consolidation would avoid duplicate trials, with possibly inconsistent results. Teperman v Atcos Baths, Inc. (1959) 7 AD2d 858, 182 NYS2d 759, reh den 7 AD2d 874, 184, NYS2d 579.

Plaintiff's action in Supreme Court to have check issued by her declared void and returned to her, was consolidated with Municipal Court action on check in which she was defendant, since the Municipal Court could not grant her affirmative relief and the issues were the same in both actions. Gitter v Schiff (1960) 20 Misc 2d 610, 195 NYS2d 101.

Negligence action against city was consolidated with malpractice action against hospital since city, if negligent, would be liable for the subsequent malpractice and same medical testimony would be involved in both actions. Echevarria v New York (1962) 34 Misc 2d 405, 227 NYS2d 480.

21. —Actions for death or personal injuries

Six actions, four pending in New York county, one in Queens and one in Bronx, arising out of two-car collision and involving passengers, operators and owners of such vehicles, including death action, were consolidated, despite claim that jury would be confused. Maiorano v William Sherman, Inc. (1949) 196 Misc 659, 94 NYS2d 768.

Consolidation of two actions arising out of automobile accident was denied where defendant in second action was suing in first action both as an individual and as representative of infants and a decedent, since a finding of negligence against him, though it would bar his individual action, was probably prejudice the parties he represented. Ramsay v Fier (1961) 32 Misc 2d 97, 222 NYS2d 894.

22. — —By several plaintiffs

Where twenty-five actions involve identical issues of negligence arising out of fire in Sullivan County and nineteen of such plaintiffs originally had actions pending in New York City area where they reside, consolidation of all such actions with venue in Albany County where consolidated action can be tried sooner there than in metropolitan area, was proper. Pomerantz v Grossinger Realty Corp. (1956) 2 AD2d 628, 152 NYS2d 138.

Four actions arising from collision between truck and automobile; consolidated, where facts were same. Maurice Slater Trucking Co. v Maus (1947, Sup) 70 NYS2d 828.

Where four automobile actions arise from same accident when tractor collided with several motor vehicles and where defendants are practically same in all actions, such actions were consolidated to avoid multiplicity of trials. Wilzin v Sarlitt (1950, Sup) 119 NYS2d 609.

Order consolidating five actions for damages growing out of one automobile accident merged all issues into single action. Keim v Orel (1941) 263 AD 779, 31 NYS2d 321, app dismd 287 NY 837, 41 NE2d 165.

Substantial identity of factual issues in three actions makes consolidation desirable and proper, despite application of different rules of contributory negligence to three plaintiffs. Winn v Zone Oil Trucking Corp. (1950, Sup) 117 NYS2d 189.

Where three actions for personal and property injury, arising from collision of automobiles, present same issues of negligence and contributory negligence, fact that parties are represented by different attorneys, did not bar consolidation. Shea v Benjamin (1949) 275 AD 1003, 91 NYS2d 745.

Two actions in municipal court, one by owner and other by driver of automobile, against same defendant driving second car, should be consolidated with pending supreme court action by passenger of second car against all parties in municipal court action, where all involve same automobile collision. Hartmann v Dakins (1953, Sup) 123 NYS2d 441.

Where six separate actions were brought as result of collapse of building under construction, and there are thirteen separate causes of action, ten for personal injuries and three for wrongful death, and all injured plaintiffs were employees of subcontractor, and some actions have 31 named defendants and each action contains third-party complaint by several defendants against employer, consolidation was denied. Stolle-D. Corp. v Rizzi Constr. Co. (1955) 144 NYS2d 564.

Five actions for negligence causing personal and property injury due to gas explosion, of which one was brought in New York county, two in Sullivan and two by different plaintiffs against same defendant, were consolidated into one action triable in Kings, where all actions were brought within period of few weeks. Pasher v Reisenberg (1949, Sup) 87 NYS2d 872.

Three negligence actions in the municipal court consolidated where all involved the same transaction and the damages sought in each did not exceed the jurisdictional amount. Agostinacci v Brooklyn C. R. Co. (1931) 141 Misc 908, 254 NYS 485.

Death actions involving same issues, except contributory negligence and damages, were properly consolidated. Kelly v John Vogel, Inc. (1952) 279 AD 797, 109 NYS2d 282.

Fact that there are different issues as to contributory negligence and damages does not bar consolidation, where plaintiffs are not prejudiced by joint trial. Nilson v Hudson Transit Corp. (1952, Sup) 110 NYS2d 893.

Death and personal injury actions are properly consolidated, though issues of negligence, contributory negligence, burden of proof and damages in death action are not same as in actions for personal injury. Lowery v Perner (1950, Sup) 117 NYS2d 102.

Where two actions arose out of same automobile action, and plaintiffs in first action were granted summary judgment and date had been set for assessment of damages, court denied motion for plaintiffs in second action for permission to intervene, or for consolidation, or joint trials, or for stay of assessment until second action was brought to judgment, since to do so would prejudice rights of plaintiffs in first action. David v Bauman (1960) 24 Misc 2d 67, 196 NYS2d 746.

23. — —Against several defendants

Plaintiff suffered injuries when the automobile in which he was a passenger collided with two others; his action against the two drivers was consolidated with a later action against the driver of the vehicle in which he was riding. Boyce v Mariano (1928) 132 Misc 623, 230 NYS 408.

But where rights of respective defendants in separate actions involving same collision of automobiles can more easily be presented to jury, it is better practice to try together such actions rather than to consolidate them. McNamara v Penner (1953, Sup) 123 NYS2d 576.

Where five different actions arise out of same accident, and in some actions parties are same while in other actions additional or other parties appear and issues have not been joined in some actions, consolidation would not save time in trial since confusion would very likely arise where plaintiffs in one action become defendants in another action. Garber v Glassman (1956, Sup) 154 NYS2d 479.

24. —Actions for injuries to person and damages to property

Where defendant was sued by the same plaintiff in separate actions for injuries to the person and damages to property due to the same accident, he could in each case set up the pendency of the other, or, on motion, secure a consolidation of the actions. McAndrew v Lake S. & M. S. R. Co. (1893) 70 Hun 46, 23 NYS 1074.

Where driver of car sued for personal injury, and his employer sued for injury to car, sustained in collision of two trucks, both actions were consolidated. Kubran v Acme Brick Corp. (1945) 268 AD 1046, 52 NYS2d 232. Cf. Pierce v Mutual Life Ins. Co. (1921, Sup) 190 NYS 50.

Denial of consolidation of actions for personal injuries, property injuries and loss of services was improvident exercise of discretion. Haber v Newton (1952) 280 AD 822, 113 NYS2d 777.

Action by administratrix suing for death of pedestrian killed in collision between fire truck and commercial truck, consolidated with action by fire truck owner and fire patrolmen for property damage and for personal injuries, and counterclaim by commercial truck owner for damages to his truck. Peters v New York Board of Fire Underwriters (1949) 276 AD 846, 93 NYS2d 146.

Actions growing out of the same accident could not be consolidated where one of the plaintiffs was sister of the defendant and guest passenger in her sister's car, and the other plaintiff owned property on the street which was damaged in the collision. Cevera v De Gregorio (1938) 169 Misc 233, 7 NYS2d 265.

Although a consolidation of property damage action arising from unauthorized use of plaintiff's automobile with negligence action against him for bodily injuries sustained by passenger in second car was denied, a joint trial was ordered. Dasheff v Bath & Tennis Club (1959) 25 Misc 2d 13, 206 NYS2d 733.

25. —Action for personal injuries and action for loss of services and expenses

Wife's action for personal injury from negligence and that of husband for loss of services should be tried together. Stahl v Niagara De Luxe Cab Co. (1930) 135 Misc 859, 239 NYS 710.

An action in the supreme court by an infant plaintiff to recover damages for personal injuries and an action in the county court by the infant's father to recover for loss of services and expenses consolidated where both actions arose out of the same accident and, except for the question of damages, involved precisely the same issues. Tascio v Citizens Bank of White Plains (1938) 254 AD 881, 5 NYS2d 35.

26. Owner of parts of single claim

Where several actions have been brought by owners of parts of a single claim they may be consolidated. Porter v Lane Const. Corp. (1925) 212 AD 528, 209 NYS 54, affd 244 NY 523, 155 NE 881.

27. Identity of parties in different actions

CPA § 96 liberalized the practice in relation to consolidation of actions and it was no longer essential that there be identity of parties in the actions consolidated. Gibbs v Sokol (1926) 216 AD 260, 214 NYS 533; Philip Shlansky & Bro., Inc. v Grossman (1948) 273 AD 544, 78 NYS2d 127.

Consolidation of actions will not be denied merely because some of parties are different. Edelstein v Hacker (1956, Co Ct) 152 NYS2d 525.

The consolidation of the causes of action of separate plaintiffs against the same defendants was permitted where it did not appear that any substantial injustice would be done the defendants by allowing proof of false representations to one plaintiff to be made at the same trial at which the other plaintiff was seeking to recover. Crandall v A. B. Leach & Co. (1927) 222 AD 292, 225 NYS 649.

It is no bar to consolidation that parties in two actions are different. Scarfe v Lorom (1955, Sup) 141 NYS2d 196.

Motion by plaintiff, suing in different capacities, to consolidate actions by him in Supreme Court and City Court may be consolidated before issues are fully framed, where court can plainly see what issues are to be. Pansy v Massola (1955) 207 Misc 908, 140 NYS2d 417.

In view of § 258, subd 9, Civil Practice Act, CPA § 96 construed not to authorize consolidation of an action in the Supreme Court by the lessee of premises against his lessor and its president for conspiring to cause and causing a third person to breach his agreement to sublease the premises, with an action thereafter commenced in the City Court of New York by the lessor's assignee to recover rent due under the lease to plaintiff. Brody v Madison Lunch, Inc. (1922) 199 AD 640, 192 NYS 10.

Two separate actions by same plaintiff against two separate defendants involving two independent accidents occurring nine months apart, where issues are not precisely same and where liability problem in each accident is unique and separate, should not be consolidated. Gamble v Fraleigh (1955) 1 Misc 2d 347, 146 NYS2d 146.

Where actions pending in City Court and in Municipal Court involve different plaintiffs and one action involves additional defendant and where settlement by one defendant would prejudice settling defendant in trial of actions brought against him by "remaining defendant" as plaintiff, consolidation was improper. Witzke v Doyle (1955) 3 Misc 2d 323, 146 NYS2d 515.

Where substantial right of plaintiff might be prejudiced by consolidation since plaintiff in action one is defendant in action three and attorneys for defendant in action one are defending attorneys in action three and will cross-examine the plaintiff in action one, consolidation denied. Resnick v Resnick (1957) 9 Misc 2d 65, 169 NYS2d 393.

Where two actions present common questions of law and fact, and the witnesses on the issues are the same, consolidation thereof will not be barred because the parties thereto are different. Vernon v Ama Electronics, Inc (1960, Mun Ct) 207 NYS2d 312.

28. Status of parties in different actions

That plaintiff in one action is the defendant in the other is no objection to consolidation. Dexter Sulphite Pulp & Paper Co. v Hearst (1923) 206 AD 101, 200 NYS 413; Scott v Patten (1951) 278 AD 1038, 106 NYS2d 893.

CPA § 96 and § 97 were held to authorize the consolidation of an action in the Supreme Court to recover damages for negligence on the part of the defendant as an architect in planning and supervising the erection of a building for plaintiff, and an action in the Municipal Court by the defendant in the former action against the plaintiff therein, to recover for services rendered in connection with the erection of the same building. Zapfe v Werner (1923) 120 Misc 326, 199 NYS 293.

Under CPA § 96 and § 97, the Supreme Court had authority to consolidate with an action pending before it for the dissolution of an alleged partnership and for an accounting between the alleged partners and the sale of the partnership assets, another action subsequently commenced in Municipal Court by defendant in the former action against the plaintiff therein based upon a breach of an alleged agreement between the parties governing the same relations described in the former action as constituting a partnership. Goldey v Bierman (1922) 201 AD 527, 194 NYS 373.

In an action by a city against a surety on a bond given by contractors with the city to recover an alleged balance due the plaintiff, the defendant surety may be entitled to a consolidation of such action with an action brought by its principals, the contractors, against the city for a breach of the contract. New York v Fidelity & Deposit Co. (1938) 253 AD 676, 3 NYS2d 714.

Action by payee against maker of note for balance due wherein maker alleged affirmative defenses of limitations and agreement by payee to cancel note in consideration of maker's consent to transfer certain corporate stock, was consolidated with action by maker of note against payee to rescind agreement by former to pay latter certain sum and to enjoin transfer of note and to compel restoration to plaintiff of stock shares pledged as collateral security to note. First Trust & Deposit Co. v Dent (1942, Sup) 36 NYS2d 664.

Fact that plaintiffs in some of the actions are also defendants in some of the other actions is not an insuperable obstacle to consolidation of the actions. Upon consolidation, all plaintiffs who are not defendants in any of the actions can be listed as plaintiffs in the consolidated action and plaintiffs who are also defendants can be listed as defendants in the consolidated action, their complaints then becoming cross-claims against other defendants. On joint trial positions and pleadings of parties would remain unchanged. Smith v Witteman Co. (1960) 10 AD2d 793, 197 NYS2d 877.

Consolidation of automobile accident actions in which same issues of negligence and contributory negligence are present will not be denied merely because party, who is both plaintiff and defendant, will be represented by different attorneys in each capacity. Pembroke v Sarkisian (1961, Sup) 219 NYS2d 424.

29. Consolidation of legal and equitable causes

Actions at law and in equity may be consolidated. Sutton Carpet Cleaners, Inc. v Firemen's Ins. Co. (1947, Sup) 68 NYS2d 218, affd 273 AD 944, 78 NYS2d 565, app dismd 298 NY 633, 82 NE2d 28 and affd 299 NY 646, 87 NE2d 53.

Equity and law actions arising from same transaction consolidated, where relief in one action would offset that in second action. Philip Shlansky & Bro. v Grossman (1948) 273 AD 544, 78 NYS2d 127.

Equitable action for foreclosure of mechanic's lien consolidated with two actions at law for breach of contract in connection with the same construction brought by another plaintiff against the same defendants. Warren Foundry & Pipe Corp. v Board of Water Comrs. (1932) 146 Misc 323, 261 NYS 236, affd 237 AD 844, 261 NYS 918.

Contractor's action to foreclose mechanic's lien wherein owner cross-complained against architect for breach of contract to supervise work, was consolidated with architect's action for services against owner who counterclaimed for such breach of contract. Slutzky v Hinderstein (1950, Sup) 97 NYS2d 255.

Where actions are independent of each other and issues are separate and distinct, consolidation is improper. Miller v Lewis (1947, Sup) 77 NYS2d 285.

Where law action was entitled to preference and equity action may be delayed by motions, consolidation was improper. Miller v Lewis, supra.

Error to change place of trial and consolidate an action at law with one in equity where both did not grow out of the same transaction. Joseph H.

Meyer Bros., Inc. v Higgins (1930) 231 AD 832, 246 NYS 235.

Action at law in supreme court, Kings county, would not be consolidated with action in equity in supreme court, New York county, where central issues in actions were not same and plaintiffs in law action in Kings county should not be deprived of right to jury trial. Lexington Concrete Corp. v William P. McGarry Co. (1938) 170 Misc 233, 9 NYS2d 296.

Actions were not consolidated where equity action was ready for trial and fraud action had not been noticed for trial and jury trial was sought. Mandel v Silverstein (1943, Sup) 46 NYS2d 586, app dismd 50 NYS2d 680.

In an action on a policy of life insurance, the defendant insurer's cross-motion for consolidation of the present action with an earlier action as plaintiff for rescission of the policy is denied. Wolff v Mutual Life Ins. Co. (1935) 154 Misc 431, 276 NYS 339, affd 241 AD 869, 271 NYS 1006.

Where declaratory judgment is action in equity and will shortly be reached for trial, and personal injury is non-jury action which failed to be preferred, and where issues are completely independent of each other and two trials will not involve duplication, motion to consolidate was denied. Macpherson v Macpherson (1956) 1 Misc 2d 1049, 149 NYS2d 525.

Action by buyer against seller of home freezer for reformation of conditional sales agreement was properly consolidated in court's discretion with action against buyer by bank to which seller had discounted buyer's note. Anderson v Nolan (1956) 2 AD2d 629, 151 NYS2d 770.

30. Consolidation of jury and non-jury causes

Jury and non-jury causes may be consolidated. Meuer v Horowitz (1940, Sup App T) 20 NYS2d 780.

The fact that one action is triable by a jury and the other without a jury is not a bar to consolidating the actions for a jury trial since the right to a non-jury trial is not a substantial right within the contemplation of this section. O'Brien v Jefts (1957) 3 AD2d 787, 160 NYS2d 22.

Defendant may not consolidate a jury case with a non-jury case and have the consolidated action tried before a jury because the result would be the trial of two cases upon payment of only one jury fee. Rubenstein v Cohen (1930) 138 Misc 305, 246 NYS 692.

That defendant is entitled to jury trial in municipal court, and not in Supreme Court, is not a fatal objection to consolidation with latter. Parsons & Whittemore, Inc. v Kenton (1945, Sup) 58 NYS2d 688.

Nonjury city court case consolidated with jury supreme court case on motion of plaintiff in latter, where objecting party demanded jury, where both actions were based on same written contract and involved identical facts and issues. Edgewater Machine Co. v Weiss (1948) 1 Misc 2d 862, 85 NYS2d 655.

Where two of three automobile accident cases were commenced in municipal court and third in supreme court, and jury has been demanded in one action in municipal court but not yet demanded in others, cases were consolidated in supreme court, with right to jury trial preserved. Denton v Koshfer (1951) 201 Misc 394, 106 NYS2d 385.

Where one action is on non-jury calendar and trial is imminent, and other action is on jury calendar and trial cannot occur for long time, consolidation would prejudice substantial right of plaintiff in non-jury action. Lichtenstein v Lapadula & Villani Trucking Corp. (1954) 283 AD 721, 127 NYS2d 357.

See also Lexington Concrete Corp. v William P. McGarry Co. (1938) 170 Misc 233, 9 NYS2d 296, in 31, supra.

Plaintiffs' action at law against corporation for salary, wherein they had demanded a jury trial, was consolidated with corporation's equity action for accounting against plaintiffs, as officer and director of corporation, for alleged waste and malfeasance and plaintiffs were held entitled to a jury trial on issues in their action for salary. Teperman v Atcos Baths, Inc. (1959) 7 AD2d 858, 182 NYS2d 759, reh den 7 AD2d 874, 184 NYS2d 579.

Where action for brokerage commissions pending in New York City was consolidated with action for rescission commenced in Supreme Court, the consolidated action was to be tried in Supreme Court before a jury, with the jury deciding the factual issues and the trial justice disposing of the equity issues. No. 123 Lafayette Ave. Corp. v Lipstein (1959) 18 Misc 2d 394, 185 NYS2d 845.

Order consolidating Municipal Court jury action with Supreme Court nonjury action may provide that trial of jury action precede trial of nonjury action in Supreme Court, and that trial of nonjury action then proceed before the same justice hearing the jury issue. Gitter v Schiff (1960) 20 Misc 2d 610, 195 NYS2d 101.

31. Actions for concurrent remedies

Although the remedies sought by the plaintiff in two actions were concurrent and each action was properly brought, yet as the facts involved were identical and no substantial harm would be done by consolidation, it was held they should be consolidated. Dee Jay Holding Corp. v Fleming (1927) 220 AD 783, 222 NYS 795.

32. Foreclosure actions

In view of CPA § 96 and § 8 (§ 103(a) herein), § 258 (§§ 601, 603, Rule 3014 herein) several actions to foreclose mortgages were consolidated. Down Town Realty Co. v Simpson (1929) 227 AD 803, 237 NYS 228.

Where the same person held two mortgages upon substantially the same premises, but the descriptions were not identical, the court refused to consolidate two separate actions of foreclosure, but intimated that there could be but one bill of costs. Wooster v Case (1890, Sup) 12 NYS 769.

Actions to foreclose mortgages on different lots, although the respective parties are identical, cannot be consolidated. Selkirk v Wood, 9 Civ Proc 141; and see Wooster v Case, supra.

33. Partition proceedings

Supreme court has no power to consolidate actions for partition where the lands to be partitioned are in different counties. Mayor v Coffin (1882) 90 NY 312.

Two actions for partition of lands in different counties cannot be consolidated where some of the defendants in one action are not parties to the other, and have no interest in the subject of the latter action. Mayor v Coffin, supra.

34. Special proceedings

The supreme court has no authority to consolidate two special proceedings which are based on different facts and are, in part, against different respondents. People ex rel. Collins v Ahearn (1911) 146 AD 135, 130 NYS 497.

Two separate proceedings against separate corporations may not be joined. Re Hafter (1946, Sup) 79 NYS2d 782, affd 270 AD 995, 62 NYS2d 861, affd 296 NY 808, 71 NE2d 774.

Arbitration is a special proceeding and, since the Supreme Court has power to consolidate special proceedings, it has power to consolidate arbitration proceedings. Application of Adam Consol. Industries, Inc. (1958) 6 AD2d 515, 180 NYS2d 507.

Arbitration proceedings may be consolidated as any special proceeding. Symphony Fabrics Corp. v Bernson Silk Mills, Inc. (1962) 16 AD2d 473, 229 NYS2d 200, affd 12 NY2d 409, 240 NYS2d 23, 190 NE2d 418.

35. Actions in Municipal Court of New York

This section applies to such court. Structural Waterproofing, Inc. v Deutsch (1941, AD) 34 NYS2d 233.

Consolidation of actions properly brought in different districts of the municipal court was approved. Melker v Guarino (1929) 135 Misc 548, 238 NYS 569.

It does not authorize a justice of the Municipal Court of New York presiding in one district to make by consolidation of actions a transfer of a case pending in another district to the district in which he is presiding. Ralph M. Levey Co. v Fox (1923) 121 Misc 113, 200 NYS 274.

Although the plaintiffs brought separate actions in the Municipal Court, if they involved common questions the court had power to unite them notwithstanding the separate claims aggregated more than $1,000. Dilworth v Yellow Taxi Corp. (1926) 127 Misc 543, 216 NYS 513, revd on other grounds 220 AD 772, 221 NYS 813.

The Municipal Court of New York City is without jurisdiction to entertain an action in which several plaintiffs joined and demanded separate judgments exceeding in the aggregate the limitation of Municipal Court Code § 6. Dilworth v Yellow Taxi Corp. (1927) 220 AD 772, 221 NYS 813.

Consolidation of Municipal Court action with Supreme Court action granted on condition that nonresident seeking consolidation appear for examination. Reuss v Moiseenko (1959) 17 Misc 2d 424, 184 NYS2d 494.

Where plaintiff brought an action in supreme court, and another in municipal court, and both arose out of same transaction, consolidation would be granted despite plaintiff's objection that consolidation would jeopardize his rights since he might lose preferred position over other creditors with respect to claim involved in municipal court action due to calendar congestion in supreme court. General Crushed Stone Co. v Central New York Contracting Co. (1960) 25 Misc 2d 572, 206 NYS2d 73.

Plaintiff's action in Supreme Court to have check issued by her declared void and returned to her was consolidated with Municipal Court action on check in which she was defendant, since the Municipal Court could not grant her affirmative relief and the issues were the same in both actions. Gitter v Schiff (1960) 20 Misc 2d 610, 195 NYS2d 101.

36. New York City Court

Several actions may be consolidated in the city court of New York and a single judgment rendered for the aggregate of the several claims, provided the sum sued for in any one of the actions does not exceed $2,000. Gillen v Canary (1897) 19 Misc 594, 44 NYS 313, overruling Bush v Abrahams (1888, City Ct) 18 NYSR 919, 2 NYS 391.

37. Action for separation and habeas corpus

Since wife's separation action necessarily involved the custody of a child of the parties, there was no error in consolidating it with husband's habeas corpus proceedings for child's custody. Comfort v Comfort (1929) 227 AD 1, 236 NYS 544.

38. Action for price and guaranty of payment

Action for price of goods sold may be joined with one on guaranty of payment of price. Winter v Maple City Mfg. Co. (1928) 132 Misc 631, 230 NYS 458.

39. Before issue joined in both actions

Where issue and nature of actions are not in doubt, consolidation is proper though one action is not at issue. Maurice Slater Trucking Co. v Maus (1947, Sup) 70 NYS2d 828; Edelstein v Hacker (1956, Co Ct) 152 NYS2d 525.

Where common questions of fact are involved in two actions and each party will undoubtedly swear same witnesses in each action, fact that action in one county is not presently at issue is not factor fatal to consolidation. Watkins Body Corp. v Arditi Limited (1951) 279 AD 619, 107 NYS2d 430.

But where the defendant seeks to consolidate two actions brought against him by the same plaintiff, it is the better practice to wait until answers have been interposed in each action from which the court can better determine the issues involved and the propriety of consolidating the actions. Boyle v Staten Island & S. B. Land Co. (1895) 87 Hun 233, 33 NYS 836.

An action for compensation for medical services and an action for malpractice have inter-related issues. Hence, an action for compensation by a physician against a parent could be removed from Municipal Court of the City of New York to the Supreme Court and consolidated therein with an action for malpractice against the doctor notwithstanding that the issues have not been joined in the malpractice action. Geller v Ticktin (1957) 6 Misc 2d 16, 161 NYS2d 628.

Where the pleadings do not show such similarity as would merit consolidation and it was premature to direct consolidation on the basis of defenses that were the subject of an undetermined motion to strike for insufficiency, order granting consolidation reversed. Weistrop v Necchi Sewing Machine Sales Corp. (1957) 3 AD2d 743, 160 NYS2d 910, reh and app den 3 AD2d 906, 163 NYS2d 370.

Although consolidation may be granted even though issue has not been joined, where the papers show that there will be an issue and its nature is not in doubt, the granting of such motion before complaint has been served in one of the actions is premature. Hoff v Buttenwieser (1961, Sup) 219 NYS2d 422.

40. Where one action partly tried

An action which has been partly tried should not be joined with one in which the issues have just been joined. Eckenroth v Egan (1897) 20 Misc 508, 46 NYS 666.

41. Actions in different courts

The language of former sections 96, 97 and 209 of the Civil Practice Act, providing for consolidation of actions and joinder of parties plaintiff, while very broad, did not confer upon the court power to make such order, even upon notice, when such plaintiffs had exercised their right of election and brought their several suits separately and in different courts. Brennan v National Equitable Inv. Co. (1924) 210 AD 426, 206 NYS 280.

Supreme court had no power under CPA § 96 to consolidate actions pending in other courts. Application of Comfort-Zone Corp. (1955, Sup) 140 NYS2d 76.

Where two parties to an automobile collision each sought to recover damages sustained in the collision by reason of the negligence of the other, one bringing his action in the County Court and the other in a Justice Court, held that neither §§ 96 and 97 nor § 130 (§§ 2212, 2213, Rule 2214(b) herein) of the Civil Practice Act, authorized the Supreme Court to make an order consolidating the two actions. Curry v Earll (1924) 209 AD 205, 203 NYS 750.

Where defendant in an action in the City Court of New York for breach of warranty upon a contract of sale thereafter brought action against plaintiff therein, in the Municipal Court for the purchase price of the goods covered by the same contract, and defendant in the Municipal Court action set up as a defense and counterclaim the same cause of action relied upon in the City Court action, the latter court was without authority, under CPA § 96 or § 97 and § 1572 (§ 101 herein) Civil Practice Act, to order consolidation of the actions in the City Court. T. Blumenthal & Co. v Theo. Tiedemann & Sons (1922) 118 Misc 560, 194 NYS 86.

Action by bondholder for accounting against trustee is consolidated with foreclosure action in which complete account will be had, where latter action is pending in tribunal of concurrent jurisdiction. Haber v Chase Nat. Bank (1934) 153 Misc 393, 275 NYS 776.

See also Weis v Coe (1943) 265 AD 471, 39 NYS2d 470, and Sommer v Kenin (1945, Sup) 58 NYS2d 536, both in 19, supra.

42. —Action in city or municipal court with action in Supreme Court

Municipal court action was properly consolidated with supreme court action where plaintiff in municipal court action would not be prejudiced thereby. Surasky v Morgan (1943) 266 AD 741, 40 NYS2d 908.

Municipal court action by seller against subsequent buyer on note given for part of purchase price, and subsequent Supreme Court action by buyers assignees against seller for breach of warranty, were consolidated in Supreme Court, on ground that they arise from same transaction, that questions of law and fact are substantially same, and can be tried together without prejudice to substantial rights of parties, and would prevent injustice which may result from divergent decisions in each separate case. Scarfe v Lorom (1955, Sup) 141 NYS2d 196.

An action begun in a city court for goods sold and delivered after the defendant therein had begun an action in the supreme court for return of the money he had paid for the goods on the ground of misrepresentation was ordered consolidated with the prior action in the supreme court. Lutus v Labor (1927) 222 AD 132, 226 NYS 108.

In view of CPA § 96 and § 97, where defendant in an action pending in the Rochester City Court has a counterclaim for an amount exceeding the jurisdiction of that court, on which he had instituted an action in the Supreme Court against the plaintiff in the City Court action, as well as other defendants, the City Court action would be consolidated with that in the Supreme Court to permit the determination of all the issues in a single action. Borzilleri v Brockway Motor Truck Corp. (1925) 124 Misc 905, 210 NYS 17.

See also Hartmann v Dakins (1953, Sup) 123 NYS2d 441, 17, supra.

Municipal and supreme court cases were consolidated where latter was first begun and both cases involved same automobile accident. Spevack v Dropkin (1949, Sup) 88 NYS2d 92.

Where parties to city court, municipal court and supreme court actions were identical, all actions resulted from transactions between the parties in supreme court action, and common questions of fact and law existed, the other actions were consolidated with the supreme court action. Hassid v Kay (1956) 6 Misc 2d 240, 163 NYS2d 311, affd 3 AD2d 904, 163 NYS2d 401.

Where plaintiff brought an action in supreme court, and another in municipal court, and both arose out of same transaction, consolidation would be granted despite plaintiff's objection that consolidation would jeopardize his rights since he might lose preferred position over other creditors with respect to claim involved in municipal court action due to calendar congestion in supreme court. General Crushed Stone Co. v Central New York Contracting Co. (1960) 25 Misc 2d 572, 206 NYS2d 73.

43. —Action in Justice Court with action in county court or Supreme Court

In view of CPA § 96 and § 97 and § 1572, the county court had power to consolidate an action brought in a justice's court with one pending in the county court, the causes of which arose out of the same transaction and the same parties were involved. Sternberg v Bergman (1931) 140 Misc 569, 250 NYS 134.

Action based on collision between automobiles commenced in Municipal Court of City of New York against two defendants will be consolidated with action in Nassau County Court based on same collision and brought by said defendants against plaintiff, where plaintiff in first action is resident of Nassau county and within jurisdiction of County Court. Woodruff v Cohen (1936) 158 Misc 332, 285 NYS 622.

A county court has power to consolidate an action subsequently commenced in the Justice's Court with an action pending in the county court between the same parties. Datz v Economy Cotton Goods Stores, Inc. (1934) 263 NY 252, 188 NE 728; Greene v Beacorn (1932) 145 Misc 870, 262 NYS 349.

Where plaintiff commenced action in justice court for $20 and later defendant commenced action in supreme court for $85, motion to consolidate actions in supreme court was denied because plaintiff, if successful in recovering $20 (less than $50), would have to pay defendant's costs which would exceed $50, unless defendant stipulated against applicability of CPA § 1472. Dadabo v Cartino (1943) 180 Misc 337, 41 NYS2d 794.

44. —Proceeding in surrogate's court with action in supreme court

Neither CPA § 96 nor CPA §§ 96-a and 190-a, (§ 325(d), Rule 326(b) herein) authorized the removal of a proceeding from the surrogate's court

to the supreme court. Budd v Schriver (1960) 22 Misc 2d 206, 203 NYS2d 291.

45. Consolidation requiring transfer to another county

Where five of seven actions for personal injuries and property damages resulting from automobile accident in Sullivan county, where commenced in such county, and one was commenced in Bronx county and another in New York county, all seven actions were consolidated in Sullivan county, since inconvenience to Bronx and New York plaintiffs will not amount to injustice to them. Balz v Kauffman & Minteer, Inc. (1955) 285 AD 1206, 140 NYS2d 902.

Equitable action on a contract to enforce a vendor's lien and for an accounting held improperly consolidated with an equitable action for a rescission of the same contract where a consolidation would have resulted in the transfer of the fundamental subject of controversy from one county to another and neither the convenience of witnesses nor the ends of justice required a change of venue. Dexter Sulphite Pulp & Paper Co. v Hearst (1923) 206 AD 101, 200 NYS 413.

Action for damages based on rescission of contract for fraud, commenced in Kings county, could not be consolidated with special proceeding to compel arbitration of contract, commenced in Queens county by defendant in former action. Big W. Const. Corp. v Horowitz (1951) 278 AD 977, 105 NYS2d 827.

46. Where one action entitled to preference

Where about a month after the commencement of an action in the City Court of New York for breach of a contract to manufacture shirts, based upon a claim of defective workmanship, the defendant therein commenced an action in the same court based upon the same contract, but for recovery of the compensation therein stated as for labor and goods sold and delivered and the defendant therein counterclaimed upon the breach which he had made the basis of the action first mentioned, it was error to consolidate the second action with the first in view of the fact that under the rules of that court the second action was entitled to a preference, while the first would not be reached within a year. Paparo v Shulman (1922) 117 Misc 690, 192 NYS 70.

47. Where delay would be caused

Where sufficient security has been posted in replevin action to protect moving party's interest in property involved, and where it would not serve ends of justice to unduly delay replevin action pending in New York City Court, motion in conversion action in Supreme Court to consolidate with it replevin action was denied. Turner v Finkelstein (1955, Sup) 145 NYS2d 328.

Action at issue in New York county is improperly consolidated with action not at issue in Westchester county, as prejudicial to substantial rights of plaintiff in New York action which was about to be reached for trial. Casanave v Robbins (1941) 262 AD 873, 28 NYS2d 588.

Rule that municipal court action for property damage should be consolidated with supreme court action for personal injuries growing out of collision of two cars on highway, does not apply where action for property damages can be speedily tried and where supreme court action involving claim of negligence of motorist to guest would delay trial. Friedman v Kleinman (1949) 275 AD 715, 87 NYS2d 201.

Both parties to eight separate contracts for the sale of goods claimed breach thereof by the other party. Plaintiff commenced three actions in the Supreme Court of New York county on six of such contracts, and thereafter defendant started a single action in Rockland County Supreme Court covering all eight contracts. Following the denial of the New York county plaintiff's motion at Rockland Special Term for a change of venue in the action started in that county to New York county, he moved and secured an order in the New York County Court removing the Rockland county action to New York county and consolidating the same with the three actions there pending. On appeal this order was reversed on the ground that while it was within the discretion of the court to order such removal and consolidation, the order was improvident in this instance because effective only to cause a delay in the trial of the issues, to the prejudice of the Rockland county plaintiff. Tenenbaum v Dunlop (1922) 200 AD 604, 193 NYS 407.

Consolidation of derivative stockholders' actions wherein the issues are identical will be denied where it will result in the loss of a speedy trial, and an indeterminate delay in the trial because of a stay operating in one of the actions. Richman v Felmus (1959) 20 Misc 2d 46, 188 NYS2d 608, app dismd 8 AD2d 985, 190 NYS2d 922.

Consolidation will not be permitted when to do so will prejudice litigant's right to an early trial as plaintiff in one of actions, and there is no showing that such early trial will prejudice the other litigant. Biederman v Yorks (1959) 9 AD2d 764, 192 NYS2d 447.

State's motion to consolidate claims against state for taking of property for highway purposes, or for joint trial thereof, was denied where some of the claimants showed that they would be prejudiced by resulting delay. Levin v State (1960) 22 Misc 2d 443, 201 NYS2d 915.

Where plaintiff brought an action in supreme court, and another in municipal court, and both arose out of same transaction, consolidation would be granted despite plaintiff's objection that consolidation would jeopardize his right since he might lose preferred position over other creditors with respect to claim involved in municipal court action due to calendar congestion in supreme court. General Crushed Stone Co. v Central New York Contracting Co. (1960) 25 Misc 2d 572, 206 NYS2d 73.

Defendant's motion to consolidate an action in which he does not genuinely dispute liability with one subsequently brought by him against plaintiff, which will result in delaying first action, was denied. Royaloy, Inc. v General Moving & Storage, Inc. (1959) 25 Misc 2d 255, 207 NYS2d 569.

48. Effect of consolidation

Where actions are consolidated, all the different actions are united and merged into one, the same as if the different causes of action had originally been joined in one. Hull v Shannon (1931) 139 Misc 564, 249 NYS 33, mod 234 AD 648, 251 NYS 960.

Where parties desire organic consolidation, joinder for all purposes of litigation, new title is one in which litigants are merged, with only one group of plaintiffs and only one group of defendants; in such case party must be plaintiff or defendant, as he cannot be both, and either he or his adversary should have his cause of action (originally pleaded in complaint) considered either by way of complaint or counterclaim. Vidal v Sheffield Farms Co. (1955) 208 Misc 438, 141 NYS2d 82.

In consolidated action only one judgment will be rendered. Vidal v Sheffield Farms Co., supra.

In organic consolidation of action, determination whether party should be cast in role of plaintiff or of defendant must be made by Special Term when formulating order of consolidation. Vidal v Sheffield Farms Co., supra.

Defendant in consolidated action is co-defendant of another defendant in that action, irrespective of whether or not that was their status in separate prior actions, and now being on "same side", certain remedies become available to them vis-a-vis each other. Vidal v Sheffield Farms Co., supra.

On removal and consolidation of City Court action with prior County Court action, plaintiffs in County Court will continue as plaintiffs. Right to be plaintiff preserved to the party who first commenced action in absence of exceptional situations. Simmons v Goldsmith (1933) 149 Misc 793, 269 NYS 417.

Consolidation will not give plaintiff in either action jurisdiction over parties upon whom he never served process. Baker v Thea (1961, Sup) 223 NYS2d 523.

49. Right to open and close in consolidated claim

The right to open and close is a substantial one of which one may not be deprived in the exercise of sound discretion under this section. Gallagher v Barth (1944) 268 AD 865, 50 NYS2d 473.

Privilege of opening and closing is a substantial and important right given to the party having affirmative of issue. Brink's Express Co. v Burns (1930) 230 AD 559, 245 NYS 649; Hartmann v Dakins (1953, Sup) 123 NYS2d 441.

Order of consolidation will determine who is entitled to open and close. Vidal v Sheffield Farms Co. (1955) 208 Misc 438, 141 NYS2d 82.

Where New Rochelle City Court action was consolidated with Westchester County Supreme Court action and former action was commenced first, plaintiff in such action was given right to open and close in consolidated action. Edelstein v Hacker (1956, Co Ct) 152 NYS2d 525.

Considered are priority of respective actions, place of origin of alleged causes of action, condition of calendar and character of parties. Leising v Norton (1954) 206 Misc 459, 133 NYS2d 262.

In absence of exceptional situations right to open and close in consolidated action is given to party who first brings his action. Kappa Frocks, Inc. v Alan Fabrics Corp. (1942) 263 AD 326, 32 NYS2d 985; Phil-or Textile Shrinking Corp. v Monarch Textile Shrinking Corp. (1936) 160 Misc 610, 290 NYS 377.

Where one action is commenced and issue joined long before other, plaintiff in first action is generally given right to open and close, subject to modification by trial justice. Hartmann v Dakins (1953, Sup) 123 NYS2d 441.

Exceptional situation must be shown to warrant departure from rule of priority. Desga Realty Corp. v Rupmor Realty Corp. (1945) 269 AD 766, 55 NYS2d 119.

The order, whereby two causes of action arising out of the same transaction were consolidated and giving the movant the right to open and close, was modified, so as to give the right to open and close to the corporate appellant in the combined action, where while the movant's action was commenced eight days prior to that of the appellant, the latter's case was at issue thirty-one days sooner. The rule giving heed to the rights of the party who first brings his action is not a controlling factor to be followed in all cases involving consolidation. Van Devort v K. & H. Evaporating Co. (1937) 252 AD 8, 297 NYS 277.

Where two actions are consolidated one for specific performance and the other to recover the deposit, the purchaser will have the right to open and close where such action was commenced first. Brunner v Steinhardt (1952) 4 Misc 2d 923, 111 NYS2d 887.

Where plaintiff instituted action by service of summons without complaint and moved for consolidation of action later brought by defendant in prior action against plaintiff, he waived right to open and close in consolidated actions. Diesel Installation Corp. v Nu-Boro Park Cleaners, Inc. (1941) 262 AD 969, 30 NYS2d 207.

In action consolidating seller's action to recover price of goods sold, wherein buyer denied acceptance and agreed price and counterclaimed for breach of warranty, with buyer's action for breach of warranty commenced by summons without complaint few hours before seller's action was commenced, seller was given right to open and close where he alone filed note of issue and obtained preference and buyer did nothing. Kappa Frocks, Inc. v Alan Fabrics Corp. (1942) 263 AD 326, 32 NYS2d 985.

Priority of action governs right to open and close; where city and supreme court actions were consolidated, and plaintiff in latter instituted prior action, he was awarded right to open and close.

Edgewater Machine Co. v Weiss (1948) 1 Misc 2d 862, 85 NYS2d 655.

Where municipal court action, first instituted, was consolidated with supreme court action on plaintiff's motion in prior action, plaintiff's right to open and close was not waived by motion to consolidate. Grafman v Coal Heat & Fuel Oil, Inc. (1949, Sup) 88 NYS2d 390.

Where eight actions arising from same automobile accident were tried together, trial court had discretion to determine order in which cases should proceed, with accompanying right to open and close. Dwyer v Divine (1950) 277 AD 807, 96 NYS2d 728.

In three separate actions arising from automobile collision, right to open and close was given to plaintiff who first served summons and verified complaint, and not to plaintiff who first served summons without complaint. Sullivan County Bldg. Material Co. v Berkman (1954) 283 AD 910, 130 NYS2d 99.

Where order consolidating jury and nonjury actions directed trial of jury issue before trial of nonjury action, the question of who shall have the right to open and close at the trial was reserved for the trial court. Gitter v Schiff (1960) 20 Misc 2d 610, 195 NYS2d 101.

Absent special factors, plaintiff whose action was first commenced is given the right to open and close in consolidated action. Pembroke v Sarkisian (1961, Sup) 219 NYS2d 424.

50. Place of trial of consolidated action

Order of consolidation of actions triable in different counties must fix place of trial of consolidated action; such determination rests in discretion of court and is not subject to any arbitrary or inflexible rule. Wegner Canning Corp. v Wegner (1942, Sup) 33 NYS2d 443.

Where consolidation of actions begun in different counties is had, venue should be in county whose jurisdiction was first invoked. Cross & Brown Co. v Cimbar Corp. (1949) 275 AD 680, 86 NYS2d 481; Bril v Storm (1949) 275 AD 954, 89 NYS2d 659.

Where the issues presented by two actions are the same, a motion to consolidate may be granted with a direction that the trial take place in the county where the real property is located where an early trial can be obtained in such county. Brunner v Steinhardt (1952) 4 Misc 2d 923, 111 NYS2d 887.

Consolidated action should be tried in county wherein one of actions consolidated was first brought, in absence of proof that witnesses would be convenienced by change. Funk v Nelson (1942) 264 AD 876, 35 NYS2d 503.

Consolidated action was ordered tried in Wayne county wherein action was first commenced and corporate parties principally operated and witnesses resided and whose trial calendar was less congested than New York county calendar. Wegner Canning Corp. v Wegner (1942, Sup) 33 NYS2d 443.

Action by "elected" officers of local union against other "elected" officers thereof was consolidated with another action by defendants (as plaintiffs) in first action and local union, against plaintiffs (as defendants) in first action and also international union and its officers, and trial was ordered in county where second action was pending, where similar action had been tried. Doolittle v Canfield (1943, Sup) 40 NYS2d 763.

Transferring trial of consolidated actions to Kings county was abuse of discretion in view of calendar conditions and fact that Queens county action was first begun. Karpel v Roberts (1948) 273 AD 896, 77 NYS2d 58.

Village Law, § 341-3, requiring all actions against village to be tried in county where village is situated, is controlled by this section, and so plaintiff's action against defendant village, commenced in Nassau county, was consolidated with his action against individual defendant, arising out of same accident, commenced in Kings county, though village was in Nassau county. Rubenstein v Silbert (1951) 200 Misc 399, 106 NYS2d 304, mod 279 AD 878, 110 NYS2d 289.

Where automobile accident occurred in Sullivan county, and first action was commenced in New York county and second action was commenced in Sullivan county, there was no abuse of discretion in fixing place of trial in Sullivan county, where cause arose and convenience of witnesses would be promoted. Hobbs v San Filippo (1953) 281 AD 929, 119 NYS2d 644.

Where three separate actions arising from same automobile collision were commenced in three different counties, it was proper to fix venue in county where accident occurred and cause arose. Edwards v Lewin (1954) 284 AD 28, 130 NYS2d 49.

Where father and son commenced actions for personal injuries in Erie where injury occurred, and defendant sued son in Monroe county, and all actions arose from same automobile collision, such actions were consolidated for trial in Erie county. Leising v Norton (1954) 206 Misc 459, 133 NYS2d 262.

In the absence of special circumstances, the venue of a consolidated action is the venue of the action first instituted. Pembroke v Sarkisian (1961, Sup) 219 NYS2d 424.

51. Counsel

Where ten stockholders' derivative actions against corporation are consolidated and all were commenced within month of each other, attorneys who commenced first action, who proposed to employ outside counsel, were designated as general counsel for plaintiffs in consolidated action. Clayton v Standard Oil Co. (1942, Sup) 37 NYS2d 259.

Dispute as to what attorneys should act as general counsel for plaintiffs barred consolidation. Price v Creole Petroleum Corp. (1944, Sup) 51 NYS2d 783.

Where substantial right of plaintiff might be preju-diced by consolidation, since plaintiff in one action is defendant in the other and attorneys for defendant in action one are defending attorneys in the other action and will cross-examine the plaintiff in action one, consolidation denied. Resnick v Resnick (1957) 9 Misc 2d 65, 169 NYS2d 393.

52. Costs upon consolidation

In a consolidated action, costs are taxes as a whole. Vidal v Sheffield Farms Co. (1955) 208 Misc 438, 141 NYS2d 82.

CPA § 96 permitted only the costs of the consolidated action unless the right to tax the costs of the individual actions was reserved in the order of consolidation. P. V. Baranowsky Co. v Guaranty Trust Co. (1936) 247 AD 169, 286 NYS 997; Hull v Shannon (1931) 139 Misc 564, 249 NYS 33, mod 234 AD 648, 251 NYS 960.

Where actions are consolidated for reasons of convenience and economy and not because of lack of jurisdiction in one of the courts in which the actions were brought, the rules relating to costs in the first court apply to all the parties for such time as they remain within the jurisdiction of said court. All parties become subject to rules relating to costs in the second court when the order removing the actions to that court becomes effective. Benjamin v Walch (1936) 160 Misc 39, 288 NYS 458.

Where an order consolidating an action in aid of an attachment with a prior action to recover an alleged deposit from the defendant trust company made no reservation in respect to costs in the individual actions, and the verdict in the consolidated action was directed in favor of the defendant, but no costs were awarded to it, the defendant is not entitled to tax the costs already accrued in the prior individual action and is not entitled to mandatory costs against the plaintiff in the action in aid of an attachment. P. V. Baranowsky Co. v Guaranty Trust Co. (1936) 247 AD 169, 286 NYS 997.

Where two actions are consolidated and no provision made for costs accrued, a party is entitled to costs in the consolidated action only from the time of consolidation. Hiscox v New Yorker Staats-Zeitung & Ottendorfer (1893) 3 Misc 110, 23 NYS 682.

When two or more actions are consolidated they are at an end and are deemed discontinued, and no costs in such actions can be taxed upon the final judgment, unless it is so provided in the order of consolidation. Kelley v Kelley (1924) 123 Misc 583, 205 NYS 737.

Where defendant fails to take an appeal from an order consolidating actions he cannot, upon appeal from an order denying resettlement of an order in the consolidated action, contend that costs should have been imposed as a condition to granting the order of consolidation. Train v Davidson (1896) 11 AD 627, 42 NYS 1133.

The question of costs should always be adjusted, if possible, at the time of the consolidation of actions. Saraceno v Eastern Cab Co. (1938) 168 Misc 631, 6 NYS2d 178.

The reasonable disbursements necessarily incurred by the successful coplaintiff in a consolidated action in prosecuting the appeal were allowed. Robinson v Terminal Freight Transport, Inc. (1958) 14 Misc 2d 1085, 180 NYS2d 458.

D. CONSOLIDATION OF CASES PENDING IN DIFFERENT COURTS

53. Generally

Consolidation of default action is not within meaning or intent of this section. Stafford v Johnson (1953, Sup) 122 NYS2d 779.

Where City Court action could be tried in day or two and Supreme Court action could not be tried for several years, consolidation would be prejudicial to plaintiff in City Court action. Dorney v Wasmuski (1956, Sup) 149 NYS2d 688.

Administratrix' proceeding for settlement of her account and action on judgment against decedent may be consolidated. Re Murray's Estate (1936) 272 NY 228, 5 NE2d 717.

Where an action in the Municipal Court can be consolidated with a Supreme Court action, without prejudice to any substantial right, a motion to consolidate the actions should be granted. White v Richmond L. & R. Co. (1924) 211 AD 861, 206 NYS 872.

In view of CPA §§ 96 and 97 and § 1572 (§ 101 herein), the county court had power to consolidate an action brought in a justice's court with one pending in the county court, the causes of which arose out of the same transaction and the same parties were involved. Sternberg v Bergman (1931) 140 Misc 569, 250 NYS 134.

County Court may order consolidation of action brought in Justice's Court with action previously instituted in County Court. Greene v Beacorn (1932) 145 Misc 870, 262 NYS 349.

Actions in the Municipal Court may be removed to the Supreme Court and consolidated with an action at issue therein where there are common questions of law and fact in all the actions and the consolidation will promote the prompt dispatch of litigated business and avoid a multiplicity of suits without prejudice to the parties. Weinstein v Cohen (1932) 235 AD 734, 255 NYS 942.

A county court has power to consolidate an action subsequently commenced in the Justice's Court with an action pending in the county court between the same parties. Datz v Economy Cotton Goods Stores, Inc. (1934) 263 NY 252, 188 NE 728.

Common questions of law and fact involved in two actions should be disposed of in one consolidated action without prejudice to substantial rights of either party. Corcoran v Scolaro (1944) 267 AD 871, 46 NYS2d 377.

The language of CPA §§ 96, 97 and CPA § 209, providing for consolidation of actions and joinder of parties plaintiff, while very broad, did not confer upon the court power to make such order,

even upon notice, when such plaintiffs had exercised their right of election and brought their several suits separately and in different courts. Brennan v National Equitable Inv. Co. (1924) 210 AD 426, 206 NYS 280.

Municipal court action at law was not consolidated with supreme court action in equity, where jury of 6 was authorized in former action, whereas in latter jury of 12 was authorized. Simon v Waltman (1945) 185 Misc 967, 58 NYS2d 249.

Where parties to city court, municipal court and supreme court actions were identical, all actions resulted from transactions between the parties in supreme court action, and common questions of fact and law existed, the other actions were consolidated with the supreme court action. Hassid v Kay (1956) 6 Misc 2d 240, 163 NYS2d 311, affd 3 AD2d 904, 163 NYS2d 401.

Consolidation was denied where inferior court calendar was five years ahead of Supreme Court calendar. Audiographic of New York Corp. v Thermionic Corp. of America (1960, Sup) 198 NYS2d 508.

Consolidation was denied where though all controversies arose out of same contract, issues in lower court actions were not the same issues as in Supreme Court action. Audiographic of New York Corp. v Thermionic Corp. of America, supra.

Defendant's motion to consolidate an action in which he does not genuinely dispute liability with one subsequently brought by him against plaintiff, which will result in delaying first action, was denied. Royaloy, Inc. v General Moving & Storage, Inc. (1959) 25 Misc 2d 255, 207 NYS2d 569.

Supreme Court has no power to order a consolidation of tenant's City Court action against landlord for treble damages with landlord's summary proceeding in Municipal Court. Application of Elliotte (1960) 28 Misc 2d 677, 209 NYS2d 506.

54. Courts to which applicable

By CPA § 1572, (§ 101 herein), CPA § 97 was made applicable to all courts of record, so that the city court of New York could remove to itself an action pending in any district court to consolidate it with an action pending in the city court between the same parties. McKay v Reed, 12 Abb NC 58 note, and the court of common pleas could remove an action brought in a district court of New York city into the common pleas. Sire v Kneuper (1888, CP Ct) 3 NYS 533.

The superior court of the city of New York has the same right of removal under this section as the supreme court, and may remove an action from the New York city court and consolidate it with one pending therein. Carter v Sully (1892, Super Ct) 19 NYS 244.

The city court of the city of New York has power to remove to itself and consolidate with an action pending in it an action brought in the municipal court of said city, and should exercise the power where the parties in both actions are the same, the causes of action identical, arise out of the same transaction, are provable by the same evidence and are contested upon the same defense. Curley v E. & M. Schaefer Brewing Co. (1901) 35 Misc 131, 71 NYS 318.

A Supreme Court action cannot be removed and consolidated with actions pending in City Court. Sam Chan v Martin (1955, Sup) 143 NYS2d 269.

Where the Municipal Court is competent to pass on all the issues raised by a final order either granting or dismissing a petition in a summary proceeding, no declaration or consolidation or stay by the Supreme Court is necessary for the protection of the parties. Picto Corp. v Marburt Holding Corp. (1957) 9 Misc 2d 407, 166 NYS2d 798.

The supreme court has no power, either statutory or inherent, to consolidate and remove to itself actions pending in different courts of inferior jurisdiction, where neither of such actions is pending in supreme court. Molampy v Valestian (1959) 20 Misc 2d 561, 191 NYS2d 416.

District Court of Nassau County is without power to remove action from City Court of Long Beach, and consolidate it with action pending in District Court. Lloyd v Karp (1959) 17 Misc 2d 872, 191 NYS2d 720.

Plaintiff's action in Supreme Court to have check issued by her declared void and returned to her was consolidated with Municipal Court action on check in which she was defendant, since the Municipal Court could not grant her affirmative relief and the issues were the same in both actions. Gitter v Schiff (1960) 20 Misc 2d 610, 195 NYS2d 101.

55. Place for motion

A party could not change the place of trial of an action triable in the first judicial district by procuring an order in the second judicial district in an action there pending to consolidate the two actions. Rule of Practice 69, subd 2, formerly provided that such motion had to be made in the first district. Dupignac v Van Buskirk (1887) 44 Hun 45; and see Dupignac v Dupignac (1887) 107 NY 629, 13 NE 940.

56. Discretion of court

The consolidation of actions between the same parties, under CPA §§ 96 and 97 rested in the sound discretion of the court to which application was made. Argyle Co. v Griffith (1908) 128 AD 262, 112 NYS 773.

No abuse of discretion for the supreme court to remove to itself an action in the county court, consolidate it with the action pending there and make plaintiff in the pending action defendant in the consolidated action. Brink's Express Co. v Burns (1930) 230 AD 559, 245 NYS 649.

Discretion of court properly exercised and order consolidating actions affirmed. Lebowitz v Leach Steel Corp. (1929) 227 AD 761, 236 NYS 485.

Where action in City Court for personal injuries received in automobile collision is ready for trial, and action in Supreme Court for injuries from same collision will not be reached for four years, it was abuse of discretion to consolidate such actions. Miro v Gottheim (1955) 285 AD 834, 137 NYS2d 31.

Determination that actions in Supreme Court and City Court for property injury from blasting should be jointly tried was improvident exercise of discretion where issues were not similar and where there were no facts showing dates when blasting occurred or that claimed damages arose from same negligent acts by defendant contractor. Imp v Tully & Di Napoli, Inc. (1955) 286 AD 841, 142 NYS2d 212.

Application to transfer from County Court to Supreme Court action for injuries arising from automobile accident and to consolidate said action with two actions in Supreme Court for death of passengers in same accident denied in exercise of discretions. McAllister v Drislane (1933) 239 AD 85, 266 NYS 809.

The supreme court has no power, either statutory or inherent, to consolidate and remove to itself actions pending in different courts of inferior jurisdiction, where neither of such actions is pending in supreme court. Molampy v Valestian (1959) 20 Misc 2d 561, 191 NYS2d 416.

Supreme Court has no power to order a consolidation of tenant's City Court action against landlord for treble damages with landlord's summary proceeding in Municipal Court. Application of Elliotte (1960) 28 Misc 2d 677, 209 NYS2d 506.

57. Condition on removal

Where an action is pending in the supreme court and another action between the same parties is pending in another court, and the causes of action might be joined in one action, an order for removal and consolidation will be made by the supreme court; in case of prejudice to plaintiffs, terms may be imposed as a condition of the consolidation of the actions. Soloman v Belden, 12 Abb NC 58.

Where an action is pending in the supreme court and another action is pending in another court between the same parties for causes of action which might be joined in one action, the supreme court will remove to itself the action in the other court, and in case of prejudice to plaintiffs, terms may be imposed as a condition of such removal. Soloman v Belden, supra; and see McKay v Reed, footnote to this case, 58 note.

Defendant's Municipal Court action to recover balance due for professional services was consolidated with plaintiff's Supreme Court malpractice action on condition that plaintiff deposit with court a sum to secure payment of alleged fee due for professional services. Gordon v Lifschitz (1960) 10 AD2d 669, 196 NYS2d 1007, resettlement den 11 AD2d 938, 207 NYS2d 230.

58. Right to open and close

Where complaint in Supreme Court action contained vague and general allegations, alleging no facts showing merit, created suspicion that Supreme Court action was instituted solely to delay trial of Municipal Court action and to wrench from plaintiff therein its right to open and close, and required denial of motion to consolidate actions without prejudice. Sealtite Mfg. Corp. v Jansa Woodworking Corp. (1955) 286 AD 875, 142 NYS2d 257.

59. Transfer to another district

This section does not authorize a justice of the Municipal Court of New York presiding in one district to make by consolidation of actions a transfer of a case pending in another district to the district in which he is presiding. Ralph M. Levey Co. v Fox (1923) 121 Misc 113, 200 NYS 274.

60. Particular matters—Contracts

Action was removed from city court and consolidated with action in supreme court where both causes related to the contract relation of client and attorney between parties. W. N. Britton Realty Co. v Clay (1938) 255 AD 930, 8 NYS2d 751.

An action begun in a city court for goods sold and delivered after the defendant therein had begun an action in the supreme court for return of the money he had paid for the goods on the ground of misrepresentation, was ordered consolidated with the prior action in the supreme court. Lutus v Labor (1927) 222 AD 132, 226 NYS 108.

Nonjury city court case was consolidated with jury supreme court case, where both actions were based on same written contract and involved identical facts and issues. Edgewater Machine Co. v Weiss (1948) 1 Misc 2d 862, 85 NYS2d 655.

Supreme court action for specific performance of oral agreement to convey to plaintiff realty later leased by defendant to plaintiff's husband and city court action by landlord to dispossess tenant, were properly consolidated, though some of parties are different. Hannigan v Diamond (1953, Sup) 125 NYS2d 423.

Supreme Court has no power to remove to itself or to County Court action on contract pending in Nassau District Court, where neither action is pending in Supreme Court or County Court. Application of Comfort-Zone Corp. (1955, Sup) 140 NYS2d 76.

Seven actions against husband for necessaries furnished wife, one in Supreme Court, one in City Court and five in Municipal Court, were properly consolidated, where all involved common issues, especially where valuable policy was served by consolidating in such type of action. Hartman, Sheridan & Tekulsky v Hale (1955) 285 AD 949, 139 NYS2d 344.

City court action by subcontractor against contractor and owner to foreclose mechanic's lien was consolidated with supreme court action by owner for damages caused by contractor and subcontractor for negligently constructing roof tank. Blu-Strike Realty Co. v North Eastern Iron Works, Inc. (1947, Sup) 75 NYS2d 4.

Municipal court action for labor and materials was not consolidated with supreme court action for damages for improper work, where purpose of latter was to delay former and where no merit was shown. Ivel Furs, Inc. v Air Distribution Co. (1948) 274 AD 66, 80 NYS2d 72.

Municipal court action by administratrix of deceased insured to recover benefits under life policy was not consolidated with supreme court action to rescind action for fraud. Manhattan Life Ins. Co. v Kerzner (1952, Sup) 112 NYS2d 872.

Justice court action for oil sold and delivered was consolidated with county court action having four causes of action for oil spilled and for commissions for oil sold, though issue had not been joined in county court action. Monticello Gas & Oil Co. v Lhevan (1954, Just Ct) 133 NYS2d 573.

Where defendant in an action in the City Court of New York City for breach of warranty upon a contract of sale thereafter sued plaintiff therein, in Municipal Court, for the purchase price of the goods covered by such contract, and defendant in the Municipal Court action set up as a defense and counterclaim the alleged breach of warranty aforesaid, the City Court had no authority, notwithstanding CPA §§ 96, 97 and CPA § 1572 (§ 101 herein), to order consolidation of the actions in that court. T. Blumenthal & Co. v Theo. Tiedemann & Sons (1922) 118 Misc 560, 194 NYS 86.

61. —Counterclaim

In view of CPA §§ 96, 97 where defendant in an action pending in City Court had a counterclaim for an amount exceeding the jurisdiction of the City Court, on which he had instituted an action in the Supreme Court against the plaintiff in the City Court action as well as other defendants, the City Court action was consolidated with that in the Supreme Court to permit determination of all the issues in a single action. Borzilleri v Brockway Motor Truck Corp. (1925) 124 Misc 905, 210 NYS 17.

Action in Municipal Court of City of New York in which plaintiff herein interposed counterclaim beyond jurisdiction of said court consolidated with plaintiff's subsequent action in Supreme Court between same parties and based upon same facts. Martin v Bull (1932) 236 AD 637, 260 NYS 814, reh den 261 NYS 963.

62. —Partnership

CPA §§ 96, 97 authorized the Supreme Court to direct the consolidation with an action pending before it for the dissolution of an alleged partnership and for an accounting between the alleged partners and the sale of the partnership assets, of an action subsequently commenced in Municipal Court by defendant in a former action against plaintiff therein, based upon breach of an alleged agreement between the parties governing the same relations described in the former action as constituting a partnership, the actions being so intimately related that the disposal of one necessarily involved the other. Goldey v Bierman (1922) 201 AD 527, 194 NYS 373.

63. —Real property

Action in replevin in City Court consolidated with action in Supreme Court for foreclosure of mortgage where both actions involve title to certain fixtures attached to and connected with real property—the plaintiff in the foreclosure action claiming under the terms of the mortgage, and the plaintiff in the replevin action claiming by virtue of a chattel mortgage. Herold v Cohrone Boat Co. (1936) 248 AD 589, 287 NYS 379.

64. —Torts

CPA §§ 96, 97 were held to authorize the consolidation of an action in the Supreme Court to recover damages for negligence on the part of the defendant as an architect in planning and supervising the erection of a building for plaintiff, and an action in the Municipal Court by the defendant in the former action against the plaintiff therein, to recover for services rendered in connection with the erection of the same building. Zapfe v Werner (1923) 120 Misc 326, 199 NYS 293.

Where two city court actions and one supreme court action arose from same automobile collision, all involve common questions of law and fact, it was abuse of discretion to deny removal of city court actions to supreme court and to consolidate all three actions. Yammerino v Surdi (1954) 283 AD 995, 130 NYS2d 291.

Though municipal and supreme court actions arose out of the same collision of two cars but former can be tried in few months and latter cannot be tried for three years, such actions were not consolidated. Stein v Sax (1954, Sup) 133 NYS2d 780.

Action brought in City Court of New York consolidated with action in Supreme Court, where both arose out of same accident and witnesses are identical except for medical testimony. Goltz v Art Awning Mfg. Co. (1932) 145 Misc 754, 260 NYS 162.

Consolidation of Supreme Court actions by automobile passengers for personal injuries against owners and operators of injuring automobiles, with Municipal Court action by insurer as subrogee of owner of automobile involved for property damage, was denied as prejudicial to insurer, unless parties stipulated to try personal injury actions without reference to property damage action, and that property injury action be determined by such verdict and by assessment of damages. Kutnerian v Sagui (1955) 285 AD 1134, 140 NYS2d 759.

Where taxicab driver brought action in supreme court for injuries against owners of car alleged to have struck taxicab, and in municipal court, insurance company, subrogated to rights of car owners on payment of collision damages, brought action against owner of taxicab, driver's employer, motion by plaintiff, taxicab driver, to consolidate municipal court action with action in supreme

court was granted. Weiss v Fox (1938) 254 AD 662, 4 NYS2d 378.

Where two parties to an automobile collision each sought to recover damages sustained in the collision by reason of the negligence of the other, one bringing his action in the County Court and the other in a Justice Court, it was held that neither CPA §§ 96 and 97 nor CPA § 130 (§§ 2212, 2213, Rule 2214(b) herein) of the Civil Practice Act authorized the Supreme Court to make an order consolidating the two actions. Curry v Earll (1924) 209 AD 205, 203 NYS 750.

Personal and property injuries, resulting from same accident; denial of consolidation was abuse of discretion. Alexander v Odgis (1947) 272 AD 917, 71 NYS2d 139.

Where county and supreme court actions involve same issues of negligence, namely, of colliding automobiles, they should be tried together by supreme court. Vandermark v Novickey (1946) 187 Misc 733, 65 NYS2d 606.

Action in Utica city court for property damage consolidated with supreme court action for personal and property injuries, both arising from some collision. Harrigan v Stiefvater (1947, Sup) 78 NYS2d 255.

Municipal court action by passenger in insured automobile against insurer was consolidated with supreme court action by insurer for judgment declaring policy was no longer in force, since such actions present common questions of law and fact with relation to breach of conditions of policy by insured. General Acc. Fire & Life Assur. Corp. v Margolis (1952, Sup) 116 NYS2d 209.

An action for compensation for medical services and an action for malpractice have inter-related issues. Hence, an action for compensation by a physician against a parent could be removed from Municipal Court of the City of New York to the Supreme Court and consolidated therein with an action for malpractice against the doctor notwithstanding that the issues have not been joined in the malpractice action. Geller v Ticktin (1957) 6 Misc 2d 16, 161 NYS2d 628.

Defendant's Municipal Court action to recover balance due for professional services was consolidated with plaintiff's Supreme Court malpractice action on condition that plaintiff deposit with court a sum to secure payment of alleged fee due for professional services. Gordon v Lifschitz (1960) 10 AD2d 669, 196 NYS2d 1007, resettlement den 11 AD2d 938, 207 NYS2d 230.

Personal injury action pending in Nassau County Supreme Court and property damage action pending in Nassau County District Court, both arising out of same accident, were ordered consolidated and tried in Supreme Court, since separate actions were held to amount to a splitting of claims and would unnecessarily subject courts and defendant to multiple trials and possible inconsistent awards. McNichols v Weiss (1960) 12 AD2d 646, 208 NYS2d 721.

FORMS

Form   1—Notice of motion for consolidation of actions
Form   2—Notice of motion to consolidate actions pending in different counties
Form   3—Affidavit on motion to consolidate
Form   4—Affidavit on motion to consolidate action pending in different counties
Form   5—Order to show cause on application for consolidation
Form   6—Order consolidating actions
Form   7—Order consolidating actions pending in different counties
Form   8—Notice of motion for joint trial of actions
Form   9—Order to show cause on motion of party both defendant in first and a third
            party defendant in second action, for consolidation or in the alternative
            joint trial of actions
Form 10—Affidavit to support motion for joint trial of actions
Form 11—Affidavit in opposition to motion for joint trial
Form 12—Order directing joint trial of actions
Form 13—Provision in order for joint trial directing separation and prior trial of a
            common issue
Form 14—Notice of motion for removal and consolidation of lower court action
Form 15—Affidavit in support of motion for removal and consolidation of action
Form 16—Affidavit in support of motion for removal and consolidation of lower court
            action—another form
Form 17—Order to show cause on motion for removal and consolidation of lower
            court action
Form 18—Order removing and consolidating lower court action
Form 19—Notice of motion to remove to county court and consolidate lower court
            action
Form 20—Affidavit in support of motion to remove to County Court and consolidate
            lower court action
Form 21—Order granting motion to remove to county court and consolidate lower
            court action
Form 22—Notice of motion to remove justice court action to county court for joint
            trial without consolidation
Form 23—Affidavit of party in support of motion
Form 24—Order removing action from inferior court for trial together with Supreme
            Court action without consolidation

Form 1

Notice of Motion for Consolidation of Actions

SUPREME COURT, __1_____ COUNTY

__2_____, Plaintiff,
  against   Index No. __3_ [if assigned]
__4_____, Defendant.

SUPREME COURT, __5_____ COUNTY   Notice of Motion
__6_____, Plaintiff,
  against   Index No. __7_ [if assigned]
__8_____, Defendant.

    PLEASE TAKE NOTICE that on the affidavit of __9_____, sworn to the __10__
day of __11_____, 19_12_ and upon all the pleadings and proceedings in the above-
entitled actions, the defendant named in the above-entitled actions will move this court
at a motion term thereof to be held in and for the County of __13_____, at the county
court house in the City of __14_____, on the __15_ day of __16_____, 19_17_ at
__18__ o'clock in the __19__ noon of that day or as soon thereafter as counsel can be

heard for an order consolidating the above-entitled actions and for such other and further relief as may be just and proper together with the costs of this motion.

Dated: __20_____, 19_21_

__22_____
Attorney for Defendant
Office and Post Office Address
Telephone No.

To: __23_____
    Attorney for Plaintiff __24_____
    Office and Post Office Address
    __25_____
    Attorney for Plaintiff __26_____
    Office and P.O. Address

Form 2

Notice of Motion to Consolidate Actions Pending in Different Counties

SUPREME COURT, __1_____ COUNTY

__2_____, Plaintiff,
    against   Index No. __3__ [if assigned]
__4_____, Defendant.

SUPREME COURT, __5_____ COUNTY   Notice of Motion
__6_____, Plaintiff,
    against   Index No. __7__ [if assigned]
__8_____, Defendant.

PLEASE TAKE NOTICE that upon the annexed affidavit of __9_____, sworn to the __10__ day of __11_____, 19_12_ and upon all the pleadings and proceedings in the above-entitled actions, the defendant in the said actions will make a motion at a motion term of this court to be held in and for the County of __13_____, at the County Court House in the City of __14_____, on the __15__ day of __16_____, 19_17_, at __18__ o'clock in the __19__ noon of that day or as soon thereafter as counsel can be heard for an order consolidating the above actions, fixing the County of __20_____, as the place of trial of the consolidated action and for such other and further relief as may be just and proper together with the costs of this motion.

Dated: __21_____, 19_22_.

__23_____
Attorney for Defendant
Office and Post Office Address
Telephone No.

To: __24_____
    Attorney for Plaintiff __25_____
    Office and Post Office Address
    __26_____
    Attorney for Plaintiff __27_____
    Office and Post Office Address

Form 3

Affidavit on Motion to Consolidate

[Title of court and cause
in both actions as in Form 1]   Affidavit

__1_____, being duly sworn, deposes and says: 1. He is the defendant in the first above-entitled action in which __2_____ is the plaintiff and is the plaintiff in the second above-entitled action in which __3_____ is the defendant.

2. The first named action above was commenced by the service of the summons and [verified] complaint on the __4__ day of __5_____, 19_6_. The complaint, a copy of which is hereto annexed, made a part hereof and marked Exhibit "A" sets forth a cause of action for __7_____. The [verified] answer was served on the __8__ day of __9_____, 19_10_, and contains a general denial and separate defenses as follows: __11_____ [set forth the substance]. A copy of said answer is hereto annexed and marked Exhibit "B."

3. Thereafter on the __12__ day of __13_____, 19_14_, deponent commenced the second named action above by the service of the summons and [verified] complaint on defendant, [or as the case may be], a copy of which complaint is hereto annexed and marked Exhibit "C," and which sets forth a cause of action for __15_____. The verified answer, a copy of which is hereto annexed, made a part hereof and marked Exhibit "D" is a general denial besides the following separate defenses: __16_____ [set forth the substance of any such defenses].

4. Neither of the above actions has yet been noticed for trial [or, if noticed, set forth facts as to condition of cases on the calendar].

5. Each of the above-entitled actions is now pending in this court.

6. The actions involve a common question of law or fact, in that __17_____ [show in detail the common question of law or fact in both actions].

7. Considerable time and expense will be saved by the consolidation of the two actions [state facts to show any other reason for consolidation].

8. The consolidation of the above actions will not be prejudicial to any substantial right in that __18_____ [state facts to show that no prejudice will result].

9. The deponent applies for an order to show cause to bring on this motion for the reason that the above-entitled action first set out is now on the ready jury calendar of this court and is likely to be reached very shortly, possibly before this motion could be heard and determined if brought on by notice of motion.

10. [If order to show cause is sought] No previous application for the relief herein prayed for or for any similar relief has heretofore been made to any court or judge.

Wherefore, deponent asks that an order be granted consolidating the above actions, pursuant to section 602 of the Civil Practice Law and Rules [if order to show cause sought, deponent may also ask for a stay of proceedings in the action first brought or as desired].

__19_____

[Print signer's name below signature]

[Jurat]

Form 4

Affidavit on Motion to Consolidate Actions Pending in Different Counties

[Title of court and causes
as in Form 2]   Affidavit

STATE OF NEW YORK
COUNTY OF __1_____   ss.:

__2_____, being duly sworn, deposes and says:

1. Deponent is the plaintiff in the action first set out above and is the defendant in the action second set out.

2. The action first set out above was commenced on the __3__ day of __4_____, 19_5_ by the service of a summons and complaint on the defendant therein. On the __6__ day of __7_____, 19_8_ the defendant therein served his answer on deponent's attorney. Thereafter and on the __9__ day of __10_____, 19_11_ deponent caused a

note of issue to be filed and the action is now on the general trial calendar of the Supreme Court, County of __12_____ as Case No. __13__.

3. The second action set out above was commenced on the __14__ day of __15_____, 19_16_ by the plaintiff therein by the service of a summons and complaint on deponent. Thereafter, and on the __17__ day of __18_____, 19_19_ deponent caused his answer to be served on the attorney for the plaintiff. No further proceedings have been taken in the said action.

4. The action first set out above was commenced by the deponent to recover for personal injuries suffered by him as a result of the negligence of the defendant therein. The second above-entitled action was commenced by the plaintiff therein to recover for personal injuries allegedly sustained by him as a result of the negligence of deponent. Both causes of action are based upon an automobile collision which occurred on the __20__ day of __21_____, 19_22_ in the Village of __23_____, County of __24_____ and State of New York. The said collision occurred when an automobile owned and operated by the defendant in the first above-entitled action collided with an automobile owned and operated by the plaintiff.

5. Both of the above-entitled actions involve common questions of law and fact, namely the automobile collision heretofore described and both actions involve the question of the negligence and contributory negligence of the parties thereto.

6. Deponent believes that time and expense will be saved by the consolidation of the two actions because such consolidation would avoid a multiplicity of suits. Deponent further believes that none of the parties will be prejudiced by the consolidation for the reason that the issues involved in each action are identical and that it is to the benefit of each of the parties to avoid a multiplicity of suits and to have a determination of all issues in one trial.

7. Deponent requests that if the consolidation which is requested on this motion is granted, provision should be made for the trial of the actions in the County of __25_____ because the action commenced in the County of __26_____ has not yet been noticed for trial, the deponent is a resident of the said County of __27_____ and the cause of action arose in the said County of __28_____. Further, deponent believes that a speedier trial can be obtained in the said County of __29_____.

__30_____

[Print signer's name below signature]

[Jurat]

Form 5

Order to Show Cause on Application for Consolidation

SUPREME COURT, __1_____ COUNTY

[Title of both causes]   Order to Show Cause

Present: Hon. __2_____, Justice.

Upon the annexed affidavit of __3_____, duly sworn to the __4__ day of __5_____, 19_6_, and upon all the pleadings and proceedings had in the above entitled actions, let __7_____, the plaintiff named in the first above entitled action, or his attorney, show cause before me, or one of the justices of this court, at a motion term to be held in and for the County of __8_____ at the County Court House in the City of __9_____, on the __10__ day of __11_____, 19_12_, at __13__ o'clock of the forenoon of that day, or as soon thereafter as counsel can be heard, why an order should not be made herein, consolidating the above entitled actions, now pending in this court, and granting the defendant named in the first above entitled action such other and further relief as to the court may seem just and proper, and, sufficient reason appearing therefor, it is

ORDERED that the action first above-entitled pending in the Supreme Court, County of __14_____, and entitled __15_____, Plaintiff against __16_____, Defendant be and the same is hereby stayed until the entry of an order deciding the motion for consolidation, and, sufficient reason appearing therefor it is

ORDERED that service of a copy of this order and a copy of the papers on which the same was made, on the attorneys for the respective parties, on or before the __17__ day of __18_____, 19_19_ by leaving a copy at the office of the respective attorneys be good and sufficient service of notice of this application.

Signed this __20__ day of __21_____, 19_22_ at __23_____, New York.

__24_____

[Print signer's name below signature]
Justice, Supreme Court
__25_____ County

Form 6

Order Consolidating Actions

SUPREME COURT, __1_____ COUNTY.

[Title of both causes]   Order

Present: Hon. __2_____, Justice.

The defendant in the first above-entitled actions having moved for an order to consolidate said actions, now pending in this court, and said motion having come on regularly to be heard,

NOW, on reading and filing the notice of motion dated the __3__ day of __4_____, 19_5_, and the affidavit of __6_____, sworn to the __7__ day of __8_____, 19_9_, with due proof [or "admission"] of service of said papers, and on the pleadings and proceedings in both said actions, in support of said motion, and the affidavit of __10_____, sworn to the __11__ day of __12_____, 19_13_, in opposition thereto, and after hearing __14_____, attorney for the defendant above, in support of said motion and __15_____, attorney for the plaintiff above, in opposition thereto, and due deliberation having been had,

NOW, on motion of __16_____, attorney for the defendant, and on the decision of the court filed herein, it is hereby

ORDERED that the motion to consolidate the two actions entitled as above be and the same is hereby granted, and it is further,

ORDERED that the clerk of the County of __17_____ be, and he is hereby directed and authorized to consolidate the files of said two actions above-entitled under the file number of the action entitled __18_____, plaintiff against __19_____, defendant, and it is further

ORDERED, that the costs of the actions hereby consolidated up to the date of this order abide the event of this consolidated action.

Signed this __20__ day of __21_____, 19_22_ at __23_____, New York.

Enter

__24_____

[Print signer's name below signature]
Justice, Supreme Court
__25_____County

Form 7

Order Consolidating Actions Pending in Different Counties

SUPREME COURT, __1_____ COUNTY.

[Title of both causes]   Order

PRESENT: Hon. __2_____, Justice.

The plaintiff in the above-entitled action first set out having moved for an order to consolidate said actions, the first of which actions is now pending in the New York Supreme Court, County of __3_____ and the second of which actions is now pending in the New York Supreme Court, County of __4_____, to fix the County of __5____ as the place of trial of the consolidated action and for such other and further relief as may be just and proper with costs, and said motion having come on regularly to be heard,

NOW, on reading and filing the notice of motion dated the __6__ day of __7_____, 19_8_ and the affidavit of __9_____, sworn to the __10__ day of __11_____, 19_12_ with due proof of service of said papers in support of the said motion and the affidavit of __13_____, sworn to the __14__ day of __15_____, 19_16_ in opposition thereto, and on all the pleadings and proceedings in both of the aforesaid actions, and after hearing __17_____, attorney for the plaintiff in the above-entitled action first set out in support of the motion and __18_____, attorney for the defendant in the above-entitled action first set out in opposition thereto and due deliberation having been had,

NOW, on motion of __19_____, attorney for the plaintiff in the above-entitled action first set out it is

ORDERED that the motion be and the same hereby is granted and it is further

ORDERED that the said action now pending in the Supreme Court, __20_____ County entitled __21_____, plaintiff, against __22_____, defendant, and the action now pending in the Supreme Court, __23_____ County entitled __24_____, plaintiff, against __25_____, defendant, be and the same hereby are consolidated into one action and that the respective pleadings in the action hereby consolidated stand as the pleadings in the consolidated action and it is further

ORDERED that the place of trial of the consolidated actions be and the same is hereby fixed as the Supreme Court, County of __26_____, and it is further

ORDERED that in the said consolidated action, __27_____ shall be deemed plaintiff and have the right to open and close and __28_____ shall be deemed defendant and it is further

ORDERED that the cost of the actions hereby consolidated up to the date of this order abide the event of the consolidated action.

Signed this __29__ day of __30_____, 19_31_ at __32_____, New York.

Enter

__33_____
[Print signer's name below signature]
Justice, Supreme Court
__34_____ County

Form 8

Notice of Motion for Joint Trial of Actions

SUPREME COURT, __1_____ COUNTY

__2_____, Plaintiff,
　against　　　　　　Index No. __3__ [if assigned]
__4_____, Defendant.

SUPREME COURT, __5_____ COUNTY　　　　　　　　Notice of Motion
__6_____, Plaintiff,
　against　　　　　　Index No. __7__ [if assigned]
__8_____, Defendant.

PLEASE TAKE NOTICE that upon the annexed affidavit of __9_____, sworn to the __10__ day of __11_____, 19_12_ and upon all the pleadings and proceedings had and taken in the above-entitled actions the undersigned will move this court at a motion term thereof to be held in and for the County of __13_____, at the County Court House in the City of __14_____ on the __15__ day of __16_____, 19_17_ at __18__ o'clock in the __19__ noon of that day or as soon thereafter as counsel can be heard for an order directing that the above-entitled actions be tried together, without consolidation, and for such other and further relief as to the court may seem just and proper with the costs of this motion.

Dated: __20_____, 19_21_.

_____22_____

Attorney for __23_____
Office and Post Office Address
Telephone No.

To: __24_____
Attorney for __25_____
Office and Post Office Address

Form 9

Order to Show Cause on Motion of Party Both Defendant in First and a Third Party Defendant in Second Action, for Consolidation or in the Alternative Joint Trial of Actions

SUPREME COURT, __1_____ COUNTY.

[Title of both actions]   Order to Show Cause

Present: Hon. __2_____, Justice.

Upon the complaint and answer in the first above entitled action, and the complaint, answer, and answer of the third party defendant, __3_____, to the counterclaim set forth against it in the said answer, and upon the annexed affidavit of __4_____, sworn to __5_____, I do hereby

ORDER that __6_____ as plaintiff in the first above-entitled action and as a third party defendant in the second above-entitled action __7_____ as plaintiff in the second above-entitled action, and __8_____ as defendants and third party plaintiffs in the second above-entitled action, or their attorneys, show cause, at a motion term, Part __9__, of the Supreme Court of the State of New York, County of __10_____, at the courthouse thereof, __11_____, on the __12__ day of __13_____, at __14__ o'clock in the __15_____ [forenoon] of that day, or as soon thereafter as counsel can be heard,

1. why an order should not be made herein consolidating the first above entitled action with the second above entitled action, now pending in this Court, or, in the alternative

2. why there should not be a joint trial of the first above entitled action, in this court, and

3. why such other and further relief should not be granted in the premises as may be just and proper.

Sufficient reason appearing therefor, I do hereby further order

Let service of this and of the annexed affidavit, by leaving copies thereof at the office of __16_____, as attorneys for __17_____ [opposing parties], at their office, __18_____, on or before the __19__ day of __20_____, 19_21_, be deemed good and sufficient service thereof.

Signed this __22__ day of __23_____, 19_24_ at __25_____, New York.

_____26_____

[Print signer's name below signature]
Justice, Supreme Court
__27_____ County

[Adapted from the record in Abelow v Equitable Life Assur. Soc. 9 AD2d 745, 192 NYS2d 663 (1959).]

Form 10

Affidavit to Support Motion for Joint Trial of Actions

[Title of court and cause in
both actions as in Form 8]   Affidavit

STATE OF NEW YORK
COUNTY OF __1_____   ss.

__2_____, being duly sworn, deposes and says:

1. He is the defendant in both of the above-entitled actions.

2. The first above-entitled action was commenced by the service of a summons and complaint upon deponent on the __3__ day of __4_____, 19_5_. The action is by __6_____ against deponent to recover __7_____ [state briefly nature of cause of action], as more fully appears from a copy of the complaint in said action which is annexed hereto and made a part hereof. Issue was joined therein by the service of an answer on the __8__ day of __9_____, 19_10_, said answer containing a denial of __11_____ [or "general denial"] and an affirmative defense of __12_____. A copy of said answer is annexed hereto, and made a part hereof.

3. The second above-entitled action was commenced by the service of a summons and complaint upon deponent on the __13__ day of __14_____, 19_15_. The action was commenced by __16_____, the plaintiff therein to recover __17_____ [state briefly nature and cause of action] as more fully appears from a copy of the complaint in said action which is annexed hereto and made a part hereof. Issue was joined therein by the service of an answer of the __18__ day of __19_____, 19_20_. The said answer contained a denial of __21_____ [and an affirmative defense of __22_____] all as more fully appears from a copy of said answer which is annexed hereto, and made a part hereof.

4. Each of the above actions involve common questions of law and [or] fact as appears from the facts stated above and from the pleadings in the two actions.

5. These two actions can be tried together, without consolidation, without inconvenience or prejudice to any substantial right of the parties in the above actions.

                              __23_____
                              [Print signer's name below signature]

[Jurat]

Form 11

Affidavit in Opposition to Motion for Joint Trial

[Title of court and action   Affidavit
and venue of affidavit]   Index No. __1__ [if assigned]

__2_____, being duly sworn, deposes and says that he is an attorney and counsellor at law associated with __3_____, attorneys for the defendant in action No. 2.

That this is a motion to consolidate action No. 1 within action No. 2 for the purpose of a joint trial. The facts are briefly these:

The plaintiff was injured on __4_____ street about __5_____ [11:30 a.m.] while he was riding a bicycle on __6_____ [street] in __7_____ [city] when he was struck by an automobile owned by __8_____, the defendant in action No. 1. As a result of this accident an ambulance was summoned from __9_____ hospital, defendant No. 2, and the plaintiff who was injured as a result of the first accident was put on a stretcher and placed in the ambulance which was proceeding on __10_____ [street] on the way to the hospital when a collision occurred between the ambulance in which the plaintiff was riding and an oil truck as a result of which the plaintiff claims he sustained further injuries. The oil truck in question is alleged to have been owned by defendant __11_____ and operated by defendant __12_____ and used in the business of defendant __13_____, all of whom, together with __14_____, the owner of the ambulance, are named codefendants.

The attorneys for the defendant __15_____ hospital object to the consolidation of these actions for the purpose of a joint trial on the grounds that the defendant __16_____ hospital will be prejudiced by such action. It will be necessary for the plaintiff to establish what injuries he sustained as a result of the first accident and what injuries he also sustained as a result of the second accident. If a joint trial is had the jury will be given the medical testimony of the doctor which the plaintiff may produce and undoubtedly will be left to speculate as to which of the injuries were sustained in the original accident and which were sustained in the second accident, all to the prejudice of the defendants in the second action. The court is well aware that the jury may not speculate as to which accident caused what injury but that this must be proven by medical testimony on the part of the plaintiff.

__17_____

[Print signer's name below signature]

[Jurat]

[Adapted from the record in Abbatepaolo v Blumberg, 7 AD2d 847, 182 NYS2d 83 (1959).]

Form 12

Order Directing Joint Trial of Actions

SUPREME COURT, __1_____ COUNTY.

[Title of both causes]   Order

PRESENT: Hon. __2_____, Justice

The defendant in the above-entitled actions having moved this court for an order directing that the said actions be tried together without consolidation and for such other and further relief as may to the court seem just and proper, and said motion having come on regularly to be heard,

NOW, on reading and filing the notice of motion dated the __3__ day of __4_____, 19_5_ and the affidavit of __6_____, sworn to the __7__ day of __8_____, 19_9_ and the exhibits thereto attached with proof of due service thereof in support of said motion and on reading and filing the affidavit of __10_____, sworn to the __11__ day of __12_____, 19_13_ in opposition thereto and upon the pleadings and other proceedings heretofore had in said actions, and after hearing __14_____, attorney for the defendant in support of said motion and no one having appeared in opposition thereto and it appearing to my satisfaction that the said above-entitled actions involve common questions of law and [or] fact and that said actions can be tried together without inconvenience or prejudice to a substantial right of any party to the said actions, and due deliberation having been had, it is

ORDERED that the motion be and the same is hereby granted and it is further

ORDERED that the two above-entitled actions be tried together without consolidation.

Signed this __15__ day of __16_____, 19_17_ at __18_____, New York.

Enter

__19_____

[Print signer's name below signature]
Justice, Supreme Court
__20_____ County

Form 13

Provision in Order for Joint Trial Directing Separation and Prior Trial of a Common Issue

That, to avoid prejudice, the issue of __1_____ [fraud in connection with the insurance policies], common to both actions, be separated and first tried.

[Adapted from the record in Abelow v Equitable Life Assur. Soc. 9 AD2d 745, 192 NYS2d 663 (1959).]

Form 14

Notice of Motion for Removal and Consolidation of Lower Court Action

SUPREME COURT, __1_____ COUNTY

__2_____, Plaintiff,
　against
__3_____, Defendant.

Notice of Motion
Index No. __4__ [if assigned]

PLEASE TAKE NOTICE that upon the annexed affidavit of __5_____, plaintiff in the above entitled Supreme Court action, sworn to the __6__ day of __7_____, 19_8_, and upon the pleadings and proceedings in the above-entitled action and an action pending in the __9_____ Court, __10_____ of __11_____ entitled __12_____, Plaintiff against __13_____, Defendant a motion will be made, at a motion term, of the Supreme Court, held in and for the County of __14_____, at the county court house in the City of __15_____, on the __16__ day of __17_____, 19_18_, at the opening of court on that day, or as soon thereafter as counsel can be heard, for an order removing into the Supreme Court the above entitled action now pending in the __19_____ court and consolidating that action with the above-entitled action, and for such other, further and different relief as may be proper, with costs.

Dated: __20_____, 19_21_.

　　　　　　　　　　　　　　　　　　　__22_____
　　　　　　　　　　　　　　　　　　　Attorney for __23_____
　　　　　　　　　　　　　　　　　　　Office and P. O. Address
　　　　　　　　　　　　　　　　　　　Telephone No.

To: __24_____
　　　Attorney for __25_____
　　　Office and P. O. Address

Form 15

Affidavit in Support of Motion for Removal and Consolidation of Action

SUPREME COURT, __1_____ COUNTY

[Title of cause]

Affidavit
Index No. __2__ [if assigned]

STATE OF NEW YORK
COUNTY OF __3_____　　　　　　　ss.:

__4_____, being duly sworn, deposes and says:

1. He is the plaintiff in the above-entitled action pending in the Supreme Court, which was commenced by the service of the summons and verified complaint on the __5__ day of __6_____, 19_7_. The complaint sets forth a cause of action for __8_____ [give details], and a copy is hereto annexed and made a part hereof. The answer was served on the __9__ day of __10_____, 19_11_, and contains a general denial of the allegations of the complaint [or set forth nature of answer]. A copy of said answer is hereto annexed and made a part hereof.

2. On the __12__ day of __13_____, 19_14_, defendant herein commenced an action

189

in the __15_____ Court of the __16_____ of __17_____, by the service of a summons and verified complaint alleging in substance a cause of action for __18_____ [set forth details] a copy of said complaint annexed hereto and made a part hereof. The verified answer in said action was served on the __19__ day of __20_____, 19_21_ and pleads a general denial and by way of a separate defense __22_____. A copy of said answer is hereto annexed and made a part hereof.

3. An examination of the pleadings in said two actions shows that they involve common questions of law and [or] fact. In support of this statement deponent further states __23_____ [state in detail the facts, circumstances and issues that are common to the two actions].

4. The removal of the action pending in the __24_____ Court of the __25_____ of __26_____ and its consolidation with the action pending in the Supreme Court will not prejudice any substantial right of any party to either of the said actions for the reason that __27_____ [state facts].

5. Much time and expense will be saved by the trial of these two actions at the same time. Further, it will be inequitable to try the action in the __28_____ Court which, deponent is advised can be tried before the Supreme Court case by being placed on the Commercial Calendar, for the reason that deponent believes that his liability on __29_____ directly depends upon the outcome of the issues in the Supreme Court action.

__30_____
[Print signer's name below signature]

[Jurat]

Form 16

Affidavit in Support of Motion for Removal and Consolidation of Lower Court Action—Another Form

SUPREME COURT __1_____ COUNTY

[Title of cause]	Affidavit Index No. __2__ [if assigned]

STATE OF NEW YORK
COUNTY OF __3_____   ss.

__4_____, being duly sworn, deposes and says:

1. She is the plaintiff in the above-entitled action pending in the Supreme Court, __5_____ County.

2. On the __6__ day of __7_____, 19_8_ a motor vehicle collision occurred near the Village of __9_____, in the County of __10_____, State of New York, between an automobile owned and operated by deponent and an automobile owned and operated by __11_____, the defendant in the above-entitled Supreme Court action. As a result of the said collision, deponent's car was greatly damaged and deponent received severe and permanent personal injuries and it is claimed by the said __12_____ that his car was somewhat damaged.

3. The injuries sustained by deponent as a result of the said collision compelled the confinement of deponent at a hospital in the City of __13_____, New York for a period of several weeks. While the deponent was so confined and on or about the __14__ day of __15_____, 19_16_, a summons and complaint in an action in the __17_____ Court of the __18_____ of __19_____ action was served upon her at the said hospital. The said action was brought to recover the sum of __20_____ Dollars on account of damages allegedly caused to the automobile owned by the said __21_____ as a result of the aforesaid collision.

4. Thereafter, and on or about the __22__ day of __23_____, 19_24_, deponent served his answer in the said __25_____ court action, denying generally the allegations of the complaint and specifically denying that she was guilty of any negligence at the time of

the said collision. The said __26_____ court action is now at issue and deponent is informed that it may be moved for trial during the __27_____ term of the said __28_____ court of the __29_____ of __30_____.

5. After answering the complaint of the said __31_____ in the __32_____ court action, deponent commenced an action in the Supreme Court, __33_____ County against the said __34_____ to recover the sum of $__35__ on account of personal injuries and property damage arising out of the aforesaid collision. The said __36_____ duly appeared in the said action by his attorney and filed an answer to the cause of action set out in deponent's complaint consisting of a general denial and a specific denial of any negligence on the part of the said __37_____ at the time of the aforesaid collision. A note of issue in the Supreme Court action was filed on the __38__ day of __39_____, 19_40_.

6. Each of said actions involve common questions of law and fact, that is, they arise out of the collision of the two automobiles as above set forth and the question of negligence to be determined in each action is substantially the same.

7. Deponent is informed and believes that both of the above-entitled actions can be tried together and that they could be properly consolidated by this court and that the action pending in the __41_____ Court of the __42_____ of __43_____ can be moved therefrom to this court and consolidated with and tried with the action pending therein.

8. The removal of the said action pending in the __44_____ Court of the __45_____ of __46_____ and its consolidation with the action pending in the Supreme Court will not inconvenience any party nor prejudice any substantial rights of any party to either of said actions.

WHEREFORE, deponent respectfully requests that an order be entered removing the above-entitled action pending in the __47_____ Court of the __48_____ of __49_____ to the Supreme Court and consolidating it with the above-entitled action pending in the Supreme Court.

__50_____

[Print signer's name below signature]

[Jurat]

Form 17

Order to Show Cause on Motion for Removal and Consolidation of Lower Court Action

SUPREME COURT, __1_____ COUNTY.

Order To Show Cause
[Title of cause]   Index No. __2__ [if assigned]

Present: Hon. __3_____, Justice.

Upon reading and filing the affidavit of __4_____, sworn to the __5__ day of __6_____, 19_7_, and the affidavit of __8_____, sworn to the __9__ day of __10_____, 19_11_, the pleadings in the above entitled action, and the pleadings in the action in the __12_____ Court of the __13_____ of __14_____, entitled __15_____, plaintiff, against __16_____, defendant, hereto annexed; and upon all the proceedings heretofore had herein,

Let __17_____, the defendant above named, or his attorney, show cause before this court, at a motion term, to be held in and for the County of __18_____ at the county court house in the City of __19_____, on the __20__ day of __21_____, 19_22_, at __23__ o'clock in the forenoon of that day, or as soon thereafter as counsel can be heard, why an order should not be made herein removing into this court the action pending in the __24_____ Court of the __25_____ of the __26_____, wherein the above named defendant is plaintiff and the above named plaintiff is defendant, and consolidating the said __27_____ court action with the above entitled action, and for such other and further relief as to this court may seem just and proper in the premises; and

The said defendant is hereby directed to serve answering affidavits upon this application, if any, upon the attorney for the plaintiff above named, on or before the __28__ day of __29_____, 19_30_.

In the meantime and until the determination of this motion and the entry of an order thereon,

Let all proceedings in the action pending in the __31_____ court of the __32_____ of __33_____, entitled __34_____, plaintiff, against __35_____, defendant, on the part of the plaintiff therein, his agents, servants, and attorneys, be and they hereby are stayed.

Satisfactory reasons appearing therefor, let service of a copy of the within affidavits, copies of the pleadings, and order to show cause, upon the attorney for the defendant above named, who is also attorney for the plaintiff in the said __36_____ court action between the same parties herein, if made on or before the __37__ day of __38_____, 19_39_, by leaving a copy at the office of such attorney, be deemed good and sufficient service.

Signed this __40__ day of __41_____, 19_42_ at __43_____, New York.

Enter

__44_____

[Print signer's name below signature]
Justice, Supreme Court
__45_____ County

Form 18

Order Removing and Consolidating Lower Court Action

SUPREME COURT, __1_____ COUNTY.

[Title of cause]   Order
               Index No. __2__ [if assigned]

PRESENT: Hon. __3_____, Justice

The plaintiff in the above-entitled action having moved this court for an order removing the action now pending in the __4_____ Court of the __5_____ of __6_____ entitled __7_____, plaintiff against __8_____, defendant, to this court and consolidating said __9_____ Court action with the above-entitled action and the said motion having regularly come on to be heard,

NOW, on reading and filing the order to show cause made by Mr. Justice __10_____, dated the __11__ day of __12_____, 19_13_ with proof of due service thereof and the affidavit of __14_____, sworn to the __15__ day of __16_____, 19_17_ in support of said motion and the affidavit of __18_____, sworn to the __19__ day of __20_____, 19_21_ in opposition thereto and upon reading the summons and complaint and other proceedings in this action and the pleadings in the action pending in the __22_____ Court of the __23_____ of __24_____ and after hearing __25_____, attorney for the plaintiff in support of this motion and __26_____, attorney for the defendant in opposition thereto, and due deliberation having been had, it is

On motion of __27_____, attorney for the plaintiff,

ORDERED that the action now pending in the __28_____ Court of the __29_____ of __30_____ entitled __31_____, plaintiff against __32_____, defendant be and the same hereby is removed to this court and consolidated with the above-entitled action and it is further

ORDERED that the clerk of the __33_____ Court of the __34_____ of __35_____, upon being served with a certified copy of this order, shall transfer to the clerk of this court all of the papers in the action pending in the said __36_____ Court of the

__37_____ of __38_____ entitled __39_____, plaintiff against __40_____, defendant and it is further

ORDERED that a copy of this order shall be served upon the calendar clerk of this court.

Signed this __41__ day of __42_____, 19_43_ at __44_____, New York.

Enter.

__45_____
[Print signer's name below signature]
Justice, Supreme Court
__46_____ County

Form 19

Notice of Motion to Remove to County Court and Consolidate Lower Court Action

COUNTY COURT, __1_____ COUNTY

Notice of Motion

[Title of cause]   Index No. __2__ [if assigned]

PLEASE TO TAKE NOTICE that upon the annexed affidavit of __3_____, sworn to the __4__ day of __5_____, 19_6_, and the pleadings herein, the undersigned will move this court at a term for motions to be held at the county court house in the City of __7_____, New York, on the __8__ day of __9_____, 19_10_, at __11__ o'clock in the forenoon of that day or as soon thereafter as counsel can be heard, for an order consolidating the above action with an action pending between the same parties instituted before Hon. __12_____, Justice of the Peace of the Town of __13_____, County of __14_____, by a summons dated the __15__ day of __16_____, 19_17_, and for such other and further relief as to the court may seem just and proper.

Dated: __18_____, 19_19_.

__20_____
Attorney for Plaintiff
Office and P. O. Address
Telephone No.

To __21_____
     Attorney for Plaintiff
     Office and P. O. Address

Form 20

Affidavit in Support of Motion to Remove to County Court and Consolidate Lower Court Action

COUNTY COURT, __1_____ COUNTY

Affidavit

[Title of Action]   Index No. __2__ [if assigned]

STATE OF NEW YORK
COUNTY OF __3_____   ss.:

__4_____, being duly sworn, deposes and says:

1. He is the secretary and treasurer of __5_____, Inc., the plaintiff named in the above-entitled action.

2. The above action was commenced in this court by the service of a summons and complaint on the defendant therein on the __6__ day of __7_____, 19_8_. The action was brought to recover the sum of $__9__, rent alleged to be due under a lease between the defendant and the __10_____, Inc. Defendant has answered the said complaint, denying the allegation that this rent is due and has set up as a separate defense that

plaintiff breached the conditions of the lease agreement in that he refused to furnish heat as was allegedly required by the terms of the lease.

3. After the commencement of the above action, the defendant, on the __11__ day of __12_____, 19_13_ commenced an action before Honorable __14_____ in Justice of the Peace Court, Town of __15_____, County of __16_____, entitled __17_____, plaintiff against __18_____, defendant. This action was commenced to recover damages in the sum of $__19__ for an alleged breach by the defendant therein of the lease between the parties.

4. The defense interposed by the defendant to the above-entitled action is identical to and based upon the same facts as the cause of action now pending in the Justice of the Peace Court.

5. Deponent makes his motion to remove the action pending in the Justice of the Peace Court and consolidate it with this action in order to avoid a multiplicity of actions. Deponent is informed and believes that the action brought in this court involves difficult legal questions relating to the law on leases and that a judgment in the Justice of the Peace Court would be res judicata and prevent deponent from continuing with the prosecution of the above action in the county court. By reason of the quicker trial in the Justice of the Peace Court, the entire controversy between the parties will be disposed of there and the trial of the action in the Justice of the Peace Court will decide all issues between the parties. It is submitted, without reflection upon the Justice of the Peace before whom this case will be tried, that he is not an attorney at law and is therefore not familiar with the difficult legal questions pertinent to the issue involved. For that reason, deponent believes that in a fair exercise of the discretion in this court, the action pending in the Justice of the Peace Court should be removed to the county court and consolidated with the above-entitled action.

6. The removal and consolidation of the action pending in the Justice of the Peace Court will not affect any substantial rights of the parties.

WHEREFORE, deponent respectfully requests that this motion be granted.

__20_____
[Print signer's name below signature]

[Jurat]

Form 21

Order Granting Motion to Remove to County Court and Consolidate Lower Court Action

COUNTY COURT, __1_____ COUNTY

[Title of cause]   Order
        Index No. __2__ [if assigned]

Present: Hon. __3_____, Judge.

A motion having been regularly made by the plaintiff in the above-entitled action for an order consolidating the above-entitled action with an action pending in the Justice of the Peace Court, Town of __4_____, County of __5_____, entitled __6_____, plaintiff against __7_____, defendant and said motion having come on regularly to be heard,

NOW, on reading and filing the notice of motion dated the __8__ day of __9_____, 19_10_, and the affidavit of __11_____, sworn to the __12__ day of __13_____, 19_14_, with due proof of service of said papers and after hearing __15_____, attorney for the plaintiff in support of said motion and no one having appeared in opposition thereto, and due deliberation having been had,

NOW, on motion of __16_____, attorney for the plaintiff it is

ORDERED that the action now pending in the Justice of the Peace Court, Town of __17_____, County of __18_____, entitled __19_____, plaintiff, against __20_____, defendant, be and the same is hereby removed to this court and consolidated with the above-entitled action and it is further

ORDERED that the plaintiff in the above-entitled action be deemed the plaintiff in the consolidated action and have the right to open and close upon the trial of the said consolidated action.

Enter

Signed this __21__ day of __22_____, 19_23_ at __24_____, New York.

__25_____

[Print signer's name below signature]
Judge, County Court
__26_____ County

Form 22

Notice of Motion to Remove Justice Court Action to County Court for Joint Trial Without Consolidation

[Title of both courts and causes]   Notice of motion for removal
                         and joint trial
                         Index No. __1__

PLEASE TAKE NOTICE that upon the annexed affidavit of __2_____, sworn to the __3__ day of __4_____, 19_5_, and the pleadings herein, the undersigned will move this court at a term for motions held at the county courthouse in the Village of __6_____, New York, on the __7__ day of __8_____, 19_9_, at __10__ o'clock in the __1f__ noon of that day or as soon thereafter as counsel can be heard, for an order pursuant to CPLR 602(b) removing to this Court an action pending between the same parties before Hon. __12_____, Justice of the Peace of the Town of __13_____, County of __14_____, by a summons dated __15_____, 19_16_, and directing that the two actions be jointly tried without consolidation, and for such other and further relief as to this Court may deem just.

Dated __17_____, 19_18_.

__19_____

Attorney for __20_____
Office and P. O. Address
__21__ [Telephone No.]

To: __22_____
     Attorney for __23_____
     Office and P. O. Address
     __24_____

Form 23

Affidavit of Party in Support of Motion

[Title of court and cause]   Affidavit in support of motion
                       Index No. __1__

[Venue]

__2_____, being duly sworn, deposes and says:

1. I am the plaintiff in the above-entitled action pending in the Supreme Court, county clerk's number __3_____, which was commenced by the service of the summons and verified complaint on the __4__ day of __5_____, 19_6_. The complaint sets forth a cause of action for __7_____ [give details], and a copy is hereto annexed, made a part hereof, and marked Exhibit "A." The answer was served on the __8__ day of __9_____, 19_10_, and contains denials [or set forth nature of answer]. A copy of said answer is hereto annexed and marked Exhibit "B."

195

2. On the __11__ day of __12_____, 19_13_, defendant herein commenced an action in the __14_____ Court, by the service of a summons and verified complaint alleging in substance a cause of action on __15_____. The verified answer in said latter action pleads a general denial and by way of a separate defense __16_____ a copy of said last-mentioned complaint is hereto annexed and marked Exhibit "C." The last-mentioned answer is hereto annexed, and marked Exhibit "D."

3. An examination of the pleadings in said two actions will show that they are based upon the same facts, issues, and transactions. In support of this statement I further state __17_____ [state in detail the facts, circumstances, and issues that are common to the two actions].

4. Much time and expense will be saved by the trial of these two actions at the same time. I further state that it will be inequitable to try the action in the __18_____ Court which, I am advised can be tried before the Supreme Court case by being placed on the Commercial Calendar, for the reason that deponent believes that his liability on __19_____ directly depends upon the outcome of the issues in the Supreme Court action.

[Signature, with name printed underneath]

[Jurat]

Form 24

Order Removing Action from Inferior Court for Trial Together With Supreme Court Action Without Consolidation

[Title of Supreme Court and cause]

Order
Index No. __1__

Present: Hon. __2_____, Justice.

The plaintiff in the above-entitled action, having moved for an order removing to this Court an action pending in the __3_____ Court, and directing that it be tried jointly with the above-entitled action, without consolidation, and said motion having come on regularly to be heard,

Now, on reading and filing the affidavit of __4_____, sworn to the __5__ day of __6_____, 19_7_, the affidavit of __8_____, sworn to the __9__ day of __10_____, 19_11_, and on the pleadings and proceedings in both said actions, in support of said motion, the affidavit of __12_____, sworn to the __13__ day of __14_____, 19_15_, in opposition thereto, and after hearing __16_____, one of the attorneys for the plaintiff above, in favor of said motion, and __17_____, one of the attorneys for the defendant above, in opposition thereto, and due deliberation having been had,

NOW, on motion of __18_____, attorneys for plaintiff, it is

ORDERED that the said motion be and the same hereby is granted, and it is further

ORDERED that the clerk of the __19_____ Court be and he hereby is directed upon service of a copy of this order and payment of his lawful fees therefor, to forward the papers in the action pending in said __20_____ Court, entitled __21_____, plaintiff against __22_____ defendant, and bearing index number __23__, to the Clerk of the County of __24_____, and it is further

ORDERED that the Clerk of the County of __25_____ be and he is hereby directed and authorized to consolidate the files of the said two actions under the index number of the action presently pending in the Supreme Court, No. __26__, and it is further

ORDERED that the costs of the actions hereby ordered to be tried together, up to the date of this order, abide the event of this consolidated action.

Signed this __27__ day of __28_____, 19_29_, at __30_____, New York.

Enter

[Signature, with name printed underneath]
J.S.C.

§ 603. Severance and separate trials

In furtherance of convenience or to avoid prejudice the court may order a severance of claims, or may order a separate trial of any claim, or of any separate issue. The court may order the trial of any claim or issue prior to the trial of the others.

HISTORY:
> Add, L 1962, ch 308, eff Sept 1, 1963.
> Earlier statutes: CPA §§ 258, 443; CCP §§ 484, 966, 967, 973; Code Proc §§ 251, 258.

ADVISORY COMMITTEE NOTES:
> This section incorporates the relevant provisions of CPA §§ 85, 96, 258, 262, 443, 474, 475 and 702.

CROSS REFERENCES:
> As to reference in special proceedings, CPLR 407.

FEDERAL ASPECTS:
> Pleadings and motions, generally, Rules 7 through 16 of Federal Rules of Civil Procedure, USCS Court Rules.
> Consolidation and separate trials in United States District Courts, Rule 42 of Federal Rules of Civil Procedure, USCS Court Rules.
> Motion day in Federal District Courts, Rule 78 of Federal Rules of Civil Procedure, USCS Court Rules.

RESEARCH REFERENCES AND PRACTICE AIDS:
> 1 NY Jur, Adjoining Landowners § 51.
> 14 NY Jur (Rev ed), Damages §§ 26, 32.
> 24 NY Jur, Fraud and Deceit § 229.
> 2 Carmody-Wait 2d, Limitation of Actions § 13:287.
> 3 Carmody-Wait 2d, Severance of Actions §§ 18:1, 18:3.
> 5 Carmody-Wait 2d, The Answer § 30:78.
> 5 Carmody-Wait 2d, Counterclaim § 31:10.
> 7 Carmody-Wait 2d, Order of Disposition of Issues; Joint and Separate Trials §§ 52:2, 52:4, 52:5.
> 21 Carmody-Wait 2d, Actions Against Persons Jointly Liable § 123:22.
> 25 Carmody-Wait 2d, Fundamentals of Practice in the Surrogate's Court § 149:327.
> 26 Carmody-Wait 2d, Probate Proceedings § 152:79.
> 1 Am Jur 2d, Actions §§ 127 et seq.
> 20 Am Jur 2d, Counterclaim, Recoupment, and Setoff § 155.
> 75 Am Jur 2d, Trial §§ 12, 13.
> 1 Am Jur Pl and Pr Forms (Rev ed), Actions, Forms 41 et seq.
> 23 Am Jur Pl and Pr Forms (Rev ed), Trial, Forms 41–51.
> 3 Am Jur Trials p 553, Selecting the Forum—Plaintiff's Position.

Annotations:
> Right to appellate review, on single appellate proceeding, of separate actions consolidated for trial together in lower court. 36 ALR2d 823.
> Tort: separate trial of issues of liability and damages in tort. 85 ALR2d 9.
> Right of plaintiff suing jointly with others to separate trial or order of severance. 99 ALR2d 670.

—Propriety of separate trials of issues of tort liability and of validity and effect of release. 4 ALR3d 456.

Appealability of state court order granting or denying consolidation, severance, or separate trials. 77 ALR3d 1082.

Separate trials, under Rule 42(b) of Federal Rules of Civil Procedure, of claims or issues in suits involving Federal Antitrust Laws. 12 ALR Fed 831.

Appealability of federal court order granting or denying consolidation, severance, or separate trials. 30 ALR Fed 393.

Law Reviews:

The quarterly survey of New York practice: CPLR 603: court grants separate trial for severable issues. 41 St. John's L Rev 300.

Forms:

See "FORMS" heading following "CASE NOTES", infra.

CASE NOTES

1. In general
2. Motion and notice
3. Claims or issues tried prior to others
4. Avoidance of confusion and prejudice
5. Issues and claims severable
6. Issues and claims not severable
7. Third party practice
8. Appeals

1. In general

A broad discretion is given court to make determinations as to which claims should be tried together and which should be severed, and as a general principle all issues having common questions of law or fact should be tried together; however, issues which might prejudice proper consideration of other issues or which by their very nature will inconvenience the court and the principal litigation should be severed. Axelrod & Co. v Telsey (1973) 77 Misc 2d 1035, 353 NYS2d 596.

2. Motion and notice

In action by employee of lessee against lessor for injuries sustained on leased premises wherein lessor filed third-party action against lessee, lessee's motion to discontinue third-party action would be considered as a motion for an order of severance and order would be granted. Tymann v National Sav. Bank (1968) 30 AD2d 881, 291 NYS2d 598.

Special term improperly granted order directing separate trial of one of two related contract actions absent a motion with appropriate notice to interested parties. W. J. McEvily Plumbing & Heating Contractor, Inc. v Rochester (1975) 50 AD2d 1083, 376 NYS2d 753.

No time limitation is fixed in the CPLR § 603 for making a motion for severance. Bonavita v Enright (1966) 25 AD2d 472, 266 NYS2d 192.

3. Claims or issues tried prior to others

If trial justice finds at trial that surviving actions which had been consolidated cannot be conveniently tried together, he may order trial of one or more causes of action or issues prior to trial of the other. Maigur v Saratogian, Inc. (1975) 47 AD2d 982, 367 NYS2d 114.

Separate trial of affirmative defenses of release and statute of limitations would be ordered where disposition thereof favorably to the defendant would terminate litigation and proof on such issues would not duplicate proof on cause of action if trial proved necessary. Mirabella v Banco Industrial De La Republica Argentina (1968) 29 AD2d 940, 289 NYS2d 474.

In a negligence action in which defendant asserted a release as a defense, that defense was stricken and ordered to be tried before a separate jury prior to the trial of the negligence action where the insurer named as a defendant in an action in an adjoining county to determine the validity of the release moved to dismiss the negligence action. Polmanteer v Nationwide Mut. Ins. Co. (1969) 60 Misc 2d 371, 303 NYS2d 146.

Separate trial of issue of damages, preceding trial of other issues, would be ordered where right to disclosure depended upon the amount of recovery. Harari-Raful v Trans World Airlines, Inc. (1973) 41 AD2d 753, 341 NYS2d 655.

The court's discretion may be exercised to sever a counterclaim and to order a trial of the issue thus severed prior to the trial of the other issues, when such a counterclaim does not involve the merits of plaintiff's cause of action, and if defendant's recovery thereon will not defeat plaintiff's claim and render trial thereof unnecessary. Fulmer v Sovocool (1966) 26 AD2d 889, 274 NYS2d 215.

4. Avoidance of confusion and prejudice

Where complaint alleges six causes of action for libel, the first being alleged solely against one newspaper, the second, third and fourth against the same newspaper and its affiliated broadcasting company, the fifth against another newspaper, and the sixth against still another newspaper, there is no allegation that the defendants had acted jointly, and the libelous statements of the newspapers are different, the causes of action should be severed and separate trials had, to avoid confusion and prejudice. Schneph v New York Times Co. (1964) 21 AD2d 599, 252 NYS2d 931.

Where defendant automobile-owner's insurer refused to defend the driver on grounds that he was operating the automobile without the owner's permission, plaintiff's motion for severance in order to assess damages separately against the driver was granted, the court holding that any prejudice to the owner resulting from the severance would ultimately fall on the insurer and would be caused by its arbitrary refusal to defend. Gallivan v Pucello (1971) 68 Misc 2d 713, 328 NYS2d 37, affd 40 AD2d 749, 338 NYS2d 411.

Where the plaintiff, injured in an accident while a passenger on a truck owned by the corporate defendant and operated by its employee, moves for an order severing the action against the individual defendant because of his default in answering, the motion is properly denied where the possibility of the plaintiff obtaining a default judgment against the individual defendant could prejudice the rights of the other defendant and its insurance carrier. Young v Peone (1965) 47 Misc 2d 698, 263 NYS2d 156.

Although the negligence of the dead man is at issue in both an action for wrongful death brought by the administratrix of his estate and in an action for property damages to the vehicle which was being operated by the deceased, and there is a possibility the jury might have some difficulty with the different rules of proof applicable to contributory negligence issues, this was not a sufficient reason to sever the actions. Crossett v Natali (1969) 60 Misc 2d 312, 303 NYS2d 428.

A severance upon the ground that it would be prejudicial to the rights of an infant plaintiff to be compelled to proceed to trial was properly granted, where an orthopedic specialist made an affidavit stating that although most of the infant plaintiff's injuries had responded to treatment, aseptic necrosis had developed and there was a possibility that further surgery might be necessary, and that 6 months to a year would be required before the nature and extent of permanent disability could be determined. Noble v Kowalenko (1969) 32 AD2d 703, 299 NYS2d 889.

Although a counterclaim will be severed where the issues presented are unrelated to the main suit and substantial rights will be prejudiced and confusion arise if all the issues are tried together, plaintiff's motion to sever a counterclaim was denied where during the present stage of the action there could be no proper appraisal as to possible prejudice or confusion in permitting the defamation counterclaim to remain. Inland Credit Corp. v Puro (1967) 27 AD2d 657, 276 NYS2d 830.

Where it appeared that it would be necessary for plaintiff, in establishing liability in wrongful death action, to offer medical evidence of injuries and of force necessary to cause such injuries and possibly other expert testimony based upon admitted facts as to what was competent to produce such force, it appeared that nature of injuries would have an important bearing on issue of liability, and separate trial on issues of liability and damages would not be ordered for purpose of avoiding prejudice to defendant from any sympathy for widow and children. Williams v Adams (1974) 46 AD2d 952, 362 NYS2d 68.

5. Issues and claims severable

The severance of the issues of liability and damages in negligence litigation has become acceptable procedure in appropriate cases. Hacker v New York (1966) 25 AD2d 35, 266 NYS2d 194.

In an action by an infant who was allegedly injured on two separate occasions while a patient in the defendant's hospital, the events of each occasion being separate and distinct, as well as the injuries claimed, plaintiff ordered to serve complaints separately, stating and numbering each cause of action with plain and concise statements therein. Garland v Memorial Hospital (1969) 60 Misc 2d 34, 301 NYS2d 144.

Where a complaint consisted of two separate and distinct causes of action in negligence for injuries sustained by a plaintiff-tenent in two different parts of the premises owned by the defendant-landlord, the first cause being predicated upon an accident which occurred in the public portion of the building and the second upon an action which occurred in the kitchen of the rented housing accommodation, a motion by the defendant for an order directing a severance was granted to the extent of directing separate trials of the two causes of action. Giummo v Julab Realty Corp. (1965) 48 Misc 2d 419, 265 NYS2d 235.

Where question of negligence in main action arising out of automobile accident was different in character, involved different rules of law and different measures of damage than issues raised in defendant's third-party action against codefendant's insurer to recover damages arising from alleged conversion of third-party plaintiff's automobile after accident and where inferences jury might draw from proof of destruction or mutilation of automobile might impair its impartial consideration of negligence question, severance was required with conversion action being tried and concluded prior to trial of negligence action. Hoff v State Farm Ins. Co. (1975) 48 AD2d 1001, 369 NYS2d 256.

The defendant's counterclaims for conversion of underground gas and trespass to land in an action to condemn underground storage space beneath defendant's land could and should be severed. Home Gas Co. v Banach (1966) 26 AD2d 758, 272 NYS2d 183.

Counterclaim interposed by defendant in a proceeding pending in the Justice Court severed where it appeared that the defendant did not intend to waive its claim of any amount in excess of $1,000 as it had an action pending thereon in the Supreme Court. Harlee-Mitchell Camp Corp. v

Granite Lake Camp, Inc. (1970) 35 AD2d 551, 313 NYS2d 184.

Although action for divorce and counterclaim that certain real property in Nassau County, which property was held by the parties as tenants by the entirety, be the sole property of the defendant could have been tried in the matrimonial proceeding in Warren County, special term did not abuse its discretion in severing the real property cause of action and transferring it to Nassau County for trial. Forde v Forde (1976) 53 AD2d 779, 384 NYS2d 547.

6. Issues and claims not severable

While a severance of legal and equitable issues under this section may be done, where legal and equitable issues are so intertwined and related that one trial of all issues is both desirable and necessary, the trial justice at the jury trial of the legal issues should at the same time try the equitable issues without the jury and it is incumbent upon the trial justice to regulate and direct the sequence of the issues as is proper under the circumstances then prevailing. Vinlis Constr. Co. v Roreck (1965) 23 AD2d 895, 260 NYS2d 245.

In a declaratory action to fix the insurer's liability following its disclaimer, the insurer's motion to sever the causes of action asserted by plaintiff, who sued the insured codefendants in a negligence action, was denied, since the injured persons had an independent right to proceed directly against the liability insurer. Birnbaum v New Amsterdam Casualty Co. (1966) 54 Misc 2d 72, 281 NYS2d 458.

Where a truck driver was injured when he stopped at a traffic light and his vehicle was struck in the rear by two separate cars only minutes apart, there was no error in joining the two defendants in a single joint trial, but plaintiff's two claims for damage were separated, since the jury might more fairly apportion damages against each defendant in a separate verdict after hearing testimony regarding plaintiff's separately acquired injuries. Mullett v Sacco (1965) 47 Misc 2d 441, 262 NYS2d 796.

Right to severance of counterclaim for wilful exaggeration, in an action to foreclose a mechanic's lien, which counterclaim was inextricably related to the plaintiff's cause of action so that separate trials would involve largely the same facts, was properly denied. Fulmer v Sovocool (1966) 26 AD2d 889, 274 NYS2d 215.

Where it was by no means certain that recovery on counterclaim based on fraud, which did not demand rescission, but alleged and asked unliquidated damages, would completely defeat plaintiff's claim and end the litigation, severance of the counterclaim was properly denied. Fulmer v Sovocool (1966) 26 AD2d 889, 274 NYS2d 215.

In action by 25 property taxpayers for review of tax assessments, Special Term's denial of assessor's motion to sever was not abuse of discretion, in view of fact that taxpayers all alleged that their assessments were unequal and that they were made at higher proportionate valuation than assessments of other properties on the same roll.

Blank v Becker (1976) 50 AD2d 418, 377 NYS2d 792.

In negligence action to recover damages for personal injuries, a complete trial embracing both liability and damage issues was required, without being bifurcated, where plaintiffs needed to show a causal connection between certain of negligent acts alleged and injury sustained and medical proof was necessary. Castelli v Regina Center, Inc. (1976) 54 AD2d 954, 388 NYS2d 632.

Trial court did not abuse its discretion in refusing to sever nonmatrimonial causes of action from divorce suit, in that failure of court to sever would not place substantial right in jeopardy. Fisher v Fisher (1977) 56 AD2d 547, 391 NYS2d 598.

7. Third party practice

The third party plaintiff's opposition to a severance based on delay in making the motion is entitled to consideration, but is not controlling in view of the prejudice to which the third party defendant would be subjected by denial of the motion. Bonavita v Enright (1966) 25 AD2d 472, 266 NYS2d 192.

Where third-party complaint was grounded on an insurance policy allegedly indemnifying the defendant third-party plaintiff against a tort claim such as that underlying plaintiffs' complaint, the fact of the existence of insurance relative to the occurrence complained of would have been prejudicial as a matter of law to third party defendants, and thus denial of third party defendant's motion to sever under CPLR § 603 was an improvident exercise of discretion. Schwartz v Jonathan Woodner & Co. (1972) 40 AD2d 1027, 339 NYS2d 145.

Where no justification existed for defendants' three-year delay in serving impleader complaint until the eve of trial after the note of issue and statement of readiness had been filed, and where allowing impleader would result either in prejudice to plaintiff by necessary delay to allow impleaded defendants to engage in discovery and examine prior voluminous disclosure or in severe prejudice to third-party defendants, severance was the least relief that court below should have granted. Vita Food Products, Inc. v A. Epstein & Sons, Inc. (1976) 52 AD2d 522, 381 NYS2d 677.

In exercise of discretion, court properly severed third-party indemnity action, based on medical malpractice, from personal injury action, and referred third-party action to medical malpractice panel; such severance was not mandated but was proper in view of early trial preference granted to injured party and in interests of simplifying cases for jury. Henderson v Wein Hardware Co. (1976) 51 AD2d 696, 379 NYS2d 414.

Third-party defendant who sought to sever third-party malpractice action from main automobile negligence action was required to show that convenience of trying both cases together was overridden by prejudice in delay and where, inter alia, it was not established that short additional delay to allow third-party defendant to prepare, his case would prejudice plaintiff in main action, motion to sever was denied. Coppola v Robb (1976) 55 AD2d 634, 390 NYS2d 167.

8. Appeals

The judgment upon a separate trial on the issue of liability in a personal injury action is appealable as of right. Hacker v New York (1966) 25 AD2d 35, 266 NYS2d 194.

An appeal lies from the Special Term order grant-ing a separate trial of the issue of liability. Dillenbeck v Bailey (1969) 32 AD2d 735, 301 NYS2d 900.

CPLR 5519 (a)(1) imposes a stay of the trial on the issue of damages without a court order, pending defendant's appeal from a judgment entered in a separate trial on the issue of liability in a personal injury action. Hacker v New York (1966) 25 AD2d 35, 266 NYS2d 194.

CASE NOTES

UNDER FORMER CIVIL PRACTICE LAWS

1. Generally; purpose
2. Disposal of preliminary issues generally
3. Res judicata
4. Validity of release
5. —Laches and waiver
6. Separate trial of issues generally
7. Time for making motion
8. Separate jury trial discretionary
9. Separate trial as to some defendants
10. Issues of law and issues of fact
11. Equitable issues in law action
12. Law issues in equitable action
13. Contract issues
14. Malpractice
15. Matrimonial issues
16. Personal injuries
17. Probate and decedents' estates
18. Stock and stockholders
19. Counterclaims
20. Miscellaneous

1. Generally; purpose

The primary purpose of CPA § 443 subdivision 3 was to provide a speedy trial of such pleas in bar as the Statute of Limitations, discharge in bankruptcy, former adjudication, jurisdiction and such matters as could be properly disposed of without going into the real merits of the cause. Kye v Stearns (1927) 130 Misc 28, 223 NYS 582.

CPA § 443 was designed to avoid unnecessary delay, and the court had discretion to determine where delays might possibly be avoided. New York v Interborough Rapid Transit Co. (1929) 134 Misc 827, 236 NYS 449.

Whether Court of Claims had power, in view of CPA § 443, to order separate trial of one or more issues, questioned but not decided. Rockaway Pacific Corp. v State (1922) 200 AD 172, 193 NYS 62.

CPA § 443 permitted surrogate to order one or more issues to be separately tried prior to trial of other issues. Re Fox's Estate (1915) 166 AD 718, 152 NYS 431.

The primary purpose of CPA § 443 was to provide a speedy trial of dilatory pleas, which could be properly disposed of without going into the merits of the case, and should be so administered as to make the provision remedial and beneficial rather than burdensome. Johnson v Methodist Hospital of Brooklyn (1960) 27 Misc 2d 1050, 210 NYS2d 888.

2. Disposal of preliminary issues generally

The procedure outlined in CPA § 443 subdivision 3 was ordinarily adopted in a case where there were preliminary or jurisdictional issues, not involving the merits. Sayer v Wilstrop (1922) 200 AD 364, 193 NYS 4.

Where plaintiff's affidavit in opposition to defendant's motion to dismiss raises an issue of fact it should be disposed of under the provisions of RCP 108 (Rule 3211 herein) instead of CPA § 443. Rizzuto v United States Shipping Board Emergency Fleet Corp. (1925) 213 AD 326, 210 NYS 482.

If plaintiff wished to have issues raised by affirmative defense tried out in advance of other issues, he might move for a severance and separate trial of that issue pursuant to CPA § 443. Baker v Matthews (1959) 8 AD2d 585, 183 NYS2d 569.

Motion for separate trial of issue of statute of limitations denied since such procedure would prejudicially limit defendant's cross-examination of witnesses. Baxter v Swanton (1931) 141 Misc 479, 252 NYS 272.

Either party, plaintiff or defendant, may move for separate trial of issues raised by affirmative defense in answer. Williams v Donyluk (1946, Sup) 66 NYS2d 242, app dismd 90 NYS2d 125.

Separate trial of affirmative defense will be ordered where its determination will destroy plaintiff's cause of action and thus render unnecessary its trial, but where merits of plaintiff's action are still required to be resolved, court will not usually order separate trial as to affirmative defense. Winthrop Products Corp. v Damsky (1953, Sup) 119 NYS2d 235, revd on other grounds 282 AD 1016, 126 NYS2d 251.

In a personal injury action, trial court's order that a separate trial be held first upon issue of liability was not an abuse of discretion where nature and extent of plaintiff's injuries did not have an important bearing upon the liability question, and where plaintiff was not prejudiced by such separate trial.

Berman v H. J. Enterprises, Inc. (1961) 13 AD2d 199, 214 NYS2d 945.

3. Res judicata

Where the answer in proceedings to review an assessment sets up what in effect is a plea of res adjudicata, it is proper for the court to require the determination of the issue thus raised in advance of the other questions involved. People ex rel. New York C. R. Co. v Bissell (1923) 207 AD 705, 201 NYS 865.

Motion should be made at Special Term for order directing separate trial of issue of res adjudicata prior to trial of other issues in case. Calva v J. Laskin & Sons Corp (1952) 279 AD 907, 113 NYS2d 223, affd 304 NY 770, 109 NE2d 75.

Defendants were entitled to separate trial on pleas of res judicata and limitation before trial of other issues. Reich v Cochran (1916) 171 AD 113, 157 NYS 130.

4. Validity of release

Issues raised by reply to plea alleging release that release was obtained by fraud or mistake should be first tried. Warner v Star Co (1914) 162 AD 458, 147 NYS 803.

Where plaintiff seeks to avoid a general release pleaded by defendant, the court at Special Term should, as a general rule, direct a separate trial of the issues as to the release. Carmosin v New York C. R. Co. (1921) 198 AD 810, 190 NYS 864.

Separate trial of issue as to release is properly refused where it would result in two trials involving substantially the same facts. Romania v Lamport & Holt, Ltd. (1923) 207 AD 861, 202 NYS 216.

In an action for negligence in which the defendant pleads a release as a defense, an order for a separate trial of such a defense is denied. Wood v Hagaman & Co., Inc. (1935) 245 AD 890, 282 NYS 351.

Appellant, to whom respondent gave general release in settlement of negligence action, is entitled to a separate trial of the issues of release where respondent claims that release was obtained by mutual mistake of fact and fraud. Spencer v Hunt (1936) 247 AD 503, 286 NYS 767.

Separate and prior trial of the issues raised by the affirmative defense of a general release in an action for negligence is granted where the reply alleges fraud and misrepresentation in the procurement of the release and mutual mistake as to the extent of the plaintiff's alleged illness. Langone v Gaetjens, Berger & Wirth, Inc. (1936) 248 AD 591, 287 NYS 357.

Order directing separate trial of issues raised as to validity of two releases pleaded as separate defense was discretionary, and such discretion was not abused. Hughes v New York C. R. Co. (1951) 278 AD 885, 104 NYS2d 275.

Cause of action to rescind release settling claim for injuries should be tried separately from cause of action for personal injuries, where principal issue of former is whether there was mutual mistake of fact. Burton v Niagara Mohawk Power Corp. (1952) 280 AD 356, 113 NYS2d 483.

Separate trial of issue as to validity of general release of all claims was ordered, where there was no claim of lack of knowledge of nature of injury at time of execution of general release. Dienstag v Kiamesha-Concord, Inc. (1954) 283 AD 736, 127 NYS2d 908.

In action for personal injuries where answer of codefendant alleges release of cause of action and reply alleges release was fraudulently obtained and unconscionable, it was improvident exercise of discretion to deny separate trial of issue or release. Landes v Mitchell (1955) 285 AD 1163, 140 NYS2d 398.

In action for personal injuries wherein defendant pleaded affirmative defense that it had paid plaintiff $750 which plaintiff accepted in full accord and satisfaction of claim stated in complaint and wherein plaintiff interposed reply in which she alleged acceptance of said payment was procured by defendant's fraud, defendant's motion for prior and separate trial of issue of release was granted. Balaka v Stork Restaurant, Inc. (1955) 286 AD 1018, 146 NYS2d 676.

Separate trial of general release in negligence action should be denied where a trial of the issues relating to the release will necessarily involve much if not all of the same evidence relating to main issues of negligence, contributory negligence and damages. House v Scheffler (1940, Sup) 27 NYS2d 681, affd 261 AD 1088, 27 NYS2d 1002.

Where in action for personal injuries, answer pleaded denial and release and reply alleged that plaintiff was induced by fraud to sign paper as receipt by insurer's agent, prior and separate trial of issue as to release was proper. Parham v Hellebush (1942, Sup) 36 NYS2d 21.

Separate trial of wife's release was denied where, if sustained, it would not bar action by plaintiff husband for loss of services. Tierney v O'Toole (1949, Sup) 95 NYS2d 40, affd 276 AD 922, 94 NYS2d 829.

The issue of the validity of release was ordered tried separately although the merits of the action were to some extent involved. Burton v Niagara Mohawk Power Corp. (1952) 280 AD 356, 113 NYS2d 483.

Where defendant moved to dismiss complaint on ground that plaintiff had released her cause of action, and plaintiff in opposing affidavit alleged mutual mistake in settling her claim, court denied motion and ordered separate trial of issue of mistake in signing release, in advance of trial of issues of negligence. Harkins v Gilkey (1953, Sup) 123 NYS2d 120, affd 285 AD 848, 137 NYS2d 639.

Though release was executed on same day on which plaintiff was injured, denial of motion for separate trial of issue of release was abuse of discretion. Williams v Doyle (1954, Sup App T) 136 NYS2d 488.

In personal injury action, court abused its discretion in denying a motion for a separate trial on issue of release. Terryberry v Lehigh V. R. Co. (1915, Sup) 152 NYS 450.

In action for personal injuries, it was within the discretion of the court to separate and first try issue as to validity of release. O'Donnell v Thompson-Starrett Co. (1915) 92 Misc 710, 156 NYS 342.

Generally negligence cases do not call for separate trial of an issue therein and the validity of a release which is much involved with the merits of the action will not be so tested. Kye v Stearns (1927) 130 Misc 28, 223 NYS 582.

Where an action was brought against a county and the trial court had assumed that service of the notice of claim was actually made or the person to be served actually received the notice, and if this was not so the matter should be raised by answer, and a separate trial of that issue might be applied for after issue was joined under CPA § 443, and if such separate trial was granted, the question could readily be disposed of without complicating the main issues. Bronson v Westchester County (1957) 10 Misc 2d 293, 168 NYS2d 735.

Where issue of waiver requires proof of facts involving main issues and the trial judge may have to hear a substantial portion if not all of the facts of the case as a whole and it is not shown that time will be saved if matter is preliminarily tried, prior trial of such issue denied. Sillman v Twentieth Century-Fox Film Corp. (1958) 12 Misc 2d 775, 177 NYS2d 818.

In action in federal court to recover for negligence, defendants are entitled to separate trials of issues of release and negligence. Hoad v New York C. R. Co. (1933, DC NY) 3 F Supp 1020.

In action to recover difference between what would be a fair settlement and what was accepted by reason of misrepresentation, separate trial on validity of release was not warranted as it would involve much of same matters as entire action. Griffel v Belfer (1960) 12 AD2d 609, 209 NYS2d 67, affd 10 NY2d 902, 223 NYS2d 517, 179 NE2d 518.

Denial of separate trial of validity of release was justifiable where two trials would impose undue hardship on 88-year-old plaintiff suffering from the aftermath of numerous injuries. Duch v Giacquinto (1961) 15 AD2d 20, 222 NYS2d 101.

5. —Laches and waiver

In an action to recover damages for personal injuries in which defendant sets up a general release, a separate trial as to the release is properly denied where defendant waits over three years before moving for a separate trial. Carmosin v New York C. R. Co. (1921) 198 AD 810, 190 NYS 864.

6. Separate trial of issues generally

A motion for a separate trial of an issue should be granted, where it appears that the trial of said issue, if determined adversely to the plaintiff, will end the litigation and render a trial of the merits unnecessary. Hmar v Texas Co. (1932) 235 AD 731, 255 NYS 944.

Only where trial of one issue, if determined adversely to plaintiff, will end litigation and render trial of merits unnecessary, should there be separate trial. Flynn v Royal Development Co. (1943) 265 AD 592, 40 NYS2d 418.

In consolidated actions for wrongful death and personal injuries against the operator and the owner of a motor vehicle, denial of defendant-owners motion for a separate trial of the issue that the motor vehicle was being operated with its knowledge and consent was improvident where the record indicated that the trial of this issue would be short whereas the trial of the other issues would be protracted and where the determination of this issue would expedite the trial of the other issues. Mihalchik v Schepis Constr. Co. (1959) 8 AD2d 618, 185 NYS2d 99.

Court should not hesitate to sever issues or grant separate trials when by doing so it expedites the findings embraced in the controversy. Gould v Gould (1924) 124 Misc 240, 207 NYS 137.

CPA § 443 subdivision 3 authorized a separate trial of segregated issues where their determination in one way would render trial of the remaining issues unnecessary, thus ending the litigation. New York v Interborough Rapid Transit Co. (1929) 134 Misc 827, 236 NYS 449.

Failure to move for separate trial of certain issues until after three futile trials was not ground for denial of the motion. Franklin v Leiter (1912) 149 AD 678, 134 NYS 399.

Joinder of 15 separate claims for fire damage, totaling $20,000, did not warrant separate trial of damages before trial of liability. Rabin v Brooklyn Trust Co. (1947) 191 Misc 321, 77 NYS2d 614.

Application for separate trial of certain issues made before completion of all pretrial procedures was denied as premature without prejudice to renewal at trial when issues would be more clearly defined. Gothar Allgemeine Versicherung A. G. v A/S Santa Martha (1961) 12 AD2d 917, 210 NYS2d 610.

Generally, where different causes of action against different defendants are stated in one complaint, severance or separate trials as to defendants who have no interest in any cause of action but one will be ordered. Hessol v Hathaway (1941) 177 Misc 336, 30 NYS2d 600.

Severance of tort claims based on unrelated accidents where prejudice might result, see Stein v Baff (1950) 197 Misc 509, 95 NYS2d 298.

7. Time for making motion

Motion for separate trial of an issue made before issue has been joined is premature and should be denied without prejudice. Hamm v Richards (1961) 12 AD2d 953, 210 NYS2d 871.

8. Separate jury trial discretionary

Where separation of issues will result in two or more jury trials, court should consider hardship to either party and great additional expense which would be incurred. McGurty v Delaware, L. & W. R. Co. (1916) 172 AD 46, 158 NYS 285.

Separate trial of the issue as to whether one of the defendants was a partner of the other defendants should be granted where on three previous trials judgment was reversed and great difficulty was encountered in instructing the jury and qualifying the admission of evidence competent as to some but not all of the parties. Franklin v Leiter (1912) 149 AD 678, 134 NYS 399.

The granting of a separate jury trial of issues is addressed to the sound discretion of the court. Spencer v Hunt (1936) 247 AD 503, 286 NYS 767.

Where no clear right to separate trial was shown, denial was proper. Palmer v Socony-Vacuum Oil Co. (1948) 273 AD 925, 77 NYS2d 450.

Where summary proceedings, action at law and two equitable actions were consolidated without prejudice to jury trial of any issue, motion by tenant for jury trial of summary proceeding and action at law was granted. Foreman v De Costa (1950) 276 AD 969, 94 NYS2d 710.

Where there will be no prejudice by severance and separate trial of one of two causes of action in stockholders' derivative action, and only answering defendant did not oppose motion, separate trial was directed. La Vin v La Vin (1953) 281 AD 1032, 121 NYS2d 1.

Waste of time may bar separate trial. Rabin v Brooklyn Trust Co. (1947) 191 Misc 321, 77 NYS2d 614.

Where tendered issues are multiple and confusing and duplicate issues which would have to be considered at later trial and where granting defendant's motion for separate trial of several issues would duplicate trials and require attendance of witnesses from distant points, separate trials should be denied. Morton v Maryland Casualty Co. (1954, Sup) 134 NYS2d 209, revd on other grounds 1 AD2d 116, 148 NYS2d 524, affd 4 NY2d 488, 176 NYS2d 329, 151 NE2d 881.

At opening of trial in negligence action court may direct that issue of liability be tried first without medical proof as to extent of plaintiff's injuries where calendar congestion presented sufficient reason for court in its discretion to make such direction. Schollmeyer v Sutter (1956) 2 Misc 2d 215, 151 NYS2d 795, dismd 3 AD2d 665, 158 NYS2d 354.

Where in an action to recover damages for personal injuries, in the exercise of discretion, issues raised by defenses that plaintiff had executed and delivered general release should be tried separately and prior to trial of negligence action. Caswell v New Manlius Park Corp. (1958) 11 Misc 2d 769, 175 NYS2d 473.

The court should exercise its discretion in ordering separate trials only where the trial of the issues involved will be brief, and the trial of the main issue may be prolonged and expensive. Johnson v Methodist Hospital of Brooklyn (1960) 27 Misc 2d 1050, 210 NYS2d 888.

Denial of separate trial of validity of release was justifiable where two trials would impose undue hardship on 88-year-old plaintiff suffering from the aftermath of numerous injuries. Duch v Giacquinto (1961) 15 AD2d 20, 222 NYS2d 101.

9. Separate trial as to some defendants

Separate trials may be accorded to each defendant in the interest of justice on a motion before an answer has been interposed. Metropolitan Life Ins. Co. v Union Trust Co. (1938) 167 Misc 262, 5 NYS2d 99.

The motion of the defendants in an action for negligence for a separate and prior trial of the defense of general release was granted, where it appeared that the issues raised by the defense would not involve the same issues or evidence as would be presented by the main issues. Winokur v Quaker City Bus Co. (1938) 255 AD 273, 7 NYS2d 380.

An order directing a separate trial between the plaintiff and one or more defendants is a discretionary one. National Exchange Bank v McFarlan (1891, Sup) 13 NYS 202.

10. Issues of law and issues of fact

In an action in equity by a principal against his agent for an accounting when there is an issue as to the basis of the agent's compensation, the trial of the main issue should be had before the court before the case is sent to a referee. If on such trial it appears that an accounting is necessary, the reference should be provided for in the interlocutory decree. Prince Line v John C. Seager Co. (1907) 118 AD 697, 103 NYS 677.

Where there arises an issue of law and an issue of fact, the issue of law shall be first tried, unless the court otherwise directs. Municipal Gas Co. v Public Service Com. (1918) 184 AD 757, 172 NYS 563.

A motion for a preference for the trial of an issue of fact will be denied where an issue of law remains undisposed of. New York Contracting & Trucking Co. v Hawkes (1903) 41 Misc 125, 83 NYS 919.

The plaintiff may put the case on the calendar for the trial of issues of fact without waiting for the determination of the issue of law. Palmer v Smedley, 13 Abb Pr 185.

11. Equitable issues in law action

In an action to redeem a certificate of membership in an exchange, where the defendant merely demanded a trial by jury, although thereby intending to question the equitable nature of the proceeding, upon refusal without objection by the defendant the plaintiff's action was narrowed down to an equitable one, and the defendant could not raise the question on appeal. Powell v Waldron (1882) 89 NY 328.

It matters not that a cause really equitable being in the nature of a creditor's bill, and tried as such, was noticed for trial at the jury term. Murtha v Curley (1882) 90 NY 372.

An order withdrawing certain issues, equitable in their nature, from the consideration of the jury and directing that they be tried before another judge without a jury, is not justified where none of the parties to the action consent thereto. Reed v Provident Sav. Life Assur. Soc. (1903) 79 AD 163, 79 NYS 665.

Where, in an action at law, the defendant has a second separate defense and by way of counterclaim sets up an equitable cause of action which, if established, would entitle him to an affirmative judgment appropriate only to a suit in equity, the proper practice is to move for an order directing separate trials of the separate issues in the appropriate form and the order of trial thereof. Goss v C. S. Goss & Co. (1908) 126 AD 748, 111 NYS 115.

Where, in answering the complaint in an action on a promissory note, the defendant, among other things, sets up an equitable counterclaim, the equitable issues may be sent to special term for trial. Hubbard v Heinze (1911) 145 AD 828, 130 NYS 542.

Where allegations contained in the complaint make out an action in equity for equitable relief, while certain of the allegations as to some of the defendants show an action at law for legal relief, the issues as to equitable relief are to be first tried at special term, and if the equitable cause fails the other issues are to be tried by a jury. Hennequin v Butterfield (1879) 76 NY 598.

In an action of ejectment, where the answer contains an equitable counterclaim praying reformation of the lease, and the latter issue was tried and dismissed, and the former resulted subsequently in a verdict for the plaintiff, the defendant's appeal from the judgment does not entitle him to a new trial of the equitable issue. Post v Moran, 10 Daly 502.

12. Law issues in equitable action

Where legal counterclaim is set up in equity action, defendant timely moving for settlement of issues is entitled to jury trial of legal issues, but court ordinarily will not order such issues tried first. Maag v Maag Gear Co. (1920) 193 AD 759, 184 NYS 630.

Separation for jury trial through framed issues, of questions of misfeasance, where incidental to other questions properly triable by the court, is not favored. Cantor v Sachs (1932) 154 Misc 429, 276 NYS 324.

13. Contract issues

In customer's action against broker to recover money used in fictitious transactions for plaintiff's account, in which accounts stated, if established, would defeat recovery, the issue as to accounts stated should first be tried. Cohen v Rothschild (1914) 162 AD 611, 147 NYS 915.

In action upon guaranty contract, plaintiff was entitled to separate trial of affirmative issues of limitation and discharge in bankruptcy. Schleestein v Cohn (1919) 188 AD 48, 175 NYS 890.

Where complaint alleges cause of action in contract and cause for malicious prosecution, action should be severed and causes be tried separately. Berger v American Nat. Fire Ins. Co. (1952) 279 AD 335, 109 NYS2d 696.

Code of Civil Procedure § 973 (CPA § 443), held to authorize the court, in an action for rent, to sever issues relative to the execution of the lease and the reasonableness of the rent, and to direct a jury issue of the former issue in advance of a determination as to the other. A. C. & H. M. Hall Realty Co. v Eisler (1921, Sup App T) 190 NYS 701.

In suit to restrain defendant from violating its contract to charge not more than a five cent fare, which defendant claimed was confiscatory and that plaintiff was estopped to enforce it, a severance and prior trial of the issues of the binding force of the contract and of the question of estoppel, was granted, leaving for subsequent trial, if necessary, the question of reasonableness of the contract rate of fare. New York v Interborough Rapid Transit Co. (1929) 134 Misc 827, 236 NYS 449.

14. Malpractice

In negligence and malpractice action against hospital, hospital was denied a separate trial of issue of statute of limitations, where plaintiff claimed that the statute had been tolled by her incompetency which had resulted from defendant's acts, as it would necessitate going into merits of main issue, with resultant duplication of effort, evidence, and expense. Johnson v Methodist Hospital of Brooklyn (1960) 27 Misc 2d 1050, 210 NYS2d 888.

15. Matrimonial issues

In husband's action for divorce, denial of separate trial of wife's affirmative defense that she had obtained Nevada divorce was abuse of discretion. Ferrer v Ferrer (1945) 269 AD 1038, 58 NYS2d 621.

Where defendant sets up condonation of adultery occurring after commencement of action, court should order such issue tried first. Hulse v Hulse (1920, Sup) 181 NYS 83.

In annulment of marriage for fraud, separate trial of wife's defense of condonation was improvident. Levine v Levine (1947) 272 AD 820, 70 NYS2d 209.

In wife's action for separation and to set aside separation agreement, separate trial of second cause of action was improper. Widera v Widera (1951) 200 Misc 753, 104 NYS2d 698.

16. Personal injuries

In a personal injury action, trial court's order that a separate trial be held first upon issue of liability was not an abuse of discretion where nature and extent of plaintiff's injuries did not have an important bearing upon the liability question, and where plaintiff was not prejudiced by such separate trial. Berman v H. J. Enterprises, Inc. (1961) 13 AD2d 199, 214 NYS2d 945.

17. Probate and decedents' estates

That preliminary issues, such as the right of certain parties to contest a will, should be heard separate and apart from the probate proceedings, was not only justified by CPA § 443, but apparently had been the uniform practice in the Surrogate's Court. Re Cook's Will (1926) 244 NY 63, 154 NE 823, 55 ALR 806.

In proceeding by executor to compel reputed widow of deceased to execute deeds pursuant to settlement agreement, surrogate may order her legal status as widow tried separately in advance of trial. Re Estate of Albright (1955) 309 NY 126, 127 NE2d 910.

Where the alleged widow offered objections to probate of husband's will, it was proper to order the issue of marriage to be first tried, but examination of witnesses before such trial was not authorized. Re Erlanger's Will (1930) 231 AD 70, 246 NYS 275.

Where probate of a will is contested in the surrogate's court by a person claiming to be the lawful widow, it is the practice to determine her status at a preliminary hearing. Re Erlanger's Estate (1930) 136 Misc 784, 242 NYS 257, affd 229 AD 778, 242 NYS 910.

Where the right of a legatee to compel an executor to account was challenged, her status as a person interested was established by the evidence in a proceeding under CPA § 443, subdivision 3, as amended in 1921. Re Fein's Will (1928) 132 Misc 613, 230 NYS 308.

Ordinarily there is no constitutional right to jury trial of any issue of fact incident to surrogate's power to determine preliminary status of parties to such proceeding. Re Fehringer's Will (1944) 183 Misc 438, 48 NYS2d 948.

Preliminary hearing of objections of legatees named in prior will not duly revoked was denied, where identical objections had been interposed by other parties, thus making two contests instead of one. Re Aims' Estate (1950) 199 Misc 185, 97 NYS2d 140.

Surrogate may, in his discretion, order trial of preliminary issue of contestant's status if that would result in saving of time and expense to estate. Re Hendrickson's Will (1950, Sur) 99 NYS2d 664, app dismd (AD) 107 NYS2d 579.

Where petitioners have challenged the status of the widow to question the validity of the alleged will and codicil where such widow was not named as a legatee in either instrument, the court properly directed a preliminary hearing to pass upon the status of objectant as a distributee of decedent. Re Will of Cohen (1958) 13 Misc 2d 384, 176 NYS2d 67.

A hearing to determine status of a contestant to file objections to a probate proceeding in Surrogate's Court is a separate trial of an issue within the purview of CPA § 443. Re Will of Sakel (1959) 9 AD2d 763, 193 NYS2d 163.

18. Stock and stockholders

In stockholder's derivative action, motion for separate trial of issue of futility of demand of directors to sue on behalf of corporation, was granted. Marco v Sachs (1954) 283 AD 1096, 131 NYS2d 678, reh and app den 284 AD 851, 134 NYS2d 276.

A stockholder, in an action against corporate officers and directors founded on conspiracy to defraud investors, in a series of transactions designed to cause losses to investors for the aggrandizement of the defendant officers and directors, is declared not to be entitled to have issues framed for the jury as to fraud and negligence. Cantor v Sachs (1932) 154 Misc 429, 276 NYS 324.

Under subdivision 3 of CPA § 443 an administrator was entitled to a separate trial to determine the character of a document bearing upon the question of ownership of corporate stock which came to respondent from decedent. Re Pritchard (1929) 226 AD 272, 235 NYS 122.

19. Counterclaims

Where dismissal of counterclaim was not upon the merits but upon the ground that matters set up did not constitute a counterclaim, although they might be sufficient to constitute a defense, it was improper to direct judgment to be entered by such decision, as application for judgment must be made either at trial term at which last issue was tried or on motion after that trial. McElroy v Floral Park Villa Co. (1916) 176 AD 106, 162 NYS 467.

Where in an action by the assignee of a policy of credit insurance for a loss under such policy the defendant insurer pleaded both a defense and a counterclaim based upon the alleged fraud of the individual defendants in procuring the assignment of the policy, asking in the defense the cancellation of the assignment and in the counterclaim the cancellation of the policy, in view of CPA § 443 and CPA § 424 (§ 603 herein) the insurer was entitled to a separate trial of its counterclaim at Special Term, since the court could not give the relief sought on its law side. Samuel Strauss & Co. v American Credit Indem. Co. (1922) 203 AD 361, 196 NYS 708.

Where same facts alleged as counterclaim were pleaded as defense and, if established on trial, would necessitate dismissal of complaint and give defendant full relief, separate trial was denied. Diamond v Polivnick (1946) 270 AD 854, 60 NYS2d 681.

Where counterclaim is sufficient to state cause of action, issues raised thereby should be separately tried before trial of plaintiff's claim. Albert A. Volk Co. v Cauldwell-Wingate Co. (1947) 272 AD 290, 70 NYS2d 662.

In action for work and labor, where matters alleged in counterclaim are directly connected with cause of action alleged in complaint and all pleaded issues between parties are involved in one continuous transaction, separate trial was denied as prejudicing substantial right of defendant. Moniz v National Constructors, Inc. (1951) 278 AD 855, 104 NYS2d 487.

Reformation issue, tendered in counterclaim, was separately triable before issues involved in complaint. Winthrop Products Corp. v Damsky (1952) 279 AD 775, 109 NYS2d 283.

A counterclaim will not be stricken on motion if it is connected with the subject of the action set forth in the complaint, and although no affirmative relief against the plaintiff can be had, may be determined at a separate trial prior to the other issue. Smith v Triangle Silk Mfg. Co. (1927) 129 Misc 669, 222 NYS 353.

Where a counterclaim or cross-action sets up equitable issues the proper practice is to move for an order directing separate trials in the appropriate forum of the separate issues and the order of trial thereof. Golran Realty Corp. v James Butler Grocery Co. (1930) 230 AD 661, 245 NYS 492.

In action on notes where defendants counterclaim for their return as procured by duress, separate trial was required. Perlman v Cohen (1947, Sup) 68 NYS2d 882.

20. Miscellaneous

In an estate tax proceeding a direction that the issue of domicile be separately tried is fully warranted. Re Trowbridge's Estate (1935) 266 NY 283, 194 NE 756.

In an action under the Federal Employers' Liability Act the better practice is for the court to submit special questions to the jury, and to require a specific finding on the percentage of negligence of the respective parties. Sherry v Pennsylvania R. Co. (1936) 248 AD 439, 290 NYS 17.

Where cause of action stated in complaint necessarily calls for an adjudication upon the rights of defendant not properly before the court, case cannot be tried, and complaint can only be dismissed upon motion for delay in prosecution. Simon v Gibralter Constr. Co. (1917) 179 AD 273, 166 NYS 466.

Where there are five separate causes of action, and one of them is adjudged not sufficient, judgment dismissing the complaint as to it with costs was irregular, but the remedy of the plaintiff was by application to the court at special term and not by appeal to the general term. Robinson v Hall (1885) 35 Hun 214.

FORMS

Form   1—Notice of motion for severance of action

Form   2—Affidavit in support of motion for severance

Form   3—Order directing severance of action

Form   4—Notice of motion to sever causes of action

Form   5—Affidavit in support of motion to sever causes of action

Form   6—Order severing action

Form   7—Order of severance where part of cause of action admitted

Form   8—Order of severance where all defendants severally liable not served

Form   9—Order of severance where separate liability of one defendant established

Form 10—Notice of motion for separate prior trial of issue

Form 11—Affidavit on motion for separate prior trial of issues

Form 12—Another form of affidavit on motion for separate prior trial of issues

Form 13—Notice of motion for separate trial where there are two or more plaintiffs

Form 14—Notice of motion for separate trial—another form

Form 15—Affidavit in support of motion for separate trial

Form 16—Order directing separate trials

Form 17—Order for prior trial of issue

Form 18—Order directing prior separate trail of defense of release

Form 19—Order to show cause on motion in legal action for order directing separate trial of equitable counterclaim

Form 20—Order on motion in legal action for order directing separate trial of equitable counterclaim

Form 1

Notice of Motion for Severance of Action

SUPREME COURT, __¹_____ COUNTY

Notice of Motion

[Title of cause]   Index No. __²__ [if assigned]

     PLEASE TAKE NOTICE that, upon the complaint herein, and the annexed affidavit of __3_____ sworn to the __4__ day of __5_____, 19_6_ the undersigned will move this court at a motion term to be held in and for the County of __7_____ at the county court house in the City of __8_____, on the __9__ day of __10_____, 19_11_, at __12__ o'clock in the forenoon of that day or as soon thereafter as counsel can be heard, for an order directing the severance of the alleged causes of action of the respective plaintiffs herein, and the separate prosecution and trial thereof, including the service by each plaintiff of a separate complaint wherein the alleged cause or causes of action of such plaintiff will be stated, upon the ground, among others, that:

1. The alleged cause of action of each plaintiff differs in material and essential elements and respects from the alleged cause of action of the other plaintiff; and

2. The joining in one action and in one complaint of the alleged causes of action of both plaintiffs above named, as set forth in the complaint herein, is prejudicial to the defendants [or that the severance of the causes of action stated in the complaint will be in furtherance of convenience];

And for such other and further relief as may be just, together with the cost of this motion.

Dated: __13_____, 19_14_.

__15_____
Attorneys for Defendants
Office and P. O. Address
Telephone No.

To: __16_____
    Attorneys for Plaintiffs
    Office and P. O. Address

Form 2

Affidavit in Support of Motion for Severance

SUPREME COURT, __1_____ COUNTY

                Affidavit
[Title of cause]   Index No. __2__ [if assigned]

STATE OF NEW YORK
COUNTY OF __3_____   ss.:

__4_____, being duly sworn, deposes and says:

1. He is one of the defendants in the above entitled action.

2. The action was commenced by the service of the summons and complaint on deponent on the __5__ day of __6_____, 19_7_ and on the defendant __8_____ on the __9__ day of __10_____, 19_11_.

3. The said complaint contains two causes of action, one against the deponent for __12_____, and the second against the defendant __13_____ to recover on __14_____. A copy of said complaint is annexed hereto.

4. The defendant __15_____, on the __16__ day of __17_____, 19_18_ interposed a verified answer containing denials and a separate defense of __19_____. A copy of said answer is hereto annexed.

5. Deponent interposed a verified answer herein on the __20__ day of __21_____, 19_22_, a copy of which is hereto annexed which said answer contains a general denial and by way of a separate defense alleges that __23_____.

6. Deponent believes the causes of action should be severed and separately tried because __24_____ [state facts in detail].

__25_____
[Print signer's name below signature]

[Jurat]

Form 3

Order Directing Severance of Action

SUPREME COURT, __1_____ COUNTY.

[Title of cause]

Order

Index No. __2__ [if assigned]

Present: Hon. __3_____, Justice.

The above named defendant having moved this court for an order directing the severance of the alleged causes of action of the respective plaintiffs herein, and the service by each plaintiff of a separate complaint wherein the alleged cause or causes of action of such plaintiff will be stated, and for such other and further relief as may be proper; and the said motion having duly come on to be heard,

NOW, upon reading and filing the notice of said motion, dated the __4__ day of __5_____, 19_6_, with proof of service thereof, the affidavit of __7_____, sworn to the __8__ day of __9_____, 19_10_, and the complaint herein, in support of the said motion and the affidavit of __11_____, sworn to the __12__ day of __13_____, 19_14_ in opposition thereto, and after hearing __15_____, of counsel for the defendant, in support of said motion, and __16_____, of counsel for the plaintiffs, in opposition thereto, and due deliberation having been had thereon [and upon filing the opinion of the court], it is

ORDERED that the alleged causes of action of the respective plaintiffs set forth in the complaint herein, be severed, and that within __17__ days after the service of a copy of this order upon the plaintiffs with notice of entry thereof, each plaintiff serve upon the attorneys for the defendant herein an amended complaint, setting forth his alleged cause of action, now contained in the original complaint.

Signed this __18__ day of __19_____, 19_20_ at __21_____, New York.

Enter

__22_____

[Print signer's name below signature]

Justice, Supreme Court

__23_____ County

Form 4

Notice of Motion to Sever Causes of Action

Notice of Motion

[Title of court and cause]

Index No. __1__ [if assigned]

Please take notice that upon the annexed affidavit of __2_____ ["one of the defendants herein," or as the case may be], sworn to __3_____, 19_4_, and upon the complaint herein and upon all the proceedings had in this action, a motion will be made by defendant [or "defendants"] at a motion term [Part __5__] of the Supreme Court, for the County of __6_____, at the county courthouse in the City of __7_____, on the __8__ day of __9_____, 19_10_, at the opening of court on that day [or "at __11__ o'clock in the __12_____ noon of that day"], or as soon thereafter as counsel can be heard, for an order, pursuant to section 603 of the Civil Practice Law and Rules, directing a severance of this action into two [or as the case may be] actions, one for __13_____ and one for __14_____ [etc., if more than two causes of action sought to be severed], and for such other, further and different relief as may be proper.

[Date]

__15_____

Attorney for Defendant

Address __16_____

Telephone No. __17__

To __18_____, Attorney for Plaintiff

Address __19_____

Form 5

Affidavit in Support of Motion to Sever Causes of Action

Affidavit

[Title of court and cause]   Index No. __1__ [if assigned]

[Venue of affidavit]

__2_____, being duly sworn, deposes and says:

1. That he is one of the defendants in the above-entitled action.

2. That this action was commenced by the service of the summons and complaint on the __3__ day of __4_____, 19_5_, which complaint contains two causes of action, one against defendant A, for rent due upon a lease, the second against defendant B, upon a guarantee of the carrying out of the terms of the lease by said A. A copy of said complaint is hereto annexed, and marked "Exhibit A."

3. That defendant A has interposed a verified answer containing denials and a separate defense of constructive eviction. A copy of said answer is hereto annexed and marked "Exhibit B."

4. That deponent has interposed a verified answer herein, a copy of which is hereto annexed, made a part hereof and marked "Exhibit C" which said answer contains a general denial and by way of separate defenses that the action as to B is prematurely brought and also pleads an estoppel.

5. That deponent believes the causes of action should be severed and separately tried because the deponent's liability can not be properly determined until it appears that the defendant A is liable to the plaintiff herein. [State facts in detail.]

[Signature]

[Print signer's name below signature]

[Jurat]

Form 6

Order Severing Action

SUPREME COURT, __1_____ COUNTY.

Order

[Title of cause]   Index No. __2__ [if assigned]

Present: Hon. __3_____, Justice.

A motion having been duly made by the above-named defendant for an order severing the above-entitled action, pursuant to section 603 of the Civil Practice Law and Rules and said motion having come on regularly to be heard,

Now, on reading and filing the notice of motion dated the __4__ day of __5_____, 19_6_, and the affidavit of __7_____, sworn to the __8__ day of __9_____, 19_10_, with due proof of service thereof, and on the pleadings herein, in favor of said motion, and the affidavit of __11_____, sworn to __12_____, 19_13_, in opposition thereto, and after hearing __14_____, attorney for defendant, in favor of said motion and __15_____, attorney for plaintiff in opposition thereto, and there being no other appearance, and due deliberation having been had,

Now, on motion of __16_____, attorney for defendant, and on the decision of the court filed herein, it is hereby

Ordered that the causes of action stated in the complaint herein be and they hereby are severed, and it is further

Ordered that the said two causes of action so severed be tried separately when reached for trial in this court with the same force and effect as if separately brought.

[Or:] Ordered that within twenty days after the entry of this order, plaintiff serve separate amended complaints against defendant in each of said actions, setting forth his alleged cause of action therein.

Signed this __17__ day of __18_____, 19_19_ at __20_____, New York.

Enter.

__21_____
[Print signer's name below signature]
Justice, Supreme Court
__22_____ County

Form 7

Order of Severance Where Part of Cause of Action Admitted

SUPREME COURT, __1_____ COUNTY.

Order
[Title of cause]   Index No. __2__ [if assigned]

Present: Hon. __3_____, Justice.

The plaintiff having moved this court for an order rendering judgment as to a part of the above-entitled action, and that the action proceed as to the remaining issues, and for a severance of the action, and on reading and filing the notice of motion, dated the __4__ day of __5_____, 19_6_, with proof of due service thereof, and upon the pleadings and proceedings in this action, and __7_____, the defendant herein, having by his answer, admitted that __8_____ dollars are due the plaintiff, and after hearing __9_____, attorney for the plaintiff, in support of this motion, and __10_____, attorney for the defendant, in opposition thereto,

Now, upon motion of __11_____, attorney for the plaintiff, it is

Ordered, that the above-named action be severed, and that judgment be entered for the plaintiff for __12_____ dollars, and that the action may be continued against the defendant the same as if it had been originally brought for the balance of the claim set forth in the complaint and not admitted to be due.

Signed this __13__ day of __14_____, 19 15_ at __16_____, New York.

Enter.

__17__ _____
[Print signer's name below signature]
Justice, Supreme Court
__18_____ County

Form 8

Order of Severance Where All Defendants Severally Liable Not Served

SUPREME COURT, __1_____ COUNTY.

Order
[Title of cause]   Index No. __2__ [if assigned]

Present: Hon. __3_____, Justice.

It appearing to the court that in the above entitled action the summons has been issued against all the above named defendants, and that they are alleged in the complaint to be severally liable, and that the summons has been duly served on __4_____ and __5_____, as parties, as appears by the affidavit of service of __6_____, the other of said defendants, and judgment having been herein entered pursuant to law in favor of the plaintiff and against the defendants __7_____ and __8_____,

Now on motion of __9_____, attorney for the plaintiff, it is

Ordered that the action be severed and that the plaintiff may proceed against the defendant, __10_____, as if he were the only defendant named herein.

Signed this __11__ day of __12_____, 19_13_ at __14_____, New York.

Enter.

__15_____

[Print signer's name below signature]

Justice, Supreme Court

__16_____ County

Form 9

Order of Severance Where Separate Liability of One Defendant Established

SUPREME COURT, __1_____ COUNTY.

[Title of cause]

Order

Index No. __2__ [if assigned]

Present: Hon. __3_____, Justice.

An application having been made in this action on the part of the plaintiff for an order directing judgment against __4_____, one of the defendants in the above entitled action, and directing that this action be severed and proceed against __5_____ and __6_____, as the only defendants herein, and for such other and further relief as may be proper;

Now, on reading and filing the summons and complaint, verified __7_____, 19_8_, the answer verified __9_____, 19_10_, the notice of motion, dated __11_____, 19_12_, with proof of due service thereof, the affidavit of __13_____, sworn to __14_____, 19_15_, the affidavits of __16_____, and __17_____, sworn to __18_____, 19_19_, on the part of the plaintiff, and the affidavit of __20_____, sworn to __21_____, 19_22_, on the part of the defendants, and on hearing __23_____, Esq., of counsel for the plaintiff, in support of the application, and __24_____, of counsel for the defendants, opposing, and it appearing to the satisfaction of the court that the answer served presents no defense as to the defendant, __25_____, and that he is liable herein; it is

Ordered and Adjudged that the plaintiff, __26_____, in this action, recover against the defendant __27_____ herein, the sum of __28_____ dollars, the debt, principal and interest demanded in the complaint, with the costs of the action as to him, and that the plaintiff have and he hereby has judgment for the said sum of __29_____ dollars with the costs against the said defendant, __30_____; and it is hereby

Further Ordered that as to the defendants, __31_____ and __32_____, the action be severed and prosecuted against them as the plaintiff may be advised, and that they be permitted and are hereby authorized to put in and serve an amended answer, and that such amended answer of the defendants, __33_____ and __34_____, must be served within ten days after the service of this order with notice of entry thereof, upon the attorney for such defendants.

Signed this __35__ day of __36_____, 19_37_ at __38_____, New York.

Enter.

__39_____

[Print signer's name below signature]

Justice, Supreme Court

__40_____ County

[Adapted from the records in Stedeker v Bernard, 102 NY 327, 6 NE 791. In this case, an action was brought on a check against a partnership consisting of three partners, and the answer served denied the making of the check by the partnership, alleging that it was made by one partner as his individual obligation. The court gave judgment against such partner and directed that the action be severed and prosecuted against the other defendants with leave to them to amend their answer.]

Form 10

Notice of Motion for Separate Prior Trial of Issue

Notice of Motion

[Title of court and cause]　　　　Index No. _1_ [if assigned]

Please take notice that upon the annexed affidavit of _2_____, sworn to the _3_ day of _4_____, 19_5_, and the pleadings in this action, the undersigned will move this court at a motion term [Part _6_ thereof], on the _7_ day of _8_____, 19_9_, at _10_ o'clock in the _11_ noon of that day, or as soon thereafter as counsel can be heard, for an order that, prior to any trial of the other issues in this action, issues of law and issues of fact alleged in the answer of the defendant, be tried, to wit: [State issue of which prior trial is desired.]

At the same time, the defendant will move for such other relief as may be just.

[Date]

_12_____

Attorney for Defendant

Address _13_____

Telephone No. _14_

To _15_____

Attorney for Plaintiff

Address _16_ ____

[Adapted from the records in Smith v Western Pac. R. Co. 144 AD 180, 128 NYS 966, affd 203 NY 499, 96 NE 1106, 40 LRA NS 137, Ann Cas 1913B 264.]

Form 11

Affidavit on Motion for Separate Prior Trial of Issues

Affidavit

[Title of court and cause]　　　　Index No. _1_ [if assigned]

STATE OF NEW YORK

COUNTY OF _2_____　　　　ss.:

_3_____, being duly sworn, deposes and says:

1. I am the defendant herein, and I submit this affidavit in support of my application for an order directing a separate prior trial of my defense of general release.

2. Plaintiff has instituted this action against me to recover for personal injuries allegedly sustained by reason of an accident arising out of the operation of one of my automobiles. I operate a newspaper delivery business, and use over fifty trucks. Sometime in June, 1960, _4_____, one of my drivers told me that plaintiff had hitched a ride on his truck and had fallen off; that from all appearances he had not been hurt, because _5_____ _6_____ saw him an hour later bowling in a bowling alley near my building at _7_____. My driver asked me what to do, and I told him to get in touch with our attorneys. I was informed by my attorneys, whose affidavit is annexed, that they had settled plaintiff's claim, and had taken a general release from him.

3. I interposed the defense of general release to this action, and obtained an order directing plaintiff to serve a reply thereto. Plaintiff in his reply admits having signed the release, but pleads that he had been forced to sign it on the threat of jail for having stolen a ride on one of my trucks.

4. This case is at issue, and has been noticed for trial and bears calendar #_8_.

5. I respectfully submit that if the issue of release is determined favorably to me, it will end the litigation and render a trial upon the merits unnecessary thereby saving the court and the litigants time and money. If I will be compelled to go to trial on the other issues, it will be a prolonged and expensive trial, judging from the nature of the injuries plaintiff alleges he suffered from the alleged accident.

Wherefore I respectfully pray for an order that the issue arising upon the defense of release be tried separately prior to any trial of the other issues in this action, for which no previous application has heretofore been made.

[Jurat]

___9_____

[Print signer's name below signature]

Form 12

Another Form of Affidavit on Motion for Separate Prior Trial of Issues

[Title of court and cause]

Affidavit in support of motion
Index No. __1__

__2_____, being duly sworn, deposes and says:

1. I am the defendant in this action.

2. On __3_____ __4_____, 19_5_, the summons and complaint in this action were served upon me. This action is on account of services alleged to have been performed by the plaintiff, __6_____ [set forth services alleged to have been performed] which said services, it is alleged, were of the value and were reasonably worth the sum of __7_____ dollars.

3. On __8_____, 19_9_, I served my answer in which I __10_____ [set forth nature of answer, as: interposed a general denial, and a defense of general release].

4. The issues which I seek to have first tried are raised by the said defense of __11_____ [as, general release]. I have not interposed this defense for delay, and as appears from a copy of said release, annexed hereto, it is a valid and meritorious defense.

5. A trial of the issues raised by this defense will not involve a trial of the merits of the action, and if determined in my favor will end the litigation, and render a trial on the merits unnecessary.

WHEREFORE I pray for an order directing a prior trial of the issues raised by my said defense.

[Jurat]

[Signature, with name printed underneath]

Form 13

Notice of Motion for Separate Trial Where There are Two or More Plaintiffs

[Title of court and cause]

Notice of Motion
Index No. __1__ [if assigned]

PLEASE TAKE NOTICE that upon the pleadings herein and the annexed affidavit of __2_____ ("one of the defendants herein,") sworn to the __3__ day of __4_____, 19_5_, a motion will be made at a motion term (Part __6__) of the Supreme Court to be held in and for the County of __7_____, at the County Court House, in the City of __8_____, on the __9__ day of __10_____, 19_11_ at __12__ o'clock in the __13__ noon of that day, or as soon thereafter as counsel can be heard, for an order directing the separate trial of the respective causes of action alleged by the plaintiff __14_____ and the plaintiff __15_____, on the ground that such an order is necessary to prevent the defendant from being prejudiced [or in furtherance of convenience] and for such other and further relief as to the court may seem just and proper.

Dated: __16_____, 19_17_.

Yours, etc.,

__18_____

[Print signer's name below signature]
Attorney for Defendant
Address and telephone number

Form 14

Notice of Motion for Separate Trial—Another Form

Notice of Motion

[Title of court and cause]　　　　Index No. __1__ [if assigned]

PLEASE TAKE NOTICE that upon the complaint herein, and the annexed affidavit of __2_____, duly sworn to the __3__ day of __4_____, 19_5_, a motion will be made at a motion term of this court (Part __6__) to be held in and for the County of __7_____, at the County Courthouse in the City of __8_____ on the __9__ day of __10_____, 19_11_ at __12__ o'clock in the __13__ noon of that day or as soon thereafter as counsel can be heard, for an order directing a separate trial of the causes of action alleged in the complaint made and filed in the above entitled action [including the service by each plaintiff of a separate complaint where each alleged cause of action of such plaintiff will be separately stated and numbered], upon the ground, among others, that:

1. The alleged cause of action of each plaintiff differs in material and essential elements and differs from the alleged cause of action of the other plaintiff;

2. The joining in one action and one complaint of the alleged causes of action of both plaintiffs above named, as set forth in the complaint made and filed herein, is prejudicial to the defendants and will embarrass and delay the trial, and is not permitted or authorized by the laws of this State or by the rules of practice and procedure of this court;

(Or) the joining in one action and one complaint of the alleged causes of action of both plaintiffs above named will be inconvenient because [state reasons for inconvenience].

And for such other and further relief as may be just and proper, together with the costs and disbursements of this motion.

Dated: __14_____, 19_15_.

Yours, etc.,

__16_____

[Print signer's name below signature]
Attorney for Defendant

Form 15

Affidavit in Support of Motion for Separate Trial

Affidavit

[Title of court and cause]　　　　Index No. __1__ [if assigned]

[Venue of affidavit]

__2_____, being duly sworn, deposes and says:

1. He is the attorney for the defendant herein.

2. This action was commenced by the service of a summons and complaint on the defendant on the __3__ day of __4_____, 19_5_ and issue was joined herein by the service of an answer on the attorneys for the plaintiff __6_____, and the plaintiff

—7—— on the —8— day of —9———, 19—10—. No further proceedings have been had in this action [or state the further proceedings which have been had].

3. The complaint herein contains two causes of action. The first cause of action is for —11—— [insert nature of cause of action] and demands judgment in favor of the plaintiff —12——. The second cause of action is for —13—— [insert nature of cause of action] and demands judgment in favor of the plaintiff —14——.

4. The answer of the defendant sets forth as a defense that —15—— [insert nature of defense set forth in answer].

5. [State facts to show why joint trial would prejudice, or why separate trials would be in furtherance of convenience.]

6. The defendant in the above entitled action has stated the facts to the deponent and deponent believes therefrom that defendant has a good and substantial defense on the merits to each of the causes of action stated in the complaint.

[Signature of deponent]
[Print signer's name below signature]

[Jurat]

Form 16

Order Directing Separate Trials

SUPREME COURT, —1—— COUNTY.

                    Order
[Title of cause]   Index No. —2— [if assigned]

Present: Hon. —3——, Justice.

The defendant [or as the case may be], —4——, having moved this court for an order directing the severance of the causes of action of the respective plaintiffs [or as the case may be] alleged in the complaint herein, and for separate prosecution and trial thereof [including the service by each plaintiff of a separate complaint wherein each cause of action will be separately stated and numbered and extending the time for said defendant to answer and make any motion herein until twenty days after the service upon his attorney of a copy of the order to be entered upon this motion], and said motion having regularly come on to be heard,

NOW, upon reading and filing the notice of motion, dated the —5— day of —6——, 19—7— and the affidavit of —8——, sworn to the —9— day of —10——, 19—11— and upon the pleadings herein, all in support of said motion, and upon reading and filing the affidavit of —12—— —13——, duly sworn to the —14— day of —15——, 19—16— in opposition thereto and after hearing —17——, Esq., attorney for defendant in support of said motion and —18——, Esq., attorney for plaintiffs [or as the case may be] in opposition thereto, and it appearing to the court that the joint trial of the causes of action alleged in the complaint may prejudice the rights of the defendant [or that separate trials of the causes of action alleged in the complaint will be in furtherance of convenience].

NOW, on motion of —19——, attorney for the defendant, it is

ORDERED that the several causes of action alleged in the complaint herein be separately tried and that the plaintiffs herein serve upon the defendant and file separate complaints wherein each alleged cause of action of each respective plaintiff will be separately stated and numbered.

Signed this __20__ day of __21_____, 19_22_ at __23_____, New York.
Enter.

__24_____
[Print signer's name below signature]
Justice, Supreme Court
__25_____ County

Form 17

Order for Prior Trial of Issue

[Title of court and cause]	Order
	Index No. __1__

PRESENT: Hon. __2_____, Justice.

[Defendant] having moved for an order that prior to the trial of the other issues in this action, the issues raised by the defense of __3_____ interposed by him in this action be tried,

Now on reading and filing the notice of motion of defendant, dated the __4__ day of __5_____, 19_6_, and the affidavit of __7_____, sworn to __8_____, 19_9_, in support thereof, and the affidavit of __10_____, sworn to __11_____, 19_12_, in opposition thereto, and after reading the pleadings, and hearing the attorneys for the respective parties hereto [and upon filing the opinion of this court], it is

ORDERED that the said motion be and the same hereby is granted, and that the separate trial of the issue contained in the defense set forth in defendant's answer to the complaint herein [to wit: the settlement of plaintiff's cause of action set forth in the complaint, and the execution and delivery of a release thereof by the plaintiff to the defendant], be and the same hereby is set for the __13__ day of __14_____, 19_15_, in __16_____ County, and the clerk is hereby directed to place the trial of such issue upon the calendar for said date without further order or notice.

Signed this __17__ day of __18_____, 19_19_, at __20_____, New York.

Enter

[Signature, with name printed underneath]
Justice, Supreme Court

Form 18

Order Directing Prior Separate Trial of Defense of Release

SUPREME COURT, __1_____ COUNTY.

	Order
[Title of cause]	Index No. __2__ [if assigned]

Present: Hon. __3_____, Justice.

The defendant in the above entitled action having duly moved this court for an order directing that the issue contained in the separate defense set forth in defendant's answer to the amended complaint herein, to wit, the settlement of plaintiff's cause of action set forth in the amended complaint, and the execution and delivery of a release thereof by the plaintiff to the defendant, __4_____, be tried separately from the plaintiff's cause of action for personal injuries set forth in the amended complaint, and that the issue of settlement for release be tried first and before the trial of the issues of the accident and the cause of action relating thereto, as set forth in the amended complaint, and for such other and further relief as to the court may seem proper.

Now, after reading and filing the notice of said motion dated __5_____ __6_____, 19_7_, and the affidavit of __8_____, sworn __9_____ __10_____, 19_11_, and after hearing __12_____ of counsel for defendant in support of said motion and __13_____ of counsel for the plaintiff in opposition thereto [the plaintiff not opposing the separate trial moved for, but asking that such separate trial be set for immediate trial to the end that the principal issue may be tried when the case is reached in regular order], and due deliberation having been had, and the decision of the court having been made, it is

Ordered that the said motion be and the same hereby is granted, and that the separate trial of the issue contained in the separate defense set forth in defendant's answer to the amended copy herein to wit, the settlement of plaintiff's cause of action set forth in the amended complaint, and the execution and delivery of a release thereof by the plaintiff to the defendant, be and the same hereby is set for the __14__ day of __15_____, 19_16_, in __17_____ County, and the clerk is hereby directed to place the trial of such issue upon the calendar for said date without further order or notice.

Signed this __18__ day of __19_____, 19_20_ at __21_____, New York.

Enter.

__22_____

[Print signer's name below signature]

Justice, Supreme Court

__23_____ County

Form 19

Order to Show Cause on Motion in Legal Action for Order Directing Separate Trial of Equitable Counterclaim

[Title of court and cause]   Order

Index No. __1__

PRESENT: Hon. __2_____, Justice.

Upon reading and filing the annexed affidavit of __3_____, sworn to __4_____, 19_5_, and copy of the pleadings thereto annexed, it is on motion of __6_____, attorney for defendant,

ORDERED that plaintiff show cause before this Court at a __7_____ Term, Part __8__ thereof, at the Courthouse thereof at __9_____, on the __10__ day of __11_____, 19_12_, at __13__ o'clock in the __14__ noon of that day, or as soon thereafter as counsel can be heard, why an order should not be granted herein setting down for trial the equitable issues raised by the defendant's counterclaim in its answer herein and plaintiffs' reply thereto, at a __15_____ Term of this court for the trial of equity causes and issues, and further directing that the issues raised by plaintiffs' complaint herein and defendant's answer thereto (except said counterclaim) be stayed meanwhile until the said equitable issues have been tried and disposed of at said __16_____ Term of this court, and for such other and further relief in the premises as this court may deem just, equitable, and proper.

Service of a copy of this order and of said affidavit upon plaintiffs' attorney on or before __17_____, 19_18_, shall be deemed sufficient notice of this motion.

Signed this __19__ day of __20_____, 19_21_, at __22_____, New York.

Enter

[Signature, with name printed underneath]

Justice, Supreme Court

Form 20

Order on Motion in Legal Action for Order Directing Separate Trial of Equitable Counterclaim

[Title of court and cause]   Order

Index No. __1__

PRESENT: Hon. __2_____, Justice.

The defendant, __3_____, having moved by order to show cause for an order directing that the equitable issues herein raised by said defendant's counterclaim in its answer and the plaintiffs' reply thereto be set down for trial at a Special Term of this court, and directing that the issues raised by the complaint herein and the answer thereto be stayed until the trial of said equitable issues, and said motion having regularly come on to be heard, Now upon reading and filing the order to show cause dated __4_____, 19_5_, and the affidavit of __6_____ sworn to __7_____, 19_8_, in support of said motion, and the affidavit of __9_____, duly sworn to __10_____, 19_11_, in opposition to said motion, and after hearing __12_____, attorney for the defendant, in support thereof, and __13_____, attorneys for the plaintiffs, in opposition thereof, and after reading the pleadings, and due deliberation having been had thereon, and upon filing the opinion of the court, it is

ORDERED that said motion for a separate prior trial of the equitable issues arising under said counterclaim and the plaintiffs' reply thereto be and the same is hereby granted, and it is further

ORDERED that trial of the issues raised by the complaint and answer be stayed pending the trial of the equitable issues arising under the said counterclaim and the reply thereto, and it is further

ORDERED that the equitable issues arising under said counterclaim and the reply thereto be tried at a Special Term of this Court, and that the Clerk of this Court place this cause on the Special Term calendar for __14_____, 19_15_.

Signed this __16__ day of __17_____, 19_18_, at __19_____, New York.

Enter

[Signature, with name printed underneath]
Justice, Supreme Court

[Adapted from the records in Caesar v American Corp. for International Commerce, 202 AD 733, 194 NYS 921, mem dec.]

§ 604. Change by supreme court of place of trial of action pending in another court

Upon motion of any party, the supreme court may order that an issue of fact in an action pending in another court, except an action relating to real property pending in a county court, be tried in the supreme court in another county upon such terms as may be just. After the trial, the clerk of the county in which it has taken place shall certify the minutes thereof, which shall be filed with the clerk of the court in which the action is pending. Subsequent proceedings shall be the same as if the issue had been tried in the court in which the action is pending.

HISTORY:

Add, L 1962, ch 308, eff Sept 1, 1963.
Earlier statutes: CPA § 189; CCP §§ 218, 343, 344.

ADVISORY COMMITTEE NOTES:

This provision is derived from CPA § 189, with only minor language changes. It provides for change of the place of trial without removal of the action; after the trial the case proceeds in the lower court where it has always remained pending. See Report of the Joint Legislative Committee on the Simplification of Civil Practice 148 (1919). But cf. 21 NY Jud Council Rep 169–75 (1955). It should be considered with new CPLR § 511, in the article on venue, which allows change of the place of trial of actions pending in the Supreme Court. This provision serves an additional purpose, in allowing trial of a lower court case within a county where witnesses reside who could not be reached by the territorially-limited process of the lower court. See 21 NY Jud Council Rep 171–72 (1955). It has been placed here rather than in article 5 since the latter applies only to venue in Supreme Court actions while this provision involves inter-court changes.

FEDERAL ASPECTS:

Removal of cases from state court to United States District Courts, 28 USCS §§ 1441 et seq.

Pleadings and motions, generally, Rules 7 through 16 of Federal Rules of Civil Procedure, USCS Court Rules.

Joinder of claims and remedies, Rule 18 of Federal Rules of Civil Procedure, USCS Court Rules.

Motion day in Federal District Courts, Rule 78 of Federal Rules of Civil Procedure, USCS Court Rules.

Civil actions removable from state court to Federal District Court under 28 USCS § 1443, 28 ALR Fed 488.

RESEARCH REFERENCES AND PRACTICE AIDS:

7 Carmody-Wait 2d, Place of Trial or Venue § 48:17.

Forms:

See "FORMS" heading following "CASE NOTES", infra.

CASE NOTES

The necessity of resort to CPLR 604 has been substantially diminished by the constitutional change providing for state-wide service of process and its local implementation, the section's present applicability being to a situation where the convenience of witnesses to one or some of the issues of a case might be served by a transfer of those issues for trial with said convenience yet not being of sufficient weight to warrant a change of venue under CPLR 510. Mia's Boutique, Inc. v Mia's Boutique, Inc. (1968) 56 Misc 2d 811, 291 NYS2d 392.

CASE NOTES

UNDER FORMER CIVIL PRACTICE LAWS

Surrogate cannot make order changing place of jury trial in contested probate proceeding to another county. Re Corey's Will (1949) 275 AD 53, 87 NYS2d 208.

Change of place of trial from City Court, Kings County, to Supreme Court, Queens County, granted where City Court lacked authority to subpoena necessary witness. Equitable Life Assur. Soc. v Sugarman (1959) 8 AD2d 941, 190 NYS2d 488.

A motion to remove an action into the supreme court and to change the place of trial is within the discretion of the court, but an order in such cases is reviewable by the court of appeals. Knowlton v Trimble, 11 Rep 65.

Where plaintiff in personal injury action waits until 18 months after becoming aware of the severity of his injuries to move for removal of action from City to Supreme Court, absent explanation for the unreasonable delay, motion will be denied. Crown v Lepper (1960) 26 Misc 2d 874, 210 NYS2d 169.

FORMS

Form 1—Notice of motion to change place of trial of proceeding in court other than supreme court

Form 2—Affidavit in support of motion to change place of trial of proceeding in court other than supreme court

Form 3—Order changing place of trial of proceeding in court other than supreme court

Form 1

Notice of Motion to Change Place of Trial of Proceeding in Court Other Than Supreme Court

SUPREME COURT, __1_____ COUNTY.

                    Notice of Motion
[Title of action]　　　Index No. __2__ [if assigned]

PLEASE TAKE NOTICE that upon the pleadings in the above entitled action and upon the annexed affidavit of __3_____ sworn to the __4__ day of __5_____ , 19_6_, a motion will be made at a Motion Term of this Court to be held in and for the County of __7_____ at the County Court House in the City of __8_____ , on the __9__ day of __10_____ , 19_11_ at __12__ o'clock in the __13__ noon of that day or as soon thereafter as counsel can be heard for an order directing that the issues of fact joined in an action pending in the __14_____ Court of the County of __15_____ entitled __16_____ , Plaintiff, against __17_____ , Defendant be tried at a term of the Supreme Court for the County of __18_____ on the grounds that the convenience of witnesses and the ends of justice will be promoted by a change of the place of trial to the County of __19_____ , together with such other and further relief as may be just and proper.

Dated, __20_____ , 19_21_.

                                          __22_____
                                          Attorney for Defendant
                                            __23_____ Address
                                          Telephone No. __24__

To: __25_____ Attorney for Plaintiff
    __26_____ Address

Form 2

Affidavit in Support of Motion to Change Place of Trial of Proceeding in Court Other Than Supreme Court

SUPREME COURT, __1_____ COUNTY.

                    Affidavit
[Title of action]　　　Index No. __2__ [if assigned]

STATE OF NEW YORK
COUNTY OF __3_____　　　　　ss.:

__4_____ , being duly sworn, deposes and says:

1. He is the defendant in an action now pending in the __5_____ Court in the County of __6_____ , entitled __7_____ , Plaintiff, against __8_____ , Defendant.

2. The said action was brought to recover for goods allegedly sold and delivered by the plaintiff to the defendant [or otherwise state nature of action].

3. The said action was commenced by the service of a summons and complaint upon the petitioner on the __9__ day of __10_____ , 19_11_. Issue was joined therein by the service of an answer by petitioner upon the attorney for the plaintiff on the __12__ day of __13_____ , 19_14_. A note of issue was filed in the action but no further proceedings have been had therein.

4. The answer of deponent admits that the goods specified in the complaint were sold and delivered to the deponent but denies that the agreed and reasonable value of the goods was $__15__ and as an affirmative defense alleges that the amount of $__16__ which was paid by deponent to the plaintiff was in full payment of the merchandise sold and delivered. [Or otherwise state nature of defense.]

5. A copy of the complaint, verified the __17__ day of __18_____ , 19_19_ and a copy of the answer in said action, verified the __20__ day of __21_____ , 19_22_ are annexed hereto and made a part hereof.

6. Deponent has fully and fairly stated the facts and circumstances of the said action

to __23____, his attorney, and is advised by said attorney that deponent has a good and substantial defense on the merits to the action.

7. Deponent will show as a defense to the said action that __24____ [state facts to show a meritorious defense].

8. [State facts to show why place of trial should be changed. The statute does not specifically state the grounds for such a change but the grounds are usually the same as in an application to change the place of trial of an action in the Supreme Court, i.e., (1) action brought in wrong county, (2) convenience of witnesses, or (3) inability to have an impartial trial.]

WHEREFORE, deponent requests that an order be made directing that the issues of fact joined in the said action be tried at a term of the Supreme Court in the County of __25____ on such terms and under such regulations as this court deems just and proper.

__26_____
[Print signer's name below signature]

[Jurat]

Form 3

Order Changing Place of Trial of Proceeding in Court Other Than Supreme Court

SUPREME COURT, __1____ COUNTY.

Order

[Title of action]   Index No. __2__ [if assigned]

Present: Hon. __3____, Justice.

The defendant, __4____, in the above entitled action, pending in the __5____ Court of the County of __6____, having moved for an order directing that the issues of fact joined in the said action be tried at a term of the Supreme Court in the County of __7____,

Now, on reading and filing the notice of motion herein dated the __8__ day of __9____, 19_10_ with proof of due service thereof, and the affidavit of __11____, sworn to the __12__ day of __13____, 19_14_, in support of said motion, and the papers and pleadings annexed thereto, and the affidavit [if any] of __15____ sworn to the __16__ day of __17____, 19_18_ in opposition thereto, and after hearing __19____, attorney for the petitioner in support of said petition and __20____ attorney for __21____, in opposition thereto, now, on motion of __22____, attorney for the petitioner, it is

ORDERED that the issues of fact arising upon the pleadings in an action pending in the __23____ Court of __24____ County entitled __25____, Plaintiff against __26____, Defendant be tried at a trial term of this court to be held in and for the County of __27____ on the __28__ day of __29____, 19_30_.

Signed this __31__ day of __32____, 19_33_ at __34____, New York.

Enter.

__35_____
[Print signer's name below signature]
Justice, Supreme Court
__36____ County

[CPLR 605–900 have been reserved for future use.
Please check your supplement.]

ARTICLE 9

Class Actions

HISTORY:

Add, L 1975, ch 207, eff Sept 1, 1975.

CROSS REFERENCES:

This article referred to in Pub Health Law § 2801-d.

3 Carmody-Wait 2d Parties §§ 19:170, 19:171, 19:174; 19:175, 19:181, 19:182.

3 Carmody-Wait 2d Stays § 22:5.

7 Carmody-Wait 2d Voluntary Discontinuance § 47:9.

20 Carmody-Wait 2d Actions and Proceedings By or Against, or in Reference to, Partnerships and Associations § 122:16.

15 Am Jur 2d, Civil Rights § 75.

15 Am Jur 2d, Compromise and Settlement § 9.

24 Am Jur 2d, Dismissal, Discontinuance, and Nonsuit § 49.

48 Am Jur 2d, Labor and Labor Relations §§ 318, 328, 1313.

59 Am Jur 2d, Parties §§ 47 et seq., 267.

61 Am Jur 2d, Pollution Control § 129.

16 Am Jur Pl & Pr Forms (Rev ed), Labor and Labor Relations, Forms 91, 334.

19 Am Jur Pl and Pr Forms (Rev ed), Parties, Forms 31–39.

21 Am Jur Trials p 1, Employment Discrimination Action Under Federal Civil Rights Acts.

21 Am Jur Trials, p 453, Franchise Litigation.

21 Am Jur Trials, p 625, Preparation and Trial of Federal Class Actions.

§ 901. Prerequisites to a class action

a. One or more members of a class may sue or be sued as representative parties on behalf of all if:

1. the class is so numerous that joinder of all members, whether otherwise required or permitted, is impracticable;

2. there are questions of law or fact common to the class which predominate over any questions affecting only individual members;

3. the claims or defenses of the representative parties are typical of the claims or defenses of the class;

4. the representative parties will fairly and adequately protect the interests of the class; and

5. a class action is superior to other available methods for the fair and efficient adjudication of the controversy.

b. Unless a statute creating or imposing a penalty, or a minimum measure

223

of recovery specifically authorizes the recovery thereof in a class action, an action to recover a penalty, or minimum measure of recovery created or imposed by statute may not be maintained as a class action.

HISTORY:
Add, L 1975, ch 207, eff Sept 1, 1975.

CROSS REFERENCES:
This section referred to in 902.

FEDERAL ASPECTS:
Class actions in United States District Courts, Rule 23 of Federal Rules of Civil Procedure, USCS Court Rules.

Prerequisites to class action in United States District Courts, Rule 23(a) of Federal Rules of Civil Procedure, USCS Court Rules.

Class actions maintainable in United States District Courts, Rule 23(b) of Federal Rules of Civil Procedure, USCS Court Rules.

Derivative actions by shareholders in United States District Courts, Rule 23.1 of Federal Rules of Civil Procedure, USCS Court Rules.

Actions in United States District Courts relating to unincorporated associations, Rule 23.2 of Federal Rules of Civil Procedure, USCS Court Rules.

RESEARCH REFERENCES AND PRACTICE AIDS:
24 NY Jur, Fraudulent Conveyances § 144.
57 NY Jur, Suretyship and Guaranty § 264.
3 Carmody-Wait 2d, Parties § 19:167.1
59 Am Jur 2d, Parties §§ 55 et seq.
19 Am Jur Pl & Pr Forms (Rev ed), Parties, Forms 31 et seq.

Annotations:
Joinder of representation of several claimants in action against carrier or utility to recover overcharge. 1 ALR2d 160.

Attorneys' fees in class actions. 38 ALR3d 1384.

Maintainability in state court of class action for relief against air and water pollution. 47 ALR3d 769.

Consumer class actions based on fraud or misrepresentations. 53 ALR3d 534.

Appealability of order denying right to proceed in form of class action. 54 ALR3d 595.

Validity of express statutory grant of power to state to seek, or to court to grant, restitution of fruits of consumer fraud. 59 ALR3d 1222.

Propriety of class action in state courts to assert tenants' rights against landlord. 73 ALR3d 852.

Propriety of state court class action by holders of bonds against indenture trustee. 73 ALR3d 880.

Maintenance of class action against governmental entity as affected by requirement of notice of claim. 76 ALR3d 1244.

Right, in suit brought as class action, to aggregate claims or interests of members of class in order to satisfy minimum jurisdictional amount requirement in Federal District Court. 3 ALR Fed 372.

Propriety, under Rules 23(a) and 23(b) of Federal Rules of Civil Procedure, as amended in 1966, of class action for violation of federal antitrust laws. 6 ALR Fed 19.

Propriety, under Rules 23(a) and 23(b) of Federal Rules of Civil Procedure, as amended in 1966, of class action seeking relief against pollution of environment. 7 ALR Fed 907.

Propriety, under Rules 23(a) and 23(b) of Federal Rules of Civil Procedure, as amended in 1966, of class action seeking relief from racial discrimination. 8 ALR Fed 461.

Propriety, under Rule 23(a) and 23(b) of Federal Rules of Civil Procedure, as amended in 1966, of class action for violation of federal securities law. 9 ALR Fed 118.

Absent class members in class action under Rule 23 of Federal Rules of Civil Procedure as subject to discovery. 13 ALR Fed 255.

Maintenance of class action in United States Court of Claims. 14 ALR Fed 760.

Appealability of determination adverse to confirmation of action as class action under Rule 23 of Federal Rules of Civil Procedure. 17 ALR Fed 933.

Propriety, under Rule 23 of Federal Rules of Civil Procedure, of class action for injuries and death in airplane crash. 28 ALR Fed 719.

Law Reviews:

Class actions in New York. 38 Albany L Rev 865.

Social utility of class actions. 42 Brooklyn L Rev 189.

Availability of class actions to consumer for fraudulent misrepresentation by seller. 21 Buffalo L Rev 233.

The 1975 New York Judicial Conference package: class actions and comparative negligence. 25 Buffalo L Rev 415.

Aggregation of claims in class actions. 68 Colum L Rev 1554.

Interlocutory appeal from orders striking class action allegations. 70 Colum L Rev 1292.

Class actions and federal securities laws. 55 Cornell L Rev 78.

State class actions and the federal rule. 71 Colum L Rev 609.

Appealability of class action determinations. 44 Fordham L Rev 548.

Group action in the pursuit of justice. 44 NYU L Rev 661.

Fluid class recovery as a consumer remedy in antitrust cases. 47 NYU L Rev 477.

Condominium class actions. 48 St. John's L Rev 1168.

Forms:

See "FORMS" heading following "CASE NOTES", infra.

CASE NOTES

1. In general
2. Common questions of law or fact
3. Typical claims or defenses
4. Fair and adequate representation; manageability of class
5. Actions to recover penalty imposed by statute

1. In general

New class action statute vests in the courts the discretion to make a determination of the feasibility and desirability of permitting the action to proceed as a class action. Shook v Lavine (1975) 49 AD2d 238, 374 NYS2d 187.

Since respondent's answer had not been served and since 60 days had not passed since answer was due, application for class action status was premature. People ex rel. Kaufmann v Goldman (1976) 86 Misc 2d 776, 384 NYS2d 935.

Where, in action seeking order in nature of mandamus and injunctive relief directing prison authorities to maintain separate detention facilities for youths and adults at New York city criminal court, authorities assured that final court determination would be complied with, class action was not necessary. Brito v Ross (1976) 53 AD2d 414, 385 NYS2d 783.

Man with wife and six children whose application for medical assistance was denied because monthly net income, including amount representing social security taxes taken from his wages, exceeded statutory limitation for family of eight individuals, but who would be eligible for such assistance if social security taxes were excluded from his net income, was entitled to individual relief in proceeding by him challenging denial of his application; however, class action relief was inappropriate. Dumbleton v Reed (1976) 40 NY2d 586, 388 NYS2d 893, 357 NE2d 363.

Plaintiffs' conclusory allegation of the prerequisites contained in class action rule did not, on the record presented, furnish a sufficient basis upon which to predicate an order allowing a class action. Jennings v Domestic Finance Corp. (1976) 55 AD2d 832, 390 NYS2d 316.

2. Common questions of law or fact

Where there were factual determinations unique to each fair hearing with respect to denial of AFDC benefits because of past transfers of assets, where class action order would pose conceptual and enforcement problems which could not reasonably be foreseen, and where there was no reason why stare decisis could not achieve all which the

AFDC recipients would hope to achieve by some form of class action, class action status would be denied. Shook v Lavine (1975) 49 AD2d 238, 374 NYS2d 187.

Where over 90% of tenants of limited dividend housing corporation organized under Private Housing Finance Law were members of tenant organization and approximately half of tenants had air conditioners, organization had standing to bring proceedings to vacate order of the division of housing and community renewal permitting increase in monthly air conditioning charges and to require public hearing on increase. Boulevard Gardens Tenants Action Committee, Inc. v Boulevard Gardens Housing Corp. (1976) 88 Misc 2d 98, 388 NYS2d 215.

Class action could not be maintained by labor class employees of Department of Transportation challenging layoff procedures and seeking restoration to positions held prior to layoff, in that there were facts individual to each employee, such as veteran of volunteer fireman status, as well as questions relating to existence of vacancies in position which each member of class would be qualified to fill, which would determine their status as to relief. Jones v Carey (1976) 55 AD2d 260, 389 NYS2d 921.

3. Typical claims or defenses

Fact named plaintiffs seek damages in different amounts or even a remedy of different character will not impair their ability to fairly represent the class; if at any stage of action a question should arise as to adequacy of class representation the trial court can then take appropriate action. Vickers v Home Federal Sav. & Loan Asso. (1977) 56 AD2d 62, 390 NYS2d 747.

4. Fair and adequate representation; manageability of class

Question of possible conflicts of interest between class representatives, bringing suit to collect penalties under Truth in Lending Act against savings and loan association on behalf of all who received inadequate disclosures in mortgage transactions between specified dates, and the class members need not be resolved at stage of litigation involving threshold determination of maintenance of a class action. Vickers v Home Federal Sav. & Loan Asso. (1977) 56 AD2d 62, 390 NYS2d 747.

In action for declaratory and injunctive relief on claim of invalidity of statute imposing additional eligibility requirements for home relief benefits on certain needy children, certification of class was unnecessary, since, not only were governmental operations involved, but court was satisfied that it could adequately protect interests of alleged class by issuing a final order which, by its terms, would run to benefit of each person affected by statute involved. Tucker v Toia (1977) 89 Misc 2d 116, 390 NYS2d 794.

Matter involving charges of medical malpractice which allegedly resulted in development of retrolental fibroplasia in various classes of proposed plaintiffs who were prematurely born infants between 1953 and 1975, who were treated by defendant doctors between 1953 and 1975, or who were subject babies enrolled in cooperative study during period of July 1, 1953 through June 30, 1954, would be unmanageable as class action, in view of potential claims of class arising in various jurisdictions, at different times, at a time when status of medical knowledge was different, when dissemination of medical knowledge was at best questionable, when defenses and legal applications varied from case to case, and where proximate cause and existence of damage in each case was an individual variable. Kanon v Brookdale Hospital Medical Center (1975) 87 Misc 2d 816, 386 NYS2d 274.

5. Actions to recover penalty imposed by statute

Plaintiffs in class action acted properly in moving within 60 days after time to serve responsive pleading had expired for order of discovery to obtain facts necessary to satisfy prerequisites of class action, and for order, pending discovery, staying determination of whether class action status was appropriate, and trial court should have ruled on such motion before dismissing petition on its finding that class action was prohibited. Knapp v Michaux (1977) 55 AD2d 1025, 391 NYS2d 496.

CASE NOTES

UNDER FORMER CIVIL PRACTICE LAWS

A. UNDER FORMER CPLR § 1005

I. IN GENERAL

1. Generally

One seeking relief on behalf of public cannot invoke theory of class action, since "class" and "public" are mutually exclusive. Werfel v Fitzgerald (1965) 23 AD2d 306, 260 NYS2d 791.

Attorney seeking mandamus against clerk of court to permit inspection of public records under control of clerk was actually claiming relief as a citizen and a member of the public where his theory was that records were public and open to inspection by anyone. Werfel v Fitzgerald (1965) 23 AD2d 306, 260 NYS2d 791.

A class action may not be maintained where the wrongs asserted are individual to the different persons involved and each of the persons aggrieved may determine for himself the remedy which he will seek and may be subject to a defense not available against others. Neely v Hogan (1970) 62 Misc 2d 1056, 310 NYS2d 63.

Class actions may not be maintained when the asserted wrongs are individual to the different persons and each aggrieved person may determine for himself the remedy he will seek and may be subject to a defense not available to the others. Fisher v Health Ins. Plan (1971) 67 Misc 2d 674, 324 NYS2d 732.

Traditional articulations of class action learning paraphrase the difficult notion that separate wrongs to separate persons, even though committed pursuant to a single plan, are not alone sufficient to create a common or general interest, and that class members must possess a substantive unity of interest. Summers v Wyman (1970) 64 Misc 2d 67, 314 NYS2d 430.

Former CPLR § 1005(a) requires the plaintiff to demonstrate as a condition precedent to a class suit not only that plaintiff has a cause of action, but that he is bound by a "unity of interest" with other members of the alleged class, and identical contracts, contract provisions, or even identical wrongs are insufficient to support such requirement. Zachary v R. H. Macy & Co. (1971) 66 Misc 2d 974, 323 NYS2d 757, affd in part and vacated in part on other grounds 39 AD2d 116, 332 NYS2d 425, revd, in part, on other grounds app dismd, in part 31 NY2d 443, 340 NYS2d 908, 293 NE2d 80.

A group of students who were individually suspended from various public schools could not maintain a class action challenging the validity of their transfers to and retention in an allegedly inadequate "tutoring center", where a determination on the merits would have necessitated consideration of the particular circumstances surrounding each suspension. Hunt v Wilson (1972) 72 Misc 2d 360, 339 NYS2d 287.

Article 78 proceeding to compel care and treatment of mentally defective children was not a proper case for a class action pursuant to CPLR § 1005, subd a, where class which included all indigent, minor, mentally retarded, handicapped, violent, and emotionally disturbed persons, as to whom various unrelated remedies or treatments may have been applicable, and against whom separate defenses may well have been asserted, was far too broad and indefinite to be encompassed by the statute. Usen v Sipprell (1973) 41 AD2d 251, 342 NYS2d 599.

Prospective legislation, as opposed to judicial development, should be allowed to more clearly define the limits of class action. Cummings v Regan (1974) 45 AD2d 415, 358 NYS2d 556, revd on other grounds 36 NY2d 969, 373 NYS2d 563, 335 NE2d 864.

Discretion of courts persists to reconsider advisability of a class action at any stage if it develops that class is unwieldy, representation ineffective or that principal issue is not appropriate for adjudication in a class action. Ray v Marine Midland Grace Trust Co. (1974) 35 NY2d 147, 359 NYS2d 28, 316 NE2d 320, 73 ALR3d 871.

Statute providing that where the question is one of a common or general interest of many persons or where persons who might be made parties are very numerous and it may be impracticable to bring them all before the court, one or more may sue or defend for benefit of all was intended to be as broad as the class action remedy fashioned and available in equity. Ray v Marine Midland Grace Trust Co. (1974) 35 NY2d 147, 359 NYS2d 28, 316 NE2d 320, 73 ALR3d 871.

Plaintiff customers of electric utility, suing utility for damage resulting when ice storm left them without heat or electricity for several days, were not entitled to maintain a class action on behalf of countless customers of the defendant utility, since each aggrieved customer was entitled to determine for himself the appropriate remedy and each individual claim might be subject to certain defenses available against others. Dennis v Long Island Lighting Co. (1974) 78 Misc 2d 400, 357 NYS2d 633.

Class action statute is limited in application to persons who have common grievance as to which only a common defense may be asserted. Cummings v Regan (1974) 45 AD2d 222, 357 NYS2d 260, revd on other grounds 36 NY2d 969, 373 NYS2d 563, 335 NE2d 864.

Corporation, which operated cable television systems in state, was not a proper representative of a class so as to maintain action, in which constitutionality of statute providing that expenses of cable television commission shall be allocated among cable television companies in proportion to their gross receipts was challenged and in which judgment setting aside commission order implementing such statute was sought, where some of services provided by corporation were not provided by a majority of cable operators and corporation's sources of revenue differed from the majority of cable operators. Ceracche Television Corp. v Kelly (1974) 80 Misc 2d 956, 364 NYS2d 276, affd 50 AD2d 134, 376 NYS2d 217.

Where mother who sought to enjoin school officials from failing to provide alternative instruction for pupil suspended from school for five days or less indicated that neither she nor any person whom she sought to have included in class when she sought to represent were questioning the validity of the suspension or the underlying grounds therefor, case presented question of common or general interest of many persons and was maintainable as a class action. Turner v Kowalski (1975) 80 Misc 2d 597, 364 NYS2d 91, mod on other grounds 49 AD2d 943, 374 NYS2d 133.

II. Particular Actions and Proceedings

2. Associations

Members of a club cannot bring a class action against club to impose a constructive trust on the total of membership fees paid by 50,000 members of club and to recover damages for breach of contract whereby club undertook to provide a private key club in New York City for the exclusive use of the 50,000 members. Onofrio v Playboy Club of New York, Inc. (1965) 15 NY2d 740, 257 NYS2d 171, 205 NE2d 308.

3. Creditors

Unpaid creditor may not proceed under Surr Ct A § 217 on behalf of himself as well as other unpaid creditors, whose claims were also not rejected, since, if the estate is insolvent, the claimants will be contending against each other for payment of their respective claims, and therefore there is no "class" within the contemplation of CPLR § 1005 to be represented. Re Scheiner's Will (1963) 40 Misc 2d 181, 242 NYS2d 875.

Action by holder of debentures for negligence and breach of trust with regard to indenture trustee's alleged failure to act affirmatively to protect debenture holders at appropriate time prior to chapter X proceedings could be maintained as class action on behalf of all debenture holders particularly, in that, though there were variations in harm sustained and in applicability of waiver or estoppel defenses, there were predominant common issues of breach of duty and neglect, and in that class was of an appropriate size and named plaintiff would be fair representative. Ray v Marine Midland Grace Trust Co. (1974) 35 NY2d 147, 359 NYS2d 28, 316 NE2d 320, 73 ALR3d 871.

4. Labor unions

Individual Negro citizens had no right to bring a class action on behalf of all state Negro citizens allegedly illegally discriminated against by construction labor unions. Gaynor v Rockefeller (1965) 15 NY2d 120, 256 NYS2d 584, 204 NE2d 627.

In class action by five members of labor union to rescind collective bargaining agreement it was duty of plaintiffs' to plead bona fide offer to return all benefits received by all parties to agreement and where plaintiffs conceded that they did not have authorization from rest of union members to make such an offer motion to dismiss complaint would be granted. Missler v Pan American World Airways, Inc. (1966) 50 Misc 2d 197, 270 NYS2d 30.

5. Partners

When limited partners, who instituted suit in partnership name as an entity, amended caption of action to sue as individuals in class action rather than as an entity, they insulated themselves from liability as general partners, but thereby came within limitation and prohibition of § 15 of the Partnership Law which provides that a limited partner, unless he is also a general partner, is not a proper party to the proceedings by or against the partnership, and an action could not thereafter be maintained. Riviera Congress Associates v Yassky (1966) 25 AD2d 291, 268 NYS2d 854, affd 18 NY2d 540, 277 NYS2d 386, 223 NE2d 876.

Limited partners may bring a class action on behalf of other limited partners where the question is one of a common or general interest to them. Lichtyger v Franchard Corp. (1966) 18 NY2d 528, 277 NYS2d 377, 223 NE2d 869; Riviera Congress

Associates v Yassky (1966) 18 NY2d 540, 277 NYS2d 386, 223 NE2d 876.

Limited partners, although not permitted to interfere in any manner with the conduct of the partnership business, may bring a class action on behalf of others similarly situated based upon alleged mismanagement of the partnership property by the general partners resulting in impairment of the rate of return on the investment of the limited partners. Lichtyger v Franchard Corp. (1966) 18 NY2d 528, 277 NYS2d 377, 223 NE2d 869.

CPLR 1005 neither extends or limits the rights of a limited partner as defined by the Partnership Law. Millard v Newmark & Co. (1966) 24 AD2d 333, 266 NYS2d 254.

An action by approximately 30 percent of the limited partners seeking general damages for all limited partners, the return of their investment, an accounting, and expenses precluded any conclusion that the "question is one of common or general interest" or that the interests of each and every partner was common or identical so as to authorize a single common action. Millard v Newmark & Co. (1966) 24 AD2d 333, 266 NYS2d 254.

6. Stockholders

Ex parte application for discontinuance with prejudice of stockholders' derivative action against certain of the directors named as defendants, even though based on stipulation signed by all the attorneys for all the parties, must be denied where there is no decisive showing that there is no cause of action against them. Borden v Guthrie (1964) 42 Misc 2d 879, 248 NYS2d 913.

Where a corporation in whose right a derivative shareholders' action is brought seeks to be substituted as plaintiff, the corporation should establish that notwithstanding its prior declination, it will now prosecute the action in good faith; and the court should direct that all shareholders receive an appropriate notice of the application, similar in purpose and effect to the notice contemplated by Bus Corp L § 626(d) for the discontinuance or compromise of such an action. Lazar v Merchants' Nat. Properties, Inc. (1964) 22 AD2d 253, 254 NYS2d 712.

Where stock tender offer was made to purchase shares of stock in defendant corporation, suit by shareholders who tendered shares, on ground that defendant corporation and defendant directors hampered and delayed plaintiffs in receipt of purchase price due, was properly maintainable as class action, being grounded on fiduciary relationship rather than on individual stock sale contracts, in which price per share, time of payment and manner of transfer were all definite, the only difference in such contracts being number of shares to be tendered by each party. Reeves v Texas Gulf, Inc. (1974) 78 Misc 2d 579, 357 NYS2d 662.

Action by holder of debentures for negligence and breach of trust with regard to indenture trustee's alleged failure to act affirmatively to protect debenture holders at appropriate time prior to chapter X proceedings could be maintained as class action on behalf of all debenture holders particularly, in that, though there were variations in harm sustained and in applicability of waiver or estoppel defenses, there were predominant common issues of breach of duty and neglect, and in that class was of an appropriate size and named plaintiff would be fair representative. Ray v Marine Midland Grace Trust Co. (1974) 35 NY2d 147, 359 NYS2d 28, 316 NE2d 320, 73 ALR3d 871.

Class allegations based, primarily, on asserted fraudulent omissions and representations relied on by purchasers of common stock did not form proper basis for class action. MFT Invest. Co. v Diversified Data Services & Sciences, Inc. (1976) 52 AD2d 761, 382 NYS2d 770.

7. Welfare beneficiaries

A recipient of public assistance with six dependent children could not bring a class action to compel a county commissioner of social services and the New York State Commissioner of Social Services to withhold from her monthly assistance grant funds sufficient to pay her utility bills because of her previously demonstrated inability to handle cash. Summers v Wyman (1970) 64 Misc 2d 67, 314 NYS2d 430.

An Article 78 proceeding was appropriately brought as a class action under CPLR § 1005, subd a to compel the Department of Social Services to render decisions on application for Aid to Families with Dependent Children within the mandatory 60-day period. Cisco v Lavine (1973) 72 Misc 2d 1009, 340 NYS2d 275, on reh 72 Misc 2d 1087, 341 NYS2d 719.

Suit by welfare recipients to enforce federal and state regulations requiring local social services department to reinstate individuals dropped from eligibility for full medical benefits by reason of social security increases was a proper class action, in that the issues raised were of common and general interest to all persons lawfully entitled to such benefits. Lutsky v Shuart (1973) 74 Misc 2d 436, 342 NYS2d 709, affd 43 AD2d 1016, 351 NYS2d 946.

In proceeding seeking to establish as a matter of law that replacement of essential furniture fell within category of essential assistance pursuant to Social Services L § 350-j was proper class action where issues were not limited to whether named petitioners were eligible for emergency assistance but whether commissioner's refusal as a matter of policy to consider their applications was proper under regulations. Baumes v Lavine (1973) 74 Misc 2d 1046, 347 NYS2d 355, revd on other grounds 44 AD2d 336, 355 NYS2d 477, affd 38 NY2d 296, 379 NYS2d 760, 342 NE2d 543.

Policy of applying income tax refunds to reduce public assistance grants was common wrong remediable by class action, but part of petition which sought reimbursement for all members of class was directed at curing separate wrongs, committed by similar means to separate persons, and thus was not properly a part of class action. Richards v Lavine (1974) 78 Misc 2d 801, 357 NYS2d 982.

Recipient of public assistance in the aid to dependent children category was entitled to maintain as class action, on behalf of that class of persons in Erie County who were in immediate need of public assistance and who had applied for such assistance at the county department of social services, an Article 78 proceeding for declaration that local agency actions in refusing to issue immediate interviews for the class members were in conflict with regulation that requires interviews to be conducted within five working days. Sauls v Sipprell (1974) 80 Misc 2d 240, 362 NYS2d 719.

In view of vast number of people in New York City who might be in need of public welfare assistance during period between application for and receipt of social security benefits, action to compel local public welfare official to provide such assistance could be brought as class action. Szanto v Dumpson, (1974) 77 Misc 2d 392, 353 NYS2d 683.

Inasmuch as action challenging validity of regulations authorizing recovery of advance assistance payments involved governmental operations, and persons other than petitioners who were similarly situated would be adequately protected under principles of stare decisis, consideration of petitioners' claim of entitlement to class action status was unnecessary. Adkin v Berger (1976) 50 AD2d 459, 378 NYS2d 135.

Action challenging proration of fuel and shelter costs when a supplemental security income recipient was a member of a household which was receiving payments in category of aid to families with dependent children would not be certified as a class action since every member of the class had administrative remedy available; furthermore, new class action rules, as effective subsequent to commencement of the action, were not to be applied retroactively since the statute is procedural in nature and there is no legislative intent that it be applied to pending proceedings. Barton v Lavine (1976) 54 AD2d 350, 389 NYS2d 416.

8. Taxpayers

Redress may be had in a taxpayer's action only when the acts complained of are fraudulent, or a waste of public property in the sense that they represent a use of public property or funds for entirely illegal purposes. Murphy v Erie County (1970) 34 AD2d 295, 310 NYS2d 959, affd 28 NY2d 80, 320 NYS2d 29, 268 NE2d 771.

Article 78 proceeding in which 250 property owners challenged the validity of a special assessment levied against their respective properties was properly treated as a class action. Acca v Bureau of Assessors (1972) 73 Misc 2d 50, 340 NYS2d 476, affd 45 AD2d 1005, 358 NYS2d 213, revd on other grounds 36 NY2d 1015, 374 NYS2d 614, 337 NE2d 127.

9. Tenants

Tenants who were non-purchasers under plan to convert to co-operative apartment could properly maintain class action for declaring their right to renewal of leases on ground that plan never became legally operative due to flagrant misrepresentation resorted to by sponsor-landlord in obtaining required percentage of purchasers. Richards v Kaskel (1973) 32 NY2d 524, 347 NYS2d 1, 300 NE2d 388.

Non-purchasing tenants who occupied building which sponsor proposed to convert to a co-operative association clearly had standing to challenge, in a plenary court action, the methods by which sponsor procured purchase agreements under the plan of co-operative association, and such tenants were entitled to renewal of their leases if they established that such agreements were executed as a result of discriminatory inducements, improper pressures, or false representations, and tenants were not required to present such contentions to the attorney general under General Business Law § 352-e. Richards v Kaskel (1973) 32 NY2d 524, 347 NYS2d 1, 300 NE2d 388.

Proceeding brought by tenant of apartment complex subject to rent control on behalf of himself and all others similarly situated to review and annul Attorney General's acceptance for filing purposes of offering plan for conversion of portion of complex to condominium presented question of common interest affecting rights of every nonpurchasing tenant in complex and thus there was no obstacle to class action treatment of such proceeding. Whalen v Lefkowitz (1975) 36 NY2d 75, 365 NYS2d 150, 324 NE2d 536.

10. Prisoners and persons in confinement

Under CPLR § 1005, subd a, prison inmate properly and successfully commenced Article 78 class action to compel parole board to give inmates meaningful reasons for denial of parole. Cummings v Regan (1973) 76 Misc 2d 137, 350 NYS2d 119, affd 45 AD2d 222, 357 NYS2d 260, revd on other grounds 36 NY2d 969, 373 NYS2d 563, 335 NE2d 864.

Prisoners properly and successfully commenced Article 78 class action to compel parole board to state ultimate ground for denial of parole with sufficient particularity to enable prisoners to understand how they were expected to regulate their behavior, and to enable a reviewing court to determine whether inadmissible factors influenced the board's decision, and whether discretion was abused. Cummings v Regan (1973) 76 Misc 2d 357, 350 NYS2d 842, revd 45 AD2d 415, 358 NYS2d 556, revd on other grounds 36 NY2d 969, 373 NYS2d 563, 335 NE2d 864.

Complaint brought by individuals detained while placing criminal charges seeking declaratory judgment that bail system was violative of their constitutional rights could not be brought as a class action as there are individual determinations to be made in every bail application. Bellamy v Judges & Justices Authorized to Sit in New York City Criminal Court (1973) 41 AD2d 196, 342 NYS2d 137, affd 32 NY2d 886, 346 NYS2d 812, 300 NE2d 153.

Prospective legislation, as opposed to judicial development, should be allowed to more clearly define the limits of class action. Cummings v Regan (1974) 45 AD2d 415, 358 NYS2d 556, revd on other grounds 36 NY2d 969, 373 NYS2d 563, 335 NE2d 864.

Action by inmates of state correctional facilities who had attained parole eligibility but not release was appropriate for class action for injunctive and declaratory relief to require that parole board state reasons for denial of parole. Cummings v Regan (1974) 45 AD2d 222, 357 NYS2d 260, revd on other grounds 36 NY2d 969, 373 NYS2d 563, 335 NE2d 864.

Judgment vacating parole delinquency detainer warrant and dismissing declaration of delinquency with prejudice, based upon failure to give defendant parole revocation hearing for two and one-half years after the warrant was issued, did not apply as class relief to other parolees similarly situated. Wright v Regan (1974) 46 AD2d 163, 361 NYS2d 437.

11. Zoning determinations

Residents of an R-1 zone were prevented from bringing a class action to enjoin establishment in such zone of a home for youths in need of rehabilitation, where the wrongs asserted were individual to the different persons aggrieved. Nowack v Department of Audit & Control (1973) 72 Misc 2d 518, 338 NYS2d 52.

12. Public employees

No class action lay for recovery of interest under General Municipal Law § 3-a on city employees' delayed retirement benefits, even though it was common knowledge that New York City Employees Retirement System was unresponsive to employees' inquiries and generally inefficient. Post v New York City Employees' Retirement System (1973) 41 AD2d 606, 340 NYS2d 416.

Article 78 proceeding to restrain police commissioner and department from reducing petitioner from rank of deputy inspector to rank of captain, in which petitioner sought declaratory relief for benefit of an unspecified class claimed to be similarly situated, could not be deemed a class action since the allegations in the petition applied only to petitioner. Foran v Cawley (1973) 77 Misc 2d 809, 354 NYS2d 757.

State employee's action for reimbursement for services of psychologist pursuant to group health policy provided by state did not warrant bringing of class action. Moore v Metropolitan Life Ins. Co. (1973) 33 NY2d 304, 352 NYS2d 433, 307 NE2d 554.

Action seeking declaration that various public officials were in violation of laws forbidding political influence and prohibiting assessments in connection with civil service employment or promotion could not be maintained as class action, on behalf of civil service employees "similarly situated", to the four named civil service employee plaintiffs, since wrongs asserted, i.e., coercion into contributing funds to political party to secure promotion, were individual to the different persons involved, different remedies were available to each member of the alleged class and varied defenses were available to defendants on any individual claim asserted. Cullen v Margiotta (1975) 81 Misc 2d 809, 367 NYS2d 638.

B. UNDER FORMER CPA § 195

I. IN GENERAL

13. Generally

The right to bring representative action arises from necessity where parties are too numerous to be joined; theory of representation is one of implied agency. Brill v Blakeley (1953) 281 AD 532, 120 NYS2d 713.

In cases where many persons have claims and are prosecuting, or are about to prosecute them at law, against one defendant, or class of defendants, or a fund liable in equal degree to all those persons and to others, a court of equity, to forestall a multiplicity of actions, has jurisdiction of an action for a general accounting and adjustment of all the rights, and to restrain separate and individual actions at law in the same or other courts, thus bringing all the litigation into one suit. It is immaterial whether the rights of action arise from general principles of law or from particular provisions of constitution or statute. Pfohl v Simpson (1878) 74 NY 137.

Where a bill in equity is filed on behalf of a class, every member of that class is entitled to come in and enjoy its benefits on contributing to the expense, whether he has some other qualification or not. Rogers v New York & T. Land Co. (1888) 17 NYSR 131, 1 NYS 908, revd on other grounds 134 NY 197, 32 NE 27.

The word "many," as used in former CPA § 195 did not necessarily contemplate "very numerous persons." Farnam v Barnum, 2 How Pr NS 396.

Where all questions of fact and law are common to all claimants, and there is no basis for discriminating between them, a basis exists for a representative action. Jones v Healy (1945) 185 Misc 400, 56 NYS2d 349.

Apart from accounting action, there is no requirement of a common fund, from which claimants seek payment, as condition to bringing representative action. Jones v Healy, supra.

Where each plaintiff's claim stems from his own contract with defendant, there is no common fund or other community of interest on which to predicate representative action. McCord v Broadcast Music (1948) 84 NYS2d 185.

A tenant may not maintain, a representative action "on behalf of himself and others similarly situated", proceeding to enjoin landlord from evicting tenants in housing project and restrain collection of increase in rentals for housing accommodations, pending final determination of federal court action. Dinkes v Glen Oaks Village (1954) 206 Misc 143, 132 NYS2d 138.

As to application generally, see Berle v Dawkins (1934) 150 Misc 911, 271 NYS 579.

Under the Conformity Act (US Code, tit 28, § 724) CPA § 195 applied to actions at law in the federal courts, but not to suits in equity. Brusselback v Cago Corp. (1936) 14 F Supp 993, revd on other grounds 85 F2d 20, cert den 299 US 586, 81 L Ed 432, 57 S Ct 111.

Unity of interest: is not required; community of interest is sufficient. Borg v New York Majestic Corp. (1954) 139 NYS2d 72.

Purpose of class actions is to avoid multiplicity of suits, but such purpose is not served by uniting in single action controversies concerning numerous expense deductions. Von Roebel v Sesac (1955) 145 NYS2d 679, affd 1 AD2d 822, 150 NYS2d 152.

Persons do not become united in interest merely because of factual similarity and a question of law is not sufficient per se to inject such causes with a representative character. Guterman v New York (1958) 10 Misc 2d 259, 172 NYS2d 76.

Where plaintiff commenced an action against the third party not the city of New York which action was settled and plaintiff had also commenced an action against the city and paid a jury fee, since it was a personal injury action, plaintiff could not recover in a representative capacity for other individuals since such an action does not fall within those defined as having a common or general interest under CPA § 195 and only the plaintiff could have an interest in the recovery of the jury fee paid. Guterman v New York, supra.

An action to have uniform players' contract in the International Baseball League declared void cannot be maintained by some of the signatories as representatives of all signatories, even though not employed by the defendants, solely because their common interest is that they all signed the same type of contract, and allegations of representative character will be directed deleted. Blake v Frick (1959) 20 Misc 2d 520, 191 NYS2d 177.

14. Effect of section

Section permits of an adjudication binding upon all without which the rights of all parties to the controversy could not be determined for want of the presence of some of them. New York State R. Co. v Security Trust Co. (1929) 135 Misc 456, 238 NYS 354, affd 228 AD 750, 238 NYS 887.

A representative action may not be brought in behalf of all persons who might under former CPA § 209 be joined as parties plaintiff. Brenner v Title Guarantee & T. Co. (1937) 276 NY 230, 11 NE2d 890, 114 ALR 1010.

In action for accounting under agreement requiring defendant to obtain licenses for use of plaintiff's musical works, wherein plaintiff claimed that defendant had improperly deducted expenses, plaintiff could not sue on behalf of other publishers similarly situated having similar agreements with defendant. Von Roebel v Sesac (1956) 145 NYS2d 679, affd 1 AD2d 822, 150 NYS2d 152.

15. Fair Labor Standards Act

Fair Labor Standards Act permits representative action to be brought, but such action may not be continued in so far as it affects employees who do not consent thereto. Thomas v Keystone Silver, Inc. (1940) 174 Misc 733, 22 NYS2d 796.

While on proper showing all employees of defendant might unite in single action under Fair Labor Standards Act to recover overtime wages, three plaintiffs may not maintain a representative action on behalf of other employees under CPA § 195. Simmons v Rudolph Knitting Mills (1942) 264 AD 871, 35 NYS2d 494.

16. Courts

The provisions of CPA § 195 permitting one or more parties to defend for the benefit of all, are not applicable to the municipal court of the city of New York. Reed v Wiley, Harker & Camp Co. (1906) 51 Misc 574, 101 NYS 39.

17. Right of defendant to invoke section

Defendant has no right to invoke CPA § 195 on behalf of parties suing. General Ins. Co. v Goldstein (1943) 182 Misc 419, 45 NYS2d 570, affd 267 AD 898, 48 NYS2d 322.

II. PLEADINGS AND CONDUCT OF ACTION

18. Generally

One of a class, for whose benefit an action has been brought but who has not been named in the summons or complaint, and who has not been made a party to the action is not to be regarded as a party for the purpose of influencing the disposition of a motion to change the venue of the action. Brown v Bache (1901) 66 AD 367, 72 NYS 687.

Where one intervened in representative action and his name was entered on the title of the summons and complaint and all subsequent proceedings as one of the plaintiffs, the fact that the former plaintiff dropped out of the case was of no consequence, and the action continued. Leighton v New York R. Co. (1915) 169 AD 553, 155 NYS 444.

19. Pleading

Where one sues for all, the various allegations in the complaint in relation to the damages which will be caused to the other parties are not irrelevant. Astor v New York Arcade R. Co. 3 NYSR 188.

An action may be construed as a representative one if the complaint so shows though does not so allege. Palmarito De Cauto Sugar Co. v Warner (1929) 225 AD 261, 232 NYS 569.

A representative action cannot be maintained unless it appears from the complaint that plaintiff not only has a cause of action but that he is representative of a common or general interest of others. Complaint dismissed because insufficient in that respect. Brown v Werblin (1930) 138 Misc 29, 244 NYS 209.

A statement at the beginning of the complaint in a creditor's suit, that the plaintiffs sue for themselves and all others similarly situated, is sufficient. Cochran v American Opera Co. 20 Abb NC 114, affd (1890) 30 NYSR 13, 8 NYS 558.

Where complaint states that action is brought by plaintiffs in behalf of themselves and all other stockholders and scripholders of a corporation similarly situated, it means the same as though it stated "all other stockholders or scripholders." Rogers v New York & T. Land Co. (1888) 17 NYSR 131, 1 NYS 908, revd on other grounds 134 NY 197, 32 NE 27.

Independent jobbers may join in one complaint for injunctive relief against labor union, seeking redress for individual wrongs and illegal acts committed against them, but they should set forth their grievances in separately pleaded causes of action, and omit references to other jobbers similarly affected. Reinman v Jaffe (1952) 116 NYS2d 366, affd 281 AD 833, 118 NYS2d 475.

Telephone subscriber, alleging class action against telephone company for declaratory judgment and for account of sales taxes collected on non-taxable telephone calls, must define class of consumers represented and specify relief sought. Goodman & Co. v New York Tel. Co. (1954) 133 NYS2d 1.

Where plaintiff sues on behalf of herself and all others interested, this must be pleaded as part of the cause of action and not merely recited in the title. Grofsick v De Angelis (1956) 156 NYS2d 878.

20. Control of action

Upon prosecution to judgment the plaintiff ceases to have control over the action. Brinckeroff v Bostwick (1885) 99 NY 185, 1 NE 663.

In an action brought by a stockholder for herself and all others, against trustees of a corporation for malfeasance, making the receiver a party, he having refused to bring the action, no other stockholder having joined, and no affirmative relief being demanded as between the defendants, held, that plaintiff might, without notice to the receiver, settle and discontinue the action before entry of judgment. Beadleston v Alley (1889) 28 NYSR 89, 7 NYS 747.

21. Right to jury trial

CPA § 195 cannot be used to deprive party of constitutional right to jury trial. General Ins. Co. v Goldstein (1943) 182 Misc 419, 45 NYS2d 570, affd 267 AD 898, 48 NYS2d 322.

22. Judgment

As to a form of judgment in an action to vacate an assignment brought on behalf of plaintiff and all others similarly situated, where no other persons apply to be made parties plaintiff, see Knell v Buffalo (1889) 54 Hun 80, 7 NYS 233.

Where a judgment creditor seeking to reach a fund in the hands of a third person states in her complaint that she sues on her own behalf and for such other creditors, similarly situated, who may come in, etc., this limitation does not prevent a judgment in favor of the plaintiff alone, if no other creditors have come in. Green v Griswold (1888) 4 NYS 8.

23. Coming in after decree or judgment

Right of other creditors to come in after judgment and prove their claims, in an action to compel an accounting by a general assignee. Lewis v Hake (1886) 42 Hun 542.

III. Particular Actions and Parties

24. Associations

One or more members of an unincorporated association may sustain an action, on behalf of themselves and all other members, to restrain an infringement of a device adopted by them, if the whole number of members is large. Strasser v Moonelis, 11 NYSR 270, affd 13 NYSR 288.

Individual members of unincorporated associations may sue in their own names on behalf of themselves and associates. Bloete v Simon, 19 Abb NC 88, 7 NYSR 87.

CPA § 195 applied to an action brought by one of a number of members of an unincorporated association. Boston Base Ball Asso. v Brooklyn Base Ball Club (1902) 37 Misc 521, 75 NYS 1076.

A holder of certificates in a cemetery association, seeking an accounting, should bring an action representative in character, or in behalf of the plaintiff and all others similarly situated, since the action is one of common or general interest to many persons. Tyndall v Pinelawn Cemetery (1910) 198 NY 217, 91 NE 591.

Action by member of New York Annual Conference of African Methodist Episcopal Church, on behalf of self and other members, against such Conference for accounting held representative and not derivative action, and was maintainable under CPA § 195. Re Taylor (1942) 265 AD 858, 37 NYS2d 675.

Acting president cannot sue for labor union. Hogan v Williams (1944) 185 Misc 338, 55 NYS2d 904, affd on other grounds 270 AD 789, 59 NYS2d 331.

Persons owning real property in the vicinity of property for which variance is sought have been held to be "specially and beneficially interested" in the determination to be reviewed so as to be permitted to intervene in an Article 78 proceeding, and they may be represented by an association. Virgo v Zoning Board of Appeals (1961) 28 Misc 2d 886, 212 NYS2d 586.

25. Bondholders

Bondholders could maintain representative action for damages for breach of contract to purchase entire issue from all bondholders. Atkins v Trowbridge (1914) 162 AD 161, 147 NYS 275.

Where large number of bondholders united in executing reorganization agreement and an agreement of defendant to purchase the bonds was breached and some of the bondholders brought action, judgment could only be rendered for those who sued or joined as plaintiffs during the action before judgment. Atkins v Trowbridge, supra.

Where right, if any, of bondholders suing trustee under trust indenture to relief from wrongful receipt by defendant of moneys, securities and income, which were specifically exempted from coverage of mortgage and were not part of mortgaged res, there was no injury to bondholders as a class, entitling them to maintain a representative action. Elkind v Chase Nat. Bk. (1940) 259 AD 661, 20 NYS2d 213, affd 284 NY 726, 31 NE2d 198.

Where all bondholders had notice and about half of them in amount participated in proceeding by trustee in mortgage for instructions as to disposition of insurance moneys, it was proper for court to make finding that all bondholders should be bound by judgment. United States Mortg. & T. Co. v New York Dock Co. (1919) 108 Misc 120, 177 NYS 455.

Class suit by bondholders could have been brought at law under CPA § 195. Savings Bank of New London v New York Trust Co. (1941) 27 NYS2d 963.

If a representative action is fairly brought and honestly conducted for the benefit of all bondholders, the judgment therein is conclusive against the plaintiffs. Stevens v Union Trust Co. (1890) 57 Hun 498, 11 NYS 268.

An action may be maintained by bondholders for themselves and the other bondholders against a trustee of a mortgage acting in bad faith to the bondholders, for its removal as trustee and for an injunction restraining further action by the trustee until the question should be decided, and this although the mortgaged premises were in another state. Gibson v American Loan & T. Co. (1890) 58 Hun 443, 12 NYS 444.

26. Certificate holders, guaranteed mortgage

In action by three plaintiffs to recover amounts paid by them respectively for the purchase from defendants of certificates of undivided shares in a bond secured by a mortgage on real property, alleged to have been induced by false representations made by defendant to each plaintiff, motion to strike from the complaint all allegations that the action was also brought on behalf of other holders of guaranteed mortgage certificates issued by the defendant, should have been granted. Brenner v Title Guarantee & T. Co. (1936) 276 NY 230, 11 NE2d 890, 114 ALR 1010.

27. Certificate holders, receivership

One of three persons holding receiver's certificates could have sued for all three under the provisions of CPA § 195. Hilton Bridge Constr. Co. v Foster (1899) 26 Misc 338, 57 NYS 140, affd 42 AD 630, 59 NYS 1106.

28. City as representative of citizen

A city which is not bound by a schedule of rates filed by a public utility company may not sue to enjoin their collection as the representative of consumers affected thereby. Oswego v Peoples' Gas & E. Co. (1921) 116 Misc 354, 190 NYS 39.

29. Civil service employees

Ten civil service employees, may sue for 400

others similarly situated to compel restoration to seniority rights. Sippell v Dowd (1948) 191 Misc 558, 76 NYS2d 440, affd 274 AD 1027, 86 NYS2d 478.

30. Creditors

Where several have received injury from the same accident and the wrongdoer is insolvent, action by a judgment creditor on the casualty bond should be in equity for the benefit of himself and all similarly situated, praying for proportionate division of the proceeds. Bleimeyer v Public Serv. Mut. Casualty Ins. Corp. (1929) 250 NY 264, 165 NE 286.

Where administrators, upon application of a creditor of their intestate, refuse to exercise the power conferred upon them to disaffirm a transfer made by said intestate to one of the administrators in fraud of the rights of creditors, and to reclaim the property fraudulently conveyed, and where the estate in the hands of the administrators proved insufficient to pay the debts, the creditor may bring an action for his own benefit and that of the other creditors to reclaim the property, making all the administrators parties. Harvey v McDonnell (1889) 113 NY 526, 21 NE 695. See also, Cochran v American Opera Co. 20 Abb NC 114, affd (1890) 30 NYSR 13, 8 NYS 558.

Creditors who have not obtained judgments until after the commencement of the action cannot come in. Claflin v Gordon (1886) 39 Hun 54.

A creditor may in his own name and for his own benefit sue directors for loans of corporate funds to stockholders (Stock Corp L § 59), but creditors similarly situated may intervene or be joined. If they do not intervene or fail to be joined, it is no objection to the maintenance of the action by the single creditor that he will thereby reap the full statutory benefit to the exclusion of other creditors. American Broadcasting-Paramount Theatres, Inc. v Frye (1960) 8 NY2d 232, 203 NYS2d 850, 168 NE2d 669.

31. Depositors

Although it was alleged in an action by two depositors that upwards of five thousand persons were, like the plaintiffs, wronged by the defendant banks, such persons were not, merely because of that fact, united in interest with either plaintiff, and the plaintiffs could not maintain a representative action, pursuant to CPA § 195 in their behalf. Society Milion Athena v National Bank (1939) 281 NY 282, 22 NE2d 374.

32. Distributees and next of kin

Distributee of intestate may sue individually and for other distributees to impress trust on realty, where there were 18 other distributees, many of whom resided outside state or United States. Costa v Pratt (1949) 197 Misc 252, 98 NYS2d 115.

One next of kin may maintain an action for the benefit of all. If the consent of any one who ought to be joined as a plaintiff cannot be obtained, he may be made a defendant, the reason therefor being stated in the complaint. Farnam v Barnum, 2 How Pr NS 396.

CPA § 195 was not applicable to an action to determine the validity of the probate of a will, but all interested persons had to be made parties. Brinkerhoff v Tiernan (1908) 61 Misc 586, 114 NYS 698.

Surviving brother of purchaser of cemetery plot may, at request of other brother and sisters, sue undertaker for burial of stranger in such plot. O'Shanghnessy v Barrett, Inc. (1946) 186 Misc 1040, 66 NYS2d 4.

33. Fraudulent conspiracy

An action for damages for a fraudulent conspiracy was not within CPA § 195. Cavanagh v Hutcheson (1931) 140 Misc 178, 250 NYS 127, affd 236 AD 794, 259 NYS 967.

34. Injunction action

Class representation will not be permitted in injunction actions, so that one who has been given no notice of the proceeding and no opportunity to defend himself will not be enjoined merely because others whose interests may be identical were given such notice and opportunity. Pan American World Airways, Inc. v Air Line Pilots Asso. (1960) 22 Misc 2d 148, 206 NYS2d 98.

35. Insurance beneficiaries

Under fire policy for benefit of customers of cleaning concern which had gone into bankruptcy and trustee claimed insurance as belonging to bankrupt, representative action on behalf of customers against him was allowed. Morrison v Warren (1940) 174 Misc 233, 20 NYS2d 26, affd 260 AD 998, 24 NYS2d 988.

36. Insurance policyholders

Beneficiary of life policy, relating to optional methods of settlement, cannot sue insurer on behalf of self, other beneficiaries and insureds, to have determined their rights to such methods of settlement. Kahn v New York L. Ins. Co. (1945) 184 Misc 417, 53 NYS2d 575.

Where a life insurance company agrees to pay a sum at a future day or at death, and then transfers its assets to another company and ceases to do business, the policyholder may rescind the contract and sue for all similarly situated to recover all that he has paid. Meade v St. Louis Mut. Life Ins. Co. 51 How Pr 1.

One of a numerous class of policyholders holding the same legal positions may sue on behalf of all to compel the officers of a company to make a proper division of dividends. Luling v Atlantic Mut. Ins. Co. 45 Barb 510, 30 How Pr 69, revd on another point 50 Barb 520, affd (1872) 51 NY 207.

37. Libeled parties

Where book libeled several persons as traitors during war time, plaintiff could not maintain action in representative capacity. Hart v E. P.

Dutton & Co. (1949) 197 Misc 274, 93 NYS2d 871, affd 277 AD 935, 98 NYS2d 773.

38. Licensees

In action by several licensees or franchise holders against licensor for accounting, suing on behalf of plaintiff and all other franchise holders, mere fact that there may be numerous plaintiffs and that all of them have similar contract relationship is not sufficient to entitle plaintiffs to sue for other licensees, since right to bring representative action depends on common interest in subject matter. Noel H. Corp. v Carvel Dari-Freeze Stores (1955) 140 NYS2d 640, affd 286 AD 1066, 146 NYS2d 663.

39. Lien Law action

Where subcontractors and materialmen sued in their representative capacity on behalf of all creditors to recover for conversion by several defendants of trust funds arising out of a common transaction, it was unnecessary to separately state each claim against each defendant, inasmuch as the claims grew out of the same transaction and the decision of the common point of litigation presented would settle the rights of all the parties. United Lakeland Air Conditioning Co. v Ahneman-Christiansen, Inc. (1959) 22 Misc 2d 80, 194 NYS2d 84.

40. Life estates

Where the question is whether taxes and assessments upon the premises, during a life estate therein, are chargeable upon the rents and profits of the real estate; and when the burden of payment, if they are not, falls upon the estate in remainder, the question is one of common interest of the many heirs and one of them can sue for the benefit of all. Clarke v Clarke (1894) 8 Misc 339, 29 NYS 338.

41. Nuisance

Persons holding their respective lands in severalty, though having a common or general interest respecting the invasion of their rights by the wrongful act of the defendant which would authorize them all to join as plaintiffs, may sue alone, or one may sue for all where three or more persons or corporations have a common interest. Climax Specialty Co. v Seneca Button Co. (1907) 54 Misc 152, 103 NYS 822.

Property owners may sue in behalf of themselves and others similarly situated to enjoin dumping odorous refuse into stream. Greer v Smith (1913) 155 AD 420, 140 NYS 43.

42. Public officers

Generally, all public officers have capacity to sue commensurate with their public trusts and duties. Rowlee v Durfey (1929) 227 AD 219, 237 NYS 539.

43. —Overseer of the poor

Overseer of the poor in his official capacity may take assignment of a cause of action from a poor person, and in enforcement of a judgment may bid in real estate on sale under an execution. Rowlee v Durfey (1929) 227 AD 219, 237 NYS 539.

44. Subscribers to fund

In an action against a large number of defendants to recover proceeds of subscriptions to aid the cause of the Irish Republic, in which many thousands of subscribers were interested, representative committees were brought in and others permitted to intervene. Irish Free State v Guaranty Safe Deposit Co. (1925) 126 Misc 269, 212 NYS 421.

45. Stockholders

Where the action is for recovery on a claim belonging to a corporation because of a wrong or injury the action must be brought either in the name of the corporation or by a stockholder in behalf of himself and other injured stockholders. Brown v Deposit Nat. Bank, (1925) 125 Misc 247, 211 NYS 366, affd 234 AD 524, 256 NYS 82.

In a stockholder's action against the directors of the corporation, wherein he sues "individually and for the benefit of all others similarly situated," the term "individually" has no reference to plaintiff except as an individual stockholder. Security Trust Co. v Pritchard (1922) 201 AD 142, 194 NYS 486.

Where plaintiff, as stockholder of a corporation, was entitled to bring an action for the benefit of himself and others similarly situated against the directors because of certain transfers in fraud of the corporation, his complaint was not open to demurrer for misjoinder of parties because he mistakenly stated therein that he sued also for the benefit of creditors, none of such creditors having in fact intervened in the action. Security Trust Co. v Pritchard, supra.

Where an action was brought by a stockholder on behalf of himself and others who came in and contributed to the expenses, to set aside a sale of railroad property, another stockholder, who had knowledge of the facts and acquiesced in the litigation for ten years and until the statute of limitations had run against his right to maintain a separate action for the same relief, will not be made a party plaintiff upon his own motion, particularly where he offers no explanation of the delay. MacArdell v Olcott (1901) 62 AD 127, 70 NYS 930.

Where there were 1000 stockholders holding 50,-000 shares, residing in nearly every state in United States, 119 of them, holding 11,192 shares, were

held sufficient to protect interests of all stockholders in their action to compel lessee telegraph company to apply rental to payment of income taxes assessed against plaintiff telegraph company. Northwestern Tel. Co. v Western Union Tel. Co. (1950) 197 Misc 1075, 99 NYS2d 331.

A stockholder may maintain an action in behalf of himself and others to set aside a fraudulent transaction of the directors. Butts v Wood (1867) 38 Barb 181, affd 37 NY 317.

A stockholder, if the corporation declines to sue is made a defendant, can maintain in his own name, in behalf of all similarly situated, an action to recover of a trustee property of the corporation which he has converted to his own use. Greaves v Gouge (1877) 69 NY 154.

A class action does not lie for fraudulently inducing the purchase of securities. White v Ludwig (1961) 32 Misc 2d 120, 223 NYS2d 316.

46. Tax assessments, proceedings to review

Class suits are not maintainable in proceedings to review tax assessments. Ploss v Board of Assessors (1959) 17 Misc 2d 283, 186 NYS2d 301.

47. Taxpayers

An action may be maintained by one or more of the persons assessed in behalf of themselves and others similarly situated to restrain the collection and enforcement of assessments for a local improvement made by the assessors upon an erroneous principle whereby other properties benefited were omitted. Kennedy v Troy (1878) 14 Hun 308, revd on another point, 77 NY 493.

48. Uniform contracts

An action to have uniform players' contract in the International Baseball League declared void cannot be maintained by some of the signatories as representatives of all signatories, even though not employed by the defendants, solely because their common interest is that they all signed the same type of contract, and allegations of representative character will be directed deleted. Blake v Frick (1959) 20 Misc 2d 520, 191 NYS2d 177.

49. Water consumers

One water consumer may sue for all to restrain threatened severing of connections with customers unless they signed an agreement to pay an increased rate. Whitmore v New York Inter-Urban Water Co. (1913) 158 AD 178, 142 NYS 1098.

FORMS

Form 1—General form of title and contents of complaint in class action

Form 2—Affidavit of attorney attesting to qualifications to represent class adequately

Form 1

General Form of Title and Contents of Complaint in Class Action

[Title of court]

__1_____, __2_____, and on behalf
of themselves and all others
similarly situated,
     Plaintiffs,   Complaint
        v   Index No. __6__ [if assigned]
__3_____, Inc., a __4_____ corporation,
and __5_____ [individual defendants],
     Defendants.

Plaintiffs, for themselves and all other members of the class hereinafter described, allege:

I.

JURISDICTION

The jurisdiction of this court arises under __7_____ [specify constitutional or statutory provisions conferring jurisdiction].

II.

PARTIES

The named plaintiffs are all residents of the City of __8_____, State of New York.

III.

Defendant __9_____, Inc. is a corporation organized and existing under the laws of the State of New York, having its principal office and place of business in the City of __10_____, in the State of New York, within the territorial jurisdiction of this court, and is engaged in __11_____ [describe business of corporation]. The individual defendants, __12_____ and __13_____, are residents of the same city and state and are respectively the __14_____ and __15_____ [titles of offices or positions in defendant corporation held by individual defendants] of defendant corporation.

CLASS ACTION ALLEGATIONS
IV.

This action is brought by plaintiffs as a class action, on their own behalf and on behalf of all others similarly situated, under the provisions of section 901 of the Civil Practice Law and Rules, for __16_____ [set forth relief sought, as for example: damages, injunctive and declaratory relief, and relief incident and subordinate thereto, including costs and attorneys' fees].

V.

The class so represented by plaintiffs in this action, and of which plaintiffs are themselves members, consists of __17_____ [identify and characterize class].

VI.

The exact number of members of the class, as hereinabove identified and described, is not known, but it is estimated that there are not less than __18_____ members. The class is so numerous that joinder of individual members herein is impracticable.

VII.

There are common questions of law and fact in the action that relate to and affect the rights of each member of the class and the relief sought is common to the entire class, namely, __18_____ [set forth common questions of law and fact].

VIII.

The claims of plaintiffs, who are representatives of the class herein are typical of the claims of the class, in that the claims of all members of the class, including plaintiffs, depend on a showing of the acts and omissions of defendants giving rise to the right of plaintiffs to the relief sought herein. There is no conflict as between any individual named plaintiff and other members of the class with respect to this action, or with respect to the claims for relief herein set forth.

IX.

The named plaintiffs are the representative parties for the class, and are able to, and will, fairly and adequately protect the interests of the class. The attorneys for plaintiffs are experienced and capable in litigation in the field of __20_____ [as the case may be] and have successfully represented claimants in other litigation of this nature. Of the attorneys designated as counsel for plaintiffs, __21_____ [name] and __22_____ [name] will actively conduct and be responsible for plaintiffs' case herein.

X.

This action is properly maintained as a class action inasmuch as the questions of law and fact common to the members of the class predominate over any questions affecting only individual members, and a class action is superior to other available methods for the fair and efficient adjudication of the controversy. In support of the foregoing allegations, plaintiffs show as follows: __23_____ [state facts supporting allegations of this paragraph].

FIRST COUNT

__24_____ [Allege facts constituting first claim for relief of representative plaintiffs and class.]

[Allege in a separate count, designated "SECOND COUNT," "THIRD COUNT," and so on, facts constituting each additional claim for relief]

WHEREFORE, plaintiffs pray, for themselves and all other members of the class:

1. That the rights of the class members to __25_____ [specify] be adjudicated and declared;

2. That defendants be permanently restrained and enjoined from __26_____ [specify];

3. __27_____ [That plaintiffs be awarded attorneys' fees in accordance with Rule 909 of the Civil Practice Law and Rules.];

4. __28_____ [That plaintiff class be awarded damages incident to the equitable relief requested, in the sum of $__29__]; and

5. That plaintiffs have such other relief as to the court may seem appropriate, including costs and expenses.

Dated __30_____, 19_31_.

```
__32_____
Attorney(s) for Plaintiffs
__33_____ Address(es)
__34__ Telephone No(s).
```

Form 2

Affidavit of Attorney Attesting to Qualifications to Represent Class Adequately

[Caption]

State of New York
County of __1_____

__2_____, being duly sworn, states:

1. He is attorney for the plaintiffs above-named.

2. He is a graduate of the __3_____ [Liberal Arts or other] College of the

University of __4____, having received a __5_____ Degree from such college in 19_6_ and is also a graduate of the Law School of the University of __7_____, having received a __8_____ degree from that institution in 19_9_.

3. He is admitted to practice in the courts of the States of New York and __10_____, in the United States District Courts for the Districts of New York and __11_____, and _ 12_____ [name other courts in which affiant admitted to practice, such as United States courts of appeal, and the U.S. Supreme Court].

4. He is a member of the law firm of __13_____, with offices in the City of __14_____, State of New York, and has been engaged primarily in trial practice for a period of approximately __15_ years, having in that time tried approximately __16_ [number] civil actions of various types and degrees of complexity in the various trial courts in which he is admitted to practice as above stated.

5. Since approximately __17_____, 19_18_ affiant has confined his trial practice to __19_____ [antitrust litigation or as the case may be] and, in that period, he has tried approximately __20_ such cases as chief trial attorney for his law firm, and has assisted actively in the trial of approximately __21_ additional cases in the same field.

6. Approximately __22_____ percent of the cases referred to in the preceding paragraph were class actions involving classes ranging in size from approximately __23_ members to approximately __24_ members. The total recovery in the class actions handled by affiant as chief counsel for plaintiffs amounted to $_25_, all of which resulted from settlements reached in such cases. No settlement was obtained in only __26_ cases, which were dismissed at early stages in the litigation. __27_ [Small number] cases were tried and resulted in verdicts of __28_____ and __29_____, respectively. At the present time affiant is engaged in approximately __30_ class actions which are pending in the New York courts in __31_____ and __32_____.

7. Of all the class actions referred to in the preceding paragraphs approximately __33_____ percent were brought in federal district courts and approximately __34_____ percent in state courts.

8. __35_____ [Add further particulars as appropriate].

[Signature]

Subscribed and sworn to before me on this __36_ day of __37_ ____, 19_38_.

[Signature and title]

§ 902. Order allowing class action

Within sixty days after the time to serve a responsive pleading has expired for all persons named as defendants in an action brought as a class action, the plaintiff shall move for an order to determine whether it is to be so maintained. An order under this section may be conditional, and may be altered or amended before the decision on the merits on the court's own motion or on motion of the parties. The action may be maintained as a class action only if the court finds that the prerequisites under section 901 have been satisfied. Among the matters which the court shall consider in determining whether the action may proceed as a class action are:

1. the interest of members of the class in individually controlling the prosecution or defense of separate actions;

2. the impracticability or inefficiency of prosecuting or defending separate actions;

3. the extent and nature of any litigation concerning the controversy already commenced by or against members of the class;

4. the desirability or undesirability of concentrating the litigation of the claim in the particular forum;

5. the difficulties likely to be encountered in the management of a class action.

HISTORY:

Add, L 1975, ch 207, amd, L 1975, ch 474, eff Sept 1, 1975.

FEDERAL ASPECTS:

Pleadings and motions, generally, Rules 7 through 16 of Federal Rules of Civil Procedure, USCS Court Rules.

Determination by order whether class actions to be maintained, Rule 23(c) of Federal Rules of Civil Procedure, USCS Court Rules.

Motion day in Federal District Courts, Rule 78 of Federal Rules of Civil Procedure, USCS Court Rules.

RESEARCH REFERENCES AND PRACTICE AIDS:

24 NY Jur, Fraudulent Conveyances § 144.

57 NY Jur, Suretyship and Guaranty § 264.

3 Carmody-Wait 2d, Parties § 19:167.2.

59 Am Jur 2d, Parties § 80.

Annotations:

Propriety of class action in state courts to assert tenants' rights against landlord. 73 ALR3d 852.

Propriety of state court class action by holders of bonds against indenture trustee. 73 ALR3d 880.

Law Reviews:

Interlocutory appeal from orders striking class action allegations. 70 Colum L Rev 1292.

Forms:

See "FORMS" heading following "CASE NOTES", infra.

CASE NOTES

In action for declaratory and injunctive relief on claim of invalidity of statute imposing additional eligibility requirements for home relief benefits on certain needy children, certification of class was unnecessary, since, not only were governmental operations involved, but court was satisfied that it could adequately protect interests of alleged class by issuing a final order which, by its terms, would run to benefit of each person affected by statute involved. Tucker v Toia (1977) 89 Misc 2d 116, 390 NYS2d 794.

Although motion for order permitting action to be maintained as class action was made more than 60 days after time to serve responsive pleading had expired, motion was not untimely where procedural statute governing class action motions did not become effective until after action was commenced. Long Island College Hospital v Whalen (1975) 84 Misc 2d 637, 377 NYS2d 890.

Action challenging decision of commissioner of department of health that hospitals may no longer be reimbursed by Medicaid or Blue Cross for litigation expenses they incur in course of their operations could be maintained as class action on behalf of 382 nonprofit hospitals located in New York State, each of which received reimbursement from the state and Blue Cross. Long Island College Hospital v Whalen (1975) 84 Misc 2d 637, 377 NYS2d 890.

Where class action statute became effective subsequent to commencement of proceedings and where persons who sought to challenge denial of AFDC benefits did not make class action motion within 60 days, as required by statute, class action certification was not required. Shook v Lavine (1975) 49 AD2d 238, 374 NYS2d 187.

Trial court erred in entertaining proceeding for order directing county commissioner of social services to pay heat allowances for 1975–1976 season to public assistance recipients who resided in federally aided public housing as a class action, where statutory requirements for class action had not been complied with and where interests of persons allegedly similarly situated would be protected without a class action. Turner v Reed (1976) 52 AD2d 739, 382 NYS2d 391.

Class actions in cases where governmental operations are involved are not necessary, since comparable relief would adequately flow to others similarly situated under principles of stare decisis. Beekman-Downtown Hospital v Whelan (1976) 88 Misc 2d 324, 387 NYS2d 758, revd on other grounds 57 AD2d 1, 392 NYS2d 878.

Plaintiffs in class action acted properly in moving within 60 days after time to serve responsive pleading had expired for order of discovery to obtain facts necessary to satisfy prerequisites of class action, and for order, pending discovery, staying determination of whether class action status was appropriate, and trial court should have ruled on such motion before dismissing petition on its finding that class action was prohibited. Knapp v Michaux (1977) 55 AD2d 1025, 391 NYS2d 496.

FORMS

Form 1—Motion for order determining that action proceed as a class action

Form 2—Motion to compel answers to interrogatories relating to size of class

Form 3—Objection to maintenance of action as class action

Form 4—Motion for order determining that action shall not be maintained as class action

Form 5—Notice of hearing on motions to certify or dismiss action as class action

Form 6—Order allowing class action

Form 1

Motion for Order Determining That Action Proceed as a Class Action

[Caption]

Plaintiffs above-named, pursuant to section 902 of the Civil Practice Law and Rules, hereby move the court for an order determining that this action shall be maintained as a class action for the benefit of the class consisting of __1_____ [describe class generally].

This motion is made on the following grounds:

1. This action was brought and is now maintained by the named plaintiffs, the moving parties, as a class action on behalf of themselves and all other persons similarly situated, comprising the class hereinabove and in the complaint described.

2. Plaintiffs are informed and believe and so declare that there are approximately __2__ members of the class herein described, so that joinder of all members of the class in this action is impracticable.

3. Claims of the named plaintiffs are typical of the claims of all members of the class herein described.

4. Named plaintiffs will fairly and adequately represent and protect the interests of all members of such class.

5. There are common questions of law and fact affecting rights of each member of the class, as against the defendants named herein, as more fully set forth in plaintiffs' complaint.

6. The common questions of law and fact predominate over any questions affecting individual members only, and a class action is superior to other available methods for the fair and efficient adjudication of the controversies between the class herein described and the named defendants. __3_____ [Add if appropriate: Memorandum of plaintiffs in support of this motion is attached hereto].

Dated __4_____, 19_5_.

__6_____

Attorney for Plaintiffs
__7_____ Address
__8__ Telephone No.

Form 2

Motion to Compel Answers to Interrogatories Relating to Size of Class

[Caption]

Plaintiffs, by __1_____, their attorney, move this court for an order compelling defendants to answer certain interrogatories heretofore served upon them by plaintiffs, and show as follows:

1. On or about __2_____, 19_3_, plaintiffs served their first set of interrogatories on defendants. Although more than __4__ days have elapsed since that date, defendants have failed to answer or to object to certain of the interrogatories, hereinafter enumerated, and have failed to respond to a written communication from plaintiffs' counsel demanding an answer to the such interrogatories.

2. The interrogatories in question are Interrogatory Nos. __5__, __6__, and __7__, the purpose of which was to ascertain the number of members of the class defined in plaintiffs' complaint, so as to enable this court to determine whether joinder of all such members as parties to this action is impracticable, and Interrogatory Nos. __8__, __9__, and __10__, the purpose of which was to establish that there are common questions of law and fact affecting all members of the class, so as to demonstrate that the requirements of section 901(2) of the Civil Practice Law and Rules are satisfied.

This motion is based on the affidavit of the undersigned attached hereto, and is further supported by the memorandum of law filed and served by plaintiffs herewith.

Dated __11_____, 19_12_.

__13_____

Attorney for Plaintiff

__14_____ Address

__15__ Telephone No.

[Affidavit of plaintiffs' attorney attached]

Form 3

Objection to Maintenance of Action as Class Action

[Caption]

Defendants __1_____, __2_____, and __3_____ oppose plaintiffs' motion for an order determining that this action shall be maintained as a class action, on the following grounds:

I

The named plaintiffs cannot fairly and adequately represent the interests of the alleged class since they have interests adverse to other members of the alleged class, and some of the plaintiffs are not in fact members of the class described in plaintiffs' complaint and in their present motion and allege no injury to themselves. The foregoing allegations are supported by the affidavit of __4_____ attached hereto, to which reference is hereby made.

II

The individuals comprising the alleged class are not so numerous as to make it impractical to bring them all before the court as named parties. As shown by the affidavit of __5_____, referred to in the preceding paragraph hereof, the number of such persons does not exceed __6_____.

III

Some of the members of the alleged class are named as individual plaintiffs against these defendants in an action commenced on or about __7_____, 19_8_ in the __9_____ Court for the County of __10_____, State of New York, being File No. __11__ of that court, and the issues of fact and law alleged therein are substantially the same as those alleged in the present action. A copy of the complaint in such court action is attached hereto as Exhibit __12__.

IV

__13_____ [Set forth additional grounds and supporting papers, as appropriate].

Dated __14_____, 19_15_.

__16_____
Attorney for Defendants
__17_____ Address
__18__ Telephone No.

[Attach affidavit and exhibit(s)]

Form 4

Motion for Order Determining That Action Shall Not Be Maintained as Class Action

[Caption]

__1_____ [Name], one of the defendants named herein as representatives of the class of defendants described in plaintiff's complaint, by __2_____, his attorney, moves this court for an order determining that this action shall not be maintained as a class action, and as grounds for said motion alleges:

[Set forth grounds separately, such as one or more of the following:]

1. The class of defendants described in plaintiff's complaint is not so numerous that the joinder of all members is impracticable.

2. The defenses of the representative defendants named in plaintiff's complaint are not typical of the defenses of the class.

3. The moving defendant and the other representative defendants named cannot, under the facts and circumstances of the case, fairly and adequately protect the interests of the members of the class not named as individual parties.

Argument and authorities in support of this motion are set forth and cited in the memorandum served and filed herewith.

Oral argument is requested on this motion.

Dated __3_____, 19_4_.

__5_____
Attorney for Defendants
__6_____ Address
__7__ Telephone No.

Form 5

Notice of Hearing on Motions to Certify or Dismiss Action as Class Action

[Caption]

To: All persons who are, or who claim to be, members of __1_____ [describe class], represented by the named __2_____ [plaintiffs or defendants] in this action:

I

Pursuant to the order of this court, dated __3_____, 19_4_, notice is hereby given of a hearing to be held on __5_____, 19_6_, before the Honorable __7_____ in his Courtroom in Room __8__ of the __9_____ Court House, __10_____ [address], beginning at __11__ o'clock __12__.m. on that day, for the presentation of oral argument on the motion of plaintiffs for certification of this action as a class action and on the motion of defendants to dismiss so much of the complaint herein as alleges __13_____ [claims on behalf of the class of persons, other than plaintiffs, described in plaintiffs' complaint herein or claims against defendants as representatives of the class described in plaintiffs' complaint as the case may be].

II

Plaintiffs above named all reside in the City of __14_____, State of New York, and are represented in this action by __15_____ [name of attorney], whose address is __16_____. The defendants, on all of whom personal service has been effected and who are now parties to this action, are __17_____ [names]. Such defendants are represented by the following attorneys: __18_____ [list names and addresses of attorneys for respective defendants]. No other persons have intervened or been joined as parties to this action.

III

This action was commenced on or about __19_____, 19_20_ by the plaintiffs above named __21_____ [on behalf of themselves and "all persons similarly situated" who __22_____ (describe class) or against the defendants above named, individually, and as representatives of __23_____ (describe class)]. The claims set forth in plaintiffs' complaint are substantially as follows: __24_____ [summarize claims]. The defendants' answers deny any wrongdoing on their part as alleged in the complaint.

IV

__25_____ [Defendants have objected to plaintiffs' motion for certification of this action as a class action on the following grounds: __26_____ (Summarize grounds, such as a claim that representative plaintiffs or defendants, as the case may be, are unable to provide fair and adequate representation of the class, that class is too small to satisfy requirement of impracticability of joinder, that methods of litigation other than class action provide means for efficient and fair adjudication of controversy comparable to a class action, and the like) or The grounds of defendants' motion to dismiss the class action allegations of the complaint are as follows: __27_____ (Summarize grounds as previously indicated)].

V

This notice is given for the purpose of affording an opportunity to all interested parties, and any persons who might qualify as members of the class hereinabove referred to, to appear and present arguments relative to the pending motions, to seek, if they deem it necessary, substitution of other persons in the place of the __28_____ [plaintiffs or defendants] above named as representatives of the class, to propose additional persons to act as such representatives, and to support or oppose either of the pending motions. Any person desiring to appear for any such purpose may file an appearance with the clerk of this court on or before __29_____, 19_30_, with proof of service on __31_____ [names and addresses of attorneys for plaintiffs and defendants]. Such appearance shall state the capacity in which, and purposes for which, the person appears, and the relief which he seeks.

Reference is hereby made to the pleadings, motion papers, affidavits, briefs, memoranda and other documents filed in this action for a more detailed statement of the same. All of such papers and documents may be inspected in the office of the clerk of this court at __32_____ [address] during regular business hours.

Dated __33_____, 19_34_.

[Signature and title]

Form 6

Order Allowing Class Action

[Caption]

This matter having come on to be heard on the motions of plaintiffs and certain intervening defendants for an order pursuant to section 902 of the Civil Practice Law and Rules and on the answers of the respective parties filed herein; and the court having considered the motions, argument and briefs of the parties, hereby finds:

1. The class represented by plaintiff in this action consists of all persons __¹_____ [identify class];

2. The members of the class represented by plaintiff are so numerous that joinder of all members is impractical;

. 3. There are questions of law and fact common to the class represented by plaintiffs;

4. The claims of plaintiffs are typical of the claims of the class they represent;

5. The plaintiffs will fairly and adequately protect the interests of the class represented by them;

6. The questions of law and fact common to the members of the class represented by plaintiff predominate over any questions affecting only individual members, and a class action is superior to other available methods for the fair and effective adjudication of the controversy herein; therefore,

It is ordered, adjudged and decreed:

The claim for relief set forth in the complaint is properly pursued as a class action as above-defined and shall be so continued and maintained as a class action.

Dated __²_____, 19_³_.

[Signature]

§ 903. Description of class

The order permitting a class action shall describe the class. When appropriate the court may limit the class to those members who do not request exclusion from the class within a specified time after notice.

HISTORY:
>Add, L 1975, ch 207, eff Sept 1, 1975.

FEDERAL ASPECTS:
>Determination by order whether class actions to be maintained, Rule 23(c) of Federal Rules of Civil Procedure, USCS Court Rules.

RESEARCH REFERENCES AND PRACTICE AIDS:
>24 NY Jur, Fraudulent Conveyances § 144.
>57 NY Jur, Suretyship and Guaranty § 264.
>3 Carmody-Wait 2d, Parties §§ 19:167.2, 19:179, 19:182.

>**Annotations:**
>>Propriety of class action in state courts to assert tenants' rights against landlord. 73 ALR3d 852.
>>Propriety of state court class action by holders of bonds against indenture trustee. 73 ALR3d 880.

§ 904. Notice of class action

(a) In class actions brought primarily for injunctive or declaratory relief, notice of the pendency of the action need not be given to the class unless the court finds that notice is necessary to protect the interests of the represented parties and that the cost of notice will not prevent the action from going forward.

(b) In all other class actions, reasonable notice of the commencement of a class action shall be given to the class in such manner as the court directs.

(c) The content of the notice shall be subject to court approval. In determining the method by which notice is to be given, the court shall consider

I. the cost of giving notice by each method considered

II. the resources of the parties and

III. the stake of each represented member of the class, and the likelihood that significant numbers of represented members would desire to exclude themselves from the class or to appear individually, which may be determined, in the court's discretion, by sending notice to a random sample of the class.

(d) I. Preliminary determination of expenses of notification. Unless the court orders otherwise, the plaintiff shall bear the expense of notification. The court may, if justice requires, require that the defendant bear the expense of notification, or may require each of them to bear a part of the expense in proportion to the likelihood that each will prevail upon the merits. The court may hold a preliminary hearing to determine how the costs of notice should be apportioned.

II. Final determination. Upon termination of the action by order or judgment, the court may, but shall not be required to, allow to the prevailing party the expenses of notification as taxable disbursements under article eighty-three of the civil practice law and rules.

HISTORY:

Add, L 1975, ch 207, eff Sept 1, 1975.

FEDERAL ASPECTS:

Notice of class actions, Rule 23(c) of Federal Rules of Civil Procedure, USCS Court Rules.

RESEARCH REFERENCES AND PRACTICE AIDS:

24 NY Jur, Fraudulent Conveyances § 144.
57 NY Jur, Suretyship and Guaranty § 264.
3 Carmody-Wait 2d, Parties §§ 19:167.3, 19:179, 19:182.
59 Am Jur 2d, Parties § 81.
19 Am Jur Pl & Pr Forms (Rev ed), Parties, Form 39.

Annotations:

Maintenance of class action against government entity as affected by requirement of notice of claim. 76 ALR3d 1244.

FORMS

Form 1—Provision in order directing notice to be given to members of class
Form 2—Affidavit that individual notice to class members is not practicable
Form 3—Notice of class action

Form 1

Provision in Order Directing Notice to be Given to Members of Class

IT IS FURTHER ORDERED that notice of this determination shall be given in the form of notice attached hereto by mailing a copy of such form of notice to each member of the class whose name and address can be determined by reference to the books and records of defendant __[1]_____, and by publication of the notice once each week for __²____ consecutive weeks in a daily or weekly newspaper of __³____ [statewide or national] circulation.

IT IS ALSO ORDERED that upon completion of service of notice as aforesaid, plaintiffs shall file affidavits attesting to compliance with the terms of this order.

[Attach form of notice]

Form 2

Affidavit That Individual Notice to Class Members is not Practicable

[Caption]

State of New York
County of __¹____

__²____ being duly sworn, deposes and says:

1. He is one of the attorneys for the representative plaintiffs in this action and makes this affidavit in support of plaintiffs' motion for determination that this action be maintained as a class action, served and filed on __³____, 19_⁴_.

2. This action is brought pursuant to section 901 of the Civil Practice Law and Rules and under the provisions of section 904 of said Rules, plaintiffs must give class members reasonable notice.

3. Such notice in this action should not include individual notice to all members, or to any members, of the class, for the reason that, although the class is identifiable and certain, the individual members thereof cannot be identified through reasonable effort. In this connection, affiant states that he has personally examined the books and records of defendant __⁵____ and all other available sources of information concerning the identity of individual class members and has concluded and verily believes that the identity of individual members cannot be determined by reasonable means, but on the contrary such identification would require an extensive, protracted, and highly expensive investigation.

4. Accordingly, affiant respectfully suggests to the court that the best notice practicable under the circumstances would be publication of a notice in __⁶____, a daily newspaper published and circulated __⁷____ [throughout the County of __⁸____ or as the case may be] for such period and for such number of insertions as the court may deem necessary.

[Signature of affiant]

Subscribed and sworn to before me this __⁹____ day of __¹⁰____ 19_¹¹_.

[Signature and title]

Form 3

Notice of Class Action

[Caption]

NOTICE OF PENDENCY OF CLASS ACTION
AND OF RIGHTS OF CLASS MEMBERS

To: __¹____ [describe members of class generally, for example:
All proprietors of retail hardware stores and other establishments handling products of defendant corporation, doing business in the Counties of __²____ and __³____, State of New York, from __⁴____, 19_⁵_ to __⁶____, 19_⁷_].

Notice is hereby given to you that the plaintiffs above named have filed a suit in the above entitled court in behalf of themselves and all members of the class herein addressed.

By order dated __⁸____, 19_⁹_, the court in this action determined that the action should be maintained as a class action under the provisions of Sections 901(a)(1) and

901(a)(5) of the Civil Practice Law and Rules and directed the giving of this notice to class members.

Notice is further given as follows:

1. The plaintiffs' complaint alleges conduct on the part of the above named defendants which they contend caused damage to the class, for which recovery is sought herein, in that __10_____ [summarize allegations of complaint]. Defendants have denied any wrongdoing, and have denied any liability to plaintiffs or any member of the class. This notice is not to be construed as an expression of any opinion by the court with respect to the merits of the respect claims or defenses of the parties. This notice and the attached "Exclusion Request" are sent merely to advise you of the pendency of the action and the rights which you have with respect to it.

2. The court will exclude any member of the class to whom this notice is addressed on written request for such exclusion on the attached form, postmarked on or before __11_____, 19_12_. Persons who request such exclusion will not be entitled to share in the benefits of the judgment if it is favorable to plaintiff, and will not be bound by the judgment if it is adverse to the plaintiffs. All requests for exclusion should be mailed by first class mail or delivered to the Clerk of the __13_____ Court for __14_____, at __15_____ [address]. A form and envelope for this purpose are enclosed with each of these notices given to individual class members, and may also be secured from the clerk. All class members who fail to return the exclusion form above referred to in the manner and within the time specified above will automatically be included in this action as members of the class represented by plaintiffs.

3. All members of the class who do not request exclusion as prescribed in the preceding paragraph, and who are therefore deemed to have elected to participate in this action, will be entitled to share pro rata in the benefits of any judgment favorable to the class or in any settlement of their claims, after deduction of attorney fees and disbursements, but they will also be bound by any judgment unfavorable to the class. Included class members will also be subject to the orders and notices hereafter given in this action with reference to the furnishing of statements and other matters of that nature.

4. If any class member does not desire to be excluded but does wish to appear in his own behalf, such class member may enter an appearance through counsel of his own choosing. All members who do not request exclusion or who do not enter an appearance through counsel of their own choosing will be represented by plaintiffs through their counsel hereinafter named.

5. Counsel for the plaintiffs and for the members of the class included in this action are __16_____ [names of attorneys] whose addresses are __17_____, and whose telephone numbers are __18_____. All communications and questions concerning this notice should be sent to the such attorneys, and should not be addressed to the clerk of this court.

6. If the address of any class member changes or is different than the address stated on the envelope enclosing this notice, advice concerning such change or a correction should be sent by mail to the attorneys above named.

7. This court has retained jurisdiction in this action to correct, modify, annul, vacate, or supplement its order determining that this cause shall be maintained as a class action, at any time before the __19_____ [trial of this action or the decision on the merits herein as the case may be].

8. The pleadings and other papers filed in this action are available for inspection in the office of the clerk of this court.

Dated __20_____, 19_21_.

[Signature and title]

§ 905. Judgment

The judgment in an action maintained as a class action, whether or not favorable to the class, shall include and describe those whom the court finds to be members of the class.

HISTORY:

Add, L 1975, ch 207, eff Sept 1, 1975.

FEDERAL ASPECTS:

Judgment in class actions, Rule 23(c) of Federal Rules of Civil Procedure, USCS Court Rules.

RESEARCH REFERENCES AND PRACTICE AIDS:

24 NY Jur, Fraudulent Conveyances § 144.
57 NY Jur, Suretyship and Guaranty § 264.
3 Carmody-Wait 2d, Parties §§ 19:167.3, 19:179, 19:182.
59 Am Jur 2d, Parties § 90.

Law Reviews:

Settlement of class actions for damages. 71 Colum L Rev 971.
Appealability of class action determinations. 44 Fordham L Rev 548.

§ 906. Actions conducted partially as class actions

When appropriate,

1. an action may be brought or maintained as a class action with respect to particular issues, or

2. a class may be divided into subclasses and each subclass treated as a class.

The provisions of this article shall then be construed and applied accordingly.

HISTORY:

Add, L 1975, ch 207, eff Sept 1, 1975.

FEDERAL ASPECTS:

Actions conducted partially as class actions in United States District Courts, Rule 23(c) of Federal Rules of Civil Procedure, USCS Court Rules.

RESEARCH REFERENCES AND PRACTICE AIDS:

24 NY Jur, Fraudulent Conveyances § 144.
57 NY Jur, Suretyship and Guaranty § 264.
3 Carmody-Wait 2d, Parties §§ 19:167.4, 19:179, 19:182.

Annotations:

Propriety of class action in state courts to assert tenants' rights against landlord. 73 ALR3d 852.
Propriety of state court class action by holders of bonds against indenture trustee. 73 ALR3d 880.

FORMS

Provision in Order Limiting Class Action to Litigation of Particular Issues

This action shall be maintained as a class action only with respect to the following issues: __1_____ [list issues as, for example: (1) The determination, as nearly may be, of the identity of the members of the class, and (2) the liability of the defendants __2_____ (names) to the members of the class]. The remaining issues including

___3____ [list remaining issues, such as: the issues as to (1) the special defenses asserted by defendants to the claims of individual class members and (2) the amounts of individual claims of class members] shall be determined in subsequent proceedings in this action or in separate actions as the court may hereafter direct.

Rule 907. Orders in conduct of class actions

In the conduct of class actions the court may make appropriate orders:

1. determining the course of proceedings or prescribing measures to prevent undue repetition or complication in the presentation of evidence or argument;

2. requiring, for the protection of the members of the class, or otherwise for the fair conduct of the action, that notice be given in such manner as the court may direct to some or all of the members of any step in the action, or of the proposed extent of the judgment, or of the opportunity of members to signify whether they consider the representation fair and adequate, or to appear and present claims or defenses, or otherwise to come into the action;

3. imposing conditions on the representative parties or on intervenors;

4. requiring that the pleadings be amended to eliminate therefrom allegations as to representation of absent persons, and that the action proceed accordingly;

5. directing that a money judgment favorable to the class be paid either in one sum, whether forthwith or within such period as the court may fix, or in such installments as the court may specify;

6. dealing with similar procedural matters.

The orders may be altered or amended as may be desirable from time to time.

HISTORY:

    Add, L 1975, ch 207, eff Sept 1, 1975.

FEDERAL ASPECTS:

    Orders in conduct of class actions in United States District Courts, Rule 23(d) of
        Federal Rules of Civil Procedure, USCS Court Rules.

RESEARCH REFERENCES AND PRACTICE AIDS:

    24 NY Jur, Fraudulent Conveyances § 144.
    57 NY Jur, Suretyship and Guaranty § 264.
    3 Carmody-Wait 2d, Parties §§ 19:167.4, 19:179, 19:182.
    59 Am Jur 2d, Parties § 88.

Law Reviews:

    Interlocutory appeal from orders striking class action allegations. 70 Colum L
        Rev 1292.

Rule 908. Dismissal, discontinuance or compromise

A class action shall not be dismissed, discontinued, or compromised without the approval of the court. Notice of the proposed dismissal, discontinuance, or compromise shall be given to all members of the class in such manner as the court directs.

HISTORY:
Add, L 1975, ch 207, eff Sept 1, 1975.

FEDERAL ASPECTS:
Dismissal or compromise of class actions in United States District Courts, Rule 23(e) of Federal Rules of Civil Procedure, USCS Court Rules.

RESEARCH REFERENCES AND PRACTICE AIDS:
24 NY Jur, Fraudulent Conveyances § 144.
57 NY Jur, Suretyship and Guaranty § 264.
3 Carmody-Wait 2d, Parties § 19:167.4.

Annotations:
Right of class member, in class action under Rule 23 of the Federal Rules of Civil Procedure, to appeal from order approving settlement with class. 30 ALR Fed 846.

Law Reviews:
Settlement of class actions for damages. 71 Colum L Rev 971.

FORMS

Form 1—Motion by representative plaintiffs to dismiss class action
Form 2—Motion by defendants to decertify and dismiss class action
Form 3—Motion to dismiss action as class action, or to strike class action allegations, or for summary judgment
Form 4—Allegation in motion to dismiss class action that members of class are so numerous and widespread that plaintiffs cannot fairly and adequately represent the class
Form 5—Notice to class members of hearing on motion to dismiss action as class action
Form 6—Order for hearing on proposed settlement and prescribing notice to class members
Form 7—Notice of hearing on proposed settlement
Form 8—Class members' objections to settlement
Form 9—Stipulation for settlement of class action

Form 1

Motion by Representative Plaintiffs to Dismiss Class Action

[Caption]

Plaintiffs __1_____ [names] by __2_____, their attorney, move the court to dismiss this action as a class action, and in support of their motion respectfully show:

1. The court __2.5_____ [certified this action as a class action by order dated __3_____, 19_4_ or has not yet acted upon plaintiffs' motion to certify this action as a class action].

2. The grounds and reasons believed by plaintiffs to exist for the maintenance of this action as a class action __5_____ [add, if appropriate and for the certification of the action as a class action by the court] have now been determined by plaintiffs to be unwarranted and insubstantial, as more fully set forth in plaintiffs' memorandum served and filed herewith.

3. Plaintiffs believe that proper and adequate notice of the proposed dismissal of this action as a class action can be given to the class members by __6_____ [specify method of giving notice]. Plaintiffs are willing and will undertake to pay the costs of such notice, as directed by the court.

Dated __7_____, 19_8_.

__9_____
Attorney for plaintiffs
__10_____ Address
__11__ Telephone No.

[Memorandum attached]

<h1 style="text-align:center">Form 2</h1>

Motion by Defendants to Decertify and Dismiss Class Action

[Caption]

Defendants above named, by __1_____, their attorney, move the court to decertify and dismiss this action as a class action, and as grounds therefor allege as follows:

1. On __2_____, 19_3_, this court entered an order determining that this action be maintained as a class action, conditional, however, on discovery proceedings having been held to determine whether the class, and the interests of its individual members, were such that the action could reasonably be managed and administered by the court as a class action.

2. Discovery proceedings were thereafter had on the part of both the plaintiffs and the defendants herein, from which it appears that the members of the class number in excess of __4_____, and that the interests of the individual members are so diverse and varied that the action cannot properly be maintained as a class action either on behalf of the class designated in the complaint and by this court's order, or on behalf of subclasses carved out of such class.

3. This motion is based on the affidavit of __5_____, the undersigned attorney for defendants, as to the number of persons in the designated class, based on defendant corporation's books and records which the undersigned has personally examined, as indicated in his affidavit, and on the depositions of __6_____ and __7_____, two of the representative plaintiffs herein, of __8_____ and __9_____, two other members of the designated class, and of __10_____, the __11_____ [title of office] of defendant corporation, heretofore filed in this cause. The pertinent portions of such depositions, which substantiate the allegations made herein, are set forth in defendants' memorandum filed and served herewith.

4. If the court deems it necessary to give notice of the instant motion to members of the designated class other than the representative parties, defendants will give and pay for such notice as the court may direct. However, defendant believes that such notice, if ordered, should be in the form of publication in a newspaper of general circulation, and not individual notice to the class members.

Dated: __12_____, 19_13_.

__14_____
Attorney for Defendants
__15_____ Address
__16__ Telephone No.

[Affidavit and memorandum attached]

<h1 style="text-align:center">Form 3</h1>

Motion to Dismiss Action as Class Action, or to Strike Class Action Allegations, or for Summary Judgment

[Caption]

Defendants __1_____ and __2_____, by __3_____, their attorney, move the court to dismiss this action to the extent that it purports to allege a claim for relief as a class action, or to strike the allegations of the complaint relative to such action, or for summary judgment in their favor with respect thereto, on the following grounds:

__4_____ [Set forth grounds separately].

A brief in support of this motion is filed herewith.

Dated __5_____, 19_6_.

__7_____

Attorney for Defendants

__8____ Address

__9__ Telephone No.

Form 4

Allegation in Motion to Dismiss Class Action That Members of Class are so Numerous and Widespread That Plaintiffs Cannot Fairly and Adequately Represent the Class

[Caption]

The representative plaintiffs will not fairly and adequately represent the class defined in their complaint for the following reasons:

1. The interests of the individual members of the class are so diverse and the geographical areas in which such members are located are so numerous and widespread, as shown by the affidavit of __1_____ attached hereto, that the plaintiffs cannot under any reasonable hypothesis fairly or adequately represent the class.

2. As further appears from the affidavit of __2_____, referred to in the preceding paragraph, the named plaintiffs do not have the requisite resources to prosecute this litigation, which undoubtedly will be protracted and costly.

3. Moreover, plaintiffs __3_____, __4_____, and __5_____, who are __6__ [number] of the __7__ [number] representative plaintiffs named in plaintiffs' complaint, lack both the interest and knowledge requisite to a fair and adequate representation of the class and the vigorous pursuit of its interests, as is evident from the testimony of such plaintiffs in their depositions on file with this court.

As alleged in paragraph __8__ of plaintiffs' complaint, the members of the class defined therein exceed __9__ in number. The size, as well as the geographical spread, of the class renders this class action inherently and inevitably unmanageable.

Form 5

Notice to Class Members of Hearing on Motion to Dismiss Action as Class Action

[Caption]

NOTICE OF MOTION TO DISMISS ACTION AS CLASS ACTION

To: All members of the class in the above-entitled action, namely, __1_____ [define class as stated in court's order certifying action as class action].

Notice is hereby given that __2_____ [plaintiffs or defendants] above-named have filed a motion to dismiss this action as a class action, and that the same will be heard by the undersigned judge, in his courtroom in __3_____ [address], on __4_____, 19_5_, at __6__ o'clock __7__.m.

Any member of the class may appear and be heard in support of or opposition to the motion at the time and place fixed, either personally or by counsel.

Any class member desiring to be heard on the motion is requested to file a notice of his intended appearance, together with a short written statement of his position and reasons in support thereof, with the Clerk of the Court, not later than __8_____ days before the hearing date.

Dated __9_____, 19_10_.

[Signature and title]

Form 6

Order for Hearing on Proposed Settlement and Prescribing Notice to Class Members

[Caption]

The representative plaintiffs and the defendants having entered into a settlement of this action, subject to the approval of the court, as set forth in the __1_____ [Stipulation for Settlement and/or Settlement Agreement] dated __2_____, 19_3_, heretofore filed in this cause, and the court having duly considered the proposed settlement and the arguments and documentation presented in support thereof by both sides, and it appearing to the court that the proposed settlement merits consideration as to its fairness and reasonableness and that a hearing should be held thereon to determine whether the settlement should be approved by the court, and that notice of the hearing should be given to the members of the plaintiff class.

IT IS ORDERED AS FOLLOWS:

1. A hearing shall be held before the undersigned judge, in Room __4__, Court House, __5_____ [address], on __6_____, 19_7_, at __8__ o'clock __9__.m., for the purpose of determining whether the proposed settlement of this action is fair and reasonable and should be approved by the court, and whether a final judgment should be entered in accordance with the terms and provisions of the settlement; and to consider the application for fees and reimbursement of expenses of counsel for plaintiffs, and to fix the amount of any fees and expenses to be awarded to such counsel.

2. Notice of the hearing shall be given to the members of the plaintiffs' class by __10_____ [mailing a copy of the annexed Notice of hearing to all __11_____ [designate class] on or before __12_____, 19_13_, such notice to be given by and at the expense of __14_____.

3. Proof of the giving of such notice as hereinabove directed shall be filed in this court prior to the date of hearing.

4. All briefs, memoranda, and other papers in support of the proposed settlement, and the application for counsel fees and reimbursement of costs shall be served and filed not later than __15_____, 19_16_, and all reply papers and briefs shall be served and filed no later than __17_____, 19_18_.

5. Any member of the class who objects to the proposed settlement, or the final judgment to be entered thereon, or to the award of counsel fees and expenses, may appear and present such objections at the hearing, provided that a member so objecting serves upon __19_____ [name and address of principal attorneys for plaintiff] and __20_____ [name and address of principal attorneys for defendants], and files with this court, (a) a written statement containing the name and address of the member so objecting and the nature extent of his claims together with notice of his intention to appear, and (b) copies of any brief and papers he intends to submit in support of his objections. No person shall be heard, and no briefs or papers shall be received or considered, unless the foregoing documents have been served and filed as hereinabove provided, except as this court in its discretion may otherwise direct.

Dated __21_____, 19_22_.

[Signature and title]

Form 7

Notice of Hearing on Proposed Settlement

[Caption]

NOTICE OF HEARING ON PROPOSED SETTLEMENT

To: __1_____ [designate class members]:

You are hereby notified, pursuant to Rule 908 of the Civil Practice Law and Rules, that a hearing will be held on __2____, 19_3_, at __4__ o'clock __5__.m., before the Honorable __6____, Judge __7____, in Courtroom No. __8__ of the Court House, __9____ [address].

The hearing was scheduled by order of the court dated __10____, 19_11_. The purpose of the hearing is to determine whether a settlement agreed to by the above-named parties is fair, reasonable, and adequate, and should be approved by the court and judgment entered thereon. At the hearing the court will also either consider the applications of attorneys for plaintiffs for allowance of fees and expenses, or direct that such application be considered at a latter date without further notice. The hearing may be adjourned by the court from time to time by an announcement at the hearing, or at any adjournment thereof, without further notice.

You may be a member of the class designated above. If so, your rights may be affected by the settlement of this action. The giving of this notice is not to be understood as expressing any opinion by this court as to the merits of any of the claims or defenses asserted by any party herein, and is for the sole purpose of informing all the class members as hereinafter defined, of the proposed settlement, so that individual class members may make whatever decisions they may deem appropriate for the protection of their interests.

HISTORY OF THE LITIGATION

A. This litigation was begun on __12____, 19_13_, by the filing of a complaint in this court by plaintiffs. The defendants in the action, who are named in the heading above, are charged with __14____ [specify]. The defendants have denied all charges of wrongdoing, and further deny that the members of the class are entitled to any relief. Defendants further contend __15____ [specify other contentions, including affirmative defenses, if any].

B. No court has yet passed on the merits of either the plaintiffs' claim or the defendants' defenses.

C. This court, by order entered __16____, 19_17_, determined that this action should be maintained as a class action under section 901 of the Civil Practice Law and Rules and notice of such determination was given to members of the class, as then ascertained from examination of defendants' records.

D. Plaintiffs have engaged in extensive discovery proceedings, have examined a very large number of documents, and have taken the depositions of the individual defendants and other persons concerned in this matter. Plaintiffs, without conceding any infirmity in their claims or those of the other members of the class, but recognizing the risks inherent in litigation as well as the economic risks in collecting a substantial judgment should one be obtained in this action, have agreed to settlement of the class action on the terms stated in the Settlement Agreement. Plaintiffs believe that the settlement is fair, reasonable and adequate and beneficial to class members and should be approved.

E. Defendants, while denying all liability on the charges made against them and any wrongdoing, and without conceding any infirmity in any defense asserted in their answer herein, consider it desirable that the action be settled. They desire settlement to avoid further expense, to preserve and protect their business reputations, to dispose of burdensome and protracted litigation and to permit the continued operation of their business unhampered by this litigation. Accordingly defendants have agreed to the settlement on the terms stated in the Settlement Agreement.

PROPOSED SETTLEMENT OF CLASS ACTION

1. The terms of the proposed settlement are set forth in the Stipulation For settlement dated __18____, 19_19_, and in the Settlement Agreement of the same date, executed by counsel for the respective parties in their behalf. In substance, the stipulation of settlement provides as follows: __20____ [set forth provisions of settlement in condensed form].

2. On approval of the settlement by the court, final judgments of dismissal will be

entered, with prejudice, and the plaintiffs, and all class members who have not timely excluded themselves from this action, will be conclusively bound by such dismissal.

3. The attorneys for the plaintiffs have made application for reimbursement of costs and expenses in the sum of $___21___, and for fees in the amount of $___22___, being ___23___ percent of the gross amount of the settlement stated in paragraph 1 above.

4. The total sum available for distribution among members of the class will be the gross amount of the settlement less costs, expenses, and fees allowed, which are to be paid from the settlement proceeds under the terms of the stipulation of settlement and Settlement Agreement.

PROCEDURE FOR PRESENTING OBJECTIONS

Any member of the class who has not heretofore elected to be excluded from this action may appear and show cause, if he has any, why the proposed settlement should not be approved by the court as fair, reasonable, and adequate, and why this action should not be dismissed on the merits, with prejudice, and any such member of the class may also object to the allowance of the costs, expenses and fees requested by plaintiffs' counsel; provided that no such person shall be heard, and no papers or briefs shall be submitted by him to the court, unless he files a notice of intention to appear and a statement of the basis of his objections, together with a memorandum of authorities, with the clerk of the court, and serves a copy thereof on ___24_____ [names], at ___25_____ [address], attorneys for plaintiffs, and on ___26_____ [names], at ___27_____ [address], attorneys for defendants, personally or by mail, on or before ___28_____, 19_29_ [date substantially in advance of date set for hearing].

Objections filed and served in accordance with the foregoing procedure will be considered by the court whether or not the objecting class member appears personally or by counsel at the hearing to argue the same.

EXAMINATION OF PLEADINGS AND PAPERS

The references in this notice to the Settlement Agreement and other papers are only summaries of those documents. The complete texts are on file with the clerk of the court, at the address of the court above stated, and are available for inspection there. Copies of documents produced during discovery proceedings, and not on file with the clerk of the court, will be available for inspection by any class member not excluded from this action and his attorney at the offices of counsel for each of the parties during regular business hours.

PROOF OF CLAIM

Each class member desiring to participate in the proceeds of the settlement is requested to complete, sign and file a written proof of claim, together with photocopies of relevant supporting documents. Forms for such proof of claim accompany this notice, and may also be obtained at the office of the clerk of this court at ___30_____ [address]. All class members are urged to complete and file claim forms, presenting the requested information concerning their individual claims. Failure to do so may result in exclusion from the proceeds of the settlement, if approved by the court. The proof of claim form is self-explanatory.

Proof of claim may not be filed by any member who has elected to be excluded from the action.

Each proof of claim form will be reviewed by a claims committee consisting of ___31_____ [names] who have been designated by the court to serve on such committee and who are co-counsel for the class. Any claimant whose claim is rejected or objected to, or as to which any question is raised, will be so advised and may obtain a hearing with respect thereto by filing application therefor within ___32_____ days following the date notice of rejection, or objection, was mailed to the claimant. If no such application for hearing is made such claimant shall be deemed to have consented to rejection of or objection to his claim.

If the total amount of authorized claims for all claimants is less than the amount of the available settlement fund, after payment of fees, costs and expenses as allowed by the court, each authorized claim will be increased pro rata. If the total amount of authorized claims exceeds the amount of the available settlement fund, then each authorized claim will be reduced pro rata.

SUBSEQUENT HEARINGS

At the hearing on the proposed settlement set for __33_____, 19_34_ the court may schedule such further hearings as it may deem necessary without the necessity of further notice to the class. The matters considered at such future hearings may include, but shall not be limited to, further consideration of the fairness and adequacy of the proposed settlement, determination and settlement of individual claims filed by class members, consideration of the applications for fees and costs of plaintiffs' counsel, and the form and entry of the final judgment of dismissal in the event the proposed settlement is approved by the court.

Dated __35_____, 19_36_.

[Signature and title]

Form 8

Class Members' Objections to Settlement

[Caption]

OBJECTIONS OF __1_____ [NAMES] TO PROPOSED SETTLEMENT OF CLASS ACTION

__2_____ and __3_____, members of the class heretofore determined by the court in this action, appear herein by the undersigned, __4_____, their attorney, and object to the proposed settlement of this action and to its approval by the court on the following grounds:

1. The notice of hearing addressed to the class members is deficient in that it fails to present to the class members sufficient facts to enable them to determine whether the amount of the proposed settlement is fair and reasonable, as it purports to be.

2. There is no mention in the notice of any provision in the proposed settlement for prorating the amount of the settlement among the various members of the class who file claims in the event that the available fund proves to be insufficient to pay such claims in full, or of any provision for reservation of jurisdiction by the court, after judgment of dismissal is entered, to assure that the terms of the settlement are complied with.

3. The proposed settlement is not definite and certain, but is, rather, contingent upon certain future events, namely: __5_____ [specify, for example: the securing of financing by the defendant corporations to enable it to pay the amount of the settlement]. If such contingency does not occur, the parties and the court will have gone to considerable trouble and expense, and will have spent a great deal of time in considering approval of the proposed settlement to no good purpose. In lieu of such contingency, proof should be submitted to the court prior to the hearing date that __6_____ [state action required to be taken to eliminate contingency, for example: The necessary financing has been secured by defendant corporations].

4. The proposed settlement provides for payment by all the corporate defendants of the fees and expenses allowed to plaintiffs' counsel without any apportionment of the amounts involved among the defendants. Such apportionment should be made and notice thereof given in advance of the hearing, so that the members of the class may be apprised of the specific burden that will be assumed by each defendant.

Wherefore, objectors pray that the proposed settlement be not approved, unless it is amended prior to hearing to the extent and in the particulars hereinabove set forth.

Dated __7_____, 19_8_.

___9_____

Attorney for Class
__10_____ Address
__11__ Telephone No.

Form 9

Stipulation for Settlement of Class Action

[Caption]

PRELIMINARY STATEMENT

A. The above-entitled action was brought by plaintiffs __1_____ [names], on behalf of themselves and all other persons similarly situated, being __2_____ [describe class generally] as a class action under Section 901 of the Civil Practice Law and Rule.

B. Plaintiffs' complaint herein, as amended and supplemented, charged in substance that __3_____ [summarize charging allegations], and that as a result plaintiffs and other members of the class were damaged.

C. In this action, plaintiffs request __4_____ [state relief requested, generally, for example: an award of damages to each member of the class for the damages sustained by him, together with injunctive and declaratory relief]. Plaintiffs also pray for reimbursement of their costs and expenses and for the allowance of reasonable counsel fees to their attorneys for prosecuting this action.

D. The named defendants have appeared and answered and have denied the material allegations of the plaintiffs' complaint, as amended and supplemented. Defendants have also pleaded that the claims asserted by plaintiffs are barred by certain affirmative defenses, namely, __5_____ [specify].

E. The court, by order dated __6_____, 19_7_, determined that this action is properly maintained as a class action under the provisions of Rules Section 901 of the Civil Practice Law and Rule, and that plaintiffs are proper representatives of the class.

F. In order to bring to rest the controversy between plaintiffs and the class represented by plaintiffs, and defendants, to secure total and final settlement of all claims against defendants arising out of the purported acts and omissions set forth in plaintiffs' complaint, as amended and supplemented, and to avoid further expense, inconvenience, and the distraction and hazard of burdensome and protracted litigation, the parties desire to settle, compromise, and terminate this action and all claims asserted therein, as well as any and all other claims against the defendants which are based upon or might be based upon or arise from any of the matters alleged in plaintiffs' complaint, as amended and supplemented, regardless of the legal theory on which such claims may be based.

STIPULATION

Now, therefore, for the reasons hereinabove set forth,

IT IS HEREBY STIPULATED AND AGREED, by and between the parties hereto, through the undersigned, their respective counsel, subject to the approval of the court and notice and an opportunity to be heard to be accorded to all class members, as follows:

1. An order and final judgment may be entered by the court __8_____ [in accordance with the provisions of paragraphs __9__ and __10__ of the Settlement Agreement annexed hereto and incorporated herein by reference or specify all terms and provisions of settlement agreement].

2. Each party will comply fully and promptly with all terms and provisions of the

settlement __11_____ [as hereinabove provided or as provided in the attached Settlement Agreement].

3. All claims asserted in this action, and any and all other claims against the defendants or any of them, which are based on or could be based on, or could arise from any of the matters alleged in plaintiffs' complaint, as amended and supplemented, regardless of the legal theory on which they are based, shall be dismissed by the court with prejudice.

4. To accomplish dismissal, this stipulation for settlement will be submitted by the parties jointly to the court, with the request that it be approved pursuant to Section 908 of the Civil Practice Law and Rules. A form of order, a copy of which is annexed hereto as Exhibit __12__, providing that a hearing shall be held to determine whether the settlement is adequate, proper, fair and reasonable, and providing that notice, in the form annexed to the proposed order as Exhibit __13__, shall, if approved by the court, be printed or otherwise reproduced and mailed to all members of the class described in paragraph A above, as directed in the proposed order. The expense of such publication, reproduction, and mailing shall be paid __14_____ [jointly by defendants __15_____ and __16_____ or as the case may be].

5. On approval of the settlement by the court, following notice and hearing, an order and final judgment shall be entered approving the settlement, adjudging the terms thereof to be adequate, proper, fair and reasonable, and directing consummation of the settlement in accordance with its terms and provisions, including dismissal of plaintiffs' complaint, as amended and supplemented on the merits, with prejudice and without costs to any party, except as otherwise specially provided in __17_____ [this stipulation or the Settlement Agreement].

6. Settlement shall be consummated pursuant to the terms of this stipulation __18_____ [add, if appropriate: and the Settlement Agreement] on approval of the court as herein provided.

7. Plaintiffs and defendants, and their counsel, will use their best efforts to secure the court's approval of the settlement as herein __19_____ [add, if appropriate: and in the Settlement Agreement] set forth.

8. Nothing incident or relating to this stipulation or any provision hereof __20_____ [add, if appropriate: or to the Settlement Agreement], including but not limited to negotiations and public announcements, may be used by any party against any other party in this action or in any other action, except to enforce the rights and obligations of the respective parties arising out of the provisions of this stipulation __21_____ [add, if appropriate: or the Settlement Agreement]. The limitation set forth in this paragraph shall survive the termination of the settlement prior to its final consummation, if such should occur.

9. After the entry of final judgment approving the settlement, and after such judgment is no longer subject to appeal or other review, counsel for plaintiffs will apply to the court for allowances of attorneys' fees and expenses relating to this litigation, to be paid __22_____ [out of the proceeds of the settlement or as otherwise agreed].

10. This stipulation is not, and shall not be construed to be, either an admission by defendants of the validity of any of the claims asserted in this action, or of their liability for any thereof, or of any wrongdoing whatsoever, nor shall the stipulation be construed as an admission by plaintiffs of any lack of merit in their allegations. Any statements or arguments made on behalf of any plaintiff or defendant at the settlement hearing or in support of the settlement shall not be used as evidence in any way in any subsequent trial, proceeding, or hearing either in this action or in any other action or proceeding between the parties thereto should such occur.

11. If the settlement, as herein __23_____ [add, if appropriate: and in the Settlement Agreement] provided, is not approved by the court, then this stipulation, except paragraphs 8 and 10 hereof, and all proceedings hereunder shall be considered as canceled and void and of no force or effect; and all parties to this action and to this

stipulation shall stand in the same position without prejudice as if the stipulation had not been entered into and submitted to the court for its consideration and approval.

Dated __24_____, 19_25_.

_____26_____

Attorneys for Parties
__27_____Addresses
__28_____Telephone Nos.

[Separate Settlement Agreement, if any, and proposed order attached]

Rule 909. Attorneys' fees

If a judgment in an action maintained as a class action is rendered in favor of the class, the court in its discretion may award attorneys' fees to the representatives of the class based on the reasonable value of legal services rendered and if justice requires, allow recovery of the amount awarded from the opponent of the class.

HISTORY:

Add, L 1975, ch 207, eff Sept 1, 1975.

FEDERAL ASPECTS:

Fees and costs, 28 USCS §§ 1911 to 1929.

Fees in United States Court of Claims, 28 USCS § 2520.

Costs in United States Supreme Court, Rule 51 of United States Supreme Court Rules, USCS Court Rules.

Fees in United States Supreme Court, Rule 52 of United States Supreme Court Rules, USCS Court Rules.

Costs in United States Court of Appeals, Rule 39 of Federal Rules of Appellate Procedure, USCS Court Rules.

Class actions, Rule 23 of Federal Rules of Civil Procedure, USCS Court Rules.

Costs of previously-dismissed action, Rule 41(d) of Federal Rules of Civil Procedure, USCS Court Rules.

Costs and judgments, Rule 54(d) of Federal Rules of Civil Procedure, USCS Court Rules.

Costs and condemnation of property, Rule 71A(l) of Federal Rules of Civil Procedure, USCS Court Rules.

RESEARCH REFERENCES AND PRACTICE AIDS:

24 NY Jur, Fraudulent Conveyances § 144.

57 NY Jur, Suretyship and Guaranty § 264.

3 Carmody-Wait 2d, Parties § 19:183.

Annotations:

Attorneys' fees in class actions. 38 ALR3d 1384.

Validity of statute allowing attorneys' fees to successful claimant but not to defendant, or vice versa. 73 ALR3d 515.

Award of counsel fees to prevailing party based on adversary's bad faith, obduracy, or other misconduct. 31 ALR Fed 833.

Validity of statute allowing attorneys fees to successful claimant but not to defendant, or vice versa. 73 ALR3d 515.

Forms:

See "FORMS" heading following "CASE NOTES", infra.

CASE NOTES

Although petitioners, residents of community hospital, successfully applied to court in class action for declaratory judgment requiring commissioners of county board of elections to register and enroll them and all residents of publicly supported institutions to establish their voting residences in such institutions under Election Law, where it had been long-standing practice that resident of public institution must vote from his former residence, there was no bad faith on commissioners' part in denying petitioners' right to vote from hospital until court ordered them to permit it and special term did not abuse its discretion in denying attorneys' fees to petitioners. Brazie v Chiavaroli (1976) 53 AD2d 1057, 385 NYS2d 953.

FORMS

Form 1—Notice of motion for allowance of attorneys' fees and expenses
Form 2—Affidavit in support of motion for attorneys' fees and expenses

Form 1

Notice of Motion for Allowance of Attorneys' Fees and Expenses

[Caption]

To: __1_____ [names and addresses of all attorneys for defendants]

Please take notice that on the annexed affidavit of __2_____, and all the pleadings, records, and files of this action, the undersigned will move, the Honorable __3_____ [name], in courtroom No. __4__ of the Court House, __5_____ [address], on __6_____, 19_7_, at __8__ o'clock __9__.m., or as soon thereafter as counsel can be heard, for an order allowing legal fees in the sum of $__10__, and expense disbursements in the sum of $__11__, to the undersigned, and directing their payment __12_____ [by defendants __13_____ (names) or from the settlement proceeds], and for such other relief as may be appropriate.

Dated __14_____, 19_15_.

         __16_____

                    Attorney
       __17_____ Address
      __18__ Telephone No.

[Attach affidavit]

Form 2

Affidavit in Support of Motion for Attorneys' Fees and Expenses

[Caption]

State of New York
County of __1_____

__2__ _____, being duly sworn, deposes and says:

1. I am a member of the law firm of __3_____, __4_____ [address], attorneys for __5_____ [names] who are __6_____ [the or among the] plaintiffs above named. I submit this affidavit in support of the application of my law firm for allowance of fees and reimbursement of expenses in this action.

2. This action was commenced on __7_____, 19_8_, and since that time has been continuously active as shown by the court file herein. The action has been settled, subject to the court's approval on hearing and due notice to the members of the class, pursuant to a stipulation of settlement dated __9_____, 19_10_, __11_____ [heretofore filed or filed herewith]. The terms of the settlement are as follows: __12_____ [summarize settlement terms].

3. Based upon the showing made herein, it is submitted that an allowance of attorney fees in the sum of $__13__ would be reasonable, and is accordingly requested herewith. In addition, reimbursement of actual out-of-pocket expenses is requested in the sum of $__14__. Such expenses are set forth in detail in Exhibit A hereto attached.

4. Economic benefit of settlement to class. Under the terms of the foregoing

proposed settlement, the economic benefit to the plaintiff class, as determined by independent and competent expert witnesses presented by plaintiffs, will be in the range from $__15__ to $__16__. The experts referred to, whose qualifications and opinions are before the court, are __17_____ [names].

5. Time expended by counsel. The settlement negotiations between the parties commenced on or about __18_____, 19_19_ and concluded with the drafting and signing of the settlement stipulation on __20_____, 19_21_. Such negotiations required approximately __22_____ meetings and the expenditure of __23_____ hours by affiant and the other members of his firm, as shown by table of time expenditures hereto attached as Exhibit A. For the convenience of court, such Exhibit contains a summary month-by-month of such services. The attention of the court is also respectfully invited to the clerk's docket of this action for an index to the proceedings herein, which corroborated many of the entries in said Exhibit. A copy of such index has been reproduced and is hereto attached as Exhibit C.

6. Special difficulties encountered. From the outset counsel for plaintiffs have encountered unusual difficulties and have surmounted barriers which ordinarily would not be expected in litigation of this nature. Such matters may be summarized as follows: __24_____ [specify].

7. Contingent nature of the fee. For reasons which are clear from the entire record in this proceeding, counsel for plaintiffs undertook this litigation entirely on a contingent basis. There is no other practical way in which the class members could have been represented and their rights vindicated.

8. Burden of establishing case prior to serious settlement negotiations with defendants. In order to enter a phase of serious settlement negotiations it was essential that counsel for plaintiff undertake and prosecute a lengthy and complicated investigation into the facts and explore and present evidence in support of the claims for relief set out in the complaint. By way of summary, it is pointed out to the court that plaintiffs' counsel have attended the examination before trial of approximately __25_____ witnesses, on more than __26_____ separate occasions, in __27_____ separate cities or towns. Counsel have had to examine thousands of pages of transcript so produced and additional thousands of pages of other documents. A summary of deposition days is hereto attached as Exhibit D. It was further necessary to do extensive research into highly specialized areas of law as well as to become familiar with the technical phases of the litigation and its extremely complex financial aspects.

9. Experience and qualifications of plaintiffs' counsel. The background of the principal attorneys for the plaintiff class in litigation of this general nature, including participation in other actions in this field, is as follows: __28_____ [summarize for each individual attorney].

10. Reasonableness of fees requested. Based upon the economic benefits to the plaintiff class produced by the settlement of this action, the complexity of the legal and factual issues involved, the experience of counsel, and the amount of time spent by counsel in preparing for trial and in settling this action, together with the fact that this cause was taken on a contingency fee basis, it is submitted that allowance of the requested fee in the amount of $__29_____ would be reasonable. Such a fee is commensurate with the fees that have been allowed in similar actions by federal district courts within the past __30_____ years. A summary of such cases and fee allowances is attached as Exhibit E.

13. Accordingly, in the light of the facts presented and the entire record of this case it is respectfully requested that the court find the request of plaintiffs' counsel for legal fees to be reasonable and allow fees in the amount of $__31_____. It is further requested that the court approve and allow reimbursement of expenses to counsel in the sum of $__32_____.

[Signature of affiant]

Subscribed and sworn to before me this ___33_____ day of __34_____, 19_35_.

[Signature and title]

[Attach exhibits]

[CPLR 910–1000 have been reserved for future use.
Please check your supplement.]

ARTICLE 10

Parties Generally

HISTORY:

Add, L 1962, ch 308, eff Sept 1, 1963.

ADVISORY COMMITTEE NOTES:

Most of the matters covered in this article have been subjects of studies and recommendations of the Judicial Council resulting in recent amendments to the CPA. They have, in the main, been followed with minor changes to conform

265

language. Thus, the new CPLR sections embody former provisions on permissive joinder of parties, interpleader, third-party practice and intervention.

The new provisions on compulsory joinder of parties express what the courts are now doing more accurately than the existing sections of the CPA.

The first part of CPA § 210, which requires that actions be prosecuted in the name of the real property in interest, is omitted. This omission will not change the law in any respect. Rather, it will clarify matters by removing the implication that the beneficial party may always bring the action and that he is the only party who may do so.

The Judicial Council did not deal with substitution of parties. The former statutes are scattered and some are verbose or archaic. The new provisions state the essential principles in brief fashion, *viz.:* that substitution of the proper parties may be ordered by the court on its own motion or on motion of any party or of the person who should be substituted, and that the consequence of failure to substitute is dismissal of the action as to the party for whom substitution should have been made.

RESEARCH REFERENCES AND PRACTICE AIDS:
3 Carmody-Wait 2d, Parties §§ 19:1 et seq.
26 Carmody-Wait 2d, Claims § 159:101.

§ 1001. Necessary joinder of parties

(a) Parties who should be joined. Persons who ought to be parties if complete relief is to be accorded between the persons who are parties to the action or who might be inequitably affected by a judgment in the action shall be made plaintiffs or defendants. When a person who should join as a plaintiff refuses to do so he may be made a defendant.

(b) When joinder excused. When a person who should be joined under subdivision (a) has not been made a party and is subject to the jurisdiction of the court, the court shall order him summoned. If jurisdiction over him can be obtained only by his consent or appearance, the court, when justice requires, may allow the action to proceed without his being made a party. In determining whether to allow the action to proceed, the court shall consider:

1. whether the plaintiff has another effective remedy in case the action is dismissed on account of the nonjoinder;

2. the prejudice which may accrue from the nonjoinder to the defendant or to the person not joined;

3. whether and by whom prejudice might have been avoided or may in the future be avoided;

4. the feasibility of a protective provision by order of the court or in the judgment; and

5. whether an effective judgment may be rendered in the absence of the person who is not joined.

HISTORY:
Add, L 1962, ch 308, eff Sept 1, 1963.
Sub (a), amd, L 1963, ch 532, § 9, eff Sept 1, 1963.
Earlier statutes: CPA §§ 193, 194, 475; CCP §§ 446, 456, 457, 488; Code Proc § 136.

NOTE:

Laws 1963, ch 532, made two types of changes: first, some provisions were designed to correct the typographical errors which existed in the CPLR. Second, other provisions incorporated into the CPLR, without any change in substance, all pertinent amendments to the C.P.A. which were passed and approved during the 1962 legislative session. In this connection, only changes in language were made to conform to the style and format of the CPLR. Those C.P.A. amendments of 1962 essentially covered by original provisions of the CPLR, and those C.P.A. amendments pertaining to areas transferred on September 1, 1963, to laws other than the CPLR, were not incorporated into this act.

ADVISORY COMMITTEE NOTES:

It is believed that this section expresses the actual practice in the courts although it differs in language from the CPA provisions. The colorless and misleading expression "united in interest" is eliminated in favor of other language which closely follows that found in CPA § 193(1), and which may be traced to § 102 of the original Field code. The term "conditionally necessary" is also eliminated, although the new CPLR section does recognize that there are some persons who must be joined if it is possible to do so, but whose joinder is excused if jurisdiction over them cannot be obtained. See generally 12 NY Jud Council Rep 45, 163–191 (1946). Cf. CPA § 194 ("real party in interest"); Fed R Civ P 19(a) ("having a joint interest").

The provision for making a person a defendant when he refuses to join as a plaintiff is found in § 194 of the CPA, being derived from the Field code which borrowed it from the chancery practice. The wording follows Federal rule 19(a).

Subd (a) is, of course, subject to the provisions of subdivision (b) and to the provisions of § 1005 governing class actions.

Subd (b) classifies the persons described in subdivision (a) into those who are indispensable and whose absence will result in the dismissal of the action, and those who are not indispensable and whose joinder is excused if jurisdiction over them cannot be obtained. Cf. Fed R Civ P 19(b); CPA § 193(2). This subdivision is principally devoted to the case of the necessary party who is not indispensable. It provides that he must be brought in if he is subject to the jurisdiction of the court, but that if he cannot be brought in, the court in its discretion can proceed without him. This is essentially the same provision which is found in CPA § 193(2) which excuses the joinder if the person cannot be "brought in without undue delay."

A new feature of the section is the enumeration of five criteria for determining whether a person is so important as a party that the action must be dismissed if he is not joined. A germ of the idea may be present in CPA § 193(1), where there is reference to an absentee who "would be inequitably affected by the judgment." This language is borrowed from the Iowa rule. 12 NY Jud Council Rep 168, 178 n 57 (1946). The considerations enumerated are those emphasized in the case law, which, on analysis, indicates that the subject defies definitive statement and that decision must rest in the sound discretion of the court. The fundamental philosophy is that indispensability should be determined in the light of all the factors and interests involved including those of the court, and that there is no single certain criterion for determining whether a person is an indispensable party. Not only should the effect of nonjoinder be considered, but also the question of who might avoid or minimize its consequences. The reference in (5) of subd (b) is to the possibility that a judgment rendered in the absence of some person would, on account of that absence, be so hollow or inconclusive that it would be a waste of the court's and the parties' time to proceed with the litigation.

The wording of the subdivision permits the court to postpone the determination of indispensability until the trial or judgment stage is reached. This may be desirable in cases where it cannot be determined at a preliminary stage whether it is safe or reasonable to enter a judgment in the absence of some person who may have an interest. Of course, no one is legally bound by a judgment unless he is a party to the action or is represented by a party, but a dispensable person is sometimes affected by a judgment in some practical way without being legally bound by it.

Provisions, like those of Federal rule 19(b), excusing the joinder if it would deprive the court of its jurisdiction, are not included, since they are significant only in connection with the diversity jurisdiction of the Federal courts and have no place in state procedure. A provision like that of Federal rule 19(b) which speaks of persons "subject to the jurisdiction of the court as to both service of process and venue" has been omitted in view of proposed § 502 of the article on venue. Cf. CPA § 193.

CROSS REFERENCES:

This section referred to in 1003; Exec Law § 808.
Joinder of causes of action, CPLR 601.
Permissive joinder of parties, CPLR 1002.
Actions on mechanics' liens, Lien Law § 62.
Real property actions, Real P Actions & Pr Law § 241.

FEDERAL ASPECTS:

Parties in actions in United States District Courts, Rules 17 to 25 of Federal Rules of Civil Procedure, USCS Court Rules.

Real party in interest in actions in United States District Courts, Rule 17(a) of Federal Rules of Civil Procedure, USCS Court Rules.

Joinder of persons needed for just adjudication, Rule 19 of Federal Rules of Civil Procedure, USCS Court Rules.

Misjoinder and nonjoinder of parties, Rule 21 of Federal Rules of Civil Procedure, USCS Court Rules.

RESEARCH REFERENCES AND PRACTICE AIDS:

10 NY Jur, Contracts § 235.
15 NY Jur (Rev), Domestic Relations §§ 256–268.
31 NY Jur, Insurance §§ 1634–1636.
57 NY Jur, Suretyship and Guaranty § 268.
3 Carmody-Wait 2d, Parties §§ 19:1, 19:55, 19:56, 19:58, 19:60, 19:63, 19:82, 19:87, 19:169.
6 Carmody-Wait 2d, Bills of Particulars and Copies of Accounts § 36:4.
6 Carmody-Wait 2d, Pretrial Motions to Dismiss § 38:22.
13 Carmody-Wait 2d, Real Property Actions Generally § 86:5.
13 Carmody-Wait 2d, Notice of Pendency of Actions § 87:78.
14 Carmody-Wait 2d, Partition §§ 91:51 et seq., 91:68.
21 Carmody-Wait 2d, Actions Against Persons Jointly Liable §§ 123:2, 123:4.
25 Carmody-Wait 2d, Fundamentals of Practice in the Surrogate's Court § 149:206.
6 Am Jur 2d, Assignments §§ 35, 133.
6 Am Jur 2d, Associations and Clubs §§ 54 et seq.
18 Am Jur 2d, Cooperative Associations § 39.
19 Am Jur 2d, Corporations § 910.
42 Am Jur 2d, Infants §§ 172, 207.
44 Am Jur 2d, Insurance §§ 1849–1856.
48 Am Jur 2d, Labor and Labor Relations §§ 318, 355.
59 Am Jur 2d, Parties §§ 12, 96.
60 Am Jur 2d, Partnership §§ 325, 326.
66 Am Jur 2d, Receivers § 477.
2 Am Jur Pl and Pr Forms (Rev ed), Assignments, Forms 71–77.
19 Am Jur Pl and Pr Forms (Rev ed), Parties, Forms 51–57.

Annotations:

Joinder or representation of several claimants in action against carrier or utility to recover overcharge. 1 ALR2d 160.

Change in party after statute of limitations has run. 8 ALR2d 6.

Trust beneficiaries as necessary parties to action relating to trust or its property. 9 ALR2d 10.

Joinder as defendants, in tort action based on condition of sidewalk or highway, of municipal corporation and abutting property owner or occupant. 15 ALR2d 1293.

Joinder of insurer and insured under policy of compulsory indemnity or liability insurance in action by injured third person. 20 ALR2d 1097.

Corporation as necessary or proper party defendant in proceedings to determine validity of election or appointment of corporate director or officer. 21 ALR2d 1048.

Necessary parties defendant to action to set aside conveyance in fraud of creditors. 24 ALR2d 395.

One party to intended sale of land as necessary or indispensable defendant in action by the other party to recover deposit from broker or agent. 33 ALR2d 1090.

Joinder, in injunction action to restrain or abate nuisance, of persons contributing thereto through separate and independent acts. 45 ALR2d 1284.

Right to join principal debtor and guarantor as parties defendant. 53 ALR2d 522.

Necessary parties defendant to independent action on injunction bond. 55 ALR2d 545.

Right to join master and servant as defendants in tort action based on respondent superior. 59 ALR2d 1066.

Proper party plaintiff, under real party in interest statute, to action against tortfeasor for damage to insured property where insured has paid part of loss. 13 ALR3d 140.

Proper party plaintiff, under real party in interest statute, to action against tortfeasor for damage to insured property where loss is entirely covered by insurance. 13 ALR3d 229.

Necessary or proper parties to suit or proceeding to establish private boundary line. 73 ALR3d 948.

Joinder of indispensable parties as affecting venue and process in civil actions against federal officers, employees, or agencies. 9 ALR Fed 744.

What constitutes "proper case" within meaning of provision of Rule 19(a) of Federal Rules of Civil Procedure that when person who should join as plaintiff refuses to do so, he may be made involuntary plaintiff "in a proper case." 20 ALR Fed 193.

Validity, construction, and application of Rule 19(b) of Federal Rules of Civil Procedure, as amended in 1966, providing for determination to be made by court to proceed with or dismiss action when joinder of person needed for just adjudication is not feasible. 21 ALR Fed 12.

Who must be joined in action as person "needed for just adjudication" under Rule 19(a) of Federal Rules of Civil Procedure, 22 ALR Fed 765

Law Reviews:

New York Civil Practice Law and Rules: parties. 27 Albany L Rev 182.

Parties and pleading under the CPLR. 31 Brooklyn L Rev 98.

Collateral estoppel, mutuality and joinder of parties. 68 Colum L Rev 1457.

A biannual survey of New York practice: Section 1001: necessary joinder of parties. 38 St. John's L Rev 417.

Biannual survey of New York practice: Part III. 39 St. John's L Rev 178.

Biannual survey of New York practice: Part IV. 39 St. John's L Rev 408.

Biannual survey of New York practice: Part V. 40 St. John's L Rev 125.

1975 survey of New York law—civil practice. 27 Syracuse L Rev 425.

Forms:

See "FORMS" heading following "CASE NOTES", infra.

CASE NOTES

1. In general
2. Who are necessary parties
3. —Actions involving government and public officials
4. —Actions involving husband and wife
5. —Actions involving landlord and tenant
6. Dismissal
7. Excusing nonjoinder and continuing with action

1. In general

The general policy of the CPLR is to limit the scope of indispensable parties to those cases where the determination of the court will adversely affect the rights of nonparties. Castaways Motel v Schuyler (1969) 24 NY2d 120, 299 NYS2d 148, 247 NE2d 124, adhered to 25 NY2d 692, 306 NYS2d 692, 254 NE2d 919.

Where plaintiff purported to sue as agent of a disclosed principal, and without showing any legal or equitable title or interest in the claim, nor that it was assigned to him, nor that he was a general agent, plaintiff failed to show that he was the real party in interest and complaint would be dismissed. Martin Fein & Co. v Sealomatic Electronics Corp. (1967) 57 Misc 2d 187, 290 NYS2d 808.

Since arbitrations are no longer considered special proceedings, the courts have been deprived of the statutory power, formerly authorized under the CPA, to consolidate arbitrations of controversies and arbitrations are also exempt from such procedural regulation as third party practice for the joinder of parties. Met Food Corp. v M. Eisenberg & Bros., Inc. (1969) 59 Misc 2d 498, 299 NYS2d 696.

Where a corporation in whose right a derivative shareholders' action is brought seeks to be substituted as plaintiff, the corporation should establish that notwithstanding its prior declination, it will now prosecute the action in good faith; and the court should direct that all shareholders receive an appropriate notice of the application, similar in purpose and effect to the notice contemplated by Bus Corp L § 626(d) for the discontinuance or compromise of such an action. Lazar v Merchants' Nat. Properties, Inc. (1964) 22 AD2d 253, 254 NYS2d 712.

Evidence in mortgage foreclosure proceeding on motion by mortgagor's widow who had been personally served and her 2 sons, who lived with her, seeking to vacate order of publication, judgment of foreclosure, and to cancel referee's deed on the grounds that the sons should have been personally served and joined as parties established that sons, one of whom signed receipt for service on mother, had adequate notice. Levy v Robinson (1973) 41 AD2d 558, 340 NYS2d 48, app dismd 33 NY2d 636, 347 S2d 585, 301 NE2d 553.

2. Who are necessary parties

Where complete relief may be accorded between the parties and the absent party will not be inequitably affected, the absentee is not a necessary party. Figari v New York Tel. Co. (1969) 32 AD2d 434, 303 NYS2d 245.

In an action against a telephone company by subscribers to a recorded announcement service seeking a judgment that a tariff requiring the individual subscriber to state his name and address on the recording was unconstitutional, the Public Service Commission is not a necessary party. Figari v New York Tel. Co. (1969) 32 AD2d 434, 303 NYS2d 245.

Implicit in any assignment of claim for security is a reservation to assignor of right to pursue claim if assignee chooses not to do so, since such action is pursued for joint benefit of assignor and assignee the assignee is also a necessary party to action so that the parties' respective equities can be determined. Fifty States Management Corp. v Pioneer Auto Parts, Inc. (1974) 44 AD2d 887, 355 NYS2d 856.

Defendant, co-maker of promissory note with plaintiff's son, was entitled under this section to compel plaintiff to join son as defendant in action on notes, or in the alternative to have action dismissed under CPLR 3211 subsection (a)(10), since equities could not otherwise be balanced. Such v Alsing (1966) 51 Misc 2d 639, 273 NYS2d 650.

A university construction fund was a person "who might be inequitably affected" as described in CPLR § 1001, subdivision a, and was thus a necessary party in Article 78 proceeding brought by students to compel acceptance of sums less than those fixed as consolidated fees, where judgment directing payment to fund of monies allegedly received from students by the college as trustee would have subjected fund to risks of litigation by contributing students and to conflicting duty to use monies for non-trust purposes pursuant to Education L § 6273 and 6278. Fellner v McMurray (1973) 41 AD2d 853, 342 NYS2d 992.

Where one of three owners, tenants in common, of cottage brought action for ejectment of defendant who took up residence in cottage as condition of his employment the other two owners must be joined before judgment could properly be rendered, inasmuch as resolution of dispute could well adversely affect the rights of remaining tenants in common. Vicario v Raymond (1974) 44 AD2d 863, 355 NYS2d 481.

One joint tortfeasor sued alone by the injured party cannot bring in as a party defendant to the action a second tortfeasor jointly liable for the injury. Musco v Conte (1964) 22 AD2d 121, 254 NYS2d 589.

In action to foreclose second mortgage first mortgagee is not a necessary party, since he does not have such interest in the property involved which must necessarily be passed on if the controversy is to be settled. Commercial Trading Co., Inc. v Little N. Parkway Realty Corp. (1963) 41 Misc 2d 472, 245 NYS2d 731.

In an action by assembly district leaders of a political party to enjoin their predecessors in office and the political club to which such predecessors belong from describing themselves in such a way as to lead to the belief that such predecessors still occupy their former official party positions and that such club is the "regular organization", the political club to which the plaintiffs belong is not a necessary party under the terms of subd a of this section. Shein v Horatio Seymour Democratic Club, Inc. (1964) 44 Misc 2d 729, 254 NYS2d 918.

In an action by the income beneficiary and remaindermen of a trust against the trustee to set aside defendant's sale to himself of stock that had been part of the trust principal, to remove defendant as trustee and to require an accounting, nonresident contingent remaindermen were not necessary persons to be joined pursuant to CPLR 1001 subdivision a, and even if they were, justice required that the court permit the action to proceed in their absence pursuant to CPLR 1001, subdivision b. O'Hayer v De St. Aubin (1965) 24 AD2d 604, 262 NYS2d 225.

Where title company commenced interpleader action and obtained order by which it was discharged from liability upon payment of escrowed funds into court, person who was entitled to claim funds jointly with a named defendant was a necessary, although not indispensable, party to the action and, since the plaintiff had been discharged, a defendant who claimed fund as assignee of a third named defendant should have brought the necessary party into action as a party. Monroe Abstract & Title Corp. v Giallombardo (1976) 54 AD2d 1084, 388 NYS2d 966.

3. —Actions involving government and public officials

An appointee to a position with a board of education, as incumbent in position sought by plaintiff in a declaratory judgment action challenging validity of the appointment, and whose right to the position was under direct attack was both a person who should have been a party if complete relief was to be accorded and one who might be inequitably affected by judgment in the action, and he should have been made a party in the action, but, even if not regarded as a necessary party, denial of appointee's request to intervene in the action would be an abuse of discretion. Kirkland v Board of Education (1975) 49 AD2d 693, 370 NYS2d 761.

City of Syracuse was necessary party to action seeking reapportionment of county board of supervisors since city might seek to question the validity of county local law or city local law that might be required therein and a multiplicity of suits could thereby be avoided. Barzelay v Board of Supervisors (1965) 47 Misc 2d 1013, 263 NYS2d 854.

In an action pursuant to Article 15 of the Real Property Actions and Proceedings Law to determine plaintiffs' title to certain real property on the ground, inter alia, that a certain tax deed from the county treasurer to defendant was void as to said lot, since the county treasurer is the official who makes and delivers tax deeds, and the county enjoys certain monetary rights under the tax sale which may be jeopardized by the voiding of the sale, the county must be made a party to the proceeding. Costa v Harris (1966) 26 AD2d 933, 274 NYS2d 434.

Public officer whose conduct is to be controlled must be made a respondent and is an indispensable party to the proceeding. Brown v Lavine (1974) 78 Misc 2d 1085, 358 NYS2d 579.

City and deputy commissioner of city human resources administration, although not charged with wrongful acts, were necessary party defendants in action to restrain interference with administrative director of day-care center in that they were source of funds which allegedly motivated wrongful acts of other defendants. Davis v New York (1975) 49 AD2d 874, 373 NYS2d 189.

In action by private bus operators challenging school bus and charter transportation activities of suburban bus authority under contract with county, absence, as plaintiffs, of other private companies in county presented no bar to deciding rights of parties, and missing bus operators would not be barred from bringing their own suits by any adjudication in case. New York State School Bus Operators Asso. v County of Nassau (1974) 79 Misc 2d 352, 357 NYS2d 641, mod on other grounds 48 AD2d 671, 367 NYS2d 825, affd 39 NY2d 638, 385 NYS2d 263, 350 NE2d 593.

In an action by the Commissioners of the State Insurance Fund to recover the proceeds of a settlement reached by the insured and third parties in a negligence action, there was no necessity to make the insured a party by service of process, and the fact the insured disputed plaintiffs' lien and claimed all or part of the fund held by his attorney did not make him a necessary party. Commissioners of State Ins. Fund v Schell (1965) 23 AD2d 556, 256 NYS2d 638.

In an action for damages for mental suffering brought by a brother and a sister of a patient in a state mental hospital whose identity was confused by the hospital officials at the time of her death so that her relatives were not notified thereof and she was buried according to the rites of a religion other than that to which she belonged, another sister who did not join in the action would have been a proper party plaintiff under § 1002 but was not a necessary party under this section. Weingast v State (1964) 44 Misc 2d 824, 254 NYS2d 952.

State and town which might have interest in disputed land which was located between plaintiff's and defendant's properties were required to be joined in plaintiff's action to determine location of common boundary line since title to the land between the properties of plaintiff and defendant and the determination of a common boundary line could not be established without joinder of the city and state. Leach v Gary (1976) 54 AD2d 688, 387 NYS2d 276.

In action brought against board of education by teachers' association on behalf of certain terminated school nurse teachers and dental hygiene teachers, seeking reinstatement of the named teachers on grounds that "vertical" tenure constituted an unconstitutional classification and that the terminated teachers had greater seniority than certain other teachers in broader general academic area, those teachers of general academic subjects who would have been adversely affected if requested relief had been granted were "indispensable parties." Crystal v Board of Education (1976) 87 Misc 2d 632, 385 NYS2d 701.

Where district attorney brought Article 78 proceeding to compel correctional and parole authorities to recompute parole eligibility dates of four prisoners, prisoners should have been named as respondents. Vergari v Ward (1977) 88 Misc 2d 911, 390 NYS2d 390.

Joinder of successful bidders was not required in consolidated Article 78 proceedings on three petitions to enjoin the award of contracts to anyone other than petitioners, in light of fact that contracts had not been awarded to such bidders and that there was no question of fact as to their relative bidding status, and, thus, such bidders' interest, though affected by such proceedings, was not affected "inequitably." CPLR 1001, 7801 et seq. Spinney Hill Collision, Inc. v Caso (1977) 56 AD2d 655, 391 NYS2d 903.

4. —Actions involving husband and wife

In an action by the plaintiff husband to recover the down payment made for the purchase of a house pursuant to a contract signed by the husband and wife prior to their separation, the wife is a necessary party and the complaint filed only by the husband was dismissed without prejudice to the institution of a new action in which the separated wife should be joined either as a plaintiff with her consent, or as a defendant if she failed to consent. Mechta v Scaretta (1967) 52 Misc 2d 696, 276 NYS2d 652.

Where plaintiff's second husband sought a declaratory judgment to the effect that plaintiff's marriage to her third husband was void, the third husband was a necessary party, and the court could on its own motion raise the issue of his nonjoinder. Roe v Roe (1966) 49 Misc 2d 1070, 269 NYS2d 40.

In an action to recover arrearages in support payments, the infant is a party who should be joined, and in the absence of joinder plaintiff's complaint was dismissed without prejudice to a new proceeding to be brought pursuant to Domestic Relations Law § 244. Gage v Rentze (1969) 59 Misc 2d 334, 299 NYS2d 98.

Where the plaintiff sought to have a Mexican divorce declared invalid, a child born to her alleged husband and a woman he had married following the Mexican divorce was not a necessary party to the proceeding. Chittenden v Chittenden (1965) 46 Misc 2d 347, 259 NYS2d 738.

5. —Actions involving landlord and tenant

Where agreement, which covered only warehousing, storage and commercial moving, with union local had no bearing on lease agreement, union was not necessary party defendant in proceeding seeking preliminary injunction after named defendants allegedly prevented plaintiff from removing its goods from leased space. Mitsubishi International Corp. v Century Moving & Warehouse Co.-Franklin Fireproof Warehouse Corp. (1975) 50 AD2d 788, 377 NYS2d 510.

Where lessee consented to motion to join it as party plaintiff in lessor's action for damage to buildings and property allegedly caused by negligent performance by defendant of contract to repair roofs, appropriate statute under which to seek joinder would be that pertaining to permissive joinder, rather than that pertaining to necessary joinder. Northeastern Industrial Park, Inc. v James Ackroyd & Sons, Inc. (1976) 51 AD2d 614, 377 NYS2d 802.

Where lessee would seek recovery for damage arising out of same transaction as lessor, original plaintiff, who sought to recover for damage to buildings and personal property because of defendant's negligent performance of contract to repair roofs, permitting joinder of lessee as party plaintiff was not an abuse of discretion, in absence of showing that such joinder would preclude defendant from asserting statute of limitations as an alleged defense. Northeastern Industrial Park, Inc. v James Ackroyd & Sons, Inc. (1976) 51 AD2d 614, 377 NYS2d 802.

Any indemnification of sublessee promised by lessees should be tried in action other than lessor's action against lessees for rent or in a third-party action by lessees against sublessee. John Malasky, Inc. v Mayone (1976) 54 AD2d 1059, 388 NYS2d 943.

6. Dismissal

Under CPLR it is proper practice to move to dismiss for nonjoinder of indispensable parties, without first moving for their joinder. Challette, Inc. v Brookhaven (1964) 43 Misc 2d 264, 250 NYS2d 165.

Motion to dismiss stockholder's derivative action involving nonresident beneficiary corporation would be held in abeyance pending determination as to whether there was jurisdiction of nonresident corporation and whether action could proceed in absence of corporation; former requirement of motion to add corporation as indispensable party is no longer prerequisite to motion to dismiss under this section. Blumenthal v Allen (1965) 46 Misc 2d 688, 260 NYS2d 363.

In action to declare zoning law invalid brought by owner of less than 10% of property affected, failure to join all owners who might be affected by result, in the absence of prejudice to defendant, does not warrant dismissal for nonjoinder. Challette, Inc. v Brookhaven (1964) 43 Misc 2d 264, 250 NYS2d 165.

Proceeding wherein petitioner sought, inter alia, a

grant of "emergency assistance" and declaration of invalidity of six-month recoupment provision contained in applicable regulation was improperly dismissed as against State Commissioner, where validity of one of his regulations was in issue. Dunn v Bates (1975) 50 AD2d 561, 374 NYS2d 677, motion den, in part, motion gr, in part 38 NY2d 1023, 384 NYS2d 449, 348 NE2d 925 and motion den 39 NY2d 1011, 387 NYS2d 244, 355 NE2d 298.

Since it was apparent that the New York State Tax Commission would not be prejudiced if not joined as a party to suit by an executor to construe decedent's will to correct alleged inadvertent error relating to the funding of marital deduction and residuary trust established, but Commission's joinder could be prejudicial since United States government declined to accept New York court's determination, Commission was neither a necessary or indispensible party and its motion to be dismissed as a party was granted. Will of Leddy (1975) 84 Misc 2d 264, 375 NYS2d 998.

Motion to dismiss for failure to join necessary parties was properly denied where none of the parties defendant sought to have joined was necessary for complete relief to be accorded between the persons who were parties to the action, nor would any be inequitably affected by a judgment in the action. Flanagan v Board of Education (1977) 56 AD2d 574, 391 NYS2d 180.

7. Excusing nonjoinder and continuing with action

The plaintiff was directed to serve the prior owner of premises as a defendant in an action to foreclose a mechanic's lien, where the owner at the time notice of the lien was filed had not been named as a party in the action instituted to foreclose the lien against a subsequent owner of the property, with a direction that if the prior owner were unavailable for process or not subject to the jurisdiction of the court, plaintiff could move for leave to continue the action without joinder. Admiral Transit Mix Corp v Sagg-Bridgehampton Corp. (1968) 56 Misc 2d 47, 287 NYS2d 751.

Failure to join state comptroller in Article 78 proceeding against civil service commission by discharged attorney seeking reinstatement to former position with department of audit and control would be excused so as not to require dismissal of petition where interests of the comptroller would be protected by the civil service commission, any possible prejudice to comptroller could be avoided by his intervention in the proceeding, and an effective order could be rendered in his absence. Greaney v Poston (1975) 50 AD2d 653, 374 NYS2d 815.

Although board of education ought to have been joined as a party to Article 78 proceeding brought by discharged tenured English teacher following affirmance of board's decision by Commissioner of Education the board was not indispensable party and failure to joint it would be excused in the interest of justice since if proceeding were terminated for failure to join the board, which was not served within the four-month statutory limitations, petitioner would have no other effective remedy and no apparent prejudice would result to the board since its interest would be adequately protected by the Commissioner. Sandor v Nyquist (1974) 45 AD2d 122, 356 NYS2d 703.

Failure to join state comptroller as a party in Article 78 proceeding against the civil service commission by discharged attorney seeking reinstatement to former position with the Department of Audit and Control would be excused so as not to require dismissal of petition in that interests of the comptroller would be protected by the Commission, any possible prejudice to comptroller could be avoided by his intervention in the proceeding and an effective order could be rendered in absence of the comptroller. Greaney v Poston (1975) 50 AD2d 653, 374 NYS2d 815.

CASE NOTES

UNDER FORMER CIVIL PRACTICE LAWS

A. IN GENERAL

1. Generally

CPA § 193-a (§§ 1007, 1008, 1011, 1020, 3012(a), Rule 4111(c) herein) warranted opinion that real party in interest need not rely on CPA § 194. Schwartz v Klein (1947) 188 Misc 665, 72 NYS2d 386.

The test of the unity in interest is that joint connection with, or relation to, the subject matter which, by the established practice of the common-law courts, will preclude a separate action. Jones v Felch, 16 Super Ct (3 Bosw) 63.

Parties in the larger legal sense are all persons having a right to control a proceeding, to make defense, to adduce and cross-examine witnesses and to appeal from a decision if an appeal lies. Knickerbocker Trust Co. v Tarrytown, W. P. & M. R. Co. (1910) 139 AD 305, 123 NYS 954.

A person does not become a party to an action by the mere naming of him in the title of the action. Bennett v Bird (1933) 237 AD 542, 261 NYS 540.

Impleading defendant is an adverse party, and not a plaintiff. O'Connor v Byrndun Corp. (1943) 182 Misc 952, 47 NYS2d 51.

Corespondent in divorce action is not specifically named in summons either as party plaintiff or defendant. Simons v Simons (1943) 182 Misc 860, 49 NYS2d 929.

A town must sue and be sued by its name, except where its officers are specially authorized by law to sue in their name of office for its benefit. Duanesburgh v Jenkins, 46 Barb 294.

The Seneca Indians may sue and be sued by that name. Seneca Nation of Indians v Tyler, 14 How Pr 109.

2. Application

CPA § 194 did not apply to parties without the State who could not have been served or effectually brought into the action. Keene v Chambers (1936) 271 NY 326, 3 NE2d 443.

3. Failure to join

Where an unincorporated association is made defendant without joining the individual members there is no party before the court capable of being sued. Andrews v Local Union, J. P. G. S. & S. F. (1929) 133 Misc 899, 234 NYS 208.

B. PROCEDURE

4. Generally

The act does not require that a party, who should be a plaintiff, must be asked to become such before being joined as defendant. Wallach v Dryfoos (1910) 140 AD 438, 125 NYS 305.

5. Joinder as plaintiff or defendant

Where it was the duty of a corporation to bring an action against directors for misappropriation, and on its failure so to do, the action was brought by a stockholder for the benefit of himself and others similarly situated, under CPA § 195, the corporation should have been joined as party defendant, in view of CPA § 194. Security Trust Co. v Pritchard (1922) 201 AD 142, 194 NYS 486.

Where plaintiff and president of defendant corporation formed partnership and sold gasoline to defendant corporation, plaintiff was not required to ask his partner to join as plaintiff but could join him as defendant. Hofer v H. E. Swezey & Son (1950, Sup) 98 NYS2d 145.

Maker of note is not necessary party to action by assignee of accommodation indorser against defendant payee of notes for whom plaintiff assignor indorsed said notes. Vetri v Johnston (1952, Sup) 112 NYS2d 822.

Where an action of ejectment is brought to recover possession of land upon a breach of a condition subsequent, all the original grantees or their heirs must join. One of the former tenants in common cannot maintain an action to recover his undivided interest therein. Cook v Wardens & Vestry of St. Paul's Church (1875) 5 Hun 293, affd 67 NY 594.

In wife's action to enforce oral agreement by her father-in-law to convey house to her and her husband when they renovated it, she was ordered to join husband as coplaintiff or defendant, despite pending action by her for separation. Rougas v Rougas (1948, Sup) 86 NYS2d 484.

Persons might be joined as parties defendant only in compliance with CPA § 194 and pleadings were required to allege their interest as plaintiffs and their failure to consent to join as such. Edwards Hotel, Inc. v Surrey Holding Corp. (1955, Sup) 145 NYS2d 653.

In action for brokers' commissions plaintiff may join cobroker as defendant and demand judgment in favor of plaintiff and defendant cobroker, as involuntary plaintiff. Lane v Smith (1955, DC NY) 136 F Supp 905.

The brothers and sister of a husband who are all signatories to an agreement to support his wife, which agreement does not indicate an intention that liability be joint and several, are joint obligors united in interest and must be joined as parties defendant with the husband in the wife's action on the agreement. Indursky v Indursky (1958) 7 AD2d 709, 180 NYS2d 61.

6. —Hostile coplaintiff

If any one refuses to join as plaintiff, he may be made a defendant. Hasbrouck v Bunce (1875) 62 NY 475; and see De Puy v Strong (1867) 37 NY 372.

In an action by a mortgagor to recover upon a fire insurance policy, the mortgagee to whom the loss is payable to the extent of his interest is a necessary party, and if such mortgagee refuses to join as a plaintiff he may be made a party defendant. Lewis v Guardian Fire & Life Assur. Co. (1905) 181 NY 392, 74 NE 224.

CPA § 194 did not require joinder of hostile partner as coplaintiff where he is joined as defendant. Hofer v H. E. Swezey & Son (1950, Sup) 98 NYS2d 145.

Coexecutrix, characterized by other executrix as hostile to success of action, should be made defendant. Prygocki v Prydatko (1951, Sup) 105 NYS2d 205.

7. Bill of particulars

Defendant, impleaded as such by plaintiff because he refused to join as plaintiff, may demand bill of particulars within limits of his liability. Cohen v City Bank Farmers Trust Co. (1946, Sup) 65 NYS2d 841.

C. PARTICULAR ACTIONS AND PARTIES

8. Accounting

In an action to compel an accounting, all persons interested in obtaining the account must be made parties. Petrie v Petrie, 7 Lans 90.

9. Annulment of marriage

Father could sue to annul daughter's marriage under CPA § 1139 (Dom. Rel. Law 140(e) herein) but he was required to join her as party plaintiff or defendant. Feldman v Intrator (1941) 175 Misc 632, 24 NYS2d 665.

10. Assignors and assignees

An assignee for the benefit of creditors is not a necessary party to an action to enforce a lien on funds in his hands. Wells v Knox (1889) 55 Hun 245, 8 NYS 58.

Where plaintiffs sue as assignees of the original obligee it is error to award a judgment in favor of one of the assignees, who, refusing to join in the suit, was made defendant, but demanded no affirmative relief from his codefendant, and when the respective interests of the assignees were not shown. Blewett v Hoyt (1907) 118 AD 227, 103 NYS 451.

Where assignor retained interest in contract, assignee suing thereon should have joined in as a party. Natter v Isaac H. Blanchard Co. (1912) 153 AD 814, 138 NYS 969.

Where assignor and assignee both had interest in contract, assignee should have joined assignor as a party when suing on the contract. Natter v Isaac H. Blanchard Co. supra.

A partial assignee may sue at law, and in such legal action can bring in all proper and necessary parties. Grosner v Abramson (1937) 162 Misc 731, 295 NYS 372.

Owner of undivided interest in bond and mortgage may sue in equity as partial assignee by joining owner of remaining interest in mortgage as party defendant. Frank v Jaffa (1943) 181 Misc 517, 41 NYS2d 104.

As result of assimilation of law practice to equity procedure, suit for money only by partial assignee of claim may be brought at law, provided plaintiff bring in his coassignees. Blake v Weiden (1943) 291 NY 134, 51 NE2d 677, 149 ALR 1050.

A plaintiff assignor of a partial assignment of a mortgage is not required in joining assignees of the partial interest in the mortgage as defendants to show that consent to sue as plaintiffs was refused where the assignment provided that the plaintiff should have the sole and exclusive right of foreclosure. New York Lien Corp. v Huntcamp Bldg. Corp. (1957) 9 Misc 2d 798, 168 NYS2d 63.

11. Corporation

In an action against officers of a corporation for misappropriation by one or more of the directors, the corporation is a necessary party defendant, but creditors and persons entitled to sue under Gen Corp Law § 90 are not necessary parties. Miller v Barlow (1903) 78 AD 331, 79 NYS 964.

In an action against the president of a new corporation which took over the stock and assets of an old corporation for stock alleged to be held in trust for the plaintiff, a stockholder in the old corporation, it was held that the new corporation was a necessary party and that the other stockholders were also necessary parties as the plaintiff had sued individually and not on behalf of himself and other stockholders. Knickerbocker v Conger (1905) 110 AD 125, 97 NYS 127.

Fact that corporate stock is largely held by plaintiff stockholders does not constitute the stockholders rather than the corporation the proper party to sue for misconduct by corporate officers. Brock v Poor (1915) 216 NY 387, 111 NE 229.

In a stockholder's derivative action, it is not necessary to join a defunct corporation. Schaler v Feder (1959) 16 Misc 2d 668, 184 NYS2d 933.

12. —Creditors

An action to charge a trustee assenting to a company's contracting debts in excess of its capital stock, under Laws 1848, ch 40, § 23, can only be brought by all the creditors jointly, or by one creditor in behalf of himself and all the other creditors of the company. Anderson v Speers (1880) 21 Hun 568.

13. Executors and administrators

In an action by the executrix to construe a will as to her rights under it, a coexecutor although having no pecuniary interest in the litigation is

"united in interest" with plaintiff in the subject of the action within the meaning of this section and must be made a party to the action. Benner v Benner (1890, Sup) 12 NYS 472.

14. Insurance

In an action by a mortgagor to recover upon a fire insurance policy, the mortgagee to whom the loss is payable, to the extent of his interest, is a necessary party and if such mortgagee refuses to join as a plaintiff, he may be made a party defendant. Lewis v Guardian Fire & Life Assur. Co. (1905) 181 NY 392, 74 NE 224.

15. Joint promisees

Where the interests of two or more promisees are several, several actions may be maintained by them, although the language of the promise is joint. Emmeluth v Home Ben. Ass'n (1890) 122 NY 130, 25 NE 234.

16. Labor dispute

Fair Labor Standards Act permits representative action to be brought by properly designated agent or representative, but such action cannot be continued in so far as it affects employees who do not consent thereto. Thomas v Keystone Silver, Inc. (1940) 174 Misc 733, 22 NYS2d 796.

17. Legatees and next of kin

The general rule is that one legatee may sue alone for his legacy, but if the fund will not suffice to pay all legatees interested, they should all be made parties by an action in the names of all, or by one for all. Towner v Tooley, 38 Barb 598; and see McKenzie v L'Amoureux, 11 Barb 516.

18. Mortgage foreclosure

One or two trustees under a mortgage executed by a railroad company to secure its bonds may sue alone to foreclose the mortgage, making his cotrustee a party defendant, without alleging that he requested the cotrustee to join as plaintiff, where the complaint states that the cotrustee is a director of the defendant, mortgagor. Cumming v Middleton, U. & W. G. R. Co. (1911) 147 AD 105, 131 NYS 710.

In foreclosure action all parties interested in ownership of lien to be foreclosed must be joined either as plaintiffs or as defendants. 418 Trading Corp. v Moon Realty Corp. (1955) 285 AD 444, 931, 137 NYS2d 513.

Surveyors whose lien was prior to the execution of the mortgage were not necessary parties to the mortgage foreclosure action. Sayville Federal Sav. & Loan Asso. v Schons (1958) 17 Misc 2d 54, 183 NYS2d 106.

19. Negotiable instrument

There is a defect of parties in an action on a promissory note made by the defendant and a third person, not made a defendant, where only a joint liability is alleged; nor can it be asserted on demurrer that the form of the note created a joint and several liability against the makers of the note, if the note is not set forth in the complaint. Trusts & Guarantee Co. v Sawyer (1911) 146 AD 63, 130 NYS 582.

Bank as pledgee of collateral and holder of draft substituted for collateral may sue in its own name to collect the proceeds of the draft, holding any surplus in trust for payees, and latter are not necessary parties. Trade Bank & Trust Co. v Equitable Fire & Marine Ins. Co. (1945, Sup App T) 56 NYS2d 495.

20. Partner

Where a member of a firm refuses to join with the other members as plaintiffs in an action brought by the firm, he may be made a defendant, and his right to become a plaintiff is lost by his own misconduct. Schnaier v Schmidt (1891, Sup) 13 NYS 728, affd 128 NY 683, 29 NE 149.

An action against a copartner for conversion does not lie in the name of an individual partner although he joins his copartner as defendant, under this section in the absence of any allegation showing why the copartner was joined as defendant rather than plaintiff, and it is not shown that his consent to act as plaintiff could not be obtained. Baron v Lakow (1907) 121 AD 544, 106 NYS 243.

Where a partnership has been dissolved and an account, stated between the two partners, shows one of them to be the creditor of the other, the creditor partner, on paying an outstanding firm debt, will be entitled in equity to be subrogated to the firm creditor's rights in mortgages which the debtor partner gave him to secure the firm debt; parties, to whom the firm creditor has since conveyed the equity of redemption, need not and should not be made defendants in the action. Schuyler v Booth (1902) 37 Misc 35, 74 NYS 733, affd 76 AD 619, 79 NYS 1146.

21. Sealed instrument

No person can sue to enforce the covenants of an instrument under seal, except those named as parties and those who signed and sealed the same; where the party of the first part consists of several persons, no one of them may maintain an action in his individual capacity without joining the others. Porter v Baldwin (1910) 139 AD 278, 123 NYS 1043.

22. Trusts

It seems that where there is a pressing need to enforce a lien for the benefit of the trust, one of several trustees, as sole plaintiff, may bring an action for that purpose, when his associates will not join; in which case they may be made defendants. Bockes v Hathorn (1879) 78 NY 222.

The principle of courts of equity that in cases of breach of trust, where no general rule or order of the court interferes, and where the facts call for a contribution or recovery over all persons who should be before the court to enable it to make complete and final judgment, is not abrogated by the Code. Sherman v Parish (1873) 53 NY 483.

In case a trust fund is misappropriated, the beneficiary may prosecute an action for the vindication of the trust for the trustee, in case the latter refused to sue, but cannot sue the trustee for recovery of the property of the trust estate until after the expiration of the trust, unless the trustee is shown to be a participant in the dealings by which the trust estate had been depleted. Copper v Weston (1888, Sup) 1 NYS 601; and see King v Barnes (1888) 109 NY 267, 16 NE 332.

In action to impress constructive trust on realty owned by defendant who agreed to convey same to plaintiff daughter-in-law on completion of dwelling thereon paid for by plaintiff, defendant's son, plaintiff's husband, was not necessary party. Petrukevich v Maksimovich (1955) 140 NYS2d 318, mod on other grounds 1 AD2d 786, 147 NYS2d 869.

In beneficiaries' action to enforce trust, settlor was conditionally necessary party and was ordered to be joined as defendant. Rothenberg v Wolfman (1958) 16 Misc 2d 124, 183 NYS2d 139.

When the interest of the issues under the trust is adverse to that of the ancestor, the issue is a necessary party to a proceeding involving the trust. Re Lachlan's Trust (1959) 24 Misc 2d 323, 193 NYS2d 408.

23. —Reformation and revocation of trust

In an action to reform and revoke a deed of trust, the beneficiaries are necessary parties. Conkling v Davies, 53 How Pr 409.

D. JUDGMENT IN ACTION AGAINST DEFENDANTS SEVERALLY LIABLE

24. Generally

CPA § 475 did not apply to defendants whose liability was joint. Oneida County Bank v Lewis (1898) 23 Misc 34, 51 NYS 826, affd 35 AD 631, 55 NYS 1144.

Under CPA § 475 where cause of action stated in complaint necessarily called for an adjudication upon the rights of defendant not properly before the court, case could not be tried, and complaint could only be dismissed upon motion for delay in prosecution. Simon v Gibralter Const. Co. (1917) 179 AD 273, 166 NYS 466.

CPA § 475 applied in the federal district court in an action on a bail bond where the liability was joint and several and all of the defendants were not in court. United States v Giacolone (1929, DC NY) 36 F2d 252.

25. Severance

Under CPA § 475 severance and continuance could be had in actions where defendants were severally liable. See Chippewa Credit Corp. v Strozewski (1940) 259 AD 187, 19 NYS2d 457.

Form of order of severance. Weston v Citizens' Nat. Bank (1903) 88 AD 330, 84 NYS 743.

Failure to sever action. Donner v White (1933) 149 Misc 709, 268 NYS 56.

26. Appeal

Where a plaintiff had brought an action against a corporation and its president, who had been conducting an individual business, jointly for labor and services rendered both, he could not on appeal invoke the provisions of CPA § 475 in relation to actions severally liable, where he had failed to make an election under said section on the suggestion of the court below. Stein v Woodward Pub. Co. (1904) 45 Misc 613, 91 NYS 17.

A reversal as to one defendant in an action for personal injuries brought against three defendants did not necessitate a reversal as to all where the acts of negligence with which each defendant was charged, while contributing to the injury, were separate and distinct. Draper v Interborough Rapid Transit Co. (1908) 124 AD 357, 108 NYS 691.

Under CPA § 475 a person who had principally advised and directed the transaction, although not a grantee, was a proper party defendant in an action to set aside a deed as procured by fraud, and was chargeable with the costs. Pritchard v Palmer (1895) 88 Hun 412, 34 NYS 787.

In an action against three persons, as partners, one not being served with the summons, nor appearing, the plaintiff was entitled to judgment against the other two upon evidence that they alone constituted the partnership. Pruyn v Black (1860) 21 NY 300.

Under CPA § 475 where a partner had not been served in an action against his firm, and no individual judgment had been entered against him, he was not entitled to a cancellation of the judgment on his discharge in bankruptcy, where there was no adjudication in that proceeding as to the partnership debt. Re Gruber (1908) 129 AD 297, 113 NYS 923.

27. Particular causes

Under CPA § 475 where a plaintiff in a negligence action had a right to sue either or both of two defendants and to hold them either severally or jointly liable he could at any time, by leave of court, discontinue the action as to any or all of such defendants as he might elect. Bohnhoff v Fischer (1911) 147 AD 672, 132 NYS 603.

Proceeding by attorney seeking to fix lien for services rendered to labor union client was maintainable under CPA § 475 where attorney charged that client and labor union officials had conspired to deprive him of his fee by discontinuing client's action against union. Application of Dimin (1943, Sup) 41 NYS2d 797.

Parties to an action by the creditor of an insolvent corporation, whose debt was created in 1900, to enforce in an action at law commenced in 1902, the joint and several liability of the holders of stock not paid in full, conferred by the Stock Corporation Law, chap 688 of 1892. Lang v Lutz (1905) 180 NY 254, 73 NE 24.

E. DECISIONS UNDER FORMER CPA § 193 SUBSEQUENT TO SEPT. 1, 1946, AND PRIOR TO SEPT. 1, 1963

28. Generally

Purpose of CPA § 193 was to liberalize third-party practice and to remove rigid requirements theretofore existing in connection with practice of impleading. J. A. Ewing & McDonald, Inc. v Municipal Warehouse Co. (1948) 193 Misc 173, 81 NYS2d 559.

One of the reasons for the enactment of CPA § 193 was to eliminate confusion which had previously existed in reference of decisions to joinder of parties as "necessary" without establishing whether such parties were, in fact, "indispensable" to the conduct of the litigation or whether they were "conditionally necessary" in the sense that their participation was desirable if complete relief was to be accorded between those already parties. Impellizzeri v Impellizzeri (1954, Sup) 133 NYS2d 44.

CPA § 193-a (§§ 1007, 1008, 3012(a) herein) warranted opinion that real party in interest did not need to rely on CPA § 193. Schwartz v Klein (1947) 188 Misc 665, 72 NYS2d 386.

CPA § 264 was identical with CPA § 193 subd 2, in respect of right of indemnification. Tangney v Skapof (1948, Sup) 81 NYS2d 831.

Notice of appeal may not restrict review by stating limitation as to matters or parties, since all parties to proceeding in surrogate's court to construe will are parties to appeal from appellate division. Re Burk's Will (1949) 298 NY 450, 84 NE2d 631.

CPA § 193 did not alter rule that complaint must allege present, immediate and existing right to relief. Sherman Plastering Corp. v R. & R. Co. (1953) 281 AD 293, 121 NYS2d 69.

Purpose and effect of CPA § 193 was to render inapplicable common-law rule under which plaintiff was privileged to select his opponents and control action. Harrison v Mary Bain Estates, Inc. (1956) 2 Misc 2d 52, 152 NY2d 239, aff'd 2 AD2d 670, 153 NYS2d 552.

Unless absentees came within statutory definitions of CPA § 193, plaintiff was entitled to proceed upon his theory of action and defendant was properly required to avail himself of other remedies. China Sugar Refining Co. v Andersen, Meyer & Co. (1956) 6 Misc 2d 184, 152 NYS2d 507.

Where a complaint asserted no claim against a defendant sought to be joined such party was neither an indispensable nor conditionally necessary party and CPA § 193 did not prohibit a party maintaining a tort action from electing to proceed against any of those he claimed to be liable whether or not others might also have been liable. Hall v Wood (1958) 11 Misc 2d 805, 174 NYS2d 16.

Since under Civil Practice Act, Section 192, no action would have been defeated by nonjoinder or misjoinder of parties except as provided in CPA § 193, it followed that if the cause of action as pleaded was otherwise sufficient, the mere fact that one or more of the plaintiffs was not entitled to the relief sought would not be a ground for dismissal. Majestic Loose Leaf, Inc. v Cannizzaro (1957) 10 Misc 2d 1040, 169 NYS2d 566.

Objection as to nonjoinder of parties may be raised only by motion to add parties; it cannot be pleaded as an affirmative defense. Bleakney v Schrauff (1959) 18 Misc 2d 919, 186 NYS2d 412.

29. Bringing in additional party

To warrant impleading third party, causes of action must be same or, at least, be based on same grounds, though arising out of different relationships. Schutrum v Horton (1946) 188 Misc 13, 67 NYS2d 6.

Contingent claim against party may not be pleaded. Atlantic Gulf & West Indies S.S. Lines v New York (1947) 271 AD 1008, 69 NYS2d 796.

Coexecutrix, characterized by other executrix as hostile to success of action, may be dropped as plaintiff and brought in as defendant. Prygocki v Prydatko (1951, Sup) 105 NYS2d 205.

Where the original action for negligence was brought within the statutory period, the third party complaint may be served although more than three years after the occurrence of the action; and the third party defendant cannot interpose a defense to the statute of limitations since it would not be available to the third party plaintiff. Giudice v New York (1954, Sup) 128 NYS2d 890.

Where defendant moves to compel plaintiff to bring in an indispensable party the fact that the party sought to be brought in is a nonresident does not preclude the granting of the motion. Presberg v Presberg (1954) 205 Misc 653, 128 NYS2d 612.

An agent who acts for an undisclosed principal in making a contract in his own name is liable on that contract and should be made a party defendant in an action based thereon. Consequently the plaintiff should be given a definite time within which to join such agent in an action for breach of the contract question. Western Woodworking Co. v Kaskel (1954, Sup) 133 NYS2d 632.

Where action for declaratory judgment brought to determine legitimacy of child and child mentioned in papers had not been served nor had a guardian ad litem been appointed, any objection defendants had in relation to nonjoinder of necessary or indispensable parties had to be the subject initially of a motion to add parties pursuant to former RCP 102 (Rule 3024(a) herein) and could not be raised by a motion to dismiss the complaint since CPA § 192 (§§ 401, 1003 herein) expressly prohibited defeat because of nonjoinder or misjoinder except as provided in subdivision 2 of former CPA § 193. Hines v Hines (1957) 12 Misc 2d 486, 169 NYS2d 1003.

Where the parties sought to be joined are not indispensable parties since the issues as constituted will permit complete relief between the present parties and will not inequitably affect the interest of any other party motion denied. Hall v Wood (1958) 11 Misc 2d 805, 174 NYS2d 16.

Where third-party complaint makes no specific request for judgment but merely attempts to bring in an additional defendant whom plaintiff had not elected to sue, it is insufficient. L. Luria & Son, Inc. v Brown (1960) 26 Misc 2d 718, 210 NYS2d 58.

Tenants are necessary parties to an Article 78 proceeding in the nature of prohibition to direct Municipal Court justice to vacate stay of execution of warrant of eviction. Rycard Realty Corp. v Rosenberg (1961) 28 Misc 2d 594, 212 NYS2d 198.

30. —Who are indispensable

In action to determine adverse claim to realty, where complaint alleges that plaintiff is in possession of premises, it is unnecessary to make grantor party defendant. Croft v Richards (1953, Sup) 123 NYS2d 792.

Successive owners of buildings are not indispensable to action for rental of shoring material on theory that they assumed defendant's liability for such rental. Heydt-Mugler Co. v Westerman Const. Corp. (1947) 188 Misc 546, 68 NYS2d 361, adhered to 189 Misc 199, 71 NYS2d 385, affd 190 Misc 990, 77 NYS2d 356.

President and stockholder were indispensable parties to action for specific performance of sales agreement whereby seller's president and controlling stockholder covenanted not to engage in competing business. Reo Stores, Inc. v Kent Stores, Inc (1953, Sup) 119 NYS2d 296, affd 283 AD 1086, 131 NYS2d 910, app den 284 AD 851, 134 NYS2d 275.

Where action for insurance proceeds was purely in personam to collect debt in which foreign government had no interest, such government was not necessary or proper party. Federal Motorship Corp. v Johnson & Higgins (1948) 192 Misc 401, 77 NYS2d 52, affd 274 AD 1034, 85 NYS2d 915, affd 274 AD 1034, 85 NYS2d 916, vacated 275 AD 660, 86 NYS2d 667.

In action to direct conveyance of property in accord with express parol trust, where complaint alleged that grandmother of plaintiffs and mother of individual defendants received property under agreement, personal representatives of estates of promisor and of mothers of plaintiffs were not indispensable parties. Goldstein v Brockstein (1953) 281 AD 762, 118 NYS2d 280.

In action by wife to enforce oral agreement of father-in-law to convey house to her and her husband when they renovated it, husband was indispensable party plaintiff or defendant, despite pending action for separation by wife against husband. Rougas v Rougas (1948, Sup) 86 NYS2d 484.

Surviving spouse is neither indispensable nor conditionally necessary party to discovery proceeding under SCA § 205 where value of property discoverable exceeds statutory value of exempt property. Re Korowitz's Estate (1953, Sur) 120 NYS2d 498.

In an action by wife to declare husband's divorce from her invalid and his subsequent marriage void, the person claiming to be the second wife is a necessary and "indispensable" party without whose presence a complete adjudication cannot be had. Impellizzeri v Impellizzeri (1954, Sup) 133 NYS2d 44.

In a wife's action to declare her husband's divorce from her invalid, and his subsequent marriage to another void, the infant son of the husband and of the wife by the second marriage is neither a necessary, a "conditionally necessary" nor an "indispensable" party, and should not be brought into the action. Impellizzeri v Impellizzeri, supra.

The state was only conditionally necessary party to action by river regulating district, state agency, to declare right to condemn land to construct reservoir. Black River Regulating Dist. v Adirondack League Club (1953) 282 AD 161, 121 NYS2d 893, revd on other grounds 307 NY 475, 121 NE2d 428.

Where state comptroller and members of state civil service commission will be required to perform certain acts if mandamus petition is granted, such officials are both proper and necessary parties. Leeman v O'Connell (1952, Sup) 115 NYS2d 163.

Equity will not consider party to be indispensable where its only function is to perform a ministerial act. Rabinowitz v Kaiser-Frazer Corp. (1952, Sup) 111 NYS2d 539.

Tenant is necessary party to summary proceeding to dispossess subtenant. Stephen Estates, Inc. v Kaplan (1950) 198 Misc 948, 100 NYS2d 455.

Maker of note is not necessary party to action by assignee of accommodation indorser against defendant payee of notes for whom plaintiff's assignor indorsed said notes. Vetri v Johnston (1952, Sup) 112 NYS2d 822.

Where each of three brokers claims commission for selling realty and one broker sues second broker, third broker should be added as party. Cohen v Douglas L. Elliman & Co. (1951) 279 AD 161, 108 NYS2d 386.

All persons who may be affected by declaratory judgment should be joined as parties to action therefor. Central Westchester Humane Soc. v Hilleboe (1952) 202 Misc 873, 115 NYS2d 769.

Guiding principle in determining indispensability is whether absentees have such interest in subject matter before court that their interests must necessarily be passed on if controversy is settled, or whether determination in their absence will nevertheless have element of finality for protection of those before court. China Sugar Refining Co. v Andersen, Meyer & Co. (1956) 6 Misc 2d 184, 152 NYS2d 507.

Test of indispensability is such legal unity of interest or joint connection with relation to subject matter that separate action involving less than all such persons should be precluded. China Sugar Refining Co. v Andersen, Meyer & Co., supra.

Persons to whom or against whom cause of action has accrued jointly, or parties jointly interested in fund, are indispensable parties. China S. R. Co. v Andersen, M. & Co., supra.

Party complaining of nonjoinder must initially move for addition of such parties and only if order directing joinder of missing party is made and such party is not joined within time therein specified, may motion to dismiss complaint be made. Marsico v Tramutolo (1954, Sup) 135 NYS2d 258.

In action for accounting as to partnership affairs, all partners must be made parties and personal representatives of any deceased partner. Gardiner v Hyde (1955, Sup) 144 NYS2d 426.

In action by lessor against lessee under television rental agreement requiring latter to purchase hotel installations at stipulated price and to obtain written assumption of rental agreement if hotel be sold, plaintiff need not join transferee as party, since defendant may have recourse against transferee in independent action. Tel-Hotel Corp. v Windsor Park Hotel Corp. (1955, Sup) 143 NYS2d 24.

In stockholder's derivative action for issuance of certificate of stock of corporation whose wholly owned subsidiary owned 50% of its stock, both of which had been dissolved, both corporations were indispensable parties to such action for issuance of stock certificate to plaintiff for 7% of stock of original corporation. Charlop v Cohen (1955) 4 Misc 2d 1015, 147 NYS2d 348.

In action by taxpayer to restrain village trustees from taking steps to consummate contract to sell land for park purposes, contract purchaser was indispensable party, and where he was not joined as party, mistrial was directed. O'Shea v Hanse (1955) 3 Misc 2d 307, 147 NYS2d 792.

Where defendant is sued as trustee, pleadings may be amended to strike out words "as trustee" and action permitted to proceed against defendant individually, in action for personal injuries to plaintiff when he fell down stairs. Martin v Talcott (1955) 1 AD2d 679, 146 NYS2d 784.

Where action brought for declaratory judgment to declare void marriage between defendant husband and another woman, the joining of such woman as a co-defendant as a party defendant is necessary in order to properly determine and declare the rights of the parties as no efficacious declaratory judgment could be rendered in her absence. Johnson v Johnson (1956, Sup) 157 NYS2d 328.

In an action for a judgment declaring that a foreign divorce which defendant husband procured is invalid, the woman whom the defendant husband subsequently married is an indispensable party and it is immaterial that neither party to the action moved to join such indispensable party and such defect is not waived by such failure and the action will be dismissed without prejudice and dismissal will be ordered even where the indispensable defendant is a nonresident. Lauricella v Lauricella (1957) 13 Misc 2d 799, 178 NYS2d 559.

Where action brought against union and facts showed that union not named as party whose internal affairs were the matter in controversy, such union should be party to the litigation and in the absence of such union, local adjudication could not bind or prevent such local from relitigating the same controversy and such locals are viewed as indispensable parties. Crawford v Newman (1958)

11 Misc 2d 322, 174 NYS2d 667, affd 5 AD2d 859, 174 NYS2d 881.

A defendant sued as an individual should be added as a party defendant in his capacity as president of a trade union local where rights of such local were involved and could not properly be adjudicated unless it was made a party and permitted to answer. Crawford v Ehrlich (1958) 11 Misc 2d 328, 172 NYS2d 2.

Where the absence of proposed defendants as parties to litigation will in no way prevent the effective determination of controversies between present plaintiffs and present defendants, such defendants are not indispensable or conditionally-necessary parties. Robinson v Glens Falls Ins. Co. (1957) 9 Misc 2d 841, 168 NYS2d 161.

The brothers and sister of a husband who are all signatories to an agreement to support his wife, which agreement does not indicate an intention that liability be joint and several, are joint obligors united in interest and must be joined as parties defendant with the husband in the wife's action on the agreement. Indursky v Indursky (1958) 7 AD2d 709, 180 NYS2d 61.

In action on promissory note, where defendant trustees, who as stakeholders had deposited moneys representing income of trust for benefit of codefendant equivalent to the amount claimed by plaintiff under an assignment of trust income, opposed plaintiff's motion for summary judgment on the ground that a judgment creditor and an attachment creditor, whose claims might be entitled to priority over plaintiff's were indispensable parties and had not been joined in the action, it was held that since these creditors had no legal unity of interest or joint connection with subject matter of the litigation they were not indispensable parties and their omission did not preclude summary judgment for plaintiff. Preiss v Bourne (1960) 24 Misc 2d 55, 203 NYS2d 124.

Joint tortfeasor is not an indispensable party. Siskind v Levy (1961) 13 AD2d 538, 213 NYS2d 379.

Co-adventurers with plaintiff and defendant in joint venture were indispensable parties to plaintiff's action to impress trust on secret profits allegedly acquired by defendant in breach of his duty under joint venture. Henshel v Held (1961) 13 AD2d 771, 216 NYS2d 41.

Doctor who has been given lien in fixed amount is not an indispensable party to patient's personal injury action. Kellogg v Michaels (1961) 31 Misc 2d 156, 219 NYS2d 913.

31. —Who are conditionally necessary

Where complaint charged that defendant acted as attorney in fact for his brother and sister in wrongfully depriving plaintiff or broker's commissions, they should be added as parties defendant. Malcolm E. Smith, Inc. v Zabriskie (1948, Sup) 84 NYS2d 362.

In action by stockholder to compel corporation to declare dividend, director is proper defendant. Davidoff v Seidenberg (1949) 275 AD 784, 88 NYS2d 5.

Proper parties are not for that reason conditionally necessary, where new parties would not aid complete relief between those already parties. Heydt-Mugler Co. v Westerman Const. Corp. (1947) 189 Misc 199, 71 NYS2d 385, affd 190 Misc 990, 77 NYS2d 356.

Owners of certificates of indebtedness issued by state agency, river regulation district, are not conditionally necessary to district's action for judgment declaring its right to condemn land to construct reservoir. Black River Regulating Dist. v Adirondack League Club (1954) 307 NY 475, 121 NE2d 428.

In a wife's action to declare husband's divorce from her invalid and his subsequent marriage to another invalid, the infant son of the husband and the second wife is neither a necessary, conditionally necessary nor indispensable party, and should not be brought into the action. Impellizzeri v Impellizzeri (1954, Sup) 133 NYS2d 44.

Presence of conditionally necessary party is required only if he is subject to jurisdiction of court and can be brought in without delay. China Sugar Refining Co. v Andersen, Meyer & Co. (1956) 6 Misc 2d 184, 152 NYS2d 507.

Conditionally necessary parties must be subject to the jurisdiction of the court before their presence will be ordered, hence children and grandchildren resident in a sister state cannot be joined by order. Schwartz v Equitable Life Assur. Soc. (1957) 9 Misc 2d 27, 167 NYS2d 660.

Where the absence of proposed defendants as parties to liquidation will in no way prevent the effective determination of controversies between present plaintiffs and present defendants, such defendants are not indispensable or conditionally-necessary parties. Robinson v Glens Falls Ins. Co. (1957) 9 Misc 2d 841, 168 NYS2d 161.

In action by wife to recover monthly payments which husband failed to make, children are not indispensable or conditionally necessary parties even though separation agreement provided for support of wife and infant children since recovery by the wife would discharge any obligation of defendant to the children and the children would be bound by such payment. Seligmann v Mandel (1958) 11 Misc 2d 714, 171 NYS2d 417, affd 5 AD2d 974, 173 NYS2d 243.

In an action to recover commissions for sale of real property the action against one of the defendants who held certain money in escrow was properly joined with the action against the person who sold the property and the stakeholder was properly before the court as a conditionally necessary party. Cammarata v Conley (1958) 13 Misc 2d 349, 179 NYS2d 923.

In deciding whether to dismiss for absence of conditionally necessary party, court will consider his interest, among other things. China Sugar Refining Co. v Andersen, Meyer & Co. (1956) 6 Misc 2d 184, 152 NYS2d 507.

In action by realty broker against lessors and lessees for rental commission, where complaint alleges that defendants conspired with each other to defeat commission, and defendants' answer disclosed that nonparty, who was owner of leased premises, had not been joined, latter was held to be conditionally necessary party in order to accord complete relief to all parties. Quinn v Tucker (1955, Misc) 141 NYS2d 902.

In action by tenant against landlord for rent overcharge, where plaintiff had assigned his cause of action to commissioner of welfare from whom plaintiff had received public assistance, but had retained sufficient interest in proceeds of cause of action in excess of amount to satisfy debt to commissioner, plaintiff may maintain such action without joining assignee. Marrero v Levitt (1956) 3 Misc 2d 555, 152 NYS2d 802.

In action to obtain specific performance of stock-holders' agreement whereby deceased stockholder's representative was required to transfer stock to the corporation, the corporation which was signatory to the agreement was a conditionally necessary party. Greenberg v Fischer (1956, Sup) 156 NYS2d 350.

In beneficiaries' action to enforce trust, settlor is a conditionally necessary party whose presence is necessary for protection of parties before the court. Rothenberg v Wolfman (1958) 16 Misc 2d 124, 183 NYS2d 139.

Joint tortfeasor is not a conditionally necessary party. Siskind v Levy (1961) 13 AD2d 538, 213 NYS2d 379.

32. —Where motion made

Application to bring in party must be made before trial at Special Term. Acetate Box Corp. v Johnson (1948) 193 Misc 54, 80 NYS2d 134.

33. —Determination of indispensability or necessity

Where question raised on motion to dismiss as to indispensability of person not party to agreement on which action brought, question of indispensability should be determined on trial and plaintiff allowed opportunity to establish at trial facts tending to show controversy can be decided without such absent parties. Morgenstern v Freudenberg (1958) 10 Misc 2d 69, 171 NYS2d 611.

34. Corporations

Corporation, in whose right and behalf stockholder's derivative action is brought, is necessary defendant. Carruthers v Jack Waite Mining Co. (1953) 306 NY 136, 116 NE2d 286.

In action where parties are stockholders, officers and directors of corporation, wherein plaintiff seeks to compel accounting by defendant for corporate assets coming into latter's hands, corporation was indispensable party. Meier v Holmes (1953) 282 AD 1030, 126 NYS2d 655.

In action for conspiracy against individuals and corporate defendant to defraud plaintiff of stock in defendant corporation to be formed to take title to plant to be purchased, defendant corporation was indispensable or conditionally necessary party.

Grene v Bailey (1953) 282 AD 857, 124 NYS2d 740.

In action to compel corporation to declare mandatory dividends, directors need not be joined. Koppel v Middle States Petroleum Corp. (1946, Sup) 66 NYS2d 496, affd 272 AD 790, 69 NYS2d 784.

In action to rescind transfer of stock on ground of fraud, corporation is conditionally necessary party. Bronstein v Bronstein (1948, Sup) 80 NYS2d 568.

In action between two groups of stockholders to enforce compromise agreement, all obligees should be brought in as plaintiffs or defendants. Witenberg v Banca Commerciale Italiana (1948) 273 AD 888, 78 NYS2d 593.

Directors need not be joined in action with corporation to compel it to set aside sums as mandatory dividends to stockholders. Koppel v Middle States Petroleum Corp. (1947) 272 AD 790, 69 NYS2d 784.

Where controversy could not be effectively determined without presence of corporation, defendant was entitled to have it made party defendant. Heitler v Opal (1947, Sup App T) 75 NYS2d 210.

Where defendant acted for self and for corporation in making contract, such corporation was not indispensable or necessary in action on such contract. Rabinovitch v Auerbach (1950) 200 Misc 77, 100 NYS2d 923.

Where plaintiff brought a stockholder's derivative action against the corporation in which plaintiff held stock another defendant corporation was not a conditionally necessary party under Section 193, since stock issued by plaintiff's corporation to the defendant corporation even if wrongfully issued was not a wrong to plaintiff's corporation. Schectman v Baker (1958) 11 Misc 2d 1, 173 NYS2d 688.

35. Municipality

In action against city for injury to pedestrian who fell on jagged sidewalk, city may not implead abutting owner who allowed tree root to undergrow and disrupt sidewalk. Van Pelt v New York (1947) 188 Misc 995, 69 NYS2d 116.

In an action involving the validity of a county tax sale certificate and tax deed given by the county treasurer, the county and county treasurer are not necessary and proper parties where neither plaintiff nor defendant can make a claim against them. Home & Land Co. v Mietlicki (1958) 10 Misc 2d 307, 174 NYS2d 751.

36. Indemnitor

In county's action against surety on official bond, surety may bring in county officials who agreed to indemnify surety against loss. Oswego County v American Surety Co. (1946) 63 NYS2d 723, affd 272 AD 862, 70 NYS2d 927.

37. Actions involving mortgages

Where plaintiff's action was based on mortgage entered into between plaintiff and defendant, and defendant's counterclaim was based on contract between him and another, latter was unnecessary party. Truman Homes v Lane Holding Corp. (1949, Sup) 88 NYS2d 406.

Where plaintiff sought to enjoin defendant from interfering with use of right of way to which mortgage by defendant was subject, his mortgagee who recognized such right was not necessary party. Bruno v Picchi (1950, Sup) 99 NYS2d 207.

Mortgagee is necessary party to suit to recover for fire loss brought by owner against insurer, if judgment is to bind mortgagee. Syracuse Sav. Bank v Yorkshire Ins. Co. (1950) 301 NY 403, 94 NE2d 73.

In mortgage foreclosure by assignee of junior interest in second mortgage, holder of senior participating interest in second mortgage was indispensable party to proceeding, either as coplaintiff or as defendant. 418 Trading Corp. v Moon Realty Corp. (1955) 285 AD 444, 931, 137 NYS2d 513.

In action to foreclose mortgage on realty solely owned by mortgagor's wife, where no deficiency was sought against mortgagor, he is neither indispensable nor conditionally necessary party. Steinlauf v Camporese (1955, Sup) 142 NYS2d 166.

Mortgagees barred by CPA § 47-a (§ 213(4) herein) from recovering either principal or interest, did not need to be served with notice to redeem in action by holder of tax deed to realty to cancel defendants mortgage of record as cloud on title. Connolly v Schild (1954, Sup) 136 NYS2d 898.

Surveyors whose lien was prior to the execution of the mortgage were not necessary parties to the mortgage foreclosure action. Sayville Federal Sav. & Loan Asso. v Schons (1958) 17 Misc 2d 54, 183 NYS2d 106.

38. Particular actions

In an accounting action there may be properly joined as parties plaintiff one who is suing in his individual capacity and that same person as administrator of the estate of a decedent. Szarf v Blumenfeld (1957) 7 Misc 2d 181, 163 NYS2d 249, revd on other grounds 5 AD2d 887, 172 NYS2d 984.

In an action under the Election Law even though failure to join the successful candidate as a party was not fatal to the proceeding, the defect could not be cured after the time limited for the institution of the proceeding namely ten days after the primary election in question. Suthergreen v Westall (1958) 6 AD2d 1014, 178 NYS2d 546.

In a proceeding under Election Law where a committee on vacancies are necessary parties and service was made on only one member and the time within which parties can be served or added under the Election Law has passed to add a necessary party thereafter would defeat the purpose and effect of the Election Law and extend the statute of limitations and proceeding dismissed. Lawler v Power (1958) 13 Misc 2d 344, 178 NYS2d 198.

In a wife's action to recover accidental death benefits the insured's children and grandchildren were neither indispensable nor conditionally necessary parties where the insured's wife is living and insured's children and grandchildren were beneficiaries only if she was dead. Schwartz v Equitable Life Assur. Soc. (1957) 9 Misc 2d 27, 167 NYS2d 660.

The joint will of a husband and wife constitutes an irrevocable contract if one dies and it is probated and it will be enforced against the executor and beneficiaries of a subsequent will made by the survivor and suit may be commenced in the supreme court without first filing a claim with the executor and the estate of the deceased life beneficiary under the joint will is not an indispensable or conditionally necessary party defendant. Re Elwyn's Estate (1957) 8 Misc 2d 704, 173 NYS2d 192, affd 5 AD2d 748, 168 NYS2d 942.

Since joint tortfeasors or conspirators are jointly and severally liable, the plaintiff may sue as many or as few as he chooses and the others are not indispensable or conditionally necessary parties. McManus v Ryan (1958) 10 Misc 2d 528, 175 NYS2d 338, revd on other grounds 7 AD2d 639, 179 NYS2d 574.

In an action for rescission of a contract, all parties are indispensable and must be brought before the court and such action will be stayed until an indispensable party has been properly served with process. Morgenstern v Freudenberg (1958) 10 Misc 2d 69, 171 NYS2d 611.

In an action for construction of an express trust, holders of the "res" were necessary parties. Application of Young (1959) 7 AD2d 946, 181 NYS2d 985.

In an action by city against cemetery for disinterment and removal of monuments plot owners are indispensable parties defendant. New York v Washington Cemetery (1959) 17 Misc 2d 847, 188 NYS2d 52.

F. Decisions Prior to Sept. 1, 1946 (earlier CPA § 193)

(Note: See note under § 1003, infra, Case Notes, subd "A".)

a. In General

39. Generally

Former CPA §§ 192, 193(1)(3)(4) were derived mainly from the English Rules of the Supreme Court (commonly known as the English Practice Act), the New Jersey Practice Act of 1912 and in part from CCP § 452, but subdivision 2 was new. Hailfinger v Meyer (1925) 215 AD 35, 212 NYS 746.

The statute was remedial and was liberally construed. Hejza v New York C. R. Co. (1930) 230 AD 624, 246 NYS 34; 125 West 45th St. Restaurant Corp. v Framax Realty Corp. (1936) 249 AD 589, 293 NYS 216; Franklin v Meredith Co. (1933, CA2 NY) 64 F2d 109; Lowry & Co. v National City Bank (1928, DC NY) 28 F2d 895.

In view of CPA § 1569 (§ 10003 herein), the provisions of former CPA § 193 being remedial, applied in a proper case to an action pending when the Act became effective. Neuss, Hesslein & Co. v National Aniline & Chemical Co. (1923) 120 Misc 164, 197 NYS 808.

Former CPA § 192 construed with former CPA § 193 in holding that complaint was not insufficient for failure to join necessary defendants. Pickhardt v First Nat. Bank & Trust Co. (1943) 266 AD 781, 41 NYS2d 502.

Former CPA § 264 (§§ 3012(a), 3019(b), 3020(a) herein) was identical with former CPA § 193, subd 2, though pleading requirements of the two sections may have differed. Patterson v New York (1945) 185 Misc 610, 57 NYS2d 427.

CPA § 264 (§§ 3012(a), 3019(b), 3020(a) herein), distinguished from subd 2 of former CPA § 193 as being less stringent than latter. McCreech v Howard R. Ware Corp. (1945, Sup) 53 NYS2d 192.

As to jurisdiction to dispose of entire controversy. See People v Hydrostatic Paper Co. (1882) 88 NY 623; Wager v Wager (1882) 89 NY 161.

The power of the supreme court to compel a plaintiff to bring into an action a third party upon his own application could be exercised only in the instances and subject to the requirements of former CPA § 193, the general powers conferred upon courts by CPA § 105 (§§ 2001, 3025(b), Rules 305(c), 2101(f) herein) being nothing more than a declaration of the inherent powers of the supreme court. Draper v Pratt (1904) 43 Misc 406, 89 NYS 356.

The true valuation of subd 4 of former CPA § 193 should not be overstressed. Hejza v New York C. R. Co. (1930) 230 AD 624, 246 NYS 34.

Under former CPA §§ 105 (§§ 2001, 3025(b), Rules 305(c), 2101(f) herein) and 193, a plaintiff in an action of partition, who had commenced his action in good faith and had been regular in his practice but who, without any fault on his part, omitted to make certain parties defendants, was entitled to an order to issue a supplemental summons and to amend his complaint. Hall v Campbell (1894) 77 Hun 567, 28 NYS 1031.

Former CPA § 193 was to be construed as requiring only such parties to be brought in who would have been, by reason of their interest, either proper or necessary parties at the time the suit was brought. Callanan v Keeseville, A. C. & L. C. R. Co. (1905) 48 Misc 476, 95 NYS 513.

When former CPA §§ 192 and 193 were read in connection with CPA § 211-a (§ 1401 herein), a legislative scheme was constituted for the determination of all the rights and liabilities of the parties in one action. Davis v Hauk & Schmidt, Inc. (1931) 232 AD 556, 250 NYS 537.

40. Purpose

The purpose of subdivision 2 of former CPA § 193 was to avoid delay and circuity of actions and to enable a controversy relating to the same subject matter to be disposed of in one suit. Michigan Alkali Co. v Bankers Indem. Ins. Co. (1937, DC NY) 19 F Supp 9.

41. Municipal court

The Municipal Court had power to render judgment against a defendant in favor of his codefendant against whom judgment had been rendered for the plaintiff, all judgments being in the same amounts. McCrorken v Spiegel (1926) 127 Misc 496, 216 NYS 561.

42. Federal court

Former CPA § 193 was not applicable to actions by materialmen or laborers under Heard Act. United States use of Johnson v Morley Const. Co. (1935, DC NY) 20 F Supp 606.

43. Legal and equitable actions generally

Former CPA § 193 applied to legal as well as to equitable actions. Graves Elevator Co. v Masonic Temple Ass'n (1895) 85 Hun 496, 33 NYS 362; contra, Rosenberg v Courtney (1894) 8 Misc 616, 29 NYS 327.

In an equitable action for accounting, additional defendants against whom the original defendant claimed right to recover over were permitted to be brought in. Gilliland v Lincoln-Alliance Bank & Trust Co. (1930) 137 Misc 709, 244 NYS 241.

It was held that in proper cases courts of equity should exercise their power to bring before them all parties whose presence was necessary to the decision of the controversy. Luitweiler v Luitweiler Pumping Engine Co. (1921, Sup) 191 NYS 111.

Application in an equity action by one defendant to join a third party as a defendant, so as to obtain cross relief, was granted where neither the plaintiff nor the third party objected, and the only objection made was by two other defendants who made no attempt to show prejudice by the presence of such third party as a defendant. Dwelle v Central Union Trust Co. (1925) 214 AD 424, 212 NYS 417.

There was a well-defined distinction between necessary and proper parties defendant in suits in equity, and where a complete determination of the controversy could not be had without the presence of other parties, it was held that the court should direct them to be brought in pursuant to former CPA § 193, and it was error for the court to proceed to judgment in the absence of such necessary parties although no objection had been previously taken. Mawhinney v Bankers' Trust Co. (1908) 124 AD 609, 109 NYS 332, aff'd 194 NY 590, 88 NE 1134.

In equity the assignee of a part of a claim might maintain a suit to enforce the same, and it was held that the court might direct other parties to be brought in in order that there might be a complete determination of the controversy. Dickinson v Tysen (1908) 125 AD 735, 110 NYS 269.

It was held that a complaint in action in equity should not be dismissed because the judge believed persons not parties might be prejudiced by the judgment, but he should direct that they be made parties. Anton Larsen & Son, Inc. v Newmark & Davis, Inc. (1918) 182 AD 724, 170 NYS 268.

44. Effect of waiver of defect of parties

Although the defect of parties appearing on the face of the complaint was waived by failure to demur on that account, the court could bring in the person omitted where his presence was necessary to a complete determination of the matter in suit. Continental Trust Co. v Nobel (1894) 10 Misc 325, 30 NYS 994.

Although the defendant in an action, by omitting to raise an objection of defect of parties by demurrer or answer, must be deemed to have waived it, yet where the granting of relief against the defendant would prejudice rights of others who were not parties to the action, and their rights could not be saved by the judgment, and the controversy could not be completely determined without their presence, it was held that the court must direct them to be made parties before proceeding to judgment, and a failure so to do was fatal to the judgment. Osterhoudt v Board of Supervisors (1885) 98 NY 239; Bear v American Rapid Tel. Co. 36 Hun 400.

The executor of a decedent to whom the assets sought to be reached by an action primarily belonged, if they existed at all, was a necessary party to the action and should have been brought in as such, although no objection on the ground of defect of parties was taken. Duane v Paige (1894) 82 Hun 139, 31 NYS 310.

Where objection to a defect of parties was not raised by answer or demurrer, or taken at the trial, the strict legal right to have the parties brought in was lost; but, it seems, where the suit was in equity and a complete determination of the controversy could not be had without the presence of other parties, the court of its own motion could direct them to be brought in and a party might urge that the presence of other parties was necessary for the first time on appeal, for the court would not render a fruitless judgment. City Equity Co. v Elm Park Realty Co. (1909) 135 AD 856, 120 NYS 437.

A partner sued upon a partnership obligation alleged to create a joint liability was entitled to have his copartners joined in the action, but he waived this right by failing to take objection. Alaska Banking & Safe Deposit Co. v Van Wyck (1911) 146 AD 5, 130 NYS 563.

45. Unrelated causes of action

It was improper to permit plaintiff to bring in as defendants, parties liable under different contracts and circumstances concerning which the facts involved were separate, distinct and unrelated as to time and subject-matter. Stern v George P. Ide & Co. (1925) 212 AD 714, 209 NYS 473.

Former CPA § 193 would not permit a plaintiff to bring in as a party defendant one against whom plaintiff might have another and distinct cause of action of an entirely different nature and which would be governed by entirely different rules. Stern v George P. Ide & Co. supra.

Where there was not sufficient measure of identity between plaintiff's cause of action against defendant and cross-claim of defendant against impleaded defendant to justify inclusion in one action, order impleading defendant was properly vacated. New York Merchandise Co. v McGraw-Hill Pub. Co. (1943) 265 AD 995, 39 NYS2d 453.

The depositor of goods in a warehouse was no proper party in an action by the party to whom the warehouse receipt was given as security, against the warehouse owner, since the transactions between the latter and the depositor were wholly unrelated to plaintiff's claim. Williams v Flagg Storage Warehouse Co. (1927) 128 Misc 566, 220 NYS 124, affd 221 AD 788, 223 NYS 925.

In an action to recover damages for defendant's alleged breach of warranty in the installation of a boiler and generator for the plaintiff, defendant was not entitled to bring in as a party defendant a person who, defendant claimed, negligently constructed and installed the boiler. Feuer v Fenton (1937) 162 Misc 887, 295 NYS 918.

In an action for the balance of a loan made to respondent in the course of a building project, the latter was not entitled to an order impleading appellant on the theory that he and not plaintiff was the real party in interest, where it appeared that that issue had been properly raised and could be determined at the trial without impleading appellant, whose alleged liability to respondent arose out of a different claim wholly unrelated to respondent's liability to plaintiff for a loan. Kalish v National Bldg. Corp. (1940) 259 AD 258, 18 NYS2d 871.

Where claims by plaintiff and by original defendant against proposed codefendant were not the same, and judgment for plaintiff could be based entirely or partly upon sole negligence of original defendant, such codefendant should not be brought in. Schwartz v Crawford (1941) 261 AD 825, 24 NYS2d 494.

One who was not yet party could not bring into litigation another who, in event of plaintiff's success, would be liable to it on a claim different in kind from that which plaintiff was pressing against present defendant. Colburn v Geneva Nursery Co. (1941, Sup) 29 NYS2d 892.

In action for breach of express warranty of fitness of material for certain purpose, defendant could not by supplemental pleading assert claim against another person for breach of warranty of merchantability, since respective claims were not same. Bancroft Bldg. Corp. v Eisner (1942) 263 AD 877, 32 NYS2d 166.

In action for personal injuries against owner and driver, driver might not implead owner who allegedly breached contract to carry liability insurance to protect driver. Darcey v Greater New York Brewery (1943) 179 Misc 1088, 40 NYS2d 950.

In action by insured for judgment declaring policy was in force when accident occurred, insurer could not implead injured individuals who might sue and recover judgments against insured and then sue insurer. Follins v Liberty Mut. Ins. Co. (1942) 179 Misc 489, 39 NYS2d 241, affd 266 AD 660, 41 NYS2d 209.

Seamen interested in cargo of oil under agreement between the owner of the vessel and themselves, were not necessary parties to an action upon contract as to transporting the oil made in plaintiff's own name. Swift v Pacific Mail S. S. Co. (1887) 106 NY 206, 12 NE 583.

46. Agreed controversy

Former CPA § 193 did not apply to an agreed controversy. Trustees of Hobart College v Fitzhugh (1863) 27 NY 130.

47. Special proceedings

Former CPA § 193 related to actions and judgments, and had no application to special proceedings. People ex rel. Steingoetter v Board of Canvassers (1888, Sup) 2 NYS 561.

Former CPA § 193 was not applicable to summary proceedings. Liberty Place Holding Corp. v Adolph Schwob (1930) 136 Misc 405, 241 NYS 438, affd 229 AD 841, 242 NYS 860.

48. Condemnation proceedings

The provisions of former CPA § 193 were made applicable to condemnation proceedings by Condemnation Law, § 26. New York C. & H. R. R. Co. v Matthews (1911) 70 Misc 567, 128 NYS 138, affd 144 AD 732, 129 NYS 828.

49. Delay or undue prejudice to plaintiff

Bringing in of additional parties should not be permitted to delay plaintiff in prosecuting his claim or enforcing any judgment he might obtain. Jersey Shore Trust Co. v Sebring (1930) 228 AD 756, 239 NYS 788.

Maker of note could not delay collection of note by moving to bring in other parties whom he claimed had indemnified him against any loss on note. National City Bank v Walker (1940) 176 Misc 68, 25 NYS2d 590.

It appearing that the administration of litigated business might be promoted without too great a sacrifice of plaintiff's rights, parties would be brought in on the defendant's motion; but in determining a motion by the defendant, the latter's convenience was not alone to be considered. Greenhouse v Rochester Taxicab Co. (1926) 218 AD 224, 218 NYS 167.

Where it was apparent that the litigation might be promoted without too great a sacrifice of plaintiff's rights parties would be brought in on defendant's motion. Davis v Hauk & Schmidt, Inc. (1931) 232 AD 556, 250 NYS 537.

Where it would be confusing, one defendant should not be permitted to try an affirmative claim against another. Murray v Mastroeni (1930) 137 Misc 708, 244 NYS 180.

Motion of defendant gas works in an action founded on negligent construction, inspection, and repair of its gas mains, whereby an explosion occurred, to bring in as defendant a municipality, whose negligence it claimed was responsible for the injury and which it claimed would be liable over to it, was denied, where under the complaint the gas works might be held liable without showing the cause of the defect in the main, and injection into the case of proof as to such cause would tend to becloud and confuse the issue tendered by the plaintiff. Blizard v Binghamton Gas Works (1935) 157 Misc 96, 282 NYS 919.

50. Discretion as to separate trials

The discretion with reference to separate trials ran through the provisions of the act, where confusion might have resulted from a common trial. Murray v Mastroeni (1930) 137 Misc 708, 244 NYS 180.

b. BRINGING IN PARTIES NECESSARY OR PROPER FOR COMPLETE DETERMINATION

51. Generally

Where controversy could not be determined without presence of certain persons, court could not dispense with their presence but must order them to be brought in. Norman v General American Transp. Corp. (1943) 181 Misc 233, 47 NYS2d 390, affd 267 AD 758, 45 NYS2d 929.

Where cause of action stated in complaint necessarily called for an adjudication upon the rights of defendant not properly before the court, case could not be tried, and complaint could only be dismissed upon motion for delay in prosecution. Simon v Gibralter Const. Co. (1917) 179 AD 273, 166 NYS 466.

Complete relief: where there was no showing that complete determination could not be had without presence of absent party or that such party was or would be liable to defendant for claim against it, defendant could not bring in such party as co-defendant. Pascuzzi v Car & General Ins. Corp. (1946) 270 AD 976, 62 NYS2d 891.

Motion to bring in additional parties defendant was granted in action by corporation against director and officer for accounting, where order would avoid multiplicity of suits and would bring all matters at issue to speedy determination. Silver Creek Preserving Corp. v Porter (1937) 164 Misc 818, 299 NYS 678, affd 254 AD 814, 5 NYS2d 512.

52. Bringing in new plaintiff

An order permitting a third party to be brought in as a plaintiff, after trial, where the suit must fail for want of a proper plaintiff, was erroneous. Davis v Mayor, etc., of New York (1856) 14 NY 506.

Defendant learning of assignment of cause of action to trustees for creditors could not compel the plaintiff to join the trustees as plaintiffs. Rothbarth v Herzfeld (1913) 159 AD 732, 144 NYS 974.

Former CPA § 193 only contemplated the bringing of parties as defendants and not as plaintiffs. Union Trust Co. v Boker (1899) 26 Misc 85, 56 NYS 550.

Trustee of a bankrupt corporation was properly brought in as party plaintiff in an action by stockholder to set aside license agreements transferring corporate rights under patents, and for an accounting. Muller v Pero (1929) 135 Misc 424, 237 NYS 591.

53. Substitution of parties defendant

Purpose of former CPA § 193 was to authorize the bringing in of a new defendant, not as a substitute for the original defendant, but to enable the mutual rights of the two defendants as well as those of the plaintiff to be determined in one action. Bozzuffi v Darrieusecq (1925) 125 Misc 178, 210 NYS 455.

The plaintiff having sued the wrong person could not cure the error by a motion in the action to substitute the right person as defendant. Spence v Griswold (1889, CP Ct) 7 NYS 145.

A trustee appointed, pending an action of foreclosure, in place of the trustee holding the equity of redemption who had resigned, could not be added as a new party, but should have been substituted in place of the former trustee. Griswold v Caldwell (1895) 14 Misc 299, 35 NYS 1057.

Former CPA § 193 did not contemplate nor authorize the dropping out of the original parties defendant. Testing Laboratories of New York, Inc. v Krainin (1925) 124 Misc 667, 208 NYS 801.

The bringing in of a new defendant could not operate to compel plaintiff to accept the alleged liability of a stranger, to his debtor, on substitution of the latter's obligation to him. Bozzuffi v Darrieusecq (1925) 125 Misc 178, 210 NYS 455.

If the new party was the undisclosed principal of the original party, the plaintiff should not have been compelled to substitute for the party on the strength of whose credit he had depended, a total stranger with whom he had no dealings. Federal Lighterage Co. v Italia-America Shipping Corp. (1925) 125 Misc 181, 210 NYS 458.

54. Powers of referee

Where, during a trial before a referee, it appeared that other persons were necessary parties, whereupon the referee directed the cause to stand over, with leave to the plaintiff to apply to the court to bring in the other parties, and he refused to make such application, it was held that the referee properly dismissed the complaint. Peyser v Wendt (1882) 87 NY 322.

The court alone had power to order a party brought in. A referee had no such power. Newman v Marvin (1877) 12 Hun 236.

55. Dismissal of complaint

If, after timely objection of want of parties, plaintiff did not bring them in, the complaint could in the discretion of the court be dismissed, but without prejudice to a new action. Sherman v Parish (1873) 53 NY 483.

Broker's action to recover earned commissions due from one party, against the other party who failed to consummate the deal after having agreed to do so, was dismissed because of wrong party defendant. Eichenbaum v Taxicab Independent Owners' Auto Mut. Cas. Co. (1929) 135 Misc 339, 237 NYS 506, adhered to 136 Misc 58, 240 NYS 499.

56. Corporations

In an action to have a receiver appointed for a corporation, the corporation was a necessary party defendant. Miller v Barlow (1903) 78 AD 331, 79 NYS 964.

In an action against the president of a new corporation which took over the stock and assets of an old corporation for stock alleged to have been held in trust for plaintiff, a stockholder in the old corporation, it was held that the new corporation was a necessary party and that the other stockholders were also, as the plaintiff had sued individually and not on behalf of himself and other stockholders. Knickerbocker v Conger (1905) 110 AD 125, 97 NYS 127.

On the merger of a railroad corporation with other corporations, an action existing, but not commenced, before the merger was perfected must have been brought against the new corporation. Lee v Stillwater & M. S. R. Co. (1910) 140 AD 779, 125 NYS 840.

In action by officers and directors, the corporation itself was a proper party and denial of defendant's motion to have it brought in was not proper exercise of discretion. Ress v Margolies (1930) 231 AD 843, 246 NYS 388.

Where corporation was a necessary party to an action against its trustees, see Greaves v Gouge (1877) 69 NY 154.

The provisions of former CPA § 193, that "the court may determine the controversy, as between the parties before it, where it can do so without prejudice to the rights of others or by saving their rights," did not apply to an action in which the corporation was not made a party, brought by a stockholder against an officer of the corporation for misappropriation of corporate funds or for damages for waste of corporate property through misfeasance in office, unless the corporation refused to sue, and in case of such refusal the corporation must have been made a defendant. Stromeyer v Combes (1888, CP Ct) 15 Daly 29, 2 NYS 232.

In an action for damages for deceit in inducing plaintiff to purchase shares of corporate stock and to expend moneys for the corporation against the persons alleged to have practiced the deception, the corporation was not a necessary party; in such an action, where the deceit was practiced by an agent, it might be alleged to have been done by the principal. Harlow v Haines (1909) 63 Misc 98, 116 NYS 449, affd 137 AD 892, 121 NYS 1135.

57. Corporate directors and officers

In an action brought by a stockholder of a corporation for an accounting, the necessary defendants were the defaulting officials and the directors or the trustees who were responsible for the corporation. McCrea v Robertson (1908) 192 NY 150, 84 NE 960.

In stockholder's action on behalf of the corporation, alleging mismanagement of corporate affairs, the corporation and directors were necessary parties, and the court properly ordered the directors brought in under this and former CPA § 192. Jones v Van Heusen Charles Co. (1930) 230 AD 694, 246 NYS 204.

58. Corporate stockholders

Whether one stockholder in a plank road company could sue the other stockholders less than the whole, to recover a debt due him from the corporation. See Simmons v Sisson (1863) 26 NY 264.

As to the rule in courts of equity that all persons could be brought in having any claim or interest in the subject matter, as applied to actions of stockholders of a construction company for an accounting by its officers and joining third persons, etc. Meyers v Scott (1888, Sup) 2 NYS 753.

The remedy of a creditor under Laws 1850, ch. 140, § 10, was not by a separate action against one or more of the stockholders, but by a suit in equity against all stockholders similarly situated. Wellington v Continental Const. & Imp. Co. (1889) 52 Hun 408, 5 NYS 587.

A creditor of a corporation, who was suing in equity on behalf of all creditors of the corporation to enforce the liability of stockholders for unpaid subscriptions to the capital stock, must join as defendants all stockholders who were liable under the statute as well as the personal representatives of those who had died. Warth v Moore Blind Stitcher & Overseamer Co. (1911) 146 AD 28, 130 NYS 748, affd 207 NY 673, 100 NE 1128.

59. Corporate creditors

An action to reach unpaid subscriptions for stock might be brought by a judgment creditor of the corporation without joining other stockholders or creditors. Wheeler v Millar (1882) 90 NY 353.

In action by administrator of deceased stockholder in three corporations, on behalf of his estate, other stockholders and creditors and corporations were indispensable parties. Mulligan v Mulligan (1946) 270 AD 836, 60 NYS2d 501.

The mere failure of a creditor suing under § 28 of the Stock Corporation Law to describe the action as representative was no ground for dismissing the complaint, since if it should be made to appear that there were any other creditors similarly situated they might be brought in under former CPA §§ 192 (§§ 401, 1003 herein) and 193. Aktieselskabet Christianssand v Federal S. S. Corp. (1923) 121 Misc 627, 201 NYS 504.

60. Municipal corporations

In an action for a declaratory judgment as to the validity of a zoning ordinance, the county, which in the event of the ordinance being declared invalid would have been called upon to pay an additional award, was a necessary party defendant. MacEwen v New Rochelle (1933) 149 Misc 251, 267 NYS 36.

Trustees of a village were neither necessary nor proper parties plaintiff or defendant in an action by the village to restrain gas company from enforcing increased rate. Mt. Morris v Pavilion Nat-ural Gas Co. (1920, Sup) 183 NYS 792, affd 196 AD 918, 187 NYS 957.

In action to enforce specific performance of congregation's contract to purchase realty in village, congregation might implead village in order to obtain judgment declaring right of congregation to maintain religious school on such property allegedly prohibited by zoning ordinance. Levy v Congregation Beth Sholom, Inc. (1943) 181 Misc 877, 42 NYS2d 891.

61. Unincorporated associations

Where an unincorporated association was made defendant under General Associations law, § 13, the action was against the president who represented the members and he was bound to protect their rights. Andrews v Local Union J. P. G. S. & S. F. (1929) 133 Misc 899, 234 NYS 208.

62. Assignors and assignees

The holder of a note with collateral securities for its payment, assigned the securities to a third party. It was held that both the holder of the note and the assignee of the securities were necessary parties to the debtor's suit for an accounting. See Inman v Corwin (1890, Sup) 9 NYS 195.

In an action on a life insurance policy, the alleged assignee of such policy was a necessary party. Hasberg v Mutual Life Ins. Co. (1903) 81 AD 199, 80 NYS 867.

A plaintiff, which had taken an assignment of a mortgage, when its validity was questioned in a prior action brought by the committee of an incompetent against several defendants to set aside the instrument as procured by fraud, should not have been granted leave to join the incompetent as a party defendant in an action of foreclosure, to which all the persons involved in the alleged fraud were not parties, but should have been left to defend its rights in the prior action. City Real Estate Co. v MacFarland (1907) 121 AD 652, 106 NYS 333.

Assignor retaining interest in a contract was necessary party in action by assignee. Natter v Isaac H. Blanchard Co. (1912) 153 AD 814, 138 NYS 969.

It was held that creditors who had assigned their claims need not be cited upon judicial settlement of account of administratrix. Re Freije's Estate (1915) 90 Misc 246, 152 NYS 726.

63. Grantors and grantees, purchasers and transferees

The grantee of a portion of the lands might properly be joined with the heirs for the purpose of ascertaining what his rights were, and to give him an opportunity of defending them. Hauselt v Fine, 18 Abb NC 142, 3 NYSR 191.

Where pending an action to restrain defendants from developing water power on a river in which plaintiffs had power rights and to determine the water rights of the several parties, the plaintiffs sold their rights without reservation to a corporation which in turn mortgaged such rights to secure an issue of bonds, and plaintiffs also personally guaranteed to the corporation and to the purchasers of the bonds the validity of their title to the water power conveyed, the court had power, under former CPA §§ 83 (§§ 1015(b), 1018, herein), 192 (§§ 401, 1003 herein), and 193, to join as parties defendant the vendee corporation, the trustee under the mortgage, and the executor of one of the plaintiffs who died pending the action. Dunlop v Sweet Bros. Paper Mfg. Co. (1925) 211 AD 363, 208 NYS 54.

64. Landlord and tenant

In tenant's action to cancel the security bond, lessor having died, his executors were proper defendants. Halstead v Globe Indem. Co. (1930) 138 Misc 717, 246 NYS 601, revd on other grounds 232 AD 576, 251 NYS 181, affd 258 NY 176, 179 NE 376.

65. Life tenant and remaindermen

In action to determine whether life tenant had right to dispose of real property remaindermen were necessary parties. Baumgrass v Brickell, 7 NYSR 685.

66. Partners

In any proceeding by one partner after the death of a copartner for an accounting, a surviving partner was a necessary party. Arnold v Arnold (1882) 90 NY 580.

Where an action was brought against an individual partner, in order to take the defense that his copartner was not joined, he must show not only that the partnership existed but that the plaintiff had knowledge thereof. Shanley v Merchant (1910) 140 AD 797, 125 NYS 587.

Where members of a partnership and two others owned the stock of a corporation, and, while the partnership was in course of preparation for dissolution, the two owners sold their stock to one of the members of the partnership under an agreement that the purchaser was not to resell it without first offering it back to the sellers, such sellers were necessary parties to a proceeding brought against the purchasing partner by the other partners to have him declared a trustee for the partnership as to the stock so purchased. Bayer v Bayer (1926) 215 AD 454, 214 NYS 322.

It was held that owners of vessels should all join in an action for freight. Merritt v Walsh (1865) 32 NY 685; Donnell v Walsh (1865) 33 NY 43.

67. Personal representatives

An executor to whom letters had been granted in this state could recover assets, and it was not necessary to join as a party a coexecutor to whom letters had been granted in another state. Lawrence v Townsend (1882) 88 NY 24.

The legal representatives of a deceased insured were held to be necessary parties to a complete determination of an action by a creditor of the insured to reform the insurance policy so as to name the creditor as beneficiary rather than the representatives, and failure of the defendant insurance company to raise the objection by demurrer or answer did not waive the defect. Steinbach v Prudential Ins. Co. (1902) 172 NY 471, 65 NE 281.

Representatives of the estate of an interested party might be brought in. Corporation Holding Co. v Wieber (1930) 230 AD 636, 246 NYS 109.

Until accounts of executors had been settled by the surrogate, they were necessary parties to an action brought against the trustee to enforce the payment of any deficiencies in the legacies. Scott v Stebbins (1882) 27 Hun 335, affd 91 NY 605.

Where during pendency of suit by the receivers of a corporation one died, the court might order the continuing of the action, bringing in his executors, and they could be bound by such orders as might be made in the suit. Re Columbian Ins. Co. (1883) 30 Hun 342, affd 94 NY 636.

On revival of action of replevin, executor of deceased defendant was properly made a party. Gueli v Lennihan (1890, Sup) 8 NYS 453.

Where a judgment creditor sued to set aside transfer made by one judgment debtor to another, and when the transferor died and appointed the transferee his administratrix, she should have been made a defendant in her capacity as administratrix. Vietor v Goodman (1899) 26 Misc 545, 57 NYS 599.

The executors of a deceased debtor were not necessary parties defendant. Hauselt v Fine, 18 Abb NC 142, 3 NYSR 191.

A coadministrator was not a necessary party to an action which sought to charge an administrator as trustee for acts not done in a representative capacity. Abell v Bradner, 11 NYSR 246.

Plaintiff was employed as an accountant in settling up the affairs of an estate by two executors, subject to the approval of a third executor, who thereafter consented, and throughout his employment he consulted with all three executors, and the services rendered by him were for their benefit. It was held that he could recover in an action brought for such services against one of the executors alone, another being living. Douglas v Leonard (1892, Sup) 17 NYS 591.

68. Heirs, devisees and legatees

Where one of several heirs of a deceased grantor brought an action to set aside a deed executed to their father during minority, the failure to bring the other heirs of the deceased children in as parties was not fatal to the maintenance of the action as the judgment preserved the rights of all the parties. O'Rourke v Hall (1899) 38 AD 534, 56 NYS 471.

A residuary legatee who brought an action for his share of the residue, must join all persons interested in the residue as defendants. The heir was a necessary party defendant in such action. See Trustees of Theological Seminary v Kellogg (1857) 16 NY 83.

69. Principal and agent

Where certain claims were collected by an agent,

the fact that the principals were joint owners of the original claims against the debtor did not prevent either of them from maintaining an action to recover his share of the money collected thereon by the agent. Allen v Brown (1870) 44 NY 228.

In action to rescind contract to purchase realty, plaintiff was permitted to add, as party codefendant, defendant's alleged agent, where defendant disclosed he might claim lack of authority in agent. Olshan v Buffalo Merchandising Co. (1943, Co Ct) 44 NYS2d 758.

70. Prior encumbrancers in second mortgage foreclosure

Prior encumbrancers whose rights could be effectively adjudged in a foreclosure action by a second mortgagee which would affect or destroy their priority were necessary parties to such foreclosure action. P. T. McDermott, Inc. v Lawyers' Mortg. Co. (1922) 232 NY 336, 133 NE 909.

71. Tenants in common

In an action for the recovery of lands owned by tenants in common, it was held that all such tenants must join to recover the whole premises, or each must bring a separate action for his own share. Hasbrouck v Bunce (1875) 62 NY 475.

Where one tenant in common might recover for use and occupation, from a cotenant who excluded him from the possession of the premises, see Muldowney v Morris & E. R. Co. (1886) 42 Hun 444.

It was held in an action for logging services that other tenants in common with defendant in the lands need not be joined where plaintiff had no knowledge or information as to their interests. Baley v Henderson (1890, Sup) 9 NYS 345.

In proceeding on claim against state by one tenant in common for damages to flooded realty owned in common, cotenant was not necessary party. Slocum v State (1941) 177 Misc 114, 29 NYS2d 993.

72. Guardian ad litem

Petition for the appointment of a guardian ad litem did not bring the application within former CPA §193 unless the petition showed the existence of an interest of the infant in property, although it did show the possibility of such interest. Van Williams v Elias (1905) 106 AD 288, 94 NYS 611.

The guardian ad litem of a plaintiff who recovered a judgment in a foreign state was not a necessary party plaintiff in an action on the judgment in this state. Finn v Post (1908) 61 Misc 136, 112 NYS 1046.

73. Assignees for benefit of creditors

Neither as assignor for the benefit of creditors, nor his personal representative, was a necessary party in an action for the settlement of an attorney's account against the assignee. Wells v Knox (1889) 55 Hun 245, 8 NYS 58.

74. Trustees and beneficiaries

The equitable rule in cases of breach of trust where no general rule or order of court interfered and where the facts of the case called for a contribution of recovery over, that all persons who should be before the court to enable it to make complete and final judgment were necessary parties, was not abrogated by the Code. Sherman v Parish (1875) 53 NY 483.

Under the circumstances it was held not necessary to join plaintiff trustees in their individual capacities. Zimmerman v Kinkel (1888) 108 NY 282, 15 NE 407.

All persons living who were beneficially interested should have been made parties in an action to set aside or revoke an instrument or deed of trust; all the designated beneficiaries and the trustees were necessary parties. McKnight v Bank of New York & Trust Co. (1930) 254 NY 417, 173 NE 568.

Judgment creditors of the settlor of a trust who had brought a suit against her to have their judgments declared a lien upon lands which were part of the trust estate were not necessary parties to a suit brought by the settlor against her trustees and the beneficiaries to have the trust declared null and void. Herzig v Herzig (1910) 140 AD 514, 125 NYS 402.

Under former CPA §193 it was held proper for the court before which proceedings for distribution of a trust fund were pending to order the summoning of a beneficiary not joined, or, if he were dead, his personal representatives and next of kin, notwithstanding his unexplained absence for more than seven years and the fact that his estate was being administered. Bering v United States Trust Co. (1922) 201 AD 35, 193 NYS 753.

Whether the interest of one under a trust agreement was a vested or contingent remainder cannot be determined so as to bind her personal representatives and heirs in their absence. Johnson v Guernsey (1923) 206 AD 788, 200 NYS 929.

The alleged absence of necessary parties was held not properly before the court on appeal from an order permitting plaintiff settlor to amend complaint for rescission of trust and for an accounting, as under former CPA §193 the trial court had full power to direct them to be brought in. Warren v Putnam (1942) 263 AD 474, 33 NYS2d 635.

The general rule was that all persons materially interested in the subject matter of the suit, including the trustee and cestuis que trust, should be brought in, so as to make the performance of the decree safe, and avoid necessity of relitigation. Brokaw v Fairchild (1929) 135 Misc 70, 237 NYS 6, affd 231 AD 704, 245 NYS 402, affd 256 NY 670, 177 NE 186.

A trustee of an express trust might be sued without uniting the parties in interest. Mead v Mitchell (1858) 17 NY 210.

A party who had under the provisions of the will received a portion of a trust estate was not a necessary party to an action against the trustees to recover a balance of a claim for services. Stanton v King (1876) 8 Hun 4, affd 69 NY 609.

A trust to convey to the surviving children of the life beneficiary after her death was good as a power in trust, and such children were necessary parties to a foreclosure suit. Graham v Fountain, 2 NYS 598. But see, contra, United States Trust Co. v Roche (1889) 116 NY 120, 22 NE 265.

Beneficiaries under a will devising the residue in trust, and directing a conversion of real property and investment of proceeds, the income to be divided among the beneficiaries, took no interest in the lands and were not necessary parties to a foreclosure. Mutual Life Ins. Co. v Woods (1889, Sup) 4 NYS 133, affd 121 NY 302, 24 NE 602.

In an action to set apart an amount for a testamentary trust, it was held that legatees to whom the money would go otherwise should be made parties, but that persons entitled to the property in remainder in any event need not be joined. Stevens v Melcher (1889, Sup) 6 NYS 811.

A suit by the holders of a quarter part in value of bonds secured by deposit of securities in the hands of a trustee, under an instrument of trust, to remove the trustee for misconduct, and appoint another to administer the trust without making the holders of the rest of the bonds parties, could not be maintained. Farrington v American Loan & Trust Co. (1890, Super Ct) 9 NYS 433.

75. Accounting

In cases where many persons had claims and were prosecuting, or about to prosecute, them at law against one defendant, a class of defendants, or a fund liable in equal degree to all those persons and to others, a court of equity, to prevent a multiplicity of actions, had jurisdiction of an action for a general accounting and adjustment of all the rights, and to restrain separate and individual actions at law in the same or other courts, thus bringing all the litigation into one suit. Pfohl v Simpson (1878) 74 NY 137.

Where one of the associates in a joint enterprise was a nonresident, he was not a necessary party in a suit by another of the associates for an accounting. Angell v Lawton (1879) 76 NY 540.

In action for accounting as to profits of a joint adventure, a third person who received such profits for the use and benefit of the defendant was not a necessary party. Lardizabal v Valentine (1918) 185 AD 124, 172 NYS 863.

In an action by trustees for an accounting, persons whose interests would be injuriously affected by the litigation must be made parties to the action before a determination in it could be secured. Stevens v Melcher (1889, Sup) 6 NYS 811.

An equitable action for an accounting, and the recovery of land alleged to have been conveyed to a decedent in his lifetime as security for a debt, being brought against his executrix, who was also his legatee, both individually and in her representative capacity, should on her death pending the action be revived, not only against the administrator of the decedent and the devisees of a portion of the land remaining unsold, but also against the personal representatives of the executrix. Benedict v Cobb (1889, Sup) 7 NYS 916.

76. —By fiduciary

The widow and administratrix of a deceased son of the testator was a necessary party in an action by a legatee against the executor for an accounting. Peyser v Wendt (1882) 87 NY 322.

In an action to compel an accounting by remaining executors and to charge them with liability for losses alleged to have been caused through their negligence, it was found that at the time of the removal of one of the executors the estate had sustained no loss, and that none was sustained by reason of any investment made by them. It was held that he was not a necessary party to the action. Earle v Earle (1883) 93 NY 104.

In an action by an administrator for an accounting, a legatee of a deceased legatee was not a necessary party. Sheldon v Whitehouse (1908) 60 Misc 161, 112 NYS 1079.

In proceeding to settle executor's account, wherein claim was filed by county under Public Welfare L § 125 for money advanced to decedent's son prior to his death, son's wife was held necessary party to be brought in on motion of executor. Re Wicks' Will (1941) 176 Misc 818, 29 NYS2d 829.

An action to compel an executor to account for funds held in trust by his testator not being a final accounting, the widow and devisees of such testator were not necessary parties. Price v Brown, 10 Abb NC 67.

77. Bonds and undertakings

Joinder of executor and other parties interested in estate, in suit on executor's bond. See Hood v Hood, 6 NYSR 684.

One of two joint obligees of a bond could not bring an action for its breach. See Pearce v Hitchcock (1849) 2 NY 388.

In a suit on a receiver's bond the obligees referred to in the bond should be made parties, either plaintiff or defendant, for their interest was not common or joint. People ex rel. Colton v Ransom, 2 NYSR 78.

Where undertaking was for the benefit of defendants jointly, and not several to each, one of them could not bring action thereon until both had recovered judgment or it had been decided that plaintiff was not entitled to the order of arrest as to both. At all events the other should have been made a party so that the rights of all might be determined. Miller v Herlich, 5 NYSR 909.

Where an injunction was dissolved as to one of several defendants, and his damages were computed on a reference, he might sue on the undertaking to recover the amount of the damages so awarded without making the other persons who were codefendants in the first action parties. Fourth Nat. Bank v Scott (1883) 31 Hun 301.

The attorney for the plaintiff was not a necessary party to an action on an undertaking upon appeal, even though his lien should extend to the whole amount of the recovery. Wadley v Poucher (1890, Sup) 9 NYS 50.

78. —Action to cancel bond

As to necessary parties in action to cancel a bond, see Zimmerman v Kinkel (1888) 108 NY 282, 15 NE 407.

79. Bailment

The owner of a bonded warehouse was liable for the goods lost while in such bonded warehouse, although in the joint custody of the owner of the bonded warehouse and a U.S. officer, and the U.S. officer need not be joined as defendant. Schwerin v McKie (1872) 51 NY 180.

80. Cloud on title

In an equitable action to prevent a cloud upon title, based upon a tax sale, the purchaser under the tax sale was a necessary party. Sanders v Yonkers (1875) 63 NY 489.

Where property was bid in by the mortgagee under an agreement to sell at an advance and give the mortgagor the benefit of the surplus, and such sale was made and completed before the entry of a judgment for deficiency, neither the mortgagor nor in case of his death, the persons interested in his estate, were necessary parties to an action by a grantee of other lands to set aside such judgment as a cloud on his title. Harris v Graham (1895) 90 Hun 198, 35 NYS 732, affd 154 NY 754, 49 NE 1097.

81. Conversion

As to necessary parties to an action to recover hypothecated bonds or their value, see Thompson v St. Nicholas Nat. Bank, 9 NYSR 363.

82. Action to recover deposit

Where a savings bank account was in the joint names of husband and wife and the signatures of both were required to draw, the husband was a necessary party defendant in an action by the wife to recover deposit. Murphy v Franklin Sav. Bank (1909) 131 AD 759, 116 NYS 228.

For dissolution of bank account, see Wicks v Walters (1941) 262 AD 780, 28 NYS2d 57.

83. Ejectment

In ejectment, occupant of real property was to be made defendant—effect of not joining others claiming title. Bradt v Church (1888) 110 NY 537, 18 NE 357.

Infant remaindermen neither claiming title to nor the right to the possession of the land nor doing any act in hostility to the plaintiff's title were not proper parties to an action of ejectment. Sisson v Cummings (1887) 106 NY 56, 12 NE 345.

84. Fraud

In an action brought by a receiver in supplementary proceedings to set aside as fraudulent an assignment of a chose in action made by the judgment debtor, the latter was a necessary party. Miller v Hall (1877) 70 NY 250.

In an action to set aside a fraudulent conveyance the court was not required to bring in other judgment creditors not originally made parties. White's Bank of Buffalo v Farthing (1886) 101 NY 344, 4 NE 734.

In a creditor's action to recover property fraudulently transferred by the debtor, the debtor was a necessary party defendant. Lathrop, Shea & Henwood Co. v Byrne (1906) 115 AD 846, 100 NYS 1041.

In an action to set aside proceedings by which an infant's real estate was sold under a fraudulent judgment, the party to such proceedings, who was alleged to have profited by the fraud, was a necessary party. Wiedersum v Naumann, 10 Abb NC 149, 62 How Pr 369.

In an action to set aside fraudulent conveyances, the alleged fraudulent grantor was a necessary party defendant. Hubbell v Merchants' Nat. Bank (1886) 42 Hun 200.

85. Injunction

Where persons having easements in common over a strip of land had not been made parties to a suit brought by one owner to restrain another from interfering with the right of way, the court could not determine that the defendant was justified in altering the condition of the land, as those having rights therein should be heard upon the question. Alexander Smith & Sons Carpet Co. v Ball (1911) 143 AD 83, 127 NYS 974.

In an action for an injunction and damages to plaintiff's lands based on the alleged wrongful obstruction of the waters of a stream, appellant county was properly joined as a party defendant, where it appeared that if the demands for money damages were withdrawn, as respondents indicate, all that remained was a cause of action in equity asserted against the county. Realty Associates, Inc. v Stoothoff (1940) 258 AD 462, 17 NYS2d 52.

Labor union made party to action by maintenance association to compel defendant to discharge employees retained in violation of closed shop agreement, where such labor union claimed that such closed shop agreement was made to evade jurisdiction of Labor Relations Board. Johnson v Bee Line, Inc. (1941, Sup) 28 NYS2d 18.

In action by apartment tenants and telephone company to enjoin landlord from preventing installation of telephone wires, landlord was held not entitled to bring in electrical workers union or telephone workers union in order to settle jurisdictional dispute between them. Bourianoff v Metropolitan Life Ins. Co. (1941, Sup) 29 NYS2d 54.

86. Taxpayer's action

In an action by a taxpayer against the board of supervisors, the collector of taxes, etc., to restrain the payment of certain accounts which had been audited by said board, it was proper to make each person claiming a part thereof a party. McCrea v Chahoon (1889) 54 Hun 577, 8 NYS 88; see also, Osterhoudt v Board of Supervisors (1885) 98 NY 239; Weeks v Cornwall (1886) 39 Hun 643, affd

104 NY 325, 10 NE 431; Mahler v Schmidt (1887) 43 Hun 512.

In a taxpayer's action to restrain a city from entering into a contract with the successful bidder for the paving of a street, the latter was a necessary party and the court would order the bidder brought in as a party defendant. Jensen v Board of Contract & Supply (1911) 74 Misc 641, 134 NYS 630.

As to necessary parties in action under taxpayer's act of 1881 to enjoin municipal corporation from paying out public moneys. Smith v Crissey, 13 Abb NC 149.

87. Insurance

The divorced wife of an insured, who was the original beneficiary under the policy, was held neither a necessary nor a proper party to a proceeding by the insured's children, who had procured their substitution as beneficiaries under § 1160, after the divorce was granted. Wilcox v Mutual Life Ins. Co. (1923) 235 NY 590, 139 NE 746.

88. Mortgage foreclosure

In an action to foreclose a mortgage where a judgment for deficiency was demanded against a grantee who set up that the assumption clause in the deed was fraudulently inserted by grantor, and prayed a reformation, the grantor simply setting up bankruptcy proceedings, it was held that a complete determination of the controversy between plaintiff and defendant could be made without the presence of any other party. Albany City Sav. Institution v Burdick (1881) 87 NY 40.

Unsecured creditors of a railroad were not necessary parties in an action to foreclose a mortgage of its property and franchises; any adjudication against the mortgagor being binding upon them. Herring v New York L. E. & W. R. Co. (1887) 105 NY 340, 12 NE 763.

Where, in action to foreclose a mortgage, it appeared that rights and priorities of a third party were involved which must be ascertained and settled, motion to bring in that party as a defendant should have been granted. 330 Bleecker Street Corp. v Mutual Tile Corp. (1932) 260 NY 258, 183 NE 381.

As to heir and next of kin of mortgagor let in to defend in foreclosure, see Zundel v Tacke (1888) 47 Hun 239.

In actions of foreclosure, person in possession should always be a party. Kopp v Kopp (1888) 48 Hun 532, 1 NYS 261.

Prior mortgagee was not a necessary party to foreclosure suit and if he died pending action the suit might proceed without reviving it against his successor. Ferris v Hard (1888, Super Ct) 4 NYS 9, revd on other grounds 135 NY 354, 32 NE 129.

In an action to foreclose a mortgage, a person should not be brought in as a party upon motion of a defendant, unless such person had some pecuniary interest in the subject of the action, and the moving party would be prejudiced by the

refusal to bring him in. Gano v Potter (1918) 105 Misc 482, 173 NYS 528.

89. Enforcement of liens

In action involving lien, an additional party, whether proper or necessary, was properly brought in so that all rights of interested parties could be determined in single action. Mitchell v Maynard (1941, Sup) 32 NYS2d 496.

The client was a necessary party in an action to enforce an attorney's lien. Oishei v Metropolitan S. R. C. (1906) 110 AD 709, 97 NYS 447.

In action against county to foreclose tax liens sold to plaintiff by village and claimed by county to be void, village was not necessary party in order to make complete determination of controversy, since if plaintiff succeeded against county, his cause of action against village failed, and if unsuccessful against county, he could still have remedy against village. Hessol v Hathaway (1941) 177 Misc 336, 30 NYS2d 600.

90. Mandamus

In proceeding for order annulling petitioner's removal as civil service commissioner, court on its own motion brought in substituted appointee. Hall v Scanlon (1942, Sup) 35 NYS2d 697.

91. Matrimonial actions

In an action brought by the mother of an infant under § 1139 to have the infant's marriage annulled on the ground that his consent was obtained by force, duress, or fraud, the infant was a necessary party. Fero v Fero (1901) 62 AD 470, 70 NYS 742.

In an action by a daughter to annul the marriage of her mother upon the ground that at the time of the marriage the mother was a lunatic and that the marriage was procured by the fraud and undue influence of the defendant, the incompetent was a necessary party and should be brought in upon her own motion. Coddington v Larner (1902) 75 AD 532, 78 NYS 276.

In action between a husband and wife to set aside a separation agreement on the ground of fraud, it was held that the court should require child and trustee to be made parties. Ducas v Ducas (1912) 150 AD 397, 135 NYS 35.

In action to declare invalid Nevada divorce and marriage between defendant and second husband, latter was necessary defendant. Varrichio v Varrichio (1945) 269 AD 678, 53 NYS2d 326.

92. Negligence

In an action to recover for damages to goods caused by the leakage of water pipes, all the owners of the goods must be joined as parties and the action could not be maintained by one of several owners. Moppar v Wiltchik (1907) 56 Misc 676, 107 NYS 594.

93. Notes

Where defense of usury, offset, and nonownership of note in suit were available to defendant without bringing in proposed party defendant, order therefor was improper. Erhardt v Stacy-Bush (1940) 259 AD 984, 20 NYS2d 429.

94. Nuisance

Where it appeared to the trial court that the defendant was not the owner of the property upon which it was alleged a nuisance existed, the court could suspend the trial and direct the plaintiff to bring in the present owner. Ackerman v True (1907) 120 AD 172, 105 NYS 12.

95. Partition

Where the will vested title in the executors, with directions to sell and divide the proceeds, legatees were not necessary parties in an action in partition, as their interest was in the proceeds only. Delafield v Barlow (1887) 107 NY 535, 14 NE 498.

In an action of partition persons not necessary parties could not be brought in by a motion of one of the defendants under CPA § 1017 (Real Prop. Actions & Proc. Law 903 herein), the plaintiff not having elected to bring such party in and said party opposing the motion; but the court could bring them in under CPA § 105 (§§ 2001, 3025(b), Rules 305(c), 2101(f) herein). Johnson v Aleshire (1909) 130 AD 178, 114 NYS 398.

In partition person in possession should always be a party. Kopp v Kopp (1888) 48 Hun 532, 1 NYS 261.

Where in an action of partition, S., one of the owners, had conveyed his interest subject to a claim of J. to be paid out of the proceeds, it was held that the interest of J. was no more than a personal right to receive a sum of money, and did not create in J. the sort of interest which made him a necessary party to such an action. Smith v Siblich (1891, Super Ct) 12 NYS 905.

S. claimed at the trial that she held possession as mortgagee and was entitled to hold possession until the mortgage was paid, and that consequently the decree for partition was improperly made. It was held that as she had not served her answer upon her codefendants she was not entitled as against them, to a judgment deciding as to the validity of the mortgage. Weston v Stoddard (1891) 60 Hun 290, 14 NYS 580, affd 137 NY 119, 33 NE 62.

96. Replevin

Under CPA § 1107 (§§ 7102(f), 7193(a), 7196(b) herein), which provided for the claim of a chattel in replevin by third parties, a claim must be made against the defendant and must be made before the chattel is actually delivered to either party; an application under former CPA § 193 would not be granted where the controversy between the parties could be completely determined without the intervention of others. Reimers v Schmitt (1902) 68 AD 299, 74 NYS 122.

97. Setting aside release

Where plaintiff sought to set aside releases signed by two persons not parties thereto, they were indispensable parties. Mannaberg v Culbertson (1942, Sup) 35 NYS2d 642, affd 265 AD 922, 39 NYS2d 984, revd 266 AD 765, 41 NYS2d 951.

98. Slander

An incompetent person was a necessary party defendant to an action for a slander alleged to have been uttered prior to a determination that he was insane, although a committee had been appointed. Capen v Delaney (1908) 128 AD 648, 113 NYS 50.

99. Specific performance

The personal representatives of a deceased vendor were necessary parties to an action for specific performance of a contract of sale. Potter v Ellice (1872) 48 NY 321.

In action for specific performance of contract by defendant's decedent to leave all his property on death to plaintiff, proof as to amount of estate must be made in order to determine if it was necessary to bring in decedent's heirs so that title to realty involved might not be adversely affected. Brindisi v Stallone (1940) 259 AD 1080, 21 NYS2d 29.

Where a vendor for the sale of land had entered into a new contract for the sale of the same land, the second vendee was a necessary party to an action for specific performance of the first contract. Fullerton v McCurdy (1873) 55 NY 637.

In vendee's action for specific performance, a third person to whom the vendor had sold the property subsequent to the contract was a necessary party. Kantrowitz v Rothweiler, 15 NYSR 297.

A subsequent purchaser was a necessary party to action for specific performance. Kantrowitz v Rothweiler, supra.

100. —Sale of corporate stock

Where complaint in action for specific performance alleged that defendant, owning majority of stock of defendant corporation, agreed on behalf of self and corporation to transfer one third of its stock to plaintiff, such corporation was necessary party. Plumbridge v Sweeney (1943, Sup) 42 NYS2d 463.

101. Wills

In an action between executors to construe a will, it was held that the court properly directed the beneficiaries to be brought in as parties. Power v Cassidy (1880) 79 NY 602.

A purchaser of the share of a defendant after judgment in an action to construe a will creating a trust could be made a party to the trustee's accounting. Savage v Sherman (1882) 87 NY 277.

In an action for the construction of a will, as to a power of appointment of property devised in trust, the persons who would have taken, had not such power been exercised, were necessary parties to the action and the record, on appeal, must disclose this fact. Pirsson v Gillespie (1889, Sup) 4 NYS 691.

The heirs and next of kin were necessary parties in an action against an administrator to enforce agreement of decedent to leave property by will, and the court must order them to be brought in. Williams v Williams (1890, Sup) 12 NYS 599.

c. THIRD-PARTY DEFENDANTS

102. Generally

Purpose of subdivision 2 of former CPA § 193 was to permit a party who was charged with some sort of liability to bring in another party liable to contribute or indemnify the party charged. Stern v George P. Ide & Co. (1925) 212 AD 714, 209 NYS 473; Driscoll v Corwin (1929) 133 Misc 788, 233 NYS 483.

The purpose of former CPA § 193 was to permit a defendant to frame a supplemental pleading in the nature of a complaint against the party sought to be brought in, which, if sustained, would entitle him to a judgment against the latter. Federal Lighterage Co. v Italia-America Shipping Corp (1925) 125 Misc 181, 210 NYS 458.

It was held that an application under former CPA § 193 to have a third person made a party should be granted, (1) where the third person was liable to the plaintiff jointly or severally with the defendant, or where either he or the defendant was so liable, for the claim sued upon, or (2) where, irrespective of the third person's liability to the plaintiff for the claim sued upon, he was liable to indemnify the defendant thereon. Lewis H. May Co. v Mott Ave. Corp. (1923) 121 Misc 398, 201 NYS 189.

The purpose of subdivision 2 of former CPA § 193 was to avoid multiplicity of suits. Mirsky v Seaich Realty Co. 256 AD 658, 11 NYS2d 191; Lepel High Frequency Laboratories, Inc. v Capita (1938) 168 Misc 583, 6 NYS2d 171, affd 256 AD 804, 9 NYS2d 896.

Former CPA § 193 would not permit plaintiff to bring in as a party defendant any party who might ultimately be liable to the plaintiff in the event that the original defendant successfully defended the action. Stern v George P. Ide & Co. (1925) 212 AD 714, 209 NYS 473.

The mere denial by the third party showing that a defense might exist would not defeat an application under subdivision 2 of former CPA § 193 which was designed to avoid circuity of action. Franklin v Meredith Co. (1933, CA2 NY) 64 F2d 109.

A party named as a defendant in the title of an action, who had not been served with a summons and complaint and never voluntarily appeared as a defendant, could be brought in by a supplemental summons pursuant to former CPA § 193. Bennett v Bird (1933) 237 AD 542, 261 NYS 540.

Evidence of plaintiff in a previous case involving the same cause of action as the instant case, but to which she was not a party, did not estop her from impleading as defendant one in whose favor such evidence was given. Jackson v Bickelhaupt (1927) 128 Misc 610, 219 NYS 601.

In an action by plaintiff for breach of contract consisting of the alleged failure of the defendant to return to the plaintiff skins delivered to the defendant to be dressed and dyed, the defendant was not entitled, under former § 193, to an order directing that certain other parties to whom the defendant claimed to have delivered the skins be brought in as parties defendant. New Netherland Bank v Goodman (1923, Sup) 201 NYS 188.

In action for breach of contract to deliver machinery free from defects, original defendant seller could implead as codefendant person employed by plaintiff buyer before purchase to inspect and approve machinery purchased from manufacturer by defendant seller. Du Rite Laundry v Washington Electric Co. (1942) 263 AD 396, 33 NYS2d 925.

In action by stockholders on guaranty by defendant of marginal trading account, plaintiffs' customer was brought in as party defendant pursuant to subdivision 2 of former CPA § 193. Fenner v Cahn (1933) 146 Misc 210, 261 NYS 528.

In action by Superintendent of Insurance, motion by defendant to interplead third party granted on conditions. Broderick v White (1933) 148 Misc 632, 266 NYS 223.

Where defendant was liable to plaintiff in tort, plaintiff's employer was brought in, defendant being liable to him under contract. Hejza v New York C. R. Co. (1930) 230 AD 624, 246 NYS 34.

Where party properly brought in and permitted to serve cross-pleading. Lo Dolce v United States Fidelity & Guaranty Co. (1929) 225 AD 883, 232 NYS 657.

103. Necessity for possible liability of original defendant

It was held that there must exist in first instance possible liability on part of original defendant for which impleaded defendant was primarily at fault. Gioscia v Weyerhaeuser S. S. Co. (1944) 267 AD 875, 46 NYS2d 447.

104. Necessity that third party be liable over to original defendant

Motion was denied where person sought to be brought in as additional party defendant was not a person who was or would be liable over to the defendant within the meaning of former § 193. Merritt v Rhodes (1931) 232 AD 422, 252 NYS 114; Kalinowski v Rock Asphalt & Constr. Co. (1932) 235 AD 657, 255 NYS 833; St. John v Thomas (1932) 235 AD 856, 257 NYS 896; Walden Arms, Inc. v Bernstein (1932) 236 AD 780, 258 NYS 1031; Katz v Bernstein (1932) 236 AD 780, 258 NYS 1026.

The bringing in of a party under former CPA § 193 was predicated upon the possibility that such party could or would be required to respond to a present defendant for the claim. Zauderer v Market St. Long Beach Realty Corp. (1926) 128 Misc 364, 218 NYS 669, affd 221 AD 760, 222 NYS 925.

Impleaded parties were determined not to be liable to the defendant for the claim made by plaintiff.

Franco-Belgian Importing Co. v Emigrant Industrial Sav. Bank (1940) 259 AD 803, 19 NYS2d 776.

Defendant could only implead third party against whom defendant had a claim based on primary or secondary liability. Brown v Cranston (1942, CA2 NY) 132 F2d 631, 148 ALR 1178, cert den 319 US 741, 87 L Ed 1698, 63 S Ct 1028.

105. Discretion of court

The amendment by chap. 512 of 1901 did not make it mandatory upon the court to grant an application of the plaintiff to have his grantee made a party to an action brought to restrain the operation of the elevated railroad in front of premises formerly owned by the plaintiff. Peope v Manhattan R. Co. (1903) 79 AD 583, 80 NYS 316.

It was within the discretion of the court, under former CPA § 193 to order the bringing in of an additional party defendant, in an action for damages for personal injuries. Fisher v Bullock (1923) 204 AD 523, 198 NYS 538; Hailfinger v Meyer (1925) 215 AD 35, 212 NYS 746; Schenck v Bradshaw (1931) 233 AD 171, 251 NYS 316; Irwin v New York Tel. Co. (1923) 121 Misc 642, 202 NYS 81; Hughes v Charles Schweinler Press (1936) 161 Misc 713, 293 NYS 259; Lepel High Frequency Laboratories, Inc. v Capita (1938) 168 Misc 583, 6 NYS2d 171, affd 256 AD 804, 9 NYS2d 896.

The discretion as to bringing in additional parties must be exercised in respect of rights under CPA § 211-a (§ 1401 herein), since it should not be exercised so as to impair or destroy a substantial right. La Lone v Carlin (1931) 139 Misc 553, 247 NYS 665.

By the 1923 amendment of former CPA § 193, the word "may" was substituted in place of the mandatory word "must," in subdivision 2. Zauderer v Market St. Long Beach Realty Corp. (1926) 128 Misc 364, 218 NYS 669, affd 221 AD 760, 222 NYS 925; and this substitution was intended to leave to the discretion of the court, the bringing in of a third party. Van Cott v Marion De Vries, Inc. (1930, CA2 NY) 37 F2d 48.

Former CPA § 193 authorized the court in its discretion to bring in parties in action at law at instance of defendant, where there was liability over, either through indemnity, contribution or otherwise, provided it appeared to the satisfaction of the court that the party brought in was or would be ultimately liable for the claim made by the plaintiff. 125 W. 45th St. Restaurant Corp. v Framax Realty Corp. (1936) 249 AD 589, 293 NYS 216.

106. Defenses and cross-claims by impleaded third party

The third party brought in under subdivision 2 of former CPA § 193 did not become a party to the original controversy and could defend only against the claim for indemnification or contribution, made against him by the original defendant. Mu-

nicipal Service Real Estate Co. v D. B. & M. Holding Corp. (1931) 257 NY 423, 178 NE 745, 78 ALR 323.

The defense that a trustee in bankruptcy had obtained title to a fund could not be asserted collaterally by anyone other than the trustee who was not a party to the action. Redondo S. S. Co. v Irving Bank-Columbia Trust Co. (1927) 219 AD 825, 221 NYS 83.

Under subdivision 2 of former CPA § 193 the party brought in could only plead with regard to the averments of the answer served upon him by the original defendant. Travlos v Commercial Union of America, Inc. (1930) 135 Misc 895, 238 NYS 692.

A defendant brought in by the original defendant under subdivision 2 of former CPA § 193 was confined to litigation of matters between the original defendant and himself; he could not litigate with the plaintiff; such a proceeding was not contemplated by the statute and it could not be exceeded nor departed from. Marsh v Standard Acci. Ins. Co. (1931) 141 Misc 484, 252 NYS 206, mod 235 AD 652, 254 NYS 1042.

107. Negligence

In an action against an insurance broker to recover damages a party whom the broker engaged to procure the insurance and whose negligence caused the loss to plaintiff, could properly be brought in as a party under subdivision 2 of former CPA § 193. Travlos v Commercial Union of America, Inc. (1926) 217 AD 352, 217 NYS 459.

In an action for negligence, a third party could be joined as a party where it was shown that he was or might be liable to the defendant or for claim made against defendant. Hotel Antlers, Inc. v Standard Oil Co. (1932) 144 Misc 781, 259 NYS 351.

108. —Party independently negligent

In a taxicab passenger's action against the taxicab company for injuries sustained in a collision between a taxicab and a streetcar, it was error, on motion of the defendant, to compel the streetcar company to come in as a defendant, thus raising issues as between the defendants. Greenhouse v Rochester Taxicab Co. (1926) 218 AD 224, 218 NYS 167.

Where neither complaint nor cross complaint alleges negligence as to impleaded defendant, order of impleader was improper; and where original defendant could be held liable to plaintiff independent of any acts of impleaded defendant, order was improper. Lumber Mut. Casualty Ins. Co. v Roberts (1943) 266 AD 749, 41 NYS2d 232.

It was held that if an accident might have happened due to the negligence, separately and not as joint tortfeasors, of two defendants, the one not sued should not be impleaded without notice to him. Jackson v Bickelhaupt (1927) 128 Misc 610, 219 NYS 601.

109. —Operator of motor vehicle in action against owner

In an action to recover for injuries suffered by the plaintiff while a passenger in an automobile owned by the appellant and driven by the plaintiff's husband, a motion by the appellant to add the driver as a party defendant was denied, where it appeared that negligent operation of the automobile, and operation knowing the automobile to be defective, were alleged against the appellant, but there was no allegation that the driver knew of the defect. Parness v Halpern (1939) 257 AD 678, 15 NYS2d 199.

In action for damages resulting from collision of defendant's truck with plaintiff's automobile in which she was riding, driven by third person, motion to bring in such person as defendant, on the ground that defendant might adduce evidence to defeat plaintiff's claim rather than to recover a joint judgment was denied. Shuler v Whitmore, Rauber & Vicinus (1930) 138 Misc 814, 246 NYS 528, affd 233 AD 892, 251 NYS 886.

The defendant owner of a motor vehicle was entitled to an order bringing in as an additional defendant the operator thereof at the time of the accident. Kurzon v Union R. Co. (1939) 172 Misc 37, 14 NYS2d 530.

In automobile guest's action for injuries in collision between streetcar and automobile owned by defendant, plaintiff's husband, and driven by their son, against insured husband and streetcar company, attorney for husband and his insurer, against former's wishes, obtained order permitting service of cross complaint on defendant's son, motion to dismiss cross complaint because obtained against wishes of defendant husband and because insurer was real party in interest, was denied. Kurzon v Union R. Co. (1940, City Ct) 21 NYS2d 310.

110. —Employees

The clause added to former CPA § 193 by the amendment of 1922 required the court, on motion of an employer sued for personal injuries alleged to be due to the negligence of an employee, to direct the joinder of such employee as party defendant upon the employer's affidavit that such employee would be wholly liable to him for the amount of any recovery in the action. Fedden v Brooklyn Eastern Dist. Terminal (1923) 204 AD 741, 199 NYS 9.

An employee sued as a codefendant with his employer in an action to recover damages for personal injuries alleged to have been sustained by the plaintiff through the negligence of the employee could not be stricken out as a party defendant on motion of the plaintiff, over the objection of the employer, where the liability of the employer was predicated solely upon the doctrine respondeat superior. Bessey v United States Shipping Board Emergency Fleet Corp. (1923) 204 AD 641, 199 NYS 15.

111. —Joint tortfeasor

Where a joint tortfeasor whom plaintiff had released from liability was brought in by the one

sued, under subdivision 2 of former CPA § 193, order dismissing him was proper, since a joint judgment for plaintiff was precluded. Fox v Western New York Motor Lines, Inc. (1931) 257 NY 305, 178 NE 289, 78 ALR 578.

The court had power under CPA § 105 (§§ 2001, 3025, Rules 305(c), 2101(f) herein), after an action was at issue as to two joint tortfeasors, to grant the plaintiff's motion to make a third joint tortfeasor a party defendant, and to allow the plaintiff to serve a supplemental summons and an amended complaint; relation between CPA §§ 105, 193 considered. Schun v Brooklyn H. R. Co. (1903) 82 AD 560, 81 NYS 859.

A defendant in a negligence action could not bring in a joint tortfeasor not made a party to the action by the plaintiff and not otherwise liable over to the defendant, and CPA § 211-a (§ 1401 herein) did not extend or modify former CPA § 193(2) in this regard. Fox v Western New York Motor Lines, Inc. (1931) 257 NY 305, 178 NE 289, 78 ALR 578, disapproving Haines v Bero Engineering Const. Corp. (1930) 230 AD 332, 243 NYS 657. As to cases where a joint tortfeasor could be brought in see McLaughlin v Syracuse (1945) 269 AD 382, 56 NYS2d 594.

By reading former CPA §§ 193, 211-a (§ 1401 herein) together a substantial right was given a defendant, in a tort action, to bring in another defendant, with which right the plaintiff might not interfere. Dee v Spencer (1931) 233 AD 217, 251 NYS 311; Blauvelt v Nyack (1931) 141 Misc 730, 252 NYS 746. (But see Fox v Western New York Motor Lines, Inc. (1931) 257 NY 305, 178 NE 289, 78 ALR 578.)

A joint tortfeasor could not be brought in on the application of a defendant in the action unless the party to be brought in was liable over to the defendant by reason of contract or status. Rhynders v Greene (1938) 255 AD 401, 8 NYS2d 143.

The rule that former CPA § 193 did not permit the bringing in of a third party as a joint tortfeasor was unaffected by the 1928 amendment of CPA § 211-a (§ 1401 herein). Rowe v Denler (1929) 135 Misc 286, 238 NYS 9.

The liability contemplated by subdivision 2 of former CPA § 193 could exist by virtue of CPA § 211-a (§ 1401 herein). Shuler v Whitmore, Rauber & Vicinus (1930) 138 Misc 814, 246 NYS 528, affd 233 AD 892, 251 NYS 886.

Purpose of subdivision 2 of former CPA § 193 was that where plaintiff had not joined tortfeasors, one of them could bring in others so that contribution could be had under CPA § 211-a (§ 1401 herein). Riley v Wood (1931) 139 Misc 314, 248 NYS 326.

In an action against the shipper of chlorine, alleging injuries from gas escaping from defective tank car, a motion by the defendant under subdivision 2 of former CPA § 193 to bring in the railway company which was transporting the chlorine, was denied in the court's discretion, where it appeared that the defendant was not the passive and secondary wrongdoer and that the railway company was not the active and primary wrongdoer. DeMarchi v Electro Bleaching Gas Co. (1935) 155 Misc 143, 278 NYS 571.

112. —Actions by automobile passengers

The plaintiff in an action had the right to join or not to join joint tortfeasors, and, after joinder, to discontinue or settle with any of them at any stage of the proceeding without consulting the other joint tortfeasor. The rights of joint tortfeasors to contribution, as against each other, did not arise until the entry of judgment against them and the payment thereof. Piratensky v Wallach (1937) 162 Misc 749, 295 NYS 581.

Where plaintiff, when injured, was riding as a guest in an automobile with which defendant's car collided, defendant's motion to bring in plaintiff's host was denied. Rothman v Byron (1931) 141 Misc 770, 253 NYS 812.

The driver and his passenger suffered damages in an automobile accident; the driver recovered of the negligent parties; in the passenger's suit against the same parties the driver was brought in; his defense of res judicata was sustained. Boice v Pallette (1931) 140 Misc 763, 252 NYS 40, affd 234 AD 644, 251 NYS 922.

It was ultimately held contrary to some earlier decisions, among them actions by passengers (Davis v Hauk & Schmidt, Inc. (1931) 232 AD 556, 250 NYS 537; Schenck v Bradshaw (1931) 233 AD 171, 251 NYS 316; Ackerson v Kibler (1931) 138 Misc 695, 246 NYS 580, affd 232 AD 306, 249 NYS 629), that former CPA § 193 did not permit the impleading of one joint tortfeasor by another, regardless of CPA § 211-a (§ 1401 herein). Fox v Western New York Motor Lines, Inc. (1931) 257 NY 305, 178 NE 289, 78 ALR 578; and see 85, supra.

113. Indemnitors

Landlord was entitled to an order, under subdivision 2 of former CPA § 193, bringing in the impleaded defendants as parties defendant in this action to recover a sum deposited as security under a written lease, where defendants had executed agreements of indemnity in favor of appellant relative to the security in question. 125 W. 45th St. Restaurant Corp. v Framax Realty Corp. (1936) 249 AD 589, 293 NYS 216.

In action for personal injuries against city and impleaded defendant, latter's motion to dismiss city's cross complaint was denied, where contract warranting impleader was broad enough to include liability over to city. Langellotti v New York (1941) 262 AD 1027, 30 NYS2d 353.

Property owner could be brought in by city, sued for personal injuries from icicle falling from roof of former, where city was entitled to indemnity from property owner. McLaughlin v Syracuse (1945) 269 AD 382, 56 NYS2d 594.

In negligence action against the owner of property, the defendant could not bring in as indemnitor a utility company which had paid the plaintiff a certain sum and had obtained a release in full of all claims. Handelman v Dime Sav. Bank (1937) 164 Misc 651, 300 NYS 17.

In action for negligence, defendant sued could not implead indemnifying defendant, although plaintiff could have sued both. Roxy Theatre, Inc. v Queensboro Farm Products, Inc. (1943) 180 Misc 707, 43 NYS2d 128.

Where defendant sheriff was indemnified against plaintiff's claim, in connection with a levy made by him, the principal and surety on the indemnity bond were brought in. Driscoll v Corwin (1929) 133 Misc 788, 233 NYS 483.

In an action against the surety by the principal's creditor defendant was denied permission to bring in the principal as a defendant. Scripture v Buckley (1930) 137 Misc 155, 241 NYS 635.

114. Contractors and subcontractors

In an action against the owner for negligent injury he could bring in an independent contractor alleged to be responsible for the defective condition of the premises. Hailfinger v Meyer (1925) 215 AD 35, 212 NYS 746.

In action against the owner of a building under construction for damages for negligent death, contractors doing the work should have been brought in. Day v Fifth Ave. & 43rd Street Bldg. Corp. (1931) 231 AD 89, 246 NYS 380.

Contractor's answer in action by injured employee of subcontractor did not authorize bringing in subcontractor. Hodges v Bewley Truesdale Contracting Co. (1931) 231 AD 495, 247 NYS 414.

In action for death of employee of masonry subcontractor against contractor and carpentry subcontractor for latter's negligence, masonry subcontractor could not be brought in by contractor. Di Benedetto v Albert A. Lutz Co. (1941) 261 AD 1080, 26 NYS2d 872.

In action by contractor against owner of building on contract for alteration, owner counterclaimed for breach by contractor, and plaintiff contractor brought in subcontractor as party, claiming latter would be liable for such breach. Capitol Motion Picture Supply Corp. v Joan of Arc Pictures, Inc. (1939) 173 Misc 773, 19 NYS2d 116.

115. —For municipality

Contractor was brought into action against city for damage from subway excavation. Judgment was reversed because the proper measure of damages was not applied. Evelyn Bldg. Corp. v New York (1931) 257 NY 501, 178 NE 771.

In suit to restrain a city from interfering with plaintiff's business by constructing a subway, contractor constructing was brought in. Eighth & N. A. R. Co. v New York (1928) 224 AD 467, 231 NYS 259. See also Eighth & N. A. R. Co. v New York (1928) 224 AD 470, 231 NYS 262.

In an action to recover damages from delay of the defendant city in completing contract to construct a pier, the defendant was not entitled to bring in the contractors where its contract with them contained no provision by which they agreed to indemnify the city for any damages caused by delay in their completion of the work. New York

Dock Co. v New York (1935) 246 AD 620, 283 NYS 2.

In an action for injuries by the plaintiff wife while a passenger in an automobile which was precipitated into an opening in the street of the defendant municipal corporation, defendant was entitled to bring in the contractor. While it did not appear that the defendant sought to be impleaded was liable over "by reason of contract," it did appear that such defendant could be liable over "by reason of status." Branch v Eastchester (1939) 258 AD 727, 14 NYS2d 863.

In an action against the defendant village for negligence in leaving an open ditch during the construction of new sewers by independent contractors, the defendant was entitled, in the court's discretion, to implead the independent contractors as defendants under subdivision 2 of former § 193. Wade v Livonia (1940) 174 Misc 893, 21 NYS2d 1020.

116. Warrantors and manufacturers

In action for damages from explosion of soda water bottle purchased from defendant retailer, he could not bring in bottler as party defendant without proper allegations. Host v Minkowitz (1945, Sup App T) 53 NYS2d 251.

In an action to recover for goods sold and delivered, defended on the ground that the goods were imperfect, it was improper to permit plaintiff to bring in as defendants, parties who furnished and delivered the goods to the principal defendant on orders from plaintiff, so that plaintiff might recover of the parties brought in any damages because of the imperfections. Stern v George P. Ide & Co. (1925) 212 AD 714, 209 NYS 473.

In a suit for personal injuries against the retailer for breach of warranty in selling impure food, the manufacturer could be brought in by defendant by supplemental summons and pleading. Cohen v Dugan Bros., Inc. (1929) 134 Misc 155, 235 NYS 118.

In action by indorsee of note given for purchase price of a machine with answer setting up breach of warranty, motion under subdivision 2 of former CPA § 193 to bring in the seller of the machine and counterclaim against him was denied. Levin v Lax & Abowitz (1930) 137 Misc 132, 241 NYS 486.

In an action to recover damages from fire caused by defect in plan for heating system, the manufacturer of the insulating material was improperly brought in as a party where it was not shown that it would be liable to the defendant upon the theory of false representations for any damages recovered. Nichols v Clark, MacMullen & Riley, Inc. (1933) 261 NY 118, 184 NE 729.

In action for breach of warranty of fitness of a dress bought by the plaintiff, the retailer defendant was entitled to bring in its vendor. Deal v Lilyan Bertell, Inc. (1938) 168 Misc 254, 5 NYS2d 772.

In action for breach of express warranty of house shingles, original defendant pleaded written contract which limited plaintiff's claim to implied warranty of merchantability; cross complaints of contractor against seller and of seller against manufacturer, for breach of warranty of merchantability, were sufficient as alleging same claims as plaintiff's claim. Cirulli v Heaphy (1943, Sup) 44 NYS2d 822.

117. Insurer

An insurer of the owner of premises against liability under a policy conditioned that insured shall have paid any loss, could not be brought into an action against the owner for negligence, under former CPA § 193, since the liability of the insurer might never accrue; and evidence that defendant was insured was incompetent and, when admitted, might constitute ground for reversal even when stricken out. Kromback v Killian (1925) 215 AD 19, 213 NYS 138.

Plaintiff was entitled to a mechanic's lien, the building burned and the land was valueless. In action against the owner, plaintiff alleged that the building had been insured for his benefit; an order bringing in the insurer, filing a supplemental complaint against him and obtaining an order restraining payment of the insurance until determination of the controversy was proper practice. R. Prescott & Son, Inc. v Nye (1928) 223 AD 356, 228 NYS 156.

In action for injuries from negligent maintenance of scaffold by defendant contractor, defendant could not bring in another for breach of contract to cause defendant to be insured against liability. Weissman v Spencer, White & Prentis, Inc. (1941) 262 AD 155, 28 NYS2d 278.

In action to recover damages for the death of the plaintiff's intestate, the defendant was not permitted to bring in its insurer and its insurance agent as parties defendant, where there was an issue as to the liability of the insurer to its insured, under an accident policy, and where no negligence of proposed defendants would be raised in regard to the accident. Jacobs v Pellegrino (1935) 154 Misc 651, 277 NYS 654.

In action brought to recover damages caused by a collision between motor trucks owned by the respective parties, where it appeared that defendants' insurer had advanced the amount of its policy covering damages, taking in return a loan receipt, such advance constituted a payment by the insurer under the terms of the policy and, to that extent, the insurer became subrogated to the rights of the defendants and was a necessary party to prevent a multiplicity of actions. Simpson v Hartranft (1935) 157 Misc 387, 283 NYS 754.

In action on policy of liability insurance, the defendant was entitled to interplead another insurer. Michigan Alkali Co. v Bankers Indem. Ins. Co. (1937, DC NY) 20 F Supp 424.

118. Indorsers or others liable on notes

In suit or promissory notes, parties alleged by defendants to be eventually liable to pay the same, were held properly brought in as defendants. Williams v Edward De V. Tompkins, Inc. (1924) 211 AD 17, 206 NYS 637.

In action against a bank on a certified note, defendant's motion was granted to have the maker interplead and have litigated the question of who was entitled to the proceeds of the note. Greenberg v World Exch. Bank (1929) 227 AD 413, 237 NYS 200.

In action on a note, maker's counterclaim stated no action against plaintiff by parties he sought to bring in. National City Bank v Holzworth (1931) 231 AD 688, 248 NYS 584.

Defendant, the maker of a note, could not against plaintiff's protest bring in drawee indorsers as parties defendant to try out against them a claimed cause of action for damages based on wrongful diversion of the note. Hayes Nat. Bank v Chynoweth (1932) 235 AD 890, 257 NYS 561.

An action by holder against indorsers of promissory note was joint or several, as the plaintiff might elect, and no right existed on the part of indorsers sued to bring in the other indorsers as parties defendant. Citizens Trust Co. v Zoller (1923) 121 Misc 451, 201 NYS 179.

In action by depositor to recover amounts paid on altered checks, the original complaint as well as complaints of defendant against other banks brought in by it under subdivision 2 of former CPA § 193 were dismissed, the alterations not being apparent on the face of the checks, and plaintiff being estopped by his own negligence. Weiner v Chase Nat. Bank (1931) 142 Misc 124, 253 NYS 203.

119. Assignors, assignees, grantees

A motion by the owner of two lots who had sued to enjoin the maintenance of a railroad on a street in front thereof to bring in as a party his grantee of one of such lots should have been denied. Welde v New York & H. R. Co. (1905) 108 AD 286, 95 NYS 728.

Motion by defendant under subdivision 2 of former CPA § 193 to implead plaintiff's assignor was denied in an action by plaintiff as an assignee to recover a balance due her from defendant under assignments. Cullen v New York (1940) 259 AD 799, 18 NYS2d 792.

In suit by assignee of mortgage defendant mortgagee could not compel plaintiff to join assignor. Cohen v Lane (1889, Sup) 4 NYS 228.

In an action by an assignee for work, labor, services and materials furnished, in which the defense was that the work was badly done, a motion, under subdivision 2 of former CPA § 193 to bring in as defendant the assignor of the plaintiff on the claim on which action was brought was denied. The motion was granted, however, with respect to a proposed defendant, which had given the order for the work to the original defendant, which had given the identical order in turn to the plaintiff's assignor. Hughes v Charles Schweinler Press (1936) 161 Misc 713, 293 NYS 259.

120. Lessee

In an action against a landlord and one of two colessees for injuries suffered on defective stairs,

the motion of the landlord to bring in the other lessee was granted. Booth v Silverman (1935) 157 Misc 93, 283 NYS 35.

In action against owner of building for injuries to tenant's employee from defective freight elevator, defendant could bring in as codefendants lessee of entire building and plaintiff's employer, who as tenant had agreed to indemnify landlord against claims from operation of building. Garrambone v Beekman Operating Co. (1946, Sup) 63 NYS2d 655.

121. Principal and agent

Where the primary defendant claimed that he contracted as agent for the benefit of his principal who was bound to reimburse him for the liability assumed, it was not error to bring in the alleged principal under former CPA § 193, but it was improper to order plaintiff to serve a supplemental pleading upon the third party. Federal Lighterage Co. v Italia-America Shipping Corp. (1925) 125 Misc 181, 210 NYS 458.

In an action for the down payment on a contract for the sale of real estate by plaintiff, an infant, the defendants, pleading a counterclaim, were not entitled under former CPA § 193 to bring in third parties on the theory that such parties were the principals and plaintiff was merely their agent. Zauderer v Market St. Long Beach Realty Corp. (1926) 128 Misc 364, 218 NYS 669, affd 221 AD 760, 222 NYS 925.

Where drafts were drawn by stockbrokers upon themselves payable through trust company which, on receipt of checks to cover from stockbrokers, marked drafts "paid" and permitted them to clear through its account, trust company merely acted as agent and guaranteed no prior indorsement and so could not be impleaded by stockbrokers sued on forged indorsement of drafts. Popkin v Gilmour (1942) 178 Misc 1074, 37 NYS2d 747.

122. Purchaser of realty in action by broker for commission

Former CPA § 193 was no basis for a claim by a real-estate broker to recover commissions from the purchaser under a clause in a contract of sale whereby purchaser agreed to indemnify the seller for commissions recovered. Warsawer v Burghard (1932) 234 AD 346, 254 NYS 749.

In a suit by plaintiff for commissions as a real-estate broker for securing a purchaser, the defendant was not entitled to have the purchaser brought in as a party defendant on the ground that the latter was liable to the defendant if the defendant was held liable to the plaintiff because in the contract of sale the purchaser represented that there was no broker. Lewis H. May Co. v Mott Ave. Corp. (1923) 121 Misc 398, 201 NYS 189.

123. Real-estate broker in action by another broker for commission

In action by real-estate broker to recover commissions, vendor could bring in as party another broker to whom commissions have been paid.

Franklin v Meredith Co. (1933, CA2 NY) 64 F2d 109.

124. Carriers and consignees

In a suit upon a special agreement of the defendants to forward and deliver merchandise at a certain time, the defendants could under former CPA § 193 have the railroad shipping the goods made a party defendant for having delayed the shipment. Wichert, Inc. v Gallagher & Ascher (1923) 201 NYS 186, affd 206 AD 756, 200 NYS 957.

If consignor of goods shipped sued carrier for breach of duty to collect purchase price, carrier could implead consignee. Novick v Kirschbaum (1944, City Ct) 50 NYS2d 279.

125. Municipal corporations

In pedestrian's action for injuries by city automobile driven by policeman, city was properly joined as defendant, since it would be liable over in event of recovery. Kosiba v Syracuse (1940) 260 AD 557, 24 NYS2d 37, reh den 261 AD 884, 25 NYS2d 1021 and affd in part and revd in part 287 NY 283, 39 NE2d 240.

In mandamus to compel the superintendent of highways to repair a highway, it was assumed the court would have power to bring in the town as defendant and that then mandamus to repair would necessarily imply a command to the town to provide the necessary funds. People ex rel. Johnson v Keesler (1930) 138 Misc 607, 245 NYS 534.

126. Conversion

In action for conversion against bank by corporation payee of checks transferred by its president without authority to its vice president who deposited them with bank and received their proceeds, bank impleaded its depositor, plaintiff's vice president. L. W. Cox & Co. v Chemical Bank & Trust Co. (1941) 175 Misc 1063, 26 NYS2d 38.

127. Ejectment

Motion by defendants in action for ejectment for order directing that plaintiff's grantor be made a party defendant denied, since it did not appear that such grantor would be liable to the defendants for the identical relief sought against them by the plaintiff. Gilbert v Mehrtens (1936) 159 Misc 702, 287 NYS 657.

128. Mortgage foreclosure

Where counterclaims in foreclosure alleged that defendant's mortgages were superior to plaintiff's mortgages and in cross complaints against respondents, defendants alleged respondents sold consolidated mortgages to plaintiff and represented them to be first liens, there was sufficient identity of subject matter to warrant impleading of respondents and cross complaints against them. Mayer v Borough Hall Holding Corp. (1942) 263 AD 971, 1001, 33 NYS2d 179.

Where purchaser of mortgaged premises assumed payment of mortgage, relationship of principal and surety existed between him and mortgagor; and in action on mortgage bond, mortgagor could bring in such purchaser grantee as party to action. Marks v Follow (1941) 177 Misc 108, 29 NYS2d 1019.

129. Replevin

Plaintiff in action in replevin was not entitled, under either former CPA §§ 192, 193 to an order bringing in as a party defendant a third party who had served on the sheriff a notice of claim of ownership. McLaughlin v McLaughlin (1932) 237 AD 1, 260 NYS 357, affd 261 NY 573, 185 NE 743.

d. PROCEDURE ON BRINGING IN THIRD PARTIES

130. Generally

In action to foreclose a mortgage, plaintiff's right to a judgment for a deficiency was withheld pending the bringing in, pursuant to former CPA § 193 of defendants' grantees. Albany Exchange Sav. Bank v Winne (1938) 168 Misc 853, 6 NYS2d 699.

A motion by a defendant in default to bring in additional defendants could not prevail, but the defendant could pay into court the amount claimed and then was entitled to an order substituting in his place any claimants to the fund and the sheriff who attached it and to be discharged from his liability. American Trust & Sav. Bank v Thalheimer (1898) 29 AD 170, 51 NYS 813.

When the time within which a complaint might be amended had not expired, an amendment could be made bringing in a defendant who was shown by the allegations of the answer to be a proper and necessary party for a complete determination of the controversy. McDonald v McDonald (1907) 120 AD 367, 105 NYS 277.

131. Time for bringing in; laches

Defendant's motion to bring in another party who was liable was improperly denied on the ground of laches, since the delay did not preclude consideration of the application upon the merits. Davis v Hauk & Schmidt, Inc. (1931) 232 AD 556, 250 NYS 537.

A party might even be brought in after judgment in order to test the validity of the judgment by an appeal. H. Koehler & Co. v Brady (1903) 82 AD 279, 81 NYS 695.

In an action to recover damages for a sale of merchandise alleged to have been induced by fraud, a judgment dismissing the complaint should not be opened and the plaintiff permitted to bring in an additional defendant who appeared upon the trial to have been the most active participator in the alleged fraud, where it appeared that the plaintiff knew that fact before the action was commenced. Lederer v Adler (1906) 51 Misc 572, 101 NYS 53.

After appeal, see Davis v Mayor, etc., of New York (1856) 14 NY 506.

Claim of laches was disallowed. Hejza v New York C. R. Co. (1930) 230 AD 624, 246 NYS 34.

132. —Limitation of actions

The court had no power to deprive a party of a statute of limitations which had run in his favor, by bringing him in as a party to an action already pending. Re Phalen's Will (1889) 51 Hun 208, 4 NYS 408; Harris v Simpson (1930) 137 Misc 809, 243 NYS 457.

133. Notice

Notice of application to bring in additional parties was generally, but not universally, required as to existing and proposed parties. Hodges v Bewley Truesdale Contracting Co. (1931) 231 AD 495, 247 NYS 414; Schultze v Ocean Acci. & Guarantee Corp. (1933) 239 AD 309, 267 NYS 284; Testing Laboratories of New York, Inc. v Krainin (1925) 124 Misc 667, 208 NYS 801; Jackson v Bickelhaupt (1927) 128 Misc 610, 219 NYS 601; Seaman v Colon (1927) 130 Misc 568, 224 NYS 338; Globe Indem. Co. v MacDougal (1928) 133 Misc 263, 231 NYS 643; Urban v Bifulco (1930) 138 Misc 506, 240 NYS 760; Danziger v Amalgamated Bank of New York (1932) 143 Misc 126, 255 NYS 344; Morbito v Rupp (1932) 143 Misc 385, 256 NYS 605.

The general provisions of CPA § 105 (§§ 2001, 3025, Rules 305(c), 2101(f) herein) as to adding names of parties were held inapplicable under former CPA § 193. Horan v Bruning (1906) 116 AD 482, 101 NYS 986.

134. Affidavit

To bring in new party, application had to be based upon a moving affidavit containing sufficient probative facts. Nichols v Clark, MacMullen & Riley, Inc. (1933) 261 NY 118, 184 NE 729; George A. Moore & Co. v Heymann (1923) 207 AD 416, 202 NYS 99; Hailfinger v Meyer (1925) 215 AD 35, 212 NYS 746; Irwin v New York Tel. Co. (1923) 121 Misc 642, 202 NYS 81; Ladue v Goodhead (1943) 181 Misc 807, 44 NYS2d 783.

A defendant moving to bring in an additional party defendant was required to make a prima facie showing that the defendant sought to be impleaded was or would be liable to the moving defendant. Leonardi v Bassett (1936) 161 Misc 324, 291 NYS 947; Hines v National Gum & Mica Co. (1925) 124 Misc 511, 208 NYS 460.

Affidavit forming basis for application for order to bring in additional party defendant should have been made by defendant, not by attorney, or reasons given why not so made. George A. Moore & Co. v Heymann (1923) 207 AD 416, 202 NYS 99; Urban v Bifulco (1930, Sup) 138 Misc 506, 240 NYS 760.

135. Vacation of order

Rules as to vacation of order under former CPA § 193 stated. Booth v Carleton Co. (1932) 236 AD 296, 258 NYS 159; Wichert, Inc. v Gallagher & Ascher (1923) 201 NYS 186, affd 206 AD 756,

200 NYS 957; Jackson v Bickelhaupt (1927) 128 Misc 610, 219 NYS 601.

136. Appealability of order

An order bringing in new parties, made under former CPA § 193 was appealable. Testing Laboratories of New York, Inc. v Krainin (1925) 124 Misc 667, 208 NYS 801.

137. Removal from trial calendar

Where new parties who were guarantors were brought in, the cause should have been stricken off the trial calendar until issue was joined between all the parties upon service of additional pleadings. Weinrich v Rosenblatt (1928) 133 Misc 484, 233 NYS 131.

138. New pleadings

Statute contemplated that the claim by the original defendant against an indemnitor should be alleged in a supplemental pleading, to which the indemnitor could only interpose an answer. Municipal Service Real Estate Co. v D. B. & M. Holding Corp. (1931) 257 NY 423, 178 NE 745, 78 ALR 323.

Single trial of issues raised by complaints, answers, and cross complaints warranted cross complaints against co-defendants. Arroway v De Franco (1940) 260 AD 988, 23 NYS2d 340.

In action for damages arising from the death of plaintiff's intestate as the result of a collision between automobiles driven by the individual defendant and by the intestate, respectively, in which the defendant company, as owner, was impleaded and interposed an answer, a motion by the impleaded defendant to amend its answer should have been allowed in the discretion of the court. Newman v Goldberg (1937) 250 AD 431, 294 NYS 211.

Proper pleading after defendants had been brought in. Davis v Hauk & Schmidt, Inc. (1931) 232 AD 556, 250 NYS 537.

Under subdivision 2 of former CPA § 193, a third person was brought in to meet a claim asserted against him by one of the original parties. Where plaintiff made no claim against the additional defendant, latter could create no controversy with plaintiff by serving an answer, and order granting plaintiff's motion to strike his answer was affirmed. Municipal Service Real Estate Co. v D. B. & M. Holding Corp. (1931) 257 NY 423, 178 NE 745, 78 ALR 323.

Drawing of new pleadings when change in parties was made fell upon attorneys of the respective parties. Urban v Bifulco (1930, Sup) 138 Misc 506, 240 NYS 760.

An order granted upon a motion made at the close of the plaintiff's case, making a third person a party defendant without any actual amendment of the pleadings or any allegation therein relating to him, or any appearance for him on the record, did not make him a party to the record so as to be bound thereby. Lehrer v Walcoff (1905) 47 Misc 112, 93 NYS 540. See also Saragovitz v Cohen (1933) 147 Misc 557, 264 NYS 201.

139. —Allegations

In action for injuries from bottle explosion, retailer could not implead bottler without alleging that bottle was in the same condition when he sold it as when he bought it. Host v Minkowitz (1945, Sup App T) 53 NYS2d 251.

Where one who claimed to have a subsequent lien served an answer and alleged that he had a prior equitable lien, his answer should not have been stricken out as frivolous. Older v Russell (1896) 8 AD 518, 40 NYS 892.

Sufficiency of answer pleading nonjoinder in action to determine validity of probate of will was immaterial. Judson v Staley (1914) 163 AD 62, 148 NYS 733.

140. Judgment

The provision of former CPA § 193 that a claim should proceed to a judgment "as may be proper" indicated that the form of judgment in each instance was dependent upon the facts of the particular case presented to the court. Provisional judgment entered in this case provided that the indemnitors should be required to satisfy the judgments against them when payment should have been made by their next succeeding indemnitee. First Nat. Bank v Bankers' Trust Co. (1934) 151 Misc 233, 271 NYS 191.

If a second defendant was brought into the action by the original defendant, judgment for plaintiff had to be against the latter and not the former who would have judgment directed against him in favor of the original defendant. Otis Elevator Co. v Miller (1926) 127 Misc 421, 216 NYS 320.

In action against original and impleaded defendants as joint tortfeasors, it was held that plaintiff should be granted judgment on jury's verdict, without having to await undecided issues between defendants. Schroeder v City & County Sav. Bank (1943) 267 AD 206, 46 NYS2d 46, mod on other grounds 293 NY 370, 57 NE2d 57.

The result of the litigation, if favorable to the claim of the plaintiff and to the position of the defendant as against his codefendant, should have been a judgment for the plaintiff against the party defendant sued in the first instance, and a judgment by the latter against the codefendant as if separately tried. Bozzuffi v Darrieusecq (1925) 125 Misc 178, 210 NYS 455.

Statute did not provide that a judgment in favor of plaintiff against one defendant should constitute a binding adjudication against an additional third-party defendant. Municipal Service Real Estate Co. v D. B. & M. Holding Corp. (1931) 257 NY 423, 178 NE 745, 78 ALR 323.

141. —Costs

Where plaintiff was a stranger to the issue between an original defendant and another brought in by him without notice to plaintiff, judgment against plaintiff for costs in favor of the defendant brought in was improper under subdivision 2 of former CPA § 193. Pagliaro v Mabey (1929) 227 AD 275, 237 NYS 599.

A defendant, impleaded under former CPA § 193 by the original defendant, was entitled to costs against the original defendant, who, in a position akin to that of a plaintiff, sought recovery on a groundless claim against the impleaded defendant. Strudler v Libray Realty Corp. (1938) 166 Misc 617, 2 NYS2d 857.

Impleaded defendant was properly denied discretionary costs against impleading defendant, where former was denied recovery from latter. O'Connor v Byrndun Corp. (1943) 182 Misc 952, 47 NYS2d 51. See Fish v Frick Co. (1944, Sup) 49 NYS2d 46.

e. INTERVENTION

142. Generally

Circumstances under which intervention was justified under former CPA § 193 stated. Touhey Co. v Shongo Const. Co. (1917) 100 Misc 181, 165 NYS 420.

A corporation which had submitted a bid for bus operations in a city could not intervene in injunction proceedings by a railroad company against the city to prohibit the granting of franchises to bus corporations, since such corporation was not a necessary or proper party. However, its counsel could be heard as amicus curiae. Yonkers R. Co. v Yonkers (1926) 128 Misc 107, 217 NYS 685.

In an action to recover broker's commissions a party who did not actively engage in the transaction, but who participated in settlement of the case was thereafter estopped from intervening by the stipulation to discontinue the case. Fankhauser v Smith (1928) 223 AD 35, 227 NYS 373.

143. Effect of right to interplead

Even though a party might be entitled to an order of interpleader, yet he could be entitled under former CPA § 193 to an order making the person a party defendant. Helene v Corn Exchange Bank (1904) 96 AD 392, 89 NYS 310.

144. Interest in controversy

The interest which necessitated the bringing in of one not a party, on his application, was a property interest or some duty or right developing upon or belonging to the party to be brought in. Morrell v Brooklyn Borough Gas Co. (1921) 231 NY 405, 132 NE 130; Corcoran v Scolaro (1943, Sup) 46 NYS2d 278, revd on other grounds 267 AD 871, 46 NYS2d 377; Bush Terminal Bldgs. Co. v Bush T. R. Co. (1945, Sup) 55 NYS2d 686.

A person not a party to an action could be brought in on his own motion under former CPA § 193 only where he had an interest in the subject of the action, or in real property title to which might be affected by the judgment, or for injury to which relief was demanded. Tysen v Tysen (1910) 137 AD 134, 121 NYS 962.

As to nature of interest see Dechert v Pratt (1943) 182 Misc 515, 44 NYS2d 475.

The fact that plaintiffs had lost their own rights in an action could not deprive a party who had an interest in the subject of the action from intervening for the mandatory relief to which he was entitled under former CPA § 193. Maas v Sullivan (1924) 124 Misc 295, 207 NYS 181, affd 213 AD 820, 208 NYS 895.

Where one owing money to a contracting company under a contract had interpleaded a judgment creditor of the contracting company, whose execution had been returned unsatisfied, the creditor had such an interest in the subject matter of the action as to give him the right to be brought in as a party defendant. Edison Illuminating Co. v Horace E. Frick Co. (1911) 146 AD 605, 131 NYS 125.

In action to have a deed from plaintiff's assignor to another declared a mortgage and that plaintiff be allowed to redeem, a third party claiming to be the owner of the fee had an absolute right to intervenc as a defendant. Mulholland v Reid (1915) 165 AD 862, 150 NYS 784.

An action at law to recover damages for entering and cutting and removing timber was held to involve title to property, and a grantor under a warranty deed who might be liable on her covenant was entitled to be made a party. Brooklyn Cooperage Co. v Sherman Lumber Co. (1916) 175 AD 246, 161 NYS 514, revd 220 NY 642, 115 NE 715.

In action on an insurance policy, pending which plaintiff died, surviving wife claiming as tenant by entirety was properly brought in. Scutella v County Fire Ins. Co. (1931) 231 AD 343, 247 NYS 689.

The State Labor Relations Board was not entitled to intervene in an action by a company to enjoin the defendant union from violating a contract made between the parties with the consent and knowledge of the Board. United Baking Co. v Bakery & Confectionery Workers' Union (1939) 257 AD 501, 1085, 14 NYS2d 74.

In an action by a foreign city to recover of a firm for the value of city bonds which the firm had wrongfully sold, and as to which the city offered to restore what it had been paid by the firm, the application of bondholders to whom the bonds had been sold to intervene should have been denied. Ironwood v Coffin (1902) 39 Misc 278, 79 NYS 502.

Guarantors of owner who had made advances had no absolute right to intervene. Van Etten v Sphinx Holding Corp. (1921) 114 Misc 436, 186 NYS 595, affd 196 AD 960, 188 NYS 956.

"An interest in the subject" of the action, within the meaning of subdivision 3 of former CPA § 193 was individual and not public, direct and not indirect, present and not remote. Petitioner, resident taxpayer of Monroe County, had no such "an interest in the subject" of actions by certain towns against the county to recover the difference between amount of taxes levied for town purposes and amount of taxes actually collected and returned to the county treasurer and actions by the county to recover money or bonds which represented advances made by the county to said towns.

Irondequoit v Monroe County (1939) 171 Misc 125, 11 NYS2d 933.

In action to recover rentals collected under assignment of rents, trustee under declaration of trust of premises was held entitled to intervene under agreement between plaintiff and trustee. Shulsky v Title Guarantee & Trust Co. (1940, Sup) 23 NYS2d 827, affd 260 AD 868, 23 NYS2d 844.

In action by city for judgment declaring right to make closed shop agreement with Transport Workers Union, transit employees were held not entitled to intervene, since judgment in action would determine their rights. New York v Transport Workers Union (1941, Sup) 28 NYS2d 290.

145. —Action to set aside sale of leasehold

A title insurance company had no such interest in real property, the title to which they have insured, to entitle them to be made defendants in an action to set aside the sale of a leasehold. Russ v Stratton (1894) 8 Misc 6, 28 NYS 392.

146. —Action to vacate railroad charter

In action by the attorney general to vacate charter of a railroad company, which had leased a portion of its road to another railroad company, the lessee had such an interest as to entitle it to be made a party defendant. People v Albany & V. R. Co. (1879) 77 NY 232.

147. —Action to restrain services for third person

In an action to restrain the performance of services by defendant for a third party, in violation of a restrictive contract, such third party had an interest in the subject within the meaning of former CPA § 193. Strobridge Lithographing Co. v Crane (1890, Sup) 12 NYS 834.

148. —Easement

Where persons who had easements in common over a strip of land had not been made parties to a suit brought by one owner to restrain another from interfering with the right of way, the court could not determine that the defendant was justified in altering the condition of the land, as those having rights therein should have been heard upon the question. Alexander Smith & Sons Carpet Co. v Ball (1911) 143 AD 83, 127 NYS 974.

149. —Proceeding to wind up insurance company

In proceedings by the attorney general to wind up an insurance company, parties in interest might be permitted to appear and represent their own interests. Atty. Gen. v North American Life Ins. Co. (1879) 77 NY 297.

150. —Restraining revocation of license

In an action by a licensee to restrain a commissioner of licenses from revoking its license, a person who had preferred charges with the commissioner against the licensee could not intervene as defendant, where he showed no other interest than that of a private citizen. Hapgoods v Bogart (1908) 124 AD 875, 109 NYS 537.

151. —Principal in action on surety bond

The principal in a surety bond, who had a defense on the ground of fraud in the procurement of the contract it was given to secure, had an interest in the subject matter of an action to enforce the bond against the surety, and should have been brought in on his application. Nevins v Fidelity & Casualty Co. (1895) 12 Misc 77, 33 NYS 43.

Where the defendant in an action in which an attachment had been granted, sued, after vacation of the attachment, upon the undertaking given to procure it, and made only the surety a party, the principal in the undertaking was entitled to be made a party defendant as he "has an interest in the subject" of the action and where he had been notified by the surety to defend it, would be concluded by the result of it. Feinburg v American Surety Co. (1900) 33 Misc 458, 67 NYS 868.

152. —Stockholders in action affecting corporation or stockholders

Where a corporation was the real party in interest, the granting of an application by stockholders to be allowed to intervene and be made parties rested in the discretion of the court. Atlantic Trust Co. v Haskinwood Vulcanizing Co. (1895) 85 Hun 219, 32 NYS 956.

In action by representatives of bondholders, of creditors and of stockholders of a surety corporation in the hands of the Superintendent of Insurance for purposes of liquidation, brought by direction of a court against former directors and officers, the court had complete supervision of the action and, in the exercise of its discretion, could refuse to permit a minority stockholder to intervene. National Bondholders Corp. v Joyce (1937) 276 NY 92, 11 NE2d 552.

Stockholders of an insolvent savings and loan association were not allowed to intervene, where the object of such intervention was modification or rejection of a plan of sale which had to be passed upon by the court. People v Anglo-American Sav. & Loan Ass'n (1901) 66 AD 9, 72 NYS 1021.

The mortgagor corporation, having consented to foreclosure without opposition, a stockholder, who was an officer of the corporation, was not permitted to intervene, since he made no showing of conspiracy to defraud. Schmidt v A. M. Schwartz Bldg. & Constr. Co. (1931) 232 AD 549, 250 NYS 732.

Exchange of stock certificates by stockholder for voting trust certificates was held not to bar his intervention in stockholders' derivative action. Hayman v Morris (1941, Sup) 36 NYS2d 754.

Stockholders of defendant were allowed to intervene and oppose plaintiff's motion for order pendente lite enjoining consummation of plan of merger of defendant with another corporation. Wilson v Rensselaer & S. R. Co. (1945) 184 Misc 218, 52 NYS2d 847, affd 53 NYS2d 306.

Where an action was brought by a stockholder on behalf of himself and others who came in and contributed to the expense, to set aside a sale of railroad property, another stockholder, who had knowledge of the facts and acquiesced in the litigation for ten years and until the statute of limitations had run against his right to maintain a separate action for the same relief, would not be made party plaintiff upon his own motion, particularly where he offered no explanation of the delay. MacArdell v Olcott (1901) 62 AD 127, 70 NYS 930.

153. —Beneficiary in action concerning trust

The beneficiaries of a testamentary trust claiming certain bonds belonging to the trust estate were entitled to be brought in as parties defendant in a suit brought by a legatee against the executor to impress a trust upon the bonds. Beck v Staudt (1910) 140 AD 481, 125 NYS 430, later app 149 AD 35, 133 NYS 529, affd 208 NY 566, 101 NE 1095.

154. —Municipal corporation

The city of New York had no interest which entitled it to intervene in an action by one of its residents to enjoin a gas company from collecting for gas the rate fixed by the public commission. Morrell v Brooklyn Borough Gas Co. (1921) 231 NY 405, 132 NE 130.

As to city as intervening in action by consumer to enjoin enforcement of unreasonable rate, see Morrell v Brooklyn Borough Gas Co. (1920) 113 Misc 72, 184 NYS 656, affd 195 AD 899, 185 NYS 890, revd 231 NY 405, 132 NE 130 and affd 195 AD 899, 185 NYS 890, revd 231 NY 617, 132 NE 911, remittitur den 232 NY 538, 134 NE 562.

City was without legal interest in controversy between water company and city residents sufficient to give it standing to enjoin the discontinuance of water service, no contract to supply water to the city itself being involved. New York v Citizens' Water Supply Co. (1921) 199 AD 169, 191 NYS 430, affd 235 NY 584, 139 NE 744.

In action by gas company against Public Service Commission to test constitutionality of a statute, city of New York was entitled to intervene as an interested party. Jamaica Gaslight Co. v Nixon (1920) 110 Misc 494, 181 NYS 620.

City was not allowed to intervene in action to restrain contractor from prosecuting public improvement in negligent manner and to recover damages. Youhey Co. v Shongo Constr. Co. (1917) 100 Misc 181, 165 NYS 420.

A city had no absolute right to intervene in an injunction suit by an individual against a contractor with the city to restrain defendant from operating its plant as a nuisance, and intervention would be denied where application was not made until after unanimous affirmance by the Appellate Division. Reid v Products Mfg. Co. (1921) 116 Misc 424, 190 NYS 403.

155. —Assignors and assignees

In action on assigned claim, assignor was entitled to intervene and contest the validity of the assignment. Bulova v E. L. Barnett, Inc. (1920) 194 AD 418, 185 NYS 424.

The assignor of the plaintiff in a stockholder's derivative action for waste of corporate funds and for an accounting was entitled to intervene as a party plaintiff in the action after the trial had progressed, but prior to judgment. Donovan v Atlas Corp. (1936) 249 AD 115, 291 NYS 518.

In action by assignee of cause of action, assignor corporation was entitled to be made a party defendant on the ground that the assignment was invalid. Bulova v E. L. Barnett, Inc. (1920) 194 AD 418, 185 NYS 424.

156. —Interest acquired pending action

The filing of a notice of the pendency of an action against real estate of the defendant entitled his legal representatives, and those purchasing from him, even after judgment had been rendered against him, to be made parties to the action, and to move the court and be heard in reference to any judgment rendered therein affecting their rights. Ladd v Stevenson (1889) 112 NY 325, 19 NE 842.

The right to be made a party to an action was not limited to one who had an interest at the time of the commencement of the action, but extended to one who had an interest at the time the application was made; accordingly the trustee in a trust deed transferring certain securities which the grantor had previously pledged to the third party as collateral to the loan was entitled to be made a party defendant in an action brought to replevin the securities. Michaelis v Towne (1900) 51 AD 466, 64 NYS 751.

When a judgment creditor, whose judgment was entered after the action of partition was commenced, would be allowed to become a party to the partition action. Flamm v Perry (1903) 78 AD 603, 80 NYS 125.

Former CPA § 193 referred to such persons as were proper or necessary parties from the commencement of the action, and not those upon whom an interest had subsequently devolved. Griswold v Caldwell (1895) 14 Misc 299, 35 NYS 1057.

The right of a person having an interest in the subject of an action at the time of the filing of the lis pendens to be admitted as a party was absolute, while the right of one who acquired his interest subsequently to the filing of the lis pendens depended upon the sound discretion of the court. Bowers v Denton (1903) 41 Misc 133, 83 NYS 942.

157. Discretion of court

An application to intervene could be granted by the court although the party had no absolute right to so intervene. Mertens v Mertens (1903) 87 AD 295, 84 NYS 352.

Permitting intervention was discretionary with the court, and the discretion could be exercised before or after judgment. Meyer v Title Guarantee & Trust Co. (1929) 227 AD 818, 237 NYS 838.

Granting of application under subd 3 of former CPA § 193 rested in sound discretion of court, despite apparent mandatory language of subdivision. Dechert v Pratt (1943) 182 Misc 515, 44 NYS2d 475.

The special term must exercise its discretion in allowing persons to intervene, and such discretion could be reviewed and reversed on appeal. Atty. Gen. v Globe Mut. Life Ins. Co. 15 NY Week Dig 306.

Where parties to the suit were numerous, advancing many varied and conflicting claims, with a large number of interested parties, motions for leave to intervene were granted and representatives of others ordered brought in, with short stay of proceedings to permit doing so. Irish Free State v Guaranty Safe Deposit Co. (1925) 126 Misc 269, 212 NYS 421.

It was in discretion of court below to allow a receiver of an original defendant to intervene in place of the defendant. Dunlop v Patterson Fire Ins. Co. (1878) 74 NY 145.

158. Assignments for benefit of creditors

In an action, brought by a judgment creditor to compel a general assignee to account, the other creditors were not entitled to be brought in as additional plaintiffs. Lewis v Hake (1886) 42 Hun 542.

In an action against an assignee for the benefit of creditors, a creditor of the assignor could not intervene unless misconduct of the assignee was shown. Davies v Fish (1888) 47 Hun 314.

159. Attachment

A plaintiff in an attachment suit had sufficient interest on the bond which was given to obtain the attachment so that he could intervene in an action brought against the sureties on said bond. Kinney v Reid Ice Cream Co. (1901) 57 AD 206, 68 NYS 325.

Where the sheriff, after having levied an attachment, sued, in the name of the defendant, a debtor of defendant, it was held that attaching creditors ought not to be made parties. See Glenville Woolen Co. v Ripley, 29 Super Ct (6 Robt) 530.

160. Collusion

In an action by a teacher against a trustee of a school district, an application was made to intervene upon the ground that the parties were acting collusively. It was held that the order to intervene should not require the intervening party to employ the attorney retained by the defendant, but the court might require the intervening defendants to stipulate that in the event of their success they would not tax costs against the plaintiff. O'Connor v Hendrick (1904) 90 AD 432, 86 NYS 1.

161. Action for money judgment

Former CPA § 193 did not authorize intervention in an action for a sum of money only (although former CPA § 193-b did subsequently). Bauer v Dewey (1901) 166 NY 402, 60 NE 30; Hoffman v Bardusch (1930) 229 AD 210, 241 NYS 561; Colburn v Geneva Nursery Co. (1941, Sup) 29 NYS2d 892.

162. Action by or against personal representatives

Where it appeared that an executor whose appointment dated back ten years could not account until the determination of an action brought by him to determine the testator's interest in a former partnership, and that the action had been pending for four years, a beneficiary under the will who had petitioned for an accounting should have been granted leave to intervene as defendant in the action in order that she could protect her ultimate interests. Schlesinger v Bear (1908) 128 AD 494, 112 NYS 826.

Where an administrator continued the business of the decedent and died, in an action by his surety against his executor for an accounting and to determine the extent of the liability of the surety upon the administrator's bond, a creditor of the business carried on by the administrator was entitled to be made a party to the action, since the profits of the business, if any, would have been applicable in equity to the payment of the liabilities incurred by the administrator in carrying it on. American Surety Co. v McGuire (1907) 54 Misc 79, 103 NYS 753.

163. Action of interpleader

One who had an interest in the subject of an action of interpleader might, in the court's discretion, come in and defend. Hood Rubber Co. v Banque Belge Pour L'Etranger (1927) 219 AD 464, 219 NYS 639.

164. Matrimonial actions

A third wife could intervene in an action by the husband against the second to declare the marriage void. Anonymous, 15 Abb Pr NS 171, 307.

As to third person not a party to a divorce suit intervening. See Simmons v Simmons (1884) 32 Hun 551.

165. Mortgage foreclosure

It was the duty of the court upon the application by a party in interest to a mortgage foreclosure suit, to direct that he be brought in as a party to the action by proper amendment, without the imposition of any conditions. Lawton v Lawton (1889) 54 Hun 415, 7 NYS 556. See also, Re Petition of New York L. & W. R. Co. (1882) 26 Hun 194.

The real owner of the mortgaged premises, although he had omitted to record his deed, was entitled to be made a defendant if he applied in time. Johnston v Donvan (1887) 106 NY 269, 12 NE 594.

A person who, subsequent to filing of lis pendens in foreclosure action, docketed judgment, which became a lien subject to that of mortgage lien against premises sought to be foreclosed, was entitled to intervene as party defendant. Henderson v Moran (1932) 235 AD 818, 256 NYS 857.

In action to foreclose leasehold mortgage against a corporation, one claiming an interest in the mortgaged premises had a right to intervene on affidavit that the corporation was formed as a cloak for usurious loans. Anam Realty Co. v Delancey Garage (1920) 190 AD 745, 180 NYS 297.

166. Partition

Where plaintiff in partition complained that a defendant had entered into an agreement to sell and assign to parties unknown, on identification of third party, court properly permitted it to intervene. Glaser v Burns (1915) 170 AD 321, 155 NYS 936.

167. Replevin

One claiming a lien on chattel sought to be replevied was allowed to come in as a party defendant. Friedman v Schreiber (1906) 50 Misc 617, 98 NYS 235.

Where persons who claimed to own goods which a sheriff had levied upon commenced an action of replevin against the sheriff and the debtors applied to the court under former CPA § 193 for leave to intervene and defend, the court should have granted the application and not imposed terms. Uhlfelder v Tamsen (1897) 15 AD 436, 44 NYS 484.

The judgment debtor against whose property the execution was issued had an interest in the subject of an action of replevin against the sheriff, brought by a claimant of goods levied upon, and the court had power to grant his application to be allowed to come in and defend. Rosenberg v Salomon (1894) 144 NY 92, 38 NE 982.

168. Specific performance

Purchaser of property subject to an option of a third party had right to intervene in action against vendor by holder of option for specific performance. Mandel v Guardian Holding Co. (1920) 192 AD 390, 182 NYS 686.

169. Effect of intervention on action

Where one intervened in representative action and his name was entered on the title of the summons and complaint and all subsequent proceedings as one of the plaintiffs, the fact that the former plaintiff dropped out of the case was of no consequence, and the action was continued. Leighton v New York R. Co. (1915) 169 AD 553, 155 NYS 444.

Impleaded parties were determined not to be liable to the defendant for the claim made by plaintiff within the meaning of subdivision 3 of former CPA § 193. Franco-Belgian Importing Co. v Emigrant Industrial Sav. Bank (1940) 259 App Div 803, 19 NYS2d 776.

f. PROCEDURE ON INTERVENTION

170. Generally

Before appellant who was not a party to an action could be heard to assert title to the property involved he had to make application under the provisions of former CPA § 193. Bram v International Mutoscope Reel Co., Inc. (1925) 215 AD 719, 212 NYS 388.

171. —Mode of application

An application to be made a party to an action could be made by petition specially entitled. Nevins v Fidelity & Casualty Co. (1895) 12 Misc 77, 33 NYS 43.

Consent of defendant to motion made by person not party to intervene in action did not convert such motion into one by defendant. Block Drug Co. v United States & Guaranty Fidelity Co. (1940, Mun Ct) 24 NYS2d 31.

172. —Sufficiency of moving papers

A motion to intervene as defendant was denied on the ground of insufficiency of moving papers. Goff v O'Rourke (1908) 123 AD 918, 107 NYS 1041.

173. —Imposition of conditions

Under former CPA § 193, it is the duty of the court upon the application of a person having an interest in the subject matter of the action to direct that he be brought in as a party to the action by a proper amendment and that no condition be imposed. Uhlfelder v Tamsen (1897) 15 AD 436, 44 NYS 484.

In action against bankrupt's wife to recover property claimed as part of his estate, delayed application to intervene by a party who claimed to have bought the property before the action had been brought, was granted conditionally. Lowenstein v Reikes (1931) 140 Misc 645, 251 NYS 618.

The court could impose terms on granting application of persons to be made a party to an action. Wall v Wall (1897) 20 AD 480, 47 NYS 33.

The imposition of a proportion of plaintiff's costs and expenses as a condition of allowing other creditors to come in and prove claims was unauthorized, but a proper allowance of such costs and expenses could be made by final judgment, payable out of the fund. Lewis v Hake (1886) 42 Hun 542.

g. Party with Possessory or Future Interest in Real Property

174. Generally

Subdivision 4 of former CPA § 193 did not apply where new parties had been brought in who had not been served with notice of trial. Weinrich v Rosenblatt (1928) 133 Misc 484, 233 NYS 131.

In an equitable action to enjoin the keeping of bees on adjoining premises as a nuisance, the owner of the fee was not a necessary party. Olmsted v Rich (1889, Sup) 6 NYS 826.

Where the plaintiff in an action against an elevated railroad was a tenant for life or so long as she remained unmarried, the persons interested in the fee should have been brought in so that there could be a complete determination of the matter at issue, and the proper award made as a condition of refusing an injunction. Bach v New York E. R. Co. (1891) 60 Hun 128, 14 NYS 620.

In cotenant's action for nuisance on land owned by tenants in common, all cotenants were necessary parties. Java Lake Colony, Inc. v Institute of Sisters of St. Joseph (1941) 262 AD 808, 28 NYS2d 33.

FORMS

Form 1—Consent to be added as party plaintiff

Form 2—Stipulation of new party as to bringing him in as coparty

Form 3—Order adding representative of deceased as coplaintiff on consent of added plaintiff

Form 4—Notice of motion by defendant to add necessary party

Form 5—Affidavit in support of motion to add necessary party

Form 6—Order granting motion to add necessary party

Form 7—Allegation in complaint as to person made defendant rather than coplaintiff

Form 1

Consent To Be Added as Party Plaintiff

SUPREME COURT, —[1]—— COUNTY.

[Title of Cause]   Consent To Be Added as Party Plaintiff

     The undersigned, —[2]——, hereby consents to be joined as a party plaintiff in this action and consents that the annexed proposed supplemental complaint be served and filed as his complaint herein.

     Dated: —[3]——, 19—[4]—.

[Signature]

[Print signer's name below signature]

[Acknowledgment]

Form 2

Stipulation of New Party As to Bringing Him in as Coparty

[Title of court and cause]

It is hereby stipulated that John Doe voluntarily appears in court upon this application to bring in new parties, and hereby consents and requests that he be brought in as a party defendant to this action without prejudice to proceedings already had herein, and upon permission of the court and the proper order being granted hereby appears as a party defendant to said action without prejudice to proceedings heretofore had in this action.

Dated, __1_____, 19_2_.

__3_____
Attorney for John Doe
[Executor of the will of
__4_____, deceased]
Office and P. O. Address
Telephone No.

Form 3

Order Adding Representative of Deceased as Coplaintiff on Consent of Added Plaintiff

[Caption of court order]

[Title of cause]

A motion having been regularly made by the plaintiff A, in which motion the other plaintiffs herein have joined, to bring in as an additional party to this action, Jane Doe, as executrix of the last will and testament of John Doe, deceased, and said proposed additional party, having, by affidavit and stipulation in writing, voluntarily appeared in court upon said application and joined therein, and consented and requested that she be brought in as a party to this action without prejudice to proceedings already had therein, and having further stipulated that upon the granting of this order she voluntarily appear by John Brown, her attorney, as party to this action, and said motion coming on regularly to be heard and the plaintiffs and proposed additional party appearing by George Blue, of counsel, and the defendant X appearing by Robert Black, its attorney, and all other defendants herein appearing by Paul White, their attorney,

Now, on reading and filing the affidavit of __1_____, sworn to the __2__ day of __3_____, 19_4_, together with the aforesaid stipulation of the proposed additional party, dated __5_____, 19_6_, mentioned in and annexed to said affidavit, and on the pleadings and all other papers and proceedings had in this action, and after hearing George Blue, of counsel for plaintiffs and proposed additional party, in support of said motion, and Robert Black, attorney for defendant X, and Paul White, attorney for all other defendants, in opposition thereto, and having considered the arguments and briefs of counsel, and due deliberation having been had thereon, it is hereby

Ordered, that Jane Doe, as executrix of the last will and testament of John Doe, deceased, is hereby brought in as party plaintiff in this action and that the plaintiffs A, B, C, and D remain as parties plaintiff herein. And it is further

Ordered, that this order is granted without prejudice to proceedings already had in this action, and that all pleadings and proceedings had in this action be amended accordingly. This order is granted without costs.

__7_____
J.S.C.

[From the records in Dunlop v Sweet Bros. Paper Mfg. Co. 211 AD 363, 208 NYS 54.]

Form 4

Notice of Motion by Defendant to Add Necessary Party

Notice of Motion

[Title of court and cause]   Index No. — [if assigned]

PLEASE TAKE NOTICE that upon the affidavit of __1____, sworn to the __2__ day of __3_____, 19_4_, and upon the pleadings in this action, a motion will be made at a motion term of this Court to be held in and for the County of __5____, at the County Courthouse in the City of __6____, on the __7__ day of __8____, 19_9_, at __10__ o'clock in the __11__ noon of that day or as soon thereafter as counsel can be heard, for an order directing that __12____ be joined in this action as a party defendant [if living, or if dead, his executors or administrators appointed by any court in any jurisdiction and his heirs at law and next of kin], upon the ground that the absence of the said __13____, [or if dead, his executors, administrators, heirs at law and next of kin] will prevent complete relief from being accorded in the controversy [or, "that the interests of the said __14____, if living, or his executors, administrators, heirs at law and next of kin, if dead, would be inequitably affected by a judgment rendered between the parties before the Court"].

Dated: __15____, 19_16_.

Yours etc.,

__17_____

Attorneys for Defendants
Office and Post Office Address
Telephone No.

Form 5

Affidavit in Support of Motion to Add Necessary Party

Affidavit

[Title of court and cause]   Index No. — [if assigned]

[Venue of affidavit]

__1____, being duly sworn, deposes and says:

1. He is the defendant in the above-entitled action.

2. This action was commenced by the service of the summons and complaint on deponent on the __2__ day of __3____, 19_4_, and issue was joined herein by the service of an answer by deponent on plaintiff's attorney on the __5__ day of __6____, 19_7_. No further proceedings have been had in this action.

3. [State nature of cause of action.]

4. [State facts tending to show that new defendant is a necessary party, such as: Complete relief cannot be accorded between those already parties to this action in the absence of __8____, for the reason that __9____.]

5. The said __10____ resides at No. __11__, __12____ Street in the City of __13____ and is subject to the jurisdiction of this Court.

WHEREFORE, deponent prays for an order directing that the said __14____ be brought into this action as a party defendant.

[Signature of deponent]
[Print signer's name below signature]

[Jurat]

Form 6

Order Granting Motion to Add Necessary Party

SUPREME COURT, __1_____ COUNTY.

Order

[Title of cause]   Index No. — [if assigned]

Present: Hon. __2_____, Justice.

On reading and filing the complaint in this action and the answer of the defendant, __3_____, and on reading and filing the affidavit of __4_____, sworn to the __5__ day of __6_____, 19_7_, and the notice of motion for this order with proof of due service thereof upon __8_____, attorney for the plaintiff herein, heretofore filed, and the said motion coming on to be heard on the __9__ day of __10_____, 19_11_, and after hearing __12_____ in support of said motion and __13_____ in opposition thereto, and due deliberation having been had and the court having made and filed its opinion that the said motion should be granted,

Now on motion of __14_____, attorneys for the defendant, __15_____, it is

ORDERED that this motion be and the same is hereby in all respects granted; and it is further

ORDERED, that the plaintiff be and he hereby is required to bring in the said __16_____, as a party defendant within __17__ days after service of a copy of this order with notice of entry upon the attorney for the plaintiff, and it is further

ORDERED, that the complaint be amended accordingly and that the plaintiff be and he hereby is required to serve a copy of said amended complaint upon the said __18_____ at the time of serving a supplemental summons as aforesaid and that within __19__ days thereafter a copy of said amended complaint be served upon the attorney for the defendant herein, and it is further

ORDERED, that until the provisions of this order are complied with all proceedings in this action on the part of the plaintiff or his attorney be stayed.

Signed this __20__ day of __21_____, 19_22_ at __23_____, New York.

Enter.

__24_____

[Print signer's name below signature]

Justice, Supreme Court

__25_____ County

Form 7

Allegation in Complaint As to Person Made Defendant Rather Than Coplaintiff

__1_____ is made a party defendant herein because his consent to join as a plaintiff cannot be obtained.

§ 1002. Permissive joinder of parties

(a) Plaintiffs. Persons who assert any right to relief jointly, severally, or in the alternative arising out of the same transaction, occurrence, or series of transactions or occurrences, may join in one action as plaintiffs if any common question of law or fact would arise.

(b) Defendants. Persons against whom there is asserted any right to relief jointly, severally, or in the alternative, arising out of the same transaction, occurrence, or series of transactions or occurrences, may be joined in one action as defendants if any common question of law or fact would arise.

(c) Separate relief; separate trials. It shall not be necessary that each plaintiff be interested in obtaining, or each defendant be interested in defending against, all the relief demanded or as to every claim included in an action; but the court may make such orders as will prevent a party from being embarrassed, delayed, or put to expense by the inclusion of a party against whom he asserts no claim and, who asserts no claim against him, and may order separate trials or make other orders to prevent prejudice.

HISTORY:

Add, L 1962, ch 308, eff Sept 1, 1963.
Earlier statutes: CPA § 212

ADVISORY COMMITTEE NOTES:

The original provisions of the CPA on permissive joinder, though somewhat complicated, were liberal on the whole. Thus, 193 plaintiffs were permitted to join their separate claims for damages arising out of a false prospectus inducing sales of stock. Akely v Kinnicutt, 238 NY 466, 144 NE 682 (1924). However, the provisions for joinder of defendants in the alternative were not liberal, with the result that joinder of the person causing plaintiff's injury and the physician who attended him was disallowed in Ader v Blau, 241 NY 7, 148 NE 771 (1925). An amendment to CPA § 258 relative to joinder of causes of action remedied this lamented ruling. Great Northern Telegraph Co. v Yokohama Specie Bank, 297 NY 135, 76 NE2d 117 (1947). Under this decision and the then existing statutes, the New York holdings as to permissive joinder were at least fairly satisfactory. However, the subject was covered by five sections of the CPA (§§ 209, 211, 212, 213, 216) which indicated varying degrees of liberality toward the several aspects of the problem. Accordingly, in 1949 the Judicial Council recommended that the subject be treated in full in a new § 212. 15 NY Jud Council Rep 56, 209 (1949). This recommendation was enacted NY Laws 1949, c. 147. As a whole the new section did not depart greatly from the repealed sections in either effect or language. However, it followed Federal rule 20 more closely than did the earlier statutes.

Since the enactment of CPA § 212, there has been virtually no litigation involving permissive joinder carried to the appellate courts. Cf. Trillard v Horowitz, 1 AD2d 680, 146 NYS2d 512 (2d Dept 1955). Trial court decisions in the main apply the section liberally to allow the joinder. Gasperini v Manginelli, 196 Misc 547, 92 NYS2d 575 (Sup Ct 1949); Larsen v Ridge Terrace, Inc. 95 NYS2d 569 (Sup Ct 1950); Metropolitan Opera Ass'n v Wagner-Nicholas R. Corp. 101 NYS2d 483 (Sup Ct 1950); Ross v Ross, 108 NYS2d 675 (Sup Ct 1951); Better v Butoula, 203 Misc 723, 115 NYS 139 (NY Munic Ct 1952); see also Tannenbaum v Baskin, 131 NYS2d 760 (NY Munic Ct 1954) (single bill of costs for all successful parties). On the other hand there are two decisions which are somewhat retrogressive. O'Hara v Gannon, 198 Misc 929, 103 NYS2d 913 (Sup Ct 1951); Tankoos v Levine, 135 NYS2d 195 (Sup Ct 1954). Of these it may be said that the same result could have been reached by allowing separate trials in the court's discretion under subd 3 of CPA § 212. Nothing in these cases suggests that an amendment of the CPA provision for permissive joinder is called for.

Accordingly, the new section follows CPA § 212. The last sentence of subd 1 and the last sentence of subd 2 of § 212 are omitted. In so far as they authorize separate judgments they are covered by the general judgment article. The statement that liability may be found "upon all of the evidence, without regard to the party by whom it has been introduced" is unnecessary. Cf. People v Kelly, 302 NY 512, 518, 99 NE2d 552, 554 (1951). Such matters are within the court's broad discretion to control the manner of trial. Cf. new CPLR § 603, allowing the court to order separate trials of claims or issues and control the order of their trial.

CROSS REFERENCES:

Real property actions, Real P Actions & Pr Law § 241.

FEDERAL ASPECTS:

Permissive joinder of parties, Rule 20(a) of Federal Rules of Civil Procedure, USCS Court Rules.

Separate trials in actions in United States District Courts, Rule 20(b) of Federal Rules of Civil Procedure, USCS Court Rules.

Misjoinder and nonjoinder of parties, Rule 21 of Federal Rules of Civil Procedure, USCS Court Rules.

RESEARCH REFERENCES AND PRACTICE AIDS:

1 NY Jur, Adjoining Landowners § 51.

10 NY Jur, Contracts §§ 235, 236.

31 NY Jur, Insurance §§ 1635, 1636.

3 Carmody-Wait 2d, Parties §§ 19:1, 19:64, 19:66–19:69, 19:71, 19:74, 19:77, 19:87.

13 Carmody-Wait 2d, Notice of Pendency of Actions § 87:78.

22 Am Jur 2d, Declaratory Judgments § 86.

59 Am Jur 2d, Parties §§ 95–101.

74 Am Jur 2d, Torts § 71.

75 Am Jur 2d, Trial §§ 11 et seq.

19 Am Jur Pl and Pr Forms (Rev ed), Parties, Forms 51–57.

5 Am Jur Trials p 1, Whom to sue—Multiple Defendants.

Annotations:

Joinder of insurer and insured under policy of compulsory indemnity or liability insurance in action by injured third person. 20 ALR2d 1097.

Joinder, in injunction action to restrain or abate nuisance, of persons contributing thereto through separate and independent acts. 45 ALR2d 1284.

Validity, construction, and application of Rule 19(b) of Federal Rules of Civil Procedure, as amended in 1966, providing for determination to be made by court to proceed with or dismiss action when joinder of person needed for just adjudication is not feasible. 21 ALR Fed 12.

Law Reviews:

New York Civil Practice Law and Rules: parties. 27 Albany L Rev 182.

Parties and pleading under the CPLR. 31 Brooklyn L Rev 98.

Collateral estoppel, mutuality and joinder of parties. 68 Colum L Rev 1457.

Forms:

See "FORMS" heading following "CASE NOTES", infra.

CASE NOTES

1. In general
2. Plaintiffs
3. Defendants
4. Separate relief or separate trials

1. In general

The failure to incorporate the last sentence of former CPA § 212(2) into CPLR § 1002 was inadvertent, and a plaintiff may rely upon any evidence in the case against any defendant, whether or not said defendant continues to participate in the trial after his motion to dismiss at the end of plaintiff's case is denied or decision reserved thereon. Shaw v Lewis (1968) 55 Misc 2d 664, 286 NYS2d 758, affd 58 Misc 2d 1072, 299 NYS2d 615.

2. Plaintiffs

The court may not substitute appellant's mother-in-law as the petitioner in a paternity suit, but may consider whether to join her as an additional petitioner. Lebowitz v Lebowitz (1967) 28 AD2d 721, 281 NYS2d 437.

Joinder of 18 petitioners in a single habeas corpus petition, where one common ground, i.e., undue delay in entering rehabilitation program, is asserted, is proper and should be permitted. Supreme Court ex rel. Cardona v Singerman (1970) 63 Misc 2d 509, 312 NYS2d 229.

Where lessee consented to motion to join it as party plaintiff in lessor's action for damage to buildings and property allegedly caused by negligent performance by defendant of contract to repair roofs, appropriate statute under which to seek joinder would be that pertaining to permissive joinder, rather than that pertaining to necessary joinder. Northeastern Industrial Park, Inc. v James Ackroyd & Sons, Inc. (1976) 51 AD2d 614, 377 NYS2d 802.

Where lessee would seek recovery for damage arising out of same transaction as lessor, original plaintiff, who sought to recover for damage to buildings and personal property because of defendant's negligent performance of contract to repair roofs, permitting joinder of lessee as party plaintiff was not an abuse of discretion, in absence of showing that such joinder would preclude defendant from asserting statute of limitation as an alleged defense. Northeastern Industrial Park, Inc. v James Ackroyd & Sons, Inc. (1976) 51 AD2d 614, 377 NYS2d 802.

In an action for damages for mental suffering brought by a brother and a sister of a patient in a state mental hospital whose identity was confused by the hospital officials at the time of her death so that her relatives were not notified thereof and she was buried according to the rites of a religion other than that to which she belonged, another sister who did not join in the action would have been a proper party plaintiff under § 1002 but was not a necessary party under § 1001. Weingast v State (1964) 44 Misc 2d 824, 254 NYS2d 952.

3. Defendants

Substituted attorneys were properly made parties to action by former attorney to recover for legal services and disbursements where such attorneys had received in settlement the sum upon part of which former attorneys claimed an equitable lien, notwithstanding that substituted attorneys had, pursuant to an order made in the negligence action, deposited a part of the settlement monies in escrow in a bank account. Dempscy v Kirschner (1968) 30 AD2d 697, 291 NYS2d 931.

One joint tortfeasor sued alone by the injured party could not bring in as a party defendant to the action a second tortfeasor jointly liable and culpable for the injury. Musco v Conte (1964) 22 AD2d 121, 254 NYS2d 589.

Occupant of mortgaged premises was properly joined as party in mortgage foreclosure action in order to cut off his interest as occupant in possession of apartment in premises, and service upon him therefore commenced foreclosure action. Empire Sav. Bank v Towers Co. (1976) 54 AD2d 574, 387 NYS2d 138.

Owner of equity of redemption need not be served in foreclosure action before receiver is appointed; service upon another proper party also commences action so as to permit appointment of receiver. Empire Sav. Bank v Towers Co. (1976) 54 AD2d 574, 387 NYS2d 138.

Where a truck driver was injured when he stopped at a traffic light and his vehicle was struck in the rear by two separate cars only minutes apart, there was no error in joining the two defendants in a single joint trial, but plaintiff's two claims for damage were separated, since the jury might more fairly apportion damages against each defendant in a separate verdict after hearing testimony regarding plaintiff's separately acquired injuries. Mullett v Sacco (1965) 47 Misc 2d 441, 262 NYS2d 796.

4. Separate relief or separate trials

Interest of all parties would best be served by a joint trial of action for declaration as to which of the defendant insurers was obligated to defend claim and the pending negligence action. Tucker v Pernell (1975) 50 AD2d 946, 377 NYS2d 188.

Where a truck driver was injured when he stopped at a traffic light and his vehicle was struck in the rear by two separate cars only minutes apart, there was no error in joining the two defendants in a single joint trial, but plaintiff's two claims for damage were separated, since the jury might more fairly apportion damage against each defendant in a separate verdict after hearing testimony regarding plaintiff's separately acquired injuries. Mullett v Sacco (1965) 47 Misc 2d 441, 262 NYS2d 796.

CASE NOTES

UNDER FORMER CIVIL PRACTICE LAWS

21. Partner
22. Physicians and surgeons
23. Tenants under different holdings
24. Tortfeasors
25. Trustee
26. Unincorporated association

A. IN GENERAL

1. Generally

CPA § 212(c) was derived from the English Practice Act (Rules of the Supreme Court, Order XVI, rule 5), which was liberally construed by the English courts. Bossak v National Surety Co. (1923) 205 AD 707, 200 NYS 148 (construing former §§ 211, 212).

A complaint will not be dismissed for improperly joining causes of action as other remedies are now furnished. New Amsterdam Casualty Co. v Parsons (1927) 219 AD 486, 220 NYS 340.

Policy of law is to encourage joinder of causes of action arising out of same or similar circumstances. Republic of Italy v De Angelis (1958, DC NY) 111 F Supp 216.

The proposed joinder of parties, as authorized by L. 1949 ch. 147, was permissive. St. James Realty Corp. v Level Realty Corp. (1956) 3 Misc 2d 934, 155 NYS2d 44.

2. Construction

Liberal construction required. Larsen v Ridge Terrace, Inc. (1950, Sup) 95 NYS2d 569.

L. 1949 ch. 147, amending § 212, gave equal freedom to joinder of parties and joinder of causes of action. St. James Realty Corp. v Level Realty Corp. (1956) 3 Misc 2d 934, 155 NYS2d 44.

This section, as amended, allows complete freedom in the joinder of parties if the matters may conveniently be tried together subject to the right of severance or separate trials in the interest of justice. St. James Realty Corp. v Level Realty Corp., supra.

3. Courts

Former CPA § 212 held not to apply to actions in Municipal Court, in view of former CPA §§ 15 and 27, Municipal Court Code. S. L. & Co. v Bock (1922) 118 Misc 756, 194 NYS 773.

Under former CPA §§ 211 and 212 two or more defendants could be joined in an action in which some causes of action did not run against all defendants, but the rule probably did not obtain in federal courts. D'Allesandro v United Marine Contracting Corp. (1928, DC NY) 30 F2d 718.

4. Prejudice from joinder

The party objecting to the joinder had the burden, under former CPA §§ 211 and 212, of showing undue prejudice and it was not merely a matter of discretion with the court. Bossak v National Surety Co. (1923) 205 AD 707, 200 NYS 148.

5. Disclaimer

In view of former CPA §§ 211 and 213, a verified complaint in equity on a bond and mortgage alleging right to relief as against several defendants prevailed against a mere disclaimer of interest in a brief on the part of some of such defendants, especially upon a motion to dismiss the complaint upon equitable grounds under rule 106, Rules of Civil Practice. Robinson v Whitaker (1923) 205 AD 286, 199 NYS 680.

6. Counterclaim

In an action to recover damages for personal injuries resulting from an automobile collision, brought jointly by the one injured and his insurer by virtue of a pro tanto assignment of the cause of action following payment of the insurer's liability on the policy, defendant held entitled to interpose a counterclaim for damage to his automobile. Gilboy v Lennon (1922) 118 Misc 467, 193 NYS 606.

7. Costs

The joinder of actions contemplated by former CPA §§ 211, 212 and 258, was permissible and not mandatory, and where such joinder was neither made by plaintiff nor sought by defendant as to several causes, the plaintiff was entitled to recover costs as to each of such actions, although by stipulation the question of fact common to all was tried in but one, and verdicts directed in the remainder pursuant to the determination in the one tried. Kranzer v Automobile Ins. Co. (1925) 124 Misc 866, 209 NYS 566.

Where the same question of law and fact as to defendant's negligence is common to all parties even though there may be differences on the question of contributory negligence or the form of the complaint, the plaintiffs or either of them may recover but one bill of costs and the same rule applies to the defendants or either of them. Tannenbaum v Baskin (1954, Mun Ct) 131 NYS2d 760 (municipal court of New York City).

B. JOINDER OF PLAINTIFFS

8. Generally

Opera company and recording company may join to enjoin another recording company from recording radio broadcasts and selling records in violation of agreement between plaintiffs. Metropolitan Opera Ass'n v Wagner-Nichols Recorder Corp. (1950) 199 Misc 786, 101 NYS2d 483, affd 279 AD 632, 107 NYS2d 795.

In father's action against psychiatrist for libel, and son's action to recover fees for services not rendered and for malpractice, father and son were properly joined. Gasperini v Manginelli (1949) 196 Misc 547, 92 NYS2d 575.

In action to dissolve partnership, where it is obvious that if assertions in complaint be true, that each plaintiff has individual basis of action against defendant and that such respective rights arise from different legal relationships as between each plaintiff and defendant, there is no common question of law or fact, but merely community of interest in that plaintiffs assert different rights with respect to same property, CPA § 212 applies. Perlman v Schor (1954, Sup) 132 NYS2d 888.

Where complaint asserts claim for breach of warranty in alternative for one company and with another company, right to single recovery is stated, so that permissive joinder is appropriate. Amalgamated Packaging Industries, Ltd. v National Container Corp. (1953, DC NY) 14 FRD 194.

Where individual and corporate plaintiffs were brothers and sought to recover commissions from defendant for procuring stock sales to defendant, under separate agreements and on different theories arising out of defendant's breach of agreements, each plaintiff was required to serve complaint alleging individual cause of action. Tankoos v Levine (1954, Sup) 135 NYS2d 195.

9. Numerous plaintiffs

Five separate employers, owning separate shops, may join in one complain to enjoin labor union from picketing their places of business. Klein v Freedman (1952, Sup) 119 NYS2d 257.

10. Insurance

Under a liberal construction of a complaint against the purchasing defendant and an insurance company, its allegations in the alternative that defendant breached its contract to cover a sugar shipment by insurance or else converted the insurance received for the loss thereof need not, on defendant's motion, be set forth separately. Cuban-Canadian Sugar Co. S. A. v Arbuckle (1926) 127 Misc 64, 215 NYS 176.

Insurer is not proper party plaintiff to action by insurer who received advance of money as loan under agreement, and not as payment for loss sustained. Schwartz v Maygreen Piece Dye Works, Inc. (1942, Sup App T) 36 NYS2d 169 affd in part and revd in part 265 AD 931, 38 NYS2d 412.

11. Realty action

Adjoining landowners, whose properties were undermined by construction of building by another property owner and his contractor, may join as plaintiffs in one action to enjoin encroachment, where they will have same witnesses. Larsen v Ridge Terrace, Inc. (1950, Sup) 95 NYS2d 569.

Life tenant suing adjoining owner for damage to real property was entitled to bring in owner of the remainder interest who consented to be joined as party-plaintiff. Abschagen v Goldfarb (1959) 8 AD2d 750, 185 NYS2d 339.

Where plaintiff and proposed additional plaintiff own neighboring property, and it is alleged that defendant erected a dock in front of both properties, and has continuously trespassed thereon, the application to bring in the additional plaintiff would be granted upon showing that both plaintiffs would call the same witnesses and common questions of fact and law would be involved. Bresler v Brunt (1959) 9 AD2d 596, 189 NYS2d 246.

C. Joinder of Defendants

12. Generally

Plaintiff in doubt as to which defendants are liable, extent of liability, and in what capacity, could join all under former CPA §§ 211–213. Winslow Bros. & Smith Co. v Grace S.S. Co. (1929) 133 Misc 902, 233 NYS 448.

Joinder of defendants liable to plaintiff on different causes of action is allowable if claims arise out of same transaction or series and if separate trials will involve common questions of law and fact. Great Northern Tel. Co. v Yokohama Specie Bank, Ltd. (1948) 297 NY 135, 76 NE2d 117.

Conditions required for joinder of defendants are assertion against defendants of right to relief arising out of same transaction and there must be presented common question of law or fact. O'Hara v Gannon (1951) 198 Misc 929, 103 NYS2d 913.

Complaint failed to show consistent relationship between the parties. Coons v Florentine (1930) 229 AD 532, 242 NYS 519.

Former CPA § 211 construed with § 212 in permitting joinder of defendants. Great Northern Tel. Co. v Yokohama Specie Bank, Ltd. (1948) 297 NY 135, 76 NE2d 117.

Merged and possessor corporations may be joined as defendants in action for breach of contract, in "anticipation of claim of nonjoinder and avoidance of multiplicity of suits". Kopitko v J. T. Flagg Knitting Co. (1953, DC NY) 111 F Supp 549.

Action by landlord to compel tenant's performance of agreement to execute lease at rental higher than registered rent and to compel Rent Commission to register rent in agreed amount as maximum rent, was in effect attempt to review act of such Commission in plenary action, and complaint was dismissed. Kellas Real Estate Corp. v Gluckmann (1955) 207 Misc 517, 137 NYS2d 755.

Where there is doubt as to which of defendants is liable, determination of liability after trial may be appropriate, but such rule presupposes that cause of action exists. American Surety Co. v Manufacturers Trust Co. (1956) 3 Misc 2d 363, 154 NYS2d 260, affd 3 AD2d 831, 162 NYS2d 334, app den 3 AD2d 990, 163 NYS2d 370.

Where complaint states facts in one count which are sufficient to constitute separate cause of action against one defendant and separate cause of action against another defendant who before answering did not move to have causes separately stated but did move against whole complaint, such motion was properly denied. Trillard v Horowitz (1955) 1 AD2d 680, 146 NYS2d 512.

Plaintiff's claim that injuries received in first automobile accident were aggravated by second automobile accident which occurred 13 months later did not justify joinder of causes of action against different defendants based on respective accidents, and a severance will be ordered. Cipolla v La Franco (1960) 24 Misc 2d 30, 202 NYS2d 337.

Parties named as defendants have the right to defend regardless of the reasons why they were named as defendants. H. D. S. Trading Co. v Redisch (1959) 19 Misc 2d 716, 186 NYS2d 696.

13. Liability in differing amounts

Defendants may be joined although they may be liable in different amounts. Virdone v Globe Bank & Trust Co. (1932) 235 AD 125, 256 NYS 421.

Where causes of action for fraud and for breach of contract are united in same complaint, defendants may be joined, though liable in different amounts. Warner Bros. Picture Distributing Corp. v Endicott Circuit, Inc. (1945, Sup) 55 NYS2d 300, affd 269 AD 934, 58 NYS2d 344.

In action upon two marine insurance policies whereby each company insured the same vessel on the same valuation although for different proportions, it was held that former CPA §§ 211 and 212 would authorize joinder of defendants. Munson Inland Lines, Inc. v Insurance Co. of North America (1929, DC NY) 36 F2d 269.

14. Liability for active and passive negligence

Where two cars collided on highway and owner of one and occupants of second were injured, and all filed claims in Court of Claims alleging dangerous highway, state could not add owner as third-party defendant in claims of occupants, on theory that owner was actively negligent and state was only passively negligent. Dunn v State (1950) 197 Misc 627, 95 NYS2d 640, affd 304 NY 774, 109 NE2d 76.

15. Defendants not all interested in each defense

The old rule, under § 484 of the Code of Civil Procedure, that only causes of action which affected all the parties to the action could be joined, was abrogated by the Civil Practice Act, and under such act the fact that the defendant was not interested in all the relief demanded did not prevent his being joined in an action, provided he was otherwise a proper party defendant. Ellicott v Archibald McNeil & Sons Co. (1923) 206 AD 441, 201 NYS 500.

The fact that all the defendants may not be liable on all the causes of action set out in the complaint is no ground for objection to their joinder as defendants. First Const. Co. v Rapid Transit Subway Const. Co. (1923) 122 Misc 145, 203 NYS 359, affd 211 AD 184, 206 NYS 822.

All persons may be joined as defendants against whom the right to any relief is alleged to exist, whether jointly, severally, or in the alternative, and judgment may be given against such one or more of the defendants as may be found liable, according to their respective liabilities; it is not necessary that each defendant should be interested as to all the relief prayed for or as to every cause of action. Sherlock v Manwaren (1924) 208 AD 538, 203 NYS 709; Metropolitan Life Ins. Co. v Union Trust Co. (1938) 167 Misc 262, 5 NYS2d 99.

In action by two plaintiffs suing defendant for negligence, and where judgment was granted for one plaintiff and for defendant against other plaintiff, only single bill of costs was allowed, since same question of law and fact as to defendant's negligence was common to all parties. Tannebaum v Baskin (1954, Mun Ct) 131 NYS2d 760.

16. Fraudulent conveyance

In a suit to set aside an alleged fraudulent conveyance, the custodian of a sum arising therefrom, who was a participant in the scheme to defraud the plaintiff, may be made a party defendant. Miller-Schlott, Inc. v Title Guarantee & Trust Co. (1932) 237 AD 859, 261 NYS 372.

17. Guarantor

Cause of action for price of goods sold and delivered may be joined with one against guarantor of payment, but should be separately stated and numbered. Winter v Maple City Mfg. Co. (1928) 132 Misc 631, 230 NYS 458.

18. Insurance

Two insurance companies insuring the same goods against loss by burglary may be joined as defendants, though the policies are separate, each of the defendants being liable only pro rata for the loss. Bossak v National Surety Co. (1923) 205 AD 707, 200 NYS 148.

Plaintiff was entitled to a mechanic's lien, the building burned and the land was valueless. In action against the owner plaintiff alleged that the building had been insured for his benefit; bringing in the insurer, filing a supplemental complaint against him and obtaining an order restraining payment of the insurance until determination of the controversy, were proper practice. R. Prescott & Son, Inc. v Nye (1928) 223 AD 356, 228 NYS 156.

In action for insurance loss, plaintiff may join insurer and broker. Chason Bros., Inc. v Insurance Co. of North America (1952, Sup) 114 NYS2d 92.

Where parked automobile and owner were injured when struck by codefendant's car and where injured car was burned while being towed away, it is proper to join driver of injuring car and insurer of burned car. Better v Butuola (1952) 203 Misc 723, 115 NYS2d 139.

19. Nuisance

Where a complaint against two railroad companies stated separately acts, which combined, caused the damage and created the nuisance complained of, judgment against one or both as the evidence showed their respective liabilities, was proper. Schenectady Holding Co. v New York C. R. Co. (1929) 225 AD 479, 233 NYS 495.

20. Partition

Former CPA § 212(3) construed with former CPA § 1013 did not require the dismissal of a complaint in partition on the ground that causes of action were improperly joined, although certain of the defendants had no interest in part of the lands of which partition was sought. Hoyt v Ruge (1922) 119 Misc 544, 197 NYS 527.

21. Partner

In view of former CPA §§ 211 and 212(3) a plaintiff charging conversion of securities by a firm was prima facie entitled to join the members of said firm in a single action, although the firm personnel changed from time to time during the transactions in suit, the burden was upon the defendants to show prejudice. Brokaw v Lage (1922) 203 AD 155, 196 NYS 531.

22. Physicians and surgeons

In proceedings against many physicians to revoke for their misconduct, authorization to render medical care under Workmen's Comp. Act involving common questions of fact, all physicians affected may be grouped in single proceeding and on hearing witnesses may testify only once. Sacharoff v Murphy (1943) 182 Misc 235, 44 NYS2d 117, affd 268 AD 765, 50 NYS2d 168, revd on other grounds, Sacharoff v Corsi (1945) 294 NY 305, 62 NE2d 81, cert den 326 US 744, 90 L Ed 445, 66 S Ct 59.

23. Tenants under different holdings

Former CPA §§ 209, 211–213 authorized the joinder in a single action of a landlord's causes of action for varying rental values of apartments in a building against the several tenants. S. L. & Co. v Bock (1922) 118 Misc 756, 194 NYS 773.

24. Tortfeasors

Administrator suing to recover damages for the wrongful death of his intestate cannot join as defendants two or more parties who are alleged to have been responsible for such death, but whose alleged wrongful acts, neglect or breeches of duty are separate and distinct. Ader v Blau (1925) 241 NY 7, 148 NE 771, 41 ALR 1216 (changed by statute as stated in Great Northern Tel. Co. v Yokohama Specie Bank, Ltd. 297 NY 135, 76 NE2d 1171).

Where separate actions were instituted against different defendants to recover damages alleged to have been sustained by plaintiff by reason of injuries to his property caused by the failure of the defendants properly to shore up and protect the property during the course of construction of buildings on both sides of it, the damages being caused by separate acts of the respective defendants at different periods of time, held that plaintiff's motion to consolidate the actions should be granted. Cowles v Marc Eidlitz & Son, Inc. (1923) 121 Misc 340, 201 NYS 254, affd 210 AD 871, 206 NYS 895.

Court would not sever causes of action where plaintiff was injured in automobile accident and then injured again when ambulance which was transporting her was in an accident, since the two causes had a common question of fact of personal damages. Wilson v Algeria (1957) 5 Misc 2d 520, 165 NYS2d 190.

25. Trustee

Trustee of inter vivos trust may be joined individually as defendant in beneficiary's action for accounting, where complaint alleged that beneficiary knowingly participated with trustee in wrongful diversion of trust income. Ross v Ross (1951, Sup) 108 NYS2d 674.

26. Unincorporated association

In view of CPA § 1569 (§ 10003 herein) the right of plaintiff in an action based upon a contract with an unincorporated association for the sale on consignment of the product of its members, to join as defendants the president of such association and the individual members, was governed by former CPA §§ 192, 211–213. Mandell v Moses (1923) 204 AD 655, 198 NYS 583.

Doubt as to person liable (former CPA § 213)

Decisions applying CPA § 213, prior to its repeal are segregated at this point for such application as they may have under § 1002.

A. In General

1. Generally

The source of former CPA § 213 was rule 7 of order 16 of the English Rules of Supreme Court, 1883, which was taken from rule 6 of order 16 of the Rules of Court as contained in the English Supreme Court of Judicature Act, 1875 (38 & 39 Vict Ch 77, §§ 16 et seq., and First Schedule, order XVI, rule 6), known as the English Practice Act. Schectman v Salaway (1923) 204 AD 549, 198 NYS 851. See also Zenith Bathing Pavilion, Inc. v Fair Oaks S.S. Corp (1925) 211 AD 492, 207 NYS 306, affd in part and revd in part 240 NY 307, 148 NE 532.

2. Validity

Validity of former CPA § 213 upheld. Zenith Bathing Pavilion, Inc. v Fair Oaks S.S. Corp (1925) 211 AD 492, 207 NYS 306, affd in part and revd in part 240 NY 307, 148 NE 532.

3. Construction

Former CPA §§ 211 and 213 were liberally construed to effectuate the purpose of their enactment, and in accordance with the construction placed upon the English rules from which they were derived. Thermoid Rubber Co. v Baird Rubber & Trading Co. (1925) 124 Misc 774, 209 NYS 277.

Former CPA § 213 gave a purely statutory remedy, nonexistent at common law, and presupposed existence of an action of which the court had jurisdiction of the parties and subject matter. Norton v Southern R. Co. (1930) 138 Misc 784, 246 NYS 676.

While former § 213 could, in view of CPA § 1569 (§ 10003 herein), be applied to actions pending at the time of the adoption of the act, it was within the discretion of the court to deny the relief sought thereunder if deemed inconsistent with prior proceedings and not in the interest of justice. Hernandez v Brookdale Mills (1922) 119 Misc 824, 198 NYS 277, affd 206 AD 653, 198 NYS 925.

Former CPA §§ 211 and 213 construed together in permitting joinder of defendants under CPA § 211. Great Northern Tel. Co. v Yokohama Specie Bank, Ltd. (1948) 297 NY 135, 76 NE2d 117.

4. Courts

The provisions of former CPA § 213 applied to actions in Municipal Court, in view of §§ 15 and 27, Municipal Court Code. S. L. & Co. v Bock (1922) 118 Misc 756, 194 NYS 773.

B. Propriety of Joinder

5. Generally

Former CPA § 213 applied only where the plaintiff was in doubt as to which of several persons was liable and not where the plaintiff's only doubt was whether a particular defendant was or was not liable. Nicholson v Close (1940) 258 AD 488, 17 NYS2d 83. Also Garrett v McAllister (1930) 137 Misc 721, 244 NYS 283; and Empreza De Comer-cio Sul-Americana, Ltds. v Fimex, Inc (1947, Sup) 80 NYS2d 562.

Former CPA § 213 could only be invoked where plaintiff was in doubt as to which defendant was liable for the redress of a single wrong. Freund Coat Corp. v Lipschutz (1929) 135 Misc 553, 238 NYS 239.

Where plaintiff proceeded on theory of joint and several liability of both defendants, former CPA § 213 had no application. Margady v Weissman (1947, Sup) 74 NYS2d 280, affd 272 AD 922, 72 NYS2d 412.

Plaintiff in doubt as to which defendant was liable, or how far liable, or whether as agent or principal, disclosed or undisclosed, could join all as defendants, under former CPA §§ 211, 213 and § 212 as then applicable. Winslow Bros. & Smith Co. v Grace S.S. Co. (1929) 133 Misc 902, 233 NYS 448.

Attachment against two defendants upheld under former CPA § 213 where there was uncertainty as to which defendant was liable. Whitman v Dayton Rubber Mfg. Co. (1925) 214 AD 794, 210 NYS 937.

Plaintiff suing to recover commissions for procuring a customer to purchase property and naming as defendants, persons who, on employing him, represented that they were the owners of the property, could join as defendant a corporation which, after issue had been joined, was found to be the true owner. Schectman v Salaway (1923) 204 AD 549, 198 NYS 851.

Joinder of parties defendant was sanctioned where, in a suit to recover wages, plaintiff was in doubt as to which of the defendants operated, managed, and controlled a certain boat during the period of his employment thereon. Lonnberg v Knox (1924) 123 Misc 148, 204 NYS 852.

Where plaintiff in attachment joined several parties as defendants for the purpose of discovering who were liable, evidence was reviewed and attachment sustained as to but one of them. Zenith Bathing Pavilion, Inc. v Fair Oaks S.S. Corp. (1925) 240 NY 307, 148 NE 532.

Where it was originally alleged that a party was principal and had assigned his claim to plaintiff, and amended complaint alleged that plaintiff was principal and the assignee his agent, defendant properly served his pleadings on both. Cramerton Mills, Inc. v Nathan & Cohen Co. (1930) 231 AD 28, 246 NYS 259.

In action on contract, two corporations were properly joined under former CPA § 213. Fox Film Corp. v Wirth & Hamid Realty Corp (1930) 231 AD 37, 246 NYS 246.

It was the plaintiff's duty to bring in all parties necessary to a complete determination and the court should aid him. Clark v Flinn & Co. (1930) 230 AD 698, 246 NYS 399.

6. Relationship between defendants and their acts

Defendants were improperly joined where claim against one was for work, labor and service, and against the other for breach of warranty. Freund

Coat Corp. v Lipschutz (1929) 135 Misc 553, 238 NYS 239.

In an action to recover for damage to and loss of certain fur pieces, one defendant had dressed some of them, one had dyed some, and a number of pieces were never returned; under these facts a motion to sever the cause of action would be granted, notwithstanding former CPA § 213, since plaintiff dealt with each of the defendants separately, and alleged no relationship between them or their acts. Klein v Betzold (1922) 119 Misc 505, 197 NYS 501.

In an action to recover for goods lost either by the carrier or a warehouseman to whom the carrier asserted it delivered them, plaintiff must make prima facie proof that it suffered loss which might reasonably be charged to one or the other of the defendants, and defendants were then called upon to exhibit their conduct in the custody of the goods and thus fix the liability as between themselves. S. & C. Clothing Co. v United States Trucking Corp. (1926) 216 AD 482, 215 NYS 349.

7. Similarity of names

Where plaintiff was in doubt whether his claim was against one or the other of two corporations, because of the similarity of names, officers, and interests of the corporations, he could not be required to elect which party he would pursue, but could join both corporations in one action. Ellicott v Archibald McNeil & Sons Co. (1923) 206 AD 441, 201 NYS 500.

8. Uniformity of liability unnecessary

The fact that all the defendants may not be liable on all the causes of action set out in the complaint was no ground for objection to their joinder as defendants. First Const. Co. v Rapid Transit Subway Const. Co. (1923) 122 Misc 145, 203 NYS 359, affd 211 AD 184, 206 NYS 822.

9. Separate torts by different defendants

Administrator suing to recover damages for the wrongful death of his intestate could not join as defendants two or more parties who were alleged to have been responsible for such death, but whose alleged wrongful acts were separate and distinct. Ader v Blau (1925) 241 NY 7, 148 NE 771, 41 ALR 1216 (changed by statute as stated in Great Northern Tel. Co. v Yokohama Specie Bank, Ltd. 297 NY 135, 76 NE2d 117).

In view of former CPA § 213, where a plaintiff has made out a prima facie case of liability for the loss of merchandise through the default of either the defendant truckman or the defendant railroad company, the railroad company was not entitled to a dismissal as to it at the close of the plaintiff's case, although the proof did not establish which of such defendants had been ultimately liable for the loss. Thermoid Rubber Co. v Baird Rubber & Trading Co. (1925) 124 Misc 774, 209 NYS 277.

Where separate actions were instituted against different defendants to recover damages for injuries to property caused by the failure of the defendants properly to shore up and protect the property during the course of construction of buildings on both sides of it, the damages being caused by separate acts of the respective defendants at different periods of time, plaintiff's motion to consolidate the actions should have been granted. Cowles v Marc Eidlitz & Son, Inc. (1923) 121 Misc 340, 201 NYS 254, affd 210 AD 871, 206 NYS 895.

In suit to recover for injuries from collision between automobile and taxicab, former CPA § 213 authorized an allegation in complaint that the owners of both cars were sued because plaintiff had been unable to determine which of the two was liable for the collision. Jacobs v Barron (1926) 215 AD 560, 214 NYS 261.

10. Separate contract breaches by different defendants

Action against one defendant for goods sold and against another for breach of contract, did not warrant joinder of defendants. Shiowitz v Fisher (1946) 187 Misc 897, 65 NYS2d 599.

11. Tenants under different holdings

Former CPA §§ 209, 211 and 212, as then applicable, authorized the joinder in a single action of a landlord's causes for rental value of apartments in a building against the several tenants thereof, although the several apartments had different rental values. S. L. & Co. v Bock (1922) 118 Misc 756, 194 NYS 773.

C. PROCEDURE

12. Generally

In view of former CPA §§ 211 and 213, and § 212 as then applicable a verified complaint in equity on a bond and mortgage alleging a right to relief as against several defendants prevailed against a mere disclaimer of interest in a brief on the part of some of such defendants, especially upon a motion to dismiss the complaint upon equitable grounds under RCP 106 (Rule 3211(a) herein). Robinson v Whitaker (1923) 205 AD 286, 199 NYS 680.

13. Pleading

Where defendants were joined under former CPA § 213, the pleading dealing with each defendant must show some basis of liability as against him. Best Foods, Inc. v Mitsubishi Shoji Kaisha, Ltd. (1928) 224 AD 24, 229 NYS 364.

A pleading under former CPA § 213 had to contain some allegation showing that the plaintiff was in doubt as to the person from whom he was entitled to redress. Totten v United States Lines (1936, DC NY) 16 F Supp 57.

In action for money deposited by plaintiff with one or more or all defendants, allegations were sufficient despite use of "and/or." Becker v Burkes (1941) 262 AD 893, 28 NYS2d 850.

14. —In alternative

Plaintiff need not allege that both defendants were liable, but that either might be. Fox Film Corp. v

Wirth & Hamid Realty Corp (1930) 231 AD 37, 246 NYS 246; Abelow v Chazen (1947, Sup) 75 NYS2d 128, affd 277 AD 973, 100 NYS2d 227.

In an action against several to recover money expended on behalf of one or more defendants, pleading in the alternative was proper. Reeve v Cromwell (1929) 227 AD 32, 237 NYS 20.

Under a liberal construction of a complaint against a purchaser and an insurance company, allegations in the alternative that purchaser had breached its contract to insure a sugar shipment or else converted insurance received need not be set forth separately. Cuban-Canadian Sugar Co. S. A. v Arbuckle (1926) 127 Misc 64, 215 NYS 176.

Where facts were pleaded under which two alternatives existed, proof of either of which would result in holding one defendant liable, it was unnecessary that both should have been liable. Garrett v McAllister (1930) 137 Misc 721, 244 NYS 283.

Action to recover for breach of contract between plaintiff and the individual defendant, who purported to act as a duly authorized agent of the corporate defendants in making the contract. Without an allegation of repudiation by the corporate defendants of the authority of the individual defendant, the facts pleaded did not show the existence of two alternatives, the proof of either of which would have resulted in holding one of the defendants liable. Wertheim v Lehigh Valley Coal Co. (1936) 249 AD 597, 293 NYS 233.

15. Counterclaim

In an action to recover damages for personal injuries resulting from an automobile collision, brought jointly by the one injured and his insurer by virtue of a pro tanto assignment of the cause of action following payment of the insurer's liability on the policy, defendant was held entitled to interpose a counterclaim for damage to his automobile, in view of former CPA §§ 211, 213, 266, 270, and CPA §§ 192, 212, 270 and 271 as then applicable, and CPA §§ 192, 209, 211, 212, and 266, 270 and 271. Gilboy v Lennon (1922) 118 Misc 467, 193 NYS 606.

16. Judgment

Plaintiff could have alternative judgment against any party provided all were joined whose liability was in doubt at close of case. Yatter v Mathies (1930) 139 Misc 26, 246 NYS 548. See also (1932) 236 AD 786, 258 NYS 1050.

D. PARTICULAR PARTIES AND RELATIONSHIPS

17. Banks

In action by foreign telegraph company against superintendent of banks and Japanese bank in liquidation on latter's agreement to make payments in dollars to plaintiff's order at its New York Agency, plaintiff could join as additional defendant another foreign corporation which agreed to but failed to collect and hold such payments within times limited. Great Northern Tel. Co. v Yokohama Specie Bank, Ltd. (1948) 297 NY 135, 76 NE2d 117.

18. Carriers

In an action for damages to a shipment originating at interior United States points moving by rail to seaboard, thence by water by the United States Shipping Board Merchant Fleet Corporation to a foreign country, said corporation was not a proper party defendant. Norton v Southern R. Co. (1930) 138 Misc 784, 246 NYS 676.

19. Corporation and officer or individual

Complaint on a promissory note praying judgment in the alternative against the corporation whose instrument it purported to be or the officer executing it if signed without authority, was sufficient to charge the individual defendant. New Georgia Nat. Bank v Lippmann (1928) 249 NY 307, 164 NE 108, 60 ALR 1344.

In an action against the corporate maker of a note and the president who signed it, praying judgment in the alternative under former CPA § 213, defense of the individual defendant that he was not liable, since he acted without authority, was contrary to the provisions of Consolidated Laws, ch. 39, § 39. New Georgia Nat. Bank v Lippmann (1928) 222 AD 383, 226 NYS 233, affd 249 NY 307, 164 NE 108, 60 ALR 1344.

Complaint of stockholder in a corporation for fraud and mismanagement of the officers was insufficient. Coons v Florentine (1930) 229 AD 532, 242 NYS 519.

Where a corporation and individuals were made defendants under former CPA § 213, latter were denied costs on dismissal of the complaint as to them. Sanitary Brass Works Co. v Marcus (1930) 135 Misc 664, 239 NYS 332.

20. Husband and wife

In actions for commissions in selling realty, plaintiff could join husband and wife as tenants by entirety, despite husband's claim that he was sole owner. Williams v Donyluk (1946, Sup) 62 NYS2d 766.

21. Landlord and tenant

Control of leased building, which drained water onto adjoining building, should have been alleged sufficiently to make either defendant lessor or lessee liable. Georges Marie Binon, Inc. v New York Lumber & Panel Co. (1947, City Ct) 67 NYS2d 766.

22. Negotiable instruments

Drawer and payee of checks, paid by payee bank after receipt of stop-payment order, could not be joined as defendants by bank in action to recover amount of check, without alleging ratification by drawer. Chase Nat. Bank v Battat (1948) 297 NY 185, 78 NE2d 465.

23. Partnership

In an action against plaintiff's copartner for a dissolution of the firm and an accounting, a third party who, with one of the partners, had wrongfully deprived the partnership of some of its assets could be brought in as a defendant. Schoner v Koeppel (1932) 237 AD 860, 261 NYS 458.

24. Principal and agent

A complaint against two defendants, one alleged to have acted as agent, the other to have been principal, which set forth the essential facts entitling plaintiff to recover against one or the other, depending upon the agent's authority to act as such, was not open to attack. Jamison v Lamborn (1923) 207 AD 375, 202 NYS 113.

In a real-estate broker's action for commissions, it was proper to join the repudiating corporate defendant and its duly authorized agent as defendants, with whom the plaintiff had dealt. Geer v Blemton Realty Corp. (1926) 218 AD 102, 218 NYS 162.

Where a purchaser of goods through one purporting to be the agent of the seller was in doubt as to whether an agency existed he could, in an action for failure to deliver the goods, ask for a judgment in the alternative against the supposed seller or the supposed agent. Stein, Hall & Co. v A. M. Alison & Co. (1924) 123 Misc 382, 205 NYS 422.

Where suit was brought on a contract executed by an alleged agent on behalf of an alleged principal, former CPA § 213 applied, since if the agent was authorized he would not be liable, but otherwise if unauthorized. Garrett v McAllister (1930) 137 Misc 721, 244 NYS 283.

Former CPA § 213 authorized impleading as defendants an agent and his assumed principal, in an action on a contract for the manufacture and sale of merchandise entered into following representations on the part of the agent as to his authority to bind his principal, but the defendant principal's motion for judgment on the pleadings was granted on the ground that the complaint failed to show an intent on the part of the plaintiff to contract with the said principal. Bristol Mfg. Co. v Zahn (1922, Sup) 199 NYS 260.

Where a plaintiff, under former CPA § 213 joined as parties defendant in an action upon a contract, the agent through whom it negotiated the contract and the principal for whom such agent asserted authority to negotiate, and judgment was given against principal but in favor of agent, court had discretion, in view of CPA §§ 1476 and 1477 (§ 8101 herein) to award costs to the successful defendant against the codefendant. Dailey Bros. v W. A. Clements Co. (1923) 120 Misc 310, 198 NYS 387.

Where plaintiff is in doubt as to who was liable, or how far liable, or whether as agent or as principal, disclosed or undisclosed, express or implied, he should have joined all such persons as defendants. Olshan v Buffalo Merchandising Co. (1943, Co Ct) 44 NYS2d 758.

Complaint alleging that individual defendant assumed to act for corporate defendant, which repudiated his authority to act, warranted their joinder as defendants. Dean Liquor Distributors v Somerset Importers (1943) 265 AD 727, 40 NYS2d 573.

25. Unincorporated association

In view of CPA § 1569 (§ 10003 herein), the right of plaintiff in an action based on a contract with an unincorporated association for the sale on consignment of the product of its members, to join as defendants the president of such association and the individual members, was governed by former §§ 211, 213 and §§ 192 and 212 as then applicable. Mandell v Moses (1923) 204 AD 655, 198 NYS 583.

FORMS

Form 1—Complaint where plaintiffs assert right to relief in alternative—skeleton form

Form 2—Complaint where plaintiffs assert right to relief jointly—skeleton form

Form 3—Complaint where plaintiffs assert right to relief severally—skeleton form

Form 4—Complaint asserting right to relief against defendants in alternative—skeleton form

Form 5—Complaint asserting right to relief against defendants in alternative—another form

Form 6—Complaint where right to relief is asserted against defendants severally—skeleton form

Form 7—Complaint asserting right to relief against defendants jointly—skeleton form

Form 8—Complaint against two foreign corporations with prayer for judgment in the alternative

Form 9—Complaint in action against two corporations where plaintiff in doubt as to which of the two the agent was acting for in making of contract sued on

Form 10—Complaint where plaintiff in doubt whether claim is against one or the other of two corporations because of similarity of names, etc.

Form 11—Complaint in action against corporate and individual defendants on a promissory note where authority to execute note disputed

Form 12—Complaint in action against principal and agent where principal denied agent's authority

Form 13—Complaint in action against carrier and warehouseman for goods lost while in possession of one or the other

Form 14—Complaint in action against carrier and manufacturer for machinery damaged in transit

Form 15—Complaint in action against guarantor and others

Form 16—Complaint in action against two insurance companies

Form 17—Complaint in action against president of unincorporated association and individual members thereof

Form 18—Complaint in action against owner and driver of automobile for damages from collision

Form 19—Complaint against owner of taxicab in which plaintiff was injured and against owner of automobile which taxicab collided with

Form 20—Complaint in action against two railroad companies for nuisance

Form 1

Complaint Where Plaintiffs Assert Right to Relief in Alternative—Skeleton Form

Complaint

[Title of court and cause]   Index No. — [if assigned]

Plaintiffs, by their attorneys, __1_____, complaining of the defendant, allege:

[Set forth facts constituting causes of action in regular form.]

12. Upon the facts hereinbefore set forth, a cause of action exists against the defendant herein in favor of the plaintiff __2_____, or the plaintiff __3_____, in the alternative, and said plaintiffs are joined as plaintiffs herein pursuant to the provisions of Section 1002 of the Civil Practice Law and Rules of the State of New York.

WHEREFORE, plaintiffs demand that judgment be granted in favor of the plaintiff __4_____, or the plaintiff __5_____, in the alternative, against the defendant in the sum of $__6__, with interest from the __7__ day of __8_____, 19_9_, together with the costs and disbursements of this action.

__10_____

Attorneys for Plaintiffs
Office and P. O. Address
Telephone No.

Form 2

Complaint Where Plaintiffs Assert Right to Relief Jointly—Skeleton Form

Complaint

[Title of court and cause]   Index No. — [if assigned]

Plaintiffs, by their attorneys, __1_____ complaining of the defendant, allege:

1. At all times hereinafter mentioned the plaintiffs were, and still are, co-partners doing business under the name and style of __2_____.

[Allege other facts constituting cause of action.]

WHEREFORE, plaintiffs demand judgment against the defendant in the sum of $__3__ with interest from the __4__ day of __5_____, 19_6_, together with the costs and disbursements of this action.

__7_____

Attorneys for plaintiffs
Office and P. O. Address
Telephone No.

Form 3

Complaint Where Plaintiffs Assert Right to Relief Severally—Skeleton Form

Complaint

[Title of court and cause] Index No. — [if assigned]

Plaintiffs, by their attorney, __1_____, complaining of the defendant, allege:

FOR A FIRST CAUSE OF ACTION, THE PLAINTIFF __2_____ ALLEGES:

[Allege facts constituting cause of action.]

9. By reason of the premises, the plaintiff __3_____ has been damaged in the sum of $__4__, for which the plaintiff demands judgment against the defendant, together with interest from the __5__ day of __6_____, 19_7_, and the costs and disbursements of this action.

FOR A SECOND CAUSE OF ACTION, THE PLAINTIFF __8_____ ALLEGES:

10. The plaintiff __9_____ repeats and re-alleges as part of this separate and complete cause of action each and all of the allegations contained in paragraphs numbered 1, 2, 3, and 4 of this complaint with like effect as if herein fully set forth.

[Allege other facts constituting cause of action.]

16. By reason of the premises, the plaintiff __10_____, has been damaged in the sum of $__11__, for which judgment is demanded against the defendant, together with interest from the __12__ day of __13_____, 19_14_, and the costs and disbursements of this action.

WHEREFORE, judgment is demanded against the defendant in favor of the plaintiff __15_____ in the sum of __16_____ Dollars with interest from the __17__ day of __18_____, 19_19_, and in favor of the plaintiff __20_____ in the sum of __21_____ Dollars with interest from __22__ day of __23_____, 19_24_, together with the costs and disbursements of this action.

__25_____

Attorney for Plaintiffs
Office and P. O. Address
Telephone No.

Form 4

Complaint Asserting Right to Relief Against Defendants in Alternative—Skeleton Form

Complaint

[Title of court and cause] Index No. — [if assigned]

Plaintiff, by his attorney, __1_____, complaining of the defendants, alleges:

[Allege facts constituting cause of action in regular manner.]

8. Plaintiff joined the two defendants named in this action and is seeking relief in the alternative for the reason that he is in doubt as to which defendant is, or whether both are, liable for plaintiff's damages as hereinbefore set forth.

WHEREFORE, plaintiff demands judgment against the defendants, or either of them, for the sum of $__2__, together with the costs and disbursements of this action.

__3_____

Attorney for plaintiff
Office and P. O. Address
Telephone No.

Form 5

Complaint Asserting Right to Relief Against Defendants in Alternative—Another Form

Complaint
[Title of court and cause]   Index No. — [if assigned]

Plaintiff, by his attorney, __1_____, complaining of the defendants, alleges:

FOR A CAUSE OF ACTION AGAINST THE DEFENDANT __2_____:

[Set forth facts constituting cause of action in regular manner.]

FOR A SECOND, ALTERNATIVE CAUSE OF ACTION AGAINST THE DEFENDANT __3_____:

8. Plaintiff repeats and re-alleges, as part of this cause of action, each and every allegation contained in paragraphs numbered 1, 2, 3, 4, and 5 of this complaint, with like effect as if herein fully set forth and repeated.

WHEREFORE, plaintiff demands judgment against the defendant __4_____, or the defendant __5_____, in the alternative, in the sum of $__6__, together with the costs and disbursements of this action.

__7_____
Attorney for Plaintiff
Office and P. O. Address
Telephone No.

Form 6

Complaint Where Right to Relief is Asserted Against Defendants Severally—Skeleton Form

Complaint
[Title of court and cause]   Index No. — [if assigned]

Plaintiff, by his attorney, __1_____, complaining of the defendants, alleges:

FOR A CAUSE OF ACTION AGAINST THE DEFENDANT __2_____:

[Allege facts constituting cause of action.]

7. As a result of the premises, the defendant __3_____ is indebted to the plaintiff in the sum of $__4__, which sum the defendant has refused and neglected to pay although due demand has been made therefor.

FOR A CAUSE OF ACTION AGAINST THE DEFENDANT __5_____:

8. Plaintiff repeats and re-alleges as part of this cause of action each and every allegation contained in paragraphs numbered 1, 3, and 4 of this Complaint with the same effect as if herein fully set forth and repeated.

[Allege other facts constituting cause of action.]

13. By reason of the premises the defendant __6_____, is indebted to the plaintiff in the sum of $__7__, which sum said defendant has refused and neglected to pay although due demand has been made therefor.

WHEREFORE, plaintiff demands judgment against the defendant __8_____ in the sum of $__9__ with interest from the __10__ day of __11_____, 19_12_, and against the defendant __13_____ in the sum of $__14__ with interest from the __15__ day of __16_____, 19_17_, together with the costs and disbursements of this action.

__18_____
Attorney for Plaintiff
Office and P. O. Address
Telephone No.

Form 7

Complaint Asserting Right to Relief Against Defendants Jointly—Skeleton Form

Complaint

[Title of court and cause]   Index No. — [if assigned]

     Plaintiff, by his attorney, ___1_____, complaining of the defendants, alleges:

[Allege facts constituting cause of action.]

     WHEREFORE, plaintiff demands judgment against the defendants in the sum of $__2__, with interest from the __3__ day of __4_____, 19_5_, together with the costs and disbursements of this action.

__6_____

Attorney for Plaintiff
Office and P. O. Address
Telephone No.

Form 8

Complaint Against Two Foreign Corporations With Prayer for Judgment in the Alternative

Complaint

[Title of court and cause]   Index No. — [if assigned]

     Plaintiff, by his attorneys, ___1_____, complaining of the defendants, alleges:

FOR A FIRST CAUSE OF ACTION AGAINST THE __2_____ MANUFAC-TURING COMPANY OF DELAWARE:

     1. Plaintiff is, and at all times hereinafter mentioned was, a resident of the City of __3_____, __4_____ County, New York.

     2. On information and belief, the defendant __5_____ manufacturing company of __6_____ is, and at all times hereinafter mentioned was, a foreign corporation organized and existing under and by virtue of the laws of the State of Delaware, and at all such times was and is now doing business in the State of New York.

     3. Plaintiff is, and at all times hereinafter mentioned was, the owner of "Ranwhit Phonelet," an improvement in the hearing mechanism of telephone receivers, radio earpieces, and the like, and is, and at all such times was the sole and exclusive owner of United States patents therefor, and has and at all such times had the exclusive right to make, use and vend "Ranwhit Phonelets" throughout the United States.

     4. On or about the month of __7_____, 19_8_, plaintiff and the defendant entered into an agreement in writing wherein and whereby in consideration of the plaintiff's agreement to extend to the defendant the sole rights covering the manufacture and sale of the "Ranwhit Phonelet" in the United States for a period of five years from the date of contract; and in consideration of the plaintiff's further agreement to furnish the defendant such manufacturing equipment as was then owned by the plaintiff, and help and cooperate in solving manufacturing and sales problems, the defendant agreed to dispose of a minimum of __9__ "Ranwhit Phonelets" during the first year in which the agreement was to be in force, and __10__ "Ranwhit Phonelets" during each succeeding year, and in default of disposing of the stipulated number of "Ranwhit Phonelets" to pay to the plaintiff such royalty as would have been due plaintiff upon the sale of the quantities named, or, in the alternative, at the election of the plaintiff, to pay the agreed royalty based upon actual sales; and defendant further agreed to pay plaintiff on each "Phonelet" sold during the first year in which said agreement was to remain in force a royalty of __11_____ cents each, a royalty of __12_____ cents each during the second year, and a royalty of __13_____ cents each during the third, fourth and fifth years; and the plaintiff and defendant further agreed in consideration of the premises to draw up and sign a formal memorandum embodying the provisions of the said agreement.

5. The plaintiff has been at all times ready, able and willing to perform all the terms and conditions on the part of the plaintiff to be performed under the said agreement, and has offered to execute the memorandum agreed upon and has requested the defendant to execute said memorandum.

6. Nevertheless, the defendant on or about the __14__ day of __15_____, 19_16_, wrongfully repudiated the said agreement and definitely notified plaintiff that it would not thereafter perform the same, and defendant has refused to execute the memorandum agreed upon, to the plaintiff's damage in the sum of __17_____ dollars.

FOR A SECOND ALTERNATIVE CAUSE OF ACTION AGAINST DEFENDANT __18_____ MANUFACTURING COMPANY:

7. Plaintiff repeats the allegations contained in the paragraphs of this complaint marked 1, 3, 4, 5 and 6.

8. On information and belief, the defendant __19_____ manufacturing company is, and at all times hereinafter mentioned was, a foreign corporation organized and existing under and by virtue of the laws of the State of Ohio, and at all such times was and is now doing business in the State of New York.

9. The agreement set forth in paragraph 4 hereof was entered into on behalf of defendant __20_____ manufacturing company [by its duly authorized agent] and the repudiation of said agreement and refusal to perform the terms of said agreement were made by defendant __21_____ manufacturing company [by its duly authorized agent] to the plaintiff's damage in the sum of __22_____ dollars.

WHEREFORE, plaintiff prays judgment against defendant __23_____ manufacturing company of Delaware or defendant __24_____ manufacturing company in the alternative for the said amount of __25_____ dollars with interest from the __26__ day of __27_____, 19_28_, together with the costs and disbursements of this action.

_____29_____

Attorneys for Plaintiff
Office and P. O. Address
Telephone No.

Form 9

Complaint in Action Against Two Corporations Where Plaintiff in Doubt as to Which of the Two the Agent was Acting for in Making of Contract Sued on

Complaint
[Title of court and cause]   Index No. — [if assigned]

The plaintiff, by __1_____, its attorney, for its complaint, respectfully shows to this court and alleges:

FOR A FIRST CAUSE OF ACTION:

1. At all times hereinafter mentioned, the plaintiff was and now is a corporation, organized and existing under and by virtue of the laws of the State of New York.

2. At all times hereinafter mentioned, the defendants were and still are domestic corporations, organized and existing under and by virtue of the laws of the State of New York.

3. On or about the __2__ day of __3_____, 19_4_, one W, acting on behalf of the defendant __5_____ realty corporation or the defendant __6_____, Inc., or for both, entered into written contracts, pursuant to which the plaintiff licensed and agreed to furnish for a period commencing on or about __7_____, 19_8_, and terminating on or about __9_____, 19_10_, positive prints of certain feature motion pictures mentioned in said contracts, to be exhibited at the __11_____ Theatre, at __12_____, and either of said defendants, or both, agreed to accept and publicly exhibit the said motion pictures within said period, and for such license and privileges, either of said defendants, or both, agreed to pay to the plaintiff the various license fees enumerated in said contracts.

4. Thereafter, in violation of said contracts, either of said defendants, or both, failed and refused to exhibit and pay for the following feature motion pictures mentioned therein, at the agreed license fee herein set forth, pursuant to the terms and provisions of the said contracts, viz.: __13_____.

5. Plaintiff has duly performed all the terms and conditions of said contracts, on its part to be performed.

6. The reason the plaintiff has joined the above named defendants is that it is in doubt as to which defendant, or both, is liable for said breach of contracts.

7. By reason thereof, the plaintiff has been damaged in the sum of __14_____ dollars, no part of which has been paid, although duly demanded.

FOR A SECOND CAUSE OF ACTION:

8. At all times hereinafter mentioned, the plaintiff was and now is a corporation, organized and existing under and by virtue of the laws of the State of New York.

9. At all times hereinafter mentioned, the defendants were and still are domestic corporations, organized and existing under and by virtue of the laws of the State of New York.

10. On or about the __15__ day of __16_____, 19_17_, one W, acting on behalf of the defendant __18_____ realty corporation, or the defendant __19_____, Inc., or for both, entered into a written contract, pursuant to which the plaintiff licensed and agreed to furnish, for a period commencing on or about __20_____, 19_21_, and terminating on or about __22_____, 19_23_, positive prints of weekly issues, known as "Odd" and "Even" Issues of "Fox News," to be exhibited at the __24_____ Theatre, at __25_____, and either of said defendants, or both, agreed to accept and publicly exhibit each week one "Odd" and one "Even" issue of said "Fox News," and for such license and privilege, either of said defendants, or both, agreed to pay to the plaintiff the sum of $__26__ for the "Odd" issues and the sum of $__27__ for the "Even" issues.

11. Thereafter, in violation of said contract, and on or about __28_____, 19_29_, either of said defendants, or both, failed and refused to exhibit and pay for the remaining weekly issues of said "Fox News," pursuant to the terms and provisions of the said contract.

12. The plaintiff has duly performed all the terms and conditions of said contract, on its part to be performed.

13. The reason the plaintiff has joined the above named defendants is that it is in doubt as to which defendant, or both, is liable for said breach of contract.

14. By reason thereof, the plaintiff has been damaged in the sum of __30_____ dollars, no part of which has been paid, although duly demanded.

WHEREFORE, plaintiff demands judgment against the defendants, or either of them, for the sum of __31_____ dollars, together with the costs and disbursements of this action.

__32_____

Attorney for Plaintiff
Office and P. O. Address
Telephone No.

Form 10

Complaint Where Plaintiff in Doubt Whether Claim is Against One or the Other of Two Corporations Because of Similarity of Names, Etc.

Complaint

[Title of court and cause]   Index No. — [if assigned]

The above named plaintiff, for a complaint herein by __1_____, his attorneys, alleges:

1. The plaintiff is, and at all the times hereinafter mentioned was, a resident of the State of New York.

2. The defendant Archibald McNeil & Sons Co. is a corporation, organized and existing under the laws of the State of Connecticut, and will be hereinafter referred to as the Connecticut corporation; the said defendant at all times herein mentioned was engaged in the business of producing, buying, selling, shipping and distributing coal, and at all such times had, and still has, an office for the transaction of its said business in the City of __²____, State of New York.

3. The defendant Archibald McNeil & Sons Co. Inc., of New York is a domestic corporation, and will be hereinafter referred to as the New York corporation. Upon information and belief, that said defendant was organized in or about the month of __³____, 19_4_, and was thereafter engaged in the business of producing, buying, selling, shipping and distributing coal, with an office for the transaction of its said business in the City of __5____, State of New York.

4. Between about __6____, 19_7_, and __8____, 19_9_, the plaintiff, at the special instance and request of the defendant Connecticut corporation, rendered services to said corporation in connection with the purchase, sale, shipping and distribution of coal for and on behalf of the said corporation, and the said corporation agreed to pay plaintiff, as compensation for such services, a commission equal to one-half of the gross profits realized by the corporation upon any and all coal bought or sold by the plaintiff, for, on behalf of, or for the account of the said corporation.

5. Between the said dates, and pursuant to the agreement above stated, the plaintiff did, from time to time, buy and sell for, on behalf, and for the account of the said corporation, various quantities of coal, upon which the said defendant realized large gross profits.

6. Between about __10____, 19_11_, and __12____, 19_13_, the plaintiff, at the special instance and request of the defendant New York corporation, rendered services to said corporation in connection with the purchase, sale, shipping and distribution of coal for and on behalf of the said corporation, and the said corporation agreed to pay plaintiff, as compensation for such services, a commission equal to one-half of the gross profits realized by the corporation upon any and all coal bought or sold by the plaintiff for, on behalf of, or for the account of the said corporation.

7. Between the said dates, and pursuant to the agreement above stated, the plaintiff did, from time to time, buy and sell for, on behalf, and for the account of the said corporation, various quantities of coal, upon which the said defendant realized large gross profits.

8. From the time of the organization of the defendant New York corporation, the two defendants were controlled by the same group of stockholders, had the same directors, officers and employees, shared the same offices in the City of __14____, carried on the same character of business in the State of New York and elsewhere, dealt with and for each other in numerous business transactions, and generally sustained such intimate intercorporate relations, and so commingled their records and affairs that the plaintiff never knew, and does not now know, and is therefore unable to state, as to any given transaction between the plaintiff and the defendants during the period from __15____, 19_16_, to __17____, 19_18_, whether the plaintiff was dealing with or for the Connecticut corporation, or with or for the New York corporation, or both. From time to time during said period, the plaintiff received checks of the New York corporation in payment or part payment of commissions due him for coal bought or sold by him under the agreements hereinabove set forth, but the plaintiff is unable to state whether such payments were made for the account of the New York corporation or for the account of the Connecticut corporation.

9. Upon information and belief, upon the coal bought or sold as aforesaid by the plaintiff, for, on behalf, or for the account of, the defendant corporations, the said defendants realized gross profits aggregating a sum in excess of $__19__, one-half of which, to wit, the sum of at least $__20__, became due and payable to the plaintiff as commissions, pursuant to the agreements above stated.

10. No part of said commissions has been paid to the plaintiff, except the sum of $__21__.

11. The plaintiff has duly performed all the covenants and conditions of each of the aforesaid agreements on his part to be performed.

12. By reason of the facts and circumstances above stated, the plaintiff is in doubt as to what extent he is entitled to redress from the defendant New York corporation and to what extent he is entitled to redress from the defendant Connecticut corporation.

WHEREFORE, the plaintiff demands judgments against each of the said defendants for the sum of __22_____ dollars with interest from __23_____, 19_24_, together with the costs and disbursements of this action.

__25_____

Attorneys for Plaintiff
Office and P. O. Address
Telephone No.

Form 11

Complaint in Action Against Corporate and Individual Defendants on a Promissory Note Where Authority to Execute Note Disputed

Complaint

[Title of court and cause]　　　　Index No. — [if assigned]

The plaintiff above named, by __1_____, its attorneys, complaining of the above named defendants, alleges as follows:

1. At all the times hereinafter mentioned plaintiff was and now is a corporation organized and carrying on business as a national bank under the laws of the United States, and has its principal place of business in __2_____, Georgia.

2. At all times hereinafter mentioned the defendant __3_____, Inc., was and now is a corporation organized and carrying on business under the laws of the State of New York, and has its principal place of business at No. __4_ _5_____ Street, __6_____ City.

3. On or about __7_____, the defendant __8_____, Inc., by L, purporting to act as the duly authorized agent of the defendant, executed to B its promissory note in writing, as follows:

"$6,400.00　　　　　　　　　　　　　　　　　　　　　Nov. 4, 1925.

Four Months after date we promise to pay to the order of Ben Adler Sixty Four Hundred and No/100 __9_____ Dollars at Georgia National Bank of Albany, Ga.

Value received.

J. & G. Lippmann
L. J. Lippmann,
Pres.

Endorsed: Ben Adler."

4. Thereafter the said B endorsed and transferred the same for a valuable consideration before maturity and the plaintiff is the owner and holder thereof and there is due to the plaintiff on account of said note from either __10_____, Inc., or L, individually, the sum of __11_____ dollars which the plaintiff claims.

5. On the __12_ day of __13_____, 19_14_, at the maturity of said note, the same was duly presented for payment to the defendant __15_____, Inc., and payment thereof demanded of it, but the said defendant refused to pay the same.

6. Said note was duly protested for nonpayment on said __16_____, 19_17_, and the cost of said protest was __18_____ dollars which plaintiff was obliged to pay and did pay.

7. No part of said note or the cost of protest has been paid.

8. The legal rate of interest under the laws of the State of Georgia is __19_____ per cent.

9. The said __20_____, Inc., denies that it authorized L to execute the note and plaintiff does not know whether or not L was so authorized.

WHEREFORE, plaintiff demands judgment against defendant __21_____, Inc., or in the alternative against L, individually, for the sum of __22_____ dollars, together with __23_____ per cent interest on __24_____ dollars from the __25__ day of __26_____, 19_27_, together with the costs of this action.

__28_____

Attorneys for Plaintiff
Office and P. O. Address
Telephone No.

Form 12

Complaint in Action Against Principal and Agent Where Principal Denied Agent's Authority

Complaint
[Title of court and cause]   Index No. — [if assigned]

Plaintiffs, by their attorneys __1_____, for their complaint herein allege:

1. At all times hereinafter mentioned, the plaintiffs, A and B, were and still are co-partners doing business under the firm name and style of __2_____, with their principal place of business at No. __3__ __4_____ street, in the City of __5_____, state of New York.

2. Upon information and belief at all the times hereinafter mentioned, the defendants C, D and E were and still are co-partners doing business under the firm name and style of __6_____ as sugar brokers in the City of __7_____.

3. Upon information and belief, at all the times hereinafter mentioned, the defendant __8_____ company was and still is a domestic corporation existing under and by virtue of the laws of the State of New York, doing business as a wholesale grocer at __9_____.

4. On or about the __10__ day of __11_____, 19_12_, the defendants __13_____ [name of partnership], assuming to act as broker and agent on behalf of the defendant __14_____ company, entered into an agreement with these plaintiffs whereby the plaintiffs agreed to sell __15_____ pounds of sugar, f.o.b. New York, to the defendant __16_____ company, delivery to be made on or about __17_____, 19_18_, for which the defendant __19_____ company agreed to pay the sum of $__20__, which was the reasonable value of the said sugar.

5. Upon entering into the aforementioned agreement, the defendants __21_____ [name of partnership] represented to the plaintiffs that they were duly authorized and empowered by the said defendant __22_____ company, so to enter into the aforementioned agreement on its behalf.

6. Relying upon said representations and said supposed authority of the defendants __23_____ [name of partnership], the plaintiffs, pursuant to the aforementioned agreement, on or about __24_____, 19_25_, loaded car __26_____ with the said __27_____ pounds of sugar, and shipped it at __28_____, covered by bill of lading issued by the __29_____ railroad, and thereafter said __30_____ railroad tendered delivery of said sugar to the defendant __31_____ company at __32_____.

7. The defendant __33_____ company declined to receive or pay for the said sugar, and denied that the defendants __34_____ [partnership] had authority to enter into the aforementioned agreement on its behalf.

8. Thereupon these plaintiffs sold the said sugar at New York for the sum of $__35__, being the best price obtainable at the said place, and such place being a proper

market at which to sell the same; that the cost of effecting the sale of the said sugar was $__36__.

9. By reason of the premises, these plaintiffs have been damaged in the sum of $__37__, being the difference between the contract price under the aforementioned agreement, and the sum realized from the resale of the said sugar, plus the cost of effecting the said sale.

10. These plaintiffs have duly demanded the amount of the aforesaid sum, and that the defendants have failed and refused to pay the same or any part thereof.

11. The plaintiffs have duly performed all the conditions on their part to be performed.

WHEREFORE plaintiffs demand judgment against the defendants in the sum of $__38__ with interest thereon from the __39__ day of __40_____, 19_41_, together with the costs and disbursements of this action.

__42_____

Attorneys for Plaintiffs
Office and P. O. Address
Telephone No.

Form 13

Complaint in Action Against Carrier and Warehouseman for Goods Lost While in Possession of One or the Other

Complaint

[Title of court and cause]   Index No. — [if assigned]

The plaintiff above named, by __1_____, its attorneys, complaining of the defendants, respectfully shows to the court and alleges:

1. At all the times hereinafter mentioned the plaintiff was and still is a domestic corporation.

2. Upon information and belief, that at all the times hereinafter mentioned, the defendant, A, was and still is a domestic corporation.

3. Upon information and belief, that at all the times hereinafter mentioned, the defendant B was and still is a domestic corporation.

4. Upon information and belief, that at all the times hereinafter mentioned, the defendant A was and now is a common carrier of goods for hire in the City of __2_____.

5. Upon information and belief, that at all the times hereinafter mentioned, the defendant B conducted a warehouse known as a public warehouse at Nos. __3__ and __4__ __5_____ Street, in the City of __6_____, for the storing of goods for hire.

6. At all the times hereinafter mentioned, the plaintiff was the owner of twelve certain cases containing certain goods, wares and merchandise.

7. On or about the __7__ day of __8_____, 19_9_, at the City of __10_____, in consideration of a reasonable compensation then agreed to be paid to it by the plaintiff, the plaintiff delivered to the defendant A and the said defendant A received from the plaintiff, the said twelve cases containing certain goods, wares and merchandise, which the said defendant A agreed safely to deliver to the said defendant B at Nos. __11__ and __12__ __13_____ Street, in the City of __14_____, to be there stored for the account of the plaintiff.

8. Upon information and belief that the defendant A delivered said cases to defendant B on or about __15_____, 19_16_, but defendant B claims that the said cases did not contain all the goods contained in them when delivered to defendant A by the plaintiff.

9. The defendant A claims it delivered to defendant B the said cases, and that at the

time of said delivery by it to the defendant B the said cases contained all the goods that were in them when they were delivered to the defendant A by said plaintiff.

10. The delivery of said cases and the contents thereof to defendant B was under and pursuant to an agreement whereby in consideration of a reasonable compensation agreed to be paid to defendant B by the plaintiff, B agreed to store and safely keep in its warehouse said cases and merchandise, the property of the plaintiff, until the same should be called for, and then safely to deliver said goods to the plaintiff or its order, at request.

11. There was duly paid and tendered to defendant B its charges for said storing, and due demand made by the plaintiff on B for delivery to it or its order of said goods.

12. This demand was made on or about the __17__ day of __18_____, 19_19_.

13. In attempted compliance with said demand by the plaintiff, the defendant B did deliver certain portions of said goods, but failed to deliver all thereof, there being a shortage therein of certain goods of the fair and reasonable value of $__20__.

14. The only reason given by defendant B for not delivering said goods was a claim on the part of the defendant B that said goods had not been delivered to it by defendant A.

15. Thereupon plaintiff duly demanded from defendant A a delivery to it [the plaintiff] of the said missing goods, but the defendant A disclaimed liability therefor, and asserted as its sole excuse for such nondelivery the fact that it claimed to have delivered said missing goods to defendant B.

16. Either the defendant A failed safely to deliver the said goods to defendant B and has converted all or part of said missing merchandise to its own use, or the defendant B failed to store and safely keep said merchandise in its warehouse as agreed, and has converted all or part of said missing merchandise to its own use, and that either both, or each in part, of said defendants have failed to perform their respective agreements, as hereinbefore set forth.

17. Plaintiff is in doubt as to the defendant from whom it is entitled to redress and has, therefore, made both the defendants herein parties defendant to the action, to the intent that the question as to which if any of the defendants is liable, and to what extent, may be determined as between the parties.

WHEREFORE plaintiff demands judgment against the defendants, or such one of them as may be liable, for the sum of $__21__, with interest thereon from __22_____, 19_23_, together with the costs and disbursements of this action.

__24_____

Attorneys for Plaintiff
Office and P. O. Address
Telephone No.

Form 14

Complaint in Action Against Carrier and Manufacturer for Machinery Damaged in Transit

Complaint
[Title of court and cause]   Index No. — [if assigned]

Plaintiff, complaining of the defendants, alleges:

1. __1_____ railway company now is and at all times hereinafter mentioned was a corporation organized and existing under and by virtue of the laws of the State of __2_____, and is a common carrier engaged in the business of carrying passengers and freight for hire in the State of __3_____ and between points in the State of __4_____ and points in other states.

2. __5_____ machinery company now is and at all times hereinafter mentioned was

a corporation organized and existing under and by virtue of the laws of the State of __6_____.

3. On or about __7_____, 19_8_, the plaintiff purchased from __9_____ Connell Company, of __10_____, a certain drag line hereinafter more particularly referred to, which was then located in or near the City of __11_____, __12_____, one of the terms of said purchase being that said drag line was to be loaded by __13_____ Connell Company for shipment on a car at __14_____, __15_____, in proper manner.

4. Plaintiff alleges upon information and belief that __16_____ Connell Company was not then the owner of said drag line, but that it subsequently and on or about __17_____, 19_18_, purchased the same from __19_____ machinery company under a written contract, one of the terms of which was that the said drag line was to be shipped f.o.b. __20_____ to __21_____, loaded on cars by the __22_____ machinery company, and said contract, together with all claims thereunder against the defendant __23_____ machinery company, was assigned to the plaintiff by __24_____ Connell Company.

5. Pursuant to the said contract between __25_____ Connell Company and __26_____ machinery company, said __27_____ machinery company loaded said drag line on cars at __28_____, and on or about __29_____, 19_30_, procured from the defendant __31_____ Railway Company a bill of lading pursuant to the terms of which said drag line was consigned by said __32_____ machinery company to its own order with directions to notify __33_____ at __34_____, and said bill of lading provided that said drag line should be shipped to __35_____, and said __36_____ railway company issued said bill of lading and thereby agreed and undertook to ship the said drag line from __37_____ to __38_____. Upon the issuance of said bill of lading by __39_____ machinery company, the said bill of lading was indorsed in blank by said __40_____ machinery company and as so indorsed was forwarded to __41_____, with directions to deliver said bill of lading to __42_____ upon the payment of the draft thereto attached, and said __43_____ did on or about __44_____, 19_45_, pay said draft and the bill of lading was thereupon delivered to him.

6. The defendant __46_____ railroad company, after the issuance of the bill of lading and on or about __47_____, 19_48_, or soon thereafter, proceeded to ship the said drag line to __49_____, but on or about the said day, and while the said drag line was still in the possession of said defendant railroad company and while it was in transit from __50_____ to __51_____, the said drag line was damaged to such an extent that it became and was a total wreck and without value.

7. On or about __52_____, 19_53_, and after the payment by the plaintiff of the draft above mentioned, the defendant __54_____ railway company notified the plaintiff that the said drag line was damaged, and such notice was the first notice that the plaintiff obtained of the fact that said drag line had been damaged while in transit.

8. It is the claim of the defendant __55_____ machinery company that the said drag line was properly loaded by it and that the loss or damage arising from the wreck of said drag line while in transit as aforesaid occurred without any negligence on its part in the loading thereof, and that the loss and damage thereto arising from the wreck thereof occurred through the negligence and carelessness of the railroad company, its servants, agents, and employees in the handling of the said shipment, and that said railroad company inspected or undertook the inspection of the loading of said drag line and approved the method and manner and sufficiency of such loading and accepted the said drag line for shipment and issued its bill of lading as aforesaid after such inspection and after causing the __56_____ machinery company to understand that it had inspected and approved the method, manner, and sufficiency of the loading of such shipment.

9. It is the claim of the defendant __57_____ railway company that the said drag line was improperly and insecurely loaded, and that the __58_____ machinery company or those who acted for it in the loading thereof loaded the said drag line in an improper, negligent, and careless manner, and that by reason thereof the said drag line became loosened from its fastenings and from the car upon which it was loaded,

and that as a result thereof said drag line was damaged, and that the said __59_____ railway company, its agents, servants, and employees were without negligence in the handling and shipment of the same.

10. Plaintiff is in doubt and is unable to determine whether the matters set forth in the claim made by the __60_____ machinery company or the matters set forth in the claim of the __61_____ railway company are true and correct and the facts in the case, and alleges upon information and belief that either the matters claimed by __62_____ machinery company to be the facts are true and correct or the facts set forth in the claim of the __63_____ railway company are true and correct, and that it is entitled to relief and judgment against the __64_____ machinery company if the facts are as set forth in the claim of the __65_____ railway company as herein set forth, or is entitled to relief and judgment against the __66_____ railway company if the facts are as set forth in the claim of the __67_____ machinery company as herein set forth, and that the __68_____ railway company and the __69_____ machinery company are joined as defendants in this action for the reason that the right of the plaintiff to relief exists in the alternative against them.

11. Claim for loss and damage to the said drag line was duly given to the __70_____ railway company in accordance with the terms and conditions of the bill of lading.

12. Said drag line at the time of the damage to it was of the value of __71_____ dollars, and by reason of the loss thereof and damage thereto plaintiff has suffered damages in the sum of __72_____ dollars.

WHEREFORE, plaintiff prays for judgment against the __73_____ railway company and __74_____ machinery company in the alternative in the sum of __75_____ dollars, together with interest thereon from __76_____, 19_77_, and his costs and disbursements in this action.

__78_____
Attorney for Plaintiff
Office and P. O. Address
Telephone No.

Form 15

Complaint in Action Against Guarantor and Others

Complaint

[Title of court and cause]   Index No. — [if assigned]

Plaintiff, complaining of the defendants, by __1_____, his attorneys, for his complaint, respectfully shows to this Court and alleges:

AS AND FOR A FIRST CAUSE OF ACTION:

1. On or about and between the __2__ day of __3_____, 19_4_, and the __5__ day of __6_____, 19_7_, defendant C requested, authorized and employed the plaintiff to purchase on behalf of and for the defendant C, a certain tract of land consisting of __8__ acres, situated in section __9__, township __10_____, South Range __11_____ East, __12_____ County, State of __13_____, and requested the plaintiff to permit the legal title to said property to be vested in the said plaintiff upon the completion of said purchase, and further requested of said plaintiff that he execute in his, plaintiff's, name and deliver to the vendors of said tract certain purchase money obligations, represented by promissory notes, a schedule of which is hereto annexed and made a part hereof and marked Exhibit A.

2. At the time of requesting plaintiff to execute the aforesaid promissory notes, defendant C promised and agreed that in consideration of such performance, the defendant C would guarantee plaintiff against and relieve plaintiff from any and all liability arising from the making and delivery of said promissory notes.

3. In reliance of and in consideration of the aforesaid promises, plaintiff made,

executed and delivered the notes set forth in Schedule A hereof, and has duly performed all the conditions on his part to be performed.

4. The defendant C utterly failed and refused to pay the said notes according to the terms thereof, and no part of the said notes has ever been paid although duly presented for payment.

5. On or about the __14__ day of __15__, 19_16_, actions were begun in the Supreme Court for the County of __17__ by __18__, __19__ and __20__ to recover from plaintiff on the aforesaid notes; that plaintiff at once notified defendant C of the commencement thereof, and requested him to defend against the same, and on the __21__ day of __22__, 19_23_, judgments were therein duly given by said court against the plaintiff herein, there the defendant, aggregating the sum of __24__ dollars, being the amount of the said notes, with interest thereon at the rate of __25__ per cent per annum, together with costs.

6. The legal rate of interest in the State of __26__, pursuant to statutes made and provided, is __27__ per cent per annum.

7. On or about the __28__ day of __29__, 19_30_, plaintiff was compelled to pay and did pay to the said __31__, __32__ and __33__, the sum of $__34__, being the amount of said judgment, and no part of the same has been repaid to the plaintiff, although duly demanded.

FOR A SECOND CAUSE OF ACTION, PLAINTIFF ALLEGES:

8. He repeats and re-alleges each and every allegation mentioned and contained in paragraph numbered 1 of the within complaint.

9. At the time of requesting the plaintiff to execute and deliver the aforesaid promissory notes, defendant C promised that in consideration of such performance, the defendant C would guarantee plaintiff against any loss and hold plaintiff harmless for any damages or losses which plaintiff might sustain by reason of the execution and delivery of the said promissory notes.

10. In reliance on and in consideration of the aforesaid promises, plaintiff made, executed and delivered the notes set forth in Schedule A hereof.

11. On or about the __35__ day of __36__, 19_37_, actions were begun in the Supreme Court for the County of __38__, by __39__, __40__ and __41__, to recover from plaintiff on the aforesaid notes; plaintiff at once notified defendant C of the commencement thereof, and requested him to defend against the same, and that on the __42__ day of __43__, 19_44_, judgments were therein duly given by the said court against the plaintiff, therein the defendant, aggregating the sum of $__45__, being the amount of the said notes, with interest thereon at the rate of __46__ per cent per annum, together with costs.

12. The legal rate of interest in the State of __47__, pursuant to statutes made and provided is __48__ per cent per annum.

13. On or about the __49__ day of __50__, 19_51_, plaintiff was compelled to pay and did pay to the said __52__, __53__ and __54__, the sum of $__55__, being the amount of said judgment, and that no part of the same has been paid to the plaintiff, although duly demanded.

FOR A THIRD CAUSE OF ACTION, PLAINTIFF ALLEGES UPON INFORMATION AND BELIEF:

14. All the defendants were co-adventurers and were members of a syndicate whose purpose was to purchase and sell real property in the State of __56__.

15. In or about and between the __57__ day of __58__, 19_59_, and the __60__ day of __61__, 19_62_, the defendants requested, authorized and employed the plaintiff on their behalf to purchase a certain tract of land consisting of __63__ acres, situated in section __64__, township __65__, South Range __66__ East, __67__ County, State of __68__, and requested the plaintiff to permit the legal title to said property to be vested in the said plaintiff upon the completion of said

purchase, and further requested of said plaintiff that he execute in his, plaintiff's, name and deliver to the vendors of said tract, certain purchase money obligations represented by promissory notes, a schedule of which is annexed hereto and made a part hereof and marked Exhibit A.

16. At the time of requesting the plaintiff to execute the aforesaid promissory notes, defendants promised and agreed that in consideration of such performance, defendants would guarantee plaintiff against and relieve plaintiff from any and all liability arising from the making and delivery of said promissory notes.

17. In reliance on and in consideration of the aforesaid promises, plaintiff made, executed and delivered the notes set forth in Schedule A hereof, and has duly performed all the conditions on his part to be performed.

18. Defendants failed and refused to pay the said notes according to their terms and no part of the same has been paid although duly presented for payment.

19. On or about the __69__ day of __70_____, 19_71_, actions were begun in the Supreme Court for the County of __72_____, by __73_____, __74_____ and __75_____ to recover from plaintiff on the aforesaid notes; that plaintiff at once notified defendants of the commencement thereof and requested them to defend against the same, and that on the __76__ day of __77_____, 19_78_, judgments were therein duly given by the said court against the plaintiff herein, therein the defendant, aggregating the sum of $__79__, being the amount of the said notes, with interest thereon at the rate of __80_____ per cent per annum, together with costs.

20. The legal rate of interest in the State of __81_____, pursuant to statutes made and provided, is __82_____ per cent per annum.

21. On or about the __83__ day of __84_____, 19_85_, plaintiff was compelled to pay and did pay to the said __86_____, __87_____ and __88_____, the sum of $__89__, being the amount of the judgment, and that no part of the same has been repaid to the plaintiff although duly demanded.

FOR A FOURTH CAUSE OF ACTION, PLAINTIFF ALLEGES UPON IN-FORMATION AND BELIEF:

22. He repeats and realleges each and every allegation mentioned and contained in paragraphs numbered 14 and 15 of the within complaint.

23. At the time of requesting the plaintiff to execute the aforesaid promissory notes, defendants promised and agreed that in consideration of such performance, defendants would guarantee plaintiff against any loss and hold plaintiff harmless for any damages or losses which plaintiff might sustain by reason of the execution and delivery of the said promissory notes.

24. In reliance of and in consideration of the aforesaid promises, plaintiff made, executed and delivered the notes set forth in Schedule A hereof, and has duly performed all the conditions on his part to be performed.

25. The defendants failed and refused to pay the said notes according to their terms and that no part of the same has been paid although duly presented for payment.

26. On or about the __90__ day of __91_____, 19_92_, actions were begun in the Supreme Court for the County of __93_____ by __94_____, __95_____ and __96_____, to recover from plaintiff on the aforesaid notes; that plaintiff at once notified defendants of the commencement thereof and requested them to defend against the same, and that on the __97__ day of __98_____, 19_99_, judgments were therein duly given by said Court against the plaintiff herein, therein the defendant, aggregating the sum of $__100__, being the amount of the said notes, with interest thereon at the rate of __101_____ per cent per annum, together with costs.

27. The legal rate of interest in the State of __102_____, pursuant to statutes made and provided is __103_____ per cent per annum.

28. On or about the __104__ day of __105_____, 19_106_, plaintiff was compelled to

pay and did pay the said __107_____, __108_____ and __109_____, the sum of $__110__, being the amount of the judgment, and that no part of the same has been repaid to the plaintiff although duly demanded.

WHEREFORE, plaintiff demands judgment against the defendant C, and/or __111_____, __112_____, __113____ and __114_____, in the sum of $__115__, with interest from the __116__ day of __117_____, 19_118_, together with the costs and disbursements of this action.

                   __119_____

                       Attorneys for Plaintiff
                     Office and P. O. Address
                           Telephone No.

Form 16

Complaint in Action Against Two Insurance Companies

Complaint

[Title of court and cause]   Index No. — [if assigned]

Plaintiffs complaining of the defendants and by their attorneys, __1_____, respectfully allege:

FOR A CAUSE OF ACTION AGAINST N SURETY COMPANY OF NEW YORK:

1. Plaintiffs are co-partners doing business under the name of __2_____.

2. Defendant is a New York corporation and among other things is in the business of issuing burglary insurance policies and that at all times herein mentioned was authorized so to do in the State of New York.

3. On or about the __3__ day of __4_____, 19_5_, and in consideration of the premium of $__6__ which was duly paid, defendant issued its policy of burglary insurance to the plaintiffs, being policy No. __7__ for all loss of property as described in the schedule thereof attached to said policy, consisting of furs and other merchandise in the place of business of plaintiffs at No. __8__ __9_____ Street, City of __10_____, occasioned by any person or persons who shall have made felonious entry in the premises by actual force and violence when the premises were not open for business, of which force and violence there shall be visible marks upon the place of such entry, by tools, explosives, electricity or chemicals; the amount of said policy was $__11__ and that its term of expiration was the __12__ day of __13_____, 19_14_.

4. On or about __15_____, 19_16_, the premises described in said policy were burglarized and there was stolen from the plaintiffs' premises property of the value of $__17__, all by force and felonious entry when the premises were not open for business, of which force and violence there were visible marks upon the place of said entry.

5. Plaintiffs duly complied with and duly performed all the conditions by them required to be performed by the terms of said policy.

6. Plaintiffs had other insurance protecting them against burglary with defendant M Insurance Company in the sum of $__18__, so that the total insurance was in the sum of $__19__.

7. Pursuant to the terms of the policy the defendant was liable to a pro rata share of the whole insurance and the defendant's pro rata share of said insurance is $__20__.

8. The said sum of $__21__ is now due and payable to the plaintiffs but the defendant has refused and still refuses to pay the said loss to the plaintiff although the time for the defendant to do so has elapsed.

FOR A CAUSE OF ACTION AGAINST M INSURANCE COMPANY:

9. Plaintiffs are co-partners doing business under the name of __22_____.

10. Defendant is a Massachusetts corporation and among other things is in the

business of issuing burglary insurance policies and at all times herein mentioned was authorized so to do in the State of New York.

11. On or about the __23__ day of __24_____, 19_25_, and in consideration of the premium of $__26__ which was duly paid, defendant issued its policy of burglary insurance to the plaintiffs, being policy No. __27__ for all loss of property as described in the schedule thereof attached to said policy, consisting of furs and other merchandise in the place of business of plaintiffs at No. __28__ __29_____ Street, City of __30_____, occasioned by any person or persons who shall have made felonious entry into the premises by actual force and violence when the premises were not open for business, of which force and violence there shall be visible marks upon the place of such entry, by tools, explosives, electricity or chemicals; that the amount of said policy was $__31__ and its term of expiration was the __32__ day of __33_____, 19_34_.

12. On or about __35_____, 19_36_, the premises described in said policy were burglarized and there was stolen from the plaintiffs' premises property of the value of $__37__, all by force and by felonious entry when the premises were not open for business, of which force and violence there were visible marks upon the place of said entry.

13. Plaintiffs duly complied with and duly performed all the conditions by them required to be performed by the terms of said policy.

14. The plaintiffs had other insurance protecting them against burglary with defendant N Surety Company in the sum of $__38__, so that the total insurance was in the sum of $__39__.

15. Pursuant to the terms of the policy the defendant was liable to a pro rata share of the whole insurance and that the defendant's pro rata share of said insurance is $__40__.

16. The said sum of $__41__ is now due and payable to the plaintiffs but that the defendant has refused and still refuses to pay the said loss to the plaintiff although the time for the defendant so to do has elapsed.

WHEREFORE, plaintiffs demand judgment against the defendant N Surety Company of New York in the sum of $__42__ and against defendant M Insurance Company in the sum of $__43__, all with interest thereon from the __44__ day of __45_____, 19_46_, together with the costs and disbursements of this action.

__47_____
Attorneys for Plaintiffs
Office and P. O. Address
Telephone No.

Form 17

Complaint in Action Against President of Unincorporated Association and Individual Members Thereof

Complaint
[Title of court and cause]   Index No. — [if assigned]

The plaintiff, complaining of the defendants, by his attorneys, __1_____, alleges on information and belief:

1. At all the times hereinafter mentioned the __2_____ County Sheep Breeders Association, hereinafter referred to as the association, was and now is an unincorporated association consisting of more than seven persons.

2. That M, at the time of the commencement of this action, was the president of the association.

3. At all the times hereinafter mentioned the defendants M and __3_____ were members of the association and the defendants __4_____ and __5_____, hereinafter referred to as the defendant non-members, were not members of the association.

4. At all the times hereinafter mentioned __6_____ and __7_____ were co-partners doing business under the firm name and style of M & Co., having a place of business in the City of __8_____, County of __9_____, and State of New York, and they are hereinafter referred to as M & Co.

5. During the month of __10_____, 19_11_, the association entered into a certain contract in writing with M & Co., a copy of which is hereunto annexed marked Schedule A and made a part of this complaint.

6. The said contract was executed and delivered by the association as the duly authorized agent of certain undisclosed principals, to wit, the defendant members and the defendant non-members who delivered to the association their 19_12_ clip of wool to be consigned to M & Co. for their account by the association in accordance with the terms and provisions of the said contract.

7. Between the __13_ day of __14_____, 19_15_, and the __16_ day of __17_____, 19_18_, the association delivered to M & Co. a certain quantity of wool amounting in the aggregate to __19_____ pounds, which was the 19_20_ clip of wool delivered to the association by the defendant members and the defendant non-members of the association to be consigned as aforesaid. The said wool was accepted by said M & Co. as consignees, agents and factors under said contract as aforesaid for the purpose of selling such wool in the open market for the account of said principals, at the best price obtainable.

8. The said M & Co., pursuant to the terms and provisions of the said contract, made certain advances for the account of said principals in the amount of $__21__, which advances were to bear interest at the rate of __22_% per annum, as therein provided. In addition M & Co. incurred expenses for freight, cartage, storage and insurance.

9. Thereafter and on or about the __23_ day of __24_____, 19_25_, M & Co., having sold a part of said consignment, pursuant to said contract, and at the best price obtainable in the open market, notwithstanding the said advances and expenses incurred, and believing that the balance of said consignment remaining unsold was amply sufficient to secure the said M & Co. for any balance that might be shown due them on a final accounting, made a further payment to the association for the account of the said principals of $__26__. The said payment of $__27__ was received and accepted by the association for the account of said principals and was thereafter distributed to the said principals who had delivered the said wool in proportion to the quantity and quality of wool so delivered by each. Between the __28_ day of __29_____, 19_30_, and the __31_ day of __32_____, 19_33_, M & Co. sold the balance of said wool, pursuant to said contract and at the best price obtainable in the open market. There is annexed hereto marked Schedule B a statement showing the names and post office addresses of each of said principals, the amount and quality of wool of the 19_34_ clip delivered by each to the association to be consigned to M & Co. for their account as aforesaid, the amount advanced to each for the wool delivered at the time it was delivered and the proportion of the further payment of $__35__ paid to each as aforesaid.

10. The said __36_____ and __37_____, composing the said firm of M & Co., duly performed all the conditions of such contract on their part.

11. The said M & Co., by reason of the foregoing, became entitled to commissions on said sale of wool to the amount of __38_% of the purchase price and to the repayment of moneys advanced to said association for the account of said principals with interest thereon as aforesaid, and to the repayment of moneys expended for the account of said principals for freight, cartage, insurance and storage. Annexed hereto and marked Schedule C is a true and complete statement of the account of said M & Co. as consignees, agents and factors, as aforesaid, with the association, as agent for the defendant members and the defendant non-members, as aforesaid, showing the sales of said consigned wool made by M & Co. under the said contract with dates, quantities, prices and amounts received therefor and also showing the cash advances and payments made by said M & Co. to the association for the account of its said

principals, as aforesaid, together with expenditures of said M & Co. at the time of the assignment of this claim to the plaintiff, as hereinafter alleged, upon as final accounting under said contract as set forth in the statement of account marked Schedule C hereunto annexed, the sum of $__39__. M & Co. duly demanded the payment of the said sum of $__40__, but that no part thereof has been paid to M & Co. or to the plaintiff herein.

12. The defendant members and the defendant non-members have received from M & Co. the sum of $__41__, to which they are not entitled, either in justice or equity, and the said principals have unjustly retained and are unjustly retaining the said sum and are unjustly enriched by said retention to the extent of said sum of $__42__.

13. On the __43__ day of __44_____, 19_45_, M & Co. duly assigned to the plaintiff for value said contract between M & Co. and the association and all their rights thereunder.

14. There is now justly due and owing to the plaintiff from the defendants the sum of $__46__ with interest from the __47__ day of __48_____, 19_49_.

WHEREFORE plaintiff demands judgment against the defendants for the sum of $__50__, with interest thereon from the __51__ day of __52_____, 19_53_, together with the costs and disbursements of this action.

                                   __54_____

                                     Attorneys for Plaintiff
                                   Office and P. O. Address
                                   Telephone No.

Form 18

Complaint in Action Against Owner and Driver of Automobile for Damages From Collision

                          Complaint
[Title of court and cause]   Index No. — [if assigned]

Plaintiff complaining of the defendants alleges:

AS AND FOR A FIRST CAUSE OF ACTION:

1. Upon information and belief at all times hereinafter mentioned the defendant R was the owner of a motor vehicle bearing 19_1_ New York Registration Number __2__.

2. Upon information and belief at all times hereinafter mentioned the defendant T operated and controlled the said motor vehicle.

3. Upon information and belief at all times hereinafter mentioned the defendant T operated and controlled the said motor vehicle with the permission of the defendant R.

4. Heretofore and on the __3__ day of __4_____, 19_5_, the said motor vehicle collided with a motor vehicle owned and operated by the plaintiff, at or about the intersection of __6_____ Street and __7_____ Avenue, City of __8_____.

5. Said accident was caused by the negligence and carelessness of the defendant T in operating said motor vehicle at an excessive rate of speed, in traveling on the wrong side of the road, in traveling against the right of way, in cutting in, in passing on the wrong side, and in being otherwise careless and negligent.

6. Plaintiff in no wise contributed to the happening of the said accident.

7. As the result of said accident, the plaintiff was seriously and severely injured in and about the legs, hands, face, head, and other parts of his body, to his damage in the sum of $__9__.

WHEREFORE the plaintiff demands judgment against the defendants in the sum of $__10__, and the costs and disbursements of this action.

__11_____
Attorney for Plaintiff
Office and P. O. Address
Telephone No.

Form 19

Complaint Against Owner of Taxicab in Which Plaintiff was Injured and Against Owner of Automobile Which Taxicab Collided With

Complaint
[Title of court and cause]   Index No. — [if assigned]

Plaintiff, by her attorney __1_____, complaining of the defendants, respectfully shows to this Court and alleges for her complaint, as follows:

1. At all times hereinafter mentioned, defendant B was and still is the owner of an automobile taxicab bearing license No. __2__, issued to him by the State of New York, for the year 19_3_.

2. At all times hereinafter mentioned, defendant D was and still is the owner of an automobile bearing license No. __4__, issued to him by the State of New York, for the year 19_5_.

3. At all times hereinafter mentioned, the Street known as __6_____ Avenue in the vicinity of __7_____ Street, was and still is a public highway in the City of __8_____, State of New York.

4. On the __9__ day of __10_____, 19_11_, at about __12__ A.M. of that day, plaintiff was a passenger for hire in the taxicab of the defendant B, bearing license No. __13__, which taxicab was owned and controlled, at the time of the accident, upon information and belief by the defendant B.

5. The said taxicab of the defendant B, in which the plaintiff was a passenger, was being driven in a northerly direction on __14_____ Avenue, in the City of __15_____, and as it approached __16_____ Street, a collision occurred between the automobile owned by the defendant D, under the control of this defendant, his agent, servants, or employees, and the taxicab of the defendant B.

6. As a result of the said collision plaintiff received severe internal and external injuries and upon information and belief, some of these injuries will be permanent.

7. As a result of the said severe injuries, received by the plaintiff herein, plaintiff was put to great medical expenses and suffered loss of earnings.

8. The accident and injuries as aforesaid were caused solely by the negligence of the defendants, and plaintiff in no wise contributed thereto.

9. By reason of the foregoing, the plaintiff has been damaged in the sum of __17_____ dollars.

WHEREFORE plaintiff demands judgment against the defendants, D and B, or either of them, for the sum of __18_____ dollars, together with the costs and disbursements of this action.

__19_____
Attorney for Plaintiff
Office and P. O. Address
Telephone No.

Form 20

Complaint in Action Against Two Railroad Companies for Nuisance

Complaint
[Title of court and cause]   Index No. — [if assigned]

Plaintiff for a complaint herein alleges upon information and belief:

1. Plaintiff is and at all the times herein mentioned was a corporation, organized and existing under and by virtue of the laws of the State of New York and engaged among ogher things in conducting a hotel business in the City of __1_____, New York.

2. The defendant N Railroad Company is a corporation duly organized and existing under and by virtue of the laws of the State of New York, and engaged as a common carrier of passengers and freight by railroad among other places in and through the City of __2_____, New York.

3. The defendant D Company is and at all the times herein mentioned was a corporation duly organized and existing under and by virtue of the laws of the State of New York and engaged as a common carrier of passengers and freight by railroad among other places in and through the City of __3_____, New York.

4. On or about __4_____, 19_5_, plaintiff became and still is the owner of premises known as the __6_____ hotel, situate at No. __7__ __8_____ Street in the City of __9_____, New York. Since that time, plaintiff has conducted and still is conducting a hotel business on said premises.

5. Prior to __10_____, 19_11_, and since the year 19_12_, plaintiff has conducted a hotel business on said premises as tenant, for which purpose plaintiff had continuously leased said hotel premises and appurtenances including the furnishings, fixtures and personal property therein from the owner thereof, pursuant to written agreements between said parties.

6. Said premises are more particularly described as follows: __13_____.

7. The rear of said property hereinbefore described is adjoining the tracks of the defendant D Company. West of and adjacent and practically parallel to said tracks are the tracks of the defendant N Railroad Company. To the adjacent southwest and west of plaintiff's premises are the freight yards of the defendant N Railroad Company. To the adjacent north and west are the passenger depot and passenger platform of the defendant N Railroad Company.

8. For six years immediately prior to the commencement of this action and for some time prior thereto, defendant N Railroad Company has used its tracks in the neighborhood of plaintiff's premises so as to constitute a nuisance. The yards of this defendant were laid out many years ago. By the great general increase in railroad traffic and the rapid growth of the City of __14_____, these yards have been long and notoriously inadequate. Incoming freight trains destined to these yards are most often left on main line tracks on account of the inability of said yards to receive them. These incoming freight trains are mainly unclassified as to any regular or orderly scheme of yard movement, and ensuing movement is almost wholly haphazard: The making place in said grossly inadequate yards for reception and classification of these incoming trains is so evidently and badly hampered by yard movements and locations of incoming trains already received as to cause utterly needless noises and endless turmoil. The breaking up and classifying of said incoming trains consumes an apparent and habitual carelessly negligent use of time and a gross exaggeration of noise. When to incoming train movements there is added the classifying and making up of outward train movements, hampered constantly by back and forth city movements, of loaded and empty freight, perishable and otherwise, a notoriously long time is required. These operations consist of hundreds of movements of the switching engine and cars from the yards north, past plaintiff's premises on the track leading from the yard, then onto the main line track, south on the main line track past plaintiff's premises, then north on the main line track past plaintiff's premises, then onto the track leading to the yard, south past plaintiff's premises and into the yards; that said operations consume

practically the entire night. Due to the inadequate and defective construction of defendant's yards, few out going freight trains are made up in the daytime, which is spent in placing incoming trains on the yard tracks and in making deliveries to places in ___15_____.

Incident to such switching and classifying operations are abnormal and continuous noises consisting of the puffing of the locomotives, the unnecessary escape of steam, the slipping of wheels, the ringing of bells, the blowing of whistles, the shouting of orders and an endless and needless crashing together particularly the whole night through of cars and trains of cars.

For and during said operations, this defendant uses old and defective switch engines which unnecessarily, wastefully and loudly let off steam and make an excessive and unnecessary noise particularly the whole night through because of their worn-out condition. Because of the defective condition of said engines and that soft coal is used therein, plaintiff's said hotel is constantly covered and filled with smoke, and soft coal refuse laden with unhealthy and incidental coal tar products. This defendant's switch engines and the engines of through freight trains and passenger trains unnecessarily and almost continuously ring their bells and blow their whistles, particularly during the entire night and in violation of the ordinances of the City of ___16_____.

9. For six years prior to the commencement of this action and for some time prior thereto, the defendant D Company has used its tracks in the rear of plaintiff's premises so as to constitute a nuisance. The tracks of this defendant are on an upgrade toward the north. Frequently during the nighttime, northbound freight trains of defendant pass the hotel. Said freight trains contain an excessive number of heavily loaded freight cars and have an insufficient number of engines thereon to pull said trains up the grade, with the result that said engines make an excessive and unnecessary amount of noise. Frequently pusher engines are used to get said trains up the grade and said pusher engines again repeat the noise blast of the pulling engine. Often, during the night particularly, said northbound trains are unnecessarily stopped on the upgrade directly in the rear of plaintiff's premises, and in starting up again with an excessive number of cars and an inadequate number of engines, said trains make loud and excessive and insufferable noises and cause a considerable and distinct vibration of the hotel building. The passenger and freight trains of this defendant blow their whistles and ring their bells loudly directly in the rear of plaintiff's premises, particularly during the nighttime and in violation of the ordinances of the City of ___17_____, and plaintiff's said hotel is constantly covered and filled with smoke and soot from the negligent operation of defective engines of defendant.

10. By reason of defendants' wrongful and unlawful acts aforesaid, the reasonable enjoyment by the plaintiff of its said property and the reasonable enjoyment of life thereon is seriously impaired; that plaintiff's hotel business has been and will be greatly diminished; that plaintiff by reason of said nuisance has been forced to rent the rooms in its hotel at a much lower rate than similar rooms elsewhere. The interior of said premises, walls, ceilings, drapes, carpets, paint and paper are blackened and discolored by reason of said coal tar smoke and dirt and other smoke, dirt and soot; that the walls and ceilings of said hotel have been injured; that said hotel building has greatly diminished in value; said building has been otherwise damaged and plaintiff has lost the otherwise available regular use of a considerable part thereof, all to its damage in the sum of ___18_____ dollars.

11. The aforesaid acts of the defendants constitute and are a nuisance which is a special injury to the plaintiff and which is continuous and will cause great and irreparable loss to the plaintiff unless restrained by injunction. Plaintiff has no adequate remedy at law.

WHEREFORE, plaintiff demands judgment against the defendants as follows:

I. That the defendants and each of them, their servants, agents and employees be permanently restrained and enjoined from any of the uses hereinbefore complained of and from continuing any of the aforesaid acts of nuisance, and any of the aforesaid trespasses upon plaintiff's said property and rights.

II. That the plaintiff recover of defendants the sum of ___¹⁹___ dollars damages.

III. That plaintiff recover its costs and disbursements in this action and have such other and further judgment and relief in the premises as may be just and equitable.

___²⁰_____

Attorneys for Plaintiff
Office and P. O. Address
Telephone No.

§ 1003. Nonjoinder and misjoinder of parties

Nonjoinder of a party who should be joined under section 1001 is a ground for dismissal of an action without prejudice unless the court allows the action to proceed without him under the provisions of that section. Misjoinder of parties is not a ground for dismissal of an action. Parties may be added or dropped by the court, on motion of any party or on its own initiative, at any stage of the action and upon such terms as may be just. The court may order any claim against a party severed and proceeded with separately.

HISTORY:

Add, L 1962, ch 308, amd, L 1964, ch 388, eff Sept 1, 1964.
Earlier statutes: CPA §§ 192, 193; CCP § 1588; 2 RS 387, §§ 6, 7.

ADVISORY COMMITTEE NOTES:

Cf. CPA § 192; RCP 102; Fed R Civ P 21. The objection of nonjoinder of an indispensable party is never waived since the court should protect the interests of such persons no matter how or when their nonjoinder is pointed out. Cf. Fed R Civ P 12(h). While there is no specific time provision for other party objections, the permissive language in the next to last sentence allows these to be overruled on the ground of unreasonable delay. See 3 Moore, Federal Practice 2905–06 (Supp 1955). The last three sentences were taken verbatim from Federal rule 21. The first sentence is included here, since it is contemplated that the rules relating to motion practice will not deal with party motions.

CROSS REFERENCES:

Substitution on consolidation, of corporations, Bus Corp Law § 906.
Executors and administrators, EPTL §§ 11-4.1, 11-4.4.
Defendant as representative, RPTL § 11-4.2.
Creditor's action against distributees and testamentary beneficiaries, EPTL §§ 12-1.1 et seq.
Unincorporated associations, Gen Assn Law §§ 13, 16, 17.
Actions on mechanic's liens, Lien Law § 62.
In action for nuisance, Real P Actions & Pr Law § 841.

FEDERAL ASPECTS:

Misjoinder and nonjoinder of parties, Rule 21 of Federal Rules of Civil Procedure, USCS Court Rules.

RESEARCH REFERENCES AND PRACTICE AIDS:

3 Carmody-Wait 2d, Severance of Actions § 18:1.
3 Carmody-Wait 2d, Parties §§ 19:1, 19:55, 19:82, 19:91.
6 Carmody-Wait 2d, Pretrial Motions to Dismiss § 38:22.
7 Carmody-Wait 2d, Dismissal of Claim for Want of Prosecution § 44:1.
10 Carmody-Wait 2d, Appeals in General §§ 70:16, 70:285.
14 Carmody-Wait 2d, Partition §§ 91:68, 91:69.
14 Carmody-Wait 2d, Foreclosure of Mortgages on Real Estate § 92:126.

21 Carmody-Wait 2d, Actions Against Persons Jointly Liable §§ 123:6, 123:7, 123:22.
24 Carmody-Wait 2d, Proceeding Against a Body or Officer § 145:287.
42 Am Jur 2d, Injunctions § 262.
59 Am Jur 2d, Parties §§ 259, 273.
1 Am Jur Pl & Pr Forms (Rev ed), Actions, Forms 41 et seq.

Annotations:

What constitutes, under 28 USCS § 1359, improper or collusive making or joinder of parties to invoke Federal District Court's jurisdiction. 75 ALR 2d 717.

Propriety of dismissal, under Rule 41(a), of action as against less than all of several defendants. 3 ALR Fed 569.

Validity, construction, and application of Rule 19(b) of Federal Rules of Civil Procedure, as amended in 1966, providing for determination to be made by court to proceed with or dismiss action when joinder of person needed for just adjudication is not feasible. 21 ALR Fed 12.

Law Reviews:

New York Civil Practice Law and Rules: parties. 27 Albany L Rev 182.
Parties and pleading under the CPLR. 31 Brooklyn L Rev 98.
Collateral estoppel, mutuality and joinder of parties. 68 Colum L Rev 1457.
A biannual survey of New York practice: Section 1003: Nonjoinder and misjoinder of parties. 38 St. John's L Rev 418.

Forms:

See "FORMS" heading following "CASE NOTES", infra.

CASE NOTES

1. In general
2. Nonjoinder; time for raising issue
3. —Dismissal of complaint
4. —Declaratory judgment action
5. Misjoinder and dropping of parties
6. Who are necessary parties
7. Who may be joined
8. Late motion to join
9. Right to discontinue
10. Matrimonial actions
11. CPLR and CPA construed together

1. In general

Addition of city housing authority as a party to neglect proceeding, in which court was requested to order the authority to provide housing adequate for mother and children, would not remove family court's power to treat a violation of any prospective order which might be rendered as a contempt punishable accordingly. Re O (1974) 80 Misc 2d 242, 362 NYS2d 688.

Fact that a motion by an appointee to a position with a board of education did not move to intervene in an action challenging his right to the appointment until after action had been determined on the merits through grant of a partial summary judgment did not preclude favorable disposition of appointee's intervention application. Kirkland v Board of Education (1975) 49 AD2d 693, 370 NYS2d 761.

A party can be added to a pending action or proceeding only on timely motion and an order of court in which action or proceeding is pending. Muka v Sturgis (1976) 53 AD2d 716, 383 NYS2d 933.

One-year period of limitations contained in Lien Law ran from time plaintiffs made final adjustments on corporate defendant's boiler and, since period had expired at time plaintiffs sought to join president of corporation individually as a defendant, joinder, being tantamount to a de novo assertion of a claim, was time barred. Tabolt v KMZ Enterprises, Inc. (1976) 52 AD2d 995, 383 NYS2d 452.

2. Nonjoinder; time for raising issue

The court may raise the nonjoinder of necessary parties at any stage of the proceedings. Figari v New York Tel. Co. (1969) 32 AD2d 434, 303 NYS2d 245.

Respondents in Article 78 proceeding were permitted to raise non-joinder of necessary parties on appeal, even though they failed to raise non-joinder at trial. Fellner v McMurray (1973) 41 AD2d 853, 342 NYS2d 992.

Rule pertaining to nonjoinder and joinder of parties is appropriate to the family court pursuant to criteria delineated in section of Family Court Act pertaining to procedure. Re O (1974) 80 Misc 2d 242, 362 NYS2d 688.

3. —Dismissal of complaint

Under CPLR it is proper practice to move to dismiss for nonjoinder of indispensable parties, without first moving for their joinder. Challette, Inc. v Brookhaven (1964) 43 Misc 2d 264, 250 NYS2d 165.

Either county department of social services or commissioner of department was indispensable party in Article 78 proceeding to review Commissioner of State Department of Social Services' upholding of county department's failure to fully replace cash stolen from petitioner; thus proceeding could not be maintained in absence of either county department or its commissioner as a party. Brown v Lavine (1974) 78 Misc 2d 1085, 358 NYS2d 579.

Dismissal of an action or proceeding for failure to join a necessary party may not be conditioned upon movant's stipulating to submit to a foreign jurisdiction. Cushing-Murray v Adams (1975) 49 AD2d 874, 373 NYS2d 191.

4. —Declaratory judgment action

In action to declare zoning law invalid brought by owner of less than 10% of property affected, failure to join all owners who might be affected by result, in the absence of prejudice to defendant, does not warrant dismissal for nonjoinder. Challette, Inc. v Brookhaven (1964) 43 Misc 2d 264, 250 NYS2d 165.

5. Misjoinder and dropping of parties

By reason of the provisions of Surrogate's Court Act § 316, the Surrogate could upon his own initiative drop any unnecessary parties from a proceeding as provided in CPLR § 1003. Re O'Brien's Will (1965) 24 AD2d 87, 264 NYS2d 26, motion to dismiss app den 17 NY2d 721, 269 NYS2d 971, 216 NE2d 834.

6. Who are necessary parties

Motion to add corporation as indispensable party in stockholders' derivative action involving nonresident beneficiary corporation is no longer prerequisite to motion to dismiss, and motion to dismiss would be held in abeyance pending determination of whether there was jurisdiction of nonresident corporation and whether action could proceed in absence of corporation. Blumenthal v Allen (1965) 46 Misc 2d 688, 260 NYS2d 363.

In an action pursuant to Article 15 of the Real Property Actions and Proceedings Law to determine plaintiffs' title to certain real property on the ground, inter alia, that a certain tax deed from the county treasurer to defendant was void as to said lot, since the county treasurer is the official who makes and delivers tax deeds, and the county enjoys certain monitary rights under the tax sale which may be jeopardized by the voiding of the sale, the county must be made a party to the proceeding. Costa v Harris (1966) 26 AD2d 933, 274 NYS2d 434.

In an action against a telephone company by subscribers to a recorded announcement service seeking a judgment that a tariff requiring the individual subscriber to state his name and address on the recording was unconstitutional, the Public Service Commission is not a necessary party. Figari v New York Tel. Co. (1969) 32 AD2d 434, 303 NYS2d 245.

Even though parkway authority had jurisdiction over area where accident occurred, claim was improperly dismissed as being defective for failure to join authority as a necessary and indispensable party, where claim alleged that park and recreation commission and state designed, constructed and maintained median guardrails, and since allegations were to be taken as true, authority and commission were to be treated as joint tort-feasors so as to preclude authority from being an indispensable party. Littanzi v State (1976) 54 AD2d 1043, 388 NYS2d 686.

7. Who may be joined

This section allows the addition of the receiver of a partnership as a party plaintiff subject to the exercise of a sound discretion, but the amended complaint should differentiate between the alleged wrong and damages according to the partnership and which would pass to the receiver, and that done by and for which redress would adhere to the individuals. Hochschartner v Schneider (1964) 22 AD2d 867, 254 NYS2d 427.

In proceeding to review determination of city board of standards and appeals which denied request for variance for auto laundries, commissioner of buildings was proper party, since commissioner had revoked permit after it had been issued by department of buildings and after borough superintendent had confirmed compliance with zoning resolution and commissioner's interpretation of zoning resolution was crux of controversy. Natchev v Klein (1974) 45 AD2d 725, 356 NYS2d 346, later app 51 AD2d 573, 378 NYS2d 634, affd 41 NY2d 833, 393 NYS2d 395, 361 NE2d 1043.

Additional party defendant in action for real estate brokerage commission was improperly joined where plaintiff failed to comply with provisions of CPLR 1003; plaintiff attorney's affirmation, in opposition to defendant's motion to dismiss, that amended complaint was served on added defendant after obtaining consent of the then existing defendants was a judicial admission of noncompliance with the statute. Catanese v Lipschitz (1974) 44 AD2d 579, 353 NYS2d 250.

Where lessee consented to motion to join it as party plaintiff in lessor's action for damage to buildings and property allegedly caused by negligent performance by defendant of contract to repair roofs, appropriate statute under which to seek joinder would be that pertaining to permissive joinder, rather than that pertaining to necessary joinder. Northeastern Industrial Park, Inc. v James Ackroyd & Sons, Inc. (1976) 51 AD2d 614, 377 NYS2d 802.

Where lessee would seek recovery for damage arising out of same transaction as lessor, original plaintiff, who sought to recover for damage to buildings and personal property because of defendant's negligent performance of contract to repair roofs, permitting joinder of lessee as party plaintiff was not an abuse of discretion, in absence of showing that such joinder would preclude defendant from asserting statute of limitations as an alleged defense. Northeastern Industrial Park, Inc. v James Ackroyd & Sons, Inc. (1976) 51 AD2d 614, 377 NYS2d 802.

8. Late motion to join

After the statute of limitations barred plaintiff's action for false arrest, she could not by virtue of timely notice of suit served upon the county join as party to defendants the sheriff and deputy sheriff against whom her claims were time barred. Brenon v County of Oneida (1966) 52 Misc 2d 795, 276 NYS2d 393.

Delayed motion to join commissioner of social services as copetitioner in mother's filiation proceeding was granted where respondent failed to establish actual prejudice arising therefrom, and where delay was not deliberate. Mores v Feel (1973) 73 Misc 2d 942, 343 NYS2d 220.

9. Right to discontinue

Provisions of CPLR 1003 are permissive, and after a party has appeared in a proceeding and presented issues affecting his rights, the other party no longer has an absolute right to discontinue the action as to him, but the matter rests in the sound discretion of the court. Re Cowles' Will (1965) 22 AD2d 365, 255 NYS2d 160, affd 17 NY2d 567, 268 NYS2d 327, 215 NE2d 509.

10. Matrimonial actions

Where plaintiff's second husband sought a declaratory judgment to the effect that plaintiff's marriage to her third husband was void, the third husband was a necessary party, and the court could on its own motion raise the issue of his nonjoinder. Roe v Roe (1966) 49 Misc 2d 1070, 269 NYS2d 40.

11. CPLR and CPA construed together

While CPLR §§ 1008 and 3011 mandate an answer to a third-party complaint, in view of the provisions of this section that the CPLR also applies to further proceedings in pending actions, but former procedure applies where the new procedure would not be feasible or would work injustice, a third-party complaint served pursuant to § 193-A of the Civil Practice Act, which made an answer to a third-party complaint clearly permissive, would be subject to the provisions of § 193-A of the CPA where the CPLR provisions would indeed work injustice. Multari v Glalin Arms Corp. (1966) 51 Misc 2d 1019, 274 NYS2d 827.

CASE NOTES

UNDER FORMER CIVIL PRACTICE LAWS

A. Decisions Subsequent to Sept. 1, 1946, and Prior to Sept. 1, 1963.

1. Generally

In action for slander, complaint cannot be dismissed for misjoinder of plaintiffs. Moran v Singer (1947, Sup) 75 NYS2d 874.

Coexecutrix, characterized by other executrix as hostile to success of action, should be joined as codefendant, which defect was correctable without defeating action. Prygocki v Prydatko (1951, Sup) 105 NYS2d 205.

A defect of parties defendant is no longer a reason for dismissal of the complaint unless a party fails or neglects to bring in a party after the making of an order directing a joinder. Re Elwyn's Estate (1957) 8 Misc 2d 704, 173 NYS2d 192, affd 5 AD2d 748, 168 NYS2d 942.

2. Effect of nonjoinder

Dismissal of complaint for nonjoinder of parties defendant was improper without order directing joinder. Wolff v Brontown Realty Corp. (1953) 281 AD 752, 118 NYS2d 74.

A motion to dismiss the complaint cannot raise, in the first instance, the objection of defective parties. Newton Jackson Co. v Barclays Bank (1954, Sup) 133 NYS2d 726.

Declaratory judgment may not be granted to restrain boards and agencies not made parties defendant and not before court. Cadman Memorial Congregational Soc. v Kenyon (1953) 306 NY 151, 116 NE2d 481.

In order that judgment in action against unincorporated labor union bind its members it was necessary that president or treasurer be made party, but absence of such party from suit did not deprive trial court of jurisdiction to render judgment on merits in respect of appearing defendants, in action to void determination of international labor organization suspending plaintiffs from holding office in local union. Carpentieri v Redmond, (1954) 284 AD 897, 134 NYS2d 410.

Under CPA § 193, subd 2, as amended, an action might not be dismissed, in the first instance, for nonjoinder of an indispensable party; the objection had to be raised by a motion made under RCP 102 (Rule 3024(a) herein), to add the necessary party. Carruthers v Jack Waite Mining Co. (1953) 306 NY 136, 116 NE2d 286.

Motion to add necessary party was exclusive manner of objecting to nonjoinder of necessary defendant pursuant to RCP 102 (Rule 3024(a) herein). Motyka v Motyka (1952, Sup App T) 113 NYS2d 892.

Where indispensable party is lacking, deficiency cannot be remedied by simply inserting name of corporation as additional party in his answer, but he must move in first instance for addition of indispensable party. Meier v Holmes (1953) 282 AD 1030, 126 NYS2d 655.

Dismissal of action for nonjoinder of indispensable party is authorized only if party fails to bring in omitted party after reasonable period granted to him to do so. Rispoli v Manufacturers Casualty Ins. Co. (1950, Sup) 99 NYS2d 22.

The fact that an indispensable party is a nonresident and jurisdiction cannot be obtained over him

is not a defense to a motion by the defendant to compel the plaintiff to bring him in. Presberg v Presberg (1954) 205 Misc 653, 128 NYS2d 612.

If party fails or neglects to bring in indispensable party after reasonable time granted to him to do so, court shall dismiss action without prejudice. Marsico v Tramutolo (1954, Sup) 135 NYS2d 258.

Motion to add parties pursuant to RCP 102 subd 2 (Rule 3024(a) herein) was "exclusive" manner in which to raise objection of nonjoinder of parties, and it could not properly be raised by motion to dismiss under RCP 106 (Rule 3211(a) herein), since CPA § 192 expressly prohibited defeat of action for nonjoinder or misjoinder except as provided in CPA § 193 subd 2, which required first order on motion under RCP 102 subd 2, directing party to be brought in within specified reasonable time fixed in such order. Lo Galbo v Lo Galbo (1955, Sup) 145 NYS2d 641.

An efficacious declaratory judgment cannot be rendered as to the marital status of a person not made a party to the action. Johnson v Johnson (1956, Sup) 157 NYS2d 328.

In action to recover accidental death benefits due under 7 life endowment policies issued on the life of plaintiff's husband, court would not order joinder of insured's children and grandchildren where some were residents of Illinois. Schwartz v Equitable Life Assur. Soc. (1957) 9 Misc 2d 27, 167 NYS2d 660.

Where person was merely conditionally necessary party and resided outside court's jurisdiction and her joinder would unduly delay trial, motion was denied. Urquhart v Urquhart (1949) 196 Misc 664, 92 NYS2d 484, affd 277 AD 752, 97 NYS2d 200.

The fact that a party sought to be brought in by defendant is without the jurisdiction, or that jurisdiction cannot be secured without undue delay, is material only when such party is a "conditionally necessary" party. Presberg v Presberg (1954) 205 Misc 653, 128 NYS2d 612.

Where at most there was a defect of parties, an action or proceeding would not be dismissed for nonjoinder or misjoinder of parties except as provided in CPA § 193, and then only when the objection had been raised as set forth in RCP 102 (Rule 3024(a) herein). Where that procedure not followed motion to dismiss made at trial properly denied. Taylor v Creary (1958) 5 AD2d 876, 171 NYS2d 560.

3. —Dismissal of complaint

Defect of parties plaintiff is not ground for dismissal of complaint; proper procedure is to raise objection to defect of parties in case of nonjoinder of even indispensable party by motion to add such party pursuant to Rule 102. Marrero v Levitt (1956) 3 Misc 2d 555, 152 NYS2d 802.

Dismissal of complaint, even though conditional, for failure to serve one of defendants is premature absent a prior order directing such service and a failure to comply therewith. Siskind v Levy (1961) 13 AD2d 538, 213 NYS2d 379.

4. —Mistrial

Court may not dismiss cause of action for failure of plaintiff to join indispensable party, but it will direct mistrial with respect thereto and will sign order severing it. O'Shea v Hanse (1955) 3 Misc 2d 307, 147 NYS2d 792.

5. Bringing in new parties

Right of defendant to interplead another party under CPA §§ 192, 193 and 193-a (§§ 1001(a)(b), 1003, 1007, 1008, 1020, 3012(a) herein), has been said not to be for the purpose of permitting third parties to come in in order to sue the plaintiff in the action. Acetate Box Corp. v Johnson (1948) 193 Misc 54, 80 NYS2d 134.

Where a motion is made to amend a pleading, at the opening of trial, to bring in an additional defendant, although the court has broad powers with regard to such motion, it must be denied in the interests of justice where such individual defendant would have substantial personal rights to defend and would be entitled to make his defense as an individual, to answer the complaint in such manner as he thought best and to employ his own counsel to represent him, and making him an individual defendant at the time of trial would deprive him of such rights. Foster v Webster (1943) 8 Misc 2d 61, 44 NYS2d 153.

Joinder of a party-plaintiff, by consent, in a pending action was contemplated by CPA § 192. Abschagen v Goldfarb (1959) 8 AD2d 750, 185 NYS2d 339.

Fact that plaintiff had made prior motion to add defendant but withdrawn it without prejudice prior to any determination thereon did not preclude plaintiff from making later motion for same relief. Cohen v Gordon (1959) 21 Misc 2d 1056, 196 NYS2d 165.

6. —Who must be brought in

Where each of three brokers claims commissions for selling realty and one broker sues second broker, third broker should be added as party. Cohen v Douglas L. Elliman & Co. (1951) 279 AD 161, 108 NYS2d 386.

In action by distributee of intestate to impress constructive trust on realty, other distributees are not necessary plaintiffs. Costa v Pratt (1949, Sup) 98 NYS2d 148, affd 277 AD 806, 96 NYS2d 868.

Where rumors were not sufficient to put plaintiff on notice that announced business was to be similar to his own he was not required or even warranted in joining such person as party in action to enjoin competing business, and such nonjoinder did not constitute laches. Weiss v Mayflower Doughnut Corp. (1956) 1 NY2d 310, 152 NYS2d 471, 135 NE2d 208.

Where pleading alleged that both State of New York and Saratoga Springs Authority, through their respective officers and employees, participated in tortious acts against claimant who had sued State, Saratoga Springs Authority was added as party defendant with State. Kanner v State (1956) 1 Misc 2d 666, 149 NYS2d 97.

7. —Who may be joined

President of corporation, who was sole stockholder, was not dropped as party plaintiff, in an action by him and his corporation against bank for refusal to honor checks signed by plaintiffs. Schwertfeger v Bank of Manhattan Co. (1946) 187 Misc 998, 67 NYS2d 84.

Where complaint charged that defendant acted as attorney in fact for brother and sister in wrongfully depriving plaintiff of broker's commissions, they should be joined as parties defendant. Malcolm E. Smith, Inc. v Zabriskie (1948, Sup) 84 NYS2d 362.

Where plaintiff corporation was dissolved and succeeded by partnership before cause of action pleaded in complaint arose, partners added as parties plaintiff on plaintiff's motion. Princeton Textile Printing Corp. v Walter Peek Paper Corp. (1949) 195 Misc 955, 91 NYS2d 443, affd 275 AD 1024, 91 NYS2d 827.

Special Term order, requiring suing stockholders holding less than 5% of shares to give security for litigation expenses but allowing application to vacate or modify order if 5% of stockholders be joined, was authorized. Baker v MacFadden Publications, Inc. (1949) 300 NY 325, 90 NE2d 876.

A life tenant suing adjoining owner for damage to real property was entitled to bring in owner of the remainder interest who consented to be joined as party-plaintiff. Abschagen v Goldfarb (1959) 8 AD2d 750, 185 NYS2d 339.

8. Substitution

Partnership cannot be substituted for dissolved corporation, as party defendant. Safrin v Joe Friedman Hat Co. (1949) 195 Misc 387, 91 NYS2d 372.

Change of title from individuals, residents, who sued as copartners under trade name to that of foreign corporation of same name, was substitution of new party, and required commencement of new action. Air Conditioning Training Corp. v Di Marzio (1948) 190 Misc 1033, 76 NYS2d 597.

In action against a town sewer district for damages as a result of the negligent construction of sewer pipes, Special Term had power to bring in the town board as a party defendant where the action was dismissed against the sewer district on the grounds it was not a corporate entity. Berean v Lloyd (1957) 3 AD2d 585, 962, 162 NYS2d 534.

9. Misjoinder of and dropping parties

After an action has been instituted and a party defendant has appeared and presented issues, plaintiff's application to drop the party is equivalent to a motion to discontinue, the granting of which rests in the discretion of the court. Re Cowles' Will (1965) 22 AD2d 365, 255 NYS2d 160, affd 17 NY2d 567, 268 NYS2d 327, 215 NE2d 509.

RCP 102 (Rule 3024(a) herein) provided that objection that there is nonjoinder or misjoinder of parties should be raised by motion to add or drop parties. New York v Draper (1951) 201 Misc 957, 107 NYS2d 789.

Dismissal of action for nonjoinder of party is authorized only if party fails to bring in omitted party after reasonable period granted to him to do so. Rispoli v Manufacturers Casualty Ins. Co. (1950, Sup) 99 NYS2d 22.

Nonjoinder of indispensable party is not ground for dismissal of complaint in first instance. Marsico v Tramutolo (1954, Sup) 135 NYS2d 258.

Action is not defeated by nonjoinder or misjoinder of parties, and neither is ground for dismissal of complaint. Pittman v March Service Co. (1955, Sup) 141 NYS2d 74.

Where defendant employed plaintiff as broker to sell realty and plaintiff hired another broker as cobroker, latter was improperly joined as party plaintiff in action for broker's commissions, where no facts were pleaded to show that original broker had either actual or implied authority to hire another broker, and cobroker was dropped as party plaintiff. Hosinger & Bode v Lembo (1955, Sup) 142 NYS2d 583.

Since under CPA § 192 no action would be defeated by nonjoinder or misjoinder of parties except as provided in CPA § 193 it follows that if the cause of action as pleaded was otherwise sufficient, the mere fact that one or more of the plaintiffs was not entitled to the relief sought would not be a ground for dismissal. Majestic Loose Leaf, Inc. v Cannizzaro (1957) 10 Misc 2d 1040, 169 NYS2d 566.

Defense that one plaintiff had not authorized attorney for other plaintiff to institute action on his behalf, and thus was not a proper party to action, was insufficient since fact that one plaintiff may not be entitled to relief does not defeat an otherwise sufficient cause of action. Senft v Neuer (1960, Sup) 198 NYS2d 142.

10. —Waiver of defect of parties

Where amended complaint added new defendants who served notice of general appearance and where original defendants answered amended complaint, latter submitted themselves to jurisdiction of court and thereby waived their rights to object to any irregularity in process. Pittman v March Service Co. (1955, Sup) 141 NYS2d 74.

11. Remedy by motion

Dismissal of complaint for nonjoinder of parties defendant was improper before making order directing joinder. Wolff v Brontown Realty Corp. (1953) 281 AD 752, 118 NYS2d 74.

Motion to add is exclusive remedy for objecting to nonjoinder of necessary defendant. Motyka v Motyka (1954, Sup App T) 113 NYS2d 892.

A motion to dismiss the complaint cannot raise, in the first instance, the objection of defective parties. Newton Jackson Co. v Barclays Bank (1954, Sup) 133 NYS2d 726.

Motion to add parties pursuant to RCP 102 subd. 2 was "exclusive" manner in which to raise objection of non-joinder of parties, and it could not

properly be raised by motion to dismiss under former RCP 106 (Rule 3211(a) herein), since former CPA § 192 expressly prohibited defeat of action for nonjoinder or misjoinder except as provided in former CPA § 193 subd. 2, which required first order on motion under RCP 102 subd 2, directing party to be brought in within specified reasonable time fixed in such order. Lo Galbo v Lo Galbo (1955, Sup) 145 NYS2d 641.

Where action for declaratory judgment brought to determine legitimacy of child and child mentioned in papers had not been served nor had a guardian ad litem been appointed, any objection defendants might have had in relation to nonjoinder of necessary or indispensable parties had to be the subject initially of a motion to add parties pursuant to former RCP 102 (Rule 3024(a) herein) and could not be raised by a motion to dismiss the complaint since former CPA 192 expressly prohibited defeat because of nonjoinder or misjoinder except as provided in subdivision 2 of former CPA 193. Hines v Hines (1957) 12 Misc 2d 486, 169 NYS2d 1003.

In action for slander where plaintiff contended that defendant made false and defamatory statements, motion by plaintiff to add newspaper reporter and owners and publishers of newspaper wherein alleged defamatory remarks published as defendants granted. Albano v Michaelsen (1958) 14 Misc 2d 76, 175 NYS2d 949.

Plaintiff's motion to discontinue action as to defendant-lienors was granted where it appeared that they were not necessary parties to the mortgage foreclosure action. Sayville Federal Sav. & Loan Asso. v Schons (1958) 17 Misc 2d 54, 183 NYS2d 106.

Objection as to nonjoinder of parties may be raised only by motion to add parties; it cannot be pleaded as an affirmative defense. Bleakney v Schrauff (1959) 18 Misc 2d 919, 186 NYS2d 412.

Where after plaintiff had served summons on city as sole defendant, and thereafter served summons and complaint on corporate defendant, naming corporation and city as codefendants, corporate defendant was not entitled to dismissal of complaint on ground that complaint was a supplemental complaint issued without leave of court, since corporate defendant would not be entitled to notice of application for leave to serve supplemental complaint. Solomon v New York (1959) 21 Misc 2d 836, 194 NYS2d 123, affd 15 AD2d 927, 226 NYS2d 679.

12. —Time of motion

Application to bring in additional parties must be made before trial, by motion at Special Term. Acetate Box Corp. v Johnson (1948) 193 Misc 54, 80 NYS2d 134.

In derivative action by stockholder of foreign corporation, motion by defendant to dismiss complaint for nonjoinder of corporation as indispensable party is premature where no motion is made to add such party. Carruthers v Jack Waite Mining Co. (1953) 306 NY 136, 116 NE2d 286.

13. —Necessity for order

When amending his complaint as matter of course, plaintiff does not have right to "add or drop parties at will"; where it is desired to add new parties defendant, court order on notice to original defendants must be given. Pittman v March Service Co. (1955, Sup) 141 NYS2d 74; Cohen v Gordon (1959) 21 Misc 2d 1056, 196 NYS2d 165.

B. DECISIONS PRIOR TO SEPT. 1, 1946.

14. Generally

CPA § 192 and subdivisions 1, 3 and 4 of former CPA § 193 were derived mainly from the English Rules of the Supreme Court (commonly known as the English Practice Act), the New Jersey Practice Act of 1912 and in part from § 452 of New York Code of Civil Procedure, but subdivision 2 of former CPA § 193 was new. Hailfinger v Meyer (1925) 215 AD 35, 212 NYS 746.

Statute was designed to permit parties in equity actions to bring in all conflicting claimants to the same property, for a complete determination of the question of title, in the one proceeding. Cinema Corp. of America v Bercovici (1931) 233 AD 88, 251 NYS 130.

When former CPA §§ 192 and 193 were read in connection with CPA § 211-a, a legislative scheme was constituted for the determination of all the rights and liabilities of the parties in one action. Davis v Hauk & Schmidt, Inc. (1931) 232 AD 556, 250 NYS 537.

Sole directors of dissolved corporation could not sue as liquidation trustees on non-negotiable note of corporation; hence complaint was dismissed, as here was no mere defect of parties remediable under former CPA § 193. Parish-Watson v Chalom Art Gallery, Inc. (1943) 181 Misc 299, 43 NYS2d 179.

The difficulties relating to joinder of parties under common-law rules, where all persons having separate interests could not be joined, probably disappeared under the Code of Civil Procedure and no longer existed under the still broader and more flexible provisions of the Civil Practice Act. Porter v Lane Const. Corp. (1925) 212 AD 528, 209 NYS 54, affd 244 NY 523, 155 NE 881.

Procedural difficulties were of little moment. Wikoff v Hirschel (1931) 232 AD 193, 249 NYS 690, affd 258 NY 28, 179 NE 249.

The fact that the plaintiff was not the real party in interest did not constitute a defense to the action, since the court might, in its discretion, afford relief by adding or substituting parties at any stage of the proceeding, notwithstanding the objection had not been raised within the time limited by RCP 105 (Rule 3024(c) herein). United States Trust Co. v Greiner (1925) 124 Misc 458, 209 NYS 105, affd 215 AD 659, 212 NYS 931.

15. Effect of nonjoinder

Nonjoinder of all necessary defendants did not defeat an action. Pickhardt v First Nat. Bank & Trust Co. (1943) 266 AD 781, 41 NYS2d 502.

A complaint would not be dismissed for defect of parties since other remedies were furnished. New Amsterdam Casualty Co. v Parsons (1927) 219 AD 486, 220 NYS 340.

Nonjoinder of parties did not defeat the action. The necessary and proper party could have been brought in under former CPA § 193. Rice v Miner (1923, Sup App T) 202 NYS 256; Sisson v Hassett (1935) 155 Misc 667, 280 NYS 148.

16. —Dismissal without prejudice

Dismissal of complaint, without prejudice, was proper since plaintiff could begin new action. McAllister v Watson (1946) 187 Misc 393, 61 NYS2d 698.

17. Bringing in new parties; generally

Where there was a nonjoinder of necessary parties, the court had authority to order that the necessary parties be brought in. Porter v Lane Const. Corp. (1925) 212 AD 528, 209 NYS 54, affd 244 NY 523, 155 NE 881.

Motion to amend answer by pleading defect of parties having been granted, motion by plaintiff to bring in the additional party should also have been granted even though it made adjournment necessary. Schneidman v Shapiro (1924) 125 Misc 892, 211 NYS 647.

Applications to bring in additional parties defendant are ordinarily granted as a matter of course, especially when the other parties to the action cannot be injured thereby. Hennenlotter v Norwich Union Fire Ins. Soc. (1924) 124 Misc 626, 207 NYS 588.

At any stage of the action a process or pleading could be amended by striking out or adding the name of a party, as where the party was referred to as the wife of one of the defendants, Riley v Stern (1889, City Ct) 10 NYS 8; but not by adding an entirely new defendant. New York State Monitor Milk Pan Asso. v Remington Agricultural Works (1882) 89 NY 22, and see Davis v Mayor, etc., of New York (1856) 14 NY 506.

Where husband filed claim against state for damages to realty owned by him and his wife as tenants by entirety, his motion to amend claim by bringing in wife as party claimant was denied, where limitations had run against her claim, since no existing action would be defected by failure to join her. MacFarland v State (1941) 177 Misc 117, 29 NYS2d 996.

Claim against state for damages to flooded realty owned by two tenants in common could not be dismissed for failure to join cotenant whose claim was not timely filed. Slocum v State (1941) 177 Misc 114, 29 NYS2d 993.

Where it appeared futile to order necessary parties defendant to be brought in, the better practice was to suspend trial and afford plaintiff reasonable time, determined by circumstances, to secure their presence. Mannaberg v Culbertson (1942, Sup) 35 NYS2d 642, affd 265 AD 922, 39 NYS2d 984, revd on the ground that court complaint should be dismissed if court believes that plaintiff is unable to obtain jurisdiction over necessary defendants, in 266 AD 765, 41 NYS2d 951, app dismd 290 NY 656, 49 NE2d 619.

In action involving lien, additional party, whether proper or necessary, was properly brought in so that all rights of interested parties might be determined in single action. Mitchell v Maynard (1941, Sup) 32 NYS2d 496.

In action to enforce specific performance of congregation's contract to purchase realty, congregation could implead village whose ordinance prohibited use of such property for congregational purposes. Levy v Congregation Beth Sholom, Inc. (1943) 181 Misc 877, 42 NYS2d 891.

18. —Who are necessary parties

Plaintiffs were receivers of a trust company, defendant, bank was depository of proceeds of checks, fraudulently drawn against the trust company by payee, an officer of the trust company, through whose secret connivance the checks had been collected; payee was not a necessary party to the suit. Newhall v Longacre Bank (1928) 248 NY 252, 162 NE 23.

In action against the trustee to set aside a conveyance of a part of the properties upon which bonds had been issued, it was unnecessary to bring in the bondholders since they were represented by the trustee. Empire State Pickling Co. v Bennett (1929) 135 Misc 482, 238 NYS 344.

The makers of a bond and mortgage alleged by defendant to have been pledged as collateral security for the note should be brought in that plaintiff may be protected should it be adjudged that defendant is entitled to the collateral upon payment of the note. National Bank of Rochester v Erion-Haines Realty Co. (1925) 213 AD 54, 209 NYS 522.

In stockholder's action on behalf of the corporation, alleging mismanagement of corporate affairs, the corporation and directors were necessary parties, and the court properly ordered the directors brought in under former CPA §§ 192 and 193. Jones v Van Heusen Charles Co. (1930) 230 AD 694, 246 NYS 204.

Personal representatives of deceased partner not necessary parties to action by one claiming to be a surviving partner to compel an accounting by a third person in possession of the partnership assets. Kade v Sanitary Fireproofing & Contracting Co. (1931) 257 NY 203, 177 NE 421. See also 256 NY 371, 176 NE 428.

Bringing in parties is an idle ceremony when not essential to establishment of rights or granting relief. Van Decar v Streeter (1930) 136 Misc 206, 240 NYS 492.

In action by landlord and tenant for judgment declaring that insurer was bound under liability policy, person injured on leased premises, although a proper party, was not a necessary party. Spiewok v United States Casualty Co. (1942, Sup) 34 NYS2d 63.

Stockholders' derivative action against directors for their misconduct to detriment of dissolved

corporation was not defeated by inability to serve corporation with summons in New York. Cohen v Dana (1942) 287 NY 405, 40 NE2d 227.

Elections: See Cross v Cohen (1944) 183 Misc 611, 50 NYS2d 42.

19. —Who may be joined

Plaintiff in replevin held entitled, in view of former CPA § 192 and §§ 211–213 (§ 1022 herein) to bring in as parties any who had made or might make claim to the property, or to have a lien upon it. Robinson v Whitaker (1923) 205 AD 286, 199 NYS 680.

Where a guaranty was made as a part of the contract making the debt, the guarantor could be made a party to an action for the principal debt. Winter v Maple City Mfg. Co. (1928) 132 Misc 631, 230 NYS 458.

An action by holder against indorsers of promissory note is joint or several, as the plaintiff may elect, and no right existed to bring in other indorsers as parties defendant. Citizens' Trust Co. v Zoller (1923) 121 Misc 451, 201 NYS 179.

The mere failure of a creditor suing under former § 28 of the Stock Corporation Law to describe the action as representative was no ground for dismissing the complaint, since if it should be made to appear that there were any other creditors similarly situated they could be brought in under former CPA §§ 192 and 193. Aktieselskabet Christianssand v Federal S.S. Corp. (1923) 121 Misc 627, 201 NYS 504.

It was error, in a taxicab passenger's action against a taxicab company for injuries sustained in a collision with a street car, to grant defendant's motion to make the street car company a defendant also, thus raising issues between the joint tortfeasors. Greenhouse v Rochester Taxicab Co. (1926) 218 AD 224, 218 NYS 167.

In action to restrain the city and board of transportation from injuring the tracks and structures of a railroad by construction of a subway, the contractors doing the construction work were properly brought in on motion of defendant. Eighth & N. A. R. Co. v New York (1928) 223 AD 316, 228 NYS 201.

A Russian corporation was brought in as an additional party defendant, notwithstanding objection that it was an agency of the Soviet government. Hennenlotter v Norwich Union Fire Ins. Soc. (1924) 124 Misc 626, 207 NYS 588.

In an action against the executrix and trustee of the estate of a decedent for an accounting and for the removal of such executrix and trustee on the ground that an investment in the stock of a certain corporation was improper, the application of the corporation for leave to intervene as a party defendant held improperly denied. Lyons v Wylde (1926) 216 AD 116, 214 NYS 666.

Where pending an action to restrain defendants from developing power on a river and to determine water rights, the plaintiffs had sold their rights without reservation to a corporation which mortgaged such rights to secure bonds, and plaintiffs had guaranteed to purchaser and bondholders the validity of their title to the water power, the court could, under CPA § 83 (§§ 1015b, 1018 herein) and former CPA §§ 192 and 193, join as defendants the vendee, the trustee under the mortgage, and the executor of one of the plaintiffs whose death occurred pending the action. Dunlop v Sweet Bros. Paper Mfg. Co. (1925) 211 AD 363, 208 NYS 54.

Where it was reasonably apparent that a majority stockholder made a contract with plaintiff for his company or for himself to sell the corporation, in action for broker's commissions, plaintiff's motion to bring in should have been granted. Clark v Flinn & Co. (1930) 230 AD 698, 246 NYS 399.

When it was alleged that two or more persons were responsible for certain acts, where the circumstances permit or warrant it, all could be joined, leaving the determination of liability to the trial. First Const. Co. v Rapid Transit Subway Const. Co. (1924) 211 AD 184, 206 NYS 822.

One who knowingly participated in and aided a trustee in the commission of a breach of trust and misappropriation of trust funds was properly joined with the trustee in an action to recover the money. Public Shoe Stores, Inc. v Goldstein (1929) 225 AD 350, 233 NYS 73.

In view of CPA § 1569 (§ 10003 herein), the right of plaintiff in an action based upon a contract with an unincorporated association for the sale on consignment of the product of its members, to join as defendants the president of such association and the individual members, was governed by former CPA §§ 192, 211–213 (§§ 1002, 5012 herein). Mandell v Moses (1923) 204 AD 655, 198 NYS 583.

Two separate causes of action against different defendants could not be united in one complaint. William C. Will Co. v Canadian N. R. Co. (1926) 216 AD 239, 214 NYS 513.

Parties charged with participation in the acts of tortious nature alleged against the original defendants, aiding and abetting them, were properly brought in. Manufacturers' Trust Co. v American Nat. Fire Ins. Co. (1931) 232 AD 535, 252 NYS 88.

Plaintiff, in an action in replevin, was not entitled, under former CPA § 192, or § 193, to an order bringing in as party defendant a third party who had served on the sheriff notice of claim of ownership. McLaughlin v McLaughlin (1932) 237 AD 1, 260 NYS 357, affd 261 NY 573, 185 NE 743.

Plaintiff executor ordered to join his coexecutors as parties defendant and serve upon them supplemental summons and complaint in an action to set aside a fraudulent conveyance. Berardini v Berardini (1932) 236 AD 850, 260 NYS 935.

The court or a referee had power to amend the summons and complaint by adding a party defendant. Magovern v Robertson (1891, Sup) 14 NYS 114, affd 129 NY 636, 29 NE 1031.

Former CPA § 193 applied to cases in which the party sought to be brought in was a necessary party or interested in the event of the action in connection with the original parties thereto, which is not the case where two tortfeasors are severally liable. Heffern v Hunt (1896) 8 AD 585, 40 NYS 914.

Under former CPA §§ 192 and 193 a plaintiff in an action of partition who had commenced his action in good faith, and had been regular in his practice but who without any fault on his part omitted to make certain parties defendants, was entitled to an order to issue a supplemental summons and to amend his complaint. Hall v Campbell (1894) 77 Hun 567, 28 NYS 1031.

Court had no power to direct that persons then in court be brought in as parties. Hood v Hood (1881) 85 NY 561.

In an action at law for a money judgment where a party elected to sue one only of parties jointly liable on a contract and the defendant objected to the complaint upon the ground that the other parties liable had not been joined, the court had power to allow an amendment bringing in the other parties if the plaintiff showed an adequate excuse for not joining them and the defendants would not be prejudiced especially where it was doubtful whether the plaintiff was entitled to sue the original defendant alone. Haskell v Moran (1907) 118 AD 810, 103 NYS 667.

When a motion to amend a complaint by adding a party defendant had been denied without leave to renew the motion, a second motion brought without leave was denied; however, when it appeared that the defendant, as administrator of a deceased partner, did not demur to the first complaint because of a failure to join the surviving partner as party defendant, but demurred to an amended complaint on the ground of defect of parties, the court should grant a further amendment bringing in the surviving partner as defendant. Haskell v Moran (1907) 117 AD 251, 102 NYS 388.

The power of the supreme court to compel a plaintiff to bring into an action a third party upon his own application could be exercised only in the instances and subject to the requirements of former CPA § 193, the general powers conferred upon courts by CPA § 105 (§§ 2001, 3025(b), Rule 305(c), 2101(f) herein) being nothing more than a declaration of the inherent powers of the supreme court. Draper v Pratt (1904) 43 Misc 406, 89 NYS 356.

Where several persons were jointly liable and a suit is brought against a part only of the persons so liable, the court had power to amend the process, pleading or proceedings by bringing in the omitted parties. Boyd v United States Mortg. & Trust Co. (1904) 94 AD 413, 88 NYS 289, later app 110 AD 866, 95 NYS 1123, affd 187 NY 262, 79 NE 999.

An order bringing in a third party as an additional defendant in an action to recover money damages for personal injuries made without notice to such party, was improper. Although former CPA § 192 gave to the court the power to amend pleadings by adding the name of a party, it did not authorize the above order and former CPA § 193 related primarily to equitable actions. Horan v Bruning (1906) 116 AD 482, 101 NYS 986.

Where, at the commencement of a replevin action and the levy under the writ, a third party files a claim to the property with the sheriff, the plaintiff was not entitled over the objection of the third party, to have the third party brought in as a defendant. Goldstein v Shapiro (1903) 85 AD 83, 82 NYS 1038.

Former CPA § 192 applied only to cases where the party was necessary to, or interested in, the defense of the action which is not a case where two or more joint tort-feasors are severally liable. Hinds, Noble & Eldredge v Bonner (1907) 52 Misc 461, 102 NYS 484.

In an action on a check, on showing that defendant had assigned said check to his wife as collateral, and that she consented to join as party plaintiff and be bound by the complaint, the plaintiff was entitled to an amendment bringing in the assignee as plaintiff. Pfister v Heins (1910) 136 AD 457, 121 NYS 173.

Former CPA § 192 changed the common-law rule that the court was without power to bring in additional defendants on the plaintiff's motion; such section applied to suits in equity and actions at law; former CPA § 193 did not restrict its scope, applying to equity actions only. Gittleman v Feltman (1907) 122 AD 385, 106 NYS 839, affd 198 AD 885, 191 NYS 205.

Former section pertained to actions at law and to equity actions; the court could direct any person who could have been joined as a party to be brought in, provided a satisfactory reason was given, except in cases where the rights of parties had been changed after the bringing of the action by subsequent transactions, in which case the provisions as to supplemental amendments and pleadings applied. Gittleman v Feltman (1908) 191 NY 205, 83 NE 969.

In an action of partition the court could direct that persons not necessary parties to the action be brought in as parties, on the motion of one of the defendants, in order that conflicting claims to the property could be determined. Johnson v Aleshire (1909) 130 AD 178, 114 NYS 398.

Name could be added in place of designation. Bannerman v Quackenbush, 11 Daly 529.

Where a party was brought in by amendment, the defense of the statute of limitations was available to him, if the statute had run when he was actually brought in. Newman v Marvin (1877) 12 Hun 236.

20. Substitution

Court under former CPA § 192, could substitute a corporation as plaintiff instead of an individual doing business under the corporate name. Kelly v Carson Petroleum Co. (1924) 123 Misc 918, 206 NYS 590.

Where a state official was a party and was later succeeded in office by another, name of latter should be substituted; courts take judicial notice of such changes of state officials. Metropolitan Life

Ins. Co. v Beha (1929) 226 AD 408, 235 NYS 501, affd Metropolitan L. Ins. Co. v Conway (1930) 252 NY 449, 169 NE 642.

One denied access to the courts of this state because suing as administratrix by appointment of a court of a foreign country whose government was unrecognized by the United States, could not move to amend her complaint by substituting as plaintiff herself as administratrix by appointment of a court of this state, whether such subsequent appointment be deemed ancillary to the foreign administration or an independent appointment. Pelzer v United Dredging Co. (1922) 200 AD 646, 193 NYS 676.

In an action to recover for the death of an intestate in an automobile collision with a railway train, occurring in a foreign state in which the law permitted only the spouse or heir but not the representative to prosecute the action, the courts of this state would not permit such allowed persons to be substituted for the representatives who began the action. Sapone v New York C. & H. R. R. Co. (1927) 130 Misc 755, 225 NYS 211.

Where a summons and complaint naming two railroad companies as parties defendant were served upon officers of such companies, but the cause of action arose while the railroads in question were under government control, former CPA § 192 did not authorize the granting of a motion to substitute as defendant the agent designated by the government pursuant to Transportation Act 1920, § 206(a), such agent not having been named as a defendant in the original summons and complaint. Fischer v Wabash R. Co. (1923) 235 NY 568, 139 NE 738, cert den 263 US 706, 68 L Ed 516, 44 S Ct 34; Weil v New York C. R. Co. (1923) 235 NY 570, 139 NE 738.

And where action is against the defendants as sureties it was error to allow amendment charging them as principals also. Smith v Staag, 47 Super Ct (15 Jones & S) 514.

The original representative of an estate having died, the new one should have been substituted as defendant. Re Des Anges' Estate (1931) 234 AD 715, 253 NYS 1.

Where an unincorporated association had been inadvertently sued by its name and alleged to be a domestic corporation and the summons had been served on its president, the court had power to allow an amendment to the summons and complaint by making the president defendant and changing the allegation to conform to the fact. Munzinger v Courier Co. (1894) 82 Hun 575, 31 NYS 737.

In an action for negligently allowing a schoolhouse to be out of repair, an amendment striking out the names of the defendants, the trustees of the school district, and substituting their corporate name, was not proper, as the corporation had not been brought into court; nor was one striking out all the defendants but the one who was in fault for the negligence sued upon. Bassett v Fish (1878) 75 NY 303.

The court had no power to make an order substituting a corporation as defendant in place of an individual, the president thereof, where the statute of limitations was a bar to the maintenance of an independent action against the corporation. Licausi v Ashworth (1903) 78 AD 486, 79 NYS 631.

The court had no power to amend a complaint by substituting a new defendant in place of the one sued. Fassy v Jacobs (1911) 71 Misc 145, 127 NYS 1062.

A complaint could not be amended by substituting a new plaintiff in place of the one by whom the action was brought. Concrete Pub. Co. v Reed (1910) 70 Misc 22, 126 NYS 653.

No construction can be given to former CPA § 192 which will authorize the substitution of a party defendant for a sole party plaintiff against his wishes, and where one was appointed administrator and brought action to foreclose mortgage, and subsequently a will was found and an executor appointed and the executor was made a defendant, court could not by amendment substitute the name of the executor as plaintiff without his consent. Morris v Morris (1916) 172 AD 719, 158 NYS 361.

Court was not authorized to strike out name of plaintiff and substitute his assignee in place thereof, as it would be in effect the bringing of a new action. Williams v Arthur H. Crist Co. (1919) 190 AD 29, 179 NYS 679.

Where it appears upon the trial of an action brought by plaintiff, as administrator, to recover the value of services rendered by his deceased daughter, that she was a minor at the time the services were rendered, an amendment of the complaint virtually allowing him to prosecute the action also in his individual capacity is not authorized by former CPA § 192, since such amendment "changes substantially" the cause of action. Doyle v Carney (1907) 190 NY 386, 83 NE 37.

The city court of the city of New York had power by amendment to turn an action against them as trustees to one against them as individuals, but both the summons and complaint should have been amended; an amendment to the complaint alone was ineffectual. Southack v Gleason (1906) 49 Misc 445, 98 NYS 859.

An administratrix, who had brought an action in her representative capacity, would not, to meet the requirements of the statute, be allowed to amend the summons and complaint so as to change the action to one in her own name as consort, after the statute of limitations had run. Bowen v Phoenix Bridge Co. (1909) 134 AD 22, 118 NYS 93, revd 198 NY 615, 92 NE 1079.

Where the action was commenced against the receiver of a corporation for services rendered to him, and, before the commencement thereof, a new corporation had been formed, and the defendant discharged from his receivership under a special act of the legislature which forbade actions against the receiver, and rendered the new company liable for all claims against the receiver, the complaint might be amended by substituting the new company as defendant. Abbott v Jewett (1881) 25 Hun 603.

21. Amendment of title of action

Court could permit amendment of title of action by striking out words "as trustee." McKenzie v Lavine (1936) 249 AD 755, 291 NYS 1011.

The special term had power to strike out from the title of an action the words "as substituted trustee under the will of —." Boyd v United States Mortg. & Trust Co. (1903) 84 AD 466, 82 NYS 1001.

The court at special term had power to allow the summons and complaint to be amended before trial so as to designate a defendant in his representative, instead of in his individual, capacity. Alker v Rhoads (1902) 73 AD 158, 76 NYS 808.

The supreme court had power under former CPA § 192 to permit the amendment of the summons and complaint in an action of negligence by changing the designation of the defendant from trustee to that of an individual. Boyd v United States Mortg. & Trust Co. (1907) 187 NY 262, 79 NE 999.

A plaintiff, suing on a policy of fire insurance in compliance with a provision thereof, brought his action against an individual as attorney in fact of a certain association of underwriters; he had the right after judgment, on discovering that only certain of the underwriters underwrote his policy, to substitute the names of the individuals who underwrote his policy in place of the name of the association; parties could not be substituted, but the name of a defendant could be corrected. Becker v Woodcock (1910) 136 AD 589, 121 NYS 71.

A court had power to amend a summons and complaint by substituting a company receiver where it appears that the cause of action was vested in a receiver, but through inadvertence the papers were entitled in the name of the company. Hulbert v Hohman (1898) 22 Misc 248, 49 NYS 633.

Where copartners were made defendants and trade name under which they were doing business was also named as defendant, court should have stricken out the trade name even though not requested. Calumet & Hecla Mining Co. v Equitable Trust Co. (1919) 186 AD 328, 174 NYS 317.

22. Misjoinder and dropping parties

In an action to rescind a contract for fraud, a person not a party to the contract was improperly joined. Alexander City Bank v Equitable Trust Co. (1928) 223 AD 24, 227 NYS 403.

In an action to rescind contract of sale of corporate bonds on the ground of false and fraudulent representations, the individual defendant, not being a party to the contract, was improperly joined, and his motion to dismiss for misjoinder or strike the allegations concerning him should have been granted. Alexander City Bank v Equitable Trust Co., supra.

Where it was stipulated on trial of an action by partners that the partnership had been dissolved prior to the indebtedness sued on, the court was not required to dismiss on the ground one partner had been improperly joined as plaintiff, but could render judgment for the partner to whom the debt was due. Comerford v Fahy Market (1923) 204 AD 533, 198 NYS 353.

A defendant should not be dropped from a suit to enforce a contract of his testator to devise certain estate to plaintiff, in his capacity as executor and devisee under the will of the devisee of said testator. Milliner v Morris (1927) 219 AD 425, 219 NYS 166.

Where plaintiff consented to the bringing in of an additional defendant upon the express condition that the case should retain its place on the calendar as a preferred case and be tried in Erie county, held that on change of place of trial to another county plaintiff should be permitted to discontinue the action against such defendant. Fisher v Bullock (1924) 208 AD 565, 204 NYS 425.

In suit for specific performance or return of payments on a land contract, the party to whom the land had been subsequently sold was improperly joined. Perlman v East Annadale Beach Corp. (1931) 233 AD 599, 253 NYS 775.

Court could strike out defendant's name added by mistake. Bartholomae v Kaufmann (1883) 91 NY 654.

Persons who were made parties to an action to construe a will were entitled to have their names stricken from the summons when they resigned as trustees and the supreme court would grant the application to resign. Rothschild v Goldenberg (1901) 33 Misc 646, 68 NYS 955, revd 58 AD 293, 68 NYS 1095.

Where two defendants were improperly joined in the summons, it could be amended by striking out the name of one of them. Trow's Printing & Book-Binding Co. v New York Book-Binding Co. (1888, City Ct) 3 NYS 59.

But not by striking out the name of a sole defendant and the insertion in lieu thereof of the names of other persons as defendants. New York State Monitor Milk Pan Asso. v Remington Agricultural Works (1882) 89 NY 22.

The name of one of the plaintiffs, who died before summons served, was stricken out. Fink v Manhattan R. Co. (1890, CP Ct) 8 NYS 327.

Dead coplaintiff's name could not be stricken out at trial; representatives of deceased parties had to be substituted. Hasbrouck v Bunce (1875) 62 NY 475. See Phillips v Melville (1877) 10 Hun 211.

Striking out name of defendant. See Shaw v Cock (1879) 78 NY 194.

Name of plaintiff, who died before service of summons, stricken out. Fink v Manhattan R. Co. (1890, CP Ct) 8 NYS 327.

In action against city and policeman for injuries to pedestrian struck by municipal car driven by policeman, dismissal of complaint was improper. Kosiba v Syracuse (1942) 287 NY 283, 39 NE2d 240.

Nonjoinder of copartner did not permit dismissal of complaint, since defendant's remedy was motion

to correct pleading under RCP 102 (Rule 3024(a) herein). Becker v Hercules Foundries, Inc. (1942) 263 AD 991, 33 NYS2d 367.

Action for personal injury originally commenced against city and policeman as joint tort-feasors but continued only against city, was not defeated by dropping him as party. Bernardine v New York (1944) 268 AD 444, 51 NYS2d 888, affd 294 NY 361, 62 NE2d 604, 161 ALR 364.

Foreign corporation was held improvidently added in action for price of merchandise. Stainless Metals, Inc. v Food Machinery Corp. (1946) 270 AD 910, 61 NYS2d 418.

In conspiracy action against corporation and individual defendants, corporation was improper party, but such defect was not ground for dismissal. Jones v Demuth Glass Works, Inc. (1946) 271 AD 840, 66 NYS2d 12.

23. Waiver of defect of parties

Nonsuit for defect of parties defendant in that mortgagee whose interests were protected under New York standard mortgage clause attached to policy sued on was not made party to action was denied for failure to object before trial. Peterson v Utica Fire Ins. Co. (1941, Sup) 27 NYS2d 51.

Objection that the party defendant to a counterclaim was a department of a sovereign government had to be made by an accredited representative of that government. Kunglig Jarnvagsstyrelsen v Dexter & Carpenter, Inc. (1929, CA2 NY) 32 F2d 195, cert den 280 US 579, 74 L Ed 629, 50 S Ct 32.

Where, under former CPA § 278 defect of parties who might have been brought in was waived, the case properly proceeded without them. Talmadge v United States Shipping Board Emergency Fleet Corp. (1931, CA2 NY) 54 F2d 240.

24. Remedy by motion

Where a plaintiff desired to strike out a party as neither necessary nor proper he should have moved to be allowed to discontinue the action, but he should not have moved to dismiss his own complaint. Hewitt v Farmers' Loan & Trust Co. (1923) 204 AD 797, 198 NYS 744.

25. —Time of motion

Defect in parties plaintiff could be remedied at any stage. Scutella v County Fire Ins. Co. (1931) 231 AD 343, 247 NYS 689.

New parties would not be added or substituted after limitation period had run. Scutella v County F. Ins. Co., supra.

Where in action against town highway superintendent he would have substantial personal rights as individual to defend motion at opening of trial to amend complaint to add him also as individual was denied. Foster v Webster (1943) 8 Misc 2d 61, 44 NYS2d 153.

26. —Notice of motion

A plaintiff was not required to give notice to the

party whom he intended to join as a defendant in an action then pending with others. Schultze v Ocean Acci. & Guarantee Corp. (1933) 239 AD 309, 267 NYS 284.

Where plaintiff sought to add a party, original defendant should have had notice. Harris v Simpson (1930) 137 Misc 809, 243 NYS 457.

Notice to the party to be brought in did not need to be given. Seaman v Colon (1927) 130 Misc 568, 224 NYS 338; Harris v Simpson (1930) 137 Misc 809, 243 NYS 457.

27. —Necessity for order

The provision of former CPA § 192 that new parties could be added by order of the court was not mandatory as to the necessity for an order. Wolford v Copelon (1934) 242 AD 91, 273 NYS 186.

28. —Vacation of order bringing in party

An application could be made under former CPA § 192 to vacate an order making a party a defendant under former CPA § 193. Wichert, Inc. v Gallagher & Ascher (1923) 201 NYS 186, affd 206 AD 756, 200 NYS 957.

The wide discretion of the court would have warranted vacating an order impleading a new defendant, but not without showing whether the order was made on notice to him, and that he did not appeal therefrom. Jackson v Bickelhaupt (1927) 128 Misc 610, 219 NYS 601.

29. Counterclaim

Where a negligence action arising out of an automobile collision was brought by an injured party and his insurer under a personal accident policy, the insurer holding a pro tanto assignment after payment under the policy, the defendant could counterclaim for damages to his automobile. Gilboy v Lennon (1922) 118 Misc 467, 193 NYS 606.

C. Decisions Under RCP 102

30. Generally

A complaint will not be dismissed for defect of parties since other remedies are now provided. McKnight v Bank of New York & Trust Co. (1930) 254 NY 417, 173 NE 568; Spaulding v First Nat. Bank (1924) 210 AD 216, 205 NYS 492, affd 239 NY 586, 147 NE 206; New Amsterdam Casualty Co. v Mobinco Brokerage Co. (1927) 219 AD 486, 220 NYS 340; Rice v Miner (1923, Sup App T) 202 NYS 256; Newtown Jackson Co. v Barclays Bank (1954, Sup) 133 NYS2d 726.

Where defendant moved to dismiss complaint for defect of parties and court heard proof and denied motion, court's determination that plaintiff has shown basis of action in his own right and that there was no defect of parties, did not preclude defendant from realleging issue by way of proffered defense. Charles v Murphy (1954) 284 AD 987, 135 NYS2d 285.

Misjoinder of parties is not ground for dismissal of

complaint, but only for its correction. Briggs v Technocracy, Inc. (1948, Sup) 85 NYS2d 735.

Defect of parties defendant was curable under RCP 102. R. & L. Goldmuntz Sprl v Fischer (1945, Sup) 54 NYS2d 635.

Nonjoinder of necessary defendants does not render complaint insufficient. Pickhardt v First Nat. Bank & Trust Co. (1943) 266 AD 781, 41 NYS2d 502.

A motion to dismiss complaint because causes of action by different plaintiffs were not joined in accordance with former Civil Practice Act, § 209, was denied, but each plaintiff was required to serve a separate amended complaint stating his individual cause of action. Kelso v Cavanagh (1930) 137 Misc 653, 244 NYS 90.

Hostile party may be joined as defendant, without asking him to join as co-plaintiff. Hofer v H. E. Swezey & Son (1950, Sup) 98 NYS2d 145.

Defendants who may properly be joined are such only as would be affected by causes of action arising out of the same transaction or series of transactions, and requiring the consideration of a common question of law or fact. 137 East 66th Street v Lawrence (1922) 118 Misc 486, 194 NYS 762.

Defect of parties plaintiff is not ground for dismissal of complaint; proper procedure is to raise objection to defect of parties in case of nonjoinder of even indispensable party by motion to add such party. Marrero v Levitt (1956) 3 Misc 2d 555, 152 NYS2d 802.

Where defendant contends that claimant's rights are joint, motion to add party under this rule, and not motion to consolidate actions under CPA § 96 (CPLR §§ 407, 602) was proper remedy. Donzella v New York State Thruway Authority (1958) 7 AD2d 771, 180 NYS2d 108.

31. Particular actions or proceedings

In action on note against one of two makers, nonjoinder can be raised by motion to correct pleading. Welch v Campbell (1950) 197 Misc 165, 94 NYS2d 860, affd 278 AD 605, 102 NYS2d 51.

Where complaint to recover money had and received alleged an obligation to three plaintiffs jointly, one of them could not be dropped in the absence of amended complaint. Wiener v Benson Bldg. Co. (1925) 213 AD 347, 210 NYS 484.

Coexecutrix, characterized by other executrix as hostile to success of action, may be dropped as plaintiff and be brought in as defendant. Prygocki v Prydatko (1951, Sup) 105 NYS2d 205.

Plaintiff's complaint for brokerage commission will not be dismissed for nonjoinder of all the parties concerned, but the court will order a supplementary summons to be served on all the parties, with time fixed to plead. O'Connell v Ryan (1926) 127 Misc 350, 216 NYS 590.

Motion for nonsuit for defect of parties defendant in that mortgagee, whose interests were protected under New York standard mortgage clause attached to policy sued on, was not party to action should be denied because such objection should have been raised before trial. Peterson v Utica Fire Ins. Co. (1941, Sup) 27 NYS2d 51.

In action for conspiracy to breach contract, plaintiff may not add as another defendant another contracting party who breached agreement. Toffel v Odzer (1956, Sup) 154 NYS2d 1002.

The brothers and sister of a husband who are all signatories to an agreement to support his wife, which agreement does not indicate an intention that liability be joint and several, are joint obligors united in interest and must be joined as parties defendant with the husband in the wife's action on the agreement. Indursky v Indursky (1958) 7 AD2d 709, 180 NYS2d 61.

In action by lessee and owner of property against electric company to recover as damages the amount expended by tenant in constructing a conduit to permit combined billing for electricity consumed, the fact that owner had agreed to bear part of the cost of installation did not give it standing to maintain the action, and it was ordered dropped as a party plaintiff. Equitable Paper Bag Co. v Consolidated Edison Co. (1958) 18 Misc 2d 118, 183 NYS2d 366.

Adjoining landowners who, subsequent to the recording of plaintiff's mortgage, began action against mortgagor-owner for trespass because of water, dirt and silt flowing from mortgaged premises onto their land, and filed a lis pendens, were properly made parties defendant in plaintiff's mortgage foreclosure action, since the filing of the lis pendens constitutes a claim affecting the title to, or the possession or use of the property involved. Cornell Associates, Inc. v White Plains Colony Estates, Inc. (1961, Sup) 212 NYS2d 825.

32. —Corporations

In action for conspiracy against corporation and individuals, latter is improper party, but such defect is not ground for dismissal. Jones v Demuth Glass Works, Inc. (1946) 271 AD 840, 66 NYS2d 12.

On failure of plaintiffs adequately to excuse their nonjoinder of the president of an issuing company with the trust company selling its bonds on action for rescission of purchase contract, or to show the latter cannot respond to judgment for the purchase price, their motion to join the president as a party defendant must be denied. Continental Ins. Co. v Equitable Trust Co. (1926) 127 Misc 50, 215 NYS 287.

Where corporation is improperly joined in stockholders' derivative action, remedy is to drop corporation, but not to dismiss complaint. Timely Drive-In Cleaning Corp. v Jacobs (1959) 21 Misc 2d 1052, 190 NYS2d 194.

A creditor may in his own name and for his own benefit sue directors for loans of corporate funds to stockholders (Stock Corp L § 59), but creditors similarly situated may intervene or be joined. If they do not intervene or fail to be joined, it is no objection to the maintenance of the action by the single creditor that he will thereby reap the full statutory benefit to the exclusion of other credi-

tors. American Broadcasting-Paramount Theatres, Inc. v Frye (1960) 8 NY2d 232, 203 NYS2d 850, 168 NE2d 669.

33. —Partnerships

In action for accounting of affairs of two successive law partnerships against surviving member, representative of second deceased member ordered brought in. Jones v Gogolick (1941) 262 AD 960, 29 NYS2d 961.

Copartner, in action against partnership for work and labor, could have been brought in as party defendant by motion under RCP 102. Becker v Hercules Foundries, Inc. (1942) 263 AD 991, 33 NYS2d 367.

34. —Real property

In action by wife to enforce oral agreement to convey house to her and her husband, plaintiff was ordered to join husband as coplaintiff or defendant, despite pending action for separation by her against husband. Rougas v Rougas (1948, Sup) 86 NYS2d 484.

Claim against state for injuries to realty owned in common could have been filed by cotenant, who could move to bring in other cotenant, but state could not have claim dismissed for nonjoinder of latter. Slocum v State (1941) 177 Misc 114, 29 NYS2d 993.

Where church pastor as committee of regular congregation members sued in ejectment president of religious association and both plaintiff and defendant incorporated as church association after action was commenced, motion to substitute incorporated associations as parties was granted. Laszczuk v Opechi (1954, Sup) 133 NYS2d 279.

In partition action, the son of one of the tenants in common who brought a partition action was properly made a party defendant in his capacity as executor of his father's estate. Levine v Gottlieb (1957) 8 Misc 2d 1017, 166 NYS2d 639.

35. —Stockholder's actions

In derivative action by stockholder of foreign corporation, motion by defendant to dismiss complaint for nonjoinder of corporation as indispensable party is premature where no motion is made to add such party. Carruthers v Jack Waite Mining Co. (1953) 306 NY 136, 116 NE2d 286.

In a stockholder's action brought to restore to the defendant corporation property which it is claimed has been diverted from the corporation by the negligent or other wrongful acts of the defendants, there is no defect of defendants where parties have been made defendants who participated in the transfer of the property and whose presence is necessary to its restoration and to a complete determination of the controversy. Baker v Baker (1924) 122 Misc 757, 204 NYS 11, affd 212 AD 850, 207 NYS 809.

There is no nonjoinder of defendants in a stockholder's representative action, where one of the directors is not included as a defendant. Baker v Baker, supra.

Where the complaint joined as plaintiffs both a corporation and its stockholders, it was held that there was a misjoinder of parties and either the individual plaintiffs or the corporate plaintiffs should be dropped, depending whether the action was intended to be a derivative stockholder's action. Bolmer Const. Co. v 9 Kew Gardens Road Corp. (1948, Sup) 82 NYS2d 632.

36. —Trusts

In an action by the settlor of a trust against the trustee to compel recognition of the revocation of the trust, the defendant is entitled to implead as additional parties an unmarried son and grandson and representative of after-born next of kin or settlor. Mayer v Chase Nat. Bank (1932) 143 Misc 714, 257 NYS 161, affd 236 AD 778, 258 NYS 1046, affd 240 AD 877, 267 NYS 939.

In action by husband to impose trust on moneys withdrawn by wife from joint savings account and deposited in own name in trust for their son, objection to nonjoinder is properly made by motion to add party and not by wife's answer. Motyka v Motyka (1952, Sup App T) 113 NYS2d 892.

In action against the trustee to set aside a conveyance of a part of the properties upon which bonds had been issued, motion to bring in the bondholders was denied, since they were represented by the trustee. Empire State Pickling Co. v Bennett (1929) 135 Misc 482, 238 NYS 344.

37. Waiver of defect

Defect of parties waived. Day v Mills (1928) 133 Misc 220, 231 NYS 235.

Any question as to nonjoinder of codefendant, which might have been raised by plaintiff or defendant, was waived by failure of both parties to raise objection either before or during trial. Cash v Diamond (1955) 208 Misc 712, 144 NYS2d 627.

Where two parties who signed releases were indispensable parties to action to set aside such releases but were not joined, and they were named but not served, such defect did not appear on face of pleadings so that failure to move under former RCP 102 did not operate as waiver of such defect. Mannaberg v Culbertson (1942, Sup) 35 NYS2d 642, affd 265 AD 922, 39 NYS2d 984, revd 266 AD 765, 41 NYS2d 951, on the ground that as it was apparent that jurisdiction of the parties was not obtainable, so if the court believes the complaint should be dismissed upon the ground of defect of parties, judgment accordingly should be entered without delay.

38. Procedure

RCP 102 expressly required that objection of nonjoinder be raised by motion to add parties. Marsico v Tramutolo (1954, Sup) 135 NYS2d 258.

Objection to misjoinder or nonjoinder of parties had to be raised by motion to add or drop parties. New York v Draper (1951) 201 Misc 957, 107 NYS2d 789.

Where there is a nonjoinder of defendants because plaintiff was in doubt as to who were liable, extent of liability, and in what capacity, motion to make more definite and certain was denied, bill of particulars being proper. Winslow Bros. & Smith Co. v Grace S. S. Co. (1929) 133 Misc 902, 233 NYS 448.

Objection to misjoinder of a party plaintiff comes too late when not made until the trial. Russian Reinsurance Co. v Stoddard (1925) 211 AD 132, 207 NYS 574, revd on other grounds 240 NY 149, 147 NE 703, reh den 240 NY 682, 148 NE 757.

Objection as to nonjoinder of parties may be raised only by motion to add parties; it cannot be pleaded as an affirmative defense. Bleakney v Schrauff (1959) 18 Misc 2d 919, 186 NYS2d 412.

An objection of non-joinder can only be raised by a motion to add parties. A defendant who does not raise a question of nonjoinder of parties in an action in equity until the trial and submission of the same for decision must be determined to have waived the objection provided the court may effect an effective decree as between the parties. Re Elwyn's Estate (1957) 8 Misc 2d 704, 173 NYS2d 192, affd 5 AD2d 748, 168 NYS2d 942.

D. CASE NOTES UNDER FORMER SCA § 289

39. Generally; necessary parties

Under this section each party who has appeared in a special proceeding must be made a party to an appeal and is a party before the Court of Appeals. Re Winburn's Will (1936) 270 NY 196, 200 NE 784.

Where an application to have the applicant appointed general guardian of an infant is denied, the infant and not the relative of the infant who objected to the appointment must be made a party to the appeal taken by the applicant. Kellinger v Roe, 7 Paige 362.

It is not necessary on an appeal from an order appointing a guardian that the appeal should be in the name of the infant, but it is proper that he should be made a party to the appeal. Underhill v Dennis, 9 Paige 202.

All parties to the proceedings before the surrogate who are interested in sustaining the order or decree appealed from should be made parties to the appeal. Kellett v Rathbun, 4 Paige 102; Gardner v Gardner, 5 Paige 170; Gilchrist v Rea, 9 Paige 66; Brown v Evans, 34 Barb 594.

So also persons to whom sums are awarded by the surrogate although they are not parties to the proceedings before the surrogate. Jauncey v Rutherford, 9 Paige 273; Re Thompson, 11 Paige 453; Wilcox v Smith, 26 Barb 316.

The heirs, next of kin and legatees of a decedent, in addition to the executors, are necessary parties to an appeal from an order admitting a will to probate. Gilman v Gilman, 35 Barb 591; Pruyn v Brinkerhoff, 57 Barb 176, 7 Abb Pr NS 400.

Under this section a special guardian is a necessary party to an appeal, and the special guardian has the right to take and prosecute an appeal himself. Re Stewart (1897) 23 AD 17, 48 NYS 999.

An appeal in an action to probate a will, held to bring in the necessary parties under SCA § 289. Williams v Supreme Council of Royal Arcanum (1907) 120 AD 883, 105 NYS 339.

Notice of appeal may not restrict review by stating limitation as to matters or parties since all parties to proceeding in surrogate's court to construe will are parties, since all parties to proceeding in interests of all must be considered. Re Burk's Will (1949) 298 NY 450, 84 NE2d 631, remittitur amd 299 NY 308, 86 NE2d 759 and motion to dismiss app den 300 NY 498, 88 NE2d 725.

Where special guardian participated in probate proceeding and notice of appeal from decree probating will was by mistake not served upon him, notice of appeal was amended to add his name at foot of notice, with permission to serve amended notice upon him, thus making him party to appeal. Re Donahue's Estate (1948) 193 Misc 685, 84 NYS2d 48.

In appeal from proceedings involving validity of assignment of interest in estate, assignee is a necessary party to assignor's appeal therefrom, and should be brought in. Re Brener's Will (1960) 12 AD2d 452, 206 NYS2d 449.

40. Supplying defect in parties

Where a creditor, appealing from an order of a surrogate fixing the amount of his claim, in proceedings to sell real property, has omitted to make the heirs parties to the appeal, the appeal must be dismissed. The time to appeal having elapsed, held, under the former statute, that the court had no power to allow the appellant to amend by bringing in the heirs. Patterson v Hamilton (1882, NY) 26 Hun 665.

Held, under the former statute, that the right of a party to apply for an order, directing him to be brought in, as a respondent, to a pending appeal from a surrogate's decree, is not affected by the fact that his own time to appeal has elapsed. Cox v Schermerhorn (1877, NY) 12 Hun 411.

A surrogate's court has no power to make an order allowing the intervention of new parties to a contest over the probate of a will where the decree

has been rendered in the matter, and an appeal therefrom is pending; the application for such an order must be made to the appellate court. Re Dunn, 1 Dem 294.

Where there is a defect of parties, if no motion is made to stay or dismiss the appeal on that ground, and the absent parties have neither taken an appeal themselves, nor applied to be made parties to the appeal, the appellate court cannot, upon the appeal, reverse the decree appealed from, even though it should come to the conclusion that the surrogate had erred in his view of the rights of the parties. Brown v Evans, 34 Barb 594.

Legatees may intervene in proceedings for probate, and upon appeal from the surrogate's order. Marvin v Marvin, 11 Abb Pr NS 97.

It seems that a person interested in proving the will may make himself a party to an appeal from the decision of the surrogate, although he was not a party to the proceedings in the court below. Foster v Foster, 7 Paige 48.

Where the surrogate makes an allowance to counsel for contestant of a will they are properly made parties to an appeal taken by the executrix. Peck v Peck (1880, NY) 23 Hun 312, affd 99 NY 608.

For old practice in regard to dismissing appeals for omission of parties, see Gardner v Gardner, 5 Paige 170; Suffern v Lawrence, 4 How Pr 129.

A motion to amend a notice of appeal from a surrogate's decree on probate by adding the names of persons who had not appeared, but who have, or claim to have, a right or interest in the subject matter of the decree, and for leave to serve the amended notice upon all parties nunc pro tunc, is not a motion to perfect an appeal under SCA § 297, but is one under SCA § 289, and should be made in the appellate court and not before the surrogate. Re Marks' Will (1908) 128 AD 775, 113 NYS 104.

Where attorney for the administratrix of an estate was aggrieved by an order made in the judicial settlement of an accounting, surrogate granted his application to be made a party thereto for the purposes of an appeal from such order. Re Polizzo, 25 Misc 2d 587, 204 NYS2d 275.

FORMS

Form 1—Notice of motion by plaintiff to add party defendant

Form 2—Affidavit in support of plaintiff's motion to add party defendant

Form 3—Order permitting plaintiff to add party defendant

Form 4—Notice of motion to drop party defendant

Form 5—Affidavit in support of motion to drop party defendant

Form 6—Order granting motion to drop party defendant

Form 1

Notice of Motion by Plaintiff to Add Party Defendant

Notice of Motion

[Title of court and cause]　　　Index No. — [if assigned]

PLEASE TAKE NOTICE that upon the complaint (and answer) herein, and upon the annexed affidavit of __1_____, sworn to the __2__ day of __3_____, 19_4_, a motion will be made at a Motion Term of this Court, to be held in and for the County of __5_____, at the County Courthouse in the City of __6_____, on the __7__ day of __8_____, 19_9_ at __10__ o'clock in the __11_____ noon of that day, or as soon thereafter as counsel can be heard, pursuant to Section 1003 of the Civil Practice Law and Rules, for an order permitting plaintiff to amend his complaint herein by adding the name of __12_____ as a party defendant in this action, and further permitting plaintiff to serve a supplemental summons directed to the said __13_____, as provided by Section 305(a) of the Civil Practice Law and Rules, and for such other and further relief as to this court may seem just and proper, together with the costs of this motion.

　　Dated: __14_____, 19_15_.

　　　　　　　　　　　　　　　　　　　　　__16_____
　　　　　　　　　　　　　　　　　　　　　　　　　Attorney for Plaintiff
　　　　　　　　　　　　　　　　　　　　　Office and Post Office Address
　　　　　　　　　　　　　　　　　　　　　　　　　　Telephone No.

To: __17_____, Attorney for Defendant

Form 2

Affidavit in Support of Plaintiff's Motion to Add Party Defendant

　　　　　　　　　　　　　　　　Affidavit
[Title of court and cause]　　　Index No.—[if assigned]

[Venue of affidavit]

　__1_____, being duly sworn, deposes and says:

1. I am the plaintiff in the above-entitled action.

2. This action was commenced by the service of a summons and complaint herein on the defendant __2_____, on the __3__ day of __4_____, 19_5_; on the __6__ day of __7_____, 19_8_, the said defendant duly appeared herein by __9_____, his attorney, and issue was joined by the service of an answer to the complaint herein; the action was placed on the Trial Term Calendar of this Court for the __10_____, 19_11_ Term thereof by service of a Note of Issue dated the __12__ day of __13_____, 19_14_; the case now bears No. __15__ on the General Trial Calendar of this Court.

3. This action was brought by me for the recovery of damages in the sum of $__16__ for personal injuries sustained by me when struck by a certain motor vehicle bearing New York State registration No. __17__ for the year 19_18_ which vehicle was at the time of the said accident being operated by __19_____, the defendant herein.

4. The complaint alleges that __20_____, the defendant herein, was at the time of the said accident the owner of the aforedescribed vehicle, which allegations were denied by the said defendant in his answer made and filed herein.

5. Since the service of the said complaint I have discovered that the record owner of the vehicle described in the complaint herein is __21_____, the wife of the defendant __22_____, and that the said __23_____ was the owner of the said vehicle at the time the accident described in the complaint occurred, and that the defendant __24_____, does not, and did not at the time of the said accident, own any right, title or interest in or to the said vehicle.

6. At the time I commenced the said action I did not know the foregoing facts and acted upon an admission made by the defendant __25_____ at the time of the accident that he was the owner of the said vehicle.

7. I am informed by my attorney, __26_____, that __27_____, the owner of the said vehicle, is liable to me for my damages sustained in the said accident if at the time of the said accident the defendant __28_____ was operating the vehicle with the permission and consent of the said __29_____.

8. I am further advised by __30_____, my attorney, that it is desirable and necessary

that __31____ be joined as a party defendant herein to the end that all parties liable to me for damages sustained by reason of the aforesaid accident may be joined in one cause of action.

9. The joinder of __32____ in this action as a party defendant will not operate to the prejudice of either __33____ or the defendant __34____ and will not inconvenience any of the parties herein.

WHEREFORE, I request that an order be granted, pursuant to Section 1003 of the Civil Practice Law and Rules, permitting me to amend the complaint herein by adding the name of __35____ as a party defendant and permitting the service of a supplemental summons upon the said __36____.

[Signature of deponent]
[Print signer's name below signature]

[Jurat]

Form 3

Order Permitting Plaintiff to Add Party Defendant

SUPREME COURT, __1____ COUNTY.

[Title of cause]

Order
Index No. — [if assigned]

PRESENT: HON. __2____, Justice.

Plaintiff herein having moved this Court for an order pursuant to Section 1003 of the Civil Practice Law and Rules permitting the joinder as a party defendant herein of __3____, permitting plaintiff to amend the complaint made and filed herein accordingly and permitting plaintiff to serve a supplemental summons and amended complaint and for such other and further relief as may be just and proper;

Now, therefore, upon reading and filing notice of motion herein dated the __4__ of __5____, 19_6_, the affidavit of __7____, sworn to the __8__ day of __9____, 19_10_, and the complaint and answer made and filed herein all in support of said motion, and upon reading and filing the affidavit of __11____, duly sworn to the __12__ day of __13____, 19_14_, in opposition thereto and after hearing __15____, Esq., attorney for the plaintiff, in support of said motion, and __16____, Esq., attorney for defendant, in opposition thereto, and due deliberation having been had, now, on motion of __17____, attorney for the plaintiff, it is

ORDERED, that said motion be and the same hereby is in all respects granted, and it is further

ORDERED, that __18____, be and he hereby is joined as a party defendant in this action, and it is further

ORDERED, that the plaintiff be and he hereby is authorized to serve an amended complaint upon the defendant herein naming the said __19____ as an additional party defendant, and it is further

ORDERED, that the plaintiff be and he hereby is permitted to serve a supplemental summons and amended complaint upon the said __20____, said supplemental summons and amended complaint together with a copy of this order with notice of entry thereof to be served upon __21____, and upon the attorney for __22____, the defendant herein, within twenty days from the date of the signing and entry of this order, and it is further

ORDERED, that all the said defendants shall have twenty days from the date of service of the supplemental summons and amended complaint within which to put in such answers to said amended complaint as they may be advised.

Signed this __23__ day of __24_____, 19_25_ at __26_____, New York.
Enter.

__27_____
Justice, Supreme Court
__28_____ County

Form 4

Notice of Motion to Drop Party Defendant

Notice of Motion

[Title of court and cause]   Index No. — [if assigned]

PLEASE TAKE NOTICE that upon the complaint herein and upon the annexed affidavit of __1_____, sworn to the __2__ day of __3_____, 19_4_, a motion will be made at a Motion Term of this Court to be held in and for the County of __5_____, at the County Courthouse in the City of __6_____, on the __7__ day of __8_____, 19_9_ at __10__ o'clock in the __11_____ noon of that day or as soon thereafter as counsel can be heard for an order amending the complaint herein by striking out the name of __12_____ as a party defendant on the ground that there is a misjoinder of party defendants in that the said __13_____, named as a defendant in this action, is not a necessary or a proper party defendant, and for such other and further relief as may be just.

Dated: __14_____, 19_15_.

__16_____
Attorney for Defendant __17_____
Office and Post Office Address
Telephone No. __18__

To: __19_____, Attorney for defendant

Form 5

Affidavit in Support of Motion to Drop Party Defendant

Affidavit

[Title of court and cause]   Index No.   [if assigned]

[Venue of affidavit]

__1_____, being duly sworn, deposes and says:

1. He is one of the defendants named in the above-entitled action.

2. This action was commenced against the deponent by the service of a summons and complaint upon him on the __2__ day of __3_____, 19_4_. The deponent duly appeared in the action by __5_____ and __6_____, his attorneys, on the __7__ day of __8_____, 19_9_, and issue was joined herein on the __10__ day of __11_____, 19_12_, by the service of an answer upon the attorneys for the plaintiff.

3. [Set forth facts showing the nature of the action and deponent's defense thereto as set forth in his answer.]

4. [Set forth facts showing that deponent is neither a necessary nor a proper party defendant or that the hardship and prejudice to defendant's rights outweigh the desirability of joining him in the action.]

5. The rights of the plaintiff herein and the other defendants will not be prejudiced or injured by the granting of the relief sought herein.

[Signature of deponent]
[Print signer's name below signature]

[Jurat]

Form 6

Order Granting Motion to Drop Party Defendant

SUPREME COURT, __1_____ COUNTY.

[Title of cause]
Order
Index No. — [if assigned]

PRESENT: HON. __2_____, Justice.

A motion having been made by the defendant __3_____, for an order amending the complaint herein by striking out the name of __4_____ as a defendant in this action on the ground that there has been a misjoinder of party defendants and said motion having come on regularly to be heard,

Now, upon reading and filing the notice of motion dated the __5__ day of __6_____, 19_7_, with proof of due service thereof, the affidavit of __8_____, sworn to the __9__ day of __10_____, 19_11_, and the pleadings and proceedings heretofore had herein in support of said motion, and the affidavit of __12_____, sworn to the __13__ day of __14_____, 19_15_, in opposition thereto, and after hearing __16_____, attorney for the defendant __17_____ in support of said motion, and __18_____, attorney of plaintiff in opposition thereto, and due deliberation having been had,

Now, on motion of __19_____, attorney for the defendant __20_____, it is

ORDERED, that the said motion be and the same hereby is in all respects granted, and it is further

ORDERED, that the complaint in this action be and the same hereby is amended by striking out __21_____ as a party defendant in this action and it is further

ORDERED, that the said defendant __22_____, have $__23__ costs of this motion.

Signed this __24__ day of __25_____, 19_26_ at __27_____, New York.

Enter.

__28_____
[Print signer's name below signature]
Justice, Supreme Court
__29_____ County

§ 1004. When joinder unnecessary

Except where otherwise prescribed by order of the court, an executor, administrator, guardian of the property of an infant, committee of the property of a judicially declared incompetent, trustee of an express trust, insured person who has executed to his insurer either a loan or subrogation receipt, trust agreement, or other similar agreement, or person with whom or in whose name a contract has been made for the benefit of another, may sue or be sued without joining with him the person for or against whose interest the action is brought.

HISTORY:

Add, L 1962, ch 308, amd, L 1963, ch 532, § 10, eff Sept 1, 1963.
See 1963 note under § 1001.
Earlier statutes: CPA § 210; CCP § 449.

ADVISORY COMMITTEE NOTES:

The first part of CPA § 210, relating to real party in interest, is omitted for the following reasons: (1) it is unnecessary since the law would be the same without any express rule, (2) it is an inept statement of an obvious principle of substantive law, (3) it misleadingly seems to say that the action must be brought by the party to be benefited, and (4) the second part of the section is not an exception to the first part as therein stated.

This section preserves the second part of CPA § 210 and, indeed, extends it by declaring that the beneficiary need not be joined in actions against, as well as by, the enumerated fiduciaries. Cf. Wis State § 260.15 (1945); NJ R Civ P 40:30-1. The entire rule is declaratory and hence not vital, but, unlike the "real party in interest" provision, it is helpful and not misleading. The advisory committee considered but did not accept the suggestion that the section be extended to general and testamentary guardians and committees. Cf. CPA §§ 1377, 1523; Fed R Civ P 17(a).

There is authority in New York that the beneficiaries of a trust should be joined with the trustee in an action to set aside the trust, although it is doubtful if the beneficiaries are indispensable. See McKnight v Bank of New York & Trust Co. 254 NY 417, 173 NE 569 (1930). With this possibility in mind, it is provided in this section that the rule excusing joinder of the beneficiary does not apply if the court orders otherwise. The court might even be justified in ordering joinder of the beneficiaries when the action is brought *by* the fiduciary. No reason is apparent why different general rules should apply for plaintiffs and defendants.

The entire category of persons authorized by statute has been eliminated as unnecessary, since, if a particular statute authorizes the name action, no further authority is necessary.

The concluding clause of Federal rule 17(a) is "and when a statute of the United States so provides, an action for the use or benefit of another shall be brought in the name of the United States." This provision is related to the real party in interest portion of the rule rather than the provision excusing joinder of beneficiaries. It is entirely unnecessary in view of the fact that the portion of the New York section relating to the real party in interest has been eliminated.

CROSS REFERENCES:
Executors and administrators, EPTL §§ 11-4.1, 11-4.4.
Holder of negotiable instrument, UCC § 3-301.

FEDERAL ASPECTS:
Pleading reasons for nonjoinder, Rule 19(c) of Federal Rules of Civil Procedure, USCS Court Rules.

RESEARCH REFERENCES AND PRACTICE AIDS:
3 NY Jur, Assignments §§ 12, 15.
9 NY Jur, Contractors' Bonds § 27.
31 NY Jur, Insurance §§ 1622, 1634.
3 Carmody-Wait 2d, Parties §§ 19:28, 19:29, 19:44, 19:46, 19:55.
7 Carmody-Wait 2d, Disclosure § 42:34.
44 Am Jur 2d, Insurance §§ 1849 et seq.
59 Am Jur 2d, Parties §§ 95 et seq.
3 Am Jur Pl and Pr Forms (Rev ed), Automobile Insurance, Forms 181–191.
10 Am Jur Legal Forms 2d, Insurance, Forms 149:191–149:194.

Annotations:
Insured as indispensable or necessary party in federal court action between his liability insurer and actual or potential tort-claimants. 8 ALR Fed 738.

Law Reviews:
New York Civil Practice Law and Rules: parties. 27 Albany L Rev 182.
Parties and pleading under the CPLR. 31 Brooklyn L Rev 98.

Forms:
See "FORMS" heading following "CASE NOTES", infra.

CASE NOTES

1. In general; real parties in interest
2. Fiduciaries
3. Insureds
4. Third party beneficiaries

1. In general; real parties in interest

Although the statute governing practice no longer requires that an action must be prosecuted by the real party in interest, that requirement has not been stricken from the law and the failure to allege facts showing that the plaintiff is the real party in interest still renders the complaint fatally defective. Carvel Farms Corp. v Bartomeo (1965) 50 Misc 2d 1073, 272 NYS2d 507.

The plaintiff could maintain its action against the defendant carrier for failure to deliver a property shipment received from the plaintiff where the allegation that the plaintiff was not the real party in interest was presented only in the opposing affidavit, was not supported by any factual background and was not set forth in the answer, and even if the defense had been properly presented, CPLR § 1004 covered the point and permitted such action. David Crystal, Inc. v Ehrlich-Newmark Truck Co. (1970) 64 Misc 2d 325, 314 NYS2d 559.

2. Fiduciaries

An escrow agent to whom a house buyer delivered a check to secure principal's performance of repairs to a new house under escrow agreement was a "holder" under UCC § 1-201 subd 20 and entitled to sue on subsequently dishonored check under CPLR § 1004 not only as the promisee of a third party beneficiary contract, but also as trustee for the principal. Helman v Dixon (1972) 71 Misc 2d 1057, 338 NYS2d 139 (1972).

3. Insureds

Bailor of goods destroyed by fire was entitled to maintain action against bailee despite contention that real party was bailor's insurance company, and bailee was in no position to complain so long as it was not subjected to double recovery. Philip Wick Co. v Lee Dyeing Co. (1972) 71 Misc 2d 82, 335 NYS2d 619, affd 41 AD2d 905, 343 NYS2d 595.

To establish the defense that the plaintiff is not the real party in interest it must appear that the plaintiff was divested of his cause of action by payment of his claim in full, but where only a portion of the claim is paid, the insured remains the real party in interest entitled to prosecute an action against the wrongdoer. Skinner v Klein (1965) 24 AD2d 433, 260 NYS2d 799.

Motion to dismiss under CPLR § 3211, subd a(10) for failure to join alleged real party in interest, plaintiff's subrogated insurance carrier, was denied pursuant to CPLR § 1004. Feeter v Van Scott Bros., Inc. (1973) 74 Misc 2d 388, 345 NYS2d 374.

Affirmative defense that electric corporation, by virtue of partial recovery from its insurance carrier, was no longer real party in interest, must fail because of electric corporation's subrogation-type agreement authorized under CPLR 1004. Rockaway Boulevard Wrecking & Lumber Co. v Raylite Electric Corp. (1966) 25 AD2d 842, 270 NYS2d 1.

Automobile buyer had no cause of action under CPLR 1004 to recover for his own benefit third party claims for property damage paid by his insurer, which claims had arisen out of an accident caused by failure of the brakes on his automobile. Kracker v Myrtle Motors Corp. (1972) 70 Misc 2d 365, 332 NYS2d 757.

4. Third party beneficiaries

An escrow agent to whom a house buyer delivered a check to secure principal's performance of repairs to a new house under escrow agreement was a "holder" under UCC § 1-201 subd 20 and entitled to sue on subsequently dishonored check under CPLR § 1004 not only as the promisee of a third party beneficiary contract, but also as trustee for the principal. Helman v Dixon (1972) 71 Misc 2d 1057, 338 NYS2d 139.

Where the sponsor of a television program canceled its contract with the network, the network had a right to sue for the total amount due under the contract notwithstanding that it was required to pay a substantial portion of those charges to independent affiliated stations and it was unnecessary to invoke the authority of the provisions of CPLR 1004. American Broadcasting-Paramount Theatres, Inc. v American Mfrs. Mut. Ins. Co. (1965) 48 Misc 2d 397, 265 NYS2d 76, affd 24 AD2d 851, 265 NYS2d 577, affd 17 NY2d 849, 271 NYS2d 284, 218 NE2d 324, cert den 385 US 931, 17 L Ed 2d 213, 87 S Ct 291.

In action by former husband against former wife and her present husband to compel an accounting for moneys supplied by him to them for the support of their infant children pursuant to the terms of a foreign divorce incorporating a separation agreement, the court deemed that in the interest of justice the infants should be joined through a guardian ad litem as party plaintiff, whether or not they were necessary parties, but in no event should the complaint be dismissed for nonjoinder of infants. Rosenblatt v Birnbaum (1963) 20 AD2d 556, 245 NYS2d 72, affd 16 NY2d 212, 264 NYS2d 521, 212 NE2d 37.

Where, by agreement between plaintiff and brother, brother undertook to make certain irrevocable testamentary provisions for the benefit of named sisters and nephews, joinder of sisters and nephews was not mandatory in action alleging that deceased brother's probated will violated agreement and for specific performance thereof, nor was such joinder required by the circumstance that plaintiff was prosecuting other, unrelated, causes of action against the estate of deceased brother for his own benefit. Katsh v Katsh (1965) 23 AD2d 494, 255 NYS2d 916, affd 17 NY2d 453, 266 NYS2d 811, 213 NE2d 891.

Membership corporation which was bargaining representative of noncommissioned state policemen and which entered agreement with state under which state contracted to introduce legislation qualifying certain class of state policemen for additional salary benefits could sue state only for specific performance of agreement; right to maintain action for money damages against state for breach of agreement belonged to association members who have been damaged by state's action. Police Benev. Asso. of New York State Police, Inc. v State (1974) 79 Misc 2d 334, 358 NYS2d 280.

CASE NOTES

UNDER FORMER CIVIL PRACTICE LAWS

1. Generally
2. Actions under particular statutes
3. Agents
4. —For collection
5. —Attorneys in fact
6. Aliens
7. Annulment of marriage
8. Assignee and assignor
9. —Assignment for benefit of creditors
10. Association of employers
11. Attorneys at law
12. Auctions and auctioneers
13. Bailment
14. Banks
15. —Bank absorbed by foreign government
16. Bills and notes
17. —Checks and coupons
18. Bondholders' committee
19. Bonds and undertakings by sureties
20. Brokers
21. Carriers
22. Civil Damage Act
23. Committee of incompetent
24. Consignor and consignee
25. Contract
26. Contract for benefit of another; generally
27. —Beneficiary of policy
28. —Beneficiary of trust
29. —Unilateral contract
30. —Wager
31. Conversion of property
32. Corporations
33. —Stockholders
34. —Municipal corporations
35. Covenants
36. Derivative action
37. Executors and administrators
38. —Foreign representatives
39. Factor
40. Forcible entry and detainer
41. Foreign government
42. Guardians and wards

43. Heirs, devisees and legatees
44. Injunction
45. Insurance; generally
46. Insurer suing third party
47. Insurer with loan or subrogation receipt or trust agreement
48. —Decisions prior to 1950 amendment
49. Insurance carrier; workmen's compensation
50. Master of vessel
51. Partners
52. Penalties
53. Performance of public duty
54. Pledges and collaterals
55. Public officers
56. Real property actions
57. Receivers
58. Restraining nuisance
59. States
60. Statutes
61. Subscriptions
62. —To corporate stock
63. Tenants in common
64. Trustees of an express trust
65. —Testamentary trustees
66. —Several trustees
67. —Agents as trustees
68. Trust beneficiaries
69. Widow suing to set aside husband's fraudulent transfer

1. Generally

Where plaintiff is shown to be without a justiciable right capable of enforcement, he has no status in an action and no legal capacity to sue and his complaint must be dismissed. Revici v Conference of Jewish Material Claims Against Germany, Inc. (1958) 11 Misc 2d 354, 174 NYS2d 825.

2. Actions under particular statutes

An action to set aside an order of labor department, under Labor Law, former § 52a, could not be prosecuted by an agent. Scheier v Mitchell (1919) 188 AD 182, 176 NYS 597.

It was assumed that three employees of defendant may sue on behalf of other employees to recover overtime wages under Fair Labor Standards Act, as being authorized to do so by such Act. Simmons v Rudolph Knitting Mills, Inc. (1942) 264 AD 871, 35 NYS2d 494.

3. Agents

A principal can enforce the contracts of his agent, although upon the face of the papers the agent was the apparent party. Indianapolis P. & C. R. Co. v Tyng (1876) 63 NY 653.

When a contract, not under seal, was made with an agent in his own name, for an undisclosed principal, whether he described himself as agent or not, either the agent or principal could sue upon it. Ludwig v Gillespie (1887) 105 NY 653, 1 NE 835.

Selling agents who make a contract for the sale of merchandise in their own name and with whom all the dealings with regard to the contract are had, including claims and adjustments, as well as part payments, may sue on the contract as plaintiffs. Watts v Phillips-Jones Corp. (1925) 211 AD 523, 207 NYS 493, affd 242 NY 557, 152 NE 425, reh den 242 NY 601, 152 NE 445.

An action to recover commissions under a contract for sale of real estate entered into between defendant and plaintiff, named as agent for a named principal, cannot be brought by the agent in his own name, the pleading and proof indicating a lack of identity between plaintiff and the principal and failing to indicate that plaintiff was subrogated to the rights of the principal, and the complaint alleging that plaintiff made the contract solely in his own interest, plaintiff not being trustee of an express trust. Wells v Merrill (1923) 204 AD 696, 198 NYS 496.

Where a contract, not under seal, was made with an agent in his own name, for an undisclosed principal, whether he described himself as agent or not, either the agent or principal could sue upon it. Ludwig v Gillespie (1887) 105 NY 653, 11 NE 835.

Where contract was between author and producer, one who was merely agent in this country and whose only interest was a stipulated percentage of collections and 50 per cent of the profits was not a "person with whom or in whose name a contract is made for the benefit of another." Karczag Pub. Co. v Shubert Theatrical Co. (1918) 181 AD 529, 169 NYS 1.

Donee of power of attorney may not maintain in his own name proceedings supplementary to judgment, formerly required. Catrakis v Jaris (1952) 280 AD 414, 114 NYS2d 225.

As to actions by agents. See Poor v Guilford (1851) 10 NY 272; Clark v Chase Nat. Bank (1942) 45 F Supp 820.

An agent for one of the parties to a sales contract did not have implied authority to compel arbitration under the contract. Re Application of Eimco Corp. (1957) 6 Misc 2d 422, 163 NYS2d 273.

Where a complaint alleged that the plaintiff was an agency of Argentina and it was dismissed since it was defective on its face since it did not appear that plaintiff was a person or a corporation and thus there was no showing that plaintiff had capacity to sue, a new allegation in an amended complaint that under the laws of Argentina plaintiff had the right to sue does not cure the defect, such allegation is both conclusory and irrelevant. Argentine Airlines v Aircraft Dynamics Corp (1957) 9 Misc 2d 272, 170 NYS2d 600.

4. —For collection

The fact that an individual assignee is constituted a collecting agent does not disable him to sue upon and collect in his own name. Gellens v 11 West 42nd Street, Inc. (1940) 259 AD 435, 19 NYS2d 525, overruling Federal Credit Bureau v Zelkor Dining Car Corp. (1933) 238 AD 379, 264 NYS 723.

Where one joint owner of a claim employs, with the assent of the others, an agent to collect it, an action is properly brought in his name alone to recover the sums collected. Noe v Christie (1873) 51 NY 270.

An agent or attorney to whom a claim is transferred as collateral to a note which he holds for collection, may sue on such claim. Poor v Guilford (1851) 10 NY 272.

5. —Attorneys in fact

Attorney in fact, without personal interest in litigation, may sue in name of principal, but not in own name; such rule applies to action for declaratory judgment. Jurnas v National City Bank (1947) 190 Misc 854, 76 NYS2d 330.

One who is merely authorized to collect a claim belonging to a party, solely for the latter's benefit, and to transmit it to him, is an attorney in fact not authorized to sue in his own name. Spencer v Standard Chemicals & Metals Corp. (1924) 237 NY 479, 143 NE 651.

6. Aliens

An alien friend may sue to protect his literary property. Palmer v De Witt (1872) 47 NY 532.

But the rule that alien enemies could not sue during the rebellion, applied to citizens of the seceded states. Sanderson v Morgan (1868) 39 NY 231.

7. Annulment of marriage

While CPA § 210 permitted a parent to maintain an action on behalf of the child without making the latter a plaintiff, it did not justify the prosecution of an action for annulment of a marriage without joining the child as a defendant. Feldman v Intrator (1941) 175 Misc 632, 24 NYS2d 665.

8. Assignee and assignor

To sue on an assigned claim in his own name the assignee must have some title, legal or equitable, to the thing assigned; if he has such title the consideration paid, the purpose of the assignment, or the use to be made of any proceeds collected, is immaterial. Spencer v Standard Chemical & Metals Corp. (1924) 237 NY 479, 143 NE 651.

Court may join assignee as coplaintiff where cause of action has been assigned since the commencement of the action. Buck Ridge Coal Mining Co. v Rosoff Engineering Co. (1926) 215 AD 441, 214 NYS 60.

Assignee of claim in favor of one of two joint executors may maintain action thereon against them. Snyder v Snyder (1884) 96 NY 88.

Paupers could assign chose in action to overseer of the poor to indemnify him in his official capacity for expenses he might incur in pauper's behalf. Officers could bring action thereon. Church v Fanning (1887) 44 Hun 302.

A recovery upon a claim which originally belonged to another is not justified where there is no proof of an assignment. Vestner v Findlay (1894) 10 Misc 410, 31 NYS 138.

A plaintiff, who has assigned his claim against the defendants, who have had notice of the assignment, cannot maintain an action thereon, as there is no claim then existing in his favor; nor will a reassignment of said claim to plaintiff after the commencement of his action create such cause of action, as the reassignment has no retroactive effect. Walsh v Woarms (1905) 109 AD 166, 95 NYS 824.

When a person has transferred his entire interest in a cause of action to another, he cannot be joined with such transferee as a party plaintiff. Alexander v Gloversville (1906) 110 AD 791, 97 NYS 198.

Assignee must sue in his own name after assignment of entire claim to him. Massi v Alben Builders, Inc. (1946) 270 AD 482, 60 NYS2d 494, affd 296 NY 767, 70 NE2d 746.

Absolute assignment makes assignee proper party. Heitzmann v Willys-Overland Motors, Inc. (1946, DC NY) 68 F Supp 873.

Under CPA § 210 and § 41 of the Personal Property Law, an assignment of a chose in action for the purpose of suit only and obligating the assignee to account for the proceeds to another enables the assignee to sue in his own name. Titus v Wallick (1939) 306 US 282, 83 L Ed 653, 59 S Ct 557.

Assignee is proper party, though assignment recites transfer is merely for purposes of suit and obligates assignee to account for proceeds to another. Heitzmann v Willys-Overland Motors, Inc. (1946, DC NY) 68 F Supp 873.

Under the Penal Law a corporation is prohibited from accepting assignment of a claim for the purpose of bringing an action thereon, but an assignment for that purpose to an individual is legal provided he is not engaged directly or indirectly in the business of collection and adjustment of claims. Gellens v 11 West 42nd St. Inc. (1940) 259 AD 435, 19 NYS2d 525.

Assignee of an absolute and complete assignment is the real party in interest and may maintain an action thereon without joining the assignor. Dumpson v Cohen (1961) 14 AD2d 871, 221 NYS2d 762.

9. —Assignment for benefit of creditors

While an assignment for the benefit of creditors remains in force, the right to attack previous conveyances executed by the assignor on the ground that they are fraudulent as against creditors, rests not in the creditors themselves, but in the assignee. It is only by virtue of a valid assignment, that the assignee acquires that right. Loos v Wilkinson (1888) 110 NY 195, 18 NE 99, later app 113 NY 485, 21 NE 392; Webster v Lawrence, 15 NYSR 140; Smith v Payne (1889) 56 NY Super Ct 451, 3 NYS 826; Strickland v Laraway (1890, Sup) 9 NYS 761.

It seems, that if an assignee for creditors refuses, in a proper case, to proceed and get in the assigned property, the creditors collectively, or one in behalf of all who may come in and join, may compel the execution of the trust in equity, or may cause the removal of the assignee and the appointment of another. Crouse v Frothingham (1884) 97 NY 105.

An assignee of a demand in trust to pay certain credits of the assignor and the balance to the assignor himself, may bring an action in his own name, to recover loss on insurance policy. Mellen v Hamilton Fire Ins. Co. (1858) 17 NY 609.

Until an assignee for the benefit of creditors has qualified, his refusal to sue to set aside as fraudulent a subsequent conveyance by the debtor cannot give the judgment creditors the right to maintain such suit. Mills v Goodenough (1890, Sup) 9 NYS 764.

After a valid assignment for benefit of creditors, a judgment creditor who has acquired no lien on the personal property of the assignors, cannot maintain an action to set aside chattel mortgages executed in good faith for valid consideration by the assignor prior to the assignment, but which are void as against plaintiff because of nonfiling. Kitchen v Lowery (1891) 127 NY 53, 27 NE 357.

The purchaser under execution of property assigned for the benefit of creditors, has no right to contest prior encumbrances on the property, as the assignment remains in force, notwithstanding the sale of the assignor's interest in the property, and such right is in the assignee. Tremaine v Mortimer (1889) 57 NY Super Ct 340, 7 NYS 681, affd 128 NY 1, 27 NE 1060.

An action may be maintained by creditors at large to restrain the sheriff who has levied upon the property of an assignee for creditors, under judgments confessed on the same day of the assignment, from disposing of the proceeds, to have the judgments declared void; and the property levied upon declared a part of the assigned estate. Spelman v Jaffray (1888, Sup) 6 NYS 570, affd Spelman v Freedman, 54 Hun 409, 7 NYS 698, affd 130 NY 421, 29 NE 765.

10. Association of employers

Plaintiff, an incorporated association of employers had legal capacity to sue for an injunction. Associated Painting Employers, Inc. v Kessler (1939) 257 AD 986, 13 NYS2d 631.

11. Attorneys at law

Plaintiff is entitled to maintain the action where the complaint alleges that without the consent of his client he delivered to defendant, also an attorney, a release of a mortgage to be held in escrow and that, in violation of the escrow agreement by defendant, an innocent purchaser acquired the property, whereupon plaintiff became obligated to pay his client the sum claimed as damages. Marks v Rubinton (1932) 144 Misc 324, 258 NYS 719.

In an action for compensation under two manager-agent contracts made between plaintiff's assignor and defendant, defense that plaintiff was an attorney and had received assignment of the causes of action for the purpose of bringing action thereon was sufficient. Broder v Brasselle (1957) 7 Misc 2d 13, 164 NYS2d 142.

12. Auctions and auctioneers

Where the terms of sale made by an auctioneer require the fees to be paid by the purchaser, he may maintain an action against the purchaser, for such fees in his own name. Miller v Burke (1877) 68 NY 615.

13. Bailment

A common carrier may sue for an injury to property entrusted to him to be carried. Merrick v Van Santvoord (1866) 34 NY 208.

Either the general owner of property, or a bailee having a special interest therein can maintain an action for an injury to or conversion of it. Green v Clarke (1855) 12 NY 343.

A hotel guest who is a gratuitous bailee of property has an action against the hotel keeper for its loss. Kellogg v Sweeney (1871) 46 NY 291.

14. Banks

A banking association formed under a general banking law may sue in the name of its president, or in its corporate name. Leonardsville Bank v Willard (1862) 25 NY 574.

15. —Bank absorbed by foreign government

In an action by directors of a Russian bank, the assets and liabilities of which had been merged with another, which in turn had been abolished and its functions transferred to the Soviet government, defense that plaintiff had no juristic existence was sustained and complaint dismissed. Banque Internationale v National City Bank (1929) 133 Misc 527, 233 NYS 255, affd 226 AD 866, 235 NYS 862, revd 253 NY 23, 170 NE 479.

16. Bills and notes

A colorable title to a note will support action upon it. Green v Swink, 9 NYSR 646, 26 NY Week Dig 574.

To entitle a party to maintain an action upon a promissory note he must be the legal owner and have the right of possession of the instrument; such ownership must be sufficient to protect the defendant upon a recovery against him, from a subsequent action thereon. Hays v Hathorn (1878) 74 NY 486; Freeman v Falconer, 45 Super Ct (13 Jones & S) 383.

Where a promissory note is, by its terms, made payable to a party who is the agent of the real owner thereof, such payee of the note becomes a trustee of an express trust, and an action is properly brought in his name to enforce payment thereof. Hollingsworth v Moulton (1889) 53 Hun 91, 6 NYS 362, affd 119 NY 612, 23 NE 1143.

Payee in note given to payee for the benefit of another may bring action in his own name. Hoxie v Kennedy, 10 NYSR 786.

Where an attorney, employed to collect judgments, obtains from the judgment debtor promissory notes aggregating the amount of the judgments and the expenses of collection upon his representation to the debtor that the creditors will not accept less, and subsequently induces the judgment creditors to satisfy the judgments upon the receipt of a portion only of such notes, representing that such is the best settlement he can obtain, and the attorney subsequently transfers the notes retained to one not a bona fide holder for value, such transferee may maintain an action upon the notes. Crouch v Wagner (1901) 63 AD 526, 71 NYS 607.

Where principal under agreement had title to machines furnished agent until settled for, and agent sold machine and took note payable to principal but later paid the principal for the machine, the principal, though having no interest in the machine or its proceeds, could have maintained an action under CPA § 210 on the note for the benefit of the agent. International Harvester Co. v Champlin (1913) 155 AD 847, 140 NYS 842.

Payee's indorsement and delivery of note in blank and its production by plaintiff, constitute prima facie evidence of plaintiff's ownership and capacity to sue. Kots v Sachs (1945) 185 Misc 224, 57 NYS2d 622.

17. —Checks and coupons

Where a bank accepted a check for deposit with the restriction "Checks credited subject to payment," it nevertheless was a holder of the check within the meaning of Negotiable Instruments Law §§ 2 and 90, and as such entitled to maintain an action thereon in its own name. Mechanics & Metals Nat. Bank v Termini (1921) 117 Misc 309, 191 NYS 334.

Bonds and interest coupons construed in connection with the resolution providing for their issuance, and held that the holder of interest coupons could maintain an action to enforce collection of interest in default. Goodjohn v United Bond & Bldg. Corp. (1929) 226 AD 137, 234 NYS 522.

18. Bondholders' committee

For right of committee representing a small minority of railroad bonds to maintain an action against the opposition of the trustees alleging defaults under the indenture securing the bonds, see Campbell v Hudson & M. R. Co. (1954) 307 NY 618, 120 NE2d 827.

19. Bonds and undertakings by sureties

An action upon an official bond of a treasurer and tax receiver of a city for an alleged misappropriation of moneys belonging to the school fund is properly brought by and in the name of the board of education, although the city was named as obligee. Board of Education v Quick (1885) 99 NY 138, 1 NE 533.

An action on the bond of a county treasurer to recover moneys of an infant, converted by him to his own use, is properly brought in the name of the board of supervisors, for the benefit of the infant. Board of Supervisors v Bristol (1885) 99 NY 316, 1 NE 878.

A failure of the county treasurer to invest railroad taxes in a sinking fund for the payment of bonds issued by a town in aid of such railroads is an injury to a property right of such town, and an action therefor is maintainable by its supervisor. Strough v Board of Supervisors (1890) 119 NY 212, 23 NE 552; Wood v Board of Supervisors (1888) 50 Hun 1, 2 NYS 369.

When actions on undertaking on appeal cannot be brought by attorney in his client's name. Kipp v Rapp, 7 Civ Proc 385.

An action upon the promise or undertaking of a putative father to support a child may be brought by the child in her own name. Todd v Weber (1884) 95 NY 181.

The attorney for plaintiff is not a necessary party to an action on an undertaking given upon appeal, even though his lien should extend to the whole amount of his recovery. Wadley v Poucher (1890, Sup) 9 NYS 50.

A public administrator who has succeeded to the rights of a special administrator, and to whom the bond of the latter has been duly assigned for prosecution, may bring an action as public administrator on the bond. Dayton v Johnson (1877) 69 NY 419.

As to the party plaintiff in an action upon an administrator's bond, see Nanz v Oakley (1890) 122 NY 631, 25 NE 263.

The people may sue on a trustee's bond. People v Norton (1853) 9 NY 176. See Dayton v Johnson (1877) 69 NY 419.

After leave obtained to prosecute, one of the parties for whose benefit the bond of an executor and testamentary trustee was given, may maintain an action thereon in his own name. Haight v Brisbin (1885) 36 Hun 579, revd 100 NY 219, 3 NE 74.

Where special circumstances exist, legatees under a will may enforce by order of the Surrogate, a bond given by a nonresident executor, although the legacies are not immediately payable, but where the legacies have been assigned the assignees are necessary parties. Hood v Hood (1881) 85 NY 561.

20. Brokers

Where broker contracts as such for named principal and alleges no special interest in such contract, he cannot sue for breach of contract or for fraud. Moise Prod. Co. v William Faehndrich, Inc. (1955, Sup) 140 NYS2d 49.

Where broker contracts as such for named principal, benefit and obligations attach only to principal, who alone has right to sue, and absent showing of special interest in contract, broker cannot sue. Moise Prod. Co. v William Faehndrich, supra.

21. Carriers

Plaintiff carrier was a proper party plaintiff notwithstanding it did not own or operate vessel involved in accident where contract was made by plaintiff carrier in its own name and all dealings were had with it. Ibrandtsen Co. v Lyncroft Grain Corp. (1957) 8 Misc 2d 521, 166 NYS2d 721.

22. Civil Damage Act

Anyone may bring an action, under Laws 1873, ch 646, known as the Civil Damage Act (now Civ RL § 16) against the persons therein named, who is injured in person, property or means of support by any intoxicated persons, or in consequence of such intoxication. Jackson v Brookins (1875) 5 Hun 530.

Married women are within the class of persons authorized to maintain actions under the Civil Damage Act (Civ RL § 16). Morenus v Crawford (1889) 51 Hun 89, 5 NYS 453.

23. Committee of incompetent

All suits affecting the person or property of a lunatic must be prosecuted in his own name, except those which are authorized by statute to be brought in the name of the committee. McKillip v McKillip, 8 Barb 552. See also Petrie v Shoemaker, 24 Wend 85; Lane & Gros v Schermerhorn, 1 Hill 97.

The committee may sue in his own name on promissory note received as such committee. Davis v Carpenter, 12 How Pr 287.

The son of a grantor who alleges that transfer of real property was made while the grantor was incompetent is not a proper party to bring the action to set aside the conveyance and only the grantor or subsequent appointed committee may move to set aside such conveyance. Roens v Ratkin (1958) 11 Misc 2d 855, 173 NYS2d 101.

24. Consignor and consignee

The consignee is the presumptive owner of goods shipped, but an action may be maintained by the consignor, if he remains the owner. Price v Powell (1850) 3 NY 322.

Where goods purchased under a contract, void by the statute of frauds, were delivered at a railroad depot marked for the purchaser at another station on the road, but were destroyed by fire with the depot before shipment, held, that the shipper could maintain an action for the loss, but the consignee could not, as he acquired no title. O'Neill v New York, C. & H. R. R. Co. (1875) 60 NY 138.

Where an agent traveling with goods of his principal to sell, contracts for their transportation, and pays therefor, in his own name but on account of and in the conduct of the business of his principal, the latter may sue in his own name for loss of such goods. Sloman v Great Western R. Co. (1876) 67 NY 208.

The forwarder of money collected for another cannot maintain an action against an express company for its nondelivery. Thompson v Fargo (1872) 49 NY 188.

25. Contract

Party to contract, where made by and in his name, may sue thereon, though arrangement may have been in part for benefit of partnership. Roth v Ward (1952) 112 NYS2d 154.

Contract giving agent power to sell lot to any purchaser, as specified price, did not entitle agent to sue for specific performance of contract. Presbrey-Leland, Inc. v Semple (1952) 200 Misc 1116, 109 NYS2d 259.

Plaintiff may sue for balance due under contract for sale of his stock of corporation organized by his father and defendant, who counterclaimed for accounting on theory that plaintiff acted only as father's agent. Kelly v Rathburn (1942) 265 AD 883, 38 NYS2d 391.

Lawyer who paid excessive charges to official stenographer for transcript could recover in action in his own name, though he represented another. Hale v McDermott (1912) 78 Misc 52, 137 NYS 975.

Declaratory judgment serves legitimate purpose only when all persons who may be affected thereby and who may question in court existence and scope of rights declared are parties to action and have opportunity to be heard. Cadman Memorial Congregational Soc. v Kenyon (1952) 279 AD 1015, 1074, 111 NYS2d 808, affd 306 NY 151, 116 NE2d 481.

26. Contract for benefit of another; generally

Where the consideration of a bond proceeds from a third party, who is acting in the name and for the benefit of the obligee, such obligee is a party to the contract in such a sense as to be entitled to the proper remedies to reform or to collect the same. Nevius v Dunlap (1865) 33 NY 676.

Person named in contract may sue thereon, though contract was for benefit of another. Fleschner Bros. v Consolidated Edison Co. (1950) 202 Misc 617, 117 NYS2d 212, revd on other grounds 279 AD 69, 107 NYS2d 598, affd 304 NY 815, 109 NE2d 471.

Where a plaintiff seeks to base his right to maintain his action upon a contract made between defendant and another it must appear by the contract that it was made or intended for his benefit. Beveridge v New York El. R. Co. (1889) 112 NY 1, 19 NE 489, 2 LRA 648. The mere fact that some benefit might result to the third party

by performance of the contract is insufficient. Simson v Brown (1887) 68 NY 355.

An individual injured by breach of contract made by another individual with the state, may sue such contractor for damages. Little v Banks (1881) 85 NY 258.

If one person contract, whether with or without seal, with another, for the benefit of a third person, such third person may maintain an action in his own name on the assessment. Lawrence v Fox (1859) 20 NY 268; Coster v Albany (1871) 43 NY 399.

A person for whose benefit a promise is made cannot, within the case of Lawrence v Fox (1859) (20 NY 268), maintain an action to enforce the promise when the promise is void as between the promisor and the promisee. Dunning v Leavitt (1881) 85 NY 30.

Where an agreement was entered into between two insurance companies by which one company agreed to pay whatever became due to policy holders in the other, held that a policy holder could maintain an action thereon. Glen v Hope Mut. L. Ins. Co. (1874) 56 NY 379; Fischer v Hope Mut. L. Ins. Co. (1877) 69 NY 161.

The purchaser of lands on sale under execution after the expiration of a year from the day of sale without redemption, acquires an equitable title, which entitles him to maintain an action for the cancellation of instruments which, within the definition of courts of equity, are clouds on title. Remington Paper Co. v O'Dougherty (1880) 81 NY 474.

A creditor of a firm cannot maintain an action upon an agreement made with the firm by one not a member, to pay a portion of its indebtedness as no one creditor can show from the contract that it was intended for his benefit, or covers any part of his debt. Wheat v Rice (1884) 97 NY 296.

A promise made by one person for a good consideration paid by another, to pay the debts of the latter, is in legal effect a promise to pay creditors who are such at the time the promise is made. Barlow v Myers (1876) 64 NY 41.

Where a life policy is held in trust for a person, and such holder agrees at the request of the insured to pay from its proceeds a debt due from the insured to a third party, the latter may maintain an action against the holder therefor. Hutchings v Miner (1871) 46 NY 456.

Husband could sue in his own name for specific performance of promise made to husband to cancel judgment recovered against wife upon payment of sum less than that stated in judgment. Weill v Paradiso (1921) 188 NYS 287.

Where there is no privity of contract, to enable a third party to maintain an action upon the theory of a beneficial promise, there must be a promise, based upon a consideration, made by some one who has the power and is capable of making the promise. Rule was not applicable to instant case. Atlantic Terra Cotta Co. v Guthy, Inc. (1930) 138 Misc 76, 244 NYS 331.

An agreement merely that the proceeds of the

recovery be paid to another does not make the person to whom the proceeds are to be paid a necessary party plaintiff. Warshauer v Webb, 9 NYSR 529.

Person named in contract may sue thereon. Morgan v Andreae (1946) 295 NY 723, 65 NE2d 429.

27. —Beneficiary of policy

The beneficiary, alone, of a life insurance policy can sue upon it, but insurer may sue to rescind under the incontestable clause, without waiting for the beneficiary to sue. New York Life Ins. Co. v Faillace (1930) 138 Misc 182, 244 NYS 426, affd 231 AD 826, 246 NYS 893.

28. —Beneficiary of trust

The beneficiary of a trust who has received the income of the trust estate through the hands of the creator of the trust cannot charge the trustee therefor. Miller v Parkhurst, 9 NYSR 759.

29. —Unilateral contract

Right to maintain action for breach of unilateral contract the consideration for which was supplied by a third party, sustained. Coleman v Dorsen (1932) 234 AD 255, 254 NYS 771.

30. —Wager

Where money has been deposited by different persons with a stakeholder, as a wager on a horse race, which has been paid over to the winner, each depositor may recover of the winner the amount which he deposited, and separate actions can be brought by each, for such amounts. And this although the bet was made by another person, in his own name, but for the benefit of the plaintiff, who furnished the money to be staked. Ruckman v Pitcher (1859) 20 NY 9.

31. Conversion of property

Plaintiff in execution cannot maintain an action to prevent, or recover for, the taking away and conversion of property levied upon by the sheriff under such execution. Steffin v Steffin (1883) 30 Hun 312.

The state has such a title or interest in a draft indorsed to the state treasurer and delivered into his office by a county treasurer for the payment of taxes due the state that an action may be maintained in the name of the people for a conversion thereof. People v Bank of North America (1879) 75 NY 547.

An action for money or property fraudulently or tortiously obtained or taken, can only be maintained by the individual or corporation to whom it belongs, either as general owner or as having a special property therein. People v Ingersoll (1874) 58 NY 1.

32. Corporations

The power of corporations to sue is limited to actions relating to their corporate interests. Board of Education v Board of Education (1902) 76 AD 355, 78 NYS 522, affd 179 NY 556, 71 NE 1128.

Circumstances under which one trustee of a corporation may bring suit on behalf of the corporation. Recamier Mfg. Co. v Seymour (1889) 24 NYSR 54, 5 NYS 648.

It seems that a corporation whose property has been sequestrated by judgment and a receiver appointed, cannot prosecute an action brought by it, or subsequently appeal from a judgment recovered therein. Parry v American Opera Co. 12 Civ Proc 194.

On the merger of a railroad corporation with other corporations, an action existing, but not commenced, before the merger is perfected must be brought against the new corporation. Lee v Stillwater & M. S. R. Co. (1910) 140 AD 779, 125 NYS 840.

Action entitled "City of New York, to use and benefit of" specified corporation upon completion bond given to city by general contractor to recover for materials supplied to subcontractor, was properly brought by such corporation and not by city. New York use of J. K. Larkin & Co. v Standard Acci. Ins. Co. (1940) 23 NYS2d 939.

An incorporated labor organization may proceed by representation to secure an injunction. United Cloak & Suit Designers' Mut. Aid Asso. v Sigman (1926) 218 AD 367, 218 NYS 483.

33. —Stockholders

As to whether an action can be brought by an individual member of religious corporation against its trustees to restrain use for other religious purposes of property granted for religious purposes, see Watkins v Wilcox, 66 NY 654.

A stockholder cannot ordinarily maintain an action at law on behalf of the corporation. Hubbard v Kensington Bank (1930) 228 AD 790, 240 NYS 45, affd 254 NY 587, 173 NE 878.

Where the officers of a corporation refuse to prosecute an action in a proper case, or the corporation itself is under the control of its officers whose misconduct is to be made the subject of action, the stockholders may sue in their own names, making the corporation a defendant. Currier v New York, W. S. & B. R. Co. (1885) 35 Hun 355; Sheridan v Sheridan Elec. Light Co. (1886) 38 Hun 396; Brewster v Hatch, 4 NY SR 617, revd on other grounds (1890) 122 NY 349, 25 NE 505; Kelsey v Sargent (1886) 40 Hun 150; Anderton v Wolf, 41 Hun 571; Frothingham v Broadway & Seventh Ave. R. Co. 9 Civ Proc 304.

A mere stockholder or corporator has no right to maintain an action against a person who has wrongfully converted the property of the corporation, without showing failure or neglect on the part of the corporation, or its directors or officers, to take steps to prosecute. Werthim v Page, 10 Week Dig 26.

As to when application to officers of a corporation to bring action need not be made by shareholders before suit may be maintained by them, see Meyers v Scott (1888) 20 NYSR 35, 2 NYS 753.

Right of resident plaintiffs who are shareholders of

foreign railroad corporation to maintain action. Ives v Smith (1888) 19 NYSR 556, 3 NYS 645, affd 28 NYSR 917, 8 NYS 46.

A portion of the stockholders of a manufacturing corporation cannot maintain an action to dissolve it. Denike v New York & R. Lime & Cement Co. (1880) 80 NY 599.

As to right of one obtaining a transfer of the stock of a corporation, for the purpose of using it to maintain the suit. Ervin v Oregon R. & Nav. Co. (1885) 35 Hun 544.

34. —Municipal corporations

City cannot sue to enjoin collection of rates by public utility company as the representative of consumers affected, it not being bound by such rates. Oswego v People's Gas & E. Co. (1921) 116 Misc 354, 190 NYS 39.

City of New York was proper plaintiff in action against a transit company to compel specific performance of the fare clauses of contracts. New York v Interborough Rapid Transit Co. (1930) 136 Misc 569, 240 NYS 316, affd 232 AD 233, 249 NYS 243, affd 257 NY 20, 177 NE 295.

An action lies at the suit of the county to recover back its moneys wrongfully paid out. Richmond County v Ellis (1875) 59 NY 620.

Where a county treasurer issued notes to an amount greatly exceeding his authority, it was held that the county which was liable to the extent of his authority could maintain an action in the nature of a bill of peace against all the holders, to have it decided which were valid. Saratoga County v Deyoe (1879) 77 NY 219.

Moneys paid from the treasury of a municipal corporation, by its financial officer, without authority of law, may be recovered back by action in the name of such corporation. People v Ingersoll (1874) 58 NY 1; People v Fields (1874) 58 NY 491.

The supervisor of a town has authority to maintain an action against persons who, by their wrongful and fraudulent conduct, have created a debt which the town will be compelled to pay. Mitchell v Strough (1885) 35 Hun 83.

An action in behalf of a town to recover moneys belonging to such town may properly be brought in the name of its supervisor. Hathaway v Cincinnatus (1875) 62 NY 434. As to town bounties to volunteers, see Carver v Creque (1872) 48 NY 385; Decker v Saltzman (1874) 59 NY 275.

Action to recover town moneys must be brought by supervisors. Hathaway v Homer, 5 Lans 267, revd on another point, (1873) 54 NY 655.

A supervisor of a town may sue on a bond given to the town clerk. Sutherland v Carr (1881) 85 NY 105.

An action cannot be maintained by the supervisor of a town in his name of office against his predecessor for omitting moneys from his account, and converting the same to his own use. Hagadorn v Raux (1878) 72 NY 583.

An action is properly brought by the supervisor of the town in his own name, as supervisor, against the railroad commissioners of the town, to require them to account for moneys received by them on sale of the stock of said railroad belonging to the town (Laws 1867, ch 747). Griggs v Griggs (1874) 56 NY 504.

Boards of health in villages may under Laws 1885, ch 270, maintain actions to restrain nuisances. Board of Health v Casey (1888) 18 NYSR 251, 3 NYS 399.

Where the proper officers refuse to sue to enjoin a threatened nuisance or public destruction, the owner of property imperiled may bring an action against the wrongdoer, joining the municipality or officers as codefendants. Overton v Olean (1885) 37 Hun 47.

35. Covenants

A remote grantee may maintain action upon covenant against encumbrances. Andrews v Appel (1880) 22 Hun 429.

A covenant to pay mortgage may be enforced by assignee of mortgage. Boyle v Youmans (1890) 29 NYSR 888, 9 NYS 14, affd 134 NY 614, 31 NE 629.

A covenant in a deed, absolute on its face but intended as a mortgage, by which the grantee assumes and agrees to pay a prior mortgage, is in effect an agreement between the parties that the grantee will advance the amount of the prior lien upon security of the land, and gives no right of action against the grantee to the holder of the mortgage, as he is neither a party to the contract nor the one for whose benefit it was made. Root v Wright (1881) 84 NY 72.

36. Derivative action

Where a corporate director had brought a derivative action and during the pendency of the action failed at re-election and lost his status as a director the fact he was not re-elected did not abate the cause of action for the benefit of the corporation. Tenney v Rosenthal (1958) 6 AD2d 510, 179 NYS2d 728, affd 6 NY2d 204, 189 NYS2d 158, 160 NE2d 463.

In a stockholder's derivative action where the plaintiffs have established prima facie that they were the beneficial and equitable owners of the stock at the time of the transaction of which they complained, the law seems clear that they do have legal capacity to join in the commencement of the action. Croen v Gottlieb (1957) 8 Misc 2d 628, 166 NYS2d 278.

37. Executors and administrators

An executor can maintain a suit, either in his own name, or as executor, upon a note given to him as executor for a debt due to the testator at the time of his decease. Merritt v Seaman (1852) 6 NY 168.

So on a demand due to the testator before his decease. Merrit v Seaman, supra.

Where executor sells part of the estate on credit he may bring action in his own name to recover the debt. Thompson v Whitmarsh (1885) 100 NY 35, 2 NE 273.

Where the policy runs to the assured, his executors, or administrators, the personal representatives may maintain an action as trustee, for those beneficially interested in the real estate. Wyman v Wyman (1863) 26 NY 253.

A husband's right to administer upon the estate of his deceased wife, confers upon the husband's legal representatives capacity to sue for a chose in action which belonged to her at the time of her death, and was not reduced to possession by him in his lifetime. Gilman v McArdle, 12 Abb NC 414, revd on other grounds (1885) 99 NY 451, 2 NE 464.

After settlement of the account, executor may as heir at law or next of kin maintain an action against coexecutor for property unaccounted for. Guibert v Saunders, 10 NYSR 43.

One of two executors may maintain an action in equity, to call his coexecutors to account. Creditors, legatees, and next of kin, are not necessary parties except in case of a final accounting. Wood v Brown (1866) 34 NY 337. But see Burt v Burt (1869) 41 NY 46.

An action may be maintained by one executor against the surety on the bond given by the executors jointly, to recover for the conversion by the coexecutor of assets which came exclusively into his possession. Nanz v Oakley (1890) 120 NY 84, 24 NE 306.

The wife of one of two joint executors may maintain an action against them on a claim due her from their intestate, and it is immaterial whether the debt accrued to her by contract with the testator or by assignment from her husband. Snyder v Snyder (1884) 96 NY 88.

Where executors are given a mere power of sale unaccompanied by title they are not entitled to be substituted as parties plaintiff in an action for partition begun by the testator during his lifetime. Hamilton v Hamilton (1909) 135 AD 454, 119 NYS 986.

Specific performance of contract between administrator and intestate's son to distribute stock shares in family corporation to other heirs may be enforced by administrator. Kennedy v Kennedy (1949) 91 NYS2d 294.

Where by a will a mortgagor to the testator is directed to pay legacies amounting to less than the mortgage and giving the mortgagor the balance, the executor may foreclose the mortgage for the amount of the legacies. Newton v Stanley (1863) 28 NY 61.

The executors or administrators of a deceased lunatic are alone entitled to bring an action for an accounting against his committee, and unless they refuse to perform their duty in this respect, an action therefor cannot be brought by the next of kin of the lunatic. Schultz v Cookingham (1883) 30 Hun 443.

A complaint by the successor of defaulting administrators, who failed to pay distributive shares, against their surety in the court of the surrogate, was not demurrable upon the ground that the distributees should sue. Flanagan v Fidelity & Deposit Co. (1900) 32 Misc 424, 66 NYS 544.

Ancillary executor is vested with the legal right to bring suit or defend in connection with any matter pertaining to the estate over which he functions, where the executor is appointed in a foreign country. Gibb v Chisholm (1953) 204 Misc 892, 126 NYS2d 150.

Although a fiduciary cannot traffic in claims outside an estate and usually has no capacity to sue, where the estate of the deceased joint payee is entitled to participate in a judgment award to the extent of rights under a contract made by a decedent and while it is not within the legitimate scope of an executor in the ordinary case to purchase claims, where under circumstances in the proper performance of her duties an executrix should acquire and enforce an obligation due to the decedent, the estate has legal capacity to sue. Goddard v Gladstone (1957) 8 Misc 2d 624, 168 NYS2d 99.

38. —Foreign representatives

Absent special statute, executor or administrator cannot sue in official capacity outside the state without there obtaining grant of administration. Farmers' Trust Co. v Bradshaw (1930) 137 Misc 203, 242 NYS 598.

The rule that a foreign executor cannot sue or be sued in this state applies only to claims and liabilities resting wholly upon the representative character, i. e., suits brought upon debts due to or by the testator in his lifetime or based upon some transaction with him; it does not prevent such executor from suing or being sued upon a contract made with him as executor. Johnson v Wallis (1889) 112 NY 230, 19 NE 653.

39. Factor

A factor to whom grapes were consigned for sale had a special property interest in the subject-matter and could, under CPA § 210, sue a common carrier in his own name. Hewitt v New York, N. H. & H. R. Co. (1937) 166 Misc 186, 1 NYS2d 292, affd 258 AD 712, 14 NYS2d 991, affd 284 NY 117, 29 NE2d 641.

40. Forcible entry and detainer

An action for forcible entry and detainer is a cause of action in tort reposing only in the person who had possession of the property. Novick v Washington (1919) 110 Misc 379, 176 NYS 387.

41. Foreign government

Suits may be brought in our courts by foreign governments in the federative name. Republic of Mexico v De Arangoiz, 11 How Pr 1, affd 11 How Pr 576.

An officer of a foreign government authorized to sue for government property, may bring an action herein his own name. Peel v Elliott, 16 How Pr 481.

42. Guardians and wards

If rights of other creditors are not involved, a complaint should not be dismissed merely because it was not brought in a representative capacity but in the name of the infant plaintiff by her guardian. Feigenbaum v Narragansett Stables Co. (1926) 127 Misc 114, 215 NYS 328, affd 219 AD 729, 219 NYS 811, affd 245 NY 628, 157 NE 886.

The right of a general guardian of an infant to bring an action to recover money belonging to his ward, is not an exclusive one, and the infant himself may, by a guardian ad litem duly appointed, bring an action to recover the same. Segelken v Meyer (1884) 94 NY 473.

CPA § 210 (Code of Civil Procedure § 449), while authorizing an action by a trustee of an express trust to be brought without joining the beneficiaries thereof, was merely permissive and did not prevent an action by holders of warehouse receipts without joining the trustee as coplaintiff. Lewis v Home Ins. Co. (1922) 199 AD 556, 192 NYS 170, affd 234 NY 498, 138 NE 421.

One who has an equitable right to an action may sue in his own name, if he so desires, or the legal owner may sue for the benefit of the one who has the equitable title. Herald Nathan Press, Inc. v Bourges (1936) 161 Misc 208, 291 NYS 650.

A general guardian cannot maintain an action in his own name to recover personal property of his ward. It must be brought in the name of a guardian ad litem. Buermann v Buermann, 17 Abb NC 391, 9 Civ Proc 146.

The general guardian may bring an action in his own name to recover a debt due his ward. Harnett v Morris, 10 Civ Proc 223. See Bayer v Phillips, 10 Civ Proc 227, 17 Abb NC 425.

A general guardian may collect and sue for his ward's share of rent collected from premises owned in part by his ward. Coakley v Mahar (1885) 36 Hun 157.

Though a guardian can sue on an award made by commissioners appointed to appraise land, taken by the right of eminent domain in his own name alone, it is proper to join the owner as plaintiff. Lent v New York & M. R. Co. (1889) 55 Hun 180, 7 NYS 729, revd 130 NY 504, 29 NE 988.

The general guardian of an infant, entitled under a will to receive during the infant's life the rents and profits of a trust fund created by the will, should not be joined with the infant as a party plaintiff in the action brought to obtain a judicial construction of the will, as he has no interest in the matter. Wead v Cantwell (1885) 36 Hun 528, affd Horton v Cantwell (1888) 108 NY 255, 15 NE 546.

In action by guardian, residence and citizenship of guardian controls, not that of ward on question of diversity of citizenship; but in action by infant, by a guardian ad litem, the citizenship of the infant is controlling. Merritt v Greenberg (1933) 4 F Supp 655.

43. Heirs, devisees and legatees

Persons to whom lands have been devised in trust may maintain an action for trespass causing an injury to the inheritance notwithstanding the premises are in possession of a tenant under a lease. Mortimer v Manhattan R. Co. (1890) 29 NYSR 262, 8 NYS 536, affd 129 NY 81, 29 NE 5.

Where land was conveyed in fee, reserving a rent charge, with right of reentry in case of nonpayment of rent, the heir of the grantor could maintain ejectment, under such right of reentry, and if there were more than one heir, each could maintain ejectment for his share without joining the others as plaintiffs. Cruger v McLaury (1869) 41 NY 219.

An action to recover the possession of lands held under a grant in fee, in which a yearly rent was reserved, with a right of entry in case of breach, as a condition of the estate, could be maintained by the devisee of the grantor, upon a breach of the condition by the grantee or his heirs or assigns. Van Rensselaer v Barringer (1868) 39 NY 9.

A legacy of the income of the residuary estate to testator's widow in lieu of dower does not abate as other legacies, and hence other residuary legatees are not necessary parties to her action to recover the legacy of the executor. Pittman v Johnson (1885) 35 Hun 38, affd 102 NY 742.

An heir at law or next of kin claiming in hostility to a will, cannot maintain an action for its construction. Chipman v Montgomery (1875) 63 NY 221.

A devisee who claims a mere legal estate in the real property of the testator, when there is no trust, cannot maintain an action for the construction of the devise, but must assert his legal title by a legal action, or if, in possession, must await an attack upon it and set up the devise in answer to the hostile claim. Weed v Weed (1883) 94 NY 243.

A devisee of the legal estate, in possession of the property desired, cannot maintain an action to establish the will against the heirs at law. Anderson v Anderson (1889) 112 NY 104, 19 NE 427.

The devisee in remainder of premises out of which rents issue may maintain a joint action against the executor of the life tenant for rent collected by him, which became due after the termination of the life estate. Marshall v Moseley (1860) 21 NY 280.

While a person may not, as next of kin simply, sue to recover personal property of a deceased person, a recovery by next of kin may be permitted without the intervention of an administrator, under special circumstances, and where his right to the property is clear and has been admitted by defendant. Segelken v Meyer (1884) 94 NY 473.

A widow under the designation of next of kin in the statute (2 RS 114, §§ 9 and 19) could maintain an action to recover a distributive share of an estate which the statute clearly gave her. Betsinger v Chapman (1882) 24 Hun 15, affd 88 NY 487.

Where the will of testatrix gave an estate for life to her husband and after his death the property was to be equally divided among her children, held that a child might as legatee bring an action during the husband's lifetime, against the former executor of the will for a devastavit and against the life tenant for alleged overpayments to him. Hayward v Place (1889) 27 NYSR 115, 7 NYS 523.

A legatee may sue in his own name to recover specific securities given by a legacy, with the assent of the executor, and, if there are no debts, the latter may be compelled to assent. Sere v Coit, 5 Abb Pr 481.

One of several heirs at law may maintain an action against an administrator, who has wrongfully converted assets of the estate, and the person receiving the same with knowledge of the misappropriation, to recover such assets or their value upon the administrator's refusal and neglect to bring such action. Randel v Dyett (1885) 38 Hun 347.

In action for wrongful death of automobile driver, real plaintiffs are those who may be entitled to distributive share of any judgment that may be obtained. Re Maryland (1955) 285 AD 1078, 139 NYS2d 746.

44. Injunction

Under Home Rule Act of the City of New York, Laws 1913, ch 247, city cannot bring an action on behalf of inhabitants to enjoin raise of water rates where the city used no water of the defendant. New York v Citizens' Water Supply Co. (1921) 189 NYS 929, affd 199 AD 169, 191 NYS 430, affd 235 NY 584, 139 NE 744.

45. Insurance; generally

Where an insurance company elected to rebuild and gave notice accordingly, and failed to do so, the insured owner was the proper plaintiff to enforce compliance although the mortgagee would have been entitled to the money if paid. Heilmann v Westchester F. Ins. Co. (1878) 75 NY 7.

One who has control of property, either as owner, consignee or agent, may effect insurance thereon in his own name, on account of whom it may concern, loss payable to him, and in case of loss may maintain an action thereon. Sturm v Atlantic Mut. Ins. Co. (1875) 63 NY 77.

A policy of insurance issued "on account of whom it may concern," ordinarily inures to the benefit of all the owners; and an action may be maintained by the party to whom it issued, suing in his own name. Walsh v Washington Marine Ins. Co. (1865) 32 NY 427.

General contractor, sued for personal injury, may as third-party plaintiff sue third-party defendant for indemnity without joining person for whose benefit action is prosecuted, namely, general contractor's liability insurer paying under trust agreement. Pike v Balmar Constr. Co. (1951) 200 Misc 371, 106 NYS2d 641, affd 279 AD 590, 107 NYS2d 99.

Agents, commission merchants or others having the custody of and being responsible for property may insure in their own names, and recover the full amount named in the policy. Waring v Indemnity F. Ins. Co. (1871) 45 NY 606.

As to actions on insurance policies where property is mortgaged, see Grosvenor v Atlantic F. Ins. Co. (1858) 17 NY 391; Bidwell v Northwestern Ins. Co. (1859) 19 NY 179.

Where a policy is issued to the owner of premises, loss, if any, payable to a mortgagee, the latter alone can sue, and has the right to recover the whole loss sustained to the owner's insurable interest, holding the surplus, if any, above his claim as trustee for the owner. Cone v Niagara F. Ins. Co. (1875) 60 NY 619.

A part owner of a vessel may sue on a marine insurance policy which runs "on account of whom it may concern," and which policy was procured by an agent. McLaughlin v Great Western Ins. Co (1892) 46 NYSR 759, 20 NYS 536.

A person taking out an insurance policy on his own life for the benefit of his wife was a trustee within the meaning of CPA § 210. Kerr v Union Mut. L. Ins. Co. (1893) 69 Hun 393, 23 NYS 619.

This action is permissive merely and does not prevent the joinder of a beneficiary. Cassidy v Sauer (1906) 114 AD 673, 99 NYS 1026, affd 187 NY 540, 80 NE 625.

The insured in an endowment policy payable to his wife may sue for accrued dividends under this section, upon exercising the option contained in the policy, but cannot recover where she has been vouched in as a party defendant. Fuchs v Mutual Life Ins. Co. of New York (1917) 164 NYS 105.

Where policy of fire insurance was payable to live stock exchange for the benefit of members of exchange, purchasers, shippers or brokers, a member of the exchange suffering loss could not sue upon it. Wilson & Co. v Hartford F. Ins. Co. (1920) 190 AD 506, 179 NYS 867, affd 229 NY 612, 129 NE 929.

Motor express carrier may, in its own name, sue insurer on fire policy covering its vehicles damaged by fire, where claimed hazard of possible double payment directly to shipper or consignee is unsubstantial. York-Buffalo Motor Exp. v National Fire & M. Ins. Co. (1943) 181 Misc 518, 43 NYS2d 483, affd 268 AD 855, 50 NYS2d 845, revd on other grounds 294 NY 467, 63 NE2d 61.

In spite of the permission given by this section to the owner to sue, the action is a single cause of action brought for the benefit both for the plaintiff and the insurance carrier so that articles in the possession of the insurance carrier may be the subject of discovery and inspection on motion of the defendant. Leone v Lohmaier (1954) 205 Misc 467, 128 NYS2d 618.

Defense that the insurer is the real party in interest having paid in full under the policy, will defeat an action by the insured. Purdy v McGarity (1941) 262 AD 623, 30 NYS2d 966; Sisson v Hassett (1935) 155 Misc 667, 280 NYS 148; Yezek v Delaware, Lackawanna & W. R. Co. (1941) 176 Misc 553, 28 NYS2d 35.

In action for automobile damage in collision, amendment of answer to allege that plaintiff had assigned his cause of action to collision insurer who was real party in interest was denied, as injecting question of insurance before jury. Butera v Donner (1942) 177 Misc 966, 32 NYS2d 633.

46. Insurer suing third party

Owner of damaged automobile, not indemnified in full by insurer, was the only person who could sue wrongdoer for full amount of loss. Henderson v Park Central Motors Service, Inc. (1930) 138 Misc 183, 244 NYS 409.

In this action for all the damages to plaintiff's automobile caused by the automobile of defendant, the defendant is entitled to an order requiring the plaintiff to amend her complaint and to bring in, as a necessary and proper party, the insurer of the plaintiff, which paid the plaintiff part of her damage. Sisson v Hassett (1935) 155 Misc 667, 280 NYS 148.

Mere fact that automobile owner was paid by insurance company and assigned part of his right of action to the insurance company did not prevent him suing in his own name, though he sued for the same amount that the insurance company paid him. Steinhaus v New York (1919) 179 NYS 195.

Motorist, who has assigned his cause of action for automobile damages to his insurer, is no longer real party in interest, and cannot maintain action thereon. Purdy v McGarity (1941) 262 AD 623, 30 NYS2d 966. See also Scarborough v Bartholomew (1941) 263 AD 765, 30 NYS2d 971.

Where plaintiff retains legal ownership of part of indivisible claim, he is only person who can prosecute action. Van Romapaye Trucking Corp. v Heebner (1948) 85 NYS2d 347.

47. Insurer with loan or subrogation receipt or trust agreement

The principle underlying the Amendment of 1950 is that of nondisclosure that the insurance carrier has paid the insured or settled the case. Pike v Balmar Constr. Co. (1951) 200 Misc 371, 106 NYS2d 641, affd 279 AD 590, 107 NYS2d 99.

The purpose of the 1950 amendment to CPA § 210 permitting an insured person who has executed a loan receipt to sue without joining the person for whose benefit the action is prosecuted was to prevent the disclosure of the fact of plaintiff's insurance to the jury. Leone v Lohmaier (1954) 205 Misc 467, 128 NYS2d 618.

Where the insurance company has advanced the amount of the loss and the owner has given a loan receipt the action to recover from a third party for the loss may properly be brought in the name of the owner without joining the insurance company. Leone v Lohmaier, supra.

Where employer satisfies a judgment against employer and employee for injuries to a pedestrian resulting from employee's negligence in loading a motor vehicle the fact that the funds used in satisfaction of the judgment were obtained from the plaintiff's liability carrier as a loan, did not prevent the bringing of the action in the name of the employer rather than of the insurance carrier.

Bond Stores, Inc. v American Fidelity & Cas. Co. (1954) 133 NYS2d 297.

In action for damage to plaintiff's premises caused by blasting on defendant's premises, plaintiff's insurer was not necessary party, though insurer had settled plaintiff's claim and paid him sum less than amount sued for in instant action, and though plaintiff executed loan agreement to repay loan from proceeds of action if she recovered amount of loan. Beasley v Huntley Ests (1955) 285 AD 887, 137 NYS2d 787.

Where insured has settled with insurer and has been given loan receipt, insured may sue on claim in his own name. Rosenfeld v Continental N. O. Co. (1955) 135 F Supp 465.

48. —Decisions prior to 1950 amendment

Prior to the amendment of CPA § 210 in 1950 permitting an insured to sue the negligent party although the insured had executed a loan receipt or similar instrument to the insurer, it was held in many cases that such insurer was either the real party in interest, or a necessary party, in such an action. Mersereau v Binghamton Gas Works (1948) 273 AD 97, 76 NYS2d 435; Scarborough v Bartholomew (1940) 22 NYS2d 635, affd 263 AD 765, 30 NYS2d 971; Yezek v Delaware L. & W. R. Co. (1941) 176 Misc 553, 28 NYS2d 35; Barrett v Matson (1942) 177 Misc 863, 32 NYS2d 59; Arnold v Kensington Plaza Garages (1943) 179 Misc 697, 42 NYS2d 118.

Other decisions held that the insured could sue the wrongdoer without joining an insurer who had advanced sums under a loan receipt or similar instrument executed by the insured and designed to prevent subrogation of the insurer with the resulting injection of the insurance feature into the jury trial. Balish v Advance Fuel Oil Co. (1943) 266 AD 683, 40 NYS2d 410; Anderson v Socony-Vacuum Oil Co. Inc. (1943) 266 AD 817, 42 NYS2d 574; Par-X Uniform Serv. Corp. v Emigrant Industrial Sav. Bank (1945) 268 AD 699, 53 NYS2d 16; Franklin v Hussman Refrigeration (1948) 274 AD 937, 83 NYS2d 730; Schwartz v Maygreen Piece Dye Works (1942) 36 NYS2d 169, affd in part and revd in part 265 AD 931, 38 NYS2d 412; Bagley & S. Co. v Shell Oil Co. 44 NYS2d 531, revd on other grounds 268 AD 888, 50 NYS2d 784; Gorman v Baltimore Drive-It-Yourself Co. (1944) 46 NYS2d 530; Koop v General American Transp. Corp. (1944) 47 NYS2d 628; Home Ins. Co. v Rosenfeld (1945) 56 NYS2d 454; Morton Coal Co. v Garcia (1945) 57 NYS2d 67; Bruner-Ritter v Town Park Garage (1949) 91 NYS2d 873. See Merrimack Mfg. Co. v Lowell Trucking Corp. (1944) 182 Misc 947, 46 NYS2d 736.

It was suggested in some cases that if the loan receipt or similar instrument was a mere device to disguise what in fact was a payment under the policy that the insurer was the real party in interest. See Cocoa Trading Corp. v Bayway Terminal Corp. (1943) 290 NY 697, 49 NE2d 632; Kulheim v Bayza (1944) 45 NYS2d 869.

49. Insurance carrier, workmen's compensation

Where employee injured by negligence of third person failed to commence action against latter within six months from date of first award of compensation made to and accepted by plaintiff, his cause of action became property of person paying compensation, and thereafter plaintiff lacked capacity to sue. Nelson v Buffalo Niagara Electric Corp. (1942) 264 AD 941, 36 NYS2d 205, affd 292 NY 600, 55 NE2d 371.

Employee covered by compensation law who fails to commence an action for his injuries within six months after award of compensation to him or within one year from date of accrual of his cause of action is not divested thereof where he has not accepted compensation. Gillette v Allen (1942) 264 AD 599, 36 NYS2d 306.

50. Master of vessel

The master who signs a charter party, payable to himself, may collect or assign the charter moneys and claims for demurrage, etc., in his own name. Rupp v Lobach, 4 E. D. Smith 69.

Master of a vessel who sails it under a contract to find crew, etc., and pay half expenses and receive half the net freight, is the proper person to sue to collect the freight. Clendaniel v Tuckerman, 17 Barb 184.

51. Partners

Upon dissolution of a firm, one of the two partners assigned all his interest in the assets of the firm to plaintiff, the other partner, who was to pay the firm debts, held that plaintiff might sue in his own name for a firm debt. Phillips v Clark (1872) 48 NY 677.

Where one engaged in business enters into partnership with another for the purpose of continuing the business and transfers business assets to the firm in consideration of an agreement by the firm to pay certain debts and to apply the assets first to the payment of said debts, a creditor holding one of the claims may maintain an action against the firm on the agreement. Arnold v Nichols (1876) 64 NY 117.

Managing partner cannot sue solely in his own name on contract of partnership. Natter v Isaac H. Blanchard Co. (1912) 153 AD 814, 138 NYS 969.

A partner, holding bonds purchased with partnership funds is a trustee of an express trust, and may maintain an action thereon without joining his copartners as plaintiff. Davidge v Guardian Trust Co. (1909) 136 AD 78, 120 NYS 628, revd on other grounds 203 NY 331, 96 NE 751.

Where a surviving partner makes a general assignment with preferences, the executor of the deceased partner may bring an action to set it aside, and for a receiver. Nelson v Tenney (1885) 36 Hun 327.

Where a member of a firm dies, the legal title of the partnership contracts, debts and property vests in the survivors, and the personal representatives of the deceased partner are not proper parties to an action in relation thereto. Matthews v Stietz, 5 Civ Proc 235.

Although a contract was made with plaintiffs under the name of "syndicate managers," held that they were entitled to sue thereon as a partnership, such relationship existing, to the knowledge of the defendant, at the time the contract was executed. Redfield v National Petroleum Corp. (1922) 199 AD 442, 191 NYS 794.

52. Penalties

The health department cannot maintain an action for a penalty. New York Health Dept. v Knoll (1877) 70 NY 530. But see Laws 1874, ch 636, § 4.

53. Performance of public duty

A taxpayer upon his own motion and in his own behalf has no right as such taxpayer to take action to compel the assessors of the town to perform their duties. People ex rel. Stevens v Hayt (1876) 66 NY 606.

54. Pledges and collaterals

One holding choses in action as collateral security may enforce payment of them and thus satisfy the principal debt. Nelson v Edwards, 40 Barb 279. Such action may be continued in his name notwithstanding his having received the debt for which the securities had been assigned to him. Greene v Tallman (1859) 20 NY 191.

Where the owner of a mortgage has pledged it as collateral for a debt less than the mortgage, he has an interest which entitles him to bring an action for foreclosure. Simson v Satterlee (1876) 64 NY 657.

A person who pledges the money of his partner as security for an obligation may sue for its recovery. Meinhardt v Excelsior Brewing Co. (1904) 98 AD 308, 90 NYS 642.

55. Public officers

Public officers should sue in their own names with the name of their office added. Paige v Fazackerly, 36 Barb 392.

An action lies in the name of the sheriff on a bond to the principal, taken by a deputy to indemnify him and all persons assisting him. Stillwell v Hurlbert (1858) 18 NY 374.

Commissioner of highways cannot by an equitable action compel the removal of an obstruction. Rozell v Andrews (1886) 103 NY 150, 8 NE 513.

An action cannot be maintained by an individual to determine his right to a municipal office, when it does not appear that any person claims the office in hostility to him, or that defendant has interfered with his legal rights as such officer. Demarest v Wickham (1875) 63 NY 320.

Action may be maintained by a person entitled to hold an office against one who has wrongfully obtained possession of the same, for the emoluments or salary attached to such office. Nichols v McLean (1886) 101 NY 526, 5 NE 347.

56. Real property actions

One in possession under claim of title may maintain an action to remove cloud upon title. Schroeder v Gurney (1877) 10 Hun 413, affd 73 NY 430.

The owner of land in a street affected by a railroad crossing may maintain an action to remove the track crossing the street, if illegally there. Clarke v Blackmar (1871) 47 NY 150.

An owner of premises upon which a house is being built under contract can maintain an action against a city for injuries caused by the bursting of a public sewer, even though the contractors were bound to deliver him a complete house notwithstanding the injury. Nims v Mayor, etc., of Troy (1875) 59 NY 500.

The reversioner may sue for injury to his reversionary interest, notwithstanding any intervening estate. Van Deusen v Young (1864) 29 NY 9.

A tenant and not the lessor, has a right of action for injury to the possession of property. Tobias v Cohn (1867) 36 NY 363.

One in possession of land under a contract of purchase can maintain an action for injury to it. Honsee v Hammond, 39 Barb 89; Sparks v Leavy, 19 Abb Pr 364.

57. Receivers

Although the receiver of a partnership undergoing dissolution does not have title to the partnership property, he has sufficient interest therein to maintain an action for conversion in his own name against one unlawfully withholding it from him. Rogers v Landers (1926) 128 Misc 208, 218 NYS 98.

As to action by a receiver of a savings bank against the trustees of such bank for losses through their failure to exercise care in managing its business, see Hun v Cary (1880) 82 NY 65.

Where his possession is not interfered with a receiver of rents and profits, or a sequestrator of real estate in divorce proceedings, cannot maintain an action to set aside a conveyance of real estate. Foster v Townshend (1887) 68 NY 203.

A receiver in supplementary proceedings to whom a widow conveys "her dower and right of dower," is entitled to have the dower admeasured and applied by a partition sale of the premises. Payne v Becker (1881) 87 NY 153.

The receiver of a dissolved corporation represents the corporation, and its creditors and stockholders, and may maintain an action to set aside illegal or fraudulent transfers and recover misappropriated funds. Atty. Gen. v Guardian Mut. L. Ins. Co. (1879) 77 NY 272.

A subscription to stock may be enforced by a receiver. Phoenix Warehousing Co. v Badger (1876) 67 NY 294.

A receiver of a manufacturing corporation may maintain an action to set aside a mortgage executed by it without the requisite assent of stockholders. Vail v Hamilton (1881) 85 NY 453.

A receiver of a savings bank may maintain an action to charge the trustees with damages for misfeasance. Hun v Cary (1880) 82 NY 65.

A receiver of a national bank may bring an action against its directors to recover damages, at least when no proceeding is pending for the forfeiture of its charter. Brinckerhoff v Bostwick (1882) 88 NY 52.

Receivers and trustees appointed in other states may sue here by comity, but cannot maintain an action for a claim conflicting with rights given by our laws. Pugh v Hurtt, 52 How Pr 22.

58. Restraining nuisance

One maintaining a common nuisance is liable to an action at the suit of another who has sustained special damage. Adams v Popham (1879) 76 NY 410.

The people can maintain an action to secure the removal of a telegraph pole which is an obstruction in the street. People v Metropolitan Tel. & Tel. Co. (1884) 31 Hun 596.

Where the proper officers, having the right to sue to enjoin a threatened nuisance, refuse on request to do so, an owner of property in the municipality imperiled may bring an action against the wrongdoer joining the municipality or officer as a co-defendant. Overton v Olean (1885) 37 Hun 47.

The operation of a manufacturing establishment by which plaintiff's occupation of her premises as a dwelling house is interfered with by the emission of vapor, smoke and cinders is a nuisance, which may be abated at the suit of plaintiff. Beir v Cooke (1885) 37 Hun 38.

Where a person for several years unnecessarily and unreasonably obstructs a public street or sidewalk to the detriment of another, it is not essential to prove great damage to warrant an abatement of the nuisance. Slight special injury is sufficient to give such injured party standing in court for redress. Flynn v Taylor (1891) 127 NY 596, 28 NE 418.

One entitled to the use of air or water in its natural condition, and who is injured by its pollution, may maintain an action against the party causing it, whether an individual or a corporation. Chapman v Rochester (1888) 110 NY 273, 18 NE 88.

59. States

The several states of the Union may sue in their corporate names in the courts of another state. Michigan v Phoenix Bank (1865) 33 NY 9.

60. Statutes

Where a statute imposes a duty upon a citizen, any person having a special interest in the performance thereof may sue for a breach, causing him injury. Willy v Mulledy (1879) 78 NY 310.

61. Subscriptions

When a subscriber to a fund to build a church, payable to a treasurer to be appointed by the subscribers, is liable to a religious corporation formed to use the edifice built with the funds. See Presbyterian Soc. v Beach (1878) 74 NY 72.

An agreement signed by several to pay sums subscribed to a person named, to be expended in repairing a road, creates no liability to a third person who has done the work, and to whom, after its completion, the payee assigned the right to recover. Van Rensselaer v Aikin (1870) 44 NY 126.

62. —To corporate stock

As to action by a railroad corporation against a subscriber for stock for the amount of his subscription, see Lake Ontario Shore R. Co. v Curtiss (1880) 80 NY 219.

A subscription to stock may be enforced by the receiver of the corporation. Phoenix Warehousing Co. v Badger (1876) 67 NY 294.

63. Tenants in common

Extent of right to sue cotenant. Stall v Wilbur (1879) 77 NY 158.

64. Trustees of an express trust

Trustee of an express trust may sue in its own name. Banca Commerciale Italiana Trust Co. v Clarkson (1937) 274 NY 69, 8 NE2d 281, 110 ALR 1105.

Trustees in whom is the title to a trust fund are the proper parties plaintiff to maintain an action to protect it. Western R. Co. v Nolan (1872) 48 NY 513.

The nominal proprietor of an individual bank is, as respects others interested with him, trustee of an express trust, and may sue in his own name on a security taken in the course of the business. See Bank of Havana v Magee (1859) 20 NY 355.

The fact that the cashier of a bank, who was named individually as grantee in a deed did not furnish the consideration does not prevent him from enforcing it; the provisions of this section covers such a case. Mutual L. Ins. Co. v Nicholas (1911) 144 AD 95, 128 NYS 902.

A bank as trustee had legal capacity to sue under this section for a judicial construction of the trust agreement, and for a declaration with respect to the payment of sums into the sinking fund provided for. City Bank Farmers Trust Co. v National Cuba Hotel Corp. (1954) 133 NYS2d 8.

A person who invests his own money and also the money of others in the purchase of certain stock, may bring an action in relation thereto in his own name. Parker v Paine (1902) 37 Misc 768, 76 NYS 942.

A corporation, to which property has been assigned as a pledge for its protection and the protection of others who became the assignor's sureties on the faith of the pledge, may, as a trustee of an express trust, maintain an action to reclaim the property pledged from the assignor, who had appropriated it to his own use, if any of the obligations, for the benefit of which the pledge was made, remain undischarged. Hoffman House v Foote (1902) 172 NY 348, 65 NE 169.

Where creditors, a debtor and three persons as trustees, agree that the creditors are to forbear prosecuting their claims, the debtor is to made stated payments and turn over certain policies to the trustees, and they are to distribute the funds to the creditors, the trustees are trustees of an express trust within this section, and on default of the debtor the trustees may maintain an action against him. Heppenstall v Baudouine (1908) 60 Misc 620, 113 NYS 849, affd 129 AD 901, 113 NYS 851, affd 198 NY 635, 92 NE 1086.

Where plaintiff and his brother took bond from bank for transmission of money, receipt to be made in the name of either and receipt was made to plaintiff, plaintiff could sue the surety in his own name as trustee of an express trust. Portoghese v Illinois Surety Co. (1913) 81 Misc 211, 142 NYS 500.

Provision in franchise that gas company should not charge consumers of gas in village more than certain amount constituted a contract for the benefit of the consumers, and the village as trustee of an express trust could maintain an action for its enforcement. Freeport v Nassau & S. Lighting Co. (1920) 111 Misc 671, 181 NYS 830.

A definite ascertained interest of a party in the proceeds of real estate in the hands of a quasi trustee not depending upon any privity or community of interest with him, or requiring any accounting, may be recovered in an action against said trustee. Penman v Slocum (1869) 41 NY 53.

An auctioneer who in his own name sells goods for another, is a trustee of an express trust. Minturn v Main (1852) 7 NY 220.

An indorsee of a bill of lading, to whom the merchandise is consigned for sale, may maintain an action for damages to the goods while in the course of transportation as "a trustee of an express trust" without joining the person for whose benefit the action is prosecuted. Robertson v National S.S. Co. (1891) 14 NYS 313, revd 42 NYSR 694, 17 NYS 459, revd 139 NY 416, 34 NE 1053.

In an action brought against a life insurance company to reform an insurance policy and to recover the surrendered value, the insurer acts as trustee of an express trust in relation to the beneficiary. Hunt v Provident Sav. Life Assur. Soc. (1902) 77 AD 338, 79 NYS 74.

Successor trustee of corporate bondholders may maintain action against former trustee to recover trust estate assets and for accounting. Newmark v National B. & T. Co. (1955) 2 Misc 2d 1021, 147 NYS2d 565.

65. —Testamentary trustees

A testamentary trustee may assert a counterclaim in his individual capacity for the difference between fair rental value and amount actually paid by plaintiff for premises occupied by himself. Haag v Turney (1934) 240 AD 149, 269 NYS 317.

Testamentary trustees having incidental power to collect outstanding choses in action may maintain an action on notes in which the decedent was payee. Bamberger v Morris (1932) 144 Misc 4, 257 NYS 696.

66. —Several trustees

A trustee of a fund for the security of an indebtedness to others, who as such is plaintiff in an action to enforce such indebtedness, may appeal from a judgment which reduces the number of those who are creditors upon the fund. One of several trustees, as sole plaintiff, may bring an action to enforce a lien for the benefit of the trust, when his associates will not join; in which case they may be made defendants. Bockes v Hathorn (1879) 78 NY 222.

67. —Agents as trustees

Complaint containing no allegation that plaintiff as an agent entered into a contract for an alleged principal either in his own name or otherwise, failed to state facts sufficient to bring him within definition of a trustee of an express trust. Novick v Washington (1919) 110 Misc 379, 176 NYS 387.

Where there is a promise to pay a person "as executive agent" of foreign company named, the agent can maintain the action as the trustee of an express trust. Considerant v Brisbane (1860) 22 NY 389.

An agent selling goods upon commission may maintain in his own name an action to recover the purchase price of goods sold by him for his principal as trustee of an express trust. Middleton v Wohlgemuth (1910) 141 AD 678, 126 NYS 734.

Agents of a syndicate to whom notes are delivered and made payable are trustees of an express trust and may maintain an action thereon. Coffin v Grand Rapids Hydraulic Co. (1893) 136 NY 655, 32 NE 1076.

Syndicate managers, with respect to handling of corporate bonds, had legal capacity to sue for subscriptions as trustees of express trust. Gallogly v Whitmore (1916) 172 AD 381, 158 NYS 830.

A power of attorney, in the usual form, to manage real estate, make leases and collect rents creates an express trust and authorizes the maintenance of an action for rent by the attorney in his own name, without joining his principals. Fargo v Owen (1894) 79 Hun 181, 29 NYS 611.

Where insurance is effected by an agent for a principal known to the insurer, but not named in the policy, the agent becomes a trustee of an express trust, and an action may be brought either in the name of the principal or agent. Pitney v Glens Falls Ins. Co. (1875) 65 NY 6.

Where a contract for the purchase of land was made by the agent of the plaintiff individually, and the deed of conveyance was to the plaintiff as "trustee" and to his heirs and assigns, the word "trustee" was merely descriptio personae, and the plaintiff was entitled under CPA § 210 to recover an excessive payment. Armour v Sound Shore Front Imp. Co. (1911) 71 Misc 253, 128 NYS 331, affd 144 AD 928, 129 NYS 1112.

68. Trust beneficiaries

Beneficiary may not intervene as plaintiff where trustee is willing plaintiff. Security Trust Co. v John Hancock Mut. L. Ins. Co. (1947) 189 Misc 259, 70 NYS2d 9.

Surviving trustee was held authorized to prosecute claim for commissions on behalf of beneficiaries and heirs of deceased cotrustee without joining them with it. United States Trust Co. v Bingham (1950) 301 NY 1, 92 NE2d 39.

Trustee to whom a claim has been assigned, after suit brought for the benefit of the attorneys, is trustee of an express trust, and may maintain the action without joining with him the other persons beneficially interested in the claim. Wetmore v Hegeman (1882) 88 NY 69.

In an action by trustees under express trust against a stranger to recover personal property belonging to the trust it was not necessary to make the beneficiaries of the trust parties to the action under CPA § 210, and in the absence of fraud the beneficiaries were bound by the result. Re Straut (1891) 126 NY 201, 27 NE 259; and so as to an action for damages to real estate. Korn v New York El. R. Co (1891) 37 NYSR 630, 13 NYS 514, affd 129 NY 648, 29 NE 1032.

An action for the funds against the personal representative of the depositor, may be prosecuted with the consent of the beneficiary and for her benefit, by a trustee appointed to succeed the depositor, though she could have sued in her own name. Macy v Williams (1890) 55 Hun 489, 8 NYS 658, affd 125 NY 767, 27 NE 409.

Beneficiaries and remaindermen of trust created for benefit of trustees as well as their surviving heirs, were parties interested in condemnation award. Bacorn v People (1949) 195 Misc 917, 88 NYS2d 628.

Where the purchase of trust property is of real estate, and the title has been vested in the trustee, the cestui que trust may maintain an action to compel a conveyance to him or in trust for him by the trustee, and it is no objection to the granting of the relief sought that the defect in his title appears upon the records. Dodge v Stevens (1883) 94 NY 209.

A bondholder, after requesting the trustee under a mortgage to foreclose it, and a refusal, may himself bring foreclosure. Davies v New York Concert Co. (1886) 41 Hun 492.

69. Widow suing to set aside husband's fraudulent transfer

A motion to dismiss a cause of action to set aside a transfer of interest by plaintiff widow's husband as illusory and in fraud of her rights under section 18 of the Decedent Estate Law must be denied since surviving widow may challenge transfer made inter vivos upon charge that it is illusory and fraudulent and plaintiff is not without capacity to sue. Katz v Katz (1958) 13 Misc 2d 953, 178 NYS2d 795.

FORMS

Form 1—Complaint in action by executor

Form 2—Complaint in action by administrator

Form 3—Complaint in action by trustee of express trust

Form 4—Complaint in action by insured person, etc.

Form 5—Complaint in action by person in whose name a contract is made for the benefit of another

Form 6—Complaint in action by guardian of the property of an infant

Form 7—Complaint in action by committee of incompetent

Form 1

Complaint in Action By Executor

SUPREME COURT, __¹_____ COUNTY.

[Title of cause]   Complaint
Index No. — [if assigned]

The plaintiff, as executor of the estate of __²_____, deceased, complaining of the defendant, respectfully alleges:

1. On or about the __³_ day of __⁴_____, 19_⁵_, __⁶_____ died leaving a last will and testament wherein and whereby the plaintiff was appointed the sole executor.

2. On or about the __⁷_ day of __⁸_____, 19_⁹_ said will was duly admitted to probate by the surrogate of the County of __¹⁰_____, and letters testamentary upon said will were thereafter and on the __¹¹_ day of __¹²_____, 19_¹³_ duly issued and granted by said surrogate to the plaintiff as executor of the estate of the said __¹⁴_____, deceased, and the plaintiff thereupon duly qualified as such executor and has ever since been and now is acting as such executor.

[Allege facts constituting cause of action.]

WHEREFORE, plaintiff demands judgment against the defendant in the sum of __¹⁵_____ dollars with interest thereon from the __¹⁶_ day of __¹⁷_____, 19_¹⁸_, together with the costs and disbursements of this action.

_____¹⁹_____
Attorney for Plaintiff
Office and P. O. Address
Telephone No.

Form 2

Complaint in Action by Administrator

SUPREME COURT, __¹_____ COUNTY.

[Title of cause]   Complaint
Index No. — [if assigned]

The plaintiff, as administrator of the estate of __²_____, deceased, complaining of the defendant, respectfully alleges:

1. On or about the __³_ day of __⁴_____, 19_⁵_, __⁶_____, died intestate in the County of __⁷_____, New York and was at the time of his death a resident thereof.

2. On or about the __⁸_ day of __⁹_____, 19_¹⁰_ by an order duly made by the surrogate of the County of __¹¹_____, the plaintiff was appointed administrator of the goods, chattels and credits of __¹²_____, deceased, and plaintiff has duly qualified as such administrator, and ever since his appointment has been and now is acting as such administrator.

[Allege facts constituting cause of action.]

WHEREFORE, the plaintiff demands judgment against the defendant in the sum of ___13_____ dollars together with the costs and disbursements of this action.

___14_____
Attorney for Plaintiff
Office and P. O. Address
Telephone No.

Form 3

Complaint in Action By Trustee of Express Trust

SUPREME COURT, ___1_____ COUNTY.

Complaint
[Title of cause]   Index No. — [if assigned]

The plaintiff, by ___2_____, his attorney, complaining of the defendant, alleges:

1. On or about the ___3__ day of ___4_____, 19_5_, ___6_____ and the plaintiff made and executed a trust agreement, a copy of which is annexed hereto and marked "Exhibit A".

2. Pursuant to the terms and provisions of the said trust agreement, ___7_____, at the time of the execution of the said agreement and for the purposes of creating and maintaining a trust fund, assigned and transferred to the plaintiff, as trustee, personal property consisting of bonds, mortgages, securities and cash, all of which the plaintiff accepted and held as a trust fund.

3. Plaintiff accepted the trust created by the trust agreement, and now holds the trust fund subject to the terms and provisions of the said trust agreement.

[Allege facts constituting cause of action.]

WHEREFORE, plaintiff demands judgment against the defendant in the sum of ___8_____ dollars, with interest from the ___9__ day of ___10_____, 19_11_ together with the costs and disbursements of this action.

___12_____
Attorney for Plaintiff
Office and P. O. Address
Telephone No.

Form 4

Complaint in Action by Insured Person, Etc.

SUPREME COURT, ___1_____ COUNTY.

Complaint
[Title of cause]   Index No. — [if assigned]

The plaintiff, by his attorney, ___2_____, complaining of the defendant, alleges:

1. On or about the ___3__ day of ___4_____, 19_5_ the ___6_____ insurance company for a valuable consideration issued to plaintiff a certain policy of insurance, insuring the plaintiff against loss by reason of collision of a motor vehicle described as follows: [insert description of motor vehicle.] A copy of said policy is annexed hereto and made a part hereof.

2. On or about the ___7__ day of ___8_____, 19_9_ the said ___10_____ insurance company loaned to the plaintiff the sum of ___11_____ dollars on the security of the said policy and plaintiff at said time executed to the ___12_____ insurance company a loan or subrogation receipt.

[Allege facts constituting cause of action.]

WHEREFORE, plaintiff demands judgment against the defendant in the sum of __13_____ dollars together with the costs and disbursements of this action.

__14_____

Attorney for Plaintiff
Office and P. O. Address
Telephone No.

Form 5

Complaint in Action by Person in Whose Name a Contract is Made For the Benefit of Another

SUPREME COURT, __1_____ COUNTY.

[Title of cause]

Complaint
Index No. — [if assigned]

The plaintiff, by __2_____, his attorney, complaining of the defendant, alleges:

1. On or about the __3__ day of __4_____, 19_5_, the plaintiff entered into an agreement with the defendant whereby [describe nature of agreement], which agreement was for the benefit of __6_____.

[Set forth facts constituting cause of action.]

WHEREFORE, the plaintiff demands judgment against the defendant for the sum of __7_____ dollars with interest thereon from the __8__ day of __9_____, 19_10_, together with the costs and disbursements of this action.

__11_____

Attorney for Plaintiff
Office and P. O. Address
Telephone No.

Form 6

Complaint in Action by Guardian of the Property of an Infant

[Title of court and cause]

Complaint
Index No. — [if assigned]

The plaintiff, as guardian of the property of __1_____, an infant, complaining of the defendant, respectfully alleges:

1. On or about the __2__ day of __3_____, 19_4_ he was duly appointed guardian of the property of __5_____, the infant above named, by the __6_____ court of the County of __7_____, and he thereafter duly qualified and acted in that capacity and is still acting as such guardian of the property of __8_____.

2. The said __9_____ is an infant under the age of __10__ years, having become __11__ years of age on the __12__ day of __13_____, 19_14_, last past, and resides with __15_____ at __16_____ [address].

[Allege facts constituting cause of action.]

WHEREFORE, plaintiff demands judgment against the defendant in the sum of __17_____ dollars with interest thereon from the __18__ day of __19_____, 19_20_, together with the costs and disbursements of this action.

__21_____

Attorney for Plaintiff
Office and P. O. Address
Telephone No.

Form 7

Complaint in Action by Committee of Incompetent

Complaint

[Title of court and cause]   Index No. — [if assigned]

The plaintiff, as committee of __1_____, an incompetent, complaining of the defendant, respectfully alleges:

1. On or about the __2__ day of __3_____, 19_4_ he was duly appointed committee of __5_____, the incompetent above named, by the __6_____ court of the County of __7_____, and he thereafter duly qualified and acted in that capacity and is still acting as such committee.

2. The said __8_____ is an incompetent, having been judicially declared to be an incompetent on or about the __9__ day of __10_____, 19_11_ by the __12_____ court of the County of __13_____, and resides at __14_____ [address].

[Set forth facts constituting cause of action.]

WHEREFORE, plaintiff demands judgment against the defendant in the sum of __15_____ dollars with interest thereon from the __16__ day of __17_____, 19_18_, together with the costs and disbursements of this section.

__19_____

Attorney for Plaintiff
Office and P. O. Address
Telephone No.

§ 1005. [Repealed]

HISTORY:

> Add, L 1962, ch 308, amd, L 1962, ch 318, § 4, repealed, L 1975, ch 207, eff Sept 1, 1975. See now CPLR 901–909.

NOTE:

> [1975] Section 1005 of the civil practice law and rules, repealed by this act, related to class actions.

§ 1006. Interpleader

(a) Stakeholder; claimant; action of interpleader. A stakeholder is a person who is or may be exposed to multiple liability as the result of adverse claims. A claimant is a person who has made or may be expected to make such a claim. A stakeholder may commence an action of interpleader against two or more claimants.

(b) Defensive interpleader. A defendant stakeholder may bring in a claimant who is not a party by serving upon such claimant a summons and interpleader complaint and all prior pleadings served in the action.

(c) Effect of pendency of another action against stakeholder. If a stakeholder seeks to bring in a claimant pursuant to subdivision (b) and there is pending in a court of the state an action between the claimant and the stakeholder based upon the same claim, the appropriate court, on motion, upon such terms as may be just, may dismiss the interpleader complaint and order consolidation or joint trial of the actions, or may make the claimant a party and stay the pending action until final disposition of the action in which interpleader is so granted, and may make such further order as may be just.

(d) Abolition of former grounds for objection. It is not ground for objection to interpleader that the claims of the several claimants or the titles on which their claims depend do not have a common origin or are not identical but are adverse to and independent of one another, or that the stakeholder avers that he is not liable in whole or in part to any or all of the claimants.

(e) Issue of independent liability. Where the issue of an independent liability of the stakeholder to a claimant is raised by the pleadings or upon motion, the court may dismiss the claim of the appropriate claimant, order severance or separate trials, or require the issue to be tried in the action.

(f) Discharge of stakeholder. After the time for all parties to plead has expired, the stakeholder may move for an order discharging him from liability in whole or in part to any party. The stakeholder shall submit proof by affidavit or otherwise of the allegations in his pleading. The court may grant the motion and require payment into court, delivery to a person designated by the court or retention to the credit of the action, of the subject matter of the action to be disposed of in accordance with further order or the judgment. An order under subdivision (g) shall not discharge the stakeholder from liability to any claimant until an order granted under this subdivision is complied with. The court shall impose such terms relating to payment of expenses, costs and disbursements as may be just and which may be charged against the subject matter of the action. If the court shall determine that a party is entitled to interest, in the absence of an agreement by the stakeholder as to the rate of interest, he shall be liable to such party for interest to the date of discharge at a rate no greater than the lowest discount rate of the Federal Reserve Bank of New York for discounts for, and advances to, member banks in effect from time to time during the period for which, as found by the court, interest should be paid.

(g) Deposit of money as basis for jurisdiction. Where a stakeholder is otherwise entitled to proceed under this section for the determination of a right to, interest in or lien upon a sum of money, whether or not liquidated in amount, payable in the state pursuant to a contract or claimed as damages for unlawful retention of specific real or personal property in the state, he may move, either before or after an action has been commenced against him, for an order permitting him to pay the sum of money or part of it into court or to a designated person or to retain it to the credit of the action. Upon compliance with a court order permitting such deposit or retention, the sum of money shall be deemed specific property within the state within the meaning of paragraph two of section 314.

HISTORY:
   Add, L 1962, ch 308, eff Sept 1, 1963.
   Earlier statutes: CPA §§ 285, 286; CCP § 820-a.

ADVISORY COMMITTEE NOTES:
   Except for formal or minor changes, this section follows § 285 of the CPA which was recommended by the Judicial Council. See 20 NY Jud Council Rep 271, 319 (1954). Cf. Fed R Civ P 22.
   As to § 287 on the interpleader compact, see Zimmerman, Wendall and Heller,

Effective Interpleader via Interstate Compacts, 55 Colum L Rev 56 (1955). However, no other jurisdiction has entered into a compact with New York. See also CPA §§ 51-a, 51-b; Frumer, On Revising the New York Interpleader Statutes, 25 NYUL Rev 737 (1950); Note, 24 NYUL Rev 894 (1949).

Subd (g) is derived from CPA § 286, which was enacted in 1954 as part of the Judicial Council's revision of the interpleader provisions. NY Laws 1954, c. 561; see 20 NY Jud Council Rep 267, 281–84 (1954). Subd 1 of CPA § 286 simply affirms that interpleader may be based on in rem or quasi in rem jurisdiction where the subject matter is specific real or personal property within the state; it is covered by the specific reference to an action of interpleader or defensive interpleader in new CPLR § 314. Subd 2 of § 286, however, represents an innovation; it provides for the creation of a res upon which interpleader jurisdiction may be based, by segregation pursuant to a court order of a sum of money representing the amount of the stakeholder's obligation. Like the interpleader compact (see CPA § 287), it is designed to meet the problem of affording the stakeholder a complete adjudication though some of the claimants are nonresidents and not subject to personal jurisdiction. As the Council recognized, there may be some question concerning its constitutionality (see 20 NY Jud Council Rep 284 (1954)), but this apparently has not yet been determined in any reported decision. Subd (g) retains this provision with only minor changes of language.

CROSS REFERENCES:

Impleader in action to enforce liability of distributees and testamentary beneficiaries, EPTL § 12-2.2.

As to jurisdiction over nonresident defendants, CPLR 314.

Pleadings in interpleader actions, CPLR 3011, 3012(a), 3017(a).

As to orders directing sale or other disposition of property interpleaded, CPLR 2701, 2702.

In certain courts, Ct Cl Act §§ 9, 14; NYC Civil Ct Act §§ 205, 901, 902. See also Bank Law §§ 134, 239, Condem Law § 22; Gen Bus Law §§ 103, 229-j; UCC § 7-603.

FEDERAL ASPECTS:

Moneys paid into court, 28 USCS §§ 2041 et seq.

Interpleader, 28 USCS § 2361.

Interpleader, Rule 22 of Federal Rules of Civil Procedure, USCS Court Rules.

RESEARCH REFERENCES AND PRACTICE AIDS:

2 Carmody-Wait 2d, Actions and Proceedings § 9:14.

3 Carmody-Wait 2d, Stays § 22:15.

6 Carmody-Wait 2d, Interpleader §§ 40:3–40:7, 40:9, 40:11, 40:13, 40:18 et seq., 40:20–40:22, 40:28, 40:31, 40:32, 40:34–40:37, 40:39, 40:49, 40:53.

14 Carmody-Wait 2d, Foreclosure of Mortgages on Real Estate § 92:129.

45 Am Jur 2d, Interpleader §§ 21 et seq., 44–49.

59 Am Jur 2d, Parties § 113.

1 Am Jur Pl and Pr Forms (Rev ed), Actions, Forms 1 et seq., 41 et seq.

15 Am Jur Pl and Pr Forms (Rev ed), Interpleader, Forms 41 et seq.

Annotations:

Allowance of interest on interpleaded or impleaded disputed funds. 15 ALR2d 473.

Jurisdiction and venue of federal court, under federal interpleader statutes, to entertain cross-claim by one interpleaded party against another. 17 ALR2d 741.

Corporation's right to interplead claimants to dividends. 46 ALR2d 980.

Allowance of attorneys' fees to party interpleading claimants to funds or property. 48 ALR2d 190.

Federal interpleader proceeding as in rem or in personam in context of problem of service of process upon particular claimant. 17 ALR Fed 447.

Availability of interpleader to insurance company for resolving dispute as to insurance policy under Federal Interpleader Act (presently 28 USCS §§ 1335, 1397, 2361) and Rule 22 of Federal Rules of Civil Procedure. 19 ALR Fed 166.

Law Reviews:

New York Civil Practice Law and Rules: parties. 27 Albany L Rev 182.

Parties and pleading under the CPLR. 31 Brooklyn L Rev 98.

A biannual survey of New York practice: Part IV: CPLR 1006: use of interpleader does not preclude jury trial. 39 St. John's L Rev 426.

Forms:

See "FORMS" heading following "CASE NOTES", infra.

CASE NOTES

1. In general
2. Where interpleader proper
3. Summary judgment
4. Deposit and discharge
5. Costs and fees; punitive damages

1. In general

An action involving conflicting claims to a bank deposit was not, properly speaking, an interpleader so as to give the New York City Civil Court jurisdiction under § 205 of the New York City Civil Court Act. Kwoczka v Dry Dock Sav. Bank (1966) 52 Misc 2d 67, 275 NYS2d 156.

Action against escrowee to recover money escrowee failed to turn over, is one at law, even though escrowee interpleads non-party claimants to money, and escrowee and interpleaded defendant are entitled to jury trial. Geddes v Rosen (1965) 22 AD2d 394, 255 NYS2d 585, affd 16 NY2d 816, 263 NYS2d 10, 210 NE2d 362.

Defendant escrowee, asserting a claim based on an alleged agreement against both plaintiff-claimant and interpleaded claimant, can counterclaim therefor and reduce the fund in litigation by set-off. Geddes v Rosen (1965) 22 AD2d 394, 255 NYS2d 585, affd 16 NY2d 816, 263 NYS2d 10, 210 NE2d 362.

2. Where interpleader proper

Absent an adjudication that they have been derived from illegal activities, disposition of monies seized pursuant to search warrant in the possession of the District Attorney of Orange County, who has been served after an arrest with a notice of levy for Federal taxes and a warrant for state taxes owed by the defendant, is best determined in an interpleader action. 1973 Ops Atty Gen Dec 14.

A claimant who is not a party may properly be brought into the action by the defendant stakeholder under the provisions of subd (b) of CPLR § 1006. Geddes v Rosen (1965) 22 AD2d 394, 255 NYS2d 585, affd 16 NY2d 816, 263 NYS2d 10, 210 NE2d 362.

Where an escrowee is faced with the prospect of exposure to multiple liability, he may properly bring in non-party claimant. Geddes v Rosen (1965) 22 AD2d 394, 255 NYS2d 585, affd 16 NY2d 816, 263 NYS2d 10, 210 NE2d 362.

Insurer's action to determine to whom it should make payment of proceeds of life policy was properly brought in interpleader where insurer had been presented with adverse claims to the proceeds and the claims were not patently without substance. Connecticut General Life Ins. Co. v Boni (1975) 48 AD2d 621, 368 NYS2d 1, app dismd 37 NY2d 917, 378 NYS2d 388, 340 NE2d 748.

Bank, which had drawn cashier's check payable to its customer, who, in turn, negotiated check to alleged swindler in allegedly fraudulent stock purchase transaction, and which was given stop payment order by customer on day check was received by bank, but before check had been paid, came within definition of "stakeholder," within meaning of interpleader rule and rule relating to payment of monies or securities into court, and bank could easily insulate itself without difficulty or expense against exposure of multiple liability. Dziurak v Chase Manhattan Bank, N.A. (1976) 88 Misc 2d 641, 388 NYS2d 496.

Life insurance company, against which conflicting claims for payment of life policy proceeds were made by the deceased insured's brother and widow, should have been allowed to pay the insurance proceeds into court and to be discharged from liability as a stakeholder, and special term, which denied the insurer's motion, erred in deciding the motion as though it had been for summary judgment as between the parties in interest. Bankers Secur. Life Ins. Soc. v Shakerdge (1976) 55 AD2d 568, 390 NYS2d 75.

3. Summary judgment

The absence of other claimants does not entitle a claimant in the interpleader to a summary judgment since he must succeed upon his own rights to the fund. District Attorney of Nassau County v Farrington (1967) 56 Misc 2d 904, 290 NYS2d 132.

Where there are conflicting claims to the proceeds

of a life insurance policy by persons who have been named beneficiaries of such policy at different times, summary judgment will be denied, and interpleader relief will be granted to the insurance company upon the payment into court of the face amount of the policy together with interest thereon from the date of the insured's death. Jensen v Metropolitan Life Ins. Co. (1967) 27 AD2d 934, 278 NYS2d 781, app dismd 20 NY2d 739, 283 NYS2d 102, 229 NE2d 699.

4. Deposit and discharge

Where the interpleading plaintiff has knowledge of material facts, the court may deny his discharge so that the rival claimants may have the advantage of full pretrial disclosure. Manacher v Sterling Nat. Bank & Trust Co. (1956) 4 Misc 2d 1077, 160 NYS2d 217.

Where insurer admitted its liability on a life insurance policy, and there was a dispute between two claimants as to their status as beneficiaries, the insurer was entitled to an order permitting it to pay the proceeds of the policy into court, and discharging the insurer from further liability. Mann v John Hancock Mut. Life Ins. Co. (1963) 20 AD2d 608, 245 NYS2d 433, am on other grounds 27 AD2d 990, 246 NYS2d 1019.

Ordinarily, a court must afford a party moving for a discharge as a stakeholder pursuant to interpleader practice the most liberal interpretation of the applicable statute. Even a "colorable" adverse claim may be sufficient to permit payment into court and the discharge of a stakeholder and for the purpose of the motion, the court should assume the truth of the allegations in the respective pleadings. MacQueen Realty Co. v Emmi (1968) 58 Misc 2d 54, 294 NYS2d 566.

Where life insurer filed a stakeholder's action against administrator of decedent's estate and named contingent beneficiaries, and court directed policy proceeds to be paid over to county treasurer so as to discharge insurer from any liability to any of parties to action, action was determined insofar as stakeholder-insurer was concerned, but continued between different defendants for determination of their respective and conflicting claims. Re Estate of Bach (1975) 81 Misc 2d 479, 365 NYS2d 454, affd 53 AD2d 612, 383 NYS2d 653.

Where insurer admitted its liability on a life insurance policy, and there was a dispute between two claimants as to their status as beneficiaries, the insurer was entitled to an order permitting it to pay the proceeds of the policy into court, and discharging the insurer from further liability. Mann v John Hancock Mut. Life Ins. Co. (1963) 20 AD2d 608, 245 NYS2d 433, am on other grounds 27 AD2d 990, 246 NYS2d 1019.

Since furrier's $12,000 fire policy would not be sufficient to cover all of its customer's claims resulting from fire which destroyed premises, it was error for special term to vacate order staying and consolidating all pending or contemplated proceedings and permitting furrier to be discharged from all liability on deposit of policy proceeds; circumstances called for equitable intervention to avoid granting of improper preferences and multiplicity of actions. Hartford Fire Ins. Co. v Weiss (1974) 44 AD2d 807, 355 NYS2d 597.

5. Costs and fees; punitive damages

Where order recognizes the status of a bank as a mere stakeholder, the court was empowered to impose terms relating to payment of expenses, costs and disbursements. Silber v Lachs (1969) 33 AD2d 544, 304 NYS2d 289, affd 28 NY2d 554, 319 NYS2d 447, 268 NE2d 126.

While a stakeholder ordinarily is entitled to reimbursement for expenses, including reasonable attorneys' fees, the granting of costs including attorneys' fees rests in the sound discretion of the court and should not be granted where the relief requested is denied. MacQueen Realty Co. v Emmi (1968) 58 Misc 2d 54, 294 NYS2d 566.

The interpleading insurance carrier was entitled to its legal expenses and disbursements to be paid out of the proceeds of the insurance policies. Re Kaplan's Estate (1966) 49 Misc 2d 335, 267 NYS2d 345.

Plaintiff warehousemen's attorneys' fees for defending counterclaims asserted by defendants, who were interpleaded in an action by the public warehousemen after several claims had been asserted to goods stored with the warehousemen, could not be charged against the deposited fund, since a disinterested stakeholder may recover only those expenses directly incurred in affecting a deposit and discharge, but not expenses incurred in defending an independent claim. National Cold Storage Co. v Tiya Caviar Co. (1966) 52 Misc 2d 289, 276 NYS2d 57.

While life insurance company, against which conflicting claims for payment of life policy proceeds were made by decedent's widow and his brother, the named beneficiary, refused to pay out the policy proceeds and instead commenced an interpleader action, there was no actionable or wanton breach by the company vis-a-vis the brother, and thus no basis for an award of punitive damages, nor was there any basis for a claim against the company for counsel fees. Bankers Secur. Life Ins. Soc. v Shakerdge (1976) 55 AD2d 568, 390 NYS2d 75.

CASE NOTES

UNDER FORMER CIVIL PRACTICE LAWS

A. IN GENERAL

1. Generally

Interpleader is procedure by which one who may be exposed to multiple liability may require adverse claimants to litigate their claims in one action or proceeding. Horoch v State (1955) 286 AD 303, 143 NYS2d 327, resettled on other grounds 286 AD 977, 144 NYS2d 721.

At least two adverse claimants are necessary for interpleader. Woodley v National Trans. Co. (1955) 208 Misc 732, 142 NYS2d 879.

Where rights of interpleaded defendants to property involved in plaintiff's action are at stake, it is error to dismiss at the instance of plaintiff the interpleading complaint bringing them into action. Isacowitz v Isacowitz (1959) 8 AD2d 837, 190 NYS2d 405.

Where stockholder was sued as sole defendant for return of deposit he was holding as escrow agent under contract providing that if purchasers could not secure mortgage, monies deposited on house were to be returned, fact that he could interplead sellers did not prevent him from raising defense, available to sellers, that plaintiffs in applying for mortgage, had misrepresented their financial status so as to get out of the contract. Falk v Goodman (1959) 7 NY2d 87, 195 NYS2d 645, 163 NE2d 871.

The independent action of interpleader as it formerly existed is not ousted by the new statutory practice. O'Donnell v Vanecek (1956) 3 Misc 2d 20, 150 NYS2d 819.

At trial of interpleader action, issues of plaintiff's own independent liability to those who appear and make claim to the fund involved may also be adjudicated. Becker v United States (1961) 216 NYS2d 971.

2. Impleader and interpleader distinguished

Impleader was not to be confused with interpleader under CPA § 285 which was procedure to determine adverse claims made against same person, whereas in impleader there were no adverse claims to be settled. Blonstein v 241 Fifth Ave. Corp. (1956) 154 NYS2d 602.

3. Prerequisites of interpleader; necessity for "stakeholder"

To afford a stakeholder protection against adverse

claims, the right to interplead is only available to the stakeholder. Casolaro v Blau (1956) 4 Misc 2d 206, 158 NYS2d 589.

In order to obtain interpleader order under CPA § 285, there had to be showing that "stakeholder" existed, who asserted that he had no interest in fund among rival claimants and sought to secure adjudication as to rightful owner of fund, and stakeholder in usual case requested that he be permitted to deposit fund in court to be paid over to rightful claimant. Stern v Stern (1955) 145 NYS2d 337.

To sustain an interpleader, the alleged claim of a third person must have some reasonable basis on which to rest. A prerequisite to the maintenance of interpleader is that the same thing, debt or duty is claimed by more than one person. Re Harris (1957) 8 Misc 2d 541, 167 NYS2d 106.

Under present practice the complaint in an action of interpleader cannot be attacked on the ground either that plaintiff asserts a personal claim to the fund involved, or that the claims thereto of those he impleads are not mutually exclusive. Plaintiff qualifies as a stakeholder so long as he shows that he is exposed to multiple liability as a result of adverse claims. Becker v United States (1961) 216 NYS2d 971.

4. —Stakeholder defined

A stakeholder is a person who is or may be exposed to double or multiple liability as the result of adverse claims. Casolaro v Blau (1956) 4 Misc 2d 206, 158 NYS2d 589.

Where defendant and interpleading plaintiffs fulfilled statutory definitions of stakeholder, under CPA § 285 subd 1 they could institute defensive interpleader under subd 3. Cerrone v Trans World Airlines, Inc. (1955) 148 NYS2d 162.

Where divorced wife commenced action against divorced husband as in fraud of plaintiff to set aside his transfer to second wife of chattel mortgage, person claiming to be real owner of chattel mortgage and claiming that husband was only nominal owner cannot be interpleaded as stakeholder and codefendant by defendant husband. Stern v Stern (1955) 145 NYS2d 337.

Where moneys of a church were deposited in two banks on resolutions authorizing withdrawals on signatures of three vestrymen and thereafter new vestrymen were elected and this election and the election of a rector are in litigation and one of the banks brought an action of interpleader against both vestries, it was authorized to deposit its moneys in an account subject to judgment of the court. Rector, Church of the Holy Trinity v Manufacturers Trust Co. (1957) 8 Misc 2d 869, 166 NYS2d 713.

5. Application of decisions under former sections

In determining whether to grant stakeholder discharge pursuant to CPA § 285 subd 7, court should have been mindful of former grounds of objection to interpleader abolished by CPA § 285

subd 5. Leventhal v Roslyn Manor, Inc. (1955) 142 NYS2d 478.

Discharge of the stakeholder, under CPA § 285(7), was denied in a case similar to those in which interpleader was denied under the former practice. Leventhal v Roslyn Manor, Inc., supra.

For decisions under former sections, see ¶¶ 18–58.

B. PRACTICE AND PROCEDURE

6. Service of summons and interpleading complaint

Where defendants alleged that they had impleaded distributees who made adverse claims to bank passbook by service upon them of summons and interpleading complaint, together with copy of original summons and complaint served upon them in action, service complied with CPA §§ 285 and 286, by bringing other persons so served into action without necessity for court order to that end. O'Donnell v Vanecek (1956) 3 Misc 2d 20, 150 NYS2d 819.

7. Jurisdiction of nonresident defendants

Where defendant and interpleading plaintiffs fulfilled statutory definitions of stakeholder under CPA § 285 subd 1, they might have instituted defensive interpleader under subd 3, and stakeholders might have proceeded to obtain quasi in rem jurisdiction over nonresidents under CPA § 232 subd 2. Cerrone v Trans World Airlines (1955) 148 NYS2d 162.

Where action involved ownership of stock certificates within state and one of the claimants was a nonresident, impleading parties as stakeholders under CPA § 286 could obtain jurisdiction under CPA § 232(2) and serve nonresident personally without the state under CPA § 235 (§§ 313, 3012(c), Rule 320(a) herein), even though such nonresident was an administrator of an estate in another state. Cerrone v Trans World Airlines, supra.

8. Stay of other actions

Although a plaintiff in an interpleader action may during the pendency thereof obtain a stay of an action brought against him by one of the defendants, yet where the effect of such stay will be to change the venue of the other action, which had been started first, court may in its discretion order a stay for thirty days to enable plaintiff to interplead in the other action. Heene v Sewell (1959) 19 Misc 2d 118, 189 NYS2d 924.

In interpleader action, temporary injunction to restrain defendant from bringing or proceeding with any action against plaintiff was denied as to the defendant who would have been seriously prejudiced if restrained from proceeding with municipal court action wherein early trial could be had. Gulf Oil Corp. v Helmus Constr. Corp. (1960) 23 Misc 2d 816, 198 NYS2d 855.

9. Examinations before trial

A stakeholder can be examined before trial as an adverse party in the discretion of the court. Casolaro v Blau (1956) 4 Misc 2d 206, 158 NYS2d 589.

10. Withdrawal of interpleaded defendant

Interpleaded defendant cannot, without consent of others, withdraw from case, though it may withdraw its answer. Kaufman v Eagle Lion Classics (1955) 285 AD 931, 138 NYS2d 463.

11. Discharge of stakeholder

After the changes in interpleader statutes in 1954, interpleader no longer necessarily involves the discharge of the stakeholder; it now means the procedure by which a stakeholder may require adverse claimants to litigate their claims in one action, but with or without the presence of the stakeholder as the court may determine. Leventhal v Roslyn Manor, Inc. (1955) 142 NYS2d 478.

Under CPA § 285 the questions of the appropriateness of interpleader relief and a discharge of the stakeholder were no longer inextricably bound together, and dependent upon one another, but could have been treated as separate problems. Nelson v Cross & Brown Co. (1959) 9 AD2d 140, 192 NYS2d 335.

In determining whether to grant stakeholder discharge pursuant to CPA § 285 subd 7, court was required to be mindful of former grounds of objection to interpleader abolished by CPA § 285 subd 5. Leventhal v Roslyn Manor, Inc. (1955) 142 NYS2d 478.

Although inconsistent claims, not mutually exclusive, no longer bar interpleader, they may be considered in determining the propriety of discharging stakeholder. Nelson v Cross & Brown Co. (1959) 9 AD2d 140, 192 NYS2d 335.

Where parties stipulated an extension of the stakeholder's time to answer, in anticipation of settlement, objection that stakeholder had not answered and so might not be discharged under CPA § 285(7) was merely technical and would not defeat such discharge. Rubin v Queensboro Farm Products, Inc. (1954) 135 NYS2d 546.

To be eligible for a discharge, stakeholder must show that resting on some reasonable basis he will be exposed to double or multiple liability as a result of adverse claims to the money involved. Nelson v Cross & Brown Co. (1959) 9 AD2d 140, 192 NYS2d 335.

Where either by virtue of stakeholder's denial of plaintiff-claimant's right to any part of the money involved, or by virtue of his offer to deposit a fraction of the sum claimed by plaintiff on the theory that he may be entitled to much more, the stakeholder cannot claim to stand indifferent to the amount in dispute, he should not be discharged. Nelson v Cross & Brown Co., supra.

Where defendant stakeholder denies plaintiff's right to recover any part of money involved, and in addition alleges that it is liable for only one-fifth thereof to either plaintiff or interpleaded defendant, it would be improper to permit stakeholder to be discharged upon deposit of only one-fifth, for stakeholder will still have to defend its right to the remaining four-fifths either as a defendant or as an interested stakeholder. Nelson v Cross & Brown Co., supra.

If stakeholder pays into court whole amount of debt, he is thereby discharged from all and further liability, and trial proceeds between claimants without his participation; if stakeholder deposits in court part of amount of debt and there is dispute as to balance, he is discharged to extent of amount deposited and remains in action to defend his interest in balance; sole issue insofar as stakeholder is concerned is whether he is liable for balance of debt; and claimants contend for amount in dispute between "them", the part of the debt deposited in court. Bisgeier v Prudential Ins. Co. (1956) 2 Misc 2d 857, 150 NYS2d 625.

Where an action was brought against two corporations which had issued certificates of indebtedness to plaintiff and a conflicting claim to ownership of the certificates was asserted on behalf of plaintiff's sons and the corporate defendants interposed an answer interpleading a certain person as trustee for plaintiff's sons, the corporate defendants' request for discharge should be denied on the ground that they were not mere stakeholders but had an interest in the action. Manacher v Sterling Nat. Bank & Trust Co. (1956) 4 Misc 2d 1077, 160 NYS2d 217.

Under CPA § 286(2) a stakeholder who was the defendant in an action for payment of the stake to the claimants, could at any time during the action apply for an order permitting him to deliver or pay the stake into court subject to further order or judgment. Casolaro v Blau (1956) 4 Misc 2d 206, 158 NYS2d 589.

Escrow agent uncertain as to which of two or more claimants was entitled to payment could interplead them, deposit the fund in court, and be relieved of liability, under CPA §§ 285, 286. Lindley v Robillard (1955) 208 Misc 532, 144 NYS2d 33.

12. Judgment; costs and allowances

Where action is one to recover upon a contract of insurance, interpleader does not make it an action in equity which would deprive the plaintiff of the right to move for summary judgment. Hunt v Unity Life & Acci. Ins. Asso. (1956) 7 Misc 2d 830, 160 NYS2d 415.

Where money had been deposited in court by a stakeholder and on the record presented it did not appear that the issues raised in answers concerning the rights and priorities of the respective defendants in relation to the fund on deposit had been tried, distribution of the fund was required to await the entry of a final judgment or an order pursuant to CPA § 285 after adjudication of all issues raised by the pleadings. John A. Johnson & Sons, Inc. v National City Bank (1958) 6 AD2d 1055, 179 NYS2d 541.

This section permits the allowance of reasonable attorney's fees as "expenses" to a plaintiff stockholder out of funds involved in interpleader action. Metropolitan L. Ins. Co. v Brody (1962, Sup) 228 NYS2d 312.

C. Particular Applications

13. Brokers

Where broker sued vendor for broker's commission and vendor paid amount thereof into court and interpleaded another broker who filed two counterclaims for commission, claiming he was procuring cause and that vendor and purchaser conspired to deprive him of commission, vendor was necessary, in one capacity or another, to all future proceedings, and his discharge as stakeholder was denied. Leventhal v Roslyn Manor, Inc. (1955) 142 NYS2d 478.

In an action to recover commissions for sale of real property where stakeholder holding money in escrow had been joined as defendant, defendant might apply for appropriate relief under the provisions of CPA § 285. Cammarata v Conley (1958) 13 Misc 2d 349, 179 NYS2d 923.

14. Escrow agreement

Where escrow agent was uncertain as to which of claimants was entitled to payment, it had available a remedy in nature of interpleader by which it could have deposited fund into court and been relieved of further liability to parties. Lindley v Robillard (1955) 208 Misc 532, 144 NYS2d 33.

Where an escrow agent denies fulfillment of the terms of the escrow agreement and is uncertain as to which claimant is entitled to the fund, interpleader is a means by which he could have deposited the fund into court and be relieved of further liability to the parties, and the action thereupon would have been equitable in nature to determine the rights of the parties to the fund. But by pleading all claimants as parties defendant and alleging that they had laid claim to all or part of the escrow fund, plaintiffs avoided the necessity of interpleader but brought before the court all the parties to enable the court to adjudicate their respective rights, otherwise impossible had the action sounded in law for liquidated damages against the escrow agent. West End Homes, Inc. v Soldinger (1958) 12 Misc 2d 342, 172 NYS2d 1012.

15. Insurance

In action against insurer and assignee of policy, where complaint indicated that plaintiffs were asserting claim against insurer, latter was stakeholder entitled to benefits of CPA § 285. Rubin v Queensboro Farm Products, Inc. (1954) 135 NYS2d 546.

In action to recover proceeds of two life insurance policies, where husband assigned policies to plaintiff and designated him as beneficiary in place of his wife previously designated, plaintiff was awarded proceeds of policies, and answer of interpleaded wife and creditors of decedent was dismissed. Kandel v New York Life Ins. Co. (1955) 143 NYS2d 458.

Where estranged wife as beneficiary of life policy sues insurer for insurance proceeds and insurer receives claim to proceeds by insured's administrator who claimed that plaintiff had released her interest by separation agreement, such conflicting claims cannot be determined in absence of administrator and cross-motion for order of interpleader was granted. Molfetta v Connecticut Gen. Life Ins. Co. (1954) 134 NYS2d 924.

Where original beneficiary of life policy sued insurer which interpleaded substituted beneficiary and paid life insurance proceeds into court, such interpleader was authorized by CPA § 285 and MCC § 27 subd 3, when construed together. Campbell v Metropolitan Life Ins. Co. (1956) 2 Misc 2d 657, 154 NYS2d 580.

Where wife of insured sued insurer who interpleaded insured's daughter and claimed life insurance proceeds, and insurer deposited in court amount of policies, insurer was discharged from liability except for deductions made for loans and unpaid premiums, which were disputed by daughter. Bisgeier v Prudential Ins. Co. (1956) 2 Misc 2d 857, 150 NYS2d 625.

Where an insurance company seeks to have interpleader but it has not shown that it is ignorant or in doubt as to which party is entitled to the awards of the insurance or that it is in real danger or hazard by means of such debt, application to interplead denied. Re Harris (1957) 8 Misc 2d 541, 167 NYS2d 106.

Where insurer paid money into court pursuant to interpleader under CPA § 285, insurer was required to pay interest from date of receipt by it of proof of death. Rubin v Queensboro Farm Products, Inc. (1954) 135 NYS2d 546.

16. Municipal corporations

Insurer of automobile owner could interplead city against whom same judgment had been rendered as against insured. It could also interplead the judgment creditor. United States Fidelity & Guarantee Co. v Hotkins (1956) 6 Misc 2d 1027, 158 NYS2d 580.

17. Vendor and purchaser

Provision in contract to purchase real property, signed by both vendor and purchaser, that a named person was the broker who brought about sale, will not preclude vendor from bringing interpleader action against named person and another broker-claimant. Heene v Sewell (1959) 19 Misc 2d 118, 189 NYS2d 924.

D. Decisions Under Former CPA §§ 285–287i

(Repealed L 1954, Ch 561. While the remedy and practice of interpleader were substantially affected by the 1954 provisions, decisions under the former sections are set out below for such application as they may have.)

18. Generally

Former § 287 was substituted for the old action of interpleader and is governed by the same principles. Windecker v Mutual L. Ins. Co. (1896) 12 AD 73, 43 NYS 358; Schell v Lowe (1894) 75 Hun 43, 26 NYS 991.

Interpleader under former § 287 was only a substitute for the old action of interpleader, and the question to be determined was the ownership of the fund. O'Rourke v Patterson (1913) 157 AD 284, 142 NYS 195.

Former § 287 was intended to prevent the cumbersome procedure by action, and substitute that by motion, and none but a stakeholder could obtain relief under this section which recognized the same rule which had prevailed in actions of interpleader. Wenstrom Electric Co. v Bloomer (1895) 85 Hun 389, 32 NYS 903.

The provisions of § 287 for interpleader by order were intended not as a new but as a concurrent and more simple remedy than the older action of interpleader; either remedy may be granted or withheld in accordance with the sound discretion of the court. Rosen v Equitable Life Assur. Soc. (1942) 289 NY 333, 45 NE2d 899.

Purpose of former § 287b was to relieve escrowee or stakeholder from subjecting himself to risk of suit or liability by reason of assertion of adverse claim and to relieve him of responsibility of making determinations of conflicting claims and issues. Hencer Corp. v Stolz (1941) 176 Misc 460, 26 NYS2d 754.

Former § 287 gave a right of interpleader, when the defendant had an interest in the fund in suit, and desired to interplead another party to the end that the whole matter might be adjudicated, but a defendant was not entitled to an order of interpleader merely because two claims were made against him for the same debt. Mitchell v Catlin & Powell Co. (1911) 71 Misc 450, 128 NYS 692.

In case of true interpleader, fund is subject of action, and rights of various claimants to fund present only issues. Keating v Astor Theatre Corp. (1950) 277 AD 52, 97 NYS2d 843.

In interpleader action, court is court of equity. Harris Motors, Inc. v Csontos (1947) 190 Misc 733, 76 NYS2d 55.

The provisions of the Code relating to interpleader were permissive, not mandatory. Hemmerich v Union Dime Sav. Institution (1911) 144 AD 413, 129 NYS 267, affd 205 NY 366, 98 NE 499.

See also, as to the general doctrine of interpleader. Dows v Kidder (1881) 84 NY 121; Barnes v New York (1882) 27 Hun 236.

Third-party claimant may intervene in any interpleader proceeding to assert claim to property, though original pleadings do not indicate existence of such claim or name him as party to action. Stern v Newton (1943) 180 Misc 241, 39 NYS2d 593.

Former § 287 was inapplicable to notice pursuant to CPA § 51-a. Solicitor v Bankers Trust Co. (1952) 304 NY 282, 107 NE2d 448.

Recourse to section (former § 287-b) should be encouraged, and in view of its beneficent object and purpose it should be liberally construed. Hencer Corp. v Stolz (1941) 176 Misc 460, 26 NYS2d 754.

Banking L § 239, subd 6(a) and this section (former § 287-b) are statutes in pari materia, and so may be read and construed together as constitut-

ing one law. Marshall v Friedman (1941) 176 Misc 32, 26 NYS2d 756.

It was not purpose of former § 287-a to permit fiduciary to deposit balance in court and be cleared of all liability for accounting for its actions. Newton v Simon (1947) 188 Misc 669, 68 NYS2d 611, affd 272 AD 871, 72 NYS2d 261.

In both replevin and conversion, court is required to exonerate stakeholder, on complying with statute (former § 287-d), from liability for damages for unlawful detention. Smith v Associated Lerner Shops (1947) 70 NYS2d 106.

19. Who may bring interpleader

Former §§ 285, 287 did not authorize one of claimants to bring action against debtor and other claimant to determine adverse claim. Brown v Arbogast & B. Co. (1914) 162 AD 603, 147 NYS 998.

Former § 287 applied only to proceedings by motion and by a defendant. Baltimore & O. R. Co. v Arthur (1882) 90 NY 234.

A motion by a defendant in default under former § 193 to bring in additional defendants could not prevail, but the defendant might under former § 287 pay into court the amount claimed and then would be entitled to an order substituting any claimants to the fund and the sheriff who attached it in his place and be discharged from liability. American Trust & Sav. Bank v Thalheimer (1898) 29 AD 170, 51 NYS 813.

Assignor and assignee: see Bergman v Liverpool & London & Globe Ins. Co. (1945) 269 AD 103, 54 NYS2d 204.

Different plaintiffs, suing same defendant, cannot be interpleaded in place of defendant, but actions should be consolidated. Melnick v Jewish Nat. Workers' Alliance (1940) 21 NYS2d 98.

By rendering itself liable to a corporation in allowing the latter's officer to indorse his company's checks to his own account, a trust company secures the right to interplead hereunder and be freed from liability for the funds from said checks by depositing the money in court. New York Trust Co. v Braham (1926) 126 Misc 462, 213 NYS 678.

When two brokers each claimed a right to commissions, and there was no pretense that the defendant was liable to both, he could, upon paying the amount into court, interplead the claimants to litigate the issues between themselves. Trembley v Marshall (1907) 118 AD 839, 103 NYS 680.

Brokers claiming commissions for the same sale of a piece of property from same defendant, he could deposit the money in court and the brokers would be required to interplead. Shipman v Scott, 14 Daly 233.

Where sheriff, under sequestration order pursuant to CPA § 406-a against witness adjudged in contempt for disobeying subpoena, seized stock owner's equity in account with brokerage firm, and after lapse of 20 years City of New York and assignee of said stock owner claimed his property so seized, stockbroker could maintain action of interpleader to determine title thereto. Hornblower & Weeks v Sherwood (1953) 124 NYS2d 322, affd 282 AD 931, 125 NYS2d 647, affd 307 NY 204, 120 NE2d 790.

By rendering itself liable to a corporation in allowing the latter's officer to indorse his company's checks to his own account, a trust company secured the right to interplead under former § 285 and be freed from liability for the funds from said checks by depositing the money in court. New York Trust Co. v Braham (1926) 126 Misc 462, 213 NYS 678.

A depositary, holding money in dispute between two or more claimants, was allowed to pay the money into court, while the claimants could properly be restrained from prosecuting actions against such depositary where the claims of the claimants rested on doubtful questions of law which the depositary could not himself determine. Mercantile Trust Co. v Calvet-Rogniat (1904) 46 Misc 16, 93 NYS 238.

20. Complaint

The complaint in an action of interpleader must allege positively that conflicting claims to substantially the same thing, fund, debt or duty are set up by the defendant; that the defendant claims no interest in the subject matter; that he is indifferent between the claimants, and is ready and willing to deliver the thing or fund, or pay the debt, or render the duty to the rightful claimant, but that he is ignorant or in doubt which is the rightful one, and is in real danger or hazard by means of such doubt from their conflicting demands. Pouch v Prudential Ins. Co, (1912) 204 NY 281, 97 NE 731.

Complaint by receivers of corporation, failing to allege dissipation of corporate funds in declaring and paying dividend or that corporation was defrauded party by virtue of actions of named conspirators, was insufficient. Amen v Black-Marshall Oil Co. (1950) 100 NYS2d 39.

21. Adequate remedy at law

The complaint was dismissed in action in equity for a money judgment against defendant bank and for an equitable decree against the individual defendant that she had no right, title or interest in a savings bank trust account, the proceeds of which plaintiff, as administratrix, was attempting to reach, where the record showed that the plaintiff had an adequate remedy at law against the savings bank either for conversion or for money had and received, provided an effective revocation of the trust could be established on the trial. Nathan v Bernstein (1937) 252 AD 497, 299 NYS 733.

22. Objections to interpleader

The amount due from a plaintiff could not be the subject of a controversy in an action of interpleader, the action could only be maintained when plaintiff admitted liability for the full amount claimed, to one or the other of the claimants.

Baltimore & O. R. Co. v Arthur (1882) 90 NY 234; and see New England Mut. Life Ins. Co. v Odell (1885) 50 Hun 279, 2 NYS 873; Delaware, L. & W. R. Co. v Corwith (1889) 5 NYS 792.

Provision of former § 285 permitting person sued on claim to bring in third party claimant applied only where claim was on "same debt" and defendant disputed liability. Thus defendant sued on agreement with customs attorneys could not interplead second attorney with whom it made similar agreement, where claim as to him was admitted. Strauss v Grande Maison De Blanc, Inc. (1932) 237 AD 83, 260 NYS 368.

Insurer must fully admit liability, as pro tanto admission of liability will not suffice, as where insurer claimed right to reduce insurance because of insured's misstatement as to age in his application for insurance. Goodman v New York Life Ins. Co. (1941) 177 Misc 14, 28 NYS2d 860.

To maintain an action of strict interpleader it was necessary to allege and show that two or more persons had preferred a claim against the plaintiff; that they claimed the same thing; that plaintiff had no beneficial interest in the thing claimed, and that it could not be determined to which of the defendants the thing belonged; he also had to offer to bring the money or thing into court. Bassett v Leslie (1890) 123 NY 396, 25 NE 386.

Interpleader could not be maintained by one disputing the amount of the fund. Empire Engineering Corp. v Mack (1916) 217 NY 85, 111 NE 475.

Interpleader was formerly unauthorized when the holder of the fund denied that the full amount demanded by the claimant sought to be substituted was due. Du Bois v Union Dime Sav. Inst. (1895) 89 Hun 382, 35 NYS 397.

A defendant could not procure an order of interpleader upon allegations that another person claimed the same money as the plaintiff unless he admitted liability to one party, etc. Cohen v Cohen (1901) 35 Misc 206, 71 NYS 481.

In an action brought under former § 285 by an insurer, where plaintiff set forth as amount involved the sum of $2,000, the real parties in interest were the defendants, notwithstanding contention by some of the defendants that $2,000 was not the correct amount because interest should be added, the plaintiff admitting that some interest was due. Supreme Lodge Knights & Ladies of Honor v Stapf (1916) 160 NYS 1051.

It was essential that the person seeking to interplead show that he was unable to determine, without hazard, to whom the funds in his hands belonged, and that the claims of the parties to same were identical and existed by virtue of the same set of facts. Wood, Dolson Co. v Leonett Realty Co. (1930) 227 AD 552, 238 NYS 342.

A prerequisite to interpleader is that the same thing, debt or duty should be claimed as owing to the applicant by each claimant, or that the claims must be mutually exclusive. Order of interpleader denied where the claims are separate and distinct, both of which may be established. Clark v Childs (1932) 234 AD 561, 256 NYS 69.

An application for an order of interpleader was addressed to the discretion of the court, and its granting was not a matter of right. Where one claimant sued to recover broker's commissions in the sale of real property, and the other for services rendered on such sale, they would not be interpleaded. Taylor v Satterthwaite (1893) 2 Misc 441, 22 NYS 187.

Where the complaint was founded on contract and the third party's claim was in tort against the same defendant, and each claim a different sum, an order of interpleader should not have been granted. Dodge v Lawson (1892) 19 NYS 904.

Where there are several claims arising from the sale of certain securities held by a bank as collateral, each being separate and distinct and having no inherent connection with each other, plaintiff could not by suit compel claimants to interplead. Fulton Bank of Brooklyn v Chase (1889) 25 NY SR 711, 6 NYS 126.

Section 287 was not applicable where there were two claimants besides the plaintiff, whose claims were not alike, and where there was a contest between the plaintiff and the other claimants, and also between the claimants themselves. New England Mut. Life Ins. Co. v Keller, 7 Civ Proc 109.

The movant was not entitled to an interpleader by motion under § 287 where the establishment of the movant's liability to one of two persons would not necessarily defeat its liability to the other. McNevin v Metropolitan Life Ins. Co. (1936) 160 Misc 468, 290 NYS 44.

Objections specifically abolished by subdivision 5 of CPA § 285, enacted in 1954, might thereafter still be considered on discharge of stakeholder under subdivision 7. Leventhal v Roslyn Manor, Inc. (1955) 142 NYS2d 478, ¶ 5, supra.

23. Jurisdiction of courts

This section applies to an action moved to a county court from a justice's court. Rundle v Gordon (1898) 27 AD 452, 50 NYS 353.

The city court of the city of New York has jurisdiction of an action of interpleader under this section. United States Mortg. & Trust Co. v Vermilye & Power (1911) 72 Misc 375, 130 NYS 303.

The city court of New York had jurisdiction to determine the ownership of a fund or interpleader under former § 287. Katz v Witt (1911) 74 Misc 582, 134 NYS 675.

The city court of New York had power to grant an order of interpleader. Krugman v Hanover F. Ins. Co. (1904) 45 Misc 346, 90 NYS 448.

While the city court of New York had no power to proceed with an action after the entry of an order of interpleader, it had power to grant an order of interpleader and proceed with the action when the order of interpleader was granted under § 115 of the Banking Law in an action brought against a savings bank to recover money on deposit. Gottschall v German Sav. Bank (1904) 45 Misc 27, 90 NYS 896.

In proper cases the municipal court of the city of New York had authority to grant an order of interpleader. Englander v Fleck (1906) 51 Misc 567, 101 NYS 125.

It was said to be doubtful whether the municipal court of the city of New York had power to grant an order of interpleader under former § 287 as it appeared in the Code. Jacobs v Lieberman (1900) 51 AD 542, 64 NYS 953.

Notwithstanding former § 287, municipal court, under Municipal Court Code, § 27, subd 3, had no power to make an order bringing in an additional defendant in an action for fraud and conversion. Beach v Bongartz (1920) 180 NYS 420.

By interpleader of additional defendant, action was changed to one equitable in nature, ousting municipal court of jurisdiction. Joseph v Corsi (1950) 277 AD 351, 100 NYS2d 49; Kornreich v Russo, 99 NYS2d 929.

Court of claims has no jurisdiction to try action by State against individual, and without showing that such person has some interest in realty or some claim on sum to be awarded in payment therefor, such party may not be interpleaded in action for damages for realty condemned. Gagliardi v State (1949) 196 Misc 813, 92 NYS2d 589.

Former § 287-a prescribed place for bringing action in nature of interpleader by person in possession of personalty to determine adverse claims thereto. Monarch Sales Co. v Vollmer (1946) 188 Misc 281, 65 NYS2d 647.

24. —Nonresident defendants

Court could not acquire jurisdiction by service of notice on nonresident outside the state either by personal service or by substituted service, the action being personal. Devoy v Nelles (1921) 197 AD 628, 189 NYS 492.

25. Grounds of relief in general

A right of action of interpleader existed at common law when a thing, debt or duty was claimed by two or more persons to be owing by the plaintiff. This rule of the common law will not be deemed repealed unless the clear meaning of the language of §§ 285 and 287 of the Civil Practice Act absolutely require such construction. Brockport Nat. Bank v Webaco Oil Co. (1939) 257 AD 68, 12 NYS2d 652.

An action of interpleader is justified, as against one of the claimants, by a finding that such claimant was not entitled to the property. Mercantile Safe Deposit Co. v Huntington (1895) 89 Hun 465, 35 NYS 390.

Interpleader granted on the application of an answering defendant, setting up no adverse claim, but the other defendants (one of them answering) claiming adversity to the plaintiff. Sibley v Equitable Life Assur. Soc. (1888) 56 Super Ct (24 Jones & S) 274, 3 NYS 8.

Where two actions by different plaintiffs against the same defendant cannot be finally settled and determined in a contest between the plaintiffs, the court properly exercised the discretion granted by this section and denied a motion to interplead. Carroll v Demarest (1899) 42 AD 155, 58 NYS 1028.

The provisions of this section are a substitute for the common-law action of interpleader and apply where facts exist which would support such an action; it is necessary to show that two persons have preferred a claim against him, that he has no beneficial interest in the thing claimed and cannot determine without hazard to himself to whom it would be delivered and that there is no collusion with any party to the action. Helene v Corn Exchange Bank (1904) 96 AD 392, 89 NYS 310.

In an action to recover a balance due for goods sold and delivered to defendant by plaintiff's assignors, an Austrian partnership, defendant's motion for interpleader is denied where the moving affidavit alleges that the defendant received a letter stating that the business of the plaintiff's assignors is in the possession of certain persons and that the assets have been seized "on account of legal reasons which require these measures." Johnson v Briggs, Inc. (1939) 12 NYS2d 60.

26. Necessity for showing reasonable basis for claims

The old rule in granting an interpleader has been modified and the rule became that it was necessary to prove that the claims had some reasonable foundation, and there was a reasonable doubt whether or not the stakeholder would be safe in paying the money. Thurber v Blanck (1872) 50 NY 80; Baltimore & O. R. Co. v Arthur (1882) 90 NY 234; Nassau Bank v Yandes (1887) 44 Hun 55; Williams v Aetna Life Ins. Co. 8 NYSR 567.

Former § 287 was not intended to introduce any new rule in reference to interpleader; an order of interpleader ought not to be made unless a claim had been presented against that which another has claimed, and the claim must have had some reasonable foundation. Stevenson v New York L. Ins. Co. (1896) 10 AD 233, 41 NYS 964.

The court should not under the discretionary power granted by § 158 of the Code allow a person to interplead upon a mere statement that a demand had been made by the party sought to be interpleaded; it was necessary to show that the claim made by the party sought to be interpleaded had some reasonable foundation. Steiner v East River Sav. Inst. (1901) 60 AD 232, 70 NYS 223.

The claim contemplated by former § 287 as the ground for an interpleader, had to be based upon such facts and circumstances as would indicate, to the satisfaction of the court, that there existed a reasonable doubt as to which of two or more claimants of the property was entitled thereto. Michigan Sav. Bank v Coy, Hunt & Co. (1904) 45 Misc 40, 90 NYS 814.

Under former § 287, a defendant, at any time before answering, upon proof by affidavit that a person, not a party to the action, was making a demand against him for the same property, without collusion with him, might apply to have such

person substituted as defendant in his place and no proof as to the validity or sufficiency of his claim was required. Dreyfus v Casey (1889) 52 Hun 95, 5 NYS 65; Bowery Nat. Bank v New York, 4 NYSR 565.

The question on a motion of this character was as to whether or not there was a reasonable doubt as to the safety of the stakeholder in paying over the money. Feldman v Grand Lodge, A. O. U. W. (1892) 46 NYSR 122, 19 NYS 73.

The application was addressed to the discretion of the court, and ought not to be granted where it appeared, on the face of the papers, that the claim of one of the claimants was clearly unfounded. Pustet v Flannelly, 60 How Pr 67; see Barry v New York Mut. L. Ins. Co. (1873) 53 NY 536.

Where in an action to recover the proceeds of checks deposited with the defendant for the purchase of securities the defendant moved for an order under former § 287, showing that the securities so purchased were claimed both by plaintiff and another, that there was a reasonable basis for the claim of each, that there was no collusion between defendant and such adverse claimant, and that defendant claimed no beneficial interest in the securities, the motion should have been granted. Brook v Randolph (1922) 201 AD 30, 193 NYS 565.

A defendant in an action of interpleader need only show a reasonable foundation for his claim in order to remain a party, and is not required to set forth the basis of his claim. Hood Rubber Co. v Banque Belge Pour L'Etranger (1927) 219 AD 464, 219 NYS 639.

Compare requirements for affidavit, 33, infra.

27. Effect of collusion

Former § 287 only authorized the substitution of a party as defendant, or the bringing in of an additional party, where a demand had been made upon the original defendant by the parties sought to be substituted for the same debt; a defendant who by collusion induced another to lay claim to the property was not entitled to have him brought in as a defendant. Boskowitz v Boskowitz (1908) 124 AD 849, 109 NYS 490.

28. Interpleading claimant of part of fund

Interpleader was granted where one person claimed the entire fund and the other a portion of it. Van Zandt v Van Zandt (1889) 26 NYSR 963, 7 NYS 706.

The defendant did not have to show that the claimant claims the whole fund; if he claims a portion of it he may be interpleaded. Koenig v New York Life Ins. Co. 14 Civ Proc 269, 14 NYSR 250.

29. Equitable interpleader

Courts of equity have jurisdiction to entertain an action of interpleader in a proper case, but a party could only be interpleaded by motion in accordance with former § 287; a party so brought in was entitled to personal notice of the motion or the equivalent thereto; a nonresident could not be substituted as a defendant, unless the service of notice of motion be made personally within this state, or he voluntarily appears and submits to the jurisdiction of the court; service of notice by mail or personal service without the state was insufficient to vest the court with jurisdiction. Bullowa v Provident Life & Trust Co. (1908) 125 AD 545, 109 NYS 1058. (Compare present § 286, subd 1.)

Equity will permit bill of interpleader where defendants are being sued in separate actions and relief may dispose of all issues in one action and save them from double recovery. Svenska Taendsticks Fabrik Aktiebolaget v Bankers' Trust Co. (1933) 239 AD 467, 268 NYS 186, affd 268 NY 73, 196 NE 748.

One of the material allegations in a bill of interpleader is that the applicant cannot determine without hazard to himself which of the rival claimants is the rightful claimant. Martin v Barker (1925) 125 Misc 486, 211 NYS 696.

Equitable interpleader, see Crane v McDonald (1890) 118 NY 648, 23 NE 991.

30. Order for deposit in court

An order of interpleader ought not to be granted under former practice releasing the defendant unless it provided that he pay into court that which was the subject of the action, particularly where the defendant did not admit liability to any one for the property which was the subject of the action. Mason v Rice (1903) 85 AD 315, 82 NYS 541.

Order requiring plaintiff to pay the money into court was not authorized under former practice where he did not show by complaint or affidavit the basis of the claims of some of the defendants. Sulzberger v Seklir (1912) 153 AD 749, 138 NYS 691.

In an action by a tenant to recover the face value and accrued interest of bonds deposited as security for the lease, motion of defendant under former § 287 to substitute as defendant his grantee, the present landlord, who claims right to reimbursement for a breach of the lease by plaintiff out of the deposited security, granted on condition that defendant deposit in court a sum sufficient to cover the present landlord's claim pending the determination of the action, and deliver to plaintiff the balance of the securities. Pollack v Jackson (1925) 124 Misc 608, 209 NYS 120.

The order under former practice of leave to pay the fund into court in a suit on a life insurance policy should require the payment into court of the interest from the date claimed by plaintiff as well as the principal. Sibley v Equitable Life Assur. Soc. (1888) 56 Super Ct (24 Jones & S) 274, 3 NYS 8; and see Koenig v New York Life Ins. Co. 14 Civ Proc 269, 14 NYSR 250.

Where pursuant to order properly obtained under (former) § 287-a, plaintiffs instituted action to determine claims to personalty, their application to retain specific personalty to credit of action and to be discharged from liability, was granted. Roths-

child v Clawans (1951) 279 AD 224, 108 NYS2d 800, affd 304 NY 557, 106 NE2d 616.

31. Time for application for order

Application for an order of interpleader must be made before answer. Martin v Barker (1925) 125 Misc 486, 211 NYS 696.

32. Notice

Persons proposed as additional parties defendant may not be brought in without notice. Danziger v Amalgamated Bank of New York (1932) 143 Misc 126, 255 NYS 344.

An order of interpleader was not granted where the moving party failed to give the party making the claim notice of application and where the moving affidavit did not allege any fact which denied the right of plaintiff to recover. Roberts v Vanhorne (1897) 21 AD 369, 47 NYS 448.

An order made pursuant to former § 287 substituting a third party as defendant in an action to recover a chattel could not be sustained where no notice of the application was given to the third party, and the moving affidavit failed to show that the third party's claim to the chattel was without collusion. O'Connor v Lock (1911) 148 AD 765, 133 NYS 320.

An order that third party be brought in could not be sustained under former § 287 in absence of proof of service of notice on the third party. United Shoe Repairing Mach. Co. v Dotchermann Storage Warehouse Co. (1919) 186 AD 359, 174 NYS 284.

Notice for application for an order of interpleader had to be served in the same manner as a summons. Devoy v Nelles (1921) 197 AD 628, 189 NYS 492.

CPA § 286 was inapplicable to notice pursuant to CPA § 51-a (§ 216(a) herein). Solicitor for Affairs of His Majesty's Treasury v Bankers Trust Co. (1952) 304 NY 282, 107 NE2d 448.

33. Affidavit

An affidavit containing statements which furnished no evidence on which either the defendant or the court was authorized to presume a gift, was insufficient, on an application for an order of interpleader. Mars v Albany Sav. Bank (1893) 69 Hun 398, 23 NYS 658.

Affidavit upon which motion was made for order of interpleader had to allege facts showing foundation for rival claims. Mars v Albany Sav. Bank (1892) 64 Hun 424, 19 NYS 791.

Affidavit, disclosing making of claim by third person without showing its reasonable basis, was insufficient. Goodstein v Contower Realty Corp. (1945) 53 NYS2d 350.

In an action by a vendor against brokers who conducted a sale for him to recover part of the purchase price, an application by said brokers was not granted on affidavits showing that the purchaser repudiated the sale because of false representations made by the brokers where there was nothing to show that the vendor made or authorized such false representations. Sullivan v Crowe (1902) 72 AD 5, 76 NYS 98.

It is necessary that the moving papers set forth facts showing that the defendant would be placed in peril by paying to either claimant. Pouch v Prudential Ins. Co. (1912) 204 NY 281, 97 NE 731.

Affidavits need only satisfy the court that there is a reasonable basis for claims in order to warrant an application for interpleader. Singer v New York Life Ins. Co. (1916) 160 NYS 442.

See necessity for showing basis of claims, 26, supra.

34. Service on interpleaded defendant

Service upon adverse claimants of summons and interpleading complaint, with copy of original summons and complaint served on interpleader, complied with §§ 286 and 287 and brought in such claimants without the necessity of a court order. O'Donnell v Vanecek (1956) 3 Misc 2d 20, 150 NYS2d 819.

After the entry of an order of interpleader, the action becomes an equitable one and the practice of courts of equity in cases of interpleader should be followed; the practice, after an order of interpleader has been made, is for the plaintiff to apply to the court under § 245 for leave to serve a supplemental complaint containing substantially the allegations of the former complaint and such further facts as may be necessary to show the facts preceding the making of the order of interpleader, etc. Greenblatt v Mendelsohn (1905) 46 Misc 554, 92 NYS 963.

Plaintiff is not required to serve supplemental summons and complaint on each party brought in by defendant. Danziger v Amalgamated Bank of New York (1932) 143 Misc 126, 255 NYS 344.

35. Answer by person brought in

Where an interpleader is ordered in a district court in the city of New York, the order should require the party brought in by the interpleader to appear and answer a complaint served upon him with the order, in the same time that a defendant is required to answer a summons. McElroy v Baer, 13 Daly 442.

An impleaded defendant who wishes to assert a claim against the plaintiff, may not implead the plaintiff as a defendant. National Surety Corp. v Federal Reserve Bank (1936) 161 Misc 308, 292 NYS 611.

36. Withdrawal of answer

The court has no power to allow the defendant to withdraw his answer served upon the plaintiff several months before application for interpleader was made. Martin v Barker (1925) 125 Misc 486, 211 NYS 696.

Where defendant desires to withdraw from a contest upon the ground of no interest he must move with diligence or his application will be denied. United States Land & Invest. Co. v Bussey (1889)

27 NYSR 185, 7 NYS 495, revd on other grounds 53 Hun 516, 6 NYS 416.

For withdrawal of answer of impleading defendant in mortgage foreclosure, see Best v New York City Waterfront Co. (1913) 158 AD 555, 143 NYS 814, ¶ 52, infra.

37. Counterclaim

In interpleader under former § 287-d by brokers for authority to deposit in court moneys from sale of securities, counterclaimed for conversion of securities in greater amount than deposit was authorized. Newton v Simon (1947) 188 Misc 669, 68 NYS2d 611, affd 272 AD 871, 72 NYS2d 261.

Where escrow agent brought interpleader action, and one claimant counterclaimed against escrow agent and other claimant made and won motion to set aside service of summons and complaint, latter was not necessary to counterclaim, though both claimants were necessary parties to interpleader. Bensonhurst Nat. Bank v Flynn (1953) 122 NYS2d 394, vacated on other grounds 124 NYS2d 205.

38. Intervention

One who has an interest in the subject of an action of interpleader may, in the court's discretion, come in and defend. Hood Rubber Co. v Banque Belge Pour L'Etranger (1927) 219 AD 464, 219 NYS 639.

39. Preference of trial

An action at law becomes equitable and triable by the court where the sole original defendant, an insurance company holding a fund all of which the plaintiff claims and none of which the insurance company claims, interpleads and makes defendant another claimant of the fund; and where the sole plaintiff is an administrator he is thereafter entitled to put the case on the special term calendar and have it preferred. Vandewater v Mutual Reserve L. Ins. Co. (1904) 44 Misc 316, 89 NYS 845.

40. Jury trial

Where an action at law, brought in the city court of the city of New York, became an equitable one, by interpleader proceedings under former § 287, it was triable by the court without a jury at any trial term when regularly reached in its order upon the calendar. Schreiber v Dry Dock Sav. Inst. (1908) 59 Misc 408, 112 NYS 360.

When an order was made substituting bailor for bailee as defendant, the action became an equitable one triable by court, and neither party had right to a trial by jury, but the parties could treat it as a common-law action. Gleason v Bush (1915) 166 AD 865, 152 NYS 54.

41. Appeal

The holder of a fund being sued by two parties having conflicting claims thereto, brought the same into court, and was discharged from litigation. There was no formal substitution of either claimant as defendant, but a reference was ordered and the fund was awarded on the report coming in: Held, a final determination of the action from which an appeal will lie to the court of appeals. Kirby v Fitzpatrick (1859) 18 NY 484.

An order granting or refusing leave to interplead was discretionary, and not appealable to the Court of Appeals. Barry v New York Mut. L. Ins. Co. (1873) 53 NY 536.

42. Effect of failure to interplead

The defendants took upon themselves a contest between plaintiff and her daughter as to the ownership of the bonds. When the action was commenced they could have relieved themselves from liability by applying for leave to interplead the daughter, pursuant to this section. Having gone to trial relying on the daughter's title as their defense, they should not complain if the same testimony were held admissible against them as would be admitted against the daughter. Hildick v Williams (1888) 21 NYSR 166, 3 NYS 817.

43. Injunction

Though former § 287 allowed interpleader only in action upon contract, ejectment and replevin in the supreme court, yet the inability of a plaintiff to obtain an interpleader in an action in the municipal court was not sufficient ground for an injunction restraining the prosecution of the action. La Femina v Arsene (1902) 69 AD 285, 74 NYS 749.

44. Action in which authorized, generally

When an action upon a contract was brought by a sheriff, and thereafter an action was brought by a receiver to recover the same money from the same defendants, and the latter applied for an order of interpleader, such order should provide for bringing the receiver into the sheriff's suit, and not the sheriff into the receiver's suit. Sickles v Wilmerding (1891) 59 Hun 375, 13 NYS 43.

Order of interpleader could be granted where two or more persons had a preferred claim against applicant, claimed the same thing, and applicant had no beneficial interest in the thing claimed and could not determine without hazard to himself to which of the rival claimants the thing belongs, and there was no collusion. Singer v New York Life Ins. Co. (1916) 160 NYS 442.

Stock interest in corporation, where ownership was disputed by third person, warranted interpleading in pending action by person claiming adversely to plaintiff. Jacobs v Thompson-Starrett Co. (1946) 61 NYS2d 9.

In action by brother of absentee against surety to recash deposit as collateral security for issuance of bail bond for absentee, which was claimed by absentee's estate, estate was interpleaded by surety which claimed only lien or setoff against fund. Re Scharf (1942) 178 Misc 1012, 36 NYS2d 912.

In action against employer for return of union dues improperly checked off by employer, union was substituted as defendant in place of employer. Barbein v Superior Meter Co. (1949) 275 AD 962, 90 NYS2d 29.

In action for return of improper deduction of union dues, defendant employer should be permitted to implead union and deposit dues in court. Barbein v Superior Meter Co., supra.

In action against trustees of pension fund to recover pension of deceased city employee, they cannot interplead other beneficiaries unless they show reasonableness of cross claim to fund, that claims are not mutually exclusive, that they were indifferent between claims and in doubt as to rightful one. Flanagan v O'Dwyer (1949) 86 NYS2d 559, revd and interpleader granted 88 NYS2d 903.

In action for proceeds of settled action for personal injuries, defendant was entitled to order interpleading persons not parties to action, who demanded such proceeds without collusion with defendant. Eddis v Union R. Co. (1942) 34 NYS2d 218.

Action by insured's widow for damages for maliciously inducing breach of contract sounds in tort, and interpleader in such action is improper. Cramer v Travelers Ins. Co. (1934) 180 Misc 464, 40 NYS2d 934.

45. Arbitration

There was no ground for interpleader where plaintiff sued on an award of arbitrators but made no claim upon any particular fund. Applebaum v Rosenblum (1914) 150 NYS 472.

46. Banks and banking

Where a deposit in a savings bank is claimed by a stranger and the bank is sued therefor by the depositor, the court may order the fund into court and direct an interpleader between the claimants. Smith v Emigrant Industrial Sav. Bank (1888) 17 NYSR 852, 2 NYS 617.

An action of interpleader could not be maintained under former § 285 by a savings bank to obtain permission to pay into court the amount of a deposit claimed by two adverse parties where in a prior action brought by one of the parties to recover the amount of the deposit the other set up a counterclaim asserting title and demanding judgment against the bank, and, after a trial and submission of the issues, the court directed judgment on the counterclaim against the bank. Williamsburgh Sav. Bank v Bernstein (1938) 277 NY 11, 12 NE2d 551.

In an action against a savings bank to recover a deposit brought by a person in whose name the account stands the defendant could, under § 259, chap 409 of 1882, interplead a claim to the fund, even though such claimant did not actually claim the whole of the deposit. Progressive Handlanger Union v German Sav. Bank (1890) 57 Super Ct (25 Jones & S) 594, 8 NYS 545.

Where a mother before her death gave a savings bankbook to her daughter and where she left a husband and children, but no creditors, the bank was not, under the Banking Law nor under former § 287, nor under § 193, entitled to have the next of kin or administrator of the donor made parties to the action brought by the daughter against said savings bank. Cosgriff v Hudson City Sav. Inst. (1898) 24 Misc 4, 52 NYS 189.

The discretion to grant interpleader under § 115 of the Banking Law, chap 689 of 1892, should be more liberally exercised than under former § 287. McGuire v Auburn Sav. Bank (1902) 78 AD 22, 79 NYS 91.

The provisions of § 115 of the Banking Law, chap 689 of 1892, allowing a savings bank to interplead claimants to a deposit did not apply to an action against such bank by the payee of a note. Former § 287 did not apply to such a case. Master v Bowery Sav. Bank (1900) 31 Misc 178, 63 NYS 964.

In an action by the holder of a certificate of deposit to recover the amount from the trust company issuing the same, the fact that the receiver of a corporation to which it was originally issued claimed that the amount was more than sufficient to cover the indebtedness for which it was transferred, and has protested to the trust company against payment, does not entitle the trust company to interplead where the plaintiff denies the contentions of the receiver. Hanna v Manufacturers' Trust Co. (1905) 104 AD 90, 93 NYS 304.

Where drawee bank refused to pay check certified at drawer's request on notice from drawer, on bank's motion drawer was interpleaded as defendant in payee's action against bank. Welch v Bank of Manhattan Co. (1942) 264 AD 906, 35 NYS2d 894.

A bank may not resort to interpleader merely because the holder of an unaccepted draft or uncertified check asserts a claim to bank deposits as against the record depositor. It may, however, interplead claim of corporation that depositor, a corporate officer, illegally deposited corporate check in his individual account. New York Trust Co. v Braham (1926) 126 Misc 462, 213 NYS 678.

Where drawee bank stopped payment on certified check when payee notified bank that holder had illegally obtained its possession, and both payee and holder separately sued bank, bank was discharged from liability and plaintiff holder was made defendant in plaintiff payee's action. Llop v First Nat. Bank (1942) 178 Misc 436, 35 NYS2d 867.

Where the drawer on a check delivered it to the agent of the payee who forged the indorsement of his principal, secured payment of the check upon the forged indorsement and absconded with the money, held that the bank when sued by the drawer was not entitled to have the payee of the check interpleaded. Greenwald v State Bank (1924) 124 Misc 176, 207 NYS 214, affd 213 AD 810, 208 NYS 870.

Where trust company undertook to receive deposits of joint adventurers, and paid them out in certain proportions, and one of the joint adventurers brought action against the trust company for his share, the defendant had the right to interplead other claimants. Evans v Guaranty Trust Co (1919) 187 AD 30, 175 NYS 118.

In action by assignee of purchaser of bungalows against purchaser, seller and escrow holder to recover escrow for $1000 deposited to secure health violations, wherein seller counterclaimed for escrow deposit, court ordered escrow holder to deposit $1000 in court, but refused to discharge purchaser or seller. Shapiro v Dorfeld (1953) 282 AD 796, 122 NYS2d 593.

In an action involving a fund on deposit in a bank, in which the plaintiff claimed an interest as partial assignee, and his assignor was not made a party, the court was not authorized to enter judgment on an order interpleading a claimant to the entire fund with respect to that portion of the fund not claimed by plaintiff. Basile v Basile (1922) 120 Misc 63, 197 NYS 668.

Plaintiff was employed by defendant to obtain some property of an estate in which he was interested, and was successful, the executor, on his accounting, being directed to pay a certain sum to defendant, who had drawn a draft on the executor in favor of a bank which draft had been accepted by the executor but not paid when this action was brought by plaintiff, who claimed a lien on the fund for his services. Held, that an order interpleading the bankers in place of the executor was properly granted. Davis v Benedict (1891) 37 NYSR 588, 14 NYS 178.

Where an action is brought against a bank and one of its depositors by a judgment creditor of the depositor, and subsequently an assignee of the depositor demands the deposit, the bank is entitled to an order of interpleader. Wells v Corn Exchange Bank (1904) 43 Misc 377, 87 NYS 480.

An action for strict interpleader may be maintained by a bank, against parties making conflicting claims to a deposit, if there is a real doubt as to the person entitled thereto, as where the deposit was made by public officers, and in consequence of a change in the officers there is a conflict as to the right to draw it out. German Exch. Bank v Commissioners of Excise, 57 How Pr 187, 6 Abb NC 394.

In an action by a membership corporation to recover a bank deposit standing in the name of its predecessor, a community volunteer fire company, the defendant, a national bank, is entitled, under ¶ (a) of subdivision 6 of § 134 of the Banking Law, to an order interpleading former members of the volunteer fire company, an unincorporated association. In view of the language of the statute, "without proof as to the merits of the claim," bank need show only that an adverse claim has been made without collusion on its part. Community Volunteer Fire Co. v City Nat. Bank (1939) 171 Misc 1027, 14 NYS2d 306.

47. Brokers

Defendant's motion to interplead as another defendant a realty broker who claims the same commission claimed by the plaintiff will be allowed. Stinson v 6–8 West 57th Street Corp. (1926) 127 Misc 69, 215 NYS 252.

Action for broker's commissions held proper cause for order of interpleader where rival workers claimed same commission. Vought, Campbell, Ward & Co. v Rowland (1941) 261 AD 971, 25 NYS2d 816.

The defendant is entitled to interpleader in a broker's action for commissions where two brokers are claiming the right to the commissions and only one of them could have been the procuring cause and there is no special contract. Steinfeld v Goess (1938) 9 NYS2d 460; Finkel v Affom Holding Corp. (1944) 46 NYS2d 378; Fanslow v Manufacturers Trust Co. (1943) 181 Misc 272, 47 NYS2d 396.

Where causes of action by two different real estate brokers to recover commissions on the sale of real property were substantially identical, the defendant was entitled to an order of interpleader. Pell & Tibbits, Inc. v Bedford (1933) 238 AD 856, 263 NYS 32.

Where two brokers claim commissions for the purchase of property from the one vendor, they may be interpleaded. Bickart v Hoffmann (1892) 46 NYSR 886, 19 NYS 472.

In an action to recover commissions for services rendered as a broker in securing a tenant where another broker interpleaded and claimed the compensation, finding and judgment for the latter was sustained by the evidence. Doyle v Meeker (1925) 125 Misc 105, 210 NYS 134.

In broker's actions for commissions, order granting permission to interplead was reversed; the claims of the parties not being identical. Wood, Dolson Co. v Leonett Realty Co. (1930) 227 AD 552, 238 NYS 342.

In action for commissions for selling realty, defendant's motion for interpleader, permitting it to pay into court amount in litigation and discharging its liability to plaintiff and rival broker, was denied, where record required determination of defendant's good faith in recognizing both brokers as claimants. Wagner v Suffolk County Trust Co. (1943) 266 AD 967, 44 NYS2d 115.

In action by broker for commissions for negotiating long term lease of defendant's premises, where lease recited that "landlord and tenant agreed that another named broker was sole broker who consummated lease, and where defendant disputes any liability to plaintiff, plaintiff was warranted in joining second broker. Robert Joseph & Co. v Hirsch (1953) 283 AD 86, 126 NYS2d 340.

In action for brokerage commission, where second broker's claim is for half of plaintiff's on contention that they were joint brokers and that person produced by second broker as lessee was supposed to be partner of persons who leased property, defendant was granted interpleader of second broker, where plaintiff admitted that there was working arrangement between him and second broker. Wm. A. White & Sons v Loew (1953) 283 AD 1, 126 NYS2d 211.

In action for broker's commissions, defendant was entitled to order of interpleader where third person claimed commissions despite existence of writing recognizing plaintiff as broker. Salamon v Brooklyn Sav. Bank (1943) 180 Misc 941, 44 NYS2d 420.

48. Construction contracts

In suit by chief building contractor against owners, sublienors could be brought in so that dependent or competing claims could be heard together and finally adjudicated, though contract enabled owner to withhold sum to cover liens of subcontractors or sublienor. Morgan v Sagamore Development Co. (1920) 193 AD 475, 184 NYS 311.

Where one owing money to a contracting company under a contract had interpleaded, a judgment creditor of the contracting company, whose execution had been returned unsatisfied, had such an interest in the subject matter of the action as to give him the right to be brought in as a party defendant. Edison Electric Illuminating Co. v Horace E. Frick Co. (1911) 146 AD 605, 131 NYS 125.

In an action brought by a receiver, appointed in supplementary proceedings against a building contractor, to recover a sum alleged to be due the judgment debtor from the defendant upon a building contract, the defendant answered that the amount owing by him on the contract had been, by due proceedings under the mechanic's lien law, subjected to liens in favor of various persons named, which liens were prior to plaintiff's title and were filed and in existence "at and prior to the commencement of this action," and exceed in amount the sum due on the building contract. Plaintiff's objection to this defense for insufficiency was overruled: Held, error—that as defendant had taken no steps for an interpleader the sufficiency of the answer must be determined by the test whether it alleges facts that plaintiff has no cause of action. McCorkle v Herrman (1889) 117 NY 297, 22 NE 948.

In action by assignee of subcontractor against general contractor for sum admittedly due, which sum was claimed by U. S. Government, assignee's motion for summary judgment was denied to permit defendant as stakeholder to bring in as party U. S. Government. Rosenberg v Paul Tishman Co. (1952) 118 NYS2d 337.

49. Conversion

Order of interpleader in action in conversion denied. Svenska Taendsticks Fabrik Akticbolaget v Bankers' Trust Co. (1933) 239 AD 467, 268 NYS 186, affd 268 NY 73, 196 NE 748.

50. Executors and administrators

An application to require adverse claimants to interplead should not be denied merely because one of them is an executor or administrator, so that the other, although he might testify in his own behalf in his action against stakeholder, may be incompetent to do so in the interpleader suit against the executor or administrator, by reason of § 347. Flanery v Emigrant Industrial Sav. Bank (1889) 7 NYS 2.

Where an executrix loaned money of the estate, taking a mortgage therefor in her own name and not as executrix, on her death her administrator brought suit on the mortgage, and the administrators de bonis non of the first decedent claiming the money, the court granted an interpleader to determine to which administrator the defendant should pay the money. Caulkins v Bolton (1885) 98 NY 511.

Defendant executors in action on claim against estate were not entitled to interplead creditors of their testator because they were not subjected to any double hazard, loss or damage with respect to plaintiff's claim. Denniston v Snyder (1916) 98 Misc 44, 162 NYS 271.

Where a trust in a bond and mortgage was held by executors, who were ready to pay, and attorneys of another party gave notice that they claimed a lien on the fund for services, a motion to interplead was granted. See Friedman v Platt (1889) 21 NYSR 190, 4 NYS 125.

If various parties file conflicting claims against each other and against the representative of an estate to bonds to which he lays claim as belonging to his estate, the dispute should be determined on interpleader and not on discovery in the surrogate court. Re Brennan (1927) 129 Misc 283, 221 NYS 462.

51. Insurance

In an action brought by one of two beneficiaries of an insurance policy where defendant denies liability to plaintiff the defendant is not entitled to have the other beneficiary made a party defendant upon its application. Montague v Jewelers' & Tradesmen's Co. (1899) 41 AD 530, 58 NYS 715.

In an action of interpleader to determine the plaintiff's right to a policy as against a rival claimant, such rival claimant is a proper party. Hasberg v Moses (1903) 81 AD 199, 80 NYS 867.

Where an insurance company holding moneys demanded by adverse claimants brings an action of interpleader under this section, it is entitled to pay the money into court and to be discharged from liability to the various claimants; it need not establish the validity of the adverse claimants. Western Commercial Travelers' Asso. v Langeheineken (1910) 139 AD 592, 124 NYS 182.

In action for death benefits of retirement annuity policy by assignee against insurer, where plaintiff's right to recover is seriously questioned by both insurer and another claimant, interpleader was proper. Rosen v Equitable Life Assur. Soc. (1942) 289 NY 333, 45 NE2d 899.

Where beneficiary of group insurance policy, after insured's death, held balance due on policy above beneficiary's claim for relief furnished to insured, and such balance was claimed by former beneficiary and wife and administratrix of insured, motion for interpleader by named beneficiary was granted. Boden v Arnstein (1944) 293 NY 99, 56 NE2d 65.

When an insurance company is sued by two plaintiffs upon the same policy, upon motion of the company one of them will be brought into the other action, and the amount of the policy will be allowed to be paid into court, and the company discharged. Pierce v Mutual Life Ins. Co. (1921) 190 NYS 50.

Motion by plaintiff insurance company in action of interpleader to be discharged from further liability on payment of money into court denied, where it is not impossible that there may be double liability and plaintiff may not be free from blame in respect to causing controversy. American Motorists Ins. Co. v Oakley (1939) 172 Misc 319, 14 NYS2d 883.

Where the widow and an assignee of a deceased policyholder claimed the amount insured upon the life of the deceased by a life insurance company, and the latter sued the company, the widow was substituted as defendant by an order of interpleader. Fowler v Butterly (1879) 78 NY 68.

In an action on an insurance policy issued to the plaintiff's husband and payable to his executors, a person who claims that the plaintiff gave him the policy should be interpleaded as a defendant in the action. Lateer v Prudential Ins. Co. (1901) 64 AD 423, 72 NYS 235.

In an action against an insurance company on a policy, defendant was entitled to an order for interpleader where a third party also claimed the proceeds of the policy, the insurer admitting its liability. Singer v New York Life Ins. Co. (1916) 160 NYS 442.

Where holder of endowment policy assigned all of his rights to his wife if living, if not, to children, wife at maturity could recover value without joining children as defendants. Eisenbach v Mutual L. Ins. Co. (1914) 162 AD 595, 147 NYS 962, affd 212 NY 593, 106 NE 1033.

Insurance proceeds, claimed by various judgment creditors of insured, warranted interpleader. Meyerhardt v Heinzelman (1947) 71 NYS2d 692, affd 272 AD 800, 71 NYS2d 925.

Where both husband and wife claimed proceeds on her matured endowment policy, and wife sued insurer who, after five years' search, located husband, insurer impleaded husband, and was not required to pay interest because of delay due to husband. Wallace v Metropolitan L. Ins. Co. (1947) 78 NYS2d 727.

An insurance company sued on a policy payable to the insured at the end of fifteen years or, if he died before that time, to plaintiff as his wife, or such other beneficiary as might be designated, is entitled to an order substituting the personal representatives of the deceased as defendants in place of the insurance company. St John v Union Mut. L. Ins. Co. (1909) 132 AD 515, 117 NYS 1077.

Interpleader refused in action on insurance policy issued by a fraternal benefit association. Fowler v Eastman Council (1908) 58 Misc 14, 108 NYS 1017.

In an action on a policy of insurance wherein on an order of interpleader the wife of decedent was substituted as defendant, a supplemental complaint was served demanding judgment against such defendant, and the latter filed a supplemental answer thereto, demanding equitable relief, and asking that the court declare affirmatively that the plaintiff had no right to the avails of the policy and that the same be paid to said defendant, held that the nature of the action was changed from one at law to an action in equity. White v White (1922) 194 NYS 114.

Motion by defendant insurer for order substituting the insured's wife as defendant, and discharging defendant insurer from action to recover on policy on life of insured, on payment of money into court, denied. McNevin v Metropolitan Life Ins. Co. (1936) 160 Misc 468, 290 NYS 44.

In an action brought against an insurance company on a policy of insurance, the defendant set up that the defendant's intestate also claimed the amount of the policy; and defendant paying the money into court, the plaintiff was required to substitute the defendant's intestate as defendant to determine the conflicting claim of the plaintiff and defendant to the fund in court. Clark v Mosher (1887) 107 NY 118, 14 NE 96; Mahr v Bartlett (1889) 53 Hun 388, 7 NYS 143, revd on other grounds Mahr v Norwich Union F. Ins. Soc. (1891) 127 NY 452, 28 NE 391.

In an action brought to determine the right of plaintiff to a certain fund and to require a life insurance company to pay the same to plaintiff, against the life insurance company and also against a party claiming the fund, leave was granted to the insurance company to pay the money into court and to have the suit discontinued as to the company. Lane v New York L. Ins. Co. (1890) 56 Hun 92, 9 NYS 97.

In an action on a policy of life insurance, motion by defendant to interplead the administrator of the estate of the plaintiff's claimed assignor and other claimants under the insurance policy granted. Mercandande v Prudential Ins. Co. (1939) 258 AD 283, 16 NYS2d 475.

Where in equity action insurer has deposited money in court, and contest is solely between rival claimants to insurance fund, court of equity will seek to do what insured apparently intended to have done, and to award fund to that claimant having strongest claim. McPherson v Equitable Life Assur. Soc. (1952) 114 NYS2d 695.

52. Mortgages

Where a bond and mortgage under foreclosure are claimed by a third person, he may be made a party on his own application; and the owner of the equity of redemption may have leave to pay into court the amount secured by the mortgage, and compel the adverse claimants to litigate their rights between themselves. Van Loan v Squires (1889) 7 NYS 171.

Where mortgage was foreclosed by one claiming as assignee, and defendant answered denying the validity of the assignment, and assignor applied to be and was made party defendant and attacked the assignment and asked for affirmative relief, original defendant had right to withdraw answer and pay the amount of the mortgage into court and be discharged from all liability. Best v New York City Waterfront Co. (1913) 158 AD 555, 143 NYS 814.

Where a bond and mortgage under foreclosure were claimed by a third person, he could be made

a party on his own application. The owner of the equity could have leave to pay into court and let the claimants litigate. Van Loan v Squires (1889) 7 NYS 171.

53. Municipal corporations and officers

Where land is taken by the city for opening a street and a third person claims an interest in the award to the extent of amount due on a mortgage on the land, he may be substituted as a defendant in place of the city. Barnes v New York (1882) 27 Hun 236.

Where the board of supervisors of a county brought an action against a large number of persons, holding notes signed by the county treasurer in behalf of the county, alleging that the treasurer had fraudulently issued such notes, held, that the plaintiffs were entitled to maintain an action to settle the rights of the defendants and the liability of the county. Saratoga County v Deyoe (1879) 77 NY 219.

Maintainable by owner and occupant of a farm against two tax collectors, for the purpose of determining in which town his farm is properly taxed. Dorn v Fox (1874) 61 NY 264.

An action to recover the salary of a public officer under an assignment thereof is not an action "upon a contract" within the meaning of this section. Walker v New York (1911) 72 Misc 97, 129 NYS 1059.

A party who is in the position of a receiptor to the sheriff, who has made a valid levy upon a certain stock of goods, and is, therefore, a bailee thereof, cannot by filing a bill of interpleader compel other parties to come into court and litigate their claims with the sheriff. Such a party does not stand in the position of a person who has come into the possession of property innocently, and has been unexpectedly assailed, without any instrumentality on his part, by different claimants of the property. Cromwell v American Loan & T. Co. (1890) 57 Hun 149, 11 NYS 144.

In action against bank and depositor for moneys allegedly stolen by depositor's principal from plaintiff and attached by sheriff under judgment for plaintiff in prior action, bank may interplead sheriff as party defendant. Marshall v Friedman (1941) 176 Misc 32, 26 NYS2d 756.

54. Patents

A defendant to an action for royalties has a right to demand that the original holder of the patent be impleaded if he is the real party interested as defendant; but the plaintiff, claiming to have no demand against said holder, should not be required to allege a claim against him. Eastern Optical Co. v General Optical Co. (1927) 219 AD 294, 219 NYS 692.

55. Replevin

Defendant in replevin failing to interplead third party claimants before answer was not entitled to relief under Civ Prac Act § 98. Sophian v Fidelity & D. Co. (1918) 184 AD 553, 172 NYS 392.

In an action of replevin the property was taken by the sheriff and not reclaimed by defendant. Thereafter on motion of defendant an order was granted substituting one K as defendant on the ground that he claimed title to the property and directing its delivery to him, to hold subject to the order of the court: Held, error. Pelham Hod Elevating Co. v Baggaley (1890) 34 NYSR 691, 12 NYS 218.

Where in an action of replevin the sheriff, after taking possession of the property, delivers it to the plaintiff, upon the latter giving the usual undertaking, if a third party interposes a claim to the possession of the property, under § 1107, and the defendant makes no claim whatever to the property, the court will make an order interpleading the third party in the place of the defendant but will make no direction as to the disposition of the property pending the action. Wright Steam Engine Works v New York Kerosene Oil Engine Co. (1904) 44 Misc 580, 90 NYS 130.

In action to recover stock from defendant holding same for third person and disclaiming all interest except as custodian, proper procedure (under former § 287-b) is for defendant to bring in such third person as party defendant. Birnbaum v Irving Trust Co. (1942) 178 Misc 206, 33 NYS2d 551.

In wife's replevin for shares of stock on which pledgee had lien, such pledgee as stakeholder may bring in claimant husband as party defendant, and be discharged from liability (under former § 287-b). Smith v Associated Lerner Shops (1947) 70 NYS2d 106.

56. Sales

And where two firms each claim the price of goods alleged to have been sold by them respectively to the defendant and each sues therefor, the purchaser is entitled to interplead them. Tynan v Cadenas, 3 How Pr NS 7.

In action for moneys received by defendant for plaintiff's use, being the proceeds of a sale of lemons, held that defendant was entitled to interplead one who had attached the property as that of a third person. San Fernando Heights Lemon Co. v Fruit Auction Co. (1919) 174 NYS 156.

57. Specific performance

In action to compel defendant stakeholder to specifically perform escrow agreement and deliver security documents to plaintiffs, where defendant alleges he was notified by claimant that plaintiffs had not performed agreement and not to turn over property to plaintiffs, defendant was entitled (under former § 287-b) to bring in such claimant as party defendant. Hencer Corp. v Stolz (1941) 176 Misc 460, 26 NYS2d 754.

58. Warehouseman

In action by assignor of warehouse receipt to recover stored goods, defendant which had issued another receipt to a third person upon representation of plaintiff's assignor that the goods had been transferred to such third person, had the right to interplead the third person as a defendant. Rosenberg v P. Viane, Inc. (1919) 109 Misc 215, 179 NYS 447.

Where a person brings an action against a warehouse company to recover possession of goods, the fact that the warehouse company may have a good defense to the action under chap. 633 of 1895 does not deprive it of its right to interplead and have rival claimants of the property substituted for it as defendants. Follett Wool Co. v Albany Terminal Warehouse Co. (1901) 61 AD 296, 70 NYS 474.

FORMS

Form   1—Interpleader; general form
Form   2—Interpleader complaint
Form   3—Complaint for interpleader and declaratory relief
Form   4—Interpleader; claimants to contents of safe deposit box
Form   5—Interpleader; claimants to deposit in bank
Form   6—Interpleader; real estate brokers claiming commission
Form   7—Interpleader; by warehouseman
Form   8—Interpleader; answer of claimant
Form   9—Answer and defensive interpleader
Form 10—Answer of stakeholder
Form 11—Notice of motion to consolidate or for joint trial
Form 12—Affidavit in support of motion to consolidate or for joint trial
Form 13—Order to consolidate or for joint trial
Form 14—Interpleading summons
Form 15—Interpleading complaint
Form 16—Answer of interpleaded defendant
Form 17—Notice of motion to dismiss interpleader action, issue of independent liability

Form 1

Interpleader; General Form

Interpleader Complaint

[Title of court and cause]   Index No. — [if assigned]

Plaintiff complaining of defendants, alleges:

1. That before the making of the claims hereinafter mentioned one A deposited with plaintiff __1___ [describe property] for safekeeping.

2. That defendant B claims the same under an alleged assignment thereof to him from said A.

3. That defendant C also claims the same under an order of said A transferring the same to him.

4. That plaintiff is ignorant of the respective rights of defendants and cannot determine, without hazard to himself, to which of the claimants the property belongs.

5. That plaintiff has no claim upon the said property and is ready and willing to deliver it to such persons as the court shall direct.

6. That this action is not brought by collusion with either of the defendants.

Wherefore, plaintiff demands judgment:

1. That defendants be restrained, by injunction, from taking any proceedings against plaintiff in relation thereto.

2. That they be required to interplead together concerning their claims to the said property.

3. That some person be authorized to receive the said property pending such litigation.

4. That upon delivering the same to such receiver plaintiff be discharged from all liability to either of defendants in relation thereto.

5. And that plaintiff's costs be paid out of the same.

__2_____

Attorney for Plaintiff

Address __3_____

Telephone No. __4__

[Verification]

Form 2

Interpleader Complaint [Official Form 18]

SUPREME COURT OF THE STATE OF NEW YORK

COUNTY OF NEW YORK

A.B., Plaintiff,
  against
C.D., Defendant

C.D., Defendant and Inter-   Interpleader Complaint
  pleading Plaintiff.   Index No.
  against
E.F., Interpleaded Defendant.

1. Defendant and interpleading plaintiff C.D. was the owner of certain premises commonly known as No. 1716, West 24th Street, New York, New York.

2. A.B. and E.F. are licensed New York real estate brokers.

3. On or about June 1, 1966, C.D. listed the premises for sale with A.B. and E.F.

4. C.D. separately agreed with A.B. and with E.F. to pay for all services rendered in connection with the sale a commission equal to five percent of the purchase price if such broker became the procuring cause of the sale, and A.B. and E.F. each undertook to sell the premises upon those terms.

5. On or about July 1, 1966, C.D. sold the premises to X.Y.Z., Inc., for four hundred thousand dollars.

6. On or about December 1, 1966, A.B. commenced an action against C.D. in which A.B. claims a commission of twenty thousand dollars for procuring the purchaser for the premises. A copy of the complaint is attached hereto.

7. E.F. claims that the sale of the premises was brought about by his sole efforts and demands from C.D. the sum of twenty thousand dollars as commission.

8. C.D. admits he owes a commission to either A.B. or E.F.

9. By reason of the claims of A.B. and E.F., C.D. is or may be exposed to multiple liability.

Wherefore C.D. demands judgment:

1. That C.D. be authorized to pay into court or to a person designated by the court the sum of twenty thousand dollars, less C.D.'s costs and disbursements, which shall be retained by and awarded to C.D.

2. That, upon such payment, C.D. be discharged from liability either to A.B. or E.F.

[Print name]

_____

Attorney for Defendant and
Interpleading Plaintiff
Address:
Telephone Number:

Form 3

Complaint for Interpleader and Declaratory Relief [Official Form 16]

SUPREME COURT OF THE STATE OF NEW YORK
COUNTY OF NEW YORK

U.V.W., Inc., Plaintiff,
   against   Complaint
C.D., E.F., and X.Y., Defendants.   Index No.

1. [Allegation as to plaintiff's incorporation.]

2. On or about June 1, 1966, plaintiff issued to G.H. a policy of life insurance whereby plaintiff promised to pay to K.L. as beneficiary the sum of twenty thousand dollars upon the death of G.H. The policy required the payment by G.H. of a stipulated premium on June 1, 1966, and annually thereafter as a condition precedent to its continuance in force.

3. No part of the premium due June 1, 1966, was ever paid and the policy ceased to have any force or effect on July 1, 1966.

4. On September 1, 1966, G.H. and K.L. died as the result of a collision between a locomotive and the automobile in which G.H. and K.L. were riding.

5. Defendant C.D. is the executor of the will of G.H.; defendant E.F. is the executor of the will of K.L.

6. Defendant X.Y. claims to have been designated as beneficiary of the above-mentioned policy in place of K.L.

7. Each of defendants C.D., E.F., and X.Y. is claiming that the above-mentioned policy was in full force and effect at the time of the death of G.H.; each of them is claiming to be the only person entitled to receive payment of the amount of the policy and has made demand for payment thereof.

8. By reason of these conflicting claims of the defendants, plaintiff is in doubt as to which defendant is entitled to be paid the amount of the policy, if it was in force at the death of G.H.

Wherefore plaintiff demands that the court adjudge:

(1) That none of the defendants is entitled to recover from plaintiff the amount of the above-mentioned policy or any part thereof.

(2) That as further or consequential relief each of the defendants be restrained from instituting any action against plaintiff for the recovery of the amount of the policy or any part thereof, and if the court shall determine that the policy was in force at the death of G.H., that the rights of the defendants to the money due under the policy be determined by the court and the plaintiff be discharged from liability under the policy except to the person whom the court shall adjudge entitled to the amount due thereunder.

(3) That the court grant such other further relief as may be just and proper.

(4) That plaintiff recover its costs and disbursements.

[Print name]

_____

Attorney for Plaintiff
Address:
Telephone Number:

Form 4

Interpleader; Claimants to Contents of Safe Deposit Box

| [Title of court and cause] | Interpleader Complaint |
| | Index No. — [if assigned] |

Plaintiff, complaining of defendants, alleges:

1. That plaintiff is and at the times hereinafter mentioned was a corporation duly organized and existing under the laws of the State of New York, and engaged in the business of safe deposit company.

2. That heretofore one S hired the use of a safe or a safe deposit box in plaintiff's vault, and stored certain property and valuables therein; that said S died intestate, as plaintiff is informed and believes, on or about __1_____, 19_2_; and that at the time of his death there was deposited in his said safe or safe deposit box the following described moneys and property, which moneys and property are still in the custody of plaintiff, viz: __3_____.

3. That thereafter defendant, C, claiming to be the duly appointed administrator of said S, deceased, applied to plaintiff for leave to enter said safe or safe deposit box and remove the contents thereof, and demanded that plaintiff deliver to him, as such administrator, the aforesaid moneys and property therein contained.

4. That at or about the same time, defendant M notified plaintiff that she claimed to be the owner of said moneys and property, and demanded that plaintiff deliver the

same to her; that defendant M also displayed in her possession the keys of said safe or safe deposit box, and served upon plaintiff a notice in writing in the following terms, viz:

"Please take notice that S, who was the lessee of a safe in the vaults of your company, died on __4_____, 19_5_; that I, the undersigned, am the sole owner of and entitled to the immediate possession of all and singular the chattels and property contained in said safe of S, deceased, and that I hold the keys to said safe; and that I hereby demand that you forthwith surrender and deliver to me the possession of all the chattels and property contained in said safe.

"And you are also notified that none of the chattels and property contained in said safe constitute or form a part of, or belong to, the estate of S, deceased, and you are hereby warned and notified not to deliver the same or any part thereof to the administrator of the estate of said S, deceased, or to any person other than the undersigned; and that for a failure to comply with this notice and demand, the undersigned will hold you liable for all damages she may sustain."

5. That plaintiff has no claim upon nor any beneficial interest in said moneys and property, and is ready and willing to deposit the same in court or deliver possession thereof to such person as the court may direct. That plaintiff is ignorant of the respective rights of defendants in said moneys and property, and cannot determine without hazard to itself to which of said defendants the same belong.

6. That the claims of defendants have been made without any collusion of plaintiff with said defendants, or either of them, and plaintiff brings this suit of its own free will and solely to avoid the dangers, injustice and expense of being compelled to defend actions or proceedings on the part of both of said defendants.

Wherefore, plaintiff demands judgment as follows:

1. That during the pendency of this suit, and until the further order of the court, the defendants, and each of them, their agents and attorneys, be enjoined and restrained from commencing or prosecuting any action or proceeding in any court against plaintiff for the recovery of said moneys and property, or any part thereof.

2. That plaintiff may deposit said moneys and property in court, or deliver possession thereof to such person as the court directs, and that thereupon plaintiff may be discharged from any and all claims of defendants, or either of them, by reason of said moneys and property, and that defendants and each of them, their agents and attorneys, may be forever enjoined and restrained from commencing or prosecuting any action or proceeding in any court against plaintiff upon their said claims or for the recovery of said moneys and property, or any part thereof.

3. That defendants interplead each with the other to determine their respective rights in said moneys and property, and that it be adjudicated to whom the same belong.

4. That plaintiff be allowed its just costs, disbursements and allowances herein out of said moneys and property, and have such other and further relief in the premises as shall seem just and equitable.

__6_____
Attorney for Plaintiff
Address __7_____
Telephone No. __8__

[Verification]

[From the records in Mercantile Safe Deposit Co. v Dimon, 55 AD 538, 67 NYS 430, in which a judgment was rendered giving plaintiff the relief it sought.]

Form 5

Interpleader; Claimants to Deposit in Bank

Interpleader Complaint

[Title of court and cause]　　　　Index No. — [if assigned]

Plaintiff complaining of defendants alleges:

1. That at all the times hereinafter mentioned plaintiff was, and still is, a domestic corporation organized and existing under and by virtue of the Banking Law of the state of New York, with its principal place of business at __1____, New York.

2. That on the __2__ day of __3____, 19_4_, there was deposited with plaintiff a certain sum of money and thereupon plaintiff at the request of the depositor opened an account in the name of "James Murphy for grandson Thomas C. Igo" and issued its pass book number __5____ in the name of "James Murphy for grandson Thomas C. Igo," as representing said account; that there is now to the credit of said account including the interest allowed by plaintiff, the sum of __6____ dollars; that said deposit was received and said account was opened upon the agreement that said account was opened subject to the by-laws of plaintiff, printed on the first and last pages of said pass book; and that prior to the opening of said account the following bylaw had been duly adopted by plaintiff and was printed on the last page of said pass book:

"14. On the decease of any depositor, the amount to the credit of the deceased shall be paid to his or her legal representatives."

3. That said bylaw had, prior to the opening of said account, been duly posted as required by the Banking Law of the State of New York.

4. That on the __7__ day of __8____, 19_9_, said James Murphy departed this life in the City of __10____, County of __11____, State of New York, and that thereafter defendant A was duly appointed by the Surrogate of the County of __12____, administratrix of the goods, chattels and credits of James Murphy, deceased, and she is now acting as such administratrix.

5. That subsequent to the death of said James Murphy plaintiff was informed that the said James Murphy had no grandson named Thomas C. Igo, but that he did have a stepson, the son of defendant A, whose name is Thomas C. Igo, and that the said Thomas C. Igo has a son named Thomas J. Igo, a step-grandson of the said James Murphy, deceased; that plaintiff was also informed since the death of James Murphy that the bank book representing said account was found among the effects of the said James Murphy after his death.

6. That subsequent to the death of said James Murphy as aforesaid, a claim for the said fund was made and asserted by defendant Thomas J. Igo, who claims to be the beneficiary named in said account and to be entitled to the whole of said sum of __13____ dollars, and likewise, since the death of said James Murphy, defendant Thomas C. Igo made a claim against plaintiff for the whole of said sum of __14____ dollars; that on or about the __15__ day of __16____, 19_17_, an action was commenced in the Supreme Court, County of __18____, against this plaintiff by the defendant, Thomas C. Igo, for the recovery of the amount standing to the credit of said account; that this plaintiff has not answered in said action; that defendant A as administratrix of James Murphy, deceased, would be entitled to the amount standing to the credit of said account if no trust was established by the depositor in relation to said account in favor of either of the other defendants; that no evidence has been furnished plaintiff that any trust was established; and that defendant A as administratrix, as aforesaid, claims said fund.

7. That plaintiff is now and has at all times been ready and willing to pay said fund to whomsoever is legally and lawfully entitled thereto, but there are conflicting claims made to said fund; that plaintiff is a mere stakeholder and has no interest in the controversy between the several defendants, but stands ready, and has always stood ready, to pay said fund to whomsoever of defendants is lawfully entitled to receive the same.

8. That plaintiff does not in any respect collude with any or either of defendants, nor do any of its officers or agents collude with either or any of defendants, touching the matters in question in this action, and plaintiff has not asked, and does not ask this relief, nor any relief herein, at the request of either or any of defendants, but solely of

its own, free will, and to avoid being molested and injured touching the matters herein set forth.

9. That plaintiff is ignorant of the respective rights of said defendants, and cannot determine, without hazard to itself, to which of said defendants the moneys due upon and under the said account of right belong; that it is in doubt as to which of said defendants is right in his claim, and has no means of satisfactorily ascertaining what are the facts of the several transactions which are relied upon by said defendants as the foundation of their respective claims; and plaintiff cannot pay over the moneys due upon the said account to any or either of defendants, without taking upon itself the responsibility of determining doubtful questions of law and of fact, and without incurring the risk of being subjected to great cost and expense in defending itself and to a double payment of the same indebtedness, if it should finally appear that plaintiff had wrongfully determined in favor of any one claimant at the expense of the others, and without being involved in a multiplicity of suits.

Wherefore plaintiff prays that, upon the payment by it of the said sum of __19_____ dollars into this court to the credit of this action, to abide the further order and judgment of this court herein, a perpetual injunction be issued and granted restraining the said defendants, __20_____, __21_____ and __22_____, as administratrix of the goods, chattels and credits of James Murphy, deceased, or any or either of them or their successors, from commencing, continuing or prosecuting any action in any court whatsoever, whether in the State of New York, or elsewhere, against plaintiff for the recovery, or to enforce the payment, of the said sum of __23_____ dollars or any part thereof, or any sum whatever which may be due, or which may be alleged to be due, upon the said account or from instituting or continuing any proceeding or proceedings whatever for that object; and that said defendants be ordered to interplead among themselves to determine their respective rights to the said moneys, and that it be adjudicated to whom, in accordance with the terms of said account and the results of the transactions hereinbefore referred to, said moneys of right belong; that upon such payment being made into this court as aforesaid, plaintiff be discharged of and from all claim by said defendants, or any or either of them, to the said sum of money or any part thereof; and that plaintiff may be allowed its costs, and its disbursements and allowances, out of the said sum of __24_____ dollars and may have such other and further relief herein as to this court shall seem just and meet, and that it may have a judgment accordingly, and may be hence dismissed.

__25_____

Attorney for Plaintiff

Address __26_____

Telephone No. __27__

[Verification]

See also Bank L § 239.

Form 6

Interpleader; Real Estate Brokers Claiming Commission

Interpleader Complaint

[Title of court and cause]   Index No. — [if assigned]

Plaintiff complaining of defendants alleges,

1. Defendant A is a duly licensed real estate broker in the state of New York.

2. Defendant B is a duly licensed real estate broker in the state of New York.

3. At the times herein mentioned plaintiff was the owner of premises known as and by [12 West 13th Street] in the city of __1_____, state of New York.

4. On or about __2_____, 19_3_, plaintiff listed his said property for sale with several real estate brokers in said city of __4_____, among whom were defendants A and B, upon the following terms [set forth terms].

5. Plaintiff agreed with said brokers to pay such broker only as should be the procuring cause of the sale of said premises, for all services rendered in connection therewith, a commission of [five] per cent of the purchase price of said property.

6. Defendants A and B each undertook to sell said property upon said terms, and said agreement as to payment of commissions.

7. On or about __5_____, 19_6_, plaintiff sold said premises to __7_____, for __8_____ dollars.

8. Defendants A and B each claim that said sale to __9_____ was brought about by his sole efforts.

9. Defendants A and B each has demanded from plaintiff the sum of __10_____ dollars, as the amount of the commissions plaintiff agreed to pay to the broker who was the procuring cause of said sale.

10. Plaintiff is ignorant of, and unable to ascertain which of defendants was the procuring cause of said sale, and is unable to determine to whom the said commissions are due and payable.

11. Plaintiff admits he owes said commissions to one of the defendants and makes no claim to any part thereof, but by reason of the foregoing may be exposed to double liability as a result of said adverse claims.

12. Plaintiff is ready and willing to pay said commissions to whomever the court shall adjudge is entitled thereto.

Wherefore, plaintiff demands judgment:

1. That the defendants, and each of them be restrained by injunction from commencing or prosecuting any action or proceeding against plaintiff in relation to said claims.

2. That plaintiff be authorized to pay said money into court, or to some person appointed by the court authorized to receive the same.

3. That defendants be required to interplead together concerning their claims to said money.

4. That upon the payment by plaintiff of said money into court, or as otherwise directed, plaintiff be discharged from all liability to either of defendants in relation thereto.

5. That plaintiff's costs and disbursements be paid out of said money paid into court, or as otherwise directed.

6. That plaintiff have such other, further, and different relief as to the court may seem just.

__11_____

Attorney for Plaintiff
Address __12_____
Telephone No. __13__

[Verification]

Form 7

Interpleader; By Warehouseman

[Title of court and cause,   Interpleader Complaint
and introductory paragraph]   Index No. — [if assigned]

1. Plaintiff is a warehouseman, doing business at __1_____ in this State, and as such has on storage __2_____ [describe the goods in a general way, such as: certain personal property, consisting of rugs, antiques, embroideries and other works of art, inclosed in boxes and barrels].

2. Said property was deposited with plaintiff by defendant A.B., on or about the __3__ day of __4_____, 19_5_.

3. Subsequent thereto defendant C.D. claimed and now claims to be the owner, by virtue of an assignment from defendant A.B. and has demanded possession from plaintiff, and has threatened to hold plaintiff responsible if delivery be not made in accordance with the demand.

4. Defendant E.F., also claims to be the owner of the property, and has demanded possession of the same from plaintiff.

5. Defendant G.H., as sheriff of the county of __6____, also claims to be entitled to the possession of the property by virtue of a warrant of attachment issued in an action pending in the __7____ Court between defendant C.D. and defendant E.F., and has levied upon said property by virtue of said warrant of attachment, claiming it to be the property of the defendant in said action.

6. There are now pending several actions between the various defendants with reference to the title and possession of the goods, and plaintiff retains and has possession of the goods as a warehouseman, and is unable to determine who is the true owner, or to whom the delivery of the said goods should be made.

WHEREFORE, plaintiff demands judgment that

1. Defendants and each of them be restrained by injunction from enforcing or attempting to enforce their claims against plaintiff touching the said property and from taking any proceedings against plaintiff in relation thereto.

2. Defendants be required to interplead herein and settle their rights to the said __8____ above specified.

3. Some person or persons be authorized to receive the said property pending such litigation.

4. Upon delivering the said property to such person or persons as the court shall direct, plaintiff be discharged from all liability to either or any of defendants thereto.

5. Plaintiff's costs and charges be paid out of the same, and that such other or further relief be granted to plaintiff as shall be equitable.

__9_____

Attorney for Plaintiff
Office __10____
Telephone No. __11__

[Verification]

Form 8

Interpleader; Answer of Claimant

Answer
[Title of court and cause]   Index No. — [if assigned]

Defendant A, answering the complaint [see Form 2:114, supra]

1. [Set forth such denials as may be proper]

AS A COMPLETE DEFENSE AND COUNTERCLAIM TO THE [FIRST CAUSE OF ACTION SET FORTH IN THE] COMPLAINT, ALLEGES:

1. Plaintiff listed the property described in the complaint with defendant A for sale, and employed defendant A as broker to sell the same for the price and on the terms set forth in the complaint [or, if on different terms, set them forth].

2. Defendant A accepted said listing, and agreed to use his best efforts to bring about the sale of said property.

3. Solely through the efforts of defendant A, defendant A obtained [XYZ Co., Inc.] as a purchaser for said property, and said [XYZ Co., Inc.] on or about __1____, 19_2_, entered into an agreement with plaintiff for the purchase and sale of said property for the sum of $__3__.

416

4. Defendant A has duly performed all the conditions of said contract with plaintiff on his part.

5. By reason of the foregoing defendant A became and is entitled to commissions, for the sale of said property in the sum of $__4__ , no part of which has been paid, although duly demanded.

WHEREFORE defendant A demands judgment against plaintiff, dismissing the complaint, with costs; that defendant A have judgment against plaintiff for the sum of $__5__, with interest thereon from __6_____, 19_7_, together with the costs and disbursements of this action.

__8_____

Attorney for defendant A

Address __9_____

Telephone No. __10__

[Verification]

Form 9

Answer and Defensive Interpleader [Official Form 18]

SUPREME COURT OF THE STATE OF NEW YORK
COUNTY OF NEW YORK

A.B., Plaintiff,
  against
C.D., Defendant

C.D., Defendant and Inter-   Answer
    pleading Plaintiff.   Index No.
  against
E.F., Interpleaded Defendant.

[For form of responsive pleadings addressed to the allegations of a complaint, see Form 2 of CPLR 3018.]

Interpleader Defense

1. On or about June 1, 1966, defendant listed the premises referred to in the complaint with A.B. and E.F., licensed New York real estate brokers.

2. Defendant separately agreed with A.B. and E.F. to pay for all services rendered in connection with the sale a commission equal to five percent of the purchase price if such broker were the procuring cause of the sale, and A.B. and E.F. each undertook to sell the premises on those terms.

3. On or about July 1, 1966, defendant sold the premises to X.Y.Z., Inc., for four hundred thousand dollars.

4. A.B. and E.F. each now claims that the sale of the premises was brought about by his sole efforts and demands from defendant the sum of twenty thousand dollars as commission.

5. Defendant admits that he owes a commission to either A.B. or E.F.

6. By reason of the claims asserted by A.B. and E.F., defendant is or may be exposed to multiple liability.

7. Defendant has interpleaded E.F. in this action. A copy of the interpleader complaint is attached to this answer.

Wherefore defendant demands judgment:

1. That defendant be authorized to pay into court or to a person designated by the court the sum of twenty thousand dollars, less defendant's costs and disbursements, which shall be retained by and awarded to defendant.

2. That upon such payment defendant be discharged from liability to either A.B. or E.F.

[Print name]

_____

Attorney for Defendant
Address:
Telephone Number:

Form 10

Answer of Stakeholder

Answer

[Title of court and cause]   Index No. — [if assigned]

Defendant answering the complaint alleges,

1. [Set forth such denials as may be proper]

AS A COMPLETE DEFENSE AND COUNTERCLAIM TO THE [FIRST CAUSE OF ACTION SET FORTH IN THE] COMPLAINT, DEFENDANT ALLEGES,

2. At all the times herein mentioned defendant was the owner of premises known as and by [12 West 13th Street] in the city of __1_____, state of New York.

3. On or about __2_____, 19_3_, defendant listed his said property for sale with several real estate brokers in said city of __4_____, among whom were plaintiff and one B upon the following terms [set forth terms].

4. Upon information and belief plaintiff and said B each is a duly licensed real estate broker in the state of New York.

5. Defendant agreed with plaintiff and said B to pay them for all services rendered in connection with the sale of said premises a commission of [five] per cent of the purchase price of said property only if plaintiff or said B were the procuring cause of the sale of said premises.

6. Plaintiff and said B each undertook to sell said property upon said terms, and said agreement as to payment of commissions.

7. On or about __5_____, 19_6_, defendant sold said premises to __7_____, for __8_____ dollars.

8. Plaintiff and said B each claims that said sale to __9_____ was brought about by his sole efforts.

9. Plaintiff and said B each has demanded from defendant the sum of __10_____ dollars as the amount of the commissions defendant agreed to pay to the broker who was the procuring cause of said sale.

10. Defendant is ignorant of, and unable to ascertain which of said claimants was the procuring cause of said sale, and is unable to determine to whom said commissions are due and payable.

11. Defendant admits he owes said commissions to either plaintiff or said B, and makes no claim to any part thereof, but by reason of the foregoing is or may be exposed to double liability.

12. Defendant is ready and willing to pay said commissions to whomever the court shall adjudge is entitled thereto.

13. That after the commencement of this action, and on or about __11_____, 19_12_, defendant as interpleading plaintiff caused to be served upon said B, as interpleaded defendant, a summons and interpleading complaint, and thereby has brought said B into this action as a party thereto.

WHEREFORE, defendant demands judgment

1. That the complaint be dismissed.

2. That plaintiff and said B be required to interplead together concerning their respective claims to said commissions.

3. That defendant be authorized to pay said money into court, or to some person appointed by the court authorized to receive the same.

4. That upon the payment by defendant of said money into court, or as otherwise directed, defendant be discharged from all liability to either plaintiff or said B in relation thereto.

5. That defendant's costs and disbursements be paid out of said money paid into court, or as otherwise directed.

6. That defendant have such other, further, and different relief as to the court may seem just.

__13_____
Attorney for defendant
Address __14_____
Telephone No. __15__

[Verification]

Form 11

Notice of Motion to Consolidate or for Joint Trial

Notice of Motion

[Title of court and cause]　　　　Index No. __1__

Please take notice that upon the annexed affidavit of __2_____, sworn to the __3__ day of __4_____, 19_5_, and the pleadings herein, the undersigned will move this court at a term for motions held at the County Courthouse in the City of __6_____, New York, on the __7__ day of __8_____, 19_9_, at __10__ o'clock in the __11__ noon of that day or as soon thereafter as counsel can be heard, for an order pursuant to CPLR 1006, removing to this court and consolidating with the above-entitled action, an action pending in the __12_____, Court of __13_____ County between __14_____ and the defendant, and for such other and further relief as to the court may seem just and proper.

Dated: __15_____.

__16_____
Attorney for defendant
[Address and Telephone Number]

To: __17_____
　　Attorney for plaintiff AB
　　[Address]

To: __18_____
　　Attorney for plaintiff CD
　　[Address]

Form 12

Affidavit in Support of Motion to Consolidate or For Joint Trial

Affidavit

[Title of court and cause]　　　　Index No. __1__

[Venue]

__2_____, being duly sworn deposes and says:

1. That he is __3_____ of the __4_____, Inc., the defendant above named which is

419

a corporation duly organized and existing under and by virtue of the laws of the State of New York.

2. That defendant is a holder of certain funds payable under a draft which on its face appears to be payable to the plaintiff by one A B.

3. That said A B demanded payment of defendant on the __5__ day of __6_____, 19_7_, pursuant to the terms of said draft; that payment was refused by the defendant on the ground that one C D had presented credentials under which he claimed to be entitled to payment of the funds held by the defendant.

4. That defendant is ignorant of the respective rights of the parties and cannot determine, without hazard to itself, to which of the claimants the funds are payable.

5. That defendant has no claim upon the said property and is merely a stakeholder and is ready, willing, and able to deliver the funds to such person or persons as the court may direct.

6. That the actions hereinafter mentioned, commenced against the defendant, were not brought by collusion with either of the parties.

7. That heretofore and on the __8__ day of __9_____, 19_10_, the plaintiff A B commenced an action in the above-entitled court against the defendant demanding payment of the sums so held by the defendant.

8. That on the __11__ day of __12_____, 19_13_, the defendant C D commenced an action in the __14_____ Court of the County of __15_____ against the defendant demanding the payment of the sums so held by the defendant.

9. This motion is made for the purpose of having the above-entitled action of A B and the action of C D consolidated in the above-entitled court or jointly tried in the above-entitled court.

10. That this motion is made for the purpose of disposing of all the issues herein in one trial, thereby saving the time of the court and the parties hereto.

Wherefore defendant asks that this motion be granted.

__16_____

[Signature, with name printed underneath]

[Jurat]

Form 13

Order to Consolidate or For Joint Trial

[Caption]

Order

[Title of cause]   Index No. __1__

The defendant in the above-entitled action, having moved for an order to consolidate in the above-entitled action pending in this court and the __2_____ Court, pursuant to CPLR 1006, and said motion having come on regularly to be heard,

Now, on reading and filing the notice of motion with proof of service thereof, the affidavit of __3_____, sworn to the __4__ day of __5_____, 19_6_, the affidavit of __7_____, sworn to the __8__ day of __9_____, 19_10_, in support of the motion [in case of opposition state opposing papers], and after hearing __11_____, attorney for the defendant in support of said motion and __12_____, and __13_____, attorneys for the respective plaintiffs in opposition thereto [or there being no opposition thereto] and due deliberation having been had,

Now on motion of __14_____, attorney for the defendant, and on the decision of the court filed herein, it is hereby

ORDERED that the motion to consolidate the two actions pending in the __15_____ Court of __16_____ and the __17_____ ___ Court of __18_____ entitled as appears herein is hereby granted and it is further

ORDERED that the clerk of the __19_____ Court be and he is hereby directed, upon service of the copy of this order and payment of requisite fees therefor, to forward the papers in the action pending in the __20_____ Court of __21_____, to the clerk of the County of __22_____, and it is further

ORDERED that the clerk of the County of __23_____, be and he is hereby directed and authorized, to consolidate the files of such two actions above entitled under the file number of the action presently pending in this court under number __24_____, and it is further

ORDERED that all papers in the action bearing the title of the action be entitled in this court, and it is further

ORDERED that the costs of the actions hereby consolidated up to the date of this order abide the event of this consolidated action.

Enter

__25_____

Justice of the Supreme Court
[Signature, with name
printed underneath]

Form 14

Interpleading Summons

Supreme Court
County of __1_____

__2_____
A., Plaintiff
  v
C., Defendant
_3_____
C., Defendant and
    interpleading plaintiff
  v
B., Interpleaded defendant
__4_____

                              Summons
                              Index No. — [if assigned]

To the above named interpleaded defendant B:

You are hereby summoned to answer the complaint of defendant and interpleading plaintiff C, in this action, copies of which are herewith served upon you, and to serve copies of your answer upon the undersigned attorney for said C, and upon John Smith, attorney for above named plaintiff, whose address is __5_____, within twenty days after the service of this summons and interpleading complaint, exclusive of the date of service. In case of your failure to appear or answer the complaint of defendant and interpleading plaintiff C, judgment will be taken against you by default for the relief demanded in the interpleading complaint.

Dated __6_____, 19_7_.

__8_____

Attorney for defendant and
interpleading plaintiff C
Office and P. O. address
__9_____
Telephone No. __10__

Form 15

Interpleading Complaint

[Title of court]

[Title of cause, as in Form 14]	Interpleading Complaint Index No. — [if assigned]

Defendant and interpleading plaintiff C, complaining of interpleaded defendant B, alleges

1. At all the times herein mentioned defendant C was the owner of premises known as and by [12 West 13th Street] in the city of __1_____, state of New York.

2. On or about __2_____, 19_3_, defendant C listed his said property for sale with several real estate brokers in said city of __4_____, among whom were plaintiff and interpleaded defendant B upon the following terms [set forth terms].

3. Upon information and belief plaintiff, and interpleaded defendant B, each is a duly licensed real estate broker in the state of New York.

4. Defendant C agreed with plaintiff and interpleaded defendant B to pay them for all services rendered in connection with the sale of said premises a commission of [five] per cent of the purchase price of said property only if plaintiff or said B were the procuring cause of the sale of said premises.

5. Plaintiff, and interpleaded defendant B, each undertook to sell said property upon said terms, and said agreement as to payment of commissions.

6. On or about __5_____, 19_6_, defendant C sold said premises to __7_____, for __8_____ dollars.

7. Plaintiff, and interpleaded defendant B, each claims that said sale to __9_____ was brought about by his sole efforts.

8. Plaintiff, and interpleaded defendant B, each has demanded from this defendant C the sum of __10_____ dollars as the amount of the commissions defendant C agreed to pay to the broker who was the procuring cause of said sale.

9. Defendant C is ignorant of, and unable to ascertain which of said claimants was the procuring cause of said sale, and is unable to determine to whom said commissions are due and payable.

10. Defendant C admits he owes said commissions to either plaintiff or interpleaded defendant B, and makes no claim to any part thereof, but by reason of the foregoing is or may be exposed to double liability.

11. Defendant C is ready and willing to pay said commissions to whomever the court shall adjudge is entitled thereto.

WHEREFORE defendant and interpleading plaintiff C demands judgment

1. That defendant C be authorized to pay said money into court, or to some person appointed by the court authorized to receive the same.

2. That upon the payment by defendant C of said money into court, or as otherwise directed, defendant C be discharged from all liability to either plaintiff or interpleaded defendant B in relation thereto.

3. That defendant C's costs and disbursements be paid out of said money paid into court, or as otherwise directed.

4. That defendant C have such other, further, and different relief as to the court may seem just.

__11_____

Attorney for defendant and
interpleading plaintiff C
Address __12_____
Telephone No. __13__

[Verification]

Form 16

Answer of Interpleaded Defendant

[Title of court and cause,　　　　　　Answer
as in Form 14]　　　　　　　　　　Index No. — [if assigned]

Interpleaded defendant B answering the complaints of plaintiff A and of interpleading plaintiff C,

1. [Set forth desired denials.]

AS A COMPLETE DEFENSE AND COUNTERCLAIM TO THE COMPLAINTS OF PLAINTIFF A, AND OF INTERPLEADING PLAINTIFF C, INTERPLEADED DEFENDANT B ALLEGES,

2. Interpleading plaintiff C listed the property described in the complaint with interpleaded defendant B for sale, and employed interpleaded defendant B as broker to sell the same for the price and on the terms set forth in the complaint [or, if on different terms, set them forth].

3. Interpleaded defendant B accepted said listing and agreed to use his best efforts to bring about the sale of said property.

4. Solely through the efforts of interpleaded defendant B interpleaded defendant B obtained [XYZ Co., Inc.] as a purchaser for said property, and said [XYZ Co., Inc.] on or about __1_____, 19_2_, entered into an agreement with interpleading plaintiff C for the purchase and sale of said property for the sum of $__3__.

5. Interpleaded defendant B has duly performed all the conditions of said contract with interpleading plaintiff C on his part.

6. By reason of the foregoing interpleaded defendant B became and is entitled to commissions, for the sale of said property in the sum of $__4__, no part of which has been paid, although duly demanded.

WHEREFORE interpleaded defendant B demands judgment

1. That the complaint of plaintiff A and interpleading plaintiff C be dismissed.

2. That judgment be awarded interpleaded defendant B on his counterclaim against interpleading plaintiff C in the amount of $__5__ with interest thereon from __6_____.

3. That interpleaded defendant B be awarded the costs and disbursements of this action against both plaintiff A and interpleading plaintiff C.

4. That such other further and different relief be granted interpleaded defendant B as to this court may seem just.

__7_____
Attorney for interpleaded
defendant B
Office and P. O. address
__8___
Telephone No. __9__

[Verification]

Form 17

Notice of Motion to Dismiss Interpleader Action, Issue of Independent Liability

Notice of Motion
[Title of cause]　　　　　　Index No. — [if assigned]

PLEASE TAKE NOTICE that upon the annexed affidavit of __1_____, sworn to __2_____, 19_3_, and upon the pleadings in this action, the undersigned will move this court at a motion term, Part __4_____ thereof, to be held in and for the county of __5_____ at the County Courthouse in the city of __6_____ on the __7__ day of __8_____, 19_9_, at __10__ o'clock in the forenoon of that day, or as soon thereafter as counsel can be heard, for an order dismissing the above entitled action against defendant __11_____ on the ground that an issue of an independent liability of plaintiff to said defendant is raised by the pleadings herein, and granting to said defendant such other, further, and different relief as to this court may seem just and proper together with costs.

Dated __12_____, 19_13_.

____14_____

Attorney for defendant __15_____

____16_____

Office and P. O. Address

Telephone No.

To __17_____, Esq.
Attorney for Plaintiff
__18_____, Esq.
Attorney for Defendant __19_____

Form 18

Affidavit in Support of Motion to Dismiss Interpleader Action, Issue of Independent Liability

Affidavit
[Title of cause]   Index No. — [if assigned]

State of New York
County of __1_____   ss:

__2_____ being duly sworn, deposes and says:

1. I am one of the defendants in this action.

2. This action was commenced against me by the service of a summons and complaint on __3_____, 19_4_.

3. This action was brought to require me and __5_____, the other defendant herein, to litigate adverse claims which we are alleged to be making against plaintiff arising out of [set forth nature of claim].

4. I appeared in this action and served an answer in which, among other things, I raised an issue of the independent liability of plaintiff to me because [set forth facts in detail showing the existence of an issue of independent liability].

WHEREFORE I respectfully pray that the above entitled action be dismissed as against me with costs.

____6_____

[Print signer's name below signature]

[Jurat]

Form 19

Order Dismissing Interpleader Action, Issue of Independent Liability

SUPREME COURT, __1_____ COUNTY.

Order
[Title of cause]   Index No. — [if assinged]

Present: Hon. __2_____, Justice.

Defendant __3_____ having duly moved for an order dismissing the above entitled action as against him on the ground that an issue of an independent liability of plaintiff to him is raised by the pleadings herein,

NOW on reading and filing the notice of motion dated __4_____, 19_5_, and the affidavit of __6_____ sworn to __7_____, 19_8_, together with proof of service of said notice of motion and affidavit upon the attorney for plaintiff and the attorney for defendant __9_____ all in support of said motion, and the affidavit of __10_____ sworn to __11_____, 19_12_, in opposition thereto, and after hearing __13_____ attorney for defendant __14_____ in support of said motion and __15_____ attorney for plaintiff and __16_____ attorney for defendant __17_____ in opposition thereto and due deliberation having been had,

Now, on motion of __18_____ attorney for defendant __19_____ __20_____, and on the decision of the court filed herein, it is

ORDERED that said motion be and the same hereby is granted, and it is further

ORDERED that the above entitled action be and the same hereby is dismissed against defendant __21_____, and it is further

ORDERED that a judgment be entered herein in favor of defendant __22_____ and against the plaintiff dismissing the above entitled action against defendant __23_____ together with the costs and disbursements of this action.

Signed this __24__ day of __25_____, 19_26_ at __27_____, New York.

Enter.

__28_____

[Print signer's name below signature]
Justice, Supreme Court
__29_____ County

Form 20

Motion for Discharge of Stakeholder

[Title of court and cause. If motion is made by a stakeholder who is a defendant and interpleading plaintiff, title of both actions as in Form 14, should be used.]

Notice of Motion
Index No. — [if assigned]

PLEASE TAKE NOTICE that upon the affidavit of __1_____, sworn to __2_____, 19_3_, and upon the pleadings and proceedings heretofore had herein, the undersigned will move this court at a Motion Term, Part __4_____ to be held at the Courthouse thereof in the city of __5_____, on __6_____, 19_7_, at __8__ o'clock in the forenoon of that day or as soon thereafter as counsel can be heard for an order permitting plaintiff [or, defendant and interpleading plaintiff A] to pay into this Court [or, to deliver to this Court, or, to a person designated by this Court] the sum of $__9__, the amount in dispute in this action [or, the property involved in this action; to wit (here, set forth the property claimed)]; discharging plaintiff [or, defendant and interpleading plaintiff A] from liability in whole to any party to this action [or, discharging plaintiff (or, defendant and interpleading plaintiff A) from liability in part to defendant __10_____]; directing the payment to plaintiff [or, defendant and interpleading plaintiff A] of his costs, expenses, and disbursements and charging the same against the said amount in dispute in this action [or, the property involved in this action]; and granting plaintiff [or, defendant and interpleading plaintiff A] such further and different relief as to the court may seem just.

Yours, etc.,

Dated __11_____, 19_12_.

__13_____

Attorney for plaintiff [or, defendant and interpleading plaintiff A]
__14_____ Office and Post Office Address
Telephone No. __15__

To __16_____
    Attorney for defendant __17_____
    [or plaintiff]
    __18_____
    Attorney for defendant __19_____
    [or interpleaded defendant]

Form 21

Affidavit in Support of Motion for Discharge of Stakeholder

[Title of cause. If motion is made by a stakeholder who is a defendant and interpleading plaintiff, title of both actions as in
Form 14 should be used.]

Affidavit
Index No. — [if assigned]

[Venue of affidavit]

A, being duly sworn, deposes and says:

1. I am plaintiff in this action [or, I am defendant in the first above entitled action, and defendant and interpleading plaintiff in the second above entitled action].

2. Prior to __1_____, 19_2_, I was the owner of premises known as and by number __3_____, city of __4_____.

3. On or about __5_____, 19_6_, I listed the above mentioned premises with several real estate brokers in said city, among whom were B and C, and I gave each of these brokers the price for which I was willing to sell the premises, and the terms and conditions of any proposed sale. I also agreed to pay any of these brokers five percentum of the said purchase price for his services, if such broker were the procuring cause of the sale.

4. I told each broker that I had listed the property with his competitors in the said city, and that I would agree to list the property with him if he agreed that he was to be entitled to the commission only if he was the procuring cause of the sale.

5. On __7_____, 19_8_, I was visited by one __9_____, who told me that he was interested in buying the said premises and asked me for my price and terms. I told him what they were, giving him the same price, terms and conditions I had given the aforesaid brokers. After some unsuccessful haggling he signed a contract upon said price, terms and conditions, a copy of which contract I annex hereto and make a part hereof.

6. On __10_____, 19_11_, defendant B [or, interpleaded defendant B] came to see me, and demanded commissions for having been the sole procuring cause of the sale of my house to said __12_____. I told him that said purchaser had not mentioned that he had been sent to me by any broker, but that I would inquire and communicate with him. Immediately thereafter C [or, plaintiff C, or, interpleaded defendant C] visited me and told me that he had been the sole procuring cause of said sale. I told him also that I did not know anything about the matter, but that I would communicate with him after I had spoken to the purchaser.

7. On __13_____, 19_14_, I spoke to the said purchaser who said that although he had been told about the property by several brokers, among whom had been said B and C, he told them the price was too high, and that he had decided to negotiate with me directly; and that he felt that no broker could really be said to have been the procuring cause of the sale.

8. I respectfully submit that under the foregoing facts I may be held liable to either B or C for the commissions; that I am ignorant of the facts and unable to ascertain which of the parties is telling the truth. I desire to avoid double liability for said commissions, and respectfully pray that both be required to establish which, if either, is entitled to the commissions. I make no claim to any part of said commissions [or, if any claim is made thereto, set it forth].

9. I hereby offer to pay into court the sum of __15_____ dollars claimed to be the commissions involved herein, and to pay the same to whoever shall be adjudged entitled thereto.

10. This action was commenced against defendants B and C on __16_____ by the service of a summons and verified complaint, and they each have interposed an answer thereto in which they each make claim to said commissions [or, This action was

commenced against me by plaintiff B on __17____ to which I interposed an answer setting up the foregoing facts, and on __18____ I served said C with a summons and interpleading complaint, to which said C interposed an answer demanding the said commissions, and upon information and belief said C also answered the complaint herein]. The time for all parties herein to plead has expired.

11. [If order to show cause is requested, set forth reasons.]

12. No previous application for the relief herein prayed for has heretofore been made.

___19_____
[Print signer's name below signature]

[Jurat]

Form 22

Order Discharging Stakeholder

SUPREME COURT, __1____ County.

[Title of cause. If motion is made by a stakeholder who is a defendant and interpleading plaintiff, title of both actions as in Form 14, should be used.]	Order Index No. — [if assigned]

Present: Hon. __2____, Justice.

Plaintiff [or, defendant and interpleading plaintiff A] having moved for an order discharging him from liability in whole to any party to the above entitled action [or, actions]

NOW, ON READING AND FILING the notice of motion dated __3____, and the affidavit of __4____, sworn to __5____, 19_6_, together with proof of service thereof on all the parties to the above entitled action [or, actions], and upon all the pleadings and proceedings heretofore had therein, all in support of said motion, and the affidavits of __7____ and __8____, in opposition thereto, and after hearing __9____, of counsel, for plaintiff [or, defendant and interpleading plaintiff A] in support of said motion, and __10____, attorney for __11____ and __12____ of counsel for __13____ in opposition to said motion, it is

ORDERED that plaintiff [or, defendant and interpleading plaintiff A] be and hereby is permitted to pay into court the sum of __14____ dollars [less the amount hereinafter allowed him for his expenses, costs and disbursements] by paying same to the County treasurer of __15____ County, to be disposed of in accordance with the further order or final judgment of this court, and it is further

ORDERED that upon paying said amount into this court as herein directed, said __16____ be and he hereby is discharged from liability in whole to any party to the above entitled action [or, actions] by reason of any matter of thing set forth in the pleadings therein, and it is further

ORDERED, that there be paid to said __17____, plaintiff [or defendant and interpleading plaintiff] as his expenses, costs and disbursements the sum of __18____, which sum shall be charged against the aforesaid __19____ dollars, the amount in dispute herein, and be paid therefrom.

Signed this __20__ day of __21____, 19_22_ at __23____, New York.

Enter

___24_____
[Print signer's name below signature]
Justice, Supreme Court
__25____ County

Form 23

Interpleader; Judgment

Judgment

[Title of court and cause]   Index No. — [if assigned]

This action having been brought by plaintiff, against the above-named defendants A and B, to obtain a judgment that defendants interplead and try the questions between them as to whom a certain sum of __1_____ dollars, held by plaintiff and mentioned in the complaint, belongs, and directing payment into court of the said sum to await the determination as to the rights of defendants thereto, and an injunction to restrain the defendants from proceeding to collect the same from plaintiff during the pendency of this action and a perpetual injunction restraining defendants from collecting the same, or any part thereof, from plaintiff, with the costs to plaintiff, and issue having been joined therein and said issue having been brought to trial at motion term [Part __2_____, thereof], held in and for the County of __3_____, at the county court house therein, on the __4__ day of __5_____, 19_6_, before Hon. __7_____, justice, and findings of fact and conclusions of law having been duly made by the court, whereby he finds and decides that plaintiff is entitled to judgment for the relief demanded in said complaint, with the costs of this action, to be paid out of the funds so deposited with the court and said costs having been duly taxed at the sum of __8_____ dollars,

Now, on motion of __9_____, attorney for plaintiff, it is hereby

Adjudged and decreed that defendants A and B interplead in this court of and concerning their respective claims to the sum of __10_____ dollars, mentioned in the complaint; that the payment of said sum by plaintiff into court be and the same hereby is ratified and confirmed and that defendants A and B, be and they are hereby perpetually enjoined and restrained from collecting or attempting to collect the sum or any part thereof from plaintiff.

It is further ordered, adjudged and decreed, that plaintiff recover the sum of __11_____ dollars, his costs of this action, to be paid to plaintiff out of the said fund of __12_____ dollars so deposited by him with the court, such payment to be made by the treasurer of the County of __13_____ on presentation of a certified copy of this judgment, with the receipt of plaintiff's attorney for the same.

Judgment signed this __14__ day of __15_____, 19_16_ at __17_____, New York.

Enter.

___18_____

[Print signer's name below signature]
Justice, Supreme Court
__19_____ County

Form 24

Interpleader; Judgment Awarding Specific Personal Property

Judgment

[Title of court and cause]   Index No. — [if assigned]

The above entitled action having been commenced by plaintiff against defendants A and B for a judgment among other things determining which of said defendants is entitled to the bonds described in the complaint herein, and each of said defendants having appeared herein by their respective attorneys and having served their answers setting forth their claims to said bonds, and an order heretofore having been granted permitting plaintiff to retain said bonds to the credit of this action to be disposed of in accordance with the further judgment of this court, and plaintiff having complied with said order, and another order having been granted discharging plaintiff from liability in whole to either defendant herein and having directed that plaintiff be paid the sum of __1_____ dollars for his costs and disbursements to be charged against the subject

428

matter of this action, and the issues raised by the answers of the respective defendants having duly come on for trial before this court without a jury at a motion term, part __2_____ thereof, held at the courthouse thereof, in the city of __3_____ on the __4__ day of __5_____, 19_6_ and the proofs of the respective parties having been heard and the court having on __7_____, 19_8_, made its decision in writing by which among other things it was found that defendant A was the owner entitled to the immediate possession of said bonds and directed that a judgment be entered requiring plaintiff herein to deliver said bonds to defendant A and assessed costs in favor of defendant A as against defendant B and the costs of defendant A having been taxed in the sum of __9_____ dollars, now on motion of __10_____ attorney for defendant A, it is

ADJUDGED that defendant A at all the times set forth in the complaint was and still is the owner and entitled to the immediate possession of the bonds described in the complaint herein, to wit: [describe bonds] and it is further

ADJUDGED that upon delivery to plaintiff of a certified copy of this judgment and payment to plaintiff by defendant A of the sum of __11_____ dollars charged against the subject matter of this action as hereinbefore set forth, plaintiff deliver to defendant A the bonds hereinbefore described, and it is further

ADJUDGED that defendant A recover of defendant B his costs as taxed in the sum of __12_____ dollars and have execution therefor.

Judgment entered this __13__ day of __14_____, 19_15_.

__16_____

[Print signer's name below signature]

Clerk

§ 1007. When third-party practice allowed

After the service of his answer, a defendant may proceed against a person not a party who is or may be liable to him for all or part of the plaintiff's claim against him, by serving upon such person a summons and third-party complaint and all prior pleadings served in the action. A defendant serving a third-party complaint shall be styled a third-party plaintiff and the person so served shall be styled a third-party defendant. The defendant shall also serve a copy of such third-party complaint upon the plaintiff's attorney.

HISTORY:

Add, L 1962, ch 308, amd, L 1962, ch 315, § 2, eff Sept 1, 1963.
Earlier statutes and rules: CPA § 193-a; RCP 54.

ADVISORY COMMITTEE NOTES:

There was no provision in New York for impleader or third-party practice prior to 1922. In that year a brief statute, suggested by the English practice, was passed. This statute was amended in 1923 and until 1946 was contained in subd 2 of § 193 of the CPA. This provision was unsatisfactory in that: (1) it required leave of court for a defendant to implead, allowed the plaintiff to object to the impleader before the bringing in of the third party and permitted an objection by the latter after he was brought in, (2) impleader was only allowed if the third party "is or *will* be liable" to the defendant, causing the courts to be illiberal in the grant of impleader by insisting that there must be identity of the claim of the plaintiff and the claim of the defendant against the third party, and (3) the third party was denied the right to interpose defenses against the claim of the original plaintiff.

In 1945, the Judicial Council made a study of the subject and submitted a new provision which remedied these defects. See 11 NY Jud Council Rep 58, 370 (1945); 12 id. at 46, 192 (1946); see also 17 id. at 65 (1951). This proposal was adopted and became CPA § 193-a.

The revised New York provision contained about twice as many words as Federal Rule 14. While § 193-a embodied most of the essential provisions of the Federal practice, there were the following differences: (1) the New York provision permitted a third-party action without leave of court which was subject to dismissal only after the appearance of the third party, (2) while impleader is discretionary under both systems, subdivision 4 of the New York section indicates the considerations for the exercise of this discretion and suggests possibilities of alternative disposition. It may be noted that the Federal advisory committee proposed amendments to Rule 14 in 1954 incorporating both of these New York features, although in somewhat terser language.

The new CPLR provisions follow with little change the provisions of CPA § 193-a. However, the provisions of subd 4 relative to special findings are omitted here; they are covered by the rules for verdicts and findings. Moreover, the requirement of verification of the complaint in subd 1 is eliminated and the expression "cause of action" changed to "claim."

The 1951 amendment to CPA § 193-a providing that third-party practice applies to actions in all courts of record is omitted since such provisions are included in the general rule on scope or applicability of the new CPLR. It should be noted that it has recently been held that the state cannot bring in a third-party defendant in the Court of Claims. Haroch v New York, 286 App Div 303, 143 NYS2d 327 (3d Dept 1955).

CROSS REFERENCES:

This section referred to in 1011.
Necessary joinder of parties, CPLR 1001.
Proceedings relating to third-party practice, CPLR §§ 1008–1011.
Pleadings generally, CPLR 3011, 3012.
Demand for relief, CPLR 3017.

FEDERAL ASPECTS:

Third-party practice in United States District Courts, generally, Rule 14 of Federal Rules of Civil Procedure, USCS Court Rules.
When plaintiff may bring in third party, Rule 14(b) of Federal Rules of Civil Procedure, USCS Court Rules.

RESEARCH REFERENCES AND PRACTICE AIDS:

28 NY Jur, Indemnity § 28.
51 NY Jur, Sales § 252.
57 NY Jur, Suretyship and Guaranty §§ 255, 271.
3 Carmody-Wait 2d, Parties §§ 19:93 et seq., 19:111 et seq., 19:124.
3 Carmody-Wait 2d, Commencement of Action; Summons and Service of Process § 24:16.
6 Carmody-Wait 2d, Tender and Offer; Payment into Court § 41:4.
14 Carmody-Wait 2d, Foreclosure of Mortgages on Real Estate § 92:126.
14 Am Jur 2d, Carriers § 1135.
18 Am Jur 2d, Contribution § 73.
59 Am Jur 2d, Parties §§ 3, 196, 202–206.
62 Am Jur 2d, Process § 53.
19 Am Jur Pl and Pr Forms (Rev ed), Parties, Forms 211–223.

Annotations:

Right of defendant in action for personal injury or death to bring in joint tortfeasor for purpose of asserting right of contribution. 11 ALR2d 228.
Federal court's jurisdiction as affected by common citizenship of third party defendant with either or both of original parties. 37 ALR2d 1411.
Independent venue requirements as to cross complaint or similar action by defendant seeking relief against a codefendant or third party. 100 ALR2d 693.
Right of employer sued for tort of employee to implead the latter. 5 ALR3d 871.
Right of defendant under Rules 14(a) and 18(a) of Federal Rules of Civil

Procedure to assert against third party properly in case, claim for damages in excess of, or different from, those sought by original plaintiff. 12 ALR Fed 877.

Necessity that claim by third-party defendant against original plaintiff under Rule 14(a) of Federal Rules of Civil Procedure be supported by independent grounds of federal jurisdiction. 12 ALR Fed 402.

Exclusive remedy provision of Federal Employees' Compensation Act (5 USCS § 8116(c)) as precluding recovery of contribution or indemnity from the United States by third-party tortfeasor for sums expended in satisfying or settling suit by injured government employee. 12 ALR Fed 616.

Law Reviews:

New York Civil Practice Law and Rules: parties. 27 Albany L Rev 182.

Parties and pleading under the CPLR. 31 Brooklyn L Rev 98.

Negligence—apportionment of damages among joint tortfeasors—right of a party actively negligent to implead a co-wrongdoer. 41 Fordham L Rev 167.

Torts—New York civil practice—a joint tort-feasor accorded unlimited right to implead a co-tortfeasor for partial indeminification based on comparative responsibility in negligence. 47 NYU L Rev 815.

A biannual survey of New York practice: Section 1007 and Rule 1010—Third-party practice. 38 St. John's L Rev 419.

A biannual survey of New York practice: Part IV: indemnification between tort-feasors. 39 St. John's L Rev 428.

A biannual survey of New York practice: Part V: CPLR 1007: vouching-in notice —third-party practice. 40 St. John's L Rev 145.

Prior adjudication in favor of third-party defendant: does it preclude subsequent direct action by plaintiff? 19 Syracuse L Rev 734.

Forms:

See "FORMS" heading following "CASE NOTES", infra.

CASE NOTES

1. In general

Notwithstanding that statutory third party practice is available, it is still permissible to vouch-in one who is not named as a party to an action. Clarke v Fidelity & Casualty Co. (1967) 55 Misc 2d 327, 285 NYS2d 503.

Third-party action may be prosecuted to completion, even though severed from the principal action, and even though no actual loss has been shown. McCabe v Queensboro Farm Products, Inc. (1968) 22 NY2d 204, 292 NYS2d 400, 239 NE2d 340.

Right of defendant to implead third party for contribution is completely different type of right than right to damages in compensation for personal injuries and property damage; although procedurally defendant becomes third-party plaintiff and asserts claim against third-party defendant, right to apportionment, at least in context of interpreting general release, is more in nature of defense to plaintiff's claim than affirmative claim against other tortfeasor. Torrence v Stenson (1976) 87 Misc 2d 697, 386 NYS2d 605.

2. Prerequisites to impleader, generally

Under CPLR 1007, a claim over is proper whenever third-party defendant may be liable to third-party plaintiff, for whatever reason, for damages to which the latter may be liable to plaintiff, and the claim need not rest upon the same cause of action or the same ground as the claim against the third-party plaintiff nor need it be related to the main action by a common question of law or fact. Norman Co. v County of Nassau (1970) 63 Misc 2d 965, 314 NYS2d 44.

The test as to whether a third party complaint may be maintained is whether the third party defendant may be liable to the third party plaintiff for all or part of the plaintiff's claim against the third party plaintiff, and it is not enough that the claim rose out of the same set of facts, but the liability of the third party defendant must rise from the liability of the defendant to the plaintiff. Horn v Ketchum (1967) 27 AD2d 759, 277 NYS2d 177.

The owner of a building lot which had been conveyed to a building contractor as security and upon which the plaintiff contractor had started to construct a house could not, subsequent to the contractor's suit for alleged breach of contract, implead the bank that had granted the building loan and paid a "first draw" to the contractor. CPLR 1007 requires that as a condition to impleader the third party by its acts or omissions must have exposed the defendant to liability to plaintiff, and the bank's contract could not possibly have caused defendant to breach his contract with the plaintiff. Howarth v Brown (1968) 60 Misc 2d 587, 303 NYS2d 236.

A third party action cannot be commenced by defendants until after service of their answer. Taca International Airlines, S.A. v Rolls Royce of England, Ltd. (1965) 47 Misc 771, 263 NYS2d 269.

Insurer's third-party complaint allowed to stand despite the fact that insurer had not paid plaintiff's claim on broker's blanket bond and was in fact contesting liability. Krause v American Guarantee & Liability Ins. Co. (1967) 27 AD2d 353, 279 NYS2d 235, affd 22 NY2d 147, 292 NYS2d 67, 239 NE2d 175.

Tenant's failure to serve 30-day notice of claim on comptroller of city and to exhaust administrative remedies did not preclude tenant, who had meritorious claim and colorable right to emergency assistance in the form of rent, from impleading commissioner of department of social services as party to summary proceedings to evict tenant for nonpayment of rent. Rothbaum v Ebel (1974) 77 Misc 2d 965, 354 NYS2d 545.

3. —Service of process and papers

The procedure under this section requires not only the service of a summons and a third-party complaint, but the service of the pleadings in the main suit as well. Lynch v Flame Fuel Oil Corp. (1967) 53 Misc 2d 535, 278 NYS2d 940.

It may not be assumed that the third party plaintiff effected a simultaneous service on both the third party defendant and the plaintiff, nor is the third party defendant's failure to show the date of such service on plaintiff excused by lack of knowledge in the absence of any showing as to what steps were taken to ascertain this date from plaintiff or third party plaintiff, and consequently the third party defendant failed to show that the amended complaint was not served within 20 days after service of the third party complaint on the plaintiff. Johnson v Equitable Life Assur. Soc. (1964) 22 AD2d 141, 254 NYS2d 261, affd 18 NY2d 933, 277 NYS2d 136, 223 NE2d 562.

Third party plaintiff's failure to serve all prior pleadings when third party complaint and summons was served as required by CPLR § 1007 was not a jurisdictional error but a mistake curable under CPLR § 2001, and jurisdiction having been obtained under CPLR § 304 by service of summons, third party plaintiff was permitted, under CPLR § 305, subd c, to amend his complaint to include the appropriate pleadings. Wings & Wheels Express, Inc. v Sisak (1973) 73 Misc 2d 846, 342 NYS2d 891.

Denial of motion for adjournment of trial for the purpose of impleading a third-party defendant, was not abuse of discretion where defendant had adequate time prior to trial to do so and no notification was given to plaintiff that an adjournment of the trial would be requested. Zeitlin v Merrick Bay Park, Inc. (1968) 56 Misc 2d 1039, 290 NYS2d 851.

In action on policy by insured against insurer for loss sustained by dishonesty of employee, wherein insurer served third-party complaint against employee, and employee was an elderly lady who had been in insured's employ for many years, a separate trial of such third-party action was held warranted to avoid prejudice to insured. Sol Lenzner Corp. v Aetna Casualty & Surety Co. (1964) 20 AD2d 305, 246 NYS2d 950.

Naming persons in plaintiff's summons did not make them parties, but personal service of summons, complaint and copy of answer containing cross claim was compliance with statute and was analogous to third-party complaint insofar as third persons were concerned, and they became defendants to extent of cross claims against them. Rubin v A. C. Kluger & Co. (1976) 86 Misc 2d 1014, 383 NYS2d 828.

4. —Limitations and laches

Fact that county was not served with notice of claim within 90 days after accrual of plaintiff's original cause of action as required by General Municipal Law § 50-e would not bar third party action against county hospital commenced by another hospital which was defendant in malpractice suit. Zillman v Meadowbrook Hospital Co. (1973) 73 Misc 2d 726, 342 NYS2d 302, revd on other grounds 45 AD2d 267, 358 NYS2d 466.

No time limit for commencement of a third-party proceeding by a defendant after the service of his answer is provided by this section, but delay may be the basis for discretionary dismissal if it affected the determination of the main action or prejudices the substantial rights of any party as provided in CPLR § 1010. Murphy v Barron (1965) 45 Misc 2d 905, 258 NYS2d 139.

Defendant who impleads another tortfeasor by third-party complaint seven years after the accident and five years after the commencement of action is not guilty of laches warranting dismissal, since he could have waited until he had paid the judgment recovered in the action. Musco v Conte (1964) 22 AD2d 121, 254 NYS2d 589.

5. —Sufficiency of complaint

In action on policy by insured against insurer for loss sustained by dishonesty of employee, wherein insurer served third-party complaint against employee, insured may move to dismiss such third-party complaint for insufficiency. Sol Lenzner

Corp. v Aetna Casualty & Surety Co. (1964) 20 AD2d 305, 246 NYS2d 950.

In determining the sufficiency of a third-party complaint the allegations of the original complaint and the third-party complaint are read together and accepted as true. Musco v Conte (1964) 22 AD2d 121, 254 NYS2d 589.

Shipper's third party complaint was dismissed as to crane operator against whom no evidence was furnished to show operator's liability for loss of cargo. Luria Bros. & Co. v Associated Metals & Minerals Corp. (1972) 73 Misc 2d 937, 343 NYS2d 152.

6. —Subrogation claims

Insurer of automobile owned by corporation which was not named in personal injuries action by passenger in such automobile against corporate owner was not estopped from asserting subrogation claim against driver by reason of its failure to implead driver in passenger's original action, as only a named defendant may proceed against a non-party and not a potential subrogee such as was insurer in original action. United States Fire Ins. Co. v Gould (1974) 43 AD2d 462, 352 NYS2d 541.

An insurer who has not made payment on its policy, upon being sued by its insurer on its policy, may not implead in a negligence action the alleged tortfeasor, because until payment, it is not subrogated to the rights of the insured. Ross v Pawtucket Mut. Ins. Co. (1963) 13 NY2d 233, 246 NYS2d 213, 195 NE2d 892 (disapproved Krause v American Guarantee & Liability Ins. Co. 22 NY2d 147, 292 NYS2d 67, 239 NE2d 175).

Insurer allowed to implead party who might be ultimately liable by third-party complaint notwithstanding language of policy which provided "in the event of any payment under this policy, the company shall be subrogated to the insured's rights of recovery therefor against any person or organization," where otherwise the subrogation claim might become time-barred. Consolidated Edison Co. v Royal Indem. Co. (1973) 41 AD2d 37, 340 NYS2d 991.

7. Claims which may be subject of impleader, generally

Since arbitrations are no longer considered special proceedings, the courts have been deprived of the statutory power, formerly authorized under the CPA, to consolidate arbitrations of controversies and arbitrations are also exempt from such procedural regulation as third party practice for the joinder of parties. Met Food Corp. v M. Eisenberg & Bros., Inc. (1969) 59 Misc 2d 498, 299 NYS2d 696.

In action on policy by insured against insurer for loss sustained by dishonesty of employee, insurer can serve third-party complaint against employee seeking judgment over in the event of recovery by the insured employer. Sol Lenzner Corp. v Aetna Casualty & Surety Co. (1964) 20 AD2d 305, 246 NYS2d 950.

Language of statute authorizing impleader is sufficiently broad to permit the bringing of a third-party action on a contingent claim. Adams v Lindsay (1974) 77 Misc 2d 824, 354 NYS2d 356.

Third-party complaint of guarantor against sub-sublessee did not state a cause of action and was dismissed, where there was no privity of contract or other relationship between guarantor of performance by sublessee and sub-sublessee, and latter could not be held liable to guarantor. Thomas Industries, Inc. v Sackren (1971) 37 AD2d 601, 323 NYS2d 202.

Where one of two joint venturers was sued for injuries resulting from accident at construction site, and such joint venturers had an agreement whereby they would "bear equally any losses and expenses that might accrue as a result of the doing of the work, labor and services" at the construction site, defendant in the principal action might maintain a third-party action against his joint venturer despite the fact that he had personally paid nothing to the plaintiff, and despite the fact that he was insured against part of the loss. McCabe v Queensboro Farm Products, Inc. (1968) 22 NY2d 204, 292 NYS2d 400, 239 NE2d 340.

Where Department of Social Services withheld rent from a recipient on the ground the certain violations of law affecting life and health existed in the premises justifying the withholding of rent by the Department, the Department could be impleaded by the recipient in a summary proceeding brought by the landlord seeking an order of eviction for nonpayment of rent. Blackman v Walker (1970) 65 Misc 2d 138, 316 NYS2d 930.

Provision of New York City Civil Court Act establishing a housing part and permitting any person or city department to be joined as a party to certain actions in order to effectuate proper housing maintenance standards and to promote the public interest expanded jurisdiction of civil court, at least with respect to housing matters, to include, in effect, a review of findings of an administrative body. Rothbaum v Ebel (1974) 77 Misc 2d 965, 354 NYS2d 545.

In summary proceeding to evict tenant for nonpayment of rent, where sufficient facts were shown to indicate that tenant had meritorious claim and colorable right to emergency assistance in the form of rent under Social Services Law and implementing rules and regulations of social services administration, commissioner of department of social services could be impleaded as party to the proceeding. Rothbaum v Ebel (1974) 77 Misc 2d 965, 354 NYS2d 545.

Only defendants may implead, counterclaim or cross-claim; there is no statutory authority which permits a plaintiff to bring a third-party action. Burgundy Basin Inn, Ltd. v Watkins Glen Grand Prix Corp. (1976) 51 AD2d 140, 379 NYS2d 873.

Breadth of jurisdiction granted to the Surrogate's Court, together with powers incidental thereto, compel use of third-party practice in Surrogate's Court when the same can resolve an issue which is intertwined with an issue before the Court. Estate of Zalaznick (1975) 84 Misc 2d 715, 375 NYS2d 522.

8. —Insurers and insureds

The language of CPLR 1007, permitting a defendant to implead any person who is or may be liable to him, is broad enough to encompass contingent claims based on subrogation. Krause v American Guarantee & Liability Ins. Co. (1968) 22 NY2d 147, 292 NYS2d 67, 239 NE2d 175.

In action on policy by insured against insurer for loss sustained by dishonesty of employee, insurer can serve third-party complaint against employee seeking judgment over in the event of recovery by the insured employer. Sol Lenzner Corp. v Aetna Casualty & Surety Co. (1964) 20 AD2d 305, 246 NYS2d 950.

Insured who sought coverage for counterclaim against him in negligence action was entitled to bring third party complaint against insurer pursuant to CPLR § 1007 despite express provision in policy prohibiting joinder of insurer as codefendant "in any action against insured to determine his liability," where said express provision did not indicate insurer's intent to prevent third party practice. Banks v Triboro Coach Corp. (1973) 73 Misc 2d 833, 342 NYS2d 612.

9. —Joint tort-feasors

Defendant whose negligence caused plaintiff's injury, and hospital whose negligent treatment thereof caused his death were not joint tortfeasors in pari delicto, but tortfeasors whose wrongs were successive, and defendant can implead hospital as third-party defendant, and the jury under proper instructions and by special verdict may decide the proportions of the recovery each is to bear. Musco v Conte (1964) 22 AD2d 121, 254 NYS2d 589.

In an action brought pursuant to the Federal Employers' Liability Act by a railroad lineman to recover for injuries sustained when the utility pole upon which he was working broke, in which the railroad impleaded the power company who allegedly erected and maintained the pole upon railroad property and in which the plaintiff had served an amended complaint against the power company charging it with failure to inspect or maintain the pole, it was held that the pleadings were susceptible of charging the railroad with possible passive negligence in failing to provide the plaintiff with a safe place to work and possible active negligence in failing to inspect or examine the pole when ordering him to work upon it, and that the third party complaint and the amended complaint both stated causes of action against the power company charging negligence in the maintenance of its service wires and pole so that the third-party defendant's motion to dismiss both complaints against it was denied. Finley v New York C. R. Co. (1965) 50 Misc 2d 194, 270 NYS2d 349, affd 25 AD2d 897, 269 NYS2d 386.

The failure of a landowner to discover and remedy a dangerous condition, affirmatively created by another, is passive negligence only. But such landowner will be barred from seeking indemnity from the creator of the condition if after actual notice thereof, he acquiesces in the continuance of the condition, because he then is in pari delicto with the original wrongdoer. Jackson v Associated Dry Goods Corp. (1963) 13 NY2d 112, 242 NYS2d 210, 192 NE2d 167.

Defendant whose negligence caused plaintiff's injury, and hospital whose negligent treatment thereof caused his death were not joint tortfeasors in pari delicto, but tortfeasors whose wrongs were successive, and defendant can implead hospital as third-party defendant, and the jury under proper instructions and by special verdict may decide the proportions of the recovery each is to bear. Musco v Conte (1964) 22 AD2d 121, 254 NYS2d 589.

10. —Joint tort-feasors: Contribution or indemnity

Rule providing for apportionment of liability among joint tortfeasors does not interfere with right of a defendant to implead or joint third parties, but rather it only removes necessity for recourse to active-passive theory of negligence thereby permitting anyone to be joined who in any way participated in causing an accident. Berliner v Kacov (1974) 79 Misc 2d 891, 361 NYS2d 477.

In Dole v Dow Chemical Co. (1972) 30 NY2d 143, 331 NYS2d 382, 282 NE2d 288, 53 ALR3d 175, it was held in an action by decedent's executrix to recover for a death caused by use of a chemical to fumigate a grain storage bin against the manufacturer of the chemical, based on its failure to label the chemical properly, that the chemical manufacturer could assert a third-party claim against the decedent's employer based on its negligent failure to follow the instructions provided with the chemical. The court disregarded the distinction between active and passive negligence and in effect permitted an apportionment of the damages in the same action, rather than requiring a separate action between named codefendants under CPLR 1401.

Defendant city, which was found 15% negligent, half of which was attributable to impleaded third parties, could not require third party defendant to contribute half of liability which city's other joint feasor could not pay since plaintiff made no complaint against third-party defendants and thereby third-party defendants did not become responsive to judgment of plaintiff. Berliner v Kacov (1974) 79 Misc 2d 891, 361 NYS2d 477.

Where a wrong committed by a third-party defendant is separate and distinct and unrelated to wrong committed by third-party plaintiff, parties are successive but not joint tort-feasors and there is no cause of action for contribution or indemnity. Addiego v Interboro General Hospital (1975) 81 Misc 2d 96, 365 NYS2d 718.

Where it was alleged that mother was negligent in allowing child to drink caustic substance and that physician was guilty of malpractice resulting in aggravation of the injuries, there was no liability running from the mother to the physician for contribution or indemnity. Addiego v Interboro General Hospital (1975) 81 Misc 2d 96, 365 NYS2d 718.

Where the person not a party is sought to be sued as one liable to the named defendant for indemnification, proper impleader requires a third-party suit under CPLR 1007. Lynch v Flame Fuel Oil Corp. (1967) 53 Misc 2d 535, 278 NYS2d 940.

The procedure of impleader does not vitiate the requirement of a showing of actual loss before there may be recovery, but it does permit an indemnitee to obtain a conditional judgment fixing the potential liability without the need for payment until it is shown that the judgment in the principal action has been satisfied in whole or part.

McCabe v Queensboro Farm Products, Inc. (1968) 22 NY2d 204, 292 NYS2d 400, 239 NE2d 340.

While technically a claim for indemnity does not arise until the prime obligation to pay has been established, the CPLR, for the sake of fairness and judicial economy, allows third-party actions to be commenced in certain circumstances before they are technically ripe, so that all parties may establish their rights and liabilities in one action. Burgundy Basin Inn, Ltd. v Watkins Glen Grand Prix Corp. (1976) 51 AD2d 140, 379 NYS2d 873.

CASE NOTES

UNDER FORMER CIVIL PRACTICE LAWS

A. IN GENERAL

1. Generally
2. Courts
3. Construction
4. Recovery against defendant

B. CLAIMS ON WHICH THIRD PARTIES MAY BE BROUGHT IN

5. Generally
6. Liability over
7. Liability for all or part of claim
8. Active negligence
9. —Joint tortfeasors
10. —Proximate cause
11. Active and passive negligence
12. Active or passive negligence in the alternative
13. Passive negligence of third party
14. Claims against defendant and third party on divergent grounds
15. Indemnity

C. PROCEDURE

16. Generally
17. Service of summons and complaint
18. —Order unnecessary
19. Time for action or motion
20. Dismissal of complaint in chief
21. Pleading in third-party actions
22. —Amendments
23. Dismissal of third-party complaint
24. —Effect of dismissal
25. Motion to dismiss
26. —Time for motion
27. Notice to all parties appearing
28. Discretion of court
29. —When prejudicial
30. Separate trial
31. Examination before trial of, or by, third party
32. —Physical examination
33. Verdict
34. Special findings

35. Costs

D. PARTICULAR THIRD PARTIES AND ACTIONS

36. Agent and principal
37. Brokers
38. Building owner and window-cleaning company
39. Buyer and seller
40. Carrier and third person
41. City and abutting owner
42. City and others
43. Cloth manufacturer and clothing maker
44. Contractor and materialman
45. Contractor and subcontractor
46. Dealer and manufacturer
47. Defrauder and plaintiff's agent
48. Employer and employee
49. Employers of common employee
50. Garage owner and labor union
51. Grantor and grantee
52. Insured and insurer
53. —Insurer disclaiming liability
54. —Where policy bars joinder
55. Landlord and court clerk
56. Landlord and mover
57. Landlord and tenant
58. Landlord and refrigerator company
59. Manufacturer and employer
60. Motorist and owner
61. Motorist and physician
62. Motorist and repairman
63. Municipality and contractor
64. Owner and architect
65. Owner and bailee
66. Owner and contractor
67. Owner and subcontractor
68. Owner and elevator or escalator company
69. Owner and elevator operator
70. Owners; successive
71. Payee and drawer

72. Purchaser and broker

73. Renter and registered truck owner

74. Retailer and manufacturer

75. Retailer and packer

76. Seller and supplier

77. Ship operator and stevedore

78. Surety and subcontractor

79. Vendor and purchaser

80. Warehouseman and landlord

81. Wife in husband's action for partnership accounting

E. SUMMONS IN THIRD-PARTY PRACTICE

82. Generally

83. Courts

84. Retrospective operation

85. Service

A. IN GENERAL

1. Generally

The amendment to CPA § 193 (§§ 1001(a)(b), 1003 herein) effected by CPA § 193-a was intended to liberalize our third-party practice, and the question of what person is liable as an indemnitor is the same as in former § 193, and the guiding decisions of the past are still applicable. Franklin E. Tyrell, Inc. v Vahlsing (1947) 193 Misc 454, 69 NYS2d 602.

Rationale of cross-claims under CPA § 264 (§§ 3012(a), 3019(b), 3020(a) herein) was identical with impleader under CPA § 193-a, with exception of different pleading and procedural requirement. Seltzer v Rosenberg (1950) 199 Misc 4, 101 NYS2d 738, affd 277 AD 1138, 101 NYS2d 940.

Purpose of amendment of former CPA § 193 (§§ 1001(a)(b), 1003 herein) by CPA § 193-a was to liberalize third-party practice and to remove rigid requirements theretofore existing in connection with practice of impleading. J. A. Ewing & McDonald, Inc. v Municipal Warehouse Co. (1948) 193 Misc 173, 81 NYS2d 559.

Where a defendant as third-party plaintiff adopts the procedure authorized by former CPA § 193 (§§ 1001(a)(b), 1003 herein) repealed by the laws of 1946, and fails to conform to the requirements of CPA § 193-a, a third-party order obtained in this manner was without statutory authority and therefore a nullity. Pollaro v Bruto (1954) 283 AD 209, 126 NYS2d 882.

Provisions of third-party practice contained in CPA § 193-a were applicable to actions, not summary proceedings. Edaviel Corp. v Boykin (1954) 205 Misc 622, 129 NYS2d 149 (summary proceeding, landlord against tenant, nonpayment of rent).

Constitutionality of CPA § 193-a upheld generally. Clements v Rockefeller (1947) 189 Misc 889, 76 NYS2d 493.

The purpose of CPA § 193-a has been stated to be to eliminate multiplicity of suits and to permit disposition of all claims arising between all persons emanating from one transaction which are related one to the other but only upon the condition that justice and convenience shall not be sacrificed by doing so. Ammann & Whitney v Edgarton (1957) 12 Misc 2d 119, 175 NYS2d 536.

To justify the use of third-party practice the relationship to the controversy must be direct and involve questions common to both controversies so that there will be a clarification and avoidance of multiple actions and not confusion and complication. Ammann & Whitney v Edgarton, supra.

Where the relation of the third party claim to the original controversy is direct and involves questions common to both controversies and the impleader will not cause unreasonable delay, prejudice, or confusion of the issues or undue complications at the trial and it is properly within the ambit of CPA § 193-a. Schneiberg v Utz (1957) 8 Misc 2d 535, 167 NYS2d 832.

CPA § 264 (§§ 3012(a), 3019(b), 3020(a) herein) compared with CPA § 193-a in holding that purpose of both sections was to avoid multiplicity of litigation and to determine ultimate rights of all parties in one trial. Galka v Albany (1954) 285 AD 27, 135 NYS2d 249.

It is important to distinguish between situation embraced in CPA § 193 (§§ 1001(a)(b), 1003 herein) requiring plaintiff to bring in additional parties and those in which defendant merely shows facts which involve in some way other participants in transaction, which may be basis of defense to plaintiff's action or for defendant's impleading them pursuant to CPA § 193-a. China S. R. Co. v Andersen, M. & Co. (1956) 6 Misc 2d 184, 152 NYS2d 507.

A characterization and description of a counter-claim as a third-party action was improper where the application pertained not to third-party practice as provided in CPA § 193-a but rather to rights and remedies falling within the purview of CPA § 271 (§§ 3012(a), 3019(f) herein). Thus, where the defendant had attempted to set up a counterclaim which raised questions between himself and the plaintiff with other persons, third-party practice was not involved. Beaunit Mills, Inc. v Tanbro Fabrics Corp. (1957) 6 Misc 2d 878, 160 NYS2d 644; Bennett Excavators Corp. v Lasker Goldman Corp. (1958) 15 Misc 2d 802, 181 NYS2d 864.

Cross-claim under CPA § 264 (§§ 3012(a), 3019(b), 3020(a) herein) and impleader under CPA § 193-a were limited to liability over for all or part of the recovery of the suitor's claim against the impleader or claimant over, and the latter could not assert an affirmative claim for his own damages. Bennett Excavators Corp. v Lasker Goldman Corp. (1959) 19 Misc 2d 926, 186 NYS2d 680.

2. Courts

CPA § 193-a was inapplicable to Albany City Court Act. Hirsch v Albany Sav. Bank (1948) 192 Misc 505, 81 NYS2d 253, affd 276 AD 792, 92 NYS2d 636.

NYC Municipal Court; CPA § 193-a applied. Thomas J. Nolan, Inc. v Martin & William Smith, Inc. (1949) 193 Misc 877, 85 NYS2d 380.

Rochester City Court; CPA § 193-a inapplicable. H. G. Fischer & Co. v Lincoln Rochester Trust Co. (1949) 195 Misc 983, 88 NYS2d 565.

Third-party practice, authorized by CPA § 193-a was applicable to arbitration proceeding. Prima Products, Inc. v Aquella Products, Inc. (1952) 280 AD 109, 111 NYS2d 558, revd on other grounds 304 NY 619, 107 NE2d 95.

CPA § 193-a was inapplicable to summary proceeding in Municipal Court of New York City, for nonpayment of rent. Edaviel Corp. v Boykin (1954) 205 Misc 622, 129 NYS2d 149.

Impleader of third party, who has no claim against State, for purpose of allowing State to assert claim against such third party, is not authorized by any statute. Horoch v State (1955) 286 AD 303, 143 NYS2d 327, resettled 286 AD 977, 144 NYS2d 721.

3. Construction

Controversy, as used in CPA § 193-a implied situation in which something was asserted on one side and denied on other. Puritan Fabrics v Charm Togs (1947) 70 NYS2d 453.

Third-party plaintiff simply means defendant. Remch v Grabow (1947) 193 Misc 731, 70 NYS2d 462.

CPA § 193-a was a remedial statute and should be liberally construed. Robinson v Binghamton Constr. Co. (1950) 277 AD 468, 100 NYS2d 900; Madison Ave. Properties Corp. v Royal Ins. Co. (1953) 281 AD 641, 120 NYS2d 626; Menikoff v Chaachou (1954) 129 NYS2d 277.

CPA § 193-a was enacted to avoid multiplicity of suits and to enable several controversies to be tried at one time, thereby saving time and expense of parties and court. Madison Ave. Properties Corp. v Royal Ins. Co. (1953) 281 AD 641, 120 NYS2d 626; Van Orden v Bartnett (1950) 101 NYS2d 1008.

CPA § 193-a was procedural in scope, and did not involve fundamental policy; and it could be waived by agreement of parties. Aulisio v California Oil Co. (1952) 202 Misc 1050, 120 NYS2d 582.

CPA § 271 (§§ 3012(a), 3019(f) herein) distinguished as not pertaining to third-party practice. Fass v Ellen (1949) 94 NYS2d 746.

Third-party practice, intended to avoid multiplicity and circuity of actions as well as promote consistency in determinations of related claims involving common question of law or fact, is liberal procedural facility whose legitimate purposes should be furthered, rather than restricted by courts. Champlain Creameries v Hovey S. & Co. (1955) 141 NYS2d 271.

CPA § 193-a was not to be confused with CPA § 193 (§§ 1007, 1008, 1011, 1020, 3012(a), Rule 4111(c) herein) which specified those parties that are indispensable or who should be joined in an action in order that complete relief be afforded between those already parties thereto; where plaintiff has in a tort action proceeded against one of those who claims to be liable, while defendant could not have relief under section 193 he might

have relief under section 193-a. Hall v Wood (1958) 11 Misc 2d 805, 174 NYS2d 16.

In action for personal injury sustained in New Jersey but brought in New York, right to implead third party was governed by CPA § 193-a as procedural law of forum controls. Cardillo v Marble Bldg. (1955) 142 NYS2d 721.

CPA § 193-a simplified third party practice and permitted defendants to seek recovery over against other parties in litigation, but such procedural changes have not varied underlying principles of tort liability. Scholom v Sumers (1955) 139 NYS2d 679.

CPA § 264 (§§ 3012(a), 3019(b), 3020(a) herein) and § 193-a were both intended to accomplish same purpose, under different circumstances with somewhat different pleading and procedural requirements. Lanswer v Baumrin (1956) 2 Misc 2d 610, 151 NYS2d 466.

CPA §§ 267, subd 1 (§ 3019(c) herein) and 474 (Rule 5012, § 5011 herein) were not to be read in contravention of CPA § 193-a subd 2. Fitzgerald v Amer. S. Co. (1956) 3 Misc 2d 609, 150 NYS2d 128.

Where third-party procedure permissible under CPA § 193-a was not as effective remedy as device of declaratory judgment under CPA § 473 (§ 3001 herein) to establish respective rights of insured and insurer under liability insurance policy and to determine conflicting issues at time when their resolution will do most good, insureds, since they paid for some kind of indemnity coverage, should be entitled to invoke equitable and protective remedy of declaratory judgment in order to ascertain promptly whether they got what they thought they had purchased. Kahn v George E. Driscoll Co. (1955) 1 Misc 2d 405, 146 NYS2d 902.

Defendant in pending action against him cannot, by interposing third-party claim against another in that action, circumvent force of arbitration agreement between them, under CPA § 1451 (§ 7503(a) herein). Knolls Co-op. v Hennessy (1956) 3 Misc 2d 220, 150 NYS2d 713.

CPA § 193-a was to be liberally construed since it was intended to mitigate the strictness of the old practice which required third party plaintiff to show clear liability on the part of the third party defendant. December v Victory Carriers, Inc. (1957) 6 Misc 2d 167, 159 NYS2d 1006.

Object of CPA § 193-a was to avoid circuity of actions. Valstrey Service Corp. v Board of Elections (1957) 2 NY2d 413, 161 NYS2d 52, 141 NE2d 565.

CPA § 193-a did not enlarge plaintiff's rights in any way, nor did it extend the statute of limitations as against impleaded defendants. Henry Spen & Co. v Ocean Box Corp. (1959) 16 Misc 2d 436, 184 NYS2d 152.

Where railroad, sued by plaintiff for injuries sustained when truck in which he was riding while being driven by coemployee was struck in New Jersey by train, served third party complaint against plaintiff's employer seeking contribution, employer was granted summary judgment dismissing third party complaint because under New Jersey law when the relation between plaintiff and third party defendant at time of injury is employer-employee, there is an absence of the essential common liability between railroad and employer upon which to predicate the right of contribution. Tuffarella v Erie R. Co. (1962) 17 AD2d 484, 236 NYS2d 503.

4. Recovery against defendant

Recovery against defendant is prerequisite for recovery against impleaded defendant. Kalkin v Marken (1949) 87 NYS2d 839.

A third-party complaint cannot be sustained where it constitutes a complete disavowal of negligence on the part of the defendant and third-party plaintiff, thus eliminating any premise upon which the original plaintiff could obtain a judgment against the third-party plaintiff, as a valid basis for such judgment is an essential condition to claim over under CPA § 193-a. Kile v Riefler Bros. Contractors (1953) 282 AD 1000, 125 NYS2d 680.

Third-party plaintiff may not assert affirmative claim for his own damages against third-party defendant, beyond amount for which it is or may be liable to plaintiff. Carroll Sheet Metal Works v Mechanical Installations (1951) 201 Misc 689, 110 NYS2d 581.

A third-party complaint is sufficient where the factual situation alleged is such that the answering defendant may be held liable to plaintiff on a theory which would permit a recovery over against third-party defendant, even though the answering defendant in his answer denies any liability to plaintiff. Gallagher v Hill Greenhouse Constr. Inc. (1960) 23 Misc 2d 167, 197 NYS2d 234.

Third-party complaint must allege facts indicating that defendant might be held liable to plaintiff for defendant's passive negligence or wrongdoing, and that third party is active wrongdoer in inflicting plaintiff's damage. Goodrich v First Nat. Bank (1954) 132 NYS2d 678.

B. Claims on Which Third Parties May Be Brought In

5. Generally

Despite CPA § 193-a, impleader was limited to prosecution of "claim over". Cloud v Martin (1947) 273 AD 769, 75 NYS2d 1.

Mere desire of party to inject another into action does not warrant interpleader; relation to controversy must be direct and involve questions common to both controversies. Napack v Grubman (1947) 190 Misc 718, 75 NYS2d 67.

A proper situation for a claim over under CPA § 193-a was presented where the cross-claim was sufficiently related to the main action by a common question of law and fact. Colonial Piece Dye Works, Inc. v General Dyestuff Corp. (1953) 282 AD 858, 125 NYS2d 305; Hirsch v Schiffman (1950) 199 Misc 883, 101 NYS2d 913.

Third-party claim "must be related to main action by question of law or fact common to both controversies", but need not rest upon same cause of action or same ground as claim asserted against third party. Madison Ave. Properties Corp. v Royal Ins. Co. (1953) 281 AD 641, 120 NYS2d 626.

Where substantial questions of fact common between defendant and unjoined third person exist, third person may be joined where main action will not be unduly delayed. Fortune v Syracuse (1948) 191 Misc 738, 78 NYS2d 775.

In action against realty owner and lessee for personal injuries to employee of subtenant of premises, defendants could not confess liability and consent to judgment against themselves and thereby create legal basis for liability of third-party defendant to plaintiff. Williams v Rhode Island Corp. (1953) 281 AD 618, 121 NYS2d 187.

In action by hotel chef against hotel lessor for injuries received in hotel fire, lessor served third-party complaint on hotel lessee which alleged that it had procured public liability insurance as required by lease, on motion such defense was struck out as insufficient. Merkle v 110 Glen R. Corp. (1953) 282 AD 617, 125 NYS2d 881.

Where bank is sued by depositor for paying out of a bank account on a forgery, the bank may have the forger made a party as a third-party defendant. Booke v Dime Sav. Bank (1953) 204 Misc 840, 127 NYS2d 59.

Where plaintiffs sue for reasonable value of legal services and defendant in his third-party complaint claims a reimbursement for any judgment which may be rendered against him under a contract with one of the plaintiffs and another party to perform the services, there is a sufficient relationship between the cause of action pleaded against the defendant and the cause alleged in the third-party complaint to sustain the latter pleading. Menikoff v Chaachou (1954) 129 NYS2d 277.

A third-party complaint in action by a property owner for damages sustained by reason of a defective fuel oil tank sold him by defendant dealer, by which the dealer sought to implead as a third-party defendant the fuel company which filled the tank, will be dismissed where the third-party complaint as against the fuel company is not sufficient to allege negligence on the part of the fuel company or any obligation of the fuel company to indemnify the defendant dealer for any part of the plaintiff's claim against it. Morrell v Montgomery Ward & Co. (1954) 133 NYS2d 656.

In action against father and son for injuries caused by son's airgun, codefendant father may not implead person who lent airgun to son, since father had no right of indemnity against such third person. Sullivan v O'Ryan (1954) 206 Misc 212, 132 NYS2d 211.

Impleader is means by which primary liability of original defendant and alleged "liability over" of third party may be settled in one action. Horoch v State (1955) 286 AD 303, 143 NYS2d 327 mod 286 AD 977, 144 NYS2d 721.

To determine if a third party complaint under attack because it was unauthorized by CPA § 193-

a should be sustained, these three questions should be answered: the first two in the affirmative, the last negatively. 1. May the third party be held liable to defendant for all or part of the money for a thing which plaintiff seeks to recover from defendant. 2. Is the third party claim related to the main action by a question of law or fact common to both. 3. Will the joinder work an injustice, unduly delay the main action or unduly inconvenience plaintiff. Schneiberg v Utz (1957) 8 Misc 2d 535, 167 NYS2d 832.

Where the answer of the third party, and its third-party complaint, contained allegations which indicated it had no liability to the original plaintiff, and if liable at all would be liable for active negligence, the third-party complaint would be insufficient to form a basis for implied indemnification from the third-party defendant. Bernardo v Fordham Hoisting Equipment Co. (1958) 6 AD2d 619, 180 NYS2d 525, affd 6 NY2d 733, 185 NYS2d 817, 158 NE2d 509.

Third-party plaintiff may properly interpose a claim-over against third-party defendant based on negligence as well as breach of warranty even though the gravamen of plaintiff's complaint is breach of warranty where a sufficient relationship exists between the facts alleged in the plaintiff's complaint and those alleged in the third-party complaint. Schoenfeld v Cake Nook Inc. (1959) 17 Misc 2d 69, 185 NYS2d 729.

Third-party complaint was properly interposed where there were common questions of fact giving rise to an obligation on part of third-party defendant to exonerate or to reimburse third-party plaintiffs. Joseph v R. & M. Embroidery Co. (1959) 21 Misc 2d 150, 195 NYS2d 738.

6. Liability over

The party impleading another must show that there exists a likelihood that the impleaded one will be held responsible to the defendant in whole or in part for any recovery by plaintiff against the defendant. Schneiberg v Utz (1957) 8 Misc 2d 535, 167 NYS2d 832.

Where third party defendant establishes that any liability to the original defendant third party plaintiff would result from its contract and the contract contains no indemnity provisions, there is no sufficient proof either of a breach or damages, judgment reversed and cross complaints dismissed. Paranzino v Yonkers Raceway, Inc. (1957) 9 Misc 2d 378, 170 NYS2d 280.

A third-party complaint grounded on an express indemnity agreement, was held not sufficient to show indemnity against the third-party's own negligence. Bernardo v Fordham Hoisting Equipment Co. (1958) 6 AD2d 619, 180 NYS2d 525, affd 6 NY2d 733, 185 NYS2d 817, 158 NE2d 509.

Where action brought by note holder of corporation against director based on fraudulent act of director, third-party complaint by director against corporation for indemnification dismissed as insufficient in law where bylaws did not provide corporation would indemnify director and expressly

provided to contrary. McNeill v Succop (1957) 10 Misc 2d 608, 169 NYS2d 506.

Where third party complaint does not allege sufficient facts to show that any recovery may be had against the defendant respondent and no facts were alleged to show that the defendant respondent was in exclusive control of the area when the accident occurred or even if it were that the third party plaintiff and third party defendant were other than joint tortfeasors if actively negligent without any agreement on defendant respondent's part to indemnify the third party plaintiff for the defendant respondent's active negligence, such third party complaint dismissed. Ruffin v 89 Realty Corp. (1958) 5 AD2d 788, 170 NYS2d 772.

Where allegations of the complaint are sufficiently broad to admit a passive negligence warranting recovery over, motion by third party defendant for dismissal of third party complaint denied. Pasquale v Babcock, Hinds & Underwood, Inc. (1958) 6 AD2d 336, 176 NYS2d 884.

A third-party complaint read with the main complaint is sufficient on its face to state a cause for liability over where the main complaint contained allegations under which the third-party plaintiff might be held liable though only passively negligent and might have recourse against the "active wrongdoer". Flory v Elmira Hotel Operating Corp. (1958) 5 AD2d 315, 172 NYS2d 68.

In negligence action, defendant can bring third party action against broker for having failed to effect adequate insurance coverage, but in the interests of justice, cases should be separately tried. Thornton v New York (1959) 20 Misc 2d 838, 193 NYS2d 777.

7. Liability for all or part of claim

Under CPA § 193-a the joinder of a nonparty was permitted whether he was or might be liable to the defendant for all or part of plaintiff's claim against him. Dick v Sunbright Steam Laundry Corp. (1954) 307 NY 422, 121 NE2d 399; Monteverdi v French Realty Corp. (1947) 190 Misc 304, 75 NYS2d 69; Green v Hudson Shoring Co. (1947) 191 Misc 297, 77 NYS2d 842.

See Truman Homes v Lane Holding Corp. (1949) 88 NYS2d 406.

In an action for injuries from eating poisonous pork, defendant retailer need not prove payment of judgment against him before proceeding on third-party complaint against partner. Occhipinti v Buscemi (1947) 71 NYS2d 766.

In action against plaintiff's landlord and manufacturer of locomotives for injuries due to vibration from operation of Diesel locomotives, manufactured by defendant, on tracks operated by railroad, manufacturer may not implead as third-party defendant railroad whose indemnity agreement did not make indemnitor liable to indemnitee for latter's own negligence. Cerkowski v General Motors Corp. (1951) 201 Misc 789, 108 NYS2d 540.

In action for death of intestate who drowned in hole dug by city on premises of intestate's employer, defendant city may implead landowner as third-party defendant for allowing dangerous hazard to continue. George v Little Falls (1951) 112 NYS2d 605.

Where plaintiff sued to recover loan to defendant, and defendant's claim was predicated upon joint agreement by plaintiff and third-party defendant to pay for legal services rendered, impleader was improper. Hirsch v Schiffman (1950) 199 Misc 883, 101 NYS2d 913.

Under former CPA § 1932 which greatly simplified and expanded third party practice, joinder of nonparty was permitted whenever that party was or may have been liable to defendant for all or part of plaintiff's claim against defendant. Coviello v N. Y. Life Inc. Co. (1955) 141 NYS2d 626, affd 286 AD 1075, 146 NYS2d 667.

8. Active negligence

The enactment of CPA § 193-a simplified third-party practice but did not change underlying principles of tort liability. Dick v Sunbright Steam Laundry Corp. (1954) 307 NY 422, 121 NE2d 399.

In action against laundry tenant of building owned by City of New York, where original complaint alleged that tenant negligently operated its laundry machinery, causing waste water to seep into plaintiff's basement, such original defendant was alleged to be active tortfeasor who was not in position to compel indemnification by City because latter negligently failed to repair its sewer pipes, and third party complaint was insufficient on any theory. Dick v Sunbright Steam Laundry Corp., supra.

Where original complaint charges only active negligence of defendant, he may not implead third party charged with active negligence. Johnson v Endicott-Johnson Corp. (1951) 278 AD 626, 101 NYS2d 922.

Where complaint does not exclude common-law negligence and is not confined solely to alleging violations of the Labor Law, cross claims of designated defendant tortfeasor against third party not designated should await trial. Mut. Liability Ins. Co. v Fairchild Press (1952) 279 AD 895, 111 NYS2d 604.

See Stabile v Vitullo (1952) 280 AD 191, 112 NYS2d 693.

In action by automobile passenger injured when automobile struck parked truck, defendant automobilist could not implead person who negligently loaded projecting lumber onto automobile. Cloud v Martin (1947) 273 AD 769, 75 NYS2d 1.

A third party complaint alleging that an accident was due to primary and active negligence of third party defendant while the premises were under the alleged control of the third party defendant, as a matter of pleading, set forth sufficient facts to constitute a cause of action. December v Victory Carriers, Inc. (1957) 6 Misc 2d 167, 159 NYS2d 1006.

It is the practice in the Third Department to allow an action over to be pleaded against one charged with active negligence. Korycka v S. A. Healy Co. (1957) 5 Misc 2d 598, 160 NYS2d 24.

A third party complaint is fatally defective where it fails to allege any facts to support the conclusion that the original plaintiff's damages were caused by the primary and active negligence of the third-party defendant and a conclusory allegation of negligence against the third-party defendant is legally insufficient. Great Eastern Fuel Co. v Massey Concrete Products Co. (1957) 160 NYS2d 642, affd 4 AD2d 948, 168 NYS2d 467.

Defendant charged with active negligence cannot implead a third-party. Putvin v Buffalo Electric Co. (1959) 5 NY2d 447, 186 NYS2d 15, 158 NE2d 691.

Where the original complaint charged defendant and third-party defendant with active negligence, third-party complaint was dismissed for insufficiency in the absence of any showing that defendant had a contractual or statutory right of indemnification from third-party defendant. Morgan v Donahue (1958) 19 Misc 2d 532, 195 NYS2d 917, affd 8 AD2d 768, 187 NYS2d 339.

Owner and driver of truck sued for personal injuries alleged to have resulted solely from their negligent operation thereof are not entitled to indemnity from, and therefore cannot implead, general contractor, who was being supplied with concrete by said truck, and who it is alleged was actively responsible for the accident because its employee negligently had guided truck at time of accident. Stec v Juliano (1959) 21 Misc 2d 333, 194 NYS2d 194.

In action against town by infant who while riding in car owned by his father and driven by his mother was injured when car went off road due to town's negligence in maintaining highway, since town can be held liable in damages only on evidence that it was guilty solely of active negligence, town's cross-claim against father alleging accident due to negligent operation of car, and towns third party complaint against mother for reckless driving, were properly dismissed. Berg v Huntington (1959) 7 NY2d 871, 196 NYS2d 1001.

Where complaint in action against dock owner for injuries sustained in fall on slippery dock while assisting in docking cruiser alleged that defendant failed to provide dock attendant, failed to answer standard signal, allowed seaweed to accumulate on dock, and failed to remove seaweed, thus charging active negligence, and defendant's third party complaint against owner of boat alleged that it churned up the seaweed, which if true, would free defendant from liability, no basis for indemnity was presented, and third party complaint was dismissed. Yager v Dock & Coal Co. (1960) 11 AD2d 592, 200 NYS2d 519.

Where allegations of complaint charged active negligence the use of such blanket phrases as "among other things" and "being otherwise careless and negligent" does not justify an inference of passive negligence. Yager v Dock & Coal Co., supra.

Where plaintiff in action against city and contractor for personal injuries alleged that he fell due to debris thrown on sidewalk by contractor, third party complaint by contractor against landlord and tenant of abutting property was dismissed for insufficiency, since plaintiff's complaint charged contractor with active negligence for which there is no indemnity. Harries v New York (1960) 24 Misc 2d 1035, 205 NYS2d 282.

Driver charged with active negligence in principal complaint cannot assert claim over against third-party defendant for alleged defective repairs to brakes or breaches of warranty of fitness of vehicle for use. Cohen v Wasserman (1960) 28 Misc 2d 58, 208 NYS2d 865.

In action against manufacturer for injuries received in operating allegedly defective machine, manufacturer could not implead plaintiff's employer because its liability depended only upon proof that it had manufactured a defective machine, and this, if proven, would constitute it an active wrongdoer thus precluding it from recovering over against employer. Wegorzewski v De Mattia Machine & Tool Co. (1961) 12 AD2d 825, 210 NYS2d 426.

In action for damages to property arising out of fire on pier, where defendant-owner is charged with negligent maintenance of the pier, defendant-customer is charged with insecurely packing highly inflammable material, which defendant-owner placed on pier, and which was ignited by defendant-repairmen who carelessly used acetylene torches in the vicinity of such material, with the knowledge of defendant-owner, defendant-owner was deemed right of recovery over against customer since such owner was clearly charged with active negligence, and the alleged negligent acts of the other defendants evidenced his negligent operation and maintenance of pier. Bush Terminal Bldgs. Co. v Luckenbach S.S. Co. (1961) 9 NY2d 426, 214 NYS2d 428, 174 NE2d 516.

Where original complaint clearly charges defendant with having created the latent defect and dangerous condition, so that it is unnecessary to try the issue as to whether it is possible under its allegations to impose a liability on the third-party plaintiff for passive negligence alone, the third-party complaint must be dismissed. Gingeresky v Gifford-Wood Co. (1961) 14 AD2d 623, 218 NYS2d 339.

9. —Joint tortfeasors

Where complaint charged defendant with active negligence but did not charge him with any liability by operation of law for the wrongful act of another, the latter is a joint tortfeasor in pari delicto and may not be impleaded. Kile v Riefler Bros. Contractors (1953) 282 AD 1000, 125 NYS2d 680.

Joint tortfeasor cannot be impleaded in action for personal injury where there is no liability over, either through indemnity or contribution or otherwise, existing at time of application. Kloppenberg v Brooklyn Union Gas Co. (1948) 82 NYS2d 687.

Joint tortfeasors could not have been impleaded because of CPA § 211-a (§ 1401 herein) making contribution dependent upon recovery of a judgment against both of them. Triglianos v Henry

Moss & Co. (1947) 189 Misc 157, 71 NYS2d 618. See Verder v Schack (1948) 191 Misc 935, 79 NYS2d 700; Denau v Beatty (1949) 195 Misc 649, 91 NYS2d 190.

State cannot implead joint tortfeasor who has not been sued in Court of Claims. Dunn v State (1950) 197 Misc 627, 95 NYS2d 640.

Where two automobiles collided on state highway and owner of one and occupants of second were injured, and all filed claims in Court of Claims alleging dangerous condition of roadway, state could not add said owner as third-party defendant in claims of occupants, on theory that owner was actively negligent and state was only passively negligent. Dunn v State, supra.

Where claim of defendant in automobile negligence accident case is that third-party defendant is solely liable the third-party complaint must be dismissed for if defendant is correct plaintiff may not recover against him and if he is negligent in part the third party is at most a joint tortfeasor who cannot be brought in. Sarna v Davis (1952) 280 AD 632, 116 NYS2d 552.

Where city is sued for negligent death and injuries, it may not implead railroad trustees as being cross complaint by one joint tortfeasor against another in pari delicto. Middleton v New York (1949) 276 AD 780, 92 NYS2d 656, affd 300 NY 732, 92 NE2d 312; Poritsky v New York (1949) 276 AD 780, 92 NYS2d 657.

Where third-party complaint alleges only that third-party defendant is joint tortfeasor with third-party plaintiff, it is properly dismissed. Sannit v Buffalo Wire Works (1951) 278 AD 632, 102 NYS2d 381, affd 302 NY 820, 100 NE2d 33.

Where complaint alleges that plaintiff was injured by collision of defendant's train with lumber placed along tracks by another defendant which lumber then struck plaintiff, plaintiff was thereby charged with active negligence by first defendant who could not implead second defendant as third-party defendant, since defendants were joint tortfeasors. Kennedy v Bethlehem Steel Co. (1953) 282 AD 1001, 125 NYS2d 552.

In action for damages for collapse of wall struck by bulldozer in control of defendant, charged with active negligence, he may not implead third-party defendant allegedly liable as joint tortfeasor to indemnify original defendant. Valdale Apts. v Ercito Mazzella Constr. (1952) 115 NYS2d 59.

Admiralty as affording contribution by one joint tortfeasor against another, see Hughes v De Simone Stevedores, Inc. (1950) 277 AD 371, 100 NYS2d 241.

Subrogation of one joint tortfeasor who paid total amount of judgment against both tortfeasors, to rights of plaintiff entitled former to recover half of sum so paid from latter, regardless of active or passive negligence between them. Tron v Thime (1951) 201 Misc 85, 105 NYS2d 546.

Where it cannot be determined from the pleadings whether third-party litigants are joint tortfeasors in pari delicto, the third-party complaint should not be dismissed on the ground that the parties are joint tortfeasors. Giudice v New York (1954) 128 NYS2d 890.

In action by store customer against store for personal injuries as result of slipping on cottage cheese sample which fell on store floor when manufacturer was distributing samples, third-party complaint by store against manufacturer alleging that plaintiff's injuries were caused by active negligence of latter in passing out cheese samples in improper manner, without alleging any indemnification agreement, was dismissed, because both parties were joint tortfeasors. Burke v Wegman's Food Markets (1955) 1 Misc 2d 130, 146 NYS2d 556.

In a negligence action where both defendants are charged with being joint tortfeasors in pari delicto and the third party complaint does not indicate any facts from which the third party plaintiff could be found only passively negligent, third party complaint dismissed. Griffin v New York Cent. R. Co. (1958) 13 Misc 2d 308, 177 NYS2d 625.

In New York action by injured automobile passenger against railroad arising out of railroad crossing accident in New Jersey where right to contribution among joint tortfeasors is treated as a substantive right enforceable by impleader, railroad was held permitted to implead automobile owner, a joint tortfeasor. Tuffarella v Erie R. Co. (1960) 10 AD2d 525, 203 NYS2d 468.

In action for damages to property arising out of fire on pier, where defendant-owner is charged with negligent maintenance of the pier, defendant-customer is charged with insecurely packing highly inflammable material, which defendant-owner placed on pier, and which was ignited by defendant-repairmen who carelessly used acetylene torches in the vicinity of such material, with the knowledge of defendant-owner, defendant-owner was deemed right of recovery over against customer since such owner was clearly charged with active negligence, and the alleged negligent acts of the other defendants evidenced his negligent operation and maintenance of pier. Bush Terminal Bldgs. Co. v Luckenbach S.S. Co. (1961) 9 NY2d 426, 214 NYS2d 428, 174 NE2d 516.

Absent an indemnification agreement, defendant owner being sued for fraud cannot implead his real estate agent where the main complaint explicitly states an active participation by both in the alleged fraud. Lambert v Pratt (1961) 14 AD2d 181, 217 NYS2d 852.

Where railroad, sued by plaintiff for injuries sustained when truck in which he was riding while being driven by coemployee was struck in New Jersey by train, served third party complaint against plaintiff's employer seeking contribution, employer was granted summary judgment dismissing third party complaint because under New Jersey law when the relation between plaintiff and third party defendant at time of injury is employer-employee, there is an absence of the essential common liability between railroad and employer upon which to predicate the right of contri-

bution. Tuffarella v Erie R. Co. (1962) 17 AD2d 484, 236 NYS2d 503.

10. —Proximate cause

Where under allegations of plaintiff's complaint in action for personal injuries respondent can be held liable to plaintiff only if his active negligence is shown to have been proximate cause of such injuries, respondent has no right of indemnity from joint tortfeasor. Bankers Indemnity Ins. Co. v Cruise (1950) 277 AD 1118, 100 NYS2d 876.

Where under allegations of plaintiff's complaint, third-party plaintiff can be held liable only if its active negligence is proved to have been proximate cause of plaintiff's injuries, third-party plaintiff has no right of indemnity from alleged joint tort-feasor. Viscomi v State Elevator Co. (1955) 286 AD 994, 144 NYS2d 456.

11. Active and passive negligence

Charging defendant with both active and passive negligence causing personal injury did not destroy propriety of impleader, since subd. 5 of CPA § 193-a provided means of controlling consistency of verdict. Dalury v Lutz (1950) 198 Misc 749, 100 NYS2d 57, affd 278 AD 578, 102 NYS2d 462.

Where main complaint charges third-party plaintiff with passive as well as active negligence resulting in plaintiff's injury, it is policy of court not to dismiss third-party complaint, but to leave question of liability over until examination of facts afforded at trial. Schellhorn v N. Y. S. Elec. & Gas Corp. (1954) 283 AD 678, 127 NYS2d 182.

It was error to dismiss a third-party complaint where plaintiff alleges defendant factory owner was negligent in permitting elevator doors to remain open while elevator was at another floor, and in failing to maintain, guard, equip and operate elevator doors and approaches as required by law, and defendant alleges third-party defendant was negligent in operating the elevator at the time, the court saying that recovery against original defendant might be based on passive negligence, with third-party defendant actively negligent. Giunta v Parker, Stearns & Co. (1952) 280 AD 807, 113 NYS2d 494.

Where it appears from facts alleged that there is possibility of liability over, third-party complaint attacked on preliminary motion should be sustained and issues relegated for determination by trial court upon full development of proofs. Garger v Mt. Vernon T. Corp. (1955) 143 NYS2d 28.

Third party complaint was dismissed where, under allegations contained in the complaint, third party plaintiff could not recover against third party defendant since negligence, if any, of third party plaintiff would be active negligence. Coffey v Flower City Carting & Excavating Co. (1957) 2 NY2d 898, 161 NYS2d 149, 141 NE2d 632.

One cannot be guilty of merely passive negligence if he has been guilty of a fault of commission. It is the omission or failure to perform a nondelegable type of duty, which constitutes passive negligence entitling one to indemnity, and to impleader. Putvin v Buffalo Electric Co. (1959) 5 NY2d 447, 186 NYS2d 15, 158 NE2d 691.

Where complaint alleges that defendant was guilty of negligence in failing to supply plaintiff with a safe place to work, and it is not alleged that there is any relationship of master and servant between them, or that defendant is the owner of a building and therefore under a nondelegable obligation to supply a contractor's workmen with a safe place to work; but all that is shown is that defendant is an independent contractor working in the same building where plaintiff was employed, the complaint charges defendant with active negligence, and defendant cannot implead another tortfeasor. Putvin v Buffalo Electric Co., supra.

Third party complaint will not be dismissed as insufficient where facts show third party defendant is guilty of primary negligence, and third party plaintiff guilty merely of secondary negligence. Carvainis v Montefiore Hospital for Chronic Diseases (1959) 9 AD2d 735, 192 NYS2d 436.

Impleader is proper where complaint alleges facts upon the proof of some of which defendant might be primarily liable for active negligence and upon proof of others of which defendant might be held secondarily liable for passive negligence. Vassiliades v Joseph P. Blitz, Inc. (1959) 22 Misc 2d 51, 193 NYS2d 959, affd 13 AD2d 539, 214 NYS2d 656 (involving violations of Labor Law §§ 200, 241).

In action by third party defendant's employee against power company and telephone company for injuries sustained when truck he was driving came in contact with live wires, allegations in his complaint charging the utilities with negligent maintenance and failure to warn of dangerous condition due to sagging wires could be construed as charging passive negligence and warranted sustaining their third-party complaint against plaintiff's employer. De Lilli v Niagara Mohawk Power Corp. (1960) 11 AD2d 839, 202 NYS2d 857.

Where plaintiff in action against city and contractor for personal injuries alleged that he fell due to debris thrown on sidewalk by contractor, third party complaint by contractor against landlord and tenant of abutting property was dismissed for insufficiency, since plaintiff's complaint charged contractor with active negligence for which there is no indemnity. Harries v New York (1960) 24 Misc 2d 1035, 205 NYS2d 282.

Where main complaint indiscriminately charges all defendants with both active and passive negligence, fate of cross-claim or third-party complaint should be reserved for decision upon trial. Macrina v Scerra (1961) 28 Misc 2d 260, 211 NYS2d 799.

Where pleadings present the possibility of passive negligence the court will not dismiss third-party complaint as matter of law but will permit matter to go to trial where full inquiry into issue may be had. Romanoff v Benjamin Eisenberg Co. (1961) 35 Misc 2d 554, 219 NYS2d 127.

12. Active or passive negligence in the alternative

Where original complaint charges both active and passive negligence, or alternatively, defendant may implead third party charged with active negligence. Johnson v Endicott-Johnson Corp. (1951) 278 AD 626, 101 NYS2d 922.

Complaint alleging that defendant was owner or lessee or operator of injuring machine alleged its status in alternative, and third-party complaint of original defendant against employer alleging that latter was owner of such machine was sufficient. Robinson v Binghamton Constr. Co. (1950) 277 AD 468, 100 NYS2d 900.

13. Passive negligence of third party

Purpose of interpleader in case of status is to shift responsibility from passive to active wrongdoer. Strawn v Todd Shipyards Corp. (1948) 89 NYS2d 416.

In action for damages for contaminating well, third-party complaint, alleging only passive negligence, was dismissed. Seider v Kline (1951) 278 AD 1016, 106 NYS2d 202.

If a complaint alleges the factual situation in which the defendant could not be held liable at all unless it was guilty of active or primary negligence, there can be no basis for the recovery over and a mere conclusory allegation in a cross complaint or third party complaint that the defendant's negligence was passive or secondary adds nothing of legal significance. Brady v Stanley Weiss & Sons, Inc. (1958) 6 AD2d 241, 175 NYS2d 850.

14. Claims against defendant and third party on divergent grounds

Where grounds of negligence are divergent from those in complaint, impleader is improper. Utica Mut. Ins. Co. v Central Hudson Gas & E. Corp. (1947) 271 AD 943, 67 NYS2d 152.

Third party may not be impleaded where the wrong alleged against the original defendant arises solely from the alleged act of such defendant and not from any act of the third-party defendant so that there can be no liability over from the third-party defendant to the third-party plaintiff for all or part of the plaintiff's claim against the defendant. Pollaro v Bruto (1954) 283 AD 209, 126 NYS2d 882.

Where the plaintiff's complaint is based on an alleged conversion of chattels in which plaintiff claims an interest as mortgagee, a third party may not be brought in by the defendant upon a third-party pleading predicated upon fraud on the part of the third-party defendant in conspiring with another to defraud the third-party plaintiff, as such claim is not related to the main action by a question of law or fact common to both controversies. Pollaro v Bruto, supra.

Where third-party complaint alleges that insurance policy insures third-party plaintiff against loss from liability imposed by law resulting from bodily injuries, but action against third-party plaintiff is not based on bodily injuries, third-party complaint was dismissed. Westinghouse Electric Supply Co. v Shelton (1951) 107 NYS2d 184.

In action for injuries from improper construction and maintenance of scaffold, defendant cannot cross-complain against third-party defendants upon version of facts which would defeat any recovery by original plaintiff against defendant. Del Longo v Bennett-Brewster Co. (1948) 192 Misc 426, 80 NYS2d 901.

See Verder v Schack (1949) 90 NYS2d 801.

Defendant may bring in person not party to action who is or may be liable to him for all or part of plaintiff's claim against him, but claim against third-party defendant must be related to main action by question of law or fact common to both controversies. Blonstein v 241 Fifth Ave. Corp. (1956) 154 NYS2d 602.

Impleader is permitted when the third party is liable to defendant for all or part of the plaintiff's claim against him but impleader for affirmative relief against the third party defendant by reason of a claim which has no bearing on the claim of the main plaintiff is not allowed. Otte v Wegner (1958) 11 Misc 2d 499, 172 NYS2d 115.

Third-party plaintiff may not, in addition to damages recoverable by plaintiff against him, assert affirmative claim for his own damages. Blonstein v 241 Fifth Ave. Corp. (1956) 154 NYS2d 602.

Where alleged cause of action which accrued to defendant third-party plaintiff has no relation to claim of plaintiff, it is not proper claim to be asserted in third-party complaint. Blonstein v 241 Fifth Ave. Corp., supra.

In action against operator of hospital, and the nurse and physician engaged by him, to recover for personal injuries to newborn child, third party complaint by hospital operator against two other physicians, alleging that any injury to child was caused by their negligence, was dismissed because it did not seek to hold third party defendants for plaintiff's claim against defendants, but for entirely different acts of negligence not alleged in the primary complaint. Shea v Gitlin (1959) 20 Misc 2d 215, 190 NYS2d 792.

In negligence action, defendant can bring third party action against broker for having failed to effect adequate insurance coverage, but in the interests of justice, cases should be separately tried. Thornton v New York (1959) 20 Misc 2d 838, 193 NYS2d 777.

15. Indemnity

Third party complaint was not insufficient for failure to plead right of indemnity on part of third party plaintiff against third party defendants since such an allegation is unnecessary where third party plaintiff's action is not based on indemnity but is based upon the trust provisions of the Lien Law. Metropolitan Sand & Gravel Corp. v Lipson (1956) 4 Misc 2d 216, 158 NYS2d 360.

Although third-party complaint which contained cause of action for recovery based upon contractual indemnity need not have a copy of the contract annexed thereto, it did have to allege the legal effect of such agreement and, to be sufficient,

it had to establish that the third-party defendant undertook to indemnify the third-party plaintiff for the latter's wrongful acts. Brown v George A. Fuller Co. (1957) 3 AD2d 830, 161 NYS2d 555.

C. Procedure

16. Generally

RCP 54 stated that action by third-party plaintiff is "commenced" by serving summons on third-party defendant, whereas CPA § 193-a provided that after service of answer defendant may "bring in" person not party to action. Hirsch v Albany Sav. Bank (1948) 191 Misc 415, 81 NYS2d 250.

Since the Workmen's Compensation Law provides that an insurance carrier has a lien on recovery in a third party action to the extent of total compensation paid, the Appellate Division properly denied the attorney for the injured employee any lien on the recovery. Kussack v Ring Constr. Corp. (1958) 4 NY2d 1011, 177 NYS2d 522, 152 NE2d 540.

17. Service of summons and complaint

Service of summons by plaintiff on third-party defendant is unnecessary; plaintiff need not apply to amend original summons. Jacobs v Driscoll (1948) 78 NYS2d 813.

Foreign corporation, having no office or property and doing no business in New York, may not be served. Flanagan v Acme Scaffold Co. (1950) 277 AD 988, 100 NYS2d 15.

18. —Order unnecessary

Order is unnecessary as condition precedent to bringing in third-party defendant. Hameline Co. v Mohawk Containers (1951) 107 NYS2d 494.

Order is unnecessary to implead third party; he may be brought in by service of summons and third-party complaint. Occhipinti v Buscemi (1947) 71 NYS2d 766.

19. Time for action or motion

No time limitation is provided, and delay of six months did not bar commencing third-party action. Triglianos v Henry Moss & Co. (1947) 189 Misc 157, 71 NYS2d 618.

Third-party complaint for indemnity to defendant secondarily liable by defendant primarily liable for injuries, may be served before cause of action accrues, to avoid multiplicity. Smith v Smucker (1950) 198 Misc 944, 100 NYS2d 35.

Application to bring in party must be made before trial, at Special Term. Acetate Box Corp. v Johnson (1948) 193 Misc 54, 80 NYS2d 134.

A defendant had to answer before bringing in a third-party defendant under CPA § 193-a. Booke v Dime Sav. Bank (1953) 204 Misc 840, 127 NYS2d 59.

Claims over for indemnification are an exception to the usual rule that action can be commenced only after cause of action has accrued. Valstrey Service Corp. v Board of Elections (1957) 2 NY2d 413, 161 NYS2d 52, 141 NE2d 565.

20. Dismissal of complaint in chief

Third party defendant may challenge sufficiency of complaint in chief, which, if sufficient, necessitates dismissal of third party complaint. Boyle v Wegman (1960) 25 Misc 2d 193, 200 NYS2d 82.

21. Pleading in third-party actions

Third-party complaint, predicated upon liability over of third party, was sufficient. Triglianos v Henry Moss & Co. (1947) 189 Misc 157, 71 NYS2d 618.

Undenied allegations of defense in answer of third-party defendant are to be deemed controverted. Gorham v Arons (1947) 76 NYS2d 850.

Third-party complaint, alleging that plaintiff's injuries were caused by sole and primary negligence of third-party defendant in operation of aforementioned cellar doors, without alleging ultimate facts, was merely conclusory. Bennett v Lambert (1948) 82 NYS2d 111.

Where theory of third-party complaint is that defendant was passive wrongdoer and may be entitled to reimbursement for damages to which he may have to respond to plaintiff because of active wrongdoing of third-party defendant, it is sufficient in law as matter of pleading. Schaller v Republic Aviation Corp. (1948) 193 Misc 60, 83 NYS2d 540.

Third-party complaint, in action for personal injury, which does not proceed upon any theory of contractual right to indemnity or common-law right of indemnification based upon theories involving passive and active negligence, was defective. Coughlan v Joseph Bisceglia & Sons (1950) 100 NYS2d 738.

Absolute liability need not be alleged; it is sufficient to assert possibility of liability. Madison Ave. Properties Corp. v Royal Ins. Co. (1953) 281 AD 641, 120 NYS2d 626.

Possible liability is all that third-party complaint need allege; uncertainty of liability does not render allegations insufficient. Lerner v Banco Constr. Corp. (1951) 109 NYS2d 231.

The fact that defendants in their answer deny any liability to the plaintiff did not bar a claim over for indemnity; such hypothetical pleading was the only way in which CPA §§ 264 (§§ 3012(a), 3019(b), 3020(a) herein) and 193-a could properly be utilized. Brady v Stanley Weiss & Sons, Inc. (1958) 6 AD2d 241, 175 NYS2d 850.

There was no rule of law which prevented a defendant from denying the allegations of the complaint and then pleading that if he nevertheless was held liable to the plaintiff it would be on a ground that entitled him to recover over against another defendant. Such pleading was the only way in which CPA §§ 264 (§§ 3012(a), 3019(b), 3020(a) herein) and 193-a could properly be utilized. Brady v Stanley Weiss & Sons, Inc., supra.

Under subdivision 3 of CPA 193-a a plaintiff might amend his pleading to assert against a third party defendant any claim which the plaintiff might have asserted against the third party defendant had he been joined originally as a defendant and this might be done as of course without securing leave of the court. CPA § 193-a did not set forth any limitation of time within which such right might be exercised nor was the privilege limited by the provisions of CPA § 244 (§ 3025(a) herein). Aprea v New York (1958) 11 Misc 2d 645, 171 NYS2d 884.

In action for wrongful death from poisonous gas escaping from defective refrigerator in plaintiff's apartment in multiple dwelling, third-party complaint by landlord against gas company for negligent repairs and breach of warranty, alleging no facts to establish primary liability of gas company but only conclusory statement that any recovery by plaintiff must be based upon its negligence, was dismissed. Mandel v Criares (1956) 1 AD2d 830, 148 NYS2d 380.

In action against city for negligence in leaving uncovered manhole in street, third-party complaint by city against county for indemnity was insufficient for failure to allege service of notice of claim on county. Keesler v Peekskill (1955) 1 Misc 2d 744, 152 NYS2d 919.

In action by plaintiff to impose liability on truck owner based on negligent operation of truck and on telephone company for negligently creating dangerous condition by stretching wire struck by truck, third-party complaint by telephone company against truck owner, based on theory of passive negligence, was insufficient, where there was no allegation of special relationship between parties responsible for injuries by which one is regarded as being bound to indemnify other in negligent situation. Campigno v McQuide (1955) 286 AD 660, 146 NYS2d 83.

In action against electrical subcontractor for injury to workman of another contractor coming in contact with conduit or pipe installed by defendant in negligent manner without guards so as to constitute nuisance and trap for employees of other contractors, defendant's third-party complaint against plaintiff's employer was insufficient where it failed to state facts from which it could be determined that the defendant was other than a joint tort-feasor in pari delicto with plaintiff's employer. Focacci v New York (1956) 2 AD2d 902, 157 NYS2d 280.

Third-party complaint will not be required to spell out a cause of action against the third-party defendant with the same precision required of the main complaint, and the question whether it should stand depends upon whether the main complaint shows that liability could be fastened on the third-party plaintiff for passive negligence in circumstances occasioned by the third-party defendant's active negligence. To compel a third-party plaintiff to plead with precision could well subject him to summary judgment by the main plaintiff. Humble Oil & Refining Co. v M. W. Kellogg Co. (1961) 13 AD2d 754, 215 NYS2d 416, app gr 14 AD2d 670, 219 NYS2d 944.

22. —Amendments

After service of a pleading under subdivision 3 of CPA § 193-a any amendment was subject to the provisions of CPA § 244 (§ 3025(a) herein). Aprea v New York (1958) 11 Misc 2d 645, 171 NYS2d 884.

Where, under the terms of the insurance policy, plaintiff, as customer of defendant, could join third-party defendant insurance company as a defendant, plaintiff was granted leave to amend the complaint to state a cause of action against the third-party defendant. Levine v Arthur Rosenbaum, Inc. (1958) 16 Misc 2d 980, 182 NYS2d 135.

23. Dismissal of third-party complaint

Complaint variously alleging acts and omissions constituting primary and secondary liability should not be dismissed on motion. Logan v Bee Builders (1950) 277 AD 1040, 100 NYS2d 483.

Uncertainty as to liability on part of third-party defendant is not sufficient reason to dismiss third-party complaint. Robinson v Binghamton Constr. Co. (1950) 277 AD 468, 100 NYS2d 900.

Where third-party complaint fails to state facts showing any right of recovery over against third-party defendant, dismissal is proper. Desimone v C. J. Burgess Co. (1951) 278 AD 751, 104 NYS2d 734, affd 303 NY 930, 105 NE2d 504; Reilly v Charles Herman Constr. Co. (1949) 89 NYS2d 632.

Where employee of third-party defendant butcher sued owner of building for personal injuries caused by falling plaster, alleging that defendant owner was responsible as active tort-feasor for such defective condition, third-party complaint against butcher, alleging liability solely because of ownership of store and constructive notice of defect, was dismissed. Mileto v Polvica R. Corp. (1954) 137 NYS2d 56.

On motion by third-party defendant to dismiss third-party complaint for insufficiency, consideration must be given not only to pleading directly attacked, but also to complaint-in-chief interposed by original plaintiff as against original defendant, who, by virtue of invoking CPA § 193-a has become third-party plaintiff, with result that original complaint thus studied must bear adequate relation to charge for which original defendant (as third-party plaintiff) is seeking indemnity from third-party defendant. Atlas C. E. Corp. v Consolidated Edison Co. (1955) 4 Misc 2d 238, 136 NYS2d 822.

In action by father and minor son for injuries to son by fall on metal grating abutting premises owned by defendant, defendant may not implead minor's father who was party plaintiff to action, suing for loss of son's services. Lesser v Klein (1955) 140 NYS2d 794.

Claim over asserted in third-party complaint against impleaded defendant is insufficient in law where it contains allegations which if established would preclude liability on part of original defendant. Coffey v Flower City C. & E. Co. (1956) 2

AD2d 191, 153 NYS2d 763, affd 2 NY2d 898, 161 NYS2d 149, 141 NE2d 632.

In action against city as owner of overhead trolley system for wrongful death of lineman killed while working on such system because of city's negligence in failure to replace defective insulator, and also against manufacturer and dealer of insulator, city's third-party complaint against contractors which installed insulator and cross-claims by contractors against manufacturer and dealer were dismissed where city failed to prove negligent manufacture of insulator. Thibault v Broadway Maintenance Corp. (1956, Sup) 154 NYS2d 338, affd in part and revd in part 6 AD2d 904, 177 NYS2d 905, affd 6 NY2d 759, 186 NYS2d 658, 159 NE2d 204.

In action for personal injuries and property damages sustained when delivery truck was struck by defendant's railroad locomotive at private grade crossing, third-party complaint by railroad against summer camp licensor granted private right to cross railroad tracks for nominal consideration, based on indemnity exempting railroad from liability for all damages, even due to negligence of its employees, was sufficient. Salamy v New York Cent. System (1955) 1 AD2d 27, 146 NYS2d 814.

Where in action by subcontractor against contractor for contract price of trussed rafters, contractor served third-party complaint against owner for indemnification, alleging that owner has contract claim against contractor because of subcontractor's delay in performance and that if subcontractor prevails in its action then contractor will sustain damages by reason of its breach of contract with owner and third-party defendant to amount of judgment, contractor's third-party complaint failed to state cause of action against owner. Timber Structures v Terra-Rube C. Corp. (1955) 145 NYS2d 599.

In action against bus company by tire company's employee for injuries sustained in fall in former's garage, third-party complaint by bus company against tire company which had contracted to furnish tires for buses and to indemnify bus company from liability for death or injuries of tire company employees while engaged in tire company's work, was dismissed, as such indemnity provision did not protect bus company against liability for its own negligence. Flynn v N. Y. C. Omnibus Corp. (1955) 286 AD 1109, 146 NYS2d 265.

In action for injuries to subcontractor's employee who fell from scaffold when wall supporting it collapsed, against owner and general contractor, wherein latter impleaded subcontractor, both complaint and third-party complaint were dismissed for failure to prove actional negligence. Haddon v Engel (1956) 1 AD2d 954, 150 NYS2d 57.

Where complaint is broad enough to admit of recovery by plaintiff upon acts of negligence separate and apart from alleged failure to comply with Administrative Code provisions for maintenance of sidewalk shed, and proof upon trial may establish that third-party plaintiff was passive tort-feasor entitled to recovery over from third-party defendant as active tort-feasor, third-party complaint should not be dismissed. Klein v Bargray C. Corp. (1956) 1 AD2d 883, 149 NYS2d 926.

Where injured employee of carpentry subcontractor sued general contractor and lumber supplier, and general contractor impleaded carpentry subcontractor as third-party defendant, and latter served cross-complaint on said lumber supplier, dismissal of cross-complaint should provide leave to replead, since lumber supplier may be liable over to carpentry subcontractor for failure to inspect defective lumber supplied. Crawford v Blitman C. Corp. (1956) 1 AD2d 398, 150 NYS2d 387.

Where original action simple contract action for services rendered triable by jury and there was no single common issue that could be tried out together under either cause of action set forth in the third-party complaint, third-party complaint dismissed with leave to serve amended complaint. Ammann & Whitney v Edgarton (1957) 12 Misc 2d 119, 175 NYS2d 536.

An automobile liability insurance company which insured corporation and which is defending action instituted against corporation by said corporation's president's wife who was injured as passenger while her said husband was driving car cannot have its attorney without the corporation's consent prepare and verify a purported third-party complaint by the corporation against the president if purported third-party defendant in spite of cooperation and subrogation provision in policy and in spite of the fact that the policy does not cover injuries to spouse and such third-party complaint dismissed. Ulanoff v Croyden Shirt Co. (1958) 14 Misc 2d 13, 174 NYS2d 357.

In action against operator of hospital, and the nurse and physician engaged by him, to recover for personal injuries to newborn child, third party complaint by hospital operator against two other physicians, alleging that any injury to child was caused by their negligence, was dismissed because it did not seek to hold third party defendants for plaintiff's claim against defendants, but for entirely different acts of negligence not alleged in the primary complaint. Shea v Gitlin (1959) 20 Misc 2d 215, 190 NYS2d 792.

Where the original complaint charged defendant and third-party defendant with active negligence, third-party complaint was dismissed for insufficiency in the absence of any showing that defendant had a contractual or statutory right of indemnification from third-party defendant. Morgan v Donahue (1958) 19 Misc 2d 532, 195 NYS2d 917, affd 8 AD2d 768, 187 NYS2d 339.

In action for wrongful death of contractor's employee who was killed in fall while working on defendant's property, where, from the allegations of original complaint, it was possible that contractor's active negligence was primary cause of employee's death and defendant owner was guilty of passive negligence, owner's third-party complaint against contractor was held sufficient. Gallagher v Hill Greenhouse Constr., Inc. (1960) 23 Misc 2d 167, 197 NYS2d 234.

On motion to dismiss third-party complaint for insufficiency where the negligence charged in the main complaint might be construed as either affirmative or passive, as where one of the specifications of negligence is, that defendant permitted the sidewalk in front of his premises to become cluttered with glass from a broken window, the question of sufficiency should be resolved in favor of the third-party complaint to await final disposition as tested against additional information secured by a bill of particulars, examinations, or ultimately the facts produced at trial. Klein v Bukowski (1961) 12 AD2d 872, 210 NYS2d 161.

Where main complaint indiscriminately charges all defendants with both active and passive negligence, fate of cross-claim or third-party complaint should be reserved for decision upon trial. Macrina v Scerra (1961) 28 Misc 2d 260, 211 NYS2d 799.

Where original complaint clearly charges defendant with having created the latent defect and dangerous condition, so that it is unnecessary to try the issue as to whether it is possible under its allegations to impose a liability on the third-party plaintiff for passive negligence alone, the third-party complaint must be dismissed. Gingeresky v Gifford-Wood Co. (1961) 14 AD2d 623, 218 NYS2d 339.

24. —Effect of dismissal

Dismissal of third-party complaint for failure to state a cause of action is not a determination on the merits. Putvin v Buffalo Electric Co. (1959) 5 NY2d 447, 186 NYS2d 15, 158 NE2d 691.

25. Motion to dismiss

Dismissal of third-party complaint will not be made where plaintiff made no formal motion but merely joined in motion by third-party defendant based solely upon insufficiency of third-party complaint. Gorham v Arons (1947) 76 NYS2d 850.

Where neither third-party defendant nor plaintiff moved for discretionary dismissal of third-party complaint, without prejudice, or for separate trial of third-party claim court cannot, on application by third party to dismiss third-party complaint, consider affidavits by plaintiff, defendant or third-party plaintiff. Green v Hudson Shoring Co. (1947) 191 Misc 297, 77 NYS2d 842.

On determining motion to dismiss third-party complaint, its allegations must be deemed to be true. Van Orden v Bartnett (1950) 101 NYS2d 1008.

On motion by third party defendant to dismiss amended third-party complaint, propriety of plaintiff's pleading is not before court. Teepell v Jefferson County Sav. Bank (1956) 3 Misc 2d 508, 148 NYS2d 347.

Where upon all pleadings triable issue is presented as to whether sole proximate cause of accident was primary or active negligence of third-party defendant and whether negligence, if any, of third-party plaintiff was secondary or passive, third-party complaint is legally sufficient. Bunchez v Astoria-

Star W. Serv. (1956) 1 AD2d 947, 150 NYS2d 760.

In action for injuries to tenant struck by door of self-service elevator in multiple dwelling, wherein defendant owner served cross-complaint against service company for negligent repairs, motion by service company to dismiss both complaint and cross-complaint was denied, as to complaint, though plaintiff was not party to contract between owner and service company, and as to cross-complaint, where there was question of fact whether owner was actively or passively negligent. Wisner v Harmas H. Corp. (1956) 1 AD2d 957, 150 NYS2d 38, app dismd 3 NY2d 775, 164 NYS2d 30, 143 NE2d 788.

In action by person injured by dumb-waiter which moved while it was open, against building owner for negligent maintenance, third-party complaint by owner against elevator company for negligent repair was legally sufficient, since jury may find that act of omission was passive negligence entitling third-party plaintiff to recover over against defendant whose conduct caused dangerous condition. Solomon v Marseilles Hotel Corp. (1956) 1 AD2d 766, 149 NYS2d 581.

A motion to dismiss a third party complaint was proper procedure where the authority of the attorney to institute the third party action was challenged since a defendant has the right to raise that objection. Schiro v Catania (1957) 13 Misc 2d 1033, 174 NYS2d 353.

Where despite formal allegations in the pleading it cannot be said with any degree of certainty assuming that defendant is adjudged to be liable to the plaintiff whether such liability will be founded on such defendant's active or passive negligence, an issue of fact is presented which should be resolved by the triers of the facts on the basis of all the proof adduced at the trial and not by the court on the basis of the pleadings. Tarantino v Buck (1958) 6 AD2d 894, 177 NYS2d 557.

Where original complaint is susceptible of construction that third party plaintiff's acts were supervisory only, liability of third party defendant may not be determined from pleadings alone. Public Admr. v Rubin Constr. Corp. (1958) 6 AD2d 678, 173 NYS2d 943.

On motion to dismiss third-party complaint, its allegations must be deemed to be true. Cook v Fogelsonger (1959) 21 Misc 2d 337, 193 NYS2d 259.

Where defendant, sued for $600 in main action, claimed over against third-party defendant for $600, or in alternative for larger sum, since he could properly recover the $600, if plaintiff recovers from him, fact that alternative demand is in excess of amount in suit in main action does not make third-party complaint dismissible. Joseph v R. & M. Embroidery Co. (1959) 21 Misc 2d 392, 195 NYS2d 736.

When evidence might be adduced which would result in jury question whether defendant was passively negligent while third party defendant was actively negligent, third party complaint would not

be dismissed on motion for insufficiency. Hollant v North Shore Hospital, Inc. (1960) 24 Misc 2d 892, 206 NYS2d 177.

Third-party complaint will not be required to spell out a cause of action against the third-party defendant with the same precision required of the main complaint, and the question whether it should stand depends upon whether the main complaint shows that liability could be fastened on the third-party plaintiff for passive negligence in circumstances occasioned by the third-party defendant's active negligence. To compel a third-party plaintiff to plead with precision could well subject him to summary judgment by the main plaintiff. Humble Oil & Refining Co. v M. W. Kellogg Co. (1961) 13 AD2d 754, 215 NYS2d 416, app gr 14 AD2d 670, 219 NYS2d 944.

The sufficiency of a third party complaint depends upon the allegations of the primary complaint showing that defendant is passively negligent, and not on allegations by defendant in his third party complaint that he was passively negligent. Sigismondi v Lewis (1962) 32 Misc 2d 210, 223 NYS2d 303, revd on other grounds 18 AD 2d 762, 235 NYS2d 655.

26. —Time for motion

Motion for discretionary dismissal of third-party complaint may be made either before or after third party has pleaded to third-party complaint. Green v Hudson Shoring Co. (1947) 191 Misc 297, 77 NYS2d 842.

After issue joined on third-party complaint, third party may move to dismiss on notice to all parties. Occhipinti v Buscemi (1947) 71 NYS2d 766.

Motion to dismiss third-party complaint before answer is proper. Smith v Brown (1947) 72 NYS2d 867, affd 273 AD 809, 76 NYS2d 836, 837, 838.

Where third-party complaint specifically charges third-party defendant with active negligence and states that third-party plaintiff's actions were passive, on motion to dismiss third-party complaint, it cannot be determined whether third-party plaintiff or third-party defendant was tortfeasor in pari delicto or whether third-party plaintiff was passively negligent and motion to dismiss denied. Epstein v Empress Hotel, Inc. (1957) 11 Misc 2d 21, 169 NYS2d 878.

27. Notice to all parties appearing

Where third-party defendant has given notice of its application to dismiss third-party complaint only to third-party plaintiff, dismissal was denied, as plaintiff had no opportunity to make known his position to court. Prost v New York (1947) 190 Misc 197, 73 NYS2d 811.

Third-party defendant is entitled to notice of plaintiff's motion for summary judgment to dismiss third-party complaint, where third-party defendant had not answered and his time to do so had not expired. Mansfield Iron Works v Silveri (1951) 106 NYS2d 496.

The right of third-party plaintiffs who compromised in action with original plaintiffs to recover over against third-party plaintiff's grantor in an action to establish a prescriptive right of way depends on proof of facts which imposed initial liability as well as reasonableness of amount paid in settlement and trial to resolve such issues required and summary judgment denied. Washington v Morantz (1958) 11 Misc 2d 273, 177 NYS2d 470.

28. Discretion of court

Abuse of discretion shown in granting plaintiff's motion to dismiss third-party complaint without prejudice to separate action. Barone v Triborough Bridge & T. Authority (1949) 276 AD 775, 92 NYS2d 796.

The court in its discretion may dismiss a third party complaint without prejudice to the bringing of another action or order a separate trial or make such other orders concerning the proceedings as may be necessary to further justice or convenience and where severance will not injure any party, severance properly directed. Kelly v Yannotti (1958) 4 NY2d 603, 176 NYS2d 637, 152 NE2d 69, conformed to 6 AD2d 1046, 179 NYS2d 653.

Where the complaint in the prime action contains allegations upon proof some of which defendant might be primarily liable and it also appears from the complaint that defendant is alleged to be guilty only of passive negligence, the court in the exercise of discretion will not dismiss the third party complaint for legal insufficiency but will leave the question of liability present for disposition at the trial. Schneiberg v Utz (1957) 8 Misc 2d 535, 167 NYS2d 832.

In passenger's action for injuries against owner and driver of car, joint third party complaint by defendants against garageman, charging that plaintiff's injuries were caused by latter's failure to properly repair brakes, was dismissed as to driver since he could not assert a valid claim over, but was sustained as to car owner since her negligence was purely statutory, and driver's active negligence could not be imputed to her, and if accident were caused by brake failure she had valid claim over against garageman. Lipsman v Warren (1960) 10 AD2d 868, 199 NYS2d 761.

29. —When prejudicial

In action for personal injuries by fall on defective step in hallway of multiple dwelling, owner's third-party complaint against contractor, filed four years after action begun, was dismissed as prejudicial to plaintiff. Steiner v Esland Properties, Inc. (1952) 113 NYS2d 51.

Where landlord, sued for death of tenant's employee, filed cross complaint against tenant, such claim would unduly delay and prejudice plaintiff, and was dismissed. Clements v Rockefeller (1947) 272 AD 1002, 74 NYS2d 412.

Delay and prejudice to plaintiff warranted separate trial of third-party claim that third-party defendant had agreed to indemnify third-party plaintiff against paying commissions to anyone else on purchase of trawler. Langdon & Matule v Eureka Iron Works (1949) 85 NYS2d 478, affd 275 AD 659, 86 NYS2d 668.

Insurer, impleaded by insured landlord, sued for personal injury, cannot avoid impleader on ground of prejudice, where jury had been formally waived. Litman v Garfinkle (1948) 193 Misc 256, 81 NYS2d 296.

Where defendant impleaded injured plaintiff's employer as third-party defendant as indemnitor, plaintiff's motion to dismiss third-party complaint on ground that introduction of workmen's compensation insurance policies by third-party defendant would be permitted and so prejudiced, was denied. Schaller v Republic Aviation Corp. (1948) 193 Misc 60, 83 NYS2d 540.

Where third-party complaint would unnecessarily complicate main action, it would be dismissed without prejudice to independent action. Bank of New York v Public Nat. Bank & T. Co. (1948) 195 Misc 812, 82 NYS2d 694, 92 NYS2d 620, affd 275 AD 932, 90 NYS2d 701, mod on reh 277 AD 963, 99 NYS2d 851, affd 301 NY 503, 93 NE2d 71.

Plaintiff's contention of undue prejudice, by delay of main trial, question of workmen's compensation coverage injected into trial, plaintiff's selection of jurors hampered, cross-examination of plaintiff's witnesses, and confusion of jury by issue of indemnity, held not to show such sacrifice of rights as to require dismissal of complaint in action for personal injuries. Brewster v Gair Realty Corp. (1950) 101 NYS2d 1006.

30. Separate trial

Where in action for trespass by insured contractor latter impleaded insurer, insurer was entitled to discretionary order of severance so that existence of insurance may not be brought to attention of jurors. Caserta v Beaver Constr. Corp. (1949) 197 Wis 410, 95 NYS2d 131.

Liability insurer was granted severance and separate trial of third-party claim, in action for personal injuries, triable by jury, against motorist who impleaded liability insurer as third-party defendant. De Lany v Allen (1951) 200 Misc 734, 105 NYS2d 635.

Insurer of defendant who impleaded insurer by third-party complaint because insurer refused to defend automobile injury case, was denied dismissal if trial to be without jury, and was granted separate trial if with jury. Remch v Grabow (1947) 193 Misc 731, 70 NYS2d 462.

Partial assignee may sue at law, provided parties necessary to effective determination of issues presented are joined. Rosenberg v Paul Tishman Co. (1952) 118 NYS2d 337.

Single trial of all issues should not be had where it will tend to create great confusion and may readily prejudice plaintiff in prosecution of his claim. Schulman v Kemach & Garson (1949) 88 NYS2d 81.

In wife's action for personal injuries and husband's action for loss of services in accident on premises owned by defendant, insured owners may implead liability insurer, and latter was granted severance of third-party action from original action to avoid prejudice because of insurance. Gleason v Sailer (1952) 203 Misc 227, 116 NYS2d 409.

In wife's action for personal injuries and husband's action for loss of services in accident on premises owned by defendant, insured owners may implead liability insurer, which was denied severance on ground that issues involved in original action and in third-party action would tax jury's ability to comprehend such issues. Gleason v Sailer, supra.

The court is given substantial discretion in connection with third-party complaints to order a separate trial of the third-party claim or of any separate issue thereof or to make such other orders concerning the proceeding as may be necessary to further justice or convenience. In exercising this discretion, the court is authorized to take into consideration whether a trial of the controversy between the third-party plaintiff and defendant would unduly delay the determination of the main action or prejudice any party thereunder. Ammann & Whitney v Edgarton (1957) 12 Misc 2d 119, 175 NYS2d 536.

In action for breach of warranty, seller brought in manufacturer and manufacturer brought in its suppliers as third party defendant. Since all the claims were related to the main action by questions of law or fact, motion for separate trial was denied. Knitmode Mills, Inc. v Bantam-U. S. Toys, Inc. (1956) 5 Misc 2d 708, 165 NYS2d 967.

Where terms of an insurance policy did not constitute a waiver barring a third party action under CPA § 193-a, motion to dismiss third party complaint denied and an application by the third party defendant for severance of trial denied. Eastling v Federated Dept. Stores, Inc. (1958) 12 Misc 2d 795, 173 NYS2d 61.

Separate trials were ordered where insurer would be prejudiced if the main personal injury and property damage action against insured and insured's third-party action against insurer were tried before the same jury. Cook v Fogelsonger (1959) 21 Misc 2d 337, 193 NYS2d 259.

In negligence action, defendant can bring third party action against broker for having failed to effect adequate insurance coverage, but in the interests of justice, cases should be separately tried. Thornton v New York (1959) 20 Misc 2d 838, 193 NYS2d 777.

In automobile personal injury negligence action where defendant impleads disclaiming insurance carrier, carrier is entitled to severance and separate trial, to avoid possible prejudice, even though jury because of compulsory insurance requirement in New York would be aware that there is insurance. Santonocito v Suburban Oil Co. (1961) 27 Misc 2d 697, 211 NYS2d 571.

Insurance broker, impleaded by defendant in negligence action, for alleged breach of agreement to provide full insurance coverage, was granted a severance, since he would be prejudiced if both actions were tried before same jury. N. & E.

Greenberg's Sons, Inc. v Peter Pan Fur Co. (1961) 33 Misc 2d 453, 215 NYS2d 787.

31. Examination before trial of, or by, third party

Having elected to contest plaintiff's claim, the third-party defendant is a party adverse to the plaintiff and may be examined as such before trial. Bizzarro v Zimkot Realty Corp. (1954) 283 AD 816, 128 NYS2d 796.

Where plaintiff's complaint seeks no relief against third-party defendant which, however, opposes plaintiff's claim against defendant, plaintiff may examine third-party defendant. Anida Realty Corp. v 6145 Realty Corp. (1950) 197 Misc 157, 94 NYS2d 56.

Where a third-party defendant asserts no claims against the original plaintiff, nor raises any issues between them, and the plaintiff has sought no relief against the third-party defendant by amendment of his complaint to join the third party as a defendant in the main action, the plaintiff and third-party defendant are not adverse parties within the meaning of CPA § 288 (§ 3101(a) Rule 3106(a) herein), and the plaintiff may not examine the third-party defendant before trial as an adverse party. Salgo v Amdor Structures, Inc. (1954) 133 NYS2d 435.

Claim by third-party defendant against plaintiff entitled former to examine plaintiff before trial. Anida Realty Corp. v 6145 Realty Corp. (1950) 197 Misc 157, 94 NYS2d 56.

Defendant and third-party plaintiff may not as such party examine plaintiff who had not amended his complaint to state cause of action against third-party defendant. Deutsch v Adams (1950) 197 Misc 505, 95 NYS2d 622.

Plaintiff may not be examined by third-party defendant, where neither asserts claim against other. Gile v Sears, Roebuck & Co. (1952) 110 NYS2d 211.

Defendant may not examine plaintiff before trial where neither asserts claims against other. Gile v Sears, Roebuck & Co., supra.

Plaintiff is entitled to notice of third party defendant's motion to vacate third party plaintiff's notice of examination before trial and, where plaintiff was not given such notice, third party defendant's motion would be denied. Rivkind v Fried (1957) 13 Misc 2d 943, 159 NYS2d 861.

32. —Physical examination

A motion by a third party defendant for an order directing plaintiff in main complaint to submit to physical examination will be granted since intention of statute is that third party defendant should not be at mercy of mere formal or inept defense to plaintiff's claim by third party plaintiff. Sorrentino v New York (1958) 14 Misc 2d 78, 178 NYS2d 500.

33. Verdict

Jury may return verdict against defendant on one of various theories of liability alleged in third-party complaint, of which at least one would permit judgment over against third-party defendant. Schaller v Republic Aviation Corp. (1948) 193 Misc 60, 83 NYS2d 540.

34. Special findings

Special findings of a jury with respect to ground of third-party plaintiff's liability are not advisory, but binding upon the court even though the third-party's liability is being tried by court, not by jury, and the principal complaint is being tried by jury. Kennard v Housing Associates, Inc. (1961) 26 Misc 2d 1000, 209 NYS2d 479.

Statutory provision CPA § 459 (Rule 4111(a)(c), 4112 herein) requiring entry of judgment on special findings even though such findings were inconsistent with general verdict was mandatory, and matter could not have been resubmitted to jury. Kennard v Housing Associates, Inc., supra.

Jury's special findings, unless set aside by court as contrary to weight of evidence, are determinative of so much of cross-claims as they cover, and fact that jury is not aware of legal results of its findings does not militate against their binding effect. Kennard v Housing Associates, Inc., supra.

35. Costs

Successful third-party defendant is entitled to statutory costs against third party plaintiff, which successful defendant is allowed by statute against unsuccessful plaintiff. Butler v Gimbel Bros. (1947) 86 NYS2d 687.

Third-party plaintiff who serves third-party complaint is in same category as any other plaintiff, when matter of costs is presented. Pearlstein v James J. McCreery & Co. (1949) 194 Misc 516, 87 NYS2d 49.

D. PARTICULAR THIRD PARTIES AND ACTIONS

36. Agent and principal

In actions for goods sold and delivered, defendant buyer may allege that he made purchase for account of third-party defendant and implead latter, praying that if plaintiff recovers against defendant, latter may have same judgment for same claim against third party. Thomas J. Nolan, Inc. v Martin & William Smith, Inc. (1949) 193 Misc 877, 85 NYS2d 380.

Where under escrow agreements defendant had obligated himself to make payment in accord with judicial determinations to be brought against his clients, defendant had right to implead his clients in action on such escrow agreements. Roosin v Rodin (1955) 140 NYS2d 315.

37. Brokers

In action by realty broker for commissions, vendor may implead purchaser who had agreed to be liable over to vendor to extent of any recovery by broker. Salzberg v Raynay Holding Corp. (1947) 188 Misc 1009, 69 NYS2d 608.

In action by realty broker for commissions, vendor may implead purchaser who repudiated contract for broker's misrepresentations. Franklin E. Tyrell, Inc. v Vahlsing (1947) 193 Misc 454, 69 NYS2d 602.

In action for commissions for selling trawler for defendant, defendant impleaded another broker who agreed to indemnify former against paying commissions to any one else, though there was no common question of law or fact. Langdon & Matule v Eureka Iron Works (1948) 85 NYS2d 478, affd 275 AD 659, 86 NYS2d 668.

In negligence action, defendant can bring third party action against broker for having failed to effect adequate insurance coverage, but in the interests of justice, cases should be separately tried. Thornton v New York (1959) 20 Misc 2d 838, 193 NYS 2d 777.

Insurance broker, impleaded by defendant in negligence action, for alleged breach of agreement to provide full insurance coverage, was granted a severance, since he would be prejudiced if both actions were tried before same jury. N. & E. Greenberg's Sons, Inc. v Peter Pan Fur Co. (1961) 33 Misc 2d 453, 215 NYS2d 787.

38. Building owner and window-cleaning company

Where bank employed window-cleaning company to clean its windows and to furnish its own employees and equipment and its employee was injured while cleaning window, bank could implead window-cleaning company on theory of passive negligence. Chideckel v Dime Sav. Bank (1951) 103 NYS2d 616.

In action by window cleaner for injuries due to fall from outside of building against building owner, third-party complaint by building owner against tenant in possession and plaintiff's employer was not dismissed on motion where it alleged that accident was due to defective ladder furnished by plaintiff's employer and that tenant, knowing of such defect, permitted its use; control given to tenant should be determined on trial. Kirkland v Dibner (1953) 123 NYS2d 801.

39. Buyer and seller

Where defendant, sued for labor in installing heating system, counterclaimed for breach of warranty, plaintiff may implead seller of equipment, allegedly liable over to plaintiff, for equipment allegedly defective. Hameline v Mohawk Containers (1951) 107 NYS2d 494.

In action by several plaintiffs for breach of contract to supply carpeting, individual defendant may not implead corporation which supplied him with carpet for breach of warranty, where claimed breach of agreement by individual defendant of his contract with plaintiffs has nothing to do with alleged breach by third-party defendant corporation with said individual defendant. Goldberg v Lieberthal (1951) 203 Misc 350, 118 NYS2d 681.

In action by buyer against seller of goods used in manufacturing raincoats, for breach of warranty based on offensive odor from material used, seller's third-party complaint alleging that processor negligently used chemicals in processing which made goods unfit by reason of offensive odor sufficiently and properly alleged cause of action against processor for negligence. Debby Jr. C&S Co. v Wollman Mills (1955) 207 Misc 330, 137 NYS2d 703.

In action by buyer against seller of goods used in manufacturing raincoats, for breach of warranty based on offensive odor from material used, seller's third-party complaint alleging that processor used chemicals in processing which made goods unfit by reason of offensive odor, sufficiently alleged cause of action against processor for breach of warranty of fitness. Debby Jr. C&S Co. v Wollman Mills, supra.

Where plaintiff sues for breach of agreement of defendant to sell it all milk receipts of dairymen's association, and association agreed with defendant to deliver milk receipts to plaintiff, failure of association to deliver milk to plaintiff raises common question of fact under both agreements, justifying impleader of association by plaintiff, so that all issues may be disposed of at one trial. Champlain Creameries v Hovey, S. & Co. (1955) 141 NYS2d 271.

In action by pedestrian against automobile driver for personal injuries where complaint alleged that defendant negligently and speedily backed his car against plaintiff on sidewalk, driver cannot implead dealer who had sold car to defendant and who allegedly had improperly adjusted its operating parts, and third-party complaint was insufficient, since accident was due to driver's active negligence. Bremen v Freed (1954) 134 NYS2d 898.

In action for personal injuries to shopper in self-service store caused by her tripping over box in aisle, against store owner who impleaded third-party defendant who left food box in aisle, where no triable issue was presented as to responsibility for condition between third-party defendant and third-party plaintiff, court directed judgment over against third-party defendant. Bockette v Grand Union Co. (1955) 286 AD 941, 142 NYS2d 617.

40. Carrier and third person

In action by shipper against motor common carrier for loss of goods by fire, carrier may not implead insured and his insurer on ground that fire was caused by negligence of insured. Chapin Owen Co. v Newman (1951) 201 Misc 1072, 107 NYS2d 941.

In action for injuries to passenger in truck negligently struck by defendant's truck, third-party complaint alleging that third-party plaintiff's truck was stopped before accident and was negligently run into by truck of third-party defendant, which "may or may not" have been pushed into vehicle in which plaintiff was riding, failed to state cause of action. Anderson v Liberty F. F. Co. (1954) 284 AD 44, 135 NYS2d 559.

In action for injuries to water-proofing company employee who fell from scaffold erected by his employer in bus terminal, negligently struck by bus, third-party complaint by bus company against terminal operators, alleging latter's negligence in allowing construction of scaffold not wide enough to permit safe passage of buses, was insufficient to charge common-law indemnity since former was

actively negligent and latter only passively negligent, but third-party complaint, alleging contract between them for partial indemnity for liability for active or passive negligence, was sufficient, irrespective of demand for damages in excess of those to which party is entitled under pleadings. Ast v Public S. C. Transport (1955) 143 NYS2d 217.

41. City and abutting owner

In pedestrian's action against city for injuries from icy sidewalk-driveway, city's third-party complaint against abutting owners, alleging their failure to remove snow and ice, was insufficient, since it was also city's duty to make such removal. Mills v New York (1947) 189 Misc 291, 71 NYS2d 507.

Where it could not be determined under pleadings in action by pedestrian injured when he stepped on water shut-off appliance on sidewalk, whether city and impleaded abutting owner were in pari delicto, dismissal of third-party complaint was denied. Schlemovitz v New York (1948) 81 NYS2d 282, affd 274 AD 1064, 85 NYS2d 923.

In action against city by pedestrian injured by falling because of hole in curbstone and sidewalk, city may implead abutter who allegedly maintained curbstone and sidewalk for his special use and benefit. Rubin v New York (1950) 277 AD 1138, 101 NYS2d 171.

Where city's third-party complaint does not allege connection of defective condition of sidewalk, which caused plaintiff's fall, with condition of sidewalk created by its special use by abutter as driveway to his garage, impleader improper. Massa v New York (1951) 201 Misc 259, 109 NYS2d 141.

In action for personal injuries due solely to negligence of city in permitting to exist in sidewalk in front of specified premises hole which caused plaintiff to fall, third-party complaint by city against abutting owner, which incorporated by reference allegations of complaint and further alleged that third-party defendant negligently caused and maintained fence which encroached on sidewalk and thereby constituted nuisance and that plaintiff's injuries were caused solely by negligence of said abutting owner, was insufficient. Gross v New York (1955) 145 NYS2d 303.

42. City and others

In action against City of New York for personal injuries due to its negligence in failing properly to maintain street, manhole and manhole cover, city's third-party complaint against private corporation, alleging that corporation maintains sewer and street for special use of apartment houses, without alleging facts from which latter's negligence could be inferred, or facts to support inference that latter is one who is or may be liable to city for all or part of plaintiff's claim, was insufficient. Resnick v New York (1955) 286 AD 861, 141 NYS2d 802.

In action for personal injuries to plaintiff from fall on defective sidewalk made defective by negligent driver of truck over it, where defective condition was known to city for four months, evidence warranted recovery against city and truck owner for concurring negligence and recovery over in favor of city, which was passively negligent, against truck owner, which was actively negligent. Napoli v New York (1955) 144 NYS2d 110.

In action against City of New York by contractor's truck driver injured in course of his employment when overhead metal runner used in connection with operation of door of city garage fell on him, where complaint alleged that such runner was defective to knowledge of city, city's third-party complaint against contractor, seeking indemnification based on contract requiring contractor to save city harmless from liability for all claims for personal injuries, was insufficient, since such contract cannot be construed to indemnify city against its own negligence. Rego v New York (1955) 285 AD 834, 137 NYS2d 5.

43. Cloth manufacturer and clothing maker

In action for personal injuries to infant from burning of costume suit against cloth manufacturer and distributor, defendants may implead costume manufacturer only where they show that he may be liable over to them to extent of any recovery by plaintiff. Timberlake v M. A. Henry Co. (1951) 104 NYS2d 284, affd 278 AD 686, 103 NYS2d 452.

In action by converter of fabrics against dyer for damages in dying, dyer may implead dye manufacturer where dyer alleged that manufacturer had breached express warranties. Colonial P. D. Works v General Dyestuff Corp. (1953) 282 AD 858, 125 NYS2d 305.

44. Contractor and materialman

In action by contractor against his subcontractor for breach of contract by using defective lime, subcontractor may implead materialman who delivered wrong kind of lime, as presenting question of law and fact common to both controversies, though cause of action alleged in third-party complaint sounds partly in tort. V. B. Constr. Co. v Murray (1948) 274 AD 1019, 84 NYS2d 797.

In action for work and labor against contractor who pleaded defective performance of work, defendant may implead person who supplied him with materials. Carroll Sheet Metal Works v Mechanical Installations (1951) 201 Misc 689, 110 NYS2d 581.

45. Contractor and subcontractor

General contractor and electrical subcontractor, sued for personal injuries due to fall over temporary electrical wiring on scaffold, may implead injured employee's employer who built scaffold and also party who furnished lumber to build scaffold. Van Orden v Bartnett (1950) 101 NYS2d 1008.

Since basis of impleading new defendant is liability over by way of indemnity, in action for death of employee of subcontractor against general contractor and owner, contractor cannot implead subcontractor, as attempting to bring in active joint tortfeasor. Chandler v Glaser Contracting Co. (1948)

80 NYS2d 502. See Dolnick v Edward Donner Lumber Corp. (1949) 275 AD 954, 89 NYS2d 783, affd 300 NY 660, 91 NE2d 322; Costello v General Motors Corp. (1950) 277 AD 788, 97 NYS2d 236.

In administrator's action against board of education and general contractor for death of painter of subcontractor by fall from scaffold, general contractor may implead subcontractor by alleging that latter furnished scaffold and that such injury was due to his active negligence or contributory negligence of painter. Ellithorp v Adams-Rice Constr. Corp. (1953) 281 AD 917, 119 NYS2d 776.

In action against contractor and subcontractor by injured employee of another subcontractor, latter could not be impleaded by defendant subcontractor. Bailey v Kew Queens Corp. (1947) 78 NYS2d 509.

In action by employee of subcontractor for personal injuries sustained when he was struck by steel beam while working on building in course of construction, contractor may implead subcontractor who had agreed to perform all steel work, alleging that plaintiff's injuries were caused by latter's active and primary negligence. Pike v Balmar Constr. Co. (1951) 104 NYS2d 569.

Insurer, sued on policy of fire insurance, may contest its liability and implead electrical contractor as third-party defendant responsible to insured for casualty because of negligence and breach of contract, by alleging that it becomes subrogated to insured's rights if it is held liable and pays recovery against it. Madison Ave. Properties Corp. v Royal Ins. Co. (1953) 281 AD 641, 120 NYS2d 626.

In action against contractor by subcontractor's employee injured on vessel at pier, contractor may implead subcontractor, though latter had complied with Longshoremen's Act. Barbara v Stephen Ranson, Inc. (1948) 191 Misc 957, 79 NYS2d 438.

In action for personal injury to employee of subcontractor's employee allegedly due solely to active negligence of general contractor, latter may not implead subcontractor who had agreed to indemnify contractor solely for subcontractor's negligence. Employers Mut. Liability Ins. Co. v Fairchild Press (1951) 105 NYS2d 790, revd on facts 279 AD 895, 111 NYS2d 604.

In action against contractor by injured employee of subcontractor, where plaintiff's complaint states amorphous cause of action alleging both active and passive negligence, contractor may implead subcontractor. Pugni v Lanning & Harris, Inc. (1949) 196 Misc 335, 92 NYS2d 21.

Where in action by employee of contractor latter is charged with both active and passive negligence, contractor may implead subcontractor as sole cause of injury despite contractor's liability for passive negligence. Strawn v Todd Shipyards Corp. (1948) 89 NYS2d 416.

In action by subcontractor's employee against general contractor and bricklaying subcontractor for personal injuries by being struck by brick falling from scaffold near where plaintiff was working, general contractor may implead bricklaying subcontractor and have verdict on cross-complaint against latter. Cohen v Tomasello Masons (1954) 283 AD 1104, 132 NYS2d 346.

In action against contractors and subcontractors on highway construction job to recover for death of construction worker struck by truck carting fill, contractor defendant, not owning nor controlling injuring truck, filed third-party complaint against chauffeur driving said truck, alleging that injury was caused by chauffeur's negligence, and third-party complaint was upheld, since its allegations, coupled with allegations of original complaint, establish that accident was caused by active negligence of chauffeur. Garger v Mt. Vernon T. Corp. (1955) 143 NYS2d 28.

In action by subcontractor against lessee of pier for damages caused by lessee's agent in preventing payment of subcontractor by contractor, where it is not possible to say that owner or lessee is not in position to recover from general contractor for damages resulting from improper supervision of job in which owner or lessee induces subcontractor to violate requirements of general contract, dismissal of third-party complaint by lessee against contractor without leave to amend was error. Unity S. M. Works v Farrell Lines (1955) 285 AD 879, 138 NYS2d 39.

In action by employee of subcontractor against general contractor for personal injuries due to fall from defective scaffold supplied by subcontractor, general contractor may implead subcontractor, where former was not guilty of any actionable statutory or common-law negligence and where latter was guilty of active negligence in directing employee to get on scaffold and do his own work. Gambella v John A. Johnson & Sons (1955) 285 AD 580, 140 NYS2d 208.

In action by employee of third-party defendant, hauling steel for steel company, injured while unloading steel beams from truck furnished by defendant and third-party plaintiff, where employee's complaint charged hauler only with neglect to warn plaintiff of manner of loading truck, and where third-party complaint against steel company alleged that sole responsibility of former was to transport steel in proper truck operated by competent driver, such complaint was insufficient. Coffey v Flower City C. & E. Co. (1956) 2 AD2d 191, 153 NYS2d 763, affd 2 NY2d 898, 161 NYS2d 149, 141 NE2d 632.

Impleader is proper where complaint alleges facts upon the proof of some of which defendant might be primarily liable for active negligence and upon proof of others of which defendant might be held secondarily liable for passive negligence. Vassiliades v Joseph P. Blitz, Inc. (1959) 22 Misc 2d 51, 193 NYS2d 959, affd 13 AD2d 539, 214 NYS2d 656 (involving violations of Labor Law §§ 200, 241).

46. Dealer and manufacturer

In action for damages for breach of warranty by dealer in sale of oil, dealer may not allege cause of action against manufacturer for loss of plaintiff's future business as result of such breach. Victory Painters & Decorators v Miller (1950) 198 Misc 196, 101 NYS2d 350.

47. Defrauder and plaintiff's agent

In action for fraud practiced upon plaintiff's husband as her agent, whereby she was induced to part with her corporate stock for less than its true value, defendant may not implead plaintiff's husband under doctrine of implied indemnification. Trachtenberg v Hershbein (1949) 87 NYS2d 912.

48. Employer and employee

Employee of defendant may not be brought in by third-party defendant, in action for damages from negligence of employee of defendant; such employee was not liable to third-party plaintiff for any part of his claim in main action. Wolf v V. La Rosa & Sons (1947) 272 AD 932, 71 NYS2d 320, affd 298 NY 597, 81 NE2d 329.

In action for death of plaintiff's intestate by falling through ceiling, fact that intestate was employee of third-party defendant and that compensation has been awarded for his death, will not necessarily defeat common-law right of recovery of defendant, record owner of premises. Tabor v Stewart (1950) 277 AD 1075, 100 NYS2d 697.

In action for personal injuries to worker, who fell into mortar mixing machine, against its owner, owner may implead employer of worker, claiming that if plaintiff recovers from defendant, latter will be entitled to indemnification from third-party defendant, and alleging acts and omissions upon proof of which defendant might be held liable for passive negligence or for secondary liability, by reason of negligence or primary liability on part of third-party defendant. Marzella v Carlson Hoist & Mach. Co. (1952) 280 AD 955, 116 NYS2d 289.

Where a plaintiff recovered against defendant and defendant had impleaded floor waxer on theory that he was active wrongdoer, defendant allowed recovery over against floor waxer and floor waxer not joint tortfeasor. Seiden v Savings & Loan Asso. (1958) 10 Misc 2d 720, 172 NYS2d 403.

Where a third party complaint alleges that the plaintiff was the employee of the third party defendant and the negligence was that of the third party defendant, a motion by the defendant and third party plaintiff to amend the answer to allege that the workmen's compensation law was the exclusive remedy will be denied, since an injured employee has the choice of compensation or common-law recovery against the third party, and where the movant does not allege that he is the employer or fellow employee, he has the status of a third party and as such is not entitled to plead the proposed defense. Favale v Jackson (1957) 8 Misc 2d 143, 163 NYS2d 438.

A defendant sued by plaintiff for injuries received cannot bring in the plaintiff's employer as a third-party-defendant solely on the theory that plaintiff had been a trespasser and had committed the trespass in the course of his employment for the employer. The trespass may change the standard of care due plaintiff but it does not make his employer liable to the defendant. The third-party complaint was insufficient. Fuscaldo v Midtown Warehouses, Inc. (1958) 16 Misc 2d 324, 181 NYS2d 628.

49. Employers of common employee

Where common employee of two corporate employers sues one of them for personal injuries while riding in car owned by both employers, employer sued may not implead other employer, since there would be no liability over. New Amsterdam Cas. Co. v Kirschenbaum (1948) 194 Misc 104, 85 NYS2d 866.

50. Garage owner and labor union

In action for damages to automobile kept in defendant's garage on its removal from garage by his employee, defendant could not implead labor union officer on theory of implied warrant of fitness or honesty of employees furnished by union. Adlman v Consolidated Garage Corp. (1949) 194 Misc 793, 87 NYS2d 773.

51. Grantor and grantee

In action to enjoin use of driveway, defendant may implead his grantor, thus disposing of various claims in one trial. Acco Products v Cooperative G.L.F. Holding Corp. (1950) 96 NYS2d 541, affd 277 AD 954, 99 NYS2d 725.

In mortgage foreclosure, former record holder of title to realty may intervene to stay or defeat action and to declare purported deed to mortgagor to be forgery and void. Harrison v Mary Bain Estates, Inc. (1956) 2 Misc 2d 52, 152 NYS2d 239, affd 2 AD2d 670, 153 NYS2d 552.

52. Insured and insurer

Where trial of issues relating to liability of third-party defendant under its contract of insurance, with issues in tort actions, would be prejudicial to third-party defendant, third-party complaint was dismissed without prejudice to third-party plaintiff to bring separate action against its insurer. Taplin v Stevens (1952) 280 AD 960, 117 NYS2d 606.

Where collision insurer paid collision insurance to insured, took assignment and then sued owner of other car in collision, defendant could not implead insured and counterclaim against him for damages in accident. Travelers Ins. Co. v Foeldes (1947) 192 Misc 613, 80 NYS2d 627.

In action for trespassing on plaintiff's land in excavating for cellar, defendant contractor may implead his insurer under indemnity policy. Caserta v Beaver Constr. Corp. (1949) 197 Misc 410, 95 NYS2d 131.

In action for wife for personal injuries based upon negligent operation of automobile by her husband, defendant's employee, against defendant, latter may implead her husband and insurer which had agreed to indemnify both said employer and employee in operating same, but action against insurer was severed to avoid disclosure that defendants were insured. Kane v Kane Ship Repair Corp. (1952) 202 Misc 530, 118 NYS2d 515.

In action for personal injury against insured, insured may implead insurer though carrier agreed to indemnify third-party plaintiff against loss from liability imposed upon it for damages on account of injuries sustained. Shapiro v New York (1953) 121 NYS2d 609.

In action on insured policy, insurer cannot implead wrongdoers without alleging that plaintiffs have assigned their cause of action to defendant (third-party plaintiff) or that defendant insurer has made payment on plaintiff's claim. Atlas Factors, Inc. v Ocean A. & Guarantee Corp. (1953) 121 NYS2d 175.

Where there is no claim on the basis of negligence and there is no claim against primary wrongdoer and where claim is based strictly on insurance contract which provides for subrogation only where there has been payment, and there has been no payment, impleader is improper. Washington Assur. Co. v Duncan (1955) 207 Misc 1042, 140 NYS2d 119.

Where third-party complaint by insured against automobile liability insurer alleged that insured duly notified insurer of replacement of insured's automobile within 30 days thereafter raised issue of fact which barred motion to dismiss. Rosenberg v Cassidy (1954) 135 NYS2d 87.

Where liability policy precluded action against insurer until judgment was obtained against insured such policy provision did not prevent insured when sued for personal injuries from impleading disclaiming insurer nor from obtaining judicial declaration of rights of parties under policy. Kahn v George E. Driscoll Co. (1955) 1 Misc 2d 405, 146 NYS2d 902.

53. —Insurer disclaiming liability

In guest's action against hotel keeper for loss of personalty by fire, insured defendant may implead insurer disclaiming liability. Leconna Cuban Boys v Kiamesha Concord (1949) 276 AD 808, 93 NYS2d 113.

Insurer of defendant who impleaded insurer by third-party complaint because insurer refused to defend automobile injury case, was denied dismissal if trial be without jury, and was granted separate trial if with jury. Remch v Grabow (1947) 193 Misc 731, 70 NYS2d 462.

In action for damages by defendant's automobile, defendant may not implead insurer who denied liability under policy. Chizik v Fuchs (1948) 193 Misc 297, 76 NYS2d 437.

Where plaintiff sued for negligent breach of storage contract, insured defendant may implead insurer who disclaimed liability and refused to defend. J. A. Ewing & McDonald, Inc. v Municipal Warehouse Co. (1948) 193 Misc 173, 81 NYS2d 559.

Where insured did not waive right to implead insurer, he may be impleaded, though denying liability under policy. Koolery v Lindemann (1949) 91 NYS2d 505.

Third party complaint by tortfeasor for judgment

over against insurance company, claiming coverage under a liability policy issued by insurance company, must set forth facts to show how third party plaintiff is an insured within terms of policy. Kaisted v New York City Housing Authority (1959) 9 AD2d 729, 192 NYS2d 406.

Insured defendant's third party complaint against insurer, alleging that insurer will be liable under its policy for whatever sum plaintiff recovers against defendant, and that insurer has disclaimed liability, states a good cause of action. Cook v Fogelsonger (1959) 21 Misc 2d 337, 193 NYS2d 259.

In automobile personal injury negligence action where defendant impleads disclaiming insurance carrier, carrier is entitled to severance and separate trial, to avoid possible prejudice, even though jury because of compulsory insurance requirement in New York would be aware that there is insurance. Santonocito v Suburban Oil Co. (1961) 27 Misc 2d 697, 211 NYS2d 571.

54. —Where policy bars joinder

Insured warehouseman, sued for injury to stored goods, may implead insurer, despite policy provision prohibiting action thereon until determination of warehouseman's liability. Brooklyn Yarn Dye Co. v Empire State Warehouses Corp. (1949) 88 NYS2d 621, affd 276 AD 611, 96 NYS2d 738.

Policy provision, barring action against insured except on basis of final judgment against insured or liquidation by agreement of parties with insurer's consent, did not bar third-party complaint by insured sued for loss of insured merchandise. Judy Negligee, Inc. v Portnoy (1949) 194 Misc 508, 89 NYS2d 656. See Adelman Mfg. Corp. v New York Wood Finisher's S. Co. (1950) 277 AD 1117, 100 NYS2d 867.

In action for breach of warranty of fitness and merchantability of materials sold to plaintiff by insured defendant, insured could implead insurer although policy barred action against insurer in absence of judgment against insured or written agreement of insured, claimant and insurer. Adelman Mfg. Corp. v N. Y. Wood Finisher's Supply Co. (1950) 277 AD 1117, 100 NYS2d 867.

Liability policy, barring "right to join insured as codefendant" was valid, barred right to implead liability insurer. Borgia v Loketch, Inc. (1951) 109 NYS2d 547.

Contract between automobile liability insurer and insured, barring joinder of insurer as codefendant in any action to determine insured's liability, barred impleader by insured sued for damages for negligence in maintaining gasoline pumps. Aulisio v California Oil Co. (1952) 202 Misc 1050, 120 NYS2d 582.

In action on hospital bill by hospital against former patient over two years after patient's discharge, insured patient may not implead hospitalization insurer where insurance contract required action thereon be commenced within two years, and where waiver of limitations was not shown.

Bronx Hospital v Stella (1953) 203 Misc 1017, 120 NYS2d 782.

55. Landlord and court clerk

In action by tenants against landlord for ejectment and damages for wrongful eviction, landlord may implead trial court clerk who failed to notify tenants of date of trial of ejectment action brought by landlord against plaintiffs, there being no such "mixture of claims" which would prevent bringing in such third party. Offiong v Wilson (1951) 278 AD 705, 103 NYS2d 330.

56. Landlord and mover

In action by tenant against landlord for injuries to tenant from falling over hand truck carelessly left in hallway, landlord may not implead hand truck owner, where complaint did not allege that landlord had no active duty to keep hallway free of obstruction. Bornhorst v Lyon (1952) 279 AD 820, 109 NYS2d 194.

57. Landlord and tenant

Lessee may be impleaded by landlord, sued for injury to infant while ascending from basement of defendant's building when cellar door closed and struck infant's head, where third-party complaint alleged that accident was due to active negligence of lessee. Schoenfeld v Four Leaf Clover Realty Corp. (1948) 273 AD 824, 76 NYS2d 526.

In action for injuries to employee of lessee of first floor of building when struck by plaster falling from second floor being repaired by lessee thereof, lessee of second floor, as original defendant, may implead lessee of first floor to whom original defendant had paid money under agreement by lessee of first floor to share proceeds with employee. Fortune v Hyle Holding Corp. (1947) 188 Misc 1011, 69 NYS2d 877.

In action against landlord for death of tenant's employee on falling down elevator shaft, landlord may implead tenant in control of premises. Clements v Rockefeller (1947) 189 Misc 885, 70 NYS2d 146.

Building owners, sued for injuries from fall down elevator shaft, could not sue tenant of third floor without setting forth lease to show tenant was obligated to indemnify owner. Verder v Schack (1948) 191 Misc 935, 79 NYS2d 700.

In action by tenant's employee against landlord for personal injuries from fall on stairway, landlord may implead tenant who had reserved control of premises. Sterenfeld v Lewittes (1951) 109 NYS2d 422.

In action against landlord by tenant's employee injured while washing windows because of defective anchor, landlord could not implead tenant as third party, though landlord claimed he had no knowledge that windows were cleaned from outside. McKay v Pedigree Fabricks (1947) 74 NYS2d 385.

In action for death of tenant's employee against landlord, fact that liability insurance policy had been obtained pursuant to terms of lease between parties, was no defense to action to determine liabilities between parties under landlord's third-party complaint against tenant for indemnity. Clements v Rockefeller (1947) 189 Misc 889, 76 NYS2d 493.

In actions by tenants against landlords for damages from lack of heat, defendant may implead another tenant who had agreed to heat premises. Braun v Gardner (1948) 191 Misc 844, 79 NYS2d 299.

Where tenant's daughter brought action against landlord based upon dangerous condition of leased premises, landlord's third party complaint against tenant was dismissed where it failed to contain allegation to effect that condition complained of by plaintiff resulted from misuse or neglect by tenant. Getter v Jad Operating Co. (1956) 157 NYS2d 213.

58. Landlord and refrigerator company

In action by tenant for injuries from defective gas refrigerator supplied by landlord, landlord may implead refrigerator company which had contracted to keep it in good repair and third-party complaint was held sufficient on ground that third-party defendant will not be permitted to avoid responsibility for nonperformance or breach of contractual duty independently owing to owner landlord. Swanson v 97 Fifth Ave. Corp. (1955) 141 NYS2d 125, affd 286 AD 994, 144 NYS2d 711, affd 1 AD2d 768, 149 NYS2d 208.

59. Manufacturer and employer

In action against manufacturer for injuries received in operating allegedly defective machine, manufacturer could not implead plaintiff's employer because its liability depended only upon proof that it had manufactured a defective machine, and this, if proven, would constitute it an active wrongdoer thus precluding it from recovering over against employer. Wegorzewski v De Mattia Machine & Tool Co. (1961) 12 AD2d 825, 210 NYS2d 426.

60. Motorist and owner

In personal injury action by passenger in automobile driven by her husband against owner of car, latter may implead former for active negligence. Halpern v Four Wheels, Inc. (1950) 96 NYS2d 585.

61. Motorist and physician

Motorist, held liable to plaintiff for injuries in automobile accident, may implead physicians who treated plaintiff and who because of their malpractice allegedly increase plaintiff's recovery. Clark v Halstead (1948) 193 Misc 739, 85 NYS2d 349, affd 276 AD 17, 93 NYS2d 49.

In action by automobile passenger, injured in collision between automobile and taxicab, against owners of two vehicles, automobile owner impleaded plaintiff's husband who was operating automobile and who was officer of corporate owner of automobile, and on trial jury rendered verdict against both defendants, defendant automobile owner was entitled to judgment against third-party defendant for amount of judgment which third-party plaintiff has to pay. Chirichella v Shamrock Cab Corp. (1954) 207 Misc 371, 138 NYS2d 82.

62. Motorist and repairman

In action against motorist for negligence in driving at excessive speed, lack of control and failure to observe stationary car ahead, defendant could not implead repairman engaged to fix brakes, on claims of negligent inspection of brakes, breaches of contract and warranty. Kalkin v Marken (1949) 87 NYS2d 839.

Where automobile owner was sued by passenger for personal injuries and cause of action was predicated on ownership of vehicle, owner may implead borrower of car and his employee who was driving it, as persons actively negligent and primarily liable. Traub v Dinzler (1955) 309 NY 395, 131 NE2d 564.

In action for personal injuries against three motorists, wherein complaint alleged that named defendant did not have his car under control or maintain proper lookout, such defendant may not implead brake repair serviceman on ground of negligent failure of brakes from negligent repair, and such third-party complaint was dismissed. Gomer v Cypress Cab Corp. (1952) 116 NYS2d 773.

63. Municipality and contractor

Where motorist, injured when his automobile skidded on highway, sued city for nuisance and negligent construction, city may implead contractor who had contracted to indemnify city. Fortune v Syracuse (1948) 191 Misc 738, 78 NYS2d 775.

In action for personal injuries from stepping into road trench improperly filled by construction corporation granted permit to excavate street to construct sewer for abutting owner, village may implead construction corporation. Zeuner v Bronxville (1951) 278 AD 790, 104 NYS2d 6.

Third party practice applies to cases involving municipal or other public corporations. Valstrey Service Corp. v Board of Elections (1957) 2 NY2d 413, 161 NYS2d 52, 141 NE2d 565.

64. Owner and architect

In contractor's action to foreclose mechanic's lien, owner, counterclaiming for damages for poor workmanship, may implead architect who approved contractor's work, on ground that architect breached his contract to supervise work. Slutzky v Hinderstein (1950) 97 NYS2d 255.

65. Owner and bailee

In action for injury to defendant's employee by negligent operation of excavation crane by another employee of defendant, defendant may not implead bailee to whom defendant rented crane without alleging express or implied indemnity by such bailee. Werbowsky v Smith (1951) 106 NYS2d 671.

66. Owner and contractor

Defendant owner, sued for personal injury due to falling scaffold, may implead plaintiff's employer, painting contractor, as indemnitor, though latter may become indirectly liable for injury to employee for which there could not be direct recovery because of employer's compliance with workmen's compensation law. Schaller v Republic Aviation Corp. (1948) 193 Misc 60, 83 NYS2d 540.

In action for wrongful death from accumulation of combustible matter, defendant landlord and tenants may implead contractor employed to install dust removal system, where control and possession was taken by contractor. Monteverdi v French Realty Corp. (1948) 274 AD 945, 83 NYS2d 758.

Defendant owner, sued for personal injury to employee of contractor due to defective steel hoist, may implead injured person's employer who had contracted to do steel work, by alleging that such injury was due to affirmative and active negligence of contractor, though original complaint charged both active and passive negligence. Johnson v Endicott-Johnson Corp. (1951) 278 AD 626, 101 NYS2d 922.

In action against building owner by window washer for personal injuries by fall due to defective safety belt, owner may implead contractor, plaintiff's employer, by alleging that contractor was obligated to indemnify owner. McManus v Board of Education (1951) 106 NYS2d 51.

In action against both landlord and storekeeper for personal injuries when customer of store stepped on manhole cover and fell, landlord cannot implead contractor who repaired manhole cover, since landlord's duty to make exterior repairs rendered him joint tortfeasor with contractor. Barber v Loblaw Groceterias (1952) 113 NYS2d 699.

In action by contractor's employee for injuries due to negligence of owner's servant in causing hand truck to strike ladder on which plaintiff was working, said owner and servant as defendants may not implead contractor by alleging that he agreed to indemnify owner and employees against liability for negligence of contractor despite any contributory negligence of owner. Sorenson v Lowe (1954) 283 AD 1118, 132 NYS2d 343.

In action for personal injuries by falling on defective step in public hallway of multiple dwelling owned by defendant, latter may not implead contractor who negligently repaired premises, since MDL § 78 imposes upon owner non-delegable duty to keep premises in good repair. Steiner v Elsand Properties, Inc. (1952) 113 NYS2d 51.

In action for injuries sustained while working on defendant's transport vessel, defendant may implead contractor who agreed to perform work and furnish material for such vessel and to indemnify defendant vessel owner against liability for negligence of contractor and its employees while working on such vessel. Joseph v Atlantic B. I. Works (1954) 132 NYS2d 671.

In common-law action for negligence for injuries on steamship, owner may implead independent contractor who was plaintiff's employer repairing ship. Goodard v Shasta S. S. Co. 9 FRD 10.

Where city was held liable to pedestrian for personal injuries from fall on sidewalk on ground that city had constructive notice of dangerous condition, city could recover full amount of judgment from contractor, impleaded by city, where contractor created dangerous condition in demolishing building, since city was only passively negligent whereas contractor was actively negligent. Shapiro v New York (1955) 141 NYS2d 320.

In action against county for injuries to infant thrown from back of truck on striking depression in county road, county impleaded construction company which in turn impleaded truck owners as causing depression, and latter in turn impleaded truck owners, alleging latters' negligence in driving truck, third-party complaint against truck owners was insufficient, since construction company and truck owners were necessarily joint tort-feasors as alleged by defendant county and construction company. Fletcher v Broome (1955) 286 AD 286, 143 NYS2d 76.

In action for wrongful death of contractor's employee who was killed in fall while working on defendant's property, where, from the allegations of original complaint, it was possible that contractor's active negligence was primary cause of employee's death and defendant owner was guilty of passive negligence, owner's third-party complaint against contractor was held sufficient. Gallagher v Hill Greenhouse Constr., Inc. (1960) 23 Misc 2d 167, 197 NYS2d 234.

67. Owner and subcontractor

In action for personal injury to subcontractor's employee who fell from construction scaffold against owner and general contractor, defendants may implead subcontractor whose duty allegedly was to furnish scaffold and where defective scaffolding would be active negligence of third-party defendant. Carlson v Cross-Siclare & Sons (1951) 106 NYS2d 617.

In action by employee of subcontractor for personal injuries from fall on defendant's premises on which building was being constructed, owner may implead subcontractor where plaintiff charges owner with both active and passive negligence, and third-party complaint alleging that third-party plaintiff was merely passively negligent and that impleaded third-party defendant was affirmatively or actively negligent could not be dismissed prior to trial. Cardillo v Marble Bldg. (1955) 142 NYS2d 721.

In action by employee of subcontractor against owner and builder, general contractor and several subcontractors for personal injuries caused by fall through unguarded ventilator shaft, predicated on claim that such failure to guard was violation of statutory duty, third-party complaint by such defendants against plaintiff's employer who was also subcontractor, alleging that third-party defendant had sole control of lumber guarding shaftway and prevented third-party plaintiffs from having access to shaft, was sufficient. Coviello v N. Y. Life Ins.

Co. (1955) 141 NYS2d 626, affd 286 AD 1075, 146 NYS2d 667.

68. Owner and elevator or escalator company

In action for personal injuries to passenger alighting from elevator in apartment owned by defendant, allegedly due to defective and unlighted elevator, owner may implead elevator company who had agreed to maintain same by alleging that latter had made defective repairs. Traeger v Farragut Gardens Co. (1951) 201 Misc 18, 107 NYS2d 525.

In action by tenant against landlord for personal injuries when struck by door of self-service automatic elevator, landlord may not implead elevator company where landlord knew that door was defective and failed to remedy defect, since landlord was guilty of active negligence. Meltzer v Temple Estates (1952) 203 Misc 602, 116 NYS2d 546.

Store owner, in action for personal injuries to escalator passenger by sudden stopping of escalator, may not implead escalator company which had agreed to service escalator but had no control of it. Stafford v Sibley, Lindsay & Curr Co. (1952) 280 AD 495, 114 NYS2d 177.

Where employee of elevator company killed in defendant's building shaft by other elevator operated by defendant's employee the building owner's third party complaint cannot be dismissed in advance of trial, since the jury must determine the questions of active and passive negligence. Goodrich v First Nat. Bank (1954) 11 Misc 2d 583, 132 NYS2d 678, affd 285 AD2d 849, 137 NYS2d 641.

69. Owner and elevator operator

In action against owner of leased factory building for personal injuries to employee from improper maintenance and construction of elevator shaftway doors, owner may implead fellow employee allegedly in actual control of elevator and actively negligent. Giunta v Parker, Stearns & Co. (1952) 280 AD 807, 113 NYS2d 494.

Third party complaint properly dismissed where plaintiff in main action against owner of building alleged that defendant owner was negligent in maintenance of elevator and owner by third party complaint against tenants alleged accident was caused by tenants and such third party defendant tenants contended that according to the third party complaint they were joint tort feasors not liable to the owner or that the third party plaintiff had a complete defense to the main action. Balch v Richby Realty Corp. (1958) 4 NY2d 1006, 177 NYS2d 519, 152 NE2d 538.

70. Owners; successive (compare 79, infra, vendor and purchaser)

Successive owners of building may not be impleaded by former owner on theory that new owners assumed defendant's liability for rental of shoring material. Heydt-Mugler Co. v Westerman Constr. Corp. (1947) 188 Misc 546, 68 NYS2d 361, affd on reh 189 Misc 199, 71 NYS2d 385, affd 190 Misc 990, 77 NYS2d 356.

71. Payee and drawer

In action by bank against seller-payee for money mistakenly paid on check after buyer-drawer had stopped payment for breach of warranty, seller could not implead buyer as for breach of contract, because buyer would not be liable over if bank be successful. Chase Nat. Bank v Battat (1950) 277 AD 49, 97 NYS2d 713.

In action for injuries to plaintiff by fall through trap door hole in grocery store, defendant owner may implead purchaser of store who had possession and control when injury occurred. Bergman v Geroge (1952) 202 Misc 998, 117 NYS2d 27.

72. Purchaser and broker

In action for specific performance of contract to sell realty, defendant may not interplead broker who fraudulently induced defendant to sign contract. Schutrum v Horton (1947) 272 AD 1086, 74 NYS2d 728.

73. Renter and registered truck owner

In action for death of employee of renter against owner of defective truck, owner may implead renter as party guilty of active negligence. Elfeld v Burkham Auto Renting Co. (1949) 196 Misc 446, 92 NYS2d 249.

In action for death of decedent struck by truck driven by defendant and owned by codefendant, defendant owner may implead hirer of truck with driver, but defendant driver may not implead such hirer. Roscher v Cecere (1954) 132 NYS2d 840.

74. Retailer and manufacturer

Retailer and manufacturer of ladder which collapsed and injured plaintiff, see Flanagan v Acme Scaffold Co. (1950) 277 AD 988, 100 NYS2d 15.

75. Retailer and packer

In action for injuries from eating poisonous pork, defendant retailer need not prove payment of judgment against him before proceeding on third-party complaint against packer. Occhipinti v Buscemi (1947) 71 NYS2d 766.

76. Seller and supplier

In action by manufacturer against steel company for breach of contract to deliver steel, defendant may implead another steel company which had contracted to deliver steel to defendant. B.M.C. Mfg. Corp. v Tarshis (1951) 278 AD 266, 104 NYS2d 254.

77. Ship operator and stevedore

Where a ship operator had a contract with a warranty by stevedoring contractor to load ship in a safe and workmanlike manner, in action by stevedore's employee against ship operator for personal injuries, ship owner's third-party complaint against stevedore for indemnity based on stevedore's negligence in performance of contract, stated a cause of action. Indemnity based on the contract and not on account of the injury as the gravamen of the action. Merriweather v Boland &

Cornelius (1959) 6 NY2d 417, 190 NYS2d 65, 160 NE2d 717.

78. Surety and subcontractor

In action by contractor against surety of subcontractor for latter's default on contract, surety may implead subcontractor as being liable over to surety for plaintiff's claim. Psaty & Fuhrman, Inc. v Continental Cas. Co. (1951) 278 AD 159, 103 NYS2d 849.

79. Vendor and purchaser (compare 70, supra, owners; successive)

In action for death of plaintiff's intestate by falling through ceiling, employee of third-party defendant, complaint alleging that premises were in exclusive possession and control of third-party defendant who had purchased same under contract from defendant record owner and that negligent acts were primarily those of third-party defendant, was sufficient. Tabor v Stewart (1950) 277 AD 1075, 100 NYS2d 697.

80. Warehouseman and landlord

In action against warehouseman on warranty that warehouse was fireproof, defendant may implead landlord who alone knew that fire torches had been used on building. Cunningham v Cirker's Moving & Storage Co. (1949) 195 Misc 1005, 89 NYS2d 33.

81. Wife in husband's action for partnership accounting

Subd 4 of CPA § 193-a was declared to be broad enough to authorize wife, as real party in interest, to intervene in husband's action for family partnership accounting. Schwartz v Klein (1947) 188 Misc 665, 72 NYS2d 386.

E. Summons in Third-Party Practice

82. Generally

Relation to main action is sole requirement of third-party practice. Fortune v Hyle Holding Corp. (1947) 188 Misc 1011, 69 NYS2d 877.

Form of third-party summons, complying with Rule 54 (§ 1007 herein), held sufficient. Hameline Co. v Mohawk Containers (1951) 107 NYS2d 494.

Applied generally. Schaller v Republic Aviation Corp. (1948) 193 Misc 60, 83 NYS2d 540.

Foreign corporation, doing no business in New York, may not be served here with third-party summons. Flanagan v Acme Scaffold Co. (1950) 277 AD 988, 100 NYS2d 15.

83. Courts

Form of third-party summons prescribed by RCP Rule 54 (§ 1007 herein) was inapplicable to Albany City Court Act. Hirsch v Albany Sav. Bank (1948) 191 Misc 415, 81 NYS2d 250; Hirsch v Albany Sav. Bank (1948) 192 Misc 505, 81 NYS2d 253, affd 276 AD 792, 92 NYS2d 636.

RCP 54 (§ 1007 herein) applied to NYC municipal court, modified to MCC § 20, prescribing service of summons within five days. Thomas J. Nolan, Inc. v Martin & William Smith, Inc. (1949) 193 Misc 877, 85 NYS2d 380, affd 85 NYS2d 387.

84. Retrospective operation

This rule RCP 54 (§ 1007 herein) applied to accrued, pending and future actions. Fortune v Hyle Holding Corp. (1947) 188 Misc 1011, 69 NYS2d 877.

85. Service

Application to court is unnecessary; defendant simply serves summons in form prescribed by this rule (§ 1007), with copy of verified complaint and copies of all pleadings on person to be made third party. Van Pelt v New York (1947) 188 Misc 995, 69 NYS2d 116.

Service of summons by plaintiff on third-party defendant is unnecessary; plaintiff need only apply to amend original summons. Jacobs v Driscoll (1948) 78 NYS2d 813.

FORMS

Form   1—Summons in third-party practice
Form   2—Third-party summons, another form
Form   3—Third-party summons, another form
Form   4—Third-party summons, another form
Form   5—Third-party summons, another form
Form   6—Third-party complaint
Form   7—Third-party plaintiff's complaint—owner and lessee
Form   8—Third-party plaintiff's complaint—owner and lessee of property
Form   9—Third-party plaintiff's complaint—guarantor and maker of promissory note
Form 10—Third-party plaintiff's complaint—manufacturer of machine against employer of injured user thereof
Form 11—Verification of third-party complaint

Form 1

Summons in Third-Party Practice

SUPREME COURT, COUNTY OF __¹_____

Don Doe, Plaintiff
  against
Roy Roe, Defendant and Third-Party   Third-Party Summons
  Plaintiff,   Index No. — [if assigned]
  against
Max Poe, Third-Party Defendant

To the above-named third-party defendant:

    You are hereby summoned to answer the complaint of the third-party plaintiff and the complaint of the original plaintiff, copies of which are herewith served upon you, and to serve copies of your answer upon the undersigned attorney for the third-party plaintiff and upon __²_____, plaintiff's attorney, whose address is __³_____, within twenty days after the service of the summons and third-party complaint, exclusive of the day of service. In case of your failure to answer the complaint of the third-party plaintiff, judgment will be taken against you by default for the relief demanded in the third-party complaint.

    Dated: __⁴_____

__⁵_____ _____
Attorney for Defendant and
Third-Party Plaintiff, Roy Roe,
[Office & P. O. Address]
Telephone No.

Form 2

Third-Party Summons, Another Form

SUPREME COURT, COUNTY OF __¹_____

Don Doe, Plaintiff,
  against
Roy Roe, Defendant.
_____
                           Third-Party Summons
Roy Roe, Defendant and Third-Party   Index No. — [if assigned]
  Plaintiff,
  against
Max Poe, Third-Party Defendant.

To the above-named third-party defendant:

    You are hereby summoned [same as preceding Form 1]

Form 3

Third-Party Summons, Another Form

SUPREME COURT, COUNTY OF __¹_____

Don Doe, Plaintiff,
  against
Roy Roe, and Tom Roe, Defendants.
_____

Roy Roe, Codefendant and Third-Party
  Plaintiff,   Third-Party Summons
  against   Index No. — [if assigned]
Max Coe, Third-Party Defendant.
_____

Max Coe, Second Third-Party Plaintiff,
  against
Sam Poe, Second Third-Party Defendant.

To the above-named Sam Poe, second third-party defendant:

You are hereby summoned to answer the complaints of the original plaintiff, of the first third-party plaintiff, and of the second third-party plaintiff, copies of which are herewith served upon you, and to serve copies of your answer upon original plaintiff's attorney, whose address is __2_____, upon first third-party plaintiff's attorney, whose address is __3_____, and upon second third-party plaintiff's attorney, whose address is __4_____, within twenty days after the service of this third-party summons and third-party complaint, exclusive of the day of service. In case of your failure to answer the complaint of the second third-party plaintiff, Max Coe, judgment will be taken against you by default for the relief demanded in the second third-party complaint of Max Coe.

Dated: __5_____.

__6_____

Attorney for Second Third-
Party Plaintiff, Max Coe,
[Office & P. O. Address]
Telephone No.

Form 4

Third-Party Summons, Another Form

__1_____ Court, __2_____ County

__3_____,
Plaintiff
　against
__4_____,
Defendant and Third-Party Plaintiff
　against
__5_____

Third-Party Summons
Index No. __6__

To the above named third-party defendant:

YOU ARE HEREBY SUMMONED to answer the third-party complaint of the third-party plaintiff, and the complaint of the plaintiff, copies of which together with copies of all prior pleadings in this action are herewith served upon you, and to serve copies of your answer upon the undersigned, attorney for the third-party plaintiff and upon __7_____, attorney for plaintiff, whose address is __8_____, within twenty days after the service of this summons, third-party complaint, and complaint, exclusive of the day of service, or if service is made by any means other than by personal delivery to you within the state, within thirty days after such service is complete. In case of your failure to appear or answer, judgment will be taken against you by default for the relief demanded in the third-party complaint.

Dated: __9_____, 19_10_.

__11_____

Attorney for defendant
and third-party plaintiff
__12_____ Office and P. O. Address
Telephone No. __13__

Form 5

Third-Party Summons, Another Form [Official Form 22]

SUPREME COURT OF THE STATE OF NEW YORK
COUNTY OF NEW YORK

R.S.T., Inc. Plaintiff,
  against
U.V.W., Inc., Defendant.

U.V.W., Inc., Defendant and	Third-Party Complaint
Third-Party Plaintiff,	Index No.
against	

X.Y.Z., Inc., Third-Party Defendant.

To the above-named third-party defendant:

You are hereby summoned and required to serve upon the third-party plaintiff's attorney an answer to the annexed complaint of the third-party plaintiff, which is herewith served upon you together with all prior pleadings in the action, within twenty days after the service thereof, exclusive of the day of service, or within thirty days after service is complete if service is made by any method other than personal delivery to you within the State of New York. In case of your failure to answer, judgment will be taken against you by default for the relief demanded in the third-party complaint.

Dated:

[Print name]
_____

Attorney for Third-
Party Plaintiff
Address:
Telephone Number:

Form 6

Third-Party Complaint [Official Form 22]

SUPREME COURT OF THE STATE OF NEW YORK
COUNTY OF NEW YORK

R.S.T., Inc., Plaintiff,
  against
U.V.W., Inc., Defendant.

U.V.W., Inc., Defendant and	Third-Party Complaint
Third-Party Plaintiff,	Index No.
against	

X.Y.Z., Inc., Third-Party Defendant.

1. [For form of allegation of parties' incorporation, see Form 2 of CPLR 3015.]

2. At all times herein mentioned, third-party defendant was in the business of manufacturing and selling building supplies to wholesalers and others, and third-party plaintiff was a wholesaler engaged in the business of selling building supplies to building contractors and others.

3. On or about June 1, 1966, third-party plaintiff purchased from third-party defendant certain building supplies warranted by third-party defendant to be merchantable and fit for their ordinary use as building supplies.

4. On or about June 8, 1966, third-party sold these building supplies to plaintiff, a building contractor.

5. On or about December 1, 1966, plaintiff commenced an action against third-party plaintiff to recover damages for breach of warranty with respect to these building supplies. A copy of the complaint is attached hereto.

6. On or about December 5, 1966, third-party plaintiff gave written notice to third-party defendant of the claimed breach of warranty.

7. If plaintiff recovers judgment against third-party plaintiff, third-party plaintiff will be entitled to recover from third-party defendant the amount of such judgment.

Wherefore third-party plaintiff demands judgment against third-party defendant for all sums that may be adjudged against third-party plaintiff in favor of the plaintiff, plus costs and disbursements.

[Print name]
_____

Attorney for Third-
Party Plaintiff
Address:
Telephone Number:

Form 7

Third-Party Plaintiff's Complaint—Owner and Lessee

[Title of court and cause,   Third-party Complaint
as in Form No. 1]   Index No. — [if assigned]

Third-party plaintiff, by his attorney, __1____, as and for his third-party complaint and cause of action against third-party defendant, alleges:

1. On and prior to the __2__ day of __3____, 19_4_, defendant and third-party plaintiff, [Roy Roe], was the owner of premises No. __5____ Avenue, in the Borough of __6____, City of New York.

2. On the __7__ day of __8____, 19_9_, said premises, including the lot, building and appurtenances, were leased in their entirety to [Leo Poe], third-party defendant, for a term of years commencing on the __10__ day of __11____, 19_12_, to the __13__ day of __14____, 19_15_.

3. At the time of the leasing of the aforesaid premises, the aforesaid building contained a number of elevators, including an elevator designated by [#17382].

4. At all times hereinafter mentioned [Leo Poe] conducted a business at the aforesaid premises in connection with which it employed certain persons.

5. Upon information and belief, that on and prior to the __16__ day of __17____, 19_18_ it had in its employ [Don Doe], plaintiff in this action.

6. Upon information and belief, plaintiff alleges in his complaint that on or about the __19__ day of __20____, 19_21_, plaintiff was employed by [Leo Poe] at the premises __22____ Avenue, Borough of __23____, City of New York, as a stock clerk and porter, and that while engaged in his duties for his employer used a certain elevator located at the aforesaid premises, which elevator was designated by [#17382], and took the aforesaid elevator to the 7th floor of the premises, left the elevator there and while he was absent, the elevator was removed from the said floor to a higher point in the elevator shaft, and when plaintiff thereafter returned to the elevator shaft, upon opening the doors, fell into the shaftway through the pit, and received the injuries alleged in his complaint, to plaintiff's claimed damages in the sum of Twenty-five thousand ($25,000) Dollars.

7. Upon information and belief, at all times hereinafter mentioned in complaint and third-party complaint, third-party defendant, [Leo Poe], his agents, servants or employees, was in operation and control of the premises __24____ Avenue, Borough of __25____, City of New York, more particularly, the elevator shaftway and elevator doors of the elevator designated by [#17382].

8. Upon information and belief, any damages suffered by plaintiff at the time and place mentioned in complaint, to wit, the __26__ day of __27____, 19_28_, at the premises __29____ Avenue, Borough of __30____, City of New York, if sustained by reason of the negligence of defendant, [Roy Roe], same were due to the primary

negligence of third-party defendant, [Leo Poe], his agents, servants and employees in permitting the operation of the elevator from the place left by the intestate to a higher point in the elevator shaftway without giving notice to the plaintiff of its removal; in failing to keep the elevator keys in a safe place and under the supervision of a responsible person; and in violation of the provisions of the Labor Law of the State of New York, the Rules of the Department of Labor, the Rules of the Board of Standards and Appeals and the Rules and Ordinances of the City of New York relating to elevators; in disregarding these rules for a long time prior to __31_____ __32__, 19_33_; in failing to exercise care and caution under the circumstances then and there existing, and that the defendant negligently and carelessly failed to provide or safeguard against occurrences or accidents, which happened to plaintiff, and was otherwise careless and negligent in other respects without any negligence on the part of the defendant, [Roy Roe], contributing thereto, and if defendant, [Roy Roe], is held liable in any respect, it will be due to the primary negligence of third-party defendant, [Leo Poe], his agents, servants and employees, and that third-party defendant, [Leo Poe], is and will be liable to [Roy Roe] for any and all damages that he may sustain by reason of the aforesaid premises, together with all costs expended in the defense of the action.

WHEREFORE, third-party plaintiff, [Roy Roe], demands judgment dismissing plaintiff's complaint, together with the costs and disbursements of this action, and in the event that a judgment is rendered against said third-party plaintiff, that he have judgment over and against third-party defendant, [Leo Poe], in the same amount or such proportionate amount as is in accordance with the provisions of the Civil Practice Law and Rules, together with the costs and disbursements of this action.

> __34_____
> Attorney for Defendant and Third-
> Party Plaintiff, [Roy Roe],
> [Office & P. O. Address]
> Telephone No.

To __35_____
    Attorney for Plaintiff
    [Office & P. O. Address]

[Verification as in Form 11]

Form 8

Third-Party Plaintiff's Complaint—Owner and Lessee of Property

| [Title of court and cause, | Third-party Complaint |
| as in Form 1] | Index No. — [if assigned] |

Third-party plaintiff above-named, by his attorneys, __1_____, as and for his third-party complaint and cause of action against third-party defendant above-named, alleges:

1. At all times mentioned herein and in plaintiff's complaint, third-party plaintiff was the owner of the building and premises known as No. __2__ Avenue, Borough of __3_____, City of __4_____.

2. On or about the __5__ day of __6_____, 19_7_, third-party defendant and Apex Corporation, third-party plaintiff's predecessor in title, entered into an agreement of lease, whereby the latter leased to third-party defendant a certain store and cellar space in a building situated at the southeast corner of __8_____ Avenue and __9_____ Avenue, in the Borough of __10_____, City of __11_____, more particularly described as follows:

"The store space immediately adjoining the corner store at the southeast corner of __12_____ and __13_____ Avenues to the south and somewhat to the east of said corner store, being in width not less than 45 feet (inside measurements from wall to wall) and running to a depth of approximately 80 feet; thence northerly along a line approximately 20 feet to the southerly line of __14_____ Avenue; thence approximately 20 feet easterly along said __15_____ Avenue line; thence southerly along the lot line 100 feet; thence westerly along the building line approximately 20 feet; and thence northerly along a line approximately 35 feet; the whole forming a "T" shaped store having a floor area of approximately 5,600 square feet with the base fronting on __16_____ Avenue and running back to the rear of the lot line.

And also the cellar space directly underneath and in line with said store, plus an added area of approximately 400 square feet to the south and an added area of approximately 140 square feet to the north and west of the store lines, the whole forming a "T" shaped cellar having a floor area of approximately 6,140 square feet, its base, as in the case of the store, fronting on __17_____ Avenue.

And also an absolute and exclusive right of an entry (ingress, egress and loading) from __18_____ Avenue to the cellar space aforedescribed in front of and underneath the store immediately adjoining the Tenant's premises to the south and east.

And also an absolute and exclusive right of an entry (ingress, egress and loading) on __19_____ Avenue to the cellar space aforedescribed in front of and underneath the store immediately adjoining the Tenant's premises to the north and east," together with appurtenances to said demised premises.

3. Subsequent to the __20_ day of __21_____, 19_22_, and prior to the __23_ day of __24_____, 19_25_, the third-party plaintiff acquired all the right, title and interest of said Apex Corporation in said premises, including the aforementioned agreement of lease.

4. Said agreement of lease was in full force and effect at all times mentioned herein and in plaintiff's complaint.

5. It is alleged in plaintiff's complaint that on the __26_ day of __27_____, 19_28_, defendant (third-party plaintiff) owned, operated, maintained and controlled the building and premises known as No. __29_____ Avenue, Borough of __30_____, City of __31_____, more particularly the basement and cellar doors located on the sidewalk on the __32_____ Avenue side of the said premises; that while plaintiff, being lawfully on said premises, was ascending from the basement thereof to the sidewalk on the __33_____ Avenue side of the said premises, one of the two doors forming the said cellar doors fell and struck his head, resulting in severe injuries; that said injuries were caused by the negligence of defendant in failing to properly equip and maintain said cellar doors so as to prevent them from falling, as a result of which a nuisance was committed, without any fault on the part of the said infant plaintiff contributing thereto; that by reason thereof plaintiff was damaged in the sum of $25,000.00.

6. On the __34_ day of __35_____, 19_36_, the aforementioned cellar doors were in the possession of and operated, maintained and controlled by the third-party defendant.

7. If the allegations of plaintiff's complaint be established, and if plaintiff's damages were caused by negligence other than that of the plaintiff, such negligence was that of third-party defendant, his agents, servants or employees in failing to maintain, operate, control and equip the said cellar doors in a careful and prudent manner and in accordance with the terms and conditions of the aforesaid agreement of lease; that such negligence on the part of third-party defendant was primary and active, and that any negligence on the part of the third-party plaintiff was merely secondary and passive.

8. In the event that plaintiff recovers a judgment against third-party plaintiff by reason of the facts set forth in plaintiff's complaint, such liability on the part of third-party plaintiff, by operation of law or otherwise, will have been caused and brought about by the acts and affirmative wrongdoing and conduct and the negligence and carelessness of third-party defendant, his agents, servants and employees, and will not have been caused or brought about by any active or affirmative negligence or carelessness on the part of third-party plaintiff, his agents, servants or employees.

9. By reason of the aforesaid, third-party defendant is primarily liable for any

injuries or damages that were sustained by plaintiff, and third-party defendant is required to indemnify third-party plaintiff for any damages it may suffer on account of the occurrence mentioned in plaintiff's complaint.

WHEREFORE, third-party plaintiff demands judgment against third-party defendant for all the sums that may be adjudged against third-party plaintiff, together with the costs and disbursements of this action.

___³⁷_____

Attorney for Third-Party Plaintiff,
[Office & P. O. Address]
Telephone No.

[Verification, as in Form 11]

Form 9

Third-Party Plaintiff's Complaint—Guarantor and Maker of Promissory Note

Third-party Complaint

[Title of court and cause]   Index No. — [if assigned]

Third-party plaintiff above-named, by his attorney, _1_____, as and for his third-party complaint and cause of action against third-party defendant above-named, alleges:

1. On or about the _2_ day of _3_____, 19_4_, the third-party defendant at _5_____, made and delivered to the third-party plaintiff, for a valuable consideration received, his promissory note in writing, dated on that day, whereby said third-party defendant promised to pay to the order of the third-party plaintiff at the City of _6_____, New York the sum of $_7_ on the _8_ day of _9_____, 19_10_ with interest at the rate of _11_% per annum.

2. Thereafter, and before the maturity of the said note, and for a good and valuable consideration, the third-party plaintiff duly endorsed the said note and negotiated and delivered it to the plaintiff who is now the owner and holder thereof.

3. Upon information and belief the note was duly presented for payment at the time of the maturity thereof by the plaintiff and in accordance with the terms of the said note and payment then and there duly demanded, but payment was refused and the same was not paid.

4. Upon information and belief, thereupon, the said note was duly protested for nonpayment, and due and timely notice thereof was given to the third-party defendant.

5. No part of the said note has been paid.

6. In the event that plaintiff recovers the judgment against third-party plaintiff by reason of the facts set forth in plaintiff's complaint, such liability on the part of third-party plaintiff by operation of law or otherwise will also be the liability of the third-party defendant, and as a result of the premises the third-party defendant will be liable to the third-party plaintiff for any judgment recovered by the plaintiff against the third-party plaintiff.

WHEREFORE, third-party plaintiff demands judgment against third-party defendant for all sums that may be adjudged against third-party plaintiff, together with the costs and disbursements of this action.

___¹²_____

Attorney for Third-Party Plaintiff
Office & P. O. Address
Telephone No.

Form 10

Third-Party Plaintiff's Complaint—Manufacturer of Machine Against Employer of Injured User Thereof

Supreme Court, State of New York
County of Nassau

Eugenia Wegorzewski and
     Stanley Wegorzewski,
Plaintiffs,   Third-party Complaint
     against   Index No. __1__
DeMattia Machine & Tool Co., Inc.,
Defendant.
DeMattia Machine & Tool Co., Inc.,
Third-Party Plaintiff,
     against
R & C Maulding Company,
Third-Party Defendant

The defendant above named as and for its Third-Party Complaint against R & C Moulding Company by its attorney __2_____, respectfully shows to this Court and alleges upon information and belief as follows:

FIRST: That at all times hereinafter mentioned the Defendant Third-Party Plaintiff was and now is a corporation with its principal office for the regular transaction of its business in the State of New Jersey where it manufactures a certain plastic injector machine.

SECOND: Upon information and belief that at all times mentioned in the complaint and for some time prior thereto the R & C Moulding Company, hereinafter referred to as R & C, was doing business at __3_____, New York and was the plaintiff's employer.

THIRD: That prior to __4_____, 19_5_, R & C, the Third-Party Defendant, purchased, caused to be delivered and installed, in its plant several plastic injector machines of the type known as No. K2 and bearing Serial No. 18-4-60-H, which were used among other things, to stamp out plastic eye sockets which eye sockets were to be used in dolls' heads.

FOURTH: That each and every operation in connection with the setting up and/or installing the said machine including, among other things, hooking up the pyrometers, the heat control, running the necessary wires to the machine, connecting up the plumbing so that water may go into the machine, regulating the mould through which the plastic goes in the operation of the machine, setting the range which is regulated by an adjustable stroke which in turn regulates a certain opening and closing, making the necessary adjustments every time a different mould is put in according to the length of the piece that is about to be molded or shaped which, in turn, makes the form of the plastic, etc. all of which were made or done by the R & C, its agents, servants and/or employees.

FIFTH: That the said machine was completely installed, regulated and controlled by the R & C, the Third-Party Defendant herein including the movable parts behind and which regulated the safety gate without any assistance whatsoever from the Third-Party Plaintiff herein, its agents, servants and/or employees.

SIXTH: That on information and belief the said machine was carelessly, improperly and negligently installed by R & C, the Third-Party Defendant herein, its agents, servants and/or employees so that the safety gate did not work as a safety measure in shutting off the current when the safety gate was open and in otherwise hindering and preventing the proper functioning of the machine.

SEVENTH: That it is alleged in the complaint, among other things, that on __6_____, 19_7_ while the plaintiff was doing her normal work using the said machine for the purpose of stamping out the said plastic eye sockets, her right thumb was amputated, at a time when the safety gate was open, when the current should normally be off and that the die and moving parts behind the safety gate moved rapidly and quickly including those parts which were used for stamping out the eye sockets, thus causing the amputation of the plaintiff's right thumb, that the negligence alleged, among other things, are that the machine was so defectively designed that the safety gate did not operate properly, that the movable parts behind the safety gate would and did operate when the said gate was open, that the machine was improperly installed and thus the safety gate did not work properly so as to shut off the current and the movement of all movable parts behind the safety gate when open and the allegations of negligence set forth in paragraph designated "Thirteenth" of the complaint, which paragraph is herein incorporated by reference with the same force and effect as if the same were herein and at length set forth.

EIGHTH: That the said machine when it left the factory was in good order and condition, that it functioned properly and that if it did not do so on the date of the accident alleged in the complaint, it was due wholly, solely and entirely to the active negligence of the Third-Party Defendant in not properly installing and adjusting the machine so that its various parts would function normally and properly as said machine did upon leaving the factory.

NINTH: That by virtue of the accident alleged in the complaint the Defendant Third-Party Plaintiff has been put to considerable expense in investigating this action as well as in engaging attorneys to defend the same, no part of which has been paid by the Third-Party Defendant herein.

TENTH: That if the machine in question did not function properly because of the alleged negligence set forth in paragraph designated "Thirteenth" of the complaint, said negligence was brought about in the first instance by the Third-Party Defendant in not properly setting up the machine, in failing to adjust it properly, in not seeing to it that the safety gate operated properly and through no negligence, carelessness or want of care on the part of the Defendant Third-Party Plaintiff contributing thereto.

WHEREFORE the defendant demands judgment dismissing the complaint herein but should judgment be entered against the defendant, then and in that event the defendant Third-Party Plaintiff will demand a judgment in like amount over and against the Third-Party Defendant above named, together with the costs and disbursements of this action as well as the amount incurred for investigating and defending the same.

___8_____

Attorney for Third-Party Plaintiff
[Office and P. O. Address]
[Telephone No.]

[Adapted from record in Wegorzewski v De Mattia Machine & Tool Co. (1961) 12 AD2d 825, 210 NYS2d 426, courtesy of Edward F. Sweeney, Esq. of New York City.]

Form 11

Verification of Third-Party Complaint

STATE OF NEW YORK
COUNTY OF __1_____   ss:

__2_____, being duly sworn, deposes and says that he is the defendant and third-party plaintiff in this action, that he has read the foregoing third-party complaint and knows the contents thereof, that the same is true to his own knowledge, except as to the matters therein stated to be alleged on information and belief, and that as to those matters he believes it to be true.

___3_____

[Print signer's name below signature]
[Signature of affiant]

[Jurat]

§ 1008. Answer of third-party defendant; defenses

The third-party defendant shall answer the claim asserted against him by serving copies of his answer upon the third-party plaintiff. The third-party defendant may assert against the plaintiff in his answer any defenses which the third-party plaintiff has to the plaintiff's claim. The third-party defendant shall have the rights of a party adverse to the other parties in the action, including the right to counter-claim, cross-claim and appeal.

HISTORY:
> Add, L 1962, ch 308, eff Sept 1, 1963.
> Earlier statutes: CPA § 193-a.

ADVISORY COMMITTEE NOTES:
> This section follows CPA § 193-a(2) except that the manner of service of pleadings is omitted. See new CPLR § 3012 for the general rule as to service of pleadings.
> Requirement of service of copy of answer on plaintiff deleted as unnecessary. The plaintiff, as well as every other party who has appeared, must be served by virtue of new CPLR rule 2103(e).
> Remainder of first sentence, and phrase "For the purpose of contesting plaintiff's claim against the third-party plaintiff" in last sentence, deleted as unnecessary.
> Provision regarding assertion of counterclaim transferred to this section, with the effect of dispensing with the limitation that the third-party defendant may assert a counterclaim against the plaintiff only if the latter has amended his complaint to assert a claim against him.
> Last sentence clarified by adding language expressly indicating that the third-party defendant has the rights of a party adverse to the "other parties in the action," including the right to "cross-claim."

CROSS REFERENCES:
> When third party practice allowed, CPLR 1007.
> Pleadings against or by third parties, CPLR 1009–1011.
> Service of pleadings, CPLR 3012(a).
> Demand for relief, CPLR 3017.
> General and special verdicts, CPLR 4111.

FEDERAL ASPECTS:
> When defendant may bring in third party, Rule 14(a) of Federal Rules of Civil Procedure, USCS Court Rules.
> Third-party practice, Rule 14 of Federal Rules of Civil Procedure, USCS Court Rules.

RESEARCH REFERENCES AND PRACTICE AIDS:
> 28 NY Jur, Indemnity § 28.
> 57 NY Jur, Suretyship and Guaranty § 255.
> 3 Carmody-Wait 2d, Parties §§ 19:98, 19:121–19:123, 19:128.
> 5 Carmody-Wait 2d, The Answer § 30:76.
> 5 Carmody-Wait 2d, Counterclaim § 31:33.

Law Reviews:
> New York Civil Practice Law and Rules: parties. 27 Albany L Rev 182.
> Parties and pleading under the CPLR. 31 Brooklyn L Rev 98.
> Negligence—apportionment of damages among joint tortfeasors—right of a party actively negligent to implead a co-wrongdoer. 41 Fordham L Rev 167.
> Torts—New York civil practice—a joint tort-feasor accorded unlimited right to implead a co-tortfeasor for partial indemnification based on comparative responsibility in negligence. 47 NYU L Rev 815.
> A biannual survey of New York practice: Part IV: indemnification between tort-feasors. 39 St. John's L Rev 428.

Forms:
> See "FORMS" heading following "CASE NOTES", infra.

CASE NOTES

Where the defendant bank debited a depositor's account the amount of a previously credited welfare check upon notice by the Department of Welfare that the endorsement of the check was a forgery 6 months after the initial deposit and long after final settlement of the item, the bank did so at its own peril. However, final settlement did not preclude the bank from pursuing its remedy by way of plenary suit to hold the depositor on its endorsement and warranties, and in such a suit in which the forgery was conclusively proved by the third-party defendant, the Department of Welfare, the bank was entitled to the benefit of that evidence and to dismissal of the complaint without prejudice to an institution by the plaintiff of a new action based upon negligence in discovering the forgery. 622 West 113th St. Corp. v Chemical Bank New York Trust Co. (1966) 52 Misc 2d 444, 276 NYS2d 85.

An appeal lies from an order denying a written motion on notice to dismiss a third-party complaint following the trial of an action in which the jury was unable to reach agreement as to the merits of the main action. Berg v New York (1973) 42 AD2d 770, 346 NYS2d 465.

While this section and CPLR § 3011 mandate an answer to a third-party complaint, in view of the provision of CPLR § 1003, which provides that the CPLR also applies to further proceedings in pending actions, but former procedure applies where the new procedure would not be feasible or would work injustice, a third-party complaint served pursuant to § 193-A of the Civil Practice Act, which made an answer to a third-party complaint clearly permissive, would be subject to the provisions of § 193-A of the CPA where the CPLR provisions would indeed work injustice. Multari v Glalin Arms Corp. (1966) 51 Misc 2d 1019, 274 NYS2d 827.

A third-party defendant against whom judgment was rendered in favor of third-party plaintiff, based on judgment recovered by plaintiff against defendant-third-party plaintiff, can appeal from the judgment rendered against him, and on such appeal can challenge the judgment recovered by plaintiff against the defendant-third-party plaintiff, and if erroneous, it will be reversed even though not appealed from by the defendant-third-party plaintiff. Rome Cable Corp. v Tanney (1964) 21 AD2d 342, 250 NYS2d 304. (This is contra to ruling in Frankel v Berman (1960) 10 AD2d 838, 199 NYS2d 261.)

Where parties had stipulated to have third party indemnification claim considered as a matter of law following jury's determination of negligence action, it was reversible error to deny third party defendant an opportunity under CPLR 1008 to further participate in trial following such stipulation where third party defendant's liability was determined in part by defendant third party plaintiff's liability to plaintiff in main action. Phillips v Chevrolet Tonawanda Div. of General Motors Corp. (1974) 43 AD2d 891, 352 NYS2d 73.

Tortfeasor's action against another tortfeasor for indemnity either by an independent action or by a third-party complaint accrues from the time of payment of judgment, and not from the time of the commission of the tort for which indemnity is sought. Musco v Conte (1964) 22 AD2d 121, 254 NYS2d 589.

A third-party defendant may assert against the plaintiff any defenses which the third-party plaintiff has to the plaintiff's claim, and therefore an order dismissing a third-party complaint could be sustained if the statute of limitations had run on the main action. Lewis v Borg-Warner Corp. (1970) 35 AD2d 722, 314 NYS2d 566.

Where 81-year-old patient, who had been injured by slipping on polished wooden stairs in insufficiently lighted hall leading to tenant-doctor's office, sued the tenant-doctor after executing a release to the landowner-doctor, who was made a third-party defendant by the defendant-tenant and third-party plaintiff, the landowner-doctor's motion to dismiss the third-party action was denied as the third-party plaintiff had not been a party to the release and the release had specifically reserved the plaintiff's rights against the third-party plaintiff. Rake v Corn (1971) 67 Misc 2d 986, 325 NYS2d 614.

In personal injury action by workman against bank, employer, as third party defendant of third party plaintiff bank's cross-claim for indemnity, was not permitted to plead defense of exclusivity of workmen's compensation (Workmen's Compensation Law § 11, § 29, subd 6) since defendant third party plaintiff bank, a nonemployer, was not entitled to plead such defense in workman's main action. Bellefeuille v City & County Sav. Bank (1974) 43 AD2d 335, 351 NYS2d 738, later app 49 AD2d 323, 374 NYS2d 781, affd 40 NY2d 879, 389 NYS2d 345, 357, NE2d 1000.

In workman's third party action wherein defendant impleaded employer, CPLR § 1008 did not permit employer to amend answer to assert exclusive remedy provisions of Workmen's Compensation Law. Bellefeuille v City & County Sav. Bank (1973) 74 Misc 2d 534, 345 NYS2d 409, mod on other grounds 43 AD2d 335, 351 NYS2d 738, later app 49 AD2d 323, 374 NYS2d 781, affd 40 NY2d 879, 389 NYS2d 345, 357 NE2d 1000.

The primary plaintiff and third-party defendant are adverse parties, and mutual examinations before trial should be permitted, irrespective of whether there exist any issues, created by the pleadings, between them. Rizzo v Steiner (1964) 20 AD2d 909, 248 NYS2d 998.

CASE NOTES

UNDER FORMER CIVIL PRACTICE LAWS

1. Generally

Third-party defendant becomes party to action both as to claim asserted by third-party plaintiff and as to cause of action asserted by plaintiff against third-party plaintiff. Jacobs v Driscoll (1948) 78 NYS2d 813.

In such case, however, to protect the plaintiff's rights the court limited the summation, for a third party, to comment on argument upon the issues between plaintiff and defendant only. Vergano v New York, supra.

Third-party defendant may move for change of venue though his answer is addressed solely to third-party complaint and plaintiff does not amend his complaint to include claim against third-party defendant. Champlain Creameries v Hovey, S. & Co. (1955) 141 NYS2d 271.

Where trial in New York county for breach of contract would inconvenience third party defendants who made related contract with original defendant and who had their place of business in Clinton county, did not justify change of venue to latter county. Champlain Creameries v Hovey, S. & Co., supra.

2. Right to contest plaintiff's claim against defendant

Third-party defendant has rights of party adverse to plaintiff, and may contest plaintiff's claim against defendant. Murray Oil Products Co. v Poons Co. (1947) 190 Misc 110, 74 NYS2d 814, affd 191 Misc 1005, 80 NYS2d 28.

Third-party defendant is authorized to contest plaintiff's claim. Wischnie v Dorsch (1949) 196 Misc 679, 91 NYS2d 558.

Third-party defendant may oppose plaintiff's claims against defendant and third-party plaintiff, though plaintiff's complaint seeks no relief against third-party defendant. Anida Realty Corp. v 6145 Realty Corp. (1950) 197 Misc 157, 94 NYS2d 56.

Where injured automobilist recovered judgment for personal injuries against defendant who served third-party complaint against physician for mal-practice, such physician may defend against charge of malpractice and litigate issue of defendant's negligence. Clark v Halstead (1949) 276 AD 17, 93 NYS2d 49.

Plaintiff's motion for summary judgment made in advance of service of answer by third-party defendant should not be entertained since such answer might assert defenses to plaintiff's claim in chief entitling him to be heard, and a disposition of motion against defendant would preclude him therefrom. New York v Nadel (1960) 11 AD2d 652, 201 NYS2d 833.

3. Defenses against plaintiff

In action for breach of warranty, defense by fourth-party defendant that he did not warrant quality of goods bought by plaintiff from third-party defendant who in turn bought from fourth-party defendant, was immaterial as to plaintiff's claim against original defendant. Pichardo v Baez (1948) 79 NYS2d 151.

In action by contractor against surety of subcontractor for latter's default on contract, impleaded subcontractor may not counterclaim against contractor for breach of subcontract where contractor asserted no claim against impleaded subcontractor, but latter may set up same cause of action as affirmative defense. Psaty & Fuhrman v Continental Casualty Co. (1951) 278 AD 159, 103 NYS2d 849.

A third-party defendant may plead a defense against the plaintiff which the third-party plaintiff has lost through delay. Marrone v John A. Johnson & Sons (1954) 283 AD 1114, 131 NYS2d 853.

Where employee sues for injuries and the defendants neglect to assert the defense that the employee's cause of action had been assigned to and was vested in his employer's compensation insurer, and lose their time to plead the defense by failure to amend as of course within twenty days, and by failure to apply for leave to amend because the time has expired within which the insurer could commence an action, this defense remains available to the employer impleaded as a third-party defendant who had been guilty of no fault or neglect preventing action by the insurer, or the timely pleading of the defense by the original defendants. Marrone v John A. Johnson & Sons, supra.

Third-party defendant may assert against plaintiff only those defenses which third-party plaintiff may have to plaintiff's claim. Fitzgerald v American Surety Co. (1956) 3 Misc 2d 609, 150 NYS2d 128.

4. —Limitation of action

In action to determine claim to realty third-party defendant cannot assert six-month statute of limitations as bar because action by plaintiff against defendant was commenced within such period, and third-party defendant cannot assert defense not available to original defendant. Feldstein v Bevier (1951) 278 AD 828, 104 NYS2d 212.

Where negligence action against city was brought in time, third-party defendant cannot interpose defense of statute of limitations. Giudice v New York (1954) 128 NYS2d 890.

Cause of action for indemnity, sought under CPA § 193-a authorizing impleading of third-party defendant, does not accrue until payment of main claim, whether such payment be made pursuant to judgment, or loss or damage be voluntarily paid by innocent party, who is legally charged, without waiting for judgment. Lanswer v Baumrin (1956) 2 Misc 2d 610, 151 NYS2d 466.

Statute of limitations with respect to third-party claim is not measured from the accrual by plaintiff's original cause of action against the defendant; a third-party cause of action based on indemnity does not accrue until actual payment by third-party plaintiff of judgment recovered against it. Sheftman v Balfour Housing Corp. (1961) 30 Misc 2d 924, 219 NYS2d 461.

5. Dismissal of complaint in chief

Third-party defendant may challenge sufficiency of complaint in chief, which, if sufficient, necessitates dismissal of third party complaint. Boyle v Wegman (1960) 25 Misc 2d 193, 200 NYS2d 82.

6. Defenses against third-party complaint

In action by an employee against a stranger to recover for personal injuries, wherein the stranger served a third-party complaint against plaintiff's employer for contribution, the defense to the third-party complaint of Workmen's Compensation as being the employee's sole remedy, is insufficient, even though there is a possibility that there may be a recovery over against the employer by the stranger for more than the compensation benefits. Tuffarella v Erie R. Co. (1961) 27 Misc 2d 638, 211 NYS2d 351.

7. Counterclaim of third-party defendant against plaintiff

Counterclaim in answer of third-party defendant cannot be asserted by him against plaintiff where latter makes no claim against former. Feldstein v Bevier (1951) 278 AD 828, 104 NYS2d 212.

In view of CPA § 264 (§§ 3012(a), 3019(b), 3020(a) herein) the former disability of a third-party defendant to cross claim against the original plaintiff in the action is removed, and where a claim over by a third-party defendant against the original plaintiff is based upon a claim for which the plaintiff would be liable in the event that the third-party defendant is liable to the third-party plaintiff, such a claim need only be related to the main action by question of law or fact common to the controversy involved in the complaint and the cross claim of the third-party defendant. Commercial Trading Co. v Zeisel Machinery Co. (1954) 133 NYS2d 308.

Where controversies between a third-party plaintiff and third-party defendant on the one hand, and third-party defendant and original plaintiff on the other, both involved the same chattel mortgage, the same auction sale, and various acts and transactions relating thereto, these controversies present such common questions of law and fact as will sustain a cross claim by the third-party defendant against the original plaintiff where the plaintiff will be liable to the third-party defendant in the event the third-party defendant is liable to the third-party plaintiff who has impleaded him. Commercial Trading Co. v Zeisel Machinery Co., supra.

Third-party defendant may interpose counterclaim against plaintiff only if plaintiff amends his complaint to assert claim against third-party defendant. Fitzgerald v American Surety Co. (1956) 3 Misc 2d 609, 150 NYS2d 128.

Where plaintiffs, as assignees of husband's cause of action based on undertaking on order of arrest procured by wife in divorce action, surety for legal services to husband assignor in successfully defending against his arrest, wife as third-party defendant cannot assert counterclaim or defense against plaintiff's attorneys, for nonpayment of alimony by their assignor. Fitzgerald v American Surety Co., supra.

8. Examination before trial of, or by, third party

Having elected to contest plaintiff's claim, the third-party defendant is a party adverse to the plaintiff and may be examined as such before trial. Bizzarro v Zimkot Realty Corp. (1954) 283 AD 816, 128 NYS2d 796.

Where plaintiff's complaint seeks no relief against third-party defendant which, however, opposes plaintiff's claim against defendant, plaintiff may examine third-party defendant. Anida Realty Corp. v 6145 Realty Corp. (1950) 197 Misc 157, 94 NYS2d 56.

Where a third-party defendant asserts no claims against the original plaintiff, nor raises any issues between them, and the plaintiff has sought no relief against the third-party defendant by amendment of his complaint to join the third-party as a defendant in the main action, the plaintiff and third-party defendant are not adverse parties within the meaning of CPA § 288 (§ 3101(a), Rule 3106(a) herein), and the plaintiff may not examine the third-party defendant before trial as an adverse party. Salgo v Amdor Structures, Inc. (1954) 133 NYS2d 435.

Claim by third-party defendant against plaintiff entitled former to examine plaintiff before trial. Anida Realty Corp. v 6145 Realty Corp. (1950) 197 Misc 157, 94 NYS2d 56.

Defendant and third-party plaintiff may not as such party examine plaintiff who had not amended his complaint to state cause of action against third-party defendant. Deutsch v Adams (1950) 197 Misc 505, 95 NYS2d 622.

Plaintiff may not be examined by third-party defendant, where neither asserts claim against other. Gile v Sears, Roebuck & Co. (1952) 110 NYS2d 211.

Defendant may not examine plaintiff before trial

where neither asserts claims against other. Gile v Sears, Roebuck & Co., supra.

Plaintiff is entitled to notice of third-party defendant's motion to vacate third-party plaintiff's notice of examination before trial and, where plaintiff was not given such notice, third-party defendant's motion would be denied. Rivkind v Fried (1957) 13 Misc 2d 943, 159 NYS2d 861.

9. —Physical examination

A motion by a third-party defendant for an order directing plaintiff in main complaint to submit to physical examination will be granted since intention of statute is that third-party defendant should not be at mercy of mere formal or inept defense to plaintiff's claim by third-party plaintiff. Sorrentino v New York (1958) 14 Misc 2d 78, 178 NYS2d 500.

FORMS

Form 1—Answer of third-party defendant

Form 2—Answer of third-party defendant constituting cross complaint against an original defendant

Form 3—Answer and counterclaims of third-party defendant, including additional third-party defendant

Form 4—Answer of third-party defendant setting out affirmative defense to complaint, affirmative defense to third-party complaint and a counterclaim against plaintiff

Form 5—Notice of retainer in third-party action

Form 1

Answer of Third-Party Defendant

Answer

[Title of court and cause]   Index No. — [if assigned]

Third-party defendant above-named, by his attorney __¹_____, as and for his answer to the third-party complaint herein, alleges:

1. Denies each and every allegation contained in paragraphs named and numbered "2", "4", "5", "6", and "9".

2. Denies each and every allegation contained in the third-party complaint in paragraph named and numbered "8" except that defendant admits that __²_____.

For a first, separate and distinct defense, the third-party defendant alleges:

3. That the alleged cause of action stated in the plaintiff's complaint against the defendant therein and the third-party plaintiff herein did not accrue within three years prior to the commencement of this action.

WHEREFORE, __³_____, the third-party defendant herein demands judgment dismissing the complaint and the third-party complaint herein together with the costs and disbursements of this action.

__4_____

Attorney for Third-Party Defendant
Office and P. O. address
Telephone No.

Form 2

Answer of Third-Party Defendant Constituting Cross Complaint Against An Original Defendant

[Title of court and cause]

As for a Cross Complaint against X corp. [an original defendant]:

The third-party defendant upon information and belief alleges:

1. That at all of the times hereinafter mentioned the defendant X corp., was and still is a domestic corporation duly organized and existing under and by virtue of the laws of the State of New York.

2. That on and about __1_____, 19_2_, _3_____, the third-party defendant herein [was performing certain masonry work in a building in the course of erection at _4_____ Avenue, _5_____, New York, pursuant to a written agreement and used certain scaffolding planking in connection with the work so performed].

3. That the plaintiff in his complaint alleges that [on _6_____, 19_7_, while in the employ of the third-party defendant herein, _8_____, he was caused to fall because of a hole in the scaffolding on which he was working], without fault on his part, but due to the negligence, carelessness [and violation of the Labor Law of the State of New York] on the part of the defendants named in the complaint and that as a result thereof he sustained injuries for which damages are claimed in the sum of _9_____ Dollars.

4. That [the scaffold planks used by _10_____, the third-party defendant, in connection with the masonry work performed by him at _11_____ Avenue, _12_____ New York, were not owned by or the property of said third-party defendant].

5. That the defendant X corp. [prior to _13_____ , 19_14_, as part of its business, rented scaffold planks for an agreed price].

6. That [pursuant to agreement made on or about _15_____, 19_16_, the defendant X corp., for an agreed price rented to _17_____, the third-party defendant, approximately _18_____ used scaffold planks, for use in connection with the masonry work being performed in the building in the course of erection at _19_____ Avenue, _20_____, New York].

7. That if upon the trial of this action the plaintiff proves [that the hole in which he fell was in a scaffold plank, the same was, to the knowledge of the defendant X corp., maintained, caused or created by the said X corp., its agents, servants and employees and not by the third-party defendant or any of his agents, servants or employees].

8. That the defendant X corp., is a party defendant to this action and has been served with a copy of the plaintiff's complaint.

9. That the third-party defendant, _21_____, is a party to this action only as to the third-party plaintiff, _22_____, copy of which third-party complaint is attached hereto.

10. That if _23_____, the third-party plaintiff herein, recover against the third-party defendant, _24_____, in this action, such recovery and liability will have been brought about and caused through the negligence and carelessness of the defendant X corp., its servants, agents and employees in [failing to supply proper scaffold planks and supplying a defective scaffold plank] and because the defendant _25_____, was otherwise guilty of primary and active negligence, without any negligence on the part of the third-party defendant contributing thereto, and the third-party defendant will therefore ask for judgment over and against the defendant X corp., for any amount he is obliged to pay to the third-party plaintiff herein, together with the reasonable counsel fees and expenses and the costs that he will incur in the defense of this action.

WHEREFORE, the third-party defendant, _26_____, demands judgment as follows:

1. Dismissing the complaint of the third-party plaintiff herein as to him, together with the costs and disbursements of this action;

2. Judgment over and against the defendant X corp., and _27_____, both, or either of them, for the amount of any judgment which may be obtained herein by the third-party plaintiff against him;

3. That the ultimate rights as between him and the defendants, __28_____ and __29_____, be determined in this action.

__30_____

Attorneys for Third-Party Defendant
__31_____

Address __32_____
Telephone No. __33__

[Verification]

[Adapted from papers in Portnoy v United Engineers & Constructors, Inc. 274 AD 891, 82 NYS2d 464.]

Form 3

Answer and Counterclaims of Third-Party Defendant, Including Additional Third-Party Defendant

State of New York, Supreme Court,
County of __1_____

A Corporation,

Plaintiff,

against

B Holding Corporation,

Defendant,

B Holding Corporation,

Defendant and Third-Party Plaintiff,

against

C Corporation,

Third-Party Defendant.

By Original Summons and Third-Party Summons and between the Said C Corporation,

Impleading Plaintiff.

against

A Corporation and B Holding Corporation

Defendants,

and

X, as Trustee and for the depositing holders of bonds and/or coupons of the D Corporation,

Impleaded Defendant.

C CORPORATION, THIRD-PARTY DEFENDANT ANSWERING COMPLAINT OF THIRD-PARTY PLAINTIFF:

1. Denies that it has any knowledge or information sufficient to form a belief as to any of the allegations contained in the paragraphs of said complaint designated and numbered __2_____ and __3_____.

2. Admits the allegations contained in the paragraphs of said complaint designated and numbered __4_____ and __5_____.

3. Denies that it has any knowledge or information sufficient to form a belief __6_____ [etc.].

4. Denies each and every allegation contained in said complaint not hereinbefore specifically admitted or denied.

THIRD-PARTY DEFENDANT ANSWERING THE COMPLAINT OF THE PLAINTIFF HEREIN:

5. Denies that it has any knowledge or information sufficient to form a belief as to any of the allegations contained in the paragraphs of said complaint designated and numbered __7_____, __8_____ and __9_____.

6. Denies that it has any knowledge or information sufficient to form a belief as to any of the allegations contained in the paragraph of said complaint designated and numbered __10_____ , except admits that __11_____ [etc.].

7. Denies each and every allegation contained in said complaint, not hereinbefore specifically admitted or denied.

FOR A FIRST AFFIRMATIVE DEFENSE TO THE COMPLAINT OF THE THIRD-PARTY PLAINTIFF ALLEGES:

8. The defendant __12_____ [did not covenant that the defendant __13_____ shall quietly enjoy, nor did it warrant the title to, the easement or right of way extending from __14_____ to __15_____ of the premises of the defendant __16_____, mentioned in the deed annexed to the third-party complaint as Exhibit "A" thereof].

FOR A SECOND AFFIRMATIVE DEFENSE TO THE COMPLAINT OF THE PLAINTIFF AND THE COMPLAINT OF THE THIRD-PARTY PLAINTIFF ALLEGES:

9. On or about __17_____, 19_18_, X [as trustee for the depositing bondholders and/or coupon holders of __19_____, the last common grantor of __20_____ and __21_____, entered into a contract with the defendant __22_____, dated __23_____, 19_24_, for the sale by said __25_____ as trustee etc., state affirmative defense against plaintiff and third-party plaintiff].

FOR A THIRD AFFIRMATIVE DEFENSE TO THE COMPLAINT OF THE PLAINTIFF AND THE COMPLAINT OF THE THIRD-PARTY PLAINTIFF, AND AS AND FOR A COUNTERCLAIM AGAINST PLAINTIFF A CORPORATION ALLEGES:

10. Prior to __26_____, 19_27_, the plaintiff A Corporation and the defendant C Corporation entered into an agreement that in the event the defendant C Corporation sold the premises mentioned in the third-party complaint, to the defendant B Corporation, __28_____ [etc., stating defense and counterclaim].

11. By reason of the facts set forth in this counterclaim and the breach by plaintiff A Corporation of said agreement mentioned in paragraph 9 hereof, the defendant C Corporation is or may be liable to the defendant B Corporation wholly or in part for the claim made against it by said third-party plaintiff B Corporation in this action, and has been or may be damaged in an amount equal to the amount of the said claim of said third-party plaintiff.

FOR A FOURTH AFFIRMATIVE DEFENSE TO THE COMPLAINT OF THE PLAINTIFF AND THE COMPLAINT OF THE THIRD-PARTY PLAINTIFF AND AS AND FOR A COUNTERCLAIM AGAINST PLAINTIFF A CORPORATION AND THIRD-PARTY PLAINTIFF B CORPORATION, AND IMPLEADED DEFENDANT X, AS TRUSTEE.

12. Paragraph numbered 8 hereof is repeated and reiterated as though herein at length fully set forth and is made a part of this counterclaim and defense.

13. __29_____ [State facts of counterclaim, etc.]

14. In the event it is held in this action that __30_____ [said right of way or easement granted to the defendant C Corporation and excepted from the conveyance to the plaintiff, A Corporation, is not such full and complete right of way as represented and stated as aforesaid then by mutual mistake of the defendant X, as trustee, and the plaintiff A Corporation and the defendant C Corporation, said contract and conveyances did not embody the actual agreement theretofore made as aforesaid.]

15. The defendant C Corporation executed said writings in the belief that the same embodied in their terms the actual agreement theretofore made as aforesaid.

16. The defendant C Corporation has performed all the covenants of the said agreement on its part to be performed.

WHEREFORE, defendant C Corporation demands judgment dismissing the complaint of the defendant third-party plaintiff B Corporation, and dismissing the complaint of the plaintiff A Corporation and in the event judgment is recovered herein by the defendant third-party plaintiff B Corporation against third-party defendant C Corporation, for judgment against the plaintiff A Corporation, in the amount of any judgment so recovered and for judgment that __³¹_____ [the written agreement mentioned in paragraph 8 be reformed and corrected so as to convey to the defendant C Corporation a full and complete easement or right of way over the said roadway extending from __³²_____ to __³³_____ of the premises of the defendant __³⁴_____, known at law as a covenant running with the land, for the benefit of said C Corporation, its successors and assigns and the grantee or grantees of the whole or any part thereof, and reforming and correcting the written agreement mentioned in paragraph 8 hereof so that the same shall be subject to such right of way as aforesaid,] and for such other and further relief as to the Court may seem just and proper, together with costs and disbursements and an additional allowance as in the CPLR 8301 et seq., provided.

__³⁵_____

Attorney for Third-Party Defendant
and Impleading Plaintiff
Address __³⁶_____
Telephone Number __³⁷__

[Verification]

[Adapted from papers in Acco Products, Inc. v Cooperative G. L. F. Holding Corp. 277 AD 954, 99 NYS2d 725.]

Form 4

Answer of Third-Party Defendant Setting Out Affirmative Defense to Complaint, Affirmative Defenses To Third-Party Complaint and a Counterclaim Against Plaintiff
[Official Form 22]

SUPREME COURT OF THE STATE OF NEW YORK
COUNTY OF NEW YORK

R.S.T., Inc., Plaintiff,
    against
U.V.W., Inc., Defendant.   Answer to Third-Party
U.V.W., Inc., Defendant and   Complaint
    Third-Party Plaintiff,   Index No.
    against
X.Y.Z., Inc., Third-Party Defendant.

Affirmative Defense to Complaint

1. The cause of action set forth in the complaint did not accrue within four years next before the commencement of this action.

Affirmative Defense to Third-Party Complaint

[For form of responsive pleadings, see Form 2 in § 3018.]

Counterclaim Against Plaintiff

[Here set forth any cause of action as a counterclaim in the manner in which a claim is pleaded in a complaint.]

Wherefore third-party defendant demands judgment (1) against plaintiff and third-party plaintiff dismissing the complaint and the third-party complaint, (2) against plaintiff on the counterclaim in the sum of ___¹_____ dollars, and (3) against plaintiff and third-party plaintiff for costs and disbursements.

[Print name]

_____

Attorney for Third-
　Party Defendant
Address:
Telephone Number:

Form 5

Notice of Retainer in Third-Party Action

[Title of court and cause]　　　　　Notice of Retainer

PLEASE TAKE NOTICE that the third-party defendants above-named hereby appear in the above-entitled action and have retained the undersigned as their attorney and hereby demand that you serve a copy of the complaint and all other papers in the original action, as well as a copy of the third-party complaint and all other papers in the third-party action, upon the undersigned attorney at the address set forth below.

Dated: _ ¹_____, 19_²_.

_____³_____

Attorney for Third-Party Defendants
[Office and P. O. address]
Telephone No.

Rule 1009. Claim by plaintiff against third-party defendant

Within twenty days after service of the third-party complaint, the plaintiff may amend his complaint without leave of court to assert against the third-party defendant any claim he has against the third-party defendant.

HISTORY:

Add as § 1009, L 1962, ch 308, renumbered Rule 1009, L 1962, ch 315, § 1, amd, by Judicial Conference, eff Sept 1, 1972.

ADVISORY COMMITTEE NOTES:

This rule contains only slight verbal changes from the form of statement in CPA § 193-a.

Twenty-day provision added to conform to the time limitation governing amendment of pleadings as of right generally. See CPLR § 3025(a).

Provision relating to counterclaim transferred to CPLR § 1008.

CROSS REFERENCES:

Third party practice pleadings, CPLR 1007, 1008, 1010, 1011.
Service of pleadings, CPLR 3012(a).
General and special verdicts, CPLR 4111.

FEDERAL ASPECTS:

Third-party practice, Rule 14 of Federal Rules of Civil Procedure, USCS Court Rules.

RESEARCH REFERENCES AND PRACTICE AIDS:

28 NY Jur, Indemnity § 28.
3 Carmody-Wait 2d, Parties §§ 19:98, 19:126.

Law Reviews:

New York Civil Practice Law and Rules: parties. 27 Albany L Rev 182.
Parties and pleading under the CPLR. 31 Brooklyn L Rev 98.

Forms:

See "FORMS" heading following "CASE NOTES", infra.

CASE NOTES

1. In general
2. Timeliness of amendment
3. Right to amend, generally
4. Joinder of third-party defendant as party defendant
5. Sufficiency of claim

1. In general

No notice of amendment need be given to the proposed defendant. Johnson v Equitable Life Assur. Soc. (1964) 22 AD2d 141, 254 NYS2d 261, affd 18 NY2d 933, 277 NYS2d 136, 223 NE2d 562.

2. Timeliness of amendment

Third-party defendant's objections of untimeliness is not established by showing service of amended complaint more than twenty days after service upon third-party of third-party complaint; it must be shown to have been served more than twenty days after service of the third-party complaint upon the plaintiff. Johnson v Equitable Life Assur. Soc. (1964) 22 AD2d 141, 254 NYS2d 261, affd 18 NY2d 933, 277 NYS2d 136, 223 NE2d 562.

Where the third-party defendant claims that an amendment of plaintiff's complaint was made after the 20-day period specified in this rule, his failure to show the date of service of the third-party complaint is not excused by lack of knowledge in the absence of any showing of what steps were taken by him to ascertain this date from the plaintiff or from the third-party plaintiff. Johnson v Equitable Life Assur. Soc. (1964) 22 AD2d 141, 254 NYS2d 261, affd 18 NY2d 933, 277 NYS2d 136, 223 NE2d 562.

3. Right to amend, generally

This rule does not curtail or circumscribe a plaintiff's right to amend his pleading in the face of a third-party claim, to assert a claim against a third-party defendant. Johnson v Equitable Life Assur.

Soc. (1964) 22 AD2d 141, 254 NYS2d 261, affd 18 NY2d 933, 277 NYS2d 136, 223 NE2d 562.

4. Joinder of third-party defendant as party defendant

A third-party defendant is not entitled to be notified of or be heard on the plaintiff's intention to join it as a party defendant. Johnson v Equitable Life Assur. Soc. (1964) 22 AD2d 141, 254 NYS2d 261, affd 18 NY2d 933, 277 NYS2d 136, 223 NE2d 562.

Since plaintiff failed to serve an amended complaint asserting a claim against the third-party defendant, the latter, if liable at all, was liable only to defendant who impleaded him; hence, it was error to award judgment in favor of plaintiff and against the third-party defendant. Society of New York Hospital v Mogensen (1972) 83 Misc 2d 840, 373 NYS2d 722.

5. Sufficiency of claim

In an action brought pursuant to the Federal Employers' Liability Act by a railroad lineman to recover for injuries sustained when the utility pole upon which he was working broke, in which the railroad impleaded the power company who allegedly erected and maintained the pole upon railroad property and in which the plaintiff had served an amended complaint against the power company charging it with failure to inspect or maintain the pole, it was held that the pleadings were susceptible of charging the railroad with possible passive negligence in failing to provide the plaintiff with a safe place to work and possible active negligence in failing to inspect or examine the pole when ordering him to work upon it, and that the third-party complaint and the amended complaint both stated causes of action against the power company charging negligence in the maintenance of its wires and pole so that the third-party defendant's motion to dismiss both complaints against it was denied. Finley v New York C. R. Co. (1965) 50 Misc 2d 194, 270 NYS2d 349, affd 25 AD2d 897, 269 NYS2d 386.

CASE NOTES

UNDER FORMER CIVIL PRACTICE LAWS

See also Case Notes under
§ 1007, supra.

Appearance and answer by corporate third-party defendant subjected such party to jurisdiction of court and entitled plaintiff to amend his complaint to assert his claim against such third party. Wajtman v Brooklyn Eastern Dist. Terminal (1949) 276 AD 853, 93 NYS2d 586.

If plaintiffs wish to examine third-party defendant as party to action, they must amend complaint to assert a claim against him. Foote v Joseph Bisceg-

lia & Sons (1948) 192 Misc 19, 80 NYS2d 60.

Plaintiff was not permitted to amend complaint and serve supplemental summons and complaint where statute of limitations had run as to third-party defendant. Henry Spen & Co. v Ocean Box Corp. (1959) 16 Misc 2d 436, 184 NYS2d 152.

Where case was already on calendar when third-party defendant served his answer, third-party plaintiff must serve copy of note of issue on all adversaries and third-party defendant. Fortune v Hyle Holding Corp. (1947) 188 Misc 1011, 69 NYS2d 877.

FORMS

Form 1—Amendment of original complaint to set up claim against third-party defendants

Form 2—Plaintiff's notice of motion to amend complaint to include cause of action
against third-party defendants

Form 3—Affidavit in support of plaintiffs' motion to amend complaint to include
causes of action against third-party defendants

Form 4—Order permitting plaintiff to amend complaint to include cause of action
against third-party defendants

Form 1

Amendment of Original Complaint to Set Up Claim Against Third-Party Defendants

SUPREME COURT, COUNTY OF __1_____

Richard Roe,
Plaintiff,
  (against)
Harry Smith, John Black and
    Edward Brown,   Amendment
Defendants,   of
Harry Smith,   Complaint
Defendant and Third-   Index No. — [if assigned]
    Party Plaintiff,
  (against)
John Black and Edward Brown,
    Third-Party Defendants

Plaintiff, by his attorneys __2_____, as and for an amended complaint herein,
alleges:

For a cause of action against the defendant __3_____ [original defendant]:

[State cause of action against original defendant as stated in original complaint.]

For a cause of action against defendants John Black and Edward Brown [third-party
defendants]:

[State complete cause of action against third-party defendants.]

WHEREFORE, plaintiff demands judgment against the defendants jointly and
severally, in the sum of $__4__, together with the costs and disbursements of this
action.

                           __5_____
                           Attorney for Plaintiff
                     Office and P. O. Address
                             Telephone No.

Form 2

Plaintiff's Notice of Motion to Amend Complaint to Include Cause of Action Against Third-Party Defendants

[Title of court and cause]

Sirs:

PLEASE TAKE NOTICE, that upon the annexed affidavit of __1_____, duly
sworn to the __2__ day of __3_____, 19_4_, and upon all the papers and proceedings
heretofore had herein, the undersigned will move this Court on __5_____, 19_6_, at
_7_ M. at the courthouse for an order permitting the plaintiff to amend his complaint
to include a cause of action in damages against __8_____, __9_____, and __10_____,
now third-party defendants herein, and to serve upon said defendants an amended

complaint in the form annexed to the moving papers herein and for an order amending the title of this action to read:

SUPREME COURT

__11_____ County.

__12_____,

Plaintiff,

   against

__13_____, __14_____, __15_____

   and __16_____,

Defendants.

and for such other and further relief as to the court may seem just and proper.

Dated: __17_____, N. Y., __18_____, 19_19_.

Yours, etc.,

__20_____

Attorney for Plaintiff

Address __21_____

Telephone Number __22__

To: __23_____

   Attorney for Third-Party Plaintiff,

   Address __24_____

   Telephone No. __25__

   __26_____

   Attorney for Third-Party Defendant,

   Address __27_____

   Telephone No. __28__

[Adapted from papers in Wajtman v Brooklyn Eastern Dist. Terminal, 276 AD 853, 93 NYS2d 586.]

Form 3

Affidavit in Support of Plaintiffs' Motion to Amend Complaint to Include Causes of Action Against Third-Party Defendants

[Title of court and cause]

[Venue]

   __1_____, being duly sworn, deposes and says:

   I am counsel for __2_____, attorney for the plaintiff in the above-entitled action, have possession of the file and am familiar with all the facts and circumstances of this action.

   That this is an action brought to recover for serious personal injuries sustained by the plaintiff while he was in the yard of the defendant __3_____ when a door of a freight car fell from the freight train and struck plaintiff.

   That originally the action was brought against the following defendants: __4_____, __5_____, __6_____ and __7_____

   After the service of the summons and complaint upon the defendant __8_____ that defendant brought in as third-party defendants __9_____, __10_____ and __11_____

   These latter companies were brought into the action by the defendant __12_____ upon the theory that each of said third-party railway companies was an intervening custodian of the defendant __13_____ and owed a duty of inspection and repair during the time that the [freight car] was under their control.

   That in order to clarify the issues and in the interests of justice, it will be necessary in order to protect the interests of the plaintiff in a proper fashion to bring in as defendants __14_____, __15_____ and __16_____.

That annexed hereto is a proposed cause of action against said __17_____ companies which is to be included in the amended complaint in the event this application is granted.

It is likewise proper in the interests of clarity to amend the complaint so that the caption and all further papers shall read: __18_____ [Naming all defendants simply as "defendants"].

That the time within which to amend the complaint in such respects without leave of court has expired.

WHEREFORE, your deponent respectfully submits that an order be made permitting the plaintiff to amend his complaint to include a cause of action in damages against __19_____, now third-party defendants herein, and to serve upon said defendants an amended complaint in the form annexed to the moving papers herein; for which no previous application has been made.

[Jurat]

[Signature, with name printed underneath]

[Adapted from papers in Wajtman v Brooklyn Eastern Dist. Terminal, 276 AD 853, 93 NYS2d 586.]

Form 4

Order Permitting Plaintiff to Amend Complaint to Include Cause of Action Against Third-Party Defendants

__1_____,
Plaintiff
  against
__2_____ and __3_____,   Order
Defendants,   Index No. __6__
  and
__4_____ and __5_____,
    Third-Party Defendants.

Present: Hon. __7_____

A motion having been made herein by the plaintiff, for an order permitting the plaintiff to amend his complaint to include a cause of action in damages against __8_____, __9_____, and __10_____, third-party defendants herein, and permitting plaintiff to serve upon said defendants an amended complaint,

NOW on reading and filing said notice of motion dated __11_____, 19_12_, together with proof of due service thereof, __13_____ [recite papers and appearances], and both said third-party defendants having opposed the said motion unless the said motion be granted without prejudice to the rights of said third-party defendants to plead any statutory bar to the amended complaint, and any and all defenses to said amended complaint as though the action by the plaintiff against them had been commenced at the time of the service of the proposed amended complaint, and unless the order to be entered thereon contain a provision preserving the rights of said third-party defendants, and due deliberation having been had, and a decision having been rendered and filed herein on the __14__ day of __15_____, 19_16_, it is

ORDERED, that the motion of the plaintiff for an order permitting the plaintiff to amend his complaint to include a cause of action in damages against the third-party defendants, __17_____ and __18_____, be and hereby is granted, without prejudice to said third-party defendants to plead any statutory bar and any and all defenses to said amended complaint as said third-party defendants may have had had the causes of action alleged against said third-party defendants been commenced at the time of the service of the proposed amended complaint, and it is further

ORDERED, that the plaintiff serve said amended complaint upon the attorneys for the third-party defendants, __19_____ and __20_____, within twenty days from the date of the service of this order, with notice of entry.

Signed this __21__ day of __22_____, 19_23_ at __24_____, New York.

Enter.

> [Signature, with name printed underneath]
> Justice, Supreme Court
> __25_____ County

[Adapted from papers in Wajtman v Brooklyn Eastern Dist. Terminal, 276 AD 853, 93 NYS2d 586.]

Rule 1010. Dismissal or separate trial of third-party complaint

The court may dismiss a third-party complaint without prejudice, order a separate trial of the third-party claim or of any separate issue thereof, or make such other order as may be just. In exercising its discretion, the court shall consider whether the controversy between the third-party plaintiff and the third-party defendant will unduly delay the determination of the main action or prejudice the substantial rights of any party.

HISTORY:

Add as § 1010, L 1962, ch 308, renumbered Rule 1010, L 1962, ch 315, § 1, eff Sept 1, 1963.
Earlier statutes: CPA § 193-a.

ADVISORY COMMITTEE NOTES:

This rule is derived from CPA § 193-a(4), substantially unchanged. The provision that the bringing in of a third-party defendant shall be freely allowed has been added to discourage the dismissal of third-party complaints at the pleading stage on the ground that the principal defendant was guilty of active negligence when this point is controverted by the principal defendant. On the other hand, the principle of Fox v Western New York Motor Lines, Inc. 257 NY 305, 178 NE 289 (1931), that CPA § 211-a does not authorize enforcement of contribution against a joint tortfeasor by means of third-party practice, is not disturbed. No change is contemplated in § 211-a, which belongs in the practice act.

CROSS REFERENCES:

Third-party practice pleadings, CPLR 1007–1009, 1011.
Service of pleadings, CPLR 3012.
General and special verdicts, CPLR 4111.

FEDERAL ASPECTS:

Separate trials and separate judgments in actions in United States District Courts, Rule 13(i) of Federal Rules of Civil Procedure, USCS Court Rules.
Third-party practice, Rule 14 of Federal Rules of Civil Procedure, USCS Court Rules.

RESEARCH REFERENCES AND PRACTICE AIDS:

3 Carmody-Wait 2d, Parties §§ 19:116, 19:117.
7 Carmody-Wait 2d, Calendar Practice; Note of Issue § 50:3.
7 Carmody Wait 2d, Order of Disposition of Issues; Joint and Separate Trials § 52:1.

Law Reviews:

New York Civil Practice Law and Rules: parties. 27 Albany L Rev 182.
Parties and pleading under the CPLR. 31 Brooklyn L Rev 98.
Negligence—apportionment of damages among joint tortfeasors—right of a party actively negligent to implead a co-wrongdoer. 41 Fordham L Rev 167.

Torts—New York civil practice—a joint tort-feasor accorded unlimited right to implead a co-tortfeasor for partial indemnification based on comparative responsibility in negligence. 47 NYU L Rev 815.

A biannual survey of New York practice: Section 1007 and Rule 1010—Third-party practice. 38 St. John's L Rev 419.

A biannual survey of New York practice: Part IV: indemnification between tort-feasors. 39 St. John's L Rev 428.

Forms:

See "FORMS" heading following "CASE NOTES", infra.

CASE NOTES

1. In general
2. Disposition of primary action as affecting third-party action
3. Grounds for dismissal or severance, generally
4. —Delay or prejudice
5. —Stipulations or agreements limiting third-party actions

1. In general

In an action for injury from fall on a public sidewalk against the city which gave notice of "vouching in" to the United States, contending that U. S. government employees had driven trucks over the walk causing it to crack and break, motion by the United States to dismiss the notice of vouching in was not authorized by the statute. Urbach v New York (1965) 46 Misc 2d 503, 259 NYS2d 975.

2. Disposition of primary action as affecting third-party action

The disposition of the primary action does not necessarily require either recovery upon, or dismissal of, the third-party action, which may be prosecuted independently. Johnson v General Mut. Ins. Co. (1966) 26 AD2d 602, 271 NYS2d 428, mod on other grounds 24 NY2d 42, 298 NYS2d 937, 246 NE2d 713.

Although third-party action by automobile dealer against auctioneer of stolen vehicle could have been severed pursuant to CPLR § 3212, subd g and § 1010 following summary judgment for plaintiff on issue of dealer's liability for breach of warranty of title, trial of third-party action was to be held at same time as plaintiff was to appear for assessment of damages, unless third party action was not ready for trial at such date. Itoh v Kimi Sales, Ltd. (1973) 74 Misc 2d 402, 345 NYS2d 416.

Where plaintiff, in action for partition, was alter ego of third-party defendant and allegations of amended third-party complaint merely mirrored affirmative defenses asserted in answer, all issues arising by reason of third-party complaint could be determined in primary action and dismissal of causes of action asserted in the amended third-party complaint was not improper. Puerto Rico Holding Corp. v Gair Holding Corp. (1975) 47 AD2d 533, 363 NYS2d 610.

3. Grounds for dismissal or severance, generally

Where one of the causes of action set forth in the third-party complaint did not contain issues common to all parties and bore no relation to any alleged liability of defendant to plaintiff, it would not be dismissed but would be severed, to be tried by the same trial judge following the trial of the issues common to all parties. Siderius, Inc. v Thyssen Steel/Los Angeles, Div. of Thyssen, Inc. (1977) 56 AD2d 555, 391 NYS2d 865.

In action on policy by insured against insurer for loss sustained by dishonesty of employee, wherein insurer served third-party complaint against employee, insured may move to dismiss such third-party complaint for insufficiency. Sol Lenzner Corp. v Aetna Casualty & Surety Co. (1964) 20 AD2d 305, 246 NYS2d 950.

The granting of a severance of the third-party action from the main one was an improvident exercise of discretion where common questions of law and fact existed, pretrial discovery procedures had been substantially accomplished, and no prejudice to a substantial right of any party had been demonstrated. Huttick v Biograph Realty Corp. (1971) 37 AD2d 597, 322 NYS2d 827.

In action on policy by insured against insurer for loss sustained by dishonesty of employee, wherein insurer served third-party complaint against employee, and employee was an elderly lady who had been in insured's employ for many years, a separate trial of such third-party action was held warranted to avoid prejudice to insured. Sol Lenzner Corp. v Aetna Casualty & Surety Co. (1964) 20 AD2d 305, 246 NYS2d 950.

4. —Delay or prejudice

The court has discretionary power to determine whether the controversy between the third-party plaintiff and the third-party defendant will unduly delay the determination of the main action or prejudice substantial rights of any party. Musco v Conte (1964) 22 AD2d 121, 254 NYS2d 589.

Although a statement of readiness had been filed in malpractice action, which involved serious and permanent physical injuries and large special damages, where action had been marked off trial calendar and a third-party claim had been asserted by the defendant medical center so that there would be no trial delay, it was not an abuse of discretion for Special Term to allow discovery to proceed. Pezzella v Catholic Medical Center, Inc. (1975) 50 AD2d 867, 377 NYS2d 144.

There was no abuse of discretion in the severance of a third-party action from the main action, in view of the tardiness of the institution of the third-party action and the resultant delay and prejudice to both the plaintiff and the third-party defendant. Todd v Gull Contracting Co. (1964) 22 AD2d 904, 255 NYS2d 452.

Even though third-party complaint in tort action stated valid cause of action for partial indemnification from subsequent tortfeasors, trial court correctly dismissed third-party complaint in view of

tardiness of commencement of third-party action and resultant delay, confusion and prejudice it would engender in main action and those joined for trial therewith; dismissal should, however, have been without prejudice. Cipollina v Kent (1976) 52 AD2d 632, 382 NYS2d 548.

5. —Stipulations or agreements limiting third-party actions

Insurer's motion for dismissal under CPLR § 1010 was denied where movant's claim that insured's third-party complaint was barred by policy provision stated no ground upon which court could grant motion. Banks v Triboro Coach Corp. (1973) 73 Misc 2d 833, 342 NYS2d 612.

CASE NOTES

UNDER FORMER CIVIL PRACTICE LAWS

See also Case Notes under § 1007, supra.

1. Generally
2. Amendments
3. Dismissal of third-party complaint
4. —Effect of dismissal
5. Motion to dismiss
6. —Time for motion
7. Notice to all parties appearing
8. Discretion of court
9. —When prejudicial
10. Separate trial

1. Generally

Third-party complaint, predicated upon liability over of third party, was sufficient. Triglianos v Henry Moss & Co. (1947) 189 Misc 157, 71 NYS2d 618.

Undenied allegations of defense in answer of third-party defendant are to be deemed controverted. Gorham v Arons (1947) 76 NYS2d 850.

Third-party complaint, alleging that plaintiff's injuries were caused by sole and primary negligence of third-party defendant in operation of aforementioned cellar doors, without alleging ultimate facts, as merely conclusory. Bennett v Lambert (1948) 82 NYS2d 111.

Where theory of third-party complaint is that defendant was passive wrongdoer and may be entitled to reimbursement for damages to which he may have to respond to plaintiff because of active wrongdoing of third-party defendant, it is sufficient in law as matter of pleading. Schaller v Republic Aviation Corp. (1948) 193 Misc 60, 83 NYS2d 540.

Third-party complaint, in action for personal injury, which does not proceed upon any theory of contractual right to indemnity or common-law right of indemnification based upon theories involving passive and active negligence, was defec-

tive. Coughlan v Joseph Bisceglia & Sons (1950) 100 NYS2d 738.

Absolute liability need not be alleged; it is sufficient to assert possibility of liability. Madison Ave. Properties Corp. v Royal Ins. Co. (1953) 281 AD 641, 120 NYS2d 626.

Possible liability is all that third-party complaint need allege; uncertainty of liability does not render allegations insufficient. Lerner v Banco Constr. Corp. (1951) 109 NYS2d 231.

The fact that defendants in their answer deny any liability to the plaintiff did not bar a claim over for indemnity; such hypothetical pleading was the only way in which CPA §§ 264 (§§ 3012(a), 3019(b), 3020(a) herein) and 193-a could properly be utilized. Brady v Stanley Weiss & Sons, Inc. (1958) 6 AD2d 241, 175 NYS2d 850.

There was no rule of law which prevented a defendant from denying the allegations of the complaint and then pleading that if he nevertheless was held liable to the plaintiff it would be on a ground that entitled him to recover over against another defendant. Such pleading was the only way in which CPA §§ 264 (§§ 3012 (a), 3019(b), 3020(a) herein) and 193-a could properly be utilized. Brady v Stanley Weiss & Sons, Inc., supra.

Under subdivision 3 of CPA § 193-a a plaintiff might amend his pleading to assert against a third-party defendant any claim which the plaintiff might have asserted against the third-party defendant had he been joined originally as a defendant and this might be done as of course without securing leave of the court. CPA § 193-a did not set forth any limitation of time within which such right might be exercised nor was the privilege limited by the provisions of CPA § 244 (§ 3025(a) herein). Aprea v New York (1958) 11 Misc 2d 645, 171 NYS2d 884.

In action for wrongful death from poisonous gas escaping from defective refrigerator in plaintiff's apartment in multiple dwelling, third-party complaint by landlord against gas company for negligent repairs and breach of warranty, alleging no facts to establish primary liability of gas company but only conclusory statement that any recovery by plaintiff must be based upon its negligence, was dismissed. Mandel v Criares (1956) 1 AD2d 830, 148 NYS2d 380.

In action against city for negligence in leaving uncovered manhole in street, third-party complaint by city against county for indemnity was insufficient for failure to allege service of notice of claim on county. Kessler v Peekskill (1955) 1 Misc 2d 744, 152 NYS2d 919.

In action by plaintiff to impose liability on truck owner based on negligent operation of truck and on telephone company for negligently creating dangerous condition by stretching wire struck by truck, third-party complaint by telephone company against truck owner, based on theory of passive negligence, was insufficient, where there was no allegation of special relationship between parties responsible for injuries by which one is regarded as being bound to indemnify other in negligent situation. Campigno v McQuide (1955) 286 AD 660, 146 NYS2d 83.

In action against electrical subcontractor for injury to workman of another contractor coming in contact with conduit or pipe installed by defendant in negligent manner without guards so as to constitute nuisance and trap for employees of other contractors, defendant's third-party complaint against plaintiff's employer was insufficient where it failed to state facts from which it could be determined that the defendant was other than a joint tort-feasor in pari delicto with plaintiff's employer. Focacci v New York (1956) 2 AD2d 902, 157 NYS2d 280.

Third-party complaint will not be required to spell out a cause of action against the third-party defendant with the same precision required of the main complaint, and the question whether it should stand depends upon whether the main complaint shows that liability could be fastened on the third-party plaintiff for passive negligence in circumstances occasioned by the third-party defendant's active negligence. To compel a third-party plaintiff to plead with precision could well subject him to summary judgment by the main plaintiff. Humble Oil & Refining Co. v M. W. Kellogg Co. (1961) 13 AD2d 754, 215 NYS2d 416, app gr 14 AD2d 670, 219 NYS2d 944.

2. Amendments

After service of a pleading under subdivision 3 of CPA § 193-a any amendment was subject to the provisions of CPA § 244 (§ 3025(a) herein). Aprea v New York (1958) 11 Misc 2d 645, 171 NYS2d 884.

Where, under the terms of the insurance policy, plaintiff, as customer of defendant, could join third-party defendant insurance company as a defendant, plaintiff was granted leave to amend the complaint to state a cause of action against the third-party defendant. Levine v Arthur Rosenbaum, Inc. (1958) 16 Misc 2d 980, 182 NYS2d 135.

3. Dismissal of third-party complaint

Complaint variously alleging acts and omissions constituting primary or secondary liability should not be dismissed on motion. Logan v Bee Builders (1950) 277 AD 1040, 100 NYS2d 483.

Uncertainty as to liability on part of third-party defendant is not sufficient reason to dismiss third-party complaint. Robinson v Binghamton Constr. Co. (1950) 277 AD 468, 100 NYS2d 900.

Where third-party complaint fails to state facts showing any right of recovery over against third-party defendant, dismissal is proper. Desimone v C. J. Burgess Co. (1951) 278 AD 751, 104 NYS2d 734, affd 303 NY 930, 105 NE2d 504; Reilly v Charles Herman Contr. Co. (1949) 89 NYS2d 632.

Where employee of third-party defendant butcher sued owner of building for personal injuries caused by falling plaster, alleging that defendant owner was responsible as active tort-feasor for such defective condition, third-party complaint against butcher, alleging liability solely because of ownership of store and constructive notice of defect, was dismissed. Mileto v Polvica R. Corp. (1954) 137 NYS2d 56.

On motion by third-party defendant to dismiss third-party complaint for insufficiency, consideration must be given not only to pleading directly attacked, but also to complaint-in-chief interposed by original plaintiff as against original defendant, who, by virtue of invoking CPA § 193-a has become third-party plaintiff, with result that original complaint thus studied must bear adequate relation to charge for which original defendant (as third-party plaintiff) is seeking indemnity from third-party defendant. Atlas C. E. Corp. v Consolidated Edison Co. (1955) 4 Misc 2d 238, 136 NYS2d 822.

In action by father and minor son for injuries to son by fall on metal grating abutting premises owned by defendant, defendant may not implead minor's father who was party plaintiff to action, suing for loss of son's services. Lesser v Klein (1955) 140 NYS2d 794.

Claim over asserted in third-party complaint against impleaded defendant is insufficient in law where it contains allegations which if established would preclude liability on part of original defendant. Coffey v Flower City C. & E. Co. (1956) 2 AD2d 191, 153 NYS2d 763, affd 2 NY2d 898, 161 NYS2d 149, 141 NE2d 632.

In action against city as owner of overhead trolley system for wrongful death of lineman killed while working on such system because of city's negligence in failure to replace defective insulator, and also against manufacturer and dealer of insulator, city's third-party complaint against contractors which installed insulator and cross-claims by contractors against manufacturer and dealer were dismissed where city failed to prove negligent manufacture of insulator. Thibault v New York (1956, Sup) 154 NYS2d 338, affd in part and revd in part 6 AD2d 904, 177 NYS2d 905, affd 6 NY2d 759, 186 NYS2d 658, 159 NE2d 204.

In action for personal injuries and property damages sustained when delivery truck was struck by defendant's railroad locomotive at private grade crossing, third-party complaint by railroad against summer camp licensor granted private right to cross railroad tracks for nominal consideration, based on indemnity exempting railroad from liability for all damages, even due to negligence of its employees, was sufficient. Salamy v New York Cent. System (1955) 1 AD2d 27, 146 NYS2d 814.

Where in action by subcontractor against contractor for contract price of trussed rafters, contractor served third-party complaint against owner for indemnification, alleging that owner has contract claim against contractor because of subcontractor's delay in performance and that if subcontractor prevails in its action then contractor will sustain damages by reason of its breach of contract with owner and third-party defendant to amount of judgment, contractor's third-party complaint failed to state cause of action against owner. Timber Structures v Terra-Rube C. Corp. (1955) 145 NYS2d 599.

In action against bus company by tire company's employee for injuries sustained in fall in former's garage, third-party complaint by bus company against tire company which had contracted to furnish tires for buses and to indemnify bus company from liability for death or injuries of tire company employees while engaged in tire company's work, was dismissed, as such indemnity provision did not protect bus company against liability for its own negligence. Flynn v New York City Omnibus Corp. (1955) 286 AD 1109, 146 NYS2d 265.

In action for injuries to subcontractor's employee who fell from scaffold when wall supporting it collapsed, against owner and general contractor, wherein latter impleaded subcontractor, both complaint and third-party complaint were dismissed for failure to prove actional negligence. Haddon v Engel (1957) 1 AD2d 954, 150 NYS2d 57.

Where complaint is broad enough to admit of recovery by plaintiff upon acts of negligence separate and apart from alleged failure to comply with Administrative Code provisions for maintenance of sidewalk shed, and proof upon trial may establish that third-party plaintiff was passive tort-feasor entitled to recovery over from third-party defendant as active tort-feasor, third-party complaint should not be dismissed. Klein v Bargray C. Corp. (1956) 1 AD2d 883, 149 NYS2d 926.

Where injured employee of carpentry subcontractor sued general contractor and lumber supplier, and general contractor impleaded carpentry subcontractor as third-party defendant, and latter served cross-complaint on said lumber supplier, dismissal of cross-complaint should provide leave to replead, since lumber supplier may be liable over to carpentry subcontractor for failure to inspect defective lumber supplied. Crawford v Blitman C. Corp. (1956) 1 AD2d 398, 150 NYS2d 387.

Where original action simple contract action for services rendered triable by jury and there was no single common issue that could be tried out together under either cause of action set forth in the third-party complaint, third-party complaint dismissed with leave to serve amended complaint. Ammann & Whitney v Edgarton (1957) 12 Misc 2d 119, 175 NYS2d 536.

An automobile liability insurance company which insured corporation and which is defending action instituted against corporation by said corporation's president's wife who was injured as passenger while her said husband was driving car cannot have its attorney without the corporation's consent prepare and verify a purported third-party complaint by the corporation against the president if purported third-party defendant in spite of cooperation and subrogation provision in policy and in spite of the fact that the policy does not cover injuries to spouse and such third-party complaint dismissed. Ulanoff v Croyden Shirt Co. (1958) 14 Misc 2d 13, 174 NYS2d 357.

In action against operator of hospital, and the nurse and physician engaged by him, to recover for personal injuries to newborn child, third-party complaint by hospital operator against two other physicians, alleging that any injury to child was caused by their negligence, was dismissed because it did not seek to hold third-party defendants for plaintiff's claim against defendants, but for entirely different acts of negligence not alleged in the primary complaint. Shea v Gitlin (1959) 20 Misc 2d 215, 190 NYS2d 792.

Where the original complaint charged defendant and third-party defendant with active negligence, third-party complaint was dismissed for insufficiency in the absence of any showing that defendant had a contractual or statutory right of indemnification from third-party defendant. Morgan v Donahue (1958) 19 Misc 2d 532, 195 NYS2d 917, affd 8 AD2d 768, 187 NYS2d 339.

In action for wrongful death of contractor's employee who was killed in fall while working on defendant's property, where, from the allegations of original complaint, it was possible that contractor's active negligence was primary cause of employee's death and defendant owner was guilty of passive negligence, owner's third-party complaint against contractor was held sufficient. Gallagher v Hill Greenhouse Constr., Inc. (1960) 23 Misc 2d 167, 197 NYS2d 234.

On motion to dismiss third-party complaint for insufficiency where the negligence charged in the main complaint might be construed as either affirmative or passive, as where one of the specifications of negligence is, that defendant permitted the sidewalk in front of his premises to become cluttered with glass from a broken window, the question of sufficiency should be resolved in favor of the third-party complaint to await final disposition as tested against additional information secured by a bill of particulars, examinations, or ultimately the facts produced at trial. Klein v Bukowski (1961) 12 AD2d 872, 210 NYS2d 161.

Where main complaint indiscriminately charges all defendants with both active and passive negligence, fate of cross-claim or third-party complaint should be reserved for decision upon trial. Macrina v Scerra (1961) 28 Misc 2d 260, 211 NYS2d 799.

Where original complaint clearly charges defendant with having created the latent defect and dangerous condition, so that it is unnecessary to try the issue as to whether it is possible under its allegations to impose a liability on the third-party plaintiff for passive negligence alone, the third-party complaint must be dismissed. Gingeresky v Gifford-Wood Co. (1961) 14 AD2d 623, 218 NYS2d 339.

4. —Effect of dismissal

Dismissal of third-party complaint for failure to state a cause of action is not a determination on the merits. Putvin v Buffalo Electric Co. (1959) 5 NY2d 447, 186 NYS2d 15, 158 NE2d 691.

5. Motion to dismiss

Dismissal of third-party complaint will not be made where plaintiff made no formal motion but merely joined in motion by third-party defendant based solely upon insufficiency of third-party complaint. Gorham v Arons (1947) 76 NYS2d 850.

Where neither third-party defendant nor plaintiff moved for discretionary dismissal of third-party complaint, without prejudice, or for separate trial of third-party claim court cannot, on application by third party to dismiss third-party complaint, consider affidavits by plaintiff, defendant or third-party plaintiff. Green v Hudson Shoring Co. (1947) 191 Misc 297, 77 NYS2d 842.

On motion by third party defendant to dismiss amended third-party complaint, propriety of plaintiff's pleading is not before court. Teepell v Jefferson County Sav. Bank, 3 Misc 2d 508, 148 NYS2d 347.

Where upon all pleadings triable issue is presented as to whether sole proximate cause of accident was primary or active negligence of third-party defendant and whether negligence, if any, of third-party plaintiff was secondary or passive, third-party complaint is legally sufficient. Bunchez v Astoria-Star W. Serv. (1956) 1 AD2d 947, 150 NYS2d 760.

In action for injuries to tenant struck by door of self-service elevator in multiple dwelling, wherein defendant owner served cross-complaint against service company for negligent repairs, motion by service company to dismiss both complaint and cross-complaint was denied, as to complaint, though plaintiff was not party to contract between owner and service company, and as to cross-complaint, where there was question of fact whether owner was actively or passively negligent. Wisner v Harmas H. Corp. (1956) 1 AD2d 957, 150 NYS2d 38.

In action by person injured by dumbwaiter which moved while it was open, against building owner for negligent maintenance, third-party complaint by owner against elevator company for negligent repair was legally sufficient, since jury may find that act of omission was passive negligence entitling third-party plaintiff to recover over against

defendant whose conduct caused dangerous condition. Solomon v Marseilles Hotel Corp. (1956) 1 AD2d 766, 149 NYS2d 581.

A motion to dismiss a third party complaint was proper procedure where the authority of the attorney to institute the third party action was challenged since a defendant has the right to raise that objection. Schiro v Catania (1957) 13 Misc 2d 1033, 174 NYS2d 353.

Where despite formal allegations in the pleading it cannot be said with any degree of certainty assuming that defendant is adjudged to be liable to the plaintiff whether such liability will be founded on such defendant's active or passive negligence, an issue of fact is presented which should be resolved by the triers of the facts on the basis of all the proof adduced at the trial and not by the court on the basis of the pleadings. Tarantino v Buck (1958) 6 AD2d 894, 177 NYS2d 557.

Where original complaint is susceptible of construction that third party plaintiff's acts were supervisory only, liability of third party defendant may not be determined from pleadings alone. Public Administrator v Rubin Constr. Corp. (1958) 6 AD2d 678, 173 NYS2d 943.

On motion to dismiss third-party complaint, its allegations must be deemed to be true. Cook v Fogelsonger (1959) 21 Misc 2d 337, 193 NYS2d 259.

Where defendant, sued for $600 in main action, claimed over against third-party defendant for $600, or in alternative for larger sum, since he could properly recover the $600, if plaintiff recovers from him, fact that alternative demand is in excess of amount in suit in main action does not make third-party complaint dismissible. Joseph v R. & M. Embroidery Co. (1959) 21 Misc 2d 392, 195 NYS2d 736.

When evidence might be adduced which would result in jury question whether defendant was passively negligent while third party defendant was actively negligent, third-party complaint would not be dismissed on motion for insufficiency. Hollant v North Shore Hospital, Inc. (1960) 24 Misc 2d 892, 206 NYS2d 177.

Third-party complaint will not be required to spell out a cause of action against the third-party defendant with the same precision required of the main complaint, and the question whether it should stand depends upon whether the main complaint shows that liability could be fastened on the third-party plaintiff for passive negligence in circumstances occasioned by the third-party defendant's active negligence. To compel a third-party plaintiff to plead with precision could well subject him to summary judgment by the main plaintiff. Humble Oil & Refining Co. v M. W. Kellogg Co. (1961) 13 AD2d 754, 215 NYS2d 416, app gr 14 AD2d 670, 219 NYS2d 944.

6. —Time for motion

Motion for discretionary dismissal of third-party complaint may be made either before or after third party has pleaded to third-party complaint. Green v Hudson Shoring Co. (1947) 191 Misc 297, 77 NYS2d 842.

After issue joined on third-party complaint, third party may move to dismiss on notice to all parties. Occhipinti v Buscemi (1947) 71 NYS2d 766.

Motion to dismiss third-party complaint before answer is proper. Smith v Brown (1947) 72 NYS2d 867, affd 273 AD 809, 76 NYS2d 836, 837, 838.

Where third-party complaint specifically charges third-party defendant with active negligence and states that third-party plaintiff's actions were passive, on motion to dismiss third-party complaint, it cannot be determined whether third-party plaintiff or third-party defendant was tort feasor in pari delicto or whether third-party plaintiff was passively negligent and motion to dismiss denied. Epstein v Empress Hotel, Inc. (1957) 11 Misc 2d 21, 169 NYS2d 878.

7. Notice to all parties appearing

Where third-party defendant has given notice of its application to dismiss third-party complaint only to third-party plaintiff, dismissal was denied, as plaintiff had no opportunity to make known his position to court. Prost v New York (1947) 190 Misc 197, 73 NYS2d 811.

Third-party defendant is entitled to notice of plaintiff's motion for summary judgment to dismiss third-party complaint, where third-party defendant had not answered and his time to do so had not expired. Mansfield Iron Works v Silveri (1951) 106 NYS2d 496.

The right of third-party plaintiffs who compromised in action with original plaintiffs to recover over against third-party plaintiff's grantor in an action to establish a prescriptive right of way depends on proof of facts which imposed initial liability as well as reasonableness of amount paid in settlement and trial to resolve such issues required and summary judgment denied. Washington v Morantz (1958) 11 Misc 2d 273, 177 NYS2d 470.

8. Discretion of court

Abuse of discretion shown in granting plaintiff's motion to dismiss third-party complaint without prejudice to separate action. Barone v Triborough Bridge & T. Authority (1949) 276 AD 775, 92 NYS2d 796.

The court in its discretion may dismiss a third party complaint without prejudice to the bringing of another action or order a separate trial or make such other orders concerning the proceedings as may be necessary to further justice or convenience and where severance will not injure any party, severance properly directed. Kelly v Yannotti (1958) 4 NY2d 603, 176 NYS2d 637, 152 NE2d 69, see 6 AD2d 1046, 179 NYS2d 653.

Where the complaint in the prime action contains allegations, upon proof of some of which defendant might be primarily liable, and it also appears from the complaint that defendant is alleged to be guilty only of passive negligence, the court in the exercise of discretion will not dismiss the third party complaint for legal insufficiency but will leave the question of liability present for disposition at the trial. Schneiberg v Utz (1957) 8 Misc 2d 535, 167 NYS2d 832.

In passenger's action for injuries against owner and driver of car, joint third party complaint by defendants against garageman, charging that plaintiff's injuries were caused by latter's failure to properly repair brakes, was dismissed as to driver since he could not assert a valid claim over, but was sustained as to car-owner since her negligence was purely statutory, and driver's active negligence could not be imputed to her, and if accident were caused by brake failure she had valid claim over against garageman. Lipsman v Warren (1960) 10 AD2d 868, 199 NYS2d 761.

9. —When prejudicial

In action for personal injuries by fall on defective step in hallway of multiple dwelling, owner's third-party complaint against contractor, filed four years after action begun, was dismissed as prejudicial to plaintiff. Steiner v Esland Properties, Inc. (1952) 113 NYS2d 51.

Where landlord, sued for death of tenant's employee, filed cross complaint against tenant, such claim would unduly delay and prejudice plaintiff, and was dismissed. Clements v Rockefeller (1947) 272 AD 1002, 74 NYS2d 412.

Delay and prejudice to plaintiff warranted separate trial of third-party claim that third-party defendant had agreed to indemnify third-party plaintiff against paying commissions to anyone else on purchase of trawler. Langdon & Matule v Eureka Iron Works (1948) 85 NYS2d 478, affd 275 AD 659, 86 NYS2d 668.

Insurer, impleaded by insured landlord, sued for personal injury, cannot avoid impleader on ground of prejudice, where jury had been formally waived. Litman v Garfinkle (1948) 193 Misc 256, 81 NYS2d 296.

Where defendant impleaded injured plaintiff's employer as third-party defendant as indemnitor, plaintiff's motion to dismiss third-party complaint on ground that introduction of workmen's compensation insurance policies by third-party defendant would be permitted and so prejudiced, was denied. Schaller v Republic Aviation Corp. (1948) 193 Misc 60, 83 NYS2d 540.

Where third-party complaint would unnecessarily complicate main action, it would be dismissed without prejudice to independent action. Bank of New York v Public Nat. Bank & T. Co. (1948) 195 Misc 812, 82 NYS2d 694, 92 NYS2d 620, affd 275 AD 932, 90 NYS2d 701, mod on reh 277 AD 963, 99 NYS2d 851, affd 301 NY 503, 93 NE2d 71.

Plaintiff's contention of undue prejudice, by delay of main trial, question of workmen's compensation coverage injected into trial, plaintiff's selection of jurors hampered, cross-examination of plaintiff's witnesses, and confusion of jury by issue of indemnity, held not to show such sacrifice of rights as to require dismissal of complaint in action for personal injuries. Brewster v Gair Realty Corp. (1950) 101 NYS2d 1006.

10. Separate trial

Where in action for trespass by insured contractor latter impleaded insurer, insurer was entitled to discretionary order of severance so that existence of insurance may not be brought to attention of jurors. Caserta v Beaver Constr. Corp. (1949) 197 Misc 410, 95 NYS2d 131.

Liability insurer was granted severance and separate trial of third-party claim, in action for personal injuries, triable by jury, against motorist who impleaded liability insurer as third-party defendant. De Lany v Allen (1951) 200 Misc 734, 105 NYS2d 635.

Insurer of defendant who impleaded insurer by third-party complaint because insurer refused to defend automobile injury case, was denied dismissal if trial to be without jury, and was granted separate trial if with jury. Remch v Grabow (1947) 193 Misc 731, 70 NYS2d 462.

Partial assignee may sue at law, provided parties necessary to effective determination of issues presented are joined. Rosenberg v Paul Tishman Co. (1952) 118 NYS2d 337.

Single trial of all issues should not be had where it will tend to create great confusion and may readily prejudice plaintiff in prosecution of his claim. Schulman v Kemach & Garson (1949) 88 NYS2d 81.

In wife's action for personal injuries and husband's action for loss of services in accident on premises owned by defendant, insured owners may implead liability insurer, and latter was granted severance of third-party action from original action to avoid prejudice because of insurance. Gleason v Sailer (1952) 203 Misc 227, 116 NYS2d 409.

In wife's action for personal injuries and husband's action for loss of services in accident on premises owned by defendant, insured owners may implead liability insurer, which was denied severance on ground that issues involved in original action and in third-party action would tax jury's ability to comprehend such issues. Gleason v Sailer, supra.

The court is given substantial discretion in connection with third-party complaints to order a separate trial of the third-party claim or of any separate issue thereof or to make such other orders concerning the proceeding as may be necessary to further justice or convenience. In exercising this discretion, the court is authorized to take into consideration whether a trial of the controversy between the third-party plaintiff and defendant would unduly delay the determination of the main action or prejudice any party thereunder. Ammann & Whitney v Edgarton (1957) 12 Misc 2d 119, 175 NYS2d 536.

In action for breach of warranty, seller brought in manufacturer and manufacturer brought in its suppliers as third party defendant. Since all the claims were related to the main action by questions of law or fact, motion for separate trial was denied. Knitmode Mills, Inc. v Bantam-U. S. Toys, Inc. (1956) 5 Misc 2d 708, 165 NYS2d 967.

Where terms of an insurance policy did not constitute a waiver barring a third party action under CPA § 193-a, motion to dismiss third party complaint denied and an application by the third party defendant for severance of trial denied. Eastling v Federated Dept. Stores, Inc. (1958) 12 Misc 2d 795, 173 NYS2d 61.

Separate trials were ordered where insurer would be prejudiced if the main personal injury and property damage action against insured and insured's third-party action against insurer were tried before the same jury. Cook v Fogelsonger (1959) 21 Misc 2d 337, 193 NYS2d 259.

In negligence action, defendant can bring third party action against broker for having failed to effect adequate insurance coverage, but in the interests of justice, cases should be separately tried. Thornton v New York (1959) 20 Misc 2d 838, 193 NYS2d 777.

In automobile personal injury negligence action where defendant impleads disclaiming insurance carrier, carrier is entitled to severance and separate trial, to avoid possible prejudice, even though jury because of compulsory insurance requirement in New York would be aware that there is insurance. Santonocito v Suburban Oil Co. (1961) 27 Misc 2d 697, 211 NYS2d 571.

Insurance broker, impleaded by defendant in negligence action, for alleged breach of agreement to provide full insurance coverage, was granted a severance, since he would be prejudiced if both actions were tried before same jury. N. & E. Greenberg's Sons, Inc. v Peter Pan Fur Co. (1961) 33 Misc 2d 453, 215 NYS2d 787.

FORMS

Form 1—Notice of motion to dismiss third-party complaint for delay or prejudice to main action

Form 2—Affidavit in support of motion to dismiss third-party complaint for delay or prejudice to main action

Form 3—Order dismissing third-party plaintiff's complaint for delay or prejudice to main action

Form 1

Notice of Motion to Dismiss Third-Party Complaint for Delay or Prejudice to Main Action

SUPREME COURT, COUNTY OF __1_____

Don Doe,
Plaintiff,
 against
Roy Roe,
Defendant and Third-   Notice of Motion
  Party Plaintiff,   Index No. — [if assigned]
 against
Leo Poe,
Third-Party Defendant.

PLEASE TAKE NOTICE that upon the original summons and complaint, original answer, third-party plaintiff's summons and third-party plaintiff's complaint, and third-party defendant's answer, the affidavit of __2_____, duly sworn to __3_____, 19_4_, and all other papers and proceedings had and filed herein, the original plaintiff above-named will move this Court, at a Motion Term, Part III thereof, to be held at the Courthouse, in the Borough of __5_____, City of __6_____, on the __7__ day of __8_____, 19_9_, at the opening of court at __10__ o'clock in the __11_____ noon of that day, or as soon thereafter as counsel can be heard, for an order dismissing the third-party plaintiff's complaint herein on the ground that the interposition of the alleged third-party claim at this time will unduly delay the determination of the main action and will unduly prejudice the substantial rights of the plaintiff, and for such other and further relief as may be just.

Date: New York, __12_____, __13__, 19_14_.

              __15__ _____
               Attorney for Plaintiff,
               [Office & P. O. Address
                and Telephone No.]

To __16_____
 Attorney for Defendant and
 Third-Party Plaintiff
 [Office & P. O. Address]

To __17_____
 Attorney for Third-Party Defendant
 [Office & P. O. Address]

Form 2

Affidavit in Support of Motion to Dismiss Third-Party Complaint for Delay or Prejudice to Main Action

[Title of court and cause,   Affidavit
as in Form 1 of CPLR 1007] Index No. — [if assigned]

STATE OF NEW YORK
COUNTY OF __1_____   ss:

__2_____, being duly sworn, deposes and says:

1. I am the plaintiff and make this motion to dismiss defendant's third-party complaint on the ground that its interposition will unduly delay the determination of the main action and will prejudice the substantial rights of the plaintiff.

2. Defendant is the owner of a tenant factory building; that he leased same to third-party defendant who agreed to insure the defendant against any claims arising out of the operation of the elevators; that plaintiff was an employee of said lessee and was injured by a fall down an open elevator shaft; that defendant was negligent in failing to

keep the elevator door keys in a safe place and under the supervision of a responsible person.

3. The summons and complaint were served in October, 1943, and the answer was served within 20 days thereafter; that the third-party complaint was not served until three years later, when the cause was on the ready trial calendar.

4. On the eve of trial, after long examinations before trial and after all the issues had been settled and framed for trial, defendant served its third-party complaint herein and annexed hereto.

5. Said third-party defendant then served its combined answer to plaintiff's complaint and to third-party's complaint, covering 21 pages; that its answer to plaintiff's complaint pleads denials and five separate defenses, such as contributory negligence, statute of limitations, lack of jurisdiction, and application of Workmen's Compensation Law, and that said answer demands judgment against both original plaintiff and third-party plaintiff.

6. It will be a long time before plaintiff can get to trial, and that, instead of presenting a simple factual issue, the trial will become so complicated and intricate that there is grave danger that the main issue will be entirely lost sight of.

7. Consequently the complicated cross-issues obscuring the original issue may so confuse the main issue that substantial rights of plaintiff will be prejudiced.

WHEREFORE plaintiff prays that this motion be granted in all respects, with the costs of this motion.

[Signature of affiant]
[Print signer's name below signature]

[Jurat]

Form 3

Order Dismissing Third-Party Plaintiff's Complaint for Delay or Prejudice to Main Action

SUPREME COURT, __1_____ COUNTY.

| [Title of cause, as in | Order |
| Form 2 of CPLR 1007] | Index No. — [if assigned] |

Present: Hon. __2_____, Justice.

A motion having been made by the attorney for the plaintiff, for an order dismissing the third-party plaintiff's complaint of the defendant, __3_____, on the ground that the interposition of the alleged third-party claim at this time will unduly delay the determination of the main action and will prejudice the substantial rights of the plaintiff and upon reading and filing the notice of motion, dated __4_____ __5__, 19_6_, with proof of due service thereof, and the pleadings herein, and said motion having regularly come on to be heard on the __7_ day of __8_____, 19_9_, and after hearing __10_____, of counsel in support of the motion, and __11_____, of counsel for the defendant and third-party plaintiff, in opposition thereto, and due deliberation having been had thereon, upon reading and filing the opinion of the Court.

Now, on motion of __12_____, attorneys for plaintiff, [Don Doe], it is

ORDERED, that this motion be and the same hereby is in all respects granted.

Signed this __13_ day of __14_____, 19_15_ at __16_____, New York.

Enter,

__17_____
[Print signer's name below signature]
Justice, Supreme Court
__18_____ County

493

Rule 1011. Successive third-party proceedings; counterclaims

A third-party defendant may proceed pursuant to section 1007 against any person who is or may be liable to him for all or part of the third-party claim. When a counterclaim is asserted against a plaintiff, he may proceed pursuant to section 1007 as if he were a defendant.

HISTORY:

Add as section 1011, L 1962, ch 308, renumbered Rule 1011, L 1962, ch 315, § 1, eff Sept 1, 1963.
Earlier statutes: CPA § 193-a.

ADVISORY COMMITTEE NOTES:

This rule follows former law; it permits successive third-party proceedings and permits a plaintiff who has had a counterclaim asserted against him to bring in a third party. The rule is derived from CPA § 193-a(6), substantially unchanged.

CROSS REFERENCES:

Third party practice pleading, CPLR 1007–1010.
Demand for relief, CPLR 3017.
General and special verdicts, CPLR 4111.

FEDERAL ASPECTS:

Counterclaim and cross-claim in actions in United States District Courts: joinder of additional parties, Rule 13(h) of Federal Rules of Civil Procedure, USCS Court Rules.
Third-party practice, Rule 14 of Federal Rules of Civil Procedure, USCS Court Rules.

RESEARCH REFERENCES AND PRACTICE AIDS:

3 Carmody-Wait 2d, Parties §§ 19:93, 19:95.

Law Reviews:

New York Civil Practice Law and Rules: parties. 27 Albany L Rev 182.
Parties and pleading under the CPLR. 31 Brooklyn L Rev 98.
Negligence—apportionment of damages among joint tortfeasors—right of a party actively negligent to implead a co-wrongdoer. 41 Fordham L Rev 167.
Torts—New York civil practice—a joint tort-feasor accorded unlimited right to implead a co-tortfeasor for partial indemnification based on comparative responsibility in negligence. 47 NYU L Rev 815.
A biannual survey of New York practice: Part IV: indemnification between tort-feasors. 39 St. John's L Rev 428.

Forms:

See "FORMS" heading following "CASE NOTES", infra.

CASE NOTES

UNDER FORMER CIVIL PRACTICE LAWS

See also Case Notes under § 1007, supra.

Where several defendants are sued for personal injury, one defendant may implead third-party defendant who became party to action commenced by plaintiff, and third-party defendant may file cross complaint against another defendant. Portnoy v United Engineers & Constructors, 274 AD 891, 82 NYS2d 464.

Where in action to enjoin use of driveway defendant impleaded his grantor, latter may plead counterclaim against defendant and plaintiff and also as third-party defendant, implead his grantor as second third-party defendant. Acco Products v Cooperative G.L.F. Holding Corp. 96 NYS2d 541, affd 277 AD 954, 99 NYS2d 725.

FORMS

Form 1—Third-party summons; action by third-party defendant

Form 2—Third-party summons; action by plaintiff on counterclaim

Form 1

Third-Party Summons; Action by Third-Party Defendant

__¹_____ Court, County of __²_____

AB,
Plaintiff
  against
CD,
Defendant
CD,
Defendant and Third-Party Plaintiff
  against   Third-Party Summons
EF,   Index No. __³__
Third-Party Defendant
EF,
Third-Party Defendant and
    Third-Party Plaintiff
  against
GH,
Third-Party Defendant

TO THE ABOVE NAMED THIRD-PARTY DEFENDANT GH:

YOU ARE HEREBY SUMMONED to answer the third-party complaint of EF, the third-party defendant and third-party plaintiff, [add, if desired: and the third-party complaint of CD, the defendant and third-party plaintiff (add, if desired: and the complaint of AB, the plaintiff)] copies of which together with copies of all prior pleadings in this action are herewith served on you, and to serve copies of your answer upon the undersigned, attorney for EF [add, if answers to the complaints of CD and/ or AB are requested: and upon __⁴_____, Esq., attorney for CD, whose address is __⁵_____, and upon __⁶_____ Esq., attorney for AB, whose address is __⁷_____] within twenty days after the service of this summons, exclusive of the day of service, or if service of this summons is made by any means other than by personal delivery to you within the state, within thirty days after such service is complete. In case of your failure to answer, judgment will be taken against you by default for the relief demanded in the third-party complaint of EF, the third-party defendant and third-party plaintiff herein.

Dated: __⁸_____

__⁹_____
Attorney for EF, third-
party defendant and
third-party plaintiff
__¹⁰_____ Office and P. O. Address
Telephone No. __¹¹__

Form 2

Third-Party Summons; Action by Plaintiff on Counterclaim

___1_____ Court, County of __2_____

AB,
Plaintiff
  against
CD,
Defendant
CD,
Defendant and Third-Party Plaintiff
  against   Third-Party Summons
EF,   Index No. __3__
Third-Party Defendant*
AB,
Defendant and Third-Party Plaintiff
  against
GH,
Third-Party Defendant

TO THE ABOVE NAMED THIRD-PARTY DEFENDANT GH:

YOU ARE HEREBY SUMMONED to answer the third-party complaint of AB, the plaintiff and third-party plaintiff [add, if desired: and the complaint of AB, the plaintiff (add, if desired: and the third-party complaint of CD, the defendant and third-party plaintiff)]* copies of which together with copies of all prior pleadings in this action are herewith served on you, and to serve copies of your answer upon the undersigned, attorney for AB, plaintiff, and plaintiff and third-party plaintiff [add if answer to the complaint of CD is requested: and upon __4_____ Esq., attorney for CD, whose address is __5_____] within twenty days after the service of this summons, exclusive of the day of service, or if service of this summons is made by any means other than by personal delivery to you within the state, within thirty days after such service is complete. In case of your failure to answer, judgment will be taken against you by default for the relief demanded in the third-party complaint of AB, the plaintiff and third-party plaintiff herein.

Dated: __6_____

__7_____
Attorney for AB, plaintiff,
and plaintiff and third-
party plaintiff
__8_____ Office and P. O. Address
Telephone No. __9__

§ 1012. Intervention as of right; notice to attorney-general where constitutionality in issue

(a) Intervention as of right. Upon timely motion, any person shall be permitted to intervene in any action:

1. when a statute of the state confers an absolute right to intervene; or

2. when the representation of the person's interest by the parties is or may be inadequate and the person is or may be bound by the judgment; or

3. when the action involves the disposition or distribution of, or the title or

---

* If counterclaim is interposed in answer of CD, defendant, then the references to the proceeding entitled to "CD against EF" should be omitted.

a claim for damages for injury to, property and the person may be affected adversely by the judgment.

(b) Notice to attorney-general where constitutionality in issue. When the constitutionality of a statute of the state is involved in an action to which the state is not a party, the court shall notify the attorney-general, who shall be permitted to intervene in support of its constitutionality.

(c) Notice to comptroller of the state of New York where public retirement benefits are in issue. Where public retirement benefits, paid, payable, claimed, or sought to be paid by a state retirement system or any other retirement system established for public employees within this state or any subdivision thereof, or the interpretation of any provisions of law or rules governing any such retirement system or the operation thereof, are involved in an action to which the comptroller of the state of New York is not a party, the court shall notify said comptroller, who shall be permitted, in his discretion, to intervene in such action or to file a brief amicus curiae.

HISTORY:
>Add, L 1962, ch 308, eff Sept 1, 1963.
>Sub (c), add, L 1972, ch 360, eff Sept 1, 1972.
>Earlier statutes: CPA §§ 193-b, 687-a.

ADVISORY COMMITTEE NOTES:
>**Subd (a)** is derived from CPA § 193-b(1), substantially unchanged.
>**Subd (b)** is new.
>As to the provision for notification to the attorney general in this section, see § 71 of the Executive Law, which corresponds, in a general way, to the Federal statute referred to in Federal rule 24(c). However, there are differences between the state and the Federal statutes which prevent using the pertinent language of rule 24(c). The state statute is somewhat complicated and the simple provision incorporated in this section is believed to suffice; there is no actual inconsistency between § 71 of the Executive Law and this section.

CROSS REFERENCES:
>Intervention by permission, CPLR 1013.
>Proposed intervention pleading, CPLR 1014.
>Co-respondent as party to action for divorce, Dom Rel Law § 172(1).
>Action involving appeal from decision relating to division for youth, Exec Law 501-b.
>Real property actions, Real P Actions & Pr Law § 241.

FEDERAL ASPECTS:
>Service and special rule where constitutionality of Act of Congress is in issue, Rule 33 of United States Supreme Court Rules, USCS Court Rules.
>Cases involving constitutional questions where United States is not a party, Rule 44 of Federal Rules of Appellate Procedure, USCS Court Rules.
>Intervention as of right, Rule 24(a) of Federal Rules of Civil Procedure, USCS Court Rules.

RESEARCH REFERENCES AND PRACTICE AIDS:
>44 NY Jur, Pensions and Retirement Systems §§ 2, 27.
>55 NY Jur, State of New York §§ 20, 28, 73.1.
>57 NY Jur, Suretyship and Guaranty § 270.
>3 Carmody-Wait 2d, Parties §§ 19:135 et seq., 19:180.
>12 Carmody-Wait 2d, Action to Recover a Chattel (Replevin) § 82:128.
>13 Carmody-Wait 2d, Notice of Pendency of Actions § 87:78.
>14 Carmody-Wait 2d, Partition § 91:69.
>21 Carmody-Wait 2d, Actions By or Against the State § 126:12.

25 Carmody-Wait 2d, Fundamentals of Practice in the Surrogate's Court § 149:214.
25 Carmody-Wait 2d, Probate Proceedings § 152:32.
7 Am Jur 2d, Attorney General § 27.
9 Am Jur 2d, Bankruptcy § 192.
15 Am Jur 2d, Civil Rights § 74.
19 Am Jur 2d, Corporations §§ 591, 592.
44 Am Jur 2d, Insurance §§ 1526, 1848, 1853.
48 Am Jur 2d, Labor and Labor Relations §§ 111, 161.
54 Am Jur 2d, Monopolies, Restraints of Trade, and Unfair Trade Practices § 288.
59 Am Jur 2d, Parties §§ 129 et seq.
66 Am Jur 2d, Receivers § 336.
74 Am Jur 2d, Taxpayers' Actions § 47.
7 Am Jur Pl and Pr Forms (Rev ed), Constitutional Law, Forms 11–24.
19 Am Jur Pl and Pr Forms (Rev ed), Parties, Forms 61 et seq.
23 Am Jur Pl and Pr Forms (Rev ed), Taxpayers' Actions, Form 71.

Annotations:

Assertion of fiduciary status of party to litigation as basis for intervention by one claiming interest in fruits thereof as trust beneficiary. 2 ALR2d 227.

Appealability of order granting or denying right of intervention. 15 ALR2d 336.

Intervention by stockholder for purpose of interposing defense for corporation. 33 ALR2d 473.

Time within which right to intervene may be exercised. 37 ALR2d 1306.

Intervention by other stockholders in stockholders' derivative action. 69 ALR2d 562.

When is representation of applicant's interest by existing parties inadequate so as to be entitled to intervention as of right under Federal Rule 24(a)(2) and similar state statutes or rules. 84 ALR2d 1412.

Who may intervene in action between union and union member. 93 ALR2d 1037.

Right of insurer "uninsured motorist" coverage to intervene in action by insured against uninsured motorist. 95 ALR2d 1330.

Necessity and propriety (under 28 USCS § 2281) of three-judge Federal District Court in suit to enjoin enforcement of state statute or administrative order. 4 L Ed 2d 1931, 15 L Ed 2d 904.

Construction and effect of 28 USCS § 2403, requiring certification to Attorney General of actions involving constitutional questions, so as to permit intervention by United States. 2 ALR Fed 978.

Construction of Federal Civil Procedure Rule 24(a)(2), as amended in 1966, insofar as dealing with prerequisites of intervention as a matter of right. 5 ALR Fed 518.

Law Reviews:

New York Civil Practice Law and Rules: parties. 27 Albany L Rev 182.

Parties and pleading under the CPLR. 31 Brooklyn L Rev 98.

A biannual survey of New York practice: intervention allowed to defend constitutionality of statute granting partial tax exemption. 39 St. John's L Rev 430.

Public intervention in settlements of government antitrust cases. 39 Brooklyn L Rev 579.

Forms:

See "FORMS" heading following "CASE NOTES", infra.

CASE NOTES

1. In general; construction
2. Persons not entitled to intervene, generally
3. Persons entitled to intervene, generally
4. Statutory authority
5. Adequacy of representation of interests
6. Property interests

7. Constitutional challenge to statute
8. Excusing nonjoinder

1. In general; construction

Liberal construction and application of the intervention statutes are called for. Raymond v Honeywell (1968) 58 Misc 2d 903, 297 NYS2d 66.

Intervention should be liberally allowed, particularly with the presence of common questions of law and fact, and is permitted as of right when interest in property may be adversely affected by judgment. Teleprompter Manhattan CATV Corp. v State Board of Equalization & Assessment (1970) 34 AD2d 1033, 311 NYS2d 46.

A party can be added to a pending action or proceeding only on timely motion and an order of court in which action or proceeding is pending. Muka v Sturgis (1976) 53 AD2d 716, 383 NYS2d 933.

In disbarment proceedings, strong presumption of regularity attached to judgment convicting attorney of conspiracy, obstruction of justice, making false declarations under oath before grand jury and perjury in making false declarations under oath before United States Senate Select Committee on Presidential Campaign Activities. Mitchell v Association of the Bar (1976) 40 NY2d 153, 386 NYS2d 95, 351 NE2d 743.

2. Persons not entitled to intervene, generally

A labor union involved in a dispute with a publishing company may not intervene in a pending Article 78 proceeding between the publisher and the Board of Education, which arose over the issue of the legality of a resolution by the Board as being opposed to the purchase of any books published by the publisher where books of equal value were available. Kingsport Press, Inc. v Board of Education (1966) 50 Misc 2d 428, 270 NYS2d 773.

Foster parents had no standing to intervene in habeas corpus proceeding brought by natural mother to compel return of child from foster parent because, until formal adoption occurred the relationship under Social Services Law § 384 is exclusively between the parent or parents and the agency and the sole issue involved is the fitness and ability of the parent without any consideration with respect to the prospective adoptive parents. People ex rel. Anonymous v Saratoga County Dept. (1968) 30 AD2d 756, 291 NYS2d 526.

In a habeas corpus proceeding against an adoption agency by the natural mother to obtain the return of her child which had been placed in the custody of prospective adoptive parents, in view of the statutory scheme enacted by the Legislature to guard against disclosure of the names and identities of the parties involved, and the subtle public policy, the prospective adoptive parents were not entitled to intervene in the proceedings. People ex rel. Scarpetta v Spence-Chapin Adoption Service (1971) 28 NY2d 185, 321 NYS2d 65, 269 NE2d 787, cert den and app dismd 404 US 805, 30 L Ed 2d 38, 92 S Ct 54.

The Motor Vehicle Accident Indemnification Cor-

poration has no right to notice of litigation which might affect its ultimate liability, and the right to intervene in that litigation. Wallace v Motor Vehicle Acci. Indemnification Corp. (1969) 25 NY2d 384, 306 NYS2d 457, 254 NE2d 761.

Intervention by Motor Vehicle Accident indemnification Corporation in action growing out of automobile collision was improper where such intervention was not preceded by motion for leave to amend, and MVAIC therefore could not properly assert cross claim in its own behalf. Wynn v Wynn (1976) 51 AD2d 868, 380 NYS2d 159.

Outdoor advertising association was not entitled to intervene as a party plaintiff as of right in suit by owner of outdoor advertising signs in Catskill park challenging the constitutionality of Environmental Conservation Law provision prohibiting the erection of advertising signs in the park without a permit, since the interests of the association were adequately represented by plaintiff and the action did not involve a disposition of or claim for damages to property in which the association might be adversely affected by the judgment. Modjeska Sign Studios, Inc. v Berle (1976) 87 Misc 2d 600, 386 NYS2d 765, affd 55 AD2d 340, 390 NYS2d 945.

3. Persons entitled to intervene, generally

The state assembly speaker, who was a necessary party to proceedings to review the constitutionality of reapportionment acts, had an absolute right to intervene in further proceedings, and such intervention must be as a party respondent. Orans v Rockefeller (1965) 47 Misc 2d 493, 262 NYS2d 893, affd 24 AD2d 217, 265 NYS2d 49, mod on other grounds 17 NY2d 601, 268 NYS2d 561, 215 NE2d 682 and mod on other grounds 17 NY2d 107, 269 NYS2d 97, 216 NE2d 311, app den 17 NY2d 721, 269 NYS2d 971, 216 NE2d 834.

4. Statutory authority

Motions by abutting and adjoining property owners for leave to intervene and question the granting of special exception permit required for operation of a day care center was denied as to permissive intervention, but, provided the movants can establish that they are aggrieved persons within the meaning of Village Law § 179-b, are entitled to intervene, as of right. Unitarian Universalist Church v Shorten (1970) 64 Misc 2d 851, 315 NYS2d 506, vacated on other grounds 64 Misc 2d 1027, 316 NYS2d 837.

5. Adequacy of representation of interests

Public employees' unions which had been parties in proceedings before the Public Employment Relations Board concerning board of education's alleged violations of Public Employees' Employment Act, became parties for all purposes and should have been permitted to intervene in the Board's judicial proceeding to obtain enforcement of its order against the board of education, since the union's full intervention was required to insure complete litigation of its interests. New York State Public Employment Relations Board v Board of

Education (1975) 46 AD2d 509, 363 NYS2d 365, affd 39 NY2d 86, 382 NYS2d 965, 346 NE2d 803.

Intervention in an action to review the constitutionality of reapportionment legislation by the president pro tem of the state senate appeared to be proper under CPLR 1012(a), paragraph 2, and in any event was allowable under CPLR 1013. Orans v Rockefeller (1965) 47 Misc 2d 493, 262 NYS2d 893, affd 24 AD2d 217, 265 NYS2d 49, mod on other grounds 17 NY2d 601, 268 NYS2d 561, 215 NE2d 682 and mod on other grounds 17 NY2d 107, 269 NYS2d 97, 216 NE2d 311, app den 17 NY2d 721, 269 NYS2d 971, 216 NE2d 834.

CPLR 1012 is in the disjunctive and permits intervention where the person may be bound by the judgment or representation of the person's interest may be inadequate. Accordingly, employer was entitled to intervene in action for personal injuries by employee against third party where Connecticut statute which governed the proceedings provided for abatement of the employer's rights if the employer failed to join in such action. Nardone v Morris A. Fierberg Co. (1972) 40 AD2d 60, 337 NYS2d 884.

6. Property interests

Purchaser of realty on condition that it be rezoned is sufficiently affected by action by other property owners to declare zoning change void to be permitted to intervene therein. Levine v Oyster Bay (1963) 40 Misc 2d 605, 243 NYS2d 656.

Where Article 78 proceeding to review action of zoning board of appeals in granting variance was dismissed, motion of neighboring landowner to intervene was rendered academic. Lavere v Board of Zoning Appeals (1972) 39 AD2d 639, 331 NYS2d 141, affd 33 NY2d 873, 352 NYS2d 442, 307 NE2d 559.

In action to foreclose a mortgage where surety, who had settled claims of mechanics' lienors and received assignments from them of their liens and all causes of action, would be adequately protected by being substituted for lienors, intervention would be denied. T. J. Bettes Co. v South Falls Corp. (1967) 28 AD2d 198, 284 NYS2d 262.

Defendant's second wife was denied intervention, on behalf of the defendant's children of his second marriage, in first wife's action concerning the interpretation of her separation agreement with defendant because the children did not have sufficient interest in their father's "property" to warrant intervention. Reurs v Carlson (1971) 66 Misc 2d 968, 323 NYS2d 370.

A motion to intervene as a party defendant in an action brought for specific performance upon the alleged breach of an option contract by which the plaintiff lessee claimed a right to purchase ten acres of real estate was granted to the moving corporation that had purchased the same property from the defendant as part of a larger tract of 137 acres. Concluding the intervening corporation had entered the controversy intentionally and with full knowledge of the pending suit, the court held the intervenor's voluntary interjection was not controlling, since it apparently had concluded that the option was without legal effect. Rich v Olendorf (1967) 55 Misc 2d 307, 285 NYS2d 723.

Site tenants were interested persons entitled to intervene in action by landlord for injunction to prevent zoning board's reopening its prior determination granting it a zoning variance. 200 West 79th Street Co. v Galvin (1970) 71 Misc 2d 190, 335 NYS2d 715.

7. Constitutional challenge to statute

Court could not pass upon constitutionality of state statute without giving Attorney General opportunity to intervene in support of constitutionality. Seasons Realty Corp. v Yonkers (1975) 80 Misc 2d 601, 363 NYS2d 738.

Plaintiff's argument on appeal that no-fault Insurance Law is unconstitutional insofar as it denies plaintiff right of action against defendant could not be considered since plaintiff did not make Attorney General a party to motion and present that argument at Special Term so that issue could have been fully considered there. Colenzo v Kernan (1975) 49 AD2d 809, 373 NYS2d 426 (not followed Abbasi v Galluzzo 88 Misc 2d 926, 390 NYS2d 514).

Section 71 of the Executive Law requires that the Attorney General appear in support of the constitutionality of an attacked statute, and CPLR 1012(b) mandates that the court shall notify the Attorney General, who shall be permitted to intervene in support of the constitutionality of the act. Himmel v Chase Manhattan Bank (1965) 47 Misc 2d 93, 262 NYS2d 515.

When the constitutionality of a state statute is in question, notification of the Attorney General is required. Strongin v Nyquist (1976) 54 AD2d 1031, 388 NYS2d 683, clarified (AD) 392 NYS2d 1022.

8. Excusing nonjoinder

Although board of education ought to have been joined as a party to Article 78 proceeding brought by discharged tenured English teacher following affirmance of board's decision by Commissioner of Education the board was not indispensable party and failure to join it would be excused in the interest of justice since if proceeding were terminated for failure to join the board, which was not served within the four-month statutory limitations, petitioner would have no other effective remedy and no apparent prejudice would result to the board since its interest would be adequately protected by the Commissioner. Sandor v Nyquist (1974) 45 AD2d 122, 356 NYS2d 703.

Failure to join state comptroller as a party in Article 78 proceeding against the civil service commission by discharged attorney seeking reinstatement to former position with the Department of Audit and Control would be excused so as not to require dismissal of petition in that interests of the comptroller would be protected by the Commission, any possible prejudice to comptroller could be avoided by his intervention in the proceeding and an effective order could be rendered in absence of the comptroller. Greaney v Poston (1975) 50 AD2d 653, 374 NYS2d 815.

CASE NOTES

UNDER FORMER CIVIL PRACTICE LAWS

1. Generally
2. Inadequate representation
3. Title to property
4. Rights of intervener
5. Timely application
6. Particular actions and proceedings
7. Procedure

1. Generally

The supreme court has inherent power to grant intervention to parties whose rights will be adversely affected by the outcome of an action and the history of intervention shows a trend in the direction of the extension of the remedy rather than restriction. Central Westchester Humane Soc. v Hilleboe (1952) 202 Misc 873, 115 NYS2d 769.

To authorize intervention, applicant must have interest in subject-matter of litigation of such nature that he will gain or lose by direct legal operation and effect of judgment. Rubin v Irving Trust Co. (1951) 105 NYS2d 140.

It has been said that the old statute, § 193 of the Civil Practice Act, repealed by the laws of 1946, contained such radically different wording that decisions thereunder were not controlling under CPA § 193-b as to the right of a party to intervene. Central Westchester Humane Soc. v Hilleboe (1952) 202 Misc 873, 115 NYS2d 769.

Proposed intervener need not have direct personal or pecuniary interest in subject of action; if he would be indirectly affected by litigation in substantial manner, he may intervene. Central W. Humane Soc. v Hilleboe, supra.

Controversy as to which faction of labor union was entitled to administer grievance matters was proper case for intervention of one faction in employer's proceeding to stay arbitration under CPA § 1450 (§§ 7501, 7502(a), 7503(a) herein). Re American Machine & Foundry Co. (1948) 193 Misc 990, 85 NYS2d 456.

Where judgment creditor of bank depositor claimed portion of deposit paid into court pursuant to order under CPA § 51-a (§ 216(a) herein) and where such depositor or adverse claimant failed within one year to intervene in action or to commence action to enforce her claim to deposit, such judgment creditor was not entitled to intervene. Solicitor v Bankers Trust Co. (1952) 304 NY 296, 107 NE2d 455.

The provisions of CPA § 193-b making it mandatory for the intervening party to submit a proposed answer on his motion to intervene, and the direction in the order permitting such intervention that the answer be served within five days were special circumstances warranting consideration on the merits of a motion pursuant to RCP 90 (Rule 3014 herein) to compel plaintiff to state and number alleged causes of action although such motion

was made after answer. City Bank Farmers Trust Co. v National Cuba Hotel Corp. (1954) 133 NYS2d 8.

Where husband sued wife's parents for family partnership accounting and they pleaded facts that he was agent of his wife who was their daughter, which he denied, she may intervene. Schwartz v Klein (1947) 188 Misc 665, 72 NYS2d 386.

In action to partition lands in Adirondacks, motion of State of New York to intervene was granted, on its affidavit showing interest in such lands under tax sales and deeds and on its proposed counterclaim asserting State is seized in fee ownership of all such lands. Hatch v Turner (1953) 282 AD 818, 123 NYS2d 285.

Public Service Commission was by legislative mandate made party to proceeding to condemn utility company's property after and by service on Commission of county court's final order confirming appraisal commissioner's report, and there was no necessity for application to court under CPA § 193-b for permission to intervene. Onondaga C. W. Auth. v New York W. S. Corp. (1955) 285 AD 655, 139 NYS2d 755.

As general rule, third party will be permitted to intervene if his interests will be jeopardized by his absence, so that whole controversy may be ended in one action and by single judgment. Harrison v Mary Bain Estates, Inc. (1956) 2 Misc 2d 52, 152 NYS2d 239, affd 2 AD2d 670, 153 NYS2d 552.

Where a theft insurance policy prohibited assignment of proceeds without insurer's consent and buyer had purchased automobile under conditional sales contract which contained clause assigning proceeds of loss and conditional buyer had instituted action against insurer to recover on the theft policy, the assignee was entitled to intervene despite the policy prohibition. Fiorito v Northern Assur. Co. (1957) 158 NYS2d 818.

Where persons are not parties in a proceeding before the state commission against discrimination and they are not affected in any way, in any property or other legal rights by order of the commission, they are not persons aggrieved and may not intervene. New York State Com. against Discrimination v Pelham Hall Apts., Inc. (1958) 10 Misc 2d 346, 171 NYS2d 558.

Judgment-creditor was not entitled to intervene in existing action between judgment-debtor and third party where there was no fund in court's custody to authorize such intervention. Hocking-Hershey Associates, Inc. v Iandoli (1959) 19 Misc 2d 210, 187 NYS2d 300.

Taxpayer was not entitled to intervene in lawsuit conducted by municipality because he did not agree with officials on how to conduct the litigation where he failed to show that he had a special interest therein differentiating him from other taxpayers. Zara Contracting Co. v Glen Cove (1960) 22 Misc 2d 279, 197 NYS2d 940.

2. Inadequate representation

Default judgment, taken against corporation, established prima facie that representation of shareholder's interest by existing parties was inadequate, and he had right to intervene, since he would be bound by judgment. Stull v Terry & Tench, Inc. (1948) 81 NYS2d 43.

Waiver by liability insurer's right to intervene occurred when it refused to defend action against insured unless he executed non-waiver agreements. Krenitsky v Ludlow Motor Co. (1950) 276 AD 511, 96 NYS2d 102.

Rent administrator was allowed to intervene in proceeding by landlord to compel clerk of court to issue warrant of eviction against tenant. Re Bernklau (1951) 106 NYS2d 548.

Junior attaching creditor has right to intervene in main action, as he will be adversely affected by any distribution of attached funds in sheriff's hands. Bennett v Kazvini (1952) 279 AD 860, 110 NYS2d 358.

Where the British treasury commenced an action in New York to appropriate a bank account belonging to a British subject, and the bank served notice upon the depositor under CPA § 51-a (§ 216(a) herein) to intervene or commence an action within one year and ten days from the date of the order authorizing the notice, and the depositor failed to take action within that time, she lost her right to the deposit and her judgment creditor has no standing or interest entitling him to intervene in the action against the bank. His Majesty's Treasury v Bankers Trust Co. (1952) 304 NY 296, 107 NE2d 455.

Liability insurer may intervene in action commenced in New York against Pennsylvania insured by latter's sister injured at insured's home in Pennsylvania, to stay New York action pending determination of action in Pennsylvania to declare obligation of insured to defend New York action. Quentin v Henderson (1951) 110 NYS2d 561.

Surviving spouse was unnecessary party to discovery proceeding under SCA § 205, where it was not claimed that executor's representation may be inadequate to protect spouse's rights. Korowitz's Estate (1953) 120 NYS2d 498.

A stockholder of a judgment debtor corporation may intervene in the action to open a default judgment against the corporation, the fact that the judgment was taken by default against the corporation establishing prima facie that the representation of the stockholders' interest by the corporation has been inadequate. Stull v Terry & Tench, Inc. (1948) 81 NYS2d 43.

Stockholder of plaintiff corporation may not intervene in its action for declaratory judgment involving contract between plaintiff and defendant corporations, on ground that existing management will never force action to conclusion. General Aniline & F. Corp. v General Dyestuff Corp. (1953) 123 NYS2d 535.

In action to enforce trust agreement, person seeking to intervene as party defendant had to show that he came within provisions of subd 1 of CPA § 193-b. Kalkstein v Kalkstein (1951) 278 AD 781, 103 NYS2d 864.

In action by chattel mortgagee to replevy mortgaged automobile conveyed by mortgagor without knowledge of mortgagee to dealer who conveyed it to defendant, such dealer had right to intervene in such action under subd 1 of CPA § 193-b. Northern New York Tr. Co. v Smith (1955) 2 Misc 2d 810, 153 NYS2d 798.

Where movant does not submit proposed pleadings setting forth the defense for which intervention is sought, and fails to demonstrate that plaintiff may or will be unable, or unwilling, to contest the action adequately, his application for intervention must be denied. Moore v Oyster Bay (1961) 29 Misc 2d 169, 211 NYS2d 858.

3. Title to property

Where plaintiff village conceded that questions may be raised as to its rights, under deed of dedication sought to be reformed by lot owner, he was allowed to intervene. Island Park v Island Park-Long Beach (1947) 74 NYS2d 492, affd 272 AD 1060, 75 NYS2d 515.

Interest of petitioner must be interest known and protected by law, claim of ownership or lesser interest, sufficient and of type to be denominated lien, legal or equitable. Solicitor v Bankers Trust Co. (1950) 198 Misc 751, 100 NYS2d 131.

See Solicitor v Bankers Trust Co. (1951) 199 Misc 498, 106 NYS2d 656, revd 279 AD 571, 107 NYS2d 575, revd on other grounds, 304 NY 296, 107 NE2d 455.

Respondent was allowed to intervene in action for damages for trespass by defendants upon certain lands. O'Brien v Goldblatt (1950) 277 AD 985, 99 NYS2d 1010.

Although his rights were subordinate to the purchase rights of plaintiff, intervener-applicant who held subsequent written agreement from defendant, supported by money consideration, for purchase of the same realty, had vendee's lien entitling him to intervene in plaintiff's action for specific performance of contract to purchase realty. Cicci v Humphreys (1962) 33 Misc 2d 94, 223 NYS2d 797.

Record title owner of property was entitled, both as a matter of right and as a matter of discretion, to intervene in action to compel specific performance of binder to sell property to plaintiff. Faha Realty Corp. v Falck (1961) 32 Misc 2d 511, 223 NYS2d 584.

4. Rights of intervener

Intervening defendant has all rights of original defendant for all purposes, including right to plead statute of limitations. Island Park v Island Park-Long Beach, Inc. (1948) 81 NYS2d 407, affd 274 AD 930, 83 NYS2d 542.

In action against city for insurance premiums on policy approved by city's common council, mayor, who was not named as party in such action had no right under city charter to serve answer in behalf of city, and where he met none of statutory requirements of CPA § 193-b, his application for leave to intervene was denied. Trans-Canada A. A. v Mechanicville (1956) 2 AD2d 734, 152 NYS2d 608.

Interveners could not have their own counsel and proceed separately in stockholders' derivative action where a number of separate actions had been consolidated and a general counsel designated and the interveners' actions were interwoven with the overall picture. Fleitman v Simpson (1957) 9 Misc 2d 398, 166 NYS2d 727.

5. Timely application

Where in action to reform deed plaintiff's motion was granted on June 5, 1947 to reopen default judgment entered May 17, 1946, movant's application for same relief to intervene on June 26, 1947, was timely. Island Park v Island Park-Long Beach (1947) 74 NYS2d 492, affd 272 AD 1060, 75 NYS2d 515.

Stockholders, who individually had notice of litigation against corporation in receivership, could not intervene where they delayed application for over one year. Forker v Royal Development Co. (1947) 189 Misc 798, 72 NYS2d 59.

Where liability insurer was notified to defend action against insured but refused to do so unless he executed non-waiver agreements, insurer's application to intervene after its appearance and default, was not timely. Krenitsky v Ludlow Motor Co. (1950) 276 AD 511, 96 NYS2d 102.

Application to intervene was timely where made before original issue in the action had been joined. Cicci v Humphreys (1962) 33 Misc 2d 94, 223 NYS2d 797.

6. Particular actions and proceedings

An application by two members of a union to intervene as parties in an arbitration proceeding between the employer and the union which is their collective bargaining agent must be denied. Such members cannot be permitted to intervene unless they establish, one, that the representation of their interest by the union is or may be inadequate or, two, that they are so situated that they may be adversely affected by distribution or other disposition of property in the custody of or subject to the control or disposition by the court or an officer thereof. General Warehousemen's Union v Glidden Co. (1957) 9 Misc 2d 648, 169 NYS2d 759.

Where several stockholders' derivative actions were consolidated and general counsel was designated for all plaintiffs but two substantial stockholders who were aware of original motions for the consolidation, employed their own counsel and moved for leave to intervene and served a proposed additional complaint, the allegations of which were inseparably interwoven with the existing consolidated complaint, the application to intervene as plaintiffs was granted. Fleitman v Simpson (1957) 9 Misc 2d 398, 166 NYS2d 727.

In a summary proceeding in the Municipal Court for nonpayment of rent, the guarantor was allowed to intervene to plead a tender of payment and a subsequent action in the Supreme Court by the lessee and guarantor against the landlord for judgment declaring that the guarantor could remedy the tenant's defaults was unnecessary. Picto Corp. v Marburt Holding Corp. (1957) 9 Misc 2d 407, 166 NYS2d 798.

Where sublessee, who was obligated by the terms of the sublease to pay real estate taxes on the premises, timely instituted a proceeding for a reduction of the assessed valuation and subsequently was dispossessed by the lessee, who then had to pay the taxes, the lessee was a party aggrieved and as such was permitted to intervene in, and further prosecute, the proceeding commenced by the sublessee. Fleetair, Inc. v Tax Com. of New York (1958) 15 Misc 2d 502, 181 NYS2d 645.

A creditor of a decedent who sought to intervene in a proceeding to revoke testamentary letters was denied permission to intervene upon a failure to show a question of law or fact common to his claim and the revocation proceeding. Re Rubin (1959) 19 Misc 2d 631, 190 NYS2d 469.

In mortgage foreclosure action, fire insurers of property in favor of mortgagor and mortgagee would not be bound by the judgment of foreclosure, and therefore may not intervene therein. Lesser v West Albany Warehouses, Inc. (1959) 17 Misc 2d 461, 191 NYS2d 113.

In action by registered ophthalmic dispensers against state university, commissioner of education, and board of regents for declaratory judgment invalidating price advertising regulation applying to licensed opticians, licensed optometrists were permitted to intervene to uphold regulation, because of a common question of law between main action and defense and absence of delay or prejudice to main action. Morofsky v University of State of New York (1959) 17 Misc 2d 707, 191 NYS2d 696.

State will not be permitted to intervene in action brought by citizen against county treasurer for return of illegal gambling money, allegedly wrongfully withheld, since state has no paramount right to such money if money is proceeds of illegal gambling. Gross v County Treasurer of Orange County (1959) 19 Misc 2d 738, 192 NYS2d 405.

A creditor may in his own name and for his own benefit sue directors for loans of corporate funds to stockholders (Stock Corp L § 59), but creditors similarly situated may intervene or be joined. If they do not intervene or fail to be joined, it is no objection to the maintenance of the action by the single creditor that he will thereby reap the full statutory benefit to the exclusion of other creditors. American Broadcasting-Paramount Theatres, Inc. v Frye (1960) 8 NY2d 232, 203 NYS2d 850, 168 NE2d 669.

Association representing property owners in vicinity of property for which variance was sought was denied permission to intervene in an Article 78 proceeding to review the determination where it failed to submit a proposed pleading setting forth the claim or defense for which intervention was sought. Virgo v Zoning Board of Appeals (1961) 28 Misc 2d 886, 212 NYS2d 586.

7. Procedure

Where movant does not submit proposed pleadings

setting forth the defense for which intervention is sought, and fails to demonstrate that plaintiff may or will be unable or unwilling to contest the action adequately, his application for intervention must be denied. Moore v Oyster Bay (1961) 29 Misc 2d 169, 211 NYS2d 858.

FORMS

Form 1—Notice of motion to intervene

Form 2—Notice of motion for leave to intervene

Form 3—Affidavit in support of motion for permission to intervene

Form 4—Affidavit in support of motion for intervention

Form 5—Affidavit of applicant in support of motion for permission to intervene

Form 6—Affidavit of attorney in support of motion for permission to intervene

Form 7—Order granting permission to third person to intervene

Form 8—Notice of motion to intervene (by order to show cause)

Form 9—Affidavit in support of motion for discretionary order permitting third person to intervene

Form 10—Order granting permission to third person to intervene—another form

Form 11—Order allowing intervention

Form 1

Notice of Motion to Intervene

SUPREME COURT, COUNTY OF __1_____

Ada Doe, Plaintiff,
   against
Ann Roe, Defendant.

Notice of Motion
Index No. — [if assigned]

PLEASE TAKE NOTICE that upon the annexed affidavit of __2_____, duly sworn to __3_____, 19_4_, the notice of pendency of this action, summons and complaint herein filed in the Office of the Clerk of __5_____ County and the proposed pleading of __6_____ setting forth the claim [or defense] for which intervention is sought the undersigned will move this Court, at a Motion Term, Part I thereof, appointed to be held in and for the County of __7_____, at the Courthouse thereof, Borough of __8_____, City of New York, on the __9__ day of __10_____, 19_11_, at the opening of Court on that day, or as soon thereafter as counsel can be heard, for an order permitting __12_____, the applicant herein, to intervene in this action, directing that he be brought in as a party defendant in this action, that the summons and complaint and notice of pendency of this action be amended by adding the said applicant thereto as a party defendant, and allowing him to serve his answer upon the attorney for the plaintiff herein within twenty days after the entry of an order granting this motion, upon the grounds that applicant has an interest in real property the title to which may be affected by a judgment in this action [or otherwise state the statutory grounds under which intervention is sought] and for such other and further relief as may be just.

[Date] __13_____

Attorney of Applicant
[Office and P. O. Address]
Telephone No.

To: __14_____
   Attorney for Plaintiff
   [Office and P. O. Address]

Form 2

Notice of Motion for Leave to Intervene

Notice of Motion

[Title of court and cause]   Index No. __1__

Sirs:

PLEASE TAKE NOTICE that upon the annexed affidavit of __2____, sworn to __3_____, 19_4_, and all the proceedings heretofore had herein, the undersigned will move this court at a Special Term, Part __5__ thereof, to be held in the __6_____ Courthouse, __7_____ Street, City of __8_____, on the __9__ day of __10_____, 19_11_, at __12__ o'clock in the forenoon of that day, or as soon thereafter as counsel can be heard, for an order permitting __13_____ to intervene herein as a party intervenor, pursuant to section 353-a of the General Business Law and the orders of this court, dated __14_____, 19_15_, and __16_____, 19_17_, and directing that the annexed affidavit of __18_____ shall constitute her pleading and that the title of this action be amended by adding the name of __19_____ as a party intervenor, and for such other and further relief as to the court may seem just and proper.

Dated: __20_____, New York, __21_____, 19_22_.

Yours, etc.,

__23_____

Attorney for Interventor
[Office] __24_____
Telephone No. __25__

To: __26_____
Attorney General
[Office] __27_____

__28_____

Receiver
[Office] __29_____

[Adapted from papers in People v Monthly Income Shares, Inc. 263 AD 832, 31 NYS2d 527.]

Form 3

Affidavit in Support of Motion for Permission to Intervene

Affidavit

[Title of court and cause]   Index No. — [if assigned]

STATE OF NEW YORK
COUNTY OF __1_____   ss:

__2_____, being duly sworn deposes and says:

1. This is an action [state nature of action].

2. [State whether cause is at issue, in judgment, etc.].

3. Affiant and applicant [state facts showing that applicant is within CPLR, § 1012].

4. Annexed hereto and made a part hereof is a copy of __3_____ [applicant's] proposed pleading setting forth the claim [or defense] for which intervention is sought.

5. [If order to show cause is sought, state reason therefor, and that previous application has been made.]

WHEREFORE, affiant prays that an order be made joining him as a party defendant in this action and directing plaintiff to amend his complaint and summons so

505

as to name and join affiant as a party defendant, and for such other and further relief as may be just.

[Signature of affiant]
[Print signer's name below signature]

[Jurat]

Form 4

Affidavit in Support of Motion for Intervention

Affidavit

[Title of court and cause]   Index No. __1__

[Venue]

__2_____, being duly sworn, deposes and says:

1. I reside at __3_____ Street, City of __4_____ New York. I am __5_____ years old and a __6_____ [widow] since 19_7_. After my __8_____ [husband's] death, my sole source of support was the income from the securities which he left me. In or about the latter part of 19_9_, I commenced dealing with the defendant __10_____, alleged investment counsel brokers and securities dealers, and thereafter during __11_____ and until about __12_____, continued to deal with said company and its successors __13_____ and __14_____. In or about __15_____, 19_16_, I was informed through the Attorney General's office that said companies had been engaged in illegal and fraudulent activities.

2. In the course of my dealings with said companies I had numerous transactions as a result of which I am now informed I have lost and been deprived of approximately $__17__. As a result __18_____ [State consequences, such as: my circumstances are so reduced that I am having difficulty in obtaining the necessaries of life, I had to give up my comfortable home and move to a two-room apartment, my health has been affected severely, I have suffered from nervous shock, loss of weight, and stomach ailments, requiring doctors' care and hospitalization, and I am unable to continue to support my aged sister who was dependent on me].

3. I have not recovered a penny of my losses.

4. I am informed that this action was instituted by the People of the State of New York on __19_____, 19_20_, pursuant to section 353-a of the General Business Law (Martin Act) and that by an order of this court dated __21_____, 19_22_, __23_____, was appointed as permanent receiver pursuant to said section 353-a of any and all property derived by the defendants, __24_____, by means of the fraudulent practices described in the complaint, and that said receiver was directed to liquidate said property "for the benefit of all persons intervening in this action and establishing an interest in such property." I am informed further that said receiver now holds substantial property which has been held by order of this court dated __25_____, 19_26_, affirming the report of __27_____, referee, dated __28_____, 19_29_, to have been derived by said defendants from the fraudulent practices described in the complaint. I am informed that said order dated __30_____, 19_31_, was affirmed by the Appellate Division, __32_____ Department in __33_____, 19_34_.

5. I am entitled to share in said property held by the said receiver for the following reasons: __35_____ [State purchases of stock, give dates, amounts, certificate numbers]. I was induced to purchase said shares by said __36_____, by means of the fraudulent practices described in the complaint in this action including the following false and fraudulent representations made to me by __37_____ orally, upon which I relied in making such purchases: __38_____ [State false representations, such as: that __39_____ was an investment company organized to manage funds through carefully selected and diversified investments in the best securities and that its Class "A" stocks had been paying a monthly dividend of __40_____ a share regularly out of earnings and would continue to do so; that said stocks of __41_____ were safe, sound, and secure investments, as goods as government bonds; that I could sell them at any time

for the prices which I paid for them; that they were investments which would improve my securities holdings and be of great benefit to me and that it was wise to sell some of the securities that I then owned and invest the proceeds therein].

6. I ascertained a few days ago, for the first time, that I am entitled to share in the property held by the said receiver of these companies and derived by them by means of fraudulent practices described in the complaint. I previously was entirely unaware of that fact. I have executed two claims, one based on my purchase of the stock of __42____ and the other based on my purchase of the stock of __43____ copies of which are attached hereto as Exhibits "__44____" and "__45____" respectively, and I have instructed my attorneys to file said claims with said receiver immediately.

[Signature, with name printed underneath]

[Jurat]

[Adapted from papers in People v Monthly Income Shares, Inc. 263 AD 832, 31 NYS2d 527.]

Form 5

Affidavit of Applicant in Support of Motion for Permission to Intervene

SUPREME COURT, __1____ COUNTY.

Affidavit

[Title of court]   Index No. — [if assigned]

__2_____, being duly sworn, deposes and says:

1. I am the applicant who makes this motion for an order to be permitted to intervene as a party defendant in this pending action to foreclose a mortgage, pursuant to CPLR § 1012, upon the ground that I have an interest in real property the title to which may be affected by a judgment in this action, in that subsequent to the filing of the lis pendens herein, I docketed a judgment which became a lien subject to that of the mortgage lien against the premises herein sought to be foreclosed.

2. I have valid and meritorious defenses to said foreclosure action, namely, lack of consideration for said mortgage and fraud inducing its execution, as hereinafter set forth.

3. On __3_____, 19_4_, defendant executed and delivered to plaintiff a mortgage for $2000 on premises owned solely by said mortgagor and known as No. __5_____ Street, Borough of __6_____, and that plaintiff recorded said mortgage in the office of the County Clerk of __7_____ County on __8_____, 19_9_.

4. On __10_____, 19_11_, plaintiff filed in the office of the County Clerk of __12_____ County the notice of pendency, summons and complaint in this action to foreclose said mortgage, and on __13_____, 19 14_, said summons and complaint were served on defendant, who defaulted by not appearing or answering.

5. Said complaint demands judgment foreclosing all claims and liens against said property asserted subsequent to the filing of the lis pendens and barring all claimants of all right, claim, lien and equity of redemption in said mortgaged premises.

6. On __15_____, 19_16_, affiant duly recovered a judgment for $__17__ against defendant in the City Court of the City of New York for __18_____ County, and on __19_____, 19_20_, when first learning that this foreclosure action was pending, duly filed a transcript of said judgment and docketed same in said county, and that affiant's judgment so docketed became a lien upon said mortgaged real property, pursuant to CPLR § 5203.

7. Said mortgage was executed without any consideration therefor. On __21_____, 19_22_, plaintiff was examined as a witness in proceedings supplementary to execution under said judgment obtained by affiant against defendant, and plaintiff then admitted that defendant did not owe her any money nor was otherwise indebted to her when said mortgage was executed, plaintiff then stated that said mortgage was given to repay

moneys given to defendant's husband. On __23____, 19_24_, defendant was examined as judgment debtor in proceedings supplementary to execution and defendant then admitted that she was not indebted to plaintiff when defendant executed said mortgage.

8. Said mortgage was executed pursuant to a conspiracy to defraud the creditors of defendant judgment debtor, the owner of the equity of redemption; in __25____, 19_26_, defendant's husband called a meeting of his creditors; that on __27____, 19_28_, when said mortgage was executed, said mortgaged premises constituted defendant's sole remaining asset; when defendant executed said mortgage, she was giving "protection" to a claim against her husband without regard to the rights of her own creditors, and said mortgage was in fact executed pursuant to a conspiracy to wipe out her creditors.

9. On __29____, 19_30_, affiant first learned that this action was pending; he immediately communicated with his attorney who, as affiant is informed and believes, wrote to plaintiff's attorney on __31____, 19_32_, requesting a copy of the complaint, which was not delivered for two weeks; on __33____, 19_34_, plaintiff was examined as witness pursuant to subpoena in supplementary proceedings against defendant judgment debtor; on such examination plaintiff promised to deliver to her attorney's office, for exhibition to affiant, the original receipts in the handwriting of defendant's husband, explaining the nature of the financial relations between him and plaintiff; plaintiff's examination was adjourned at the request of plaintiff until __35____, 19_36_, plaintiff failed to appear on said adjourned date, and failed to produce said receipts.

10. Unless the relief sought herein is granted, claimant's lien herein will be foreclosed and wiped out by the judgment sought in this action; and in view of the facts aforesaid, application should not be denied.

11. Annexed hereto and made a part hereof is a copy of applicant's proposed pleading setting forth the claim [or defense] for which intervention is sought.

12. No previous application has been made for the relief requested herein.

13. The provisions of CPLR § 1012, that any person who has an interest in realty whose title may be affected by the judgment in the action "shall be permitted to intervene" therein, are mandatory, and therefore this Court has no discretion to deny this motion, but is bound to permit applicant to intervene herein.

WHEREFORE, affiant prays that this motion be granted in all respects.

[Signature of affiant]
[Print signer's name below signature]

[Jurat]

Form 6

Affidavit of Attorney in Support of Motion for Permission to Intervene

Affidavit
[Title of court and cause]   Index No. — [if assigned]

STATE OF NEW YORK,
COUNTY OF __1____,   ss:

__2____, being duly sworn, deposes and says:

1. I am the attorney mentioned in the foregoing affidavit of __3____, President of __4____.

2. I have read the foregoing affidavit and know the contents thereof; I have carefully examined into the matters set forth in said affidavit; I have personally examined the applicable provisions of the Civil Practice Law and Rules and of the law relating to the subject matter of said affidavit.

3. I am of the opinion and verily believe, and have so advised said corporation and

508

said affiant, that said corporation has a good, substantial and meritorious cause of action arising from the conspiracy alleged in the answer of the defendant, and that the said corporation is entitled to make application to this Court to be made a party to this action on account of its interest in the subject matter thereof, and that such application should be granted; and I, therefore, make this affidavit in support of this motion for an order directing said corporation to be brought in by a proper amendment as a party defendant to this action, and permitting said corporation to plead to the complaint herein, and for such other and further relief as may be just.

4. I ask for the privilege of presenting the motion by order to show cause because the litigation is very active; the bringing in of said corporation as a party defendant at the earliest possible moment will prevent a delay of the trial; as soon as said corporation is joined, it will desire to make a certain motion or motions necessary to its proper protection; and I believe necessity exists for qualifying said corporation to make such motion at the earliest opportunity.

5. Annexed hereto and made a part hereof is a copy of the proposed pleading of _5_____ Corporation setting forth the claim [or defense] for which intervention is sought.

6. No previous application for this relief or any part thereof has been made to any court or judge.

[Signature of affiant]
[Print signer's name below signature]

[Jurat]

Form 7

Order Granting Permission to Third Person to Intervene

SUPREME COURT, _1_____ COUNTY.

Order

[Title of cause]   Index No. — [if assigned]

PRESENT: HON. _2_____, Justice.

An application having been made to this court for an order permitting _3_____ to intervene in this action, directing that he be brought in as a party defendant in this action, that the summons and complaint and notice of pendency in this action be amended by adding thereto the said _4_____ as a party defendant and allowing the said _5_____ to serve his answer upon the attorney for the plaintiff herein;

NOW, after reading and filing the affidavit of _6_____, duly sworn to the _7__ day of _8_____, 19_9_, the affidavit of _10_____, duly sworn to the _11__ day of _12_____, 19_13_, in support of said motion, and the affidavit of _14_____ sworn to the _15__ day of _16_____, 19_17_, in opposition thereto, and after hearing _18_____, Esq., attorney for applicant in support of said motion and _19_____, Esq., attorney for plaintiff in opposition thereto, and due deliberation having been had thereon, and it appearing that said _20_____ has an interest in the real property to be affected by a judgment in this action, it is

ORDERED that the said _21_____ be permitted to intervene in this action as party defendant, and it is further

ORDERED that the summons and complaint and notice of pendency in this action to be amended by adding thereto the said _22_____ as a party defendant, and it is further

ORDERED that the said _23_____ be permitted to serve his answer upon the attorney for a plaintiff herein or otherwise move with respect to the complaint within twenty days from the date of the entry of this order.

his __24__ day of __25_____, 19_26_ at __27_____, New York.

__28_____

[Print signer's name below signature]

Justice, Supreme Court

__29_____ County

Form 8

Notice of Motion to Intervene (by order to show cause)

SUPREME COURT, __1_____ COUNTY

Order to Show Cause

[Title of cause]   Index No. — [if assigned]

PRESENT: HON. __2_____, Justice.

On reading and filing the annexed affidavits of __3_____, and __4_____, both sworn to __5_____, 19_6_, a copy of the proposed pleading of the __7_____ Corporation, and the summons and pleadings herein, it is

ORDERED, that the parties hereto show cause before this Court, at a motion term, Part I thereof, to be held at the County Courthouse, in the Borough of __8_____, City of New York, on the __9__ day of __10_____, 19_11_, at the opening of Court on that day, or as soon thereafter as counsel can be heard, why an order should not be made directing that the __12_____ Corporation be brought in by proper amendment as a party defendant to this action, that said Corporation be permitted to plead to the complaint herein on the grounds that applicant has a statutory right to intervene in this action in the discretion of the court [or otherwise state statutory grounds for intervention] and why the said Corporation should not be granted such other and further relief as may be just.

Signed this __13__ day of __14_____, 19_15_ at __16_____, New York.

__17_____

[Print signer's name below signature]

Justice, Supreme Court

__18_____ County

Form 9

Affidavit in Support of Motion for Discretionary Order Permitting Third Person to Intervene

Affidavit

[Title of court and cause]   Index No. — [if assigned]

STATE OF NEW YORK,

COUNTY OF __1_____,   ss.:

__2_____, being duly sworn deposes and says:

1. I am President of the __3_____ Corporation, duly organized and existing under and by virtue of the laws of the State of New York.

2. I am duly authorized by said corporation to make this application on its behalf for the relief prayed.

3. Upon information and belief, the summons and complaint in this action were served upon defendant, __4_____, on __5_____, 19_6_; the answer of defendant, __7_____, was served upon the attorneys for the plaintiff on __8_____, 19_9_; the reply of plaintiff to counterclaim contained in the answer of defendant was served upon the attorneys for defendant on __10_____, 19_11_; and the action was noticed for trial by plaintiff for __12_____, 19_13_, term.

4. The complaint in this action purports to seek the removal of one __14_____, as

Executrix and Trustee under the Last Will and Testament of her late husband, __15____, and to enjoin her from voting the stock of the said Corporation, held by the Estate, and to compel the sale of the said stock, and for other relief.

5. The answer of defendant alleges, by way of affirmative defense and by way of counterclaim, a conspiracy entered into shortly after the death of __16____ to procure voting control of the management and affairs of said Corporation; injunctive relief, permanently and during the pendency of the action, is prayed in the said answer and damages are asked for the injury suffered by the defendant on account of the said conspiracy.

6. No motion has been made challenging the sufficiency of the said affirmative defense and the said counterclaim, and, upon information and belief, the time to move has expired.

7. Said Corporation is a consolidation of two corporations; one of them organized by the said __17____, deceased, the other organized, controlled and conducted by different interests. The consolidation was initiated and consummated by the late __18____, who became President and controlling stockholder of the consolidated corporation, of which (affiant) is now President.

8. Said __19____ died in 19_20_, leaving a Last Will and Testament, a copy of which is annexed to the complaint in this action; his Estate has succeeded to his position as majority stockholder of said Corporation; and said Estate of the late __21____ owns __22_ shares of the __23____ Stock of said Corporation, representing bare voting control thereof.

9. Among the acts stated in the said answer to have been committed in furtherance of the said conspiracy are a number of acts going directly to the stability and continued success and prosperity of the said Corporation, including attempts to create dissension among the employees of said Corporation, "which seriously endangers and endangered its successful management and the proper care and management of its affairs"; enticement of its employees from its employ; withdrawal of profitable products from it, and harassing and vexing it, by the presentation of unjustified claims and demands, and by the institution of unfounded suits and litigations.

10. I have read the said answer of the defendant, __24____, and am familiar with the contents thereof; as President of said Corporation, continuously in active daily control of its business and affairs, I am thoroughly familiar with the facts and circumstances set forth in the said answer upon which the said allegations of conspiracy are based; upon information and belief, the allegations of the said answer are true in every respect; from my own personal knowledge of what has been going on since shortly after the death of the late __25____, I state that the conspiracy alleged in the answer of the defendant __26____, and having the objects and purposes therein set forth, exists and has done substantial damage to said Corporation and seriously threatens its stability and continued success and prosperity.

11. Affiant has been advised by __27____, a member of the firm of __28____, attorneys for the said Corporation, and verily believes, that said Corporation has a good, substantial and meritorious cause of action arising from the said conspiracy against the parties thereto; he is further advised by the said __29____, that if the said conspiracy is proved, said Corporation will be entitled to injunctive relief against the continuance of the conspiracy and to damages for the injury done thereby up to this time; in view of the foregoing he is also advised by the said __30____, and verily believes, that said Corporation is entitled under section 1013 of the Civil Practice Law and Rules of this State, to make application to this Court to be made a party to this action on account of its interest in the subject matter thereof; and that it is peculiarly entitled to be made a party to this action on account of the following special circumstances of this case, which should commend themselves to the conscience of a court of equity:

(a) The plaintiff is alleged to be, and affiant verily believes and states upon his information and belief that plaintiff is a party to this conspiracy; he is a resident of the State of __31____, __32____, and so is immune from the process of this Court.

(b) It would be impossible, therefore, for said Corporation to proceed against the conspirators herein in any single state, and numerous actions, some of them in states greatly distant from each other, would have to be instituted, so that the attempt to procure relief against the said conspiracy would be singularly difficult, burdensome and expensive, and would involve a multitude of actions.

(c) In the present action, however, all the parties to the said conspiracy, so far as their identity is now known to said Corporation, are before the Court, and the issue can be litigated in a single action, and relief granted which will be effectual as against all the known parties to this organized effort to destroy and disrupt the business of said Corporation.

12. The said Corporation is ready, able and willing to submit itself in every respect with regard to the issues herein to the jurisdiction of this Court, and to comply with the orders, directions, and adjudications thereof, with respect thereto.

13. Attached hereto and made a part hereof is a copy of __33_____ Corporation's proposed pleading setting forth the claim and defense for which intervention is sought.

WHEREFORE, affiant respectfully prays that an order may be made directing __34_____ Corporation to be brought in by proper amendment, as a party defendant in this action, and permitting said Corporation to plead to the complaint herein, and for such other and further relief as may be just.

[Signature of affiant]
[Print signer's name below signature]

[Jurat]

Form 10

Order Granting Permission to Third Person to Intervene—Another Form

Supreme Court, __1_____ County.

Order

[Title of cause]   Index No. — [if assigned]

PRESENT: HON. __2_____, Justice.

The motion of the __3_____ Corporation for leave to intervene as a party defendant having come on to be heard; now on reading and filing the order to show cause dated __4_____, 19_5_, a copy of the proposed pleadings of the __6_____ Corporation, sworn to __7_____, 19_8_, in support of such motion, and proof of service thereof, and the opposing affidavit of __9_____, duly sworn to and after hearing __10_____, Esq., of counsel for the __11_____ Corporation, in support of such motion, and __12_____, Esq., of counsel for plaintiff, and __13_____, of counsel for defendant __14_____, in opposition thereto, and due deliberation having been had thereon; upon filing the opinion of the Court, it is, on motion of __15_____, attorney for __16_____ Corporation,

ORDERED, that said motion be and the same is hereby in all respects granted.

Signed this __17__ day of __18_____, 19_19_ at __20_____, New York.

Enter.

__21_____
[Print signer's name below signature]
Justice, Supreme Court
__22_____ County

Form 11

Order Allowing Intervention

Order

[Title of court and cause]   Index No. __1__

Present: Hon. __2_____, Justice.

A motion having been made herein by __3_____ for an order permitting her to intervene herein pursuant to Section 353-a of the General Business Law and the orders of this court dated __4_____, 19_5_, and __6_____, 19_7_, and directing that her moving affidavit sworn to __8_____, 19_9_, __10_____ [and her supplemental affidavit sworn to __11_____, 19_12_], shall constitute her pleading, and that the title of this action be amended by adding her name, and for such other and further relief as to the court might seem just and proper, and said motion having duly come on to be heard,

Now, upon reading and filing the notice of motion dated __13_____, 19_14_, and __15_____ [Recite additional papers, such as: the moving affidavit and supplemental affidavit of __16_____, sworn to __17_____, 19_18_, and __19_____, 19_20_, respectively], with proof of due service thereof on __21_____, [Name the Martin Act receiver], on __22_____, Attorney General of the State of New York, and on __23_____, intervenor, in support of said motion, and [additional papers, such as: the affidavits of __24_____, sworn to __25_____, 19_26_, and of Assistant Attorney General __27_____, sworn to __28_____, 19_29_, submitted upon said motion but not in opposition thereto, and the affidavit of __30_____, sworn to __31_____, 19_32_, in opposition thereto], and upon all the proceedings heretofore had herein, and after hearing __33_____, by __34_____ of counsel, attorneys for __35_____, in support of said motion, and __36_____ [other appearances, such as: receiver as aforesaid appearing but not opposing, and __37_____, attorney for __38_____], in opposition thereto, and due deliberation having been had thereon, and upon filing the opinion of this court, it is

ORDERED, that the motion of __39_____ to intervene herein is hereby granted and the said affidavits of __40_____ sworn to __41_____, 19_42_, and __43_____, 19_44_, be and they hereby are constituted as her pleading herein and the title of this action is hereby amended to read as follows: __45_____.

ORDERED, that this order shall be deemed to be without prejudice to the rights of persons who were induced to purchase stock of the defendant __46_____ or the defendant __47_____, or the defendant __48_____ to challenge the right of __49_____ to participate in said property, and also without prejudice to the right of such persons to demand a more formal pleading herein by said __50_____, and such persons may apply for relief herein as against said __51_____ through a resettlement of this order; and it is further

ORDERED, that __52_____ [or __53_____ as receiver as aforesaid], may take such further steps herein as they may deem advisable for the purpose of obtaining a determination of the validity of the claim for $__54_, sworn to by said __55_____ on __56_____, 19_57_, heretofore filed with said receiver, based upon her purchase of __58_____ [5,000 shares of the Class "A" stock] of the defendant __59_____, and for the purpose of establishing her interest in the property held by said receiver; and it is further __60_____ [Insert any further ordering paragraphs, as:

ORDERED, that the objections interposed by __61_____, intervenor, against the motion of __62_____ to intervene herein are hereby dismissed, and it is hereby determined that said __63_____, intervenor, has no right to object to the claim asserted by said __64_____ in connection with her purchase of the stock of the defendant __65_____].

Signed this __66__ day of __67_____, 19_68_, at __69_____, N. Y.

[Signature, with name printed underneath]
Justice, Supreme Court

Enter

[Adapted from papers in People v Monthly Income Shares, Inc. 263 AD 832, 31 NYS2d 527.]

§ 1013. Intervention by permission

Upon timely motion, any person may be permitted to intervene in any action when a statute of the state confers a right to intervene in the discretion of the court, or when the person's claim or defense and the main action have a common question of law or fact. In exercising its discretion, the court shall consider whether the intervention will unduly delay the determination of the action or prejudice the substantial rights of any party.

HISTORY:
Add, L 1962, ch 308, eff Sept 1, 1963.
Earlier statutes: CPA §§ 193-b, 687-a.

ADVISORY COMMITTEE NOTES:
This section is derived from CPA § 193-b(2), substantially unchanged; Cf. CPA § 988 (part of first sentence).

CROSS REFERENCES:
Intervention generally, CPLR 1012.
Proposed intervention pleading, CPLR 1014.
Real property actions, Real P Actions & Pr Law § 241.

FEDERAL ASPECTS:
Permissive intervention, Rule 24(b) of Federal Rules of Civil Procedure, USCS Court Rules.

RESEARCH REFERENCES AND PRACTICE AIDS:
3 Carmody-Wait 2d, Parties §§ 19:135, 19:142, 19:143, 19:145.
12 Carmody-Wait 2d, Action to Recover a Chattel (Replevin) § 82:128.
13 Carmody-Wait 2d, Notice of Pendency of Actions § 87:78.
21 Carmody-Wait 2d, Actions By or Against the State § 126:12.
24 Carmody-Wait 2d, Proceeding Against a Body or Officer § 145:289.
25 Carmody-Wait 2d, Fundamentals of Practice in the Surrogate's Court § 149:214.
25 Carmody-Wait 2d, Probate Proceedings § 152:33.

Annotations:
Assertion of fiduciary status of party to litigation as basis for intervention by one claiming interest in fruits thereof as trust beneficiary. 2 ALR2d 227.
Appealability of order granting or denying right of intervention. 15 ALR2d 336.
Intervention by stockholder for purpose of interposing defense for corporation. 33 ALR2d 473.
Time within which right to intervene may be exercised. 37 ALR2d 1306.

Law Reviews:
New York Civil Practice Law and Rules: parties. 27 Albany L Rev 182.
Parties and pleading under the CPLR. 31 Brooklyn L Rev 98.
A biannual survey of New York practice: intervention allowed to defend constitutionality of statute granting partial tax exemption. 39 St. John's L Rev 430.
Public intervention in settlements of government antitrust cases. 39 Brooklyn L Rev 579.

CASE NOTES

1. In general
2. Motion, pleading, and practice
3. Intervention allowed
4. Intervention not allowed

1. In general

Liberal construction and application of the inter-vention statutes are called for. Raymond v Honeywell (1968) 58 Misc 2d 903, 297 NYS2d 66.

Intervention should be liberally allowed, particularly with the presence of common questions of law and fact, and is permitted as of right when interest in property may be adversely affected by judgment. Teleprompter Manhattan CATV Corp. v State Board of Equalization & Assessment (1970) 34 AD2d 1033, 311 NYS2d 46.

Where party was technically without status to appear in proceeding, her appearance by attorney should not have been filed without court order permitting same pursuant to appropriate motion for leave therefor. Re Will of Mann (1976) 86 Misc 2d 1028, 382 NYS2d 906.

2. Motion, pleading, and practice

Oral motion to intervene in Art 78 proceeding seeking to annul approval by Commissioners of Health and Environmental Conservation of sanitary landfill site was denied for failure to comply with provisions of CPLR §§ 1013 and 1014. Howard v Diamond (1974) 76 Misc 2d 809, 351 NYS2d 533.

CPLR 1013 contemplates local litigation including pleadings to be served by the party seeking intervention. 176 East 123rd St. Corp. v Fragen (1971) 67 Misc 2d 281, 323 NYS2d 737.

The court cannot consider an intervenor's motion to dismiss the complaint and must deny the intervenor's application to oppose plaintiff's motion for temporary injunctive relief until an order has been entered granting the right to intervene under CPLR § 1013. Brown v Waryas (1965) 45 Misc 2d 77, 255 NYS2d 724.

Where Article 78 proceeding to review action of zoning board of appeals in granting variance was dismissed, motion of neighboring landowner to intervene was rendered academic. Lavere v Board of Zoning Appeals (1972) 39 AD2d 639, 331 NYS2d 141, affd 33 NY2d 873, 352 NYS2d 442, 307 NE2d 559.

In an action for an injunction in which the plaintiffs sought an order permitting the addition of certain named individuals as party plaintiffs, the motion should be brought pursuant to CPLR 1013, which refers to "intervention by permission" and applies to prospective plaintiffs, and should be accompanied by proposed pleadings setting forth the claim for which intervention is sought as required by CPLR 1014. Del Prete v Lorenz Schneider Co. (1970) 33 AD2d 1021, 308 NYS2d 68.

A party can be added to a pending action or proceeding only on timely motion and an order of court in which action or proceeding is pending. Muka v Sturgis (1976) 53 AD2d 716, 383 NYS2d 933. Application made by various interns and residents in New York City hospitals to intervene in proceeding brought by New York City Health and Hospital Corporation to compel the city to comply with various monetary obligations, including tax levy payments and medicaid payments, was not barred by res judicata, notwithstanding the denial of a prior motion to intervene by the present movants' predecessors, since the basis of the Appellate Division's prior denial of intervention was not a lack of standing to intervene as a matter of law but as a matter of fact, the Appellate Division having believed that movants' interests would be protected by prosecution of the proceeding by petitioner, but since history had not borne out that prediction. New York City Health & Hospitals Corp. v New York (1976) 85 Misc 2d 501, 380 NYS2d 891, affd 56 AD2d 535, 391 NYS2d 834.

3. Intervention allowed

Where automobile liability insurer brought action to declare validity of its disclaimer of coverage, MVAIC was entitled to intervene, since it has a real and substantial interest in the matter of the determination sought. United Services Auto Asso. v Graham (1964) 21 AD2d 657, 249 NYS2d 788.

Intervention in an action to review the constitutionality of reapportionment legislation by the president pro tem of the state senate appeared to be proper under CPLR 1012(a), paragraph 2, and in any event was allowable under CPLR 1013. Orans v Rockefeller (1965) 47 Misc 2d 493, 262 NYS2d 893, affd 24 AD2d 217, 265 NYS2d 49, mod on other grounds 17 NY2d 601, 268 NYS2d 561, 215 NE2d 682 and mod on other grounds 17 NY2d 107, 269 NYS2d 97, 216 NE2d 311, app den 17 NY2d 721, 269 NYS2d 971, 216 NE2d 834.

City permitted to intervene in proceeding involving special franchise assessment inasmuch as the court's decision would materially affect the city's interest. Sterling Information Service, Ltd. v State Board of Equalization & Assessment (1969) 60 Misc 2d 45, 302 NYS2d 226.

4. Intervention not allowed

Motions by abutting and adjoining property owners for leave to intervene and question the granting of special exception permit required for operation of a day care center was denied as to permissive intervention, but, provided the movants can establish that they are aggrieved persons within the meaning of Village Law § 179-b, are entitled to intervene, as of right. Unitarian Universalist Church v Shorten (1970) 64 Misc 2d 851, 315 NYS2d 506, vacated on other grounds 64 Misc 2d 1027, 316 NYS2d 837.

Where party seeking to intervene in a proceeding by trustees for the settlement of their accounts proposes to interpose objections which had already been asserted by a necessary party to the proceeding, intervention, which is not to be granted indiscriminately and without regard to the statutes, will be denied as a matter of discretion. Re Spangenberg (1963) 41 Misc 2d 584, 245 NYS2d 501.

Intervention by motor vehicle accident indemnification corporation in death action against known tortfeasor would not be permitted where corporation's claim did not involve issues common to death action. McGee v Horvat (1965) 23 AD2d 271, 260 NYS2d 345.

A labor union involved in a dispute with a publishing company may not intervene in a pending Article 78 proceeding between the publisher and the Board of Education, which arose over the issue of the legality of a resolution by the Board as being opposed to the purchase of any books published by the publisher where books of equal value were available. Kingsport Press, Inc. v Board of Education (1966) 50 Misc 428, 270 NYS2d 773.

Outdoor advertising association was not entitled to intervene as a party plaintiff as of right in suit by owner of outdoor advertising signs in Catskill park challenging the constitutionality of Environmental Conservation Law provision prohibiting the erection of advertising signs in the park without a permit, since the interests of the association were adequately represented by plaintiff and the action did not involve a disposition of or claim for damages to property in which the association might be adversely affected by the judgment. Modjeska Sign Studios, Inc. v Berle (1976) 87 Misc 2d 600, 386 NYS2d 765, affd 55 AD2d 340, 390 NYS2d 945.

CASE NOTES

UNDER FORMER CIVIL PRACTICE LAWS

A. UNDER FORMER CPA § 193-B(2)

1. Generally
2. Discretionary intervention
3. Rights of intervener
4. Timely application
5. Particular actions and proceedings

1. Generally

The supreme court has inherent power to grant intervention to parties whose rights will be adversely affected by the outcome of an action and the history of intervention shows a trend in the direction of the extension of the remedy rather than restriction. Central Westchester Humane Soc. v Hilleboe (1952) 202 Misc 873, 115 NYS2d 769.

To authorize intervention, applicant must have interest in subject-matter of litigation of such nature that he will gain or lose by direct legal operation and effect of judgment. Rubin v Irving Trust Co. (1951) 105 NYS2d 140.

It has been said that the old statute, § 193 of the Civil Practice Act, repealed by the laws of 1946, contained such radically different wording that decisions thereunder were not controlling under CPA § 193-b as to the right of a party to intervene. Central Westchester Humane Soc. v Hilleboe (1952) 202 Misc 873, 115 NYS2d 769.

Proposed intervenor need not have direct personal or pecuniary interest in subject of action; if he would be indirectly affected by litigation in substantial manner, he may intervene. Central Westchester Humane Soc. v Hilleboe, supra.

Controversy as to which faction of labor union was entitled to administer grievance matters was proper case for intervention of one faction in employer's proceeding to stay arbitration under CPA § 1450 (§§ 7501, 7502(a), 7503(a) herein). Re American Machine & Foundry Co. (1948) 193 Misc 990, 85 NYS2d 456.

Where judgment creditor of bank depositor claimed portion of deposit paid into court pursuant to order under CPA § 51-a (§ 216(a) herein), and where such depositor or adverse claimant failed within one year to intervene in action or to commence action to enforce her claim to deposit, such judgment creditor was not entitled to intervene. Solicitor v Bankers Trust Co. (1952) 304 NY 296, 107 NE2d 455.

The provisions of this section making it mandatory for the intervening party to submit a proposed answer on his motion to intervene, and the direction in the order permitting such intervention that the answer be served within five days are special circumstances warranting consideration on the merits of a motion pursuant to RCP 90 (Rule 3014 herein) to compel plaintiff to state and number alleged causes of action although such motion is made after answer. City Bank Farmers Trust Co. v National Cuba Hotel Corp. (1954) 133 NYS2d 8.

Where husband sued wife's parents for family partnership accounting and they pleaded facts that he was agent of his wife who was their daughter, which he denied, she may intervene. Schwartz v Klein (1947) 188 Misc 665, 72 NYS2d 386.

In action to partition lands in Adirondacks, motion of State of New York to intervene was granted, on its affidavit showing interest in such lands under tax sales and deeds and on its proposed counterclaim asserting State is seized in fee ownership of all such lands. Hatch v Turner (1953) 282 AD 818, 123 NYS2d 285.

Public Service Commission is by legislative mandate made party to proceeding to condemn utility company's property after and by service on Commission of county court's final order confirming appraisal commissioner's report, and there is no necessity for application to court under CPA § 193-b for permission to intervene. Onondaga C. W. Auth. v New York W. S. Corp. (1955) 285 AD 655, 139 NYS2d 755.

As general rule, third party will be permitted to intervene if his interests will be jeopardized by his absence, so that whole controversy may be ended in one action and by single judgment. Harrison v Mary Bain Estates, Inc. (1956) 2 Misc 2d 52, 152 NYS2d 239, affd 2 AD2d 670, 153 NYS2d 552.

Where a theft insurance policy prohibited assignment of proceeds without insurer's consent and buyer had purchased automobile under conditional sales contract which contained clause assigning proceeds of loss and conditional buyer had instituted action against insurer to recover on the theft policy, the assignee was entitled to intervene despite the policy prohibition. Fiorito v Northern Assur. Co. (1957) 158 NYS2d 818.

Where persons are not parties in a proceeding before the state commission against discrimination and they are not affected in any way, in any property or other legal rights by order of the commission, they are not persons aggrieved and may not intervene. New York State Com. against Discrimination v Pelham Hall Apts., Inc. (1958) 10 Misc 2d 346, 171 NYS2d 558.

Judgment-creditor was not entitled to intervene in existing action between judgment-debtor and third party where there was no fund in court's custody to authorize such intervention. Hocking-Hershey Associates, Inc. v Iandoli (1959) 19 Misc 2d 210, 187 NYS2d 300.

Taxpayer was not entitled to intervene in lawsuit conducted by municipality because he did not agree with officials on how to conduct the litigation where he failed to show that he had a special interest therein differentiating him from other taxpayers. Zara Contracting Co. v Glen Cove (1960) 22 Misc 2d 279, 197 NYS2d 940.

2. Discretionary intervention

In action by mother for personal injuries in collision between automobiles driven by plaintiff's son and other defendant, wife and son of driver of second car in which they were riding may intervene and assert affirmative claims on their own behalf for personal injuries against driver of first car. Schwartz v Myers (1951) 104 NYS2d 609.

Stockholders' derivative action against corporation to restrain it from selling its stock to realty corporation is one against realty corporation; intervention, ostensibly on behalf of realty corporation, would prejudice stockholders' action and complicate and confuse issues. Breswick & Co. v Harrison-Rye Realty Corp. (1952) 280 AD 820, 114 NYS2d 25.

In action to determine boundary line between two towns, incorporated village, situated within boundaries of defendant town, was permitted to intervene and serve answer, in expectation of avoiding unnecessary multiplication of actions, where action may affect established boundary line of village and proposed answer raises no issue other than boundary issue. Brookhaven v Smithtown (1955) 285 AD 1172, 140 NYS2d 707. See Brookhaven v Smithtown (1955) 285 AD 1172, 140 NYS2d 706.

In action by chattel mortgagee to replevy mortgaged automobile conveyed by mortgagor without knowledge of mortgagee to dealer who conveyed it to defendant, such dealer could have intervened in such action under subd 2 of CPA § 193-b. Northern New York Tr. Co. v Smith (1955) 2 Misc 2d 810, 153 NYS2d 798.

An arbitration proceeding is a special proceeding and if an arbitration panel declines to permit an employee to intervene, he can apply to Special Term for an order directing that he be allowed to intervene over the opposition of the employer and the union. Iroquois Beverage Corp. v International Union, etc. (1955) 14 Misc 2d 290, 159 NYS2d 256.

The motion of a third-party defendant to intervene and interpose an answer and counterclaim for damages was improperly granted where the third party defendant was not a necessary party nor even a proper party and had no relationship with

the plaintiff. A. W. Peterson & Sons Die Co. v Singer (1957) 160 NYS2d 760.

CPA § 193-b applied to proceedings as well as to actions. Special term properly exercised its discretion to grant applications of certain oil corporations and an oil refiners' association for leave to intervene on an application by a trustee of a trust even though they were not beneficiaries of the trust since the proposed interveners had a real and substantial interest in the proceeding. Re Petroleum Research Fund (1956) 3 AD2d 1, 157 NYS2d 693.

A creditor of a decedent who sought to intervene in a proceeding to revoke testamentary letters was denied permission to intervene upon a failure to show a question of law or fact common to his claim and the revocation proceeding. Re Rubin (1959) 19 Misc 2d 631, 190 NYS2d 469.

Where two actions arose out of same automobile action, and plaintiffs in first action were granted summary judgment and date had been set for assessment of damages, court denied motion for plaintiffs in second action for permission to intervene, or for consolidation of joint trials, or for stay of assessment until second action was brought to judgment since to do so would prejudice rights of plaintiffs in first action. David v Bauman (1960) 24 Misc 2d 67, 196 NYS2d 746.

3. Rights of intervener

Intervening defendant has all rights of original defendant for all purposes, including right to plead statute of limitations. Island Park v Island Park-Long Beach, Inc. (1948) 81 NYS2d 407, affd 274 AD 930, 83 NYS2d 542.

In action against city for insurance premiums on policy approved by city's common council, mayor, who was not named as party in such action had no right under city charter to serve answer in behalf of city, and where he met none of statutory requirements of CPA § 193-b, his application for leave to intervene was denied. Trans-Canada A. A. v Mechanicville (1956) 2 AD2d 734, 152 NYS2d 608.

Interveners could not have their own counsel and proceed separately in stockholders' derivative action where a number of separate actions had been consolidated and a general counsel designated and the interveners' actions were interwoven with the overall picture. Fleitman v Simpson (1957) 9 Misc 2d 398, 166 NYS2d 727.

4. Timely application

Where in action to reform deed plaintiff's motion was granted on June 5, 1947 to reopen default judgment entered May 17, 1946, movant's application for same relief to intervene on June 26, 1947, was timely. Island Park v Island Park-Long Beach, Inc. (1947) 74 NYS2d 492, affd 272 AD 1060, 75 NYS2d 515.

Stockholders, who individually had notice of litigation against corporation in receivership, could not intervene where they delayed application for over one year. Forker v Royal Development Co. (1947) 189 Misc 798, 72 NYS2d 59.

Where liability insurer was notified to defend action against insured but refused to do so unless he executed non-waiver agreements, insurer's application to intervene after its appearance and default, was not timely. Krenitsky v Ludlow Motor Co. (1950) 276 AD 511, 96 NYS2d 102.

5. Particular actions and proceedings

An application by two members of a union to intervene as parties in an arbitration proceeding between the employer and the union which is their collective bargaining agent must be denied. Such members cannot be permitted to intervene unless they establish, one, that the representation of their interest by the union is or may be inadequate or, two, that they are so situated that they may be adversely affected by distribution or other disposition of property in the custody of or subject to the control or disposition by the court or an officer thereof. General Warehousemen's Union v Glidden Co. (1957) 9 Misc 2d 648, 169 NYS2d 759.

Where several stockholders' derivative actions were consolidated and general counsel was designated for all plaintiffs but two substantial stockholders who were aware of original motions for the consolidation, employed their own counsel and moved for leave to intervene and served a proposed additional complaint, the allegations of which were inseparably interwoven with the existing consolidated complaint, the application to intervene as plaintiffs was granted. Fleitman v Simpson (1957) 9 Misc 2d 398, 166 NYS2d 727.

In a summary proceeding in the Municipal Court for nonpayment of rent, the guarantor was allowed to intervene to plead a tender of payment and a subsequent action in the Supreme Court by the lessee and guarantor against the landlord for judgment declaring that the guarantor could remedy the tenant's defaults was unnecessary. Picto Corp. v Marburt Holding Corp. (1957) 9 Misc 2d 407, 166 NYS2d 798.

Where sublessee, who was obligated by the terms of the sublease to pay real estate taxes on the premises, timely instituted a proceeding for a reduction of the assessed valuation and subsequently was dispossessed by the lessee, who then had to pay the taxes, the lessee was a party aggrieved and as such was permitted to intervene in, and further prosecute, the proceeding commenced by the sublessee. Fleetair, Inc. v Tax Com. of New York (1958) 15 Misc 2d 502, 181 NYS2d 645.

In action by registered ophthalmic dispensers against state university, commissioner of education, and board of regents for declaratory judgment invalidating price advertising regulation applying to licensed opticians, licensed optometrists were permitted to intervene to uphold regulation, because of a common question of law between main action and defense and absence of delay or prejudice to main action. Morofsky v University of State of New York (1959) 17 Misc 2d 707, 191 NYS2d 696.

A creditor of a decedent who sought to intervene in a proceeding to revoke testamentary letters was denied permission to intervene upon a failure to show a question of law or fact common to his claim and the revocation proceeding. Re Rubin (1959) 19 Misc 2d 631, 190 NYS2d 469.

In mortgage foreclosure action, fire insurers of property in favor of mortgagor and mortgagee would not be bound by the judgment of foreclosure, and therefore may not intervene therein. Lesser v West Albany Warehouses, Inc. (1959) 17 Misc 2d 461, 191 NYS2d 113.

State wil not be permitted to intervene in action brought by citizen against county treasurer for return of illegal gambling money, allegedly wrongfully withheld, since state has no paramount right to such money if money is proceeds of illegal gambling. Gross v County Treasurer of Orange County (1959) 19 Misc 2d 738, 192 NYS2d 405.

A creditor may in his own name and for his own benefit sue directors for loans of corporate funds to stockholders (Stock Corp L § 59), but creditors similarly situated may intervene or be joined. If they do not intervene or fail to be joined, it is no objection to the maintenance of the action by the single creditor that he will thereby reap the full statutory benefit to the exclusion of other creditors. American Broadcasting-Paramount Theatres, Inc. v Frye (1960) 8 NY2d 232, 203 NYS2d 850, 168 NE2d 669.

Association representing property owners in vicinity of property for which variance was sought was denied permission to intervene in CPA Article 78 (Art 78 herein) proceeding to review the determination where it failed to submit a proposed pleading setting forth the claim or defense for which intervention was sought. Virgo v Zoning Board of Appeals (1961) 28 Misc 2d 886, 212 NYS2d 586.

B. UNDER FORMER SCA § 291

6. In general

Notice vacated where one served as adverse party is not adverse party. Syracuse Mortg. Corp. v Kepler (1923) 122 Misc 95, 202 NYS 193.

Where attorney intervened personally for purposes of appeal, his notice of appeal, served and filed before leave to intervene was granted, was ineffectual, and appeal was dismissed. Re Polizzo's Estate (1961) 13 AD2d 697, 213 NYS2d 931, amd 14 AD2d 537, 218 NYS2d 986.

§ 1014. Proposed intervention pleading

A motion to intervene shall be accompanied by a proposed pleading setting forth the claim or defense for which intervention is sought.

HISTORY:
Add, L 1962, ch 308, eff Sept 1, 1963.
Earlier statutes: CPA § 193-b.

ADVISORY COMMITTEE NOTES:
The common law courts were opposed to a third person intervening in an action, which was regarded as a private contest between the original parties. Intervention was allowed, however, in equity, which borrowed the device from the civil, ecclesiastical and admiralty courts. A narrow type of permissive intervention in actions for the recovery of real or personal property was added by amendment to the Field code in 1851. This was broadened somewhat in 1876. There was a further enlargement in 1901, extending the procedure to cases where the intervenor had an interest in real property for injury to which the complaint demanded relief. As so amended, the provision became part of CPA § 193 in 1920.

In 1945, the Judicial Council concluded that the state provisions for intervention were too narrow, mainly because there was, in general, no right to intervene in an action for money and because confusion had resulted from the absence of a provision outlining the proper procedure in intervention. See 11 NY Jud Council Rep 59, 396 (1945). A proposal for amendment was made, closely following Federal rule 24 both as to scope and general language. This proposal was adopted in 1946 (NY Laws 1946, c. 971) and became CPA § 193-b.

In its provision for intervention of right, CPA § 193-b included cases "(c) when the applicant has an interest in real property, the title to which may in any manner be affected by the judgment or in real property for injury to which the complaint demands relief." This language comes from the earlier New York statutory provisions and has no counterpart in Federal rule 24. It adds to the length of the intervention provision and is unnecessary. See Hatch v Turner, 282 App Div 818, 123 NYS2d 285 (3d Dept 1953); Town of Brookhaven v Town of Smithtown, 285 App Div 1172, 140 NYS2d 706 (2d Dept 1955). Another reason for elimination of this matter is that the specific enumeration weakens the scope of the provision for intervention of right. Thus, it could be argued that if the quoted words were retained there would be no intervention of right in actions for recovery of, or for injury to, personal property.

Most of the cases decided under the 1946 amended provision have been liberal in allowing intervention. Onondaga Co. Water Auth. v N. Y. Water Service Corp. 285 App Div 655, 139 NYS2d 755 (4th Dept 1955) (statutory intervention of right); Town of Brookhaven v Town of Smithtown, 285 App Div 1172, 140 NYS2d 706 (2d Dept 1955) (permissive); Hatch v Turner 282 App Div 818, 123 NYS2d 285 (3d Dept 1953) (interest in land). See also Donato v American Locomotive Co. 283 App Div 410, 127 NYS2d 709 (3d Dept 1954); cf. His Majesty's Treasury v Bankers Tr. Co. (Tennent), 304 NY 296, 107 NE2d 455 (1952) (judgment creditor cannot intervene where his debtor was in default as a claimant to money paid into court under CPA § 51-a).

Section 193-c was added to the CPA in 1946 as a part of the same bill which enacted the 1946 intervention procedure; both were the result of the same study by the Judicial Council. Section 193-c was not an intervention statute, however, but rather one requiring joinder of parties in certain actions brought to recover damages for injury to real property. CPA § 193-c has not been applied in any published opinion during the ten years it has been on the statute books. It is adequately covered by new CPLR § 1001 since the persons specified in its first sentence would be necessary parties under that section. The need for the second sentence of § 193-c is unclear since the result it provides for is an inevitable one unless the party joined discontinues without prejudice, and a judge would hardly allow such a discontinuance in this situation. The order to protect an absentee provided for by the third sentence of § 193-c is authorized without such specific provision.

CROSS REFERENCES:
Intervention as of right, CPLR 1012.
Intervention by permission, CPLR 1013.

Real property actions, Real P Actions & Pr Law § 241.

FEDERAL ASPECTS:

Pleadings and motions, generally, Rules 7 through 16 of Federal Rules of Civil Procedure, USCS Court Rules.

Procedure for intervention in actions in United States District Courts, Rule 24(c) of Federal Rules of Civil Procedure, USCS Court Rules.

RESEARCH REFERENCES AND PRACTICE AIDS:

3 Carmody-Wait 2d, Parties §§ 19:135, 19:144.

24 Carmody-Wait 2d, Proceeding Against a Body or Officer § 145:289.

25 Carmody-Wait 2d, Probate Proceedings §§ 152:32, 152:33.

Law Reviews:

New York Civil Practice Law and Rules: parties. 27 Albany L Rev 182.

Parties and pleading under the CPLR. 31 Brooklyn L Rev 98.

A biannual survey of New York practice: intervention allowed to defend constitutionality of statute granting partial tax exemption. 39 St. John's L Rev 430.

Public intervention in settlements of government antitrust cases. 39 Brooklyn L Rev 579.

Forms:

See "FORMS" heading following "CASE NOTES", infra.

CASE NOTES

Where prospective intervenor fails to include in his motion papers the required proposed pleading, the court has no power to grant leave to intervene. Carriage Hill, Inc. v Lane (1964) 20 AD2d 914, 249 NYS2d 455.

Where a prospective intervenor fails to include a motion paper as required for pleading, the court has no power to grant leave to intervene. Mohawk Maintenance Co. v Drake (1968) 29 AD2d 689, 287 NYS2d 124.

In an action for an injunction in which the plaintiffs sought an order permitting the addition of certain named individuals as party plaintiffs, the motion should be brought pursuant to CPLR 1013, which refers to "intervention by permission" and applies to prospective plaintiffs, and should be accompanied by proposed pleadings setting forth the claim for which intervention is sought as required by CPLR 1014. Del Prete v Lorenz Schneider Co. (1970) 33 AD2d 1021, 308 NYS2d 68.

Oral motion to intervene in Art 78 proceeding seeking to annul approval by Commissioners of Health and Environmental Conservation of sanitary landfill site was denied for failure to comply with provisions of CPLR §§ 1013 and 1014. Howard v Diamond (1974) 76 Misc 2d 809, 351 NYS2d 533.

CASE NOTES

UNDER FORMER CIVIL PRACTICE LAWS

Where movant does not submit proposed pleadings setting forth the defense for which intervention is sought, and fails to demonstrate that plaintiff may or will be unable or unwilling to contest the action adequately, his application for intervention must be denied. Moore v Oyster Bay (1961) 29 Misc 2d 169, 211 NYS2d 858.

FORMS

Pleading of Intervenor

SUPREME COURT, COUNTY OF __1_____

John Doe, Plaintiff,
   against   Answer
Richard Roe, Defendant,   Index No. — [if assigned]
John Smith, Intervenor.

John Smith, the intervenor above-named, as and for his Answer herein alleges as follows:

§ 1015. Substitution upon death

(a) Generally. If a party dies and the claim for or against him is not thereby extinguished the court shall order substitution of the proper parties.

(b) Devolution of rights or liabilities on other parties. Upon the death of one or more of the plaintiffs or defendants in an action in which the right sought to be enforced survives only to the surviving plaintiffs or against the surviving defendants, the action does not abate. The death shall be noted on the record and the action shall proceed.

HISTORY:

Add, L 1962, ch 308, eff Sept 1, 1963.
Earlier statutes: CPA §§ 82–86; CCP §§ 755–759; 2 RS 386, § 1; Code Proc § 121.

ADVISORY COMMITTEE NOTES:

Cf. Fed R Civ P 25(a). See also CPA §§ 82, 84, 85, 86, 88, 478. As to when an action survives, see §§ 116 to 120 of the Decedent Estate Law.

In spite of its defects (see 4 Moore, Fed Prac 510 (Supp 1955)), Federal rule 25 has some good features—notably its brevity and directness. Hence in the drafting of the rules relating to substitution, it is taken as a model as to general form and structure, and its deficiencies are corrected by incorporating the better parts of the New York procedure. The substantive provisions of the sections of the CPA cited have been omitted.

The CPA provisions dealt to a considerable degree in terms of revivor instead of utilizing a motion procedure. Here the Federal rules seem superior. The motion regarding substitution may come from (1) the plaintiff who either wants the judgment to affect the successors of the deceased party or wishes to guard against a dismissal in case of failure to substitute, (2) a surviving defendant who wishes the successors brought in, or (3) the successors who wish to protect their interests.

The unfortunate time limit features of Federal rule 25 are omitted and instead it is provided in new CPLR § 1021 that when substitution is not made within a reasonable time the court may dismiss the action as to the party for whom substitution was ordered. This provision applies to substitution in all cases and not merely in case of death.

This section follows Federal rule 25(a)(2), which was undoubtedly suggested by CPA § 85.

The provisions of CPA § 89 for "nonabatement after verdict, report or decision" are omitted as unnecessary.

CROSS REFERENCES:

Merger or consolidation, no abatement, Bank Law § 602; Bus Corp Law § 906; Ins Law § 502; Vill Law § 18-1810.

Death of person in whose favor cause of action for personal injury existed, EPTL § 11-3.2.

Unincorporated associations, actions by and against, Gen Assn Law § 14.

Effect of repeal of statute, Gen Const Law § 94.

Dissolution of corporation during action to recover tax, Tax Law § 203-a.

Proceedings as to children born out of wedlock, Family Ct Act § 518.

FEDERAL ASPECTS:

Substitution of parties upon death, Rule 43(a) of Federal Rules of Appellate Procedure, USCS Court Rules.

Substitution upon death, Rule 25(a) of Federal Rules of Civil Procedure, USCS Court Rules.

Substitution of parties: transfer of interest, Rule 25(c) of Federal Rules of Civil Procedure, USCS Court Rules.

RESEARCH REFERENCES AND PRACTICE AIDS:

2 Carmody-Wait 2d, Abatement and Survival of Actions §§ 11:6, 11:14.

3 Carmody-Wait 2d, Parties § 19:151.

10 Carmody-Wait 2d, Appeals in General §§ 70:46, 70:47, 70:50.

12 Carmody-Wait 2d, Action to Recover a Chattel (Replevin) §§ 82:87, 82:209.

14 Carmody-Wait 2d, Partition § 91:70.

17 Carmody-Wait 2d, Committee for an Incompetent or a Mental Patient § 109:12.

20 Carmody-Wait 2d, Actions and Proceedings By and Against Corporations, Their Officers, Directors, and Shareholders § 121:212.

21 Carmody-Wait 2d, Actions Against Persons Jointly Liable § 123:11.

24 Carmody-Wait 2d, Proceeding Against a Body or Officer § 145:236.

25 Carmody-Wait 2d, Fundamentals of Practice in the Surrogate's Court §§ 149:212, 149:382.

25 Carmody-Wait 2d, Probate Proceedings § 152:43.

1 Am Jur 2d, Abatement, Survival, and Revival §§ 41, 49, 136.

59 Am Jur 2d, Parties § 231.

63 Am Jur 2d, Public Officers and Employees § 536.

1 Am Jur Pl and Pr Forms (Rev ed), Abatement, Revival, and Stay, Forms 1 et seq., 251 et seq.

19 Am Jur Pl and Pr Forms (Rev ed), Parties, Forms 141 et seq.

23 Am Jur Pl and Pr Forms (Rev ed), Taxpayers' Actions, Forms 81, 82.

Annotations:

Conflict of laws as to survival or revival of wrongful death actions against estate or personal representative of wrongdoer. 17 ALR2d 690.

Construction of Federal Rule 25(a)(1) as permitting substitution, as a party, of personal representative of nonresident decedent. 79 ALR2d 532.

Validity of exception for specific kind of tort action in survival statute. 77 ALR3d 1349.

Survival of right of action for damages based on violation of federal antitrust laws. 11 ALR Fed 963.

Sufficiency of suggestion of death of party, filed under Rule 25(a)(1) of Federal Rules of Civil Procedure governing substitution of parties upon death. 12 ALR Fed 951.

Applicable time limitation for service upon persons not parties, of motion and notice of motion for substitution of parties on death under Rule 25(a)(1) of Federal Rules of Civil Procedure. 13 ALR Fed 830.

Law Reviews:

New York Civil Practice Law and Rules: parties. 27 Albany L Rev 182.

Parties and pleading under the CPLR. 31 Brooklyn L Rev 98.

Forms:

See "FORMS" heading following "CASE NOTES", infra.

CASE NOTES

1. In general
2. Substitution or appointment of representative
3. Failure of substitution or appointment of representative

1. In general

Under New York law, the death of a party to a lawsuit revokes the power of an attorney to represent the deceased party. Yonofsky v Wernick (1973, DC NY) 362 F Supp 1005.

Where it appeared that plaintiff had died more than two years prior to settlement of action and that order to show cause why settlement should not be vacated and complaint dismissed had been served upon person alleged to be daughter and sole distributee of plaintiff, as well as upon attorneys for deceased plaintiff, and no affidavit was interposed in opposition to such motion, court had no alternative but to vacate settlement and dismiss action, but if representative was appointed, such representative could then move to vacate such judgment. Flumenbaum v Hartman (1974) 79 Misc 2d 544, 360 NYS2d 394.

Prior to the enactment of the CPLR in 1962, there was no statutory authority for out-of-state service on a nonresident executor or administrator in either a plenary action or a substitution proceeding, and CPLR 1015[a] was not intended to change any former practice available under the CPA; so that accordingly, it is CPLR 302 which expressly authorizes a court to "exercise personal jurisdiction" over a nondomiciliary's executor or administrator and CPLR 313 which authorizes out-of-state service upon such a personal representative. Rosenfeld v Hotel Corp. of America (1967) 20 NY2d 25, 281 NYS2d 308, 228 NE2d 374.

Where one of two petitioners, who were appealing from the decision of the Board of Trustees which denied their application to rezone their property, was deceased, and the record did not disclose the manner in which petitioners held the property, it was held that if all the deceased's rights survived to the remaining petitioner, the action could proceed with a notation of death in the record, and that otherwise, the appeal could not be prosecuted until an executor or administrator had been appointed to represent the estate of the deceased. Heller v Rogers (1966) 26 AD2d 640, 272 NYS2d 433.

2. Substitution or appointment of representative

Although the Supreme Court had the power to appoint a representative for a deceased defendant, where the trial had not started at the time of defendant's death, the court denied a petition for summary appointment of a representative holding that an application should be made by plaintiff in the proper forum. Castrovinci v Edwards (1969) 59 Misc 2d 696, 299 NYS2d 1017.

Plaintiff husband was entitled to substitute himself as administrator of estate of deceased wife as party plaintiff in her place in malpractice actions arising out of alleged negligence of defendants in care and treatment of the wife. Davis v New York (1975) 47 AD2d 529, 363 NYS2d 599, affd 38 NY2d 257, 379 NYS2d 721, 342 NE2d 516.

Beneficiaries of Workmen's Compensation claimant, who was deemed civilly dead because he had been sentenced to life imprisonment, should be substituted for claimant, since they were entitled to posthumous claim as though the claimant were actually physically dead. Garner v Shulte Co. (1965) 23 AD2d 127, 259 NYS2d 161.

An order of substitution pursuant to CPLR 1015[a] and 1021 is effected within the discretion of the court. Rosenfeld v Hotel Corp. of America (1967) 20 NY2d 25, 281 NYS2d 308, 228 NE2d 374.

Where co-owner of real property died after the institution of condemnation proceedings but before the commencement of the trial, and condemnor failed to effect proper substitution, Special Term properly exercised its discretion in the interest of fair and orderly procedure in ordering that the coexecutors be substituted as respondents in the proceeding. Rochester Urban Renewal Agency v Salitan (1976) 52 AD2d 753, 382 NYS2d 207.

3. Failure of substitution or appointment of representative

Where respondent died prior to entry of order appealed from, and no representative is substituted for him, both the order and the notice of appeal therefrom are nullities. Rizzo v Steiner (1964) 20 AD2d 909, 248 NYS2d 998.

Where during interim between service of notice of appeal and the submission thereof plaintiff-appellant dies, in the absence of the substitution of his executor or administrator, the court may not proceed to a determination of the appeal on the merits, but will hold the appeal in abeyance for ninety days to effect such substitution, and if it is not done, the appeal will be dismissed. Price v Booth (1964) 21 AD2d 680, 249 NYS2d 1007.

Where one of defendants dies prior to trial and entry of judgment, and there has been no substitution of his executor or administrator as a party defendant, nor a severance, the judgment against the deceased defendant is a nullity. Goldbard v Kirchik (1964) 20 AD2d 725, 248 NYS2d 191.

CASE NOTES

UNDER FORMER CIVIL PRACTICE LAWS

A. IN GENERAL

I. IN GENERAL

1. Generally

The supreme court had the same power, under CPA §§ 82, 83, to continue such actions as the court of chancery possessed under the act of 1832. People v Troy Steel & Iron Co. (1894) 82 Hun 303, 31 NYS 337.

Where plaintiff dies pending an appeal from an order dismissing his complaint and awarding costs against him in a suit that from its nature abates on his death, his administratrix may have the suit revived in her name, and prosecute the appeal to relieve herself from liability for the costs. Campbell v Gallagher (1890) 9 NYS 432.

Court has no power to grant motion substituting next of kin. Simon v Noma Electric Corp. (1944) 291 NY 824, 53 NE2d 579.

The executors of a deceased defendant, in order to become parties, must seek their rights under the provisions relating to proceedings in an action after the death of a party. Callanan v Kesseville, A. C. L. C. R. Co. (1905) 48 Misc 476, 95 NYS 513.

Where a cause of action survives, the plaintiff upon the death of defendant may be entitled to a continuance under this section, although the facts do not bring the case within any specific provision, unless laches is a sufficient answer to the motion. Lyon v Park (1888) 111 NY 350, 18 NE 863.

The rule of the common law, that an action for a personal injury abates on the death of the plaintiff, was not changed by CPA except where "a verdict, report or decision" had been rendered in the case. Corbett v Twenty-third Street R. Co. (1889) 114 NY 579, 21 NE 1033.

Death of plaintiff in negligence action after judgment for defendant; when administratrix not entitled to prosecute appeal. Re Tubbiolo (1911) 146 AD 323, 130 NYS 776.

CPA § 89 only applied where there was remaining in force at the time of the death a verdict or decision in favor of the party desiring to continue the action. Pessini v Wilkins, 8 NYSR 89.

Upon a verdict the plaintiff is entitled to immediate judgment, and if he dies before that judgment is entered his right thereto will not have been in any wise affected. Re Workingmen's Pub. Asso. (1901) 62 AD 604, 71 NYS 248.

Administrator who did not make application for substitution and continuance until seven years after cause of action accrued, five years after plaintiff's death, and three years after issuance of letters of administration, and offered no satisfactory excuse therefor, was denied relief because of laches. Meier v Shively (1960) 10 AD2d 566, 195 NYS 509.

On a plaintiff's death, abatement of a negligence action may be initiated by an order to show cause but not by a notice of motion. Muller v National Transp. Co. (1958) 10 Misc 2d 800, 170 NYS2d 434.

2. Appeals

CPA §§ 82–89 (§§ 407, 1015(a)(b), 1018, 1021 herein) relating to abatement and revival of actions in replevin, applied only to the original action and not to appeals. Riley v Gitterman (1889) 28 NYSR 983, 10 NYS 38, affd 125 NY 727, 26 NE 757.

3. Arbitration proceeding

Since an arbitration proceeding is a special proceeding it does not abate by reason of the death of a partner. First Nat. Oil Co. v Arrieta (1956) 2 AD2d 590, 157 NYS2d 313.

4. Marine court

CPA § 82 was applicable to actions in the marine court of New York. People ex rel. Egan v New York Marine Court Justices (1880) 81 NY 500.

5. Surrogate's court

A discovery proceeding under §§ 205 and 206 of the Surrogate's Court Act does not abate by reason of the death of the original respondent after the petitioner's prima facie case has been completed. Re Courtade (1939) 172 Misc 1078, 16 NYS2d 974.

CPA §§ 82, 84 in relation to the abatement and revival of special proceedings, did not relate to proceedings in surrogate's courts. Re Camp (1894) 81 Hun 387, 30 NYS 884, and there was no provision of law which prevented a special proceeding from abating in a surrogate's court where a sole party to such proceeding died. Re Schlesinger (1889) 36 AD 77, 55 NYS 514.

6. Matrimonial actions

Matrimonial actions abate on the death of either party. An order setting aside a judgment of separation could not be vacated on motion after the death of the defendant. Morey v Morey (1937) 164 Misc 527, 299 NYS 161, affd 254 AD 713.

In action for separation where husband died before conclusion of trial, court was without power to make any disposition of custody of children of marriage. Hoff v Dugan (1943) 266 AD 790, 41 NYS2d 691.

An action for an absolute divorce is a personal one and abates upon the death of the plaintiff. Hunt v Hunt (1912) 75 Misc 209, 135 NYS 39, mod 154 AD 833, 139 NYS 413.

Since a cause of action for annulment on the ground of fraud survives the death of the defrauded plaintiff, a pending action therefor does not abate upon plaintiff's death, whether such death occurs before or after the entry of interlocutory judgment. Re Haney's Will (1961) 14 AD2d 121, 217 NYS2d 324.

7. Action for expenses of medical care

A cause of action for the expenses of medical care and treatment resulting from personal injury does not survive the death of the person injured. Austin v Wood (1934) 153 Misc 719, 275 NYS 710.

8. Actions for penalties

In the absence of express statutory provision, an action to recover a penalty does not survive the death of either party. People v Newcomb (1912) 75 Misc 258, 135 NYS 151.

9. Action to establish will

The power of the court to revive an action which does not abate on the death of a party is not limited to the cases specifically enumerated; an action to establish the validity of a will did not abate on the death of a party. Carolan v O'Donnell (1910) 141 AD 463, 126 NYS 551.

10. Death of party after judgment

CPA § 478 (Rules 5016(d), 5203(a) herein) held to provide exception to CPA § 82. Nicholson v McMullen (1941) 176 Misc 693, 28 NYS2d 287.

Death of plaintiff in negligence action after judgment for defendant; when administratrix not entitled to prosecute appeal. Re Tubbiolo (1911) 146 AD 323, 130 NYS 776.

11. —Prosecution of appeal for costs

Although the cause of action has abated, an executor may be permitted to continue the action for the prosecution of an appeal for the costs. Campbell v Gallagher (1890) 9 NYS 432.

12. Payment of money into court

Motion to pay money into court may be made though an original party is dead and the action has not been revived. Cazet v Hubbell (1867) 36 NY 677.

13. Necessity of substitution

Where plaintiff in divorce action died after entry of interlocutory judgment and defendant moved to vacate same and to open his default in appearance in action, there resulted suspension of activity until substitution is made for deceased party. Angelo v Angelo (1953) 282 AD 981, 125 NYS2d 621.

Where defendant died prior to plaintiff's motion to vacate dismissal of complaint pursuant to RCP 302 (§ 3215(c), Rule 3404 herein), though action did not abate since no substitution of defendant's representative had been made, order granting plaintiff's motion was void, and defendant's notice of appeal therefrom, purporting to be an appeal by the deceased defendant, was seemingly void. Solomon v Kittay (1960) 11 AD2d 725, 204 NYS2d 598.

14. Of plaintiff or petitioner

A father's action for damages for death of son, resulting from injuries suffered in Pennsylvania from defendant's negligence, does not abate by reason of father's death while action was pending and after expiration of one year statutory period of limitation under Pennsylvania statutes. Murray v New York, O. & W. R. Co. (1934) 242 AD 374, 275 NYS 10.

Proceeding by committee of testator's incompetent mother to test validity of charitable gift survived her death after opinion decision by surrogate, which was not entered until after her death. Re Sonderling (1935) 157 Misc 231, 283 NYS 568.

An action to enforce personal liability of a trustee of a corporation for its debts, or failure to file annual report, etc., does not abate on death of plaintiff, but may be continued by his personal representative. Bonnell v Griswold, 8 Civ Proc 280, 2 How Pr NS 451.

15. —Death of co-executor

An action by executors and trustees for an accounting does not abate by the death of one of the executors. Gould v Gould (1923) 122 Misc 152, 203 NYS 399, affd 211 AD 78, 207 NYS 4.

Appeal by one of two executors does not abate on death of appellant. Re Jackson's Will (1930) 231 AD 17, 246 NYS 14.

16. —Death of guardian

Where the general guardian of an infant institutes a proceeding to compel a guardian ad litem of the infant to pay over certain moneys which he has collected for the infant, and, upon the proceedings before a referee appointed to take and state the guardian ad litem's account, it appears that the general guardian is dead and that the infant, at the time the order of reference was made, had attained her majority, it is only necessary that a suggestion of these facts be made upon the record, and the proceeding will thereafter be continued in the name of the former infant. Smith v Mingey (1902) 72 AD 103, 76 NYS 194, affd 172 NY 650, 65 NE 1122.

17. —Action for deceit

A cause of action founded upon the deceit of the directors of an association does not abate by the death of the plaintiff. Squires v Thompson (1902) 73 AD 552, 76 NYS 734, affd 172 NY 652, 65 NE 1122.

18. —Action for ejectment

In action of ejectment where plaintiff died pending the action and trial, the complaint could not be amended as if the executors had been substituted before the trial; former CPA §§ 82–88 did not apply but the former practice was to amend complaint and proceed de novo. Doherty v Matsell, 53 Super Ct (21 Jones & S) 73.

19. —Proceeding to vacate assessment

A proceeding to vacate a street assessment abates with the death of the petitioner. Re Roberts (1889) 53 Hun 338, 6 NYS 195; Re Barney (1889) 53 Hun 480, 6 NYS 401; Re Marshall (1889) 27 NYSR 889, 7 NYS 861.

20. —Action for personal injury

Whether cause of action survives is governed by law of state where negligent personal injury is alleged to have been committed. Allen v Whitehall Pharmacal Co. (1953) 115 F Supp 7.

21. Of party defendant; Attachment

Where a nonresident defendant dies after an attachment upon his property and has no administrator in this state, the action may be continued against his administrator appointed in the foreign jurisdiction, and service upon him may be had by publication, if such service be begun within thirty days after the granting of the attachment. Logan v Greenwich Trust Co. (1911) 144 AD 372, 129 NYS 577, affd 203 NY 611, 96 NE 1120.

22. —Action for forcible entry or assault

Causes of action for forcible entry and detainer and for assault and battery abate on the death of the defendant, but a cause of action for the conversion of personal property does not abate and may be continued against the personal representatives of the deceased defendant; where there are codefendants jointly and severally liable in tort and one of them dies, the plaintiff may proceed against the survivors and the representatives of the deceased defendant at the same time, but it must be by separate actions, and a prior action against all must be severed. Mulligan v O'Brien (1907) 119 AD 355, 104 NYS 301.

23. —Action to quiet title

Where the original defendant in an action to quiet title dies, the action may properly be continued against his executors who have a power of sale, as they are necessary parties. Sweetland v Buell (1900) 89 Hun 543, 35 NYS 346, affd 164 NY 541, 58 NE 663.

24. —Action to enforce stockholder's liability

Stockholder's liability survived his death, and action therefor did not abate but it was necessary to obtain court's consent to continuance of action, and a proceeding by petition and order is necessary with proper service upon executors, and mere order to show cause is not sufficient. Skinner v Sullivan (1920) 112 Misc 365, 184 NYS 159.

25. —Incompetency proceedings

A proceeding for the appointment of a committee abated on the death of the alleged incompetent person. Re Frank (1940) 283 NY 106, 27 NE2d 801.

26. —Workmen's Compensation award

Where compensation award was made against uninsured employer during his lifetime for funeral expenses of employee, ascertainment of death benefits for employee's wife-widow was purely ministerial, and Industrial Board had power to make such award after employer's death. Skorepa v Capek (1943) 266 AD 898, 42 NYS2d 734.

27. —Death of one of several co-defendants

Where there was originally more than one defendant in an action and of whom one has died, that one is a sole defendant within the provisions of §§ 82–87. Palen v Bushnell (1889) 51 Hun 423, 4 NYS 63.

In an action against two copartners upon their copartnership contract, where the summons is served upon one of them and he dies before service on the other, the action does not abate, as the cause of action survives, and the plaintiff may proceed against the other, and no leave is necessary therefor. Latz v Blumenthal (1906) 50 Misc 407, 100 NYS 527, affd 116 AD 914, 101 NYS 1128.

An action by receiver of a corporation against its trustees for assets of the company which had been diverted or misapplied by them does not abate upon the death of one of the trustees, but may be continued against his personal representatives. Pierson v Morgan (1889) 23 NYSR 382, 4 NYS 898, affd 121 NY 705, 24 NE 1100.

28. —Party entitled to continuance

When action does not abate by the death of the defendant, both parties have a right to a continuance. Dalton v Sandland, 4 Civ Proc 73.

29. —Time for revival

In an action at law there is no fixed time within which the action may be revived against the executor of a deceased defendant. The time within which an action in equity can be revived is ten years. Washington Trust Co. v Baldwin (1907) 118 AD 186, 102 NYS 1105, affd 189 NY 543, 82 NE 1134.

II. CORPORATIONS

30. Generally

Stockholders' derivative action against directors for accounting survives and continues without abatement regardless of any change in status of stockholders. Smith v Bradlee (1942) 37 NYS2d 512.

31. Change in corporate officers

Suit by a director for the benefit of the corporation does not abate by reason of his removal as a director. Wangrow v Wangrow (1924) 211 AD 552, 207 NYS 132.

Action by a director and officer of a corporation against other officers and directors for mismanagement of the affairs of the corporation does not abate by reason of the fact that since its commencement plaintiff has ceased to be a director and officer. Manix v Fantl (1924) 209 AD 756, 205 NYS 174.

The foregoing case disapproves of the contrary decision in Hamilton v Gibson (1911) 145 AD 825, 130 NYS 684, as having been based on an erroneous assumption that such an action may be prosecuted by a director only in his official capacity.

A director of a corporation may continue to maintain an action brought by him while a director on behalf of corporation against fellow directors for breach of duty after he has been defeated for reelection as director, and such action may not be defeated either on theory of abatement or lack of capacity to sue. Tenney v Rosenthal (1959) 6 NY2d 204, 189 NYS2d 158, 160 NE2d 463.

32. Entry of judgment in derivative action by stockholder

Where a judgment has been entered in derivative action by a stockholder, all remaining similar actions abate. Gerith Realty Corp. v Normandie Nat. Secur. Corp. (1933) 154 Misc 615, 276 NYS 655, affd 241 AD 717, 269 NYS 1007, affd 266 NY 525, 195 NE 183.

III. TRUSTS AND ESTATES

33. Foreign administrator or executor

Upon death of foreign executrix her interest in estate passed to administrator with will annexed, and cause of action by resident creditor to have property of the testator situated within the state administered did not abate, but proceedings are stayed until the administrator is substituted as party defendant. Thorburn v Gates (1920) 191 AD 506, 181 NYS 520, affd 232 NY 544, 134 NE 565.

Where jurisdiction was obtained by service of

summons and complaint personally within this state upon a foreign executrix, and she died, it was not necessary to serve a supplemental summons and complaint to bring in as defendant foreign administrator with the will annexed. Thorburn v Mitchell (1920) 193 AD 174, 183 NYS 424.

34. Trustees

Upon the death of a trustee the action is suspended until a successor is appointed. The action survives, but there is an abatement as to the party plaintiff who died. Paget v Pease (1888) 18 NYSR 750, 2 NYS 335, affd 24 NYSR 762, 6 NYS 386.

When trustee may continue action on death of beneficiary. Farmer's Loan & Trust Co. v Pendleton (1906) 115 AD 506, 101 NYS 340.

35. Judicial settlement of account of administrator

Where the administrator of a decedent commenced special proceedings for the judicial settlement of his account and thereafter the administrator died, held proceedings abated. Re Smith's Estate, 1 How Pr NS 64.

B. Where Sole Party Dies

I. In General

36. Generally

In determining whether a cause of action survives, the statute in force at the time of an alleged wrongdoer, rather than that in force when the cause of action arose, controls. Gorlitzer v Wolffberg (1913) 208 NY 475, 102 NE 528.

CPA § 478 (Rule 5016(d), § 5203(a) herein) held to provide exception to CPA § 84. Nicholson v McMullen (1941) 176 Misc 693, 28 NYS2d 287.

The right of a party to a continuance of an action by or against the representatives of the deceased party where the action survived did not depend upon the existence of the precise circumstances stated in CPA § 84. Lyon v Park (1881) 111 NY 350, 18 NE 863.

Motion to vacate judgment after death of one of parties to action is proper practice, and not action in revivor. Dye v Dye (1949) 93 NYS2d 95.

37. Discretion of court

The right conferred by CPA § 84 was not an absolute one but it was within the discretion of the court to allow or compel the action to be continued. Shipman v Long Island R. Co. (1896) 11 AD 46, 41 NYS 1131.

A motion to continue an action upon the death of a surviving plaintiff is within the discretion of the court to grant. Shipman v Long Island R. Co. (1896) 17 Misc 102, 39 NYS 498, affd 11 AD 46, 41 NYS 1131.

"The court, must, upon motion" in CPA § 84 did not mean that the court unconditionally had to grant every application to revive that was presented. Knoch v Funke (1892) 19 NYS 242, affd 8 Misc 682, 28 NYS 1146.

The effect of CPA § 84 was to take away the discretion which the courts formerly had in equitable actions either to grant relief on motion, or to put the party to an action in the nature of a bill of revivor. But it did not compel the court to grant the motion in every case, but only where the party had the right, according to settled rules of equity, to a revivor or continuance. Coit v Campbell (1880) 82 NY 509.

The provisions of CPA § 84 were mandatory in actions at law. Lehman v Koch (1890) 30 NYSR 224, 9 NYS 302; but quaere as to equitable actions. Lehman v Koch, supra; as to proper parties to be substituted, see Benedict v Cobb (1889) 7 NYS 916.

38. Successor in interest or in office

The words "successor in interest" in CPA § 84 referred to an interest depending upon death occurring and not to an interest gained by transfer or assignment. Northrop v Smith (1890) 31 NYSR 182, 9 NYS 802.

On death of overseer of poor pending an action brought by him as such, his successor in office has control of the suit without being substituted as plaintiff. Bellinger v Birge (1889) 54 Hun 511, 7 NYS 695, 8 NYS 174.

Where there has been a transfer of interest, the right to substitute the transferee was based upon CPA § 83 and lay within the discretion of the court; the term "successor in interest" as used in this section referred to those succeeding to the right of action where the deceased party sued in the representative capacity of trustee, etc. Hale v Shannon (1901) 58 AD 247, 68 NYS 803.

Where an action for the partition of real property is brought by a husband as committee of the property of his wife, an incompetent person, and, after the action was commenced the wife died and the husband became entitled to an estate for his life in the real property sought to be partitioned as tenant by the curtesy, he is entitled to an order allowing the action to be continued by him as successor in interest to his wife. Duke v Abel (1908) 57 Misc 371, 109 NYS 662.

In an action to recover a sum of money only the term "successors in interest" of a deceased defendant as such term was used in CPA generally meant the person or persons upon whom liability devolved with respect to the cause of action pleaded and an action might not be continued as against proposed defendants merely upon the ground that they had succeeded to the title to certain real property owned by the deceased defendant at the time of the alleged accident. Cudak v Muffs (1957) 8 Misc 2d 793, 169 NYS2d 282.

In action for accounting and conversion begun by administratrix based upon transaction between her decedent and defendant, after death of administratrix, her executor in the absence of laches or prejudice might be substituted as plaintiff, and permitted to serve supplemental complaint, under CPA § 84. Haeseler v American Gas & Chemicals, Inc. (1959) 21 Misc 2d 93, 196 NYS2d 130.

39. Necessity of substitution

Death of sole defendant abated the action and precluded any further steps until substitution of successor in interest. Motion to dismiss denied; order denying motion to restore case to calendar reversed. O'Brien v Flynn (1930) 228 AD 704, 239 NYS 59.

Where counterclaim has been made, and issue joined, the action may be continued by defendant's representatives. Livermore v Bainbridge (1872) 49 NY 125.

Where defendant's representatives after judgment are substituted as parties on their own application the court will not allow them, after obtaining a new trial, to move to vacate the order of substitution. Arthur v Griswold (1875) 60 NY 143.

Where plaintiff in divorce action died after entry of interlocutory judgment and defendant moved to vacate same and to open his default in appearance in action, there resulted suspension of activity until substitution is made for deceased party. Angelo v Angelo (1953) 282 AD 981, 125 NYS2d 621.

Where defendant died before service of plaintiff's notice of motion to vacate judgment and for new trial, order denying such motion was a nullity as was the notice of appeal from such order since the action had abated with defendant's death and no further proceedings could be taken until defendant's executor had been substituted as party defendant. Reoux v Reoux (1961) 14 AD2d 648, 218 NYS2d 754.

40. Security for costs as condition

In a proper case the relief shall be granted; and the court may require the plaintiff to give security for costs as a condition. Knoch v Funke (1892) 19 NYS 242, affd 8 Misc 682, 28 NYS 1146.

Security for costs should not be imposed as a condition of continuance of an action by an executor, although the action seems unmeritorious and was delayed many years before the testator's death. Collins v Jewell (1893) 3 Misc 341, 22 NYS 716.

41. Stipulations

A stipulation for judgment absolute on appeal in case of affirmance does not prevent abatement of action on death of plaintiff after appeal. Corbett v Twenty-Third Street R. Co. (1889) 114 NY 579, 21 NE 1033.

42. Death of all parties

The provisions in CPA § 84 directing a continuance of an action by or against the representative of a party to the action, who died since the commencement of the action, did not include a case where all the parties to the action were dead at the time of the motion, and by the common law the action abated. Holsman v St. John, 48 Super Ct (16 Jones & S) 306, revd on other grounds 90 NY 461.

An action did not abate on the death of both of the original parties where it had proceeded to judgment before the death of either party. Carr v Risher (1890) 119 NY 117, 23 NE 296; and see McLachlin v Brett (1882) 27 Hun 18.

43. Death during appeal

Appeal from decree of surrogate's court, settling trustee's account survived death of appellant and order of substitution was proper. Re Jackson's Will (1930) 231 AD 17, 246 NYS 14.

A decision of the Appellate Division, whereby a judgment on appeal was reversed and judgment rendered nunc pro tunc, is valid, though the decision was made after the death of the then plaintiff and before any substitution of parties had been ordered, where the cause, one in equity for an injunction and to set aside a contract, had been fully submitted to the court prior to the death of the plaintiff. MacLean v Hart (1933) 238 AD 1, 263 NYS 704, affd 262 NY 552, 188 NE 60.

44. Proof of death

Not necessary to prove at the trial the death of original party, the order of substitution is sufficient. Gibson v National Park Bank (1885) 98 NY 87.

45. Vacation of order

When an order reviving an action was vacated because it had been granted on an ex parte application, the court could not, under former CPA, let so much of the order stand as substituted attorneys, because on vacating the order of revival the action had stood abated and no motion could have been made therein until property revived. Robinson v Thomas (1908) 123 AD 414, 107 NYS 1109.

II. Causes of Action Which Abate

46. Generally

Where final judgment is entered before death of defendant, the cause of action does not survive or continue but is merged and lost in the judgment, and this section does not apply. Leake v Bundy, 48 Hun 208.

A special proceeding to vacate an assessment must be revived on death of petitioner. Re Palmer (1887) 43 Hun 572.

In an action to restrain the defendant from entering upon and cutting timber on lots of the plaintiffs, after a temporary injunction the defendant died, held, the action abated on the defendant's death. Johnson v Elwood (1880) 82 NY 362.

An action for admeasurement of widow's dower, or for the sale of the premises and awarding a gross sum in lieu thereof, in the event of her death before the entry of interlocutory judgment determining her right of dower, etc., the action abates. McKeen v Fish (1884) 33 Hun 28, affd 98 NY 645.

In an action brought against a surviving partner by judgment creditors to reach certain lands, the legal title to which was in the defendant P but alleged to be held by him as trustee for the firm, held, that on the death of P the action could not be revived against his executors. Coit v Campbell (1880) 82 NY 509.

It seems an action against a director of a corporation organized under the general manufacturing act to recover a debt due from the company because of failure of defendant to make and file an annual report as required by the act is a penal action and abates upon the death of either party before verdict. Carr v Risher (1890) 119 NY 117, 23 NE 296.

The liability created against the directors of a corporation created under that act, by reason of their making a false report, abates on the death of the original creditors of the corporation and cannot be revived in favor of or prosecuted by his personal representatives. Sinnott v Hanan (1913) 156 AD 323, 141 NYS 505, revd on other grounds 214 NY 454, 108 NE 858; Boyle v Thurber (1888) 50 Hun 259, 2 NYS 789.

An action brought against two copartners for injuries to plaintiff's son, caused by negligence of defendant's driver, abates by death of the defendants. Pessini v Wilkins, 8 NYSR 89.

An action to recover damages for fraud, in inducing plaintiff to marry and cohabit with the defendant, by means of fraudulent representations that his first wife was dead, and that he was competent to marry, does not survive the defendant's death. The action is for injury to the person of the plaintiff, and its character is not changed by an allegation in the complaint that the defendant "promised, undertook, covenanted and warranted that he had the right and was in all respects competent to marry." Price v Price (1878) 75 NY 244.

In slander where, pending appeal, plaintiff dies, on reversal no new trial can be ordered. Spooner v Keeler (1873) 51 NY 527.

Where the cause of action arises out of the death alone and suggests no injury to the estate or property of the deceased, such a cause of action is abated by the death of the wrongdoer. Hegerich v Keddie (1885) 99 NY 258, 1 NE 787.

Action against landlord for knowingly letting unhealthy premises abates with death of defendant. Causes of action for personal injury cannot be assigned, and this characteristic is a good criterion to determine whether the action survives. Victory v Krauss, 4 NYSR 33.

Plaintiff's death terminated action to recover for money expended for medical treatment, etc., for his wife as a result of negligence of defendant. Hunter v Wittner (1932) 142 Misc 795, 256 NYS 598, in which, however, the court points out that the result was attributable to legislative inadvertence.

An action by a father for the loss of the services of an infant child, though the damages claimed include actual expenditures by the father, wholly abates on the death of the father. Bianco v Sun Oil Co. (1928) 143 Misc 764, 256 NYS 597, affd 224 AD 817, 231 NYS 698.

The effect of an exception from a survival statute

of injuries to the person "either of the plaintiff or of another," is to preclude the substitution of the personal representative of the deceased defendant in a husband's action for loss of his wife's services and expenses consequent upon personal injuries alleged to have been caused by the defendant's negligence. Gorlitzer v Wolffberg (1913) 208 NY 475, 102 NE 528.

47. Tort actions

A cause of action for personal injuries is abated by the death of the wrongdoer, and does not survive against the wrongdoer's estate. Herzog v Stern (1933) 148 Misc 25, 265 NYS 72, revd 240 AD 881, 267 NYS 968, revd 264 NY 379, 191 NE 23, cert den 293 US 597, 79 L Ed 690, 55 S Ct 112.

III. Causes of Action Which Survive

48. Generally

The representative of a deceased objectant to the probate of a will may either continue the opposition or withdraw the objections. Re Mackenzie (1934) 152 Misc 759, 274 NYS 98.

A cause of action for fraud survived the death of the person defrauded, and a complaint by the executor of the latter was sufficient which alleged that the defendant, the bigamous spouse of the executor's decedent, deceived the decedent into believing that she was competent to marry him and thereby induced him to make payable to her certain life insurance which she received on his death, when in fact she was not competent to marry the decedent, being already the wife of a living husband. Snyder v Schneider (1935) 154 Misc 26, 276 NYS 445, affd 244 AD 778, 280 NYS 777.

Action for escape against sheriff properly continued after his death against his estate. London v Hessberg (1934) 264 NY 435, 191 NE 501.

The liability of a stockholder for the debt of an insurance company which transacts business before its capital is fully paid up, survives his death. Chase v Lord (1879) 77 NY 1.

Stockholder's liability survived his death, and action therefor did not abate but it was necessary to obtain court's consent to continuance of action, and a proceeding by petition and order is necessary with proper service upon executors, and mere order to show cause is not sufficient. Skinner v Sullivan (1920) 112 Misc 365, 184 NYS 159.

An action to charge trustees of a manufacturing corporation for its debts by reason of alleged default in filing the annual report does not abate by death of the plaintiff. Zoller v O'Keeffe, 15 Abb NC 483; and such action may be continued in the name of the administrator or trustee. An administrator is deemed in law to be the assignee of the assets of the estate. Bonnell v Griswold, 15 Abb NC 470.

Where an action is brought to compel the determination of a claim to real property in which defendant obtains judgment and plaintiff, on paying all the costs, has the judgment vacated; and before the second trial is had, plaintiff dies, a devisee of plaintiff's interest in the property affected, may be substituted in the place on motion of defendant, and compelled to continue the action. Higgins v New York (1892) 136 NY 214, 32 NE 772.

An action for injunction against an elevated railroad and for damages for its maintenance is one in equity affecting rights to real estate, and does not abate on the death of sole plaintiff. Sanders v New York El. R. Co. (1889) 27 NYSR 795, 7 NYS 641.

Suit to foreclose mortgage does not abate by death of plaintiff, and where the mortgagor was one of the executors, the other one revived the action. McGregor v McGregor (1866) 35 NY 218; and see Weyh v Boylan, 63 How Pr 72.

An action brought by a grantee in the name of his grantor, against one who at the time of the execution of the deed was in possession of the premises under an adverse claim of title, does not abate by the death of the grantee. Ward v Reynolds (1881) 25 Hun 385, 62 How Pr 183.

An action by a widow under Civil Damage Act survives her death. Moriarty v Bartlett (1884) 34 Hun 272, revd on other grounds 99 NY 651, 1 NE 794.

In case of death of one of the firm plaintiffs, the entire cause of action vests in surviving plaintiffs and may be prosecuted by them. Shale v Schantz (1885) 35 Hun 622.

An action for damages for conspiracy to cheat survives. Brackett v Griswold (1886) 103 NY 425, 9 NE 438.

In an action to recover an insurance policy the assignee of the beneficiary may be substituted as plaintiff after the death of the insured. Hunt v Provident Sav. Life Assur. Soc. (1902) 77 AD 338, 79 NYS 74.

Causes of action for damages resulting from the defendant's alleged refusal to split up the plaintiff's stockholdings in the defendant company; for damages because of the failure of the defendant company to supply the plaintiff with weekly and monthly financial statements; for salary alleged to have been due to plaintiff for services; and counterclaims for damages resulting from plaintiff's inattention to duty and misconduct in office and from plaintiff having brought a groundless suit against the defendant company, all survived the plaintiff's death. Winslow v Domestic Engineering Co. (1937) 20 F Supp 578.

When judgment is rendered, the original wrong is merged therein and the judgment becomes property with all the attributes of a judgment in an action ex contractu. Carr v Richer (1890) 119 NY 117, 23 NE 296.

49. Against public officers

An action against a sheriff upon his liability as bail arising from his failure to require justification of sureties on a bail bond taken upon an order of arrest in an action for personal injuries does not abate on his death, but may be revived against his personal representatives. Hamilton v Gorman (1895) 14 Misc 114, 35 NYS 183.

Death of relator pending certiorari to review proceedings removing him from office—the action survives. People ex rel. Fairchild v Fire & Bldg. Comrs. (1887) 105 NY 674, 12 NE 179.

50. Foreclosure of mechanic's lien

An action brought to foreclose a mechanic's lien does not abate by the death of the owner of the premises during the pendency thereof, but may be revived against the successors in interest of the deceased owner, without prejudice to proceedings already had therein. Perry v Levenson (1903) 82 AD 94, 81 NYS 586, affd 178 NY 559, 70 NE 1104 (distinguishing Leavy v Gardner (1875) 63 NY 624, as having been decided under a different statute).

51. Injury to property

An action for injury to property rights or interests does not abate on the death of the wrongdoer and may be revived against his personal representatives. Miller v Young (1895) 90 Hun 132, 35 NYS 643.

52. Personal injury

Where in action against a city for damages by reason of defective sidewalk, the right of action by the city over against the owner does not abate by death of defendant. Rochester v Campbell (1889) 55 Hun 138, 8 NYS 252, revd on other grounds 123 NY 405, 25 NE 937.

When, after a verdict for the plaintiff in an action for personal injuries the trial court sets the verdict aside and directs a verdict for the defendant and the plaintiff dies pending his appeal, his representative is entitled to revive the action. Schramme v Lewinson (1908) 123 AD 662, 107 NYS 1075.

Under § 119 of the Decedent Estate Law a husband's action for loss of his injured wife's services did not abate upon his death. Friedlander v Roxy Theatre (1953) 204 Misc 740, 127 NYS2d 765, affd 283 AD 860, 129 NYS2d 896.

IV. PARTICULAR PARTIES AND PROCEEDINGS

53. Action to quiet title

Where the original defendant in an action to quiet title dies, the action may properly be continued against his executors who have a power of sale, as they are necessary parties. Sweetland v Buell (1895) 89 Hun 543, 35 NYS 346, affd 164 NY 541, 58 NE 663.

54. Assignees

When a person brings an action on a claim assigned to him by another and during the pendency of the action the claim is reassigned, the court is authorized, upon the death of the plaintiff, to allow the action to be continued in the name of the plaintiff's administrator. Betts v De Selding (1903) 81 AD 161, 80 NYS 799.

Substitution of assignees of claim after suit brought in place of deceased plaintiff. See Schell v Devlin (1880) 82 NY 333.

55. Divorce

CPA § 84 had no application to an action for divorce. Faversham v Faversham (1914) 161 AD 521, 146 NYS 569.

56. Executors and administrators

CPA § 84 did not apply in an action by a beneficiary under a will against an executor for an accounting, where the executor dies pending a rehearing after an interlocutory judgment directing an accounting. Mackey v Duryea (1889) 6 NYS 573.

The court has power to substitute as a party an administrator with the will annexed in place of the deceased executor and the case will then go on to judgment on the pleadings and evidence then in. Wood v Flynn (1883) 30 Hun 444.

Order directing substitution of executors as parties defendant in place of their decedent, though made without notice, should not be vacated, since such order would follow as a matter of course. Wiley v Moses (1943) 266 AD 801, 42 NYS2d 4.

Where final judgment required son to deliver mother's securities in his possession to trust company as custodian and she died before such delivery, her executor was entitled to amendment nunc pro tunc of such judgment to require delivery to him. Humbeutel v Humbeutel (1953) 305 NY 159, 111 NE2d 429.

The executor, also a trustee under decedent's will, should revive an action of ejectment begun by decedent in her lifetime by joining with him the residuary legatees named in the will. Motheral v Perchment (1926) 127 Misc 6, 214 NYS 495.

Where plaintiff in an action under §§ 500, 501 of the Real Property Law to determine claim to real property dies during pendency of the action his administrator cannot revive and continue the action to final determination of the title to the premises in controversy. Brandenstein v Kawecki (1925) 213 AD 574, 211 NYS 253.

Motion by administrator of deceased claimant against State to amend claim by substituting himself as claimant was granted in court's discretion, though administrator waited eight months after his appointment before he moved to amend claim, despite statute permitting Attorney General to move to dismiss claim. Pehel v State (1955) 208 Misc 742, 145 NYS2d 24.

When in an action against the indorsers of a promissory note one of the defendants dies, his executor may be substituted as defendant under former CPA § 87, such substituted defendant may be brought in by order under CPA § 85 and it is not essential that an order be made requiring such defendant to be served with a supplemental summons and complaint under former CPA § 87. Citizens' Nat. Bank v Bang (1906) 112 AD 748, 99 NYS 76.

CPA § 84 did not apply where deceased's executor was appointed outside state. Bennett v Harrisville Combing Mills (1952) 111 NYS2d 462.

Foreign executor of decedent, who died resident of foreign state and who had sued resident relative to realty, was denied substitution as sole plaintiff, where ancillary administration could easily be had. Neuberger v Hart (1943) 266 AD 612, 44 NYS2d 490.

Notwithstanding this section the court in which an action is pending is without power, on the death of the defendant, to substitute in his stead his nonresident foreign executors, without their consent, where they have not taken possession of any assets of the estate within the state, the plaintiff's remedy being to institute proceedings under the Surrogate's Court Law for the issuance of ancillary letters. McMaster v Gould (1925) 239 NY 606, 147 NE 214, 40 ALR 792.

CPA § 84, providing for the continuance of an action by or against the representatives or successors in interest of a party who died was held to relate only to representatives and successors in interest over whom jurisdiction exists in the action and did not include foreign representatives in actions at law. McGrath v Weiller (1904) 98 AD 291, 90 NYS 420.

An assignee of a foreign executor or administrator of a deceased party plaintiff may recover and continue the action in his own name, and the order which revives and continues the action in the name of such assignee need not direct the administrator or executor of the original plaintiff to be brought in. McNulta v Huntington (1901) 62 AD 257, 70 NYS 897.

Where a nonresident defendant dies after an attachment upon his property and has no administrator in this state, the action may be continued against his administrator appointed in the foreign jurisdiction, and service upon him may be had by publication, if such service be begun within thirty days after the granting of the attachment. Logan v Greenwich Trust Co. (1911) 144 AD 372, 129 NYS 577, affd 203 NY 611, 96 NE 1120.

In action where sole defendant dies, the action survives and may be continued against his personal representative though appointed in another state. German-American Coffee Co. v Johnston (1915) 168 AD 31, 153 NYS 866.

In action to declare that plaintiff continued to be wife of defendant despite his alleged divorce in Florida, plaintiff's motion to substitute foreign executors of estate of deceased defendant as defendant was denied where there was no proof that they had been appointed. Hanrahan v Hanrahan (1950) 99 NYS2d 401.

57. Foreclosure proceedings

Effect of death of plaintiff in foreclosure proceedings before entry of judgment; action should be revived before entry of judgment, but the failure to revive it does not render the judgment void, although irregular. Smith v Joyce, 11 Civ Proc 257, 3 NYSR 360.

Suit had been commenced to foreclose a mortgage and plaintiff died; but before his death defendants had put in a counterclaim much larger than the mortgage. After plaintiff's death his executor assigned the mortgage to S, and thereupon S moved to continue the suit and be substituted as plaintiff, which was granted. Dock v South Brooklyn Saw Mill Co. 6 Civ Proc 144; and see Schlichter v South Brooklyn Saw-mill Co. (1885) 35 Hun 339.

58. Partition

Revivor of an action, for the partition of real estate of copartners, in which an interlocutory judgment directing a reference has been made and the reference is pending undetermined. Jones v Jones (1902) 68 AD 5, 74 NYS 297, affd 171 NY 653, 63 NE 1118.

59. Penalties

Action to recover penalties under manufacturing companies' law does not abate on the death of sole plaintiff—but otherwise as to death of sole defendant. Bonnell v Griswold, 8 Civ Proc 280, 2 How Pr NS 451; but see Stokes v Stickney (1884) 96 NY 323; Blake v Griswold, 103 NY 429, 9 NE 434; Zoller v O'Keeffe, 15 Abb NC 483.

60. Replevin

A cause of action in replevin survives the death of plaintiff, but not that of the defendant. Potter v Van Vranken (1867) 36 NY 619; but see Burkle v Luce (1848) 1 NY 163.

In an action to recover chattels if appellant dies after appeal and before argument thereof, the action may be revived in name of appellant's assignee for benefit of creditors. Riley v Gitterman (1889) 28 NYSR 983, 10 NYS 38, affd 125 NY 727, 26 NE 757.

61. Summary proceedings

Where, after an appeal is taken by the tenant from a final order in summary proceedings, the respondent dies, the court will substitute his widow and heirs as parties in his place. Demaron v Martin (1911) 72 Misc 152, 131 NYS 46.

62. Surrogate court proceedings

CPA §§ 82 and 84, in relation to the abatement and revival of special proceedings, did not relate to proceedings in surrogate's courts. Re Camp (1894) 81 Hun 387, 30 NYS 884.

63. Tort actions

Supreme Court has no authority to appoint executor or administrator for deceased defendant in personal injury action. Robinson v Susi C. Co. (1953) 119 NYS2d 241.

64. Trustees

Death of a trustee pending action suspends the suit until his successor is appointed and there is no abatement as to the party plaintiff who died. Paget v Pease (1888) 18 NYSR 750, 2 NYS 335, affd 24 NYSR 762, 6 NYS 386.

C. Proceedings When One or More of Several Parties Die

I. In General

65. Generally

CPA § 85 [subd (b) herein] referred to abatement

as to a party, and provided for cases where one of several plaintiffs dies, and the cause of action survives in favor of the others. Paget v Pease (1888) 18 NYSR 750, 2 NYS 335, affd 24 NYSR 762, 6 NYS 386.

Under CPA § 85 [subd (b) herein], upon the death of a codefendant the plaintiff may drop the matter so far as the decedent's estate is concerned and proceed against the survivors, or, on order bring in the executor and continue the action against the executor and the surviving defendants, as codefendants, or on bringing in the executor, the court may order severance, the action proceeding then as two actions. Lane v Fenn (1912) 76 Misc 48, 134 NYS 92.

Plaintiff was given reasonable opportunity to apply for appointment of executor or administrator of estate of deceased defendant before canceling lis pendens under CPA § 123 (§ 6514(b)(c) herein). Lemma v Laurino (1932) 235 AD 628, 254 NYS 1058.

66. Discretion of court

CPA § 85 [subd (b) herein] was not mandatory. Gas Works Constr. Co. v Monheimer (1892) 48 NYSR 741, 20 NYS 501.

67. Death of unnecessary party

No order to revive a foreclosure suit is necessary in case of the death of a prior mortgagee as he was not a necessary party. Hancock v Hancock (1860) 22 NY 568.

68. Application for abatement and revival

Objection of defect of plaintiffs by reason of death must be set up by objecting to the cause proceeding until the defect is cured. Hasbrouck v Bunce (1875) 62 NY 475.

The fact that the personal representative of one of the original signers of a contract, who died before the action was commenced, was not made a party to the action, does not entitle the defendants to have the complaint dismissed upon their motion, as their remedy is to move to have the personal representative of the deceased signer brought in. O'Connor v Green (1901) 60 AD 553, 69 NYS 1097.

Stockholder's liability survived his death, and action therefore against several stockholders did not abate to him but it was necessary to obtain court's consent to continuance of action, and a proceeding by petition and order is necessary with proper service upon executors, and mere order to show cause is not sufficient. Skinner v Sullivan (1920) 112 Misc 365, 184 NYS 159.

69. Dismissal

When after the commencement of an action by two plaintiffs on behalf of themselves and other creditors of the defendant to recover for labor and materials furnished, one of the plaintiffs dies, the right of action of the surviving plaintiff and other creditors does not abate and the complaint may be dismissed for failure to appear at trial; the dismissal of the complaint does not affect the right of the personal representative of the deceased plaintiff to revive the action as to him. Hawkes v Claffy (1907) 122 AD 546, 107 NYS 534.

70. Necessity of revivor

Judgment without revivor is irregular and cannot be amended and allowed to stand against the surviving parties. Tracy v First Nat. Bank (1868) 37 NY 523.

71. Supplemental summons and complaint

When the cause of action does not survive against the other defendants but does against the representatives of deceased, supplemental summons and complaint are necessary to bring them in. Mackey v Duryea (1889) 22 Abb NC 284, 6 NYS 573.

When in an action against the indorsers of a promissory note one of the defendants dies, his executor may be substituted as defendant under former CPA § 87; such substituted defendant may be brought in by order under this section, and it is not essential that an order be made requiring such defendant to be served with a supplemental summons and complaint under former CPA § 87. Citizens' Nat. Bank v Bangs (1906) 112 AD 748, 99 NYS 76.

II. PARTICULAR CLASSES OF PARTIES

72. Infants

Infants may regularly become parties defendant to an action without the service of a summons upon them. Gruner v Ruffner (1908) 59 Misc 266, 110 NYS 873, revd on other grounds 134 AD 837, 119 NYS 942.

73. Joint obligors and partners

The legal representatives of a joint obligor, who died after the commencement of an action against the obligors, are not proper parties defendant in an action against the survivors unless it has been established that the survivors are insolvent or are unable to pay, notwithstanding the provisions of this section. Potts v Dounce (1903) 173 NY 335, 66 NE 4; Erie County v Baltz (1908) 125 AD 144, 109 NYS 304; Central Hanover Bank & Trust Co. v Vernon Estates (1933) 238 AD 565, 265 NYS 527.

A creditor may bring an action at law against a single partner without serving the summons upon the others, and upon the death of that partner is entitled to continue the action against his representative. Seligman v Friedlander (1910) 138 AD 784, 123 NYS 583, affd 199 NY 373, 92 NE 1047.

Where judgment rendered against two partners has been satisfied as against one only, and the other dies, the action may be continued in the name of the legal representatives of the latter. Hackett v Belden (1872) 40 How Pr 289, affd 47 NY 624.

In an action against two copartners upon their copartnership contract, where the summons is served upon one of them and he dies before service on the other, the action does not abate, as the cause of action survives and the plaintiff may proceed against the other, and no leave is necessary therefor. Latz v Blumenthal (1906) 50 Misc 407, 100 NYS 527, affd 116 AD 914, 101 NYS 1128.

The former rule that the representative of a deceased partner could not be sued at law by a creditor of the firm, and could be held in equity only when the surviving partners were insolvent, and the remedy against them has been exhausted by execution, was changed by this section; said section providing that an estate of a person jointly liable upon contract with others shall not be discharged by his death does not mean that his estate is discharged unless the surviving partners are insolvent. Heintz v Havemeyer (1909) 132 AD 56, 116 NYS 317.

74. Directors of corporation

Minority stockholders' suit against directors was abated as to particular director who died 60 days after service of complaint upon him. Weinstein v Behn (1946) 65 NYS2d 536, affd 272 AD 1045, 75 NYS2d 284.

A cause of action by a bank stockholder against its directors under the National Bank Act survives the death of a director and may be revived against his personal representative. Benton v Deininger (1927) 21 F2d 659.

75. Principal obligor

Where a joint obligor was a principal debtor, or received some benefit from the obligation, his estate was liable after his death. Richardson v Draper (1882) 87 NY 337.

76. Successors in interest

When party succeeds to the interest of deceased defendant, a mere suggestion upon the record to that effect is sufficient, and the action may proceed without further pleadings or statements. Stevens v Melcher (1889) 25 NYSR 978, 6 NYS 811; and see Palen v Bushnell (1889) 51 Hun 423, 4 NYS 63.

77. Sureties

The amendment of 1877 was passed to change the rule laid down in Wood v Fisk (1875) 63 NY 245; Hauck v Craighead (1876) 67 NY 432; and Risley v Brown (1876) 67 NY 160, namely, that where one of two sureties in an undertaking in the ordinary form, given upon an appeal, died, his estate was absolutely discharged, and the survivor only was liable.

Under the practice as it stood before the enactment of CPA § 758, the personal representatives could not be charged in an action with other parties, where the deceased person whom they represented was a mere surety or a joint obligor. Baskin v Andrews (1889) 53 Hun 95, 6 NYS 441, affd Baskin v Huntington (1891) 130 NY 313, 29 NE 310.

If the creditor has obtained any lien upon the property of the surety before his death, it is not discharged by the surety's death. Baskin v Andrews (1889) 53 Hun 95, 6 NYS 441, affd Baskin v Huntington (1891) 130 NY 313, 29 NE 310.

CPA § 85 could not have a retroactive effect, and where a surety died after its enactment, but the undertaking was executed before its enactment, held that his estate was discharged from liability by his death. Randall v Sackett (1879) 77 NY 480; and see Baskin v Andrews (1889) 53 Hun 95, 6 NYS 441, affd Baskin v Huntington (1891) 130 NY 313, 29 NE 310.

Without reference to CPA § 85, the death of one of two or more sureties in an undertaking did not relieve his estate from liability to contribute ratably to the other sureties, towards discharging any payment which they might make although it was made after the death of their cosurety. The rule that the deceased surety was discharged, applied only against the creditor and was changed by this section. Johnson v Harvey (1881) 84 NY 363.

Where in an action against two sureties both are served, but judgment is taken against one only, such judgment cannot be enforced for more than one half of the amount due upon the undertaking, and the other surety is released from all liability on the undertaking, or for contribution by his cosurety.

Where one of three obligors upon a bond has no beneficial interest therein, and is surety merely, his estate upon his death before the death of the principals becomes discharged from any liability under such bond in equity as well as at law. Chard v Hamilton (1890) 56 Hun 259, 9 NYS 575, affd 125 NY 777, 27 NE 409.

78. Trustees

The effect of the death of a trustee during the running of a publication of services is to suspend the action until his successor is appointed, when the publication would have to be commenced de novo. Paget v Pease (1889) 18 NYSR 750, 6 NYS 386, affd 24 NYSR 762, 6 NYS 386; and see Edwards v Woodruff (1882) 90 NY 396.

III. PARTICULAR ACTIONS

79. Ejectment

On the death of one of plaintiffs before trial, his representatives must be substituted before further proceedings. Doherty v Matsell, 53 Super Ct (21 Jones & S) 73.

80. Tort actions

An action for tortiously carrying away goods may be revised in case of death of plaintiff but not in case of death of defendant. Potter v Van Vranken (1867) 36 NY 619.

Where a complaint against three defendants sued jointly alleges a cause of action for unlawful entry and detainer, another for assault and battery and a third for conversion, the first two causes of action abate as to a defendant who dies before judgment but the third cause of action survives and may be continued separately against his executrix. Mulligan v O'Brien (1907) 53 Misc 4, 102 NYS 911, affd 119 AD 355, 104 NYS 301.

Under CPA § 85 (subd. (b) herein) and Decedent Estate Law, § 120, where in an action for tort a codefendant dies, the action might be continued against his executor and the surviving defendants. Lane v Fenn (1912) 76 Misc 48, 134 NYS 92.

Administrators of a joint tortfeasor are not jointly liable with the surviving tortfeasors but are only debtors, and a release to an administrator for damages from tortious act of decedent does not release his surviving tort-feasor. German-American Coffee Co. v O'Neil (1918) 102 Misc 165, 169 NYS 421.

81. Libel and slander

In action for libel, plaintiff's motion to substitute executors of two deceased defendants as parties defendant was granted though plaintiff sought both compensatory and punitive damages. Cullom v Kadel (1955) 208 Misc 18, 142 NYS2d 600.

IV. EFFECT OF SURVIVAL OF PART OF CAUSE OF ACTION UNDER FORMER CPA § 86

82. Generally

Where a defendant died without whose presence the issues could have been tried, a reference might proceed without bringing in the legal representative of the deceased. Lemon v Smith (1897) 20 AD 522, 47 NYS 158.

In an action to recover a sum of money only the successors in interest of a deceased defendant as such term was used in CPA generally meant the person or persons upon whom liability devolved with respect to the cause of action pleaded and an action might not be continued as against proposed defendants merely upon the ground that they had succeeded to the title to certain real property owned by the deceased defendant at the time of the alleged accident. Cudak v Muffs (1957) 8 Misc 2d 793, 169 NYS2d 282.

83. Severance

Upon the decease of one of several defendants jointly liable, an action could only be revived as a separate action against the representatives of the deceased defendant; but an order might be made therein, severing the action with leave to continue two causes of action, separately, against the surviving defendants and with leave to continue a third cause of action, separately, against the executrix of the deceased defendant. Mulligan v O'Brien (1907) 53 Misc 4, 102 NYS 911, affd 119 AD 355, 104 NYS 301.

In tort action against two defendants upon the death of one of them and the substitution of his executor for the purpose of enforcing his several liability, it was discretionary with the court whether or not to sever the action against the executor. Kasen v Morrell (1960) 11 AD2d 1050, 206 NYS2d 282.

84. Necessity for petition and order

Stockholder's liability survived his death, and action therefor did not abate but it was necessary to obtain court's consent to continuance of action, and a proceeding by petition and order was necessary with proper service upon executors, and mere order to show cause was not sufficient. Skinner v Sullivan (1920) 112 Misc 365, 184 NYS 159.

Where in action to remove encroachments one defendant died prior to trial and no application was made to substitute his executor or administrator as party defendant, judgment did not affect him or his interest in subject-matter. Schoenfeld v Chapman (1950) 200 Misc 444, 102 NYS2d 235, mod 280 AD 464, 115 NYS2d 1.

85. Supplemental summons and complaint

Where, upon the death of one or more of several defendants, the cause of action did not survive against the other defendants, but did against the representatives of the deceased, the proper remedy was to bring them in by supplemental summons and complaint; it cannot be done by motion, for CPA §§ 84–87 (this section and §§ 407, 1015(a)(b), 1021 herein) did not provide for such a case. Mackey v Duryea (1889) 6 NYS 573.

86. Matters determined on motion

When existence of cause of action not determined on motion and action could not be continued by one plaintiff as successor in interest to another. See Fink v Manhattan R. Co. (1890) 15 Daly 479, 8 NYS 327.

87. Payment of costs

An application to continue executor of deceased party, the sole plaintiff in an action of foreclosure, should have been granted even though deceased party omitted to pay certain costs awarded to defendant; the executor's motion was not "a proceeding in the action." Van Brocklin v Van Brocklin (1897) 17 AD 226, 45 NYS 541.

88. Trust funds

CPA §§ 85 and 86 were inapplicable to the case of the death of a plaintiff trustee joined with his cestui que trust in an action to protect the trust fund. Paget v Pease (1889) 24 NYSR 762, 6 NYS 386.

89. Partners

Action to charge special partner as general partner is on contract and not for a penalty, and survives his death. First Nat. Bank of Jersey City v Lenk (1890) 10 NYS 261.

FORMS

Form 1—Notice of motion by representative of deceased plaintiff for continuance and substitution

Form 2—Order to show cause why representative of deceased plaintiff should not be substituted as plaintiff

Form 3—Affidavit on motion for substitution

Form 4—Order substituting representative of deceased plaintiff

Form 5—Notice of motion for substitution as plaintiff where previously substituted representative has died

Form 6—Affidavit upon death of previously substituted representative

Form 7—Order of substitution after death of previously substituted representative

Form 8—Order to show cause why substitution should not be ordered after death of coplaintiff

Form 9—Order to show cause to compel substitution of representative of deceased defendant

Form 10—Notice of motion to compel substitution of representative of deceased defendant

Form 11—Affidavit on motion to compel substitution of representative of deceased defendant

Form 12—Order directing substitution of representative of deceased defendant

Form 13—Supplemental complaint after substitution of assignee as plaintiff

Form 1

Notice of Motion by Representative of Deceased Plaintiff for Continuance and Substitution

SUPREME COURT, —¹—— COUNTY

Notice of Motion

[Title of cause]   Index No. — [if assigned]

PLEASE TAKE NOTICE that on the annexed affidavit of —²——, sworn to the

_ ³_ day of __⁴____, 19_⁵_ and on all the pleadings and proceedings heretofore had in this action, a motion will be made at a motion term of the __⁶____ Court, County of __⁷____, to be held at the county court house in the City of __⁸____ on the __⁹_ day of __¹⁰____, 19_¹¹_ at __¹²____ o'clock in the __¹³____ noon of that day or as soon thereafter as counsel can be heard for an order substituting as plaintiff in the above-entitled action, __¹⁴____, Executor under the Last Will and Testament of __¹⁵____, deceased, in the place and stead of the said __¹⁶____, deceased, and amending the summons, pleadings and proceedings accordingly, without prejudice to any proceedings heretofore had in this action and for such other and further relief as may be just and proper together with the costs of this motion.

Dated __¹⁷____, 19_¹⁸_.

__¹⁹_____

Attorney for __²⁰____, Executor
Office and P. O. Address
Telephone No.

To: __²¹_____
     Attorney for Defendant
     Office and P. O. Address

Form 2

Order to Show Cause Why Representative of Deceased Plaintiff Should Not Be Substituted as Plaintiff

SUPREME COURT, __¹____ COUNTY

Order To Show Cause

[Title of cause]   Index No. — [if assigned]

PRESENT: HON. __²____, Justice.

On the annexed affidavit of __³____, sworn to the __⁴_ day of __⁵____, 19_⁶_ and on all the pleadings and proceedings had in this action,

LET __⁷____, the defendant herein, show cause at a motion term of this Court to be held in and for the County of __⁸____ at the County Court House in the City of __⁹____, on the __¹⁰_ day of __¹¹____, 19_¹²_ at __¹³_ o'clock in the __¹⁴____ noon of that day, or as soon thereafter as counsel can be heard, why an order should not be granted substituting as plaintiff in the above-entitled action, __¹⁵____, as Executor under the Last Will and Testament of __¹⁶____, deceased, in the place and stead of __¹⁷____, deceased, and amending the summons, pleadings and proceedings accordingly, without prejudice to any proceedings heretofore had in this action, and for such other and further relief as may be proper and sufficient cause appearing, it is

ORDERED that service of this order to show cause on the annexed affidavit upon __¹⁸____, attorney for the defendant herein, on or before the __¹⁹_ day of __²⁰____, 19_²¹_ shall be deemed good and sufficient service.

Signed this __²²_ day of __²³____, 19_²⁴_ at __²⁵____, New York.

__²⁶_____

[Print signer's name below signature]
Justice, Supreme Court
__²⁷____ County

Form 3

Affidavit on Motion for Substitution

SUPREME COURT, __¹____ COUNTY

Affidavit

[Title of cause]   Index No. — [if assigned]

STATE OF NEW YORK
COUNTY OF __²____   ss.:

__³____, being duly sworn, deposes and says:

537

1. He is the Executor under the Last Will and Testament of __4_____, the plaintiff in this action, now deceased.

2. This is an action for goods sold and delivered [or otherwise state briefly the nature of the action so that it appears that cause of action survives], and a copy of the pleadings filed herein is annexed hereto and made a part hereof.

3. This action was commenced on or about the __5__ day of __6_____, 19_7_ by the service of a summons and complaint upon the defendant. Issue was joined by the service of defendant's answer on the __8__ day of __9_____, 19_10_ and thereafter a note of issue was duly served and filed by the attorney for the plaintiff on the __11__ day of __12_____, 19_13_. The said action is now on the General Trial Term calendar of this court as No. __14__. No further proceedings have been had in this action.

4. The above-named plaintiff, __15_____, died on or about the __16__ day of __17_____, 19_18_. Thereafter, and on the __19__ day of __20_____, 19_21_ the last will and testament of the said __22_____ was duly admitted to probate in the Surrogate's Court in the County of __23_____ and letters testamentary were duly issued to deponent under the said last will and testament. Deponent has duly qualified as such executor and is still acting as such executor. [Or, where plaintiff died intestate, substitute the following clause: "After the service of the answer herein, as hereinbefore alleged, and before any further proceedings were had in this action, and on or about the __24__ day of __25_____, 19_26_, the above-named plaintiff died intestate. On or about the __27__ day of __28_____, 19_29_ deponent, by an order of the Surrogate's Court of __30_____ County was duly appointed administrator of the goods, chattels and credits of the said __31_____, and letters of administration were duly issued to deponent who has duly qualified and is still acting as such administrator."]

5. [If order to show cause is sought, add] The reason an order to show cause is sought is that the defendant is without the State of New York and cannot be personally served within the State of New York with due diligence. The said defendant has duly appeared in this action by __32_____, an attorney at law with offices at No. __33__, __34_____ Street in the City of __35_____, New York. Deponent respectfully requests that the order to show cause direct that service be made upon the said attorney for the defendant rather than upon the defendant personally.

6. [If order to show cause is sought, add] No previous application has been made for the order requested herein or for any similar order.

WHEREFORE, deponent respectfully requests that an order be made herein directing the substitution of __36_____, as executor of the last will and testament of __37_____, deceased, in the place and stead of __38_____, deceased, as plaintiff in the above-entitled action, and amending the summons, pleadings and proceedings accordingly, all without prejudice to the proceedings already had herein and for such other and further relief as may be just and proper.

__39_____
[Print signer's name below signature]

[Jurat]

Form 4

Order Substituting Representative of Deceased Plaintiff

SUPREME COURT, __1_____ COUNTY.

[Title of cause]   Order
                Index No. — [if assigned]

PRESENT, Hon. __2_____, Justice

A motion having been made by __3_____, as executor under the last will and testament of __4_____, deceased, the above-named plaintiff, to substitute the said __5_____, as executor under the last will and testament of __6_____, deceased, as party plaintiff in the above-entitled action, and said motion having come on regularly to be heard,

NOW, upon reading and filing the notice of motion dated the __7__ day of __8_____, 19_9_, the affidavit of __10_____, sworn to the __11__ day of __12_____, 19_13_ with due proof of service of said notice and affidavit personally upon the defendant herein, and after reading the pleadings herein, all in support of the said motion and after hearing __14_____, attorney for __15_____ in support of said motion and no one having appeared in opposition thereto and due deliberation having been had, it is

ON MOTION of __16_____, attorney for __17_____, executor,

ORDERED that said motion be and the same is hereby granted and it is further

ORDERED that __18_____, executor under the last will and testament of __19_____, deceased, be and he hereby is substituted as plaintiff in the said action in the place and stead of __20_____, deceased, without prejudice to any proceedings heretofore had in this action and it is further

ORDERED that the summons and complaint and all papers and proceedings heretofore had in this action be deemed amended by substituting the name of __21_____, as executor of the Estate of __22_____, deceased, as plaintiff in the place and stead of __23_____, all without prejudice to the proceedings already had herein.

Signed this __24__ day of __25_____, 19 26_ at __27_____, New York.

Enter

__28_____

[Print signer's name below signature]
Justice, Supreme Court
__29_____ County

Form 5

Notice of Motion for Substitution as Plaintiff Where Previously Substituted Representative Has Died

SUPREME COURT __1_____ COUNTY

Notice of Motion

[Title of cause]   Index No. — [if assigned]

PLEASE TAKE NOTICE, that upon the annexed affidavit of __2_____, sworn to the __3__ day of __4_____, 19_5_, and on all the pleadings and proceedings had in this action an application will be made at a motion term of this court to be held in and for the County of __6_____ at the County Court House in the City of __7_____ on the __8__ day of __9_____, 19_10_ at __11__ o'clock in the __12_____ noon of that day or as soon thereafter as counsel can be heard for an order directing the substitution of __13_____, as successor executor under the last will and testament of __14_____, deceased, as party plaintiff in the place and stead of __15_____, Executor of __16_____, deceased previously substituted as defendant in the above-entitled action and for such other and further relief as to the court may seem just and proper.

Dated __17_____, 19_18_.

__19_____

[Print signer's name below signature]
Attorney for __20_____
Office and P. O. Address
Telephone No.

To: __21_____
    Attorney for Defendant
    Office and P. O. Address
    __22_____
    Attorney for __23_____, Deceased
    Office and P. O. Address

539

Form 6

Affidavit Upon Death of Previously Substituted Representative

Affidavit

[Title of cause]   Index No. — [if assigned]

STATE OF NEW YORK
COUNTY OF __¹_____   ss.:

__²_____, being duly sworn, deposes and says:

1. The above-entitled action was brought by __³_____, as plaintiff, against the defendant, __⁴_____, to recover upon a certain promissory note alleged to have been made by the defendant to the said __⁵_____ all as more fully appears from a copy of the complaint which is annexed hereto and made a party hereof.

2. The above-entitled action was commenced by the service of a summons and complaint upon the defendant on or about the __⁶__ day of __⁷_____, 19_⁸_. Thereafter, and on or about the __⁹__ day of __¹⁰_____, 19_¹¹_ issue was duly joined by the service of defendant's answer which denied generally the allegations of the complaint, a true copy of which answer is annexed hereto and made a part hereof.

3. After the service of the answer herein and before any further proceedings were had in this action and on or about the __¹²__ day of __¹³_____, 19_¹⁴_, the said __¹⁵_____, the plaintiff in the above-entitled action, died in the County of __¹⁶_____, intestate. Thereafter, and on or about the __¹⁷__ day of __¹⁸_____, 19_¹⁹_, letters of administration of the goods, chattels and credits of the said __²⁰_____, deceased were duly issued to __²¹_____, by the Surrogate's Court of the County of __²²_____ and the said __²³_____ duly qualified as such administrator and acted as such until the time of his death as hereinafter set forth.

4. Upon the appointment and qualification of __²⁴_____, as administrator of the Estate of __²⁵_____, an order of this court was duly entered substituting as plaintiff in the above-entitled action the said __²⁶_____ in the place and stead of the said __²⁷_____, deceased.

5. Following such substitution, __²⁸_____, Esq., Attorney and Counsellor at Law of No. __²⁹__, __³⁰_____ Street in the City of __³¹_____, New York appeared for and acted as the attorney for the said __³²_____, as such administrator, as plaintiff herein.

6. On or about the __³³__ day of __³⁴_____, 19_³⁵_, the said __³⁶_____, as attorney for the said plaintiff, duly served and filed a note of issue placing the above-entitled action upon the Trial Calendar of this Court, No. __³⁷__. No further proceedings have been had herein.

7. On or about the __³⁸__ day of __³⁹_____, 19_⁴⁰_, the said __⁴¹_____, the administrator of the goods, chattels and credits of the said __⁴²_____, deceased, and the person substituted as the representative of the plaintiff, in the place and stead of the plaintiff in the above-entitled action, died in the County of __⁴³_____.

8. On or about the __⁴⁴__ day of __⁴⁵_____, 19_⁴⁶_, letters of administration, de bonis non of the goods, chattels and credits of the said __⁴⁷_____, deceased, were duly issued to deponent by the Surrogate's Court of the County of __⁴⁸_____ and deponent duly qualified as administrator de bonis non and thereafter acted and is still acting as such administrator.

9. [Set forth facts showing that the action survives the decedent.]

WHEREFORE, deponent requests that an order be entered herein substituting deponent, as administrator de bonis non of the goods, chattels and credits of __⁴⁹_____, as the plaintiff in the said action in the place and stead of __⁵⁰_____, as administrator of the goods, chattels and credits of __⁵¹_____, without prejudice to the proceedings already had herein, and for such other and further relief as to the court may seem just and proper.

___52_____
[Print signer's name below signature]

[Jurat]

Form 7

Order of Substitution After Death of Previously Substituted Representative

SUPREME COURT, __1_____ COUNTY.

Order

[Title of action]　　　Index No. — [if assigned]

PRESENT: Hon. __2_____, Justice.

Upon reading and filing the notice of motion herein dated the __3__ day of __4_____, 19_5_, the affidavit of __6_____, sworn to the __7__ day of __8_____, 19_9_, and upon all the papers and proceedings heretofore filed and had herein, and due notice of this application having been given to __10_____, the defendant herein and __11_____, attorney for __12_____, the deceased administrator of the goods, chattels and credits of __13_____, and after hearing __14____, attorney for __15_____, in support of this application and no one having appeared in opposition thereto,

NOW, on motion of __16_____, attorney for __17_____, as administrator de bonis non of the goods, chattels and credits of __18_____, it is

ORDERED, that __19_____, as administrator de bonis non of the goods, chattels and credits of __20_____, deceased, be and he hereby is substituted as plaintiff in this action in the place and stead of __21_____, above-named and that the title of this action be amended accordingly, without prejudice to the proceedings already had in this action.

Signed this __22__ day of __23_____, 19_24_ at __25_____, New York.

Enter

26_____
[Print signer's name below signature]
Justice, Supreme Court
__27_____ County

Form 8

Order to Show Cause Why Substitution Should Not Be Ordered After Death of Co-plaintiff

SUPREME COURT, __1_____ COUNTY.

Order to Show Cause

[Title of cause]　　　Index No. — [if assigned]

PRESENT: Hon. __2_____, Justice.

On the annexed affidavit of __3_____, sworn to the __4__ day of __5_____, 19_6_, let __7_____, the defendant herein, show cause at a Motion Term of this court to be held in and for the County of __8_____ at the County Court House in the City of __9_____ on the __10__ day of __11_____, 19_12_ at __13__ o'clock in the __14_____ noon of that day or as soon thereafter as counsel can be heard why an order should not be made bringing in __15_____, administrator of the estate of __16_____, as an additional party plaintiff to this action without prejudice to proceedings already had herein in the place and stead of the plaintiff __17_____, deceased, and why all pleadings and proceedings heretofore had in this action should not be deemed amended accordingly and for such other and further relief as to this court may seem just and proper, and sufficient cause appearing therefor

LET service of a copy of this order and the affidavit upon which it is based upon __18_____, attorney for the plaintiff __19_____, deceased, __20_____, the attorney for the plaintiff __21_____ and __22_____, attorney for the defendant on or about the __23__ day of __24_____, 19_25_ be good and sufficient service.

Signed this __26__ day of __27_____, 19_28_ at __29_____, New York.

__30_____

[Print signer's name below signature]
Justice, Supreme Court
__31_____ County

Form 9

Order to Show Cause to Compel Substitution of Representative of Deceased Defendant

SUPREME COURT, __1_____ COUNTY.

Order to Show Cause
[Title of cause]　　　Index No. — [if assigned]

PRESENT: Hon. __2_____, Justice.

On the annexed affidavit of __3_____ sworn to the __4__ day of __5_____, 19_6_ and on the pleadings and proceedings heretofore had herein,

LET, __7_____, as Executor of the Estate of __8_____, the deceased defendant herein, show cause at a Motion Term of this Court to be held in and for the County of __9_____ at the County Court House in the City of __10_____, on the __11__ day of __12_____, 19_13_ at __14__ o'clock in the __15_____ noon of that day, or as soon thereafter as counsel can be heard, why an order should not be granted substituting said __16_____, as Executor of the Estate of __17_____, as the party defendant herein, amending the summons and pleadings accordingly [directing that the order of reference and the evidence and exhibits admitted by the Referee and the other proceedings heretofore had herein stand and enure to the benefits of both parties herein] and for such other and further relief as to the court may seem just and proper and, sufficient cause appearing it is

ORDERED that service of this order to show cause and the annexed affidavit upon __18_____, Executor of the Estate of __19_____, deceased on or about the __20__ day of __21_____, 19_22_, shall be deemed good and sufficient service.

Signed this __23__ day of __24_____, 19_25_ at __26_____, New York.

__27_____

[Print signer's name below signature]
Justice, Supreme Court
__28_____ County

Form 10

Notice of Motion to Compel Substitution of Representative of Deceased Defendant

SUPREME COURT, __1_____ COUNTY

Notice of Motion
[Title of cause]　　　Index No. — [if assigned]

PLEASE TAKE NOTICE that upon the annexed affidavit of __2_____, sworn to the __3__ day of __4_____, 19_5_ and upon the papers and proceedings heretofore filed and had herein, an application will be made at a Motion Term of this court to be held in and for the County of __6_____, at the County Court House in the City of __7_____, on the __8__ day of __9_____, 19_10_, at __11__ o'clock in the __12_____ noon of that day or as soon thereafter as counsel can be heard for an order substituting

___13_____, as Executor of the Estate of ___14_____, deceased as party defendant in the place and stead of ___15_____, deceased and amending the summons and pleadings herein so as to make the said ___16_____, as Executor of the Estate of ___17_____ the party defendant in this action without prejudice to the proceedings already had herein and for such other and further relief as to the court may seem just and proper.

Dated: ___18_____, 19_19_.

___20_____

Attorney for Plaintiff
Office and P. O. Address
Telephone No.

To: ___21_____
Executor of the Estate of ___22_____

Form 11

Affidavit on Motion to Compel Substitution of Representative of Deceased Defendant

SUPREME COURT, ___1_____ COUNTY

Affidavit
[Title of cause]   Index No. — [if assigned]

STATE OF NEW YORK
COUNTY OF ___2_____   ss.:

___3_____, being duly sworn, deposes and says:

1. He is the attorney for the plaintiff in the above-entitled action and is duly authorized by the said plaintiff to make this motion.

2. The above-entitled action was commenced on or about the ___4__ day of ___5_____, 19_6_, by the service of a summons and complaint upon the above-named defendant. On or about the ___7__ day of ___8_____, 19_9_, issue was duly joined herein by the service of defendant's answer on deponent's attorney. A note of issue was duly served and filed by deponent on the ___10__ day of ___11_____, 19_12_. Thereafter, and on or about the ___13__ day of ___14_____, 19_15_, an order of reference to Hon. ___16_____ was made herein to determine the controversy existing between the parties. On the hearing before the said Referee ___17_____, the testimony of the defendant above-named, now deceased, and other witnesses was taken and exhibits were admitted into evidence. Said reference is not yet concluded. No further proceedings have been had herein.

3. This action was brought to recover the sum of $___18__ for the conversion of ___19_____ shares of stock of the ___20_____ Company of the City of ___21_____, loaned to defendant ___22_____, now deceased, by plaintiff on the ___23__ day of ___24_____, 19_25_ which were to be returned thereafter on demand but which were not returned after due demand was made on or about the ___26__ day of ___27_____, 19_28_ all as more fully appears by reference to the complaint which is herewith submitted. The cause of action alleged in this action survived the death of the defendant.

4. On or about the ___29__ day of ___30_____, 19_31_, the said ___32_____, deceased, being the sole defendant herein, died, leaving a last will and testament which was duly admitted to probate in the Surrogate's Court of ___33_____ County where said ___34_____ resided. The said ___35_____ was duly appointed as Executor of the Estate of ___36_____ by an order of the Surrogate's Court, ___37_____ County, dated the ___38__ day of ___39_____, 19_40_ and the said ___41_____ has duly qualified as such executor and is still acting as such.

5. The said ___42_____, as executor of the estate of ___43_____, deceased, is the representative of the above-named defendant and has not made any application for a substitution in the above-entitled action.

[If an order to show cause is sought, add]

6. An order to show cause is sought because of the difficulty of personally serving the said __44_____, due to his frequent sojourns from the State of New York and because the plaintiff is in doubt as to the manner in which service must be made.

7. No previous application has been made for the relief sought herein or for any similar relief.

WHEREFORE, deponent prays for an order directing said __45_____, as Executor of the Estate of __46_____ and __47_____, the attorney for the above-named defendant, to show cause why an order should not be granted herein directing the substitution of __48_____, as Executor of the Estate of __49_____, the deceased defendant herein in the place and stead of said __50_____, deceased, amending the pleadings and other proceedings accordingly without prejudice to any proceedings heretofore had in this action, directing that the order of reference and the evidence and exhibits admitted by such Referee and all other proceedings heretofore had herein stand and enure to the benefits of both parties herein and for such other and further relief as to the court may seem just and proper.

__51_____
[Print signer's name below signature]

[Jurat]

Form 12

Order Directing Substitution of Representative of Deceased Defendant

SUPREME COURT, __1_____ COUNTY.

Order

[Title of cause] Index No. — [if assigned]

PRESENT: Hon. __2_____, Justice.

After reading and filing the order to show cause herein made by Mr. Justice __3_____ and dated the __4__ day of __5_____, 19_6_ and the affidavit of __7_____, sworn to the __8__ day of __9_____, 19_10_ with proof of due service thereof and upon all the pleadings and proceedings heretofore had herein and after hearing __11_____, attorney for the plaintiff in support of this motion and no one having appeared in opposition thereto,

NOW on motion of __12_____, attorney for the plaintiff, it is

ORDERED that the said __13_____, as Executor of the Estate of __14_____, deceased, be and he hereby is substituted as the party defendant in this action in the place and stead of the said __15_____, and it is further

ORDERED that the summons and pleadings in this action be deemed amended so as to make the said Executor the party defendant in the said action all without prejudice to any proceedings heretofore had in said action, and it is further

ORDERED that the order of reference and the evidence taken herein before the death of said __16_____, and all other proceedings heretofore had herein, shall stand and enure to the benefit of the plaintiff as fully and completely as though said executor had been the original party defendant herein.

Signed this __17__ day of __18_____, 19_19_ at __20_____, New York.

Enter

__21_____
[Print signer's name below signature]
Justice, Supreme Court
__22_____ County

Form 13

Supplemental Complaint after Substitution of Assignee as Plaintiff

SUPREME COURT, __1_____ COUNTY

Supplemental Complaint
[Title of cause]   Index No. __2__

The above-named plaintiff, having been duly substituted as plaintiff in the above-entitled action by an order of this court made and entered in the office of the Clerk of __3_____ County on the __4__ day of __5_____, 19_6_, by this his supplemental complaint served pursuant to said order, which complaint is supplemental to the original complaint heretofore served in said action, by __7_____, his attorney, alleges:

1. On or about the __8__ day of __9_____, 19_10_, said __11_____ the original plaintiff herein, in consideration of the sum of __12_____ Dollars ($__13__) paid by this plaintiff, assigned the cause of action alleged in said original complaint to this plaintiff, who is now the lawful and sole owner of such cause of action. A copy of said assignment is hereto attached marked "Exhibit A" and made a part hereof.

2. Said assignment has since then been and is now in full force and effect, and by virtue thereof this plaintiff is entitled to everything demanded by said original complaint.

WHEREFORE, plaintiff demands judgment against defendant for the relief demanded in the original complaint heretofore served herein.

__14_____

[Print signer's name below signature]
Attorney for Plaintiff
Office and P. O. Address
Telephone No.

[Verification]

§ 1016. Substitution upon incompetency

If a party is adjudicated incompetent, the court shall order substitution of his committee.

HISTORY:

Add, L 1962, ch 308, eff Sept 1, 1963.

ADVISORY COMMITTEE NOTES:

This provision is based upon Federal rule 25(b). See notes to § 1015.

FEDERAL ASPECTS:

Substitution of parties, Rule 43 of Federal Rules of Appellate Procedure, USCS Court Rules.

Substitution upon incompetency, Rule 25(b) of Federal Rules of Civil Procedure, USCS Court Rules.

RESEARCH REFERENCES AND PRACTICE AIDS:

3 Carmody-Wait 2d, Parties § 19:147.
9 Am Jur Legal Forms 2d, Incompetent Persons, Forms 141:11–141:17.

Law Reviews:

New York Civil Practice Law and Rules: parties. 27 Albany L Rev 182.
Parties and pleading under the CPLR. 31 Brooklyn L Rev 98.

§ 1017. Substitution in case of receivership or dissolution of a corporation

If a receiver is appointed for a party, or a corporate party is dissolved, the court shall order substitution of the proper parties.

HISTORY:

Add, L 1962, ch 308, eff Sept 1, 1963.

ADVISORY COMMITTEE NOTES:

The statutory law on the subject of substitution in case of dissolution of a corporation seems to be in a state of confusion. Article 10 of the Stock Corporation Law deals with dissolution without judicial proceedings. Section 105(8) provides that such a corporation continues for the purpose of paying debts, collecting assets and winding up affairs and "may sue or be sued in its corporate name." Subd 12 of the same section provides that any pending suits at the time of dissolution "may proceed, against the surviving directors, as trustees, who may continue to be sued in the corporate name." See also Gen Corp Law § 29; Tax Law § 203-a. The general provision for receivers is § 106 of the Stock Corporation Law. See also Gen Corp Law, art 12. These provisions are not articulate on the subject of substitution in case of appointment of a receiver for a corporate party. Compare CPA § 977-b(19), where substitution is contemplated in case of appointment of a receiver for a foreign corporation.

Most of the case law regarding substitution in case of dissolution deals with the situation where a receiver is appointed for a corporation. The general rule seems to be that the receiver must be substituted in pending actions. See Matter of French, 181 App Div 719, 168 NY Supp 988 (1st Dept), affd 224 NY 555, 120 NE 863 (1918); Holmes v Camp, 186 App Div 675, 175 NY Supp 349 (1st Dept), affd 227 NY 635, 126 NE 910 (1919); Maxrice Realty Corp. v B/G Sandwich Shops, Inc. 239 App Div 472, 267 NY Supp 863 (1st Dept 1933); cf. Decker v Gardner, 124 NY 334, 26 NE 814 (1891) (temporary receiver); Honegger v Wettstein, 94 NY 252 (1884) (receiver cannot intervene); Sturges v Vanderbilt, 73 NY 384 (1878) (foreign corporation); Sinnott v Hanan, 214 NY 454, 108 NE 858 (1915) (same); Chaplin v Selznick, 293 NY 529, 58 NE2d 719 (1944) (same); Eisenstadt v Heffernan, 256 App Div 488, 10 NYS2d 868 (1st Dept 1939), affd 283 NY 478, 27 NE2d 439 (1940) (dissolution under NY Tax Law).

In this condition of the law, the framing of a specific procedural rule is difficult. This section seems desirable but its impact must await the clarification of substantive corporation law now being undertaken. See Senate Resolution No. 27, 1956.

FEDERAL ASPECTS:

Substitution of parties, Rule 43 of Federal Rules of Appellate Procedure, USCS Court Rules.

RESEARCH REFERENCES AND PRACTICE AIDS:

2 Carmody-Wait 2d, Abatement and Survival of Actions § 11:34.
3 Carmody-Wait 2d, Parties § 19:147.
20 Carmody-Wait 2d, Actions and Proceedings By and Against Corporations, Their Officers, Directors, and Shareholders § 121:212.

Law Reviews:

New York Civil Practice Law and Rules: parties. 27 Albany L Rev 182.
Parties and pleading under the CPLR. 31 Brooklyn L Rev 98.

CASE NOTES

Where party which was thereafter appointed trustee in bankruptcy had been named as party defendant and charged in pleadings with partici- pating in actions which were contrary to the interest of the corporations for which he was appointed trustee, there existed possible conflict of interest which rendered it inappropriate that trustee be substituted as party plaintiff with respect to derivative causes of action. SNR Holdings, Inc. v Ataka America, Inc. (1976) 54 AD2d 406, 388 NYS2d 909.

CASE NOTES

UNDER FORMER CIVIL PRACTICE LAWS

1. Receivers
2. Dissolution of corporations
3. Foreign corporations

1. Receivers

A receiver of a corporation was not permitted to invoke CPA §§ 82, 83 (§§ 1015, 1018 herein) in order to continue an action which the bank of which he has become receiver had no right to commence. Mutual Bank v Burrell (1899) 29 Misc 322, 60 NYS 522.

2. Dissolution of corporations

Action by corporation is not abated by the dissolution of the corporation. Platt v Ashman (1884) 32 Hun 230.

The dissolution of a corporation terminates the action, and all subsequent proceedings are void, unless it be continued by order of the court, which order must require the substitution of its successor in interest. McCulloch v Norwood (1874) 58 NY 562.

After dissolution of corporation its attorneys have no power thereafter to act for it and the stipulation signed by them will not authorize the entry of judgment against it. Re Norwood (1884) 32 Hun 196.

A corporation which has been enjoined from the exercise of its franchises and deprived of its property is not dissolved, and, until there is a judgment of dissolution, it may be sued. Kincaid v Dwinelle (1875) 59 NY 548.

An action for negligence causing death, pending against a corporation at the time of its dissolution, does not abate by reason thereof, and the court, upon a proper application, should direct its continuance against the receiver. People v Troy Steel Iron Co. (1894) 82 Hun 303, 31 NYS 337.

An action against a corporation for personal injuries cannot be revived against the trustees thereof, on dissolution of the corporation. Grafton v Union Ferry Co. 19 NYS 966; contra, Hepworth v Union Ferry Co. (1891) 62 Hun 257, 16 NYS 692.

3. Foreign corporations

The mode of continuing an action against a foreign corporation after its dissolution is a matter of practice governed by the laws of this state. Sturges v Vanderbilt (1878) 73 NY 384.

An action by a foreign corporation may be continued in its name even after the appointment of an ancillary receiver. Sigua Iron Co. v Brown (1902) 171 NY 488, 64 NE 194.

Where an action has been brought against a foreign corporation which was dissolved, the action cannot be continued against trustees or directors under this section as being the "representative or successor in interest of the corporation"; the receiver or other officer appointed to dissolve the corporation is the successor of the trustees or directors. Wamsley v H. L. Horton & Co. (1896) 12 AD 312, 42 NYS 767, affd 153 NY 687, 48 NE 1107.

§ 1018. Substitution upon transfer of interest

Upon any transfer of interest, the action may be continued by or against the original parties unless the court directs the person to whom the interest is transferred to be substituted or joined in the action.

HISTORY:

Add, L 1962, ch 308, eff Sept 1, 1963.

Earlier statutes: CPA § 83; CCP § 756; Code Proc § 121.

ADVISORY COMMITTEE NOTES:

This provision is taken from Federal rule 25(c), which was derived from CPA § 83, which in turn stems from § 101 of the Field code. The notion that a transfer of interest should not require a substitution of parties unless the court so orders has met with favor throughout the years and has not given rise to difficulty. It will be noted that the aspects of § 83 dealing with devolution on other parties to the action are covered by new CPLR § 1015(b), as in Federal rule 25(a)(2).

FEDERAL ASPECTS:

Substitution of parties, Rule 43 of Federal Rules of Appellate Procedure, USCS Court Rules.

Substitution of parties: transfer of interest, Rule 25(c) of Federal Rules of Civil Procedure, USCS Court Rules.

RESEARCH REFERENCES AND PRACTICE AIDS:
2 Carmody-Wait 2d, Abatement and Survival of Actions §§ 11:28, 11:34, 11:37.
3 Carmody-Wait 2d, Parties §§ 19:162, 19:164.
11 Carmody-Wait 2d, Attachment § 76:180.
21 Carmody-Wait 2d, Litigation By and Against Fiduciaries § 129:27.

Law Reviews:
New York Civil Practice Law and Rules: parties. 27 Albany L Rev 182.
Parties and pleading under the CPLR. 31 Brooklyn L Rev 98.

Forms:
See "FORMS" heading following "CASE NOTES", infra.

CASE NOTES

In action to foreclose a mortgage, where surety paid or otherwise settled claims of mechanics' lienors and received assignments from them of their liens and all causes of action, Special Term should order the surety substituted for lienors. T. J. Bettes Co. v South Falls Corp. (1967) 28 AD2d 198, 284 NYS2d 262.

Where corporate plaintiff obtained interest of individual in business before commencement of libel action, statute permitting court, upon transfer of interest, to direct person to whom interest is transferred to be substituted or joined in the action did not sanction granting corporate plaintiff's motion for leave to serve amended summons and complaint, to extent of joining in action the individual as added party plaintiff. Neggy Travel Service, Inc. v Sabena Belgian World Airlines (1977) 56 AD2d 537, 391 NYS2d 581.

CASE NOTES

UNDER FORMER CIVIL PRACTICE LAWS

1. Generally
2. Discretion of court
3. Conveyance pendente lite
4. Mandamus
5. Boards
6. Motion for substitution
7. Effect of substitution
8. Surrogates' courts
9. Assignment for benefit of creditors
10. Bankruptcy
11. Assignment of cause of action
12. Substitution of assignee
13. Corporations
14. Receiverships
15. Conveyance of real estate
16. Contract for labor
17. Rights of indorsers
18. Action for tort
19. Change of name
20. Attorney's lien for costs
21. Mechanics' liens
22. Partition
23. Trusts
24. Removal of trustee

25. Executors and administrators

1. Generally

CPA § 83 did not permit the substitution of a new party to an action for the original party, where the action had been terminated by the entry of a final judgment on the merits. Central Nat. Bank v Richmond (1940) 175 Misc 425, 22 NYS2d 747.

Whatever would have been sufficient to prevent relief on a bill of revivor in chancery, is sufficient now to defeat a motion to revive. The right is to be determined according to the settled rules of equity so far as established by precedent. Patterson v McCunn, 14 NYSR 385, affd (1888) 110 NY 670, 18 NE 481.

The representative of a deceased husband may, under this section, apply for modification of a divorce judgment awarding alimony where the wife remarries. Kirkbride v Van Note (1937) 275 NY 244, 9 NE2d 852, 112 ALR 243.

Distinction between actions for real property, and for the recovery of personal property in favor of persons acquiring rights or interests under one of the parties during the pendency of the litigation. Palen v Bushnell (1889) 51 Hun 423, 4 NYS 63.

If an assignor of a chose in action desires to be relieved of his responsibility as a party he should apply for a substitution in the course of the proceedings and before a judgment is entered for costs in the action. Riverside Bank v Totten (1891) 41 NYSR 166, 16 NYS 348.

Alien Property Custodian may not be joined as coplaintiff with receiver of enemy corporation, who originally brought action in its behalf, under CPA § 977-b. Propper v Taylor (1946) 270 AD 890, 62 NYS2d 601.

Insured may continue action in own name after insurer has paid plaintiff's loss in full, where such payment was made after commencement of action. Zamochnick v New York C. R. Co. (1948) 191 Misc 318, 80 NYS2d 65.

An order substituting a defendant in place of present defendant is authorized only in case of a transfer of interest or devolution of liability. Spa Baths Co. v Board of Comrs. of State Reservation (1917) 98 Misc 399, 163 NYS 775, affd 181 AD 960, 171 NYS 1100.

CPA § 83 did not apply where plaintiff's interest was transferred before action was commenced. Bernard Bake Shop v Glassman (1952) 109 NYS2d 520.

CPA § 83 did not authorize substitution of parties after entry of final judgment. Levine v Simon (1961) 212 NYS2d 888.

2. Discretion of court

Where there has been a transfer of interest, the right to substitute the transferee is based upon this section and lies within the discretion of the court. Hale v Shannon (1901) 58 AD 247, 68 NYS 803.

An order directing the substitution is usually granted, but it is discretionary and the court may withhold it. McNamara v Harris, 4 Civ Proc 76.

Under CPA § 83 the court had a very broad authority to bring in a party who may have had an interest in the suit. DeBost v Albert Palmer Co. 1 How Pr NS 508; and see Getty v Spaulding (1874) 58 NY 636; Senft v Manhattan R. Co. 57 Super Ct (25 Jones & S) 417.

A motion made by a party to intervene as an additional party plaintiff is governed by this section, which provides that a motion is discretionary with the court. Israel v Metropolitan El. R. Co. (1901) 58 AD 266, 69 NYS 218.

Motion for substitution of plaintiff on transfer of claim after action brought is one for a favor and not of right. Helfand v Massachusetts Bonding & Ins. Co. (1912) 197 AD 759, 189 NYS 246.

3. Conveyance pendente lite

Where pending an action to restrain defendants from developing water power on a river in which plaintiffs had power rights and to determine the water rights of the several parties, the plaintiffs sold their rights without reservation to a corporation which in turn mortgaged such rights to secure an issue of bonds, and plaintiffs also personally guaranteed to the corporation and to the purchasers of the bonds the validity of their title to the water power conveyed, the court had power, under this section and CPA §§ 192 and 193 (§§ 401, 1001(a), (b), 1003 herein), to join as parties defendant the vendee corporation, the trustee under the mortgage, and the executor of one of the plaintiffs whose death occurred pending the action. Dunlop v Sweet Bros. Paper Mfg. Co. (1925) 211 AD 363, 208 NYS 54.

Where pending the retrial of an action to secure reformation of a contract and deed so as to include therein a provision for a perpetual easement in adjoining property, and for an injunction restraining defendants from erecting upon the property subject to such easement any building which would obstruct the view from the property covered by such contract and deed, the plaintiff, grantee of such deed, conveyed the property to another, covenanting with his grantee to prosecute this action to judgment, in view of this section plaintiff was entitled to judgment in his favor notwithstanding such conveyance of his interest in the property. Phillips v West Rockaway Land Co. (1922) 203 AD 202, 196 NYS 723.

Defendants entitled to continue replevin action unless the court otherwise directs, even though there has been the transfer of title subsequent to the commencement of the action. Fulton Auto Exch., Inc. v Salitsky (1935) 155 Misc 696, 278 NYS 980.

4. Mandamus

Where mandamus proceedings have been instituted against the commissioners of a department of municipal government to secure the reinstatement of the relator and the respondent ceases to be the commissioner of such department, the proceedings are abated; the relator is not entitled to have the respondent's successor substituted as respondent, but his remedy is to make a demand for reinstatement upon the successor and to institute a new mandamus proceeding if such successor refuses to reinstate him. People ex rel. Hatch v Lantry (1903) 88 AD 583, 85 NYS 193.

5. Boards

A new board of education may proceed with an action brought in the name of the former board. Beck v Kerr (1903) 87 AD 1, 83 NYS 1057.

6. Motion for substitution

To substitute an assignee, a motion must be made on his behalf. Schell v Devlin (1880) 82 NY 333.

Motion for substitution should not have been entertained during stay of proceedings awaiting giving of security for costs. Helfand v Massachusetts Bonding & Ins. Co. (1912) 197 AD 759, 189 NYS 246.

7. Effect of substitution

Where the grantee of premises has been substituted under the provisions of this section in place of former owner in an action to restrain trespass by elevated road and where a supplemental complaint is served which does not ask for an injunction, the action is then only one to recover damages sustained since the property was purchased. Hutton v Metropolitan El. R. Co. (1897) 19 AD 243, 46 NYS 169.

8. Surrogates' courts

CPA § 83 did not apply to surrogates' courts. Re Tilden's Estate, 5 Civ Proc 449.

9. Assignment for benefit of creditors

Plaintiff's assignee for benefit of creditors cannot be compelled to become a party, in a suit commenced before the assignment; suit may proceed with the original plaintiff only. Lawson v Woodstock (1885) 37 Hun 352.

Where the plaintiff, after commencement of the action, made a general assignment, and afterwards his assignee was substituted as plaintiff, upon a motion made upon notice to the defendant, held, that the order of substitution was sufficient to prove the plaintiff's title, notwithstanding the defendant's objection. Smith v Zalinski (1882) 26 Hun 225, affd 94 NY 519.

An action on a promissory note may be continued in the name of the plaintiff although since the action was commenced the plaintiff has made an assignment for the benefit of creditors. Burton v Burton (1901) 57 AD 113, 67 NYS 1067.

10. Bankruptcy

In action for accounting bankrupt interposed a counterclaim; his trustee was substituted to continue the action. Weiss v Kanarek (1930) 136 Misc 848, 241 NYS 345.

Adjudication of plaintiff as a bankrupt after commencing an action he is adjudged bankrupt, may be regarded as a transfer of interest which does not compel another to be substituted for such plaintiff and in any event the plaintiff's allegation that the trustee had assigned him the claim may be looked on as a waiver by the trustee enabling the plaintiff to continue the action. Melnick v Commercial Casualty Ins. Co. (1927) 221 AD 599, 224 NYS 516.

Where an assignee in bankruptcy neglects to apply to defend an action against the bankrupt, pending at the time of his appointment, until after judgment has been rendered and executed, it is in the discretion of the court whether to let him in on motion, or to leave him to his remedy by action. Keck v Werder (1881) 86 NY 264.

It is better practice for a trustee in bankruptcy to obtain the consent of the federal court before seeking to be substituted as plaintiff in a prior action brought by the creditors against the bankrupt. Hahlo v Cole (1906) 112 AD 636, 98 NYS 1049.

After a judgment for costs has been obtained against the plaintiff by a defendant, the plaintiff cannot have his trustee in bankruptcy substituted as plaintiff in such judgment. Murtagh v Sullivan (1911) 74 Misc 517, 132 NYS 503.

Action in state court does not abate upon adjudication of bankruptcy of plaintiff, and the action may be continued in the name of the plaintiff unless the trustee in bankruptcy obtains leave of federal court and becomes substituted as plaintiff. Gilbert v Mechanics & Metals Nat. Bank (1916) 172 AD 25, 157 NYS 953.

In personal injury action, appeal by defendant from judgment for plaintiff will not be dismissed because of defendant's adjudication as a bankrupt and appointment of trustee, who was given leave to intervene but declined to take part in the appeal. Schoonmaker v Pittsburgh Contracting Co. (1916) 176 AD 48, 161 NYS 186, 1055.

Trustee in bankruptcy did not take title through plaintiff as assignee for benefit of creditors, and action could not be continued in the name of the original plaintiff nor the trustee. Gilbert v Mechanics & Metals Nat. Bank (1916) 95 Misc 364, 160 NYS 710, affd 176 AD 915, 162 NYS 1121, affd 221 NY 648, 117 NE 1068.

Adjudication of bankruptcy and appointment of trustee do not warrant dismissal of action. Colgan v Finck (1913) 159 AD 57, 144 NYS 408.

11. Assignment of cause of action

This section appears to treat question of assignments pendente lite very pragmatically, allowing continuance by assignor, or joinder of both parties "as case requires." Fox v McGrath (1945) 152 F2d 616, cert den 327 US 806, 90 L Ed 1030, 66 S Ct 966.

Where, since the commencement of an action the cause of action has been assigned, the court may join the assignee as coplaintiff. Buck Ridge Coal Mining Co. v Rosoff Engineering Co. (1926) 215 AD 441, 214 NYS 60.

An assignment by plaintiff made after the commencement of the action does not preclude recovery. Hardee v Karman (1933) 149 Misc 339, 266 NYS 601.

The devolution or transfer of a claim or cause of action by assignment or otherwise subsequent to the commencement of the action does not prevent the transferor from continuing the action in his own name for the benefit of the transferee or assignee. Herald Nathan Press, Inc. v Bourges (1936) 161 Misc 208, 291 NYS 650.

Where a plaintiff has assigned his entire cause of action, this section furnishes no authority for the continuation of the action by the plaintiff, in case his assignee has settled the claim and demands that the action be discontinued. Hirshfeld v Fitzgerald (1898) 157 NY 166, 51 NE 997.

Where defendants prevailed and obtained judgment on counterclaim, plaintiffs were entitled to continue action against defendants though they assigned their rights pending appeal. Fox v Peacock (1912) 153 AD 887, 138 NYS 535.

Defendant on learning that plaintiffs had assigned the cause of action to trustees for creditors could not compel the joining of the trustees as plaintiffs. Rothbarth v Herzfeld (1913) 159 AD 732, 144 NYS 974.

Rights of assignee of mortgage pending foreclosure were subject to those of bona fide purchasers at foreclosure sale. Clement v Saratoga Holding Co. (1914) 161 AD 898, 145 NYS 628.

Where at commencement of action plaintiff had no right to sue because he had assigned his claim, subsequent assignment by plaintiff's trustee in bankruptcy of the alleged cause of action transferred no interest within the meaning of this section. Williams v Arthur H. Crist Co. (1919) 190 AD 29, 179 NYS 679.

12. Substitution of assignee

In an action to recover on insurance policy the assignee of the beneficiary may be substituted as plaintiff after the death of the insured. Hunt v Provident Sav. Life Assur. Soc. (1902) 77 AD 338, 79 NYS 74.

The assignee of a claim under a marriage separation agreement may on motion be substituted as plaintiff and serve a supplemental complaint against the other party to such agreement. Scher v Adams (1927) 220 AD 309, 221 NYS 547.

Where Superintendent of Banks, suing for assessment against stockholders of bank in liquidation, assigned judgment pending appeal by defendant, assignee should not, in exercise of court's discretion, be substituted, where assignee opposes it. White v Hardy (1943) 180 Misc 63, 39 NYS2d 911, affd 266 AD 660, 41 NYS2d 210.

Substitution of assignee for corporation as nominal party defendant was denied, where assignee had interest in stockholder's derivative action based on alleged wrongs on defendant corporation by individual defendants as directors, but he was permitted to join as nominal party defendant. Marco v Sachs (1951) 201 Misc 928, 106 NYS2d 522.

Landlord's assignee succeeded to all rights acquired by landlord under existing final order, and was entitled to be substituted as party landlord. Jamaica Investors v Blacharsh (1950) 108 NYS2d 53.

After the commencement of action, the plaintiff assigned the cause of action; afterwards he was adjudged a bankrupt; judgment in his favor was recovered; and afterwards he died, leaving no property, and no administrator was appointed. The assignees were substituted as plaintiffs, without the appointment of an administrator. Schell v Devlin (1880) 82 NY 333.

In view of CPA § 82 (§ 1015 herein), and § 83, the motions of plaintiffs in actions against a railroad company for personal injuries sustained while its property was under federal control, to substitute the Director General of Railroads as agent under Transportation Act 1920, § 206, as defendant, will be granted, notwithstanding that the limitation provided by subdivision "a" of said § 206 has run, the injuries in suit having been sustained prior to the passage of such act and prior to the promulgation of orders of the Director General governing suits against carriers under federal control. De Witt v New York Cent. R. Co. (1922) 119 Misc 456, 196 NYS 870, affd 206 AD 638, 198 NYS 909.

13. Corporations

Assignee of a corporation need not be formally substituted in a suit pending in the corporate name. Platt v McMurray, 63 How Pr 149.

"Right of action" arises from existence of primary right and invasion of that right by some delict, and a judgment against a corporation is not part of its "property, contracts, and rights of action," within Insurance Law, § 63, providing for liquidation of business of insurance corporation. Hartigan v Casualty Co. of America (1917) 180 AD 193, 167 NYS 645.

Where delay in bringing motion for substitution of partnership in place of dissolved partnership as party plaintiff in action for injunction and damages was explained satisfactorily, substitution of partnership as party plaintiff should be allowed. Country Tweeds, Inc. v Clyde Fashions, Ltd. (1955) 286 AD 491, 145 NYS 2d 267.

Where after a suit is commenced against a corporation to enjoin it from using a trade name the defendant is merged in another corporation, the plaintiff is entitled under CPA § 83 to have the second corporation substituted in place of the original defendant. Burrow v Marceau (1909) 132 AD 797, 117 NYS 537.

The fact that one was not re-elected as a director after instituting an action against his co-directors for mismanagement does not abate the action. Manix v Fantl (1924) 209 AD 756, 205 NYS 174, disapproving a contrary decision in Hamilton v Gibson (1911) 145 AD 825, 130 NYS 684.

Suit by director for benefit of corporation may be continued after his removal as a director. Wangrow v Wangrow (1924) 211 AD 552, 207 NYS 132.

14. Receiverships

An action by a foreign corporation may be continued in its name even after the appointment of an ancillary receiver. Sigua Iron Co. v Brown (1902) 171 NY 488, 64 NE 194.

Assignment by a judgment debtor after the appointment of a receiver in supplemental proceedings is no transfer of interest in the sense of this section. Gilkey v Koch (1923) 201 NYS 703.

Under this section a receiver is at liberty to permit pending actions to proceed in the name of the judgment debtor, who may apply to be substituted as plaintiff in place of the debtor. Spencer v Berdell (1887) 45 Hun 179; and irregularities in his appointment are not grounds for denial of motion. Palen v Bushnell (1889) 51 Hun 423, 4 NYS 63.

Receiver of a corporation when not liable to a creditor who fails to present his claim, although suit pending therefor at the time of receiver's appointment. Owen v Kellogg (1890) 56 Hun 455, 10 NYS 75.

Where a receiver appointed by a U. S. court resigns, while the action is pending, the action may be continued in his name unless a substitution is applied for and ordered; the substitution is not jurisdictional. Hegewisch v Silver (1893) 140 NY 414, 35 NE 658.

An action against receivers appointed by a federal court brought in this state under the Revised Statutes was not terminated by their discharge and the transfer of the property in their hands under a decree by federal court. Baer v McCullough (1903) 176 NY 97, 68 NE 129.

Where action of ejectment was brought against receivers of corporation as occupants, court erred in ordering amendment of summons and complaint by eliminating receivers as defendants where it appeared that they had been discharged by the court appointing them, there being no devolution of liability. Barwin Realty Co. v H. Batterman Co. (1915) 169 AD 415, 155 NYS 178.

15. Conveyance of real estate

Where plaintiff conveyed the premises in question pending an action against the defendant, an elevated railroad company, but the deed reserved to the plaintiff "all damages caused or to be caused by the present, past or future maintenance and operation of the elevated railway . . . and the fee and easement," held, that the plaintiff preserved his right to continue the action by the reservation in the grant, but that he might join his grantee as coplaintiff. McGean v Metropolitan El. R. Co. (1891) 59 Super Ct (27 Jones & S) 472, 14 NYS 761, affd 133 NY 9, 30 NE 647.

Where after action is brought, and during pendency thereof, to restrain the operation of an elevated railroad in front of plaintiff's premises and for past damages, the plaintiff conveys the premises to another, and such conveyance does not affect the action, and a judgment obtained binds the assignee upon all the issues litigated, the same as though he had been substituted in place of his assignor; there is no distinction in this respect between actions at law and in equity, provided the cause of action is assignable. McGean v Metropolitan El. R. Co. (1892) 133 NY 9, 30 NE 647.

16. Contract for labor

Where a contract for labor has been assigned and is to become absolute only upon certain contingencies which do not eventuate until after the assignor may continue the action unless the court directs that the assignee be substituted as plaintiff or joined as a party to such action. Hawkins v Mapes-Reeve Constr. Co. (1904) 178 NY 236, 70 NE 783.

17. Rights of indorsers

After commencement of suit on a note against maker, the indorser paid it to the plaintiff and holder. Held, entitled to be subrogated to plaintiff's rights. Concord Granite Co. v French, 3 Civ Proc 56, affd 3 Civ Proc 445, 12 Daly 228, 65 How Pr 317.

18. Action for tort

In an action for a personal tort, the defendant's counsel may stipulate, as a condition of continuance, that the action shall not abate by the plaintiff's death, and such a stipulation will prevent an abatement, notwithstanding an intermediate verdict and judgment, which have been set aside. Cox v New York Cent. & H. R. R. Co. (1875) 63 NY 414.

Where pending an action for an accounting as to certain real and personal property alleged to have been fraudulently transferred by defendant Bange to Bushnell, Bushnell died, the action could, in the discretion of the court, be continued against the executors of Bushnell. Palen v Bushnell (1889) 51 Hun 423, 4 NYS 63.

19. Change of name

Where the name of plaintiff is changed by the legislature after suit is brought and is at issue, the court may allow substitution, and defendant is not entitled to serve a new answer. New York County v Tweed (1875) 3 Hun 682; and see New York County v Miller (1875) 4 Hun 71.

20. Attorney's lien for costs

An attorney may sue in the name of his client to enforce any lien he may have for costs. Kipp v Rapp, 7 Civ Proc 316, 2 How Pr NS 169.

21. Mechanics' liens

An action brought to foreclose a mechanic's lien does not abate by the death of the owner of the premises during the pendency thereof, but may be revived against the successors in interest of the deceased owner, without prejudice to proceedings already had therein. Perry v Levenson (1903) 82 AD 94, 81 NYS 586, affd 178 NY 559, 70 NE 1104.

22. Partition

Revivor of an action for the partition of real estate of copartners, in which an interlocutory judgment directing a reference has been made and the reference is pending undetermined. Jones v Jones (1902) 68 AD 5, 74 NYS 297, affd 171 NY 653, 63 NE 1118.

23. Trusts

Trustee of an express trust may sue in his own name. Van der Stegen v Neuss, Hesslein & Co. (1934) 243 AD 122, 276 NYS 624, affd 270 NY 55, 200 NE 577.

24. Removal of trustee

An appeal from an order removing a testamentary trustee does not prevent the substitution of his successor in his place in an action brought by a cestui que trust to enforce her rights in the testamentary trust fund. Stout v Betts (1893) 74 Hun 266, 26 NYS 809.

25. Executors and administrators

In an action against the sureties of a sheriff's bond, the administrator with the will annexed of one of them will be substituted as a party defendant in the place and stead of his executor who, pending the actions, has ceased to be the representative of the estate. Hamilton v Crawford (1911) 73 Misc 23, 132 NYS 277.

Administrators, who have settled up the estate of the intestate, and become the owners of the claims in suit by assignment from all persons interested, are entitled to be substituted individually as plaintiffs. McLachlin v Brett (1882) 27 Hun 18.

Executor of stockholder, who died after commencing derivative action and who bequeathed shares in trust to executor, was substituted as plaintiff to continue action. Salter v Columbia Concerts (1948) 191 Misc 479, 77 NYS2d 703.

The provision of Vehicle and Traffic Law § 253 for continuing an action against the executor or administrator of nonresident motorist applies only where the action was originally commenced by service on the Secretary of State and not where service was made personally within the state. Gruberger v Titus (1962) 16 AD2d 813, 228 NYS2d 899.

FORMS

Form 1—Order to show cause why assignee should not be substituted

Form 2—Affidavit in support of motion to substitute assignee as plaintiff

Form 3—Order substituting assignee as plaintiff

Form 4—Order to show cause why trustee in bankruptcy should not continue action in his name

Form 5—Affidavit of trustee in bankruptcy in support of motion for substitution and continuance of action

Form 6—Order substituting trustee in bankrupt as plaintiff

Form 1

Order to Show Cause Why Assignee Should Not Be Substituted

SUPREME COURT, __1_____ COUNTY

Order to Show Cause

[Title of cause]   Index No. — [if assigned]

On the annexed affidavit of __2_____, duly sworn to the __3__ day of __4_____, 19_5_ and the attached exhibits consisting of a copy of the complaint in the above-entitled action, a copy of an assignment dated the __6__ day of __7_____, 19_8_ and the consent of the plaintiff above-named to a substitution of parties, dated the __9__ day of __10_____, 19_11_ and on all the pleadings and proceedings heretofore had herein,

LET __12_____, the defendant above-named show cause at a special term of this court to be held in and for the County of __13_____ , at the County Court House in the City of __14_____ on the __15__ day of __16_____, 19_17_ at __18__ o'clock in the __19_____ noon of that day or as soon thereafter as counsel can be heard why an order should not be made directing that __20_____, the moving party herein, be substituted as plaintiff in the above-entitled action in the place and stead of __21_____, the present plaintiff therein and why the action should not be continued in the name of the moving party as plaintiff without prejudice to the proceedings heretofore had herein and the pleadings and other proceedings amended accordingly, and why the moving party should not have [permission to file a supplemental complaint and have] such other and further relief as to this court may seem just and proper.

Sufficient cause appearing therefor it is

ORDERED that service of a copy of this order, together with the affidavit and the exhibits upon which it is granted, made upon the attorney for the defendant on or before the __22__ day of __23_____, 19_24_ shall be deemed good and sufficient service.

Signed this __25__ day of __26_____, 19_27_ at __28_____, New York.

Enter

__29_____

[Print signer's name below signature]

Justice, Supreme Court

__30____ County

Form 2

Affidavit in Support of Motion to Substitute Assignee as Plaintiff

Affidavit

[Title of cause]   Index No. — [if assigned]

STATE OF NEW YORK

COUNTY OF __1_____   ss.:

__2_____, being duly sworn, deposes and says:

1. He is the attorney for __3_____, who is the assignee of the cause of action set forth in the complaint in the above-entitled action.

2. Deponent has been duly authorized by the said __4_____ to make this motion to substitute the said __5_____ as the plaintiff in the above-entitled action in the place and stead of __6_____, the present plaintiff therein.

3. This is an action to recover the price of goods sold and delivered by the said __7_____ to the defendant under a written contract dated the __8__ day of __9_____, 19_10_ as more fully appears from the copy of the complaint hereunto annexed and made a part hereof.

4. The above-entitled action was commenced on or about the __11__ day of __12_____, 19_13_ by __14_____, the plaintiff above-named, by the service of a summons and complaint upon __15_____, the defendant above-named. Issue was duly joined by the service of defendant's answer on the __16__ day of __17_____, 19_18_. A note of issue was duly served and filed on the __19__ day of __20_____, 19_21_. The case now appears on the general trial term calendar of this court as No. __22__. No further proceedings have been had in this action.

5. After the filing of a note of issue as aforesaid, and on or about the __23__ day of __24_____, 19_25_, the above-named plaintiff, by an instrument in writing annexed hereto and made a part hereof, duly assigned and transferred to the said __26_____, for a valuable consideration, the claim and demand constituting the cause of action set forth in the complaint in the above-entitled action. The said __27_____ has ever since been and is now the lawful owner of the said cause of action.

6. As more fully appears from a copy of an instrument dated the __28__ day of __29_____, 19_30_, the said __31_____ has consented to the substitution of the said __32_____ as the plaintiff in the above-entitled action.

7. An order to show cause is requested so that the Court may direct the method and manner of the service of notice of this motion.

8. No previous application has been made for the relief sought herein or for any similar relief.

9. The defendant cannot be prejudiced by the granting of the relief sought herein. [In particular cases, facts should be set forth to substantiate this statement.]

WHEREFORE, deponent requests that an order be made directing the defendant to show cause why an order should not be made substituting __33_____ as plaintiff in the above-entitled action in the place and stead of __34_____, continuing the said action in the name of __35_____ and amending the pleadings accordingly all without prejudice to prior proceedings had herein and why the said __36_____ should not be granted such other and further relief as to the Court may seem just and proper.

Dated: __37_____, 19_38_.

__39_____

[Print signer's name below signature]

[Jurat]

Form 3

Order Substituting Assignee as Plaintiff

SUPREME COURT, __1_____ COUNTY.

Order
[Title of cause]   Index No. — [if assigned]

PRESENT: Hon. __2_____, Justice.

Upon reading and filing the order to show cause herein made by Mr. Justice __3_____ and dated the __4__ day of __5_____, 19_6_ and the affidavit of __7_____, sworn to the __8__ day of __9_____, 19_10_ and the exhibits attached thereto consisting of the pleadings filed in this action, and assignment executed by __11_____ dated the __12__ day of __13_____, 19_14_ and the consent of __15_____ to a substitution of parties dated the __16__ day of __17_____, 19_18_ all in support of this motion and after reading and filing the affidavit of __19_____, sworn to the __20__ day of __21_____, 19_22_ in opposition thereto and upon all the pleadings and proceedings heretofore had herein, and after hearing __23_____, attorney for the moving party in support of this motion and __24_____, attorney for defendant in opposition thereto,

NOW, on motion of __25_____, of counsel for __26_____, attorney for the moving party, it is

ORDERED that said motion be and the same hereby is in all respects granted, and it is further

ORDERED that __27_____, be and he hereby is substituted as plaintiff in the above-entitled action in the place and stead of __28_____, without prejudice to the proceedings heretofore had in this action, and it is further

ORDERED that the above-entitled action be continued in the name of __29_____, as plaintiff and that the summons, pleadings and other proceedings therein be and they hereby are deemed amended by showing the said __30_____ as the plaintiff therein.

Signed this __31__ day of __32_____, 19_33_ at __34_____, New York.

Enter

__35_____
[Print signer's name below signature]
Justice, Supreme Court
__36_____ County

Form 4

Order to Show Cause Why Trustee in Bankrupty Should Not Continue Action in His Name

SUPREME COURT, __1_____ COUNTY

Order to Show Cause
[Title of cause]   Index No. __2__

PRESENT: Hon. __3_____, Justice.

On the annexed affidavit of __4_____, Trustee in Bankruptcy of the Estate of __5_____, sworn to the __6__ day of __7_____, 19_8_, the certificate of the Referee in Bankruptcy showing the moving party's appointment and qualifications as such Trustee and a certified copy of an order of the United States District Court of the __9_____ District of New York dated the __10__ day of __11_____, 19_12_ allowing the moving party as such trustee in bankruptcy to prosecute this action against __13_____, and on all the pleadings and proceedings heretofore had herein,

LET __14_____, the defendant above-named, show cause at a Motion Term of this Court to be held in and for the County of __15_____, at the County Court House in the City of __16_____ on the __17__ day of __18_____, 19_19_ at __20__ o'clock in the

555

___21_____ noon of that day or as soon thereafter as counsel can be heard why an order should not be made directing that ___22_____, Trustee in Bankruptcy in the Estate of ___23_____, be substituted as plaintiff in the action now pending in the ___24_____ Court, ___25_____ County between ___26_____, plaintiff and ___27_____, defendant in the place and stead of the present plaintiff without prejudice to the proceedings heretofore had herein and why the said action should not be continued in the name of ___28_____, Trustee in Bankruptcy of the Estate of ___29_____ and the pleadings amended accordingly and why the moving party should not have such other and further relief as to the court may seem just and proper, and sufficient cause appearing, it is

ORDERED that service of a copy of this order, together with the affidavit and exhibits upon which it is granted, made upon the attorney for the defendant on or before the ___30__ day of ___31_____, 19_32_ shall be deemed good and sufficient service.

Signed this ___33__ day of ___34_____, 19_35_ at ___36_____, New York.

___37_____

[Print signer's name below signature]

Justice, Supreme Court

___38_____ County

Form 5

Affidavit of Trustee in Bankruptcy in Support of Motion for Substitution and Continuance of Action

SUPREME COURT, ___1_____ COUNTY

[Title of cause]   Affidavit

Index No. ___2__

___3_____, being duly sworn, deposes and says:

1. On or about the ___4__ day of ___5_____, 19_6_, ___7_____, the plaintiff named in the above-entitled action was duly adjudicated a bankrupt in the United States District Court for the ___8_____ District of ___9_____. On the said date, deponent was duly elected and appointed trustee in bankruptcy of the property of the said ___10_____ and has duly qualified as such trustee.

2. The above-entitled action was commenced by ___11_____, the plaintiff therein, on the ___12__ day of ___13_____, 19_14_ by service of a summons and complaint on ___15_____, the defendant. On or about the ___16__ day of ___17_____, 19_18_ the defendant served his answer on the attorney for the plaintiff and issue was duly joined. A note of issue was filed by the attorney for the plaintiff on the ___19__ day of ___20_____, 19_21_ and the said action now appears on the general calendar of this court as Case No. ___22__. No further proceedings were had in this action.

3. The said action was brought to recover on a promissory note executed by the defendant in favor of the plaintiff and payable on the ___23__ day of ___24_____, 19_25_ or otherwise state nature of action.

4. On or about the ___26__ day of ___27_____, 19_28_ an order was duly made and entered in the United States District Court for the ___29_____ District of ___30_____ permitting the deponent, as trustee in bankruptcy of the estate of ___31_____, to prosecute the above-entitled action.

5. The defendant cannot be prejudiced by the substitution of the deponent as the plaintiff herein [if necessary state facts substantiating this statement].

6. The deponent requests an order to show cause because the defendant is without the state and cannot be personally served and so that the court may direct the manner in which notice of this application should be served upon the plaintiff and defendant herein.

7. No previous application has been made for the relief sought herein or for any similar relief.

WHEREFORE, deponent respectfully requests that an order be made substituting __32_____, as trustee in bankruptcy of the estate of __33_____, as the plaintiff herein in the place and stead of __34_____, the plaintiff herein, and that the pleadings be deemed amended accordingly and for such other and further relief as to the court may seem just and proper.

Dated __35_____, 19_36_.

_____37_____
[Print signer's name below signature]

[Acknowledgment]

Form 6

Order Substituting Trustee in Bankrupt as Plaintiff

SUPREME COURT, __1_____ COUNTY

[Title of cause]   Order
Index No. __2__

PRESENT: Hon. __3_____, Justice.

A motion by __4_____, trustee in bankruptcy of the estate of __5_____, for his substitution as plaintiff in an action now pending between __6_____, plaintiff and __7_____, defendant in the __8_____ Court of the State of New York, County of __9_____, having duly come on to be heard

NOW, upon reading and filing the order to show cause herein made by Mr. Justice __10_____, and dated the __11__ day of __12_____, 19_13_ and the affidavit of __14_____, trustee in bankruptcy of the estate of __15_____, sworn to the __16__ day of __17_____, 19_18_ in support of this motion and after reading and filing of the opposing affidavit of __19_____, sworn to the __20__ day of __21_____, 19_22_ and upon all the pleadings and proceedings heretofore had herein, and after hearing __23_____, attorney for the moving party in support of this motion and __24_____, attorney for defendant in opposition thereto,

NOW, on motion of __25_____, attorney for the moving party it is

ORDERED that said motion be and the same hereby is in all respects granted, and it is further

ORDERED that __26_____, as trustee in bankruptcy of the estate of __27_____, be and he hereby is substituted as plaintiff in the above-entitled action in the place and stead of __28_____, without prejudice to the proceedings heretofore had in this action and is further

ORDERED that the above-entitled action be continued in the name of __29_____, as trustee in bankruptcy of the estate of __30_____, as plaintiff and that the summons, pleadings and other proceedings heretofore had herein be deemed amended by showing the said __31_____, as trustee in bankruptcy of the estate of __32_____ as the plaintiff therein.

Signed this __33__ day of __34_____, 19_35_ at __36_____, New York.

Enter

_____37_____
[Print signer's name below signature]
Justice, Supreme Court
__38_____ County

§ 1019. Substitution of public officers

If a person made a party in his capacity as public officer dies or otherwise ceases to hold office, the action may be continued by or against his successor if it is shown to the court that there is need for so continuing it. Before a substitution is made his successor and, unless the court otherwise orders, the party shall be given reasonable notice of the motion and accorded an opportunity to object. When, in accordance with section 1023, an officer is described by his official title and his name is not added, no substitution is necessary.

HISTORY:

Add, L 1962, ch 308, eff Sept 1, 1963.
Earlier statutes: CPA §§ 90, 90-a; CCP §§ 766, 766-a; 2 RS 388, § 14; chap 295 of 1832, § 3.

ADVISORY COMMITTEE NOTES:

See CPA § 90. This is basically Federal rule 25(d), omitting the specific time limitation.

FEDERAL ASPECTS:

Substitution of public officers upon death or separation from office, Rule 43(c) of Federal Rules of Appellate Procedure, USCS Court Rules.
Substitution of public officers upon death or removal from office, Rule 25(d) of Federal Rules of Civil Procedure, USCS Court Rules.

RESEARCH REFERENCES AND PRACTICE AIDS:

1 NY Jur, Accountants § 2.
2 Carmody-Wait 2d, Abatement and Survival of Actions §§ 11:36, 11:37.
3 Carmody-Wait 2d, Parties § 19:147.
Carmody-Wait 2d, Proceeding Against a Body or Officer § 145:325.

Law Reviews:

New York Civil Practice Law and Rules: parties. 27 Albany L Rev 182.
Parties and pleading under the CPLR. 31 Brooklyn L Rev 98.

Forms:

See "FORMS" heading following "CASE NOTES", infra.

CASE NOTES

UNDER FORMER CIVIL PRACTICE LAWS

1. Generally
2. Notice

1. Generally

Under chap 47 of 1867, § 3, it was not necessary for the continuance of an action brought by the supervisors of a town, against railroad commissioners, to require them to account for moneys received on sale of stock of the railroad belonging to the town, that the successor of the original plaintiff be substituted. Griggs v Griggs (1874) 56 NY 504.

Under 2 R. S., 447, § 100, it was optional with the parties authorized to apply for substitution, whether they would make such application or not, and until they or the adverse parties applied, the suit was to proceed in the name of the original parties. Manchester v Herrington (1854) 10 NY 164.

An action by a sheriff for conversion of goods levied on does not abate by the death of the sheriff, but by virtue of this section may be continued by his successor in office. Dickinson v Oliver (1906) 112 AD 806, 99 NYS 432.

A proceeding against a municipal officer for the enforcement of a right against the municipality does not abate by the removal or retirement of the officer against whom it was originally instituted, but may be continued against his successor in office, and an appeal therein should be taken only in behalf and in the name of such successor. People ex rel. Walker v Ahearn (1910) 200 NY 146, 93 NE 472.

2. Notice

In an action for an accounting instituted by executors and trustees, nonresident executors of a deceased executor might be brought in and made parties on notice served either personally or by mail. Gould v Gould (1923) 122 Misc 152, 203 NYS 399, affd 211 AD 78, 207 NYS 4.

FORMS

Form 1—Notice of motion for substitution of public officer
Form 2—Affidavit on motion for substitution of public officer
Form 3—Order directing substitution of public officer

Form 1

Notice of Motion for Substitution of Public Officer

SUPREME COURT, __1_____ COUNTY

                   Notice of Motion
[Title of cause]   Index No. __2__ [if assigned]

PLEASE TAKE NOTICE that upon the annexed affidavit of __3_____, sworn to the __4__ day of __5_____, 19_6_, an application will be made at a motion term of this court to be held in and for the County of __7_____ at the County Court House in the City of __8_____ on the __9__ day of __10_____, 19_11_ at __12_____ o'clock in the __13_____ noon of that day or as soon thereafter as counsel can be heard, for an order substituting __14_____ as __15_____ of the County of __16_____ in the place and stead of __17_____, deceased, the plaintiff in this action, and for such other and further relief as to the court may seem just and proper.

Dated __18_____, 19_19_.

                                   __20_____
                                 Attorney for __21_____
                                 Office and P. O. Address
                                 Telephone No.

To: __22_____
       Attorney for Defendant
       Office and P. O. Address

Form 2

Affidavit on Motion for Substitution of Public Officer

SUPREME COURT, __1_____ COUNTY

                   Affidavit
[Title of cause]   Index No. __2__ [if assigned]

STATE OF NEW YORK
COUNTY OF __3_____   ss.:

__4_____, being duly sworn, deposes and says:

1. Deponent is the __5_____ of the County of __6_____ and makes this affidavit in support of his motion for an order directing that he be substituted in the above-entitled action in the place and stead of __7_____, the plaintiff named therein.

2. This action was commenced by the said __8_____ as the __9_____ of the County of __10_____ for the purposes of recovering on the undertaking given by the defendant to the plaintiff, above-named, to insure his faithful performance of a contract dated the __11__ day of __12_____, 19_13_ whereby the defendant agreed to erect a certain building specified in the contract and failed and refused to render the performance required by the said contract [or otherwise state nature of action].

3. This action was commenced by the service of a summons and complaint on the defendant on the __14__ day of __15_____, 19_16_. Thereafter and on or about the __17__ day of __18_____, 19_19_, the defendant filed and served his answer on __20_____, the attorney for the plaintiff. No further proceedings have been had in this action.

4. The said __21_____, the plaintiff above-named, commenced the above-entitled

action as __22_____ of the County of __23_____. On or about the __24__ day of __25_____, 19_26_ the said __27_____ died and the office of the __28_____ of the County of __29_____ was thus vacated.

5. On or about the __30__ day of __31_____, 19_32_, deponent was duly appointed as the __33_____ of the County of __34_____ by __35_____, the Governor of the State of New York. Deponent has duly qualified for the said office and has entered upon the duties of said office and still holds the same.

WHEREFORE, deponent requests that an order be entered substituting deponent as the __36_____ of __37_____ in the above-entitled action in the place and stead of __38_____, deceased, late __39_____ of the County of __40_____ and that said action be continued in the name of deponent and that such other and further relief be granted as to the court may appear just and proper.

__41_____
[Print signer's name below signature]

[Jurat]

Form 3

Order Directing Substitution of Public Officer

SUPREME COURT, __1_____ COUNTY.

[Title of cause]   Order
            Index No. __2__ [if assigned]

PRESENT: Hon. __3_____, Justice.

On reading and filing the affidavit of __4_____, as __5_____ of the County of __6_____, and the notice of motion dated the __7__ day of __8_____, 19_9_ and on reading the pleadings and other proceedings in the above-entitled action and after hearing __10_____, attorney for the said __11_____, in support of this motion and no one having appeared in opposition thereto,

NOW on motion of __12_____, attorney for __13_____, it is

ORDERED that the said motion be and the same hereby is granted and it is further

ORDERED that __14_____, as __15_____ of the County of __16_____, be substituted in this action as the plaintiff in the place and stead of __17_____, late __18_____ of the County of __19_____, now deceased and that a copy of this order be filed in the office of the clerk of the County of __20_____, for the purpose of filing the same with the judgment roll in this action and it is further

ORDERED that this action be continued in the name of the said __21_____, as __22_____ of the County of __23_____ and that the pleadings and proceedings heretofore had be deemed amended accordingly and it is further

ORDERED that a copy of this order with notice of entry thereof be forthwith served upon the defendant or his attorney.

Signed this __24__ day of __25_____, 19_26_ at __27_____, New York.

Enter

__28_____
[Print signer's name below signature]
Justice, Supreme Court
__29_____ County

§ 1020. Substitution of indemnitors for executing or attaching officer

Where an action is brought against an officer to recover a chattel levied upon by virtue of an execution or order of attachment, or to recover damages for the detention or sale of such a chattel, and an undertaking indemnifying the officer against such acts has been given, the court may order that the indemnitor be substituted for the officer.

HISTORY:
Add, L 1962, ch 308, eff Sept 1, 1963.
Earlier statutes: CPA § 699; CCP § 1421.

ADVISORY COMMITTEE NOTES:
This rule replaces CPA §§ 699, 705 and 967. The forerunners of §§ 69–705 were added as new by the authors of the Throop Code to abrogate the case law doctrine that the officer was entitled to maintain the defense of the action himself and the indemnitor's only recourse for improper management of the defense was an action against the sheriff. See CPA § 1421, note (Throop ed 1880). As originally enacted, the forerunner of § 699 required that the court "shall" order the substitution; however, when the word "shall" was changed to "may" in 1900 (NY Laws 1900, c. 115) the need for special statutory treatment of this kind of substitution ceased to exist. See 1 Report of the Board of Statutory Consolidation on the Simplification of the Civil Practice of New York 324 (1915).
The remaining provisions (§§ 700–705), detailing the procedure to be followed in making such substitution, are omitted as unnecessary. Insofar as they prescribe terms and notice requirements, they may be left to the court's discretion; and insofar as they deal with joinder and severance they are simply facets of more general rules. The sentence in § 704 relating to single costs is covered by new CPLR § 82.2. The effect of discontinuance or dismissal, dealt with by the last sentence of § 704, is governed by the ordinary rules of res judicata and new CPLR rule 5013. Cf. CPA § 1090.
Section 967, in the attachment provisions of the CPA, is also omitted as covered by the new rule. It was added by the drafters of the act simply to "recall the practitioner's attention" to sections 699–705, which are by their own terms applicable to attachments. See Report of the Joint Legislative Committee on the Simplification of Civil Practice 486 (1919).

FEDERAL ASPECTS:
Substitution of parties, Rule 25 of Federal Rules of Civil Procedure, USCS Court Rules.

RESEARCH REFERENCES AND PRACTICE AIDS:
3 Carmody-Wait 2d, Parties § 19:147.
9 Carmody-Wait 2d, Enforcement of Money Judgments §§ 64:181 et seq.
11 Carmody-Wait 2d, Attachment § 76:192.

Law Reviews:
New York Civil Practice Law and Rules: parties. 27 Albany L Rev 182.
Parties and pleading under the CPLR. 31 Brooklyn L Rev 98.

Forms:
See "FORMS" heading following "CASE NOTES", infra.

CASE NOTES

UNDER FORMER CIVIL PRACTICE LAWS

1. Generally
2. Constitutionality
3. Prerequisites
4. Motion for substitution
5. Liability of indemnitors
6. Additional security

1. Generally

CPA § 699 was in derogation of the common law and a sheriff should not be allowed to have the executors of deceased indemnitors substituted as defendants in an action brought against him. Buchner v Tamsen (1898) 26 AD 612, 50 NYS 125.

The provisions of CPA §§ 699–705, authorizing

substitution of indemnitors as defendants in place of the sheriff, were innovations in the law, and required a very clear case to be made out before the court would direct such substitution. Berg v Grant, 18 Abb NC 449.

The provisions of CPA §§ 699–703, relating to actions against public officers to recover a chattel levied upon or damages resulting from levies or sales, did not apply to a bond given by a third party claiming title to attached property. Krauss v Merklee (1907) 53 Misc 277, 103 NYS 192.

No substitution can be made when there have been several successful seizures, and there are no facts which indicate, with reasonable certainty, the property seized under the process for which the petitioner became a party to the bond of indemnity. Carter v Bowe (1888) 47 Hun 628.

CPA § 699 entitled a sheriff, against whom an action of replevin had been brought to recover property alleged to have been wrongfully levied upon by him under an execution, to procure the substitution, in his place and stead, of his indemnitors as defendants in the action. Terhune v Dunn (1898) 23 Misc 600, 51 NYS 1122.

The court may make an order of substitution of indemnitors of the sheriff even though successive levies have been made. Corn v Tamsen (1896) 16 Misc 670, 39 NYS 129.

CPA § 699 was mandatory and the indemnitors of the sheriff must be substituted; delay afforded no reason for denying the application. Rosenblum v Gorman (1897) 21 AD 618, 47 NYS 754.

Where a proper case is clearly made out, the court has no discretion to refuse the application of the sheriff, but creditors in whose favor no levy has been made need not be substituted. Cantor v Grant (1889) 10 NYS 223.

On motion to substitute indemnitor in place of sheriff, the latter was not entitled to an allowance by reason of his appearance by counsel, where such counsel was a salaried officer paid by the county. Coddington v Harburger (1912) 77 Misc 211, 137 NYS 536.

2. Constitutionality

CPA §§ 699–703 were constitutional. Hein v Davidson (1884) 96 NY 175.

Mandatory provisions as amended in 1887 were in contravention of the constitution prohibiting the taking of private property without due process of law. Levy v Dunn (1899) 160 NY 504, 55 NE 288.

3. Prerequisites

The moving papers must show that the bond was executed before the commencement of the action against the sheriff. Hayes v Davidson (1885) 98 NY 19; Pool v Ellison (1890) 56 Hun 108, 9 NYS 171.

It is not necessary, in order to authorize the substitution of the parties, that the bond given by the indemnitors should have been given prior to the levy. Hessberg v Riley (1883) 91 NY 377; Hart v Sexton (1895) 11 Misc 446, 32 NYS 222.

4. Motion for substitution

The application is properly made by the indemnitors. Jakobi v Gorman (1892) 1 Misc 222, 21 NYS 466, affd 2 Misc 190, 21 NYS 762.

An application of an executrix of a deceased sheriff to have his indemnitors substituted as defendants, in an action which was brought in the first place against her husband, should be granted even though the application was not made until two years after the death of the sheriff. Ullman v Gorman (1897) 21 AD 616, 47 NYS 756.

Motion by sheriff proper. Isaacs v Cohen (1895) 86 Hun 119, 33 NYS 188.

5. Liability of indemnitors

The provisions giving the indemnitors the right to be substituted as defendants in place of the sheriff in no way vary the rights of the injured party. Dyett v Hyman (1891) 129 NY 351, 29 NE 261.

Where the indemnitors are substituted as parties in place of the sheriff, it is not necessary to prove any cause of action against them, but only to prove the cause of action against the sheriff. Pool v Ellison (1890) 56 Hun 108, 9 NYS 171.

Where parties, after wrongful seizure of property by a sheriff, furnish him with indemnity against liability for his acts in taking, holding and disposing of it, they are as a general rule, liable for the full value of the property so seized. Hayes v Davidson (1884) 34 Hun 243, revd on other grounds 98 NY 19.

An oral notice to the sheriff by the indemnitors not to defend suit for conversion, and thereby incur costs in defending, is nugatory in face of their written bond of indemnity. The defense of the action could not be avoided by the sheriff, and the defendants were properly held liable for the expenses thereof. Grant v Tefft (1890) 29 NYSR 496, 8 NYS 465.

Upon motion for substitution, the plaintiff will not be heard to object that notice of the motion was not served upon the officer who made the levy. Hessberg v Riley (1883) 91 NY 377.

In an action brought to recover for injury suffered by reason of the seizure by the sheriff of certain property alleged to belong to the plaintiff, if the defendant, the sheriff, moves to substitute all his indemnitors as defendants in the action in his place, the court is authorized to divide the action and to limit each action to the part of the property for which each class of indemnitors is responsible. If this is not requested or done, and the substitution made is general and the whole body of indemnitors are treated as responsible for the entire trespass complained of in the original action against the sheriff, they, have chosen to assume that attitude, cannot thereafter be segregated. Issacs v Cohen (1895) 86 Hun 119, 33 NYS 188.

6. Additional security

The requiring of additional security is discretionary with the court ordering the substitution. Hessberg v Riley (1883) 91 NY 377.

CPA § 701 gave the court the right to impose

such terms for the security of either of the original parties. Rosenblum v Gorman (1897) 21 AD 618, 47 NYS 754.

Where an order substituting the indemnitors required them to give security to plaintiff in excess of the amount of his claim, they were liable thereunder. McBride v Tappen (1890) 31 NYSR 477, 10 NYS 137.

Where an application is made by the sheriff for the substitution of indemnitors, he cannot be compelled to furnish additional surety to answer the final result of the litigation. Fleig v Gorman (1892) 1 Misc 194, 20 NYS 615.

FORMS

Form 1—Notice of motion by sheriff to substitute his indemnitors

Form 2—Notice of motion by indemnitors to be substituted for sheriff as defendants

Form 3—Affidavit upon motion for substitution of sheriff's indemnitors as defendants in action for improper execution

Form 4—Affidavit of indemnitor on motion by indemnitors to be substituted for sheriff as defendants

Form 5—Order to show cause why sheriff should not be permitted to substitute indemnitors as defendants

Form 6—Order substituting sheriff's indemnitors as defendants in action for improper execution

Form 7—Clauses in amended complaint by third person against sheriff for wrongful levy on plaintiff's property, as to substitution of sheriff's indemnitors as defendants

Form 8—Clauses in answer where indemnitors substituted as defendants in place of sheriff in action for improper execution

Form 9—Consent of indemnitors to be substituted in place of defendant in action for improper execution

Form 1

Notice of Motion by Sheriff to Substitute His Indemnitors

Notice of Motion

[Title of court and cause]   Index No. __1__ [if assigned]

PLEASE TAKE NOTICE that upon the complaint [or pleadings] in this action [and the affidavit of __2_____ sworn to the __3__ day of __4_____], a motion will be made at a motion term of this court to be held in and for the county of __5___ , at the county courthouse in the city of __6_____ on the __7__ day of __8_____ at __9_____ o'clock in the forenoon of that day or as soon thereafter as counsel can be heard for an order substituting __10_____ and __11_____, indemnitors on a certain undertaking given for the purpose of __12_____ [specify] in the place and stead of __13_____, sheriff of the county of __14_____ as defendants in the above-entitled action, and for such other and further relief as may be just.

Dated __15_____.

                                  __16_____

                                  Attorney for Defendant

                  [Office and Post-Office Address, etc.]

                                    Telephone No.

To __17_____ [indemnitors or their attorney, and attorney for the plaintiff].

Form 2

Notice of Motion by Indemnitors to be Substituted for Sheriff as Defendants

Notice of Motion

[Title of court and cause]   Index No. __1__ [if assigned]

PLEASE TAKE NOTICE that upon the complaint (or pleadings) in action (and the affidavit of __2_____ sworn to the __3__ day of __4_____), a motion will be made at a motion term of this court to be held in and for the county of __5_____, at the county courthouse in the city of __6_____ on the __7__ day of __8_____ at __9_____ o'clock in the forenoon of that day or as soon thereafter as counsel can be heard for an order substituting __10_____ and __11_____, indemnitors on a certain undertaking given for the purpose of __12_____ [specify] in the place and stead of __13_____, sheriff of the county of __14_____ as defendants in the above-entitled action, and for such other and further relief as may be just.

Dated __15_____.

__16_____

(Attorney for Indemnitors)
Office and Post-Office Address, etc.
Telephone No.

To __17_____ [The attorney for each party in the action, and if the defendant has not appeared, to him personally.]

Form 3

Affidavit Upon Motion for Substitution of Sheriff's Indemnitors as Defendants in Action for Improper Execution

Affidavit
[Title of court and cause]   Index No. __1__ [if assigned]

State of New York
County of __2_____   ss.

__3_____, being duly sworn, deposes and says that on the __4__ day of __5_____, 19_6_, an action was commenced in the Supreme Court, County of __7_____, herein __8_____ was plaintiff, and __9_____ was defendant; that deponent was the attorney for the plaintiff in said action, and on the __10__ day of __11_____, 19_12_, an attachment was duly issued in said action to the sheriff, duly levied on property in the possession of said __13_____ under and by virtue of said attachment; that __14_____, the plaintiff in the above-entitled action claimed said property, and that thereupon __15_____ and __16_____, duly executed and delivered in behalf of the plaintiff in said action a bond to said sheriff to indemnify him for any loss he may sustain by reason of the levy under said attachment as aforesaid; that __17_____, the plaintiff in the above-entitled action, having sued __18_____, the sheriff because of said levy, the said indemnitors do pray this court that an order be made and entered substituting the said __19_____ and __20_____ as defendants in the above-entitled action, in the place and stead of the above-named __21_____, sheriff; that no previous application for this or a similar order has been made herein.

[Signature of deponent]
[Print signer's name below signature]

[Jurat]

[Adapted from the records in Hessberg v Riley, 91 NY 377; and Levy v Dunn, 160 NY 504, 55 NE 288, 73 Am St Rep 699.]

Form 4

Affidavit of Indemnitor on Motion by Indemnitors to be Substituted for Sheriff as Defendants

Affidavit
[Title of action against sheriff]   Index No. __1__ [if assigned]

[Venue of affidavit]

__2_____, being duly sworn deposes and says:

1. That he is one of the sureties on the undertaking hereinafter mentioned.

2. That on or about the __3__ day of __4_____ a judgment was duly recovered in the __5_____ court of __6_____ County in an action wherein __7___ was plaintiff and __8__ was defendant in favor of the said plaintiff, and against the said defendant for the sum of __9_____ dollars, which judgment was thereafter and on or about the __10__ day of __11_____ duly filed and docketed in the office of the clerk of the county of __12_____.

3. That thereafter and on or about the __13__ day of __14_____ an execution against the property of __15_____, such judgment debtor was duly issued to the sheriff of the county of __16_____ wherein the said judgment debtor then resided and still resides.

4. That thereafter and on or about the __17__ day of __18_____ acting pursuant to and under the said execution, the said sheriff of the county of __19_____ duly levied upon the following described property, to wit: __20_____ [describe property].

5. That thereafter and on or about the __21__ day of __22_____ one __23_____ duly served upon the said sheriff of the county of __24_____ and upon the judgment creditor, __25_____, a notice of petition pursuant to the provision of § 5238 of the Civil Practice Law and Rules, claiming to be the owner of the said property so levied upon.

6. That thereafter and on or about the __26__ day of __27_____, 19_28_, the said sheriff of the county of __29_____ served upon __30_____, the attorney for the plaintiff in the above-entitled action a notice that he, the said sheriff, required indemnity against the said claim.

7. That thereafter and on or about the __31__ day of __32_____, __33_____, the judgment creditor above mentioned, duly gave to the said sheriff of the county of __34_____ an undertaking with two sureties to the effect that the sureties would indemnify the said sheriff of the county of __35_____ to the amount of __36_____ dollars, that being a sum not less than twice the claimed value of the said property and damages if any over and above that value, against all damages, costs and expenses in an action to be brought against him by any person, by the claimant, his assignee or any representative by reason of the levy upon, detention or sale of any of the property by virtue of the execution.

8. That deponent and __37_____ were the sureties upon such undertaking.

9. That such sureties justified according to law and the said bond was duly filed and served upon the adverse party pursuant to the provision of § 2505 of the Civil Practice Law and Rules.

10. That on or about the __38__ day of __39_____ , __40_____, the claimant above mentioned, duly commenced in the __41_____ court of __42_____ County an action against the sheriff of the county of __43_____ to recover the property above specified so levied upon and for damages by reason of the levy, detention and sale, a copy of the complaint in which action is hereto annexed and made a part of this affidavit.

11. That no previous application has been made for the relief sought herein.

WHEREFORE, deponent asks that an order be granted substituting him and the said __44_____, as defendants in the foregoing action in the place and stead of __45_____, sheriff of the county of __46_____.

__47_____
[Signature of Surety]
[Print signer's name below signature]

[Jurat]

Form 5

Order to Show Cause Why Sheriff Should Not Be Permitted to Substitute Indemnitors as Defendants

SUPREME COURT, __1_____ COUNTY.

[Title of cause]
　　　　　　　　　　　Order to Show Cause
　　　　　　　　　　　Index No. __2__ [if assigned]

Present: Hon. __3_____, Justice.

Upon reading and filing the annexed affidavits of __4_____ and __5_____, both sworn on the __6__ day of __7_____, 19_8_, and the bonds or undertakings of indemnity mentioned and described in said affidavits, and the approval of said bonds thereon indorsed, and the complaint herein.

Let the above-mentioned plaintiff or his attorneys, and the __9_____, the indemnitors mentioned and described in said affidavit or their attorney, show cause before one of the justices of this court, at a motion term to be held at [Part __10__ thereof] in the county courthouse in the County of __11_____, on the __12__ day of __13_____, 19_14_, at __15_____ o'clock in the __16_____ noon of that day, or as soon thereafter as counsel can be heard, why the said __17_____ and __18_____ should not be substituted as defendants in the above-entitled action, in the place and stead of __19_____, the above-named defendant, and the above-named defendant released from all further liability herein, and why the said __20_____ should not pay to __21_____, attorney for said defendant, the sum of fees and expenses herein, and why the summons and complaint herein should not be amended by striking out the name of __23_____, as sheriff of the County of __24_____, in the title thereof, and substituting in lieu and place thereof, the __25_____, and a copy of the complaint amended as aforesaid and in such further particulars as may be necessary by the changed condition of this action, be served upon the said __26_____, and it have leave to serve its answer thereto, or why the defendant should not have such other, further or different relief in the premises as to the court may seem just and proper.

Sufficient reason appearing therefor, let service of a copy of this order and the annexed affidavit upon the plaintiff or his attorneys, and upon said __27_____, on or before the __28__ day of __29_____, 19_30_, be sufficient and timely service.

Signed this __31__ day of __32_____, 19_33_ at __34_____, New York.

　　　　　　　　　　　　　　　　　　__35_____
　　　　　　　　　　　　　　[Print signer's name below signature]
　　　　　　　　　　　　　　　　　　Justice, Supreme Court
　　　　　　　　　　　　　　　　　　__36_____ County

Form 6

Order Substituting Sheriff's Indemnitors as Defendants in Action for Improper Execution

SUPREME COURT, __1_____ COUNTY.

[Title of cause]
　　　　　　　　　　　Order
　　　　　　　　　　　Index No. __2__ [if assigned]

Present: Hon. __3_____, Justice.

The motion on the order to show cause dated the __4__ day of __5_____, 19_6_, why __7_____, the indemnitor on the bond given to the defendant above-named, should not be substituted as defendant in the place and stead of __8_____, the defendant above-named, coming on to be heard and after reading and filing said order to show cause and the affidavit of __9_____ and the consent of __10_____ to such substitution, and the affidavit of __11_____; and after hearing __12_____, attorney for indemnitor, in favor thereof, and the indemnitor having executed the stipulation required by the decision herein and the same having been served on the plaintiff's attorney, it is on motion of __13_____, attorney for __14_____, indemnitor.

ORDERED that said motion be and the same is hereby granted and that __15_____ be, and he is hereby substituted as defendant in this action in the place and stead of __16_____, defendant above-named, and that the summons and complaint herein be amended by substituting the names of the said __17_____ as defendant herein in the place and stead of __18_____, and that the said defendants have __19_ days after the service of the amended summons, and complaint on __20_____, their attorney, to serve their answer thereto.

Signed this __21_ day of __22_____, 19_23_ at __24_____, New York.

Enter

_25_____
[Print signer's name below signature]
Justice, Supreme Court
__26_____ County

[Adapted from the records in Hessberg v Riley, 91 NY 377; and Hein v Davidson, 96 NY 175.]

Form 7

Clauses in Amended Complaint by Third Person Against Sheriff for Wrongful Levy on Plaintiff's Property, as to Substitution of Sheriff's Indemnitors as Defendants

[Paragraphs 1–4 substantially as in form 4 above]

5. That thereafter and on or about the __1_ day of __2_____, 19_3_, this action was duly instituted in this court by the above-named plaintiff against said __4_____, sheriff of the County of __5_____, as defendant, for the recovery of the sum of __6_____ Dollars, damages suffered and sustained by plaintiff by reason of said unlawful taking and detention by said __7_____, of said chattels as aforesaid.

6. That thereafter proceedings were instituted by said __8_____ in the said action for the substitution in his place and stead as defendant in the action of __9_____, of __10_____, his indemnitors, as defendants herein, due notice of which application was given to the said __11_____ and to all other parties interested therein, which proceedings resulted in the entry of an order in said action at a motion term of this Court on the __12_ day of __13_____, 19_14_, directing the substitution of said __15_____, as defendants herein, in lieu and place of said __16_____, and directing the amendment of the summons and complaint in said action against said __17_____ by the substitution of the names of __18_____ for the name of said __19_____ as sheriff aforesaid and in such further particulars as may be necessary because of the changed condition of said action.

[From the records in Columbia Bank v American Surety Co. 178 NY 628, 71 NE 1129, affg without opinion 84 AD 487, 82 NYS 1054, in which a judgment for plaintiff was affirmed.]

Form 8

Clauses in Answer Where Indemnitors Substituted as Defendants in Place of Sheriff in Action for Improper Execution

[Title of court and cause]

The defendants, __1_____, __2_____, and __3_____, for their answer to the complaint herein, alleged:

1. That this action was originally begun against __4_____, as sheriff of the County of __5_____; that after the commencement of this action the said __6_____, the then defendant herein, made a motion in this court to procure the substitution of the present defendants in his place and stead, as his indemnitors, pursuant to section 1020 of the

Civil Practice Law and Rules, and thereupon such proceedings were duly had; that on or about the __7__ day of __8_____, 19_9_, an order was duly made and entered herein, wherein and whereby __10_____ and __11_____ were substituted as defendants in this action in the place and stead of said __12_____ as sheriff of the County of __13_____. [Continue to set forth usual allegations in defense.]

[Adapted from the records in Rogers v Pell, 47 App Div 240, 62 NYS 92, affd 168 NY 587, 60 NE 1112 mem dec.]

Form 9

Consent of Indemnitors to be Substituted in Place of Defendant in Action for Improper Execution

Consent of Indemnitors to Substitution

[Title of court and cause]   Index No. __1__ [if assigned]

I, __2_____, one of the sureties on the bond of indemnity given to __3_____, as sheriff of the County of __4_____, in a certain action, in which __5_____ was plaintiff and __6_____ was defendant, do hereby consent to be made a defendant in this action in the place and stead of __7_____, the defendant above named.

[Date]

__8_____

[Print signer's name below signature]

[Acknowledge or prove and certify in like manner as a deed to be recorded.]

[Adapted from the records in Hessberg v Riley, 91 NY 377.]

§ 1021. Substitution procedure; dismissal for failure to substitute; presentation of appeal

A motion for substitution may be made by the successors or representatives of a party or by any party. If a person who should be substituted does not appear voluntarily he may be made a party defendant. If the event requiring substitution occurs before final judgment and substitution is not made within a reasonable time, the action may be dismissed as to the party for whom substitution should have been made, however, such dismissal shall not be on the merits unless the court shall so indicate. If the event requiring substitution occurs after final judgment, substitution may be made in either the court from or to which an appeal could be or is taken, or the court of original instance, and if substitution is not made within four months after the event requiring substitution, the court to which the appeal is or could be taken may dismiss the appeal, impose conditions or prevent it from being taken. Whether or not it occurs before or after final judgment, if the event requiring substitution is the death of a party, and timely substitution has not been made, the court, before proceeding further, shall, on such notice as it may in its discretion direct, order the persons interested in the decedent's estate to show cause why the action or appeal should not be dismissed.

HISTORY:

Add, L 1962, ch 308, amd, L 1970, ch 93, L 1975, ch 25, eff Mar 25, 1975.
Earlier statutes: CPA §§ 84, 578, 579; CCP §§ 757, 1298, 1299; Code Proc § 121.

ADVISORY COMMITTEE NOTES:

This section applies to all cases of substitution. With the first two sentences, compare Federal rule 25(a). See also CPA §§ 84, 87, 192, 557, 578, 579.

Dismissal as to the sole party on one side would be equivalent to dismissal of the entire action.

CROSS REFERENCES:

This section referred to in 1022, 5016.

FEDERAL ASPECTS:

Substitution of parties, Rule 25 of Federal Rules of Civil Procedure, USCS Court Rules.

RESEARCH REFERENCES AND PRACTICE AIDS:

2 Carmody-Wait 2d, Abatement and Survival of Actions § 11:6.
3 Carmody-Wait 2d, Parties §§ 19:148, 19:150, 19:151, 19:162.
3 Carmody-Wait 2d, Extensions and Abridgements of Time § 21:3.
9 Carmody-Wait 2d, Enforcement of Money Judgments § 64:182.

Law Reviews:

New York Civil Practice Law and Rules: parties. 27 Albany L Rev 182.
Parties and pleading under the CPLR. 31 Brooklyn L Rev 98.
A biannual survey of New York practice: Part IV: nominal corporate defendant allowed substitution as plaintiff despite lack of express sanction in Article 10. 39 St. John's L Rev 431.

Forms:

See "FORMS" heading following "CASE NOTES", infra.

CASE NOTES

CPLR 1021 appears specifically to authorize the dismissal of a case against a plaintiff who has died but for whom substitution has not been made "within a reasonable time." De Rijdt v Robert Straile Co. (1968) 58 Misc 2d 543, 296 NYS2d 601.

Where it appeared that plaintiff had died more than two years prior to settlement of action and that order to show cause why settlement should not be vacated and complaint dismissed had been served upon person alleged to be daughter and sole distributee of plaintiff, as well as upon attorneys for deceased plaintiff, and no affidavit was interposed in opposition to such motion, court had no alternative but to vacate settlement and dismiss action, but if representative was appointed, such representative could then move to vacate such judgment. Flumenbaum v Hartman (1974) 79 Misc 2d 544, 360 NYS2d 394.

Where all proceedings were as matter of law stayed upon death of defendant executrix until entry of order of substitution, note of issue and statement of readiness, filed after death and prior to order of substitution, were invalid, and did not preclude previously scheduled examinations before trial from proceeding. Braynard v Morgan (1975) 50 AD2d 810, 376 NYS2d 575.

Notice of motion to continue action against deceased defendant's representative must be served on such representative, and not on the attorney for the deceased defendant, his authority to act as such attorney having terminated with the death. Lewis v Lewis (1964) 43 Misc 2d 349, 250 NYS2d 984.

Where during interim between service of notice of appeal and the submission thereof plaintiff-appellant dies, in the absence of the substitution of his executor or administrator, the court may not proceed to a determination of the appeal on the merits, but will hold the appeal in abeyance for ninety days to effect such substitution, and if it is not done, the appeal will be dismissed. Price v Booth (1964) 21 AD2d 680, 249 NYS2d 1007.

Where both defendants, who appealed from orders denying motion to dismiss certain causes of action, appeared by same attorney and one record on appeal had been filed, appeals were to be held in abeyance for period of four months on death of one defendant; however, if a personal representative should not have been appointed and substituted for deceased within four months, application could be made to dismiss appeals. Gutwein v Ungar Management, Inc. (1974) 44 AD2d 800, 355 NYS2d 392, supp op 46 AD2d 636, 360 NYS2d 254.

An order of substitution pursuant to CPLR 1015[a] and 1021 is effected within the discretion of the court. Rosenfeld v Hotel Corp. of America (1967) 20 NY2d 25, 281 NYS2d 308, 228 NE2d 374.

NOTES OF DECISIONS UNDER SCA § 1021

Where but one executor appealed and died pending same, the other was properly substituted. Re Jackson's Will (1930) 231 AD 17, 246 NYS 14.

CASE NOTES

UNDER FORMER CIVIL PRACTICE LAWS

1. Generally
2. Procedure
3. Necessity for supplemental complaint
4. Laches

1. Generally

Where a defendant dies after a judgment and during the pendency of an appeal, the appeal cannot be heard until a substitution has been made in place of the deceased defendant. Proceedings had on the appeal without such substitution are null and without effect. Bronheim v Kelleher (1940) 258 AD 972, 16 NYS2d 898.

Special term of supreme court is proper forum to which to apply for substitution of new president of labor union whose former president was removed from office, where appeal from judgment against labor union is pending in appellate division. Schwartz v Seamon (1942) 178 Misc 260, 33 NYS2d 567.

2. Procedure

Where the cause of action did not survive against the other defendants but did against the representatives of the deceased, the proper remedy was to bring them in by supplemental summons, it could not be done by motion. CPA §§ 84 to 87 and §§ 407, 1015(a)(b), and 1021 herein did not provide for such a case. Mackey v Duryea (1889) 22 Abb NC 284, 6 NYS 573.

Under CPA § 84 notice of application to continue action against representative of deceased defendant had to be given to person to be substituted. Clancy v Bernstein (1946) 66 NYS2d 52.

Under CPA § 84 the objection that the cause of action did not survive might be raised at the trial. Arthur v Griswold, 60 NY 143; so also that the representatives of deceased parties have not been brought in. Hasbrouck v Bunce (1875) 62 NY 475.

Under CPA, on a motion to revive an action upon the affidavits of an attorney, he had to show his authority to make the motion, and on such motion, the complaint had to be made part of the moving papers, or the nature of the action clearly shown. Robinson v Thomas (1908) 123 AD 411, 107 NYS 1110.

Under CPA, where claimant against state for damages for personal injuries from improper medical treatment while state prison inmate, had died during pendency of claim, and where six months had elapsed without service of order of substitution on attorney general, court might dismiss only where motion to dismiss had been made on such notice to assignee or successor of claimant as court might require. Cawthorn v State (1954) 205 Misc 234, 127 NYS2d 353.

3. Necessity for supplemental complaint

Under CPA § 84 party interested might be substituted without first filing a supplemental complaint. Garvey v Owens (1889) 9 NYSR 227, affd (1889) 115 NY 671, 22 NE 1127.

4. Laches

Under CPA §§ 82 (§§ 105(b), 1015(b), 1018 herein) and 84 the courts were given discretionary power in determining whether or not relief should be accorded where there was laches. Crowley v Murphy (1898) 33 AD 456, 54 NYS 54.

Under CPA, no mere lapse of time absolutely defeated an application for the continuance of an action at law in the name of the representative of a deceased party. Evans v Cleveland (1878) 72 NY 486; Lehman v Koch (1890) 30 NYSR 224, 9 NYS 302.

A motion to revive proceedings to vacate an assessment in the name of an administrator of a deceased petitioner, made eleven years after death of petitioner, was denied, Re Fitzpatrick, 25 NYSR 628, 6 NYS 195; this is so where there was a delay of twelve years. Re Wendell, 27 NYSR 536, 6 NYS 195.

Where there was great laches, under CPA §§ 82–85 the court might deny the application; the right to a continuance was not so absolute as to preclude the court from denying it. Lyon v Park (1888) 111 NY 350, 18 NE 863.

CPA § 84 did not mean that the granting of the motion to continue the action was compulsory in all cases. Long delay will justify a refusal to continue the action. Re Palmer (1889) 115 NY 493, 22 NE 221; Duffy v Duffy (1889) 56 Super Ct (24 Jones & S) 593, 4 NYS 533; and see Beach v Reynolds (1873) 53 NY 1; Coit v Campbell, 82 NY 509; Hayes v Nourse (1889) 114 NY 595, 22 NE 40.

Where delay has occurred, under CPA § 84 the court's discretion to refuse relief is to be guided by the statute of limitations applicable to the case. Coit v Campbell (1880) 82 NY 509.

Under CPA § 84 an executor of a deceased party, the sole plaintiff in an action of foreclosure was entitled to order of continuance even though there had been delay in making application where there was no proof that defendant's defense had been prejudiced. Van Brocklin v Van Brocklin (1897) 17 AD 226, 45 NYS 541.

Six-year delay before substitution of administrator following decedent's death warranted dismissal for lack of prosecution, absent a showing of merits even though both parties shared responsibility for the delay, since defendant could have applied for the substitution under CPA § 84. Ruderman v Feffer (1960) 10 AD2d 704, 198 NYS2d 130 (plaintiff was given leave to vacate dismissal on a proper affidavit of merits).

FORMS

Form 1—Notice of motion for substitution of representative upon death of party pending appeal

Form 2—Affidavit on motion to substitute representative upon death of party pending appeal

Form 3—Orders substituting representative upon death of party pending appeal

Form 4—Affidavit for order to show cause for dismissal or reversal on failure to apply for substitution on death of party

Form 5—Order to show cause for dismissal or reversal on failure to apply for substitution on death of party

Form 6—Order for dismissal or reversal on failure to apply for substitution on death of party

Form 1

Notice of Motion for Substitution of Representative Upon Death of Party Pending Appeal

Notice of Motion

[Title of court and cause]   Index No. __1__

PLEASE TAKE NOTICE, that upon the annexed affidavit of __2_____ sworn to the __3__ day of __4_____, 19_5_, and upon the pleadings and all proceedings heretofore had herein, the undersigned will move this court at a motion term [Part __6__] thereof, to be held in the county court house [Borough of __7_____] City of __8_____, on the __9__ day of __10_____, 19_11_, at __12__ o'clock in the __13_____ noon of that day, or as soon thereafter as counsel can be heard, for an order permitting __14_____, the executor [or administrator] of the estate of __15_____, to be substituted as a party plaintiff in the place of __16_____, deceased, and for such other and further relief as to the court may seem just and proper.

[Date]

__17_____

Attorney for Plaintiff
Address __18_____
Telephone No. __19__

To __20_____, Esq.,
     Attorney for Defendant
     Address __21_____

Form 2

Affidavit on Motion to Substitute Representative Upon Death of Party Pending Appeal

Affidavit

[Title of court and cause]   Index No. __1__

State of New York
County of __2_____   ss.

__3_____, being duly sworn, says:

1. That he is __4_____.

2. That on the __5__ day of __6_____, 19_7_, a judgment was rendered in the

above-entitled action by the __8_____ court, in favor of __9_____, against __10_____, for __11_____, which judgment was entered in the county clerk's office on the __12__ day of __13_____, 19_14_.

3. That after the rendition and entry of the said judgment, and on the __15__ day of __16_____, 19_17_, the said __18_____ died intestate [or died "leaving a last will and testament"].

4. That __19_____ was appointed administrator of the property of __20_____, on the __21__ day of __22_____, 19_23_, by the surrogate of __24_____ County, in which county the said __25_____ resided at the time of his death and that he duly qualified as such. [Or as follows: "4. That said will was admitted to probate on the __26__ day of __27_____, 19_28_, by the surrogate of __29_____ County, in which county the said __30_____ resided at the time of his death" and that __31_____ was approved as executor and thereafter accepted such appointment and qualified as such.]

5. That said __32_____ appealed from said judgment to the __33_____ court, on the __34__ day of __35_____, 19_36_.

> [Signature of deponent]
> [Print signer's name below signature]

[Jurat]

Form 3

Order Substituting Representative Upon Death of Party Pending Appeal

SUPREME COURT, __1_____ COUNTY.

	Order
[Title of cause]	Index No. __2__

Present: Hon. __3_____, Justice

On reading and filing the affidavit of __4_____, dated the __5__ day of __6_____, 19_7_, by which it appears that __8_____; and on reading and filing notice of this motion, with proof of due service thereof on __9_____; and on reading and filing [name opposing papers, if any]; and after hearing __10_____, Esq., of counsel for __11_____, in support of the motion, and __12_____, Esq., of counsel for __13_____, in opposition thereto:

NOW, on motion of __14_____, Esq., it is

ORDERED that said __15_____ [describe person substituted] be and hereby is substituted as respondent in the place of said __16_____, as the respondent in the said appeal brought by said __17_____ from the said judgment.

Signed this __18__ day of __19_____, 19_20_ at __21_____, New York.

Enter

> __22_____
> [Print signer's name below signature]
> Justice, Supreme Court
> __23_____ County

Form 4

Affidavit for Order to Show Cause for Dismissal or Reversal on Failure to Apply for Substitution on Death of Party

	Affidavit
[Title of Appellate Divison and cause]	Index No. __1__

State of New York
County of __2_____　　　　　　　　ss.

__3_____, being duly sworn, says:

1. That he is ___4_____.

2. That on the __5__ day of __6_____, 19_7_, an appeal was taken by __8_____ from judgment of the __9_____ court, entered in the above-entitled action on the __10__ day of __11_____, 19_12_, for __13_____, in favor of __14_____ against __15_____.

3. That said __16_____, the appellant [or "respondent"] died on the __17__ day of __18_____, 19_19_, before any hearing had been had of said appeal.

4. That the following are all the persons interested in the estate of said __20_____, so far as can be ascertained by deponent, to wit: __21_____; that the inquiries made to ascertain who are the persons interested in said estate are as follows: __22_____.

5. That no order has been made substituting any other person in the place of __23_____ in said appeal although more than four months have elapsed since the death of decedent.

6. That no previous application has been made for this or a similar order.

[Signature of deponent]
[Print signer's name below signature]

[Jurat]

Form 5

Order to Show Cause for Dismissal or Reversal on Failure to Apply for Substitution on Death of Party

Order To Show Cause
[Title of Appellate Division and cause]   Index No. __1__

PRESENT: Hon. __2_____, Presiding Justice
           Hon. __3_____,
           Hon. __4_____, Associate Justices
           Hon. __5_____,
           Hon. __6_____,

On reading and filing the affidavit of __7_____, dated the __8__ day of __9_____, 19_10_, showing [state, in substance, contents of affidavit as to taking of appeal, death of party pending appeal, and the failure to obtain an order of substitution within three months].

IT IS HEREBY ORDERED that all persons interested in the estate of said __11_____ show cause before this court, at a term thereof, to be held at __12_____, on the __13__ day of __14_____, 19_15_, [a day not less than six months after making this order] why the said judgment or order should not be affirmed or reversed, or why the appeal from the said judgment or order should not be dismissed on the ground that said __16_____, appellant, is now deceased, and no successor or legal representative has been substituted in his place within four months of the death of said appellant and why such other and further relief as may be just should not be granted.

AND IT IS FURTHER ORDERED that a copy of this order and a copy of said affidavit be served on [name all persons interested] by [designate mode of giving notice] on or before the __17__ day of __18_____, 19_19_.

Signed this __20__ day of __21_____, 19_22_ at __23_____, New York.

___24_____
[Print signer's name below signature]
P. J.

573

Form 6

Order for Dismissal or Reversal on Failure to Apply for Substitution on Death of Party

[Title of Appellate Division]

                                            Order
[Title of Cause]   Index No. __1__

PRESENT: Hon. [Presiding justice and associate justices].

An order having been heretofore made and entered in this action on the affidavit of __2_____, sworn to the __3__ day of __4_____, 19_5_, at a special term of this court, held at __6_____ on the __7__ day of __8_____, 19_9_, that all persons interested in the estate of __10_____ show cause at this term why the judgment [or order] entered in this action on __11_____, 19_12_, should not be affirmed [or "reversed" or "appeal dismissed"]; and on reading [name opposing papers, if any]; and on proof by the affidavit of __13_____ of service on the __14__ day of __15_____, 19_16_, of said order to show cause on or before the __17__ day of __18_____, 19_19_ [or otherwise state time], as prescribed in said order and the affidavits upon which said order was founded; and on motion of __20_____, attorney for __21_____, and after hearing __22_____, attorney for __23_____, in opposition thereto: it is hereby

ORDERED that the said judgment [or order] be, and the same hereby is, affirmed [or "reversed" or that "the appeal from said judgment or order be and the same hereby is dismissed"].

Signed this __24__ day of __25_____, 19_26_ at __27_____, New York.

Enter.

                                    _____28_____
                                    [Print signer's name below signature]
                                                                    P. J.

§ 1022. Substitution: extension of time for taking procedural steps

Unless the court orders otherwise, if the time for making a motion for a new trial or for taking an appeal or for making a motion for permission to appeal or for taking any other procedural step in the action has not expired before the occurrence of an event permitting substitution of a party, the period is extended as to all parties until fifteen days after substitution is made, or, in case of dismissal of the action under section 1021, is extended as to all parties until fifteen days after such dismissal.

HISTORY:

Add, L 1962, ch 308, eff Sept 1, 1963.
Earlier statutes: CPA § 99; CCP § 784, in part; § 785; Code Proc § 405.

ADVISORY COMMITTEE NOTES:

See CPA § 99. This section deals with the tolling of procedural limitations (not the statute of limitations), until there is an opportunity for substitution. It recognizes that time will be necessary for qualification of successors. Furthermore, the rule covers both the situation where the successor will be the moving party and that in which the other parties take the initiative. Whoever would be prejudiced by failure to substitute must take the laboring oar or run the risk of a dismissal under § 1021. The court has been given discretion to limit the extension of time for taking action. This will permit the court to prevent unnecessary delays.

CROSS REFERENCES:

This section referred to in 5514.

FEDERAL ASPECTS:

Substitution of parties, Rule 25 of Federal Rules of Civil Procedure, USCS Court Rules.

RESEARCH REFERENCES AND PRACTICE AIDS:

3 Carmody-Wait 2d, Parties § 19:150.

3 Carmody-Wait 2d, Extensions and Abridgements of Time § 21:3.

9 Carmody-Wait 2d, Judgments § 63:181.

10 Carmody-Wait 2d, Appeals in General § 70:125.

21 Carmody-Wait 2d, Litigation By and Against Fiduciaries § 129:82.

25 Carmody-Wait 2d, Fundamentals of Practice in the Surrogate's Court § 149:387.

Law Reviews:

New York Civil Practice Law and Rules: parties. 27 Albany L Rev 182.

Parties and pleading under the CPLR. 31 Brooklyn L Rev 98.

CASE NOTES

UNDER FORMER CIVIL PRACTICE LAWS

Except where party entitled to appeal dies, court is powerless to extend time for taking an appeal. Warner v Dunlap (1921) 196 AD 41, 187 NYS 374.

Under CPA § 99 both order for leave to appeal had to be entered and notice of appeal following the order had to be served within four months of death of party. Warner v Dunlap (1921) 196 AD 41, 187 NYS 374.

Where appellant died and notice of appeal was issued and served in his name before his executrix was substituted in his place as party, but permission to appeal pursuant to CPA § 99 was never granted, such service of notice of appeal was nullity. Hoberman v O'Connell (1953) 282 AD 762, 122 NYS2d 714.

NOTES OF DECISIONS UNDER SCA § 291

1. Order of substitution.

Failure to procure order of substitution. Re Lie-berman (1933) 238 AD 305, 264 NYS 303, app dismd 262 NY 678, 188 NE 117.

§ 1023. Public body or officer described by official title

When a public officer, body, board, commission or other public agency may sue or be sued in its official capacity, it may be designated by its official title, subject to the power of the court to require names to be added.

HISTORY:

Add, L 1962, ch 308, eff Sept 1, 1963.

Earlier statutes: CPA § 213.

ADVISORY COMMITTEE NOTES:

This section is a restatement of former law with no substantial change. See CPA § 213.

CROSS REFERENCES:

This section referred to in 1019.

Authority of public officials to bring and defend actions, Bank Law §§ 205, 619, 631, 632.

Actions by and against counties, County Law § 51.

Parties to lien actions, Lien Law §§ 41–44-a.

Leave to sue on bond of public officer, Pub O Law §§ 20–24.

Parties to action by Public Service Commission, Pub Ser Law §§ 74, 87, 102, 103.

A town as party, Town Law § 65.

Substitution on consolidation of villages, Vill Law § 18-1810.

FEDERAL ASPECTS:

United States as a party, 28 USCS §§ 2401 et seq.

RESEARCH REFERENCES AND PRACTICE AIDS:

23 Carmody-Wait 2d, Actions By and Against Public Bodies and Public Officers § 144:3.

24 Carmody-Wait 2d, Judicial Review of Tax Assessments and Taxes § 146:139.

Law Reviews:

New York Civil Practice Law and Rules: parties. 27 Albany L Rev 182.

Parties and pleading under the CPLR. 31 Brooklyn L Rev 98.

CASE NOTES

The statutory provision is expressly designed to encourage the use of the official title without any mention of the officer individually. Travel House of Buffalo, Inc. v Grzechowiak (1968) 31 AD2d 74, 296 NYS2d 689, affd 24 NY2d 1034, 303 NYS2d 79, 250 NE2d 355.

CASE NOTES

UNDER FORMER CIVIL PRACTICE LAWS

CPA § 213 construed with CPA § 1386 (now Real Prop Actions & Proc Law 1711) in holding that public officers were declared to be continuously in office so that actions and proceedings might be maintained against them in their official, not individual, capacities. Heslin v Schechter (1956) 3 Misc 2d 42, 148 NYS2d 625.

§ 1024. Unknown parties

A party who is ignorant, in whole or in part, of the name or identity of a person who may properly be made a party, may proceed against such person as an unknown party by designating so much of his name and identity as is known. If the name or remainder of the name becomes known all subsequent proceedings shall be taken under the true name and all prior proceedings shall be deemed amended accordingly.

HISTORY:

Add, L 1962, ch 308, eff Sept 1, 1963.

Earlier statutes: CPA § 215; CCP § 451.

ADVISORY COMMITTEE NOTES:

The chief occasion for proceeding against unknown parties is in connection with unknown heirs of deceased owners of land, and service on them is typically by publication. This section is suggested by § 215 of the CPA and New Jersey rule 4:30-4. Cf. NY Civ Prac Act §§ 232-a(6), 1036, 1055, 1064–69, 1073. To take care of possible counterclaim situations "party" is used instead of "defendant" in the title and the body of the statute. The provision of § 215 for a fictitious name is eliminated. There is no general provision in the Federal rules for unknown parties. Cf. Fed R Civ P 25(c). Several of the states which have followed the Federal rules likewise have no general provision for unknown parties.

RESEARCH REFERENCES AND PRACTICE AIDS:

3 Carmody-Wait 2d, Parties § 19:9.

14 Carmody-Wait 2d, Partition § 91:50.

22 Carmody-Wait 2d, Proceeding Relating to Express Trusts § 131:4.

25 Carmody-Wait 2d, Fundamentals of Practice in the Surrogate's Court § 149:121.

Law Reviews:
New York Civil Practice Law and Rules: parties. 27 Albany L Rev 182.
Parties and pleading under the CPLR. 31 Brooklyn L Rev 98.

Forms:
See "FORMS" heading following "CASE NOTES", infra.

CASE NOTES

This section simplifies the sections from which it is derived and indicates that no change was contemplated from the earlier practice. Kiamesha Concord, Inc. v Pullman (1966) 52 Misc 2d 210, 274 NYS2d 431.

Where landlord in petition in holdover summary proceeding clearly designated subtenant as an occupant of the premises whose possessory interest, if any, was sought to be terminated, the defect in the caption of the petition, which designated the subtenant as John Doe, was amendable nunc pro tunc. Teachers College v Wolterding (1974) 77 Misc 2d 81, 351 NYS2d 587.

Implicit in CPLR 1024 is that the unusual authority of sanctions should not be availed of in the absence of a genuine effort to learn the name of the party. Chavez v Nevell Mgmt. Co. (1972) 69 Misc 2d 718, 330 NYS2d 890.

If a party wishes to secure the restrictive benefits of CPLR 1024, it should demonstrate to the court by affidavit that the party or parties named as unknown were actually unknown at the time the papers were drawn and served and that genuine, diligent, and timely inquiry was initially made to discover the true names. Teachers College v Wolterding (1973) 75 Misc 2d 465, 348 NYS2d 286, revd on other grounds 77 Misc 2d 81, 351 NYS2d 587.

Caption in summary proceeding which named "John Doe" as respondent subtenant was amendable nunc pro tunc to include actual name of subtenant. Teachers College v Wolterding (1974) 77 Misc 2d 81, 351 NYS2d 587.

Where suit was instituted, judgment obtained, and supplementary proceedings brought against a party under a fictitious first name, without further identification, and on defendant's default in the supplementary proceedings, the judgment creditor moved to punish defendant for contempt, naming the respondent on the motion in the same fashion as

theretofore, the court, although it was not mandatory under this section, adopted as an addendum to this section provisions appearing in its predecessors which authorized a court to issue an order, upon due notice to the party involved, amending the proceedings already taken by the insertion of the true name of defendant in place of the fictitious name or part of a name, and that all subsequent proceedings be taken under the true name, and motion to punish defendant for contempt of court was denied. Kiamesha Concord, Inc. v Pullman (1966) 52 Misc 2d 210, 274 NYS2d 431.

Purpose of statutory provision that party who is ignorant, in whole or in part, of name or identity of person who may properly be made a party, may proceed against such person as an unknown party by designating so much of his name and identity as is known, is to permit cause of action known to exist to be brought against person whose name only is unknown. Orchard Park Cent. School Dist. v Orchard Park Teachers Asso. (1976) 50 AD2d 462, 378 NYS2d 511, app dismd 38 NY2d 911, 382 NYS2d 756, 346 NE2d 557.

Where school district would have had to join some 280 persons in order to name in its application for injunction all teachers who participated in strike, district's application was not improper insofar as it named John Doe and Mary Roe as teachers employed by the district. Orchard Park Cent. School Dist. v Orchard Park Teachers Asso. (1976) 50 AD2d 462, 378 NYS2d 511, app dismd 38 NY2d 911, 382 NYS2d 756, 346 NE2d 557.

Under statute allowing use of John Doe caption only where plaintiff is ignorant of name or identity of proper party defendant, dismissal of action as against one of defendants was required where his name and identity had been known to plaintiff well before lawsuit was instituted and plaintiff did not act in accordance with statute to add such defendant as a party. ABKCO Industries, Inc. v Lennon (1976) 52 AD2d 435, 384 NYS2d 781.

CASE NOTES

UNDER FORMER CIVIL PRACTICE LAWS

A. IN GENERAL

1. Generally
2. Actions to which applicable
3. Persons to which applicable

4. Necessity for ignorance of true name

B. PLEADING AND SERVICE

5. Generally
6. Remedy of defendant

7. Amendments

8. Effect of service on person not named

C. PARTICULAR APPLICATIONS

9. Assumed names

10. Defendant known by different names

11. Middle name

12. Use of trade name

13. Unincorporated associations

14. Mechanics' liens

A. IN GENERAL

1. Generally

The right to supply fictitious names does not apply in a partition action as to heirs not shown at the time to exist. Smith v R. B. I. Bldg. Corp. (1926) 126 Misc 826, 215 NYS 1.

Where in an action of foreclosure unknown owners are made defendants and are described in the summons, the addition of the words "if any" does not invalidate the suit. Abbott v Curran (1885) 98 NY 665.

In an action to foreclose a mortgage made by a sailor, who had left the country, he was made defendant and also "all persons unknown having an interest in the premises," such unknown persons being described in the complaint as the wife, widow, heirs at law, devisees, grantees, assignees or next of kin of the said defendant "and their respective husbands and wifes if any"—held that such description was sufficient. Moran v Conoma (1891) 36 NYSR 680, 13 NYS 625, affd 128 NY 591, 28 NE 251.

Plaintiff having sued wrong person cannot cure the error by a motion to substitute the right defendant. Spence v Griswold (1889) 7 NYS 145.

2. Actions to which applicable

CPA § 215 applied to all actions, including partition and all actions in which service by publication was made. Sanford v White (1874) 56 NY 359; Bergen v Wyckoff (1881) 84 NY 659; Lenehan v College of St. Francis Xavier (1900) 30 Misc 378, 63 NYS 1033, affd 51 AD 535, 64 NYS 868.

In partition where a part owner had not been heard of for 30 years, plaintiff could use fictitious names for unknown wife and heirs of such part owner. Snyder v Parezo (1912) 151 AD 110, 135 NYS 960, affd 206 NY 689, 99 NE 1118.

Actions to register titles to land. Partenfelder v People (1913) 157 AD 462, 142 NYS 915, affd 211 NY 355, 105 NE 675.

In actions under Real Property Law, art. 12, to register title, description of heirs as "all other persons, if any, having any right or interest," was insufficient. Sherman v People (1915) 169 AD 17, 154 NYS 484.

In an action to determine the validity of the probate of a will when the names of parties were unknown they could have been brought into court under CPA § 215. Brinkerhoff v Tiernan (1908) 61 Misc 586, 114 NYS 698.

3. Persons to which applicable

CPA § 215 applied to an unknown infant. Wheeler v Scully (1872) 50 NY 667.

In an action by the insurer for rescission of a life insurance policy, the infant daughter of a beneficiary named in the policy was a proper and necessary party and the fact that she merely belonged to a general class of persons who might, on the happening of various contingencies, share in the proceeds, if any, was no impediment in joining her. Prudential Ins. Co. v Markowitz (1939) 172 Misc 911, 16 NYS2d 416.

4. Necessity for ignorance of true name

CPA § 215 did not permit of a fictitious name applicable to no particular person, but adopted as an expedient to cover the name of a person whose name was known but who was not intended to be sued, but whom it might be desirable to make a defendant at a subsequent stage of the proceedings. Hancock v First Nat. Bank (1883) 93 NY 82.

B. PLEADING AND SERVICE

5. Generally

There must be an allegation that the true name is unknown. Crandall v Beach, 7 How Pr 271; Gardner v Kraft, 52 How Pr 499.

6. Remedy of defendant

In case of misnomer of party defendant, his remedy was by answer and a demurrer in such case was held frivolous. Gannon v Myars, 3 NYSR 199, 11 Civ Proc 187.

The proper remedy where it appeared that plaintiff knew the real name of the defendant, was a motion to set aside the proceedings as irregular and contrary to CPA § 215. People ex rel. Maibach v Dunn (1899) 38 AD 112, 56 NYS 627.

7. Amendments

The court may allow pleadings to be amended on the trial by striking out the words "and son" and inserting in place thereof the name of the son. Bannerman v Quackenbush, 2 How Pr NS 293.

On summons against "W. H. Williams" and served personally, complaint may be amended and judgment entered as against "William H. Williams," after time to answer had expired. Farmers' Nat. Bank v Williams, 9 Civ Proc 212.

Adding to or striking out such name, either at the trial or before or after judgment. Farmers' Nat. Bank v Williams, supra. See Skoog v New York Novelty Co. 4 Civ Proc 144.

Where a defendant is sued by a fictitious name, the real name being unknown, a judgment obtained is irregular unless the summons and judgment contain a description sufficient for the identification of the defendant for purposes of execution against his property; when the proper name is discovered, the judgment proceedings must be amended before further proceedings; a fictitious name may be used only when the real name is not known. Simon v Underwood (1908) 61 Misc 369, 115 NYS 65.

Where a summons and attachment papers were issued and served on defendant under a fictitious name, and it appears that the name used is the real name of the defendant, it is the duty of the court to amend the papers by striking out the words describing part of defendant's name as fictitious. Italian Importing Co. v Spodaro (1909) 63 Misc 320, 117 NYS 135.

8. Effect of service on person not named

Where a summons against Simon Cohn was served upon Samuel Cohn, this did not prejudice the latter or give him a status in court to make a motion to set aside the judgment. Upham v Cohn, 14 Civ Proc 27. See Smith v Jackson (1888) 12 Civ Proc 428, affd 1 NYS 13.

C. PARTICULAR APPLICATIONS

9. Assumed names

The law presumes every one to have a family name and a given name and allows two fictitious names to be inserted when the real names are unknown. Frank v Levie, 28 Super Ct (5 Robt) 599; and where a person is known as well by one name as another, he may be sued in either. Eagleston v Son, 28 Super Ct (5 Robt) 640. He may be sued by the name by which he is ordinarily known, although that is not his true name. Cooper v Burr, 45 Barb 9.

10. Defendant known by different names

If defendant is known by two names, he may be sued by either. Anderson v Horn (1889) 10 NYS 8.

11. Middle name

The law recognizes but one Christian name. The omission of a middle name or letter or insertion of a wrong one will not vitiate the proceedings. If a wrong middle letter or name is used, it may be struck out as surplusage. Van Voorhis v Budd, 39 Barb 479. See Franklin v Talmadge, 5 Johns 84; Roosevelt v Gardiner, 2 Cow 463; Milk v Christie & Todd, 1 Hill 102.

12. Use of trade name

The plaintiff in ignorance of the true names of the defendants, supposing they were a corporation by the name in which they transacted business, sued them in that name; having after suit discovered their true names and that they were not a corporation, he was allowed to substitute their names as defendants. Newton v Milleville Mfg. Co. note to 17 Abb Pr 318.

13. Unincorporated associations

Suit against the association by name; amended by adding names of the members. Skoog v New York Novelty Co. 4 Civ Proc 144.

14. Mechanics' liens

And the fact that the Mechanic's Lien Act provides that the lien shall not be invalid because of mistake in the name of the owner, does not give plaintiff the right to substitute a new defendant. Spence v Griswold (1889) 7 NYS 145.

FORMS

Form   1—Designation in title of summons and complaint of party defendant whose name is unknown

Form   2—Designation in title of summons and complaint of party defendant whose first name is unknown

Form   3—Designation in title of summons and complaint of several suppositious persons described as falling in one of several classes

Form   4—Title of action where entire name of defendant unknown

Form   5—Title of action where part of name of defendant unknown

Form   6—Allegations in complaint making unknown persons defendants

Form   7—Allegations in complaint as to certain other unknown owners

Form   8—Allegations in complaint as to certain unknown owners who claim some interest in or lien upon the real estate involved

Form   9—Allegations in complaint as to unknown heirs or devisees

Form 10—Answer by a defendant sued by a wrong name

Form 1

Designation in Title of Summons and Complaint of Party Defendant Whose Name is Unknown

SUPREME COURT, __¹_____ COUNTY.

James Smith, Plaintiff,
  against
"Richard Roe", the name "Richard Roe"

being fictitious, the real name of the defendant being unknown to plaintiff, said
fictitious name being intended to designate
__²_____ [describe person whose name is
unknown so that summons can be served
on him, for instance, "occupant of the premises at __³_____"], Defendant

Summons [or Complaint,
as the case may be]
Index No. — [if assigned]

Form 2

Designation in Title of Summons and Complaint of Party Defendant Whose First Name is Unknown

SUPREME COURT, __¹_____ COUNTY.

James Smith,　　　　　　　　　Plaintiff,
　　　　against
John [or "Mary"] Roe, the first name being
fictitious, his [or "her"] Christian name being unknown to the plaintiff, such defendant being [add description tending to iden-
tify such defendant such as "the agent of
__³_____ in charge of __⁴_____," or
"the wife of __⁵_____"],
　　　　　　　Defendant

Summons [or Complaint,
as the case may be]
Index No. — [if assigned]

Form 3

Designation in Title of Summons and Complaint of Several Suppositious Persons Described as Falling in One of Several Classes

SUPREME COURT, __¹_____ COUNTY.

James Smith,　　　　　　　　　Plaintiff,
　　　　against
John White, Richard Black, John Brown,
and Harold Gray, said names being fictitious
and the true names being unknown to the
plaintiff, and being intended to designate
the wife, if any, of the said __³_____, and
if he be dead, his widow, heirs at law, devisees and legal representatives, and their
wives, widows or husbands, if any, and the
heirs at law, devisees and legal representatives of any who may be dead,
　　　　　　　Defendants

Summons [or Complaint,
as the case may be]
Index No. — [if assigned]

Form 4

Title of Action Where Entire Name of Defendant Unknown

__¹_____ Court, __²_____

John Roberts,　　　　　　　　　Plaintiff
　　　　against
The owner of the building located
at 2 West 36th Street in the
Borough of Manhattan, City and
State of New York, whose name
is unknown
　　　　　　　Defendant.

Summons
Index No. __³__

Form 5

Title of Action Where Part of Name of Defendant Unknown

__1_____ Court, __2_____ County

John Roberts, Plaintiff	
against	Summons
Mrs. James Parks, whose name is	Index No. __3__
unknown, the wife of James Parks	
Defendant.	

Form 6

Allegations in Complaint Making Unknown Persons Defendants

There are other persons, in addition to those hereinbefore named as defendants, whose names are unknown, who do or may claim some right, title, interest or lien in, to or upon the real estate hereinbefore described, or some part or parts thereof, as heirs or devisees of __1_____, deceased, who previous to his death was or claimed to be interested in said real estate, or some part or parts thereof; but that the names of any such heirs or devisees are unknown to plaintiff.

Form 7

Allegations in Complaint as to Certain Other Unknown Owners

There are other persons, in addition to those hereinbefore made defendants, whose names are unknown, who do or may claim some right, title, interest or lien in, to or upon the real estate hereinbefore described, or some part or parts thereof, as [insert description of the unknown persons to be made defendants and the interests held or claimed by them]; but that the names of any such persons are unknown to plaintiff.

Form 8

Allegations in Complaint as to Certain Unknown Owners Who Claim Some Interest in or Lien Upon the Real Estate Involved

There are other persons, in addition to those hereinbefore made defendants, whose names are unknown, who do or may claim some interest in or lien upon the real estate hereinbefore described, or some part or parts thereof, as the owner or owners or holder or holders of certain notes [or "bonds," or as the case may be], described in and secured by that certain trust deed from __1_____ to __2_____, as trustee, dated __3_____, and recorded in the __4_____ office of __5_____ County, New York, in Book __6__, page __7__, conveying the real estate hereinbefore described, or some part or parts thereof; but that the name or names of any such persons are unknown to plaintiff.

Form 9

Allegations in Complaint as to Unknown Heirs or Devisees

There are persons, whose names are unknown, who do or may claim some right, title, interest or lien in, to or upon the real estate described in the complaint herein, or some part or parts thereof, as heirs or devisees of __1_____, deceased, who, previous to his death, was, or claimed to be, interested in said real estate, or some part or parts thereof; all of which said heirs or devisees have been made parties defendant to said complaint under the name and description of "Unknown heirs or devisees of __2_____, deceased."

Form 10

Answer by a Defendant Sued by a Wrong Name

The defendant __¹_____, sued herein as __²_____, for his answer, etc.

§ 1025. Partnerships and unincorporated associations

Two or more persons conducting a business as a partnership may sue or be sued in the partnership name, and actions may be brought by or against the president or treasurer of an unincorporated association on behalf of the association in accordance with the provisions of the general associations law.

HISTORY:

Add, L 1962, ch 308, eff Sept 1, 1963.
Earlier statutes: CPA § 222-a; CCP § 801-a.

ADVISORY COMMITTEE NOTES:

This section is a restatement of former provisions with no substantial change. See CPA § 222-a; Gen Asso Law §§ 12, 13. Article 10 seems a logical place in which to look for such provisions and hence they have been included here.

Certain matters in connection with actions against partners and joint debtors were considered by the Judicial Council in 1945. See 11 NY Jud Council Rep 40, 221 (1945). As a result of this study, CPA § 222-a was enacted, § 229-a was repealed and §§ 1185, 1187–89 and 1197–1201 were amended. See 12 NY Jud Council Rep 23 (1946). Attention should be called to § 232 of the Debtor and Creditor Law (judgment against one obligor does not release others), which is the key substantive provision on the subject. It has been concluded that these provisions and also CPA § 475, dealing with judgments against persons severally liable, do not come within the scope of Articles 6 or 10, except for the provisions of this section and of sections 1001 and 1002 dealing with joinder of parties. As to the latter, see Greenleaf v Safeway Trails, Inc. 140 F2d 889 (2d Cir 1944). However, these various provisions of the former New York law are considered in connection with Articles 3 and 50, and also with the preservation of the substantive provisions now found in the CPA.

RESEARCH REFERENCES AND PRACTICE AIDS:

20 Carmody-Wait 2d, Actions and Proceedings By or Against, or in Reference to, Partnerships and Associations §§ 122:5–122:7, 122:11, 122:16–122:26.
25 Carmody-Wait 2d, Fundamentals of Practice in the Surrogate's Court § 149:140.
6 Am Jur 2d, Associations and Clubs § 55.
59 Am Jur 2d, Parties § 87.

Annotations:

Standing to bring action relating to title in real property of condominium. 73 ALR3d 314.

Law Reviews:

New York Civil Practice Law and Rules: parties. 27 Albany L Rev 182.
Parties and pleading under the CPLR. 31 Brooklyn L Rev 98.
The quarterly survey of New York practice: CPLR 1025: limited partner cannot sue derivatively on behalf of his partnership. 41 St. John's L Rev 301.

Forms:

See "FORMS" heading following "CASE NOTES", infra.

CASE NOTES

The New York courts obtained personal jurisdiction over a limited partnership organized under New Jersey law with principal offices in New Jersey which did not transact business in this state by service of a summons upon a general partner of the defendant who resided in New York. It was also held the fact that the partnership was sued in the partnership name was of no consequence. Rait v Jacobs Bros. (1966) 49 Misc 2d 903, 268 NYS2d 750.

CPLR 1025 is permissive and not mandatory, and thus an individual partner may still sue on a debt due the partnership, but must bring the action on behalf of and for the benefit of the partnership and may not recover individually. D'Ippolito v Cities Service Co. (1967, CA2 NY) 374 F2d 643.

Although this section allows for the bringing of an action in the partnership name, it is permissive in nature and does not mandate such a course. Arlen of Nanuet, Inc. v State (1967) 52 Misc 2d 1009, 277 NYS2d 560.

When a tort is committed by a partnership, the wrong is imputable to all of the partners jointly and severally, and an action may be brought against all or any of them in their individual capacities or against the partnership as an entity. Pedersen v Manitowoc Co. (1969) 25 NY2d 412, 306 NYS2d 903, 255 NE2d 146.

Partnerships are not terminated on dissolution, but continue until the winding up of partnership affairs is completed and are still conducting business during the winding up process within the meaning of this section, and therefore a partnership may be sued in its partnership name, and personal service upon one of the partners effectively binds the partnership. Re Luckenbach's Estate (1965) 45 Misc 2d 897, 258 NYS2d 44.

Although a partnership may sue or be sued in the partnership name for purposes of pleading, a limited partner, unless he is also a general partner, is not a proper party to proceedings by or against a partnership, except where the object is to enforce a limited partner's right against or liability to the partnership; and when limited partners instituted suit in the partnership name as an entity, they assumed liability as general partners; and when they amended the caption of their action to sue as individuals in a class action, rather than as an entity, they insulated themselves from liability as general partners and could not therefore maintain the action. Riviera Congress Associates v Yassky (1966) 25 AD2d 291, 268 NYS2d 854, affd 18 NY2d 540, 277 NYS2d 386, 223 NE2d 876.

The provision of this section that a partnership may sue or be sued in the partnership name is designed to make clear that, at least for the purpose of pleading, a partnership is a legal entity. Riviera Congress Associates v Yassky (1966) 25 AD2d 291, 268 NYS2d 854, affd 18 NYS2d 540, 277 NYS2d 386, 223 NE2d 876.

The owners of real estate condemned by the state, who formed a partnership, assigned their interest in the land to the partnership, and functioned as the general partners, were entitled to file claims in their individual names against the state, but those partners designated as investing partners, who were in a legal sense limited partners, were not proper parties to the claim and their inclusion as claimants would have been erroneous. Arlen of Nanuet, Inc. v State (1967) 52 Misc 2d 1009, 277 NYS2d 560.

CASE NOTES

UNDER FORMER CIVIL PRACTICE LAWS

1. Generally
2. Effect of dissolution of partnership
3. Medical partnership
4. Effect of service of summons on partnership using name of deceased person under CPA § 223

1. Generally

Partnership may sue in its own name. Bernstein's Duck Farm v Brookhaven, 71 NYS2d 311. See also Wegman v Republic Camera Corp. (1947) 190 Misc 513, 75 NYS2d 745, affd 273 AD 757, 75 NYS2d 776.

CPA § 222-a construed with CPA § 266 (§ 3019(a) herein) in holding that partnerships, especially limited partnerships, were legal entities for procedural purposes. Ruzicka v Rager (1953) 305 NY 191, 111 NE2d 878, 39 ALR2d 288.

Partnership, having five partners, is not separate legal entity with separate residences apart from that of its partners. Koons v Kaiser (1950) 91 F Supp 511.

Where one partner was driving an automobile owned by a partnership on partnership business with his wife as a passenger and the wife was injured, she could sue the partnership as an entity without alleging that it was a partnership and without naming the partners. Travelers Indem. Co. v Unger (1956) 4 Misc 2d 955, 158 NYS2d 892.

2. Effect of dissolution of partnership

CPA § 222-a was inapplicable to dissolved partnership. Stikeman v Whitman, Requardt & Smith (1947) 272 AD 627, 75 NYS2d 73.

A partnership although dissolved and having different partners at the time of suit than at the time the cause of action arose may sue in the firm name. Hunt, Hill & Betts v A. H. Bull S.S. Co. (1957) 9 Misc 2d 274, 170 NYS2d 403.

3. Medical partnership

Where action brought against two physicians for injuries even though physicians in a partnership, it is to recover damages for malpractice and is consequently barred by the two-year statute of limitations, since although the persons comprising the partnership may be sued in the partnership name, the partnership is not a separate entity which may be held liable for negligence on the theory that it permitted the plaintiff to be treated by unskilled or incompetent employees. Golia v Health Ins. Plan (1958) 6 AD2d 884, 177 NYS2d 550.

4. Effect of service of summons on partnership using name of deceased person under CPA § 223

Service under CPA § 223 (§ 1025 herein) was authorized only when one of a partnership using the name of a deceased person was served with process and embraced a situation where process was issued against the name of the deceased but service was effected on one of the partners using the name of the deceased as a trade name. Cox Co. v Barber S.S. Lines (1936) 246 AD 238, 285 NYS 322.

Summons and complaint not validly served under CPA § 223 (§ 1025 herein). Cox Co. v Barber S.S. Lines, supra.

FORMS

Form 1—Complaint in action brought against an association in name of officer

Form 2—Complaint in action against partnership

Form 3—Complaint in action by partnership

Form 4—Allegations by members suing on behalf of all

Form 5—Affidavit of service upon president of unincorporated association

Form 1

Complaint in Action Brought Against an Association in Name of Officer

[Title of court]

__1_____, Plaintiff,
 against
__2_____,   Complaint
as __3_____ [President or Treasurer]   Index No. — [if assigned]
of the __4_____ Association, defendant.

The plaintiff for its complaint against the __5_____ Association, alleges:

1. The said __6_____ Association was, at the times hereinafter mentioned, and ever since has been, an unincorporated association; that said association was formed for the purpose of pecuniary profit __7_____. [Add particular business conducted.]

2. That the above-named __8_____, at the time of the commencement of this action, was the __9_____ [President, or treasurer] thereof.

[If provisions of the articles of association, constitution or by-laws are material, allege them thus:]

3. That the members of the said association have duly adopted and are governed by certain articles of association and by a constitution and by-laws also duly adopted; that among other things it is provided in and by the said articles of association, constitution and by-laws, as follows: [Quoting what is material].

4. [Allege cause of action against association, which must be one upon which the members will be liable either jointly or severally.]

Form 2

Complaint in Action Against Partnership

__1_____ Court, __2_____ County

__3_____, Plaintiff,
 against   Complaint
John Roberts Company,   Index No. __4__
Defendant.

Plaintiff complaining of defendant alleges:

1. Upon information and belief defendant John Roberts Company at all the times hereinafter mentioned was and still is a partnership consisting of __5_____ and __6_____, and has its principal place of business at __7_____, County of __8_____, State of New York.

[Continue with allegations of cause of action.]

Form 3

Complaint in Action by Partnership

__1_____ Court, __2_____ County

John Roberts Company, Plaintiff,

against	Complaint
__3_____, Defendant.	Index No. __4__

Plaintiff complaining of defendant alleges:

1. John Roberts Company at all the times hereinafter mentioned was and still is a partnership consisting of __5_____ and __6_____, and has its principal place of business at __7_____, County of __8_____, State of New York.

[Continue with allegations of cause of action.]

Form 4

Allegations by Members Suing on Behalf of All

This action is instituted by the plaintiffs on their own behalf and for the benefit of other similarly situated with them as members of Local Union No. __1__ of the __2_____, and on behalf of the said Local Union No. __3__ with respect to the defendants and the cause of action herein set forth.

At all the times hereinafter mentioned said Local Union No. __4__ was and now is an unincorporated voluntary labor union or association existing by virtue of a charter granted to it by the __5_____.

At all the times hereinafter mentioned __6_____, __7_____ and __8_____ [titular plaintiffs], were, and now are, members in good standing of said Local Union No. __9_____ of the __10_____, and were, and now are, president, treasurer and secretary, respectively, of said Local Union No. __11__.

[Adapted from the papers in Keller v Lindelof, 294 NY 717, 61 NE2d 452.]

Form 5

Affidavit of Service Upon President of Unincorporated Association

[Title of court]

__1_____ Plaintiff,

against	Affidavit
__2_____ as president of the	Index No. __4__
__3_____, an unincorporated Association,	
Defendant.	

[Venue]

__5_____, being duly sworn, deposes and says that he is over the age of eighteen years and is not a party to this action and that on the __6__ day of __7_____, 19_8_, at No. __9__ Street in the __10_____ of __11_____, county of __12_____, state of New York, he served the annexed __13_____ [summons or summons and complaint] on __14_____ the president of __15_____, by delivering to and leaving with the said __16_____, a true copy thereof.

Deponent further says that he knew the person so served to be __17_____, the president of __18_____, the person described in the summons as the defendant in this action.

[Signature, with name printed underneath]

[Jurat]

**[CPLR 1026–1100 have been reserved for future use.
Please check your supplement.]**

ARTICLE 11

Poor Persons

1101. Motion for permission to proceed as a poor person; affidavit; certificate; notice
      (a) Motion; affidavit
      (b) Certificate
      (c) Notice
1102. Privileges of poor person
      (a) Attorney
      (b) Stenographic transcript
      (c) Appeals
      (d) Costs and fees
1103. Distribution of recovery in favor of poor person

HISTORY:

Add, L 1962, ch 308, eff Sept 1, 1963.

ADVISORY COMMITTEE NOTES:

This article is a reorganization and consolidation of the ten sections and rules specifically relating to poor persons which were found in various parts of the CPA and RCP. It is more useful to place all of these provisions in one appropriately captioned article. In most respects, article 11 is merely a recodification of former statutes and rules. The most important changes made by this article are that the three hundred dollar limit on available property imposed by CPA § 199 is replaced by the requirement that the moving party in his motion papers state the amount and sources of his income and list his property with its value; and that any recovery had in favor of the poor person is required to be paid into court to await final distribution pursuant to court order.

RESEARCH REFERENCES AND PRACTICE AIDS:

Actions by and against poor persons, 21 C-W2d §§ 127:1 et seq.

§ 1101. Motion for permission to proceed as a poor person; affidavit; certificate; notice

(a) Motion; affidavit. Upon motion of any person, the court in which an action is triable, or to which an appeal has been or will be taken, may grant permission to proceed as a poor person. The moving party shall file his affidavit setting forth the amount and sources of his income and listing his property with its value; that he is unable to pay the costs, fees and expenses necessary to prosecute or defend the action or to maintain or respond to the appeal; the nature of the action; sufficient facts so that the merit of his contentions can be ascertained; and whether any other person is beneficially interested in any recovery sought and, if so, whether every such person is unable to pay such costs, fees and expenses. An executor, administrator or other representative may move for permission on behalf of a deceased, infant or incompetent poor person.

(b) Certificate. The court may require the moving party to file with the affidavit a certificate of an attorney stating that he has examined the action and believes there is merit to the moving party's contentions.

(c) Notice. If an action has already been commenced, notice of the motion shall be served on all parties, and notice shall also be given to the county attorney in the county in which the action is triable or the finance administrator if the action is triable in the city of New York.

HISTORY:

Add, L 1962, ch 308, eff Sept 1, 1963.

Sub (c), amd, L 1966, ch 455, L 1969, ch 407, § 114, eff May 9, 1969.

Earlier statutes and rules: CPA §§ 196, 198, 198-a; RCP 35–37; CCP §§ 458–460, 462–465; 2 RS 444; 2 RS 445 §§ 1, 2, 3, 5.

ADVISORY COMMITTEE NOTES:

Subd (a) permits a motion to be made for permission to proceed as a poor person and the granting of such permission by an appropriate court. In order to simplify and make terminology uniform, the words "motion" and "moving party" are used in preference to "application" and "applicant." The subdivision is derived from §§ 198, 198-a and 199 and part of § 196 of the CPA as well as parts of rules 35, 36 and 37 of the RCP. CPA § 197, which provides that the unpaid costs in a former action are not a bar to proceeding as a poor person after permission to do so has been granted, has been omitted as unnecessary. Under former law, permission to defend as a poor person was more restricted than leave to so prosecute. See 20 Carmody-Wait, Cyclopedia of New York Practice 82 (1955). A plaintiff seeking permission to proceed as a poor person must show only that he had a cause of action; a defendant was confronted with the stricter standard of whether the action involved his "right, title or interest in or to real or personal property." CPA §§ 196, 198. This distinction has been abolished. The first sentence of this subdivision is intended to make it clear that permission may be granted before the action has been commenced or at any time thereafter. The granting of permission is discretionary with the court. Smith v Smith, 2 NY2d 120, 123, 138 NE2d 790, 792 (1956). The court in passing upon a motion for permission to proceed as a poor person should consider the moving party's motives, for the privileges granted to a poor person are made available at the expense and inconvenience of the court, the litigants and the public. It should be noted, however, that one lower court has held motive immaterial. Ganem v Bernuth Lembcke Co. 82 NYS2d 777 (NYC Ct 1948). The standards required by this subdivision and the contents of the affidavit are derived from CPA § 199 and part of RCP 35 and 37. One important change has been made. The requirement of subparagraph 2 of rule 35 of the RCP that the petition state that "the applicant is not worth three hundred dollars in cash or available property besides the wearing apparel and furniture necessary for himself and his family" has been replaced by the requirement that the affidavit set forth "the amount and sources of his income" and list "his property with its value." The new requirement places the actual facts of the moving party's financial position before the court and enables it to ascertain more easily whether permission to proceed as a poor person should be granted. While the former provision appears to supply a simple objective standard for the court, as a practical matter the petitioner himself must decide what is "necessary" for his family. He does not need to list the items and his judgment is accepted unless the court's suspicions are aroused. Moreover, a fixed maximum sum of three hundred dollars is unnecessarily rigid. The new provision gives the court greater control as well as greater discretion. Furthermore, the words "available property" in subparagraph 2 of rule 35 raise difficulties because they are not subject to precise definition. See Smith v Smith, supra. The majority of "poor person" provisions in other states do not contain a limitation on the moving party's worth and leave the matter to the complete discretion of the trial court. See, e. g., Ill Rev Stat c. 33, § 5 (1955); Mo Rev Stat §§ 205.590, 514.040 (1949). The requirement in RCP 36 that the court to which the application is made find that the applicant has a "good cause of action" has been altered. Some courts have been overly strict in interpreting this requirement with the result that they have required a substantial probability of success. The proposed subdivision requires only that the court be satisfied that there is merit in the applicant's contentions—*i.e.,* that it is not frivolous.

The attorney's certificate, required by subdivision (b) also utilizes this standard. The last sentence of RCP 36 has been omitted, since a court always possesses the power to vacate or annul its own orders. Thus, some courts have vacated orders authorizing an applicant to proceed as a poor person in situations to which RCP 36 was not applicable. See, e.g., Rosa v Second Avenue R.R., 20 App Div 334, 46 NY Supp 807 (1st Dept 1897). It has been held that a court has no power to entertain an application for permission to proceed as a poor person if costs already awarded in the action are unpaid and a stay under CPA § 1520 has thereby become operative. See, e.g., DeRuvo v Paglia, 135 NYS2d 666 (Sup Ct 1954). Costs awarded upon appeal from an intermediate order are within this section. See, e.g., Muller v Brooklyn Heights RR., 139 App Div 727, 124 NY Supp 491 (2d Dept 1910). It would seem that such an outright prohibition is improper and that in appropriate cases the court should have the power to grant permission despite the fact that prior costs have not been paid. This problem is considered in detail in new CPLR sections on costs. Until 1941, CPA § 196 contained no reference to a representative of a deceased poor person. In 1939, the Court of Appeals held that an executor or administrator of a deceased poor person could not avail himself of its provisions. Fontheim v Third Avenue Ry., 281 NY 392, 24 NE2d 95 (1939). As a result of this case, the section was amended to allow application by a person "as the executor or administrator or other representative of a deceased person." NY Laws 1941, c. 164. The provision is continued in the new subdivision. It is broadened to permit applications by a representative of infants or other persons incompetent to sue on their own behalf. In connection with a motion by the representative of a deceased person, it should be noted that if the distributees are of sufficient financial status, the court should deny permission. But cf. Pizza v Circle Coal & Coke Co. 169 Misc 897, 9 NYS2d 261 (Sup Ct 1938); 20 Carmody-Wait, Cyclopedia of New York Practice 76 (1955). Under the new provisions, persons beneficially interested in the recovery, such as distributees, would be indicated in the affidavit. This requirement, that the affidavit state whether any other person is beneficially interested in any recovery sought and whether he is able to pay the costs, fees and expenses, is new. Its purpose is to place all relevant facts before the court. It would reveal an agreement by an attorney to handle the case on a contingent fee basis; in such an instance, the court may not grant permission to proceed as a poor person. Cf. Lawrence v Murray, 171 Misc 666, 12 NYS2d 262 (Sup Ct 1939). Similarly, when the moving party is only one of several plaintiffs or defendants the court will not ordinarily grant such permission. See 20 Carmody-Wait Cyclopedia of New York Practice 75–76 (1955).

The requirement of certification by an attorney, presently found in RCP 35, is made discretionary; it gives some assurance that the affidavit will be in proper form and that the moving party's contentions have merit. This is especially true where the attorney consents to act as attorney for the poor person. The requirement that the attorney certify that the contentions have merit, rather than that he has a "good cause of action" conforms to the requirements of the affidavit.

Subd (c) is new, but it is merely a statement of existing case law. See, e.g., Rosetano v State of New York, 208 Misc 352, 143 NYS2d 904 (Ct Cl 1955); 20 Carmody-Wait, Cyclopedia of New York Practice 81 (1955).

CROSS REFERENCES:

Privileges of poor persons, 1102.
Distribution of recovery in favor of poor person, 1103.
Appeals to court of appeals as of right, 5601.

CODES, RULES AND REGULATIONS:

Determination of eligibility for public assistance by Department of Social Services. 18 NYCRR 349 et seq.

Filing and service of records, briefs and appendices in Appellate Division, Fourth Judicial Department. 22 NYCRR 1000.5 (CLS App. Div. Rules—Fourth Judicial Dept. § 1000.5).

FEDERAL ASPECTS:

Forma pauperis proceedings in United States courts, 28 USCS § 1915.

Proceedings in forma pauperis, Rule 53 of United States Supreme Court Rules, USCS Court Rules.

Proceedings in forma pauperis in appellate courts, Rule 24 of Federal Rules of Appellate Procedure, USCS Court Rules.

Motions, § 27 of Rules of United States Court of Appeals for the Second Circuit, USCS Court Rules.

Motions in United States District Courts, Rule 7(d) of Federal Rules of Civil Procedure, USCS Court Rules.

RESEARCH REFERENCES AND PRACTICE AIDS:

10 Carmody-Wait 2d, Appeals in General § 70:59.

21 Carmody-Wait 2d, Actions and Proceedings By and Against Poor Persons §§ 127:5, 127:6, 127:9–127:12, 127:15, 127:19, 127:27.

10 Carmody-Wait 2d, Appeals in General § 70:59.

20 Am Jur 2d, Costs §§ 47–51.

21 Am Jur 2d, Criminal Law §§ 318–323.

Am Jur 2d, New Topic Service, Welfare Laws §§ 1 et seq.

7 Am Jur Pl and Pr Forms (Rev ed), Costs, Forms 51 et seq.

Annotations:

Right to sue or appeal in forma pauperis as dependent on showing of financial disability of attorney or other nonparty or nonapplicant. 11 ALR2d 607.

Right of indigent to proceed in marital action without payment of costs. 52 ALR3d 844.

Law Reviews:

Indigent defendant's rights on appeal in New York. 29 Brooklyn L Rev 261.

Parties and pleading under the CPLR. 31 Brooklyn L Rev 98.

Motion practice under the CPLR. 9 NY L F 317.

Forms:

See "FORMS" heading following "CASE NOTES", infra.

CASE NOTES

1. In general
2. Motions, affidavits, notice and the like
3. —Appeals
4. Determination of poor person status
5. —Tenants
6. —Indigent spouse

1. In general

The "poor persons" statutes are applicable to matrimonial actions. Jeffreys v Jeffreys (1968) 57 Misc 2d 416, 292 NYS2d 767, op withdrawn 58 Misc 2d 1045, 296 NYS2d 74, revd on other grounds 38 AD2d 431, 330 NYS2d 550.

The poor person's statutes (CPLR 1101, 1102) do not require the city to pay the cost of serving of summons by publication. Jeffreys v Jeffreys (1968) 58 Misc 2d 1045, 296 NYS2d 74, revd on other grounds 38 AD2d 431, 330 NYS2d 550.

2. Motions, affidavits, notice and the like

Under CPLR § 1101(c), Finance Administrator was an indispensable party to a forma pauperis petition for changes of name under Civil Rights Law § 63, and due to failure of petitioner to give Administrator statutory notice, court could not sign the ex parte petition. Application of Whyte (1972) 72 Misc 2d 116, 338 NYS2d 331.

In a matrimonial action, applications for leave to serve summons by publication under the poor person's statutes (CPLR 1101, 1102) must be made upon notice to the city treasurer or county attorney, as the case may be. Jeffreys v Jeffreys (1968) 58 Misc 2d 1045, 296 NYS2d 74, revd on other grounds 38 AD2d 431, 330 NYS2d 550.

3. —Appeals

Where Appellate Division has refused respondent permission to proceed as a poor person, but merely gave him leave to appeal on a typewritten record and briefs, Trial Term was in error in directing City Treasurer to furnish him with a free transcript. Moriarity v Butler Bin Co. (1964) 21 AD2d 865, 251 NYS2d 44, affd 15 NY2d 901, 258 NYS2d 429, 206 NE2d 361.

Where claimant's financial status brought him within the requirements of CPLR 1101 and his action was meritorious, the fact that claimant's counsel had been retained to serve on a contingent fee basis would not preclude prosecution of an appeal as a poor person, where the retainer agreement was in conformity with requirements as to reasonableness. Orman v State (1969) 59 Misc 2d 709, 300 NYS2d 379.

4. Determination of poor person status

After service of notice of appeal, the initial application for permission to proceed as a poor person and for the transcript of the stenographer's minutes should be made to the trial court, and the determination of the trial court thereon is subject to review on appeal. If such application is granted by the trial court, application can then be made to the appellate court for leave to proceed on a single copy of the record and five typewritten briefs. Jenks v Murphy (1964) 21 AD2d 346, 250 NYS2d 848.

5. —Tenants

As a matter of law, tenant whose income exceeded expenses by $126 per month was not entitled to poor person status either in landlord's summary nonpayment proceeding or on appeal from judgment for landlord. Dolan Properties, Inc. v Schoolcraft (1973) 75 Misc 2d 1084, 350 NYS2d 292.

It was error to deny the application of a tenant for leave to defend as a poor person where she made a prima facie showing of indigency by her affidavit stating that she was a recipient of public assistance and without assets, and her sworn denial that she owed any rent was a sufficient showing of merit to support the motion. Hotel Martha Washington Management Co. v Swinick (1971) 66 Misc 2d 833, 322 NYS2d 139.

Tenant in non-payment summary proceeding would be permitted to proceed as a poor person where he made a prima facie showing of indigency and of the merit of his defense and there was no opposition on the part of the landlord or finance administrator of city both of whom had been served as defendants. Rosen v Slate (1973) 76 Misc 2d 862, 353 NYS2d 86.

6. —Indigent spouse

Where husband had been found, making service by publication unnecessary, and total costs in wife's divorce action were $25, wife's application under CPLR § 1101 and § 1102 to sue as an indigent person was properly denied in the court's discretion. Kirk v Kirk (1973) 41 AD2d 594, 340 NYS2d 346, app dismd 33 NY2d 636, 347 NYS2d 584, 301 NE2d 552.

Allegations that petitioner was receiving public assistance and had no other income or property established prima facie that he was entitled to proceed as poor person pursuant to CPLR 1101 in seeking divorce from his wife. Bartlett v Kitchin (1973) 76 Misc 2d 1087, 352 NYS2d 110.

An indigent wife, seeking divorce, could not be barred by the state from access to the divorce courts by requiring her to pay the cost of service of summons by publication which was the sole statutory method available to her to secure service of process, and the cost of publication was to be borne by the wife's county of residence, rather than by the state. Deason v Deason (1972) 39 AD2d 331, 334 NYS2d 236, affd 32 NY2d 93, 343 NYS2d 321, 296 NE2d 229.

Where petitioner asked County Department of Social Services to provide him lawyer for obtaining divorce from wife or in the alternative to pay fee for lawyer of his choice and was advised that no funds were available for such purpose, action by petitioner to compel department to provide him with lawyer was not premature by reason of his failure to apply for "fair hearing" as doctrine of exclusion of administrative remedies is inapplicable where such exclusion would be futile. Bartlett v Kitchin (1973) 76 Misc 2d 1087, 352 NYS2d 110.

Where wife's complete indigency was established and she was undoubtedly a "poor person," case involving husband and wife would be remanded to trial term with direction to appoint counsel to represent wife in such action without charge for that service, without costs, and without disbursements. Yearwood v Yearwood (1976) 54 AD2d 626, 387 NYS2d 433.

CASE NOTES

UNDER FORMER CIVIL PRACTICE LAWS

A. In General

1. Generally

The right to sue as a poor person is purely statutory. Robertson v Schoonmaker (1936) 249 AD 657, 291 NYS 487.

The right of a plaintiff to sue as a poor person was given in CPA §§ 196–199 (§§ 1101(a), 1102(d) herein), which sections also gave procedure to be followed in RCP 35 (§§ 1101(a), 1102(d) herein) and 36 (§§ 1101(a), 1102(a), (d) herein). Schechter v Lichtenstein (1928) 223 AD 60, 227 NYS 245.

Bad faith in bringing the action bars leave to sue as a poor person. McNamara v Nolan (1895) 13 Misc 76, 34 NYS 178.

CPA § 198 considered with CPA §§ 196, 197, 198-a, 558 (§ 1102(c) herein), and former 593 in connection with appeal to the Court of Appeals as a poor person. Siegelbaum v Dowling (1938) 279 NY 22, 17 NE2d 409.

Record examined and proof of the facts specified in former CPA § 199 was found to be satisfactory in Brown v Willard (1951) 302 NY 839, 100 NE2d 37.

Where a party comes within the provisions of the statute permitting leave to sue as a poor person the fact that he may have an ulterior motive to avoid furnishing security for costs is irrelevant. Ganem v Bernuth Lembcke Co. (1948, City Ct) 82 NYS2d 777.

Disapproval has been expressed of earlier cases to the effect that one who retains an attorney upon a contingent basis forfeits his right to leave to sue as a poor person, especially in case of a plaintiff seaman. Ganem v Bernuth Lembcke Co., supra.

Subject of action excluded in determining worth of seaman, suing for injuries aboard employer's vessel. Ganem v Bernuth Lembcke Co., supra.

Defendant, who had pleaded guilty to burglary third degree and to an information charging him with a prior felony and who had been committed, was not entitled to relief under former CPA § 199. The only statute governing free minutes in criminal cases is Criminal Code § 308. People v Moylan (1956) 4 Misc 2d 747, 162 NYS2d 479.

Where the arrest of defendant is caused by plaintiff, leave to sue as a poor person will be refused. Friedman v Fischer, 5 NYSR 913.

An order permitting plaintiff to sue as a poor person was not granted where plaintiff's attorney had an interest in the claim, since RCP 36 (previously CCP § 460) required plaintiff's counsel to act without compensation. See Downs v Farley, 12 Civ Proc 119, 18 Abb NC 464. See also Cahill v Manhattan R. Co. (1899) 38 AD 314, 57 NYS 10.

2. Construction

CPA § 196 must be strictly construed. Robertson v Schoonmaker (1936) 249 AD 657, 291 NYS 487.

CPA §§ 196, 197, 198, 198-a considered with CPA §§ 558 (§ 1102(c) herein) and 593 in connection with appeal to the Court of Appeals as a poor person. Siegelbaum v Dowling (1938) 279 NY 22, 17 NE2d 409.

Rights to sue as a poor person were defined by CPA §§ 196, 197, 199, and the procedure which had to be followed was shown by RCP 35 and 36 (§§ 1101(a), (b), 1102(a), (d) herein). Schechter v Lichtenstein (1928) 223 AD 60, 227 NYS 245.

3. Courts

CPA §§ 196–198-a applied to court of claims. Johnson v State (1945, Ct Cl) 55 NYS2d 792; Lipschultz v State, 192 Misc 70, 78 NYS2d 731; Rosetano v State (1955) 208 Misc 352, 143 NYS2d 904.

Where Court of Claims has jurisdiction to entertain motion to permit appeal as poor person, after completion of trial and after decision dismissing claim on merits, but before entry of judgment and before filing and serving notice of appeal, such motion must be denied, for it is prematurely brought, for failure to give due notice of application and for defects in moving papers. Rosetano v State, supra.

Under Municipal Court Code, § 15, former CPA § 197 applied to proceedings in that court, and its violation was held ground for appeal prior to the appeal of subd 8 of § 154 of the Municipal Court Code. Johnson v Interborough Rapid Transit Co. (1917, Sup App T) 164 NYS 23.

Under Municipal Court Code, § 28, and former CPA § 197, one may have brought a new action as a poor person, though costs of former action were not paid. Monteforte v Aetna Life Ins. Co. (1917, Sup App T) 162 NYS 762.

Municipal Court Code, § 125, must be read in conjunction with former CPA § 197 and a person to whom leave to sue as pauper was granted could prosecute the same though he had failed to pay costs in former action between the same parties involving the same cause of action. Guttilla v Engel (1916) 95 Misc 163, 158 NYS 773.

A plaintiff could have moved in the appellate

division for leave to appeal as a poor person and an application could then have been made to the trial court under CPA §§ 196–199, and pursuant to CPA § 1493 an application could have been made to the trial court for a transcript of the stenographic minutes without charge to the appellant. Hauck v Roncone (1958) 5 AD2d 804, 169 NYS2d 915.

4. Vacation of order

The order permitting suit as a poor person can only be vacated upon a motion regularly made for that purpose, and is not invalidated by the failure of the plaintiff to serve a copy. Buccolo v New York L. Ins. Co. (1907) 117 AD 423, 102 NYS 794.

5. Appealability of order

An order granting leave to sue as a poor person is appealable, as a substantial right is affected. McNamara v Nolan (1895) 13 Misc 76, 34 NYS 178.

6. Renewal of application

Fact that previous action for same cause of action was dismissed and that plaintiff did not pay the costs is not bar to prosecution of action as poor person. Pankawicus v Nichols Copper Co. (1915) 169 AD 419, 155 NYS 123.

7. Security for costs

An order directing plaintiff to give security for costs does not debar him of his right to move at any time after action brought for leave to sue as a poor person. Shapiro v Burns (1894) 7 Misc 418, 27 NYS 980.

An infant plaintiff, suing by guardian ad litem, may be permitted to sue in forma pauperis, although the defendant requires security for costs. Trimble v Kilgannon (1895) 12 Misc 459, 34 NYS 256.

Where suit is actually begun by the guardian ad litem and an order made requiring security, it is too late to apply for permission to sue in forma pauperis and to set aside the order already made. Glasberg v Dry Dock, E. B. & B. R. Co. 12 Civ Proc 50. But see contra, Shearman v Pope (1887) 106 NY 664, 12 NE 713; Irving v Garrity, 4 Civ Proc 105.

It was formerly held that where an infant sues by guardian ad litem, security for costs to defendant being a statutory right, the court has no power to destroy it by allowing the guardian to sue as a poor person. Kleinpeter v Enell, 2 Civ Proc (Browne) 21; Re Daly, 2 Civ Proc (Browne) 22 note; but these cases are now overruled. Erickson v Poey (1884) 96 NY 669; Hotaling v McKenzie, 7 Civ Proc 320. See also, Nichols v Cammann, 2 Civ Proc (Browne) 375.

A nonresident of this state may in the discretion of the court be allowed to prosecute an action as a poor person, notwithstanding the provisions requiring a nonresident plaintiff to give security for costs. Harris v Mutual Life Ins. Co. (1890, Sup) 10 NYS 473, affd 37 NYSR 599, 13 NYS 718.

An order requiring a nonresident plaintiff to give security for costs should be vacated where an order permitting the plaintiff to sue as a poor person has been granted before the commencement of the action. Buccolo v New York L. Ins. Co. (1907) 117 AD 423, 102 NYS 794.

8. Payment of outstanding costs

Although a person suing in a representative capacity as a poor person is not to be prevented by liability for costs in a former action against the same defendant, the previous adverse result may properly be considered on the merits of plaintiff's right to sue. Re Cannice (1906) 52 Misc 6, 101 NYS 1054.

The provision of former CPA § 197 did not extend to one who was already in default as to costs incurred in the same action. Plaintiff would not be permitted leave to sue as a poor person where costs awarded by the appellate division on a motion for different relief in this action had not been paid. Hand v Equitable Life Assur. Soc. (1937) 166 Misc 785, 2 NYS2d 565.

Nonpayment by plaintiff of the costs of a former action, brought for the same cause, is not a good reason for refusing to permit the plaintiff to prosecute the second action as a poor person. Harris v Mutual Life Ins. Co. 10 NYS 473, revd on other grounds, 37 NYSR 599, 13 NYS 718.

Fact that previous action for same cause of action was dismissed and that plaintiff did not pay the costs is not bar to prosecution of action as poor person. Pankawicus v Nichols Copper Co. (1915) 169 AD 419, 155 NYS 123.

Former CPA § 197 providing that costs in "former" action should be no bar to granting leave to sue as poor person, did not apply to nonpayment of costs in "same" action which may, and in this type of action should, bar granting of such leave. De Ruvo v Paglia (1954, Sup) 135 NYS2d 666.

Rights to sue as a poor person were defined by CPA §§ 196, 197, 199, and the procedure which must be followed was shown by RCP 35 and 36 (§§ 1101(a), (b), 1102(a), (d) herein). Schechter v Lichtenstein (1928) 223 AD 60, 227 NYS 245.

CPA §§ 196, 197, 198, 198-a considered with CPA §§ 558 (§ 1102(c) herein), and former 593 in connection with appeal to the Court of Appeals as a poor person. Siegelbaum v Dowling (1938) 279 NY 22, 17 NE2d 409.

Fact that previous action for same cause of action was dismissed and that plaintiff did not pay the costs is not bar to prosecution of action as poor person. Pankawicus v Nichols Copper Co. (1915) 169 AD 419, 155 NYS 123.

9. —As condition of action by court

Leave to sue as a poor person does not deprive the court of power to impose costs against such person as a condition upon which a judgment by default will be opened. Neugrosche v Manhattan R. Co. 1 NYSR 302; Elwin v Routh, 1 Civ Proc 131.

Costs may be awarded against one suing in forma

pauperis as a condition of discontinuance. Parkinson v Scott (1893) 5 Misc 261, 25 NYS 102.

B. WHO MAY MAKE APPLICATION TO PROCEED AS POOR PERSON

10. Generally, showing of indigence

Only one of many plaintiffs would not ordinarily be granted the privilege of appealing as a poor person in the absence of a showing that all of the plaintiffs were poor persons as defined by RCP 35 (§ 1101(a), (b) herein). Orlowski v St. Stanislaus R. C. Church Soc. (1939, AD) 12 NYS2d 350. See also Ostrander v Harper, 14 How Pr 16.

To constitute one a poor person it was not necessary that he be a pauper; it was enough that he was not worth the amount specified in former CPA § 199. McNamara v Nolan (1895) 13 Misc 76, 34 NYS 178.

Where there was no proper showing of indigence or lack of funds except statement of attorney on information and belief, leave to appeal as poor person was denied. People v Latshaw (1955, AD) 136 NYS2d 852.

11. Committee of lunatic

The court is not authorized to permit the committee of a lunatic to sue as a poor person. Bechtle v Manhattan R. Co. (1894, CP Ct) 30 NYS 410.

12. Executors and administrators

Prior to 1941 amendment, an executor or administrator could not prosecute as a poor person an appeal to the Court of Appeals in an action for the death of her intestate. Fontheim v Third Ave. R. Co. (1939) 281 NY 392, 24 NE2d 95.

An executor was entitled to leave to sue as a poor person under CPA § 198-a and the financial condition of the next of kin was immaterial. Pizza v Circle Coal & Coke Co. (1938) 169 Misc 897, 9 NYS2d 261.

An administrator or an executor may make application and may sue as a poor person. Re Cannice (1906) 52 Misc 6, 101 NYS 1054.

Where an administratrix seeks to prosecute as a poor person her petition must show the financial condition of the estate. Daus v Nussberger (1898) 25 AD 185, 49 NYS 291.

13. Infants

Infant is liable for costs to successful defendant, unless infant has obtained leave to sue as poor person. Stevenson v Guardian Life Ins. Co. (1941) 175 Misc 823, 25 NYS2d 483.

After, but not before, a guardian ad litem has been appointed, the infant may apply. Glasberg v Dry Dock, E. B. & B. R. Co. 12 Civ Proc 50.

14. —Guardians ad litem

A plaintiff may sue in forma pauperis, although her guardian ad litem, her father, is a man of means; and on compliance with the statutory conditions the court must grant the right to sue as a poor person. Shapiro v Burns (1894) 7 Misc 418, 27 NYS 980.

Where the petition of an infant over fourteen years of age asks leave to sue as a poor person complies with the requirements and is verified by a guardian ad litem, the application should not be denied simply because it appears that the guardian ad litem is a responsible person. Feier v Third Ave. R. Co. (1896) 9 AD 607, 41 NYS 821.

An infant plaintiff, not possessed of any funds of his own, should not be denied leave to prosecute the action as a poor person simply because his guardian ad litem is his father, and the father, upon his application for appointment as such guardian, has shown himself to be worth more than $100 and to be of sufficient financial responsibility to answer to the plaintiff for any misconduct in prosecuting the action. Larsen v Interurban St. R. Co. (1904) 97 AD 150, 89 NYS 649.

Court should not appoint an irresponsible person as a guardian ad litem since they remain "responsible for costs" of the action. Tropeano v Grimaldi (1916) 173 AD 534, 159 NYS 1025.

The provisions of CPA § 196 applied to infants as well as adults. Tobias v Broadway & Seventh Ave. R. Co. (1891, City Ct) 14 NYS 641; thus anticipating the amendment of 1891.

A guardian ad litem may make application to sue as a poor person. Florence v Bulkley, 8 Super Ct (1 Duer) 705. See Cohen v Hautcharow (1903, Sup App T) 84 NYS 573.

A guardian ad litem, for same plaintiff in a different action dismissed before application, may not apply. Rosso v Second Ave. R. Co. (1897) 13 AD 375, 43 NYS 216.

A father of an infant, not yet appointed guardian ad litem, may not apply where no action has been commenced. Kerrigan v Langstaff (1901) 64 AD 497, 72 NYS 230.

15. Nonresidents

A nonresident may make application and may sue as a poor person. Harris v Mutual Life Ins. Co. (1891, Sup) 37 NYSR 599, 13 NYS 718. However, he may not sue as a poor person in the federal court. Thomas v Wilson, 6 Hill 257; Heckman v Mackey (1887, CC NY) 19 Abb NC 394, 32 F 574.

Leave should not be granted a nonresident to sue as a poor person except in a reasonably clear case, and the attorney making the application should not be assigned as counsel except where he certifies that he will act without compensation. Harris v Mutual Life Ins. Co. (1891, Sup) 37 NYSR 599, 13 NYS 718.

Where the action is for a tort committed in another state, of which both parties are residents, the court should not grant an order for prosecution in forma pauperis. Alexander v Meyers, 8 Daly 112.

An order requiring a nonresident plaintiff to give security for costs should be vacated where an order permitting the plaintiff to sue as a poor person has been granted before the commencement of the action. Buccolo v New York L. Ins. Co. (1907) 117 AD 423, 102 NYS 794.

16. Imprisoned persons

Application concerning one imprisoned, see Lipshultz v State (1948) 192 Misc 70, 78 NYS2d 731.

17. Married women

A married woman may sue as a poor person respecting an injury to her separate property. Roberti v Carlton, 18 How Pr 466.

Where statutory prerequisites were fulfilled, court had discretionary power to permit wife to prosecute appeal in matrimonial action as poor person, despite ownership of realty by wife and husband jointly. Smith v Smith (1956) 2 NY2d 120, 157 NYS2d 546, 138 NE2d 790.

C. APPEAL AS POOR PERSON

18. Generally

An order dispensing with the printing of the record in the appellate division does not confer upon the plaintiff the status of a poor person within the meaning of CPA §§ 196 and 558 (§ 1102(c) herein). Rocco v New York (1954) 283 AD 1056, 131 NYS2d 506.

An application for leave to proceed as a "poor person" must be on papers complying with the relevant statutory provisions of CPA §§ 196, 558 (§ 1102(c) herein) and RCP 35, 36 (§§ 1101(a), (b), 1102(a), (d) herein), and an ordinary motion to dispense with printing of papers on an appeal cannot be entertained. Re Bieder (1954) 283 AD 725, 127 NYS2d 645.

19. Decisions under former law

Prior to the 1935 amendment, the privilege of suing as a poor person did not extend to an appeal taken from an adverse determination. Hayden v Hayden, 8 AD 547, 40 NYS 865; Morse v Troy (1885, NY) 38 Hun 301.

Compliance with CPA § 198a required as condition of granting motion for leave to appeal as poor person. Commissioner of Public Welfare ex rel. Alberti v Sonsky (1940) 259 AD 831, 19 NYS2d 219.

Compliance with CPA § 558 (§ 1102(c) herein) required as condition of granting leave to appeal as poor person. Commissioner of Public Welfare ex rel. Alberti v Sonsky, supra.

Leave to appeal to the Appellate Division as a poor person denied. Re Altherr v Irving Trust Co. (1936) 249 AD 696, 291 NYS 301.

A motion in court of appeals for order permitting a party to appeal to that court as a poor person, to the extent of allowing prosecution of the appeal without the filing of the required undertaking, must be denied. The application should have been for leave to prosecute as a poor person upon proof of the facts prescribed by former CPA § 199. If leave be given, such a person would have the privileges prescribed in CPA § 558 (§ 1102(c) herein), including waiver of the undertaking. Siegelbaum v Dowling (1938) 279 NY 22, 17 NE2d 409.

Court of appeals has no power to grant leave to

appeal as poor person direct to court of appeals. People ex rel. Mark v Warden of Attica State Prison (1942) 287 NY 745, 39 NE2d 943.

Permission to prosecute appeal as poor person on typewritten record denied where question of fact only is involved. Brecher v David Eisner & Co. (1942, AD) 34 NYS2d 140.

Proper course for claimant desiring to review as poor person dismissal of his claim by Court of Claims is to appeal to Appellate Division and then make due application to said Court upon due notice to State of New York for permission to appeal as poor person and for assignment of counsel for that purpose. Rosetano v State (1955) 143 NYS2d 904.

Satisfactory proof of facts specified in former CPA § 199 warranted granting leave to appeal on record used in appellate division and to dispense with filing undertaking. Brown v Willard (1951) 302 NY 839, 100 NE2d 37.

Motion for leave to appeal to Appellate Division as poor person, on typewritten record, was denied, with leave to renew on typewritten record presenting with motion the stenographer's minutes, and brief showing the points to be raised on the appeal. People v Todak (1937) 250 AD 796, 295 NYS 748.

Leave to appeal as a poor person denied. Re Butler (1935) 246 AD 648, 284 NYS 635; People ex rel. La Pierre v Murphy (1935) 247 AD 829, 284 NYS 629; Altherr v Irving Trust Co. (1936) 249 AD 696, 291 NYS 301.

Leave to appeal on a typewritten record and brief held properly allowed. Cronin v State (1938) 1 NYS2d 669.

20. —Showing of merit of appeal

Appellate court will authorize a poor person to prosecute appeal only where there is merit to appeal. Ehdc v State (1940) 260 AD 511, 23 NYS2d 616; Rosetano v State (1955) 143 NYS2d 904.

Motion for reconsideration of motion for leave to appeal as poor person was denied where papers submitted showed there was no merit in the appeal. People ex rel. Ware v Fay (1960) 11 AD2d 733, 204 NYS2d 892.

In habeas corpus proceeding, the court is under a duty to determine whether there is any merit to the appeal before allowing appellant to prosecute it as a poor person upon typewritten papers. People ex rel. Maconi v Murphy (1960) 11 AD2d 1095, 206 NYS2d 484.

A meritorious cause of action must be shown to obtain permission to prosecute appeal as poor person. Johnson v Rochester Sav. Bank (1939) 256 AD 1043, 10 NYS2d 944. Noncompliance therewith is fatal. Wemyss v Allan (1903) 88 AD 475, 85 NYS 91; Traver v Jackman, 98 AD 287, 90 NYS 739.

Motion papers for leave to sue as poor person had

to set forth facts showing that petitioner was poor person within meaning of former CPA § 199, and had to set forth facts showing that there was merit to appeal. Rosetano v State (1955) 208 Misc 352, 143 NYS2d 904.

Motion papers for leave to sue as poor person had to set forth facts showing that petitioner was poor person within meaning of former CPA § 199 and had to set forth facts showing that there was merit to appeal. Rosetano v State, supra.

Motion for leave to prosecute appeal as poor person on typewritten papers was denied, on the ground that it did not appear that there was merit in appeal. Farkas v Washburn Wire Co. (1937) 251 AD 751, 295 NYS 589; Humienski v Foreman (1937) 251 AD 751, 295 NYS 576; People ex rel. Tomkalski v Wilkins (1960) 11 AD2d 628, 200 NYS2d 477 (habeas corpus proceeding); People ex rel. Hatzis v Martin (1955, AD) 139 NYS2d 699.

D. Application for Leave to Sue (Decisions Under RCP 35)

21. Generally

A mere request is insufficient; a formal motion is necessary. Schechter v Lichtenstein (1928) 223 AD 60, 227 NYS 245.

An order permitting plaintiff to sue as a poor person can only be made pursuant to a proper application setting forth facts constituting grounds for such relief. Schechter v Lichtenstein, supra.

The granting of leave to sue as a poor person is discretionary; only such poor persons as would otherwise be unable to prosecute their action may be granted leave. Weinstein v Schnepp (1900) 56 AD 275, 67 NYS 746.

Unless facts are set forth showing the advice of counsel, the application will be held insufficient. Weinstein v Frank, supra.

22. Nature of action

The petition must clearly state the nature of the action. Larsen v Interurban Street R. Co. (1904) 97 AD 150, 89 NYS 649. See McGillicuddy v Kings County El. R. Co. (1894) 10 Misc 21, 30 NYS 833.

A petition for leave to sue as a poor person, which refers to the complaint, sufficiently states the nature of the cause of action. McGillicuddy v Kings County El. R. Co., supra.

23. Cause of action

The alleged poor person must show to the court that he has a good cause of action. Young v Nassau Elec. R. Co. (1898) 34 AD 126, 54 NYS 600; Weinstein v Schnepp (1900) 56 AD 275, 67 NYS 746; Saltzman v Northrop (1896) 18 Misc 353, 41 NYS 547.

In a suit by a wife against her husband for separation, reasonable or probable grounds for success must be ascertained by the report of master. Robertson v Robertson, 3 Paige 387.

Before an application to sue in forma pauperis is granted the court should be satisfied that the plaintiff has a good cause of action and may receive affidavits in opposition; and the order should not be granted except in a reasonably clear case. Beyer v Clark (1892, Super Ct) 22 NYS 540.

It is not a condition precedent to the granting of the order that the plaintiff should prove his right to recover; it is only necessary that the complaint set forth facts which, if established on the trial, will entitle the plaintiff to a recovery. McNamara v Nolan (1895) 13 Misc 76, 34 NYS 178.

Where a cause of action appears on the face of the complaint, leave to sue as a poor person will not be refused, though the merits of the action are denied by affidavit. McNamara v Nolan (1895) 11 Misc 621, 32 NYS 922, affd 13 Misc 76, 34 NYS 178.

24. Inability to prosecute

An application must show that the petitioner is an object of charity. Thus, where his style of living was beyond that permitted by compensation of most judicial officers, and there was a showing of high rent and the keeping of a servant, the application was held to be insufficient. Isnard v Cazeaux, 1 Paige 39.

However, application held not to be insufficient merely because the petitioner, with his wife and child, occupied four rooms comfortably furnished on the second floor of a building and was in receipt of $15 per week in wages. McNamara v Nolan (1895) 13 Misc 76, 34 NYS 178.

Materiality of the guardian's ability to prosecute. See Feier v Third Ave. R. Co. (1896) 9 AD 607, 41 NYS 821; Rutkowsky v Cohen (1902) 74 AD 415, 77 NYS 546; Muller v Bammann, 77 AD 212, 78 NYS 1022; Sumkow v Sheinher (1903) 84 AD 463, 82 NYS 995; Wemyss v Allan (1903) 88 AD 475, 85 NYS 91; Larsen v Interurban Street R. Co. (1904) 97 AD 150, 89 NYS 649; Tobias v Broadway & 7th Ave. R. Co. (1891, City Ct) 14 NYS 641; Shapiro v Burns (1894) 7 Misc 418, 27 NYS 980; Gallagher v Geneva, W. S. F. & C. Lake Traction Co. (1903) 39 Misc 637, 80 NYS 606; Cohen v Hautcharow (1903, Sup App T) 84 NYS 573.

An administratrix, alleging her own lack of means, without alleging the condition of the estate, renders the application insufficient. Daus v Nussberger (1898) 25 AD 185, 49 NYS 291.

An application showing merely that an infant has no property by gift or bequest or inheritance held insufficient. Gallerstein v Manhattan R. Co. (1899) 26 Misc 853, 55 NYS 444.

What petitioner must show as to financial condition. See Weinstein v Frank Schnepp (1900) 56 AD 275, 67 NYS 746; Berkman v Wolf (1901) 65 AD 79, 72 NYS 661; Kaufmann v Manhattan R. Co. (1902) 68 AD 94, 74 NYS 146; Sumkow v Sheinker (1903) 84 AD 463, 82 NYS 995.

25. Consent of attorney

The consent of the attorney to act without pay is necessary and must be shown. Traver v Jackman (1904) 98 AD 287, 90 NYS 739.

Filing the attorney's consent with the moving papers is the better practice. Daus v Nussberger (1898) 25 AD 185, 49 NYS 291.

An order permitting a plaintiff to sue as a poor person must assign an attorney to prosecute the action without compensation; consent of an attorney to so prosecute, filed by him, is insufficient. Schechter v Lichtenstein (1928) 223 AD 60, 227 NYS 245.

Leave should not be granted a nonresident to sue as a poor person except in a reasonably clear case, and the attorney making the application should not be assigned as counsel except where he certifies that he will act without compensation. Harris v Mutual Life Ins. Co. (1891, Sup) 37 NYSR 599, 13 NYS 718.

An order permitting plaintiff to sue as a poor person was not granted where plaintiff's attorney had an interest in the claim since RCP 36 (previously CCP § 460) required plaintiff's counsel to act without compensation. See Downs v Farley, 12 Civ Proc 119, 18 Abb NC 464. See also Cahill v Manhattan R. Co. (1899) 38 AD 314, 57 NYS 10.

26. Time for application

As to time for making application, see Re Byrne, 1 Edw Ch 41; Florence v Bulkley, 8 Super Ct (1 Duer) 705; Ostrander v Harper, 14 How Pr 16; Friedman v Fischer, 5 NYSR 913; Glasberg v Dry Dock, E. B. & B. R. Co. 12 Civ Proc 50; Shapiro v Burns (1894) 7 Misc 418, 27 NYS 980; Sweeney v White, 10 Misc 29, 30 NYS 1051; Kahn v Singer Mfg. Co. (1896) 18 Misc 568, 42 NYS 461.

27. Verification

Leave to appeal as poor person was denied for failure of appellant to verify petition. McMenamy Application (1941, AD) 26 NYS2d 508.

The statute is explicit that it is the guardian ad litem already appointed in the action, and not the person to be appointed such guardian, who must verify the petition by his affidavit in case the infant is under the age of fourteen years. Kerrigan v Langstaff (1901) 64 AD 497, 72 NYS 230.

A petition by the father of an infant, and verified by him as petitioner, held insufficient. Cohen v Hautcharow (1903, Sup App T) 84 NYS 573.

FORMS

Form   1—Affidavit in support of motion for permission to proceed as a poor person

Form   2—Certificate of attorney in support of application for leave to sue as a poor person

Form   3—Order permitting plaintiff to sue as a poor person when application made before action brought

Form   4—Allegation in complaint where plaintiff sues as a poor person

Form   5—Notice of motion for leave to proceed as a poor person when motion made after action brought

Form   6—Order granting leave to proceed as a poor person after action brought

Form   7—Notice of motion for permission to prosecute appeal as a poor person

Form   8—Affidavit in support of motion for permission to prosecute appeal as a poor person

Form   9—Certificate of attorney in support of affidavit for permission to appeal as a poor person

Form 10—Order granting permission to prosecute appeal as a poor person

Form 1

Affidavit in Support of Motion for Permission to Proceed as a Poor Person

[Title of court and cause]   Affidavit

[Venue of affidavit]

__1____, being duly sworn, deposes and says:

1. That he resides at No. __2__, __3____ Street, City of __4____ and State of New York.

2. That he is over the age of eighteen years. [If the applicant is an infant motion must be made by the guardian of his property, parent, etc., or guardian ad litem, as provided in CPLR § 1201. See Form 1 under § 1201].

3. That the amount and sources of his income and his property and its value are as follows: [Set forth amount and sources of income and list property with its value].

4. [Set forth facts showing that applicant is unable to pay the costs, fees and expenses necessary to proceed.]

5. That he intends to bring an action against __5_____ for __6_____ [or otherwise state facts sufficient to show the nature of the action and so that the merit of his contentions can be ascertained.]

6. That the following persons [if any] are beneficially interested in the recovery sought and deponent is informed and believes that each of such persons is unable to pay such costs, fees and expenses.

7. No previous application for such an order or similar order has been made.

WHEREFORE, deponent prays that an order may be entered granting permission to deponent to bring an action [defend, or otherwise proceed, as the case may be] as a poor person against the said __7_____ on the cause of action above stated and assigning an attorney and counselor to prosecute the action.

[Signature of deponent]

[Jurat]

[Print signer's name below signature]

Form 2

Certificate of Attorney in Support of Application for Leave to Sue as a Poor Person

Certificate

I, __1_____, of No. __2__ __3_____ Street in the City of __4_____, County of __5_____, State of New York, a counselor at law duly admitted to practice in the courts of the State of New York, do hereby certify that I have examined the case set forth in the foregoing affidavit, and I am of the opinion that there is merit in the deponent's contentions; and I stipulate and agree that I will prosecute [or defend, etc., as the case may be] such action, on behalf of __6_____ without compensation except for what the court may assign to me as a reasonable sum for my services and taxable disbursements in the event of recovery.

Dated this __7__ day of __8_____, 19_9_.

[Signature]
[Print signer's name below signature]

Form 3

Order Permitting Plaintiff to Sue as a Poor Person When Application Made Before Action Brought

SUPREME COURT, __1_____ COUNTY.

Order

[Title of cause]   Index No. — [if assigned]

PRESENT: Hon. __2_____ Justice.

The above named __3_____ having duly made an application for permission to bring an action as a poor person against __4_____ [or defend, etc., or otherwise proceed as the case may be] for __5_____ [briefly state the nature of the action], now, on reading and filing the affidavit of said __6_____ duly sworn to the __7__ day of __8_____, 19_9_, [If action has been commenced, insert provisions relative to notice and service thereof] and the certificate of __10_____, an attorney and counselor at law, admitted to practice in the courts of this State, dated the __11__ day of __12_____, 19_13_, [where required by the court] and on motion of __14_____, attorney for said petitioner, and no one appearing in opposition thereto, [or if appearance made, so state] it is hereby

ORDERED that said motion be and the same hereby is granted, and said __15_____ is hereby permitted to bring an action as a poor person against __16_____ [or defend or otherwise proceed, as the case may be] for __17_____ [briefly state the nature of the action], without paying fees to any officer, and if judgment is rendered against him in said action, or his complaint is dismissed, no costs shall be awarded against him, and it is further

ORDERED that __18_____ be and hereby is assigned as attorney and counsel of said __19_____ to prosecute said action against __20_____, [or defend or otherwise proceed, as the case may be] and said __21_____ shall act as such attorney and counsel without any compensation whatever, except, that if a recovery is had the court may allow the said __22_____, a reasonable sum for his services and taxable disbursements.

Signed this __23__ day of __24_____, 19_25_ at __26_____, New York.

Enter

__27_____
[Print signer's name below signature]
Justice, Supreme Court
__28_____ County

Form 4

Allegation in Complaint Where Plaintiff Sues as a Poor Person

On __1_____, 19_2_, an order was duly made by this court allowing the plaintiff in this action to sue as a poor person, pursuant to section 1101 of the Civil Practice Law and Rules.

Form 5

Notice of Motion for Leave to Proceed as a Poor Person When Motion Made After Action Brought

Notice of Motion

[Title of court and cause]   Index No. __1__ [if assigned]

PLEASE TAKE NOTICE that on the annexed affidavit of __2_____, sworn to the __3__ day of __4_____, 19_5_, and on the pleadings made and filed herein upon all the proceedings had herein, the undersigned will move this court at a motion term [Part I thereof], to be held in the county courthouse, in the County of __6_____, on the __7__ day of __8_____, 19_9_, at __10_____ o'clock in the forenoon of that day or as soon thereafter as counsel can be heard, for an order permitting the plaintiff herein to prosecute [or defend or otherwise proceed, as the case may be] this action as a poor person, and assigning an attorney and counselor at law for that purpose, and for such other and further relief as may be just.

Dated, __11_____, 19_12_.

__13_____
Attorney for Plaintiff
Office and Post Office Address

To __14_____, Attorney for Defendant   Telephone No.

To __15_____ County Attorney
Address
   or
To __16_____
Finance Administrator of the City of New York
Address

Form 6

Order Granting Leave to Proceed as a Poor Person After Action Brought

SUPREME COURT, __1____ COUNTY.

Order

[Title of cause]   Index No. __2__ [if assigned]

PRESENT: Hon. __3_____, Justice.

On reading and filing the notice of motion served herein and dated the __4__ day of __5_____, 19_6_, the affidavit of __7_____ sworn to __8_____, 19_9_, and the certificate of __10_____, an attorney and counselor at law dated __11_____, 19_12_ [where required by the court], and upon the summons, complaint and answer and all the proceedings had herein, and after hearing __13_____ for the petitioner, and __14_____ in opposition thereto, and the court being satisfied that there is merit to the moving party's contentions; it is

ORDERED that the moving party be permitted to prosecute as a poor person, and __15_____ is hereby assigned to him to act as counsel and attorney but without compensation except such allowance as may be made by the court for his services and taxable disbursements if a recovery is had herein.

Signed this __16__ day of __17_____, 19_18_, at __19_____, New York.

Enter

__20_____

[Print signer's name below signature]

Justice, Supreme Court

__21_____ County

Form 7

Notice of Motion for Permission to Prosecute Appeal as a Poor Person

Notice of Motion

[Title of appellate court and cause]   Index No. __1__

PLEASE TAKE NOTICE that upon the annexed affidavit of __2_____, sworn to the __3__ day of __4_____, 19_5_, and on the pleadings made and filed herein and on the stenographer's transcript of the trial had herein, and upon all the proceedings had herein, the undersigned will move this court at a stated term thereof for the hearing of motions to be held at the __6_____ courthouse, __7_____ Street [Borough of __8_____] City of __9_____ on the __10__ day of __11_____, 19_12_, at __13_____ o'clock in the __14__ noon on that day, or as soon thereafter as counsel can be heard, for an order permitting the plaintiff-appellant herein to prosecute this appeal as a poor person, and assigning an attorney and counselor at law for that purpose, and for such other and further relief as may be just.

[Date]

__15_____

Attorney for Plaintiff-Appellant

Address __16_____

Telephone No. __17__

To __18_____

     Attorney for Defendant-Respondent

     Address __19_____

To __20_____

     County Attorney, County of __21_____

     Address, New York __22_____

        or

To __23_____

     Finance Administrator City of New York

     Address __23_____

Form 8

Affidavit in Support of Motion for Permission to Prosecute Appeal as a Poor Person

[Title of appellate court and cause]   Affidavit
Index No. __1__

[Venue of affidavit]

__2____, being duly sworn, deposes and says:

1. That he resides at No. __3_____ Street in the City of __4_____ and State of New York and is the plaintiff-appellant in the above entitled action.

2. That this action was commenced on or about the __5__ day of __6_____, 19_7_ by the service of a summons and verified complaint on the defendant. Issue was joined by service of a verified answer on the plaintiff's attorney on the __8__ day of __9_____, 19_10_. The cause was thereafter placed upon the Trial Calendar for a General Term of Supreme Court held in and for the County of __11_____ commencing on the __12__ day of __13_____, 19_14_. The cause was reached for trial on the __15__ day of __16_____, 19_17_ and was tried before the Hon. __18_____ and a jury on the __19__ and __20__ days of __21_____, 19_22_. On the __23__ day of __24__, 19_25_ the jury returned a verdict in favor of the defendant and against the plaintiff. Judgment was entered in the office of the clerk of __26_____ County in favor of the defendant and against the plaintiff on the __27__ day of __28_____, 19_29_, and a certified copy of such judgment, with notice of entry thereof, was served on the plaintiff's attorney on the __30__ day of __31_____, 19_32_. Plaintiff appealed to this Court from such judgment by filing a notice of appeal in the office of the clerk of __33_____ County and serving a copy of such notice on the defendant's attorney on the __34__ day of __35_____, 19_36_.

3. That deponent is informed and verily believes that his contentions for appeal to this court have merit, by reason of the numerous errors committed upon the trial of this action in regard to the admission and exclusion of evidence, the charge to the jury and the granting and denial of requests to charge the jury all of which errors were prejudicial to deponent and to deponent's cause, all of which more fully appears in the pleadings and the stenographer's transcript of the minutes of the trial herein submitted herewith.

4. That the amount and sources of deponent's income are as follows: [show amount and sources of income].

5. That deponent's property and the value thereof is as follows: [List property with its value].

6. That deponent is unable to pay the costs, fees and expenses necessary to maintain this appeal.

7. That deponent desires that __37_____, an attorney and counselor at law, be assigned to prosecute this appeal and understands that such attorney will act without compensation except as may be allowed by the court if a recovery is had.

8. No previous application for the relief sought herein has been made to this or any other court.

WHEREFORE, deponent asks permission to prosecute the appeal in the above-entitled action as a poor person and that the court assign __38_____ as attorney and counsel for that purpose and that such attorney and counsel prosecute the same without compensation except such reasonable sum for his services and taxable disbursements as may be allowed by the court if recovery is had.

[Signature of deponent]
[Print signer's name below signature]

[Jurat]

Form 9

Certificate of Attorney in Support of Affidavit for Permission to Appeal as a Poor Person

[Title of appellate court and cause]   Certificate
Index No. __1__

I, __2_____, of No. __3__ __4_____ Street in the City of __5_____, County of __6_____, State of New York, an attorney and counsellor at law duly admitted to practice in the courts of the State of New York do hereby certify that I represented the plaintiff-appellant upon the trial of the case set forth in the foregoing affidavit, that I have examined such case and the transcript of such trial and I am of the opinion that deponent's contentions for appeal have merit. I am of the opinion that the following errors committed upon such trial require a reversal of the judgment entered against deponent and should be reviewed by this court: [State alleged errors in the admission and exclusion of evidence, the charge to the jury, etc.]

I stipulate and agree that I will prosecute such appeal on behalf of __7_____ without compensation except for what the court may assign to me as a reasonable sum for my services and taxable disbursements in the event of recovery.

[Date]

[Signature]
[Print signer's name below signature]

Form 10

Order Granting Permission to Prosecute Appeal as a Poor Person

Supreme Court, Appellate Division, [First] Department.

[Title of cause]   Order
Index No. __1__

Present: Hon. [Name of justices present].

A motion for an order allowing the plaintiff-appellant to prosecute the appeal herein as a poor person and assigning an attorney and counsel for that purpose having duly and regularly come on to be heard.

NOW on reading and filing the notice of motion dated __2__, __3_____, 19_4_, the affidavit of __5_____, sworn to __6__ __7_____, 19_8_, and the certificate of __9_____, an attorney and counselor at law dated __10__ __11_____, 19_12_ and upon the summons, complaint, answer, judgment, notice of appeal, transcript of trial and all the proceedings had herein, and after hearing __13_____ for the moving party, and __14_____ in opposition thereto, and the court being satisfied that the moving party's contentions for the appeal herein have merit; it is

ORDERED that the moving party be permitted to prosecute the appeal herein as a poor person, and __15_____ is hereby assigned to him to act as attorney and counsel without compensation except such allowance as may be made by the court for his services and taxable disbursements if a recovery is had herein.

Signed this __16__ day of __17_____, 19_18_ at __19_____, New York.

Enter

__20_____
[Print signer's name below signature]

§ 1102. Privileges of poor person

(a) Attorney. The court in its order permitting a person to proceed as a poor person may assign an attorney.

(b) Stenographic transcript. Where a party has been permitted by order to appeal as a poor person, the court clerk, within two days after the filing of said order with him, shall so notify the court stenographer, who, within twenty days of such notification shall make and certify two typewritten transcripts of the stenographic minutes of said trial or hearing, and shall deliver one of said transcripts to the poor person or his attorney, and file the other with the court clerk together with an affidavit of the fact and date of such delivery and filing. The expense of such transcripts shall be a county charge or, in the counties within the city of New York, a city charge, as the case may be, payable to the stenographer out of the court fund upon the certificate of the judge presiding at the trial or hearing. A poor person may be furnished with a stenographic transcript without fee by order of the court in proceedings other than appeal, the fee therefor to be paid by the county or, in the counties within the city of New York by the city, as the case may be, in the same manner as is paid for transcripts on appeal. Notwithstanding this or any other provision of law, fees paid for stenographic transcripts with respect to those proceedings specified in paragraph (a) of subdivision one of section thirty-five of the judiciary law shall be paid by the state in the manner prescribed by subdivision four of section thirty-five of the judiciary law.

(c) Appeals. On an appeal or motion for permission to appeal a poor person may submit typewritten briefs and appendices, furnishing one legible copy for each appellate justice.

(d) Costs and fees. A poor person shall not be liable for the payment of any costs or fees unless a recovery by judgment or by settlement is had in his favor in which event the court may direct him to pay out of the recovery all or part of the costs and fees, a reasonable sum for the services and expenses of his attorney and any sum expended by the county or city under subdivision (b).

HISTORY:

Add, L 1962, ch 308, eff Sept 1, 1963.
Sub (b), add, L 1966, ch 455, amd, L 1969, ch 681, eff Sept 1, 1969.
Former sub (b), amd, L 1964, ch 576, repealed L 1966, ch 455, eff Sept 1, 1966.
Subd (c), amd, L 1965, ch 773, eff Sept 1, 1965.
Subd (d), amd, L 1965, ch 773, eff Sept 1, 1965.
Earlier statutes and rules: CPA §§ 196, 558, 1493; RCP 36; CCP §§ 458, 460–462, 466, 467; 2 RS 444 pt 3, ch 8, tit 1, § 1; 2 RS 445 §§ 3–5.

ADVISORY COMMITTEE NOTES:

This section enumerates the privileges which inure to a person who is permitted to proceed as a poor person. **Subd (a)** is taken from part of the first sentence of rule 36 of the RCP and part of the last sentence of CPA § 196. On its face, the first sentence of rule 36 could be interpreted as not requiring assignment of an attorney when permission is granted; however, it has been held that a failure to make an assignment makes the order defective. See 20 Carmody-Wait, Cyclopedia of New York Practice 87 nn. 18 & 19 (1955). The word "may" has been substituted for "shall" so that appointment of an attorney to represent a poor person will be discretionary. It was pointed out that in some counties such as Wyoming, where the number of lawyers is quite small, requiring the appointment of an attorney for all poor persons would unduly burden the bar.

Subd (b) is taken from part of the CPA § 1493. It expressly states that notice of an application for a stenographic transcript must be given to the county attorney of the county in which the case was tried. This requirement is not found in CPA § 1493 but at least one court has held that such notice is required. See Rosetano v State of New York, 208 Misc 352, 143 NYS2d 904 (Ct Cl 1955). The Court of Appeals has recently indicated that omission of a requirement of prior notice might render the first paragraph of section 1493 constitutionally invalid. Smith v Smith, 2 NY2d 120, 138 NE2d 790 (1956). While the court did not have to decide whether such notice was required, since it found that the county had had a hearing on the merits "so that in the end there was no deprivation of due process," the majority opinion stated: "However, this is not to say that, if the circumstances warrant, a county may not successfully challenge a certificate issued under section 1493." Id. at 125, 138 NE2d at 793. The insertion of the requirement of notice in the new CPLR section will clear up this constitutional doubt. A county treasurer who is required to pay the transcript fee should have the opportunity to present the relevant facts on the financial position of a moving party before paying the fee. In some cases, as in the Smith case, all parties would be quite willing to shift the financial responsibility of obtaining the transcript to the county. See ibid (dissenting opinion).

Subd (c) is taken from CPA § 558 and has been changed only to the extent of conforming it to the phraseology of the new CPLR appeal provisions.

Subd (d) is taken from part of the first paragraph of § 1493, part of the last sentence of CPA § 196 and part of the first sentence of the RCP 36. Phrase "by judgment or by settlement" added because, although "recovery" was meant to embrace settlements, it might otherwise be construed as limited to recovery by judgment after trial. In contrast to portions of § 196 and rule 36, subd (d) is not limited to "taxable" disbursements. There is no reason for such a limitation; an attorney for a successful poor person plaintiff should be able to recover all disbursements which are approved by the trial court. Moreover, the former provision seems to imply that the attorney may be reimbursed for his disbursements only if his client wins, a rule that is unsound.

CROSS REFERENCES:

Motion for permission to proceed as poor person, CPLR 1101.
Distribution of recovery in favor of poor person, CPLR 1103.

CODES, RULES AND REGULATIONS:

Filing and service of records, briefs and appendices in Appellate Division, Fourth Judicial Department. 22 NYCRR 1000.5 (CLS App. Div. Rules—Fourth Judicial Dept. § 1000.5).
Payment for transcript in Fourth Judicial Department. 22 NYCRR 1027.1 (CLS App. Div. Rules—Fourth Judicial Dept. § 1027.1).

FEDERAL ASPECTS:

Attorney's fees for counsel appointed by United States District Court, 18 USCS § 3006A(d).
Payment by Marshal of Supreme Court of certain expenses in forma pauperis proceedings, 28 USCS § 672.
Fees for transcript of reporter in United States District Courts, 28 USCS § 753.
Costs and fees in United States courts, 28 USCS §§ 1911 et seq.
Forma pauperis proceedings in United States courts, 28 USCS § 1915.
Proceedings in forma pauperis, Rule 53 of United States Supreme Court Rules, USCS Court Rules.
Appeals from District Courts, Rule 3 et seq. of Federal Rules of Appellate Procedure, USCS Court Rules.
Transcript of proceedings on appeal, Rule 10(b) of Federal Rules of Appellate Procedure, USCS Court Rules.
Proceedings in forma pauperis in appellate courts, Rule 24 of Federal Rules of Appellate Procedure, USCS Court Rules.
Fees, § 17 of Rules of United States Court of Appeals for the Second Circuit, USCS Court Rules.

Costs in United States District Courts, Rule 54(d) of Federal Rules of Civil Procedure, USCS Court Rules.

RESEARCH REFERENCES AND PRACTICE AIDS:

13 NY Jur, Counties §§ 34, 134.

1 Carmody-Wait 2d, Officers of Court § 3:126.

10 Carmody-Wait 2d, Appeals in General § 70:59.

21 Carmody-Wait 2d, Actions and Proceedings By and Against Poor Persons §§ 127:15, 127:17, 127:22–127:30.

24 Carmody-Wait 2d, Costs §§ 148:38, 148:81.

28 Carmody-Wait 2d, Costs and Allowances § 167:19.

4 Am Jur 2d, Amusements and Exhibitions §§ 345–351.

20 Am Jur 2d, Costs §§ 47–51.

Annotations:

What costs or fees are contemplated by statute authorizing proceeding in forma pauperis. 98 ALR2d 292.

Building and construction contracts: contractor's equitable lien upon percentage of funds withheld by contractee or lender. 54 ALR3d 848.

What constitute "fees" or "costs" within meaning of Federal Statutory Provision (Under 28 USCS § 1915(a) and similar predecessor statutes) permitting party to proceed in forma pauperis without prepayment of fees and costs or security therefor. 20 ALR Fed 274.

Law Reviews:

Indigent defendant's rights on appeal in New York. 29 Brooklyn L Rev 261.

Parties and pleading under the CPLR. 31 Brooklyn L Rev 98.

Appointed counsel for the indigent civil defendant: a constitutional right without a judicial remedy? 36 Brooklyn L Rev 368.

Indigent's "right" to counsel in civil cases. 43 Fordham L Rev 989.

Forms:

See "FORMS" heading following "CASE NOTES", infra.

CASE NOTES

1. In general
2. Assignment and compensation of counsel
3. —Matrimonial actions
4. Stenographic transcript; appeals
5. Costs and fees
6. —Publication
7. —Counsel fees

1. In general

CPLR § 1102 is not applicable to a criminal proceeding. Cooper v Criminal Court of New York (1972) 71 Misc 2d 367, 336 NYS2d 201.

In a matrimonial action, applications for leave to serve summons by publication under the poor person's statutes (CPLR 1101, 1102) must be made upon notice to the city treasurer or county attorney, as the case may be. Jeffreys v Jeffreys (1968) 58 Misc 2d 1045, 296 NYS2d 74, revd on other grounds 38 AD2d 431, 330 NYS2d 550.

Where husband had been found, making service by publication unnecessary, and total costs in wife's divorce action were $25, wife's application under CPLR § 1101 and § 1102 to sue as an indigent person was properly denied in the court's discretion. Kirk v Kirk (1973) 41 AD2d 594, 340 NYS2d 346, app dismd 33 NY2d 636, 347 NYS2d 584, 301 NE2d 552.

The contention that, having sued as a poor person, the plaintiff was immune from responsibility for counsel fees for his wife which were made necessary by a divorce action, was without foundation, since CPLR § 1102 makes no mention of counsel fees, dealing as it does only with charges for transcripts, appeals without printing, and costs and fees for which a poor person is not liable. Gutierrez v Gutierrez (1972) 70 Misc 2d 16, 332 NYS2d 958.

The Rockland County Clerk may defer the question of the index number filing fee until determination of an application for leave to sue as a pauper. 1967 Ops Atty Gen August 9.

2. Assignment and compensation of counsel

The court upon motion may grant permission for a defendant to proceed as a poor person in a civil proceeding and may assign an attorney upon granting such leave. Garner v Garner (1969) 59 Misc 2d 29, 297 NYS2d 463.

An attorney assigned to represent an indigent defendant on appeal will not be relieved of his assignment on the basis of his alleged inexperience or incompetence in the field of criminal law and appellate practice, or because he feels in his conscience that he is being compelled to undertake a legal matter which he should not undertake, for lack of experience does not provide a basis for such relief; the number of defendants requiring assignment of counsel is large and the burden of such assignments should not be imposed solely upon those members of the bar specializing in criminal law. People v Maybusher (1965) 24 AD2d 765, 263 NYS2d 625.

Tenant, who was granted the right to defend an action by her landlord as a poor person, was entitled to the assignment of counsel, but if counsel was available to tenant through a public or semi-public agency, tenant should be relegated to such an agency. Hotel Martha Washington Management Co. v Swinick (1971) 66 Misc 2d 833, 322 NYS2d 139.

There is no absolute right to assigned counsel in private litigation; whether in a particular case counsel shall be assigned lies instead in the discretion of the court. Re Smiley (1975) 36 NY2d 433, 369 NYS2d 87, 330 NE2d 53.

Inherent in courts and historically associated with the duty of the Bar to provide uncompensated services for the indigent has been the discretionary power of the court to assign counsel in a proper case to represent private indigent litigants without compensation. Re Smiley (1975) 36 NY2d 433, 369 NYS2d 87, 330 NE2d 53.

3. —Matrimonial actions

Indigent parties in divorce proceedings had no constitutional due process or equal protection right to appointed counsel. Menin v Menin (1974) 79 Misc 2d 285, 359 NYS2d 721.

Indigent wife, as plaintiff or defendant in a divorce action, is not entitled as a matter of constitutional right to have county provide her with counsel or compensate counsel retained by her, and there is no power in the courts to direct the provision of counsel or require compensation of retained counsel for indigent wife out of public funds, absent statutory authority. Re Smiley (1975) 36 NY2d 433, 369 NYS2d 87, 330 NE2d 53.

Courts have a broad discretionary power to assign counsel without compensation for indigent parties in divorce actions, and the Bar has a duty to respond. Re Smiley (1975) 36 NY2d 433, 369 NYS2d 87, 330 NE2d 53.

It would be injudicious to mandate in all matrimonial cases involving indigents the assignment of counsel without the possibility of provision for compensation. Re Smiley (1975) 36 NY2d 433, 369 NYS2d 87, 330 NE2d 53.

Although circumstances of defendant in action for divorce and for related relief clearly warranted assignment of counsel by court, court's assignment

of county legal assistance corporation, a federally funded agency, over objection of the corporation was an improvident exercise of discretion, in view of limitations imposed on scope of corporation's authorization to participate in the performance of legal services. Cerami v Cerami (1974) 44 AD2d 890, 355 NYS2d 861.

Fact that need and burden or representing indigent matrimonial suitors and other private litigants may overtax voluntary private resources and voluntary services available from the Bar on a noncompensated basis is a problem to be addressed to the legislature, which has the power to appropriate funds for publicly compensated counsel. Re Smiley (1975) 36 NY2d 433, 369 NYS2d 87, 330 NE2d 53.

Where petitioner asked County Department of Social Services to provide him lawyer for obtaining divorce from wife or in the alternative to pay fee for lawyer of his choice and was advised that no funds were available for such purpose, action by petitioner to compel department to provide him with lawyer was not premature by reason of his failure to apply for "fair hearing" as doctrine of exclusion of administrative remedies is inapplicable where such exclusion would be futile. Bartlett v Kitchin (1973) 76 Misc 2d 1087, 352 NYS2d 110.

Although an attorney should be assigned to represent an indigent person in a matrimonial action, court had no authority to require municipality to pay fee of assigned counsel or the fee of counsel privately retained by the indigent person. Vanderpool v Vanderpool (1973) 43 AD2d 716, 350 NYS2d 435.

Supreme Court had no authority under CPLR § 1102 to direct city to pay fees of counsel appointed or selected to represent indigent parties in divorce actions. Jacox v Jacox (1973) 43 AD2d 716, 350 NYS2d 435.

4. Stenographic transcript; appeals

The taking of a deposition before trial is not a "proceeding" within the meaning of CPLR 1102, subd (b). Lester v Lester (1972) 69 Misc 2d 528, 330 NYS2d 190.

Although appellate court may permit appeal to be prosecuted upon one typewritten record on appeal and five typewritten briefs, application for stenographic transcript without charge must be made in the first instance to the trial court. Jenks v Murphy (1964) 20 AD2d 757, 247 NYS2d 535.

After service of notice of appeal, the initial application for permission to proceed as a poor person and for the transcript of the stenographer's minutes should be made to the trial court, and the determination of the trial court thereon is subject to review on appeal. If such application is granted by the trial court, application can then be made to the appellate court for leave to proceed on a single copy of the record and five typewritten briefs. Jenks v Murphy (1964) 21 AD2d 346, 250 NYS2d 848.

An application for a stenographic transcript of the trial proceedings to be furnished at the expense of the county under subd (b) of this section should be made in the first instance to the trial court, and referred to the justice who presided at the trial. Dowell v Remmer (1965) 24 AD2d 543, 261 NYS2d 749, motion dismd 16 NY2d 864, 264 NYS2d 101, 211 NE2d 522.

One seeking to prosecute an appeal as a poor person should disclose whether or not he has sufficient assets with which to obtain a copy of the minutes of the trial. Jenks v Murphy (1964) 21 AD2d 346, 250 NYS2d 848.

Where Appellate Division had refused respondent permission to proceed as a poor person, but merely gave him leave to appeal on a typewritten record and briefs, Trial Term was in error in directing City Treasurer to furnish him with a free transcript. Moriarity v Butler Bin Co. (1964) 21 AD2d 865, 251 NYS2d 44, affd 15 NY2d 901, 258 NYS2d 429, 206 NE2d 361.

Under CPLR 1102, a party has no statutory right to have the county pay for a stenographic transcript of depositions taken before trial. Lester v Lester (1972) 69 Misc 2d 528, 330 NYS2d 190.

The legislature never intended the county to be liable for the stenographer's fee for recording and transcribing an examination before trial. Lester v Lester (1972) 69 Misc 2d 528, 330 NYS2d 190.

5. Costs and fees

The poor person's statutes (CPLR 1101, 1102) do not require the city to pay the cost of serving a summons by publication. Jeffreys v Jeffreys (1968) 58 Misc 2d 1045, 296 NYS2d 74, revd on other grounds 38 AD2d 431, 330 NYS2d 550.

Petitioner's allegation that she was the recipient of public assistance and had no available property to draw upon established prima facie that she was unable to pay the cost, fees and expenses necessary to prosecute her contemplated action. Emerson v Emerson (1970) 33 AD2d 1022, 308 NYS2d 69.

On appeal by the mother from an order awarding custody of their children to the father, she was allowed to proceed as a poor person, but if she later realized a recovery to the court's final determination that the father should pay her expenses, the county might look to that fund for reimbursement. State ex rel. Rowlee v Rowlee (1970) 62 Misc 2d 64, 307 NYS2d 901.

6. —Publication

Costs of publication are not among the items included in CPLR Article 11 for which an indigent is excused from payment and the constitutional question of whether denial of access to the courts in the matrimonial action by reason of indigency violates the equal protection clause of the Constitution will not be decided where it is raised for the first time on appeal. Brown v Brown (1970) 34 AD2d 727, 311 NYS2d 780.

Indigent plaintiff seeking divorce may not be denied access to the courts because of inability to pay court fees and cost, including the cost for publication of notice which is an auxiliary expense payable to a third person other than a public officer. Deason v Deason (1973) 32 NY2d 93, 343 NYS2d 321, 296 NE2d 229.

In the absence of legislation on the issue, court costs, including the costs of publication of notice, in divorce action brought by indigent plaintiff should be borne by the local rather than the state government. Deason v Deason (1973) 32 NY2d 93, 343 NYS2d 321, 296 NE2d 229.

The publication fees legally incurred in a matrimonial action are "costs" which may be an appropriate county charge under direction of the court when a person has been granted permission to proceed as a poor person. Brown v Wyman (1969) 59 Misc 2d 740, 300 NYS2d 254.

In the absence of specific legislative authorization, a city is not required to pay the cost of publication in a matrimonial action brought by an indigent, and the obligation to pay such expenses remains with the State. Jeffreys v Jeffreys (1972) 38 AD2d 431, 330 NYS2d 550.

Where the plaintiff has been granted permission to proceed as a poor person in a divorce action, the cost of publication is chargeable against the county as part of the cost. McCandless v McCandless (1972) 38 AD2d 171, 327 NYS2d 896.

There is no provision of law which authorizes a city to pay costs and expenses of service by publication in a matrimonial action in behalf of an indigent plaintiff. Jackson v Jackson (1971) 37 AD2d 953, 326 NYS2d 224.

7. —Counsel fees

An indigent wife in a matrimonial action has the right to private counsel of her own choosing and may apply to the court for an award of counsel fees to enable her to defend the action; that her husband is an adjudicated poor person and may be unable to pay the fees is of no consequence provided he is not thereby barred from access to the courts. Thomas v Thomas (1973) 72 Misc 2d 749, 340 NYS2d 753.

While CPLR § 1102 bars assessment of costs and fees against a poor person, assessment of auxiliary costs such as counsel fees is not proscribed. Thomas v Thomas (1973) 72 Misc 2d 749, 340 NYS2d 753.

Supreme Court had no authority under CPLR § 1102 to direct city to pay fees of counsel appointed or selected to represent indigent parties in divorce actions. Jacox v Jacox (1973) 43 AD2d 716, 350 NYS2d 435.

Although an attorney should be assigned to represent an indigent person in a matrimonial action, court had no authority to require municipality to pay fee of assigned counsel or the fee of counsel privately retained by the indigent person. Vanderpool v Vanderpool (1973) 43 AD2d 716, 350 NYS2d 435.

The contention that, having sued as a poor person, the plaintiff was immune from responsibility for counsel fees for his wife which were made necessary by a divorce action, was without foundation, since CPLR § 1102 makes no mention of counsel fees, dealing as it does only with charges for transcripts, appeals without printing, and costs and fees for which a poor person is not liable. Gutierrez v Gutierrez (1972) 70 Misc 2d 16, 332 NYS2d 958.

In absence of statutory authority for payment of assigned counsel in matrimonial actions and ap-

propriation of funds to implement such authority, trial court could not direct payment of counsel fees by county to attorney who was assigned to represent indigent plaintiff in matrimonial action. Birch v Birch (1974) 89 Misc 2d 630, 392 NYS2d 345.

CASE NOTES

UNDER FORMER CIVIL PRACTICE LAWS

See also Case Notes under § 1101, supra.

A. IN GENERAL
1. Generally
2. Applicability to court of claims
3. Applicability to federal court
4. Assignment of counsel
5. —Compensation of counsel
6. Stenographic minutes
7. Fees

B. COSTS
8. Generally
9. Allowance against poor person
10. Allowance to poor person

A. IN GENERAL

1. Generally

A poor person, referred to in CPA § 558, is one who has been allowed to sue or defend as a poor person. Siegelbaum v Dowling (1938) 279 NY 22, 17 NE2d 409; La Barbera v Hart & Crouse Co. (1936) 248 AD 261, 289 NYS 567; Robertson v Schoonmaker (1936) 249 AD 657, 291 NYS 487.

CPA § 1493 cited in Agnello v Weissglass GSD Corp. (1940) 260 AD 925, 1039, 23 NYS2d 122.

2. Applicability to court of claims

RCP 36 applied to court of claims. Johnson v State (1945, Ct Cl) 55 NYS2d 792. Followed in Lipschultz v State (1948) 192 Misc 70, 78 NYS2d 731.

Proper course for claimant desiring to review as poor person dismissal of his claim by Court of Claims is to appeal to Appellate Division and then make due application to said Court upon due notice to State of New York for permission to appeal as poor person and for assignment of counsel for that purpose. Rosetano v State (1955) 208 Misc 352, 143 NYS2d 904.

3. Applicability to federal court

RCP 36 was inapplicable to a federal court action. Re Tyndall (1907) 117 AD 294, 102 NYS 211, affd 190 NY 522, 83 NE 1133.

4. Assignment of counsel

Under former rules, order for leave to prosecute as a poor person is fatally defective where it does not assign an attorney. Pankawicus v Nichols Copper Co. (1915) 169 AD 419, 155 NYS 123.

The court is not obliged to assign the attorney designated by a party applying for leave to sue as a poor person. Helmprecht v Bowen (1895) 87 Hun 362, 34 NYS 1141.

5. —Compensation of counsel

Prior to the amendment, where leave to prosecute an action as a poor person was granted, an attorney who obtained such leave was bound to act for the plaintiff without compensation beyond costs recovered, and was not entitled to retain any portion of the recovery, notwithstanding an agreement with the plaintiff therefor, even though the costs of the action were set off against the costs recovered by defendant against his client in a former action for the same cause. Daus v Nussberger (1898) 25 AD 185, 49 NYS 291; Rutkowsky v Cohen (1902) 74 AD 415, 77 NYS 546; Sumkow v Sheinker (1903) 84 AD 463, 82 NYS 995; Schechter v Lichtenstein (1928) 223 AD 60, 227 NYS 245; Re Kelly, 12 Daly 110; Shapiro v Burns (1894) 7 Misc 418, 27 NYS 980; Helmprecht v Bowen (1895) 87 Hun 362, 34 NYS 1141.

Agreement with attorney for contingent fees as barring leave to sue as poor person. See Cahill v Manhattan R. Co. (1899) 38 AD 314, 57 NYS 10.

Where an attorney agreed to act as the attorney for a party petitioning to sue in forma pauperis "without compensation except the statutory costs," an order allowing the party to so sue should have been granted, as under CPA § 1493 (this section) costs awarded to a party, suing as a poor person were to be divided between the attorney and counsel in the case. Malkin v Postal Typewriter Co. (1904) 95 AD 205, 88 NYS 403.

6. Stenographic minutes

CPA § 1493 so far as it related to stenographic minutes, could not be invoked in the Appellate Division. Commissioner of Public Welfare v Sonsky (1940) 259 AD 831, 19 NYS2d 219.

Order denying motion for transcript of stenographer's minutes reversed where papers on appeal establish prima facie case forbidding dismissal of complaint. Skolnick v Fumo (1941) 261 AD 1002, 27 NYS2d 445.

Application by claimant, who was obtained permission to prosecute appeal from judgment of Court of Claims as poor person, for copy of stenographer's minutes of trial without cost, denied. Ehde v State, 173 Misc 1095, 19 NYS2d 674, revd 260 AD 511, 23 NYS2d 616.

The Court of Claims had jurisdiction, under CPA § 1493 to order its official stenographer to furnish the claimant, authorized by the Appellate Division to prosecute his appeal as a poor person with a transcript of the testimony taken upon the trial and to issue to him a certificate fixing the amount of his fees. Ehde v State (1940) 260 AD 511, 23 NYS2d 616.

Where Appellate Division denied plaintiff's motion for leave to appeal as poor person, but permitted appeal to be prosecuted on typewritten papers, plaintiff, never thereby acquiring status of "poor person", was not entitled to an order requiring official court stenographer to furnish him with copy of stenographic minutes of his trial. Scarpulla v Mogavero (1960) 23 Misc 2d 294, 200 NYS2d 998.

A motion by the attorney for the plaintiffs in a negligence action, under CPA § 1493 for an order directing the stenographer who took the minutes of the trial to furnish a copy thereof to the plaintiffs without charge, made after permission had been granted to the plaintiffs to prosecute their appeal as poor persons, was denied, where no disclosure had been made to the court as to the terms of the agreement between counsel and the plaintiffs as to the amount of fee to be paid. Lawrence v Murray (1939) 171 Misc 666, 12 NYS2d 262.

See Lipschultz v State (1948) 192 Misc 70, 78 NYS2d 731.

Where permission has been granted to prosecute appeal as poor person, public policy permits court to order county in which such action was tried to bear expense of furnishing stenographic minutes of trial to such poor person. County of Sullivan v Smith (1955) 286 AD 1060, 144 NYS2d 859, affd Smith v Smith, 2 NY2d 120, 157 NYS2d 546, 138 NE2d 790.

Where person has been permitted to prosecute as poor person, stenographer's minutes for use on appeal should be furnished only upon order of court or justice before whom case was tried. People v Sutliff (1956) 1 AD2d 985, 150 NYS2d 86.

Where defendant was convicted of burglary in County Court and he filed notice of motion and pauper's oath to obtain copy of stenographer's minutes of trial for appeal, County Court had power to issue certificate to official stenographer covering his statutory fees for minutes and County Treasurer was directed to pay therefor. People v Jackson (1956) 2 Misc 2d 521, 152 NYS2d 893.

On an appeal as a poor person the trial court will issue a certificate of the sum which the court must pay to the official stenographer if notice of the application is given to the county attorney and where the case is tried in one county and testimony of a medical witness taken at a session of court in another county, notice must be given to the county attorneys for both counties. Pisacano v State (1957) 8 Misc 2d 937, 938, 169 NYS2d 133, 134.

Where Appellate Division denied plaintiff's motion for leave to appeal as poor person, but permitted appeal to be prosecuted on typewritten papers, plaintiff, never thereby acquiring status of "poor person", was not entitled to an order requiring official court stenographer to furnish him with copy of stenographic minutes of his trial. Scarpulla v Mogavero (1960) 23 Misc 2d 294, 200 NYS2d 998.

Appellant permitted to appeal as poor person must make his application to obtain a transcript of the minutes at county expense before the court or judge before whom the hearing was held. People ex rel. Quinones v O'Neill (1961) 12 AD2d 980, 212 NYS2d 676.

7. Fees

Under CPA § 558, a county clerk was not required to furnish or file a judgment roll but was required to certify, without fee, the correctness of papers on file in his office. People v Straub (1958) 5 AD2d 854, 170 NYS2d 102.

Ex parte application of mental hospital inmate for order directing that subpoenas for witnesses he wished to call in his pending habeas corpus proceeding be served at county's expense would not be considered on the merits where he had failed to apply first for leave to sue as a poor person and had failed to show a meritorious ground for his proceeding. People ex rel. King v McNeill (1961) 30 Misc 2d 566, 219 NYS2d 118, cert den 370 US 932, 8 L Ed 2d 832, 82 S Ct 1599.

B. Costs

8. Generally

Admission to prosecution as poor person must be shown before trial court is authorized to transfer obligation of paying costs of stenographer's minutes from litigant to county. Rocco v New York (1954) 283 AD 1056, 131 NYS2d 506.

On affirmance by Court of Appeals of determination of Appellate Division affirming decree of Surrogate, where Court of Appeals granted appellants leave to prosecute appeal to such court, Surrogate cannot make allowance for costs for proceeding in Court of Appeals. Re Jennings' Estate (1956) 3 Misc 2d 601, 154 NYS2d 689.

9. Allowance against poor person

Successful defendant may recover costs from unsuccessful infant who can avoid such liability only by suing as poor person. Stevenson v Guardian Life Ins. Co. (1941) 175 Misc 823, 25 NYS2d 483.

The authority of the trial court under CPA § 1493, to transfer the obligation of paying the cost of the stenographer's minutes from the litigant to the county was applicable only where the litigant had been admitted to prosecute as a poor person. Rocco v New York (1954) 283 AD 1056, 131 NYS2d 506.

Where leave had been granted to prosecute or defend as a poor person, the imposition of costs was error; under such circumstance CPA §§ 1488, former CPA 1491 (§ 8107 herein) and 1520 (§ 5101 herein) were to be read in conjunction with and were limited by CPA § 1493. Waterman v Byrne (1958) 5 AD2d 822, 171 NYS2d 39.

A plaintiff who had been allowed to sue as a poor person could not be held liable for costs even though the recovery was less than $50; such a case was governed by former CPA § 461. Weltman v Posenecker (1897) 19 Misc 592, 44 NYS 406, revg 18 Misc 599, 42 NYS 699.

Interlocutory costs not to be awarded against him. Steele v Mott, 20 Wend 679.

A person who sues as a poor person may appeal from a judgment but he is chargeable if unsuccessful with costs. Hayden v Hayden (1896) 8 AD 547, 40 NYS 865.

In action in which the jury brought in a verdict for both the plaintiff and the defendant on separate causes of action in the complaint, the defendant was not entitled, under CPA § 1483 (§ 8103 herein) to include costs in its judgment against the plaintiff who sued as a poor person. Wilson v Metropolitan L. Ins. Co. 167 Misc 853, 4 NYS2d 147, mod 168 Misc 125, 5 NYS2d 310.

10. Allowance to poor person

CPA § 1470 (§ 8101 herein) construed with CPA § 196 in holding that successful plaintiff was entitled to costs as matter of right though suing in forma pauperis. Flock v Langley (1943, Co Ct) 42 NYS2d 37.

CPA § 196 made no provision regarding costs where the plaintiff was wholly or partially successful, but in such case costs followed as in an action by an ordinary litigant. Weltman v Posenecker, 18 Misc 599, 42 NYS 699, revd 19 Misc 592, 44 NYS 406.

If he recovers, costs are in the discretion of the court. Williams v Wilkins, 3 Johns Ch 65.

Not to be awarded to him on overruling informal plea, if the defense is finally established. Bolton v Gardner, 3 Paige 273.

FORMS

Form 1—Notice of motion for stenographic transcript without fee

Form 2—Certificate of justice directing payment of fees to official stenographer

Form 3—Provision in order directing furnishing of stenographic minutes to poor person

Form 1

Notice of Motion for Stenographic Transcript Without Fee

Notice of Motion

[Title of court and cause]   Index No. __1__ [if assigned]

Sir:

Please take notice that upon the order entered in the above-entitled action on the __2__ day of __3_____, 19_4_, permitting __5_____ [plaintiff or defendant] to proceed herein as a poor person, and upon all the proceedings had in this action, a motion will be made at a motion term, part __6__, of the Supreme Court, held in and for the County of __7_____, at the county courthouse in the City of __8_____, New York, on the __9__ day of __10_____, 19_11_, at __12__ o'clock in the __13_____ noon of that day, or as soon thereafter as counsel can be heard, for an order directing the furnishing of stenographic minutes of the above-entitled action to __14_____ [plaintiff or defendant], without fee, pursuant to § 1102[b] of the Civil Practice Law and Rules.

Date, __15__, __16_____ 19_17_.

__18_____

Attorney for [plaintiff or defendant]
Office and postoffice address
Telephone No.

To: __19_____
Attorney for [defendant or plaintiff]
Address __20_____

To: __21_____ County Attorney
Address
    or

To: __22_____ Finance Administrator of the City of New York
Address

Form 2

Certificate of Justice Directing Payment of Fees to Official Stenographer

Supreme Court, _____¹_____ County.

[Title of action]	Certificate of payment of stenographer's fees Index No. _²_ [if assigned]

To the county treasurer of the County of _³_____ (or the Finance Administrator of the City of New York.)

I, _⁴_____, justice of the Supreme Court of the State of New York, before whom the above-entitled action was tried, hereby certify that _⁵_____, official stenographer of this court, who took the minutes of the trial of the above-entitled action is entitled to the sum of $_⁶_, as a fee for such minutes furnished by my order to the plaintiff _⁷_____ prosecuting as a poor person and direct that said fee be paid to him by _⁸_____, county treasurer, (or Finance Administrator of the City of New York), upon the presentation of this certificate.

Signed this _⁹_ day of _¹⁰_____, 19_¹¹_ at _¹²_____, New York.

_____13_____

[Print signer's name below signature]
Justice, Supreme Court
_¹⁴_____ County

Form 3

Provision in Order Directing Furnishing of Stenographic Minutes to Poor Person

Ordered that _¹_____ [name of official stenographer], and official stenographer of this court, furnished to _²_____ [plaintiff or defendant proceeding as a poor person], or his attorney a copy of the minutes taken by him upon the trial of this action.

§ 1103. Distribution of recovery in favor of poor person

Any recovery by judgment or by settlement had in favor of a poor person, shall be paid to the clerk of the court in which the order permitting the person to proceed as a poor person was entered, to await distribution pursuant to court order.

HISTORY:

> Add, L 1962, ch 308, eff Sept 1, 1963.
> Earlier statutes: CPA § 1493; CCP §§ 461 (part), 467; 2 RS 445, § 4.

ADVISORY COMMITTEE NOTES:

> This section replaces the last two paragraphs of CPA § 1493. The provisions of these paragraphs are too inelastic; for example, when the recovery is of property necessary for the poor person or his family it may be inappropriate for the court to order that costs be paid out of the recovery. Under this section the eventual distribution of any recovery in favor of a poor person is left to the discretion of a court. The requirement that the recovery be paid into court assures the safety of the property until the court directs final distribution. The word "recovery" includes amounts received as a settlement and as costs.

FEDERAL ASPECTS:

> Forma pauperis proceedings in United States courts, 28 USCS § 1915.
> Proceedings in forma pauperis, Rule 53 of United States Supreme Court Rules, USCS Court Rules.
> Proceedings in forma pauperis in appellate courts, Rule 24 of Federal Rules of Appellate Procedure, USCS Court Rules.

RESEARCH REFERENCES AND PRACTICE AIDS:
13 NY Jur, Counties § 134.

**[CPLR 1104–1200 have been reserved for future use.
Please check your supplement.]**

ARTICLE 12

Infants and Incompetents

HISTORY:

Add, L 1962, ch 308, eff Sept 1, 1963.

ADVISORY COMMITTEE NOTES:

Generally. This article is a consolidation and reorganization of various sections of the CPA and RCP relating to infants and incompetents. It replaces §§ 201 through 208, § 492, § 980-a, §§ 1320 through 1324, the last paragraph of § 1377 and subdivision 1 of § 1448 of the CPA and rules 39 through 44 and rule 294 of the RCP.

Representative generally. The new provisions alter former law in several respects. Section 1201 eliminates the requirement that a guardian ad litem be appointed to represent the interests of an infant when there is a guardian of the property of the infant, permits a parent to represent his or her child without being appointed a guardian, and provides that a guardian ad litem should be appointed for an adult defendant who is incapable of adequately protecting his rights although he has not been judicially declared incompetent. New rule 1202(a) adds to those classes of persons who are permitted to move for the appointment of a guardian ad litem. New § 1203 eliminates the need for a guardian ad litem as a prerequisite for entry of default judgments against infants whose representatives have appeared in the action and grants to incompetent persons the same protections given to infants in respect to defaults. Cf. § 120. New § 1206 simplifies the procedure for disposing of the proceeds of claims of infants or adjudicated incompetents; it protects the proceeds of all claims and not merely those resulting from personal injuries as does CPA § 980-a.

Settlement of claims. New CPLR § 1207 expands the scope of the provision relating to the settlement of infant claims so as to permit the settlement of all claims by infants. Under former provisions only certain types of claims by infants could be settled before an action was commenced.

Section 201, stating that when an infant has a right of action he may maintain an action thereon, and the last paragraph of CPA § 1377, permitting an action on behalf of an incompetent to be brought in the name of the committee, have been omitted from this article.

In rem jurisdiction. Section 206 of the CPA provides an alternative to the method set out in § 203 for the appointment of a guardian ad litem to represent a nonresident infant defendant or an infant defendant who is temporarily absent from the state. It is omitted. Where an appointment is made in this manner the summons in the action is served upon the appointed guardian rather than upon the infant. CPA § 224. The purpose of §§ 206 and 224 was to permit a plaintiff to save costs of publication. Such a special method is unnecessary under the new CPLR because the court can acquire in rem jurisdiction by personal delivery to the infant outside the state. See new CPLR § 314.

Qualification of representative. Subparagraphs 1, 2, and 4 of RCP 40, 41, 42 and 44 have also been omitted from this article. The first part of subparagraph 1, stating that the guardian ad litem may be the general guardian of the infant, is unnecessary because of proposed new CPLR § 1201. Self-evident are the last part of subparagraph 1, stating that a person appointed must be fully competent to protect the rights of the ward, and those parts of subparagraph 2, which provide that the guardian shall have no interest adverse to the ward and that the guardian shall not be connected in business with the attorney or counsel of any adverse party. The remainder of subparagraph 2, which provides that the guardian shall not be nominated by any person having an adverse interest, is too restrictive. See new CPLR rule 1202(a), listing persons who may move for the appointment of a guardian ad litem. Subparagraph 4, permitting a trust company to be appointed guardian ad litem, is unnecessary since a trust company which is a guardian or committee of the property of the ward may represent the ward under new § 1201.

Duties and responsibilities of representative. The duties of a guardian ad litem or special guardian to examine the case, to account for all moneys received and to invest the same pursuant to court direction are self-evident and need not be set out as they are in RCP 42. RCP 44 has been eliminated for the reasons stated in the notes to new CPLR rule 1202(a).

RCP 41, providing that a guardian ad litem, special guardian or petitioner under CPA art 80 shall not be permitted to receive any money or property of his ward except for his costs and expenses allowed by the court until he has given sufficient security, has been omitted. There is no reason to prohibit distribution to such a person since new CPLR § 1206 specifically provides for the disposition of the ward's property.

RESEARCH REFERENCES AND PRACTICE AIDS:

14 Carmody-Wait 2d, Partition § 91:30.
22 Carmody-Wait 2d, Proceeding Relating to Express Trusts § 131:4.

§ 1201. Representation of infant or incompetent person

Unless the court appoints a guardian ad litem, an infant shall appear by the guardian of his property or, if there is no such guardian, by a parent having legal custody, or, if there is no such parent, by another person or agency having legal custody, or, if the infant is married, by an adult spouse residing with the infant, and a person judicially declared to be incompetent shall appear by the committee of his property. A person shall appear by his guardian ad litem if he is an infant and has no guardian of his property, parent, or other person or agency having legal custody, or adult spouse with whom he resides, or if he is an infant or person judicially declared to be incompetent and the court so directs because of a conflict of interest or for other cause, or if he is an adult incapable of adequately prosecuting or defending his rights.

HISTORY:

Add, L 1962, ch 308, amd, L 1968, ch 844, L 1974, ch 606, eff May 30, 1974.
Earlier statutes: CPA §§ 202, 208, 1389, 1390; CCP §§ 426, 428, 469, 471, 472, 1535; 2 RS 317 § 2; 2 RS 446 §§ 2, 4.

ADVISORY COMMITTEE NOTES:

(See also advisory committee notes preceding this section under subheading "Representatives generally.") This section is new. It replaces parts of CPA §§ 202 and 208. Section 202 requires that an infant appear by a guardian ad litem despite the fact that there is an appointed guardian of his property. Such a procedure is unnecessary and wasteful. The infant should appear by his already appointed guardian unless the court otherwise directs just as an incompetent person appears by the committee of his property. See NY Temp Comm'n on the Courts Rep III 228, Leg Doc 6(b) (1957). In cases where such guardian or committee has an adverse interest the court should appoint a guardian ad litem. CPA § 208; cf. new CPLR rule 1202(a). The court may direct representation by a guardian ad litem "for other cause," such as the fact that the guardian or committee is a nonresident.

Another substantial change in former law is made by permitting a parent to appear for his child if there is no appointed guardian of the child's property. In many cases the interests of the infant can be adequately protected by such representation and the expense of a guardian ad litem may be saved. If the court believes that a guardian ad litem is necessary to protect the infant's interests, the last sentence of the section gives broad authority to the court to order such representation. Representation by a guardian ad litem might well be required in actions involving the title to real property.

This section uses the words "guardian of his property." Such a guardian may be appointed in any one of three ways: by court order, by will or by deed (see Surr Ct Act § 172) and would include a "general guardian of the property" of an infant. Section 81 of the Domestic Relations Law states that a guardian by will may not lawfully act until the will is admitted to probate and that a guardian by deed likewise cannot lawfully act until the deed is executed and recorded pursuant to § 187 of the Surrogate's Court Act; therefore, a condition precedent is imposed upon such a guardian acting under this section.

The last phrase of the last sentence of this section requires that a defendant, other than an infant or judicially declared incompetent, who is incapable of adequately protecting his rights be represented by a guardian ad litem. Under former law, such a defendant's interests were protected in essentially the same manner. CPA § 226(1) permitted a court to order that a copy of a summons also be delivered to a designated person and after such an order is made service is not complete until a copy of the summons is so delivered. The designated person is required to examine the case and protect the rights of the defendant until and unless a special guardian is appointed. RCP 44. In reality, the designated person is a special guardian. If no order requiring service of process on a designated person on behalf of such a defendant is made the proper procedure is to have a guardian ad litem appointed. See 19 Carmody-Wait, Cyclopedia of New York Practice 715 (1955). There is no reason to require that the guardian ad litem for such a defendant be served with a summons. His appointment will apprise him of the action. Under new CPLR § 309 service will have already been made and this service should be sufficient in itself to give the court jurisdiction and stop the running of the statutes of limitation.

Adoption of this provision permits omission of RCP 44 and the last sentence of CPA § 203.

New CPLR rule 1202(a) permits the infant or incompetent to be protected "at any stage" of the action on the court's own initiative. Where a party has information indicating that another party is incompetent to protect his interests it should be revealed to the court so that the court can appoint a guardian. Failure to suggest the party's inadequacy to the court would constitute a fraud which could be the basis for a motion to set aside any judgment.

CROSS REFERENCES:

This section referred to in 321, 7704.
Appointment of guardian ad litem, 1202.
Compensation of guardian ad litem, 1204.
Action to determine claim to property, Real P Actions & Pr Law § 1513.
Action to register title, Real P Law § 388.

CODES, RULES AND REGULATIONS:

Service of legal process and execution of instruments by mentally ill patients. 14 NYCRR 22.

FEDERAL ASPECTS:

National banks acting as committee for incompetent persons, 12 USCS § 92a.
Magistrates' duties with respect to juvenile proceedings, 18 USCS § 5034.
Appointment of guardian under Longshoremen's and Harbor Workers' Compensation Act, 33 USCS § 911.
Infants or incompetent persons as parties in United States District Courts, Rule 17(c) of Federal Rules of Civil Procedure, USCS Court Rules.
Substitution of parties in United States District Courts, Rule 25(b) of Federal Rules of Civil Procedure, USCS Court Rules.

RESEARCH REFERENCES AND PRACTICE AIDS:

20 NY Jur, Equity § 148.
25 NY Jur, Guardian and Ward § 121.
28 NY Jur, Infants §§ 61, 62, 64.
1 Carmody-Wait 2d, Officers of Court §§ 3:58, 3:97.
2 Carmody-Wait 2d, Limitation of Actions § 13:209.
3 Carmody-Wait 2d, Steps Preliminary to Bringing Suit; Leave to Sue § 14:1.
8 Carmody-Wait 2d, Judgments § 63:71.
14 Carmody-Wait 2d, Partition § 91:31.
17 Carmody-Wait 2d, Proceeding for Disposition of Real Property of Infant or Incompetent § 106:4.
17 Carmody-Wait 2d, Committee for an Incompetent or a Mental Patient § 109:13.
18 Carmody-Wait 2d, Absolute Divorce §§ 114:80, 114:81.
19 Carmody-Wait 2d, Actions in the Court of Claims § 120:31.
21 Carmody-Wait 2d, Actions and Proceedings By and Against Infants and Incompetents §§ 124:2, 124:10, 124:13 et seq.
21 Carmody-Wait 2d, Litigation By and Against Fiduciaries § 129:40.
41 Am Jur 2d, Incompetent Persons §§ 113 et seq.
42 Am Jur 2d, Infants §§ 155 et seq.
2 Am Jur Proof of Facts p 247, Attractive Nuisance.
11 Am Jur Proof of Facts 2d p 423, Dependency of Child Who Has Attained Majority in Workmen's Compensation Cases.

Annotations:

Federal Civil Procedure Rule 17(c) relating to representation of infants or incompetent persons. 68 ALR2d 752.
Right of natural parent to withdraw valid consent to adoption of child. 74 ALR3d 421.
Carrier's liability for injury or death of infant passenger as affected by fact that child was in custody of parent or other adult. 74 ALR3d 1171.

Jurisdiction of court to permit sterilization of mentally defective person in absence of specific statutory authority. 74 ALR3d 1210.

Power of parent to have mentally defective child sterilized. 74 ALR3d 1224.

Statutory change of age of majority as affecting pre-existing status or rights. 75 ALR3d 228.

Liability for injury or death of minor or other incompetent inflicted upon himself by gun made available by defendant. 75 ALR3d 825.

Who has custody or control of child within terms of penal statute punishing cruelty or neglect by one having custody or control. 75 ALR3d 933.

Failure to give adequate notice to juvenile's parents as ground for reversal of determination of juvenile delinquency under Federal Juvenile Delinquency Act (18 USCS §§ 5031–5042). 30 ALR Fed 745.

Degree of mental competence, required of accused who pleads guilty, sufficient to satisfy requirement, of Rule 11 of Federal Rules of Criminal Procedure, that guilty pleas be made voluntarily and with understanding. 31 ALR Fed 375.

Law Reviews:

Parties and pleading under the CPLR. 31 Brooklyn L Rev 98.

A biannual survey of New York practice: appointment of guardian ad litem before action commenced. 38 St. John's L Rev 422.

Biannual survey of New York practice: Part IV: preference given to nominee of relatives of incompetent when appointing committee. 39 St. John's L Rev 433.

The biannual survey of New York practice: Part V: CPLR 1201: guardian ad litem appointed for unadjudicated-incompetent plaintiff. 40 St. John's L Rev 146.

The quarterly survey of New York practice: CPLR 1201: plaintiff must establish defendant's inability to defend and nonfeasibility of instituting proceedings for the appointment of a committee before a guardian ad litem will be appointed. 41 St. John's L Rev 137.

Forms:

See "FORMS" heading following "CASE NOTES", infra.

CASE NOTES

1. In general
2. Circumstances necessitating appointment; effect of appointment
3. —Infants
4. —Incompetents
5. Conflict of laws
6. Powers and duties of representative
7. —Appeals
8. —Accounting
9. Procedural matters
10. —Service of process and other papers

1. In general

Statutes providing that an incompetent shall appear by a committee of his property or guardian are directory only and not to be construed as restrictive of the incompetent's right of independent representation in a proceeding for appointment of committee in which representation either by a committee or a guardian ad litem might be inadequate. Re Aho (1976) 39 NY2d 241, 383 NYS2d 285, 347 NE2d 647.

The appointment of a guardian ad litem made pursuant to an order to show cause presented by a bank in connection with the judicial settlement of its account was an improvident exercise of discretion, and the Special Term should have granted petitioner's application to revoke the appointment and upon the return date petitioner's mother should have been appointed guardian ad litem, since CPLR 1201 and 1202 indicate a legislative preference for the appearance of the natural guardian. Re Leggett's Trust (1966) 25 AD2d 727, 268 NYS2d 911.

In view of the small balance, approximately $1430, remaining in the estate of an incompetent veteran allowances of $250 and $750 respectively to the guardian ad litem and to the attorney for the committee were grossly excessive and modified to the extent of reducing the allowance to the attorney for the committee to the sum of $300 and reducing the allowance to the "special guardian" to the sum of $100. Re Becan (1966) 26 AD2d 44, 270 NYS2d 923.

A default judgment was vacated where a bank brought suit on a debt, where it had notice that the defendant was under mental disability and failed to bring that fact to the court's attention and permit the court to determine whether a guardian ad litem should be appointed to protect such defendant's interests. Oneida Nat. Bank & Trust Co. v Unczur (1971) 37 AD2d 480, 326 NYS2d 458.

In contract action, motion for summary judgment based on defense of infancy was premature, even though affirmation by plaintiff's attorney was insufficient to avoid defense of infancy as based on the factual elements provided in General Obligations Law § 3-101, subd 3, where no guardian had been appointed pursuant to CPLR § 1201 to represent infants' interests. Cogen Properties, Ltd. v Griffin (1973) 42 AD2d 915, 347 NYS2d 364.

Where alleged client was adjudicated incompetent and finding of incompetence was not contested, purported attorneys for incompetent had authority to bring appeal of order appointing committee of person and property for incompetent. Re Aho (1976) 39 NY2d 241, 383 NYS2d 285, 347 NE2d 647.

Attorneys who represented alleged incompetent in proceedings which resulted in adjudication of her incompetency had authority to prosecute appeal from such adjudication and therein to seek review of the denial of motion for change of venue. Re Aho (1976) 39 NY2d 241, 383 NYS2d 285, 347 NE2d 647.

Purpose of statute which allows infant to appear by a parent without the appointment of a guardian ad litem was to eliminate an unnecessary application to the court. Villafane v Banner (1976) 87 Misc 2d 1037, 387 NYS2d 183.

2. Circumstances necessitating appointment; effect of appointment

In contract action, motion for summary judgment based on defense of infancy was premature, even though affirmation by plaintiff's attorney was insufficient to avoid defense of infancy as based on the factual elements provided in General Obligations Law § 3-101, subd 3, where no guardian had been appointed pursuant to CPLR § 1201 to represent infants' interests. Cogen Properties, Ltd. v Griffin (1973) 42 AD2d 915, 347 NYS2d 364.

A default judgment was vacated where a bank brought suit on a debt, where it had notice that the defendant was under mental disability and failed to bring that fact to the court's attention and permit the court to determine whether a guardian ad litem should be appointed to protect such defendant's interests. Oneida Nat. Bank & Trust Co. v Unczur (1971) 37 AD2d 480, 326 NYS2d 458.

Appointment of guardian was necessary for proposed conservatee who appeared to have a valid cause of action but was unable to prosecute it personally. Stane v Dery (1976) 86 Misc 2d 416, 382 NYS2d 607.

When creditor becomes aware that his alleged debtor is or apparently is incapable of protecting his own legal interests, it is incumbent upon creditor to advise court thereof so that court may make suitable inquiry and in its discretion may appoint a person to receive service of a copy of the summons and complaint in behalf of the defendant, and so that court may thereafter in its discretion appoint guardian ad litem to protect defendant's interests. Barone v Cox (1976) 51 AD2d 115, 379 NYS2d 881.

3. —Infants

Under CPLR 1201 and 1202 the appointment of a guardian ad litem should await the application of the persons entitled to move for the appointment of the guardian ad litem, and be made after due consideration of any recommendation in the absence of a showing that if such procedure were followed it would constitute a danger to the infant's interests. Re Thoms' Trust (1970) 33 AD2d 990, 307 NYS2d 312.

As a guardian ad litem does not have to be appointed for a minor defendant in a paternity action in a Family Court, service of process pursuant to CPLR 309 is not a prerequisite to the jurisdiction of the court in such an action. Anonymous v Anonymous (1972) 70 Misc 2d 584, 333 NYS2d 897.

It is the policy of the State of New York to avoid unnecessary appointments of guardians for infants whose interests may be involved in litigation by encouraging parents to act as guardians ad litem, and accordingly the father of infant children was appointed guardian ad litem of his children's possible interest in the cash surrender value and interest in the proceeds of life insurance policies owned by the father levied upon in an action to foreclose federal tax liens. United States v Noble (1967, DC NY) 269 F Supp 814.

As the intention of the legislature in enacting Family Court Act §§ 241 and 249 was to provide for representation of a minor in a Family Court proceeding by a law guardian or counsel of his own choosing and not by a guardian ad litem pursuant to CPLR 1201, failure to appoint a guardian ad litem was not a defense to infant in Family Court paternity proceedings who was represented by counsel of his own choosing. Anonymous v Anonymous (1972) 70 Misc 2d 584, 333 NYS2d 897.

In a matrimonial action seeking an adjudication of the rights of plaintiff's second husband, plaintiff's third husband, and the status of a child allegedly born to plaintiff and defendant, the child was a proper party to the action and must be represented by a guardian ad litem, where the mother who had custody of the child sought a declaration that the infant was the illegitimate offspring of the father, and the father who asserted legitimacy stated that custody should be awarded to the child's mother. Roe v Roe (1966) 49 Misc 2d 1070, 269 NYS2d 40.

A court is not required to wait for the natural guardians to appear before appointing a guardian ad litem if to do so would constitute a danger to the infant's interests. Byrn v New York City Health & Hospital Corp. (1972) 38 AD2d 316, 329 NYS2d 722, affd 31 NY2d 194, 335 NYS2d 390, 286 NE2d 887, app dismd 410 US 949, 35 L

Ed 2d 683, 93 S Ct 1414, reh den 411 US 940, 36 L Ed 2d 404, 93 S Ct 1889.

Separate guardianship and trust accounts under judicial scrutiny are the legal protection for infants so that damages awarded for their pain and suffering are not invaded to pay the parents' debt, assuming such parent is found to be contributorily negligent and required to indemnify defendant for damages. Hairston v Broadwater (1973) 73 Misc 2d 523, 342 NYS2d 787.

Although a guardian may be appointed upon proper petition to represent the interests of an infant where such action is necessary and appropriate, this section eliminates the mandatory requirement that a guardian ad litem be appointed where the infant appears by a parent who is adequately able to represent the infant's interests. Klein v Motor Vehicle Acci. Indemnification Corp. (1965) 48 Misc 2d 82, 264 NYS2d 268.

Upon an application to vacate a trust indenture it was not good practice to appoint a guardian ad litem for an infant beneficiary, where there was no conflict of interest between the infant and her mother, the trustee. Application of Pugach (1967) 29 AD2d 518, 285 NYS2d 258, affd 23 NY2d 901, 298 NYS2d 306, 246 NE2d 160.

A petition by the infant's mother in his behalf, asserting a claim under a separation agreement providing for the infant's college education, was amply authorized by the provisions of this section which in turn is authorized by § 316 of the Surrogate's Court Act. Re Chilson's Will (1966) 54 Misc 2d 51, 282 NYS2d 53, affd 28 AD2d 766, 282 NYS2d 80.

Grandmother's longstanding but informal custody of infant under the age of 14 was not "legal custody" within meaning of statute which requires that infant litigant appear either by guardian ad litem or by party having "legal custody" and, therefore, it was necessary to appoint guardian ad litem to bring action on behalf of infant whose parents resided in Puerto Rico. Villafane v Banner (1976) 87 Misc 2d 1037, 387 NYS2d 183.

4. —Incompetents

Although in a proper case the committee of an incompetent can be relied upon to protect both the incompetent and his estate from the consequences of a spurious claim of competency, and although the appointment of a guardian ad litem serves to decrease the amount of allowances to be made to the attorney, guardian ad litem and referee, appointment of such guardian in proceeding instigated by incompetent to declare competency is proper to afford the incompetent representation independent of the committee's influence. Berman v Grossman (1965) 24 AD2d 432, 260 NYS2d 736.

Director of mental health information service was appointed as guardian ad litem to represent incompetent husband in forma pauperis divorce action where proposed guardian refused to serve on basis that neither party was able to pay his fee. Rodriguez v Rodriguez (1973) 74 Misc 2d 944, 343 NYS2d 285.

Although CPLR § 1201 requires the appointment of a guardian ad litem for an incompetent adult defendant, it does not prohibit the appointment by the court of a guardian ad litem for a plaintiff who is in an unconscious state as the result of an automobile accident and who may continue in such a state for weeks or months; and CPLR Rule 1202 specifically confers upon the court a general power of appointment of a guardian ad litem at any stage in the action either upon its own initiative or upon the motion of another. Liebowitz v Hunter (1965) 45 Misc 2d 580, 257 NYS2d 434.

The motion of a guardian ad litem, appointed to protect the interests of a husband in an annulment action, for discharge was granted, upon evidence that the husband was gainfully employed, fully aware of the precise nature of the action, and did not wish to have anyone defend the action on his behalf. The mere fact the husband had previously been a patient in a mental institution from which he had received an "outright discharge" two years ago was not evidence of an existing present incompetency. Arcieri v Arcieri (1966) 49 Misc 2d 223, 266 NYS2d 1020.

Where the affairs of an incompetent veteran are brought within the purview of the Supreme Court, that court has a duty placed directly on it to protect and preserve his property, and where necessary or proper a guardian ad litem may be designated to appear for and take such proceedings as are necessary to protect the interests of the incompetent. Re Becan (1966) 26 AD2d 44, 270 NYS2d 923.

It was improper to appoint a guardian ad litem on application by attorneys for the plaintiff without notice to the defendant, an adult, and without satisfactory proof that defendant, although allegedly mentally ill, was incapable of adequately protecting his rights. Abrons v Abrons (1965) 24 AD2d 970, 265 NYS2d 381.

CPLR 1201 and 1203 are to be read together and interpreted as requiring the appointment of a guardian ad litem in every case where the defendant is an adult incapable of adequately protecting his rights before a default judgment may be entered against him. Oneida Nat. Bank & Trust Co. v Unczur (1971) 37 AD2d 480, 326 NYS2d 458.

5. Conflict of laws

Being procedural in nature, New York statutory provision controlled issue whether guardian was to be appointed for 18-year-old remainderman in New York proceedings for judicial settlement of intermediate account of trustees, notwithstanding that remainderman, who resided with her parents in Connecticut, was no longer a minor under Connecticut law. Re Riddell (1973) 78 Misc 2d 150, 355 NYS2d 36.

6. Powers and duties of representative

The functions of a guardian ad litem appointed to protect the interests of an infant are purely ministerial and not judicial or quasi judicial, and he should submit to the court for its consideration every question involving the rights of the infant. De Forte v Liggett & Myers Tobacco Co. (1964) 42 Misc 2d 721, 248 NYS2d 764.

In personal injury actions an infant remains a ward of the court until the cause of action is finally disposed of, and guardian has no power to veto proposed settlement which is fair and reasonable. De Forte v Liggett & Myers Tobacco Co. (1964) 42 Misc 2d 721, 248 NYS2d 764.

The guardian ad litem is an officer of the court with powers and duties strictly limited by law, and he may act only in accordance with the instructions of the court and within the law under which appointed. De Forte v Liggett & Myers Tobacco Co. (1964) 42 Misc 2d 721, 248 NYS2d 764.

7. —Appeals

Where alleged client was adjudicated incompetent and finding of incompetence was not contested, purported attorneys for incompetent had authority to bring appeal of order appointing committee of person and property for incompetent. Re Aho (1976) 39 NY2d 241, 383 NYS2d 285, 347 NE2d 647.

Attorneys who represented alleged incompetent in proceedings which resulted in adjudication of her incompetency had authority to prosecute appeal from such adjudication and therein to seek review of the denial of motion for change of venue. Re Aho (1976) 39 NY2d 241, 383 NYS2d 285, 347 NE2d 647.

8. —Accounting

An attorney appointed to act as a guardian ad litem in an accounting proceeding by the Committee of an incompetent veteran should report in detail his acts with respect to the performance of his duties, and whether or not the account is correct and if he disapproves of it, the nature of his objections, and as an officer of the court is bound to conscientiously perform his duties with the understanding he may be asked to accept most moderate compensation for his services. Re Becan (1966) 26 AD2d 44, 270 NYS2d 923.

Where the estate of an incompetent veteran consists mainly of a small balance of funds derived principally from the payment of benefits under the direction of the Veterans' Administration and there is no reason to believe that an account filed by the committee is wrongful, improper, or substantially inaccurate, generally there will be no need for the appointment of a guardian ad litem during settlement of the account, although notice of such settlement is required to be given to the Veterans' Administration. Re Becan (1966) 26 AD2d 44, 270 NYS2d 923.

Where 18-year-old remainderman's mother was one of the accounting parties under inter vivos trust and also a life beneficiary with power to appoint principal, there existed in law, even if not in fact, a conflict of interest between mother and daughter which, for protection of daughter, called for appointment of guardian ad litem for purpose of judicial settlement of intermediate account. Re Riddell (1973) 78 Misc 2d 150, 355 NYS2d 36.

9. Procedural matters

Under CPLR 1201 and 1202 the appointment of a guardian ad litem should await the application of the persons entitled to move for the appointment of the guardian ad litem, and be made after due consideration of any recommendation in the absence of a showing that if such procedure were followed it would constitute a danger to the infant's interests. Re Thoms' Trust (1970) 33 AD2d 990, 307 NYS2d 312.

An infant plaintiff who elects to proceed without a guardian with a personal injury action against a shipping company, as is permitted by this section, is not barred by the period of limitations provided in § 183-b of Title 46 of USC when the action is commenced within three years and eight months after the occurrence of the injury. Powell v Compagnie Generale Transatlantique, Ltd. (1965) 47 Misc 2d 670, 263 NYS2d 17.

In the absence of a judicial declaration of incompetency, a person, although mentally ill, can sue or be sued in his name. Neely v Hogan (1970) 62 Misc 2d 1056, 310 NYS2d 63.

10. —Service of process and other papers

As a guardian ad litem does not have to be appointed for a minor defendant in a paternity action in a Family Court, service of process pursuant to CPLR 309 is not a prerequisite to the jurisdiction of the court in such an action. Anonymous v Anonymous (1972) 70 Misc 2d 584, 333 NYS2d 897.

The service of motion papers, by which the moving attorney sought to withdraw as attorney for the infant defendant, upon the infant defendant in person was insufficient, and the attorney's motion to withdraw was denied. Stillwell v Giant Supply Corp. (1965) 47 Misc 2d 568, 262 NYS2d 833.

In an action seeking relief from a default judgment on the ground that at the time of making the retail instalment contract upon which the judgment was founded the defendant was an infant, it was held that service of summons upon an infant alone was insufficient and that his representation by a guardian ad litem or some other statutory representative was required, and that judgment by default could not be entered against him except after appearance by a representative or the expiration of 20 days from the appointment of a guardian ad litem. State Bank of Albany v Murray (1966) 27 AD2d 627, 275 NYS2d 985.

CASE NOTES

UNDER FORMER CIVIL PRACTICE LAWS

See also Case Notes under Rule 1202, infra.

A. In General

1. Generally

A. In General

1. Generally

Citizenship of infant, and not that of guardian ad litem, confers jurisdiction on federal court. Horzepa v Dauski (1941, DC NY) 40 F Supp 476.

Court by appointing guardian ad litem acquired jurisdiction and the responsibility of the party foreclosing the mortgage ended. Hopkins v Frey (1892) 64 Hun 213, 18 NYS 903.

CPA § 182 (§ 503(a)(b) herein) construed with CPA § 202 in holding that stockholder was party plaintiff in stockholder's derivative action against corporation and that his county residence fixed venue. Feldmeier v Webster (1955) 208 Misc 996, 145 NYS2d 365, affd 1 AD2d 938, 150 NYS2d 581.

Although appearance by a guardian is necessary, the infant remains the real party in interest, and it is improper to examine the guardian ad litem as a party. Arnold v Williams (1959) 17 Misc 2d 953, 187 NYS2d 691.

The provisions of CPA § 202 were held to relate entirely to matters of procedure, and not to affect the jurisdiction of the court. Holmes v Staib

Abendschein Co. (1921) 198 AD 354, 190 NYS 449.

Infant's guardian ad litem was not employee, or agent, or party to action within CPA § 288 (§ 3101(a), Rule 3106(a) herein) authorizing examination before trial of any party to action; at best he was merely representative of party. Alsante v Roberts (1953, Sup) 118 NYS2d 683.

While it is the duty of the court to vacate orders appointing guardians ad litem for infant defendants, appointed in violation of Court Rule, yet an error of the court in this respect does not deprive the court of jurisdiction or render an interlocutory judgment directing a sale in partition voidable. Parish v Parish (1903) 175 NY 181, 67 NE 298.

When, upon the petition of an infant defendant over the age of fourteen, a guardian ad litem has been appointed in a partition suit, the order is valid, though no summons had been previously served upon the infant. Varian v Stevens, 9 Super Ct (2 Duer) 635.

The supreme court of this state, like the former court of chancery, exercises a general control over all minors. People v Erbert, 17 Abb Pr 395; Lefevre v Laraway, 22 Barb 167; Re Mathews (1882, NY) 27 Hun 254, affd 90 NY 688.

Special guardian is not representative or "alter ego" of appointing court, but he is appointed pursuant to statutory direction to represent party who is non sui juris. Re Barc's Estate (1941) 177 Misc 578, 31 NYS2d 139, affd 266 AD 677, 41 NYS2d 213.

A guardian ad litem is an officer of the court with powers and duties limited by law. He may act only in accordance with the instructions of the court and the law under which appointed. Persons dealing with him are bound to ascertain his authority and unauthorized payments to him or unauthorized agreements with him do not bind the infant. Honadle v Stafford (1934) 265 NY 354, 193 NE 172.

A special guardian, while in a sense a representative and officer of the court, is not a judicial officer and his duty is to protect and advance the potential rights of his wards by every honorable means under penalty of damages for failure. And with respect to litigation for which he is appointed, he acts solely as attorney for those whose interests he is designated to protect. Re Schrier (1935) 157 Misc 310, 283 NYS 233; Re Barc's Estate (1941) 177 Misc 578, 31 NYS2d 139, affd 266 AD 677, 41 NYS2d 213.

The functions of a guardian ad litem appointed to protect the interests of an infant are purely ministerial and not judicial or quasi-judicial, and he should submit to the court for its consideration every question involving the right of the infant affected by the suit. Glogowski v Rapson (1959) 20 Misc 2d 96, 198 NYS2d 87.

2. Necessity of appointment of guardian

The better practice, designed for the protection of

the property of an infant, is to bring the action in the name of the infant, represented by a guardian appointed for the purposes of the particular action. Carr v Huff (1890) 57 Hun 18, 10 NYS 361.

It is not necessary, upon a trial of an action brought by an infant to prove the appointment of a guardian ad litem unless the defendant objects that no guardian has been appointed who will answer for costs; and where no such objection is taken on the trial, it cannot be successfully taken on appeal. Strong v Jenkins (1891, Super Ct) 15 NYS 120.

As to the bringing of an action by a general guardian, on behalf of the infant, see Perkins v Stimmel (1889) 114 NY 359, 21 NE 729.

Court was not required to appoint guardian ad litem for infant remainderman prior to return day of order to show cause. Re O'Malley's Trust (1955) 286 AD 869, 142 NYS2d 21.

An action relating to the personal estate of an infant can only be brought in the name of the infant by his guardian ad litem, appointed for that purpose. Buerman v Buerman, 3 How Pr NS 393, 9 Civ Proc 146. See also Segelken v Meyer (1884) 94 NY 473.

If rights of other creditors are not involved, a complaint should not be dismissed because it was not brought in a representative capacity but in the name of the infant plaintiff by her guardian. Feigenbaum v Narragansett Stables Co. (1926) 127 Misc 114, 215 NYS 328, affd 219 AD 729, 219 NYS 811, affd 245 NY 628, 157 NE 886.

3. Particular actions and proceedings

In action for infants for personal injuries, where at trial term jury rendered verdict for $90,000, court with jury present could appoint a special guardian to protect their interests. Siganoff v Metropolitan Distributors (1951, Sup) 111 NYS2d 21.

In action by People involving fraudulent practices in sale of securities, where it appeared that defendant attempted to withdraw money from bank account in name of infant son, special guardian was appointed for infant. People v Walker (1948, Sup) 82 NYS2d 307.

A special guardian would not be appointed under CPA § 207 in a proceeding under § 440 of the Correction Law for an order permitting the retention of an alleged mentally defective prisoner in a State Training School after expiration of sentence. Re Naylor (1940) 284 NY 188, 30 NE2d 468.

4. —Accounting

The denomination of the office of custodian as a personal trust with the duties of a guardian of the property of an infant (Personal Property Law, section 266, subd. 1) requires legal representation of the infant in an accounting proceeding (Personal Property Law, section 268, subd 2) following the procedure designated by CPA art 79. Re Strauss (1957) 11 Misc 2d 277, 176 NYS2d 1014.

In proceeding to settle accounts of receiver appointed in sequestration proceedings against husband suing for annulment of his marriage to

defendant who was alleged incompetent, special guardian should be appointed to protect her rights in accounting proceeding. Weisbaum v Kastenbaum (1954) 284 AD 882, 134 NYS2d 545.

5. —Annulment

In action for annulment of marriage against one confined in an asylum under an ex parte commitment, plaintiff's application for appointment of a special guardian for defendant was denied, and plaintiff was advised to propose an order under former CPA § 226 designating person to be served. Zalinsky v Zalinsky (1918) 103 Misc 308, 170 NYS 1005.

6. —Article 78 proceeding

Where proceeding is brought under Art 78 to review right of infant defendant to waive jury in criminal case, application should be made in such proceeding for appointment of a guardian ad litem or special guardian for the infant and such an appointment will be made nunc pro tunc. Scott v McCaffrey (1958) 12 Misc 2d 671, 172 NYS2d 954.

7. —Appointment on appeal

Pending an appeal where one of the parties was ascertained to be an infant, the appellate court, upon application of the other party as well as upon the infant's request, will appoint a guardian ad litem. Fish v Ferris, 3 ED Smith 567.

8. —Declaratory judgment

In action to declare status of child, such as legitimacy and parentage, guardian ad litem should be appointed to protect its interests. Melis v Department of Health (1940) 260 AD 772, 24 NYS2d 51.

In action for declaratory judgment by insurer against administratrix, who had individually and officially brought action for wrongful death against insured, to determine whether plaintiff insured was obliged to afford coverage under automobile liability policy to insured because of his alleged failure to notify insurer of insured's acquisition of automobile involved in fatal accident, guardian ad litem should have been appointed for infant daughter of decedent. Glens Falls Indem. Co. v Bellinger (1954, Sup) 142 NYS2d 401.

9. —Disclosure

Application by railroad, before commencement of action, to take deposition of witnesses of railroad crossing collision involving injured infant for use in any future action against railroad is motion, and not action or special proceeding, and court may not appoint special guardian for infant. Re New York C. R. Co. 41 NYS2d 614, revd 266 AD 904, 44 NYS2d 104.

10. —Legitimacy of infants

Where legitimacy of children was in issue, it was imperative that a guardian be appointed for the purpose of protecting their interests and proper procedure required application for joinder pursuant to RCP 102 (Rule 3024(a) herein) and compliance with RCP 39 (§ 1201 herein). Hines v Hines (1957) 12 Misc 2d 486, 169 NYS2d 1003.

In action by husband for annulment of marriage with prayer for determination of legitimacy of child, court appointed a special guardian to protect the interests of the child. Cesareo v Cesareo, 134 Misc 88, 234 NYS 44.

See Melis v Department of Health (1940) 260 AD 772, 24 NYS2d 51, ¶ 8, supra.

11. —Recovery of personalty

Domestic Relations Act § 82, construed with CPA § 202 in holding that general guardian of infant may represent infant in action for recovery of infant's personalty. Marcus v Neugarten (1942, Sup) 37 NYS2d 364.

Where alleged incompetent, through petition filed by himself, sought appointment of committee of particular portion of his property illegally retained by attorney general asserting that incompetent had fraudulently obtained said property, he was entitled to have appointed special guardian to succeed him as petitioner in such proceeding. Re King (1954) 284 AD 748, 135 NYS2d 495.

12. —Submission of controversy

There is no authority for the appointment of a guardian for the purpose of a submission of a controversy without action. An infant cannot submit a controversy. Fisher v Stilson, 9 Abb Pr 33.

13. —Summary proceedings

A guardian ad litem may be appointed for an infant defendant in summary proceedings. Jessurum v Mackie (1881, NY) 24 Hun 624.

14. —Support actions

Facts reviewed and special guardian appointed for incompetent husband where his committee was uninformed as to allegations in petition of separated wife for support for self and children. Re Warren (1924) 207 AD 793, 202 NYS 586.

15. Particular courts

The Court of Claims, instead of the Supreme Court, should appoint guardians ad litem for infant claimants in the Court of Claims. Torrey v State, 175 Misc 259, 23 NYS2d 370, revd on other grounds 266 AD 900, 42 NYS2d 567.

In action in court of claims for personal injury by infant by guardian ad litem appointed by supreme court, court of claims may appoint substitute guardian ad litem nunc pro tunc as of date of supreme court order appointing guardian or of filing of claim, for purpose of prosecution of such action. Mackney v State (1941) 177 Misc 94, 29 NYS2d 1004.

The powers conferred by the former Revised Statutes upon the court of chancery in respect to infants had not been given to the county courts, and could not be implied from mere power to sell infant's lands. Stiles v Stiles, 1 Lans 90.

A county court in exercising the authority conferred upon it to order the sale of an infant's real estate within the county had the same general powers as the old court of chancery, and the provisions of the former Revised Statutes in reference to such sales as well as the general rules of equity jurisprudence were applicable. Brown v Snell (1874) 57 NY 286, affg 3 Lans 283; but see Stiles v Stiles, 1 Lans 90.

This jurisdiction is not required to be exercised at a stated term, but the court is always open for that purpose, save as otherwise directed by the statute. Brown v Snell, 57 NY 286, affg 3 Lans 283.

When proceedings were instituted under former statute for the sale of the real estate of an infant, from the time of the application, the infant is to be considered as the ward of the court so far as relates to the property affected, its proceeds or income. Re Price (1876) 67 NY 231, affg 6 Hun 513.

SCA § 64 furnishes complete machinery required to protect interests of infants who are under age of 14 years, by directing Surrogate to appoint proper person to act as special guardian, thereby making CPA § 203 inapplicable. Vanderbilt's Will (1955) 208 Misc 5, 142 NYS2d 897.

B. NECESSITY AND EFFECT OF APPOINTMENT

16. Generally

See Bernal v Baptist Fresh Air Home Soc. (1949) 275 AD 88, 87 NYS2d 458, affd 300 NY 486, 88 NE2d 720; Hilburger v Cottman (1949) 196 Misc 106, 91 NYS2d 721.

If rights of other creditors are not involved, a complaint should not be dismissed merely because it was not brought in a representative capacity but in the name of the infant plaintiff by her guardian. Feigenbaum v Narragansett Stables Co. (1926) 127 Misc 114, 215 NYS 328, affd 219 AD 729, 219 NYS 811, affd 245 NY 628, 157 NE 886.

17. Effect of age of incompetent

The court may appoint a guardian to appear and defend for a lunatic defendant, although of full age. Legal liabilities may be enforced against lunatics. Hawley v Brennan, 9 NYSR 505.

18. Appointment where there is a general guardian

General guardian cannot maintain action against surety for negligence of its agent and against surrogate for fraud in failing to prevent waste of ward's estate, where general guardian was instructed by court to proceed against estate of deceased guardian. Dunn v Fidelity & Cas. Co. (1941) 177 Misc 365, 30 NYS2d 639.

A general guardian appointed by the surrogate cannot act for an infant defendant; there must be a guardian ad litem appointed by the court. Re Stratton, 1 Johns 509; Sharp v Pell, 10 Johns 486; Clark v Clark, 14 Abb Pr 299, 21 How Pr 479; Lansing v Gulick, 26 How Pr 250.

Where a "next friend" appointed in another state was acting in this state without primary or ancillary appointment, the court stated that seemingly a guardian ad litem should be appointed, without which the foreign judgment involved would be prima facie, invalid, if the irregularity was not seasonably corrected. Horvath v Brettschneider (1928) 131 Misc 618, 227 NYS 109.

Where mother sold stock belonging to her and her child individually and as guardian of the child, she could maintain an action to set aside the transfer and sale on the ground of fraud individually and as guardian of the child, and it was not necessary to appoint a guardian ad litem. Dold v Dold (1918) 103 Misc 86, 169 NYS 209.

Where incompetent's adjudication of competency had not yet become final, and committee, whose interests were now adverse to those of incompetent, was still functioning, court had authority to appoint guardian ad litem to bring action against committee individually to cancel deed executed by incompetent to committee. Mathews v Mathews (1960) 25 Misc 2d 250, 203 NYS2d 475.

19. Effect of failure to appoint for plaintiff

A judgment of separation in favor of a defendant husband will be vacated where it appears that the plaintiff is an infant and no guardian ad litem had been appointed; the failure to appoint such guardian is an error for which judgment may be vacated at any time within two years under CPA § 528 (§ 5015(a) herein). Byrnes v Byrnes (1905) 109 AD 535, 96 NYS 306.

Failure to appoint a guardian for an infant plaintiff does not deprive the court of jurisdiction of the action. Sims v New York College of Dentistry (1885, NY) 35 Hun 344.

Where insurer delayed ten months after infant filed claim to insurance proceeds before filing interpleader to settle adverse claims to proceeds, such delay was not excused by absence of guardian of property of infant claimant, in view of CPA §§ 202–204 and RCP 39 providing for service of process on infant. John Hancock M. L. I. Co. v Doran (1956, DC NY) 138 F Supp 47.

In Perkins v Stimmel, 42 Hun 520, revd on other grounds 114 NY 359, 21 NE 729, it was said that the objection, that the action was brought by the general guardian, was waived by failure to raise it by demurrer or answer. See Harnett v Morris, 10 Civ Proc 223.

20. —Attaining majority by infant plaintiff prior to judgment as curing defect

The irregularity in that the plaintiff was infant at the time of the commencement of the action and that no guardian ad litem had ever been appointed was cured by the fact that the infant attained his majority prior to the trial. Holm v Eastern Greyhound Lines (1937) 252 AD 778, 299 NYS 154.

Where upon the trial of an action defendant first learned, from the cross-examination of the plaintiff, that at the time of the commencement of the action she was a minor, although she had become of age before the time of the trial, held, that a motion to dismiss the complaint was properly denied. Rima v Rossie Iron Works (1890) 120 NY 433, 24 NE 940 (Imhoff v Wurtz, 9 Civ Proc 48, contra, was disapproved); Sims v New York College of Dentistry (1885, NY) 35 Hun 344.

21. Effect of failure to appoint for defendant

Where an infant defendant in an action for foreclosure of a mortgage is served with the summons, but a guardian ad litem for him is not appointed, the judgment is voidable, but not absolutely void. McMurray v McMurray (1876) 66 NY 175. Held, by the supreme court, at general term, that such an omission was not an irregularity, but an error in fact. Rogers v McLean, 31 Barb 304, revd on other grounds 11 Abb Pr 440, affd 34 NY 536.

There can be no judgment against a minor defendant unless a guardian ad litem has been appointed. Grego v Demario, 133 Misc 53, 231 NYS 130, revd on other grounds 226 AD 833, 234 NYS 805.

Jurisdiction of action for personal injuries against an infant defendant is not acquired where no guardian ad litem was appointed. Marty v Roberts (1933) 146 Misc 332, 261 NYS 144.

Where no guardian ad litem has been appointed for infant, appearance in his behalf by attorney has no legal effect. Krieger v Krieger (1950) 198 Misc 450, 99 NYS2d 80.

The facts that defendant was a minor of twenty years, and that no guardian ad litem had been appointed for her, rendered the judgment against her void or voidable depending upon the manner in which the summons was served upon her. The infant must raise the question as to whether the judgment is void or voidable either through a guardian before reaching her majority, or by her own action or motion after that event. Belcher v Haskell (1936) 249 AD 251, 292 NYS 387.

Failure to appoint a guardian ad litem for an infant defendant is an irregularity if the objection is properly and timely presented. Frost v Frost (1895) 15 Misc 167, 37 NYS 18.

Where question of infancy was not raised by pleadings but defendant testified he was twenty years of age, court properly denied defendant's motion at close of case to dismiss on ground of lack of jurisdiction over defendant, proper remedy being to move to vacate summons so as to give plaintiff opportunity to meet proof. Midland Trading Corp. v Hechtkopf (1919) 176 NYS 712.

Jurisdictional defect results from failure to have guardian ad litem appointed for infant, and is not corrected by appointment of guardian ad litem in separate action or by service of summons. Linder v Castro (1953, Sup App T) 120 NYS2d 612.

Provisions permit an incompetent to defend an action or proceeding by his committee or guardian ad litem only. Re Brown's Estate (1926) 131 Misc 420, 226 NYS 32.

Service of summons and complaint in action for divorce upon minor defendant without delivering copy to parent or guardian ad litem did not confer jurisdiction of infant's person, and judgment against him without appointment of guardian ad litem was void. Wiberg v Wiberg (1955) 1 Misc 2d 431, 145 NYS2d 785.

Where insurer delayed ten months after infant filed claim to insurance proceeds before filing interpleader to settle adverse claims to proceeds, such delay was not excused by absence of guardian of property of infant claimant in view of CPA §§ 202–204 and Rule 39 providing for service of process on infant. Re John Hancock M. L. I. Co. (1956, DC NY) 138 F Supp 47.

The court held that an order should have been, and could be, vacated where no guardian ad litem had been appointed for the infant prior to the determination of the proceeding, but that no appeal could be entertained since no guardian had been appointed to prosecute it. Anonymous v Anonymous (1959) 7 AD2d 932, 183 NYS2d 776.

Where no guardian ad litem has been appointed for an infant, an appearance in his behalf by an attorney has no legal effect. Leahy v Hardy (1929) 225 AD 323, 232 NYS 543.

An infant defendant, though over fourteen years of age, could not appear in an action even to attack the appointment of the guardian appointed for him on his adversary's application; his remedy was to apply for appointment of another guardian, pursuant to CPA 203, to make the attack. Gibson v Foster (1959) 9 AD2d 946, 195 NYS2d 726.

In action for separation by infant plaintiff against infant defendant, service was complete when summons was delivered to infant and his father; plaintiff was under no obligation to secure appointment of guardian ad litem for infant defendant prior to service of process. Gelernter v Gelernter (1959) 19 Misc 2d 25, 187 NYS2d 283.

22. —Attaining majority by infant defendant prior to trial or judgment as curing defect

A judgment rendered against one who was an infant at the time an action was commenced is void and of no effect where no guardian ad litem was ever applied for or appointed, even though the infant had attained his majority at the time the judgment was entered. Melnick v Laszio (1937) 161 Misc 791, 293 NYS 261.

An infant defendant by taking the witness stand in his defense after reaching majority and by his attorney continuing with the prosecution of the defense without objection, appeared and submitted his person to the court's jurisdiction, although no guardian ad litem had been applied for or appointed at the time the summons and complaint were served on him. Pacilio v Scarpati (1937) 165 Misc 586, 300 NYS 473.

23. Appointment of person with adverse interests

The appointment of guardian ad litem of an infant defendant of one having an adverse interest to the infant, especially of the plaintiff, is more than an irregularity. Hecker v Sexton (1887, NY) 43 Hun 593.

Adverse interest of committee must be shown to bar intervention of committee in place of incompetent defendant in separation action. Olsen v Olsen (1950) 197 Misc 451, 95 NYS2d 265.

24. Powers and duties of guardian ad litem

A guardian ad litem cannot, without the order of the court, make a settlement of the controversy so as to bind the infant. Edsall v Vandemark, 39 Barb 589; see Leggett v Sellon, 3 Paige 84; Bulkley v Van Wyck, 5 Paige 536; Litchfield v Burwell, 5 How Pr 341, 1 NY Code R NS 42.

A guardian should execute a deed by signing with the infant's name "by Josiah S. Mitchell his guardian ad litem." Hyatt v Seeley (1854) 11 NY 52.

A release on the settlement of a former action by the guardian ad litem, under order of the court, bars a subsequent action by the infant. Frehe v Schildwachter (1943) 289 NY 250, 45 NE2d 427.

25. —Sale of real estate

Where a person has been appointed a special guardian to sell infant's real estate, and at the time was himself the owner of a tax title thereto, and which, pending the proceedings, he sold, and retained the money, held, that it must be considered as for the infant's benefit after reimbursing himself his expenses. Spelman v Terry (1876, NY) 8 Hun 205, affd 74 NY 448.

A special guardian, appointed in proceedings for the sale of the infant's real estate, took a mortgage on the premises to secure a part of the purchase money; he afterwards foreclosed the mortgage, bid off the property, and took a deed of the same to himself personally. Held, that he took title as trustee for his ward. Dodge v Thompson, 13 NY Week Dig 104.

From the time of the application, the infant is considered the ward of the court, with respect to the property affected, and its proceeds or income. The special guardian is the officer of the court; and so long as the purchase money remains in his hands, and until the infant attains majority and receives it, the court has control over it and over the proceedings. Re Price (1876) 67 NY 231, affg Re Jackson, 6 Hun 513.

26. Effect of judgment

An infant is bound by a judgment, when he is duly served, and a guardian is appointed who accepts the trust as if he were an adult. Re Hawley (1885) 100 NY 206, 3 NE 68.

27. Elimination of guardian ad litem when infant becomes of age

Where no objection is made during the pendency of an action by an infant and his guardian ad litem, the validity of the proceedings will not usually be affected by failure to strike out a guardian for an infant who has become of age. Where prejudice is shown to an adverse party by the failure of the infant to make the formal correction of the record and prosecute in his own name, the remedy after judgment would seem to be a motion by the adverse party for an order nunc pro tunc, striking the guardian from the action. McCarthy v Anable (1938) 169 Misc 595, 7 NYS2d 887.

28. Substitution and intervention by committee or guardian

Where the guardian ad litem of an infant was

appointed and subsequently the infant was committed to an asylum and a committee of his property appointed, the court may order the substitution of such committee as plaintiff. Callahan v New York C. & H. R. R. Co. (1904) 99 AD 56, 90 NYS 657.

Although a guardian ad litem is not a party to an action and is not entitled to be made a party or interpose an answer, yet, he may intervene, and, to the extent that it may be advisable and proper, "conduct the defense for the incompetent defendant." Behlen v Behlen (1902) 73 AD 143, 76 NYS 747.

FORMS

Form 1—Complaint where action is brought by an infant

Form 2—Answer of guardian for infant defendant

Form 3—General answer of infant by his guardian ad litem in particular actions

Form 4—Bond of guardian ad litem or special guardian

Form 5—Affidavit for appointment of guardian for incompetent defendant for whom a committee has been appointed

Form 6—Order appointing special guardian ad litem where committee of incompetent not a fit person to protect rights of defendant

Form 1

Complaint Where Action Is Brought by an Infant

SUPREME COURT, __1_____ COUNTY *

__2_____, an infant, by
__3_____, guardian of his property
[or other proper person described in
    CPLR § 1201],
                        Plaintiff,   Complaint
        against

        __4_____,
        Defendant.

The plaintiff, complaining of the defendant alleges:

1. At all the times hereinafter mentioned plaintiff was and still is an infant under the age of 18 years.

2. By an order of this court, made on the __5__ day of __6_____, 19_7_, and entered in the office of the clerk of the County of __8_____ on the __9__ day of __10_____, 19_11_, __12_____ was duly appointed general guardian of the property of the plaintiff [or otherwise show capacity and method of appointment, if any, of person representing the infant].

3. [State facts to show cause of action as in ordinary case.]

Form 2

Answer of Guardian for Infant Defendant

[Title of court and cause.]   Answer

The defendant, __1_____, an infant under [or "over"] the age of fourteen years, by the guardian of his property [parent, guardian ad litem, etc., as the case may be], __2_____, for his answer to the complaint herein, denies that __3_____ [or as the case may be].

WHEREFORE he demands judgment that __4_____, with such other and further relief to the said infant defendant as may be just.

Dated, __5_____, 19_6_.

__7_____

Guardian ad litem and attorney for said defendant

Office and Post Office Address

Telephone No.

Form 3

General Answer of Infant by his Guardian ad Litem in Particular Actions

[Title of court and cause.]

Answer

Index No. __1__ [if assigned]

The defendant __2_____, by __3_____, his guardian ad litem, answering the complaint of the plaintiff herein, alleges that he is an infant under the age of eighteen years; that he is a stranger to all and singular the matters and things therein set forth; and claims such interest, right and estate in the real property and premises described therein as he is entitled to; and he submits his rights and interests in the matter in question to the protection of the court.

WHEREFORE the defendant prays such judgment herein as will fully protect his rights and interests in the matter in question in this action.

__4_____

Attorney for Defendant

Office and P. O. Address

Telephone No.

Form 4

Bond of Guardian ad Litem or Special Guardian

Bond

KNOW ALL MEN BY THESE PRESENTS that we, __1_____ [name of guardian], of No. __2__ __3_____ Street, City of __4_____, State of New York, attorney at law, and __5_____, [name of surety], of No. __6__ __7_____ Street, City of __8_____, State of New York, and __9_____, [name of surety], of No. __10__ __11_____ Street, City of __12_____, State of New York, are held and firmly bound unto __13_____ [the infant], of No. __14__ __15_____ Street, City of __16_____, State of New York, in the sum of __17_____ dollars, lawful money of the United States, to be paid to the said __18_____, his executors, administrators or assignees; for which sum, well and truly to be paid, we bind ourselves, our heirs, executors and administrators, jointly and severally by these presents.

Sealed with our seals. Dated the __19__ day of __20_____, 19_21_.

WHEREAS, at a motion term of the Supreme Court held at the county court house, City of __22_____, County of __23_____, and State of New York, on the __24__ day of __25_____, 19_26_, before the Hon. __27_____, one of the justices of the said court, an order was made in an action wherein __28_____, an infant [under the age of fourteen years], was plaintiff, and __29_____ was the defendant, appointing the above named __30_____ as guardian of the said infant, to appear for and prosecute said action in his behalf; and

WHEREAS judgment was rendered in such action upon the __31__ day of __32_____, 19_33_, in favor of __34_____ for __35_____ dollars;

NOW, the condition of this obligation is such that if the above bounded __36_____ shall faithfully discharge the trust committed to him as such guardian by the paying over, investing of and accounting for all money received by him, and by the observance of any provision of law or of the rules and the directions of the court in relation to the trust, then this obligation to be void, otherwise to remain in full force and effect.

[Signatures and seals]
[Print signers' name below signatures]

STATE OF NEW YORK
COUNTY OF __1_____   SS:

On this __2__ day of __3_____ 19_4_ before me personally appeared __5_____, to me personally known and known to me to be the same persons described in and who executed the within instrument, and they severally acknowledged to me that they executed the same.

__6_____
Notary Public

STATE OF NEW YORK
COUNTY OF __1_____   SS:

__2_____, being duly sworn, deposes and says:

He resides at No. __3__, __4_____ Street in the City of __5_____, New York.

He is a householder [or freeholder] within the State of New York and is worth the sum of at least __6_____ dollars [the penalty of the bond or twice the sum specified in the undertaking] over and above all the debts and liabilities which he owes or has incurred and exclusive of property exempt by law from levy and sale under an execution.

[Signature of Deponent]
[Print signer's name below signature]

[Jurat]

[The principal on the bond and each individual surety should make an affidavit as above.]

The undersigned hereby approves the foregoing bond [or undertaking] as to form and sufficiency of sureties thereon.

Dated this __7__ day of __8_____, 19_9_.

__10_____
[Print signer's name below signature]

Form 5

Affidavit for Appointment of Guardian for Incompetent Defendant for Whom a Committee has been Appointed

Affidavit

[Title of court and cause]   Index No. __1__ [if assigned]

The petition of __2_____, respectfully shows:

1. I am the attorney for the plaintiff in the above-entitled action.

2. This action was brought for the purpose of __3_____ [State nature of action].

3. This action was commenced by service of summons on the defendant and upon __4_____ as committee for the said defendant on the __5__ day of __6_____, 19_7_.

4. [Allege facts to show that the interest of the committee is adverse to that of the defendant or that the committee, for any reason, is not a fit person to protect the rights of the defendant.]

WHEREFORE, deponent respectfully requests that an order be entered appointing a guardian ad litem for the defendant __8____.

[Signature of Petitioner]
[Print signer's name below signature]

[Jurat]

Form 6

Order Appointing Special Guardian ad Litem Where Committee of Incompetent not a fit Person to Protect Rights of Defendant

SUPREME COURT, __1____ COUNTY.

Order

[Title of cause]   Index No. __2__ [if assigned]

PRESENT: Hon. __3____, Justice.

On reading and filing the affidavit of __4____, sworn to the __5__ day of __6____, 19_7_, and the summons and complaint in this action, and the affidavits of the service of said summons and a copy of the complaint on each of the defendants, __8____ and __9____, on the __10__ day of __11____, 19_12_, and the affidavit of service of said summons and complaint on __13____, as committee of the person and property of said defendants, __14____ and __15____, on the __16__ day of __17____, 19_18_; and on reading and filing a certified copy of an order of this court, made at a motion term thereof, bearing date the __19__ day of __20____, 19_21_, wherein and whereby the said __22____ was appointed committee of the person and property of defendant, __23____, an incompetent person; and also on reading and filing a certified copy of an order of this court, bearing date the __24__ day of __25____, 19_26_, wherein and whereby the said __27____ was appointed committee of the person of the said defendant, __28____, an incompetent person; and on reading and filing a certified copy of an order of this court, made at a Motion Term thereof, bearing date the __29__ day of __30____, 19_31_, wherein and whereby the said __32____ was appointed committee of the property of the said defendant, __33____;

And it appearing to the court that the said __34____, as committee of the person and property of the said __35____ and __36____, has been duly served with the summons and copy of complaint in this action, and has neither appeared nor answered in this action, and the court has, in its opinion, reasonable grounds to believe that the interests of the said defendants, __37____ and __38____, will not be protected in this action, and that a special guardian ad litem should be appointed to conduct the defense and protect the rights of the said defendants, __39____ and __40____, in this action;

NOW, on motion of __41____, attorney for the plaintiff, it is

ORDERED, that __42____, attorney and counselor-at-law, be, and he is, hereby appointed special guardian ad litem of the said defendants, __43____ and __44____, to protect and defend their rights in this action, with the same powers and subject to the same liabilities, as a committee of their property.

Signed this __45__ day of __46____, 19_47_ at __48____, New York.

Enter

__49_____

[Print signer's name below signature]
Justice, Supreme Court
__50____ County

Additional Forms:
14 Am Jur Pl and Pr Forms (Rev ed), Incompetent Persons, Forms 91–94.

Rule 1202. Appointment of guardian ad litem

(a) By whom motion made. The court in which an action is triable may appoint a guardian ad litem at any stage in the action upon its own initiative or upon the motion of:

1. an infant party if he is more than fourteen years of age; or

2. a relative, friend or a guardian or committee of the property; or

3. any other party to the action if a motion has not been made under paragraph one or two within ten days after completion of service.

(b) Notice of motion. Notice of a motion for appointment of a guardian ad litem for a person shall be served upon the guardian of his property or upon his committee or, if he has no such guardian or committee, upon the person with whom he resides. Notice shall also be served upon the person who would be represented if he is more than fourteen years of age and has not been judicially declared to be incompetent.

(c) Consent. No order appointing a guardian ad litem shall be effective until a written consent of the proposed guardian has been submitted to the court together with an affidavit stating facts showing his ability to answer for any damage sustained by his negligence or misconduct.

HISTORY:

Add, L 1962, ch 308, eff Sept 1, 1963.

Earlier statutes and rules: CPA §§ 202–204, 207, 208; RCP 39, 40; CCP §§ 426, 428, 469–472, 477-a, 1535, 2352; 2 RS 317 § 2; 2 RS 446 §§ 2, 4; Code Proc § 116; Gen Rules Pr 49, 50.

ADVISORY COMMITTEE NOTES:

Subd (a) is derived from the first sentence of CPA § 203, and parts of §§ 202, 207 and 208 and RCP § 39. The use of the term "special guardian" is abolished. RCP 40 uses the words "guardian ad litem" if the appointment is made in an action and "special guardian" if made in a special proceeding. The distinction is unnecessary. Subparagraph 1 and, insofar as it relates to infants, subparagraph 2, are derived from the first part of the first sentence of CPA § 203. One change of substance has been made—any guardian of the property may move for the appointment of a guardian ad litem. Thus, two restrictions imposed by CPA § 203 have been eliminated. That section permitted application to be made only by a general or testamentary guardian if the infant was under fourteen years of age. There is no reason to exclude a guardian of the property appointed by deed (see Dom Rel Law § 81) or to prevent any guardian from moving for the appointment of a guardian ad litem whatever the age of the infant. Subparagraph 2 permits a motion to be made by a relative or friend of the defendant for the appointment of a guardian ad litem for a defendant who is incapable of adequately protecting his rights but who is not an infant or a person judicially declared incompetent. There is no similar provision in the CPA or RCP. Such a provision will aid in protecting the rights of such a defendant when the friend but not the adverse party has knowledge of the defendant's incapacity. Subparagraph 2 also permits such a motion to be made by a committee of the property of the incompetent; there is no similar provision in the former act or rules. The committee should be allowed to make such a motion for there may be times when his interest is adverse to his ward's interest. He should be permitted—indeed, he is morally obligated—to bring his interest to the court's attention by such a motion. Subparagraph 3 is taken from the last part of the first sentence of CPA § 203 and from RCP rule 39. Two changes have been made: first, the time restriction on another party so moving has been reduced from twenty to ten days and, second, the proposed provision is made applicable to persons judicially declared incompetent and defendants incapable of adequately protecting their rights as well as to infant plaintiffs by objection of § 1201. In all these situations another party to the action should be allowed to move for appointment of a guardian ad litem since without such an appointment a judgment which is rendered may be voidable. See notes to § 1201.

Subd (b) is derived from CPA § 204. It has a broader scope than the CPA section, however, since it is not confined to actions involving infants. The subdivision requires that notice of motion be given to a defendant alleged to be incapable of adequately protecting his rights since such a person should be afforded an opportunity to contest the motion.

Subd (c) is taken from subparagraphs 3 and 5 of RCP § 40.

CROSS REFERENCES:

Compensation of guardian ad litem, 1204.

Cure of failure to appoint, see CPLR 2001.

Action to determine claim to property, Real P Actions & Pr Law § 1513.

Action to register title, Real P Law § 388.

CODES, RULES AND REGULATIONS:

Guardian ad litem's qualification and report in Surrogates' Courts, all counties, Third Judicial Department. 22 NYCRR 1940.23 (CLS Surrogates' Cts. Rules—Third Judicial Department § 1940.23).

Appointment of guardian ad litem on nomination in Surrogate's Court, Ulster County, Third Judicial Department. 22 NYCRR 2200.21 (CLS Surrogate's Ct. Rules—Ulster County § 2200.21).

FEDERAL ASPECTS:

Appointment of guardian under Longshoremen's and Harbor Workers' Compensation Act, 33 USCS § 911.

Motions in United States District Courts, Rule 7(b) of Federal Rules of Civil Procedure, USCS Court Rules.

Infants or incompetent persons as parties in United States District Courts, Rule 17(c) of Federal Rules of Civil Procedure, USCS Court Rules.

Substitution of parties in United States District Courts, Rule 25(b) of Federal Rules of Civil Procedure, USCS Court Rules.

RESEARCH REFERENCES AND PRACTICE AIDS:

1 NY Jur, Acknowledgments § 1.

28 NY Jur, Infants § 62.

57 NY Jur, Suretyship and Guaranty § 41.

17 Carmody-Wait 2d, Committee for and Incompetent or a Mental Patient § 109:13.

19 Carmody-Wait 2d, Actions in the Court of Claims § 120:31.

21 Carmody-Wait 2d, Actions and Proceedings By and Against Infants and Incompetents §§ 124:6, 124:10, 124:16–124:19, 124:21, 124:23, 124:25, 124:26.

41 Am Jur 2d, Incompetent Persons §§ 115, 116.

42 Am Jur 2d, Infants §§ 155–191.

Annotations:

Consideration and weight of religious affiliations in appointment or removal of guardian for minor child. 22 ALR2d 696.

Maintainability of bastardy proceedings against infant defendant without appointment of guardian ad litem. 69 ALR2d 1379.

Appointment of guardian for incompetent or for infant as affecting running of statute of limitations against ward. 86 ALR2d 965.

Who is minor's next of kin for guardianship purposes. 63 ALR3d 813.

Law Reviews:

Parties and pleading under the CPLR. 31 Brooklyn L Rev 98.

A biannual survey of New York practice: appointment of guardian ad litem before action commenced. 38 St. John's L Rev 422.

Biannual survey of New York practice: Part IV: preference given to nominee of relatives of incompetent when appointing committee. 39 St. John's L Rev 433.

The biannual survey of New York practice: Part V: CPLR 1201: guardian ad litem appointed for adjudicated-incompetent plaintiff. 40 St. John's L Rev 146.

The quarterly survey of New York practice: CPLR 1201: plaintiff must establish defendant's inability to defend and nonfeasibility of instituting proceedings for the appointment of a committee before a guardian ad litem will be appointed. 41 St. John's L Rev 137.

Forms:

See "FORMS" heading following "CASE NOTES", infra.

CASE NOTES

1. In general; preferences
2. Court's duties and powers
3. —Time of appointment
4. Notice of motion
5. Guardian's duties and powers
6. Discharge of guardian
7. Allowances and compensation

1. In general; preferences

The appointment of a guardian ad litem made pursuant to an order to show cause presented by a bank in connection with the judicial settlement of its account was an improvident exercise of discretion, and the Special Term should have granted petitioner's application to revoke the appointment and upon the return date petitioner's mother should have been appointed guardian ad litem since CPLR 1201 and 1202 indicate a legislative preference for the appearance of the natural guardian. Re Legget's Trust (1966) 25 AD2d 727, 268 NYS2d 911.

Even if court were to appoint guardian ad litem for children in order to permit them to bring action challenging the validity of the marriage of their parents, where it appeared that the moving figure behind such a suit was their father who was trying to establish the nullity of his Mexican divorce from his first wife, the father's brother would not be an appropriate guardian and it would be required that an objective outsider to the family be appointed. Pettas v Pettas (1976) 88 Misc 2d 955, 389 NYS2d 537.

2. Court's duties and powers

Where the affairs of an incompetent veteran are brought within the purview of the Supreme Court, that court has a duty placed directly on it to protect and preserve his property, and where necessary or proper a guardian ad litem may be designated to appear for and take such proceedings as are necessary to protect the interests of the incompetent. Re Becan (1966) 26 AD2d 44, 270 NYS2d 923.

Although CPLR § 1201 requires the appointment of a guardian ad litem for an incompetent adult defendant, it does not prohibit the appointment by the court of a guardian ad litem for a plaintiff who, is in an unconscious state as the result of an automobile accident and who may continue in such a state for weeks or months; and CPLR Rule 1202 specifically confers upon the court a general power of appointment of a guardian ad litem at any stage of the action either upon its own initiative or upon the motion of another. Liebowitz v Hunter (1965) 45 Misc 2d 580, 257 NYS2d 434.

If it appears that a suit is brought not in the best interests of the children but rather in someone else's interest in the children's name, the court must block the suit; court is the ultimate legal guardian of the children's interests. Pettas v Pettas (1976) 88 Misc 2d 955, 389 NYS2d 537.

Where uncle of two children sought to be appointed guardian ad litem so that children could bring action to establish that their parents were never legally married, and where the proposed complaint implied that children would enjoy greater social security benefits and greater estate benefits if their father was declared married to his first wife, from whom he obtained a possibly invalid Mexican divorce, and not to their mother, motion to appoint uncle of the children as their guardian ad litem would be denied. Pettas v Pettas (1976) 88 Misc 2d 955, 389 NYS2d 537.

3. —Time of appointment

In actions or proceedings involving infants and incompetents the court should await the application of the persons entitled to move for the appointment of the guardian ad litem, and after due consideration of any recommendation, to make an appointment. Where it appears that such procedure may constitute a danger to the infant's or incompetent's interests, or that his status or situation is such that waiting cannot result in anything but the appointment of a guardian without the benefit of any recommendation, the appointment can then be made at the inception of the action or proceeding, as in an order to show cause prior to the service thereof. Re Beyer (1964) 21 AD2d 152, 249 NYS2d 320.

Under CPLR 1201 and 1202 the appointment of a guardian ad litem should await the application of the persons entitled to move for the appointment of the guardian ad litem, and be made after due consideration of any recommendation in the absence of a showing that if such procedure were followed it would constitute a danger to the infant's interests. Re Thoms' Trust (1970) 33 AD2d 990, 307 NYS2d 312.

4. Notice of motion

It was improper to appoint a guardian ad litem on application by attorneys for the plaintiff without notice to the defendant, an adult, and without satisfactory proof that defendant, although allegedly mentally ill, was incapable of adequately protecting his rights. Abrons v Abrons (1965) 24 AD2d 970, 265 NYS2d 381.

5. Guardian's duties and powers

An attorney appointed to act as a guardian ad litem in an accounting proceeding by the Committee of an incompetent veteran should report in detail his acts with respect to the performance of his duties, and whether or not the account is correct and if he disapproves of it, the nature of his objections, and as an officer of the court is bound to conscientiously perform his duties with the understanding he may be asked to accept most moderate compensation for his services. Re Becan (1966) 26 AD2d 44, 270 NYS2d 923.

Only under careful judicial scrutiny should guardians, committees, or such representatives be allowed to tamper with family relationships in the name of the ward's best interest. Pettas v Pettas (1976) 88 Misc 2d 955, 389 NYS2d 537.

Guardian's primary duty is to act in his or her ward's interest. Pettas v Pettas (1976) 88 Misc 2d 955, 389 NYS2d 537.

6. Discharge of guardian

The motion of a guardian ad litem, appointed to protect the interests of a husband in an annulment action, for discharge was granted, upon evidence that the husband was gainfully employed, fully aware of the precise nature of the action, and did not wish to have anyone defend the action on his behalf. The mere fact that the husband had previously been a patient in a mental institution from which he had received an "outright discharge" two years ago was not evidence of an existing present incompetency. Arcieri v Arcieri (1966) 49 Misc 2d 223, 266 NYS2d 1020.

7. Allowances and compensation

In view of the small balance, approximately $1430, remaining in the estate of an incompetent veteran allowances of $250 and $750 respectively to the guardian ad litem and to the attorney for the committee were grossly excessive and modified to the extent of reducing the allowance to the attorney for the committee to the sum of $300 and reducing the allowance to the "special guardian" to the sum of $100. Re Becan (1966) 26 AD2d 44, 270 NYS2d 923.

CASE NOTES

UNDER FORMER CIVIL PRACTICE LAWS

See Case Notes under § 1201, supra.

A. IN GENERAL

1. Generally; courts

CPA § 207 was inapplicable to Municipal Court of City of New York. New York City Housing Authority v Pena (1953) 204 Misc 253, 123 NYS2d 62.

Where claim of a mentally defective person is to be prosecuted in Court of Claims, the better practice is to apply to that court for appointment of guardian ad litem, even though the supreme court in the exercise of its general jurisdiction over the person and property of such persons has appointed a guardian ad litem. Hawley v State (1961) 28 Misc 2d 150, 217 NYS2d 107.

The Court of Claims, instead of the Supreme Court, should appoint guardians ad litem for infant claimants in the Court of Claims. Torrey v State, 175 Misc 259, 23 NYS2d 370, revd on other grounds 266 AD 900, 42 NYS2d 567.

In action in court of claims for personal injury by

infant by guardian ad litem appointed by supreme court, court of claims may appoint substitute guardian ad litem nunc pro tunc as of date of supreme court order appointing guardian or of filing of claim, for purpose of prosecution of such action. Mackney v State (1941) 177 Misc 94, 29 NYS2d 1004.

Supreme Court does not lack jurisdiction to appoint guardian ad litem because infant is represented by general guardian, in proceeding to settle trustee's account in respect of inter vivos trust. Armour's Trust (1956) 3 Misc 2d 60, 153 NYS2d 90, affd 2 AD2d 840, 155 NYS2d 785.

2. Necessity for personal jurisdiction of infant or incompetent

Appointment of a special guardian for an incompetent was denied where the record did not disclose that she was served with process as a defendant in the action or that she appeared. Lawbaugh v Sweeney (1934) 242 AD 500, 275 NYS 869.

The court at any time on its own motion may protect the interests of a defendant adjudged incompetent by designating a special guardian, or requiring further service upon her committee if it appears that she has one, although she has been served as if competent. Jacobs v Jacobs (1926) 127 Misc 505, 217 NYS 280, affd 217 AD 753, 217 NYS 918.

Court was not required by CPA § 1313 (§ 1201, Rule 1202 herein) to appoint guardian ad litem for infant remainderman prior to return day of order to show cause. O'Malley's Trust (1955) 286 AD 869, 142 NYS2d 21.

A guardian ad litem can only be regularly appointed for an infant defendant after personal or substituted service. Ingersoll v Mangam (1881) 84 NY 622.

Appointment of a guardian ad litem cannot be sustained unless such appointment be made after service of a summons on the infant. Van Williams v Elias (1905) 106 AD 288, 94 NYS 611.

A guardian ad litem for an incompetent defendant could not be appointed ex parte where no leave to sue had been first obtained, as CPA § 208 authorized an appointment of a guardian only after the legal service of the summons upon incompetent and his committee. Smith v Ketaltas (1898) 27 AD 279, 50 NYS 471, affd 39 AD 670, 57 NYS 1148.

CPA § 208 authorized the appointment of a guardian ad litem only after the service of the summons upon the committee and the incompetents as prescribed by CPA § 225 (§§ 308, 309(a)(b) herein) and service could not be made until leave to do so was obtained from the court. Smith v Ketaltas, supra.

Court had no jurisdiction to appoint a guardian ad litem before service upon the infant defendant had been completed. Ward v Ward (1930) 136 Misc 234, 242 NYS 171.

Appearance and answer of a guardian does not waive a defect in the service of a summons. Bingham v Bingham, 3 How Pr NS 166.

The appointment of a guardian ad litem for a nonresident infant over fourteen years of age, upon the petition of such infant, together with an appearance and answer by such guardian, is sufficient to give jurisdiction to the court without service of a summons upon the infant. Shriver v Shriver, 12 NY Week Dig 328, affd 86 NY 575.

Appointment of a guardian ad litem cannot be sustained unless such appointment be made after service of a summons on the infant. Grant v Van Schoonhoven, 9 Paige 255; Ingersoll v Mangam (1881) 84 NY 622; Van Williams v Elias, 106 AD 288, 94 NYS 611; Glover v Hawes, 19 Abb Pr 161 note. But see Mace v Scott, 8 ·Civ Proc 200, 17 Abb NC 100.

Where the court had not acquired jurisdiction of the person of an infant, an order appointing a guardian ad litem was nullity. Lella v Holman (1938) 166 Misc 796, 3 NYS2d 352.

Where court had not acquired jurisdiction of the person of an infant, order appointing a guardian ad litem was nullity. Lella v Holman, supra.

The plaintiff in his action to annul his marriage may not raise the question of failure of service upon defendant for not serving her committee in charge of her as an incompetent, except to apprise the court of the facts. Jacobs v Jacobs (1926) 127 Misc 505, 217 NYS 280.

Service of a summons upon a nonresident infant defendant in partition not necessary, provided the infant voluntarily appear in the action by its guardian ad litem. Thistle v Thistle, 66 How Pr 472.

In an action for partition an order was made directing that unless an infant defendant then temporarily without the state, or some one in his behalf, procured an appointment of a guardian ad litem within ten days after service of the order upon the father of the infant that one C be appointed such guardian, and thereafter upon proof that the father of the infant had been continuously without the state for more than six months before granting the order, directing that such order be served by publication, or personally without the state in the same manner as a summons might be served, and thereafter such service was made upon the father and no guardian was procured to be appointed, and thereupon the order appointing C was made absolute: Held, that the service of such order without the state was irregular and void; that the court never acquired jurisdiction over the infant defendant. Uhl v Longhran (1888, Sup) 2 NYS 190, affd 22 NYSR 459, 4 NYS 827.

3. Necessity of adjudication of insanity

Where a person who is of full age becomes insane during the pendency of an action against him the court may appoint a guardian to appear and defend the action for him, although he has not been judicially declared insane in proceedings instituted for that purpose, and no committee of his person or estate has been appointed. Hanley v Brennan, 12 Civ Proc 147, 19 Abb NC 186.

Incompetent persons become wards of court where circumstance of such incompetency appears and whether such incompetence has been adjudicated or committee has been appointed, and proper procedure requires holding proceeding in abeyance until committee or next friend can be appointed. Re Lanham (1955) 1 Misc 2d 264, 144 NYS2d 401.

CPA § 207 was not confined by its wording to persons judicially declared incompetent under CPA § 1356 et seq., and CPA § 207 became useful only if interpreted to apply to persons who in fact were incompetent, but had not been so adjudicated. McCabe v State (1947) 208 Misc 485, 144 NYS2d 488.

A husband could bring an action against his former wife to impress a trust on real property though he had been in a mental hospital from 1944 to 1953, where he had never been adjudicated to be an incompetent and no committee of his person or property had been appointed. Anonymous v Anonymous (1957) 3 AD2d 590, 162 NYS2d 984.

Where plaintiff wife alleged that she was and continued to be mentally ill and of unsound mind, the duty of the court to protect the litigant actually incompetent but not yet judicially declared to be such was performed when the court appointed a special guardian and directed him to investigate and represent to the court the necessary steps to protect the plaintiff's interests but since the plaintiff was an unadjudged incompetent she was authorized to sue, and necessarily she was entitled to be represented by attorneys. Sengstack v Sengstack (1958) 4 NY2d 502, 176 NYS2d 337, 151 NE2d 887, 71 ALR2d 1237.

An unadjudicated incompetent who is actually an inmate of a mental institution may have a guardian ad litem appointed to prosecute her claim against the state. Re Ciena (1959) 8 AD2d 877, 187 NYS2d 59, affd 7 NY2d 939, 197 NYS2d 740, 165 NE2d 581.

Appointment of guardian ad litem for mentally defective person over twenty-one years of age, where no committee had been appointed, is proper procedure. Hawley v State (1961) 28 Misc 2d 150, 217 NYS2d 107.

4. Consent of infant

A guardian ad litem cannot be appointed for an infant over fourteen years of age without the infant's consent. E. B. v E. C. B. 28 Barb 299.

The surrogate has power to appoint a special guardian or guardian ad litem for a minor though over fourteen years of age, without the consent of the minor. This power is inherent in every court of justice, whether of inferior or general jurisdiction. Re Brick's Estate, 15 Abb Pr 12.

Affidavit, executed by infant over 14 years who was in armed forces in Texas, submitted with mother's petition to sell infant's realty, stating infant joined in petition, complied with CPA §§ 1387 (Real Prop. Actions & Proc. Law 1712)

and 1389 (§ 1201 herein). Re Lauder (1947, Sup) 73 NYS2d 15.

B. Guardian ad Litem

5. Generally; qualifications

It is the duty of the court on application for appointment of guardian ad litem to ascertain qualifications of appointee, with burden resting upon petitioner who seeks to nominate the guardian. Walter v Bernheimer (1929) 225 AD 343, 233 NYS 90.

A clerk in the office of the attorney cannot be appointed guardian ad litem of the infant. Lake v Kessel (1901) 64 AD 540, 72 NYS 311.

An attorney or officer of the court may be appointed special guardian of the incompetent. Re Warren, 207 AD 793, 202 NYS 586.

Any qualified person, such as an attorney or officer of the court, may be appointed special guardian of an incompetent. Re Warren, supra.

Administrator of estate held improper as guardian ad litem of infant legatees in a proceeding for sale of testator's real estate. Re Frits, 2 Paige 374.

6. —Financial ability

Defendant may call court's attention to pecuniary irresponsibility of the guardian and move for an order revoking appointment. Backerman v Coccola (1919) 189 AD 235, 178 NYS 423.

A financially irresponsible guardian ad litem should not be allowed to continue to act merely upon giving security for costs, especially as there is no power in the court to exact security for costs. Backerman v Coccola, supra.

Father of infant not of sufficient means to fulfill requirements of this section will not be appointed guardian ad litem. Re Maug, 5 Civ Proc 162.

RCP 40 (Rule 1202 herein) contemplated that the guardian ad litem should have been a person of sufficient responsibility to pay any costs which might be adjudged against him. Robertson v Robertson, 3 Paige 387; Cook v Rawdon, 1 NY Code R NS 382, 6 How Pr 233.

Infant's father, not of sufficient means to fulfil requirements of RCP 40 (Rule 1202 herein) would not be appointed guardian ad litem. Re Maug, 5 Civ Proc 162.

Where special guardian had been appointed to represent infants in action to reform trust indenture, had qualified and consented to act and did act as such, and where no final order has been entered in action, he was permitted to file his affidavit required by RCP 40 (Rule 1202 herein), nunc pro tunc as of time of his appointment. Guest v Bessemer T. Co. (1954, Sup) 138 NYS2d 243.

7. —Interest adverse to infant or incompetent

The appointment of guardian ad litem of an infant defendant of one having an interest adverse to the infant, especially of the plaintiff, is more than an irregularity and is a violation of rule 40. Re Cutting (1899) 38 AD 247, 56 NYS 945; Hecker v

Sexton (1887, NY) 43 Hun 593. See Grant v Van Schoonhoven, 9 Paige 255.

The court will not appoint a guardian ad litem for an infant defendant upon the nomination of the complainant. Knickerbacker v De Freest, 2 Paige 304.

Appointment of guardian ad litem for infant plaintiff on petition presented to court by defendant's attorney violated this Rule. Bose v Wehrli (1945) 186 Misc 325, 60 NYS2d 213.

Possible conflict of interest between infant's estate and mother's estate precluded appointment of general guardians of infant, who were also executors of mother's estate, as guardians ad litem for infant. Chase Manhattan Bank v De Caumont (1960) 27 Misc 2d 497, 210 NYS2d 277.

The committee of the incompetent may be appointed his special guardian, if his interest is not adverse to the incompetent; he will then have special and particular duties. Re Warren (1924) 207 AD 793, 202 NYS 586.

8. Consent of appointee

A guardian ad litem or next friend cannot be appointed against his consent. Leopold v Myers, 10 Abb Pr 40, 2 Hilt 580.

An order appointing a guardian ad litem is irregular when the consent of the person named as guardian to act as such is not acknowledged, and should be set aside, and the action brought by the guardian under such appointment dismissed. Cole v McGarvey, 6 Civ Proc 305.

But where a guardian ad litem nisi was appointed for an infant temporarily out of the state, and subsequently another guardian ad litem was appointed upon an application in the infant's behalf, the court acquired jurisdiction, although the guardian ad litem nisi did not acknowledge his consent to become such. Schell v Cohen (1889) 55 Hun 207, 7 NYS 858.

9. Liability for costs

A guardian ad litem may be charged with costs in an action and proceeding and a second action may be stayed until payment thereof. Robbins v Rogers (1936) 247 AD 603, 288 NYS 127.

10. Bond

Where summons and complaint on action of partition was served upon infants, and a guardian ad litem legally appointed the day after service of the complaint, the omission to require a bond from the guardian ad litem for the infants severally did not divest the jurisdiction of the court, but was merely an irregularity which could not be objected to by a purchaser at a sale under the judgment. Reed v Reed (1887, NY) 46 Hun 212, affd 107 NY 545, 14 NE 442.

11. Attack on appointment

The appointment of a guardian ad litem cannot be attacked collaterally upon the ground that he was unfit because adversely interested, where the appointment was made upon the application of the ward or his parents and they did not thereafter seek to vacate the appointment. Parish v Parish (1903) 175 NY 181, 67 NE 298.

Order appointing guardian for infant remaindermen named in testamentary trust was not disturbed, where no Federal statute prohibited same, though it was contended that vesting order had terminated their interest in trust property. Re Bank of New York (1948, Sup) 85 NYS2d 413.

12. Time for questioning qualifications

While defendant in an action by an infant is entitled to have the plaintiff represented by a guardian ad litem who is pecuniarily responsible, he must raise the question as to the guardian's qualifications as soon as he learns of the appointment. Wice v Commercial Fire Ins. Co. 7 Daly 258, 2 Abb NC 325.

On motion to vacate appointment of guardian ad litem in proceeding to settle trustee's account in respect of inter vivos trust, where movant, general guardian of infant, desires to be designated as guardian ad litem, it is incumbent on her to make timely application therefor and to establish facts qualifying her to act in that capacity. Armour's Trust (1956) 3 Misc 2d 60, 153 NYS2d 90, affd 2 AD2d 840, 155 NYS2d 785.

13. Revocation of appointment

The financial ability of the guardian is a question in which defendant has an interest, and he may call court's attention to pecuniary irresponsibility and move for an order revoking appointment. Backerman v Coccola (1919) 189 AD 235, 178 NYS 423.

A financially irresponsible guardian ad litem should not be allowed to continue to act merely upon giving security for costs, especially as there is no power in the court to exact such security. Backerman v Coccola, supra.

C. APPLICATION FOR APPOINTMENT

14. Generally; time for application

Where infant sued for divorce and jury decided against her on issues submitted, court erred in appointing a guardian ad litem nunc pro tunc, though judgment had not been rendered on the verdict, and the cause was stricken from the calendar. Anderson v Anderson (1914) 164 AD 812, 150 NYS 359.

Where it appears upon trial that one of the defendants is a minor, judge may enter an order appointing a guardian ad litem nunc pro tunc, but on failure to do so the judgment is defective. Seiden v Reimer (1920) 190 AD 713, 180 NYS 345, affd 232 NY 593, 134 NE 585.

An application for the appointment of a guardian ad litem for a nonresident infant defendant, made by the plaintiff after the infant had been served by publication, and the time to appear had expired, was governed by CPA § 203 rather than by former CPA § 206. Platt v Finck (1901) 60 AD 312, 70 NYS 74.

Where proceeding brought under Article 78 to

review right of infant defendant to waive jury trial in criminal case, application should be made in such Article 78 proceeding for appointment of a guardian ad litem or special guardian for the infant and such an appointment will be made nunc pro tunc. Scott v McCaffrey (1958) 12 Misc 2d 671, 172 NYS2d 954.

Pending an appeal where one of the parties was ascertained to be an infant, the appellate court, upon application of the other party as well as upon the infant's request, will appoint a guardian ad litem. Fish v Ferris, 3 ED Smith 567.

Where proceeding is brought under Art 78 to review right of infant defendant to waive jury in criminal case, application should be made in such proceeding for appointment of a guardian ad litem or special guardian for the infant and such an appointment will be made nunc pro tunc. Scott v McCaffrey (1958) 12 Misc 2d 671, 172 NYS2d 954.

15. By whom application made

Plaintiff may move for appointment of guardian ad litem for infant defendant if no one is appointed on latter's application. Krieger v Krieger (1950) 198 Misc 450, 99 NYS2d 80.

The court will not appoint a guardian ad litem for an infant defendant upon the nomination of the complainant. Knickerbacker v De Freest, 2 Paige 304.

The uncle (O'Reilly v King, 25 Super Ct (2 Robt) 587) or the general guardian may present the petition. Re Lansing, 3 Paige 265; Re Whitlock, 32 Barb 48.

16. —Mother as "next friend"

A mother, who is the natural guardian of her infant child, may, as "next friend" of such infant, present a petition for the appointment of a guardian to sell real estate of the infant. Re Whitlock, 32 Barb 48.

17. —General guardian appointed in another state

The general guardian or committee of a nonresident infant lunatic appointed in the state where the infant resides may petition for the appointment of a guardian ad litem for the infant when made a defendant in this state. Personal service upon such infant lunatic is not necessary. Rogers v McLean, 11 Abb Pr 440, affd 34 NY 536.

Where infant is a nonresident and has no general or testamentary guardian or guardian ad litem, a guardian ad litem may be appointed by the court whether the infant is over or under fourteen years old. Mace v Scott, 8 Civ Proc 200, 17 Abb NC 100.

18. —Infant defendant

An infant defendant may apply for appointment of guardian ad litem, even after twenty days, if none has been appointed. McConnell v Adams, 5 Super Ct (3 Sandf) 728.

19. —Other party

Adverse party cannot secure appointment of guardian ad litem until twenty days after service of process upon the infant. Keyes v Ellensohn (1893) 72 Hun 392, 25 NYS 693; Ward v Ward (1930) 136 Misc 234, 242 NYS 171.

An application for the appointment of a guardian ad litem for a nonresident infant defendant, made by the plaintiff after the infant had been served by publication, and the time to appear had expired, was governed by RCP 39 (Rule 1202 herein). Platt v Finck (1901) 60 AD 312, 70 NYS 74.

20. Notice requirements

Notice must be given mother with whom infant resides of application to appoint father guardian ad litem. Re Lopilato (1943) 180 Misc 699, 42 NYS2d 813.

Provision for notice to general guardian of infant pending application to appoint guardian ad litem is not jurisdictional. Armour v Armour (1953) 203 Misc 1093, 121 NYS2d 786, affd 281 AD 1022, 122 NYS2d 381.

In applying to the court for leave to dispose of the property of an insane person, his committee represents him, and is not required to give him notice of the proceedings. Agricultural Ins. Co. v Barnard (1884) 96 NY 525, revg 26 Hun 302.

21. Form and contents of application

As CPA § 1389 (§ 1201 herein) did not describe any particular form to be observed by the person who presented the application as next friend, and nothing appearing to the contrary, the court might properly assume that the ceremony was sufficiently observed, in putting the application before the court, to confer jurisdiction; that a departure from the practice prescribed by the rules of the court did not invalidate the proceedings. Aldrich v Funk (1888) 48 Hun 367, 1 NYS 541.

If CPA § 1389 (§ 1201 herein) was followed in substance, the form of the application was unimportant. O'Reilly v King, 25 Super Ct (2 Robt) 587.

Petitions in proceedings for the sale of infant's real estate should be addressed "to the supreme court of the state of New York." Re Bookhout, 21 Barb 348.

Any relation may be made a party to the proceeding when instituted by guardian. Re Stafford, 3 Misc 106, 22 NYS 706.

A sale of infant's real property is sufficiently brought under RCP 297 (Real Prop. Actions & Proc. Law 1722) by allegations of the petition that executors who have a power of sale are about to sell it and that the purchasers of said property will no doubt be strangers to the infant and apt to disregard her interest. Blanchard v Blanchard (1900) 33 Misc 284, 67 NYS 478.

A petition to sell infant's real estate is defective in failing to state the facts and particulars concerning the real and personal property of the infant, his income and the debts against his estate required by this section. Re Hopkins (1898) 33 AD 615, 53 NYS 1051.

22. Amendment of petition and affidavit

An order may be made in an action to foreclose a mortgage amending the petition and affidavit nunc pro tunc as of the time when they were made, by reciting in the petition that the infant was under and not over the age of fourteen years and directing that the affidavits showing these facts be annexed to a judgment roll. Baumeister v Demuth (1903) 84 AD 394, 82 NYS 831, affd 178 NY 630, 71 NE 1128.

23. Power of court under application

Where, following a petition under CPA § 1389 (§ 1201 herein) and CPA § 1388 (Real Prop. Actions & Proc. Law 1731) by the committee of an incompetent person, the court had authorized the execution of a lease of the property of the incompetent with an option to the lessee to purchase the same, the court thereafter had jurisdiction to direct the execution of a conveyance of the property pursuant to the terms of the option, on the application of the lessee, such application not being a new proceeding, to be instituted only by the persons specified in CPA § 1389, but merely a continuation of the former proceeding. Re Benedict (1925) 239 NY 440, 147 NE 59, revg 208 AD 823, 203 NYS 919.

24. —Appointment nunc pro tunc

Where it appears upon trial that one of the defendants is a minor, judge may enter an order appointing a guardian ad litem nunc pro tunc, but having failed to do so the judgment is defective. Seiden v Reimer (1920) 190 AD 713, 180 NYS 345, affd 232 NY 593, 134 NE 585.

Where county court instead of court of claims appointed guardian ad litem for infant to commence proceding on claim for appropriating her land, such error could be corrected and appointment would be made nunc pro tunc where no objection had been made to jurisdiction of court of claims. Walker v State (1951) 199 Misc 198, 102 NYS2d 620.

The bringing of suit upon a judgment by the guardian ad litem of the infant plaintiff without reappointment is a mere irregularity which can be cured by a nunc pro tunc order. Feigenbaum v Narragansett Stables Co. (1926) 127 Misc 114, 215 NYS 328, affd 219 AD 729, 219 NYS 811, affd 245 NY 628, 157 NE 886. See Louden v State (1943) 181 Misc 139, 41 NYS2d 455.

A guardian may be appointed at any time before verdict for an infant defendant, but after a verdict adverse to the infant a guardian nunc pro tunc cannot be appointed. Starr v MacNamara (1920) 111 Misc 242, 182 NYS 746.

Where infant sued for divorce and jury decided against her on issues submitted to it, court then erred in appointing a guardian ad litem nunc pro tunc, though judgment had not been rendered on the verdict which was for defendant, and the cause was stricken from the calendar. Anderson v Anderson (1914) 164 AD 812, 150 NYS 359.

When guardian ad litem for infant defendant cannot be appointed nunc pro tunc. See Kennedy v Arthur (1890, Sup) 11 NYS 661.

Failure to have a guardian ad litem appointed for an infant plaintiff or infant defendant is a jurisdictional defect but such defect can be cured nunc pro tunc without prejudice to the proceeding already had and the absence of the guardian ad litem does not deprive the court of jurisdiction of the subject matter. Randall v Randall (1958) 12 Misc 2d 468, 172 NYS2d 985.

Where proceeding brought under Article 78 to review right of infant defendant to waive jury trial in criminal case, application should be made in such Article 78 proceeding for appointment of a guardian ad litem or special guardian for the infant and such an appointment will be made nunc pro tunc. Scott v McCaffrey (1958) 12 Misc 2d 671, 172 NYS2d 954.

Where a guardian ad litem appointed by the Supreme Court commenced an action in the Court of Claims, since the statute requires that the guardian be appointed by the court in which the action is brought, in the absence of any objection to its jurisdiction, the Court of Claims appointed the same person guardian litem nunc pro tunc. Donoghue v State (1957) 17 Misc 2d 316, 186 NYS2d 99.

FORMS

Form 1—Order appointing guardian ad litem on court's own motion

Form 2—Affidavit in support of motion by infant of 14 or over for appointment of guardian ad litem

Form 3—Consent of proposed guardian

Form 4—Affidavit of proposed guardian

Form 5—Affidavit in support of motion by infant defendant for the appointment of guardian ad litem

Form 6—Affidavit for appointment of guardian for incompetent defendant for whom a committee has been appointed

Form 7—Notice of motion by relative or friend of infant plaintiff for appointment of guardian ad litem

Form 8—Order appointing guardian ad litem for infant plaintiff over 14

Form 1

Order Appointing Guardian ad Litem on Court's Own Motion

SUPREME COURT, ___1_____ COUNTY.

Order

[Title of cause.] Index No. __2__ [if assigned]

PRESENT: HON. __3_____ Justice.

The above entitled proceedings having duly come on to be heard before this court on the __4__ day of __5_____, 19_6_ and it appearing that __7_____, one of the defendants above named, is an infant under [or over] the age of 14 years, and that it is necessary for the proper protection of the rights and interests of the said infant that a guardian ad litem be appointed for the said infant for the reason that [set forth reasons why it appears to the court necessary for the proper protection of the rights and interests of such infant that a guardian ad litem be appointed], now on motion of this court it is

ORDERED that __8_____, Counselor at Law of __9_____ Street in the City of __10_____, County of __11_____, in the State of New York be and he hereby is appointed guardian ad litem of the said infant __12_____, to appear for and protect the interests of the said infant in this action.

Signed this __13__ day of __14_____, 19_15_ at __16_____, New York.

Enter

___17_____

[Print signer's name below signature]
Justice, Supreme Court
__18_____ County

Form 2

Affidavit in Support of Motion by Infant of 14 or Over for Appointment of Guardian ad Litem

Affidavit

[Title of court and cause] Index No. — [if assigned]

[Venue of affidavit]

__1_____, being duly sworn, deposes and says:

1. That he is an infant over the age of fourteen years; to wit, of the age of __2__ years and resides at No. __3__ __4_____ Street, in the City of __5_____, New York, with __6_____, his mother and __7_____ his father.

2. That he is about to commence an action in the __8_____ Court, County of __9_____, against __10_____ for __11_____ [state briefly the nature of the cause of action].

3. [State reasons why guardian ad litem should be appointed].

4. __12_____ who resides at __13_____ in the City of __14_____, as deponent is informed and verily believes, is a competent and responsible person, and fully competent to understand and protect the rights of the deponent and has no interest adverse to deponent, nor is he connected in business with the attorney or counsel of any adverse party.

5. That the said __15_____ is worth the sum of at least __16_____ Dollars, over and above all the debts and liabilities which he owes or has incurred, and exclusive of property exempt by law from levy and sale under an execution and is sufficient to answer for any damage which may be sustained by reason of his negligence or misconduct in the prosecution of the suit herein referred to, as will more fully appear by the affidavit of the said __17_____ hereto annexed.

6. As more fully appears from the consent of the said __18_____, annexed hereto, the said __19_____ is willing to act as guardian ad litem for deponent.

7. No previous motion for the appointment of a guardian ad litem or for similar relief has been made herein.

WHEREFORE deponent prays that an order be entered appointing __20_____ or some other competent person, guardian ad litem to bring such action for petitioner.

[Date]

[Jurat]

[Signature of Deponent]
[Print signer's name below signature]

Form 3

Consent of Proposed Guardian

I, __1_____, hereby consent to be appointed the guardian ad litem to bring the action above referred to, pursuant to the prayer of the foregoing affidavit.

[Date]

[Acknowledgment]

[Signature]
[Print signer's name below signature]

Form 4

Affidavit of Proposed Guardian

[Title of court and cause]

Affidavit
Index No. — [if assigned]

STATE OF NEW YORK
COUNTY OF __1_____   ss.

__2_____, being duly sworn, deposes and says that he resides at No. __3__, __4_____ Street, City of __5_____ and County of __6_____, New York; he is the person proposed in the foregoing affidavit as guardian ad litem for __7_____; he is fully competent to understand and protect the rights of the infant above named, and has no interest adverse to that of the infant; he is of sufficient ability to answer to said infant for any damage which may be sustained by his negligence or misconduct in the prosecution of the suit, and is worth the sum of at least __8_____ dollars over and above all the debts and liabilities which he owes or has incurred, and exclusive of property exempt by law from levy and sale under an execution.

[Signature of deponent]
[Print signer's name below signature]

[Jurat]

Form 5

Affidavit in Support of Motion by Infant Defendant for the Appointment of Guardian Ad Litem

[Title of court and cause]

Affidavit
Index No. __1__

[Venue]

__2_____, being duly sworn, deposes and says:

1. I am an infant over the age of fourteen years; to wit __3__ years old. I reside with __4_____, my uncle, at __5_____, New York, both my parents being dead.

2. I am being sued herein for the partition of certain realty more particularly described in the complaint. The summons and complaint were served on me and my uncle on __6_____, 19_7_.

3. I am informed and verily believe that I should appear and be represented in this action by a guardian ad litem. I have no general or testamentary guardian. I respectfully submit that my uncle is fully able to act for and protect my interests, and is in all respects a competent and responsible person to be appointed as such guardian ad litem, and I respectfully pray for his appointment.

4. No previous application has heretofore been made for the appointment of a guardian ad litem for me in this action.

[Signature, with name printed underneath]

[Jurat]

Form 6

Affidavit for Appointment of Guardian for Incompetent Defendant for Whom a Committee has been Appointed

Affidavit

[Title of court and cause]   Index No. __1__

__2_____, being duly sworn, deposes and says:

1. I am the attorney for the plaintiff in the above-entitled action.

2. This action was brought for the purpose of __3_____ [State nature of action].

3. This action was commenced by service of summons on the defendant and upon __4_____ as committee for the said defendant on the __5__ day of __6_____, 19_7_.

4. [Allege facts to show that the interest of the committee is adverse to that of the defendant or that the committee, for any reason, is not a fit person to protect the rights of the defendant.]

WHEREFORE, deponent respectfully requests that an order be entered appointing a guardian ad litem for the defendant __8_____.

[Signature, with name printed underneath]

[Jurat]

Form 7

Notice of Motion by Relative or Friend of Infant Plaintiff for Appointment of Guardian ad Litem

SUPREME COURT, __1_____ COUNTY.

Notice of Motion

[Title of cause]   Index No. __2__ [if assigned]

PLEASE TAKE NOTICE, that on the annexed affidavit of __3_____, sworn to the __4__ day of __5_____, 19_6_, and on the consent of __7_____, duly acknowledged the __8__ day of __9_____, 19_10_, and the affidavit of __11_____, sworn to the __12__ day of __13_____, 19_14_, a motion will be made at a motion term [Part I] of the Supreme Court, to be held in and for the County of __15_____ at the county court house therein, on the __16__ day of __17_____, 19_18_, at __19__ o'clock in the forenoon or as soon thereafter as counsel can be heard, for an order appointing __20_____ guardian ad litem of __21_____ an infant under the age of fourteen years, for the purpose of bringing an action in the Supreme Court against __22_____ for

641

__23_____ [briefly state the cause of action], and for such other, further and different relief as may be proper.

Dated, the __24__ day of __25_____, 19_26_.

__27_____
Attorney for Petitioner
Office and Post Office Address
Telephone No.

To __28_____,

Form 8

Order Appointing Guardian ad Litem for Infant Plaintiff Over 14

SUPREME COURT, __1_____ COUNTY.

	Order
[Title of action]	Index No. __2__ [if assigned]

PRESENT: Hon. __3_____, Justice.

A motion having been duly made by __4_____, an infant over fourteen years of age, for the appointment of __5_____ as his guardian ad litem for the purpose of bringing an action in the __6_____ court County of __7_____ against __8_____ for __9_____ [briefly state cause of action];

Now, on reading and filing the affidavit of said __10_____, in support of said motion, sworn to the __11__ day of __12_____, 19_13_; the consent of __14_____ to become such guardian, duly acknowledged on the __15__ day of __16_____, 19_17_; and the affidavit of __18_____, sworn to the __19__ day of __20_____, 19_21_, showing that said __22_____ is a proper person to be appointed guardian ad litem and on motion of __23_____, attorney for said infant, it is hereby

ORDERED, that __24_____ be and hereby is appointed guardian ad litem of __25_____, an infant over the age of fourteen years, for the purpose of bringing an action in the __26_____ court, County of __27_____ against __28_____ for __29_____ [briefly state cause of action].

Signed this __30__ day of __31_____, 19_32_ at __33_____, New York.

Enter

__34_____
[Print signer's name below signature]
Justice, Supreme Court
__35_____ County

Additional Forms:

13 Am Jur Pl and Pr Forms (Rev ed), Guardian and Ward, Forms 71–76.
14 Am Jur Pl and Pr Forms (Rev ed), Incompetent Persons, Forms 251–260.
14 Am Jur Pl and Pr Forms (Rev ed), Infants, Forms 21–79.

§ 1203. Default judgment

No judgment by default may be entered against an infant or a person judicially declared to be incompetent unless his representative appeared in the action or twenty days have expired since appointment of a guardian ad litem for him. No default judgment may be entered against an adult incapable of adequately protecting his rights for whom a guardian ad litem has been appointed unless twenty days have expired since the appointment.

HISTORY:
Add, L 1962, ch 308, eff Sept 1, 1963.
Earlier statutes: CPA § 492; CCP § 1218; Code Proc § 115.

ADVISORY COMMITTEE NOTES:
This section replaces CPA § 492 which states that no default judgment may be taken against an infant until twenty days after a guardian ad litem has been appointed to represent him. Since new CPLR § 1201 alters former law by permitting others to appear for the infant, their appearance is made an alternative condition for the default judgment. Furthermore, there is no reason to differentiate in the protection given an infant and that given a judicially declared incompetent. See NJ R Civ P 4:56-2. Accordingly, the section has been drafted to encompass both. The last sentence is new. It will give the guardian ad litem of a person incapable of adequately protecting his rights an opportunity to prepare the case and decide upon a course of action.

CROSS REFERENCES:
Default judgment generally, 3215.

CODES, RULES AND REGULATIONS:
Service of legal process and execution of instruments by mentally ill patients. 14 NYCRR 22.

FEDERAL ASPECTS:
Default in United States District Courts, Rule 55 of Federal Rules of Civil Procedure, USCS Court Rules.

RESEARCH REFERENCES AND PRACTICE AIDS:
20 NY Jur, Equity § 148.
28 NY Jur, Infants §§ 62, 65.
8 Carmody-Wait 2d, Judgments § 63:71.
9 Carmody-Wait 2d, Judgments § 63:181.
21 Carmody-Wait 2d, Actions and Proceedings By and Against Infants and Incompetents § 124:25.
41 Am Jur 2d, Incompetent Persons §§ 123, 126.
42 Am Jur 2d, Infants § 216.

Law Reviews:
Parties and pleading under the CPLR. 31 Brooklyn L Rev 98.

CASE NOTES

CPLR 1201 and 1203 are to be read together and interpreted as requiring the appointment of a guardian ad litem in every case where the defendant is an adult incapable of adequately protecting his rights before a default judgment may be entered against him. Oneida Nat. Bank & Trust Co. v Unczur (1971) 37 AD2d 480, 326 NYS2d 458.

The statute requires that infants must appear by a guardian ad litem in every civil case and an infant has no capacity to waive the failure to appoint such a representative to protect his interests. State ex rel. Byrnes v Goldman (1969) 59 Misc 2d 570, 302 NYS2d 926.

In an action seeking relief from a default judgment on the ground that at the time of making the retail instalment contract upon which the judgment was founded the defendant was an infant, it was held that service of summons upon an infant alone was insufficient and that his representation by a guardian ad litem or some other statutory representative was required, and that judgment by default could not be entered against him except after appearance by a representative or the expiration of 20 days from the appointment of a guardian ad litem. State Bank of Albany v Murray (1966) 27 AD2d 627, 275 NYS2d 985.

A default judgment was vacated where a bank brought suit on a debt, where it had notice that the defendant was under mental disability and failed to bring that fact to the court's attention and permit the court to determine whether a guardian ad litem should be appointed to protect such defendant's interests. Oneida Nat. Bank & Trust Co. v Unczur (1971) 37 AD2d 480, 326 NYS2d 458.

Under statutes which provide that adults who are incapable of adequately defending their rights shall appear in actions against them by their guardians, and that no default judgment may be entered against an adult incapable of adequately protecting his rights for whom a guardian ad litem has been appointed until 20 days after the appointment, an action at law against person incapable of protecting his interests, or who apparently is so incapable, and who has no committee or guardian may not proceed without notice to court of circumstances and inquiry therein by court. Barone v Cox (1976) 51 AD2d 115, 379 NYS2d 881.

Where defendant, in action on promissory note, was senile and disoriented to such an extent that she needed institutional care, and had entered county home for the aged approximately two months before service of summons and complaint, and where plaintiff knew or had reason to know that defendant was incapable of protecting her interests, it was error for special term to deny estate administrator's timely motion to vacate default judgment which had been entered against defendant 18 months prior to her death. Barone v Cox (1976) 51 AD2d 115, 379 NYS2d 861.

CASE NOTES

UNDER FORMER CIVIL PRACTICE LAWS

1. Generally
2. Effect of answer after twenty days
3. Necessity for guardian ad litem
4. Failure of guardian to serve general answer

1. Generally

CPA § 492 applied to a case where the infancy was admitted and a judgment could be entered against an infant defendant. Jackson v Brunor (1896) 16 Misc 294, 38 NYS 110.

After majority, infant, alone served, may not validate void judgment. Greenberg v Schilb (1947) 192 Misc 961, 964, 77 NYS2d 736, 84 NYS2d 437.

2. Effect of answer after twenty days

Twenty days having elapsed after appointment of guardian ad litem, plaintiff was entitled to move for judgment on the pleadings, the other defendants being also in default in serving answer, but answer of infant defendant after expiration of twenty days had the effect of requiring the court to take proof of facts and circumstances alleged in the complaint, such proof to be taken by the court itself or by referee. Kindgen v Craig (1914) 162 AD 508, 147 NYS 571.

3. Necessity for guardian ad litem

In action for annulment of marriage against an infant defendant, court was justified when plaintiff moved the case for trial without having guardian ad litem appointed for defendant, in dismissing the complaint. Lichtenstein v Belknap (1917) 100 Misc 468, 165 NYS 936.

Appointment of guardian ad litem for infants born before or after alleged adultery in action for divorce is necessary before their legitimacy can be passed upon. Cuyno v Cuyno (1945, Sup) 61 NYS2d 530.

Service of summons and complaint in action for divorce upon minor defendant without delivering copy to parent or guardian ad litem did not confer jurisdiction over his person, and judgment against him without appointment of guardian ad litem was void. Wiberg v Wiberg (1955) 1 Misc 2d 431, 145 NYS2d 785.

4. Failure of guardian to serve general answer

The failure of a guardian ad litem to serve a general answer does not invalidate the judgment in foreclosure. Hopkins v Frey (1892) 64 Hun 213, 18 NYS 903.

§ 1204. Compensation of guardian ad litem

A court may allow a guardian ad litem a reasonable compensation for his services to be paid in whole or part by any other party or from any recovery had on behalf of the person whom such guardian represents or from such person's other property. No order allowing compensation shall be made except on an affidavit of the guardian or his attorney showing the services rendered.

HISTORY:

Add, L 1962, ch 308, eff Sept 1, 1963.
Earlier statutes and rules: CPA § 207; RCP 43; CCP § 477-a; Gen Rules Pr 50.

ADVISORY COMMITTEE NOTES:

This section is derived from RCP § 43 and also from a part of CPA § 207. Rule 43 required that no order allowing compensation be made except upon an affidavit by the guardian (and in some cases also by his attorney) stating that the case had been examined and all necessary steps have been taken to protect the rights of the ward. The requirement has been preserved. Despite its imperfections, such an affidavit will furnish at least some basis for determining the value of the guardian's services.

The section gives the court three alternatives with regard to payment of compensation: (1) it may direct payment out of any recovery by the ward, or (2) if there is no recovery or an inadequate recovery, it may provide for payment from the ward's other property, or (3) it may require such compensation to be paid by any other party in the action. CPA § 207 permits the Supreme Court to order payment "from the estate of" an infant or incompetent to his guardian ad litem. RCP rule 43 omits power to provide payment from the estate but adds power to provide payment by another party. Both the second and third alternatives of the new section are sound. If the ward has assets of his own and his guardian has rendered worthwhile services there is no reason why the infant should not pay for them. The court is in a position to protect the ward against overreaching. The first alternative recognizes that the final judgment and the services of the guardian may also be of value to the party directed to compensate the guardian as where the action involves title to real property in which infants have an alleged interest. See 19 Carmody-Wait, Cyclopedia of New York Practice 692-93 (1955). As drafted this section permits the court to order payment in part from each of the three sources of funds available.

CROSS REFERENCES:

Appointment of guardian ad litem, CPLR 1202.

Allowance to guardian ad litem where proceeding is dismissed or abates, Men Hyg Law § 78.03.

RESEARCH REFERENCES AND PRACTICE AIDS:

18 Carmody-Wait 2d, Committee for an Incompetent or a Mental Patient § 109:181.

21 Carmody-Wait 2d, Actions and Proceedings By and Against Infants and Incompetents § 124:34.

24 Carmody-Wait 2d, Costs § 148:104.

42 Am Jur 2d, Infants § 190.

Annotations:

Allowance of fees for guardian ad litem appointed for infant defendant, as costs. 30 ALR2d 1148.

Forms:

See "FORMS" heading following "CASE NOTES", infra.

CASE NOTES

Where the petition for the appointment of a committee of the person and estate of an alleged incompetent was dismissed for lack of evidence, the petitioner was required, under this section, to pay the reasonable compensation of the guardian ad litem and of a psychiatrist engaged by him. Re Novohradsky (1965) 46 Misc 2d 1045, 261 NYS2d 667.

In absence of statutory authority, where no estate or fund existed, city could not be required to pay compensation of attorney appointed guardian ad litem for infant in proceedings to deprive of parental rights parent of minor child who had been responsibility of New York City Department of Social Services. Re Guardianship of V. (1975) 80 Misc 2d 986, 365 NYS2d 463.

Compensation could be granted to guardian ad litem for unsuccessful infant defendants in trust fund dispute, payable by trustees out of share of successful party, since presence of infants as defendants was necessary to determination of the dispute and they had to be represented, since even if infants' mother had acted for infants as their natural guardian without appointment of a guardian ad litem there still would have been a need for mother as guardian to have a lawyer, so that same legal fees would have been incurred, and since claim of infants was a substantial and not inequitable claim which had to be pressed. Seidel v

Werner (1975) 81 Misc 2d 1064, 367 NYS2d 694, affd 50 AD2d 743, 376 NYS2d 139.

In proceeding to declare competency, terminate committee, and restore incompetent's property, $6,000 fee for guardian ad litem held grossly excessive and reduced to $2,000. Berman v Grossman (1965) 24 AD2d 432, 260 NYS2d 736.

Considering the fact that the adjudication hearing in a proceeding to declare a person incompetent was short and uncomplicated, the allowance to the guardian ad litem would be reduced from $2,250 to $1,250. Landsman v Schutzman (1968) 29 AD2d 932, 289 NYS2d 119.

Applications of guardians ad litem for counsel fees and expenses in connection with proceeding to judicially settle the accounts of an inter vivos trust should initially be determined in the court of original instance. Re Marine Midland Bank—Western (1976) 55 AD2d 215, 389 NYS2d 705.

CASE NOTES

UNDER FORMER CIVIL PRACTICE LAWS

1. Generally
2. Courts
3. Where granted
4. —Extra allowance
5. Compensation from subject matter of action
6. Right of guardian not properly appointed

1. Generally

Guardian ad litem giving thorough and able consideration to case should be compensated. Bartos v Bartos (1930) 138 Misc 117, 244 NYS 713.

Guardian ad litem, duly and properly appointed, is entitled to fair and reasonable compensation. Re O'Malley's Trust (1955) 286 AD 869, 142 NYS2d 21; RCP 43 construed with RCP 40 (Rule 1202(c) herein) in holding that RCP 43 made no mention whatever of affidavit of qualifications or of consent as provided for under RCP 40. Guest v Bessemer T. Co. (1954, Sup) 138 NYS2d 213.

Prior to RCP 43 the compensation made to a guardian ad litem in an equitable action was not dependent upon the provisions of the statutes for an extra allowance, or any other similar provision. The court, it was said, had inherent and well established authority to award the guardian such compensation as appeared to be reasonable for the services he in fact performed, to be paid out of the subject matter of the action. Weed v Paine (1883, NY) 31 Hun 10; Roberts v New York El. R. Co. (1895) 12 Misc 345, 33 NYS 685, mod on other grounds 155 NY 31, 49 NE 262.

Prior to the amendment of RCP 43 in 1921, it was held that the compensation of the guardian ad litem could not be charged against the interest of other parties to the litigation. New York Life Ins. & T. Co. v Sands (1899) 26 Misc 252, 56 NYS 741; Brinckerhoff v Farias (1900) 52 AD 256, 65 NYS 358, affd 170 NY 427, 63 NE 437. An award to such guardian, under the former rule, was limited to taxable costs. Re Farmers' Loan & T. Co. (1900) 49 AD 1, 63 NYS 227; Re Robinson (1899) 40 AD 30, 57 NYS 523, affd 160 NY 448, 55 NE 4, affd 160 NY 692, 55 NE 1100.

2. Courts

An application by a guardian ad litem for compensation for services in conducting appeals should be made in the Supreme Court in accordance with RCP 43 and CPA § 207 (Rule 1202(a), § 1204 herein). Denials of compensation by the Court of Appeals was without prejudice to such an application. Morton v American Secur. & T. Co. (1937) 276 NY 601, 12 NE2d 596.

Under Correction L §§ 440 and 441, county court had no jurisdiction of proceeding to retain mentally defective prisoners at Albion state training school, nor power to appoint special guardian for them or to allow compensation to him. Re Naylor (1940) 284 NY 188, 30 NE2d 468.

3. Where granted

Guardians held entitled to compensation where their services were beneficial and necessary to adverse parties, even though judgment for the infants was reversed. Livingston v Ward (1928) 248 NY 193, 161 NE 468.

Where infant recovered judgment for $21,137 guardian ad litem was allowed $200 for consulting attorneys, attending trial and testifying briefly; denied claim for loss of time during trial. Scolavino v State (1947) 190 Misc 548, 74 NYS2d 573.

Finding that the infant represented by the guardian ad litem or special guardian has no interest in the property which was the subject-matter of the suit did not deprive the guardian of his compensation. Livingston v Ward (1928) 248 NY 193, 161 NE 468.

A guardian for an infant defendant, in an action for assault and battery, was entitled to compensation, though there is no fund in court out of which compensation can be directed. Richardson v Van Voorhis (1888, Sup) 3 NYS 396.

4. —Extra allowance

In action to settle accounts of trustee of inter vivos trust, guardian ad litem of infant defendant was granted extra allowance for infant's appeal from judgment settling such accounts, provided affidavit required by RCP 43 be filed by guardian. City Bank Farmers Trust Co. v Meyn (1942) 263 AD 671, 34 NYS2d 373.

5. Compensation from subject matter of action

The power of the court to provide for compensation of a guardian from the subject matter of the action is inherent in it, and does not depend upon statutory provisions. Weed v Paine (1883, NY) 31 Hun 10.

Allowance to guardian ad litem of infant defendants, in action by committee of incompetent to reach corpus of trust for incompetent's support, held properly made out of the estate. Rezzemini v Brooks (1923) 236 NY 184, 140 NE 237.

Attorney's fees were payable out of trust property, in action to settle account of trustees for infant. Steinhardt v Steinhardt (1948) 192 Misc 819, 81 NYS2d 222.

Infant's guardian in interim trust accounting proceeding of long duration was reimbursed for sums already expended by him for legal fees as to guardianship duties, chargeable half to general estate and half to infant's share. Re Harris (1950) 277 AD 1030, 100 NYS2d 784.

6. Right of guardian not properly appointed

One appointed guardian ad litem for an infant should be denied compensation where he was disqualified by adverse interest to serve in that capacity, and if he has procured payment to be made by the executors of the estate the court will order him to make restitution. Heuel v Stein (1914) 165 AD 14, 150 NYS 540.

CPA § 207 (Rule 1202(a), § 1204 herein) applied to the guardian of an infant or incompetent and not to a guardian for an alleged incompetent. Accordingly, where an alleged incompetent died during the pendency of a proceeding for the appointment of a committee, the court was without power to make an allowance to the special guardian. Re Frank (1940) 283 NY 106, 27 NE2d 801.

FORMS

Form 1—Notice of motion by guardian ad litem or special guardian for remuneration

Form 2—Affidavit in support of above motion

Form 3—Affidavit of attorney upon application by guardian for compensation

Form 4—Order granting remuneration to guardian ad litem

Form 1

Notice of Motion by Guardian ad Litem or Special Guardian for Remuneration

Notice of Motion

[Title of court and cause]   Index No. __1__ [if assigned]

PLEASE TAKE NOTICE that upon the annexed affidavits of __2____, __3____ and __4____, all sworn to __5____, 19_6_, the certificate of __7____, the referee herein, dated __8____, 19_9_, the report of said referee, dated __10____, 19_11_, his opinion duly filed herein on __12____, 19_13_, and upon all the pleadings and proceedings, an application will be made to this court at a motion term thereof to be held in the county court house in the City of __14____, County of __15____, on the __16__ day of __17____, 19_18_, at __19__ o'clock in the forenoon of that day or as soon thereafter as counsel can be heard, for an order granting __20____, the guardian ad litem of the defendant, __21____, an allowance of __22____ dollars, as reasonable compensation for his services herein as such guardian ad litem, payable out of the share or interest in the estate of the infant defendant, __23____.

Dated, __24____, 19_25_.

                                             __26_____

                             Guardian ad litem for the defendant

To __27____, Attorney for the Plaintiff

__28____, Attorney for the Defendant __29____

__30____, Attorney for the Defendant __31____

Form 2

Affidavit in Support of Above Motion

Affidavit

[Title of court and cause]   Index No. __1__ [if assigned]

STATE OF NEW YORK

COUNTY OF __2____   ss:

__3____, being duly sworn, deposes and says:

1. He is an attorney and a member of the firm of __4_____.

2. On __5_____, 19_6_, he was appointed by this court the guardian ad litem of the infant defendant, __7_____, on his petition, verified __8_____, 19_9_, and he proceeded to take steps to protect the interests of said infant.

3. This proceeding was brought by the plaintiffs as executors and trustees of __10_____, the father of the infant, for a judicial settlement of their accounts as such from his death in __11_____, 19_12_, to __13_____, 19_14_, a period of over __15_____ years. This was the first accounting which has been had. The plaintiffs filed accounts showing [show magnitude of interests involved].

4. Subsequent to his appointment deponent associated with him __16_____, of his office, who has been in charge of the case since __17_____, 19_18_, and __19_____, who had charge of it up to that date. Their affidavits of service are hereto annexed.

5. To appreciate the amount of labor expended, the issues and difficulties of the case should be borne in mind. The issues substantially were two-fold: [show issues and difficulty of case].

6. This litigation has been in active operation since __20_____, 19_21_. The filed accounts, original and supplemental, covered __22__ pages, and the vouchers numbered __23__. There have been __24__ hearings to take testimony, and [show statistics of case].

7. During the progress of this case deponent has been at all times in consultation with regard to it and in the preparation and examination of the various papers and records. He has interviewed and consulted with various persons with reference to the ascertainment of facts and the necessary evidence, and has made use of facilities of his office to that end. He has consulted with the __25_____ Trust Co., the general guardian of the infant, and has corresponded and consulted with his mother and other parties. He has personally attended __26__ of the hearings and attended court at __27__ upon an interlocutory motion.

8. Deponent has defeated the attempt to credit __28_____ with over __29_____ dollars more than rightfully belonged to him in the remaining assets of the estate, and has obtained __30_____ dollars of this amount for the infant as additional income belonging to him, and [show other results accomplished].

9. By his report, dated __31_____, 19_32_, the referee awarded deponent costs to be taxed. Such costs will amount to __33_____ dollars. Deponent's actual disbursements to date amount to __34_____ dollars, and he has incurred additional indebtedness of __35_____ dollars not yet paid.

WHEREFORE, deponent asks the court for an allowance of __36_____ dollars in addition to the foregoing costs and disbursements as a fair and reasonable compensation for his services herein as guardian ad litem for the infant, payable out of the share or interest in the estate of the infant defendant, __37_____.

[Signature of deponent]
[Print signer's name below signature]

[Jurat]

Form 3

Affidavit of Attorney Upon Application by Guardian for Compensation

Affidavit

[Title of court and cause]   Index No. __1__ [if assigned]

STATE OF NEW YORK
COUNTY OF __2_____   ss:

__3_____, being duly sworn, deposes and says:

1. He is an attorney of this court duly licensed to practice as such.

2. He has acted in this manner in behalf of __4_____, guardian ad litem [or special guardian] of __5_____, the infant defendant [or plaintiff] in the above action.

3. He has examined into the circumstances of the case and to the best of his ability has made himself acquainted with the rights of the said ward, the infant above named; the said __6_____ as guardian ad litem [or special guardian] of said infant has taken all the steps necessary for the protection of the rights of the infant, to the best of his knowledge and as he believes.

4. For the purpose of ascertaining the rights of the said __7_____, the infant plaintiff [or defendant] named in the above entitled action, your deponent has __8_____ [set forth in detail what was done].

5. Deponent believes that the reasonable value of the services rendered to the said __9_____ by __10_____, the guardian ad litem [or special guardian], is the sum of __11_____ dollars.

[Signature]
[Print signer's name below signature]

[Jurat]

Form 4

Order Granting Remuneration to Guardian ad Litem

SUPREME COURT, __1_____ COUNTY.

[Title of cause]

Order

Index No. __2__

PRESENT: Hon. __3_____, Justice.

__4_____, the duly appointed guardian ad litem of the infant defendant __5_____, having moved for an allowance of __6_____ dollars as reasonable compensation for his services as such in addition to taxable costs and his actual disbursements, payable out of the share or interest in the estate of the infant defendant, __7_____, and said motion having duly come on to be heard,

NOW on reading and filing the notice of motion, dated __8_____, 19_9_, the affidavits of __10_____, __11_____ and __12_____, sworn to __13_____, 19_14_, and the certificate of __15 ____, the referee herein, dated __16_____, 19_17_, with due proof of service thereof, and on reading the report of said referee, dated __18_____, 19_19_, his opinion and the several exhibits referred to in his report, all of which have already been duly filed herein, and on the appearance of and after hearing __20_____ in favor of said motion, and no one having appeared in opposition thereto, and due deliberation having been had, it is

ORDERED that said __21_____ be and he hereby is granted an allowance of the sum of __22_____ dollars as reasonable compensation for his services to date as guardian ad litem herein of the infant defendant __23_____, and it is further

ORDERED that said __24_____ be and he hereby is further allowed the sum of __25_____ dollars as such proper disbursements, and the clerk of this court is hereby directed to tax them as such; and it is further

ORDERED that the costs, allowances and disbursements now directed in this litigation be payable out of the share or interest in the estate of the infant defendant, __26_____.

Signed this __27__ day of __28_____, 19_29_, at __30_____, New York.

Enter

__31_____

[Print signer's name below signature]
Justice, Supreme Court
__32_____ County

Additional Forms:

13 Am Jur Pl and Pr Forms (Rev ed), Guardian and Ward, Forms 611–621.

§ 1205. Liability for costs of infant or judicially declared incompetent or representative

An infant, a person judicially declared to be incompetent, a person for whom a guardian ad litem has been appointed, or a representative of any such person, shall not be liable for costs unless the court otherwise orders.

HISTORY:

Add, L 1962, ch 308, eff Sept 1, 1963.
Earlier statutes: CPA § 205; CCP §§ 469, 477; 2 RS 446, § 2; 2 RS 447, § 12.

ADVISORY COMMITTEE NOTES:

This section is derived from CPA § 205 which is limited in scope to infants or guardians ad litem for infants. This section also encompasses judicially declared incompetents and their representatives and exempts them from costs unless the court otherwise orders. There is no sound reason for granting the exemption to one class and not to the other. Under former law, a guardian ad litem was always necessary to represent an infant and, thus, § 205 did not refer to a guardian of the property of the infant. Since new CPLR § 1201 permits representation by such a guardian he would be exempted from costs by the rule unless a court otherwise ordered. A committee of an incompetent should be treated in the same way. A court will award costs against a representative where he has been guilty of misconduct. See Gottfried v Natanson, 165 Misc 447, 300 NY Supp 777 (NYC Ct 1937).

Phrase "a person for whom a guardian ad litem has been appointed" added to include, in addition to a defendant declared incompetent for whom a committee has been appointed, a defendant not so declared for whom a guardian ad litem has been appointed under new CPLR § 1201 because he is incapable of adequately protecting his rights.

FEDERAL ASPECTS:

Costs in United States District Courts, Rule 54(d) of Federal Rules of Civil Procedure, USCS Court Rules.

RESEARCH REFERENCES AND PRACTICE AIDS:

21 Carmody-Wait 2d, Actions and Proceedings By and Against Infants and Incompetents § 124:31.
41 Am Jur 2d, Incompetent Persons §§ 25, 117.
42 Am Jur 2d, Infants § 191.

Forms:

See "FORMS" heading following "CASE NOTES", infra.

CASE NOTES

If a representative joins a claim in his individual capacity with the claim of an infant whom he represents, CPLR 1205 has no application to the resulting judgment insofar as it relates to the representative's individual claim and costs thereon may be taxed against him without a court order.

Tiano v Yaple (1968) 56 Misc 2d 44, 287 NYS2d 778.

In the absence of a court order, costs of dismissed third-party action could not be taxed against infant third-party plaintiff. Sweet v Bordis (1975) 47 AD2d 793, 365 NYS2d 917.

CASE NOTES
UNDER FORMER CIVIL PRACTICE LAWS

1. Generally
2. Construction
3. Security for costs

1. Generally

A guardian ad litem is generally not to be regarded as a party but merely the limited representative of the infant and is not liable for costs unless specifically charged therewith by the court. Alsante v Roberts (1953, Sup) 118 NYS2d 683.

CPA §§ 205, 1522 (§ 8501 herein) were to be read together and indicated that a guardian ad litem was not ordinarily liable for costs. Johnson v Board of Education (1925) 214 AD 740, 209 NYS 854.

A motion to charge a guardian ad litem of an infant daughter with liability for costs was denied where no misconduct on his part was shown. Gottfried v Natanson (1937) 165 Misc 447, 300 NYS 777.

A plaintiff suing as a trustee of an express trust will be required to file security for costs when one of the beneficiaries is a nonresident of the state, and the other is an infant whose guardian ad litem has not filed such security. Fish v Wing, 1 Civ Proc 231.

Where an action was brought in the name of an infant by his guardian ad litem, the guardian was responsible for the costs thereof; his liability was absolute and unqualified, and the costs awarded against the infant could be collected by execution or otherwise against the guardian ad litem, in like manner as if the latter was plaintiff. Miller v Woodhead (1889) 52 Hun 127, 5 NYS 88.

In action by plaintiff individually and as guardian ad litem, this section had no application to judgment in so far as it related to the plaintiff in his individual capacity, even though he joined such a cause of action with one belonging to the infant plaintiff and sought to be enforced by the same person in his capacity as guardian ad litem. Giebner v Retz (1937) 253 AD 752, 300 NYS 1050.

An infant plaintiff, who sues by her guardian ad litem for personal injuries, is not subject to costs in the defendant's favor, where the action is dismissed for the plaintiff's failure to proceed and the court makes no direction as to costs. Goishen v Samor Realty Co. (1938) 167 Misc 477, 4 NYS2d 107.

Costs against plaintiffs were disallowed without prejudice where infant plaintiff reached majority pending action by guardian ad litem and no motion was made to strike out the guardian ad litem as a party. McCarthy v Anable (1938) 169 Misc 595, 7 NYS2d 887.

It is the usual form, in the New York City Municipal Court, for a guardian ad litem for an infant plaintiff to consent "to be liable for costs if he fails in the action". Goishen v Samor Realty Co. (1938) 167 Misc 477, 4 NYS2d 107.

In federal court, guardian ad litem is liable for costs unless court otherwise directs, where judgment is for defendant. Barrett v Rosecliff Realty Co. (1950, DC NY) 9 FRD 597.

CPA § 205 had no application to a judgment insofar as it related to a plaintiff suing in his individual capacity although he joined such a cause of action with one inhering in an infant plaintiff and the selfsame person in his capacity as guardian ad litem sought to enforce it. Letson v De Long (1958) 11 Misc 2d 655, 175 NYS2d 249.

2. Construction

Mun Ct Code § 161 subd 11-a construed with CPA § 205 in holding infant liable for costs in absence of court order. Holmberg v Anderson (1942) 178 Misc 617, 35 NYS2d 478.

CPA §§ 205 and 288 (§ 3101(a) Rule 3106(a)), herein construed in holding that infant plaintiff's guardian ad litem is not employee, or agent or party to action, authorizing examination before trial of any party to action. Alsante v Roberts (1953, Sup) 118 NYS2d 683.

3. Security for costs

Although a resident guardian ad litem may no longer be required to give security for costs, yet a nonresident guardian and a nonresident infant plaintiff are compelled to do so as a matter of right upon the demand of the defendant. Maxwell v Klein (1934) 151 Misc 485, 271 NYS 886.

A resident guardian ad litem for a nonresident infant need not give security for costs. Blumenthal v Alexander (1916) 176 AD 184, 162 NYS 403.

Guardian ad litem for infant plaintiff, who is incompetent and irresponsible, may be removed or may be permitted to continue upon giving security to protect infant, but cannot be required to give security for payments of costs of defendant. McGovern v New York Tel. Co. (1917) 100 Misc 177, 165 NYS 480.

Where both guardian ad litem and infant plaintiff are nonresidents, both were required to join in giving security, since both may become liable for costs. Grindle v Westbury Food Mkt. (1954, Sup) 135 NYS2d 21.

Ordinarily any party to an action has the right to discontinue without reason upon payment of costs. But an infant or guardian ad litem for an infant is not liable for costs unless specially charged therewith by order of the court. Lo Galbo v Lo Galbo (1956, Sup) 159 NYS2d 649.

FORMS

Form 1—Notice of motion to charge guardian ad litem with costs of action

Form 2—Affidavit upon motion for order charging guardian ad litem with costs of action

Form 3—Order charging guardian ad litem with costs of action

Form 1

Notice of Motion to Charge Guardian ad Litem With Costs of Action

SUPREME COURT, __1_____ COUNTY.

Notice of Motion

[Title of cause]   Index No. __2__ [if assigned]

PLEASE TAKE NOTICE that, upon the annexed affidavit of __3_____, sworn to the __4__ day of __5_____, 19_6_ and upon the pleadings and proceedings in this action, a motion will be made at a Motion Term of this court to be held in and for the County of __7_____ at the County Court House in the City of __8_____ on the __9__ day of __10_____, 19_11_ at __12__ o'clock in the __13_____ noon of that day or as soon thereafter as counsel can be heard for an order charging __14_____ the guardian ad litem for the infant defendant in the above entitled action with the costs of this action.

Dated, __15_____, 19_16_.

__17_____

Attorney for Plaintiff
Office and P.O. Address
Telephone No.

To: __18_____
     Attorney for Defendant
     __19_____
     Guardian Ad Litem for Defendant

Form 2

Affidavit Upon Motion for Order Charging Guardian ad Litem With Costs of Action

SUPREME COURT, __1_____ COUNTY.

Affidavit

[Title of cause]   Index No. __2__ [if assigned]

STATE OF NEW YORK
COUNTY OF __3_____   ss:

__4_____, being duly sworn, deposes and says:

1. He is the attorney for the plaintiff in the above entitled action and is familiar with all the records and proceedings had and filed therein.

2. By order of this court dated the __5__ day of __6_____, 19_7_ and entered in the office of the County Clerk of the County of __8_____ on that date, __9_____, was appointed guardian ad litem for the infant defendant, __10_____, for the purpose of defending said action on behalf of the said infant defendant.

3. This action brought [state nature of cause of action].

4. This action was commenced by the service of a summons and complaint on the defendant on the __11__ day of __12_____, 19_13_ and judgment was rendered in said action in favor of the plaintiff and against the defendant, which judgment was entered in the office of the County Clerk of the County of __14_____ on the __15__ day of __16_____, 19_17_.

5. In the said judgment costs were awarded against the defendant and in favor of the plaintiff in the sum of __18_____ Dollars.

6. [Allege facts showing reason for exercise of discretion of court in charging guardian ad litem with costs of action such as misconduct, etc.].

WHEREFORE, deponent asks that an order be granted herein charging __19_____ the guardian ad litem for __20_____, the infant defendant in this action, with the costs of this action.

[Signature of deponent]
[Print signer's name below signature]

[Jurat]

Form 3

Order Charging Guardian ad Litem With Costs of Action

SUPREME COURT, __1_____ COUNTY.

Order

[Title of cause]   Index No. __2__ [if assigned]

PRESENT: HON. __3_____ Justice.

Upon reading and filing the notice of motion herein dated the __4__ day of __5_____ 19_6_, the affidavit of __7_____, sworn to the __8__ day of __9_____ 19_10_, and upon all the pleadings and proceedings heretofore had and filed herein, showing to the satisfaction of the court that __11_____, is the guardian ad litem for __12_____, the infant defendant in the above entitled action and that he was appointed to and did defend this action in behalf of the said infant defendant, and that the said guardian ad litem was guilty of misconduct in conducting the defense of the said action, and upon proof of service of said notice of motion upon __13_____, the guardian ad litem for the infant defendant herein and upon the attorney for the said infant defendant, and after hearing __14_____, Esq. in support of this motion and __15_____, guardian ad litem for the infant defendant, in opposition thereto,

Now, upon motion of __16_____, attorney for the plaintiff, it is

ORDERED that __17_____, the guardian ad litem of __18_____, the infant defendant herein, pay to the plaintiff the costs awarded to the plaintiff against the defendant by the judgment duly entered herein on the __19__ day of __20_____ 19_21_.

Signed this __22__ day of __23_____, 19_24_ at __25_____, New York.

Enter

__26_____

[Print signer's name below signature]
Justice, Supreme Court
__27_____ County

Additional Forms:

14 Am Jur Pl and Pr Forms (Rev ed), Incompetent Persons, Forms 201–215.

9 Am Jur Legal Forms 2d, Incompetent Persons, Forms 141:21–141:26.

§ 1206. Disposition of proceeds of claim of infant or judicially declared incompetent

Except as provided in EPTL 7-4.8, any property to which an infant or a person judicially declared to be incompetent is entitled, after deducting any expenses allowed by the court, shall be distributed to the guardian of his property or the committee of his property to be held for the use and benefit of such infant or incompetent, except that:

(a) in the case of an infant who is married to and resides with an adult spouse, the court may order that the property be distributed to such adult spouse for the use and benefit of the infant; or

(b) if the value of the property does not exceed one thousand dollars the court may order the property distributed to a person with whom such infant or incompetent resides or who has some interest in his welfare to be held for the use and benefit of such infant or incompetent; or

(c) the court may order that money constituting any part of the property be deposited in one or more specified insured banks or trust companies or be invested in one or more specified accounts in insured savings and loan associations subject to withdrawal only upon order of the court, except that no court order shall be required to pay over to the infant who has attained the age of eighteen years all moneys so held unless the depository is in receipt of an order from a court of competent jurisdiction directing it to withhold such payment beyond the infant's eighteenth birthday. The reference to the age of twenty-one years in any order made pursuant to this subdivision or its predecessor, prior to September first, nineteen hundred seventy-four, directing payment to the infant without further court order when he reaches the age of twenty-one years, shall be deemed to designate the age of eighteen years; or

(d) the court may order that the property be held for the use and benefit of such infant or incompetent as provided by subdivision (d) of section 1210.

HISTORY:

Add, L 1962, ch 308, amd, L 1968, ch 844, eff Sept 1, 1968.

Opening par, amd, L 1973, ch 455, eff June 5, 1973.

Sub (a), add, L 1968, ch 844, eff Sept 1, 1968.

Sub (b), formerly sub 1, so lettered, L 1968, ch 844, eff Sept 1, 1968.

Sub (c), formerly sub 2, so lettered and amd, L 1968, ch 844, L 1974, ch 924, L 1975, ch 228, eff Sept 1, 1975.

Sub (d), formerly sub 3, so lettered, L 1968, ch 844, eff Sept 1, 1968.

Laws 1975, ch 228, § 4, provides as follows:

§ 4. This act shall take effect on the first day of September next succeeding the date on which it shall have become a law, but shall not affect, impair or render ineffectual any order issued pursuant to law prior to the time this act takes effect, except insofar as an order issued pursuant to subdivision (c) of section 1206 of the Civil Practice Law and Rules, or its predecessor, designates the age of twenty-one as the age at which the infant may obtain from the depository the money held for the infant upon his demand therefor without further court order.

Earlier statutes: CPA § 980-a.

ADVISORY COMMITTEE NOTES:

This section is derived from CPA § 980-a. Several changes have been made. The scope of the rule encompasses all claims of an infant or incompetent and not merely those connected with personal injuries.

Subparagraph 1 increases the amount of property which may be held for the use and benefit of the infant or incompetent by a person with whom he resides or who has some interest in his welfare from five hundred to one thousand dollars. A one thousand dollar maximum, while arbitrary, is more realistic.

Subparagraph 2 is patterned after the second and third sentences of subdivision 1 of CPA § 980-a except that it eliminates the necessity of a guardian of the property or a committee. Adequate protection of the ward's interests is secured by the fact that the money may only be withdrawn upon order of the court. No monetary limit has been imposed on the amount of money which may be deposited or invested in the prescribed manner since the use of this procedure is discretionary with the court. The court order must specify the place where the deposit or investment is to be made. The words "one or more" are used to make possible more than one deposit or investment when the money held for the ward exceeds the maximum amount insured by the Federal Deposit Insurance Corporation or the Federal Savings and Loan Insurance Corporation.

Subparagraph 3 is new and grants to the court additional freedom in directing how a ward's property shall be held. Under this provision a court could direct the money to be invested in indebtedness of the United States of America as is permitted under subdivision 1 of CPA § 980-a.

If a court does not wish to exercise the discretion granted to it in subparagraphs 1 through 3, a guardian or committee of the property must be appointed to hold the ward's property.

CODES, RULES AND REGULATIONS:

Deposit, withdrawal, and accounting of infants' funds in Fourth Judicial Department. 22 NYCRR 1022.6 (CLS App. Div. Rules—Fourth Judicial Dept. § 1022.6).

Use of infants' funds recovered in personal injury actions, Fourth Judicial Department. 22 NYCRR 1039.8 (CLS App. Div. Rules—Fourth Judicial Dept. § 1039.8).

Compromise of actions or claims of infants in Supreme Court, Nassau County, Second Judicial Department. 22 NYCRR 785.19 (CLS Nassau County Supreme Ct. Rules § 785.19).

Approval of compromise of claims or actions belonging to infants in Supreme Court, Suffolk County, Second Judicial Department. 22 NYCRR 790.19 (CLS Suffolk County Supreme Ct. Rules § 790.19).

Settlement of infants' cases in Supreme Court, Westchester County, Second Judicial Department. 22 NYCRR 780.11(a) (CLS Westchester County Supreme Ct. Rules § 780.11(a)).

RESEARCH REFERENCES AND PRACTICE AIDS:

25 NY Jur, Guardian and Ward § 88.

63 NY Jur, Welfare and Social Security § 177.

9 Carmody-Wait 2d, Judgments § 63:140.

21 Carmody-Wait 2d, Actions and Proceedings By and Against Infants and Incompetents §§ 124:49, 124:50.

28 Carmody-Wait 2d, Payment of Testamentary Dispositions and Distributive Shares §§ 169:184, 169:185.

Forms:

See "FORMS" heading following "CASE NOTES", infra.

CASE NOTES

The law of the state of New York, exemplified by CPLR 1206 and SCPA 2220, does not sanction the granting of an application for the withdrawal of interest or withdrawal of interest or principal of the proceeds of a recovery or settlement in an action brought by or on behalf of an infant as a mere matter of routine. Levin v United Air Lines, Inc. (1967, DC NY) 279 F Supp 860.

Separate guardianship and trust accounts under judicial scrutiny are the legal protection for infants so that damages awarded for their pain and suffering are not invaded to pay the parents' debt, assuming such parent is found to be contributorily negligent and required to indemnify defendant for damages. Hairston v Broadwater (1973) 73 Misc 2d 523, 342 NYS2d 787.

In negligence action by child against third party, third party may not recover contribution against child's parent based on negligent supervision of child. Holodook v Spencer (1974) 36 NY2d 35, 364 NYS2d 859, 324 NE2d 338.

Where trust fund represented recovery by infant in personal injury action for pain and suffering, the same could not be released to pay for legal representation when infant, age 18, was charged with a felony, until the court was assured that there was no other way to provide such services and until the court was provided with a schedule of services performed and a rate compensable for such services. Franklin v Newberry (1974) 77 Misc 2d 1042, 356 NYS2d 175.

Indigent parent was not permitted under CPLR § 1206 to withdraw money from infant son's personal injury settlement to buy school clothes; Department of Social Services had the obligation to furnish necessities to such child (Social Services Law § 131) if parents were unable to do so. Application of Serrano (1973) 75 Misc 2d 1037, 349 NYS2d 952.

Funds paid in settlement of an infant's claim for personal injuries by the Motor Vehicle Accident Indemnification Corporation cannot be used to reimburse the Department of Social Services for maintenance and hospital care furnished to the infant since the occurrence of and injuries to such infant. Galante v Doe (1971) 68 Misc 2d 295, 326 NYS2d 199.

Under statute providing that no right of action shall accrue against infant by reason of assistance or care granted to him unless at time it was granted infant was possessed of money and prop-erty in excess of his reasonable requirements, where infant was already recipient of public assist-ance and was receiving medical care as necessity as result of automobile accident, no lien could be enforced against proceeds of settlement, and any lien for medical services rendered to infant was to be expunged. Washington v Beitel (1974) 77 Misc 2d 1016, 355 NYS2d 726.

CASE NOTES

UNDER FORMER CIVIL PRACTICE LAWS

1. Generally
2. Payment to unauthorized person
3. Withdrawal of petition
4. —For defense of criminal proceedings
5. —For family use
6. —For investment
7. —For religious education

1. Generally

The Supreme Court has the inherent right and duty to protect the rights and interests of an infant in an action for personal injuries. An alleged tort feasor or its insurance company should not be permitted to furnish or even suggest an attorney to carry on the necessary proceedings for the effectu-ation of a settlement agreement made though an adjuster and a parent or others who are supposed to act for the benefit of infants. De Gristina v Swift & Co. (1936) 158 Misc 91, 285 NYS 34.

Bond was required by person seeking possession of sum awarded infant and bond cannot be dispensed with in exercise of court's discretion. United States v Newhard (1954, DC Pa) 15 FRD 348.

2. Payment to unauthorized person

In an action by an infant, through his guardian ad litem, to recover for personal injuries, where an order has been entered permitting the guardian ad litem to settle and discontinue the action upon payment to him by the defendant of a stated sum, payment of the amount to the attorney for the guardian ad litem is insufficient and, where the attorney converted the money to his own use, a motion by the plaintiff for an order directing the defendant to pay to the guardian ad litem the sum specified in the order of settlement should be granted. Honadle v Stafford (1934) 265 NY 354, 193 NE 172, revg 241 AD 395, 272 NYS 444, which affd 150 Misc 412, 269 NYS 27.

The Supreme Court is without authority as a matter of chancery discretion to give direction for payment of shares of infant trust remaindermen to the infants' foreign guardian thereby dispensing with ancillary guardianship. The ancillary proce-dure is dictated by statute, Surrogate's Court Act §§ 184, 271, 314, subd 13, and there was no comparable statutory provision in the Civil Prac-tice Act governing foreign infants' estates. Re Starr (1958) 14 Misc 2d 1, 178 NYS2d 586.

3. Withdrawal of petition

A petition for withdrawal of an infant's funds should contain (1) a full explanation of the reason for the withdrawal, (2) several sworn statements by qualified persons of the estimated costs of the proposed expenditures and the necessity for work to be done, (3) the infant's age, (4) the date when and the amounts recovered, respectively, by the infant and parent, (5) the amount on hand and earned income, (6) a recital of previous withdraw-als and the reasons therefor, (7) a recital of finan-cial circumstances of the infant's family, (8) a statement that the expenditure cannot be afforded by the infant's family, (9) the nature of the infant's injury and present state of health, and (10) any other facts material to the application. Re Stack-pole (1957) 9 Misc 2d 922, 168 NYS2d 495.

See Federal Deposit Ins. Corp. v Tremaine (1940, DC NY) 37 F Supp 177.

4. —For defense of criminal proceedings

Defense of charge of grand larceny brought against delinquent infant, who was without funds, was sufficiently urgent to justify withdrawal of $250 for legal fees for the infant's chosen counsel from damages awarded in personal injury action, Hyter v Children's Village, Inc. (1957) 7 Misc 2d 1032, 166 NYS2d 667.

5. —For family use

Withdrawal of infant's funds recovered in personal injury cases and held in custodia legis should not be encouraged, and mother's application to with-draw funds for family use was denied, but reduced withdrawal was permitted with direction that it be expended for sole use and benefit of infant. Leon v Walker (1955) 1 Misc 2d 219, 147 NYS2d 331.

Money which has been deposited with the city treasurer to the credit of an infant plaintiff as the result of injuries sustained by him should not be withdrawn piecemeal by his father for infant's ordinary expenses of support. Zambrana v Railway Express Agency, Inc. (1956) 11 Misc 2d 553, 175 NYS2d 486.

6. —For investment

Application by guardian ad litem for permission to withdraw from savings bank balance in his ac-count as guardian and to purchase U. S. Defense savings bonds to be registered in his name as guardian for infant, held unauthorized. Schwartz v Kutsher (1941) 176 Misc 815, 29 NYS2d 168.

7. —For religious education
Motion granted for permission to withdraw proceeds of infant's cause of action for personal injuries for parochial school education where father of infant deeply religious and is in modest circumstances. Galvin v Feehan (1957) 10 Misc 2d 835, 170 NYS2d 54.

It is the duty of the court to protect an infant's funds and an application to withdraw such funds which were the proceeds of a cause of action for personal injuries for the purpose of paying tuition in a religious high school must be denied, notwithstanding the inability of the petitioner parent to pay the tuition. Re Stackpole (1957) 9 Misc 2d 922, 168 NYS2d 495.

FORMS

Directions in Order as to Disposition of Proceeds of Infant's or Incompetent's Claim

Ordered that the proceeds of said cause of action, the same not exceeding $1,000.00, be paid to __1_____, the father [or "mother"] of said infant [or "incompetent"] [or "to __2_____ with whom said infant (or 'incompetent') resides (or 'who has an interest in the welfare of said __3_____ because of __4_____')"] for the use and benefit of said infant [or "incompetent"].

Ordered that the proceeds of said cause of action, the same, after deductions, exceeding the sum of $1000.00, be deposited in __5_____ Bank, said bank being an insured bank [or in one or more specified banks or trust companies or specified accounts in insured savings and loan associations] subject to withdrawal only upon order of the court, except that no court order shall be required to pay over to said infant who has attained the age of eighteen years all moneys so held unless the depository is in receipt of an order from a court of competent jurisdiction directing it to withhold such payment beyond said infant's eighteenth birthday.

or

Ordered that the proceeds of said cause of action be invested in Savings Bonds of the United States of America, series __6_____.

§ 1207. Settlement of action or claim by infant or judicially declared incompetent, by whom motion made; special proceeding; notice; order of settlement

Upon motion of a guardian of the property or guardian ad litem of an infant or, if there is no such guardian, then of a parent having legal custody of an infant, or if there is no such parent, by another person having legal custody, or if the infant is married, by an adult spouse residing with the infant, or of the committee of the property of a person judicially declared to be incompetent, the court may order settlement of any action commenced by or on behalf of the infant or incompetent. If no action has been commenced, a special proceeding may be commenced upon petition of such a representative for settlement of any claim by the infant or incompetent in any court where an action for the amount of the proposed settlement could have been commenced. If no motion term is being held and there is no justice of the supreme court available in a county where the action or an action on the claim is triable, such a motion may be made, or special proceeding may be commenced, in a county court and the county judge shall act with the same power as a justice of the supreme court even though the amount of the settlement may exceed the jurisdictional limits of the county court. Notice of the motion or petition shall be given as directed by the court. An order on such a motion shall have the effect of a judgment. Such order, or the judgment in a special proceeding, shall be entered without costs and shall approve the fee for the infant's or incompetent's attorney, if any.

HISTORY:

Add, L 1962, ch 308, amd L 1969, ch 209, L 1971, ch 571, eff Sept 1, 1971.
Earlier statutes and rules: CPA §§ 1320–1324; RCP 294.

ADVISORY COMMITTEE NOTES:

(See also Advisory Committee notes preceding § 1201, under subheading "Settlement of claims.")

This section is derived from CPA §§ 1320–1324 and a part of subparagraph 1 and all of subparagraph 9 of rule 294 of the RCP. Under former law, there were two procedures for settling an infant's claim. If an action was already pending, only rule 294 was applicable. If no action was pending, sections 1320 through 1324 were applicable and were supplemented in several respects by rule 294. Because of the difference between motions and special proceedings, both procedures have been retained. Except for form, the two procedures are almost identical and they have been combined in this section.

One difference which formerly existed was in the kinds of actions or claims which might be settled. While rule 294 permitted settlements of any "claim or cause of action belonging to an infant," § 1320 was limited to cases where the infant has "a claim for damages for personal injury, injury to property or for breach of contract." The latter phraseology is more limited in application and needlessly restrictive. The new provision is taken from rule 294 and uses the words "any action" and "any claim"; the reference to "cause of action" is omitted as redundant. Neither rule 294 nor § 1320 applied to settlements of claims or actions against an infant. There seems to be no reason not to make this procedure also available as to such claims and the new provision does so. Several other states have statutes providing for settlement of claims by and against infants. See, e. g., NJ Stat Ann § 3A:14-4 (1953); Va Code Ann § 8-169 (1950); Wash Rev Code § 11.92.060 (1951). Furthermore, the procedure is equally appropriate in cases involving judicially declared incompetents and it has been extended to cover these cases.

The section differs from former law by providing that the motion or petition shall be made by a parent only if there is no guardian of the property or guardian ad litem of the infant. When there is a guardian, only he may make the motion or petition since he is specifically authorized to protect the infant's interests.

The first two sentences of the section are derived from §§ 1320 and 1321 and the opening portion of rule 294. The last sentence of § 1321 and subparagraph 4(b) of rule 294, stating that if the infant is over fourteen years of age he must join in the motion, have been omitted. It has been held as to the last sentence of § 1321 that a settlement is valid even though the infant did not so join. See Armour v Broadman, 283 App Div 351, 128 NYS2d 281 (1st Dept), affd without opinion, 307 NY 897, 123 NE2d 90 (1954). The third sentence is taken from § 1322 and the last sentence from § 1324, a part of subparagraph 1 and all of subparagraph 9 of rule 294. Section 1323 has been omitted.

CROSS REFERENCES:

This section referred to in 2213.

CODES, RULES AND REGULATIONS:

Approval of compromise of claims or actions belonging to infants in Appellate Division, First Judicial Department. 22 NYCRR 603.8 (CLS App. Div. Rules— First Judicial Dept. § 603.8).

Approval of compromise of claims or actions belonging to infants in Appellate Division, Second Judicial Department. 22 NYCRR 691.19 (CLS App. Div. Rules —Second Judicial Dept. § 691.19).

Matters heard at Special Term of Supreme Court, Erie and Niagara Counties, Fourth Judicial Department. 22 NYCRR 1155.13 (CLS Supreme Ct. Rules—Erie and Niagara Counties § 1155.13).

Compromise of actions or claims of infants in Supreme Court, Nassau County, Second Judicial Department. 22 NYCRR 785.19 (CLS Nassau County Supreme Ct. Rules § 785.19).

Approval of compromise of claims or actions belonging to infants in Supreme Court, Suffolk County, Second Judicial Department. 22 NYCRR 790.19 (CLS Suffolk County Supreme Ct. Rules § 790.19).

Approval of compromise of claims or actions belonging to infants in Suffolk County Court, Second Judicial Department. 22 NYCRR 1281.13 (CLS Suffolk County Ct. Rules § 1281.13).

Settlement of infants' cases in Supreme Court, Westchester County, Second Judicial Department. 22 NYCRR 780.11(a) (CLS Westchester County Supreme Ct. Rules § 780.11(a)).

RESEARCH REFERENCES AND PRACTICE AIDS:
15 NY Jur (Rev ed), Domestic Relations § 384.
40 NY Jur, Municipal Corporations § 1052.
59 NY Jur, Towns § 794.
21 Carmody-Wait 2d, Actions and Proceedings By and Against Infants and Incompetents §§ 124:36–124:48.
42 Am Jur 2d, Infants §§ 11, 82, 153, 217; 7 Am Jur Pl and Pr Forms (Rev ed), Compromise and Settlement, Forms 1 et seq., 11–13.
14 Am Jur Pl and Pr Forms (Rev ed), Infants, Forms 161–170.
4 Am Jur Trials p 289, Settling the Case-Plaintiff.
4 Am Jur Trials p 379, Settling the Case-Defendant.
4 Am Jur Trials p 411, Sample Settlement Brochure.
2 Am Jur Proof of Facts p 233, Attorney's Fees.

Law Reviews:
Parties and pleading under the CPLR. 31 Brooklyn L Rev 98.
The biannual survey of New York practice: Part V: CPLR 1207: settlement of action or claim by infant or incompetent. 40 St. John's L Rev 147.

CASE NOTES

The Surrogate's Court has no jurisdiction to approve a compromise of an infant's cause of action for personal injuries. A compromise order may be had only pursuant to the provisions of Article 12 of the CPLR. Where an action has been commenced in a New York court, application is made to the court in which the action was commenced. If no action has been commenced it is made in any court where an action for the amount of the proposed settlement could have been commenced. Petition of Wright (1968) 58 Misc 2d 783, 296 NYS2d 489.

Resettled order of compromise in infant's action against owner and driver of truck following accident while infant was passenger in parents' car, providing that settlement with owner and driver of truck was without prejudice to right of infant to seek recovery against any other person or persons, made on notice to all parties to that action, was not rendered without binding force and effect by fact that no notice was given to insurer of the parents, whom infant subsequently sued for their alleged negligence in the operation of their automobile. Krichmar v Krichmar (1975) 48 AD2d 515, 370 NYS2d 133, motion gr 38 NY2d 796, 381 NYS2d 871, 345 NE2d 342.

Where the issue of liability was of importance in determining the favorableness of the proposed settlement to the infant, and the mother was not represented by counsel, the court appointed a referee to determine this issue and report back on the reasonableness of the settlement. Application of Gonzalez (1972) 70 Misc 2d 38, 332 NYS2d 554.

Entry of consent judgment without an order of compromise or the protective procedures prescribed in this section and § 1208 for the settlement of an infant's actions complied with by the parties, constitutes error. Candiloro v New York (1966) 26 AD2d 693, 272 NYS2d 679.

The application in a special proceeding under CPLR § 1207 for an order approving settlement of an infant's cause of action against Motor Vehicle Accident Indemnification Corporation, although unopposed, must be denied when the petition was not accompanied by the affidavit of the physician as required by subd (c) of CPLR Rule 1208, or the affidavit or affirmed statement of the attorney as required by subd (b) of CPLR Rule 1208 and by CPLR Rule 2106, and when the infant did not personally appear before the court as required by subd (d) of CPLR Rule 1208. Bittner v Motor

Vehicle Acci. Indemnification Corp. (1965) 45 Misc 2d 584, 257 NYS2d 521.

An order fixing attorney's fees of $6,000 on a settlement recovery of $60,000 for infant plaintiff was remanded to the trial justice for further consideration with the suggestion that the factors involved in the merits of the case, the contribution made by the lawyers, the propriety of such contribution, and any other elements which might be determined to be relevant should be considered in fixing fee. Rivera v New York (1965) 23 AD2d 837, 259 NYS2d 583, later app 25 AD2d 297, 269 NYS2d 200, affd 19 NY2d 776, 279 NYS2d 530, 226 NE2d 317.

Attorney for infant could not settle a claim against

Motor Vehicle Accident Indemnification Corporation on behalf of infant, even though attorney's affidavit asserted that child's parents could not be located, where moving papers did not contain parent's approval of settlement as required by CPLR §§ 1207 and 1208, and did not contain parent's assignment of infant's claim to MVAIC as required by Insurance Law § 613. Speights v Motor Vehicle Acci. Indem. Corp. (1973) 75 Misc 2d 937, 348 NYS2d 691.

Appointment of guardian was necessary for proposed conservatee who appeared to have a valid cause of action but was unable to prosecute it personally. Stane v Dery (1976) 86 Misc 2d 416, 382 NYS2d 607.

CASE NOTES

UNDER FORMER CIVIL PRACTICE LAWS

1. Generally; purpose
2. Construction
3. Failure to obtain court approval
4. Attempts to circumvent statute
5. Order of settlement
6. Vacatur of settlement
7. Attorney's fee

1. Generally; purpose

CPA Article 80 (§§ 1320–1324) was designed to safeguard infants by empowering the courts to scrutinize the propriety and reasonableness of proposed settlements. Valdimer v Mt. Vernon Hebrew Camps, Inc. (1961) 9 NY2d 21, 210 NYS2d 520, 172 NE2d 283.

2. Construction

Although the provisions of CPA Art 80 were permissive and not mandatory, no settlement of an infant's claim could be enforced if court approval thereof had not been obtained. Valdimer v Mt. Vernon Hebrew Camps, Inc. (1961) 9 NY2d 21, 210 NYS2d 520, 172 NE2d 283.

3. Failure to obtain court approval

No settlement of an infant's claim, obtained without court approval, whether before or after the commencement of an action, is enforceable. Valdimer v Mt. Vernon Hebrew Camps, Inc. (1961) 9 NY2d 21, 210 NYS2d 520, 172 NE2d 283.

4. Attempts to circumvent statute

Since infants are the wards of the court, the practice of insurance companies of avoiding the requirements of Article 80 of the Civil Practice Act was not proper and parent's release of infant's

claims for damages was invalid. Gordon v Agaronian (1957) 10 Misc 2d 650, 171 NYS2d 131.

Agreement to settle an infant's claim for personal injuries is unenforceable without court's approval regardless of whether or not an action has been commenced, and an agreement executed by father of infant to indemnify one against damage resulting from settling infant's claim without court approval is equally unenforceable. Valdimer v Mt. Vernon Hebrew Camps, Inc. (1959) 9 AD2d 900, 195 NYS2d 24, affd 9 NY2d 21, 210 NYS2d 520, 172 NE2d 283.

5. Order of settlement

The Supreme Court was without authority as a matter of chancery discretion to give direction for payment of shares of infant trust remaindermen to the infants' foreign guardian thereby dispensing with ancillary guardianship. The ancillary procedure was dictated by statutes, Surrogate's Court Act, §§ 184, 271, 314, subd. 13, and there was no comparable statutory provision in the Civil Practice Act governing foreign infants' estates. Re Starr (1958) 14 Misc 2d 1, 178 NYS2d 586.

6. Vacatur of settlement

Settlement of infant's claim, though not accepted by guardian ad litem, would not be vacated where infant's attorney had had full authority to settle claim and application for vacatur was not made for more than 18 months after settlement. Savas v Stern (1961) 29 Misc 2d 529, 213 NYS2d 130.

7. Attorney's fee

In infants' cases an order must be obtained fixing the attorney's fee. Re Goldberg (1930) 227 AD 502, 238 NYS 273.

Rule 1208. Settlement procedure; papers; representation

(a) **Affidavit of infant's or incompetent's representative.** An affidavit of the infant's or incompetent's representative shall be included in the supporting papers and shall state:

1. his name, residence and relationship to the infant or incompetent;

2. the name, age and residence of the infant or incompetent;

3. the circumstances giving rise to the action or claim;

4. the nature and extent of the damages sustained by the infant or incompetent, and if the action or claim is for damages for personal injuries to the infant or incompetent, the name of each physician who attended or treated the infant or incompetent or who was consulted, the medical expenses, the period of disability, the amount of wages lost, and the present physical condition of the infant or incompetent;

5. the terms and proposed distribution of the settlement and his approval of both;

6. the facts surrounding any other motion or petition for settlement of the same claim, of an action to recover on the same claim or of the same action;

7. whether reimbursement for medical or other expenses has been received from any source; and

8. whether the infant's or incompetent's representative or any member of the infant's or incompetent's family has made a claim for damages alleged to have been suffered as a result of the same occurrence giving rise to the infant's or incompetent's claim and, if so, the amount paid or to be paid in settlement of such claim or if such claim has not been settled the reasons therefor.

(b) Affidavit of attorney. If the infant or incompetent or his representative is represented by an attorney, an affidavit of the attorney shall be included in the supporting papers and shall state:

1. his reasons for recommending the settlement;

2. that directly or indirectly he has neither become concerned in the settlement at the instance of a party or person opposing, or with interests adverse to, the infant or incompetent nor received nor will receive any compensation from such party, and whether or not he has represented or now represents any other person asserting a claim arising from the same occurrence; and

3. the services rendered by him.

(c) Medical or hospital report. If the action or claim is for damages for personal injuries to the infant or incompetent, one or more medical or hospital reports, which need not be verified, shall be included in the supporting papers.

(d) Appearance before court. On the hearing, the moving party or petitioner, the infant or incompetent, and his attorney shall attend before the court unless attendance is excused for good cause.

(e) Representation. No attorney having or representing any interest conflicting with that of an infant or incompetent may represent the infant or incompetent.

(f) Preparation of papers by attorney for adverse party. If the infant or incompetent is not represented by an attorney the papers may be prepared by the attorney for an adverse party or person and shall state that fact.

HISTORY:

Add, L 1962, ch 308, amd, L 1968, ch 844, eff Sept 1, 1968.

Section heading, amd, L 1968, ch 844, eff Sept 1, 1968.

Sub (a), amd, L 1968, ch 844, eff Sept 1, 1968.

Sub (a), par 5, formerly par 6, so numbered, L 1968, ch 844, eff Sept 1, 1968.

Sub (a), pars 6 and 7, formerly pars 8 and 9, so numbered, L 1968, ch 844, eff Sept 1, 1968.

Former sub (a), par 7, deleted, L 1968, ch 844, eff Sept 1, 1968.

Sub (a), par 8, add, L 1968, ch 844, eff Sept 1, 1968.

Sub (b), amd, L 1968, ch 844, eff Sept 1, 1968.

Sub (c), add, L 1968, ch 844, eff Sept 1, 1968.

Former sub (c), amd, L 1964, ch 195, deleted, L 1968, ch 844, eff Sept 1, 1968.

Sub (d), amd, L 1968, ch 844, eff Sept 1, 1968.

Sub (g), add, L 1967, ch 578, deleted, L 1968, ch 844, eff Sept 1, 1968.

Earlier rules: RCP 294.

ADVISORY COMMITTEE NOTES:

(See also Advisory Committee notes preceding § 1201 under subheading "Settlement of claims.")

Subds (a), (b) and (c) are derived from subparagraphs 4 through 8 of RCP 294. The second sentence of subparagraph 1 of rule 294, stating that a full examination may be made into the proposed settlement, has been omitted; the court always possesses this power. Paragraph 9 of subdivision a is new. It is desirable for the court to know whether reimbursement for medical or other expenses has been received from any other source. In a substantial number of instances today the parent has insurance which covers medical expenses and there is no reason to permit withdrawal of the infant's funds for such purpose. The requirements of paragraph 2 of subdivision b have been made more specific to insure that there is no conflict of interest.

Subd (d) is derived from the first two sentences of subparagraph 3 of RCP 294. The last sentence has been omitted since the court may always require further documents and information.

Subd (e) is taken verbatim from the first sentence of subparagraph 1 of RCP 294 and subd (f) is derived from subparagraph 2 of rule 294. The requirement that there be a full examination into the proposed settlement when the papers are prepared by the attorney for an adverse party is omitted. A court will look more closely at such a settlement without such a statement.

CODES, RULES AND REGULATIONS:

Approval of compromise of claims or actions belonging to infants in Appellate Division, First Judicial Department. 22 NYCRR 603.8 (CLS App. Div. Rules—First Judicial Dept. § 603.8).

Approval of compromise of claims or actions belonging to infants in Appellate Division, Second Judicial Department. 22 NYCRR 691.19 (CLS App. Div. Rules—Second Judicial Dept. § 691.19).

Matters heard at Special Term of Supreme Court, Erie and Niagara Counties, Fourth Judicial Department. 22 NYCRR 1155.13 (CLS Supreme Ct. Rules—Erie and Niagara Counties § 1155.13).

Compromise of actions or claims of infants in Supreme Court, Nassau County, Second Judicial Department. 22 NYCRR 785.19 (CLS Nassau County Supreme Ct. Rules § 785.19).

Approval of compromise of claims or actions belonging to infants in Supreme Court, Suffolk County, Second Judicial Department. 22 NYCRR 790.19 (CLS Suffolk County Supreme Ct. Rules § 790.19).

Approval of compromise of claims or actions belonging to infants in Suffolk County

Court, Second Judicial Department. 22 NYCRR 1281.13 (CLS Suffolk County Ct. Rules § 1281.13).

Settlement of infants', wrongful death, incompetents' and workmen's compensation cases in Supreme Court, Westchester County, Second Judicial Department. 22 NYCRR 780.11 (CLS Westchester County Supreme Ct. Rules § 780.11).

FEDERAL ASPECTS:

Settlement of United States Government life insurance when beneficiary is infant or incompetent, 38 USCS § 783.

RESEARCH REFERENCES AND PRACTICE AIDS:

25 NY Jur, Guardian and Ward § 142.

40 NY Jur, Municipal Corporations § 1052.

59 NY Jur, Towns § 794.

21 Carmody-Wait 2d, Actions and Proceedings By and Against Infants and Incompetents §§ 124:36, 124:38, 124:40, 124:42, 124:44, 124:46, 124:49.

6 Am Jur Proof of Facts p 131, Hospital Records.

Law Reviews:

Parties and pleading under the CPLR. 31 Brooklyn L Rev 98.

The biannual survey of New York practice: Part V: CPLR 1207: settlement of action or claim by infant or incompetent. 40 St. John's L Rev 147.

Forms:

See "FORMS" heading following "CASE NOTES", infra.

CASE NOTES

The statute requires that infants must appear by a guardian ad litem in every civil case and an infant has no capacity to waive the failure to appoint such a representative to protect his interests. State ex rel. Byrnes v Goldman (1969) 59 Misc 2d 570, 302 NYS2d 926.

Where there has been a settlement of an infant plaintiff's action for personal injuries the court must be made aware of the existence of claim for assistance previously paid of a department of social services against the recovery. Re Estate of Colon (1975) 83 Misc 2d 344, 372 NYS2d 812.

Where the issue of liability was of importance in determining the favorableness of the proposed settlement to the infant, and the mother was not represented by counsel, the court appointed a referee to determine this issue and report back on the reasonableness of the settlement. Application of Gonzalez (1972) 70 Misc 2d 38, 332 NYS2d 554.

Entry of judgment on consent without an order of compromise or the protective procedures prescribed by this section and § 1207 for the settlement of infant's actions complied with by the parties, constitutes error. Candiloro v New York (1966) 26 AD2d 693, 272 NYS2d 679.

Attorney for infant could not settle a claim against Motor Vehicle Accident Indemnification Corporation on behalf of infant, even though attorney's affidavit asserted that child's parents could not be located where moving papers did not contain parent's approval of settlement as required by CPLR §§ 1207 and 1208, and did not contain parent's assignment of infant's claim to MVAIC as required by Insurance Law § 613. Speights v Motor Vehicle Acci. Indem. Corp. (1973) 75 Misc 2d 937, 348 NYS2d 691.

The application in a special proceeding under CPLR § 1207 for an order approving settlement of an infant's cause of action against Motor Vehicle Accident Indemnification Corporation, although unopposed, must be denied when the petition was not accompanied by the affidavit of the physician as required by subd (c) of CPLR Rule 1208, or the affidavit or affirmed statement of the attorney as required by subd (b) of CPLR Rule 1208 and by CPLR Rule 2106, and when the infant did not personally appear before the court as required by subd (d) of CPLR Rule 1208. Bittner v Motor Vehicle Acci. Indemnification Corp. (1965) 45 Misc 2d 584, 257 NYS2d 521.

Appointment of guardian was necessary for proposed conservatee who appeared to have a valid cause of action but was unable to prosecute it personally. Stane v Dery (1976) 86 Misc 2d 416, 382 NYS2d 607.

Following consent at pretrial conference to $25,000 settlement by infant plaintiff's mother, who was not party to action brought by infant plaintiff and by his father, as his natural guardian, to recover damages for injuries, trial court properly denied defendants' motion for order directing execution of general release, or, in alternative, for appointment of temporary guardian for purpose of executing release and consummating settlement, where defendants had no authority to petition for appointment of guardian, defendants failed to demonstrate any authority or compelling facts to force plaintiffs to accept settlement, since they had not consented thereto, and there was failure to comply with statute outlining settlement procedure designed to protect infant's rights. Caglioti v Medi-Cab, Inc. of New York (1976) 52 AD2d 544, 382 NYS2d 311.

While strictly speaking infant plaintiff's consent to settlement might not have been required, in action brought by infant plaintiff and by his father as natural guardian to recover damages for injuries, his wishes should have been considered, especially in light of fact that infant was very intelligent 16-year-old boy. Caglioti v Medi-Cab, Inc. of New York (1976) 52 AD2d 544, 382 NYS2d 311.

CASE NOTES

UNDER FORMER CIVIL PRACTICE LAWS

1. Generally
2. Constitutionality
3. Construction
4. Necessity of compliance with rule
5. Requisites and sufficiency of application
6. Funeral expenses
7. Infant's consent
8. Guardian ad litem's refusal to compromise

1. Generally

Where rights or property of infant are involved, supreme court will exercise its protective equitable jurisdiction. Bogartz v Astor (1943, Misc 2d) 45 NYS2d 74.

Release, executed by guardian ad litem and approved by court on settlement of infant's action for personal injury, barred infant's second action therefor, where complaint did not allege fraud or ask rescission of release. Frehe v Schildwachter (1943) 289 NY 250, 45 NE2d 427.

Where infant, guardian ad litem and father stipulated in open court to settle personal injury action, and there was no fraud or overreaching, such stipulation was binding, though no order of settlement had been signed in compliance with RCP 294. Storman v New York (1953, Sup) 120 NYS2d 569.

RCP 294 did not contemplate giving guardian ad litem veto power over a proposed compromise settlement of infant's claim. Lee v Gucker (1959) 16 Misc 2d 346, 186 NYS2d 700.

2. Constitutionality

Third paragraph of RCP 294 authorizing attorney for defendants to prepare papers for application to compromise infant's claim, was held contrary to common law and unenforceable. Bose v Wehrli (1945) 186 Misc 325, 60 NYS2d 213.

Constitutionality of RCP 294 upheld as not repugnant to any statutory or constitutional provision. Carlis v Stratigos (1946) 186 Misc 337, 61 NYS2d 456.

3. Construction

Although the provision of RCP 294 were permissive and not mandatory, no settlement of an infant's claim could be enforced if court approval thereof had not been obtained. Valdimer v Mt. Vernon Hebrew Camps, Inc. (1961) 9 NY2d 21, 210 NYS2d 520, 172 NE2d 283.

4. Necessity of compliance with rule

Judges of the municipal court urged to observe the provisions of RCP 294. Re Fink (1930) 229 AD 338, 241 NYS 886.

Conduct of an attorney who misled the court with reference to compliance with RCP 294 (this rule) was disapproved. Re Wilbur (1930) 228 AD 197, 239 NYS 483.

No settlement of an infant's claim, obtained without court approval, whether before or after the commencement of an action, is enforceable. Valdimer v Mt. Vernon Hebrew Camps, Inc. (1961) 9 NY2d 21, 210 NYS2d 520, 172 NE2d 283.

5. Requisites and sufficiency of application

Requisites to be complied with by counsel making application hereunder fully set forth; affidavit of physician was too general as to infant's recovery from the injury; more complete examination ordered. Maguire v New York Rapid Transit Corp. (1931) 141 Misc 807, 253 NYS 855.

6. Funeral expenses

Guardian may pay funeral expenses of infant's father. Re Neville (1933) 147 Misc 171, 263 NYS 528.

7. Infant's consent

Sub 4(b) of RCP 294 was a procedural provision and did not require court to disapprove compromise and settlement of infant's claim in action by trustee of inter vivos trust to settle his accounts, upon sole ground that acknowledged consents of infants over fourteen years of age were withheld. Armour v Broadman (1954) 283 AD 351, 128 NYS2d 281, affd 307 NY 896, 123 NE2d 90.

8. Guardian ad litem's refusal to compromise

After a full examination into the reasonableness and propriety of the proposed offer, the court ordered the action to be compromised where guardian ad litem's stubborn refusal to compromise was prejudicial to infant's interests. Lee v Gucker (1959) 16 Misc 2d 346, 186 NYS2d 700.

After finding that guardian ad litem's refusal to consent to settlement of action was unreasonable and arbitrary, court directed the guardian to settle it. Glogowski v Rapson (1959) 20 Misc 2d 96, 198 NYS2d 87.

FORMS

Form　1—Petition for leave to settle claim of infant

Form　2—Allegation in petition for leave to settle claim of judicially declared incompetent

Form　3—Defendant's offer of settlement

Form　4—Affidavit in support of motion to settle infant's action

Form　5—Attorney's affidavit on motion to settle infant's action

Form　6—Affidavit of opposing attorney

Form　7—Affidavit of physician on motion to settle infant's claim or action

Form　8—Notice of application for leave to settle infant's claim

Form　9—Consent of parent other than petitioner or moving party

Form 10—Order settling infant's action

Form 1

Petition for Leave to Settle Claim of Infant

SUPREME COURT, COUNTY OF __1_____

In the Matter of
the Application of __2_____,
for Leave to Settle a Claim of __3_____, an Infant.　　　　　　Petition

To: Hon. __4_____, Justice, Supreme Court.

The petition of __5_ ____, respectfully shows:

1. Petitioner resides at No. __6__, __7_____ Street in the City of __8_____, County of __9_____ and State of New York.

2. Petitioner is the father of __10_____, an infant of the age of __11__ years, said infant having been born on the __12__ day of __13_____, 19_14_.

3. That no guardian of the property or guardian ad litem has been appointed for said infant.

4. The said infant resides with petitioner at No. __15__, __16_____ Street, in the City of __17_____, County of __18_____ and State of New York.

5. [Set forth circumstances giving rise to claim of infant, as—] On or about the __19__ day of __20__ _, 19_21_, the said infant went upon certain property owned, occupied and controlled by one, __22_____, and located on __23_____ Street in the City of __24_____, County of __25_____ and State of New York about __26__ feet north of the intersection of said __27_____ Street with __28_____ Street. At the said time and place the said __29_____, his agents and employees were engaged in the construction of a house on the said property and had caused an excavation to be made on the said property which was approximately __30__ feet deep and __31__ feet in diameter. At about __32__ o'clock in the __33__ noon of the said __34__ day of __35_____, 19_36_ the said excavation was unguarded and uncovered and the said infant fell into the excavation sustaining injuries hereinafter set forth.

6. [Set forth the injuries suffered by the infant as—] The injuries sustained by the said infant as a result of the aforesaid accident consisted of abrasions and contusions of the face and head and an abrasion of the left arm.

7. [Set forth the medical treatment accorded to the infant after the accident, as—] Immediately after the said accident, petitioner brought the said infant to Dr. __37_____, M.D. a physician with offices at No. __38__ __39_____ Street in the City of __40_____, New York. Medical attention was given to the said infant at that time and he was returned to his home. Thereafter, the said infant was brought to the offices of Dr. __41_____, M.D. for further medical attention on __42_____ other occasions. The expense for such medical care and attention amounted to __43_____ Dollars which sum has been paid in full by petitioner.

8. Reimbursement for medical or other expenses have not been received from any source [or as the case may be].

9. [Set forth period and nature of disability, as—] As a result of the injuries sustained as aforesaid, the infant was disabled for __44__ days following the accident and suffered a permanent scar on his upper lip as is more fully described in the affidavit of __45_____, M.D. annexed hereto and made a part hereof. The said infant has fully recovered from his said injuries except for the scar on his upper lip.

10. [Set forth whether the infant's representative or any member of infant's family has made a claim for damages alleged to have been suffered as a result of the same occurence giving rise to infant's claim and, if so, the amount paid or to be paid in settlement of such claim or if such claim has not been settled the reasons therefor].

11. [Set forth nature of proposed settlement, as—] On or about the __46__ day of __47_____, 19_48_ negotiations were entered into between __49_____, as attorney representing your petitioner and the said infant, and the __50_____ Insurance Company as the carrier of liability insurance for __51_____, for the settlement and compromise of the claims of the said infant and petitioner. On or about the __52__ day of __53_____, 19_54_ the said __55_____ Insurance Company offered to pay your petitioner and the said infant the sum of __56_____ Dollars in full settlement and discharge of their claims. It is proposed that this offer be accepted and the settlement approved on the following terms: the sum of __57_____ Dollars to be paid to petitioner in payment and satisfaction of his claim for medical expenses incurred on behalf of the infant and loss of the infant's services. Of this amount the sum of __58_____ Dollars represents compensation to petitioner for loss of the services of the infant. The sum of __59_____ Dollars to be paid to __60_____ as the reasonable value of the services rendered by him in negotiating a settlement of the claim of the infant herein. The balance, amounting to the sum of __61_____ Dollars to be paid to the infant herein.

12. Petitioner thinks and believes that the proposed settlement should be accepted since there is much uncertainty as to whether or not he and the said infant would be finally successful if an action were brought upon the said claim in that __62_____ claims that the infant was a trespasser on the said property and that the excavation had been covered but that the cover had been removed by the said infant and other children who were playing in the area. The circumstances leading up to and precipitating the infant's fall into the said excavation are unknown for the reason that there was no witness to the accident and the infant is of such tender years that he cannot fully explain the said circumstances and would not be permitted to testify in an action brought on the said claim.

13. No action has been commenced on behalf of the said infant to recover damages for the aforementioned personal injuries.

14. Petitioner believes that the said sum of __63_____ Dollars is the highest amount the said __64_____ would offer or give under any circumstances to settle and compromise the aforementioned claim and approves of the sum of __65_____ Dollars as the reasonable fee for the legal services performed by the said __66_____ in settling the claim of the infant as aforesaid.

15. [Set forth nature of security proposed to be given, as—] Petitioner respectfully asks the giving of security be dispensed with pursuant to CPLR Rule 1210(c) because the money or the value of the property to be received by the infant upon the proposed settlement does not exceed the sum of $1000.00 after payment of attorney's fees and expenses.

16. No previous application for settlement of the above described claim has been made by petitioner or by any other person.

17. No action has been commenced on the claim of the infant described herein by petitioner or by any other person.

WHEREFORE, petitioner respectfully asks that the Court approve the aforementioned settlement of __67_____ Dollars, the payment of the sum of __68_____ Dollars to petitioner in settlement of his claim for medical expenses and loss of services and the payment of __69_ __ Dollars to __70_____, as compensation for legal services rendered by him and that the court grant permission for the entry of a final judgment of settlement pursuant to the provisions of Section 1207 of the Civil Practice Law and Rules. (P)Dated __71_____ 19_72_

__73_____

[Print signer's name below signature]
Office and P.O. Address
Telephone No.

[Verification]

Form 2

Allegation in Petition for Leave to Settle Claim of Judicially Declared Incompetent

[The forms for settlement or compromise of infants' claims or actions are readily adaptable to proceedings or motions on behalf of a judicially declared incompetent.]

2. Petitioner is the duly appointed and qualified committee of __1_____, who was judicially declared to be incompetent by the __2_____ court of the County of __3_____ on the __4_ day of __5_____, 19_6_, the petitioner having been appointed [state facts showing proper appointment and qualification of committee].

Form 3

Defendant's Offer of Settlement

[Title of court and cause]

Defendant hereby offers to pay the sum of __1_____ dollars [$__2__], in full settlement of the causes of action herein, and agrees to pay the portion of the said sum determined to be in full settlement of said infant plaintiff's cause of action in accordance with the provisions of the order of settlement made herein.

Date __3_____

To __4_____, Esq.
   Plaintiffs' Attorney
   [Address]

[Signature, office and post-office
address, and telephone number
of defendant's attorney]
[Venue]

__5_____ being duly sworn says:

That he is the attorney for __6_ ____ in this action. That he is duly authorized by __7_____ to make the offer of settlement hereto annexed on his behalf.

That he has subscribed said offer in pursuance of such authority.

[Signature of deponent]

[Jurat]

Form 4

Affidavit in Support of Motion to Settle Infant's Action

SUPREME COURT, __1_____ COUNTY.

               Affidavit
[Title of cause]   Index No. __2__ [if assigned]
STATE OF NEW YORK
COUNTY OF __3_____   SS.:

__4_____, being duly sworn, deposes and says:

1. Deponent resides at No. __5__ __6_____ Street, in the City of __7_____, County of __8_____ and State of New York.

2. Deponent is the father of __9_____, the infant named in the above entitled action and no guardian of the property of the said infant or guardian ad litem for said infant has been appointed.

3. __10_____, the said infant plaintiff was born on the __11__ day of __12_____, 19_13_ and was __14__ years of age on __15_____, 19_16_. The said infant now resides with deponent at No. __17__ __18_____ Street in the City of __19_____, County of __20_____ and state of New York and has resided with deponent at the said address for a period of __21_____ years.

4. [State circumstances giving rise to the infant's claim, as—] On the __22__ day of __23_____, 19_24_ the infant plaintiff was struck by an automobile owned and operated by the defendant herein and sustained personal injuries as a result thereof. The accident occurred on __25_____ Street in the City of __26_____, New York at about __27__ o'clock in the __28_____ of that day. Deponent did not see the accident but was told by the said infant plaintiff that the infant was playing on the sidewalk on the __29_____ side of __30_____ Street and started to cross the road. When the said infant was almost in the center of the road she saw the defendant's car approaching and started to run to the __31_____ side of the Street but was struck by the front of the defendant's car at a point about __32_____ feet from the __33_____ line of the said __34_____ Street.

5. [Set forth the injuries suffered by the plaintiff, as—] The defendant, immediately after the said accident, brought the infant plaintiff to the __35_____ Hospital in the City of __36_____ where the infant was treated by Dr. __37_____, M.D. of No. __38__, __39_____ Street in the City of __40_____, New York. Thereafter, on the day of the accident the said infant was examined and treated by Dr. __41_____, M.D. of No. __42__, __43_____ Street in the City of __44_____, New York. The said infant remained at the hospital for a period of __45__ days and was released therefrom on the __46__ day of __47_____, 19_48_. The injuries sustained by the said infant plaintiff were a severe skull concussion, a laceration of the left side of the head, laceration of the upper lip, contusion of the left side of the jaw and multiple contusions and abrasions of the arms, legs, body and face. The said infant was disabled for a period of __49_____ weeks as a result of the said accident but has now fully recovered from the said injuries with the exception of a permanent disfigurement caused by a small scar about one-quarter inch in length over his left ear. The said infant was treated only by Dr. __50_____ and Dr. __51_____ but the said Dr. __52_____ had a consultation with one Dr. __53_____, M.D. of No. __54__, __55_____ Street in the City of __56_____, New York, an eye, ear, nose and throat specialist on the __57__ day of __58__, 19_59_.

6. [Set forth the medical expenses incurred in treating the infant, as—] The medical expenses incurred by deponent as a result of the said accident are as follows:

__60_____ Hospital	$__61_____
Dr. __62_____, M.D.	$__63_____
Dr. __64_____, M.D.	$__65_____
Dr. __66_____, M.D.	$__67_____
Drugs and medicines	$__68_____

7. No reimbursement for medical or other expenses has been received from any source [or as the case may be].

8. [Set forth whether the infant's representative or any member of the infant's family has made a claim for damages alleged to have been suffered as a result of the same occurence giving rise to the infant's claim and, if so, the amounts paid or to be paid in settlement of such claim or if such claim has not been settled the reasons therefor.]

9. The aforesaid action was commenced by deponent on the __69__ day of __70_____, 19_71_ and issue was joined on the __72__ day of __73_____, 19_74_. The cause is now on the general calendar of this court, No. __75__.

10. After the commencement of the said action, the said __76_____ entered into

negotiations with __77_____ the attorney for the defendant herein and on the __78__ day of __79_____, 19_80 the said __81_____ offered to settle the claim of the infant for the sum of __82_____ Dollars and the claim of the deponent as the infant's father for the sum of __83_____ Dollars.

11. Under the terms of the proposed settlement herein, the infant plaintiff will receive the sum of __84_____ dollars and deponent will receive the sum of __85_____ dollars. Of the amount received by deponent the sum of __86_____ dollars represents medical expenses incurred by the deponent in providing medical care and treatment for the infant and the sum of __87_____ dollars represents compensation to deponent for loss of services of the infant herein. [Set forth, in detail, the distribution of the settlement].

12. Deponent has read the affidavit of __88_____, M.D. sworn to the __89__ day of __90_____, 19_91_ and annexed hereto and the affidavit of __92_____, Esq. sworn to the __93__ day of __94_____, 19_95_ and annexed hereto and to the best of deponent's information and belief, the statements contained in said affidavits are true.

13. As Representative of __96_____, the infant plaintiff herein, deponent consents and recommends that the claim of the said infant be settled and compromised for the sum of __97_____ dollars and that the settlement proposed herein be accepted and approved by this court and he further recommends, subject to the approval of this court, that __98_____, Esq., be paid for his services in this action in behalf of the infant plaintiff, the sum of __99_____ dollars.

14. [Set forth security proposed to be given, as—] Deponent respectfully asks that the giving of security be dispensed with pursuant to CPLR Rule 1210(c) on the ground that the money or the value of the property to be received upon the proposed settlement does not exceed the sum of $1000 after payment of expenses and attorney's fees.

15. No previous application for settlement of this claim has been made to any court or judge thereof.

WHEREFORE deponent prays that a judgment be entered herein authorizing and empowering said Representative, __100_____, to compromise the cause of action existing in behalf of the infant plaintiff, __101_____ for __102_____ Dollars ($103__) and to compromise his own cause of action for the sum of __104_____ Dollars ($__105__) subject to the terms and conditions set forth above.

__106_____

[Print signer's name below signature]

[Jurat]

Form 5

Attorney's Affidavit on Motion to Settle Infant's Action

SUPREME COURT, __1_____ COUNTY.

	Affidavit
[Title of cause]	Index No. __2__ [if assigned]

STATE OF NEW YORK
COUNTY OF __3_____   SS.:

__4_____, being duly sworn, deposes and says:

1. Deponent is an attorney at law with offices at No. __5__ __6_____ Street in the City of __7_____. He is the attorney for the infant plaintiff herein and is fully familiar with all the facts and circumstances concerning his claim.

2. A cause of action exists in behalf of __8_____, the infant plaintiff herein for damages for personal injuries sustained by said infant on __9_____, 19_10_, when the infant, a pedestrian, was struck by an automobile owned and operated by the defendant

on __11_____ Street on or near its intersection with __12_____ Avenue, in the City of __13_____, County of __14_____, State of New York.

3. A cause of action also exists in behalf of __15_____, individually, as father of said infant, for loss of services of the said infant and for medical expenses incurred as the result of said personal injuries.

4. No guardian of the property or guardian ad litem has been appointed for said infant.

5. The above entitled action was commenced against the defendant by the personal service of a summons and verified complaint on __16_____, 19_17_, and said defendant by his attorney, __18_____, Esq., answered said complaint by serving his verified answer on your deponent on __19_____, 19_20_ a copy of said pleadings being annexed hereto and made a part hereof.

6. Deponent was retained by __21_____, the father of the infant __22_____ to represent the interests of the said infant and his father herein, on __23_____, 19_24_ [and notice of said retainer has been filed with the Appellate Division, __25_____ Department]. The terms of said retainer were that your deponent be paid __26__ per centum of all sums of money that might be collected on behalf of __27_____, individually, and that for all services rendered to __28_____, in his capacity as Representative of his infant son, __29_____, your deponent be paid the reasonable value of his services, not exceeding, however, one-third of any moneys that might be collected.

7. Immediately after your deponent was retained in this matter, your deponent secured a police report of the accident, a photostatic copy of the defendant's accident report to Albany, and also made a complete investigation of the circumstances relating to this accident. Several days were spent in an investigation and the neighborhood and vicinity of the accident was canvassed with the result that no witnesses to the accident could be found, and the police report does not report the names of any witnesses.

8. The investigation herein disclosed that the defendant __30_____ prior to the happening of the accident was driving in a westerly direction on __31_____ Street, and that the infant was crossing __32_____ Street from west to east when the accident occurred, and was found lying at a point about __33_____ feet north of __34_____ Avenue on __35_____ Street. The accident occurred at about __36_____ o'clock in the __37_____ of that day at which time it was dark and it was raining lightly at the time.

9. The infant plaintiff has told your deponent the following story of how the accident happened: "I started to cross the street. I saw the lights of the car and heard a horn blow and I started to run. I was singing when I passed the corner store. The automobile hit me."

10. The defendant's contention is that he was proceeding on __38_____ Street when he heard a thud toward the rear of his car and thought that a package which he had on the rear seat of his car had fallen to the floor, but that he stopped his car to investigate and upon getting out discovered that his car had come into contact with the infant plaintiff herein. Defendant claims not to have seen him at any time prior to the accident.

11. The defendant is insured with the __39_____ Casualty Company of No. __40__ __41_____ Street, New York City, and your deponent has negotiated with said company through __42_____, one of their investigators and adjusters, and originally received from him an offer of settlement in the amount of __43_____ Dollars ($__44__), which was refused, and which offer was ultimately raised by negotiations to __45_____ Dollars ($__46__), which amount your deponent believes fairly represents the value of the entire case upon a settlement basis.

12. On or about __47_____, 19_48_, your deponent told __49_____ the father of the infant herein, that the final and largest offer he was able to secure from the insurance carrier was __50_____ Dollars and your deponent advised said father that in your deponent's opinion it was a fair offer and should be accepted. The said father informed

your deponent that he was willing to compromise the within cause of action for the amount of ___51_____ Dollars ($___52__).

13. Subject to the Court's approval, the cause of action in behalf of the infant plaintiff herein will be compromised for the sum of ___53_____ Dollars ($___54__), subject to the deduction of counsel fees which deponent asks the Court to fix at ___55_____ Dollars ($___56__);

14. Further subject to the Court's approval, the cause of action in behalf of ___57_____, the father of said infant, will be compromised for ___58_____ Dollars ($___59__) subject to the deduction of counsel fees in the sum of ___60_____ Dollars and to payment of expenses as follows:

___61_____ Hospital	$___62_____
___63_____ M. D.	$___64_____
___65_____ M. D.	$___66_____

15. Deponent recommends approval of the proposed settlement for the reason that there were no witnesses to the accident and it would be difficult to prove that the defendant was negligent. The defendant does not admit responsibility for the accident and the infant plaintiff is of such a young age that it is possible that he could not give competent or comprehensive testimony upon a trial of the action.

16. Deponent has not directly or indirectly become concerned in this motion or its subject matter at the instance of a party or person opposing, or with interests adverse to, the infant, he has not received and is not to receive any compensation from such party directly or indirectly, nor from any person or firm in connection with this case, he has no interest, and represents no interest conflicting with that of the infant plaintiff, but is acting solely in the interest of and for the benefit of the infant plaintiff, and set forth whether or not he has represented or now represents any other person asserting a claim arising from the same occurrence.

17. No previous application for the relief herein requested has been made to any Court or Judge.

WHEREFORE deponent respectfully requests that the aforesaid proposal of settlement be approved and that a judgment be entered herein granting deponent leave to settle and compromise the claim of the said infant and discontinue the above entitled action.

_____67_____

[Print signer's name below signature]

[Jurat]

Form 6

Affidavit of Opposing Attorney

SUPREME COURT, ___1_____ COUNTY.

[Title of cause]

Affidavit

Index No. ___2__ [if assigned]

STATE OF NEW YORK
COUNTY OF ___3_____   SS.:

___4_____, being duly sworn, deposes and says:

1. Deponent is an attorney at law with offices at No. ___5__, ___6_____ Street in the City of ___7_____ and is the attorney for ___8_____, the person against whom ___9_____, the aforesaid infant has a claim [or—"the defendant herein"] and as such attorney has prepared the papers required for this application.

2. The said infant does not have a guardian ad litem or a guardian of his property and neither the petitioner, the father of the said infant nor the infant are represented by an attorney.

3. On or about the __10__ day of __11_____, 19_12_ the said infant went upon certain property owned, occupied and controlled by the said __13_____ and located on __14_____ Street in the City of __15_____ County of __16_____ and State of __17_____. At the same time and place the said __18_____, his agents and employees were engaged in the construction of a house and had caused an excavation to be made on said property. At about __19_____ o'clock in the __20__ noon of the said __21__ day of __22_____, 19_23_ the said infant fell into the excavation and sustained the injuries more particularly described in the affidavit of Dr. __24_____, sworn to the __25__ day of __26_____ 19_27_ and annexed hereto. [Continue to set forth facts concerning the claim.]

4. As more fully appears from the affidavit of __28_____, M.D. and the petition herein the said infant suffered __29_____ [set forth nature of injuries]. The infant has fully recovered from the said injuries except __30_____. The amount expended for the treatment and examination of the said injuries is $__31__ which sum the petitioner has paid.

5. Heretofore and on or about the __32__ day of __33_____, 19_34_ negotiations were entered into between deponent and __35_____, the father [or as the case may be] of the said infant, and the __36_____ Insurance Company as the carrier of liability insurance for __37_____ for the settlement and compromise of the claim of the said infant. On or about the __38__ day of __39_____, 19_40_ your deponent and said insurance company offered to pay the said infant, __41_____, and __42_____ his father, the sum of __43_____ Dollars in full settlement and discharge of their claims, the sum of __44_____ Dollars to be paid to __45_____, the father as reimbursement for medical expenses paid by him and the balance to be paid to __46_____ for the account of the said infant.

6. No action to recover on said claim has been commenced by the infant herein nor by anyone in behalf of the said infant.

7. No application for settlement of the infant's claim has been previously made.

__47_____
[Print signer's name below signature]

[Jurat]

Form 7

Affidavit of Physician on Motion to Settle Infant's Claim or Action*

SUPREME COURT, __1_____ COUNTY.

         Affidavit

[Title of cause]   Index No. __2__ [if assigned]

STATE OF NEW YORK
COUNTY OF __3_____   ss.:

__4_____, M.D., being duly sworn, deposes and says:

1. He is a physician duly licensed to practice in the State of New York, and has his office at No. __5__ __6_____ Street, in the City of __7_____, County of __8_____ and State of New York.

2. On __9_____, 19_10_, at about __11_____ o'clock in the __12_____ of that day, deponent was called to the __13_____ Hospital in the City of __14_____ to attend the infant plaintiff herein for injuries she had received.

3. Deponent saw the said infant for the first time at the said __15_____ Hospital and an examination made at that time revealed that she had suffered a laceration of the left side of her head; laceration of the upper lip; contusion of the left side of the jaw

---

* Editor's Note: CPLR 1208(c) states that "if the action or claim is for damages for personal injuries to the infant or incompetent, one or more medical or hospital reports, which need not be verified, shall be included in the supporting papers."

and multiple contusions and abrasions of the arms, legs, body and face. About twenty minutes after making his examination deponent was summoned to the infant's room where he found her unconscious, with dilated, light-fast pupils, and vomiting. The child was found to be in shock and began to have convulsions, to control which it was necessary to administer an anesthetic. A spinal tap was performed and bloody fluid obtained. Intravenous administration of 50% glucose was given and treatment of normal saline solution by hypodermoclysis was given. The child remained unconscious for many hours and was disoriented for several days. Several X-ray examinations were made of the skull, legs, chest and back, but all were negative for fractures. The child suffered a severe concussion of the brain. The child's mouth was swollen and lacerated and was treated with warm saline solution; the child's left eye was blackened and was so swollen that examination was not possible for several days, when it was found that there was a sub-scleral hemorrhage. The eye remained swollen and blackened for about seven days.

4. On the __16__ day of __17_____, 19_18_, your deponent consulted with Dr. __19_____, M.D., Eye, Ear and Nose Specialist as to the treatment of the injuries to said infant's eye. Said consultation was held at the __20_____ Hospital, __21_____ County, New York, and said specialist confirmed the diagnosis and treatment of your deponent, who believed that said consultation was necessary and advisable because of the severity of the injuries to said infant's eye.

5. There is presently a scar on the scalp over the left ear and a scar on the upper margin of the left ear which is accompanied by a small amount of keloid formation.

6. On __22_____, 19_23_ deponent made a complete final examination of __24_____, and found that she had recovered from the effect of these injuries, and that except for the scars aforementioned there were no permanent injuries and no indications of any defects or abnormality in said infant. Her injuries have healed well and she has had a good recovery.

7. It is difficult to give a prognosis as to the ultimate outcome of any brain concussion because there is always the possibility of traumatic epilepsy at a later date, provided there has been an actual brain injury. Your deponent, however, can find no evidence of any such brain injury and believes that the infant has made a full and complete recovery.

8. Deponent treated and examined the infant __25_____ times during the period of __26_____, 19_27_ to __28_ ___, 19_29_. The fair and reasonable cost and value of deponent's medical treatment of plaintiff is $__30_. Deponent has not been paid and does not expect to be paid by the defendant herein or by anyone acting on the defendant's behalf.

__31_____
[Print signer's name below signature]

[Jurat]

Form 8

Notice of Application for Leave to Settle Infant's Claim

SUPREME COURT __1_____ COUNTY

	Notice of Application
[Title of cause]	Index No. __2__ [if assigned]

Sir:

PLEASE TAKE NOTICE that on the annexed petition of __3_____ duly verified the __4__ day of __5_____, 19_6_ and the annexed affidavit of __7_____, sworn to the __8__ day of __9_____, 19_10_ an application will be made for leave to settle a claim of __11_____, an infant, against __12_____, before Hon. __13_____, Justice of the Supreme Court on the __14__ day of __15_____, 19_16_ at __17_____ o'clock in the __18__ noon of that day or as soon thereafter as counsel can be heard at the Chambers of the Hon. __19_____ in the County Court House in the City of __20_____, County of __21_____ and State of New York.

Dated, __22_____, 19_23_.

Yours, etc.,

__24_____

Attorney for Petitioner,
Office and P. O. Address.
Telephone No.

Form 9

Consent of Parent Other Than Petitioner or Moving Party

SUPREME COURT, __1_____ COUNTY.

Consent to Settlement
[Title of cause]   Index No. __2__ [if assigned]

I, __3_____ [mother] of __4_____, the infant named in the annexed application,

DO HEREBY CONSENT that an order be made by Hon. __5_____, Justice of the Supreme Court, State of New York, authorizing and empowering __6_____, the guardian ad litem [or as the case may be] of __7_____, the infant plaintiff herein, to settle and compromise the above entitled cause of action on behalf of the said infant plaintiff in accordance with the terms set forth in the affidavit of the said guardian ad litem.

Dated __8_____, 19_9_.

__10_____

[Print signer's name below signature]

[Acknowledgment]

Form 10

Order Settling Infant's Action

SUPREME COURT, __1_____ COUNTY.

Order
[Title of cause]   Index No. __2__

PRESENT: Hon. __3_____, Justice.

Upon reading and filing the annexed affidavit of __4_____, guardian ad litem [or as the case may be] of __5_____, an infant under the age of __6_____ years, sworn to the __7__ day of __8_____, 19_9_, the affidavit of __10_____, the attorney for said infant sworn to the __11__ day of __12_____, 19_13_ and the affidavit of Dr. __14_____, M.D., sworn to the __15__ day of __16_____, 19_17_ [or the medical report of Dr. __18_____, M.D. or the hospital report of the __19_____ Hospital] and this motion for the approval by this Court of the settlement of the above-entitled action having come on regularly to be heard and __20_____, the infant plaintiff herein, __21_____, her Guardian ad Litem [or as the case may be] and __22_____ the attorney making this application having appeared before me and been examined and it appearing that acceptance of the sum of $__23__ in settlement of the claim of the said infant and the sum of $__24__ in settlement of the claim of __25_____, her father, would be to the best interests of the said infant, and that the sum of $__26__ is the fair and reasonable value of the services rendered by __27_____, Esq. in prosecuting and negotiating a settlement of the said action, it is

On motion of __28_____, attorney for the plaintiff,

ORDERED that the said Guardian ad Litem [or as the case may be] be and he hereby is authorized and empowered to settle and compromise the above entitled cause of action on behalf of the infant plaintiff for the sum of __29____ dollars ($__30__), and it is further

ORDERED that __31____ the Guardian ad Litem [or as the case may be] of __32____, the infant herein, be and he hereby is directed to file a bond to the said infant conditioned for the faithful discharge of his trust for the paying over, investing of, and accounting for all monies received by him as such guardian. The said bond to be in the sum of $__33__ and it is further

ORDERED that upon the approval and filing of a bond by __34____ as aforesaid, and upon payment by __35____, the defendant herein, of the sum of __36____ dollars to __37____, as Guardian ad Litem [or as the case may be] of __38____, an infant, and upon the payment by __39____, the defendant herein, of the sum of __40____ dollars to __41____, individually as the father of __42____ an infant, and upon the payment by __43__, of the sum of __44____ dollars to __45____, the attorney for the said infant, the said __46____, be and hereby is discharged from any claim that said infant and/or Guardian ad Litem [or as the case may be] had or might have against him as a result of any injuries sustained by the said infant by reason of an accident which occurred on the __47__ day of __48____, 19_49_ at __50____ o'clock in the __51____ noon of that day on __52____ Street when an automobile owned and operated by __53____, the defendant herein, struck and collided with the said infant and it is further

ORDERED that upon the filing of the bond and payments as aforesaid, this action be and the same hereby is settled and stricken from the calendar of this court.

Signed this __54__ day of __55____, 19_56_ at __57____, New York.

__58_____
[Print signer's name below signature]
Justice, Supreme Court
__59____ County

Additional Forms:

    Drafting compromise and settlement agreements, New York Forms, §§ 15:2, 15:3.
    7 Am Jur Pl and Pr Forms (Rev ed), Compromise and Settlement, Forms 1 et seq., 11–13.
    13 Am Jur Pl and Pr Forms (Rev ed), Guardian and Ward, Forms 581–601.

§ 1209. Arbitration of controversy involving infant or judicially declared incompetent

A controversy involving an infant or person judicially declared to be incompetent shall not be submitted to arbitration except pursuant to a court order made upon application of the representative of such infant or incompetent.

HISTORY:

    Add, L 1962, ch 308, eff Sept 1, 1963.
    Earlier statutes: CPA § 1448.

ADVISORY COMMITTEE NOTES:

    This section is derived from subd 1 of CPA § 1448 with only language changes which do not affect the substance of the provision. The representative must be one mentioned in new CPLR § 1201.
    The following sentence of CPA § 1448 has been omitted:
    "But where a person capable of entering into a submission or contract has knowingly entered into the same with a person incapable of so doing, as prescribed in subdivision one of this section, the objection on the ground of incapacity can be taken only in behalf of the person so incapacitated."
    In such a situation a representative of the infant or incompetent may have the

award vacated pursuant to new CPLR § 7511(b) and equity principles would prevent a person who has knowingly entered into an arbitration with an infant or incompetent from raising the objection of incapacity.

CROSS REFERENCES:

Arbitration generally, §§ 7501 et seq.

RESEARCH REFERENCES AND PRACTICE AIDS:

10 NY Jur, Contracts § 154.

28 NY Jur, Infants § 10.

22 Carmody-Wait 2d, Arbitration § 141:15.

5 Am Jur 2d, Arbitration and Award §§ 46, 62, 63, 65, 149, 172.

42 Am Jur 2d, Infants § 138.

Forms:

See "FORMS" heading following "CASE NOTES", infra.

CASE NOTES

The provision of CPLR § 1209 that a controversy involving an infant shall not be submitted to arbitration except pursuant to a court order applies equally to statutory and common law arbitrations. Coughlin v Motor Vehicle Acci. Indemnification Corp. (1965) 45 Misc 2d 672, 257 NYS2d 549.

The statute requires that an infant's representative must first make application to the court for an order permitting him to submit the claim to arbitration. Frame v American Motorists Ins. Co. (1969) 31 AD2d 872, 297 NYS2d 247, mod on other grounds 32 AD2d 572, 300 NYS2d 542.

Failure to obtain orders with respect to submission to arbitration on behalf of each infant would not be fatal if such orders were obtained before opening of arbitration hearings. Aetna Life & Casualty Co. v Stekardis (1974) 34 NY2d 182, 356 NYS2d 587, 313 NE2d 53.

Infants cannot proceed to arbitration in their own right, but they must appear by their respective guardians ad litem or by such of their respective parents having legal custody, as provided in CPLR § 1209. Turner v Motor Vehicle Acci. Indemnification Corp. (1965) 47 Misc 2d 1097, 264 NYS2d 204.

The prohibition in CPLR § 1209 against the submission to arbitration of a controversy involving an infant except by court order applies only where an infant is a party, but a controversy between husband and wife involving the amount to be paid by the husband for support, maintenance, and education of the issue of the parties is not one to which an infant is a party and such controversy is arbitrable. Schneider v Schneider (1965) 24 AD2d 768, 264 NYS2d 9, affd 17 NY2d 123, 269 NYS2d 107, 216 NE2d 318.

This section applies only where an infant is a party, and a controversy involving the quantum of support and maintenance is not one in which the infant is a party. Goldenberg v Goldenberg (1966) 25 AD2d 670, 268 NYS2d 383, affd 19 NY2d 759, 279 NYS2d 359, 226 NE2d 185.

Provisions for the support of an infant child upon the divorce of its parents may be made by arbitration, and need not be fixed by a court. Schneider v Schneider (1966) 17 NY2d 123, 269 NYS2d 107, 216 NE2d 318.

Insured who was 17 years old at time of hit-and-run accident and who failed to provide any persuasive reason for failure to file notice of accident with automobile insurer for over two years was not entitled to arbitration of claim against the insurer. Cuzdey v American Motorists Ins. Co. (1974) 45 AD2d 134, 357 NYS2d 143, affd 37 NY2d 939, 380 NYS2d 648, 343 NE2d 287.

Infant defendant in negligence action can stay arbitration proceedings brought by plaintiff against the Motor Vehicle Accident Indemnification Corporation and such infant, since an infant defendant cannot be compelled to arbitrate unless he has sought and obtained court permission to submit to arbitration. Scheck v Motor Vehicle Acci. Indemnification Corp. (1963) 40 Misc 2d 575, 243 NYS2d 288.

An infant plaintiff need not seek permission of the court to arbitrate his claim under an uninsured automobile endorsement, but may instead bring a plenary action against the insurer based upon his claim under such endorsement. Lunger v Hartford Acci. & Indem. Co. (1972) 38 AD2d 857, 330 NYS2d 123.

This section requires that an infant's representative, whether a guardian ad litem or a parent, make application for an order of court permitting the infant's claim against the Motor Vehicle Accident Indemnification Corporation to be submitted to arbitration. Klein v Motor Vehicle Acci. Indemnification Corp. (1965) 48 Misc 2d 82, 264 NYS2d 268.

FORMS

Form 1—Petition by guardian or committee for permission to arbitrate

Form 2—Order directing entry of judgment granting permission to guardian or committee to arbitrate

Form 1

Petition by Guardian or Committee for Permission to Arbitrate

[Title of court]

In the Matter of the Application of

__1_____, plaintiff,

    against

__2_____, defendant [an infant or   Petition
person judicially declared to be incompetent], for a Judgment permitting said defendant to submit certain differences between the parties to arbitration.

To the __3_____ court of the county of __4_____:

The petition of __5_____ respectfully shows to the court.

1. That your petitioner was duly appointed general guardian [guardian ad litem or committee or, if an infant, is the parent or other relative having legal custody] of __6_____ the infant [incompetent] above named, by the __7_____ court of the County of __8_____ on or about the __9__ day of __10_____, 19_11_, and that he thereafter duly qualified and acted in that capacity and is still acting as such general guardian [committee or as the case may be].

2. That the said __12_____ is an infant [incompetent] under the age of __13_____ years, having become __14_____ years of age on the __15__ day of __16_____, 19_17_, last past, and resides with __18_____ at __19_____ [address].

3. That your petitioner desires the permission of this court to submit to arbitration on behalf of the said infant [incompetent] the matter in dispute hereafter set forth.

4. That a controversy has arisen out of the following state of facts: [state in detail the facts constituting the controversy.]

5. That the said __20_____ intends to bring an action against the said infant [incompetent] based upon the state of facts hereinbefore recited unless the said controversy is submitted to arbitration. [Or otherwise state that litigation may result from failure to arbitrate.]

6. That the said __21_____ has offered to enter into a submission to arbitration, a copy of which is hereto annexed and made a part of this petition [under which it is provided one arbitrator will be appointed by your petitioner, one by the said __22_____ and a third by the two said arbitrators, the decision of a majority of whom to be valid and binding on the parties in accordance with the provisions of the Civil Practice Law and Rules].

7. That your petitioner is fully competent to understand and protect the rights of the said infant [incompetent], has no interest adverse to that of the infant [incompetent], is not connected in business with the adverse party or his attorney and has not been appointed guardian [committee] through the application or nomination of any person having an adverse interest; that he is of sufficient financial responsibility to answer to said infant [incompetent] for any damage that may be sustained as a result of his negligence or misconduct in connection with the said matter, being worth the sum of __23_____ dollars over and above all debts and liabilities owing and incurred by him and exclusive of property exempt by law from execution. [Or has given an undertaking for the proper performance of his duties upon his appointment as guardian [committee] as aforesaid.]

8. That your petitioner believes that it is for the best interests of the said infant [incompetent] that the controversy aforesaid be submitted to arbitration for the reason that [state reasons].

9. That no previous application has been made for the order or relief sought herein.

Wherefore, your petitioner prays that a judgment be entered herein by this court granting permission to your petitioner to submit [in accordance with the annexed proposed submission] such controversy to arbitration pursuant to the provisions of the Civil Practice Law and Rules.

[Date]

[Signature of petitioner]
[Print signer's name below signature]
Office and P.O. Address
Telephone No.

[Annex proposed submission]

STATE OF NEW YORK
COUNTY OF __24_____

__25_____, being duly sworn, deposes and says that he is the petitioner in the above proceeding; that he has read the foregoing petition and knows the contents thereof; that the same is true to the knowledge of deponent except as to those matters stated to be on information and belief; and that as to those matters he believes it to be true.

[Signature of deponent]

[Jurat]

Form 2

Order Directing Entry of Judgment Granting Permission to Guardian or Committee to Arbitrate

SUPREME COURT, __1_____ COUNTY.
[Title of proceeding as

in Form No. 3:40, above]   Order Index No. — (if assigned]

PRESENT: Hon. __2_____, Justice.

__3_____, the general guardian [guardian ad litem or committee or, if an infant, the parent or other relative having legal custody] of __4_____, an infant [incompetent] having by his petition verified the __5__ day of __6_____, 19_7_, petitioned this court to approve such petition for permission to submit the controversy therein recited to arbitration, and it appearing to the court that it is for the best interests of the said infant that such controversy be submitted to arbitration,

Now on motion of __8_____, Esq., attorney for the said petitioner, it is

Ordered that the said petition for permission to submit such controversy to arbitration be and the same hereby is approved, and it is further

Ordered that a judgment be entered herein, directing that petitioner, as general guardian [guardian ad litem or committee or, if an infant, the parent or other relative having legal custody] of the said __9_____, be authorized and empowered to execute in behalf of the said __10_____ the submission to arbitration of the controversy existing between the said __11_____ and one __12_____, presented to this court and annexed to the said petition.

Signed this __13__ day of __14_____, 19_15_ at __16_____, New York.

Enter.

__17_____
[Print signer's name below signature]
Justice, Supreme Court
__18_____ County

Rule 1210. Guardian of infant

(a) Petition for appointment; by whom presented; contents. An infant, if of the age of fourteen years or more, or a relative or friend of an infant, may present a petition to the court for appointment of a guardian. The petition shall state the age and residence of the infant, the name and residence of any living parent and of the person proposed as guardian, the relationship if any which such person bears to the infant, and the nature, status and value of the infant's estate.

(b) Hearing. The court shall ascertain the age of the infant, the amount of his personal property, the gross amount or value of the rents and profits of his real estate during his minority, and the sufficiency of the security offered by the proposed guardian. If the infant is of the age of fourteen years or more, the court shall examine him as to his voluntary nomination of or preference for a suitable guardian; if he is under the age of fourteen, the court shall select and appoint a suitable guardian.

(c) Undertaking. The court shall make an order requiring or dispensing wholly or partly with an undertaking, in an amount and according to the conditions set forth in section seventeen hundred eight of the surrogate's court procedure act.

(d) Direction as to management of estate. The court in its discretion may direct that the principal of the estate or any part of it be invested in bonds of the state of New York or of the United States, or deposited with any bank, trust company, insured savings and loan association or insured savings bank which has been designated as a depository for such fund; or invested in a bond and mortgage on unincumbered and improved property within the state, having a value, to be shown to the satisfaction of the court, of at least double the amount of principal invested, for the benefit of the infant, and may direct that only the interest or income be received by the guardian.

(e) Filing of certified copy of order of appointment. Upon the appointment of a guardian of the person or property, or both, of an infant, the guardian shall file a certified copy of the order of his appointment with the clerk of the surrogate's court of the county in which he has been appointed.

HISTORY:

Add as § 1210, L 1962, ch 308, renumbered Rule 1210, L 1962, ch 318, § 5, amd by Judicial Conference, eff Sept 1, 1969.

Sub (d), amd, L 1975, ch 490, eff Sept 1, 1975.

Sub (e), add L 1966, ch 961, eff Sept 1, 1967.

Section 1210, renumbered Rule 1210, L 1962, ch 318, § 5, eff Sept 1, 1963.

Earlier rules: RCP 290–292; Gen Rules Pr 52-54.

ADVISORY COMMITTEE NOTES:

This rule is based on rules 290, 291 and 292 of the RCP. Article 10 of the Surrogate's Court Act contains more detailed and comprehensive provisions for the appointment of a general guardian in the Surrogate's Court, which has concurrent jurisdiction in this area. See Surr Ct Act §§ 172–182. These would supersede the general practice provisions where they are inconsistent. See id. § 316; 11 Carmody-Wait, Cyclopedia of New York Practice 801 (1954). Section 183 of the Surrogate's Court Act provides that where the guardian is appointed by another court, a certified copy of the order of appointment and of the undertaking must be filed in the Surrogate's Court; and that the guardian so appointed is subject to all the duties and liabilities specified in article 10 of the Surrogate's Court Act.

Subd (a) of this rule is based on RCP 290, subd (b) on rule 291 and subd (c) and (d) on rule 292. The only change that has been made is in subdivision (c). The provisions of Surrogate's Court Act, § 180 have been substituted for the undertaking requirement of rule 292, since they provide a more flexible procedure and enable the court to effect substantial savings to the estate in proper cases.

CROSS REFERENCES:

This section referred to in 1206.

Investments by custodians of gifts to minors, EPTL § 7-4.3. Letters of guardianship, SCPA § 701.

FEDERAL ASPECTS:

Appointment of guardian under Longshoremen's and Harbor Workers' Compensation Act, 33 USCS § 911.

Infants or incompetent persons as parties in United States District Court, Rule 17(c) of Federal Rules of Civil Procedure, USCS Court Rules.

RESEARCH REFERENCES AND PRACTICE AIDS:

21 Carmody-Wait 2d, Actions and Proceedings By and Against Infants and Incompetents § 124:49.

26 Carmody-Wait 2d, Guardians and Custodians §§ 155:9, 155:10, 155:28.

39 Am Jur 2d, Guardian and Ward §§ 4 et seq.

10 Am Jur Proof of Facts 2d p 635, Relinquishment of Parental Claim to Child in Adoption Proceedings.

11 Am Jur Proof of Facts 2d p 541, Parent's Failure to Supervise Children.

Annotations:

Power of guardian representing unborn future interest holders to consent to invasion of trust corpus. 49 ALR2d 1095.

Function, power, and discretion of court where there is testamentary appointment of guardian of minor. 67 ALR2d 803.

Termination of continuing guaranty by appointment of guardian or conservator for guarantor. 55 ALR3d 344.

Who is minor's next of kin for guardianship purposes. 63 ALR3d 813.

Carrier's liability for injury or death of infant passenger as affected by fact that child was in custody of parent or other adult. 74 ALR3d 1171.

Power of parent to have mentally defective child sterilized. 74 ALR3d 1224.

Who has custody or control of child within terms of penal statute punishing cruelty or neglect by one having custody or control. 75 ALR3d 933.

Failure to give adequate notice to juvenile's parents as ground for reversal of determination of juvenile delinquency under Federal Juvenile Delinquency Act (18 USCS §§ 5031–5042). 30 ALR Fed 745.

Law Reviews:

Parties and pleading under the CPLR. 31 Brooklyn L Rev 98.

Forms:

See "FORMS" heading following "CASE NOTES", infra.

CASE NOTES

NOTES OF DECISIONS UNDER SCA § 178

It is error to exclude evidence of the home and surroundings of the respective parties seeking the custody of a minor child. Brush v Brown, 20 NY Week Dig 516.

Where an application is made to a surrogate for the appointment of a guardian of an infant under fourteen years of age, he should assign a day for the hearing of the application, and after ascertaining who are the near relatives of the infant residing in the county, he should direct notice to be given to such of them as he may deem reasonable, for the purpose of having the rights of the infant properly attended to upon the application. Under-

hill v Dennis, 9 Paige 202; White v Pomeroy, 7 Barb 640.

CASE NOTES

UNDER FORMER CIVIL PRACTICE LAWS

1. Generally
2. Jurisdiction of surrogate
3. Selection of guardian
4. Bond or undertaking

1. Generally

Where a proceeding instituted for the appointment of a general guardian of an infant under the age of fourteen years proceeded from the outset as one solely to determine the custody of the child, whose mother was dead, an order awarding custody to the maternal grandmother instead of to the father, based on unsatisfactory and conflicting affidavits and without hearing testimony as to the fitness or unfitness of the parties to have the custody of the infant, should be reversed and the matter remitted to the Special Term where a general guardian of the infant should be appointed after hearing of proofs of the various parties. Re Thoemmes (1933) 238 AD 541, 264 NYS 829.

Where an infant acquires property, it is only a duly appointed guardian who is legally charged with its control and management. Decker v Pouvailsmith Corp. 225 AD 489, 233 NYS 407 (1929) revd on application of Workmen's Compensation Law 252 NY 1, 168 NE 442.

2. Jurisdiction of surrogate

A surrogate has no general jurisdiction over a guardian of an infant as trustee. His powers are only such as have been specially conferred by statute, together with incidental powers necessary to carry out that jurisdiction. Re Camp (1891) 126 NY 377, 27 NE 799.

The statutory power of a surrogate to appoint a general guardian for an infant is not affected by an order of the supreme court dismissing a father's writ of habeas corpus to obtain the custody of the

child from the guardian appointed by the mother's will, notwithstanding the fact that the letters to the guardian had been issued ex parte without notice to the father. Re Lee (1916) 176 AD 141, 161 NYS 1100, revd on ground guardian did not have right to take custody of infant in disregard of order of supreme court, 220 NY 532, 116 NE 352.

3. Selection of guardian

In the selection of a guardian the court will be guided by the moral character and future ability of the petitioners to advance and promote the interests of the infant. Re Bishop (1930) 137 Misc 496, 244 NYS 614.

It was not the intention in formulating RCP 291 to permit an infant over fourteen to absolutely prevent the court from appointing a guardian to care for his property by nominating some person who such infant knew would not be acceptable to the court. Re Wyckoff (1910) 67 Misc 1, 124 NYS 625.

Where such infant prayed for a decree appointing a general guardian of his property, by that act he submitted his property to the jurisdiction of the court and conferred upon it the right to appoint either the person nominated or any other person deemed by the court proper to act. Re Wyckoff, supra.

4. Bond or undertaking

Failure to observe the formalities of statutes relating to bonds or undertakings furnished thereunder does not relieve the surety from his common-law obligation where the instrument is supported by a valid consideration. Cohen v Fidelity & Deposit Co. (1928) 132 Misc 193, 229 NYS 296.

There is no fixed standard of time within which a guardian must liquidate "non-legals" received. Re Horton (1938) 166 Misc 768, 3 NYS2d 215.

FORMS

Form 1—Petition for appointment of general guardian for infant under 14

Form 2—Consent of parent to appointment of third person as guardian

Form 3—Decision in proceeding to appoint general guardian

Form 4—Judgment appointing general guardian

Form 1

Petition for Appointment of Guardian of Infant Under 14

SUPREME COURT, __1_____ COUNTY.

In the Matter of the Application for the Appointment of a General Guardian of the Person and Estate of __2_____ an infant under fourteen years of age.	Petition Index No. — [if assigned]

To the Supreme Court of the County of __3_____:

The petition of __4_____, residing at No. __5__ __6_____ Street, in the City of __7_____ County of __8_____, State of New York, respectfully shows:

1. That petitioner is __9_____ [a relative or friend] of __10_____, an infant.

2. That said infant is a resident of __11_____, County of __12_____, State of New York and is under fourteen years of age, to-wit, of the age of __13__ years, and was born on the __14__ day of __15_____ 19_16_, and resides with petitioner at the above address [or state other facts as to residence in a proper case].

3. That __17_____ the father of said infant, is [or is not] living, and [if alive] resides at __18_____.

4. That __19_____, the mother of said infant is [or is not] living and [if alive] resides at __20_____.

5. [If a particular person is proposed by the petitioner as guardian.] That __21_____, who resides at __22_____ and is the said infant's __23_____ [state relationship, if any, to infant].

6. The nature, status and value of the said infant's estate is as follows: [state facts with sufficient particularity to allow the court to ascertain the nature and value of the infant's personal property, the nature and value of said infant's real estate and the gross amount or value of the merits and profits therefrom during the infant's minority].

Wherefore your petitioner prays that a judgment be entered appointing __24_____ guardian of the person and estate of said infant during his infancy.

Dated this __25__ day of __26_____, 19_27_.

[Verification]

__28_____

Petitioner

Address: __29_____

Telephone No. __30__

Form 2

Consent of Parent to Appointment of Third Person as Guardian

Consent to Appointment
of Guardian

[Indorse on petition in a proper case.]

I, the undersigned, father [or "mother"] of the infant above named do hereby consent and pray that __1_____ be appointed the guardian of the person and estate of said infant.

[Acknowledgment]

[Signature]
[Print signer's name below signature]

Form 3

Decision in Proceeding to Appoint Guardian of Infant

Decision

[Title of court and cause]   Index No. __1__ [if assigned]

The issues in this proceeding having regularly come on to be heard before me, one of the Justices of this Court, at a Motion Term [Part __2__] thereof, held in and for the County of __3_____, at the Courthouse in __4_____, New York, and __5_____, 19_6_, and having read the petition and consent of __7_____, mother and sole surviving parent of __8_____, the infant named above, and having heard the proofs on the said petition of __9_____, for the appointment of a guardian of __10_____, the infant named above, and due deliberations having been had thereon,

Now, after hearing __11_____, attorney for petitioner, in support of said petition and no one having appeared in opposition thereto, and it appearing to the court that:

1. The said __12_____, is an infant, under the age of fourteen years, towit, 13_____ years of age.

2. That the said infant resides at __14__ __15_____ Street, City of __16_____, New York, with __17_____, his mother, who is the sole surviving parent of the said infant, __18_____, the father of said infant having died on the __19__ day of __20_____, 19_21_ at __22_____, New York.

3. That __23_____, the mother of said infant has consented to the appointment of __24_____ as guardian of said infant.

4. That the amount of the personal property of the said infant is __25_____, consisting of __26_____ [state nature of personal property].

5. That the value of the real estate of said infant is __27_____, consisting of __28_____ [state nature and description of real estate], and that the gross value of the rents and profits of said real estate during the minority of said infant is __29_____.

6. That the interests of the said infant will be promoted by the appointment of a guardian.

7. That __30_____, the petitioner herein is a suitable guardian for said infant.

It is hereby

Ordered, that __31_____ be appointed as guardian of the person and property of __32_____, an infant, and it is further

Ordered, that, before commencing to act as such guardian, the said __33_____ shall qualify by taking an oath or affirmation to will, faithfully and honestly discharge the duties of guardian of said infant __34_____, and execute to __35_____, said infant, his bond, with at least two sureties, in the penalty of __36_____ dollars, conditioned as prescribed by law, and approved of by the clerk of this court, and it is further

Ordered, that the clerk enter judgment in accordance with this decision and that a certified copy of such judgment and the undertaking required herein be filed in the Surrogate's Court for the County of __37_____.

[Date]

_____38_____
[Print signer's name below signature]
Justice, Supreme Court

Form 4

Judgment Appointing Guardian of Infant

Judgment
[Caption as in Form 1, supra]   Index No. __1__.

The issues in the above entitled proceeding having been regularly brought on for hearing before Mr. Justice __2_____, at a Motion Term, Part __3__ of this court held in and for the County of __4_____ at the County Courthouse in the City of __5_____, State of New York on the __6__ day of __7_____, 19_8_, upon the petition of __9_____ for the appointment of a guardian of the person and property of __10_____, an infant, under the age of fourteen years, and upon the consent of __11_____, mother and sole surviving parent of said infant, attached to said petition, and the petitioner having appeared by his attorney and the allegations and proofs having been heard and the Justice having rendered his decision thereon directing that a Judgment be entered herein appointing __12_____, the petitioner, as guardian of the person and property of __13_____, an infant under the age of 14 years, and requiring the said __14_____, before commencing to act as such guardian, to qualify by taking oath or affirmation to well, faithfully and honestly discharge the duties of guardian of said infant __15_____, and to execute to __16_____, said infant, his bond, with at least two sureties, in the penalty of __17_____ dollars, conditioned as prescribed by law, and approved of by the clerk of this court, and that a certified copy of this judgment and said undertaking be filed in the Surrogate's Court for the County of __18_____, it is accordingly

ADJUDGED, that __19_____, be and he hereby is appointed guardian of the person and property of __20_____, an infant under the age of 14 years, but before acting as such guardian the said __21_____ shall qualify by taking oath or affirmation to well, faithfully and honestly discharge the duties of guardian of said infant __22_____, and shall execute to __23_____, said infant, his bond, with at least two sureties to be approved by the clerk of this court, in the penalty of __24_____ dollars, conditioned as prescribed by law, and it is further

ADJUDGED, that a certified copy of this Judgment and the undertaking required herein be filed in the Surrogate's Court for the County of __25_____.

Judgment signed this __26__ day of __27_____, 19_28_.

__29_____
[Print signer's name below signature]
Clerk

Additional Forms:

13 Am Jur Pl and Pr Forms (Rev ed), Guardian and Ward, Forms 11 et seq.
9 Am Jur Legal Forms 2d, Guardian and Ward, Forms 133:11 et seq.

§ 1211. Allowance for infant's support

(a) Petition to supreme court, county court or surrogate's court; contents. A petition to the supreme court, county court or the surrogate's court for the application of an infant's property or a portion thereof to the infant's support, maintenance or education shall set forth in detail:

1. the amount and nature of the infant's property, where it is situated and how invested, his income from such property or any other source and any claim against the infant;

2. whether or not the infant's parents are living and, if either of them is living, all circumstances relative to their ability to support the infant, and, if neither of them is living, the names of other persons legally obligated to support the infant and the circumstances relative to their ability to support the infant; and

3. the terms of any previous order made by any court within or without the state for similar relief and the disposition made of any property pursuant thereto.

(b) Notice. Such notice as the court shall direct shall be given to:

1. the guardian of the property of the infant, if the petition is presented by a person other than such guardian;

2. the infant's father if he is living or, if not, then to the infant's mother or, if neither parent is living, then to the person with whom the infant resides; and

3. the infant if he is of the age of fourteen years or more.

HISTORY:

Add, L 1962, ch 308, eff Sept 1, 1963.
Sub (a), amd, L 1972, ch 276, eff Sept 1, 1972.
Earlier statutes: RCP 293.

ADVISORY COMMITTEE NOTES:

This rule is derived from RCP 293 with only minor stylistic changes. It should be read together with provisions in the Surrogate's Court Act and rules of particular Surrogate's Courts governing such applications. See, e.g., Surr Ct Act § 194; Kings Co Surr Ct Rule XXVIII; NY Co Surr Ct Rule XIII.

CODES, RULES AND REGULATIONS:

Deposit, withdrawal, and accounting of infants' funds in Fourth Judicial Department. 22 NYCRR 1022.6 (CLS App. Div. Rules—Fourth Judicial Dept. § 1022.6).

Use of infants' funds recovered in personal injury actions, Fourth Judicial Department. 22 NYCRR 1039.8 (CLS App. Div. Rules—Fourth Judicial Dept. § 1039.8).

Allowance for infant's support in Supreme Court (Third, Fourth and Sixth Judicial Districts) Third Judicial Department. 22 NYCRR 863.1 (CLS Supreme Ct. Rules —3d, 4th, and 6th Judicial Dists. § 863.1).

Allowance for infant's support in Surrogates' Courts, all counties in Third Judicial Department. 22 NYCRR 1940.17 (CLS Surrogates' Cts. Rules—Third Judicial Department § 1940.17).

Allowances for infants in Surrogates' Courts, all counties in Fourth Judicial Department. 22 NYCRR 2230.11 (CLS Surrogates' Cts. Rules—Fourth Judicial Department § 2230.11).

RESEARCH REFERENCES AND PRACTICE AIDS:

25 NY Jur, Guardian and Ward § 86.
26 Carmody-Wait 2d, Guardians and Custodians §§ 155:45, 155:46.
60 Am Jur 2d, Penal and Correctional Institutions §§ 50 et seq.
13 Am Jur Pl and Pr Forms (Rev ed), Guardian and Ward, Forms 261–293.
15 Am Jur Proof of Facts p 1, Child Custody.

Annotations:

Court's power in habeas corpus proceedings relating to custody of child to adjudicate questions as to child's support. 17 ALR3d 764.

Forms:

See "FORMS" heading following "CASE NOTES", infra.

CASE NOTES

UNDER FORMER CIVIL PRACTICE LAWS

1. Generally
2. Jurisdiction

1. Generally

Petition for hearing on application, pursuant to RCP 293 (this rule) and § 17 of Personal Property Law, for order applying infant's property to his past and future support, maintenance and education, denied. Re Keller (1935) 244 AD 822, 280 NYS 1007.

Where infant's whereabouts unknown, application by commissioner of welfare under RCP 293 was defective where proper notice was not given to infant. Re Abantantonio (1948, Sur) 83 NYS2d 111.

Where infant contemplates marriage, his parent and his guardian ad litem was allowed to withdraw from fund awarded infant for personal injuries sum of $100 for wedding clothes for infant, but not sums to pay accumulated bills. Re Groom (1952) 203 Misc 574, 116 NYS2d 454.

Withdrawal of infants' funds recovered in personal injury cases and held in custodia legis, under CPA § 980-a (§ 1206 herein), was not encouraged, and mother's application to withdraw funds for family use was denied, but reduced withdrawal was permitted with direction that it be expended for sole use and benefit of infant. Leon v Walker (1955) 1 Misc 2d 219, 147 NYS2d 331.

Application to withdraw an infant's funds, the proceeds of a cause of action for personal injuries, for the purpose of paying tuition in religious high school, denied, notwithstanding father's financial inability to meet payment. Re Stackpole (1957) 9 Misc 2d 922, 168 NYS2d 495.

Money which had been deposited with the city treasurer to the credit of an infant plaintiff as the result of injuries sustained by him was not permitted to be withdrawn piecemeal by his father for infant's ordinary expenses of support. Zambrana v Railway Express Agency, Inc. (1956) 11 Misc 2d 553, 175 NYS2d 486.

2. Jurisdiction

The two courts mentioned in the opening sentence of RCP 293 (this rule) were the only ones having jurisdiction of the distribution of infants' estates. Nicolosi v Olshansky (1938) 166 Misc 55, 1 NYS2d 943.

FORMS

Form 1—Petition for allowance for support of infant

Form 2—Decision in proceeding for allowance for support of infant

Form 3—Judgment directing application of money

Form 1

Petition for Allowance for Support of Infant

SUPREME COURT, __1_____ COUNTY.

In the Matter of the Petition of

     __2__,

           Guardian,

of   Petition

     __3__,   Index No. — [if assigned]

           Infant,

for leave to draw and apply money for support and education.

To the Supreme Court of __4_____ County:

The petition of __5_____ respectfully shows:

1. That petitioner resides at __6_____, County of __7_____, State of New York.

2. That petitioner was appointed guardian of __8_____, the above named infant, by a judgment of this court entered on the __9__ day of __10_____, 19_11_, and duly qualified and gave bond as such, and is still acting as such guardian.

3. That said infant is __12__ years of age and was born on the __13__ day of __14_____, 19_15_, and now resides with petitioner at the above address [or, if infant does not reside with petitioner, state the place of his residence and with whom he resides].

4. That the last annual account of said guardian was duly filed on __16__, 19_17_.

5. That the property of said infant consists of __18_____ [state amount and nature of property, where situated and how invested], and that his annual income from such property and from any other source is __19_____ dollars.

6. That the father of said infant is __20_____, residing at __21_____, and the mother of said infant is __22_____, residing at __23_____. [If either parent, or both parents, dead, state the facts.] That the resources of the parents of said infant are as follows: __24_____.

7. That petitioner deems it necessary that __25_____ dollars be applied each month for the support and education of said infant. That the reasons for requesting such allowance are as follows: __26_____.

8. That no other petition for allowance has been presented to this court except __27_____ [state facts and order made].

9. That no other order has been made by any court, either within or without this

state, for similar relief except [state facts and order made and disposition made of any property pursuant thereto].

10. That no other person than those herein above mentioned are interested in this application.

Wherefore petitioner prays that a judgment be entered herein permitting __28_____, guardian, to draw from the __29_____ the sum of __30_____ in each month during the year ending __31_____, 19_32_, to be applied to the support and education of the said infant.

[Date.]

__33_____, Petitioner
Office and P. O. Address
Telephone No.

[Verification.]

Form 2

Decision in Proceeding for Allowance for Support of Infant

Decision

[Title of court and cause]   Index No. __1__ [if assigned]

The issues in this proceeding having regularly come on to be heard before me, one of the Justices of this Court, at a Motion Term [Part __2__] thereof, held in and for the County of __3_____, at the Courthouse in __4_____, New York, on __5__ __6_____, 19_7_, and having read the petition of __8_____, guardian of the person and property of __9_____, an infant, for an allowance for the support of said infant, and having heard the proofs thereon, and due deliberation having been had thereon,

Now, after hearing __10_____, attorney for petitioner, in support of said petition and no one having appeared in opposition thereto, and it appearing to the court that:

1. The petitioner, __11_____, is the guardian of the person of __12_____, an infant of the age of __13__ years, that he has duly qualified and given bond as such guardian, and that his last annual account as such guardian was duly filed on __14_____, 19_15_.

2. The property of said infant consists of [state amount and nature of property, where situated and how invested], and that his annual income from such property is __16____ dollars, and that he has no income from any other source.

3. The said infant resides at __17_____, with __18_____ and __19_____, his father and mother, the resources of the father and mother of said infant are insufficient to provide for his support and education because [state amount of parents' resources and reasons why they are insufficient to provide for the support and education of the infant].

4. That it is necessary that __20_____ dollars be applied each month for the support and education of said infant because [state reasons for necessity of applying funds for infant's support and education].

It is hereby

Ordered, that a judgment be entered herein by the clerk of this court, directing __21_____, as guardian of the person and property of __22_____, the infant above named, to apply to the support and education of said __23_____, infant the sum of __24_____ dollars per month, for the period of __25_____ payable out of the income [or "income and principal"] of said infant's property.

[Date]

__26_____
[Print signer's name below signature]
Justice, Supreme Court

Form 3

Judgment Directing Application of Money

Judgment

[Caption as in Form 1, supra   Index No. __1__.

The issues in the above entitled proceeding having been regularly brought on for hearing before Mr. Justice __2_____, at a Motion Term, Part __3__ of this court, held in and for the County of __4_____ at the County Courthouse in the City of __5_____, State of New York on the __6__ day of __7_____, 19_8_, upon the petition of __9_____, guardian of the person and property of __10_____, an infant, and the petitioner having appeared by his attorney, and the allegations and proofs having been heard, and the Justice having rendered his decision thereon directing that a Judgment be entered herein directing __11_____, as guardian of the person and property of __12_____, the infant above named, to apply to the support and education of said __13_____, infant the sum of __14_____ dollars per month, for the period of __15_____ payable out of the income [or "income and principal", as directed] of said infant's property, it is accordingly

ADJUDGED, that __16_____, as guardian of the person and property of __17_____, an infant, be, and he hereby is directed to apply to the support and education of said __18_____, infant, the sum of __19_____ dollars per month, for the period of __20_____ payable out of the income [or "income and principal"] of said infant's property.

Judgment signed this __21__ day of __22_____, 19_23_.

                                                  __24_____
                                                  [Print signer's name below signature]
                                                  Clerk

Additional Forms:

   14 Am Jur Pl and Pr Forms (Rev ed), Incompetent Persons, Forms 181–193.
   9 Am Jur Legal Forms 2d, Incompetent Persons, Forms 141:21–141:26.

[CPLR 1212–1300 have been reserved for future use. Please check your supplement.]